Fuzzy Models for Pattern Recognition

IEEE PRESS
445 Hoes Lane, PO Box 1331
Piscataway, NJ 08855-1331

Fuzzy Models for Pattern Recognition

Methods That Search for Structures in Data

Edited by

James C. Bezdek
Division of Computer Science
University of West Florida

Sankar K. Pal
Electronics and Communications Science Unit
Indian Statistical Institute, Calcutta

IEEE
PRESS

A Selected Reprint Volume
IEEE Neural Networks Council, *Sponsor*

The Institute of Electrical and Electronics Engineers, Inc., New York

Printed in the United States of America

10 9 8 7 6 5 4 3 2

ISBN 0-7803-0422-5

IEEE Order Number: PC0317-8

Library of Congress Cataloging-in-Publication Data

Bezdek, James C.,
Fuzzy models for pattern recognition : methods that search for structures in data / by James C. Bezdek, Sankar K. Pal.
p. cm.
Includes bibliographical references and index.
ISBN 0-7803-0422-5
1. Pattern perception. 2. Fuzzy sets. 3. Cluster analysis.
I. Pal, Sankar K. II. Title.
Q327.B47 1992
006.4—dc20

91-45019
CIP

Contents

Foreword

To view the contents of this volume in a proper perspective, it is of historical interest to note that the initial development of the theory of fuzzy sets was motivated in large measure by problems in pattern classification and cluster analysis.

In the spring of 1964, I was invited by Richard Bellman to spend a part of the summer at Raud in Santa Monica to work on problems in pattern classification and systems analysis. At the time, we both felt that conventional approaches to the analysis of large-scale systems were ineffective in dealing with systems that are complex and mathematically ill-defined, as are most of the real-world systems in which human perception and intuitive judgment play important roles. The question was: What can be done to capture the concept of imprecision in a way that would differentiate imprecision from uncertainty?

A very simple idea that occurred to us at that time was to generalize the concept of the characteristic function of a set to allow for intermediate grades of membership. This, in effect, was the genesis of the concept of a fuzzy set. Although, as was noted in my 1965 paper on fuzzy sets, the concept of a grade of membership bears a close relation to the truth value of a predicate, the agenda of fuzzy set theory is quite different from that of multivalued logic. In particular, the concept of a fuzzy set fits very naturally into the framework of pattern recognition. Indeed, the papers collected in this volume provide a convincing demonstration of the effectiveness of fuzzy-set-theoretic techniques in both the formulation and solution of problems in these fields.

The starting point in the application of fuzzy set theory to pattern classification was the 1966 paper by Bellman, Kalaba, and myself. In this paper, the problem of pattern classification was formulated as the problem of interpolation of the membership function of a fuzzy set, and thereby a link with the basic problem of system identification was established. A seminal contribution to cluster analysis was Ruspini's concept of a fuzzy partition (1969). A new direction in the applications of fuzzy set theory to cluster analysis was initiated by Bezdek and Dunn in their work on fuzzy ISODATA and the fuzzy *c*-means algorithms (1973, 1974). At roughly the same time, Azriel Rosenfeld became interested in the use of fuzzy sets in image analysis in 1969; several of his earliest papers on this topic appear in this volume. S. K. Pal first applied fuzzy sets to the speech recognition problem in 1977. Subsequently, Bezdek and Pal have been major contributors to both the theory and applications of fuzzy models in image processing and pattern recognition.

This volume contains most of the prominent early contributions in the field. Taken in their totality, the papers collected herein present a remarkably complete exposition of the application of fuzzy-set-theoretic techniques to pattern classification. Furthermore, they relate very succinctly the central problem of pattern classification; namely, the problem of interpolation of the membership function, to the problem of learning from examples in neural network theory. This symbiotic relation between fuzzy set and neural network theories is already being exploited in a growing number of consumer products and industrial systems ranging from washing machines to combustion control regulators. In this regard, what we are witnessing now is probably just the beginning of a new and fundamentally important direction in the amalgamation and synthesis of parts of fuzzy set and neural network theories that center on the induction of if-then rules from observations.

Professors Bezdek and Pal have produced a very important work which will be a landmark in its own right; they deserve the congratulations and thanks of all of us for filling an important need in highlighting the evolution of the applications of fuzzy set theory to pattern recognition, and for linking fuzzy set and neural network theories through learning from examples.

Berkeley, California

Lotfi A. Zadeh

Preface

Applications of fuzzy pattern recognition have matured in the last five years, especially as they interact with and support control systems. At the same time, the theory on which these applications are based has evolved into a cohesive subject, as reflected by the papers we have collected for this volume. From a practical view then, as well as pedagogically, it is timely to introduce a unified presentation of fuzzy models for pattern recognition. From a more utilitarian viewpoint, scientists and engineers are very anxious to understand this approach because of the commercial success in recent years of Japanese products based on fuzzy technology.

This volume collects seminal papers relating to the theory and applications of pattern recognition based on fuzzy sets. Specifically, the volume begins with Zadeh's original 1965 article on fuzzy sets, and proceeds chronologically through the evolution of fuzzy algorithms for feature analysis, clustering, classifier design, neural network learning image processing and computer vision. Each of these major categories is represented by papers important to the theory or an actual application in a pattern recognition system design problem. Each chapter contains an introduction to the topic, comments on the importance of the papers selected, and a bibliography for further reading.

Scientists and engineers in academia, industry, and government that do research about, and development of, fielded systems that process sensor data for classification, prediction, and control should find this collection useful. This volume can also be used as a secondary (supplementary) text for courses in fuzzy sets, classifier design, cluster analysis, feature analysis, image processing, and computational models for uncertain reasoning. The material in most of the papers is at a level appropriate for senior undergraduates and/or first year graduate students in engineering, and the physical and computational sciences.

This volume was commissioned by the Neural Networks Council (NNC) of the IEEE. The NNC, under the guidance and vision of Bob Marks, Stamatos Kartolopoulos, Pat Simpson, and Russ Eberhart, has championed the sponsorship of fuzzy conferences, an *IEEE Transactions on Fuzzy Systems*, and books such as this one on fuzzy pattern recognition within the IEEE. Thus, we owe the NNC and their leaders a vote of thanks for their help and encouragement. Second, preliminary drafts of the original material were reviewed by perhaps a dozen readers, each of whom provided us with valuable comments that made the material more comprehensible, correct, and accessible; we acknowledge their help and constructive advice. Finally, the staff at IEEE PRESS—in particular, Dudley Kay and Karen Miller, have done an outstanding job of overseeing the production of this volume. Their patience with us at what must have been a remarkably difficult task for them (the production schedule was very, very tight; and, of course, they had to deal with us!) has been outstanding.

Chapter 1
Fuzzy Models for Pattern Recognition
Background, Significance, and Key Points

1.0 Introduction

FUZZY sets were introduced in 1965 by Lotfi Zadeh [1] as a new way to represent vagueness in everyday life. They are a generalization of conventional set theory, one of the basic structures underlying computational mathematics and models. Computational pattern recognition has played a central role in the development of fuzzy models because fuzzy interpretations of data structures are a very natural and intuitively plausible way to formulate and solve various problems. Fuzzy control theory has also provided a wide variety of real, fielded system applications of fuzzy technology. We shall have little more to say about the growth of fuzzy models in control, except to the extent that pattern recognition algorithms and methods described in this book impact control systems (cf. Fig. 21).

Collected here are many of the seminal papers in the field. There will be, of course, omissions that are neither by intent nor ignorance: we cannot reproduce all of the important papers that have helped in the evolution of fuzzy pattern recognition (there may be as many as five hundred) even in this narrow applications domain. We will attempt, in each chapter introduction, to comment on some of the important papers that have *not* been included and we ask both readers and authors to understand that a book such as this simply cannot "contain everything." Our objective in Chapter 1 is to describe the basic structure of fuzzy sets theory as it applies to the major problems encountered in the design of a pattern recognition system.

1.1 Fuzzy Sets and Membership Functions

You are approaching a red light and must advise a driving student when to apply the brakes. Would you say, "begin braking *74 feet* from the crosswalk"? Or would your advice be more like, "apply the brakes *pretty soon*"? The latter, of course; the former instruction is too precise to be implemented. Everyday language is one example of the ways vagueness is used and propagated. Imprecision in data and information gathered from and about our environment is either *statistical* (e.g., the outcome of a coin toss is a matter of chance) or *nonstatistical* (e.g., "apply the brakes pretty soon"). This latter type of uncertainty is called *fuzziness*.

Children quickly learn how to interpret and implement fuzzy instructions ("go to bed *about* 10"). We all assimilate and use (i.e., act on) fuzzy data, vague rules, and imprecise information, just as we are able to make decisions about situations that seem to be governed by an element of chance. Accordingly, computational models of real systems should also be able to recognize, represent, manipulate, interpret, and use both fuzzy and statistical uncertainties. Statistical models deal with random events and outcomes; fuzzy models attempt to capture and quantify nonrandom imprecision. The appearance of linguistic imprecision and accounting for uncertainty in the construction of mathematical models is highlighted with the following quotes, excerpted from Feynman [2] in his comments on the reliability analysis of the Challenger space shuttle (our italics):

> A mathematical model was made of the erosion. . . . Uncertainties appear everywhere in this model. *How strong* the gas stream might be was unpredictable. . . . Blowby showed that the ring *might* fail, even though it was only *partially* eroded. The empirical formula was known to be uncertain, for the curve did not go directly through the very data points by which it was determined. . . . Similar uncertainties surrounded the other constants in the formula, etc., etc.

> "When using a mathematical model, careful attention must be given to the *uncertainties* in the model"
>
> Richard P. Feynman, on the reliability of the Challenger space shuttle [2]

Conventional (or crisp) sets contain objects that satisfy *precise properties* required for membership. The set of numbers H from 6 to 8 is crisp; we write $H = \{r \in \mathcal{R} \mid 6 \leq r \leq 8\}$. Equivalently, H is described by its membership function, m_H:

$$m_H(r) = \begin{matrix} 1; & 6 \leq r \leq 8 \\ 0; & \text{otherwise}. \end{matrix} \qquad (1)$$

The crisp set H and the graph of m_H are shown in the left half of Fig. 1. Every real number r is either in H or is not in H. Because m_H maps all real numbers $r \in \mathcal{R}$ onto the two points $\{0, 1\}$, crisp sets correspond to 2-valued logic—is or isn't, on or off, black or white, 1 or 0. In logic, values of m_H are called *truth values* with reference to the question, "is r in H?" The answer is yes if and only if $m_H(r) = 1$; otherwise, the answer is no.

Fuzzy sets, on the other hand, contain objects that satisfy *imprecise* properties to varying degrees, for example, the "set" of numbers F that are "close to 7." In 1965 Zadeh [1] proposed representing F by a *membership function*, say m_F, that maps numbers into the entire unit interval [0, 1]. The value $m_F(r)$ is called the *grade of membership* of r in F. This construct corresponds to continuously valued logic; roughly speaking, all shades of gray between black (= 1) and white (= 0) can be described. In this context, $m_F(r)$ is sometimes regarded as the "truth" in the proposi-

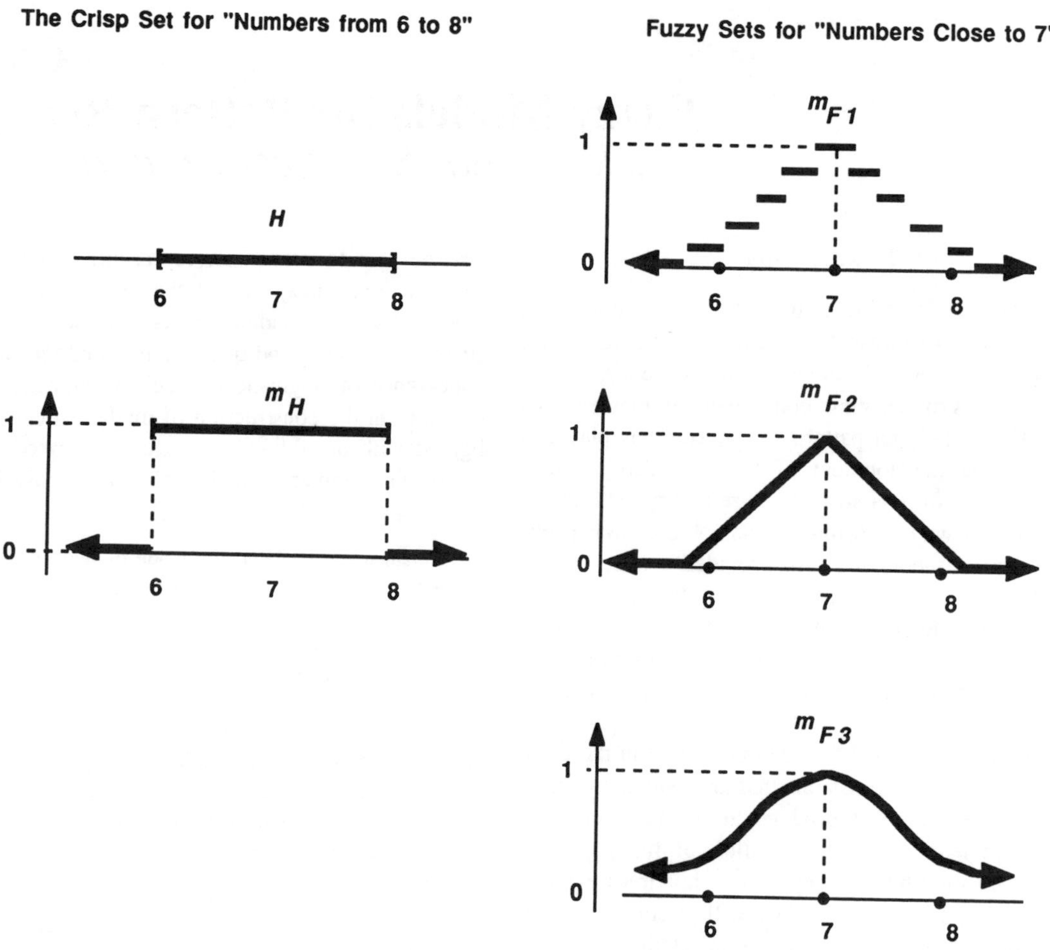

Fig. 1. Membership functions for hard and fuzzy subsets of $\mathscr{R}$.

tion that r does indeed satisfy the imprecise property (or properties) defining F.

Because the property "close to 7" is fuzzy, there is not a unique membership function for F. Rather, it is left to the modeler to decide, based on the potential application and properties desired for F, what m_F should be like (this point is discussed further in Section 1.2 of this chapter). Properties that seem plausible for this particular fuzzy set might include:

(i) Normality: $m_F(7) = 1$.
(ii) Monotonicity: The closer r is to 7, the closer $m_F(r)$ is to 1, and conversely.
(iii) Symmetry: Numbers equally far left and right of 7 should have equal memberships.

Given these intuitive constraints, any of the functions shown in the right half of Fig. 1 might be a useful representative of F. Each may be satisfactory, all are different. In the staircase graph, m_{F1} is discrete; in the triangle graph, m_{F2} is continuous but not smooth; while in the bell graph, m_{F3} is very smooth. Note that, as in the graph of m_{F3}, every number can have some positive membership in F, but we would not expect numbers "far from 7" (20,000,987, for example) to have much.

Does this scheme for describing numbers close to 7 seem practical? Sure: "How much does it cost?" "About 7 dollars." Suppose the numbers in H and F are heights of basketball players (p). If someone tells you that $m_H(p) = 1$, all you know about player p's height is that it is between 6 and 8 feet. On the other hand, knowing that $m_{F2}(q) = 0.98$ tells us that q's height is "pretty close" to 7 feet. Which piece of information seems more useful? This illustrates the important point that the *type of information* borne by hard and fuzzy models is different in both quantity and quality.

Readers new to the field often wonder what the "set" *is*, physically. In conventional set theory, any set of actual, real objects (we include numbers between 6 and 8 as "real" objects) is completely equivalent to, and isomorphically described by, a crisp membership function such as m_H (in set theory, this function is often called a characteristic or indicator function). There is, however, no set-theoretic equivalent of "real objects" corresponding to m_F, the function-theoretic representation of F. That is, fuzzy sets are always (and only) functions, from some universe of objects, say X, onto [0, 1], the range of m_F. This is depicted graphically in Fig. 2

So, the membership function is the basic idea in fuzzy set theory; its values measure degrees to which objects satisfy imprecisely defined properties. In order to manipulate fuzzy

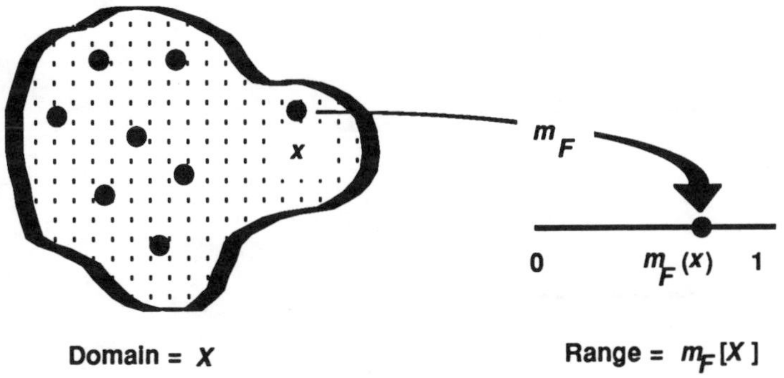

Fig. 2. Fuzzy sets are membership functions.

sets, it is necessary to have operations that enable us to combine them. Zadeh laid out "classical" operations for fuzzy sets in [1]. We characterize these operations in terms of $\mathscr{F}(X)$ = All Fuzzy Subsets of X. That is, $m \in \mathscr{F}(X) \Leftrightarrow m: X \rightarrow [0, 1]$.

Let fuzzy sets m_A, $m_B \in \mathscr{F}(X)$. We define ($\forall x \in X$: pointwise, function theoretic operations)

$$(=) \quad \text{Equality } A = B \Leftrightarrow m_A(x) = m_B(x) \tag{2}$$

$$(\subset) \quad \text{Containment } A \subset B \Leftrightarrow m_A(x) \leq m_B(x) \tag{3}$$

$$(\sim) \quad \text{Complement } m_{\tilde{A}}(x) = 1 - m_A(x) \tag{4}$$

$$(\cap) \quad \text{Intersection } m_{A \cap B}(x) = \min\{m_A(x), m_B(x)\} \tag{5}$$

$$(\cup) \quad \text{Union } m_{A \cup B}(x) = \max\{m_A(x), m_B(x)\} \tag{6}$$

Example 1: Let $P = \{\text{people}, p\}$; $x = h(p)$ = height of $p \in P$; and let $X = h[P]$ = {heights of $p \in P$} = [0, 11]. Shown in Fig. 3 are membership functions for two fuzzy sets, characterized as:

$m_A \in \mathscr{F}(X)$ = {(heights) close to 7 feet}	$(m_A \circ h) \in \mathscr{F}(P)$ = {(people) close to 7 feet (tall)}
$m_B \in \mathscr{F}(X)$ = {(heights) close to 3 feet}	$(m_B \circ h) \in \mathscr{F}(P)$ = {(people) close to 3 feet (tall)}

$m_A(3) = 3/7$ = extent to which a 3′ p is ≈ 7′ tall

$m_{\tilde{A}}(3) = 1 - (3/7) = 4/7$
= extent to which a 3′ p is NOT ≈ 7′ tall

$m_A(6) = 6/7$ = extent to which a 6′ p is ≈ 7′ tall

$m_B(6) = 5/8$ = extent to which a 6′ p is ≈ 3′ tall

$m_{A \cap B}(6) = \min\{6/7, 5/8\} = 5/8$
= extent to which p is ≈ 3′ AND 7′ tall

$m_{A \cup B}(6) = \max\{6/7, 5/8\} = 6/7$
= extent to which p is ≈ 3′ OR 7′ tall

Zadeh's paper [1] discusses these operations on fuzzy sets at length, and many writers have subsequently proposed other systems of functions for these five set operations [3, 13, 46]. Our purpose in reporting the original operations here is to familiarize readers with the basic ideas about how to combine pairs of fuzzy sets. In fact, these operations seem to be ubiquitous in real applications, and in some sense thus remain more important than many of the subsequent generalizations.

Equations (2–6) can lead to some amusing situations. Consider the membership function m_N shown in Fig. 4 and discussed in our next example.

Example 2: Let $X = [a, b]$, and suppose $m_N(x) = 0.5$ for every x in X (Fig. 4).

$m_N(x) = 0.5$ for every x in X.

Therefore, by equations (4) to (6) we have:

$m_{\tilde{N}}(x) = 1 - (0.5) = 0.5$ for every x in X.

$m_{N \cap \tilde{N}}(x) = \min\{0.5, 0.5\} = 0.5$ for every x in X.

$m_{N \cup \tilde{N}}(x) = \max\{0.5, 0.5\} = 0.5$ for every x in X.

So, for this fuzzy set, $N = \tilde{N} = N \cap \tilde{N} = N \cup \tilde{N}$. In particular, the union of N with its complement is a proper subset of X!

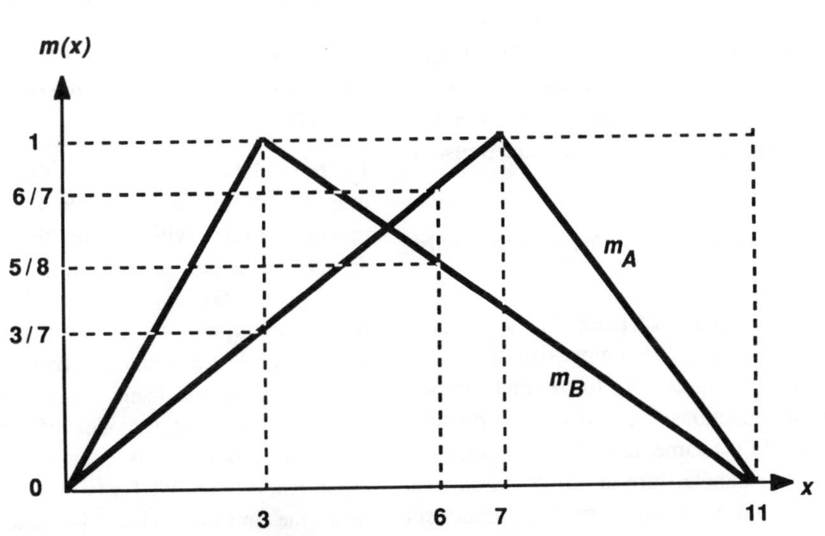

Fig. 3. Membership functions for Example 1.

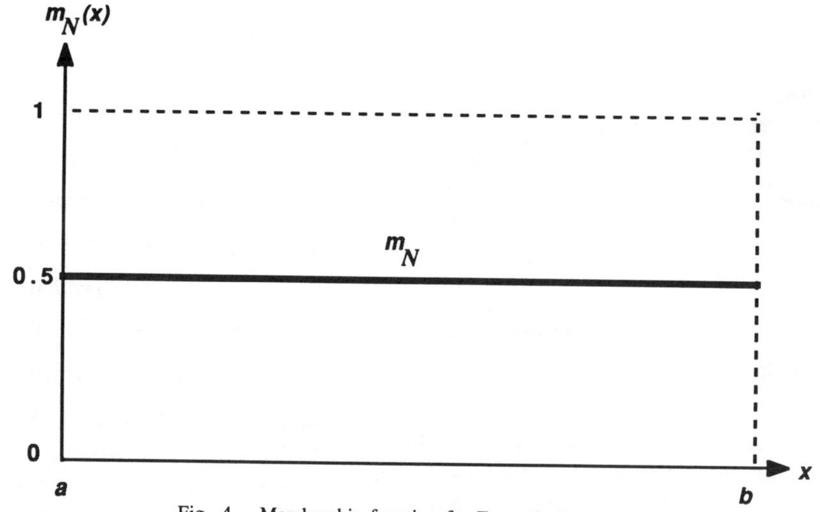

Fig. 4. Membership function for Example 2.

Readers may have some questions about fuzzy sets at this point. A first question that is often asked concerns the relationship between fuzzy sets and probability. However, we feel that answers to several preliminary questions about fuzzy sets will make this issue clearer, so we ask first:

Question 1: Membership Values – what are they?

In view of Fig. 1, this question is easy to answer. The statement $m_{F2}(q) = 0.98$ (see Fig. 1) tells us that q's height is "pretty close" to 7 feet. In short, 0.98 is a measure of the similarity of q to other objects in X that possess the imprecise property that m_{F2} represents. Note that we do not interpret this number as, "the probability is 0.98 that q is pretty close to 7." This distinction will be further discussed in Section 1.2 of this chapter.

Because fuzzy sets are a generalization of the classical set theory, the embedding of conventional models into a larger setting endows fuzzy models with greater flexibility to capture various aspects of incompleteness or imperfection (i.e., deficiencies) in whatever information and data are available about a real process. Another way to say this is to imagine that membership functions possess *elasticity*; thus, the higher the value of membership of an object to a class, the less the imprecisely defined concept of the fuzzy set must be stretched to accommodate the object. Hard membership functions, of course, are *inelastic.*

Question 2: Membership Functions – where do they come from?

Membership functions come from two places: data and people—precisely like probabilities! We emphasize that it is important, when asking this question, to remind oneself where probability density functions come from; we contend that they come from exactly the same sources as membership functions do. Data, for example, are used in parametric estimation of the means and covariances of the component densities in a mixture of normal distributions, just as data are used to find a fuzzy partition and prototypes by the fuzzy c-means clustering algorithm. But what of the normal density itself? Is it somehow different from, say, just "adopting" function m_{F2} because it seems to provide a reasonable and useful model of the process being described? Well, no. The normal distribution comes from Gauss, and we use it because it often fits the physical world. So, we do get probability density functions and membership functions in the same way. The papers in this collection exhibit both sources of fuzzy sets.

Many studies have been conducted that attempt to assess how to assign memberships to objects in fuzzy sets. Indeed, the idea of the fuzzy set has itself been generalized in various ways. For example, there are well defined concepts of Type 2, Type 3, . . . Type n fuzzy sets, ultrafuzzy sets, interval-valued fuzzy sets, L-valued fuzzy sets, and spectral fuzzy sets. Readers interested in these generalizations can consult [5–11]. In particular, spectral fuzzy sets will emerge in *Chapter 4: Image Processing and Machine Vision* as a natural and convenient way to deal with uncertainties in many computer vision problems.

Question 3: Where do fuzzy models fit in with other models?

Fuzzy models belong wherever they can provide either collateral or competitively better information about a physical process. No one will disagree that the binomial distribution is an optimal model, in some philosophically intuitive sense, for the flip of a fair coin. One could model this process with a fuzzy technique, but the results would almost certainly be less satisfying, in terms of a natural and verifiable representation of the process itself. On the other hand, while we could certainly represent the idea of "pretty close to 7" with a statistical model, it is easy to see that this is much less satisfactory than the fuzzy models exhibited above, simply from the intuitive view, because the notion of chance is absent from our naive description of the process. We exemplify this a different way in Section 1.3 of this chapter. As an example of this, we note that each of the following disciplines provides some information about the dynamics of motion:

- Newtonian Mechanics
- Relativistic Mechanics
- Statistical Mechanics
- Quantum Mechanics
- Auto Mechanics

These models provide us with different, useful, auxiliary, and sometimes contradictory information about various facets of dynamics. Each contributes something about the physcial world; so it is with various classes of models!

From a different point of view, because every hard set is fuzzy but not conversely, the mathematical embedding of conventional set theory into fuzzy sets is as natural as the idea of embedding the real numbers into the complex plane. In both cases we can expect the larger "space" to contain answers to (real) questions that cannot be found in the smaller one. Thus, the idea of fuzziness is one of *enrichment*, not replacement.

There are a number of books and collections of papers that deal with elementary notions of fuzzy sets and their generalizations. Kaufmann's early text [12] is still timely and there have been updates and extensions as the corpus of work on fuzzy models has grown. Readers can begin a general tour of the field with the excellent work of Dubois and Prade [3], and continue with related material [15–19], and with works by Klir and Folger [13] and Zimmermann [14].

1.2 Models of Uncertainty: Probability and Fuzziness

Question 4: Isn't fuzziness just a clever disguise for probability?

This is without doubt the most often asked question about fuzzy sets. It is an interesting question, and, of course, has hounded fuzzy sets since its inception. Our answer is an emphatic *no*. There is a strong philosophical argument against regarding fuzziness as a surrogate for probability. The spirit of this argument is contained in Example 3.

Example 3: Let L = set of all liquids, and let fuzzy subset $\mathscr{L}$ = {all (**potable**) liquids}. Suppose you had been in the desert for a week without drink and you came upon two bottles marked C and A as in Figure 5a.

Confronted with this pair of bottles, and given that you must drink from the one that you chose, which would *you* choose to drink from? Most readers, when presented with this experiment, immediately see that while C could contain, say, swamp water, it would not (discounting the possibility of a Machiavellian fuzzy modeler) contain liquids such as hy-

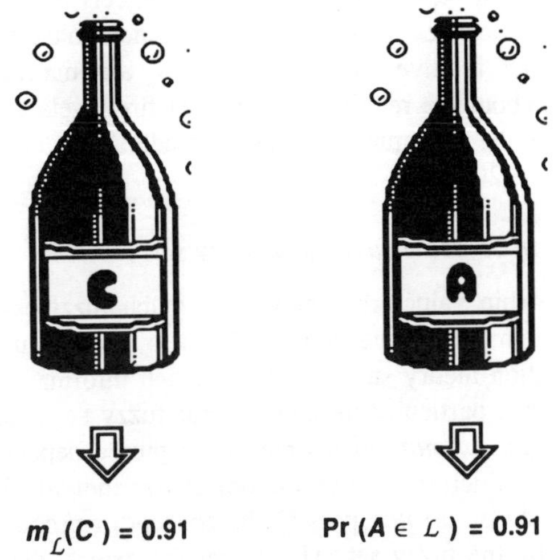

Fig. 5a. A pair of bottles for the weary traveler.

drochloric acid. That is, *membership* of 0.91 means that the contents of C are fairly similar to perfectly potable liquids (e.g., pure water). On the other hand, the *probability* that A is potable = 0.91 means that over a long run of experiments, the contents of A are expected to be potable in about 91% of the trials; in the other 9% the contents will be deadly —about 1 chance in 10. Thus, most subjects will opt for a chance to drink swamp water.

There is another facet to this example, and it concerns the idea of *observation*. Continuing then, suppose that we examine the contents of C and A and discover them to be as shown in Fig. 5b. Note that, *after observation*, the membership value for C is unchanged while the probability value for A drops from 0.91 to 0.0.

This example shows that these two models possess philosophically different kinds of information: fuzzy member-

Fig. 5b. A pair of bottles for the weary traveler (unmasked).

ships, which represent similarities of objects to imprecisely defined properties; and probabilities, which convey information about relative frequencies. There are many amusing articles about the relationship between fuzzy sets and probability in the literature. Interested readers can consult, for example, [20–31].

Question 5: How fuzzy is a fuzzy set?

Membership values determine how much fuzziness a fuzzy set contains. This question is related to similar questions in information theory such as, "how much information is contained in a particular message"? For fuzzy sets, quantification of the *amount* of imprecision captured depends on the extent to which the supporting objects (as individuals or in a group) *do* or *do not* possess the concept or property represented by the fuzzy set. The higher the extent, the lower is the fuzziness of the set, and conversely. For example, consider a fuzzy set "good football players" with 20 members, where $m(x)$ denotes the degree of goodness of a player x. If $m(x) = 1$ or 0, then there is no ambiguity in asserting that a given player is good or not. On the other hand, if $m(x) = 0.5$ (i.e., if x is a crossover point of the function m), the assertion concerning goodness (or badness) possesses a maximum amount of uncertainty. Thus, the uncertainty associated with an individual player increases monotonically in the interval [0, 0.5], and then decreases monotonically in the interval [0.5, 1]. We can, for example, average the 20 values of $m(x)$ over this fuzzy set to get a quantification of the amount of uncertainty it possesses.

Many measures of fuzziness have been proposed and investigated over the last two decades. For example, there are indices of fuzziness, crispness, entropy, certitude, ambiguity, and belief [12, 32–36]. Some of these are based on notions such as the distance between a fuzzy set and its "nearest" (furthest) crisp set, distance between a fuzzy set and its complement, or Shannon's classical entropy function. Usually, these measures have properties such as being minimum when m is crisp for x and maximum when $m(x) = 0.5$ for all x. If we "sharpen" a fuzzy set, that is, increase its contrast around the value 0.5 (or make the membership function steeper in this neighborhood), then its fuzziness will decrease. Some applications of several of these measures are reported in [37]. Papers throughout this collection address this issue in various ways.

Global measures of uncertainty on a fuzzy set are not always sufficient. Often we are interested in questions such as: if a team of, say, eleven players is formed by randomly selecting any eleven players from the twenty in the above pool, to what extent, on average, might the team be called "good"? This raises two important issues: namely, how to measure the degree to which a collection of objects, as a whole, possess the property of "goodness" and how to measure the average amount of ambiguity related to such collections.

The first issue depends on the problem at hand. For example, consider a quiz team. If $m(x)$ represents the ability of member x, then the overall ability of the team, as a whole, can be taken as $\max\{m(x)\}$, because if one of the members succeeds, the team succeeds. On the other hand, suppose a group of acrobats are positioned so that all of them will fall if any one falls. Under this situation, if $m(x)$ is the stability of member x, then the stability of the team would be $\min\{m(x)\}$. Answers to the second issue have been proposed by several writers. For example, one way to assess the average amount of imprecision associated with a given group is to compute the *rth order entropy* H^r [38] of a fuzzy set, which provides a measure of the average uncertainty (ambiguity) in making a decision on any subset with r elements as regards its possession of the imprecise property. The significance of this measure for pattern recognition and image processing problems is described in [38].

Another information measure of a fuzzy set called "hybrid entropy" H_{hy} represents the amount of difficulty in deciding whether an element belongs to a fuzzy set (or possesses a certain fuzzy property) or not by making a prevision on its probability of occurrence. This measure takes into account not only the fuzziness of a set, but also the underlying probability structure of the supporting elements. The significance of hybrid entropy in image enhancement and noise reduction problems is well described elsewhere [38].

1.3 Pattern Recognition: Models and Approaches

What is pattern recognition? There are many definitions, and many schools of thought about what constitutes the discipline itself. In 1973, Duda and Hart [34] characterized pattern recognition as a "field concerned with machine recognition of meaningful regularities in noisy or complex environments." We think a very workable definition is that *pattern recognition is the search for structure in data.* With this definition it is easy to make a case for the position that pattern recognition is in fact the basis for almost every line of scientific inquiry that humans have ever pursued. Pattern recognition is, by its very nature, an inexact science, and thus admits many approaches, sometimes complementary, sometimes competing, to the approximate solution of a given problem.

In a different vein, we can view pattern recognition as a major area of current research and development driven by the need to process data and information obtained from the interactions between scientists, technologists, and society in general. Another motivation for the spurt of activity in this field is the need for the people to communicate with computing machines in natural languages. The third and most important motivation for study in this area is that scientists and engineers are concerned with the idea of designing and making automata (intelligent machines) that can carry out certain tasks with skills comparable to human performance. Application areas for pattern recognition include, but are not limited to, man–machine communication (automatic speech recognition, script recognition, speech understanding, image understanding, natural language processing), defense (automatic target recognition, guidance, and control), medicine (medical diagnosis, image analysis, disease classification), vehicular (automobile, airplane, train, boat controllers), police and detective (crime and criminal detection from speech, handwriting, fingerprint, photograph), natural resource study and estimation (agriculture, forestry, geology, environment), industry (CAD, CAM, product testing and assembly, inspection and quality control), domestic systems (appliances), and computers (fuzzy hardware and software).

Treatments of many deterministic statistical, and fuzzy approaches to the design of *numerical* pattern recognition systems (PRSs) can be found, for example, in references [39–59]. There is another branch of pattern recognition that is also important and well represented in the literature [60]; syntactic (or structural) pattern recognition. Readers may consult Fu [61] for a nice introduction to a variety of approaches based on this idea. This approach to pattern recognition has not been well developed by researchers in the fuzzy community, however, so we are content for the present to restrict our attention (almost) entirely to numerical pattern recognition (Papers 3.6 and 3.11 are exceptions to this disclaimer).

We characterize numerical pattern recognition in terms of four major areas that collectively comprise a fielded pattern recognition system. Fig. 6 portrays the overall relationship between the four components, and encapsulates each of the steps outlined below in the context of system design. Specifically, the following steps lead to a fielded PRS. Arguably, perhaps, this is an accurate description of (1) specifically, the art and science used in the development of pattern recognition systems, and (2) more generally, the scientific method itself.

Development of a Pattern Recognition System in a Nutshell

1. Humans nominate data that hopefully capture basic relationships between the apparently important variables of a process.
2. Data are collected from humans and sensors. Data for numerical PRSs are either feature vectors (object data) or pairwise similarities or dissimilarities (relational data).
3. We search for underlying structure in the data that provides a basis for hypothesizing relationships between the variables governing the process.
4. Hypotheses are formalized by characterizing the process with equations, rules, or perhaps algorithms; in short, we propose a model of the system.
5. If possible, various theoretical aspects of the model, such as linearity, continuity, and stability, are analyzed in hopes of gaining insight into both the model and the process it represents.
6. The model is often then "trained" with labeled training

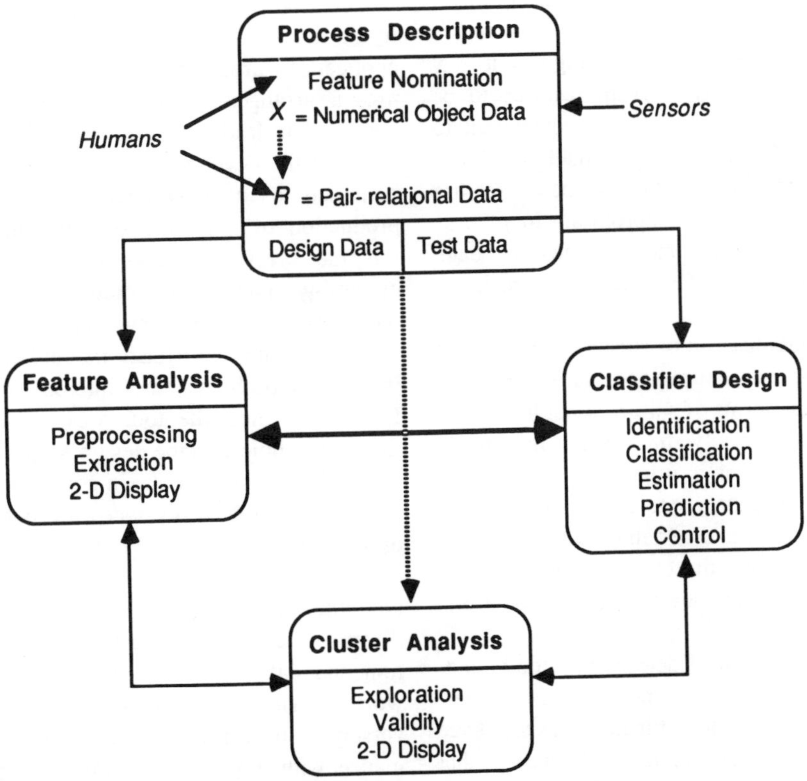

Fig. 6. Elements of a typical numerical pattern recognition system.

data (we find the parameters of the model by providing it with examples of correct instances). Classification of the labeled data can be done simultaneously with learning (decision-directed learning) or we may postpone classification until learning is complete.

7. The model is tested with labeled test data, when available, and is compared with other models of the same process for things such as relative sensitivity to perturbations of its inputs and parameters, error rate performance, and time and space complexity. (The smaller the training or design set and the larger the size of test set, the better the expected classifier design and predicted validity of its performance. Results are, at the least, biased optimistically if the same training set is used as the test set.)
8. We build, test, and place in service a system comprised of hardware and software that implements the model.
9. The model enables us to classify, predict, estimate and/or control elements of the process and its subprocesses.

Consider the case of a decision-theoretic approach to pattern classification. With conventional probabilistic and deterministic classifiers [39, 42], the features characterizing the input vectors are quantitative (i.e., numerical) in nature. Vectors having imprecise or incomplete specification are usually either ignored or discarded from the design and test sets. Impreciseness (or ambiguity) in such data may arise from various sources. For example, instrumental error or noise corruption in the experiment may lead to partially reliable information available on a feature measurement. Again, in some cases the expense incurred in extracting a very precise exact value of a feature may be high or it may be difficult to decide on the most relevant features to be extracted. For these reasons, it may become convenient to use linguistic variables and hedges (e.g., small, medium, high, very, more or less, etc.) in order to describe the feature information. In such cases, it is not appropriate to give an exact numerical representation to uncertain feature data. Rather, it is reasonable to represent uncertain feature information by fuzzy subsets.

Again, uncertainty in classification or clustering of patterns may arise from the overlapping nature of the various classes; for example, the amorphous forms of sulfur do not have clear temperature boundaries—they really *do* overlap. In conventional classification techniques, it is usually assumed that a pattern can belong to one and only one class, which is not necessarily realistic physically, and certainly not mathematically. Thus, feature vectors (and the objects they represent) can and should be allowed to have degrees of membership in more than one class.

Similarly, consider the problem of determining the boundary or shape of a class from its sampled points or prototypes. Conventional approaches attempt to estimate an exact shape for the area in question by determining a boundary that contains (i.e., passes through) some or all of the sample points. However, this property is not necessarily desirable for boundaries in real images. For example, it may be necessary to extend the boundaries to represent obscured portions not represented in the sampled points. Extended portions should have a lower membership in the boundary for such a class than the portions explicitly highlighted by the sample points. The size of extended regions should decrease with an increase in the number of sample points. This leads one to define multivalued or fuzzy (with continuum grade of belonging) shapes and boundaries of certain classes.

From these examples, we see that the concept of fuzzy sets can be used at the feature level for representing input data as an array of membership values denoting the degree of possession of certain properties, at the classification level, for representing class membership of objects, and for providing an estimate (or a representation) of missing information in terms of membership values. Therefore, fuzzy set theory can be incorporated in the handling of uncertainties (arising from deficiencies in the available information caused by, among others, incomplete, imprecise, ill-defined, not-fully-reliable, vague, and contradictory data and information) in various stages of a PRS. The utility of fuzzy sets for managing and representing the uncertainties that often arise while processing an image and designing a vision system will be described in Section 1.3E of this chapter.

In the paragraphs to follow, we discuss each of the four areas shown in Fig. 6, their relationship to each other, and their relationship to fuzzy models. We use a cartoon format to describe some of the most important considerations and choices that are associated with each of these four areas. The reader might imagine herself or himself in the situation of trying to construct a PRS by picking through the menus of an applications program for this purpose. The sequence of figures is arranged like a set of nested, interactive pull-down menus that lead one into successively deeper (and finer) levels in the development of the system. The reader may be surprised to see how many alternative routes exist in the production of a fielded system; along the way we try to integrate fuzzy approaches as a natural result of their apparent utility, rather than force them into the system because they exist. We give a few examples in this context, illustrating the usefulness of fuzzy models for handling uncertainties in various problems encountered in the design of a PRS. Figure 7 depicts the four areas of Fig. 6 as if they were first-level choices in the design program.

The first point to make in connection with Figs. 6 and 7 is that the four first-level nodes are not independent. Selection of a menu item at Level 2 under any of the bars in Fig. 7 may constrain or entail concurrent or derivative selections under the other three menus. Hence, these four root nodes are illustrated as being connected by a bus that carries information and data in both directions at all times. In the ideal world, perfect features make classifier design trivial; conversely, a universal classifier would give error-free performance with any set of features. In practice, however, the successful PRS is developed by iteratively revisiting each of

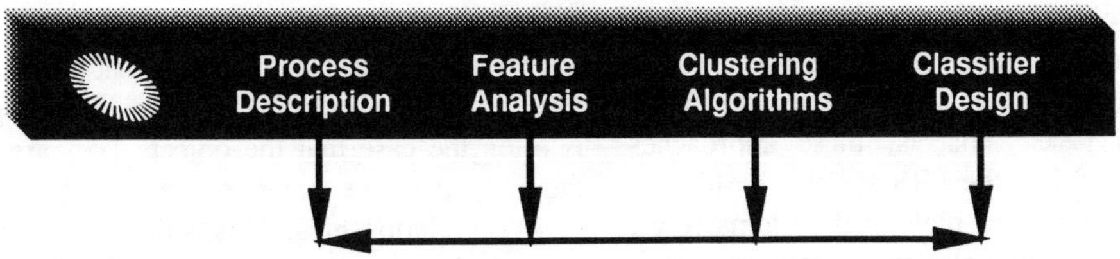

Fig. 7. Pattern recognition systems: Level 1.

the four major modules in Fig. 6 until the system satisfies (or is at least optimized for) a given set of performance requirements. Should there be a *fifth* Level 1 header bar entitled *Fuzzy Models*? No; fuzzy models provide a means for axiomatization of algorithms that attempt to solve problems under each of these headers, but they do not constitute a fundamentally new first level choice. Fuzzy models are a novel, promising, and possibly better approach toward solving certain problems that appear under each of the four Level 1 menu bars depicted in Fig. 7 but they do not, in and of themselves, constitute a new, major component of PRS design.

1.3.A Process Description

The first choice faced by the PRS designer concerns the way the process of interest will be represented for study. Very few authors write about this part of system design, and the papers collected in this volume treat the subject implicitly. Consequently, we will spend a little more time on this portion of system design in this Chapter than we will on the other three problem areas, which are well represented in the papers themselves. Figure 8 shows a menu bar that displays some of the typical items that must be considered during process description. This window itemizes a number of very important activities that must concern the designer of a fielded system and that are sometimes ignored by researchers

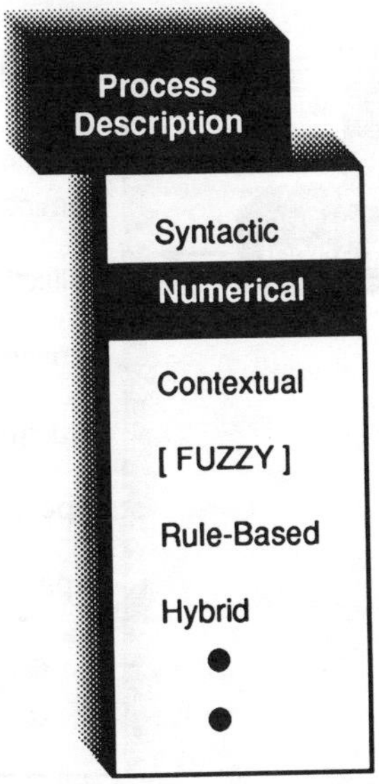

Fig. 8. Process description: Level 2.

interested in a particular algorithm or model. In pattern recognition, the usual situation is that the process is governed by, governs, or both, individual objects (possibly including as individuals the average over time of a large number of "real" individuals) and their relationships with each other. The most familiar choice is the representation of objects within the process by (sets of) numbers.

We might again ask, "should fuzzy models be included in Fig. 8 as a second level choice under process description?" Perhaps. We have shown this option as [FUZZY] to indicate that it is possible to begin system design with the intention of using fuzzy sets to describe the variables important to the process. However, as our intent is to describe fuzzy models as an option for numerical pattern recognition, we believe that a more basic choice is what data type, for example, will be the basis for system design.

Syntactic pattern recognition holds that algorithms ought to be able to decompose and reconstitute objects from representations of structural relationships between various parts of the object, much as humans apparently do [61]. Syntactic pattern recognition deals with representations of structure via sentences, grammar, and automata. Searching among such data is done by means of various kinds of parsing. The syntactic approach has incorporated the concept of fuzzy sets at two levels. First, the pattern primitives are themselves considered to be labels of fuzzy sets, that is, subpatterns such as "almost circular arcs," "gentle," "fair," and "sharp" curves are considered. Second, the structural relations among the subpatterns may be fuzzy, so that the formal grammar is "fuzzified" by weighted production rules, and the grade of membership of a string is obtained by min-max composition of the grades of the production used in the derivations. Inference of a fuzzy grammar is the problem of inferring the productions as well as the weights of these rules from the specified fuzzy language. Conventional (nonfuzzy) syntactic pattern recognition is not a mature technology; its theory is far more well developed than are fielded applications, so it is not particularly surprising that fuzzy models for the recognition of objects by structural decomposition and reconstitution has not played a dominant role in our thinking about practical models (cf., however, Papers 3.6 and 3.11 of this volume). Nonetheless, if we aim to build computers that can reason and perceive in a fashion at least roughly as humans do, the philosophical spirit engendered by this area of PRS design may be a ripe breeding ground for good ideas and the rapid development and utilization of the fuzzy logic approach.

Contextual, conceptual and rule-based approaches to

the solution of pattern recognition problems are attempts to add context, concept, and expert knowledge at some intermediate level of processing in order to capitalize on human expertise at recognition tasks. That is, these approaches attempt to capture and model in the PRS system the higher-level functions that we attribute to biological systems (e.g., human cognition, etc.). For example, the context of usage would enable prediction of the missing letter in the word "o_yx": "n" if appearing in a sentence about gemstones and "r" if in a sentence concerning antelopes. Efforts of this kind typically include elements of expert system design such as knowledge acquisition, representation, and manipulation. The systems we speak of here, however, are usually referred to as *low-level systems* because most of the processing and algorithms involve numerical data obtained from sensors, as opposed to higher-level "knowledge" or rules about how to reason with such data. Pao [44] makes the important point that the advent of symbolic processing, the basis for a large percentage of the artificial intelligence models used in this context, has driven a wedge between the low-level world engendered by conventional numerical pattern recognition and computational systems that try to model higher-level cognition in this way. Pao suggests that one of the main uses of fuzzy logic is to provide a bridge between low- and intermediate-level processing. Chapter 5 contains several papers that suggest that the impact of fuzzy pattern recognition on current trends in the use of computational neural networks (CNNs) for expert system design is an important and rapidly developing area.

Numerical Data. Generally speaking, two data structures are used in numerical PRSs: *object data* vectors (feature vectors, pattern vectors) and pairwise *relational data* (similarities, proximities). Object data, that is, sets of numerical vectors of features, are represented in the sequel as $X = \{\mathbf{x}_1, \mathbf{x}_2, \ldots, \mathbf{x}_n\}$, a set of (n) feature vectors in feature space $\mathcal{R}^p$. The jth object observed in the process (some physical entity such as a person, airplane, seismic record, photograph, etc.) has vector $\mathbf{x}_j$ as its numerical representation; $\mathbf{x}_{jk}$ is the kth characteristic (or feature) associated with object j. Object data for pattern recognition can be *labeled*, in which case the identity of each vector as belonging to one of several classes is known, or they can be *unlabeled* so that we have only the vectors themselves and, perhaps, some idea about the classes of objects they represent.

It may happen that, instead of an object data set X as described above, we have access to a set of (n^2) numerical relationships, say $\{r_{jk}\}$, between pairs of objects. That is, r_{jk} represents the extent to which objects j and k are related in the sense of some binary relation ρ. If the (n) objects that are pairwise related by ρ are called $O = \{o_1, o_2, \ldots, o_n\}$, then $\rho: O \times O \rightarrow \mathcal{R}$. It is convenient to array the relational values as an $(n \times n)$ relation matrix, $R = [r_{jk}] = [\rho(o_j, o_k)]$. R constitutes a set of *numerical relational data.* There are, as indicated in Fig. 6, two classes of relational data—natural and induced. Note several things about R. First, the objects $O = \{o_i\}$ can be anything whatsoever. In particular, they might be the physical objects that generate the numerical object data X alluded to above or they might be X itself. It is often the case that the objects $\{o_i\}$ are *implicit*—that is, the only data we have to work with is the matrix R of pairwise relationships. This is the case more often than not in numerical taxonomy, where relationships between species, families, and so on are given their numerical values by human experts, say $R = R(O;\ \eta)$, that is, $[r_{jk}] = [\eta(o_j, o_k)]$. We call η a *natural relation* to distinguish it from the other source of R, namely the derivation of R from X by some (dis)similarity function σ: $\mathcal{R}^p \times \mathcal{R}^p \rightarrow \mathcal{R}$, whereby $R = R(X;\ \sigma)$, that is, $[r_{jk}] = [\sigma(\mathbf{x}_j, \mathbf{x}_k)]$. In this case R is induced on O by σ, so we call it an *induced relation.* Many functions (σ) will convert X into relational data of this kind. For example, every metric d on $\mathcal{R}^p \times \mathcal{R}^p$ produces a (dis)similarity matrix $R(X;\ d)$ where we take $(\sigma = d)$. Relational data are to be found in many applications and systems, perhaps hiding in different semantic guises. For example, cognitive maps, influence diagrams, weighted digraphs, repertory grids, personal construct theory, and fuzzy relations all have this general form. Fuzzy models for pattern recognition problems associated with natural and induced relational data are fairly well developed; several papers in this collection illustrate how various fuzzy techniques are used to solve pattern recognition problems that involve relational data.

Each of the second level choices under "Process Description" in Fig. 8 might give rise to a different third-level menu. Selecting "numerical" as in Fig. 8 might lead to the choices displayed in Fig. 9. The performance of any PRS depends on the data used in the system, so choices made here certainly affect downstream performance. Sometimes there is little that the PRS designer can do about one of these third level choices (e.g., one must use sensors that are both available and affordable). The designer must try to ensure that each

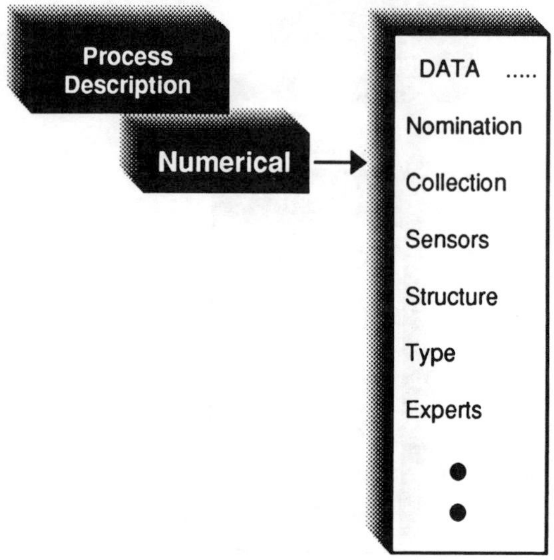

Fig. 9. Process description: Level 3.

choice is given careful thought with a view toward the overall design of the system. Sensors, for example, will produce data according to their physical characteristics. Important side issues about sensors include their reliability, cost, size, weight, and, most important for the PRS, whether they produce data that increases the overall effectiveness of the system.

1.3.B Feature Analysis

Feature analysis refers to a collection of methods that are used to explore and improve raw data, that is, the data that are nominated and collected during process description. With but few exceptions this problem area assumes the data to be object data (i.e., feature vectors). Fig. 10 shows both second and third level menus that might pop up under "Feature Analysis."

Preprocessing includes operations such as scaling, normalization, smoothing and various other "clean-up" techniques. Fuzzy models are sometimes used for these purposes, especially in fields like image processing, where problems such as blurring, noise, low contrast, and obscuration can be dealt with in a variety of ways. The utility of data for more complex downstream processing tasks such as clustering and classifier design is clearly affected by preprocessing operations, so this step in the design of a PRS is always important and should be given careful attention.

Extraction and 2-D Display techniques for object data can be cast in a single framework: any function $f_E: \mathscr{R}^p \to \mathscr{R}^q$ where $p \geq q$ is a feature extractor when applied to X. The new features are the image of X under f_E, say $Y = f_E[X]$. Feature *selection*, choosing subsets of the original measured features, is done by taking f_E to be a projection onto some coordinate subspace of $\mathscr{R}^p$.

The basic idea is that feature space can be compressed by eliminating, via selection or transformation, redundant (dependent) and unimportant (for the problem at hand) features. If $p \gg q$, time and space complexity of algorithms that use the transformed data are obviously reduced in the process. Extraction techniques can be divided into analytic (closed form for f_E) versus algorithmic; and linear versus nonlinear. Figure 10 shows some of the popular third level choices under this branch of our PRS design tree. Note that fuzzy models appear here both for general feature extraction and for 2-D display. We will highlight some of the important work in this area in Chapter 3.

2-D Display, the visual representation of d-dimensional data in a viewing plane is a way to explore structure in, and get ideas about, the measured data. Methods for 2-D display fall into two general categories: scatterplots and pictorial displays. When $q = 2$, the transformed data set Y can be displayed as a scatter diagram for visual inspection. All of the methods itemized in Fig. 10 can be used to produce 2-D scatterplots by taking $q = 2$. The other class of display techniques use analytic or algorithmic transformations of the data that result in Y being some sort of pictorial representation of X. Included in this category are, for example, Chernoff Faces, Andrews plots, Stars, Icicles, Castles, and Kohonen's Feature Maps.

What can one learn from a 2-D display of multidimen-

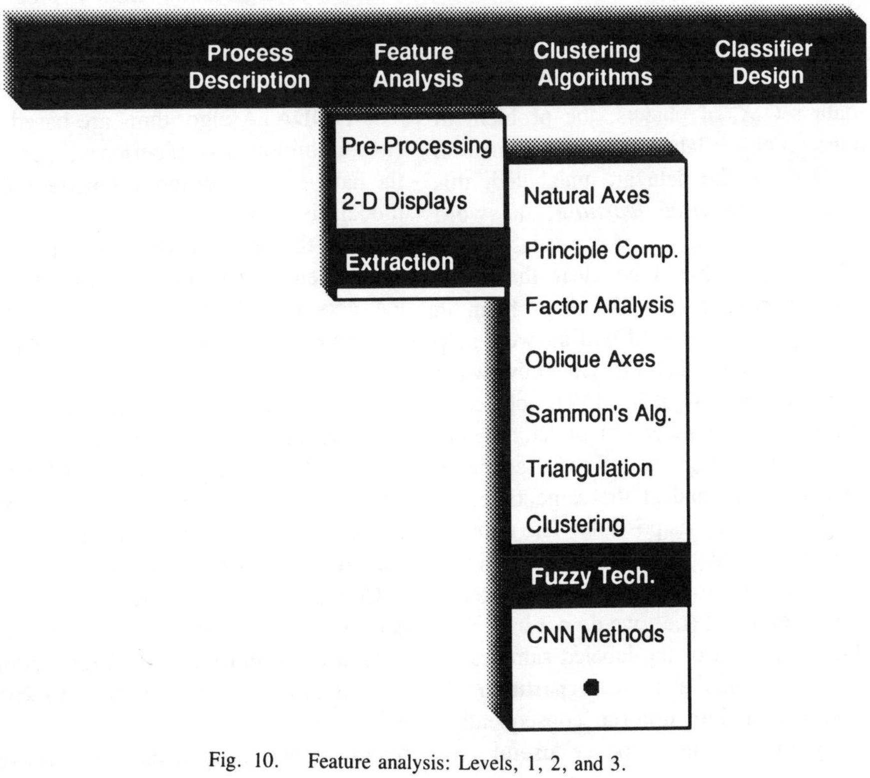

Fig. 10. Feature analysis: Levels, 1, 2, and 3.

sional data? According to Tukey [57], displays of this type are useful because, "It is important to learn what you CAN DO before you learn to measure how WELL you seem to have DONE it." Put simply, 2-D displays and diagrams afford a means for "looking" at data to see what they *seem* to say, as opposed to *confirming* from and with the data what we hold to be true about the process under study. This branch of data analysis seems to many to be a bit removed from the mainstream of pattern recognition, although designers of fielded PRSs have long since recognized the importance of the oft quoted, "keep it simple—but only as simple as it needs to be." Looking at 2-D displays of multidimensional data enables us to cast hypotheses, postulate models, reject theories; in short, get *ideas* about the data, how the data seem to be structured, what cannot be true, etc. One need look no further than Kohonen's self-organizing feature map idea, which is a 2-D Display technique that enables us to see how data seem to be structured and how this algorithm organizes its prototypes to reflect this structure to find the influence of computational neural-like network (CNN) thinking in this area. Interestingly enough, Kohonen's algorithmic technique is clearly related to the so-called hard and fuzzy ISODATA (or hard and fuzzy *c*-means) algorithms. In fact, ISODATA is an acronym for *iterative, self-organizing data analysis techniques A* [62]. Thus, this area of numerical pattern recognition is closely connected by a long history to one branch of current studies about computational neural models, namely Kohonen's self organizing clustering and feature mapping schemes. There is a rich and largely undiscovered mathematical connection between the work of Kohonen and the c-means clustering algorithms [63]. Several papers in Chapter 5 will pursue this connection.

1.3.C Cluster Analysis

Given any finite data set X of objects, the problem of clustering in X is to assign object labels that identify natural subgroups in the set. Because the data are unlabeled, this problem is often called *unsupervised learning*, the word *learning* here referring to learning the correct labels for "good" subgroups. In turn, it should be clear that good subgroups implies that we have a question or problem in mind that finding subgroups of some kind will answer, help describe the process, etc.—that is, that we will know when we have good subgroups for the task at hand. The objective is to partition X into a certain number (c) of natural and homogeneous subsets, where the elements of each set are as similar as possible to each other and at the same time, as different from those of the other sets as possible. The number (c) can be fixed beforehand, or may result as a consequence of physical or mathematical constraints. Because the technique of clustering is nonsupervised (i.e., we do not have any information on the class structures or the labeled samples of the classes), clustering algorithms attempt to partition X based on certain assumptions and/or criteria; consequently, algorithmic outputs may or may not produce useful and meaningful interpretations of structure in the data. Typical applications include image segmentation and remote sensing (e.g., LANDSAT) data analysis. For example, the number (c) of regions is taken to be unknown while segmenting (multithresholding) an image into meaningful, homogeneous subimages. The subimages can be characterized by, for example, the criteria of maximum contrast between regions, maximum homogeneity within a region, significant cluster dimension, etc. Therefore, the output partition, which includes both the number of classes (c) and the class membership structures, are dependent on the criteria that are used to control the clustering algorithm.

Example 4: Let $X = \{\text{Father, Mother, Daughter, Son}\}$, a group of four objects. Suppose that for this data set, the father has brown eyes and the mother, son, and daughter have blue eyes; that the mother has type A blood, the father and daughter have type O blood, and the son has type B blood. Depending on the criterion we select to define clusters, we will get the various hard subsets or natural groups in X shown in Fig. 11. Note especially that there are different and yet "correct" clusters at $c = 1$, 2, 3 and 4; there are also different correct clusters at, for example, $c = 2$. Thus, the criterion that defines the clusters is all-important for determining the optimality of the solution.

Many algorithms have been developed to obtain hard clusters from a given data set, such as those illustrated in Fig. 11. Among those, the *c*-means algorithms and their generalizations, the ISODATA clustering methods, are probably the most widely used. The *c*-means algorithms assume that c is known, whereas c is unknown in the case of the ISODATA algorithms. Both approaches are iterative. Hard *c*-means is based on the minimization of a performance index (i.e., the sum of squared distances from all points in each hard partitioning subset to the cluster center of the subset). The ISODATA algorithms are based on combining heuristic (i.e., intuition and experience) performance measures with the hard *c*-means criterion function. The performance of both models is influenced by the choice of c, the initial cluster centers, the order in which the samples are taken as input (in the sequential versions), the choice of distance measure, and the geometrical properties of the data. Data that exhibit compact, well-separated clusters with hyperspherical shapes are amenable to these methods but practice, extensive trial and error experiments with various values of c, distance, termination criteria, the initial cluster centers, and different orderings of samples are needed in order to find "good" natural groupings. In practice, then, the performance of any cluster-seeking algorithm depends in no small way on the cleverness of its designers and users.

Conventional clustering techniques assume that an object can belong to one and only one class. In practice, the separation of clusters is a fuzzy notion (e.g., nectarines are hybrids of peaches and plums, and will share some characteristics of both parents) and hence the concept of fuzzy subsets offers special advantages over conventional clustering by

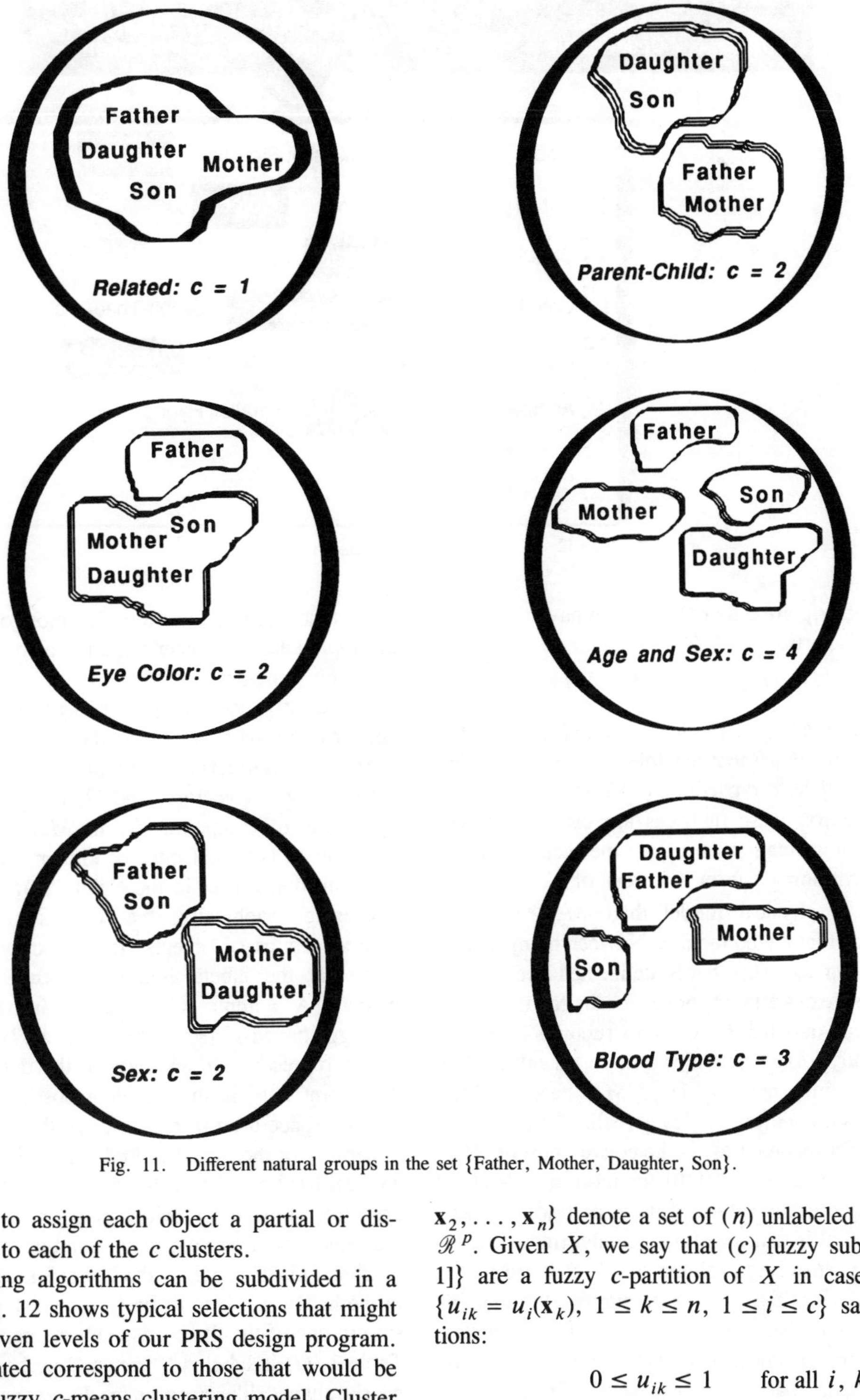

Fig. 11. Different natural groups in the set {Father, Mother, Daughter, Son}.

allowing algorithms to assign each object a partial or distributed membership to each of the c clusters.

Numerical clustering algorithms can be subdivided in a number of ways. Fig. 12 shows typical selections that might appear in the first seven levels of our PRS design program. The choices highlighted correspond to those that would be selected to use the fuzzy c-means clustering model. Cluster analysis is a large field, both within fuzzy sets and beyond it. The papers reprinted in Chapter 2 on fuzzy approaches to clustering are but a small fraction of the articles that have appeared in this area. The reason for this is that fuzzy partitions of finite data sets endow solutions to this problem with an intuitively satisfying philosophical structure. To help the reader to understand this, a brief exposition of fuzzy partition spaces follows.

Let (c) be an integer, $1 < c < n$ and let $X = \{\mathbf{x}_1, \mathbf{x}_2, \ldots, \mathbf{x}_n\}$ denote a set of (n) unlabeled feature vectors in $\mathcal{R}^p$. Given X, we say that (c) fuzzy subsets $\{u_i: X \to [0, 1]\}$ are a fuzzy c-partition of X in case the (cn) values $\{u_{ik} = u_i(\mathbf{x}_k),\ 1 \le k \le n,\ 1 \le i \le c\}$ satisfy three conditions:

$$0 \le u_{ik} \le 1 \quad \text{for all } i, k; \tag{7a}$$

$$\Sigma u_{ik} = 1 \quad \text{for all } k; \tag{7b}$$

$$0 < \Sigma u_{ik} < n \quad \text{for all } i. \tag{7c}$$

Each set of (cn) values satisfying conditions (7a–c) can be arrayed as a $(c \times n)$ matrix $U = [u_{ik}]$. The set of all such matrices is the *nondegenerate fuzzy c-partitions* of X:

$$M_{fcn} = \{U \text{ in } \mathcal{R}^{cn} \mid u_{ik} \text{ satisfies (7a–c) for all } i \text{ and } k\}. \tag{8}$$

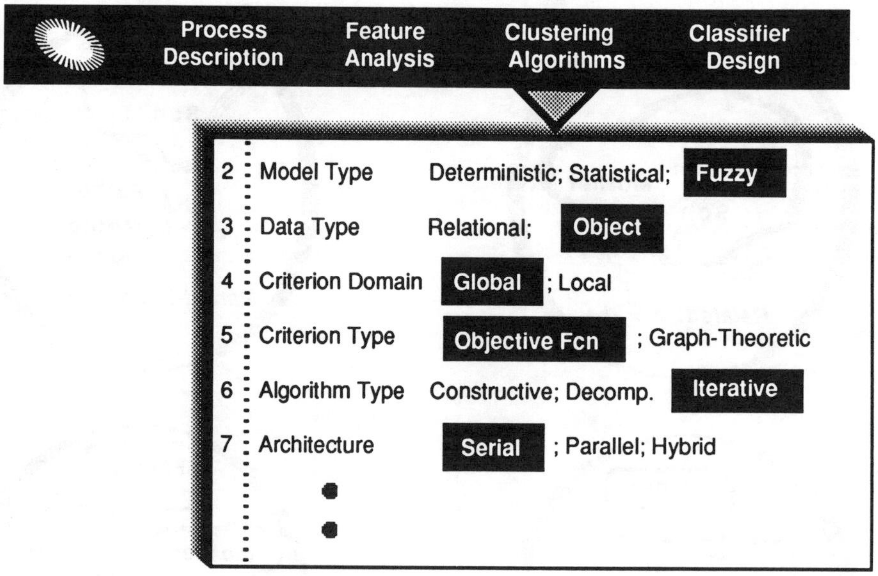

Fig. 12. Cluster analysis: Levels 1 to 7.

And in case *all* the u_{ik} are either 0 or 1, we have the subset of hard (or crisp) c-partitions of X:

$$M_{cn} = \{U \text{ in } M_{fcn} \mid u_{ik} = 0 \text{ or } 1 \text{ for all } i \text{ and } k\} \quad (9)$$

Ruspini introduced M_{fcn} in 1969; his seminal work in this area paved the way for much that has followed [58]. M_{cn} is a subset of M_{fcn}: every hard c-partition of X is fuzzy, but not conversely. The reason these matrices are called partitions follows from the interpretation of u_{ik} as the membership of $\mathbf{x}_k$ in the ith partitioning subset (cluster) of X. M_{fcn} is more realistic as a physical model than M_{cn}, for it is common experience that the boundaries between many classes of real objects are in fact very badly delineated (i.e., really fuzzy), so M_{fcn} provides a much richer means for representing and manipulating data that have such structures than does M_{cn}. Mathematically, M_{fcn} provides a more tractable set to work with than the finite but very large M_{cn} because M_{fcn} (actually, M_{fcno}, the superset of M_{fcn} realized by relaxing (7c) to have nonstrict inequalities) is the convex hull of M_{cn}. Interested readers should consult [40] for more details about the algebraic and geometric nature of these partition spaces.

The important point is that *all* clustering algorithms generate solutions to the clustering problem for X that are matrices in M_{fcn}. Clustering in X, is, quite simply, the identification of an "optimal" partition U of X in M_{fcn}—that is, one that groups together object data vectors (and, hence, the objects they represent) that share some well-defined, mathematical similarity. It is our hope and implicit belief, of course, that an optimal mathematical grouping is in some sense an accurate portrayal of natural groupings in the physical process from whence the object data are derived. We mention that (c) is assumed to be known; otherwise, its value becomes a part of the clustering problem. This facet of the problem is often called the *cluster validity* question; its resolution is also the focus of a large and active research community. Several of the papers in Chapter 2 recognize the importance of this question, but most of the work to date in *all* approaches to cluster validity has been, at best, somewhat heuristic in nature.

Apparently, two things are needed in order to make the clustering problem for object data well defined: (1) a measure (direct or indirect) of similarity between groups, usually pairs, of object vectors; and (2) a criterion that assesses the optimality of competing Us in M_{fcn}. As previously noted, the value of (c) itself must be known, of course, in order that one can look for U in the "right" M_{fcn}. Figure 13 depicts clustering graphically; the idea is simple—put labels on natural groups of objects. In the bottom half of the figure, note that the labels assigned to the objects are "hard," namely, A = apple, O = orange, and P = pear, except for the egg-shaped object, which has a (?) assigned to it. This object represents an anomaly in the data—perhaps a lemon. The point here is that all data possess troublesome points, and the space used to characterize the solution greatly affects the ability of the model to find and deal with data of this type. Typical hard and fuzzy 3-partitions for the objects in Fig. 13 are shown in Table 1, which is arranged so that all objects of the same type are in adjacent columns.

Object (?) is shown as the last column of each partition and in the hard case, it must be (erroneously) given full membership in one of the three crisp subsets partitioning this data. In Table 1, (?) is labeled "orange," perhaps because it is most nearly shaped like an orange. Fuzzy partitions enable algorithms to (sometimes!) avoid such mistakes. The final column of the fuzzy partition in Table 1 allocates most (0.60) of the membership of (?) to the orange class; but also assigns a lesser membership to (?) as a pear, and even less as an apple. Columns of this kind in fuzzy partitions serve a useful purpose—fuzzy memberships in several classes are a signal to take a second look. Hard partitions of data cannot suggest this. Thus, the fuzzy model provides a richer and more flexible solution structure, one that models the real objects

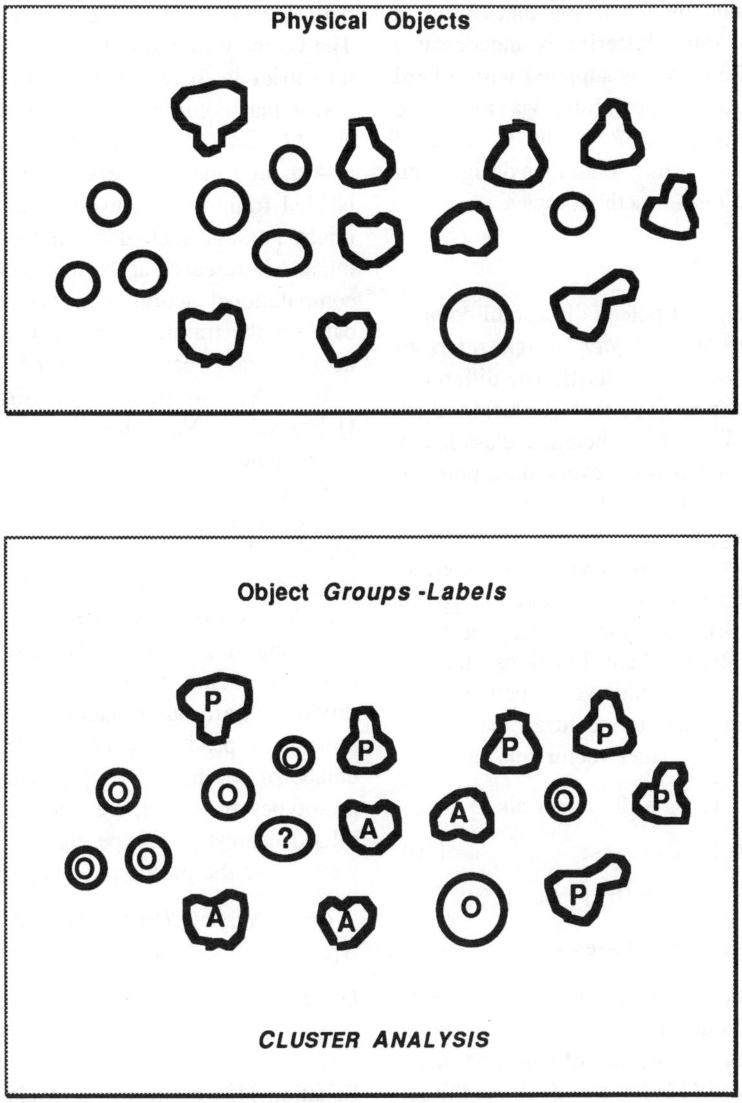

Fig. 13. Cluster analysis.

TABLE 1
HARD AND FUZZY 3-PARTITIONS OF THE OBJECT DATA IN FIG. 13

	Hard U in M_{cn}			? ↓	Fuzzy U in M_{fcn}			? ↓
A	1111	0000000	000000	0	1 . . . 0.95	0.0 . . . 0	0 0.1 . . . 0	0.15
O	0000	1111111	000000	1	0 . . . 0.05	0.8 . . . 1	0 0.2 . . . 0	0.60
P	0000	0000000	111111	0	0 . . . 0.00	0.2 . . . 0	1 0.7 . . . 1	0.25

with a finer degree of detail than the harshness that crisp models impose on the problem. Note also that some columns of the fuzzy partition are hard; these correspond to objects in the data that some labeling algorithm is certain about. We reiterate that the entries in the fuzzy matrix are not probabilities; they are similarities of individual object vectors to class paradigms. Finally, it is appropriate to note that there are many statistical clustering algorithms (e.g., unsupervised learning with maximum likelihood [39]) that usually produce solutions in M_{fcn}.

It is possible, and there are a few statistical approaches to clustering that do this, to relax constraint (7b) so that the sum of memberships (or probabilties, as the case may be) is not required to be 1. Thus, our (?) in Table 1 might receive memberships of 0.6, 0.4, and 0.4 in the three classes. This is a natural and physically appealing extension of M_{fcn} to an even larger solution space for clustering.

Numerical relational data as discussed above can also be the basis for cluster analysis. This branch of pattern recognition finds many adherents in fields such as, for example, numerical taxonomy (cf. [64]). In this case, clustering objects is accomplished implicitly by clustering groups of indices in the relational data matrix. Clustering numerical relational data with fuzzy models is less well studied than object data, perhaps because of the fact that sensors produce object data and most fielded systems are at least partially dependent on inputs from sensors. The solution space for relational clustering is still M_{fcn} and our remarks above about fuzzy partitions of the data are equally applicable in this case. Several papers in Chapter 2 approach this problem from the fuzzy viewpoint.

We conclude this subsection by remarking that X_L is a labeled data set of n_L points (and clustering is unnecessary) precisely when, and only when, X_L is supplied with a hard c-partition U_L whose kth column exhibits, via the value $u_{L,ik} = 1$, the label of $\mathbf{x}_k$ to be (i) for $k = 1$ to n_L. Labeled data are useful for supervised learning (classifier design) and for testing the validity of clustering methodologies.

1.3.D Classifier Design

A more ambitious, difficult, and potentially useful computational problem than clustering, *classifier design* refers to finding a hard or fuzzy partition of $\mathscr{R}^p$ itself. The difference between clustering and classification is that clustering algorithms label given data sets $X \subset \mathscr{R}^p$, whereas a classifier is capable, once it is defined, of labelling *every* data point in the entire space $\mathscr{R}^p$. Classifiers are usually—*but not always*—designed with labeled data, in which case we sometimes refer to this problem as *supervised learning* (in this context we are learning the parameters of a classifier function $\underline{\mathbf{D}}$). In either case, the partitioning decision functions may be computationally *explicit* (e.g., discriminant functions, nearest prototype rules) or *implicit* (e.g., multilayered perceptrons, k-nearest neighbor rules). To characterize fuzzy classifiers, we first define the hard and fuzzy label vector sets in $\mathscr{R}^c$:

$$N_c = \{\mathbf{y} \in \mathscr{R}^c \mid \Sigma y_k = 1;\ y_k \in \{0, 1\} \text{ for all } j\}$$
$$= \text{hard label vectors for } c \text{ classes}; \tag{10}$$

$$N_{fc} = \{\mathbf{y} \in \mathscr{R}^c \mid \Sigma y_k = 1;\ y_k \in [0, 1] \text{ for all } j\}$$
$$= \text{fuzzy label vectors for } c \text{ classes}. \tag{11}$$

N_c is just the usual canonical basis of Euclidean c-space, and N_{fc} is its convex hull. As usual, we have the imbedding $N_c \subset N_{fc}$. Figure 14 is a sketch of the sets of hard and fuzzy label vectors defined in (10) and (11) for $c = 3$. N_3 is the set of three vertices of the triangular portion of the hyperplane defined by (11): $N_3 = \{\mathbf{e}_1, \mathbf{e}_2, \mathbf{e}_3\}$. N_{f3} is the triangle itself. The vector $\mathbf{y}$ shown in Fig. 14 is a typical fuzzy label vector; its entries lie between 0 and 1, and sum to 1. Readers will notice that columns of hard and fuzzy c-partitions $U \in M_c$ and M_{fc} are column vectors from N_c and N_{fc}, respectively.

Although most readers are unfamiliar with the concept of labeled training data itself being fuzzy, it is clear that one might possess such data. Indeed, a topic of great current interest in research at the interface between fuzzy models and computational neural networks is the use of fuzzily labeled data for the training portion of the design of a CNN classifier. Several papers in Chapter 5 utilize or relate to this idea.

With N_{fc}, we define a *classifier* on $\mathscr{R}^p$ as any function $\underline{\mathbf{D}}$ imaged in N_{fc}. That is, classifiers are a special kind of vector field, which we shall denote as $\underline{\mathbf{D}}: \mathscr{R}^p \to N_{fc} \subset \mathscr{R}^c$. Thus, the value of $\underline{\mathbf{D}}$ at any $\mathbf{x} \in \mathscr{R}^p$ is $\mathbf{y} = \underline{\mathbf{D}}(\mathbf{x})$, the label vector for $\mathbf{x}$ in N_{fc}. With this notation, we say that $\underline{\mathbf{D}}$ is a *crisp* (or hard, or conventional) *classifier* if and only if the image of $\mathscr{R}^p$ under $\underline{\mathbf{D}}$ is N_c ($\underline{\mathbf{D}}[\mathscr{R}^p] = N_c$); otherwise, the classifier is fuzzy. Readers should distinguish carefully between the ideas of input data having fuzzy labels, outputs of classifiers being fuzzy labels, and models that are fuzzy producing hard output labels. For example, we can use fuzzy c-means to produce a set of c prototype vectors $\{\mathbf{v}_k\}$ for an unlabeled (or labeled) input data set X in $\mathscr{R}^p$. Once the prototypes are found, we can subsequently use them to define a hard nearest prototype classifier in the usual way, that is, we can use the prototypes $\{\mathbf{v}_k\}$ to define $\underline{\mathbf{D}}$ as follows:

Crisp Nearest Prototype (1-NP) Classifier. Given prototypes $\{\mathbf{v}_k \mid 1 < k \leq c\}$ and $\mathbf{x} \in \mathscr{R}^p$:

$$\text{Decide } \mathbf{x} \in i \Leftrightarrow \mathbf{e}_i = \underline{\mathbf{D}}(e, x) \Leftrightarrow \|\mathbf{x} - \mathbf{v}_i\| \leq \|\mathbf{x} - \mathbf{v}_k\| : \quad 1 \leq k \leq c \tag{12}$$

Equation (12) defines a hard classifier, even though its parameters come from a fuzzy algorithm. It would be careless

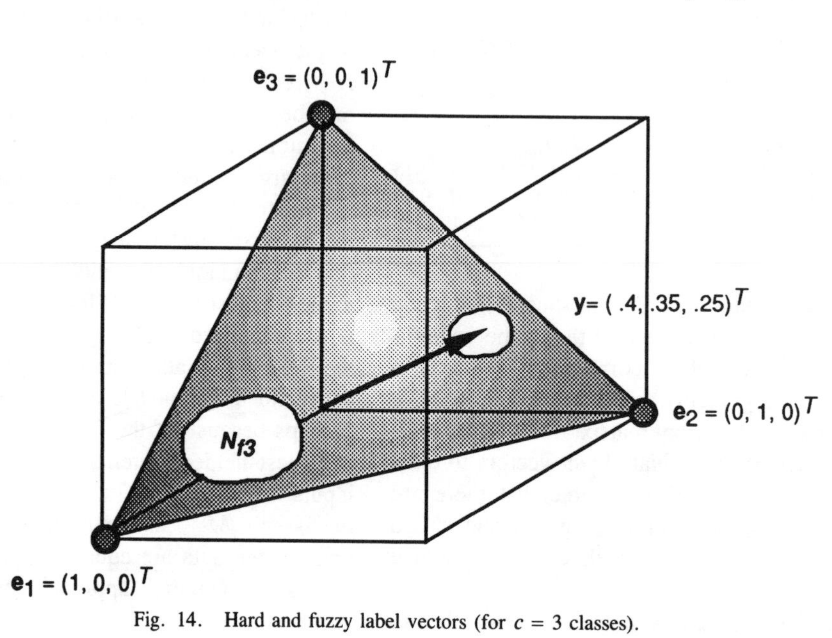

Fig. 14. Hard and fuzzy label vectors (for $c = 3$ classes).

to call $\underline{\mathbf{D}}$ in (12) a fuzzy classifier, because (12) can be implemented and has the same geometric structure, using a set of prototypes $\{\mathbf{v}_k\}$ from any clustering algorithm that produces them. For example, $\{\mathbf{v}_k\}$ can be the weight vectors attached to the nodes in the competitive layer of a Kohonen clustering network, or they can be estimates of (c) assumed mean vectors $\{\mu_k\}$ obtained by applying, for example, unsupervised maximum likelihood estimation from statistical mixture theory to unlabeled data, or they can be the centroids or crisply labeled data, and so on. While there is a certain amount of semantic hair-splitting in drawing attention to this fact, we feel it is worth pointing out because fielded pattern recognition systems inevitably require hard labels for objects being classified. One must, therefore, at some point in any design that uses the idea of fuzzy sets, reconcile this need with the fuzzy model that is being used. Most of the papers in Chapter 3 eventually ''defuzzify'' fuzzy label vectors (if this is what the classifier produces). Thus, *fuzzy classifier design* almost always means arriving at a hard classifier such as (12), but uses the idea of fuzziness somewhere upstream. Readers may wonder, given the ultimate necessity for hard labels, whether there is any advantage to using fuzzy techniques at all. The papers reprinted in Chapter 3 show, through computational examples, that incorporation of fuzzy ideas in the model leading to a hard classifier design do indeed (sometimes!) yield better hard classifiers than those that result from simply looking for a hard design to begin with. This can again be atrributed to the idea of imbedding: we find a better solution to a crisp problem by looking in a larger space at first, which has different (usually less) constraints and therefore allows the algorithm more freedom to avoid errors forced by commission to hard answers in intermediate stages. This idea and corroborating evidence for it are well documented in the papers in Chapter 3.

Figure 15 shows the same object set as Fig. 13, with boundaries that enclose each set of labeled objects. The *classifier* is the set of decision regions or, equivalently, their boundaries. The regions shown in Fig. 15 are crisp (that is, the boundaries subdivide feature space into crisply labeled regions), so this is a schematic depiction of a hard classifier. Object (?) has been arbitrarily placed in the oranges region for the purpose of illustration; alternatively, one can set up a no decision region for objects that do not seem to fit into any of the design categories. Note that the apples are in two noncontiguous regions. Also shown in Fig. 15 is an orange that happens to lie in the lower apple region. This exemplifies a hard classifier mistake because the orange will automatically receive an apple label, having landed in part of the decision region for apples.

Like clustering, there are many ways to categorize classifier designs. Figure 16 depicts possible windows for the first few levels of classifier design. The highlighted selections shown in Fig. 16 could yield, for example, a next level window for Bayesian classifier design or the k-nearest neighbor rule. There are so many algorithms that fit into each selection set in this figure that it seems impossible to attempt a listing that is worthwhile. Rather, the important point here is that each of these choices produces a different classifier function $\underline{\mathbf{D}}$ and, subsequently, a (possibly) very different solution to a particular classification problem.

1.3.E Image Processing and Machine Vision

While the application of fuzzy sets in cluster analysis and classifier design was in the process of development, an important and related effort in fuzzy image processing was evolving more or less in parallel with the general developments outlined above. This evolution was based on the

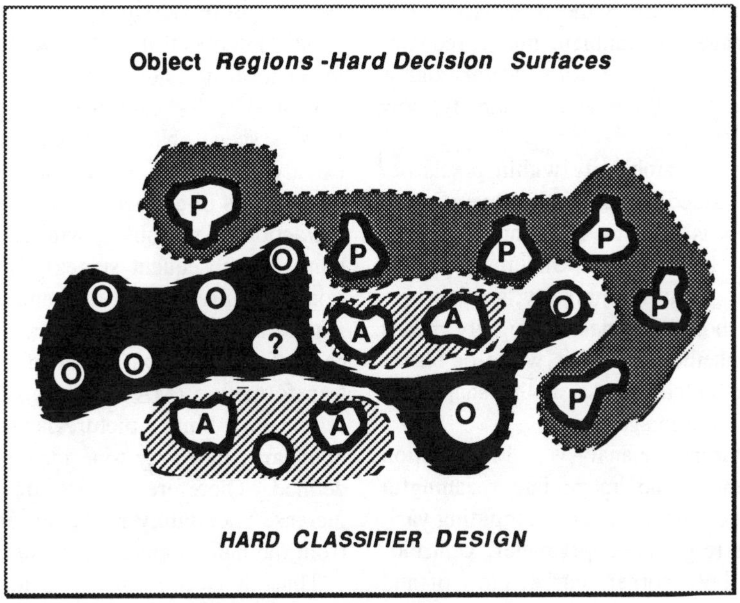

Fig. 15. (Hard) classifier design.

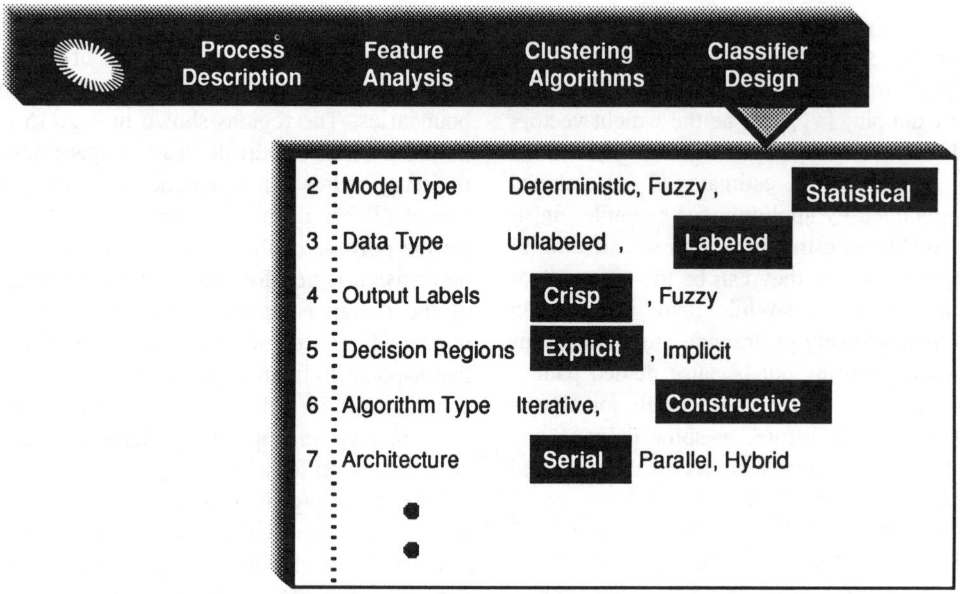

Fig. 16. Classifier design: Levels 1 to 7.

realization that many of the basic concepts in image analysis (e.g., the concept of an edge or a corner or a relation between regions) do not lend themselves well to precise definition. Chapter 4 will address this special branch of fuzzy numerical pattern recognition. This section gives a brief characterization of problems in this application domain and how they relate to the fuzzy models described above. When the input is a gray tone image, the measurement space usually involves processing tasks such as enhancement, filtering, noise reduction, segmentation, contour extraction, and skeleton extraction in order to derive salient features from the image pattern (these operations are a particular instance of feature analysis—see Section 1.3.B of this chapter). This is what is generally known as *image processing*. The ultimate aim is to use data contained in the image to enable the system to understand, recognize, and interpret the processed information available in the image. A complete image recognition/interpretation system is called a *vision system* and is usually viewed as consisting of three levels, namely, low level, mid level, and high level.

A gray tone image possesses ambiguity within pixels because of the possible multivalued levels of brightness in the image. This indeterminacy is due to inherent vagueness rather than to randomness. Incertitude in an image pattern can be explained in terms of grayness ambiguity, spatial (i.e., geometrical) ambiguity, or both. Grayness ambiguity means indefiniteness in deciding whether a pixel is white or black. Spatial ambiguity refers to indefiniteness in the shape and geometry of a region within the image.

Conventional approaches to image analysis and recognition [65, 66] consist of segmenting the image into meaningful regions, extracting their edges and skeletons, computing various features and properties (e.g., area, perimeter, centroid, etc.) and primitives (e.g., line, corner, curve, etc.) of and relationships among the regions, and finally, developing decision rules/grammars for describing, interpreting and/or classifying the image and its subregions. In a conventional system each of these operations involves crisp decisions (i.e., yes or no, black or white, 0 or 1) to make regions, features, primitives, properties, relations, and interpretations crisp.

Because the regions in an image are not always crisply defined, uncertainty can arise within every phase of the aforesaid tasks. Any decision made at a particular level will have an impact on all higher-level activities. A recognition or vision system should have sufficient provision for representing and manipulating the uncertainties involved at every processing stage (i.e., in defining image regions, features, matching, and relations among them) so that the system retains as much of the information content of the data as possible. If this is done, the ultimate output (result) of the system will possess minimal uncertainty (and, unlike conventional systems, it may not be biased or affected as much by lower-level decision components).

Consider, for example, the problem of object extraction from a scene. Now the question is, "how can one define exactly the target or object region in a scene when its boundary is ill-defined?" Any hard thresholding made for the extraction of the object will propagate the associated uncertainty to subsequent stages (e.g., thinning, skeleton extraction, primitive selection) and this, in turn, might affect feature analysis and recognition. Consider, for example, the case of skeleton extraction of a region through medial axis transformation (MAT). The medial axis transformation of a region in a binary picture is determined with respect to its boundary. In a gray tone image, the boundaries are not well defined. Therefore, errors are likely (and, hence, further increase uncertainty in the system), if we compute the MAT from the hard-segmented version of the image.

Thus, it is convenient, natural, and appropriate to avoid commission to a specific hard decision (e.g., segmentation/thresholding, edge detection, and skeletonization), by allowing the segments, skeletons, or contours to be fuzzy subsets of the image, the subsets being characterized by the possibility or degree to which each pixel belongs to them. Similarly, for describing and interpreting ill-defined structural information in a pattern, it is natural to define primitives (line, corner, curve, etc.) and relations among them using labels of fuzzy sets. For example, primitives that do not lend themselves to precise definition can be defined in terms of arcs with varying grades of membership from 0 to 1 representing their degree of belonging to more than one class. The production rules of a grammar can similarly be fuzzified to account for the fuzziness or imprecisenesss in physical relations among the primitives, thereby increasing the generative power of a grammar for syntactic recognition of a pattern.

Image Definition: An image X of size $M \times N$ with L intensity levels available for each of its MN pixels $\{x_{ij}\}$ can be considered as an array of fuzzy singletons, each having a value of membership denoting its degree of brightness relative to some brightness level λ, $\lambda = 0, 1, 2, \ldots L - 1$. We let $\{m_X(x_{ij}) \mid x_{ij} \in X\}$, where $m_X(x_{ij})$, $0 \leq m_X(x_{ij}) \leq 1$, denotes the extent to which each pixel possesses some property m_x (e.g., brightness, edginess, smoothness), or the degree of belongingness to some image subset (e.g., object, skeleton, or contour) by each pixel x_{ij}. In other words, a fuzzy subset m of an image X is, as it must be, a mapping m from X into [0, 1]. For any point $x_{ij} \in X$; $m(x_{ij})$ is called the degree of membership of x_{ij} in m. (Note that an ordinary subset of X can be regarded as a fuzzy subset for which m takes on only the values of 0 and 1.)

One can use either global or local information in an image to define membership functions characterizing various image properties. For example, brightness or darkness can be defined only in terms of the gray value of a pixel whereas edginess or textural properties need neighborhood information about a pixel to define their membership functions. Similarly, positional or coordinate information is necessary, in addition to gray level and neighborhood information, to characterize dynamic properties of an image. Membership functions that represent various fuzzy properties of images can be used in a number of ways; the papers in Chapter 4 explore many alternatives of this kind.

Basic principles and operations of image processing and recognition in the light of fuzzy set theory are available in [37]. The papers reprinted in Chapter 4 describe these issues in the context of image processing operations, ambiguity/information measures and quantitative evaluation, computing fuzzy geometrical properties, and describing/representing uncertainties in various operations and their applications.

1.3.F Computational Neural Networks

The last chapter in this volume contains papers that attempt to integrate fuzzy modeling concepts into a class of algorithms called computational neural-like networks (CNNs); conversely, there are several papers that use CNNs as part of a fuzzy model for pattern recognition. Most of these papers are very recent and in this regard we are abandoning the milestone concept to some extent because this is current research. It remains to be seen whether these papers will, over time, retain the importance they seem to have today (indeed, one can make the same assertion about CNNs and fuzzy models themselves). Nonetheless, the interface between neural models and fuzzy logic is growing rapidly at this writing, so it seems appropriate to conclude this volume with contemporary work that brings the reader to the forefront of current research in fuzzy pattern recognition.

Even a cursory glance at the contents of, for example, proceedings of a recent *International Joint Conferences on Neural Networks* (IJCNN) indicates a wide ranging interest in CNNs for solving a variety of computational problems. For example, CNNs are being used for signal and image processing of data generated by sonar, radar, ladar, infrared, and color video sensors for machine vision; robotics; and speech, character, and target recognition. Other areas exploring the problem-solving potential of CNN technologies include (to name a few) medical diagnosis, decision theory, numerical analysis, optimization, dynamic control, partial differential equations, cognitive systems, psychometry, econometrics, and various facets of expert system design. In many of these applications the CNN is asked to perform one or more of several well-known pattern recognition tasks.

The relationship between the four major areas of numerical pattern recognition (process description, feature analysis, clustering, and classifier design) and CNNs has been muddied by some misconceptions about what CNNs can and cannot be expected to do. Overviews that partially explain these relationships can be found in the excellent comparative survey by Lippman [68]. Pao [44] and Kosko [69] discuss various means for exploiting the potential interaction between fuzzy logic and CNNs as they are applied to numerical pattern recognition. Because the use of CNNs in pattern recognition is relatively new, we have decided to include Lippman's survey as the first paper in Chapter 5, even though it contains no discussion of the interface between fuzzy pattern recognition and CNNs. It is our hope that the inclusion of this paper will provide readers with additional background material on this general area, and that it will help them understand, interpret, and place in context the work reproduced thereafter. Kohonen and Arbib provide nice introductions to computational structures that draw their inspiration from neurophysiological models [70, 71].

Sometimes justification for investigating the potential of neural nets for the solution of various pattern recognition problems is obvious. On the other hand, current enthusiasm for this approach has led to the use of neural models when the apparent rationale for their use has been justified by what is best described as a feeding frenzy. The papers in Chapter 5 try to examine these issues with a view toward guessing how best to integrate and exploit the promise of the neural approach with fuzzy efforts aimed at advancing the art and science of pattern recognition and its applications in fielded systems in the next decade.

This introduction also cautions readers to concern themselves with the issue of technology transfer—have we considered the relevant issues about the practical use of CNNs in pattern recognition, and what is their potential impact to fielded performance in pattern recognition systems? When, where, how, and why can CNNs play a major role in shaping systems that depend on fuzzy pattern recognition techniques? More specifically, what pattern recognition problems seem most amenable to a combination of fuzzy logic and the CNN approach? What potential exists for CNNs to provide improvements in the way existing fuzzy algorithms solve various pattern recognition problems? And, finally, can we expect CNNs to solve problems that are currently intractable for conventional or fuzzy techniques? It is not our intent, nor do we claim to be able to, answer many questions that will surface. The objective of this introduction and, by extension, of the papers that follow it, is rather to raise these issues and point out their importance for research about and development of CNNs as they relate to fuzzy pattern recognition, and vice versa.

In order to set the stage for the papers in Chapter 5, we give a brief introduction to the basic concepts that serve as inspiration for CNNs and then present a short description of the CNN. The biological neural network (BNN) is one of the systems that enables organisms (in particular, humans) to perform various biological pattern recognition (BPR) tasks; in turn, BPR is one aspect of biological intelligence. We sometimes refer to the BNN as the *brain*, so that biological intelligence (BI) corresponds to the *mind*. Neural networks are one facilitator of pattern recognition; subsequently, pattern recognition is but one aspect of intelligence.

A BNN is, literally, a network of interconnected neurons. Figure 17 depicts the simplest ideas we have about the components and configuration of a BNN: a network of neurons, each of which has an axon (pulse generator), soma (pulse emitter), dendrites (pulse receptors), and synapses (connectors) that offer variable resistance (synaptic weights $\mathbf{w}_k$) to the conduction of packets of data (electrochemical pulses $\mathbf{x}_k$) through the network. Information (electrical, chemical, or biological in form) is generated, flows, is assimilated, and somehow is used to solve problems. Our assumption is that each neuron does some numerical computing—this gives rise to the hope that computers can be used to imitate this structure and its performance.

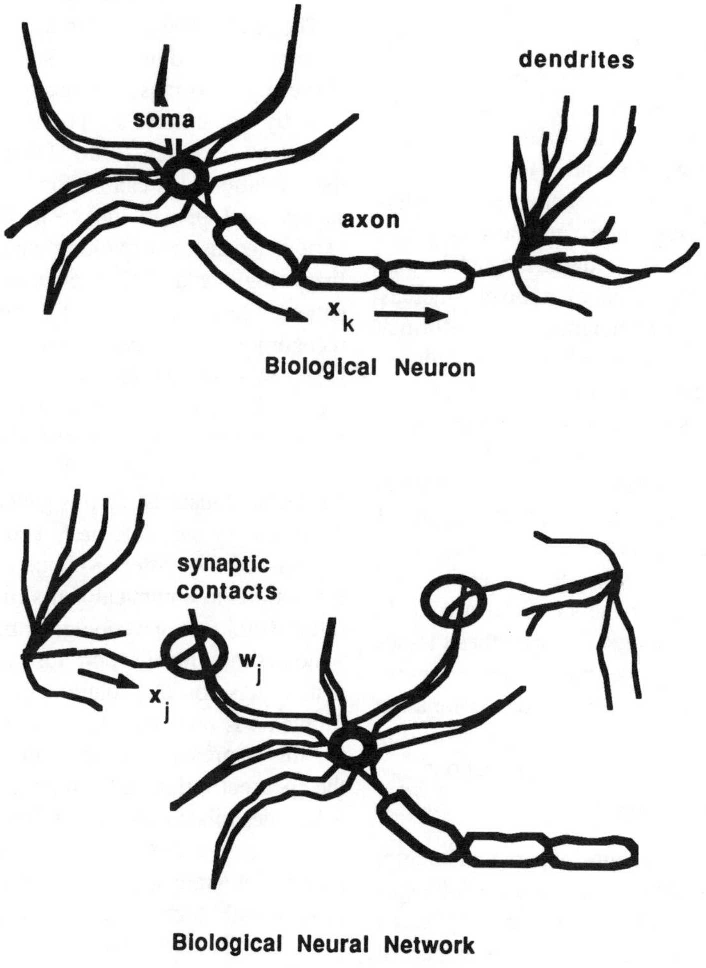

Fig. 17. The biological neural network (BNN).

Figure 18 illustrates the components of a typical electromechanical (or optical) CNN: a layout of hardware and/or software components in an architecture (i.e., arrangement) that ostensibly mirrors the biological version. We remark that hardware implementations of the CNN are very evolutionary at this writing; many researchers feel that implementation of this idea will be best realized in optical (photonic) processing. The CNN shown in Fig. 18 is very general in that it has feed-forward, feed-backward, and cyclic connections between and amongst its nodes. Most CNN architectures are feed-forward only, a simplification that seems necessary for both computational and analytical tractability.

Each "N" in Fig. 18 corresponds to a node (local processor) whose biological analog is the soma (center of the nerve cell). DARPA's definition of the neural network is "a system composed of many simple processing elements, operating in parallel, whose function is determined by network structure, connection strengths, and the processing performed at computing elements or nodes" [72, p. 60]. The *connection strengths* referred to in the DARPA definition are the weights $\{\mathbf{w}_j\}$. The synaptic weights $\{\mathbf{w}_j\}$ at a node in the BNN are believed to vary over time and it is assumed that this is one of the major mechanisms by which the brain "adapts" to changes in its information processing system (i.e., to changes in its input data and/or output requirements). Another means for achieving adaptation to system tasks is thought to be through the activation and deactivation of (sets of) nodes in the network (i.e., network reconfiguration), again on the fly. That the brain can and does adapt in real time is inarguable—it is the mechanisms for doing so that are not well understood.

From the standpoint of the BNN, then, a reasonable working definition of the word *adaptive* is the ability to adjust local processing parameters and global configurations of processors to accommodate changes in inputs or requirements without interruption of current processing. When should we call a computational scheme adaptive? If we intend for this term to connote the same property as just defined for the BNN, an algorithm should be called *computationally adaptive* if and only if it can adjust local processing parameters and global configurations of processors to accommodate changes in inputs or requirments *without interruption* of current processing.

In pattern recognition, we seem to be interested in the potential of CNNs at two very different levels. First, to replicate the computational power (i.e., low level arithmetic processing ability) of the BNN. Second, and much more ambitiously, we hope, with the CNN, to endow machines with the higher level cognitive abilities that biological organisms possess (due in part, perhaps, to their low level computational prowess). Much of the current confusion about what

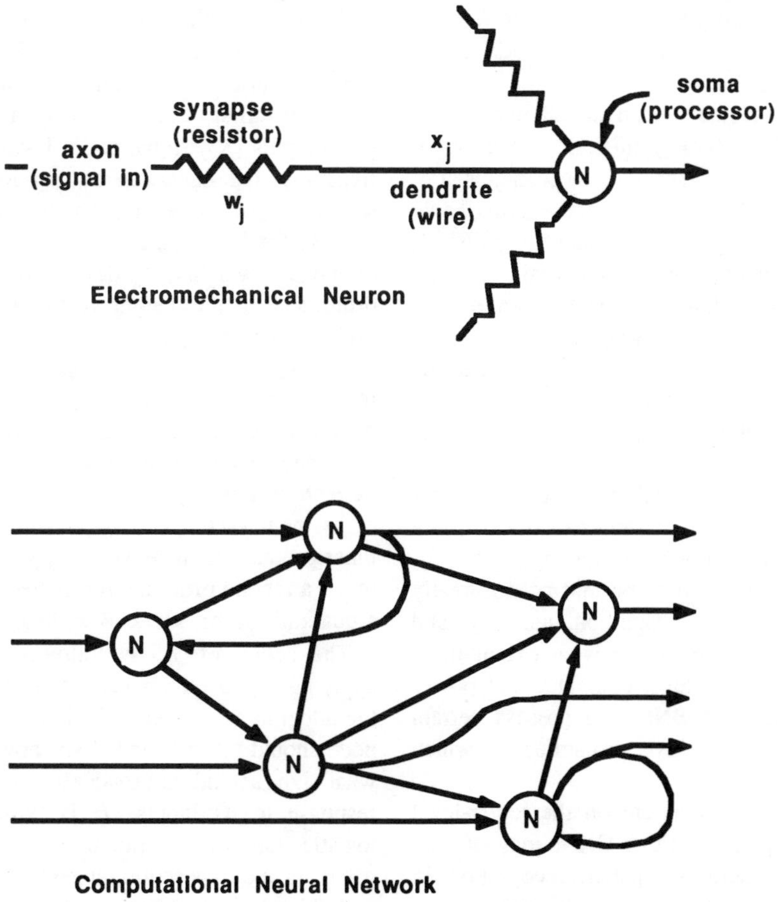

Fig. 18. The computational neural network (CNN).

CNNs can and cannot be expected to do can be avoided by carefully separating these two functions and our ability to reproduce them. In the first capacity, CNNs are often reputed to enjoy four major advantages over many classical low-level pattern recognition techniques:

- **(P1)** *adaptivity*—the ability to adjust when given new information;
- **(P2)** *speed*—via massive parallelism;
- **(P3)** *fault tolerance*—to missing, confusing and/or noisy data; and
- **(P4)** *optimality*—as regards error rates in classification systems.

With careful definitions (not yet made by workers in the pattern recognition community), each of these is a *computational property* of algorithms that can be measured objectively. About this we offer two observations. First, what reason is there for anticipating that a CNN may possess these properties to a greater extent than non-neural algorithms? Second, to what extent is the low-level computational power of the BNN, which is what the computer is best able to imitate, responsible for its higher-level abilities (i.e., perception, cognition, etc.)? Perhaps the major stumbling block to keeping the two functions of BNNs well separated is that the answer to this larger question is completely unknown. The important point to be made here is that confusion often arises precisely because the commonly held answer for *both* questions seems to lie with one's hope that the CNN really mimics the BNN in its behavior.

The BNN in general, and the human neural network in particular, certainly exhibit (P1–P4) in their execution of cognitive tasks. However, the specific mechanisms (algorithms) that enable a BNN to achieve these remarkable feats are hidden in a very complex arrangement of physical, chemical, and biological interactions in the brain that are largely, if not completely, unknown. There is an intense philosophical debate at present as to whether computers in general, and CNNs in particular, will ever possess the higher-level capabilities that we wish they could. It falls beyond our intent (and/or ability) to join the philosophical debate about this larger question, except as it seems to confuse us in attempts to understand and use CNNs for computational purposes. Interested readers can refer to any number of excellent papers and books on this topic [68–96]. An agreeable middle ground seems to be that no one really knows how perception, reasoning, cognition, memory, and thought are realized by the BNN, or to what extent these properties ensue from sheer low-level computational power (the computer's forte), but that BNNs do possess certain enviable computational and cognitive properties to which CNNs can aspire.

The papers in Chapter 5 concentrate on the lower-level computational power and properties that CNNs may or may not possess in the context of numerical pattern recognition. In this less ambitious domain it still seems overly optimistic to say (or infer), as some writers and readers do, that a certain algorithmic structure possesses any of the properties (P1–P4) in other than a strictly computational, empirically verifiable, low-level sense, simply because it has, according to its advocates, a "neural" architecture. Indeed, the word *neural* is an example of seductive semantics. Neural connotes to many *brain-like behavior*; it suggests that the computer can take on, or possess, the human ability for associative recall and deductive reasoning when and if the computer can be programmed so that it behaves in a neural manner (which, as observed above, seems far beyond our abilities, at least for the present). Most conventional architectures and algorithms for pattern recognition also provide or possess each of these four properties to a greater or lesser extent and they do so quite independent of any conscious attempt to imitate the BNN. For example, Bayesian classifiers based on parameters estimated with, say, maximum likelihood using labeled data, can be turned off and retrained if more data become available —thus, in the current jargon, they are "adaptive." An even more dramatic example is the k-nearest neighbor (k-NN) rule. When additional labeled data become available, the k-NN rule adapts to this as soon as the data are stored (i.e., the training time is *zero*!). This is as adaptive as a computational structure can get! Finally, we remark that it seems clear that low- and intermediate-level algorithms such as are described in the papers of this volume are hardly adaptive in the biological sense discussed above.

Figure 19 reflects current thinking about the processing that should be performed at local nodes. Two mathematical functions are usually active at each node. An *integrator function* f first integrates the synaptic weights $\{\mathbf{w}_j\}$ with the pulse inputs $\{\mathbf{x}_j\}$ to the node. Usually, f is an inner product (typically, the Euclidean dot product as shown in Fig. 19), say $v = f_{\mathbf{w}}(\mathbf{x}) = \langle \mathbf{w}, \mathbf{x} \rangle$. This choice can be seen geometrically in the lower half of Fig. 19. For a particular vector $\mathbf{w}$ of synaptic weights, $f_{\mathbf{w}}$ defines the hyperplane $H_{\mathbf{w}}$, which is orthogonal to the weight vector $\mathbf{w} = (\mathbf{w}_1, \mathbf{w}_2, \ldots \mathbf{w}_p)$. $H_{\mathbf{w}}$ divides $\mathscr{R}^p$ into plus and minus half-spaces, that is, regions where $f_{\mathbf{w}}$ is positive or negative; $f_{\mathbf{w}}$ is zero on $H_{\mathbf{w}}$. The term $1 \cdot \alpha = \alpha$ shown in Fig. 19 is called the offset or *bias* at this node. Geometrically, it simply translates $H_{\mathbf{w}}$ away from the origin. This arrangement is called a *first order neuron* because $f_{\mathbf{w}}$ is an affine (linear when $\alpha = 0$) function of its input vector $\mathbf{x}$. *Higher order* neurons arise when the inner product $f_{\mathbf{w}}$ is replaced by a more complicated function, (e.g., a second order neuron is realized by replacing $f_{\mathbf{w}}$ with a quadratic form, say $\mathbf{x}^t W \mathbf{x}$, in $\mathbf{x}$).

The action of $f_{\mathbf{w}}$ is followed locally at each node by applying a transfer (or activation) function F to the value of the integrator function on its inputs. F is used to decide if the node should "fire." and if so, how much "charge," and of what sign, should be broadcast to the network by this node in response to its inputs. F is typically assumed to be the logistic (sigmoidal) function $F(v) = F(f_{\mathbf{w}}(\mathbf{x})) = (1/(1 + e^{-v}))$, or the hyperbolic tangent $F(v) = \tanh(v)$.

A third important mathematical operator for the CNN is an

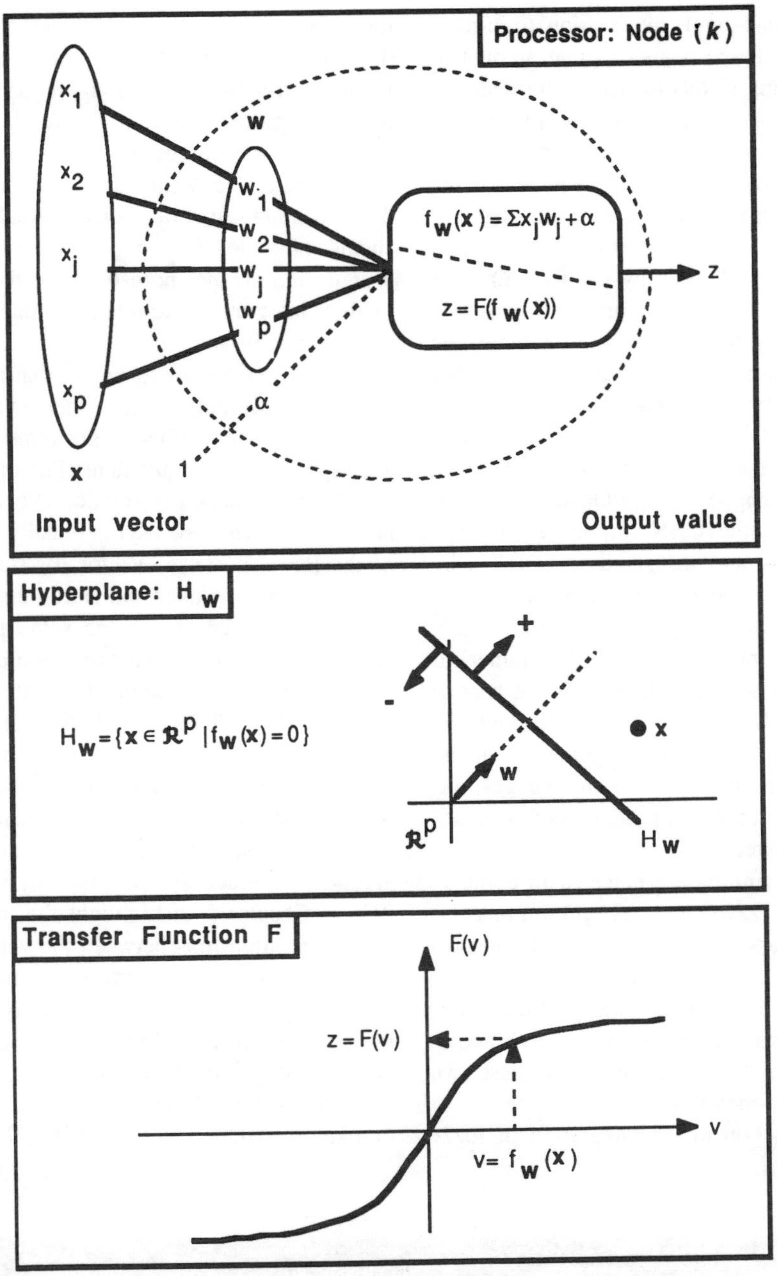

Fig. 19. The mathematical neuron.

update function or strategy U that converts the current set of weights at any node into a new or updated set. The action of the update (or learning) rule can be written symbolically as $\mathbf{w}_{t+1} = U(\mathbf{w}_t)$, where $\mathbf{w}_t = (\mathbf{w}_1, \ldots \mathbf{w}_M)$ is the *network weight vector* (the collection of all the individual weights at the M nodes in the network) at any time (iteration) t. Updating is performed during training, whenever the CNN system output(s) do not correspond well enough to the desired labeled outputs. For pattern recognition, this usually means that the CNN is operating as a classifier and in this context the CNN is simply a box, or algorithmic representation of classifier functions $\underline{\mathbf{D}}$ imaged in N_{fc} as described in Section 1.3.C of this chapter.

There are many principles that guide the choice of a learning strategy. Different update or learning rules are chosen to match a specific network architecture (layout of nodes and their interconnections); most attempt to optimize some function of the observed error(s) between the desired and observed outputs of the network. By far the most popular and pervasive CNN to date is the feed-forward, back-propagation (FFBP) network [72]; many fuzzy variants of this structure are being studied.

There are two distinct areas of integration between fuzzy pattern recognition and CNNs. First, we can use the conventional CNN for a variety of computational tasks within the larger framework of a preexisting fuzzy model. In this category, for example, are attempts to build membership function representations with CNNs and implementation of fuzzy logic operations such as union (max-nets), intersection (min-nets) and the extension principle. There is also a great amount of effort being expended in using CNNs to derive optimal rule sets for fuzzy controllers or to automate the process of membership function tuning of linguistic term sets used in both fuzzy pattern recognition and control. Several of the papers chosen for inclusion in Chapter 5 are of this type.

On the other hand, many writers are investigating ways and means of building "fuzzy CNNs" by incorporating the notion of fuzziness *into* a CNN framework as opposed to using the CNN within a fuzzy framework. For example, the target outputs of the CNN during training can be fuzzy label vectors (points in the interior of the triangle N_{fc} shown in Fig. 14). In this case, the CNN itself is functioning as a fuzzy classifier and is conceptually identical to any other fuzzy classifier function $\underline{\mathbf{D}}$ imaged in N_{fc}. Operationally, of course, $\underline{\mathbf{D}}$ is represented by the CNN implicitly. Another way to incorporate fuzziness into the standard CNN is by altering the integrator/transfer functions at each node so that they perform some sort of fuzzy aggregation (i.e., fuzzy union, weighted mean, or intersection) on the numerical information arriving at each node [100]. A different way to introduce fuzziness into the CNN framework is through the input data X to the CNN itself, which can be fuzzified in one of several ways. Moreover, there are many suggestions current in the literature about making individual neurons fuzzy—this is an active research topic.

On the third hand, some authors are engaged in comparisons of CNN techniques to fuzzy pattern recognition models. For example, several authors have compared the fuzzy *c*-means algorithms (see the papers in Chapter 2) to Kohonen's self-organizing feature map clustering strategy. References [73—92] are a small but typical selection of research activities that center around the synergism afforded by these two technologies in the areas just mentioned.

We conclude this introduction to the integration of fuzzy logic and CNNs with Fig. 20, which illustrates our view of the role played by CNNs in the overall design of a pattern recognition system. The four major areas of numerical pattern recognition (see Fig. 6) are shown as first level menu bars in a "system design applications program." The arrangement and contents of the second and third level pull-down windows are, of course, arguable. In our view, CNNs should (and do) first appear at the third level of system design, and are no more (or less) than evolving alternatives (and/or integratives) to other approaches to low-level computational models and algorithms.

Evidence continues to mount that many of the most popular CNN techniques are either exact implementations of well-known conventional algorithms or have properties that are asymptotically equivalent. For example, the well known feed-forward, back propagation (FFBP) architecture recently has been shown to be asymptotically equivalent to estimation of the Bayes posterior vector for statistical classifier design [93]. In view of Cover and Hart's classic result on the *k*-NN rules [94], which shows the same property for a different algorithm, we now have three nonfuzzy methods for doing statistical classifier design. Thus, the (FFBP) CNN is highlighted in Fig. 20 as a *statistical* classifier. This surprising result is an example of the convergence of CNN structures to models in statistical pattern recognition. We feel that results of this kind are very important, because they tend to demystify new fields, and add greatly to our knowledge of how to architect a fielded system. Indeed, we have included paper [93] in Chapter 5 to highlight the importance of constantly seeking relationships between the various and ostensibly different approaches to pattern recognition. In view of results of this type, we suggest that it is merely a matter of time before investigators show further equivalences between various fuzzy pattern recognition techniques and both CNN and conventional algorithms. Readers interested in this line of investigation are encouraged to consult [95, 97–99] for further details

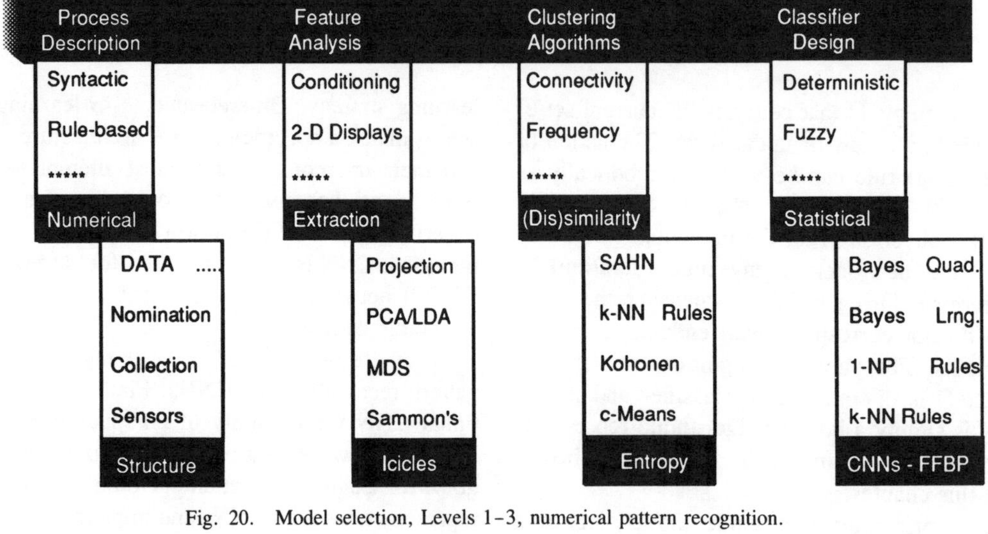

Fig. 20. Model selection, Levels 1–3, numerical pattern recognition.

on statistical mixtures and the approximation of arbitrary functions by CNNs.

SUMMARY

We have defined, mathematically and conceptually, the four main areas of pattern recognition system design. In the end, a useful system is one that satisfies its performance requirements and design constraints. It is impossible to overemphasize the importance of iteration and feedback in the evaluation of specific choices in each of the four first level nodes. The remaining chapters of this book collect papers about particular algorithms that attempt to solve various problems in pattern recognition using fuzzy models. The key features of the articles and how they relate to the development of the topic are explained in the introduction to each chapter.

Like most research, many of these papers address a specific problem—that is, they do not consider how the algorithm being studied will fit into a larger picture. We urge readers interested in systemic applications to read these papers with this larger context in mind, for although this book is specifically (mostly!) about fuzzy approaches to pattern recognition, we are well aware of the fact that no graver error can be made than to commit to a particular model ahead of time. Indeed, it is our expectation and contention that synthesis between fuzzy and other approaches to problems in this domain will continue—perhaps this will be the single most important horizon for our research in the next decade or so.

REFERENCES

[1] L. A. Zadeh, "Fuzzy sets," *Information and Control*, vol. 8, pp. 338-352, 1965.

[2] R. P. Feynman, "On the reliability of the [Challenger] shuttle," in *What Do You Care What Other People Think?* New York: Bantam, 1989, pp. 224-225.

[3] D. Dubois and H. Prade, *Fuzzy Sets and Systems: Theory and Applications*, New York: Academic Press, 1980.

[4] C. A. Murthy, S. K. Pal and D. Dutta Majumder, "Representation of fuzzy operators using ordinary sets," *IEEE Trans. Syst., Man, and Cybern.*, vol. SMC-17, no. 5, pp. 840-847, 1987.

[5] K. Hirota, "Concepts of probabilistic sets," *Fuzzy Sets and Syst.*, vol. 5, pp. 31-46, 1981.

[6] I. B. Turksen, "Interval valued fuzzy sets based on normal forms," *Fuzzy Sets and Syst.*, vol. 20, pp. 191-210, 1986.

[7] M. Mizumoto and K. Tanaka, "Some properties of fuzzy sets of type 2," *Inform. Control*, vol. 31, pp. 312-340, 1976.

[8] L. A. Zadeh, "Making computers think like people," *IEEE Spectrum*, vol. 21, pp. 26-32, August 1984.

[9] S. K. Pal and A. Dasgupta, "Spectral fuzzy sets and soft thresholding," *Inform. Sci.* (in press).

[10] C. A. Murthy and S. K. Pal, "Bounds for membership functions: Correlation based approach," *Inform. Sci.*, 1992.

[11] C. A. Murthy, S. K. Pal, and D. Dutta Majumder, "Correlation between two fuzzy membership functions," *Fuzzy Sets and Systs.*, vol. 7, no. 1, pp. 23-38, 1985.

[12] A. Kaufmann, *Introduction to the Theory of Fuzzy Subsets*, New York: Academic Press, 1975.

[13] G. Klir and T. Folger, *Fuzzy Sets, Uncertainty and Infomation*, Englewood Cliffs, NJ: Prentice-Hall, 1988.

[14] H. Zimmermann, *Fuzzy Set Theory and its Applications*, 2nd ed., Boston: Kluwer, 1990.

[15] A. Kaufmann and M. Gupta, *Introduction to Fuzzy Mathematics*, New York: Van Nostrand Co., Inc., 1985.

[16] K. Schmucker, *Fuzzy Sets, Natural Language and Computation*, Rockville, MD: Computer Science Press, 1984.

[17] V. Novak, *Fuzzy Sets and Their Applications*, Bristol: Adam Hilger, 1986.

[18] M. Smithson, *Fuzzy Sets Analysis for Behavioural and Social Sciences*, New York: Springer-Verlag, 1986.

[19] A. Kandel, *Fuzzy Mathematical Techniques with Applications*, Reading, MA: Addison-Wesley, 1986.

[20] P. Cheeseman, "An inquiry into computer understanding," *Comput. Intell.*, vol. 4, pp. 57-142, 1988.

[21] P. Cheeseman, "Probabilistic versus fuzzy reasoning," in *Uncertainty in Artificial Intelligence*, L. Kanel and J. Lemmer, Eds. New York: Elsevier, 1986, pp. 85-102.

[22] B. R. Gaines, "Fuzzy and probability uncertainty logics," *Inform. Control*, vol. 38, pp. 154-169, 1978.

[23] B. Kosko, "Fuzziness versus probability," *Int. J. General Syst.*, vol. 17(2-3), pp. 211-240, 1990.

[24] B. Y. Lindley, "Scoring rules and the inevitability of probability," *Int. Stat. Review*, vol. 50, pp. 1-26, 1982.

[25] W. Stallings, "Fuzzy set theory versus Bayesian statistics," *IEEE Trans. Syst., Man, Cybern.*, vol. SMC-7, pp. 216-219, 1977.

[26] L. A. Zadeh, "Probability measures of fuzzy events," *J. Math. Anal. and Appl.*, vol. 23, pp. 421-427, 1968.

[27] L. A. Zadeh, "Fuzzy sets as a basis for a theory of possibility," *Fuzzy Sets and Syst.*, vol. 1, pp. 3-28, 1978.

[28] R. R. Yager, "A foundation for a theory of possibility," *J. Cybern.*, vol. 10, pp. 177-204, 1980.

[29] E. Hisdal, "Are grades of membership probabilities?," *Fuzzy Sets and Syst.*, vol. 25, pp. 325-348, 1988.

[30] R. Giles, "The concept of grade of membership," *Fuzzy Sets and Syst.*, vol. 25, pp. 297-323, 1988.

[31] A. Kandel and W. J. Byatt, "Fuzzy sets, fuzzy algebra and fuzzy statistics," *Proc. IEEE*, vol. 66, pp. 1619-1639, December 1978.

[32] A. De Luca and S. Termini, "A definition of a nonprobabilistic entropy in the setting of fuzzy set theory," *Inform. Control*, vol. 20, pp. 301-312, 1972.

[33] S. K. Pal, "Fuzzy tools for the management of uncertainty in pattern recognition, image analysis, vision and expert systems, *Int. J. Syst. Sci.*, vol. 22, no. 3, pp. 511-549, 1991.

[34] B. Kosko, "Fuzzy entropy and conditioning," *Inform. Sci.*, vol. 40, pp. 165-174, 1986.

[35] S. G. Loo, "Measures of fuzziness," *Cybernetica*, vol. 20, pp. 201-210, 1977.

[36] W. X. Xie and S. D. Bedrosian, "An information measure for fuzzy sets," *IEEE Trans. Syst., Man., Cybern.*, vol. SMC-14, pp. 151-156, 1984.

[37] S. K. Pal and D. K. Dutta Majumder, *Fuzzy Mathematical Approach to Pattern Recognition*, New York: John Wiley and Sons, 1986.

[38] N. R. Pal and S. K. Pal, "Higher order fuzzy entropy and hybrid entropy of a set," *Inform. Sci.*, vol. 61, no. 3, pp. 211-231, 1992.

[39] R. Duda and P. Hart, *Pattern Classification and Scene Analysis*, New York: Wiley Interscience, 1973.

[40] J. C. Bezdek, *Pattern Recognition with Fuzzy Objective Function Algorithms*, New York: Plenum Press, 1981.

[41] A. Kandel, *Fuzzy Techniques in Pattern Recognition*, New York: Wiley Interscience, 1982.

[42] J. T. Tou and R. C. Gonzalez, *Pattern Recognition Principles*, Reading, MA: Addison-Wesley, 1974.

[43] J. Hartigan, *Clustering Algorithms*, New York: John Wiley and Sons, 1975.

[44] Y. H. Pao, *Adaptive Pattern Recognition and Neural Networks*, Reading, MA: Addison-Wesley, 1989.

[45] P. Devijver and J. Kittler, *Pattern Recognition: A Statistical Approach*, Englewood Cliffs, NJ: Prentice-Hall, 1982.
[46] D. Dubois and H. Prade, *Possibility Theory: An Approach to Computerized Processing of Uncertainty*, New York: Plenum, 1986.
[47] K. S. Fu, *Sequential Methods in Pattern Recognition and Machine Learning*, London: Academic Press, 1968.
[48] H. C. Andrews, *Mathematical Techniques in Pattern Recognition*, New York: Wiley Interscience, 1972
[49] E. A. Patrick, *Fundamentals of Pattern Recognition*, Englewood Cliffs, NJ: Prentice-Hall, 1972.
[50] K. Fukunaga, *Introduction to Statistical Pattern Recognition*, New York: Academic Press, 1972.
[51] M. R. Anderberg, *Cluster Analysis for Applications*, New York: Academic Press, 1973.
[52] W. S. Meisel, *Computer Oriented Approaches to Pattern Recognition*, New York: Academic Press, 1972.
[53] L. A. Zadeh, K. S. Fu, K. Tanaka and M. Shimura, (eds), *Fuzzy Sets and Their Applications to Cognitive and Decision Processes*, London: Academic Press, 1975.
[54] R. Di Mori, *Computerized Models of Speech Using Fuzzy Algorithms*, New York: Plenum Press, 1983.
[55] S. Watanabe, *Pattern Recognition: Human and Mechanical,* New York: John Wiley and sons, 1985.
[56] A. K. Jain and R. C. Dubes, *Algorithms for Clustering Data*, Englewood Cliffs, NJ: Prentice-Hall, 1988.
[57] J. Tukey, *Exploratory Data Analysis*, Reading MA: Addison-Wesley, 1977.
[58] E. Ruspini, "A new approach to clustering," *Inform. Control*, vol. 15, pp. 22-32, 1969.
[59] W. Pedrycz, "Fuzzy sets in pattern recognition: Methodology and methods," *Pattern Recognition*, vol. 23, no. 1/2, pp. 121-146, 1990.
[60] T. Pavlidis, *Structural Pattern Recognition*, New York: Springer-Verlag, 1977.
[61] K. S. Fu, *Syntactic Pattern Recognition with Applications*, Englewood Cliffs, NJ: Prentice-Hall, 1982.
[62] G. Ball, and D. Hall, "A clustering technique for summarizing multivariate data, *Behav. Sci.*, vol. 12, pp. 153-155, 1967.
[63] J. Bezdek, "Self-organization and clustering algorithms," in *Proc. 2nd Joint Tech. Workshop on Neural Networks and Fuzzy Logic*, R. Lea and J. Villereal, Eds. NASA #CP 10061, vol. 1, pp. 143-158, 1991.
[64] P. Sneath and R. Sokal, *Numerical Taxonomy*, San Francisco: W. H. Freeman, 1973.
[65] A. Rosenfeld and A. C. Kak, *Digital Picture Processing*, 2nd ed., New York: Academic Press, 1982.
[66] R. C. Gonzalez and P. Wintz, *Digital Image Processing*, 2nd ed., Reading, MA: Addison-Wesley, 1987.
[67] D. Marr, *Vision*, San Francisco: W. H. Freeman, 1982.
[68] R. Lippman, "An introduction to neural computing," *IEEE ASSP Mag.*, pp. 4-22, April 1987.
[69] B. Kosko, *Neural Networks and Fuzzy Systems: A Dynamical Approach to Machine Intelligence,* Englewood Cliffs, NJ: Prentice-Hall, 1991.
[70] T. Kohonen, *Self-Organization and Associative Memory*, 3rd ed., Berlin: Springer-Verlag, 1989.
[71] M. Arbib, *Brains, Machines and Mathematics*, 2nd ed., Berlin: Springer-Verlag, 1987.
[72] *DARPA Neural Network Study*, Fairfax, VA: AFCEA Press, 1988.
[73] J. M. Keller and H. Tahani, "Backpropagation neural networks for fuzzy logic," *Inform. Sci.*, 1992.
[74] J. M. Keller and D. J. Hunt, "Incorporating fuzzy membership functions into the perceptron algorithms, *IEEE Trans. Pattern Anal. Machine Intell.*, vol. PAMI-7, 693-699, 1985.
[75] C. C. Lee, "A self-learning rule-based controller employing approximate reasoning and neural net concepts," *Int. J. Intell. Sys.*, vol. 6, pp. 71-93, 1991.
[76] C. C. Lee, "Intelligent control based on fuzzy logic and neural net theory, in *Proc. Int. Conf. on Fuzzy Logic and Neural Networks*, T. Yamakawa, Ed. Iizuka, Japan, 1990, pp. 759-764.
[77] S. C. Lee and E. T. Lee, "Fuzzy Neural Networks," *Mathematical Biosciences*, vol. 23, pp. 151-177, 1975.
[78] S. Mitra, and S. C. Newton, "Leader clustering by unsupervised adaptive neural networks using a fuzzy learning rule," *Proc. SPIE Conf. on Adaptive Signal Processing*, San Diego, 1991.
[79] S. Mitra, and S. K. Pal, "Self-organizing neural network as a fuzzy classifier," *IEEE Trans. Syst., Man., Cybern.*, (in press).
[80] S. Mitra and S. K. Pal, "Layered Neural Net As A Fuzzy Classifier," *Proc. Fourth Int. Conf. Industrial & Engineering Applications of Artificial Intell & Expert Systems*, Kauai, Hawaii, June 2-5, 1991, pp. 128-137.
[81] A. Ghosh, N. R. Pal and S. K. Pal, "Self-organization for object extraction using multilayer neural network and fuzziness measures," *IEEE Trans. Fuzzy Systems*, 1992 (in press).
[82] W. Pedrycz, "Neurocomputations in relational systems," *IEEE Trans. Pattern Anal. Machine Intell.*, vol. PAMI-13, pp. 289-296, 1991.
[83] G. A. Carpenter, S. Grossberg, and D. B. Rosen, "Fuzzy ART: Fast stable learning and categorization of analog patterns by an adaptive resonance system," *Neural Networks*, vol. 4, no. 6, pp. 759-772, 1992.
[84] J. C. Bezdek, "A note on generalized self-organizing clustering algorithms," *Proc. SPIE*, vol. 1293, *Applications of AI (VIII).*, pp. 260-267, 1990.
[85] E. Sanchez, "Fuzzy connectionist expert systems," in *Proc. Int. Conf. on Fuzzy Logic and Neural Networks*, T. Yamakawa, Ed. Iizuka, Japan, 1990, pp. 31-35.
[86] E. Sanchez, "Fuzzy logic and neural networks in artificial intelligence and pattern recognition," *Proc. Int. Conf. Sto. and Neural Models*, SPIE, 1991.
[87] H. Takagi and I. Hayashi, "Artificial neural network driven fuzzy reasoning," *Int. J. Appr. Reason.*, vol. 5, pp. 191-212, 1991.
[88] W. G. Wee and K. S. Fu, "A formulation of fuzzy automata and its application as a model of learning systems," *IEEE Trans. Syst. Sci. Cyberns.*, vol. SSC-5, pp. 215-223, 1969.
[89] P. Werbos, "Neurocontrol and fuzzy logic—Connections and Designs," *Int. J. Appr. Reason.*, vol. 6, no. 2, 1992.
[90] T. Yamakawa and S. Tomoda, "A fuzzy neuron and its application to pattern recognition, *Proc. 3rd IFSA Congress*, J. Bezdek, Ed. Seattle, 1989, pp. 30-38.
[91] J. Yen, "The role of fuzzy logic in the control of neural networks," in *Proc. Int. Conf. on Fuzzy Logic and Neural Networks*, T. Yamakawa, Ed. Iizuka, Japan, 1990, pp. 771-774.
[92] J. Yen,"Using fuzzy logic to integrate neural networks and knowledge-based systems," in *Proc. 2nd NASA Workship on Neural Networks and Fuzzy Logic*, R. Lea and J. Villereal, Eds. NASA CP10061, vol. 1, pp. 217-233, 1991.
[93] D. Ruck, S. Rogers, M. Kabrisky, M. Oxley, and B. Suter, "The multi-layer perceptron as an approximation to a Bayes optimal discriminant function," *IEEE Trans. Neural Nets.*, vol. NN-1, pp. 296-298, 1990.
[94] T. Cover and P. Hart, "Nearest neighbor pattern classification," *IEEE Trans. Inform. Theory*, vol. IT-13, pp. 21-27, 1967.
[95] P. Gallinari, S. Thiria, F. Badran, and F. Fogelman-Soulie, "On the relations between discriminant analysis and multilayer perceptrons," *Neural Networks*, vol. 4, pp. 349-360, 1991.
[96] D. Hofstadter, "The turing tests: A coffeehouse conversation," in *The Mind's I*, D. Hofstadter and D. Dennett, Eds. New York: Bantam, pp. 69-91, 1981.
[97] K. Hornik, "Approximation capabilities of multilayer feedforward networks," *Neural Networks*, vol. 4, 1991, pp. 251-257.

[98] H. Traven, ''A neural network approach to statistical pattern classification by ''Semiparametric'' estimation of probability density functions,'' *IEEE Trans. Neural Networks*, vol. NN-2, pp. 366–377, 1991.
[99] D. Titterington, A. Smith, and U. Makov, *Statistical Analysis of Finite Mixture Distributions*, New York: John Wiley and Sons, 1985.
[100] R. Krishnapuram and J. Lee, ''Fuzzy connective based hierarchical aggregation networks for decision making,'' *Fuzzy Sets and Systems*, 1992 (in press).

Chapter 2
Cluster Analysis

2.0 Introduction

THIS chapter addresses various questions in clustering (also known as *unsupervised learning* or *self-organization*). We have discussed the general area in some detail in Section 1.3.C of Chapter 1. References [1–20] pertain to various aspects of clustering and are offered as general reading; we will mention specific references as we proceed. The papers in Chapter 2 cover five areas. Papers 2.1 and 2.2 concern themselves with the origins of the fuzzy set theory. Papers 2.3–2.8 deal with partitional clustering methods based on the optimization of some criterion function of the data and the desired partition; these papers also investigate both relational data and object data. Papers 2.9–2.11 are concerned with algorithmic and asymptotic convergence of fuzzy partitioning algorithms. Papers 2.12–2.16 address clustering from a different viewpoint—specifically, relational data are the basis of the methodology, and decompositional algorithms form the approach toward implicit partitioning of the objects that are pairwise related. Finally, Papers 2.17–2.20 describe various approaches to the cluster validity problem.

Paper 2.1 is, of course, Zadeh's original paper on fuzzy sets. As such, it has probably been reproduced thousands of times by now and has appeared on various occasions in several other collections of reprints. The paper is clear, concise, and, like all really great papers, contains a wealth of ideas that have led to the establishment of new branches of science. The most astonishing thing about the paper is that one can go back to it, reread it from time to time, and find good ideas for current research that to this day have not been fully exploited! Paper 2.2 contains Zadeh's introduction to the concept of a linguistic variable. This paper was also an outstanding milestone for fuzzy models; the current development of fuzzy control and, to a lesser extent, pattern recognition schemes based on linguistic term sets, have their genesis here. Nothing more needs to be said—these two papers were the point of departure for much of the work that has been done in the twenty-odd years since their publication—readers will appreciate these remarks simply by reading the papers.

Algorithms that generate matrices in M_{fcn} (fuzzy c-partitions of X) are sometimes called *partitional clustering algorithms*. In Paper 2.3, Ruspini first suggested the structure (M_{fcn}) of fuzzy c-partition spaces that we exhibited in Equation (8) in Chapter 1. Ruspini further defined and analyzed the first fuzzy objective function algorithm for generating fuzzy c-partitions of a finite set of unlabeled data. Ruspini's functional was actually based on relational data in the relational form discussed in Chapter 1, but he assumed that it was induced via some measure of dissimilarity on object data, so this paper really discusses a technique that can be used for either kind of data. Almost all of the fuzzy clustering and classification models that are currently used are based on Ruspini's idea.

Gitman and Levine (Paper 2.4) was the first attempt to decompose "mixtures," or data with multimodality, using fuzzy sets. Figure 5 of Paper 2.1 had already contained the suggestion that fuzzy sets would be useful for this problem; Gitman and Levine were the first to make use of this idea. Their idea was not related to the decomposition of statistical mixtures in any formal way. The basic method in Paper 2.4 is to augment the measured features with an additional one, namely, the *importance* of each feature vector, and subsequently to decompose the data with this added information as part of the data. Although not explicitly relevant to many later papers, this article was the first that suggested augmentation of the input data with numbers that represented linguistic characteristics of the inputs. Derivatives of this idea are much in evidence today (cf. reference [19] in Chapter 5).

The most well known objective function for clustering in $\mathbf{X}$ is the classical within groups sum of squared errors function, defined as

$$J_1(U, \mathbf{v}; X) = \Sigma_i \Sigma_k u_{ik}(\|\mathbf{x}_k - \mathbf{v}_i\|)^2 \qquad (1)$$

where $\mathbf{v} = (\mathbf{v}_1, \mathbf{v}_2, \cdots, \mathbf{v}_c)$ is a vector of (unknown) cluster centers (weights or prototypes) $\mathbf{v}_i \in \mathcal{R}^p$ for $1 \leq i \leq c$, and U is a hard or conventional c-partition of X. Optimal partitions U^* of X are taken from pairs (U^*, v^*) that are local minimizers of J_1. Dunn first generalized (1) for $m = 2$ (in equation (2) below) in Paper 2.5. This was the first formal extension of least squared error functionals from previously known conventional models and, as such, was a very important contribution to fuzzy pattern recognition. Dunn also defined and exemplified several measures of data separation and reported some results on cluster validity functionals that were defined in [21]. Subsequently, Bezdek generalized (1) to the infinite family of fuzzy c-means (FCM) functionals written as

$$J_m(U, \mathbf{v}; X) = \Sigma_i \Sigma_k u_{ik}^m(\|\mathbf{x}_k - \mathbf{v}_i\|_A)^2 \qquad (2)$$

where $m \in [1, \infty)$ is a weighting exponent on each fuzzy membership, U is a fuzzy c-partition of X, $\mathbf{v} = (\mathbf{v}_1, \mathbf{v}_2, \cdots, \mathbf{v}_c)$ are cluster centers in $\mathcal{R}^p$, A = any positive definite $(p \times p)$ matrix, and $\|\mathbf{x}_k - \mathbf{v}_i\|_A = (\mathbf{x}_k - \mathbf{v}_i)^T A(\mathbf{x}_k - \mathbf{v}_i)$ is the distance (in the A norm) from $\mathbf{x}_k$ to $\mathbf{v}_i$ [21]. The basic idea in FCM is to minimize J_m over the variables U and $\mathbf{v}$, on the assumption that matrices U that are part of optimal pairs for J_m identify "good" partitions of the data. There have been many studies on the best way to do this; the most popular set of algorithms, known variously as the FCM or fuzzy ISODATA algorithms, depend on simple Picard iteration through the necessary conditions arising from setting the Lagrangian of the gradient of J_m to 0. This function and its generalizations are, arguably, the most heavily studied fuzzy model in pattern recognition. Several papers reprinted in this chapter concern different aspects of the FCM models and/or their generalizations. Although an accurate count is impossible, we guess that perhaps as many as 300 papers have been written on extensions and generalizations of this scheme. Thus, Dunn's contribution was extremely important and has had lasting and far-reaching implications in the area of fuzzy clustering.

Paper 2.6 was one of the earliest attempts to synthesize various emerging models for pattern classification based on fuzzy models. Like Ruspini, Roubens made an important contribution in the area of relational clustering based on optimizing an objective function of the unknown fuzzy partition and the data at hand; this was perhaps the second important attempt to cast clustering with relational data into a fuzzy model suitable for analysis with optimization techniques. This paper also discusses some of the early indices of fuzziness that were being studied in the context of cluster validity.

There are two ways for algorithms of the c-means type to account for geometric shapes in different clusters: by adjusting the norm (and hence, the shape of open and closed unit balls in feature space), and by changing the fitting prototypes $\{\mathbf{v}_i\}$. There have been many studies on the effect of changing A in equation (2) on the assumption that *all* of the clusters in X have roughly the same A-norm geometry. Gustafson and Kessel, in Paper 2.7, first introduced the new and important concept of *localized* shape matching via norms that adapted to the shapes of single clusters. They proposed that the matrix A shown in equation (2) for J_m become a third set of variables by putting $\mathbf{A} = (A_1, A_2, \cdots, A_c)$, and writing J_m as a function of $(U, \mathbf{v}, \mathbf{A}; X)$. The important idea here is that the ith cluster in U might be best matched by a different hyperellipsoidal shape that was generated by the eigenstructure of the matrix A_i. The resultant algorithm carried a volume constraint on the determinant of each A_i that was subsequently seen to be unimportant. Nonetheless, this was a significant departure from the basic idea of the FCM algorithms. The idea that different substructures can be simultaneously locally matched by different pieces of the same global objective function has been studied extensively since publication of Gustafson and Kessel's paper. Work is continuing on generalizations of this idea [24, 25].

The other way to account for local variations in data substructures is to alter the prototypes $\{\mathbf{v}_i\}$ in equation (2), which are geometric objects in feature space that possess inherent shapes of their own, independent of the topology of open sets induced by the norm function used to measure dissimilarity in J_m. It is clear that minimization of J_m is, in a somewhat different context, a very generalized form of curve fitting, the data X being fit simultaneously by the c prototypes. Bezdek et al. introduced and analyzed several families of objective functions and convex combinations thereof that replaced the points $\{\mathbf{v}_i\}$ in equation (2) with linear varieties $\{\mathbf{P}_i\}$ of arbitrary dimension [22, 23]. This second method of accommodating various data geometries has also led to a wide range of extensions and generalizations. Indeed, Krishnapuram et al. and Dave have recently introduced extensions of this idea, which fit c clusters with arbitrary hyperquadrics that each use their own norm (that is, they combine the two methods discussed above) [24, 25]. Their results on very complex data structures are perhaps better than any other methods, such a B-splines or Hough transforms, known for this problem.

Windham, Paper 2.8, attempts to characterize the nature of geometric clustering algorithms in a wider perspective, thus extending the ideas of geometric matching of algorithms to data somewhat beyond the confines of fuzzy models. This line of thinking carries the original goals of fuzzy sets researchers in this application domain into a larger context, so it is an important attempt at generalization. References [26–57] are papers that pursue various themes exposed in Papers 2.5–2.8. Investigations on some of these themes are still quite active; refinements, improvements and corrections crop up often. For example, the first FCM model using non-inner-product norms is discussed in [49], references [50–55] discuss models for fuzzy clustering based on the use of objective functions that apply to relational data, and references [56, 57] are good recent "state of part of the art" surveys on fuzzy pattern recognition models.

Although no paper was included herein on the idea of synthesis between fuzzy clustering models and statistical decision theory, there have been many studies about the possibility of both theoretical as well as empirical relationships between, for example, FCM and mixture decomposition analysis [10]. This aspect of fuzzy clustering began with the work of Bezdek and Dunn in 1975 [58] and culminated, in some sense, with the results in Sabin's work (Paper 2.11, reprinted in this chapter). The relationship between mixtures and fuzzy models was mentioned briefly in connection with Gitman and Levine's article and we alert the reader that a lot of effort has been expended on elucidating relationships of this kind. (See also Paper 5.2, which pursues the same general question from an entirely different perspective, namely, that certain computational neural network structures approximate the well-known Bayesian classifier.) References [58–64] will introduce the reader to the use of and interaction between fuzzy clustering models and mixture analysis. In reference [65], the prototypes in FCM are replaced by (c) regression models in an attempt to solve the switching regression problem with unlabeled data. This is a new line of investigation that integrates ideas from fuzzy clustering with regression analysis.

Papers 2.9, 2.10, and 2.11 all address issues about convergence of the fuzzy c-means algorithms. Paper 2.9 is important because it introduced the use of Zangwill's theory of convergence for point to set maps as a basis for establishing the main result—namely, that every iterate sequence $\{U_t, \mathbf{v}_t\}$

of FCM converges (or has a convergent subsequence that does) to a local extrema of J_m, beginning from any initialization in $M_{fcn} \times \mathscr{R}^p$. There is, however, a technical flaw in Paper 2.9—convergence to local minima was presumably established but an oversight in the proof led to an incorrect result. Windham was the first to opine that this was the case, and then Tucker found a numerical counterexample to the claim [66]. This finally resulted in the collaboration that produced a clarification and correction in Paper 2.10, which gives the correct result, that is, that convergence as stated above can be to either a local minimum or saddle point of J_m.

The results of Papers 2.9 and 2.10 are numerical convergence results—the data are fixed and the limiting process is applied to t, the *number of iterations* of the optimization algorithm. Sabin's Paper 2.11 carried convergence analysis of FCM even further by providing asymptotic results about the distribution of limiting prototypes produced by FCM as n, the *number of samples* used, approached infinity. Under specific assumptions about statistical properties of the population from which the data were drawn, Sabin shows that FCM generates, in the limit, estimators based on the empirical distribution that are at least as good as those based on the true distribution. In practice, *termination* of FCM (which is a different notion from either numerical ($t \to \infty$) or asymptotic ($n \to \infty$) *convergence* has not been a problem. The reason this trio of papers seem important in the context of fuzzy pattern recognition is that they illustrate that fuzzy pattern recognition algorithms can and should be analyzed in precisely the same way that algorithms from other branches of numerical mathematics are analyzed. Readers sometimes assume that because the basic idea of membership functions is heuristic, that fuzzy models do not lend themselves well to careful mathematical analysis. Papers 2.9–2.11 are included here to exemplify that this is not the case ("careful," of course, does not exactly characterize the results of Paper 2.9!). References [67–72] contain further results on convergence of various fuzzy clustering algorithms; references [70, 71] contain general material on convergence analysis that is useful in the broader context of grouped coordinate descent techniques.

In Paper 2.12, Zadeh proposed (and thereby initiated) another branch of fuzzy pattern recognition. In this seminal article Zadeh defined the idea of fuzzy similarity relations, an extension of the well-known notion of hard or conventional equivalence relations (ERs) on a finite set of objects. Recognizing the well-known isomorphism between hard partitions and equivalence relations, Zadeh wrote a fuzzy similarity relation as the union of a finite number of weighted ERs and proved that any fuzzy similarity relation could be decomposed into a nested sequence of hard ERs. For clustering, this meant that a fuzzy similarity relation could be decomposed into a nested sequence of hard partitions (a dendogram or partition tree) of the objects, each with a level of importance that indicates, in some sense, how much credence should be attached to it. Even more important, however, was that in the process, Zadeh made the first definition of *fuzzy transitivity*. To appreciate this idea, suppose that objects i and j are related by R and that objects j and k are also R-related. In the conventional sense then, $iRj = 1$ and $jRk = 1$, so $iRk = 1$ (i.e., object j links i to k via hard transitivity). In logic, we call this method of inferencing *hypothetical syllogism*—one form of crisp logic. But what if $iRj = 0.8$ and $jRk = 0.6$, that is, j provides a partial linkage from i to k? What relationship, if any should there be between i and k? Zadeh proposed, and his decomposition theorem uses, max–min transitivity. Thus, if $iRj = 0.8$ and $jRk = 0.6$, then take $iRk = \min\{0.6, 0.8\} = 0.6$.

In a much larger sense, this was really the beginning of the field that is now known as *fuzzy approximate reasoning* (inferencing with fuzzy logic). Max–min transitivity of a fuzzy relation has subsequently been generalized in many ways. In our opinion the spirit and substance of much of the current research into the utility of different conjunction and disjunction operators (see Paper 5.9) for fuzzy reasoning in pattern recognition and control really had its origins in Paper 2.12. Zadeh further led the way in Paper 2.12 to the idea of the transitive closure of a fuzzy relation and this idea has become an important and pervasive one in pattern recognition, as well as many other fields; investigations into efficient ways to compute fuzzy transitive closures continue to this day [78, 79].

Paper 2.13 by Tamura et al. was also published in 1971, and Zadeh was aware of this group and their interest in the use of the decomposition algorithm described above for clustering and classification (see reference [14] in Paper 2.12). Zadeh proposed computing the max–min transitive closure of fuzzy relation R using simple matrix multiplication, an $\mathcal{O}(n^4)$ method, n being the number of elements in the relation. Tamura et al. gave a modified scheme that resulted in an algorithm that was somewhere between $\mathcal{O}(n^3)$ and $\mathcal{O}(n^3 \log_2 n)$; moreover, Paper 2.13 contains an example of the use of this procedure for clustering on a small but real relational data set. A few years later, Dunn provided in Paper 2.14, an alternate means for computing this transitive closure based on Prim's maximal spanning tree and showed that it was $\mathcal{O}(n^2)$. Much more important, perhaps, Dunn observed that the nested hierarchy of clusters generated by this procedure was very similar to the clusters found by the well-known (nonfuzzy) single linkage method, by noting that the crucial step in max–min transitivity was dual to the ultrametric inequality. Just a few months later, Kandel and Yelowitz published in Paper 2.15 yet another $\mathcal{O}(n^3)$ method for computing the max–min transitive closure of a fuzzy similarity relation. Their approach was based on a simple modification of Warshall's algorithm, which has been used to compute the transitive closure of a crisp ER for many years. We decided to include all three papers because of their close relationship to both each other and to the idea of decompositional clustering in fuzzy relational data.

In the last paper in this subset, Paper 2.16, the notion of fuzzy transitivity is extended beyond the max–min definition to other max–star operators, where star was one of several binary relations on [0, 1]x[0, 1]. In particular, the authors analyzed and illustrated the notion of fuzzy transitivity for the conjunction (or intersection) operator $T(x, y) = \max\{0, x + y - 1\}$, which has more recently been called the T_1 norm, and showed that every max–T_1 transitive fuzzy similarity relation induced a *pseudometric* on any finite set of objects. (Zadeh had shown earlier, in Paper 2.12, that a similar statement was true for max–min or (max–T_3) similarity relations, namely, that they did induce *ultrametrics* on the data.) Paper 2.16 also considered the convex hull of hard ERs and proposed a clustering scheme based on convex decomposition of relations having this property. Many authors have subsequently generalized the results of Papers 2.12–2.16 in various directions. The idea of different kinds of fuzzy transitivity corresponds to different ways to aggregate partial evidence in fuzzy reasoning systems, and in this context it is one of the most important areas of current research and development in fuzzy modeling [75]. References [76–80] give readers a few other entry points into literature related to the subject material of Papers 2.12–2.16.

The last group of papers in Chapter 2 concerns the problem of cluster validity—put simply, if the data are really unlabeled, how do we know if *any* algorithmically suggested c-partition is really right? Because every clustering algorithm produces c-partitions on demand, and almost all algorithms yield at least superficially different partitions when applied to the same set of unlabeled data, this is an important question. While models such as the FCM functionals shown above produce candidates for optimal Us in M_{fcn}, each candidate is optimal only in the limited sense of the model that defines and identifies it. For example, the failure of hard c-means on long, linear clusters to produce what a human would regard as the visually correct clusters is well known (see examples in reference [3]). Indeed, it is fairly easy to devise simple 2-D examples of data that "trick" every known clustering method. This is one reason fuzzy models have enjoyed some success in pattern recognition—their soft boundaries make them a little less susceptible to such traps. Ruspini's Paper 2.3 has a short discussion on "the correct number of clusters" and mentions the possible utility of a functional that is formally similar to Shannon's entropy function toward answering this question. DeLuca and Termini discussed the use of entropy as a measure of the amount of fuzziness or uncertainty contained by fuzzy sets in 1972 [80]. A measure of cluster validity for fuzzy c-partitions of data called the partition coefficient of U was introduced, analyzed, and exemplified in reference [21] and used by Dunn in Paper 2.5. Dunn also recognized the need to examine the validity of solutions and himself defined several indices of separation for hard clusters in the data. An important difference between Dunn's approach and the one suggested by Bezdek [21] was that Dunn's indices measured *properties of the data*, whereas the partition coefficient measured a property of Us produced by an algorithm *operating on the data*. As an historical aside, we note that Trauwert inadvertently identified the partition coefficient as Dunn's [85] when in fact it was first displayed in Bezdek's work [21]. Subsequently, the partition entropy of U was defined [81] and statistical parameters of both coefficients were found [82].

This brings us to an important point: measures of validity are inevitably tied somehow to properties of the data itself. Most attempts to quantify this aspect of unsupervised learning have tried to marry the idea that algorithmic clustering outputs are implicitly tied to the structure of the data with notions about null hypotheses on statistical properties of the data having assumed distributional structures of one kind or another. Readers are referred to the excellent treatment of this topic by Jain and Dubes (Chapter 4 of reference [7]) for prefatory material. Windham's treatment of validity via the uniform data function (UDF) in Paper 2.17 brought these two ideas together for the first time in the context of fuzzy clustering; although his presentation is tied to the FCM model in this paper, the general approach has utility for other fuzzy clustering models and as such, seems to be an important step toward a useful way to assess the validity of clustering algorithms.

In Paper 2.18, Backer and Jain approach the problem of cluster validity by proposing a method of ranking the optimality of different clusterings of X by a *goal directed comparison* approach, rather than through direct computations on either algorithmic partitions of the data or on the data itself. A new method of fuzzy clustering based on decomposing the data with an induced fuzzy sets affinity decomposition is given, and resultant partitions of X are subsequently compared with those produced by FCM on the same data. The significant idea in this paper is that when the output of any clustering algorithm has a well-defined purpose, that purpose can sometimes be used to decide which clusters (and clustering algorithm) are best for the purpose at hand. In the present case, the ultimate goal was a good classifier design (which always has the well-defined performance goal of minimum error rate), and this goal was in turn used as a benchmark for cluster validity.

Paper 2.19 by Gath and Geva contains three interesting ideas. First, performance measures based on densities and hypervolumes are used for assessment; second, a hybrid algorithm is proposed that combines fuzzy c-means with a fuzzy maximum likelihood method, an interplay reminiscent of the papers on mixture analysis between fuzzy and probabilistic models; and third, the number of clusters is not assumed known a priori. Although the method described is not fully dynamic (the number of clusters can only increase during a run), this represents a step toward full dynamic allocation of memberships across an optimal number of clusters and, in this sense, is an important step toward assessment strategies. Gath and Geva also incorporate the goal-directed approach reported in Paper 2.18.

In Paper 2.20 by Xie and Beni, yet another index for cluster validity that has its roots in Dunn's work (Paper 2.5) is proposed. Xie and Beni's computational strategy, like that of Gath and Geva, is monotonically dynamic in the number of clusters chosen. One interesting aspect of this article is that it ties the work of Chapter 2 to an important real problem, namely, segmentation of colored images for the detection of defects in integrated circuit wafers. This paper might just as easily have been placed in Chapter 4, which is on image processing; we decided to include it here to indicate that the validity problem is an ongoing concern in cluster analysis that has a very real impact on useful applications. Additional material on cluster validity is available [83–85].

References

[1] R. C. Tryon, *Cluster Analysis*, Ann Arbor: Edwards Bros., 1939.

[2] P. H. A. Sneath and R. R. Sokal, *Numerical Taxonomy*, San Francisco: W. H. Freeman, 1973.

[3] R. O. Duda and P. E. Hart, *Pattern Classification and Scene Analysis*, New York: Wiley-Interscience, 1973.

[4] J. T. Tou and R. C. Gonzalez, *Pattern Recognition Principles*, Reading, MA: Addison-Wesley, 1974.

[5] J. A. Hartigan, *Clustering Algorithms*, New York: John Wiley and Sons, 1975.

[6] J. W. Tukey, *Exploratory Data Analysis*, Reading, MA: Addison-Wesley, 1977.

[7] A. Jain and R. Dubes, *Algorithms for Clustering Data*, Englewood Cliffs, NJ: Prentice-Hall, 1988.

[8] K. S. Fu, *Syntactic Pattern Recognition and Applications*, Englewood Cliffs, NJ: Prentice Hall, 1982.

[9] B. S. Everitt, *Cluster Analysis*, 2nd ed., London: Heinemann, 1980.

[10] B. S. Everitt and D. J. Hand, *Finite Mixture Distributions*, New York: Chapman & Hall, 1981.

[11] M. Thomason and R. Gonzalez, *Syntactic Pattern Recognition: An Introduction*, Reading, MA: Addison-Wesley, 1978.

[12] P. A. Devijver and J. Kittler, *Pattern Recognition: A Statistical Approach*, Englewood Cliffs, NJ: Prentice-Hall, 1982.

[13] R. A. Johnson and D. W. Wichern, *Applied Multivariate Statistical Analysis*, Englewood Cliffs, NJ: Prentice-Hall, 1982.

[14] M. R. Anderberg, *Cluster Analysis for Researchers*, New York: Academic Press, 1983.

[15] M. Lorr, *Cluster Analysis for the Social Sciences*, San Francisco: Jossey-Bass, 1983.

[17] R. Dubes and A. K. Jain, "Clustering methodologies in exploratory data analysis," in *Advances in Computers*, vol. 19, M. Yovits, Ed., New York: Academic Press, 1980, pp. 113–215.

[18] G. Nagy, "Candide's practical principles of experimental pattern recognition," *IEEE Trans. Pattern Anal. Mach. Intell.*, vol. PAMI-5, pp. 199–200, 1983.

[19] E. Diday and J. C. Simon, "Clustering analysis," in *Digital Pattern Recognition*, K. S. Fu, Ed., New York: Springer-Verlag, 1976, pp. 47–94.

[20] H. H. Bock, "Statistical testing and evaluation methods in cluster analysis," *Proc. ISI*, pp. 116–146, Calcutta, 1984.

[21] J. Bezdek, *Fuzzy mathematics in pattern classification*, PhD Thesis, Cornell University, 1973.

[22] J. C. Bezdek, C. Coray, R. Gunderson, and J. Watson, "Detection and characterization of cluster substructure: I. Linear structure: Fuzzy *c*-lines," *SIAM J. Appl. Math.*, vol. 40, no. 2, pp. 339–357, 1981.

[23] J. C. Bezdek, C. Coray, R. Gunderson, and J. Watson, "Detection and characterization of cluster substructure: II. Fuzzy *c*-varieties and convex combinations thereof," *SIAM J. Appl. Math.*, vol. 40, no. 2, pp. 358–372, 1981.

[24] R. Krishnapuram, H. Frigui, and O. Nasraoui, "New fuzzy shell clustering algorithms for boundary detection and pattern recognition," *Proc. SPIE Conference on Intelligent Robotics and Computer Vision X*, 1991 (in press).

[25] R. Dave, "Fuzzy shell clustering and applications to circle detection in digital images," *Int. J. General Systems*, vol. 16, pp. 343–345, 1990.

[26] J. C. Bezdek, "Numerical taxonomy with fuzzy sets," *J. Math. Biol.*, vol. 1, no. 1, pp. 57–71, 1974.

[27] J. C. Bezdek and W. Fordon, "Analysis of hypertensive patients by the use of the fuzzy ISODATA clustering algorithms," *Proc. 1978 Joint Automatic Control Conference*, 1978, pp. 349–355.

[28] J. C. Bezdek and J. D. Harris, "Convex decompositions of fuzzy partitions," *J. Math. Anal. Appl.*, vol. 67, no. 2, pp. 490–512, 1979.

[29] J. M.Keller and J. A. Givens, "Membership function issues in fuzzy pattern recognition," *Proc. IEEE Syst., Man, Cybern. Soc.*, Tucson, AZ, 1985.

[30] E. Backer, "*Cluster Analysis by Optimal Decomposition of Induced Fuzzy Sets*," Delft, The Netherlands: Delft University Press, 1978.

[31] J. C. Bezdek, "A physical interpretation of fuzzy ISODATA," *IEEE Trans. Syst., Man, Cybern.*, vol. SMC-6, no. 5, pp. 387–389, 1976.

[32] J. C. Bezdek, "Fuzzy algorithms for particulate morphology," *Proc. 1978 Int'l. Powder and Bulk Solids Conf.*, pp. 143–150, Chicago: ISCM Press, 1978.

[33] R. W. Gunderson, "An adaptive FCV clustering algorithm," *Int. J. Man-Machine Studies*, vol. 19, no. 1, pp. 97–104, 1983.

[34] J. C. Bezdek and W. A. Fordon, "The application of fuzzy set theory to medical diagnosis," in *Advances in Fuzzy Set Theory and Applications*, Amsterdam: North Holland, 1979, pp. 445–461.

[35] B. B. Devi, "Compact clustering using fuzzy ISODATA," *Proc. NAFIPS*, Columbia: NAFIPS Press, 1986, pp. 31–37.

[36] J. C. Bezdek and K. Solomon, "Simulation of implicit numerical characteristics using small samples," *Proc. ICASRC*, G. E. Lasker, Ed., vol. VI, pp. 2773–2784, New York: Pergamon Press, 1981.

[37] R. Cannon, J. Dave, and J. C. Bezdek, "Efficient implementation of the fuzzy *c*-means clustering algorithms," *IEEE Trans. Pattern Anal. Machine Intell.*, vol. PAMI-8, no. 2, pp. 248–255, 1986.

[38] J. Bezdek and J. Harris, "Convex decompositions of fuzzy partitions," *J. Math. Anal. Appl.*, vol. 67, no. 2, pp. 490–512, 1979.

[39] W. Full, R. Ehrlich, and J. C. Bezdek, "Fuzzy QMODEL: A new approach for linear unmixing," *J. Math. Geo.*, vol. 14, no. 3, pp. 259–270, 1982.

[40] J. C. Bezdek, N. Grimball, J. Carson, and T. Ross, "Structural failure determination with fuzzy sets," *Civil Engr. Sys.*, vol. 3, pp. 82–92, 1986.

[41] G. Granath, "Application of fuzzy clustering and fuzzy classification to evaluate provenance of glacial till," *J. Math Geo.*, vol. 16, no. 3, pp. 283–301, 1984.

[42] T. Jacobsen and R. Gunderson, "Trace element distribution in yeast and wort samples: An application of the FCV clustering algorithms," *Int. J. Man-Machine Studies*, vol. 10, pp. 105–106, 1983.

[43] A. B. McBratney and A. W. Moore, "Application of fuzzy sets to climatic classification," *Ag. Forest Meteor*, vol. 35, pp. 165–185, 1985.

[44] C. Windham, M. P. Windham, B. Wyse, and G. Hansen, "Cluster analysis to improve food classification within commodity groups," *J. Amer. Diet. Assoc.*, vol. 85, no.10, pp. 1306–1314, 1985.

[45] J. Bezdek, R. Ehrlich, and R. Full, "FCM: The fuzzy *c*-means clustering algorithm," *Comp. Geo. Sci.*, vol. 10, no. 2, pp. 191–203, 1984.

[46] J. Bezdek, M. Trivedi, R. Ehrlich, and W. Full, "Fuzzy clustering: A new approach for geostatistical analysis," *Int. J. Syst., Measurement and Decision*, vol. 1, no. 2, pp. 13–24, 1981.

[47] J. Bezdek and E. W. Choiu, "Core zone scatterplots: A new approach to feature extraction for visual displays," *CVGIP*, vol. 41, pp. 186–209, 1988.

[48] M. P. Windham, "A unification of optimization-based numerical classification algorithms," in *Classification as a Tool for Research*, W. Gaul and M. Schader, Eds. Amsterdam, The Netherlands: North Holland, 1986, pp. 447–451.

[49] L. Bobrowski and J. Bezdek, "*c*-Means clustering with the $\mathscr{L}_1$ and $\mathscr{L}_\infty$ norms," *IEEE Trans. Syst., Man, Cybern.*, vol. SMC-21, no. 3, pp. 545–554, 1991.

[50] G. Libert and M. Roubens, "Non-metric fuzzy clustering algorithms and their cluster validity," in *Fuzzy Information and Decision Processes*, M. Gupta and E. Sanchez, Eds. New York: Elsevier, 1982, pp. 417-425.

[51] M. P. Windham, "Numerical classification of proximity data with assignment measures," *J. Classification*, vol. 2, pp. 157-172, 1985.

[52] J. Bezdek and R. Hathaway, "Clustering with relational *c*-means partitions from pairwise distance data," *J. Math. Modelling*, vol. 9, no. 6, pp. 435-439, 1987.

[53] J. Bezdek and R. Hathaway, "Relational duals of the *c*-means clustering algorithms," *Pattern Recognition*, vol. 22, no. 2, pp. 205-212, 1989.

[54] J. Bezdek, R. Hathaway, and M. Windham, "Numerical comparison of the RFCM and AP algorithms for clustering relational data," *Pattern Recognition*, vol. 24, no. 8, pp. 783-791, 1991.

[55] J. Bezdek and R. Hathaway, "Dual object-relation clustering models," *Int. J. General Systems*, vol. 16, no. 4, pp. 385-396, 1990.

[56] J. Keller and H. Qiu, "Fuzzy sets methods in pattern recognition," in *Pattern Recognition, Lecture Notes in Computer Science*, J. Kittler, Ed., New York: Springer-Verlag, 1988, pp. 173-182.

[57] W. Pedrycz, "Fuzzy sets in pattern recognition: Methodology and methods," *Pattern Recognition*, vol. 23, no. 1, pp. 121-146, 1990.

[58] J. C. Bezdek and J. C. Dunn, "Optimal fuzzy partitions: A heuristic for estimating the parameters in a mixture of normal distributions," *IEEE Trans. Comp.*, vol. 24, no. 8, pp. 835-838, 1975.

[59] S. Peleg and A. Rosenfeld, "A note on the evaluation of probabilistic labelings," *IEEE Trans. Syst., Man, Cybern.*, vol. SMC-11, no. 2, pp. 176-179, 1981.

[60] R. P. W. Duin, "The use of continuous variables for labelling objects," *Pattern Recognition Letters*, vol. 1, pp. 15-20, 1982.

[61] J. C. Bezdek, R. J. Hathaway, and V. J. Huggins, "Parametric estimation for normal mixtures," *Pattern Recognition Letters*, vol. 3, pp. 79-84, 1985.

[62] R. Hathaway and J. C. Bezdek, "On the asymptotic properties of fuzzy *c*-means cluster prototypes as estimators of mixture subpopulations," *Comm. Stat.*, vol. 5, no. 2, pp. 505-513, 1986.

[63] R. Redner, R. Hathaway, and J. Bezdek, "Estimating the parameters of mixture models with modal estimators," *Comm. in Stat. (A)*, vol. 16, no. 9, pp. 2639-2660, 1987.

[64] J. Davenport, J. Bezdek, and R. Hathaway, "Parameter estimation for finite mixture distributions," *Int. J. Comp. Math. Applic.*, vol. 15, no. 10, pp. 819-828, 1988.

[65] J. Bezdek and R. Hathaway, "Generalized regression and clustering," *Proc. Int. Conference on Fuzzy Logic and Neural Networks*, T. Yamakawa, Ed., Kyushu Institute of Technology, Iizuka, 1990, pp. 575-578.

[66] W. Tucker, "Counterexamples to the convergence theorm for the fuzzy ISODATA algorithms," in *The Analysis of Fuzzy Information*, J. Bezdek, Ed., Boca Raton, FL: CRC Press, 1987, pp. 109-122.

[67] S. A. Selim and M. A. Ismail, "*K*-means type algorithms: A generalized convergence theroem and characterization of local optimality," *IEEE Trans. Pattern Anal. Mach. Intell.*, vol. PAMI-6, no. 1, pp. 81-87, 1984.

[68] R. Hathaway and J. Bezdek, "Local convergence of the fuzzy *c*-means algorithms," *Pattern Recognition*, vol. 19, no. 6, pp. 477-480, 1986.

[69] M. A. Ismail and S. A. Selim, "On the local optimality of the fuzzy ISODATA clustering algorithm," *IEEE Trans. Pattern Anal. Mach. Intell.*, vol. PAMI-8, no. 2, pp. 284-288, 1986.

[70] J. Bezdek, R. Hathaway, R. Howard, and C. Wilson, "Coordinate descent and clustering," *Control Cybern.*, vol. 15, no. 2, pp. 195-203, 1986.

[71] J. Bezdek, R. Hathaway, R. Howard, M. Windham, and C. Wilson, "Local convergence analysis of a grouped variable version of coordinate descent," J. Optimization Theory and Appl., vol. 54, no. 3, pp. 471-477, 1987.

[72] R. Hathaway and J. Bezdek, "Recent convergence results for the fuzzy *c*-means clustering algorithms," *J. Classification*, vol. 5, no. 2, pp. 237-247, 1988.

[73] T. Kim, J. Bezdek, and R. Hathaway, "Optimality tests for fixed points of the fuzzy *c*-means algorithm," *Pattern Recognition*, vol. 21, no. 6, pp. 651-663, 1988.

[74] J. Bezdek and R. Hathaway, "Acelerating convergence of the fuzzy *c*-shells clustering algorithms," *Proc. 1991 IFSA Congress – Mathematics*, R. Lowen and M. Roubens, Eds. Brussels, 1991, pp. 12-15.

[75] P. Bonnisone and K. Decker, "Selecting uncertainty calculi and granularity: An experiment in trading-off precision and complexity," GE TR85.5C38, Schenectady, NY: General Electric Company, 1985.

[76] J. Bezdek, G. Biswas, and L. Y. Huang, "Transitive closures of fuzzy thesauri for information retrieval systems," *Int. J. Man-Machine St.*, vol. 25, pp. 343-356, 1986.

[77] W. Zhang, S. S. Chen, and J. Bezdek, "Pool2: A generic system for cognitive map development and decision analysis," *IEEE Trans. Syst., Man, Cybern.*, vol. SMC-19, no. 1, pp. 31-39, 1989.

[78] H. Larsen and R. Yager, "Efficient computation of transitive closures," *Fuzzy Sets and Systems*, vol. 38, pp. 81-90, 1990.

[79] S. Y. Li, "The simplest method of ascending value to find fuzzy transitive closures," *Fuzzy Sets and Systems*, vol. 38, pp. 91-96, 1990.

[80] A. DeLuca and S. Termini, "A definition of a non-probabilistic entropy in the setting of fuzzy sets theory," *Inform. Control*, vol. 20, pp. 301-312, 1972.

[81] J. Bezdek, "Cluster validity with fuzzy sets," *J. Cyber.*, vol. 3, no. 3, pp. 58-72, 1974.

[82] J. Bezdek, M. Windham, and R. Ehrlich, "Statistial parameters of fuzzy cluster validity functionals," *Int. J. Comp. and Inf. Sci.*, vol. 9, no. 4, pp. 232-336, 1980.

[83] M. Windham, "Cluster validity for fuzzy clustering algorithms," *Fuzzy Sets and Systems*, vol. 5, pp. 177-185, 1981.

[84] M. Roubens, "Fuzzy clustering algorithms and their cluster validity," *Eur. J. Op. Res.*, vol. 10, pp. 294-301, 1982.

[85] E. Trauwaert, "On the meaning of Dunn's partition coefficient for fuzzy clusters," *Fuzzy Sets and Systems*, vol. 25, pp. 217-242, 1988.

[86] S. K. Pal and S. Mitra, "Fuzzy dynamic clustering algorithm," *Pattern Recognition Letters*, vol. 11, no. 8, pp. 525-535, 1990.

[87] S. K. Pal and P. K. Pramanik, "Fuzzy measures in determining seed points in clustering," *Pattern Recognition Letters*, vol. 4, no. 3, pp. 159-164, 1986.

[88] K. Lesczynski, P. Penczek, and W. Grochulski, "Sugeno fuzzy measures and fuzzy clustering," *Fuzzy Sets and Systems*, vol. 15, pp. 147-158, 1985.

Fuzzy Sets*

L. A. ZADEH

Department of Electrical Engineering and Electronics Research Laboratory, University of California, Berkeley, California

A fuzzy set is a class of objects with a continuum of grades of membership. Such a set is characterized by a membership (characteristic) function which assigns to each object a grade of membership ranging between zero and one. The notions of inclusion, union, intersection, complement, relation, convexity, etc., are extended to such sets, and various properties of these notions in the context of fuzzy sets are established. In particular, a separation theorem for convex fuzzy sets is proved without requiring that the fuzzy sets be disjoint.

I. INTRODUCTION

More often than not, the classes of objects encountered in the real physical world do not have precisely defined criteria of membership. For example, the class of animals clearly includes dogs, horses, birds, etc. as its members, and clearly excludes such objects as rocks, fluids, plants, etc. However, such objects as starfish, bacteria, etc. have an ambiguous status with respect to the class of animals. The same kind of ambiguity arises in the case of a number such as 10 in relation to the "class" of all real numbers which are much greater than 1.

Clearly, the "class of all real numbers which are much greater than 1," or "the class of beautiful women," or "the class of tall men," do not constitute classes or sets in the usual mathematical sense of these terms. Yet, the fact remains that such imprecisely defined "classes" play an important role in human thinking, particularly in the domains of pattern recognition, communication of information, and abstraction.

The purpose of this note is to explore in a preliminary way some of the basic properties and implications of a concept which may be of use in dealing with "classes" of the type cited above. The concept in question is that of a *fuzzy set*,[1] that is, a "class" with a continuum of grades of membership. As will be seen in the sequel, the notion of a fuzzy set provides a convenient point of departure for the construction of a conceptual framework which parallels in many respects the framework used in the case of ordinary sets, but is more general than the latter and, potentially, may prove to have a much wider scope of applicability, particularly in the fields of pattern classification and information processing. Essentially, such a framework provides a natural way of dealing with problems in which the source of imprecision is the absence of sharply defined criteria of class membership rather than the presence of random variables.

We begin the discussion of fuzzy sets with several basic definitions.

II. DEFINITIONS

Let X be a space of points (objects), with a generic element of X denoted by x. Thus, $X = \{x\}$.

* This work was supported in part by the Joint Services Electronics Program (U.S. Army, U.S. Navy and U.S. Air Force) under Grant No. AF-AFOSR-139-64 and by the National Science Foundation under Grant GP-2413.

[1] An application of this concept to the formulation of a class of problems in pattern classification is described in RAND Memorandum RM-4307-PR, "Abstraction and Pattern Classification," by R. Bellman, R. Kalaba and L. A. Zadeh, October, 1964.

A *fuzzy set (class)* A in X is characterized by a *membership (characteristic) function* $f_A(x)$ which associates with each point[2] in X a real number in the interval [0, 1],[3] with the value of $f_A(x)$ at x representing the "grade of membership" of x in A. Thus, the nearer the value of $f_A(x)$ to unity, the higher the grade of membership of x in A. When A is a set in the ordinary sense of the term, its membership function can take on only two values 0 and 1, with $f_A(x) = 1$ or 0 according as x does or does not belong to A. Thus, in this case $f_A(x)$ reduces to the familiar characteristic function of a set A. (When there is a need to differentiate between such sets and fuzzy sets, the sets with two-valued characteristic functions will be referred to as *ordinary sets* or simply *sets*.)

Example. Let X be the real line R^1 and let A be a fuzzy set of numbers which are much greater than 1. Then, one can give a precise, albeit subjective, characterization of A by specifying $f_A(x)$ as a function on R^1. Representative values of such a function might be: $f_A(0) = 0$; $f_A(1) = 0$; $f_A(5) = 0.01$; $f_A(10) = 0.2$; $f_A(100) = 0.95$; $f_A(500) = 1$.

It should be noted that, although the membership function of a fuzzy set has some resemblance to a probability function when X is a countable set (or a probability density function when X is a continuum), there are essential differences between these concepts which will become clearer in the sequel once the rules of combination of membership functions and their basic properties have been established. In fact, the notion of a fuzzy set is completely nonstatistical in nature.

We begin with several definitions involving fuzzy sets which are obvious extensions of the corresponding definitions for ordinary sets.

A fuzzy set is *empty* if and only if its membership function is identically zero on X.

Two fuzzy sets A and B are *equal*, written as $A = B$, if and only if $f_A(x) = f_B(x)$ for all x in X. (In the sequel, instead of writing $f_A(x) = f_B(x)$ for all x in X, we shall write more simply $f_A = f_B$.)

The *complement* of a fuzzy set A is denoted by A' and is defined by

$$f_{A'} = 1 - f_A . \tag{1}$$

As in the case of ordinary sets, the notion of containment plays a central role in the case of fuzzy sets. This notion and the related notions of union and intersection are defined as follows.

Containment. A is *contained in* B (or, equivalently, A is a *subset of* B, or A is *smaller than or equal to* B) if and only if $f_A \leqq f_B$. In symbols

$$A \subset B \Leftrightarrow f_A \leqq f_B . \tag{2}$$

Union. The *union* of two fuzzy sets A and B with respective membership functions $f_A(x)$ and $f_B(x)$ is a fuzzy set C, written as $C = A \cup B$, whose membership function is related to those of A and B by

$$f_C(x) = \text{Max}\,[f_A(x), f_B(x)], \qquad x \in X \tag{3}$$

or, in abbreviated form

$$f_C = f_A \vee f_B . \tag{4}$$

Note that $\cup$ has the associative property, that is, $A \cup (B \cup C) = (A \cup B) \cup C$.

Comment. A more intuitively appealing way of defining the union is

[2] More generally, the domain of definition of $f_A(x)$ may be restricted to a subset of X.

[3] In a more general setting, the range of the membership function can be taken to be a suitable partially ordered set P. For our purposes, it is convenient and sufficient to restrict the range of f to the unit interval. If the values of $f_A(x)$ are interpreted as truth values, the latter case corresponds to a multivalued logic with a continuum of truth values in the interval [0, 1].

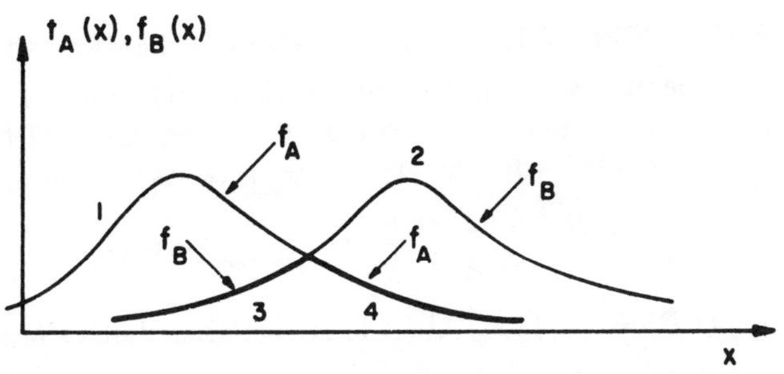

FIG. 1. Illustration of the union and intersection of fuzzy sets in R^1

the following: The union of A and B is the smallest fuzzy set containing both A and B. More precisely, if D is any fuzzy set which contains both A and B, then it also contains the union of A and B.

To show that this definition is equivalent to (3), we note, first, that C as defined by (3) contains both A and B, since

$$\text{Max}\,[f_A, f_B] \geqq f_A$$

and

$$\text{Max}\,[f_A, f_B] \geqq f_B.$$

Furthermore, if D is any fuzzy set containing both A and B, then

$$f_D \geqq f_A$$

$$f_D \geqq f_B$$

and hence

$$f_D \geqq \text{Max}\,[f_A, f_B] = f_C$$

which implies that $C \subset D$. Q.E.D.

The notion of an intersection of fuzzy sets can be defined in an analogous manner. Specifically:

Intersection. The *intersection* of two fuzzy sets A and B with respective membership functions $f_A(x)$ and $f_B(x)$ is a fuzzy set C, written as $C = A \cap B$, whose membership function is related to those of A and B by

$$f_C(x) = \text{Min}\,[f_A(x), f_B(x)], \qquad x \in X, \tag{5}$$

or, in abbreviated form

$$f_C = f_A \wedge f_B. \tag{6}$$

As in the case of the union, it is easy to show that the intersection of A and B is the *largest* fuzzy set which is contained in both A and B. As in the case of ordinary sets, A and B are *disjoint* if $A \cap B$ is empty. Note that $\cap$, like $\cup$, has the associative property.

The intersection and union of two fuzzy sets in R^1 are illustrated in Fig. 1. The membership function of the union is comprised of curve segments 1 and 2; that of the intersection is comprised of segments 3 and 4 (heavy lines).

Comment. Note that the notion of "belonging," which plays a fundamental role in the case of ordinary sets, does not have the same role in the case of fuzzy sets. Thus, it is not meaningful to speak of a point x "belonging" to a fuzzy set A except in the trivial sense of $f_A(x)$ being positive. Less trivially, one can introduce two levels α and β ($0 < \alpha < 1$, $0 < \beta < 1$, $\alpha > \beta$) and agree to say that (1) "x belongs to A" if $f_A(x) \geqq \alpha$; (2) "x does not belong to A" if $f_A(x) \leqq \beta$; and (3) "x has an indeterminate status relative to A" if $\beta < f_A(x) < \alpha$. This leads to a three-valued logic (Kleene, 1952) with three truth values: T ($f_A(x) \geqq \alpha$), F ($f_A(x) \leqq \beta$), and U ($\beta < f_A(x) < \alpha$).

III. SOME PROPERTIES OF ∪, ∩, AND COMPLEMENTATION

With the operations of union, intersection, and complementation defined as in (3), (5), and (1), it is easy to extend many of the basic identities which hold for ordinary sets to fuzzy sets. As examples, we have

$$\left.\begin{aligned}(A \cup B)' &= A' \cap B' \\ (A \cap B)' &= A' \cup B'\end{aligned}\right\} \text{De Morgan's laws} \qquad \begin{aligned}(7)\\(8)\end{aligned}$$

$$C \cap (A \cup B) = (C \cap A) \cup (C \cap B) \qquad \text{Distributive laws.} \qquad (9)$$

$$C \cup (A \cap B) = (C \cup A) \cap (C \cup B) \qquad (10)$$

These and similar equalities can readily be established by showing that the corresponding relations for the membership functions of A, B, and C are identities. For example, in the case of (7), we have

$$1 - \text{Max}\,[f_A, f_B] = \text{Min}\,[1 - f_A, 1 - f_B] \qquad (11)$$

which can be easily verified to be an identity by testing it for the two possible cases: $f_A(x) > f_B(x)$ and $f_A(x) < f_B(x)$.

Similarly, in the case of (10), the corresponding relation in terms of f_A, f_B, and f_C is:

$$\text{Max}\,[f_C, \text{Min}\,[f_A, f_B] = \text{Min}\,[\text{Max}\,[f_C, f_A], \text{Max}\,[f_C, f_B]] \qquad (12)$$

which can be verified to be an identity by considering the six cases:

$f_A(x) > f_B(x) > f_C(x), f_A(x) > f_C(x) > f_B(x), f_B(x) > f_A(x) > f_C(x),$

$f_B(x) > f_C(x) > f_A(x), f_C(x) > f_A(x) > f_B(x), f_C(x) > f_B(x) > f_A(x).$

Essentially, fuzzy sets in X constitute a distributive lattice with a 0 and 1 (Birkhoff, 1948).

An Interpretation for Unions and Intersections

In the case of ordinary sets, a set C which is expressed in terms of a family of sets $A_1, \cdots, A_i, \cdots, A_n$ through the connectives ∪ and ∩, can be represented as a network of switches $\alpha_1, \cdots, \alpha_n$, with $A_i \cap A_j$ and $A_i \cup A_j$ corresponding, respectively, to series and parallel combinations of α_i and α_j. In the case of fuzzy sets, one can give an analogous interpretation in terms of sieves. Specifically, let $f_i(x)$, $i = 1, \cdots, n$, denote the value of the membership function of A_i at x. Associate with $f_i(x)$ a sieve $S_i(x)$ whose meshes are of size $f_i(x)$. Then, $f_i(x) \vee f_j(x)$ and $f_i(x) \wedge f_j(x)$ correspond, respectively, to parallel and series combinations of $S_i(x)$ and $S_j(x)$, as shown in Fig. 2.

More generally, a well-formed expression involving $A_1, \cdots, A_n$, ∪, and ∩ corresponds to a network of sieves $S_1(x), \cdots, S_n(x)$ which can be found by the conventional synthesis techniques for switching circuits. As a very simple example,

$$C = [(A_1 \cup A_2) \cap A_3] \cup A_4 \qquad (13)$$

corresponds to the network shown in Fig. 3.
Note that the mesh sizes of the sieves in the network depend on x and that the network as a whole is equivalent to a single sieve whose meshes are of size $f_C(x)$.

IV. ALGEBRAIC OPERATIONS ON FUZZY SETS

In addition to the operations of union and intersection, one can define a number of other ways of forming combinations of fuzzy sets and relating them to one another. Among the more important of these are the following.

Algebraic product. The *algebraic product* of A and B is denoted by AB

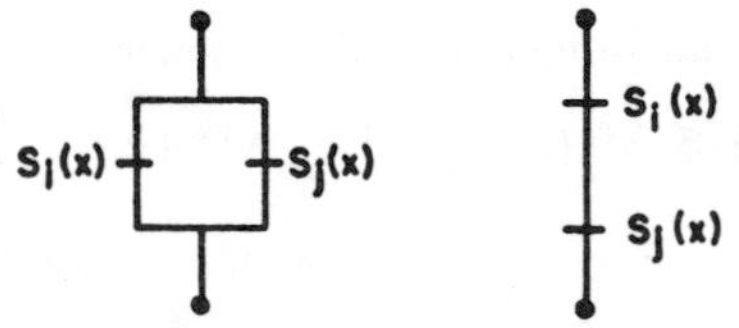

FIG. 2. Parallel and series connection of sieves simultating $\cup$ and $\cap$

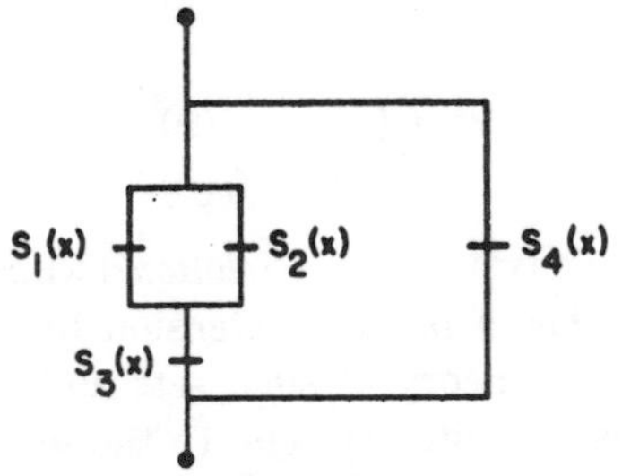

FIG. 3. A network of sieves simultating $\{[f_1(x) \vee f_2(x)] \wedge f_3(x)\} \vee f_4(x)$

and is defined in terms of the membership functions of A and B by the relation

$$f_{AB} = f_A f_B . \tag{14}$$

Clearly,

$$AB \subset A \cap B. \tag{15}$$

Algebraic sum.[4] The *algebraic sum* of A and B is denoted by $A + B$ and is defined by

$$f_{A+B} = f_A + f_B \tag{16}$$

provided the sum $f_A + f_B$ is less than or equal to unity. Thus, unlike the algebraic product, the algebraic sum is meaningful only when the condition $f_A(x) + f_B(x) \leqq 1$ is satisfied for all x.

Absolute difference. The *absolute difference* of A and B is denoted by $|A - B|$ and is defined by

$$f_{|A-B|} = |f_A - f_B|.$$

Note that in the case of ordinary sets $|A - B|$ reduces to the relative complement of $A \cap B$ in $A \cup B$.

Convex combination. By a convex combination of two vectors f and g is usually meant a linear combination of f and g of the form $\lambda f + (1 - \lambda)g$, in which $0 \leqq \lambda \leqq 1$. This mode of combining f and g can be generalized to fuzzy sets in the following manner.

Let A, B, and Λ be arbitrary fuzzy sets. The *convex combination of A, B, and Λ* is denoted by $(A, B; \Lambda)$ and is defined by the relation

$$(A, B; \Lambda) = \Lambda A + \Lambda' B \tag{17}$$

where Λ' is the complement of Λ. Written out in terms of membership functions, (17) reads

$$f_{(A,B;\Lambda)}(x) = f_\Lambda(x) f_A(x) + [1 - f_\Lambda(x)] f_B(x), \qquad x \in X. \tag{18}$$

A basic property of the convex combination of A, B, and Λ is expressed by

$$A \cap B \subset (A, B; \Lambda) \subset A \cup B \qquad \text{for all } \Lambda. \tag{19}$$

[4] The dual of the algebraic product is the *sum* $A \oplus B = (A'B')' = A + B - AB$. (This was pointed out by T. Cover.) Note that for ordinary sets $\cap$ and the algebraic product are equivalent operations, as are $\cup$ and $\oplus$.

This property is an immediate consequence of the inequalities

$$\text{Min}\,[f_A(x), f_B(x)] \leqq \lambda f_A(x) + (1 - \lambda) f_B(x) \leqq \text{Max}\,[f_A(x), f_B(x)], \qquad x \in X \quad (20)$$

which hold for all λ in [0, 1]. It is of interest to observe that, given any fuzzy set C satisfying $A \cap B \subset C \subset A \cup B$, one can always find a fuzzy set Λ such that $C = (A, B; \Lambda)$. The membership function of this set is given by

$$f_\Lambda(x) = \frac{f_C(x) - f_B(x)}{f_A(x) - f_B(x)}, \qquad x \in X. \quad (21)$$

Fuzzy relation. The concept of a *relation* (which is a generalization of that of a *function*) has a natural extension to fuzzy sets and plays an important role in the theory of such sets and their applications—just as it does in the case of ordinary sets. In the sequel, we shall merely define the notion of a fuzzy relation and touch upon a few related concepts.

Ordinarily, a relation is defined as a set of ordered pairs (Halmos, 1960); e.g., the set of all ordered pairs of real numbers x and y such that $x \geqq y$. In the context of fuzzy sets, a *fuzzy relation in* X is a fuzzy set in the product space $X \times X$. For example, the relation denoted by $x \gg y$, $x, y \in R^1$, may be regarded as a fuzzy set A in R^2, with the membership function of A, $f_A(x, y)$, having the following (subjective) representative values: $f_A(10, 5) = 0$; $f_A(100, 10) = 0.7$; $f_A(100, 1) = 1$; etc.

More generally, one can define an *n-ary fuzzy relation* in X as a fuzzy set A in the product space $X \times X \times \cdots \times X$. For such relations, the membership function is of the form $f_A(x_1, \cdots, x_n)$, where $x_i \in X$, $i = 1, \cdots, n$.

In the case of binary fuzzy relations, the *composition* of two fuzzy relations A and B is denoted by $B \circ A$ and is defined as a fuzzy relation in X whose membership function is related to those of A and B by

$$f_{B \circ A}(x, y) = \text{Sup}_v \,\text{Min}\,[f_A(x, v), f_B(v, y)].$$

Note that the operation of composition has the associative property

$$A \circ (B \circ C) = (A \circ B) \circ C.$$

Fuzzy sets induced by mappings. Let T be a mapping from X to a space Y. Let B be a fuzzy set in Y with membership function $f_B(y)$. The inverse mapping T^{-1} induces a fuzzy set A in X whose membership function is defined by

$$f_A(x) = f_B(y), \qquad y \in Y \quad (22)$$

for all x in X which are mapped by T into y.

Consider now a converse problem in which A is a given fuzzy set in X, and T, as before, is a mapping from X to Y. The question is: What is the membership function for the fuzzy set B in Y which is induced by this mapping?

If T is not one-one, then an ambiguity arises when two or more distinct points in X, say x_1 and x_2, with different grades of membership in A, are mapped into the same point y in Y. In this case, the question is: What grade of membership in B should be assigned to y?

To resolve this ambiguity, we agree to assign the larger of the two grades of membership to y. More generally, the membership function for B will be defined by

$$f_B(y) = \text{Max}_{x \in T^{-1}(y)} f_A(x), \qquad y \in Y \quad (23)$$

where $T^{-1}(y)$ is the set of points in X which are mapped into y by T.

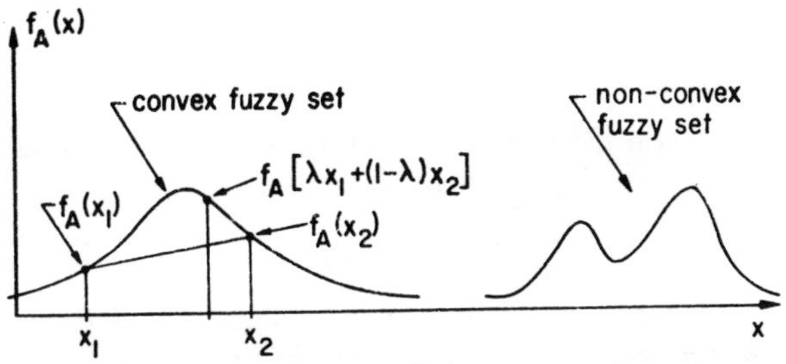

FIG. 4. Convex and nonconvex fuzzy sets in E^1

V. CONVEXITY

As will be seen in the sequel, the notion of convexity can readily be extended to fuzzy sets in such a way as to preserve many of the properties which it has in the context of ordinary sets. This notion appears to be particularly useful in applications involving pattern classification, optimization and related problems.

In what follows, we assume for concreteness that X is a real Euclidean space E^n.

DEFINITIONS

Convexity. A fuzzy set A is *convex* if and only if the sets Γ_α defined by

$$\Gamma_\alpha = \{x \mid f_A(x) \geqq \alpha\} \tag{24}$$

are convex for all α in the interval (0, 1].

An alternative and more direct definition of convexity is the following[5]: A is *convex* if and only if

$$f_A[\lambda x_1 + (1 - \lambda)x_2] \geqq \text{Min}\,[f_A(x_1), f_A(x_2)] \tag{25}$$

for all x_1 and x_2 in X and all λ in [0, 1]. Note that this definition does not imply that $f_A(x)$ must be a convex function of x. This is illustrated in Fig. 4 for $n = 1$.

To show the equivalence between the above definitions note that if A is convex in the sense of the first definition and $\alpha = f_A(x_1) \leqq f_A(x_2)$, then $x_2 \in \Gamma_\alpha$ and $\lambda x_1 + (1 - \lambda)x_2 \in \Gamma_\alpha$ by the convexity of Γ_α. Hence

$$f_A[\lambda x_1 + (1 - \lambda)x_2] \geqq \alpha = f_A(x_1) = \text{Min}\,[f_A(x_1), f_A(x_2)].$$

Conversely, if A is convex in the sense of the second definition and $\alpha = f_A(x_1)$, then Γ_α may be regarded as the set of all points x_2 for which $f_A(x_2) \geqq f_A(x_1)$. In virtue of (25), every point of the form $\lambda x_1 + (1 - \lambda)x_2$, $0 \leqq \lambda \leqq 1$, is also in Γ_α and hence Γ_α is a convex set. Q.E.D.

A basic property of convex fuzzy sets is expressed by the

THEOREM. *If A and B are convex, so is their intersection.*

Proof: Let $C = A \cap B$. Then

$$f_C[\lambda x_1 + (1 - \lambda)x_2] = \text{Min}\,[f_A[\lambda x_1 + (1 - \lambda)x_2], f_B[\lambda x_1 + (1 - \lambda)x_2]]. \tag{26}$$

Now, since A and B are convex

$$\begin{aligned} f_A[\lambda x_1 + (1 - \lambda)x_2] &\geqq \text{Min}\,[f_A(x_1), f_A(x_2)] \\ f_B[\lambda x_1 + (1 - \lambda)x_2] &\geqq \text{Min}\,[f_B(x_1), f_B(x_2)] \end{aligned} \tag{27}$$

and hence

$$f_C[\lambda x_1 + (1 - \lambda)x_2] \geqq \text{Min}\,[\text{Min}\,[f_A(x_1), f_A(x_2)], \text{Min}\,[f_B(x_1), f_B(x_2)]] \tag{28}$$

[5] This way of expressing convexity was suggested to the writer by his colleague, E. Berlekamp.

or equivalently

$$f_C[\lambda x_1 + (1 - \lambda)x_2] \geq \text{Min}\,[\text{Min}\,[f_A(x_1), f_B(x_1)], \text{Min}\,[f_A(x_2), f_B(x_2)]] \tag{29}$$

and thus

$$f_C[\lambda x_1 + (1 - \lambda)x_2] \geq \text{Min}\,[f_C(x_1), f_C(x_2)]. \quad \text{Q. E. D.} \tag{30}$$

Boundedness. A fuzzy set A is *bounded* if and only if the sets $\Gamma_\alpha = \{x \mid f_A(x) \geq \alpha\}$ are bounded for all $\alpha > 0$; that is, for every $\alpha > 0$ there exists a finite $R(\alpha)$ such that $\| x \| \leq R(\alpha)$ for all x in Γ_α.

If A is a bounded set, then for each $\epsilon > 0$ then exists a hyperplane H such that $f_A(x) \leq \epsilon$ for all x on the side of H which does not contain the origin. For, consider the set $\Gamma_\epsilon = \{x \mid f_A(x) \geq \epsilon\}$. By hypothesis, this set is contained in a sphere S of radius $R(\epsilon)$. Let H be any hyperplane supporting S. Then, all points on the side of H which does not contain the origin lie outside or on S, and hence for all such points $f_A(x) \leq \epsilon$.

LEMMA. *Let A be a bounded fuzzy set and let $M = \text{Sup}_x f_A(x)$. (M will be referred to as the* maximal grade *in A.) Then there is at least one point x_0 at which M is essentially attained in the sense that, for each $\epsilon > 0$, every spherical neighborhood of x_0 contains points in the set $Q(\epsilon) = \{x \mid f_A(x) \geq M - \epsilon\}$.*

Proof.[6] Consider a nested sequence of bounded sets $\Gamma_1, \Gamma_2, \cdots$, where $\Gamma_n = \{x \mid f_A(x) \geq M - M/(n + 1)\}$, $n = 1, 2, \cdots$. Note that Γ_n is nonempty for all finite n as a consequence of the definition of M as $M = \text{Sup}_x f_A(x)$. (We assume that $M > 0$.)

Let x_n be an arbitrarily chosen point in Γ_n, $n = 1, 2, \cdots$. Then, $x_1, x_2, \cdots$, is a sequence of points in a closed bounded set Γ_1. By the Bolzano-Weierstrass theorem, this sequence must have at least one limit point, say x_0, in Γ_1. Consequently, every spherical neighborhood of x_0 will contain infinitely many points from the sequence $x_1, x_2, \cdots$, and, more particularly, from the subsequence $x_{N+1}, x_{N+2}, \cdots$, where $N \geq M/\epsilon$. Since the points of this subsequence fall within the set $Q(\epsilon) = \{x \mid f_A(x) \geq M - \epsilon\}$, the lemma is proved.

Strict and strong convexity. A fuzzy set A is *strictly convex* if the sets Γ_α, $0 < \alpha \leq 1$ are strictly convex (that is, if the midpoint of any two distinct points in Γ_α lies in the interior of Γ_α). Note that this definition reduces to that of strict convexity for ordinary sets when A is such a set.

A fuzzy set A is *strongly convex* if, for any two distinct points x_1 and x_2, and any λ in the open interval $(0, 1)$

$$f_A[\lambda x_1 + (1 - \lambda)x_2] > \text{Min}\,[f_A(x_1), f_A(x_2)].$$

Note that strong convexity does not imply strict convexity or vice-versa. Note also that if A and B are bounded, so is their union and intersection. Similarly, if A and B are strictly (strongly) convex, their intersection is strictly (strongly) convex.

Let A be a convex fuzzy set and let $M = \text{Sup}_x f_A(x)$. If A is bounded, then, as shown above, either M is attained for some x, say x_0, or there is at least one point x_0 at which M is essentially attained in the sense that, for each $\epsilon > 0$, every spherical neighborhood of x_0 contains points in the set $Q(\epsilon) = \{x \mid M - f_A(x) \leq \epsilon\}$. In particular, if A is strongly convex and x_0 is attained, then x_0 is unique. For, if $M = f_A(x_0)$ and $M = f_A(x_1)$, with $x_1 \neq x_0$, then $f_A(x) > M$ for $x = 0.5x_0 + 0.5x_1$, which contradicts $M = \text{Max}_x f_A(x)$.

More generally, let $C(A)$ be the set of all points in X at which M is essentially attained. This set will be referred to as the *core* of A. In the case of convex fuzzy sets, we can assert the following property of $C(A)$.

[6] This proof was suggested by A. J. Thomasian.

THEOREM. *If A is a convex fuzzy set, then its core is a convex set.*

Proof: It will suffice to show that if M is essentially attained at x_0 and x_1, $x_1 \neq x_0$, then it is also essentially attained at all x of the form $x = \lambda x_0 + (1 - \lambda)x_1$, $0 \leqq \lambda \leqq 1$.

To the end, let P be a cylinder of radius ϵ with the line passing through x_0 and x_1 as its axis. Let x_0' be a point in a sphere of radius ϵ centering on x_0 and x_1' be a point in a sphere of radius ϵ centering on x_1 such that $f_A(x_0') \geqq M - \epsilon$ and $f_A(x_1') \geqq M - \epsilon$. Then, by the convexity of A, for any point u on the segment $x_0'x_1'$, we have $f_A(u) \geqq M - \epsilon$. Furthermore, by the convexity of P, all points on $x_0'x_1'$ will lie in P.

Now let x be any point in the segment x_0x_1. The distance of this point from the segment $x_0'x_1'$ must be less than or equal to ϵ, since $x_0'x_1'$ lies in P. Consequently, a sphere of radius ϵ centering on x will contain at least one point of the segment $x_0'x_1'$ and hence will contain at least one point, say w, at which $f_A(w) \geqq M - \epsilon$. This establishes that M is essentially attained at x and thus proves the theorem.

COROLLARY. *If $X = E^1$ and A is strongly convex, then the point at which M is essentially attained is unique.*

Shadow of a fuzzy set. Let A be a fuzzy set in E^n with membership function $f_A(x) = f_A(x_1, \cdots, x_n)$. For notational simplicity, the notion of the *shadow* (projection) of A on a hyperplane H will be defined below for the special case where H is a coordinate hyperplane, e.g., $H = \{x \mid x_1 = 0\}$.

Specifically, the *shadow* of A on $H = \{x \mid x_1 = 0\}$ is defined to be a fuzzy set $S_H(A)$ in E^{n-1} with $f_{S_H(A)}(x)$ given by

$$f_{S_H(A)}(x) = f_{S_H(A)}(x_2, \cdots, x_n) = \operatorname{Sup}_{x_1} f_A(x_1, \cdots, x_n).$$

Note that this definition is consistent with (23).

When A is a convex fuzzy set, the following property of $S_H(A)$ is an immediate consequence of the above definition: If A is a convex fuzzy set, then its shadow on any hyperplane is also a convex fuzzy set.

An interesting property of the shadows of two convex fuzzy sets is expressed by the following implication

$$S_H(A) = S_H(B) \text{ for all } H \Rightarrow A = B.$$

To prove this assertion,[7] it is sufficient to show that if there exists a point, say x_0, such that $f_A(x_0) \neq f_B(x_0)$, then their exists a hyperplane H such that $f_{S_H(A)}(x_0^*) \neq f_{S_H(B)}(x_0^*)$, where x_0^* is the projection of x_0 on H.

Suppose that $f_A(x_0) = \alpha > f_B(x_0) = \beta$. Since B is a convex fuzzy set, the set $\Gamma_\beta = \{x \mid f_B(x) > \beta\}$ is convex, and hence there exists a hyperplane F supporting Γ_β and passing through x_0. Let H be a hyperplane orthogonal to F, and let x_0^* be the projection of x_0 on H. Then, since $f_B(x) \leqq \beta$ for all x on F, we have $f_{S_H(B)}(x_0^*) \leqq \beta$. On the other hand, $f_{S_H(A)}(x_0^*) \geqq \alpha$. Consequently, $f_{S_H(B)}(x_0^*) \neq f_{S_H(A)}(x_0^*)$, and similarly for the case where $\alpha < \beta$.

A somewhat more general form of the above assertion is the following: Let A, but not necessarily B, be a convex fuzzy set, and let $S_H(A) = S_H(B)$ for all H. Then $A = \operatorname{conv} B$, where conv B is the convex hull of B, that is, the smallest convex set containing B. More generally, $S_H(A) = S_H(B)$ for all H implies conv A = conv B.

Separation of convex fuzzy sets. The classical separation theorem for ordinary convex sets states, in essence, that if A and B are disjoint convex sets, then there exists a separating hyperplane H such that A is on one side of H and B is on the other side.

It is natural to inquire if this theorem can be extended to convex fuzzy

[7] This proof is based on an idea suggested by G. Dantzig for the case where A and B are ordinary convex sets.

sets, without requiring that A and B be disjoint, since the condition of disjointness is much too restrictive in the case of fuzzy sets. It turns out, as will be seen in the sequel, that the answer to this question is in the affirmative.

As a preliminary, we shall have to make a few definitions. Specifically, let A and B be two bounded fuzzy sets and let H be a hypersurface in E^n defined by an equation $h(x) = 0$, with all points for which $h(x) \geqq 0$ being on one side of H and all points for which $h(x) \leqq 0$ being on the other side.[8] Let K_H be a number dependent on H such that $f_A(x) \leqq K_H$ on one side of H and $f_B(x) \leqq K_H$ on the other side. Let M_H be Inf K_H. The number $D_H = 1 - M_H$ will be called the *degree of separation of A and B by H.*

In general, one is concerned not with a given hypersurface H, but with a family of hypersurfaces $\{H_\lambda\}$, with λ ranging over, say, E^m. The problem, then, is to find a member of this family which realizes the highest possible degree of separation.

A special case of this problem is one where the H_λ are hyperplanes in E^n, with λ ranging over E^n. In this case, we define the *degree of separability* of A and B by the relation

$$D = 1 - \bar{M} \tag{31}$$

where

$$\bar{M} = \text{Inf}_H M_H \tag{32}$$

with the subscript λ omitted for simplicity.

Among the various assertions that can be made concerning D, the following statement[9] is, in effect, an extension of the separation theorem to convex fuzzy sets.

THEOREM. *Let A and B be bounded convex fuzzy sets in E^n, with maximal grades M_A and M_B, respectively* [$M_A = \text{Sup}_x f_A(x)$, $M_B = \text{Sup}_x f_B(x)$]. *Let M be the maximal grade for the intersection $A \cap B$* ($M = \text{Sup}_x \text{Min} \cdot [f_A(x), f_B(x)]$). *Then $D = 1 - M$.*

Comment. In plain words, the theorem states that the highest degree of separation of two convex fuzzy sets A and B that can be achieved with a hyperplane in E^n is one minus the maximal grade in the intersection $A \cap B$. This is illustrated in Fig. 5 for $n = 1$.

Proof: It is convenient to consider separately the following two cases: (1) $M = \text{Min}(M_A, M_B)$ and (2) $M < \text{Min}(M_A, M_B)$. Note that the latter case rules out $A \subset B$ or $B \subset A$.

Case 1. For concreteness, assume that $M_A < M_B$, so that $M = M_A$. Then, by the property of bounded sets already stated there exists a hyperplane H such that $f_B(x) \leqq M$ for all x on one side of H. On the other side of H, $f_A(x) \leqq M$ because $f_A(x) \leqq M_A = M$ for all x.

It remains to be shown that there do not exist an $M' < M$ and a hyperplane H' such that $f_A(x) \leqq M'$ on one side of H' and $f_B(x) \leqq M'$ on the other side.

This follows at once from the following observation. Suppose that such H' and M' exist, and assume for concreteness that the core of A (that is, the set of points at which $M_A = M$ is essentially attained) is on the plus side of H'. This rules out the possibility that $f_A(x) \leqq M'$ for all x on the plus side of H', and hence necessitates that $f_A(x) \leqq M'$ for all x on the minus side of H', and $f_B(x) \leqq M'$ for all x on the plus side of H'. Consequently, over all x on the plus side of H'

$$\text{Sup}_x \text{Min}[f_A(x), f_B(x)] \leqq M'$$

and likewise for all x on the minus side of H'. This implies that, over all

[8] Note that the sets in question have H in common.

[9] This statement is based on a suggestion of E. Berlekamp.

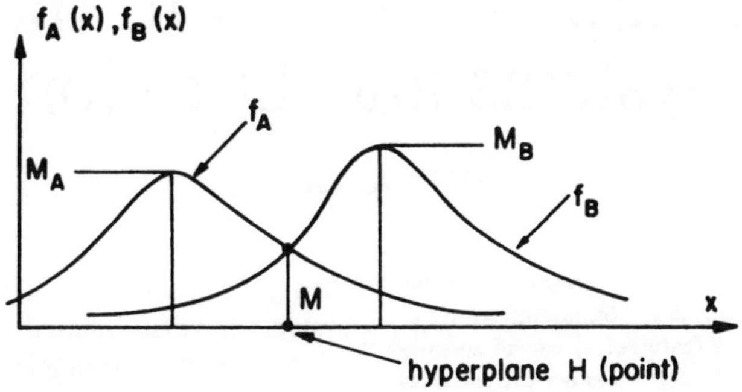

FIG. 5. Illustration of the separation theorem for fuzzy sets in E^1

x in X, $\text{Sup}_x \text{ Min } [f_A(x), f_B(x)] \leqq M'$, which contradicts the assumption that $\text{Sup}_x \text{ Min } [f_A(x), f_B(x)] = M > M'$.

Case 2. Consider the convex sets $\Gamma_A = \{x \mid f_A(x) > M\}$ and $\Gamma_B = \{x \mid f_B(x) > M\}$. These sets are nonempty and disjoint, for if they were not there would be a point, say u, such that $f_A(u) > M$ and $f_B(u) > M$, and hence $f_{A \cap B}(u) > M$, which contradicts the assumption that $M = \text{Sup}_x f_{A \cap B}(x)$.

Since Γ_A and Γ_B are disjoint, by the separation theorem for ordinary convex sets there exists a hyperplane H such that Γ_A is on one side of H (say, the plus side) and Γ_B is on the other side (the minus side). Furthermore, by the definitions of Γ_A and Γ_B, for all points on the minus side of $H, f_A(x) \leqq M$, and for all points on the plus side of $H, f_B(x) \leqq M$.

Thus, we have shown that there exists a hyperplane H which realizes $1 - M$ as the degree of separation of A and B. The conclusion that a higher degree of separation of A and B cannot be realized follows from the argument given in Case 1. This concludes the proof of the theorem.

The separation theorem for convex fuzzy sets appears to be of particular relevance to the problem of pattern discrimination. Its application to this class of problems as well as to problems of optimization will be explored in subsequent notes on fuzzy sets and their properties.

RECEIVED: November 30, 1964

REFERENCES

BIRKHOFF, G. (1948), "Lattice Theory," Am. Math. Soc. Colloq. Publ., Vol. 25, New York.

HALMOS, P. R. (1960), "Naive Set Theory." Van Nostrand, New York.

KLEENE, S. C. (1952), "Introduction to Metamathematics," p. 334. Van Nostrand, New York.

Outline of a New Approach to the Analysis of Complex Systems and Decision Processes

LOTFI A. ZADEH

Abstract—The approach described in this paper represents a substantive departure from the conventional quantitative techniques of system analysis. It has three main distinguishing features: 1) use of so-called "linguistic" variables in place of or in addition to numerical variables; 2) characterization of simple relations between variables by fuzzy conditional statements; and 3) characterization of complex relations by fuzzy algorithms.

A *linguistic variable* is defined as a variable whose values are sentences in a natural or artificial language. Thus, if *tall, not tall, very tall, very very tall*, etc. are values of *height*, then *height* is a linguistic variable. *Fuzzy conditional statements* are expressions of the form IF A THEN B, where A and B have fuzzy meaning, e.g., IF x is *small* THEN y is *large*, where *small* and *large* are viewed as labels of fuzzy sets. A *fuzzy algorithm* is an ordered sequence of instructions which may contain fuzzy assignment and conditional statements, e.g., x = *very small*, IF x is *small* THEN y is *large*. The execution of such instructions is governed by the *compositional rule of inference* and the *rule of the preponderant alternative*.

By relying on the use of linguistic variables and fuzzy algorithms, the approach provides an approximate and yet effective means of describing the behavior of systems which are too complex or too ill-defined to admit of precise mathematical analysis. Its main applications lie in economics, management science, artificial intelligence, psychology, linguistics, information retrieval, medicine, biology, and other fields in which the dominant role is played by the animate rather than inanimate behavior of system constituents.

I. Introduction

THE ADVENT of the computer age has stimulated a rapid expansion in the use of quantitative techniques for the analysis of economic, urban, social, biological, and other types of systems in which it is the animate rather than inanimate behavior of system constituents that plays a dominant role. At present, most of the techniques employed for the analysis of *humanistic*, i.e., human-centered, systems are adaptations of the methods that have been developed over a long period of time for dealing with *mechanistic* systems, i.e., physical systems governed in the main by the laws of mechanics, electromagnetism, and thermodynamics. The remarkable successes of these methods in unraveling the secrets of nature and enabling us to build better and better machines have inspired a widely held belief that the same or similar techniques can be applied with comparable effectiveness to the analysis of humanistic systems. As a case in point, the successes of modern control theory in the design of highly accurate space navigation systems have stimulated its use in the theoretical analyses of economic and biological systems. Similarly, the effectiveness of computer simulation techniques in the macroscopic analyses of physical systems has brought into vogue the use of computer-based econometric models for purposes of forecasting, economic planning, and management.

Given the deeply entrenched tradition of scientific thinking which equates the understanding of a phenomenon with the ability to analyze it in quantitative terms, one is certain to strike a dissonant note by questioning the growing tendency to analyze the behavior of humanistic systems as if they were mechanistic systems governed by difference, differential, or integral equations. Such a note is struck in the present paper.

Essentially, our contention is that the conventional quantitative techniques of system analysis are intrinsically unsuited for dealing with humanistic systems or, for that matter, any system whose complexity is comparable to that of humanistic systems. The basis for this contention rests on what might be called the *principle of incompatibility*. Stated informally, the essence of this principle is that as the complexity of a system increases, our ability to make precise and yet significant statements about its behavior diminishes until a threshold is reached beyond which precision and significance (or relevance) become almost mutually exclusive characteristics.[1] It is in this sense that precise quantitative analyses of the behavior of humanistic systems are not likely to have much relevance to the real-world societal, political, economic, and other types of problems which involve humans either as individuals or in groups.

An alternative approach outlined in this paper is based on the premise that the key elements in human thinking are not numbers, but labels of fuzzy sets, that is, classes of objects in which the transition from membership to nonmembership is gradual rather than abrupt. Indeed, the pervasiveness of fuzziness in human thought processes suggests that much of the logic behind human reasoning is not the traditional two-valued or even multivalued logic, but a logic with fuzzy truths, fuzzy connectives, and fuzzy rules of inference. In our view, it is this fuzzy, and as yet not well-understood, logic that plays a basic role in what may well be one of the most important facets of human thinking, namely, the ability to *summarize* information—to extract from the collections of masses of data impinging

Manuscript received August 1, 1972; revised August 13, 1972. This work was supported by the Navy Electronic Systems Command under Contract N00039-71-C-0255, the Army Research Office, Durham, N.C., under Grant DA-ARO-D-31-124-71-G174, and NASA under Grant NGL-05-003-016-VP3.

The author is with the Department of Electrical Engineering and Computer Sciences and Electronics Research Laboratory, University of California, Berkeley, Calif. 94720.

[1] A corollary principle may be stated succinctly as, "The closer one looks at a real-world problem, the fuzzier becomes its solution."

Reprinted from *IEEE Trans. Syst., Man, Cybern.*, vol. SMC-3, no. 1, pp. 28–44, January 1973.

upon the human brain those and only those subcollections which are relevant to the performance of the task at hand.

By its nature, a summary is an approximation to what it summarizes. For many purposes, a very approximate characterization of a collection of data is sufficient because most of the basic tasks performed by humans do not require a high degree of precision in their execution. The human brain takes advantage of this tolerance for imprecision by encoding the "task-relevant" (or "decision-relevant") information into labels of fuzzy sets which bear an approximate relation to the primary data. In this way, the stream of information reaching the brain via the visual, auditory, tactile, and other senses is eventually reduced to the trickle that is needed to perform a specified task with a minimal degree of precision. Thus, the ability to manipulate fuzzy sets and the consequent summarizing capability constitute one of the most important assets of the human mind as well as a fundamental characteristic that distinguishes human intelligence from the type of machine intelligence that is embodied in present-day digital computers.

Viewed in this perspective, the traditional techniques of system analysis are not well suited for dealing with humanistic systems because they fail to come to grips with the reality of the fuzziness of human thinking and behavior. Thus, to deal with such systems realistically, we need approaches which do not make a fetish of precision, rigor, and mathematical formalism, and which employ instead a methodological framework which is tolerant of imprecision and partial truths. The approach described in the sequel is a step—but not necessarily a definitive step—in this direction.

The approach in question has three main distinguishing features: 1) use of so-called "linguistic" variables in place of or in addition to numerical variables; 2) characterization of simple relations between variables by conditional fuzzy statements; and 3) characterization of complex relations by fuzzy algorithms. Before proceeding to a detailed discussion of our approach, it will be helpful to sketch the principal ideas behind these features. We begin with a brief explanation of the notion of a linguistic variable.

1) *Linguistic and Fuzzy Variables:* As already pointed out, the ability to summarize information plays an essential role in the characterization of complex phenomena. In the case of humans, the ability to summarize information finds its most pronounced manifestation in the use of natural languages. Thus, each word x in a natural language L may be viewed as a summarized description of a fuzzy subset $M(x)$ of a universe of discourse U, with $M(x)$ representing the meaning of x. In this sense, the language as a whole may be regarded as a system for assigning atomic and composite labels (i.e., words, phrases, and sentences) to the fuzzy subsets of U. (This point of view is discussed in greater detail in [4] and [5].) For example, if the meaning of the noun *flower* is a fuzzy subset $M(\textit{flower})$, and the meaning of the adjective *red* is a fuzzy subset $M(\textit{red})$, then the meaning of the noun phrase *red flower* is given by the intersection of $M(\textit{red})$ and $M(\textit{flower})$.

If we regard the color of an object as a variable, then its values, *red*, *blue*, *yellow*, *green*, etc., may be interpreted as labels of fuzzy subsets of a universe of objects. In this sense, the attribute *color* is a *fuzzy variable*, that is, a variable whose values are labels of fuzzy sets. It is important to note that the characterization of a value of the variable *color* by a natural label such as *red* is much less precise than the numerical value of the wavelength of a particular color.

In the preceding example, the values of the variable *color* are atomic terms like *red*, *blue*, *yellow*, etc. More generally, the values may be sentences in a specified language, in which case we say that the variable is *linguistic*. To illustrate, the values of the fuzzy variable *height* might be expressible as *tall*, *not tall*, *somewhat tall*, *very tall*, *not very tall*, *very very tall*, *tall but not very tall*, *quite tall*, *more or less tall*. Thus, the values in question are sentences formed from the label *tall*, the negation *not*, the connectives *and* and *but*, and the hedges *very*, *somewhat*, *quite*, and *more or less*. In this sense, the variable *height* as defined above is a linguistic variable.

As will be seen in Section III, the main function of linguistic variables is to provide a systematic means for an approximate characterization of complex or ill-defined phenomena. In essence, by moving away from the use of quantified variables and toward the use of the type of linguistic descriptions employed by humans, we acquire a capability to deal with systems which are much too complex to be susceptible to analysis in conventional mathematical terms.

2) *Characterization of Simple Relations Between Fuzzy Variables by Conditional Statements:* In quantitative approaches to system analysis, a dependence between two numerically valued variables x and y is usually characterized by a table which, in words, may be expressed as a set of conditional statements, e.g., IF x is 5 THEN y is 10, IF x is 6 THEN y is 14, etc.

The same technique is employed in our approach, except that x and y are allowed to be fuzzy variables. In particular, if x and y are linguistic variables, the conditional statements describing the dependence of y on x might read (the following italicized words represent the values of fuzzy variables):

IF x is *small* THEN y is *very large*
IF x is *not very small* THEN y is *very very large*
IF x is *not small and not large* THEN y is *not very large*

and so forth.

Fuzzy conditional statements of the form IF A THEN B, where A and B are terms with a fuzzy meaning, e.g., "IF John is *nice* to you THEN you should be *kind* to him," are used routinely in everyday discourse. However, the meaning of such statements when used in communication between humans is poorly defined. As will be shown in Section V, the conditional statement IF A THEN B can be given a precise meaning even when A and B are fuzzy rather than nonfuzzy sets, provided the meanings of A and B are defined precisely as specified subsets of the universe of discourse.

In the preceding example, the relation between two fuzzy variables x and y is *simple* in the sense that it can be characterized as a set of conditional statements of the form IF A THEN B, where A and B are labels of fuzzy sets representing the values of x and y, respectively. In the case of more complex relations, the characterization of the dependence of y on x may require the use of a fuzzy algorithm. As indicated below, and discussed in greater detail in Section VI, the notion of a fuzzy algorithm plays a basic role in providing a means of approximate characterization of fuzzy concepts and their interrelations.

3) *Fuzzy-Algorithmic Characterization of Functions and Relations:* The definition of a fuzzy function through the use of fuzzy conditional statements is analogous to the definition of a nonfuzzy function f by a table of pairs $(x,f(x))$, in which x is a generic value of the argument of f and $f(x)$ is the value of the function. Just as a nonfuzzy function can be defined algorithmically (e.g., by a program) rather than by a table, so a fuzzy function can be defined by a fuzzy algorithm rather than as a collection of fuzzy conditional statements. The same applies to the definition of sets, relations, and other constructs which are fuzzy in nature.

Essentially, a fuzzy algorithm [6] is an ordered sequence of instructions (like a computer program) in which some of the instructions may contain labels of fuzzy sets, e.g.:

Reduce x *slightly* if y is *large*
Increase x *very slightly* if y is *not very large and not very small*
If x is *small* then stop; otherwise increase x by 2.

By allowing an algorithm to contain instructions of this type, it becomes possible to give an approximate fuzzy-algorithmic characterization of a wide variety of complex phenomena. The important feature of such characterizations is that, though imprecise in nature, they may be perfectly adequate for the purposes of a specified task. In this way, fuzzy algorithms can provide an effective means of approximate description of objective functions, constraints, system performance, strategies, etc.

In what follows, we shall elaborate on some of the basic aspects of linguistic variables, fuzzy conditional statements, and fuzzy algorithms. However, we shall not attempt to present a definitive exposition of our approach and its applications. Thus, the present paper should be viewed primarily as an introductory outline of a method which departs from the tradition of precision and rigor in scientific analysis—a method whose approximate nature mirrors the fuzziness of human behavior and thereby offers a promise of providing a more realistic basis for the analysis of humanistic systems.

As will be seen in the following sections, the theoretical foundation of our approach is actually quite precise and rather mathematical in spirit. Thus, the source of imprecision in the approach is not the underlying theory, but the manner in which linguistic variables and fuzzy algorithms are applied to the formulation and solution of real-world problems. In effect, the level of precision in a particular application can be adjusted to fit the needs of the task and the accuracy of the available data. This flexibility constitutes one of the important features of the method that will be described.

II. Fuzzy Sets: A Summary of Relevant Properties

In order to make our exposition self-contained, we shall summarize in this section those properties of fuzzy sets which will be needed in later sections. (More detailed discussions of topics in the theory of fuzzy sets which are relevant to the subject of the present paper may be found in [1]–[17].)

Notation and Terminology

A fuzzy subset A of a universe of discourse U is characterized by a membership function $\mu_A: U \rightarrow [0,1]$ which associates with each element y of U a number $\mu_A(y)$ in the interval $[0,1]$ which represents the grade of membership of y in A. The *support* of A is the set of points in U at which $\mu_A(y)$ is positive. A *crossover point* in A is an element of U whose grade of membership in A is 0.5. A *fuzzy singleton* is a fuzzy set whose support is a single point in U. If A is a fuzzy singleton whose support is the point y, we write

$$A = \mu/y \tag{2.1}$$

where μ is the grade of membership of y in A. To be consistent with this notation, a nonfuzzy singleton will be denoted by $1/y$.

A fuzzy set A may be viewed as the union (see (2.27)) of its constituent singletons. On this basis, A may be represented in the form

$$A = \int_U \mu_A(y)/y \tag{2.2}$$

where the integral sign stands for the union of the fuzzy singletons $\mu_A(y)/y$. If A has a finite support $\{y_1,y_2,\cdots,y_n\}$, then (2.2) may be replaced by the summation

$$A = \mu_1/y_1 + \cdots + \mu_n/y_n \tag{2.3}$$

or

$$A = \sum_{i=1}^{n} \mu_i/y_i \tag{2.4}$$

in which μ_i, $i = 1,\cdots,n$, is the grade of membership of y_i in A. It should be noted that the + sign in (2.3) denotes the union (see (2.27)) rather than the arithmetic sum. In this sense of +, a finite universe of discourse $U = \{y_1,y_2,\cdots, y_n\}$ may be represented simply by the summation

$$U = y_1 + y_2 + \cdots + y_n \tag{2.5}$$

or

$$U = \sum_{i=1}^{n} y_i \tag{2.6}$$

although, strictly, we should write (2.5) and (2.6) as

$$U = 1/y_1 + 1/y_2 + \cdots + 1/y_n \tag{2.7}$$

and

$$U = \sum_{i=1}^{n} 1/y_i. \tag{2.8}$$

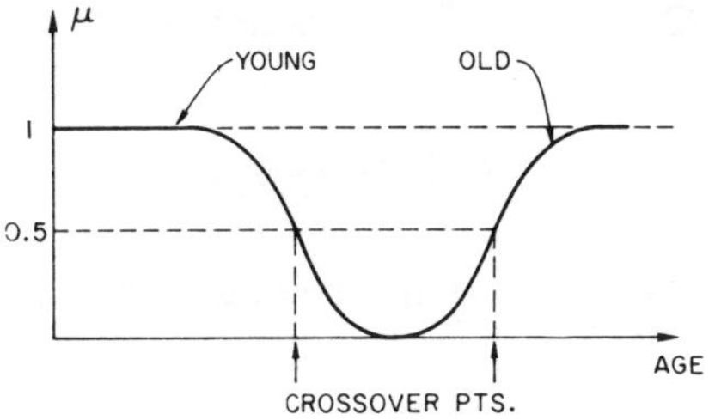

Fig. 1. Diagrammatic representation of *young* and *old*.

As an illustration, suppose that

$$U = 1 + 2 + \cdots + 10. \tag{2.9}$$

Then a fuzzy subset[2] of U labeled *several* may be expressed as (the symbol $\triangleq$ stands for "equal by definition," or "is defined to be," or "denotes")

$$several \triangleq 0.5/3 + 0.8/4 + 1/5 + 1/6 + 0.8/7 + 0.5/8. \tag{2.10}$$

Similarly, if U is the interval [0,100], with $y \triangleq age$, then the fuzzy subsets of U labeled *young* and *old* may be represented as (here and elsewhere in this paper we do not differentiate between a fuzzy set and its label)

$$young = \int_0^{25} 1/y + \int_{25}^{100} \left(1 + \left(\frac{y-25}{5}\right)^2\right)^{-1} / y \tag{2.11}$$

$$old = \int_{50}^{100} \left(1 + \left(\frac{y-50}{5}\right)^{-2}\right)^{-1} / y. \tag{2.12}$$

(see Fig. 1).

The grade of membership in a fuzzy set may itself be a fuzzy set. For example, if

$$U = \text{TOM} + \text{JIM} + \text{DICK} + \text{BOB} \tag{2.13}$$

and A is the fuzzy subset labeled *agile*, then we may have

$$agile = medium/\text{TOM} + low/\text{JIM} + low/\text{DICK} + high/\text{BOB}. \tag{2.14}$$

In this representation, the fuzzy grades of membership *low*, *medium*, and *high* are fuzzy subsets of the universe V

$$V = 0 + 0.1 + 0.2 + \cdots + 0.9 + 1 \tag{2.15}$$

which are defined by

$$low = 0.5/0.2 + 0.7/0.3 + 1/0.4 + 0.7/0.5 + 0.5/0.6 \tag{2.16}$$

$$medium = 0.5/0.4 + 0.7/0.5 + 1/0.6 + 0.7/0.7 + 0.5/0.8 \tag{2.17}$$

$$high = 0.5/0.7 + 0.7/0.8 + 0.9/0.9 + 1/1. \tag{2.18}$$

[2] A is a subset of B, written $A \subset B$, if and only if $\mu_A(y) \leq \mu_B(y)$, for all y in U. For example, the fuzzy set $A = 0.6/1 + 0.3/2$ is a subset of $B = 0.8/1 + 0.5/2 + 0.6/3$.

Fuzzy Relations

A *fuzzy relation* R from a set X to a set Y is a fuzzy subset of the Cartesian product $X \times Y$. ($X \times Y$ is the collection of ordered pairs (x,y), $x \in X$, $y \in Y$). R is characterized by a bivariate membership function $\mu_R(x,y)$ and is expressed

$$R \triangleq \int_{X \times Y} \mu_R(x,y)/(x,y). \tag{2.19}$$

More generally, for an $n$ary fuzzy relation R which is a fuzzy subset of $X_1 \times X_2 \times \cdots \times X_n$, we have

$$R \triangleq \int_{X_1 \times \cdots \times X_n} \mu_R(x_1,\cdots,x_n)/(x_1,\cdots,x_n), \quad x_i \in X_i, \quad i = 1,\cdots,n. \tag{2.20}$$

As an illustration, if

$$X = \{\text{TOM, DICK}\} \quad \text{and} \quad Y = \{\text{JOHN, JIM}\}$$

then a binary fuzzy relation of *resemblance* between members of X and Y might be expressed as

$$resemblance = 0.8/(\text{TOM, JOHN}) + 0.6/(\text{TOM, JIM}) + 0.2/(\text{DICK, JOHN}) + 0.9/(\text{DICK, JIM}).$$

Alternatively, this relation may be represented as a *relation matrix*

$$\begin{array}{c} \\ \text{TOM} \\ \text{DICK} \end{array} \begin{array}{c} \text{JOHN} \quad \text{JIM} \\ \begin{bmatrix} 0.8 & 0.6 \\ 0.2 & 0.9 \end{bmatrix} \end{array} \tag{2.21}$$

in which the (i,j)th element is the value of $\mu_R(x,y)$ for the ith value of x and the jth value of y.

If R is a relation from X to Y and S is a relation from Y to Z, then the *composition* of R and S is a fuzzy relation denoted by $R \circ S$ and defined by

$$R \circ S \triangleq \int_{X \times Z} \vee_y (\mu_R(x,y) \wedge \mu_s(y,z))/(x,z) \tag{2.22}$$

where $\vee$ and $\wedge$ denote, respectively, max and min.[3] Thus, for real a,b,

$$a \vee b = \max(a,b) \triangleq \begin{cases} a, & \text{if } a \geq b \\ b, & \text{if } a < b \end{cases} \tag{2.23}$$

$$a \wedge b = \min(a,b) \triangleq \begin{cases} a, & \text{if } a \leq b \\ b, & \text{if } a > b \end{cases} \tag{2.24}$$

and $\vee_y$ is the supremum over the domain of y.

If the domains of the variables x, y, and z are finite sets, then the relation matrix for $R \circ S$ is the max–min product[4] of the relation matrices for R and S. For example, the max–min product of the relation matrices on the left-hand side of (2.25) results in the relation matrix $R \circ S$ shown on the

[3] Equation (2.22) defines the max–min composition of R and S. Max-product composition is defined similarly, except that $\wedge$ is replaced by the arithmetic product. A more detailed discussion of these compositions may be found in [2].

[4] In the max–min matrix product, the operations of addition and multiplication are replaced by $\vee$ and $\wedge$, respectively.

right-hand side of

$$\overset{R}{\begin{bmatrix} 0.3 & 0.8 \\ 0.6 & 0.9 \end{bmatrix}} \circ \overset{S}{\begin{bmatrix} 0.5 & 0.9 \\ 0.4 & 1 \end{bmatrix}} = \overset{R \circ S}{\begin{bmatrix} 0.4 & 0.8 \\ 0.5 & 0.9 \end{bmatrix}}. \tag{2.25}$$

Operations on Fuzzy Sets

The negation *not*, the connectives *and* and *or*, the hedges *very*, *highly*, *more or less*, and other terms which enter in the representation of values of linguistic variables may be viewed as labels of various operations defined on the fuzzy subsets of U. The more basic of these operations will be summarized.

The *complement* of A is denoted $\neg A$ and is defined by

$$\neg A \triangleq \int_U (1 - \mu_A(y))/y. \tag{2.26}$$

The operation of complementation corresponds to negation. Thus, if x is a label for a fuzzy set, then *not* x should be interpreted as $\neg x$. (Strictly speaking, $\neg$ operates on fuzzy sets, whereas *not* operates on their labels. With this understanding, we shall use $\neg$ and *not* interchangeably.)

The *union* of fuzzy sets A and B is denoted $A + B$ and is defined by

$$A + B \triangleq \int_U (\mu_A(y) \vee \mu_B(y))/y. \tag{2.27}$$

The union corresponds to the connective *or*. Thus, if u and v are labels of fuzzy sets, then

$$u \text{ or } v \triangleq u + v \tag{2.28}$$

The *intersection* of A and B is denoted $A \cap B$ and is defined by

$$A \cap B \triangleq \int_U (\mu_A(y) \wedge \mu_B(y))/y. \tag{2.29}$$

The intersection corresponds to the connective *and*; thus

$$u \text{ and } v \triangleq u \cap v. \tag{2.30}$$

As an illustration, if

$$U = 1 + 2 + \cdots + 10 \tag{2.31}$$

$$u = 0.8/3 + 1/5 + 0.6/6 \tag{2.32}$$

$$v = 0.7/3 + 1/4 + 0.5/6 \tag{2.33}$$

then

$$u \textit{ or } v = 0.8/3 + 1/4 + 1/5 + 0.6/6 \tag{2.34}$$

$$u \textit{ and } v = 0.7/3 + 0.5/6. \tag{2.35}$$

The *product* of A and B is denoted AB and is defined by

$$AB \triangleq \int_U \mu_A(y)\mu_B(y)/y. \tag{2.36}$$

Thus, if

$$A = 0.8/2 + 0.9/5 \tag{2.37}$$

$$B = 0.6/2 + 0.8/3 + 0.6/5 \tag{2.38}$$

then

$$AB = 0.48/2 + 0.54/5. \tag{2.39}$$

Based on (2.36), A^α, where α is any positive number, is defined by

$$A^\alpha \triangleq \int_U (\mu_A(y))^\alpha/y. \tag{2.40}$$

Similarly, if α is a nonnegative real number, then

$$\alpha A \triangleq \int_U \alpha\mu_A(y)/y. \tag{2.41}$$

As an illustration, if A is expressed by (2.37), then

$$A^2 = 0.64/2 + 0.81/5 \tag{2.42}$$

$$0.5A = 0.4/2 + 0.45/5. \tag{2.43}$$

In addition to the basic operations just defined, there are other operations that are of use in the representation of linguistic hedges. Some of these will be briefly defined. (A more detailed discussion of these operations may be found in [15].)

The operation of *concentration* is defined by

$$\text{CON}\ (A) \triangleq A^2. \tag{2.44}$$

Applying this operation to A results in a fuzzy subset of A such that the reduction in the magnitude of the grade of membership of y in A is relatively small for those y which have a high grade of membership in A and relatively large for the y with low membership.

The operation of *dilation* is defined by

$$\text{DIL}\ (A) \triangleq A^{0.5}. \tag{2.45}$$

The effect of this operation is the opposite of that of concentration.

The operation of *contrast intensification* is defined by

$$\text{INT}\ (A) \triangleq \begin{cases} 2A^2, & \text{for } 0 \le \mu_A(y) \le 0.5 \\ \neg 2(\neg A)^2, & \text{for } 0.5 \le \mu_A(y) \le 1. \end{cases} \tag{2.46}$$

This operation differs from concentration in that it increases the values of $\mu_A(y)$ which are above 0.5 and diminishes those which are below this point. Thus, contrast intensification has the effect of reducing the fuzziness of A. (An entropy-like measure of fuzziness of a fuzzy set is defined in [16].)

As its name implies, the operation of *fuzzification* (or, more specifically, *support fuzzification*) has the effect of transforming a nonfuzzy set into a fuzzy set or increasing the fuzziness of a fuzzy set. The result of application of a fuzzification to A will be denoted by $F(A)$ or $\tilde{A}$, with the wavy overbar referred to as a *fuzzifier*. Thus $x \approx 3$ means "x is approximately equal to 3," while $x = \tilde{3}$ means "x is a fuzzy set which approximates to 3." A fuzzifier F is characterized by its *kernel* $K(y)$, which is the fuzzy set resulting from the application of F to a singleton $1/y$. Thus

$$K(y) \triangleq \widetilde{1/y}. \tag{2.47}$$

In terms of K, the result of applying F to a fuzzy set A is given by

$$F(A; K) \triangleq \int_U \mu_A(y)K(y) \tag{2.48}$$

where $\mu_A(y)K(y)$ represents the product (in the sense of (2.41)) of the scalar $\mu_A(y)$ and the fuzzy set $K(y)$, and $\int_U$ should be interpreted as the union of the family of fuzzy sets $\mu_A(y)K(y)$, $y \in U$. Thus (2.48) is analogous to the integral representation of a linear operator, with $K(y)$ playing the role of impulse response.

As an illustration of (2.48), assume that U, A, and $K(y)$ are defined by

$$U = 1 + 2 + 3 + 4 \tag{2.49}$$

$$A = 0.8/1 + 0.6/2 \tag{2.50}$$

$$K(1) = 1/1 + 0.4/2 \tag{2.51}$$

$$K(2) = 1/2 + 0.4/1 + 0.4/3.$$

Then, the result of applying F to A is given by

$$\begin{aligned} F(A; K) &= 0.8(1/1 + 0.4/2) + 0.6(1/2 + 0.4/1 + 0.4/3) \\ &= 0.8/1 + 0.32/2 + 0.6/2 + 0.24/1 + 0.24/3 \\ &= 0.8/1 + 0.6/2 + 0.24/3. \end{aligned} \tag{2.52}$$

The operation of fuzzification plays an important role in the definition of linguistic hedges such as *more or less*, *slightly*, *much*, etc. Examples of its uses are given in [15].

Language and Meaning

As was indicated in Section I, the values of a linguistic variable are fuzzy sets whose labels are sentences in a natural or artificial language. For our purposes, a language L may be viewed as a correspondence between a set of terms T and a universe of discourse U. (This point of view is described in greater detail in [4] and [5]. For simplicity, we assume that T is a nonfuzzy set.) This correspondence may be assumed to be characterized by a fuzzy *naming relation* N from T to U, which associates with each term x in T and each object y in U the degree $\mu_N(x,y)$ to which x applies to y. For example, if $x =$ *young* and $y = 23$ years, then $\mu_N(young, 23)$ might be 0.9. A term may be atomic, e.g., $x =$ *tall*, or composite, in which case it is a concatenation of atomic terms, e.g., $x =$ *very tall man*.

For a fixed x, the membership function $\mu_N(x,y)$ defines a fuzzy subset $M(x)$ of U whose membership function is given by

$$\mu_{M(x)}(y) \triangleq \mu_N(x,y), \qquad x \in T, \quad y \in U. \tag{2.53}$$

This fuzzy subset is defined to be the *meaning* of x. Thus, the meaning of a term x is the fuzzy subset $M(x)$ of U for which x serves as a label. Although x and $M(x)$ are different entities (x is an element of T, whereas $M(x)$ is a fuzzy subset of U), we shall write x for $M(x)$, except where there is a need for differentiation between them. To illustrate, suppose that the meaning of the term *young* is defined by

$$\mu_N(young, y) = \begin{cases} 1, & \text{for } y \leq 25 \\ \left(1 + \left(\frac{y - 25}{5}\right)^2\right)^{-1}, & \text{for } y > 25. \end{cases} \tag{2.54}$$

Then we can represent the fuzzy subset of U labeled *young* as (see (2.11))

$$young = \int_0^{25} 1/y + \int_{25}^{100} \left(1 + \left(\frac{y - 25}{5}\right)^2\right)^{-1} / y \tag{2.55}$$

with the right-hand member of (2.55) representing the meaning of *young*.

Linguistic hedges such as *very*, *much*, *more or less*, etc., make it possible to modify the meaning of atomic as well as composite terms and thus serve to increase the range of values of a linguistic variable. The use of linguistic hedges for this purpose is discussed in the following section.

III. Linguistic Hedges

As stated in Section II, the values of a linguistic variable are labels of fuzzy subsets of U which have the form of phrases or sentences in a natural or artificial language. For example, if U is the collection of integers

$$U = 0 + 1 + 2 + \cdots + 100 \tag{3.1}$$

and *age* is a linguistic variable labeled x, then the values of x might be *young*, *not young*, *very young*, *not very young*, *old and not old*, *not very old*, *not young and not old*, etc.

In general, a value of a linguistic variable is a composite term $x = x_1 x_2 \cdots x_n$, which is a concatenation of atomic terms $x_1, \cdots, x_n$. These atomic terms may be divided into four categories:

1) *primary terms*, which are labels of specified fuzzy subsets of the universe of discourse (e.g., *young* and *old* in the preceding example);
2) the negation *not* and the connectives *and* and *or*;
3) *hedges*, such as *very*, *much*, *slightly*, *more or less* (although *more or less* is comprised of three words, it is regarded as an atomic term), etc.;
4) *markers*, such as parentheses.

A basic problem P_l which arises in connection with the use of linguistic variables is the following: Given the meaning of each atomic term x_i, $i = 1, \cdots, n$, in a composite term $x = x_1 \cdots x_n$ which represents a value of a linguistic variable, compute the meaning of x in the sense of (2.53). This problem is an instance of a central problem in quantitative fuzzy semantics [4], namely, the computation of the meaning of a composite term. P_l is a special case of the latter problem because the composite terms representing the values of a linguistic variable have a relatively simple grammatical structure which is restricted to the four categories of atomic terms 1)–4).

As a preliminary to describing a general approach to the solution of P_l, it will be helpful to consider a subproblem of P_l which involves the computation of the meaning of a composite term of the form $x = hu$, where h is a hedge and u is a term with a specified meaning; e.g., $x =$ *very tall man*, where $h =$ *very* and $u =$ *tall man*.

Taking the point of view described in [15], a hedge h may be regarded as an operator which transforms the fuzzy set $M(u)$, representing the meaning of u, into the fuzzy set $M(hu)$. As stated already, the hedges serve the function of

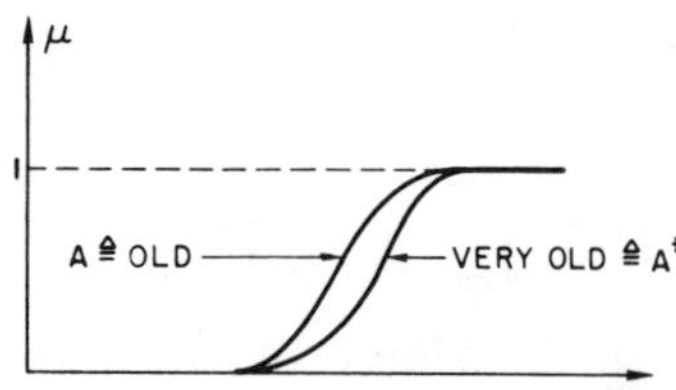

Fig. 2. Effect of hedge *very*.

generating a larger set of values for a linguistic variable from a small collection of primary terms. For example, by using the hedge *very* in conjunction with *not*, *and*, and the primary term *tall*, we can generate the fuzzy sets *very tall*, *very very tall*, *not very tall*, *tall and not very tall*, etc. To define a hedge h as an operator, it is convenient to employ some of the basic operations defined in Section II, especially concentration, dilation, and fuzzification. In what follows, we shall indicate the manner in which this can be done for the natural hedge *very* and the artificial hedges *plus* and *minus*. Characterizations of such hedges as *more or less*, *much*, *slightly*, *sort of*, and *essentially* may be found in [15].

Although in its everyday use the hedge *very* does not have a well-defined meaning, in essence it acts as an intensifier, generating a subset of the set on which it operates. A simple operation which has this property is that of concentration (see (2.44)). This suggests that *very* x, where x is a term, be defined as the square of x, that is

$$very\ x \triangleq x^2 \tag{3.2}$$

or, more explicitly

$$very\ x \triangleq \int_U \mu_x^2(y)/y. \tag{3.3}$$

For example, if (see Fig. 2)

$$x = old\ men \triangleq \int_{50}^{100} \left(1 + \left(\frac{y-50}{5}\right)^{-2}\right)^{-1} \bigg/ y \tag{3.4}$$

then

$$x^2 = very\ old\ men = \int_{50}^{100} \left(1 + \left(\frac{y-50}{5}\right)^{-2}\right)^{-2} \bigg/ y. \tag{3.5}$$

Thus, if the grade of membership of JOHN in the class of *old men* is 0.8, then his grade of membership in the class of *very old men* is 0.64. As another simple example, if

$$U = 1 + 2 + 3 + 4 + 5 \tag{3.6}$$

and

$$small = 1/1 + 0.8/2 + 0.6/3 + 0.4/4 + 0.2/5 \tag{3.7}$$

then

$$very\ small = 1/1 + 0.64/2 + 0.36/3 + 0.16/4 + 0.04/5. \tag{3.8}$$

Viewed as an operator, *very* can be composed with itself. Thus

$$very\ very\ x = (very\ x)^2 = x^4. \tag{3.9}$$

For example, applying (3.9) to (3.7), we obtain (neglecting small terms)

$$very\ very\ small = 1/1 + 0.4/2 + 0.1/3. \tag{3.10}$$

In some instances, to identify the operand of *very* we have to use parentheses or replace a composite term by an atomic one. For example, it is not grammatical to write

$$x = very\ not\ exact \tag{3.11}$$

but if *not exact* is replaced by the atomic term *inexact*, then

$$x = very\ inexact \tag{3.12}$$

is grammatically correct and we can write

$$x = (\neg exact)^2. \tag{3.13}$$

Note that

$$not\ very\ exact = \neg(\text{very exact}) = \neg(exact^2) \tag{3.14}$$

is not the same as (3.13).

The artificial hedges *plus* and *minus* serve the purpose of providing milder degrees of concentration and dilation than those associated with the operations CON and DIL (see (2.44), (2.45)). Thus, as operators acting on a fuzzy set labeled x, *plus* and *minus* are defined by

$$plus\ x \triangleq x^{1.25} \tag{3.15}$$

$$minus\ x \triangleq x^{0.75}. \tag{3.16}$$

In consequence of (3.15) and (3.16), we have the approximate identity

$$plus\ plus\ x = minus\ very\ x. \tag{3.17}$$

As an illustration, if the hedge *highly* is defined as

$$highly = minus\ very\ very \tag{3.18}$$

then, equivalently,

$$highly = plus\ plus\ very. \tag{3.19}$$

As was stated earlier, the computation of the meaning of composite terms of the form hu is a preliminary to the problem of computing the meaning of values of a linguistic variable. We are now in a position to turn our attention to this problem.

IV. Computation of the Meaning of Values of a Linguistic Variable

Once we know how to compute the meaning of a composite term of the form hu, the computation of the meaning of a more complex composite term, which may involve the terms *not*, *or*, and *and* in addition to terms of the form hu, becomes a relatively simple problem which is quite similar to that of the computation of the value of a Boolean expression. As a simple illustration, consider the computation of the meaning of the composite term

$$x = not\ very\ small \tag{4.1}$$

where the primary term *small* is defined as

$$small = 1/1 + 0.8/2 + 0.6/3 + 0.4/4 + 0.2/5 \tag{4.2}$$

with the universe of discourse being

$$U = 1 + 2 + 3 + 4 + 5. \tag{4.3}$$

By (3.8), the operation of *very* on *small* yields

$$\textit{very small} = 1/1 + 0.64/2 + 0.36/3 + 0.16/4 + 0.04/5 \tag{4.4}$$

and, by (2.26),

$$\textit{not very small} = \neg(\textit{very small})$$
$$= 0.36/2 + 0.64/3 + 0.84/4 + 0.96/5$$
$$\approx 0.4/2 + 0.6/3 + 0.8/4 + 1/5. \tag{4.5}$$

As a slightly more complicated example, consider the composite term

$$x = \textit{not very small and not very very large} \tag{4.6}$$

where *large* is defined by

$$\textit{large} = 0.2/1 + 0.4/2 + 0.6/3 + 0.8/4 + 1/5. \tag{4.7}$$

In this case,

$$\textit{very large} = \textit{large}^2$$
$$= 0.04/1 + 0.16/2 + 0.36/3 + 0.64/4 + 1/5 \tag{4.8}$$

$$\textit{very very large} = (\textit{large}^2)^2$$
$$\approx 0.1/3 + 0.4/4 + 1/5 \tag{4.9}$$

$$\textit{not very very large} \approx 1/1 + 1/2 + 0.9/3 + 0.6/4 \tag{4.10}$$

and hence

not very small and not very very large

$$\approx (0.4/2 + 0.6/3 + 0.8/4 + 1/5)$$
$$\cap (1/1 + 1/2 + 0.9/3 + 0.6/4)$$
$$\approx 0.4/2 + 0.6/3 + 0.6/4. \tag{4.11}$$

An example of a different nature is provided by the values of a linguistic variable labeled *likelihood*. In this case, we assume that the universe of discourse is given by

$$U = 0 + 0.1 + 0.2 + 0.3 + 0.4 + 0.5 + 0.6 + 0.7 + 0.8 + 0.9 + 1 \tag{4.12}$$

in which the elements of U represent probabilities. Suppose that we wish to compute the meaning of the value

$$x = \textit{highly unlikely} \tag{4.13}$$

in which *highly* is defined as (see (3.18))

$$\textit{highly} = \textit{minus very very} \tag{4.14}$$

and

$$\textit{unlikely} = \textit{not likely} \tag{4.15}$$

with the meaning of the primary term *likely* given by

$$\textit{likely} = 1/1 + 1/0.9 + 1/0.8 + 0.8/0.7 + 0.6/0.6 + 0.5/0.5 + 0.3/0.4 + 0.2/0.3. \tag{4.16}$$

Using (4.15), we obtain

$$\textit{unlikely} = 1/0 + 1/0.1 + 1/0.2 + 0.8/0.3 + 0.7/0.4 + 0.5/0.5 + 0.4/0.6 + 0.2/0.7 \tag{4.17}$$

and hence

very very unlikely

$$= (\textit{unlikely})^4$$
$$\approx 1/0 + 1/0.1 + 1/0.2 + 0.4/0.3 + 0.2/0.4. \tag{4.18}$$

Finally, by (4.14)

highly unlikely

$$= \textit{minus very very unlikely}$$
$$\approx (1/0 + 1/0.1 + 1/0.2 + 0.4/0.3 + 0.2/0.4)^{0.75}$$
$$\approx 1/0 + 1/0.1 + 1/0.2 + 0.5/0.3 + 0.3/0.4. \tag{4.19}$$

It should be noted that in computing the meaning of composite terms in the preceding examples we have made implicit use of the usual precedence rules governing the evaluation of Boolean expressions. With the addition of hedges, these precedence rules may be expressed as follows.

Precedence	Operation
First	*h, not*
Second	*and*
Third	*or*

As usual, parentheses may be used to change the precedence order and ambiguities may be resolved by the use of association to the right. Thus *plus very minus very tall* should be interpreted as

plus (*very* (*minus* (*very* (*tall*)))).

The technique that was employed for the computation of the meaning of a composite term is a special case of a more general approach which is described in [4] and [5]. The approach in question can be applied to the computation of the meaning of values of a linguistic variable provided the composite terms representing these values can be generated by a context-free grammar. As an illustration, consider a linguistic variable x whose values are exemplified by *small, not small, large, not large, very small, not very small, small or not very very large, small and* (*large or not small*), *not very very small and not very very large*, etc.

The values in question can be generated by a context-free grammar $G = (V_T, V_N, S, P)$ in which the set of terminals V_T comprises the atomic terms *small, large, not, and, or, very*, etc.; the nonterminals are denoted S, A, B, C, D, and E; and the production system is given by

$S \to A$	$C \to D$
$S \to S$ *or* A	$C \to E$
$A \to B$	$D \to$ *very* D
$A \to A$ *and* B	$E \to$ *very* E
$B \to C$	$D \to$ *small*
$B \to$ *not* C	$E \to$ *large*
$C \to (S)$.	(4.20)

Each production in (4.20) gives rise to a relation between the fuzzy sets labeled by the corresponding terminal and nonterminal symbols. In the case of (4.20), these relations are (we omit the productions which have no effect on the associated fuzzy sets)

$$S \rightarrow S \text{ or } A \Rightarrow S_L = S_R + A_R$$

$$A \rightarrow A \text{ and } B \Rightarrow A_L = A_R \cap B_R$$

$$B \rightarrow \text{not } C \Rightarrow B_L = \neg C_R$$

$$D \rightarrow \text{very } D \Rightarrow D_L = D_R^2$$

$$E \rightarrow \text{very } E \Rightarrow E_L = E_R^2$$

$$D \rightarrow \text{small} \Rightarrow D_L = \text{small}$$

$$E \rightarrow \text{large} \Rightarrow E_L = \text{large} \tag{4.21}$$

in which the subscripts L and R are used to differentiate between the symbols on the left- and right-hand sides of a production.

To compute the meaning of a composite term x, it is necessary to perform a syntactical analysis of x in terms of the specified grammar G. Then, knowing the syntax tree of x, one can employ the relations given in (4.21) to derive a set of equations (in triangular form) which upon solution yield the meaning of x. For example, in the case of the composite term

$$x = \textit{not very small and not very very large}$$

the solution of these equations yields

$$x = (\neg \textit{small}^2) \cap (\neg \textit{large}^4) \tag{4.22}$$

which agrees with (4.11). Details of this solution may be found in [4] and [5].

The ability to compute the meaning of values of a linguistic variable is a prerequisite to the computation of the meaning of fuzzy conditional statements of the form IF A THEN B, e.g., IF x is *not very small* THEN y is *very very large*. This problem is considered in the following section.

V. Fuzzy Conditional Statements and Compositional Rule of Inference

In classical propositional calculus,[5] the expression IF A THEN B, where A and B are propositional variables, is written as $A \Rightarrow B$, with the implication $\Rightarrow$ regarded as a connective which is defined by the truth table.

A	B	$A \Rightarrow B$
T	T	T
T	F	F
F	T	T
F	F	T

Thus,

$$A \Rightarrow B \equiv \neg A \vee B \tag{5.1}$$

[5] A detailed discussion of the significance of implication and its role in modal logic may be found in [18].

in the sense that the propositional expressions $A \Rightarrow B$ (*A implies B*) and $\neg A \vee B$ (*not A or B*) have identical truth tables.

A more general concept, which plays an important role in our approach, is a *fuzzy conditional statement*: IF A THEN B or, for short, $A \Rightarrow B$, in which A (the antecedent) and B (the consequent) are fuzzy sets rather than propositional variables. The following are typical examples of such statements:

IF *large* THEN *small*
IF *slippery* THEN *dangerous*

which are abbreviations of the statements

IF x is *large* THEN y is *small*
IF the road is *slippery* THEN driving is *dangerous*.

In essence, statements of this form describe a relation between two fuzzy variables. This suggests that a fuzzy conditional statement be defined as a fuzzy relation in the sense of (2.19) rather than as a connective in the sense of (5.1).

To this end, it is expedient to define first the *Cartesian product* of two fuzzy sets. Specifically, let A be a fuzzy subset of a universe of discourse U, and let B be a fuzzy subset of a possibly different universe of discourse V. Then, the Cartesian product of A and B is denoted by $A \times B$ and is defined by

$$A \times B \triangleq \int_{U \times V} \mu_A(u) \wedge \mu_B(v)/(u,v) \tag{5.2}$$

where $U \times V$ denotes the Cartesian product of the nonfuzzy sets U and V; that is,

$$U \times V \triangleq \{(u,v) \mid u \in U, v \in V\}.$$

Note that when A and B are nonfuzzy, (5.2) reduces to the conventional definition of the Cartesian product of nonfuzzy sets. In words, (5.2) means that $A \times B$ is a fuzzy set of ordered pairs (u,v), $u \in U$, $v \in V$, with the grade of membership of (u,v) in $A \times B$ given by $\mu_A(u) \wedge \mu_B(v)$. In this sense, $A \times B$ is a fuzzy relation from U to V.

As a very simple example, suppose that

$$U = 1 + 2 \tag{5.3}$$

$$V = 1 + 2 + 3 \tag{5.4}$$

$$A = 1/1 + 0.8/2 \tag{5.5}$$

$$B = 0.6/1 + 0.9/2 + 1/3. \tag{5.6}$$

Then

$$A \times B = 0.6/(1,1) + 0.9/(1,2) + 1/(1,3) + 0.6/(2,1) + 0.8/(2,2) + 0.8/(2,3). \tag{5.7}$$

The relation defined by (5.7) may be conveniently represented by the relation matrix

$$\begin{array}{c} \\ 1 \\ 2 \end{array}\begin{array}{c} \begin{array}{ccc} 1 & 2 & 3 \end{array} \\ \begin{bmatrix} 0.6 & 0.9 & 1 \\ 0.6 & 0.8 & 0.8 \end{bmatrix} \end{array}. \tag{5.8}$$

The significance of a fuzzy conditional statement of the form IF A THEN B is made clearer by regarding it as a special case of the conditional expression IF A THEN B ELSE C, where A and (B and C) are fuzzy subsets of possibly different universes U and V, respectively. In terms of the Cartesian product, the latter statement is defined as follows:

$$\text{IF } A \text{ THEN } B \text{ ELSE } C \triangleq A \times B + (\neg A \times C) \qquad (5.9)$$

in which $+$ stands for the union of the fuzzy relations $A \times B$ and $(\neg A \times C)$.

More generally, if $A_1,\cdots,A_n$ are fuzzy subsets of U, and $B_1,\cdots,B_n$ are fuzzy subsets of V, then[6]

$$\text{IF } A_1 \text{ THEN } B_1 \text{ ELSE IF } A_2 \text{ THEN } B_2 \cdots \text{ ELSE IF } A_n \text{ THEN } B_n$$

$$\triangleq A_1 \times B_1 + A_2 \times B_2 + \cdots + A_n \times B_n. \qquad (5.10)$$

Note that (5.10) reduces to (5.9) if IF A THEN B ELSE C is interpreted as IF A THEN B ELSE IF $\neg A$ THEN C. It should also be noted that by repeated application of (5.9) we obtain

$$\text{IF } A \text{ THEN (IF } B \text{ THEN } C \text{ ELSE } D) \text{ ELSE } E$$

$$= A \times B \times C + A \times \neg B \times D + \neg A \times E. \qquad (5.11)$$

If we regard IF A THEN B as IF A THEN B ELSE C with unspecified C, then, depending on the assumption made about C, various interpretations of IF A THEN B will result. In particular, if we assume that $C = V$, then IF A THEN B (or $A \Rightarrow B$) becomes[7]

$$A \Rightarrow B \triangleq \text{IF } A \text{ THEN } B \triangleq A \times B + (\neg A \times V). \qquad (5.12)$$

If, in addition, we set $A = U$ in (5.12), we obtain as an alternative definition

$$A \Rightarrow B \triangleq U \times B + (\neg A \times V). \qquad (5.13)$$

In the sequel, we shall assume that $C = V$, and hence that $A \Rightarrow B$ is defined by (5.12). In effect, the assumption that $C = V$ implies that, in the absence of an indication to the contrary, the consequent of $\neg A \Rightarrow C$ can be any fuzzy subset of the universe of discourse. As a very simple illustration of (5.12), suppose that A and B are defined by (5.5) and (5.6). Then, on substituting (5.8) in (5.12), the relation matrix for $A \Rightarrow B$ is found to be

$$A \Rightarrow B = \begin{bmatrix} 0.6 & 0.9 & 1 \\ 0.6 & 0.8 & 0.8 \end{bmatrix}.$$

It should be observed that when A, B, and C are nonfuzzy sets, we have the identity

$$\text{IF } A \text{ THEN } B \text{ ELSE } C = (\text{IF } A \text{ THEN } B) \cap (\text{IF } \neg A \text{ THEN } C) \qquad (5.14)$$

which holds only approximately for fuzzy A, B, and C. This indicates that, in relation to (5.15), the definitions of IF A THEN B ELSE C and IF A THEN B, as expressed by (5.9) and (5.12), are not exactly consistent for fuzzy A, B, and C. It should also be noted that if 1) $U = V$, 2) $x = y$, and 3) $A \Rightarrow B$ holds for all points in U, then, by (5.12),

$$A \Rightarrow B \text{ implies and is implied by } A \subset B \qquad (5.15)$$

exactly if A and B are nonfuzzy and approximately otherwise.

As will be seen in Section VI, fuzzy conditional statements play a basic role in fuzzy algorithms. More specifically, a typical problem which is encountered in the course of execution of such algorithms is the following. We have a fuzzy relation, say, R, from U to V which is defined by a fuzzy conditional statement. Then, we are given a fuzzy subset of U, say, x, and have to determine the fuzzy subset of V, say, y, which is induced in V by x. For example, we may have the following two statements.

1) x is *very small*
2) IF x is *small* THEN y is *large* ELSE y is *not very large*

of which the second defines by (5.9) a fuzzy relation R. The question, then, is as follows: What will be the value of y if x is *very small*? The answer to this question is provided by the following rule of inference, which may be regarded as an extension of the familiar rule of *modus ponens.*

Compositional Rule of Inference: If R is a fuzzy relation from U to V, and x is a fuzzy subset of U, then the fuzzy subset y of V which is induced by x is given by the composition (see (2.22)) of R and x; that is,

$$y = x \circ R \qquad (5.16)$$

in which x plays the role of a unary relation.[8]

As a simple illustration of (5.16), suppose that R and x are defined by the relation matrices in (5.17). Then y is given by the max-min product of x and R:

$$\overset{x}{\begin{bmatrix} 0.2 & 1 & 0.3 \end{bmatrix}} \circ \overset{R}{\begin{bmatrix} 0.8 & 0.9 & 0.2 \\ 0.6 & 1 & 0.4 \\ 0.5 & 0.8 & 1 \end{bmatrix}} = \overset{y}{\begin{bmatrix} 0.6 & 1 & 0.4 \end{bmatrix}}. \qquad (5.17)$$

As for the question raised before, suppose that, as in (4.3), we have

$$U = 1 + 2 + 3 + 4 + 5 \qquad (5.18)$$

with *small* and *large* defined by (4.2) and (4.7), respectively. Then, substituting *small* for A, *large* for B and *not very large* for C in (5.9), we obtain the relation matrix R for the fuzzy conditional statement IF *small* THEN *large* ELSE *not very large*. The result of the composition of R with $x =$ *very*

[6] It should be noted that, in the sense used in ALGOL, the right-hand side of (5.10) would be expressed as $A_1 \times B_1 + (\neg A_1 \cap A_2) \times B_2 + \cdots + (\neg A_1 \cap \cdots \cap \neg A_{n-1} \cap A_n) \times B_n$ when the A_i and B_i, $i = 1,\cdots,n$, are nonfuzzy sets.

[7] This definition should be viewed as tentative in nature.

[8] If R is visualized as a fuzzy graph, then (5.16) may be viewed as the expression for the fuzzy ordinate y corresponding to a fuzzy abscissa x.

small is

$$\overset{x}{[1\ \ 0.64\ \ 0.36\ \ 0.16\ \ 0.04]} \circ \overset{R}{\begin{bmatrix} 0.2 & 0.4 & 0.6 & 0.8 & 1 \\ 0.2 & 0.4 & 0.6 & 0.8 & 0.8 \\ 0.4 & 0.4 & 0.6 & 0.6 & 0.6 \\ 0.6 & 0.6 & 0.6 & 0.4 & 0.4 \\ 0.8 & 0.8 & 0.64 & 0.36 & 0.2 \end{bmatrix}}$$

$$= \overset{y}{[0.36\ \ 0.4\ \ 0.6\ \ 0.8\ \ 1]}. \qquad (5.19)$$

There are several aspects of (5.16) that are in need of comment. First, it should be noted that when $R = A \Rightarrow B$ and $x = A$ we obtain

$$y = A \circ (A \Rightarrow B) = B \qquad (5.20)$$

as an exact identity, when A, B, and C are nonfuzzy, and an approximate one, when A, B, and C are fuzzy. It is in this sense that the compositional inference rule (5.16) may be viewed as an approximate extension of *modus ponens*. (Note that in consequence of the way in which $A \Rightarrow B$ is defined in (5.12), the more different x is from A, the less sharply defined is y.)

Second, (5.16) is analogous to the expression for the marginal probability in terms of the conditional probability function; that is

$$r_j = \sum_i q_i p_{ij} \qquad (5.21)$$

where

$$q_i = \Pr\{X = x_i\}$$
$$r_j = \Pr\{Y = y_j\}$$
$$p_{ij} = \Pr\{Y = y_j \mid X = x_i\}$$

and X and Y are random variables with values $x_1, x_2, \cdots$ and $y_1, y_2, \cdots$, respectively. However, this analogy does not imply that (5.16) is a relation between probabilities.

Third, it should be noted that because of the use of the max–min matrix product in (5.16), the relation between x and y is not continuous. Thus, in general, a small change in x would produce no change in y until a certain threshold is exceeded. This would not be the case if the composition of x with R were defined as max–product composition.

Fourth, in the computation of $x \circ R$ one may take advantage of the distributivity of composition over the union of fuzzy sets. Thus, if

$$x = u \text{ or } v \qquad (5.22)$$

where u and v are labels of fuzzy sets, then

$$(u \text{ or } v) \circ R = u \circ R \text{ or } v \circ R. \qquad (5.23)$$

For example, if x is *small or medium*, and $R = A \Rightarrow B$ reads IF x is *not small and not large* THEN y is *very small*, then we can write

(*small or medium*) ∘ (*not small and not large* ⇒ *very small*)
= *small* ∘ (*not small and not large* ⇒ *very small*) *or medium* ∘ (*not small and not large* ⇒ *very small*). (5.24)

As a final comment, it is important to realize that in practical applications of fuzzy conditional statements to the description of complex or ill-defined relations, the computations involved in (5.9), (5.10), and (5.16) would, in general, be performed in a highly approximate fashion. Furthermore, an additional source of imprecision would be the result of representing a fuzzy set as a value of a linguistic variable. For example, suppose that a relation between fuzzy variables x and y is described by the fuzzy conditional statement IF *small* THEN *large* ELSE IF *medium* THEN *medium* ELSE IF large THEN *very small*.

Typically, we would assign different linguistic values to x and compute the corresponding values of y by the use of (5.16). Then, on approximating to the computed values of y by linguistic labels, we would arrive at a table having the form shown below:

Given		Inferred	
A	B	x	y
small	*large*	*not small*	*not very large*
medium	*medium*	*very small*	*very very large*
large	*very small*	*very very small*	*very very large*
		not very large	*small or medium*

Such a table constitutes an approximate linguistic characterization of the relation between x and y which is inferred from the given fuzzy conditional statement. As was stated earlier, fuzzy conditional statements play a basic role in the description and execution of fuzzy algorithms. We turn to this subject in the following section.

VI. Fuzzy Algorithms

Roughly speaking, a fuzzy algorithm is an ordered set of fuzzy instructions which upon execution yield an approximate solution to a specified problem. In one form or another, fuzzy algorithms pervade much of what we do. Thus, we employ fuzzy algorithms both consciously and subconsciously when we walk, drive a car, search for an object, tie a knot, park a car, cook a meal, find a number in a telephone directory, etc. Furthermore, there are many instances of uses of what, in effect, are fuzzy algorithms in a wide variety of fields, especially in programming, operations research, psychology, management science, and medical diagnosis.

The notion of a fuzzy set and, in particular, the concept of a fuzzy conditional statement provide a basis for using fuzzy algorithms in a more systematic and hence more effective ways than was possible in the past. Thus, fuzzy algorithms could become an important tool for an approximate analysis of systems and decision processes which are much too complex for the application of conventional mathematical techniques.

A formal characterization of the concept of a fuzzy algorithm can be given in terms of the notion of a fuzzy Turing machine or a fuzzy Markoff algorithm [6]–[8]. In this section, the main aim of our discussion is to relate the concept of a fuzzy algorithm to the notions introduced in the preceding sections and illustrate by simple examples some of the uses of such algorithms.

The instructions in a fuzzy algorithm fall into the following three classes.

1) *Assignment Statements:* e.g.,

$x \approx 5$
$x =$ *small*
x is *large*
x is *not large and not very small.*

2) *Fuzzy Conditional Statements:* e.g.,

IF x is *small* THEN y is *large* ELSE y is *not large*
IF x is positive THEN decrease y *slightly*
IF x is *much greater* than 5 THEN stop
IF x is *very small* THEN go to 7.

Note that in such statements either the antecedent or the consequent or both may be labels of fuzzy sets.

3) *Unconditional Action Statements:* e.g.,

multiply x by x
decrease x *slightly*
delete the first *few* occurrences of 1
go to 7
print x
stop.

Note that some of these instructions are fuzzy and some are not.

The combination of an assignment statement and a fuzzy conditional statement is executed in accordance with the compositional rule (5.16). For example, if at some point in the execution of a fuzzy algorithm we encounter the instructions

1) $x =$ *very small*
2) IF x is *small* THEN y is *large* ELSE y is *not very large*

where *small* and *large* are defined by (4.2) and (4.7), then the result of the execution of 1) and 2) will be the value of y given by (5.19), that is,

$$y = 0.36/1 + 0.4/2 + 0.64/3 + 0.8/4 + 1/5. \quad (6.1)$$

An unconditional but fuzzy action statement is executed similarly. For example, the instruction

$$\text{multiply } x \text{ by itself a } \textit{few} \text{ times} \quad (6.2)$$

with *few* defined as

$$\textit{few} = 1/1 + 0.8/2 + 0.6/3 + 0.4/4 \quad (6.3)$$

would yield upon execution the fuzzy set

$$y = 1/x^2 + 0.8/x^3 + 0.6/x^4 + 0.4/x^5. \quad (6.4)$$

It is important to observe that, in both (6.1) and (6.4), the result of execution is a fuzzy set rather than a single number. However, when a human subject is presented with a fuzzy instruction such as "take *several* steps," with *several* defined by (see (2.10))

$$\textit{several} = 0.5/3 + 0.8/4 + 1/5 + 1/6 + 0.8/7 + 0.5/8 \quad (6.5)$$

the result of execution must be a single number between 3 and 8. On what basis will such a number be chosen?

As pointed out in [6], it is reasonable to assume that the result of execution will be that element of the fuzzy set which has the highest grade of membership in it. If such an element is not unique, as is true of (6.5), then a random or arbitrary choice can be made among the elements having the highest grade of membership. Alternatively, an external criterion can be introduced which linearly orders those elements of the fuzzy set which have the highest membership, and thus generates a unique greatest element. For example, in the case of (6.5), if the external criterion is to minimize the number of steps that have to be taken, then the subject will pick 5 from the elements with the highest grade of membership.

An analogous question arises in situations in which a human subject has to give a "yes" or "no" answer to a fuzzy question. For example, suppose that a subject is presented with the instruction

$$\text{IF } x \text{ is } \textit{small} \text{ THEN stop ELSE go to 7} \quad (6.6)$$

in which *small* is defined by (4.2). Now assume that $x = 3$, which has the grade of membership of 0.6 in *small*. Should the subject execute "stop" or "go to 7"? We shall assume that in situations of this kind the subject will pick that alternative which is more true than untrue, e.g., "x is *small*" over "x is *not small*," since in our example the degree of truth of the statement "3 is *small*" is 0.6, which is greater than that of the statement "3 is *not small*." If both alternatives have more or less equal truth values, the choice can be made arbitrarily. For convenience, we shall refer to this rule of deciding between two alternatives as the *rule of the preponderant alternative*.

It is very important to understand that the questions just discussed arise only in those situations in which the result of execution of a fuzzy instruction is required to be a single element (e.g., a number) rather than a fuzzy set. Thus, if we allowed the result of execution of (6.6) to be fuzzy, then for $x = 3$ we would obtain the fuzzy set

$$0.6/\text{stop} + 0.4/\text{go to 7}$$

which implies that the execution is carried out in parallel. The assumption of parallelism is implicit in the compositional rule of inference and is basic to the understanding of fuzzy algorithms and their execution by humans and machines.

In what follows, we shall present several examples of fuzzy algorithms in the light of the concepts discussed in the preceding sections. It should be stressed that these examples are intended primarily to illustrate the basic aspects of fuzzy algorithms rather than demonstrate their effectiveness in the solution of practical problems.

It is convenient to classify fuzzy algorithms into several basic categories, each corresponding to a particular type of application: definitional and identificational algorithms; generational algorithms; relational and behavioral algorithms; and decisional algorithms. (It should be noted that an algorithm of a particular type can include algorithms of other types as subalgorithms. For example, a definitional algorithm may contain relational and decisional subalgorithms.) We begin with an example of a definitional algorithm.

Fuzzy Definitional Algorithms

One of the basic areas of application for fuzzy algorithms lies in the definition of complex, ill-defined or fuzzy concepts in terms of simpler or less fuzzy concepts. The following are examples of such fuzzy concepts: sparseness of matrices; handwritten characters; measures of complexity; measures of proximity or resemblance; degrees of clustering; criteria of performance; soft constraints; rules of various kinds, e.g., zoning regulations; legal criteria, e.g., criteria for insanity, obscenity, etc.; and fuzzy diseases such as arthritis, arteriosclerosis, schizophrenia.

Since a fuzzy concept may be viewed as a label for a fuzzy set, a *fuzzy definitional algorithm* is, in effect, a finite set of possibly fuzzy instructions which define a fuzzy set in terms of other fuzzy sets (and possibly itself, i.e., recursively) or constitute a procedure for computing the grade of membership of any element of the universe of discourse in the set under definition. In the latter case, the definational algorithm plays the role of an *identificational algorithm*, that is, an algorithm which identifies whether or not an element belongs to a set or, more generally, determines its grade of membership. An example of such an algorithm is provided by the procedure (see [5]) for computing the grade of membership of a string in a fuzzy language generated by a context-free grammar.

As a very simple example of a fuzzy definitional algorithm, we shall consider the fuzzy concept *oval*. It should be emphasized again that the oversimplified definition that will be given is intended only for illustrative purposes and has no pretense at being an accurate definition of the concept *oval*. The instructions comprising the algorithm OVAL are listed here. The symbol T in these instructions stands for the object under test. The term CALL CONVEX represents a call on a subalgorithm labeled CONVEX, which is a definitional algorithm for testing whether or not T is convex. An instruction of the form IF A THEN B should be interpreted as IF A THEN B ELSE go to next instruction.

Algorithm OVAL:

1) IF T is not closed THEN T is not *oval*; stop.
2) IF T is self-intersecting THEN T is not *oval*; stop.
3) IF T is not CALL CONVEX THEN T is not *oval*; stop.
4) IF T does not have two *more or less* orthogonal axes of symmetry THEN T is not *oval*; stop.
5) IF the major axis of T is not *much* longer than the minor axis THEN T is not *oval*; stop.
6) T is *oval*; stop.

Subalgorithm CONVEX: Basically, this subalgorithm involves a check on whether the curvature of T at each point maintains the same sign as one moves along T in some initially chosen direction.

1) $x = a$ (some initial point on T).
2) Choose a direction of movement along T.
3) $t \approx$ direction of tangent to T at x.
4) $x' \approx x + 1$ (move from x to a neighboring point).
5) $t' \approx$ direction of tangent to T at x'.
6) $\alpha \approx$ angle between t' and t.
7) $x \approx x'$.
8) $t \approx$ direction of tangent to T at x.
9) $x' \approx x + 1$.
10) $t' \approx$ direction of tangent to T at x'.
11) $\beta \approx$ angle between t' and t.
12) IF β does not have the same sign as α THEN T is not convex; return.
13) IF $x' \approx a$ THEN T is convex; return.
14) Go to 7).

Comment: It should be noted that the first three instructions in OVAL are nonfuzzy. As for instructions 4) and 5), they involve definitions of concepts such as "*more or less* orthogonal," and "*much* longer," which, though fuzzy, are less complex and better understood than the concept of *oval*. This exemplifies the main function of a fuzzy definitional algorithm, namely, to reduce a new or complex fuzzy concept to simpler or better understood fuzzy concepts. In a more elaborate version of the algorithm OVAL, the answers to 4) and 5) could be the degrees to which the conditions in these instructions are satisfied. The final result of the algorithm, then, would be the grade of membership of T in the fuzzy set of oval objects.

In this connection, it should be noted that, in virtue of (5.15), the algorithm OVAL as stated is approximately equivalent to the expression

$$\begin{aligned} \textit{oval} = {} & \text{closed} \cap \text{non-self-intersecting} \cap \text{convex} \\ & \cap\ \textit{more or less} \text{ orthogonal axes of symmetry} \\ & \cap \text{ major axis } \textit{much} \text{ larger than minor axis} \qquad (6.7) \end{aligned}$$

which defines the fuzzy set *oval* as the intersection of the fuzzy and nonfuzzy sets whose labels appear on the right-hand side of (6.7). However, one significant difference is that the algorithm not only defines the right-hand side of (6.7), but also specifies the order in which the computations implicit in (6.7) are to be performed.

Fuzzy Generational Algorithms

As its designation implies, a fuzzy generational algorithm serves to generate rather than define a fuzzy set. Possible applications of generational algorithms include: generation of handwritten characters and patterns of various kinds; cooking recipes; generation of music; generation of sentences in a natural language; generation of speech.

As a simple illustration of the notion of a generational algorithm, we shall consider an algorithm for generating the letter **P**, with the height h and the base b of **P** constituting the parameters of the algorithm. For simplicity, **P** will be generated as a dotted pattern, with eight dots lying on the vertical line.

Algorithm **P**(h,b)*:*

1) $i = 1$.
2) $X(i) = b$ (first dot at base).

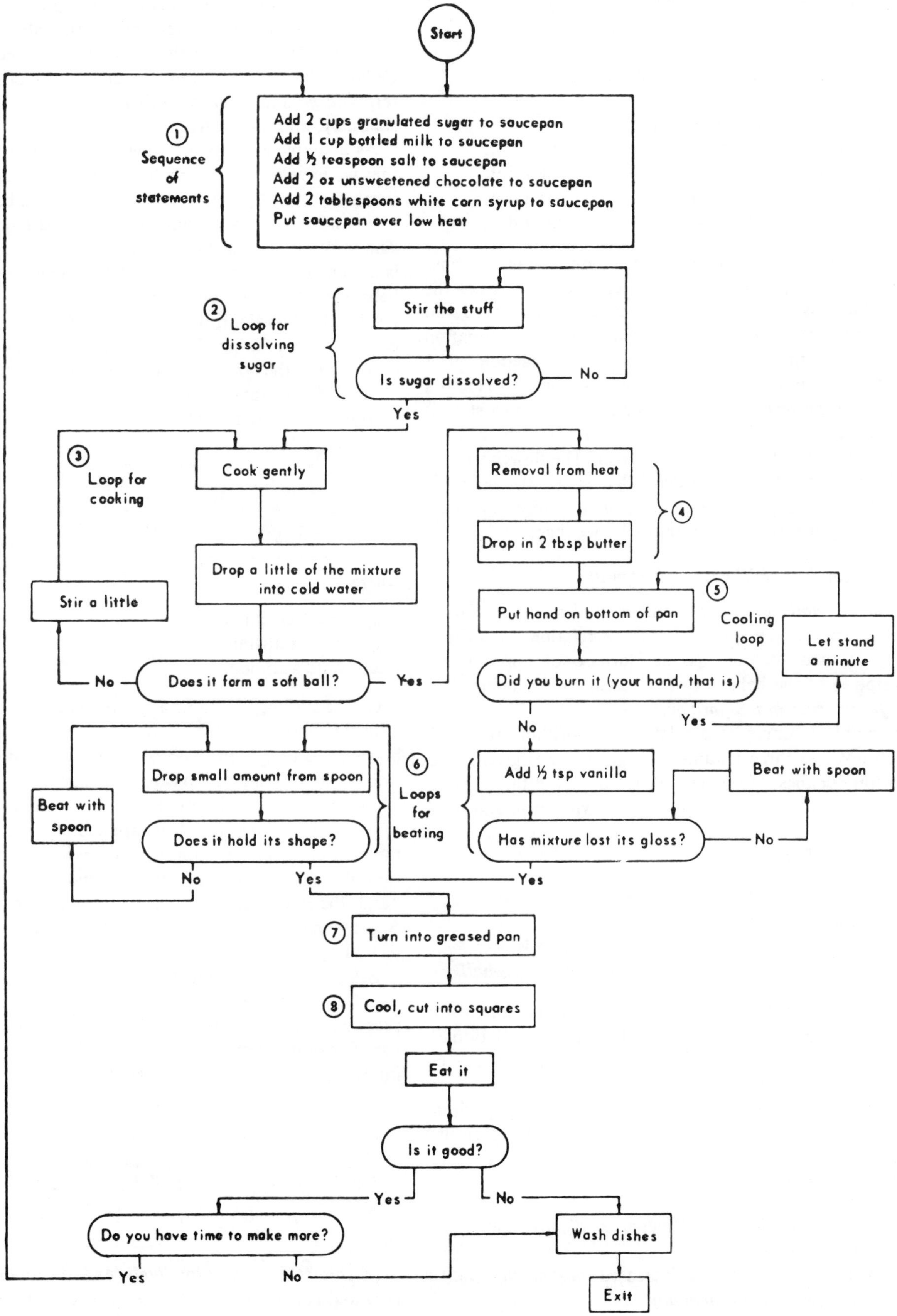

Fig. 3. Recipe for chocolate fudge (from [19]).

3) $X(i + 1) \approx X(i) + h/6$ (put dot *approximately* $h/6$ units of distance above $X(i)$).
4) $i = i + 1$.
5) IF $i = 7$ THEN make right turn and go to 7).
6) Go to 3.
7) Move by $h/6$ units; put a dot.
8) Turn by 45°; move by $h/6$ units; put a dot.
9) Turn by 45°; move by $h/6$ units; put a dot.
10) Turn by 45°; move by $h/6$ units; put a dot.
11) Turn by 45°; move by $h/6$ units; put a dot; stop.

The algorithm as stated is of open-loop type in the sense that it does not incorporate any feedback. To make the algorithm less sensitive to errors in execution, we could introduce fuzzy feedback by conditioning the termination of the algorithm on an approximate satisfaction of a specified test. For example, if the last point in step 11) does not fall on the vertical part of **P**, we could return to step 8) and either reduce or increase the angle of turn in steps 8)–11) to correct for the terminal error. The flowchart of a cooking recipe for chocolate fudge (Fig. 3), which is reproduced from [19], is a good example of what, in effect, is a fuzzy generational algorithm with feedback.

Fuzzy Relational and Behavioral Algorithms

A *fuzzy relational algorithm* serves to describe a relation or relations between fuzzy variables. A relational algorithm which is used for the specific purpose of approximate description of the behavior of a system will be referred to as a *fuzzy behavioral algorithm.*

A simple example of a relational algorithm labeled R which involves three parameters x, y, and z is given. This algorithm defines a fuzzy ternary relation R in the universe of discourse $U = 1 + 2 + 3 + 4 + 5$ with *small* and *large* defined by (4.2) and (4.7).

Algorithm $R(x,y,z)$:

1) IF x is *small* and y is *large* THEN z is *very small* ELSE z is *not small.*
2) IF x is *large* THEN (IF y is *small* THEN z is *very large* ELSE z is *small*) ELSE z and y are *very very small.*

If needed, the meaning of these conditional statements can be computed by using (5.9) and (5.11). The relation R, then, will be the intersection of the relations defined by instructions 1) and 2).

Another simple example of a relational fuzzy algorithm $F(x,y)$ which illustrates a different aspect of such algorithms is the following.

Algorithm $F(x,y)$:

1) IF x is *small* and x is increased *slightly* THEN y will increase *slightly.*
2) IF x is *small* and x is increased *substantially* THEN y will increase *substantially.*
3) IF x is *large* and x is increased *slightly* THEN y will increase *moderately.*
4) IF x is *large* and x is increased *substantially* THEN y will increase *very substantially.*

As in the case of the previous example, the meaning of the fuzzy conditional statements in this algorithm can be computed by the use of the methods discussed in Sections IV and V if one is given the definitions of the primary terms *large* and *small* as well as the hedges *slightly, substantially,* and *moderately.*

As a simple example of a behavioral algorithm, suppose that we have a system S with two nonfuzzy states (see [3]) labeled q_1 and q_2, two fuzzy input values labeled *low* and *high*, and two fuzzy output values labeled *large* and *small.* The universe of discourse for the input and output values is assumed to be the real line. We assume further that the behavior of S can be characterized in an approximate fashion by the algorithm that will be given. However, to represent the relations between the inputs, states, and outputs, we use the conventional state transition tables instead of conditional statements.

Algorithm BEHAVIOR:

u_t \ x_t	x_{t+1}: q_1	x_{t+1}: q_2	y_t: q_1	y_t: q_2
low	q_2	q_1	*large*	*small*
high	q_1	q_1	*small*	*large*

where

u_t input at time t
y_t output at time t
x_t state at time t.

On the surface, this table appears to define a conventional nonfuzzy finite-state system. What is important to recognize, however, is that in the case of the system under consideration the inputs and outputs are fuzzy subsets of the real line. Thus we could pose the question: What would be the output of S if it is in state q_1 and the applied input is *very low*? In the case of S, this question can be answered by an application of the compositional inference rule (5.16). On the other hand, the same question would not be a meaningful one if S is assumed to be a nonfuzzy finite-state system characterized by the preceding table.

Behavioral fuzzy algorithms can also be used to describe the more complex forms of behavior resulting from the presence of random elements in a system. For example, the presence of random elements in S might result in the following fuzzy-probabilistic characterization of its behavior:

u_t \ x_t	x_{t+1}: q_1	x_{t+1}: q_2	y_t: q_1	y_t: q_2
low	q_2 *likely*	q_1 *likely*	*large likely*	*small likely*^{2}
high	q_1 *likely*^{2}	q_1 *unlikely*^{2}	*small likely*^{2}	*large unlikely*^{2}

In this table, the term *likely* and its modifications by *very* and *not* serve to provide an approximate characterization of probabilities. For example, IF the input is *low* and the present state is q_1, THEN the next state is *likely* to be q_2. Similarly, IF the input is *high* and the present state is q_2 THEN the output is *very unlikely* to be *large.* If the meaning of *likely* is defined by (see (4.16))

$$likely = 1/1 + 1/0.9 + 1/0.8 + 0.8/0.7 + 0.6/0.6 + 0.5/0.5 + 0.3/0.4 + 0.2/0.3 \quad (6.8)$$

then

$$unlikely = 0.2/0.7 + 0.4/0.6 + 0.5/0.5 + 0.7/0.4 + 0.8/0.3 + 1/0.2 + 1/0.1 + 1/0 \quad (6.9)$$

$$very\ likely \approx 1/1 + 1/0.9 + 1/0.8 + 0.6/0.7 + 0.4/0.6 + 0.3/0.5 + 0.1/0.4 \quad (6.10)$$

$$very\ unlikely \approx 0.2/0.6 + 0.3/0.5 + 0.5/0.4 + 0.6/0.3 + 1/0.2 + 1/0.1 + 1/0. \quad (6.11)$$

Fuzzy Decisional Algorithms

A *fuzzy decisional algorithm* is a fuzzy algorithm which serves to provide an approximate description of a strategy or decision rule. Commonplace examples of such algorithms, which we use for the most part on a subconscious level, are the algorithms for parking a car, crossing an intersection, transferring an object, buying a house, etc.

To illustrate the notion of a fuzzy decisional algorithm, we shall consider two simple examples drawn from our everyday experiences.

Example—Crossing a traffic intersection: It is convenient to break down the algorithm in question into several subalgorithms, each of which applies to a particular type of intersection. For our purposes, it will be sufficient to describe only one of these subalgorithms, namely, the subalgorithm SIGN, which is used when the intersection has a stop sign. As in the case of other examples in this section, we shall make a number of simplifying assumptions in order to shorten the description of the algorithm.

Algorithm INTERSECTION:

1) IF signal lights THEN CALL SIGNAL ELSE IF stop sign THEN CALL SIGN ELSE IF blinking light THEN CALL BLINKING ELSE CALL UNCONTROLLED.

Subalgorithm SIGN:

1) IF no stop sign on your side THEN IF no cars in the intersection THEN cross at *normal* speed ELSE wait for cars to leave the intersection and then cross.
2) IF not *close* to intersection THEN continue approaching at normal speed for a *few* seconds; go to 2).
3) *Slow down.*
4) IF in a *great* hurry and no police cars in sight and no cars in the intersection or its *vicinity* THEN cross the intersection at *slow* speed.
5) IF *very close* to intersection THEN stop; go to 7).
6) Continue *approaching* at *very slow* speed; go to 5).
7) IF no cars *approaching* or in the intersection THEN cross.
8) Wait a *few* seconds; go to 7).

It hardly needs saying that a realistic version of this algorithm would be considerably more complex. The important point of the example is that such an algorithm could be constructed along the same lines as the highly simplified version just described. Furthermore, it shows that a fuzzy algorithm could serve as an effective means of communicating know-how and experience.

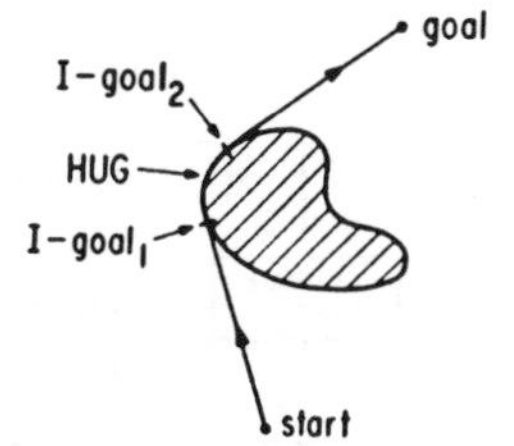

Fig. 4. Problem of transferring blindfolded subject from *start* to *goal*.

As a final example, we consider a decisional algorithm for transferring a blindfolded subject H from an initial position *start* to a final position *goal* under the assumption that there may be an obstacle lying between *start* and *goal* (see Fig. 4). (Highly sophisticated nonfuzzy algorithms of this type for use by robots are incorporated in Shakey, the robot built by the Artificial Intelligence Group at Stanford Research Institute. A description of this robot is given in [20].)

The algorithm, labeled OBSTACLE, is assumed to be used by a human controller C who can observe the way in which H executes his instructions. This fuzzy feedback plays an essential role in making it possible for C to direct H to *goal* in spite of the fuzziness of instructions as well as the errors in their execution by H. The algorithm OBSTACLE consists of three subalgorithms: ALIGN, HUG, and STRAIGHT. The function of STRAIGHT is to transfer H from *start* to an intermediate goal $I\text{-}goal_1$, and then from $I\text{-}goal_2$ to *goal*. (See Fig. 4.) The function of ALIGN is to orient H in a desired direction; the function of HUG is to guide H along the boundary of the obstacle until the goal is no longer obstructed.

Instead of describing these subalgorithms in terms of fuzzy conditional statements as we have done in previous examples, it is instructive to convey the same information by flowcharts, as shown in Figs. 5–7. In the flowchart of ALIGN, ε denotes the error in alignment, and we assume for simplicity that ε has a constant sign. The flowcharts of HUG and STRAIGHT are self-explanatory. Expressed in terms of fuzzy conditional statements, the flowchart of STRAIGHT, for example, translates into the following instructions.

Subalgorithm STRAIGHT:

1) IF not *close* THEN take a step; go to 1).
2) IF not *very close* THEN take a *small* step; go to 2).
3) IF not *very very close* THEN take a *very small* step; go to 3).
4) Stop.

VII. Concluding Remarks

In this and the preceding sections of this paper, we have attempted to develop a conceptual framework for dealing

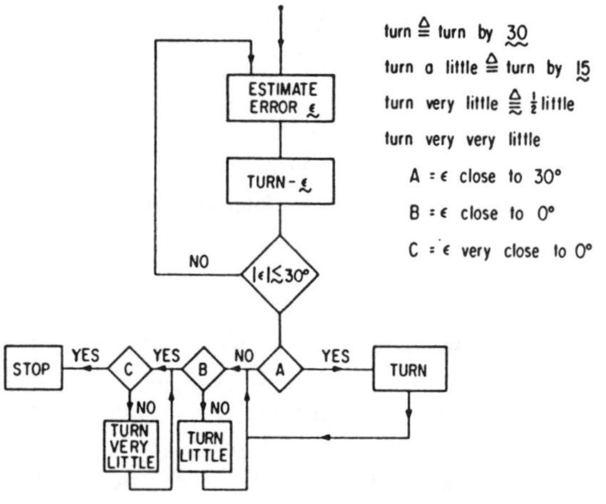

Fig. 5. Subalgorithm ALIGN.

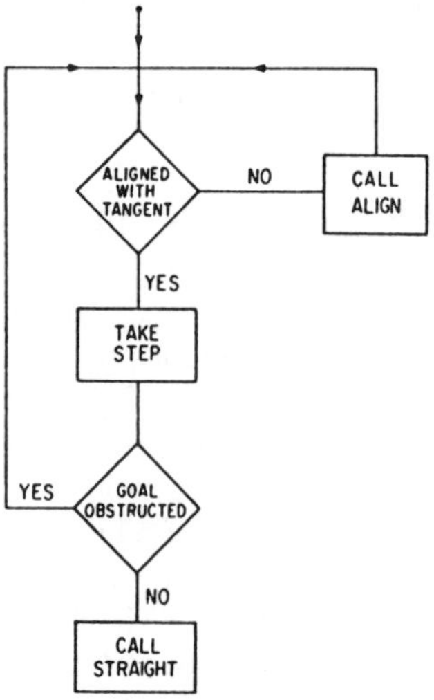

Fig. 6. Subalgorithm HUG.

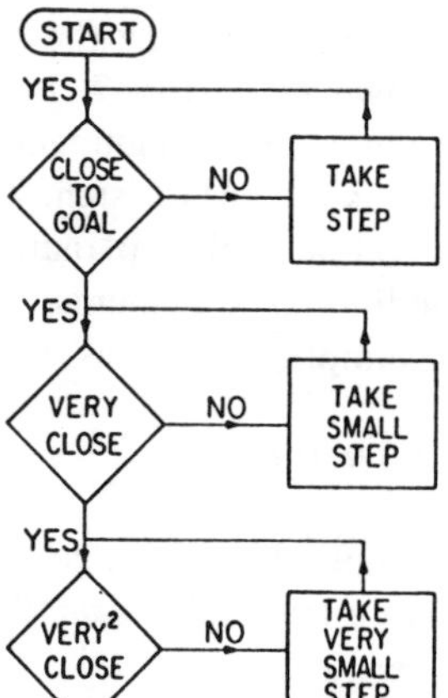

Fig. 7. Subalgorithm STRAIGHT.

with systems which are too complex or too ill-defined to admit of precise quantitative analysis. What we have done should be viewed, of course, as merely a first tentative step in this direction. Clearly, there are many basic as well as detailed aspects of our approach which we have treated incompletely, if at all. Among these are questions relating to the role of fuzzy feedback in: the execution of fuzzy algorithms; the execution of fuzzy algorithms by humans; the conjunction of fuzzy instructions; the assessment of the goodness of fuzzy algorithms; the implications of the compositional rule of inference and the rule of the preponderant alternative; and the interplay between fuzziness and probability in the behavior of humanistic systems.

Nevertheless, even at its present stage of development, the method described in this paper can be applied rather effectively to the formulation and approximate solution of a wide variety of practical problems, particularly in such fields as economics, management science, psychology, linguistics, taxonomy, artificial intelligence, information retrieval, medicine, and biology. This is particularly true of those problem areas in these fields in which fuzzy algorithms can be drawn upon to provide a means of description of ill-defined concepts, relations, and decision rules.

References

[1] L. A. Zadeh, "Fuzzy sets," *Inform. Contr.*, vol. 8, pp. 338–353, 1965.
[2] ——, "Similarity relations and fuzzy orderings," *Inform. Sci.*, vol. 3, pp. 177–200, 1971.
[3] ——, "Toward a theory of fuzzy systems," in *Aspects of Network and System Theory*, R. E. Kalman and N. DeClaris, Eds. New York: Holt, Rinehart and Winston, 1971.
[4] ——, "Quantitative fuzzy semantics," *Inform. Sci.*, vol. 3, pp. 159–176, 1971.
[5] ——, "Fuzzy languages and their relation to human and machine intelligence," in *Proc. Conf. Man and Computer*, 1970; also Electron. Res. Lab., Univ. California, Berkeley, Memo. M-302, 1971.
[6] ——, "Fuzzy algorithms," *Inform. Contr.*, vol. 12, pp. 94–102, 1968.
[7] E. Santos, "Fuzzy algorithms," *Inform. Contr.*, vol. 17, pp. 326–339, 1970.
[8] L. A. Zadeh, "On fuzzy algorithms," Electron. Res. Lab., Univ. California, Berkeley, Memo. M-325, 1971.
[9] S.-K. Chang, "On the execution of fuzzy programs using finite-state machines," *IEEE Trans. Comput.*, vol. C-21, pp. 241–253, Mar. 1972.
[10] S. S. L. Chang and L. A. Zadeh, "Fuzzy mapping and control," *IEEE Trans. Syst., Man, Cybern.*, vol. SMC-2, pp. 30–34, Jan. 1962.
[11] R. E. Bellman and L. A. Zadeh, "Decision-making in a fuzzy environment," *Management Sci.*, vol. 17, pp. B-141–B-164, 1970.
[12] J. A. Goguen, "The logic of inexact concepts," *Syn.*, vol. 19, pp. 325–373, 1969.
[13] G. Lakoff, "Hedges: a study in meaning criteria and the logic of fuzzy concepts," in *Proc. 8th Reg. Meet. Chicago Linguist. Soc.*, 1972.
[14] L. A. Zadeh, "A system-theoretic view of behavior modification," Electron. Res. Lab., Univ. California, Berkeley, Memo. M-320, 1972.
[15] ——, "A fuzzy-set-theoretic interpretation of hedges," Electron. Res. Lab., Univ. California, Berkeley, Memo. M-335, 1972.
[16] A. De Luca and S. Termini, "A definition of a non-probabilistic entropy in the setting of fuzzy sets theory," *Inform. Contr.*, vol. 20, pp. 301–312, 1972.
[17] R. C. T. Lee, "Fuzzy logic and the resolution principle," *J. Ass. Comput. Mach.*, vol. 19, pp. 109–119, 1972.
[18] G. E. Hughes and M. J. Cresswell, *An Introduction to Modal Logic*. London: Methuen, 1968.
[19] R. S. Ledley, *Fortran IV Programming*. New York: McGraw-Hill, 1966.
[20] B. Raphael, R. Duda, R. E. Fikes, P. E. Hart, N. Nilsson, P. W. Thorndyke, and B. M. Wilbur, "Research and applications—artificial intelligence," Stanford Res. Inst., Menlo Park, Calif., Final Rep., Oct. 1971.

A New Approach to Clustering

ENRIQUE H. RUSPINI

Space Biology Laboratory, University of California, Los Angeles

A general formulation of data reduction and clustering processes is proposed. These procedures are regarded as mappings or transformations of the original space onto a "representation" or "code" space subjected to some constraints. Current clustering methods, as well as three other data reduction techniques, are specified within the framework of this formulation. A new method of representation of the reduced data, based on the idea of "fuzzy sets," is proposed to avoid some of the problems of current clustering procedures and to provide better insight into the structure of the original data.

LIST OF SYMBOLS

R:	the real line
R^+:	the non-negative real numbers
R^n:	Euclidean n-dimensional space
X:	data set
$P(x)$:	density function defined in X
g:	grouping function
C:	representation set
K:	set of subindexes of constraints
T_k, V_k:	constraints on g
I:	optimality conditions
J:	relaxed constraints
δ:	distance function
λ:	Lagrange multiplier
$\mathbf{N}$:	natural numbers
ρ:	Watanabe's inter-relation function
S_j:	fuzzy sets
$P(S_j/x)$:	degree of belongingness of x to S_j
$P(S_j)$:	size of S_j or a priori probability of S_j
$P(x/S_j)$:	density function of the cluster S_j
M_j, M:	mean distances with respect to class j and the whole population respectively
H_L:	normalized local entropy
N:	number of fuzzy sets
W_k:	weights on general constraint
U:	threshold in clustering

1. INTRODUCTION

The purpose of this paper is to introduce a general formulation of data reduction techniques and to outline a new view of the problem of numerical classification or clustering. The object of cluster analysis is to classify experimental data in a certain number of sets where the elements of each set should be as similar as possible and dissimilar from those of other sets. This implies the existence of a measure of distance or similarity between the elements to be classified. The number of such classes may be fixed beforehand or may be a consequence of some constraints imposed on them.

Present clustering techniques are in a primitive stage of development and no known procedure is exempt from the difficulties detailed in Nagy (1968).

The problem of misclassifications originated by "bridges" or strays between sets, and that of pairs classified in different classes having a

Reprinted with permission from *Inform. Control*, vol. 15, no. 1, pp. 22–32, July 1969.

greater similarity than some pairs within the same set, represent two frequent difficulties. A survey of the methods and techniques of clustering may be found in Ball (1965).

To allow a comparative study of data reduction techniques, we present first a mathematical formulation of these processes in Section 2. Section 3 is dedicated to the characterization of some of the present techniques in terms of such formulation. This will serve to emphasize the differences between them. Our approach is introduced in Section 4.

2. A MATHEMATICAL FORMULATION OF DATA REDUCTION TECHNIQUES

Given a set X and a probability measure P in X, then a *data reduction technique* is a set C called the *code or representation space* and a function $g:X \to C$ called the *grouping function* that satisfies the following constraint:

For each element k of a set K there are two functions,

$$T_k:X \times X \to R, \qquad V_k:C \times C \to R, \tag{1}$$

and for all $(x, y) \in X \times X$,

$$T_k(x, y) = V_k(g(x), g(y)). \tag{2}$$

In other words, we are trying to classify a "sample" of X characterized by the density function P, and C is our set of names or representatives for our original data contained in X. The g is the function that pairs each element with its name or representation. $\{T_k, V_k\}$ is a set of constraints that requires that some properties of the elements in X should be preserved after transformation. For example, in cluster analysis "close elements should be assigned to the same class."

The set $g(X) = \{g(x):x \in X\}$ is called the *reduction* of X.

Sometimes we look not only for grouping functions that satisfy the constraints but for one that is best in some sense:

$$I:C \to R, I(g) = \min. \tag{3}$$

In other instances, the constraints are so restrictive that no grouping function exists. We can relax then some of those conditions so that they will hold approximately. For example, if we have $K = \{1, \cdots, N\}$, and we decide to relax all conditions, we can make

$$J(g) = \sum_{k=1}^{N} W_k^2 \iint [T_k(x, y) - V_k(g(x), g(y))]dP(x)\, dP(y) = \min. \tag{4}$$

The more general formulation for this K will be,

$$J \subset K, \quad T_k(x, y) = V_k(g(x), g(y)), \quad k \in J, \quad I(g) + \lambda J(g) = \min; \quad W_k = 0, \text{ if } k \in J. \tag{5}$$

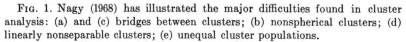

FIG. 1. Nagy (1968) has illustrated the major difficulties found in cluster analysis: (a) and (c) bridges between clusters; (b) nonspherical clusters; (d) linearly nonseparable clusters; (e) unequal cluster populations.

3. SOME SPECIFIC EXAMPLES

A. Current Clustering Methods

Here X = finite sample from R^n,
P = point probability in X,
C = $\mathbf{N}$ or a subset of it,
$g(x_i)$ = m (the number of the cluster to which x_i belongs).

The properties T_k and V_k vary greatly for each particular method but they are usually stated in terms of a distance function $\delta : X \times X \to R^+$ (the non-negative real numbers) that satisfies:

$$1.\ \delta(x, x) = 0, \qquad 2.\ \delta(x, y) = \delta(y, x).$$

A typical set of constraints can be described by

$$T = \begin{cases} 1 & \text{if } \delta(x, y) \geqq U \\ 0 & \text{otherwise,} \end{cases}$$

$$V = 0 \quad \text{if } g(x) = g(y); \qquad 1 \text{ otherwise,}$$

thus requiring that points distant more than some threshold U to be placed in different clusters. A similar set may require that points sufficiently close may be classified in the same set. Constraints of the number of elements of $g(X)$ are usual. In other cases, restricting properties are not invoked and the clumping properties of g are obtained from the optimality condition.

Usually, all the constraints are not satisfied and some sort of compromise is reached. This results in the anomalies described in Section1. Even when g exists, its determination is by no means easy; reallocation and correction processes are common (*cf.* Lance and Williams, 1967; Ball, 1965). These procedures may be used sequentially to generate hierarchical classifications.

B. Factor Analysis and Related Techniques

Factor analysis is a procedure to find linear relations between data sampled from a linear space. We shall restrict our description to finite dimensional Euclidean spaces. Let, then
X = subset of R^n,
C = R^m, $\quad m < n$.
The idea is to represent $x \in X$ as

$$x = g_1 V_1 + \cdots + g_m V_m, \quad \text{where} \quad V_i \in R^n, g_i \in R, 1 \leqq i \leqq m,$$

then

$$g : x \to (g_1, \cdots, g_m),$$

and here

$$K = R^2,$$

and

$$T_{\lambda\mu}(x, y) = \lambda x + \mu y,$$

$$V_{\lambda\mu}(u, v) = \lambda u + \mu v.$$

In other words, g is required to be linear. The constraints cannot be satisfied in general so that the relaxed forms

$$\int (x - g_1(x) V_1)^2 dP(x) = \min_{g_1(x), V_1}$$

$$\int [(x - g_1(x) V_1) - g_2(x) V_2]^2 dP(x) = \min_{g_2(x), V_2}$$

and so forth, are used.

C. The Information Theoretical Correlation Method of Watanabe

X = subset of the set of all m-tuples with binary components (0 or 1); m is finite.

$C = \mathbf{N}$.

$P(x)$ is the probability function of the elements of X. A function ρ (the inter-relation) is then defined (Watanabe, 1965). This inter-relation function measures the resemblance between the two sets, determined by the number of their similar or correlated binary components. It can be shown that the inter-relation between two sets is zero if and only if they are statistically independent.

Two points x and y are said to be *stuck* if no set Y exists such that $x \in X - Y$, $y \in Y$, and

$$\rho(X - Y, Y) = \min_{Z \subset X} \rho(X - Z, Z),$$

where the minimization is carried over all nonvoid proper subsets of X.

$$T(x, y) = 1 \quad \text{if and only if } x \text{ and } y \text{ are } \textit{stuck},$$
$$= 0 \quad \text{otherwise.}$$

V is such that

$$V(u, v) = \begin{cases} 0 & \text{if} \quad u \neq v, \\ 1 & \text{if} \quad u = v. \end{cases}$$

g is selected so that Card $g(X)$ = number of classes, is a maximum. (This is indeed a consequence of the preceding constraints and as a constraint is unnecessary.)

In this method the internal structure of each subclass determines the classification in groups that are not inter-related (or "redundant"). Watanabe (1965) gives an example using an information measure as his inter-relation. Distances are not used; rather sharing of a number of attributes by each group is the reason for the common label applied to its members. The method is then applied iteratively to produce a hierarchy.

D. The Information Measure of Wallace and Boulton

Here, as in the preceding examples, the space X is a subset of R^n and C is a set of real vectors such that

(a) the first element of $g(x) \in C$ represents the number of the class to which x belongs,

(b) the next element of $g(x)$ represents the type of class to which x belongs. This can be anyone of a predefined dictionary of classes (Ex: normal, uniform, etc.),

(c) the next r elements where r is variable are the parameters of the class to which x belongs,

(d) the next s elements are devoted to specify the position of x with respect to the class (ex.: distance of x to the mean in some units in normal distributions).

The length of the vector $g(x)$ is then variable depending on the class selected and the amount of information needed to specify that class and the position of x within that set. All the attributes are used for classification while the number of possible choices for classes is limited by the size of the dictionary of classes.

Clustering is then made trying to optimize the length of the codes, subjected to some restrictions, to insure a proper encoding and identification of each data point. An information measure is used and the analysis resembles the determination of optimal lengths of codes, as done in coding theory (here, more frequent classes have longer codes than unfrequent classes and are better specified than those).

For more details, see Wallace and Boulton (1968).

4. NEW APPROACH

A. Number of Classes Fixed

The set X is usually a finite subset of R^n; then let

$$X = \{x_1, \cdots, x_m\} \subset R^n, \text{ and}$$

$$C = \{\text{set of all } N\text{-tuples with positive elements and sum of its elements} = 1\}.$$

A distance δ as described in 3A is presumed to be defined in $X \times X$ and

$$g{:}x \to (P(S_1/x), \cdots, P(S_N/x)). \tag{6}$$

The use of the probability notation will become clearer later.

We regard numerical classification as the process of assigning to each data point a certain degree of belongingness to each class $S_1, \cdots, S_N$. In that sense, the S_j's are "fuzzy sets" in the sense of Zadeh (1966). However, our fuzzy sets have a strong probabilistic meaning and our rules of operation are not those proposed by Zadeh but those that come naturally from probability theory. Figure 2 is an idealized example of such a classification applied to a dichotomy of a simple set. Several advantages can be noted over conventional clustering representation: Points in the "core" or center of some class will have a degree $= 1$ of being members of that class, while boundary points, between the core and other classes may be identified as such. "Bridges" or stray points may be classified as undetermined points with a degree of indeterminacy proportional to their similarity to "core" points.

In this subsection, the number N of "fuzzy sets" is fixed. In subsection 4B, some thought is given to the problem of a variable number of subsets. Assuming now that X is finite, we introduce the following notations that will be useful later

$$P(S_j) = \sum_{i=1}^{m} P(x_i)P(S_j/x_i). \tag{7}$$

Note that $P(S_j) \geqq 0$ and $\sum_{j=1}^{N} P(S_j) = 1$. $P(S_j)$ is a measure of the relative size of each class.

$$P(x_i/S_j) = \frac{P(S_j/x_i)P(x_i)}{P(S_j)}. \tag{8}$$

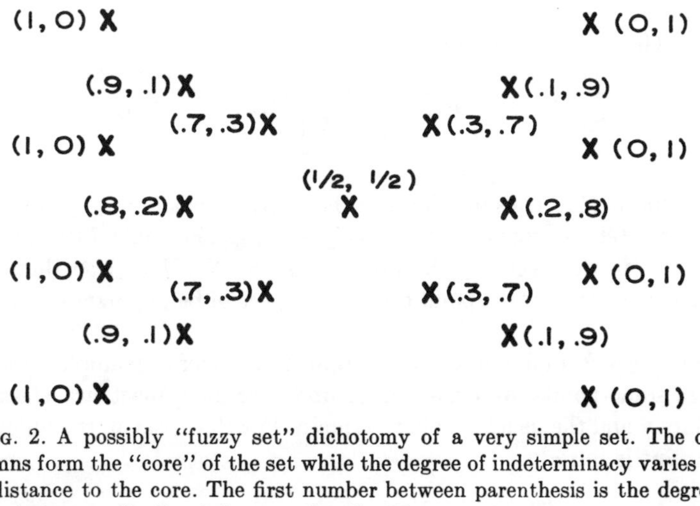

FIG. 2. A possibly "fuzzy set" dichotomy of a very simple set. The outer columns form the "core" of the set while the degree of indeterminacy varies with the distance to the core. The first number between parenthesis is the degree of belongingness to Set I and the second to Set II.

From (8) it is easy to see that

$$P(x) = \sum_{j=1}^{N} P(S_j)P(x/S_j),$$

and so the clustering process may be seen as the decomposition of the density function $P(x)$ into the weighted sum of the component cluster densities $P(x/S_j)$ with weights $P(S_j)$ (the "a priori" probability of S_j). This is the main reason for the use of the probabilistic notation. The consideration of the degrees of belongingness as probabilities is very useful for pattern recognition purposes after the fuzzy sets or classes have been established.

We now define

$$M(x_i) = \sum_{k=1}^{m} P(x_k)\delta(x_i, x_k), \tag{9}$$

(mean density of the population around x_i)

$$M_j(x_i) = \sum_{k=1}^{m} P(x_k/S_j)\delta(x_i, x_k). \tag{10}$$

(mean density of the class S_j around x_i).

From (7) we see that

$$\sum_{j=1}^{N} P(S_j)M_j(x_i) = M(x_i).$$

To insure that the density functions $P(x/S_j)$ really represent clusters, optimality conditions and constraints should be imposed.

The use of both is greatly limited by computational difficulties. The procedures to carry out the numerical optimization are sophisticated enough to be, along with our numerical experiments, the object of a forthcoming paper.

Two optimality conditions have been used so far:

(I.) For each point i, let $S_{(i)}$ be such that

$$P(S_{(i)}/x_i) = \max_{1 \leq j \leq N} \mathrm{P}(S_j/x_i).$$

The parenthetical subscript notation is then introduced to indicate the most likely cluster assignment. Then g is selected to make

$$\sum_{i=1}^{m} \left[P(x_i) \, \frac{P(S_{(i)})M_{(i)}(x_i)}{M(x_i)} \right]^2, \tag{11}$$

a minimum.

(II.) Here g is selected to make

$$\sum_{i=1}^{m} P(x_i) \sum_{j=1}^{N} P(S_j) \left[\frac{P(S_j)M_j(x_i)}{M(x_i)} \right] P(S_j/x_i), \tag{12}$$

a minimum.

Constraint (11) tries to minimize the average mean density of a point to the cluster to which it most likely belongs. Formula (12) tries to minimize (in the average) the products $P(S_j/X_i)M_j(x_i)$ so that large mean densities will correspond to small degrees of belongingness and vice versa.

These two formulas have been applied to several examples and although some points are classified as undetermined, most are classified absolutely and the usual problems remain. For that reason, the following constraint is introduced:

$$T(x, y) = F(\delta(x, y)), \tag{13}$$

$$V(g(x), g(y)) = \left(\sum_{j=1}^{n} (P(S_j/x) - P(S_j/y))^2\right)^{1/2}. \tag{14}$$

where $F:R^+ \to R^+$ is a nonnegative non-decreasing function not identically zero such that $F(0) = 0$. This constraint requires that the map g preserves the distance structure, transforming pairs of similar points into pairs of similar codes.

In general, this constraint cannot be satisfied by any g, and so the approach detailed in (4) is used. Here:

$$J(g) = \sum_{k=1}^{n} \sum_{i=1}^{n} P(x_i)P(x_k)(F(\delta(x_i, x_k)) - V(g(x_i), g(x_k)))^2. \tag{15}$$

Experiments with simple sets are encouraging and a computational technique is being developed. Numerical experience shows that the results of using constraints (11) and (12) provide a good starting point for the numerical methods used in the minimization of condition (15). The possibility of making F variable over a set of feasible functions to improve J is foreseen.

B. On the Number of Clusters

Some of the already defined quantities may be useful in determining the optimal number of clusters N.

First it may be noted that $J(g)$ as defined in the preceding paragraph is not a decreasing function of the number of clusters and is likely that for some N it may be a minimum.

Considerations on the diameter of a set and the distance between sets are invoked usually as constraints to determine N.

In our approach, a function may be useful

$$H_L = -(\log N)^{-1} \sum_{i=1}^{N} P(x_i)\left(\sum_{j=1}^{N} P(S_j/x_i) \log P(S_j/x_i)\right) \tag{16}$$

(normalized local entropy of the classification). In the ideal case depicted in Fig. 3, the local entropy of the classification in three sets is much higher than that of two sets, corresponding to a high number of undetermined points produced as a result of the dichotomy of one cluster.

5. SUMMARY

We have presented here a mathematical formulation that permits a unified view of data reduction techniques. We have also proposed a new approach to numerical classification problems. This approach is intrinsically free of the shape and size problems of other clustering methods and using proper constraints gives better information about the structure of the data set.

Furthermore, formulation of constraints and optimality conditions is easier in terms of this framework than in the usual set description.

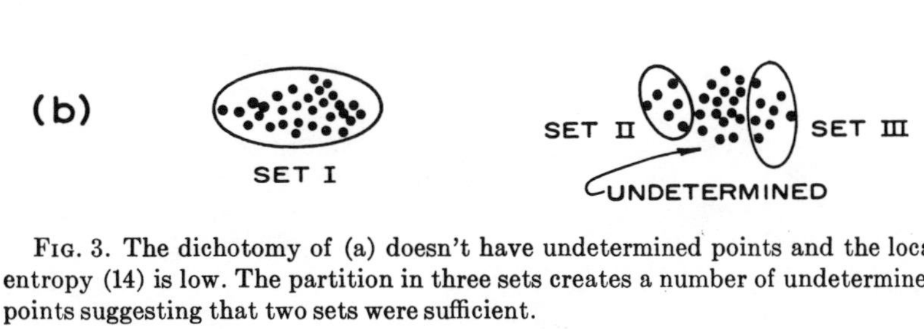

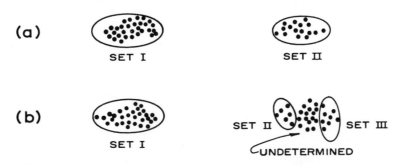

FIG. 3. The dichotomy of (a) doesn't have undetermined points and the local entropy (14) is low. The partition in three sets creates a number of undetermined points suggesting that two sets were sufficient.

ACKNOWLEDGMENTS

The author wishes to thank D. O. Walter and R. T. Kado for helpful suggestions during the development of this research; M. Maddex for the typing of the manuscript; and Mrs. J. Payne for the illustrations of the article. Computational assistance was obtained from the Health Sciences Computing Facility, UCLA, supported by NIH Grant FR-3. This research was supported by the Advanced Research Projects Agency of the Department of Defense and was monitored by U.S. Army Medical Research and Development Command under Contract No. DADA 17-67-C-7124.

RECEIVED: February 5, 1969; revised May 28, 1969.

REFERENCES

BALL, G. H. (1965), Data analysis in the social sciences: What about the details?, Proceedings, Fall Joint Computer Conference, 533–559.

LANCE, C. N. AND WILLIAMS, W. T. (1967), A general theory of classificatory sorting strategies. II. Clustering systems, *Computer Journal* **10**, 271–277.

NAGY, G. (1968), State of the art in pattern recognition, *Proc. IEEE.* **56**, 836–882.

WALLACE, C. S. AND BOULTON, D. M. (1968), An information measure for classification, *Computer Journal* **11**, 185–194.

WATANABE, S. (1965), Une explication mathematique du classement d'objets. *In* "Information and Prediction in Science" (Dockx, S. and Bernays, P., eds.). Academic Press, New York.

ZADEH, L. A., (1965), Fuzzy sets, *Inform. Control* **8**, 338–353.

An Algorithm for Detecting Unimodal Fuzzy Sets and Its Application as a Clustering Technique

ISRAEL GITMAN AND MARTIN D. LEVINE, MEMBER, IEEE

Abstract—An algorithm is presented which partitions a given sample from a multimodal fuzzy set into unimodal fuzzy sets. It is proven that if certain assumptions are satisfied, then the algorithm will derive the optimal partition in the sense of maximum separation.

The algorithm is applied to the problem of clustering data, defined in multidimensional space, into homogeneous groups. An artificially generated data set is used for experimental purposes and the results and errors are discussed in detail. Methods for extending the algorithm to the clustering of very large sets of points are also described.

The advantages of the method (as a clustering technique) are that it does not require large blocks of high speed memory, the amount of computing time is relatively small, and the shape of the distribution of points in a group can be quite general.

Index Terms—Clustering algorithms, multimodal data sets, pattern recognition, symmetric fuzzy sets, unimodal fuzzy sets.

I. Introduction

THE PRIMARY objective of clustering techniques is to partition a given data set into so-called homogeneous clusters (groups, categories). The term homogeneous is used in the sense that all points in the same group are similar (according to some measure) to each other and are not similar to points in other groups. The clusters generated by the partition are used to exhibit the data set and to investigate the existence of families as is done in numerical taxonomy or alternatively, as categories for classifying future data points as in pattern recognition. The role of cluster analysis in pattern recognition is discussed in detail in two excellent survey papers [1], [16].

The basic practical problems that clustering techniques must address themselves to involve the following:

1) the availability of fast computer memory,
2) computational time,
3) the generality of the distributions of the detected categories.

Clustering algorithms that satisfactorily overcome all of these problems are not yet available. In general, techniques that can handle a relatively large data set (say 1000 points) are only capable of detecting very simple distributions of points [Fig. 1(a)]; on the other hand, techniques that perform an extensive search in the feature space (the vector space in which the points are represented) are only able to handle a small data set.

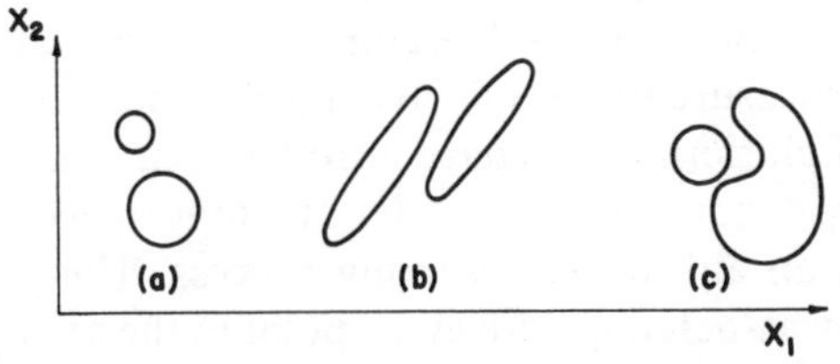

Fig. 1. Distribution of points in a two-dimensional feature space. The curves represent the closure of the sets which exhibit a high concentration of sample points.

Some authors [6], [9], [19], [20] have formulated the clustering problem in terms of a minimization of a functional based on a distance measure applied to an underlying model for the data. The clustering methods used to derive this optimal partition perform an extensive search and are therefore only applicable to small data sets (less than 200 points). In addition, there is no guarantee that the convergence is to the true minimum. Other methods [3], [12], [15] use the so-called pairwise similarity matrix or sample covariance matrix [15]. These are memory-limited since, for example, one-half million memory locations are required just to store the matrix elements when clustering a data set of 1000 points. Also, the methods in [12], [15] will generally not give satisfactory results in detecting categories for an input space of the type shown in Fig. 1(b).

It is rather difficult to make a fruitful comparison among the many clustering techniques that have been reported in the literature and this is not the aim of the paper. The difficulty may be attributed to the fact that many of the algorithms are heuristic in nature, and furthermore, have not been tested on the same standard data sets. In general it seems that most of the algorithms are not capable of detecting categories which exhibit complicated distributions in the feature space [Fig. 1(c)] and that a great many are not applicable to large data sets (greater than 2000 points).

This paper discusses an algorithm which partitions the given data set into "unimodal fuzzy sets." The notion of a unimodal fuzzy set has been chosen to represent the partition of a data set for two reasons. First, it is capable of detecting all the locations in the vector space where there exist highly concentrated clusters of points, since these will appear as modes according to some measure of "cohesiveness." Second, the notion is general enough to represent clusters which exhibit quite general distributions of points.

Manuscript received September 22, 1969; revised December 15, 1969. The research reported here was sponsored by the National Research Council of Canada under Grant A4156.

I. Gitman was with the Department of Electrical Engineering, McGill University, Montréal, Canada. He is now with the Research and Development Laboratories, Northern Electric Co. Ltd., Ottawa, Ontario, Canada.

M. D. Levine is with the Department of Electrical Engineering, McGill University, Montréal, Canada.

Reprinted from *IEEE Trans. Comput.*, vol. C-19, no. 7, pp. 583–593, July 1970.

The generated partition is optimal in the sense that the program detects all of the existing unimodal fuzzy sets and realizes the maximum separation [21] among them. The algorithm attempts to solve problems 1), 2), and 3) mentioned above; that is, it is economical in memory space and computational time requirements and also detects groups which are fairly generally distributed in the feature space [Fig. 1(c)]. The algorithm is a systematic procedure (as opposed to an iterative technique) which always terminates and the computation time is reasonable.

An important distinction between this procedure and the methods reported in the literature[1] is that the latter use a distance measure (or certain average distances) as the only means of clustering. We have introduced another "dimension," the dimension of the order of "importance" of every point, as an aid in the clustering process. This is accomplished by associating with every point in the set a grade of membership or characteristic value [21]. Thus the order of the points according to their grade of membership, as well as their order according to distance, are used in the algorithm. The latter partitions a sample from a multimodal fuzzy set into unimodal fuzzy sets.

In Section II the concept of a fuzzy set is extended in order to define both symmetric and unimodal fuzzy sets. The basic algorithm consists of the two procedures, F and S, which are described in detail in Sections III and IV, respectively. Section V deals with the application of the algorithm to the clustering of data and the various practical implications. Section VI discusses the experimental results. Possible extensions of the algorithm to handle very large data sets (say greater than 30 000 points) are presented in Section VII. The conclusions are given in Section VIII.

II. Definitions

The notion of a fuzzy set was introduced by Zadeh [21]. Let X be a space of points with elements $x \in X$. Then:

"a fuzzy set A in X is characterized by a membership (characteristic) function $f_A(x)$ which associates with each point in X a real number in the interval [0, 1], with the value $f_A(x)$ at x representing the 'grade of membership' of x in A."

In the rest of this section we shall introduce some notation and certain definitions required for the description of the algorithm.

Let B be a fuzzy set in X with the membership (characteristic) function f, and let μ be the point at which the maximal grade of membership is attained, that is,

$$f(\mu) = \sup_{x \in B} [f(x)].$$

We may define two sets in B as follows:

$$\Gamma_{x_i} = \{x | f(x) \geq f(x_i)\}^2$$

and

$$\Gamma_{x_i d} = \{x | d(\mu, x) \leq d(\mu, x_i)\}$$

where x_i is some point in B and d is a metric.

Definition: A fuzzy set B is symmetric if and only if, for every point x_i in B, $\Gamma_{x_i} = \Gamma_{x_i d}$.

Clearly, if B is symmetric, then for every two points x_i and x_k in B,

$$d(x_i, \mu) \leq d(x_k, \mu) \Leftrightarrow f(x_i) \geq f(x_k).$$

As an example of a symmetric fuzzy set, consider the set B defined as "all the very tall buildings." B is a symmetric fuzzy set, since the taller the building, the higher the grade of membership it will have in B. Any symmetric (in the ordinary sense) function, or a truncated symmetric function, can represent a characteristic function of a symmetric fuzzy set.

Definition: A fuzzy set B is unimodal if and only if the set Γ_{x_i} is connected for all x_i in B (see Fig. 2).

In order to consider the problem of clustering data points it will be necessary to define discrete fuzzy sets.

A sample point from B will be a point $x \in X$ with its associated characteristic value, $f(x)$. Further, we will denote a sample of N points from B by $S = \{(x_i, f_i)^N\}$, where x_i is a point in X and f_i its corresponding grade of membership. S can be considered as a discrete fuzzy set which includes only those points x_i given by the sample. We shall require a large sample S; in particular, S is large in comparison to the dimension of the space X, and to the number of local maxima in f.

$\{(S_i, \mu_i)^m\}$ denotes a partition of S into m subsets, where S_i is a discrete fuzzy subset and μ_i the point in S_i at which the maximal grade of membership is attained. We refer to μ_i as the mode of S_i. A mode will be called a *local maximum* if it is a local maximum of f and will then be denoted by $\hat{\nu}_i$. It will be assumed that every local maximal grade of membership is unique [21].

The notion of an interior point in a discrete fuzzy set is defined as follows.

Definition: Let S be a sample from a fuzzy set B and S_i a proper subset of S. For some point x_k in S_i we associate a point x_t in $(S - S_i)$ such that

$$d(x_t, x_k) = \min_{x_j \in (S - S_i)} [d(x_k, x_j)].$$

The point x_k is defined to be an interior point in S_i if and only if the set $\Gamma = \{x | d(x_t, x) < d(x_t, x_k)\}$ includes at least one sample point in S_i (see Fig. 3).

Note that when the sample is of infinite size, in the sense that every point in X is also in S, this definition reduces to that of an interior point in ordinary sets.

Given a sample, the algorithm to be described in the next two sections is composed of two parts: procedure F which

[1] Rogers and Tanimoto [17] introduced a certain order among the points by associating with the point i, a value which is the number of points at a *constant* finite distance from i. When the number of attributes is large, this so-called "prime mode" will be the centroid of the data set, rather than a "mode" of a cluster. A measure of inhomogeneity is used to detect clusters one at a time.

[2] This is equivalent to the set Γ_α in [21] where $\alpha = f(x_i)$.

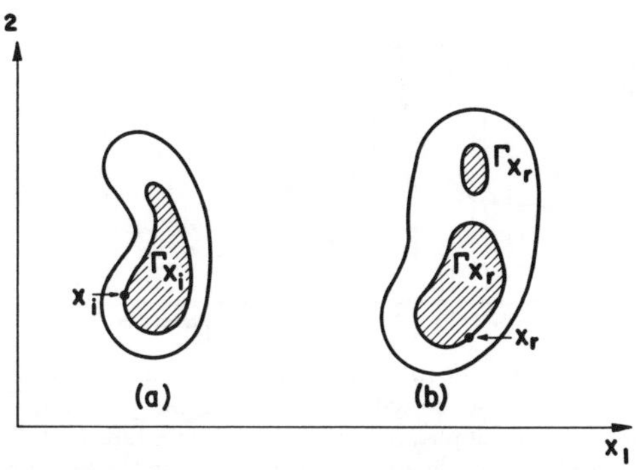

Fig. 2. An example of a unimodal fuzzy set in a two-dimensional space. The curves indicate lines of equigrade of membership. (a) A unimodal fuzzy set where for every point x_i in the set, the set Γ_{x_i} is not disjoint. (b) A multimodal fuzzy set, since there exists a point x_r for which Γ_{x_r} is disjoint.

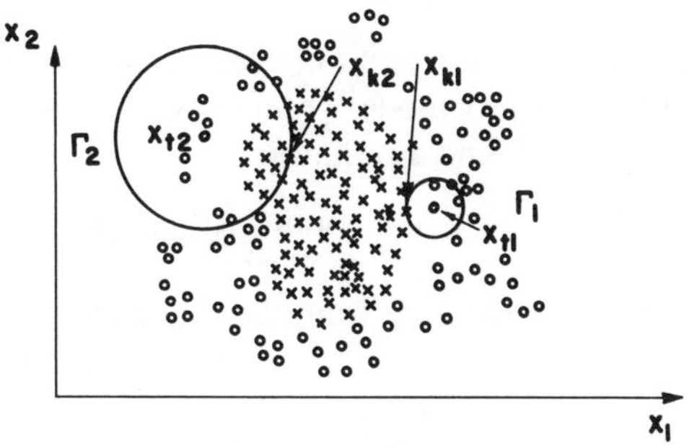

Fig. 3. The points in S_i are denoted by x. The point x_{k1} is on the boundary of S_i since Γ_1 includes no sample points in S_i. The point x_{k2} is an interior point in S_i, since Γ_2 includes points in S_i.

detects all the local maxima of f, and procedure S which uses these local maxima and partitions the given sample into unimodal fuzzy sets.

III. Procedure F

Given a sample $S=\{(x_i, f_i)^N\}$ from a multimodal fuzzy set, subject to certain conditions on f and S (see Theorem 1), procedure F detects all the local maxima of f. It is divided into two parts: in the first part, the sample is partitioned into symmetric subsets and in the second, a search for the local maxima in the generated subsets is performed.

In order to make the steps in the procedure clear, some preliminary explanations are given below. An example which demonstrates the procedure is presented later.

The number of groups (subsets) into which the sample is partitioned is not known beforehand. The procedure is initialized by the construction of two sequences: a sequence A in which the points are ordered according to their grade of membership, and a sequence A_1 in which they are ordered according to their distance to the mode of A (the first point in A). The order of the points in the sequence A is the order in which the points are considered for assignment into groups. This process will initiate new groups when certain conditions are satisfied. Whenever a group, say n, is initiated, a sequence of points A_n is formed of all the points in S which might be considered for assignment into group n. The first point in A_n is its mode and the points are ordered according to their distance to this mode. Not all the points in A_n will necessarily be assigned into group n at the termination of the procedure. At every stage of assignment, every group i displays a point from its sequence A_i, which is its candidate point, to be accepted into the group. The point of A to be assigned is compared (for identity) with each of the candidate points in turn and is either assigned into one of the existing groups (if it is identical to the corresponding candidate point) or initiates a new group. If, for example, the point is assigned into group j, then the candidate of this group is replaced by its next point in the sequence A_j. Thus a point is assigned to the group in which its order according to the grade of membership corresponds to its order according to the distance to its mode.

Part 1 of Procedure F

Let $S=\{(x_i, f_i)^N\}$ be a sample from a fuzzy set (assume, for simplicity, that $f_i \neq f_j$ for $i \neq j$).[3]

1) Initially it is required to generate the following two sequences.

a) $A=(y_1, y_2, \cdots, y_N)$ is a descending sequence of the points in the sample ordered according to their grade of membership; that is, $f_j \geq f_t$ for $j \leq t$, where f_j and f_t are the grades of membership of y_j and y_t, respectively.

b) $A_1=(y_1^1, y_2^1, y_3^1, \cdots, y_N^1)$, where $y_1^1 \equiv y_1$,[4] is the sequence of the points ordered according to their distance to y_1^1; that is, $d(y_1^1, y_j^1) \leq d(y_1^1, y_t^1)$ for $j \leq t$.[5]

We will also refer to A_1 as the sequence of ordered "candidate" points to be assigned into group 1. Thus y_2^1 is the first candidate, and if it is assigned into group 1, then y_3^1 becomes the next candidate, and so on. We can therefore state that the current candidate point for group 1, y_c^1, is the nearest point to its mode $y_1^1(\equiv y_1 \equiv \mu_1)$ except for points that have already been assigned to group 1. This will hold true for any sequence A_i; that is, $y_1^i \equiv \mu_i$ is the mode for group i, and y_c^i is its candidate point.

2) If $y_i \equiv y_i^1$, for $i=2, 3, \cdots, r-1$, and $y_r \not\equiv y_r^1$, then y_i, $i=1, 2, \cdots, r-1$, are assigned into group 1 and a new group is initiated with $y_1^2 \equiv \mu_2 \equiv y_r$ as its mode. That is, the sequence $A_2=(y_1^2, y_2^2, y_3^2, \cdots, y_p^2)$ is generated. The latter includes from among the points that have not yet been assigned, those points which are closer to y_r than the shortest distance from y_r to the points that have already been assigned; this is shown for one dimension in Fig. 4. The points in A_2 are now ordered according to their distance to y_r; that is, $d(y_r, y_j^2) \leq d(y_r, y_t^2)$ for $j \leq t$.

3) Suppose that G groups have been initiated. Thus there exist G sequences, A_i, $i=1, \cdots, G$, each of which displays a candidate point, y_c^i. Suppose that y_q in the sequence A is the point currently being considered for assignment (all the

[3] The case in which there are equal grades of membership will be discussed in Section V.

[4] We shall use the symbol "$\equiv$" to mean "is identical to."

[5] The sets A and A_1 are sequences of the same N points; however, the ordering principle is different. Thus the point y_k^i is some point in A and its label indicates that it is also in location k in the sequence A_i.

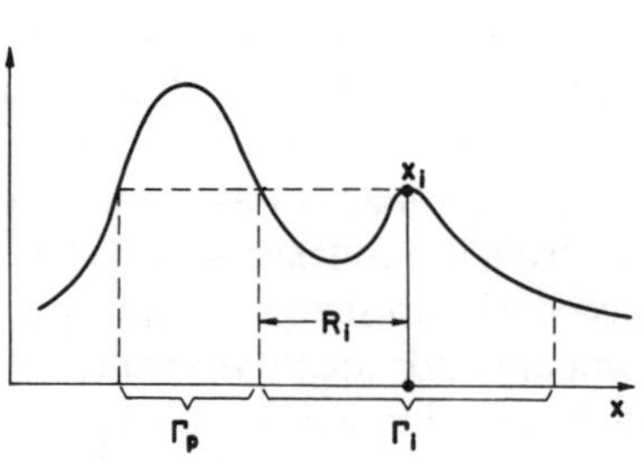

Fig. 4. At the stage where the point $x_i(=\mu_i)$ initiates a new group, all the sample points that have already been assigned are in the domain Γ_p. Thus the nearest point in Γ_p to x_i is at a distance R_i, which defines the domain Γ_i of all the points which are at a shorter distance to x_i than R_i. The sample points in Γ_i will be ordered as candidate points to be assigned into the group in which x_i is the mode.

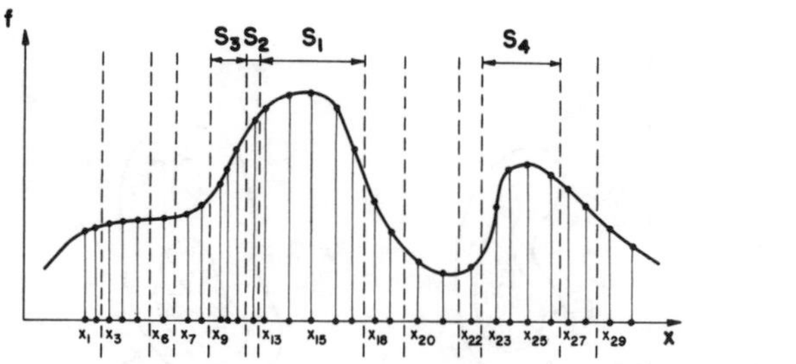

Fig. 5. The characteristic function f and the 30 point sample for the example are shown. The dotted lines indicate the partition (the sets S_i) resulting from the application of part 1 of procedure F. We can observe that x_{15} and x_{25} are the only interior modes in the partition and thus will be recognized as the local maxima points (v_i) of f.

points in A for $i<q$ have already been assigned); then the following holds.

a) If $y_q \equiv y_c^i$ and $y_q \not\equiv y_c^j, j=1, \cdots, G, j \neq i$, then y_q is assigned into group i.

b) If $y_q \equiv y_c^i$ for some $i \in I$, where I is a set of integers representing those groups whose candidate points are identical to y_q, then y_q is assigned into that group to which its nearest neighbor with a higher grade of membership, has been assigned.

c) If $y_q \not\equiv y_c^i$ for $i=1, \cdots, G$, then a new group is initiated with y_q as its mode.

Part 1 of procedure F is terminated when the sequence A is exhausted.

Theorem 1[6]: Let f be a characteristic function of a fuzzy set with K local maxima so that:

1) if v_K is a local maximum of f, then there exists a finite $\epsilon>0$ such that the set $\{x | d(v_k, x) \leq \epsilon\}$ is a symmetric fuzzy set.

Let $S=\{(x_i, f_i)^N\}$ be a large sample from f, such that:

2) for every x_i in the domain of f, the set $\{x | d(x_i, x) < \epsilon/2\}$ includes at least one point in S, and

3) $\{(v_k, f_k)^K\} \subset S$.

Let $\{(S_i, \mu_i)^m\}$ denote the partition generated by part 1 of procedure F, where S_i denotes the discrete fuzzy set, μ_i its maximal grade of membership (mode), and m the number of groups. Then μ_i is an interior point in S_i if and only if it is a local maximum of f.

Theorem 1 states the sufficient condition under which the procedure will detect all the local maxima of f. The main restriction is the requirement that every local maximum of f shall have a small symmetric subset in its neighborhood (condition 1). It is not necessary for the sample to be of infinite size; it will be sufficient if it is large in the neighborhood of a local maximum. Condition 2 indirectly relates the dimension of the space to the size of the sample set.

Using the result of Theorem 1, part 2 of the procedure is employed to check all the modes μ_i in order to detect which are interior points. This is done according to the definition given in the previous section.

Part 2

Let $\{S_i, \mu_i)^m\}$ be the partition generated by part 1 of procedure F. For every mode μ_i and set S_i, a point x_{pi} and a distance R_i can be found as follows:

$$R_i = d(\mu_i, x_{pi}) = \min_{x_k \in (S - S_i)} [d(\mu_i, x_k)].$$

R_i is the minimum distance from the mode to a point in S outside the set S_i. We say that μ_i is a local maximum if the set

$$\Gamma_{R_i} = \{x | d(x_{pi}, x) < R_i\}$$

includes points in S_i. Otherwise we decide that μ_i is not a local maximum because it is a boundary point of S_i.

To summarize this section, if f and S satisfy the conditions stated in Theorem 1, then the procedure presented detects all the local maxima of f.

Example: The following example demonstrates the various procedures associated with the algorithm. A sample of 30 points was taken from a one-dimensional characteristic function. The latter, as well as the sample points with their associated sample numbers, are shown in Fig. 5. The sequences A and A_1 are given by

$$A = (y_1, y_2, \cdots, y_{30}) = (x_{15}, x_{14}, x_{16}, x_{13}, \boxed{x_{12}}, x_{11}, x_{17}, x_{25}, x_{24}, x_{10}, x_{26}, x_9, x_{27}, x_{23}, x_{18}, x_8, x_{28}, x_7, x_6, x_5, x_4, x_3, x_{19}, x_{29}, x_2, x_{30}, x_1, x_{20}, x_{22}, x_{21}).$$

$$A_1 = (y_1^1, y_2^1, y_3^1, \cdots, y_{30}^1) = (x_{15}, x_{14}, x_{16}, x_{13}, \underline{x_{17}}, x_{12}, x_{18}, x_{11}, x_{10}, x_9, x_{19}, x_{20}, x_8, x_7, x_{21}, x_6, x_{22}, x_5, x_4, x_{23}, x_3, x_{24}, x_2, x_1, x_{25}, x_{26}, x_{27}, x_{28}, x_{29}, x_{30}).$$

Observing these sequences, we can see that the first four points in A and A_1 are pairwise identical and thus they are assigned to group 1. Thereafter, the candidate point for group 1 is $y_5^1 = x_{17}$, whereas the point to be assigned is x_{12}. Thus the latter will initiate a new group and a new sequence A_2 will be generated.

[6] The proofs of the theorems are given in Appendix I.

After the first four groups are initiated, the sequences A_i and the resulting partition to this point are as follows:

$$A = (y_1, y_2, \cdots, y_{30}) = (x_{15}, x_{14}, x_{16}, x_{13}, x_{12}, x_{11}, x_{17}, x_{25}, x_{24}, \textcircled{x_{10}}, x_{26}, \cdots, x_{21})$$

$$\begin{cases} A_1 = (y_1^1, y_2^1, \cdots, y_{30}^1) = x_{15}, x_{14}, x_{16}, x_{13}, x_{17}, \underline{x_{12}}, x_{18}, \cdots, x_{30}) \\ S_1 = (x_{15}, x_{14}, x_{16}, x_{13}, x_{17},) \end{cases}$$

$$\begin{cases} A_2 = (y_1^2) = (x_{12}) \quad \text{——} \\ S_2 = (x_{12},) \end{cases}$$

$$\begin{cases} A_3 = (y_1^3, y_2^3, y_3^3) = (x_{11}, \underline{x_{10}}, x_9) \\ S_3 = (x_{11},) \end{cases}$$

$$\begin{cases} A_4 = (y_1^4, y_2^4, y_3^4, y_4^4, \cdots, y_{13}^4) = (x_{25}, x_{24}, \underline{x_{26}}, x_{23}, x_{27}, x_{28}, x_{22}, x_{29}, x_{21}, x_{30}, x_{20}, x_{19}, x_{18}) \\ S_4 = (x_{25}, x_{24},). \end{cases}$$

In relation to the procedure described above, we note the following.

1) The sequence A_2 includes only one point (its mode) since the nearest point to x_{12} in S has already been assigned. Therefore there are no sample points in S to generate a symmetric fuzzy set whose mode is x_{12}.
2) At the stage shown, x_{10} in the sequence A is to be assigned. The candidate points for the four groups that have already been initiated are x_{12}, no candidate, x_{10}, and x_{26}, respectively. Thus x_{10} will be assigned to group 3 since it is identical with the latter's candidate point.
3) No more points will be assigned into group 1, since its candidate x_{12} has already been assigned to another group, and thus cannot be replaced as a candidate for group 1.

The resulting symmetric fuzzy sets generated by the application of part 1 of procedure F are shown in Fig. 5. Part 2 of the procedure is now applied to test each of the 13 modes to detect which of these are interior points. In Fig. 5 we can see that only the modes x_{15} and x_{25} are interior points in their corresponding sets, and therefore only two local maxima are discovered. Based on this partial result, the example will be continued at the end of the next section in order to demonstrate procedure S.

IV. Procedure S

Procedure S partitions a sample from a fuzzy set into unimodal fuzzy sets, providing the local maxima of f are known. Thus this procedure uses the information obtained from the application of procedure F; that is, the number, location, and characteristic values of the local maxima of f. The rule for assigning the points differs from the known classification rules appearing in the pattern recognition literature. Rather than an arbitrary order which is the usual case, the points are finally assigned in the order in which they appear in the sequence A.

Specifically, let $S = \{(x_i, f_i)^N\}$ be a sample from a fuzzy set, and $\{(v_i, f_i(v))^K\} \subset S$ be the sample of the K local maxima v_i of f. Assume that $f_i(x_i) \neq f_j(x_j)$ for $i \neq j$, and $f(v_i) > f(v_j)$ for $i \leq j$. Let A be the sequence of the points ordered according to their grade of membership, and suppose that the K local maxima of f are in locations p_i, $i = 1, \cdots, K$ in A. We can infer the following proposition.

Proposition: The point x_j in location j in the sequence A, $p_M \leq j < p_{(M+1)}$, $M \leq K$, can only be assigned into one of the groups $i \in I_M = \{1, 2, \cdots, M\}$.

If $f(x_{p_r})$, $r = M+1, M+2, \cdots, K$ is the local maximum of group r, then only points with a lower grade of membership can be assigned into group r. Since all the points that precede location p_r in A have higher grades of membership, none of them can be assigned into group r, $r = M+1, M+2, \cdots, K$.

This proposition implies that all the points in A which are found in the locations $p_1 \leq j < p_2$ will automatically be assigned into group 1; the points in locations $p_2 < j < p_3$ will be divided between group 1 and group 2, and so on.

Procedure S uses the following rule: assign the point x_j in location j in the sequence A into the group in which its nearest neighbor with a higher grade of membership (all the points preceding x_j in A) has been assigned. This rule applies to all the points with the exception of the local maxima that initiate new groups. Note that the rule is different from the "nearest neighbor classification rule" [5] because of the particular order in which the points are introduced.

Theorem 2: Let f be a piecewise continuous characteristic function of a fuzzy set.

Let $S = \{(x_i, f_i)^N\}$ be an infinite sample from f, such that

1) for every x_i in the domain of f and for an $\alpha \geq 0$, the set $\Gamma = \{x | d(x_i, x) < \alpha/2\}$ includes at least one sample point S.

If $\alpha \to 0$, then procedure S partitions the given sample into unimodal fuzzy sets.

Theorem 3: Let S be a sample from a fuzzy set with a characteristic function f. Let f and S be constrained as in Theorem 2.

If $\alpha \to 0$, then every final set is a union of the sets S_i generated in part 1 of procedure F.

If $X = E^1$, a more powerful result than Theorem 2 can be stated; for simplicity we will state it for the case of two local maxima.

Theorem 4: Let f be a piecewise continuous characteristic function of a fuzzy set and d the distance between its two local maxima.

Let S be a sample from f, such that,

1) for every point x_i in the domain of f and for a finite $\alpha > 0$, $\alpha \ll d$, the set $\Gamma = \{x | d(x_i, x) < \alpha\}$ includes at least one point in S, and
2) the local maxima, $(v_1, f(v_1))$, $(v_2, f(v_2))$ are in S.

Let $H=x_0$[7] be the optimal hyperplane (point) separating f into unimodal fuzzy sets and $\Gamma_v=\{x|d(x_0, x)<\alpha/2\}$.

If S does not include any points in Γ_v, then procedure S derives the optimal partition of S for any finite α, $\alpha<<d$.[8]

Theorem 2 states the sufficient conditions (but not necessary) under which procedure S derives the optimal partition into unimodal fuzzy sets. Note that when $\alpha=0$, the sample S is identically equal to the domain of f. On the other hand, given a characteristic function f, we can always find a finite α for which the result holds. Observing procedure S, we may see that the sample must be large, particularly in the neighborhood of the separating hypersurface (see Theorem 4).

Utilizing the result of Theorem 3, we can modify procedure S to assign subsets S_i, generated in part 1 of procedure F, rather than individual points of S. That is, we can first assign μ_i (the mode of S_i), and then automatically all the points in S_i to this same group. In fact no further computation is necessary since, if μ_i is a mode, it will initiate a new set (group) in part 1 of procedure F. In the latter, when evaluating the distances to the points that have already been assigned, we can record its nearest point (with a higher grade of membership). Hence procedure S reduces to an automatic classification of the points.

Theorem 4 implies that if α is finite, but $\alpha<<d$, then only points in S within a distance α to H can be misclassified.

Example: To demonstrate procedure S, we again consider the sequence A, where now it is assumed that the local maxima are known.

$$A = (\boxed{x_{15}}, x_{14}, x_{16}, x_{13}, x_{12}, x_{11}, x_{17}, \boxed{x_{25}}, x_{24}, x_{10}, x_{26}, x_9, x_{27}, \textcircled{x_{23}}, x_{18}, x_8, x_{28}, x_7, x_6, x_5, x_4, x_3, x_{19}, x_{29}, x_2, x_{30}, x_1, x_{20}, x_{22}, x_{21}).$$

All the points up to x_{25} are automatically assigned to the group in which x_{15} is the local maximum (see proposition). The other points are assigned either to the first group or to the second (where x_{25} is the local maximum) according to the classification of the nearest point to the point to be assigned.

In particular, if x_{23} is the point to be currently assigned, then the partial sets (S_1 and S_2) are given by

$$S_1 = (x_{15}, x_{14}, x_{16}, x_{13}, x_{12}, x_{11}, x_{17}, x_{10}, x_9,)$$

$$S_2 = (x_{25}, x_{24}, x_{26}, x_{27},).$$

Since the nearest point to x_{23} (among the ones that have already been assigned) is x_{24}, the former will be assigned into S_2. This stage of the process and the final partition are shown in Fig. 6.

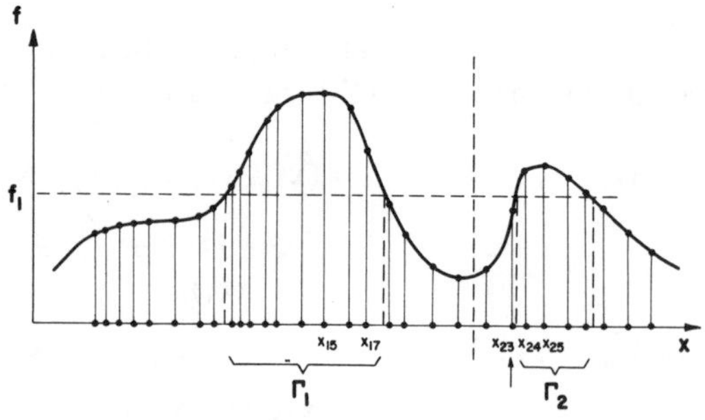

Fig. 6. This figure demonstrates procedure S. At a certain stage in the procedure, all the points in the sequence A with higher grade of membership than f_1 have been assigned, and x_{23} is the next point to be assigned. In this case, all the points in the domains Γ_1 and Γ_2 have already been assigned. The distance of x_{23} to all the points Γ_1 and Γ_2 is evaluated and this point will eventually be assigned into the group in which x_{24} is a member. The dotted line indicates the final partition for this example.

V. The Application of the Algorithm to Clustering Data

The problem we have treated so far, which can be stated as "the partition of a fuzzy set into unimodal fuzzy sets," is well defined. This is not, however, the case in the clustering problem [16] where a set of points $\{(x_i)^N\}$ is given that must be clustered into categories. In order to directly employ the algorithm it is necessary to associate with every point x_i a grade of membership f_i. In other words, a certain order of importance is introduced to facilitate the discrimination among the points not only on the basis of their location (in the vector space) but also according to their "importance." There are many possible ways to discriminate among the points. One possibility is to use a clustering model to associate with every point a membership value according to its "contribution" to the desired partition. By a clustering model, we mean functionals which describe the properties of the desired categories and the structure of the final partition [19].

In our experiments, we have used a threshold value T and associated with every point x_i, an integer number n_i which is the number of sample points in the set $\Gamma_i=\{x|d(x_i, x)\leq T\}$. It is obvious that the resulting partition is dependent on T, although for any T, a unique partition into unimodal fuzzy sets is derived. A previous knowledge about the data to be partitioned is not essential in order to choose T. The latter must be determined in such a way that there is "sufficient" discrimination among the points. For example, in the extreme, if a very large threshold is chosen, then every point will have the same number $n_i(n_i=N)$ and no discrimination is achieved; on the other hand, this is also true for a very small T, but in this case $n_i=1$. The threshold essentially controls the resolution of the characteristic function f. It is quite within the realm of possibility to automate this procedure but this was not done for the experiments reported in Section VI.

It is also necessary to consider the practical situation where many points have the same grade of membership since this was explicitly excluded in the previous theoretical developments. This problem was solved by allowing for a permutation of the points in the sequence A when they have the same grade of membership. More specifically, consider part I of the procedure F in which the symmetric fuzzy sets are derived. Suppose that G groups have already been initiated and y_q is the point in the sequence A to be assigned next. If $y_q \neq y_c^i$, for $i=1, \cdots, G$ and if $f(y_{q+1})=f(y_q)$, then

[7] If $X=E^1$, then a unimodal fuzzy set is also a convex fuzzy set [21], and the hypersurface becomes a hyperplane.

[8] Among other changes in the statement of the theorem in the case when the number of local maxima is greater than two, we must replace the distance d by the minimum distance between any two local maxima of f.

the identity between y_{q+1} and y_c^i, $i=1, \cdots, G$, is checked. Thus y_q will initiate a new group only if none of the points $y_{q+1}, y_{q+2}, \cdots$, with the same grade of membership as y_q, is identical to y_c^i, $i=1, \cdots, G$.

Another consideration is the case in which the maximal grade of membership in a set S_i is attained by a number of points. To solve this problem, we have modified part II of procedure F (in which a search for the local maxima is performed) in the following way. Let S_{ii} be the subset of points in S_i which have the same (maximal) grade of membership as μ_i; then every point in S_{ii} is examined as the mode of S_i. If at least one of these points is on the boundary of S_i, then μ_i *is not* considered as a local maximum.

VI. Experiments

Clustering techniques can be compared only if they are applied to the same data set or to data sets in which the categories are well-known beforehand. Such experiments can therefore be performed either on artifically generated data, or on data sets such as, for example, handprinted characters [4].

In order to be able to reach some significant conclusions concerning the performance of the algorithm we have applied it to artifically generated data sets. The latter consists of points in a ten-dimensional vector space and belonging to sets described by multimodal spherical and ellipsoidal distributions. The samples from each category of the former were generated by adding zero-mean Gaussian noise to a prototype vector. The ellipsoidal data sets were determined by subjecting the vectors of the spherical data sets to certain linear transformations, stretching, and rotation. This data set is a part of the version that was used in [7], [18] for pattern recognition experiments and is described in [8]. We have taken the first ten prototype vectors and generated a data set of 1000 points–100 points for each prototype vector.[9]

Two series of experiments were performed. In the first series, the algorithm was applied to six data sets; the spherical sets with $\sigma=15$, 20, and 25, and the ellipsoidal data sets derived from these. A summary of the results is given in Tables I and II. In the second series, two additional runs with the ellipsoidal data set (derived from the spherical set with $\sigma=15$) obtained with different initial conditions for the random number generator, were performed. The same threshold T as in the first series was used, thus facilitating a comparison of the results of three runs for different initial conditions of the random number generator. The results are shown in Tables III and IV.

The optimal partitions for these data sets are unknown but will be characterized by the rates of error associated with the optimal solution of the supervised pattern recognition problem. This classification is achieved by assuming a knowledge of the functional form and the parameters of the parent populations and using an optimal classifier (Bayes sense). Although these solutions are known theoretically, the computation for the ellipsoidal data sets is difficult because the hyperellipsoids which indicate the hypersurfaces of equal probability density have different shapes and orientations (see [7]). The reference partition that we have used is the partition into the original ten categories of 100 points each. It is appreciated that this partition cannot be achieved by any clustering technique because of overlapping among the categories, in particular for the case of $\sigma=25$. Two types of errors have been used to grade the partitions.

1) E_m, the mixing error, defines the error caused by some of the points of category i being assigned to category j, $i \neq j$; it is therefore a result of the possible overlapping among the categories or the linking of several categories.
2) E_t, the total error, consists of E_m plus the error produced by the generation of small clusters not in the original set of ten. These small clusters are the result of the fact that a finite sample from a Gaussian distribution can be made up of several modes.

[9] The prototype vectors which have been used for the data sets are listed in Appendix II.

TABLE I*

Group Number	Spherical			Ellipsoidal		
	$\sigma=15$	$\sigma=25$	$\sigma=25$	$\sigma=15$	$\sigma=20$	$\sigma=25$
1	100	201(100, 1)	202(99, 3)	101(1)	101(1)	271(89, 83, 2)
2	100	100	100	100	100	101(1)
3	100	100	100	100	99(1)	100
4	100	100	99	100	97(1)	93(1)
5	100	99	99(2)	100	93	88
6	99	97	97	97	80	87
7	85	96	94	95	78	62(2)
8	81	94(2)	88	71	65	62(8)
9	79(1)	81	78(1)	71	62	45
10	66	19	20	69	60	38
11	21	8	12	29	38	13
12	21	3	8	29	26	13(1)
13	19	2	3	22	24	10
14	15			7	18	9
15	13			4	12	5
16	1			3	10	3
17				2	10	
18					5	
19					4	
20					4†	

* $n(n_1, n_2, n_3)$ indicates that there is a total of n points in the corresponding group of which n_1, n_2, and n_3 are from different categories.

† In this case 5 additional groups of 4, 2, 2, 2, 2 points, respectively, were generated.

TABLE II*

Data	σ	T^2	$f(v_1)$	E_m (percent)	E_t (percent)	CPU (minute)
Spherical	15	4000	92	0.1	9.1	3.40
	20	2500	17	10.3	11.6	5.29
	25	4000	18	10.5	12.8	5.10
Ellipsoidal	15	3500	65	0.1	9.7	3.33
	20	4000	31	0.3	16.8	5.59
	25	4500	15	18.7	23.9	5.04

* $f(v_1)$ indicates the maximal grade of membership in the corresponding test. CPU is the number of minutes required to cluster the data on an IBM 360/75 and includes the time needed to generate the data set.

TABLE III

Group Number	Ellipsoidal $\sigma=15$		$T^2=3500$
1	101(1)	100	158(58)
2	100	100	100
3	100	100	100
4	100	100	100
5	100	100	100
6	97	96	100
7	95	95	100
8	71	92	100
9	71	57	63
10	69	48	42
11	29	38	16
12	29	20	11
13	22	11	10
14	7	8	
15	4	7	
16	3	5	
17	2	5	
18		5	
19		5	
20		4	
21		4	

TABLE IV

	$f(v_1)$	E_m (percent)	E_t (percent)	CPU
Ellipsoidal $\sigma=15$, $T^2=3500$	65	0.1	9.7	3.33
	70	0	11.2	3.29
	70	5.8	9.5	3.33

From Table I, we can see that nine to ten major categories as well as a number of small clusters were generated in each test. These clearly indicate that the samples of some of the categories are in fact multimodal. The experiments show that there is a small amount of overlapping among some of the categories. The major mixing error can be attributed to the fact that the algorithm did not detect a local maximum in the neighborhood of the prototype vector for some of the categories. This can be seen in Table I by the entries in the first row, columns 2, 3, and 6, where 2, 2, and 3 categories, respectively, have been linked together. The reason for this seems to be that the sample was not large enough. This is supported by the low values of $f(v_1)$ in Table II where for the above tests the entries are 17, 18, and 15, respectively. We believe that a better choice for T could have eliminated this mixing for the spherical data set with $\sigma=20$, although it is doubtful that this could be achieved for the data sets with $\sigma=25$, given the sample size. On the other hand, it is reasonable to assume that the problem could be eliminated using larger data sets.

A total of 25 experiments (3 to 5 per data set) have been performed and the best results are included in the tables. The threshold T was varied coarsely over a wide range and no fine adjustments were made in order to improve the results. The minimum value of T is constrained by the resolution, while the maximum is constrained by the possible linkage of several categories; that is, if T is very large, then a point which is not in a cluster at all, but in a space among several categories, might have the largest grade of membership. However, even in this case, the point will usually not become a local maximum, since the condition for having a symmetric fuzzy set in its neighborhood will not be satisfied. As a guide, a small T is preferred when no previous knowledge of the data set is available.

The required computing time lay between three and six minutes on an IBM 360/75 computer and this depended on the discrimination in the values of f. If it is such that many points have the same grade of membership, then procedure F requires more computer time (see Section V). The value $f(v_1)$ in Table II gives some indication as to the discrimination achieved; comparing the entries in this column with the corresponding ones in the CPU column gives some support to the above statement. This factor could be eliminated by, for example, using an additional measure for discriminating among the points which have the same grade of membership, or possibly by using an underlying model to evaluate the grade of membership and so yield a continuous variation in f. The computer program used the process of assigning a point at a time in procedure S. All of the computing time in the latter which includes $N(N-1)$ computations of distance and the search for the minimum distance for every point, could be saved by applying Theorem 3. It is estimated that this would result in an approximate 25 percent reduction in computational time.

From the results of the second series of experiments (see Tables III and IV) we can see that the partitions generated with data sets obtained for different initial conditions of the random number generator, are similar. In one of these experiments, a local maximum in the neighborhood of one of the categories was not detected, thus linking 58 points of this category with another. The difference in the error rates is within 1.7 percent.

Generally speaking, the results are quite encouraging. In the two series of experiments, 5 out of 80 local maxima in the neighborhood of the prototype vectors were not detected. This problem could be eliminated if the size of the sample were increased. In particular, the fact that the error rates for the ellipsoidal data are comparable with those for the spherical sets, indicates that the shape of distribution of the points was not a major factor in causing the error. This supports our claim that the algorithm is capable of detecting categories with general distributions of points.

VII. The Extension of the Algorithm to Very Large Data Sets

The computers available now are generally not capable of clustering very large data sets (say, greater than 30 000 points in a many dimensional space) because of both memory space and computing time limitations. We propose two ways in which such sets could be treated to derive partitions which are very similar (if not identical) to the ones discussed in the previous sections. These have not yet been tested experimentally.

Threshold Filtering

In this process we reduce the sample size before applying procedures F and S. A small threshold T_1 is employed for filtering purposes while a large value T_2 (equivalent to T in the previous section) is used to evaluate the final grade of membership.

The first point, say x_1, is introduced. Then all the other points are introduced sequentially and the distance from x_1 to every point is measured. If $d(x_1, x_i) \leq T_1$, then the grade of membership of x_1 is increased by 1; the corresponding point x_i is assigned *finally* into the group into which x_1 will later be assigned. Thus x_i is not considered further in the application of procedures F and S. On the other hand, if $d(x_1, x_i) > T_1$, then x_i will again be introduced until every point has been assigned. When this process of filtering is terminated, there remains a smaller set of points, $x_1, x_2, \cdots, x_N$ with the temporary grades of membership $n_1, n_2, \cdots, n_N$, where

$$\sum_{i=1}^{N} n_i = \text{the number of points in the original data set.}$$

Now the usual discrimination procedure is employed; for example, to evaluate $f(x_i)$, if

$$S \cap \{x | d(x_i, x) \leq T_2\} = \{x_i, x_l, x_m\},$$

then set

$$f(x_i) = n_i + n_l + n_m.$$

If N is of such a size that can be handled by the available computer, then the algorithm can be employed; if not, a further filtering stage can be imposed in the same manner. Although threshold filtering has been used before, it has a particular significance here. This is because the points which are filtered out contribute to the partition of the entire set since they are represented in the grade of membership of the points which are included for clustering.

Truncating the Sequence A

It can be observed that the major memory space limitations are governed by the requirements of part 1 in procedure F. By truncating the sequence A, part 1 of procedure F can be applied sequentially to the truncated parts. Once the sample has been partitioned into symmetric fuzzy subsets, then part 2 of procedure F and procedure S can be applied to the entire set.

First the sequence A is generated in the usual way. Then it is truncated at several points according to the desired sample size, and the truncated parts can then be introduced sequentially in order to generate the symmetric fuzzy subsets. An example of the truncation process when $X = E^1$ is given in Fig. 7. Here the sequence A is truncated at a point x_l where $F(x_l) = f_l$ and at x_{ll} where $f(x_{ll}) = f_{ll}$. This operation results in the partition (division) of the domain of f into three disjoint domains where each of the latter may be a union of several disjoint subdomains. Every subset which is produced includes sample points in only one of the above domains and the grade of membership of the points is as in the original function f. The entire domain and the three domains resulting from the truncation are shown in Fig. 7(a), (b), (c), and (d), respectively. It can be seen that a local maximum may sometimes not be detected if the truncation is done immediately after a local maximum point.

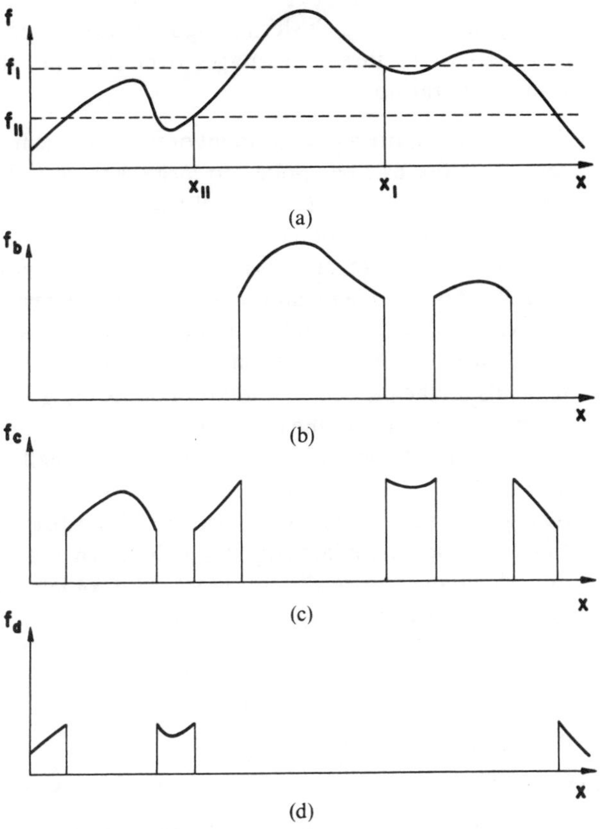

Fig. 7. The truncation process. (a) The characteristic function f, truncated at f_1 and f_{11}. (b), (c), (d). The resultant characteristic functions f_b, f_c, and f_d.

VIII. Conclusions and Remarks

An algorithm is presented which partitions a given sample from a multimodal fuzzy set into unimodal fuzzy sets. It is proven that if certain conditions are satisfied, then the algorithm derives the optimal partition in the sense treated. This partition is also optimal in the sense of maximum separation [21]. The use of this algorithm as a clustering technique was also demonstrated. Experiments on artificially generated data sets were performed and both the results and errors were discussed in detail.

The algorithm can also be applied effectively in supervised pattern recognition, in particular when the categories are multimodal and this information is not known. Such experiments have been reported in [7], [10], [18]. We can use this algorithm to first partition every category independently into unimodal fuzzy sets. In this case we associate with every point x_i the distance membership function

$$f_i = \min_{x_j \in (S - C_i)} [d(x_i, x_j)]$$

where C_i is the set of points in the category in which x_i is a member.

It is suggested that the clustering algorithm reported in this paper possesses three advantages over the ones discussed in the literature.

1) It does not require a great amount of fast core memory and therefore can be applied to large data sets. The storage requirement is $(20N+CN+S)$[10] bytes, where N is the number of points to be partitioned, $20N$ and CN are required for the fixed portion of the program and the variable length data sequences (A, A_i), respectively, and S is the number of storage locations required for the given set of data points. Obviously, S depends on the particular resolution of the magnitude of the components of the data vectors.
2) The amount of computing time is relatively small.
3) The shape of the distribution of the points in a group (category) can be quite general because of the distributions that the unimodal fuzzy sets include. This can be an advantage, especially in practical problems in which the categories are not distributed in "round" clusters.

Appendix I

Proof of Theorem 1

Lemma: The sets S_i are disjoint symmetric fuzzy sets.

Proof: Let A_{ii} define a subsequence of A, of the points that have been assigned into group i, arranged in the order that they stand in A. Let A_i be the sequence of candidate points to be assigned into group i. Bearing in mind procedure F, any two points x_p and x_q can be assigned to the same set S_i if and only if their order in A_{ii} corresponds to their order in A_i. Suppose their order does not correspond, that is,

$$A_{ii} = (\cdots x_p, \cdots, x_q \cdots)$$

and

$$A_i = (\cdots x_q, \cdots, x_p, \cdots).$$

Then x_p in A_{ii} must be assigned first. But x_q precedes x_p as a candidate to be assigned into group i; thus x_q will prevent x_p from being assigned into S_i since it is not replaced as a candidate point, unless it is assigned to S_i. Thus if N_i is the number of points that have been assigned into group i, then for every $n<N_i$:

$$\left.\begin{array}{r} f(x_n) < f(x_j) \\ d(\mu_i, x_n) > d(\mu_i, x_j) \end{array}\right\} \quad \text{for } j = 1, 2, \cdots, n-1, \quad x_j \in S_i$$

and

$$\left.\begin{array}{r} f(x_n) > f(x_r) \\ d(\mu_i, x_n) < d(\mu_i, x_r) \end{array}\right\} \quad \text{for } r = n+1, \cdots, N_i, \quad x_r \in S_i$$

which proves that S_i is symmetric.

Disjointness is demonstrated by the same argument. Suppose x_q is an interior point in S_i and has been assigned into group $j, j\neq i$. Then there exists a subset $S_{ii}\subset S_i$ which satisfies the condition $d(\mu_i, x_r)>(\mu_i, x_q)$ for $x_r\in S_{ii}$. Thus x_q precedes all the points in S_{ii} in the sequence A_i. Since x_q is assigned to group $j, j\neq i$, it will not be replaced as the candidate point in group i, and thus will block all the points in S_{ii} from being assigned into group i.

Proof of Theorem 1

The lemma implies that if μ_i is not a local maximum then it must be on the boundary of S_i. It remains to be shown that if it is a local maximum of f, then it is an interior point.

If μ_i is a local maximum, then assumption 1 of Theorem 1 implies that the subset S_i is

$$S_i = \{x_j | d(\mu_i, x_j) \le \eta\}, \quad \text{where} \quad n > \epsilon/2. \tag{1}$$

Now let x_t be the sample point such that

$$R_t = d(\mu_i, x_t) = \min_{x_k \in (S - S_i)} [d(\mu_i, x_k)].$$

Assumption 1 implies that $R_t \ge \epsilon$.

To show that the set $\Gamma=\{x|d(x_t, x)<R_t\}$ includes at least one sample point in S_i, we may consider the line segment joining x_t and μ_i, and the point x_{in} on this line such that $d(x_{in}, \mu_i)=\epsilon/2$. Defining the set $\Gamma=\{x|d(x_{in}, x)<\epsilon/2\}$, assumption 2 assures that Γ includes at least one sample point and (1) shows that this point is in S_i.

Proof of Theorem 2

Without loss of generality, let us assume that f has only two local maxima. Let H be the optimal hypersurface separating f into the two unimodal fuzzy sets, and S_1 and S_2 the optimal partition of S.

Suppose that $(n-1)$ points have already been assigned correctly, thus generating the sets $S_1^{(n-1)}\subset S_1$ and $S_2^{(n-1)}\subset S_2$, and that $x_n\in S_1$ is the point to be assigned next. It is sufficient to show that there exists a sample point $x_u\in S_1^{(n-1)}$, such that

$$d(x_n, x_u) \le \min_{x_p \in S_2^{(n-1)}} [d(x_n, x_p)].$$

Let

$$\Gamma = \{x | d(x_n, x) = \alpha/2\}, \qquad f(\mu) = \sup_{x\in\Gamma} [f(x)],$$

and $\Gamma_\mu=\{x|d(\mu, x)\le\alpha/2\}$. Clearly, $f(\mu)\ge f(x_n)$, since x_n is not a local maximum. In the limit when $\alpha\to 0$, $f(x_n)\le f(x)$ for every $x\in\Gamma_\mu$. Let x_v be the point such that

$$d(x_n, x_v) = \min_{x_j \in (\Gamma_\mu \cap S)} [d(x_n, x_j)].$$

Assumption 1 implies that $(\Gamma_\mu\cap S)$ is not empty; thus $d(x_n, x_v)\le\alpha$.

We have shown that there is a sample point $x_v\in S$ such that

$$f(x_v) \ge f(x_n) \quad \text{and} \quad d(x_n, x_v) \le \alpha.$$

$\alpha\to 0$ establishes the proof, since

$$\min_{x_p \in S_2} [d(x_n, x_p)] \le \min_{x_j \in S_1^{(n-1)}} [d(x_n, x_j)]$$

if and only if $d(x_n, H)\le\alpha$.

[10] C depends on the number of categories that the given data set represents; in our experiments, $C=5$ was found to be sufficient. Note that this estimate of the total memory space is correct for N up to 32 767.

Proof of Theorem 3

In this proof we make use of the lemma to Theorem 1. Note that in the proof of this lemma, none of the constraints of Theorem 1 were applied; thus the sets S_i generated by part 1 of procedure F are always symmetric and disjoint fuzzy sets.

Let us assume that f has only two maxima and let H be the optimal hypersurface separating f into the two unimodal fuzzy sets. It is sufficient to show that if S_i is a set generated by the above procedure, then it is on one side (either inside or outside) of H. Then the application of Theorem 2 will complete the proof.

Suppose that S_i includes points on both sides of H, say the sets S_{i1} and $S_{i2}(S_{i1} \cup S_{i2} = S_i)$ and suppose that μ_i (the mode of S_i) is in S_{i1}. Let x_2 be the point such that

$$d(\mu_i, x_2) = \min_{x_j \in S_{i2}} [d(\mu_i, x_j)].$$

Let L be the line segment joining x_2 and μ_i, and x_k be the point at which L intersects H (suppose that there is one point of intersection; if not, let x_k be the point of intersection with the lowest value f). Define the following sets:

$$\Gamma_k = \{x | d(x_k, x) \leq \alpha\}$$

and

$$S_k = S \cap \Gamma_k.$$

Condition 1 (see Theorem 2) implies that S_k is not empty. Now if $\alpha \to 0$ and x_r is any point in S_k, then

$$f(x_r) \leq f(x_2)$$

and

$$d(\mu_i, x_r) \leq d(\mu_i, x_2),$$

which implies that S_i is not symmetric. This contradicts the above assumption. An application of Theorem 2 completes the proof since if S_1 and S_2 is the optimal partition, then S_1 is on one side of H and S_2 is on its other side.

Proof of Theorem 4

Let S_1 and S_2 denote the optimal partition of S. Suppose that $(n-1)$ points have already been assigned correctly, thus generating $S_1^{(n-1)} \subset S_1$ and $S_2^{(n-1)} \subset S_2$, and suppose $x_n \in S_1$ is the next point to be assigned.

Let x_u be the point such that

$$d(x_n, x_u) = \min_{x_j \in (S_1^{(n-1)} \cup S_2^{(n-1)})} [d(x_n, x_j)].$$

Condition 1 implies that $d(x_n, x_u) \leq \alpha$. Now x_u and x_n must belong to S_1, since if there are no sample points in Γ_v, then $d(x_n, x_p) \geq \alpha$ for every x_p in S_2.

Appendix II

The following are the ten prototype vectors, given by their integer components in the ten-dimensional space, which were used to generate the data sets for the experiments discussed in Section VI. The order of the vectors bears no relation to the group numbers in Tables I and III. The vectors are the first ten of the eighty prototype vectors given in [8].

V_1	V_2	V_3	V_4	V_5	V_6	V_7	V_8	V_9	V_{10}
−77	−57	−79	−27	47	−1	29	3	99	43
−67	−57	−13	59	89	13	−59	−3	51	−35
−13	19	69	−55	−19	−37	69	35	25	11
27	−65	−11	25	−5	−43	65	−43	27	5
−63	83	65	−27	47	45	−25	51	21	−65
51	53	33	−33	−75	−71	−17	−23	29	−73
−87	67	11	−47	−93	−87	41	21	3	−97
−73	−69	67	33	−49	−21	−65	5	23	15
53	73	53	31	−71	−37	−37	87	59	−41
49	57	−1	67	−71	−91	−65	−17	43	−85

References

[1] G. H. Ball, "Data analysis in the social sciences: What about the details?" *1965 Fall Joint Computer Conf. AFIPS Proc.*, vol. 27, pt. 1. Washington, D. C.: Spartan, 1965, pp. 533–559.

[2] G. H. Ball and D. J. Hall, "ISODATA, A novel method of data analysis and pattern classification," Stanford Research Institute, Menlo Park, Calif., April 1965.

[3] R. E. Bonner, "On some clustering techniques," *IBM J. Res. and Develop.*, vol. 8, pp. 22–32, January 1964.

[4] R. G. Casey and G. Nagy, "An autonomous reading machine," *IEEE Trans. Computers*, vol. C-17, pp. 492–503, May 1968; also IBM Corp., Yorktown Heights, N. Y., Research Rept. RC-1768, February 1967.

[5] T. M. Cover and P. E. Hart, "Nearest neighbor pattern classification," *IEEE Trans. Information Theory*, vol. IT-13, pp. 21–27, January 1967.

[6] A. A. Dorofeyuk, "Teaching algorithms for a pattern recognition machine without a teacher based on the method of potential functions," *Automation and Remote Control*, vol. 27, pp. 1728–1737, December 1966.

[7] R. O. Duda and H. Fossum, "Pattern classification by iteratively determined linear and piecewise linear discriminant functions," *IEEE Trans. Electronic Computers*, vol. EC-15, pp. 220–232, April 1966.

[8] ——, "Computer-generated data for pattern recognition experiments," available from C. A. Rosen, Stanford Research Institute, Menlo Park, Calif., 1966.

[9] W. D. Fisher, "On grouping for maximum homogenity," *Amer. Stat. Assoc. J.*, vol. 53, pp. 789–798, 1958.

[10] O. Firschen and M. Fischler, "Automatic subclass determination for pattern-recognition applications," *IEEE Trans. Electronic Computers* (Correspondence), vol. EC-12, pp. 137–141, April 1963.

[11] E. W. Forgy, "Detecting natural clusters of individuals," presented at the 1964 Western Psych. Assoc. Meeting, Santa Monica, Calif., September 1964.

[12] J. A. Gengerelli, "A method for detecting subgroups in a population and specifying their membership," *J. Psych.*, vol. 55, pp. 457–468, 1963.

[13] T. Kaminuma, T. Takekawa, and S. Watanabe, "Reduction of clustering problem to pattern recognition," *Pattern Recognition*, vol. 1, pp. 195–205, 1969.

[14] J. MacQueen, "Some methods for classification and analysis of multivariate observations," *Proc. 5th Berkeley Symp. on Math. Statist. and Prob.* Berkeley, Calif.: University of California Press, 1967, pp. 281–297.

[15] R. L. Mattson and J. E. Dammann, "A technique for determining and coding subclasses in pattern recognition problems," *IBM J. Res. and Develop.*, vol. 9, pp. 294–302, July 1965.

[16] G. Nagy, "State of the art in pattern recognition," *Proc. IEEE*, vol. 56, pp. 836–862, May 1968.

[17] D. J. Rogers and T. T. Tanimoto, "A computer program for classifying plants," *Science*, vol. 132, pp. 115–118, October 1960.

[18] C. A. Rosen and D. J. Hall, A pattern recognition experiment with near-optimum results," *IEEE Trans. Electronic Computers* (Correspondence), vol. EC-15, pp. 666–667, August 1966.

[19] J. Rubin, "Optimal classification into groups: An approach for solving the taxonomy problem," IBM Rept. 320-2915, December 1966.

[20] J. H. Ward, "Hierarchical grouping to optimize an objective function," *Amer. Stat. Assoc. J.*, vol. 58, pp. 236–244, 1963.

[21] L. A. Zadeh, "Fuzzy sets," *Information and Control*, vol. 8, pp. 338–353, 1965.

A Fuzzy Relative of the ISODATA Process and Its Use in Detecting Compact Well-Separated Clusters

J. C. Dunn
Department of Theoretical and Applied Mechanics, Cornell University

Abstract

Two fuzzy versions of the k-means optimal, least squared error partitioning problem are formulated for finite subsets X of a general inner product space. In both cases, the extremizing solutions are shown to be fixed points of a certain operator T on the class of fuzzy k-partitions of X, and simple iteration of T provides an algorithm which has the descent property relative to the least squared error criterion function. In the first case, the range of T consists largely of ordinary (i.e. non-fuzzy) partitions of X and the associated iteration scheme is essentially the well known ISODATA process of Ball and Hall. However, in the second case, the range of T consists mainly of fuzzy partitions and the associated algorithm is new; when X consists of k compact well separated (CWS) clusters, X_i, this algorithm generates a limiting partition with membership functions which closely approximate the characteristic functions of the clusters X_i. However, when X is not the union of k CWS clusters, the limiting partition is truly fuzzy in the sense that the values of its component membership functions differ substantially from 0 or 1 over certain regions of X. Thus, unlike ISODATA, the "fuzzy" algorithm signals the presence or absence of CWS clusters in X. Furthermore, the fuzzy algorithm seems significantly less prone to the "cluster-splitting" tendency of ISODATA and may also be less easily diverted to uninteresting locally optimal partitions. Finally, for data sets X consisting of dense CWS clusters embedded in a diffuse background of strays, the structure of X is accurately reflected in the limiting partition generated by the fuzzy algorithm. Mathematical arguments and numerical results are offered in support of the foregoing assertions.

1. Introduction

Computer implemented partitioning algorithms have proved to be useful in many areas of applied science, beginning with Sneath's work on bacteriological taxonomy [1] and extending over a wide range of unrelated fields, including psychology, sociology, geology, medicine, experimental particle physics, operations research, and the technology of automatic reading machines. Extensive bibliographies, good general overviews of partitioning techniques, and applications can be found in [2]-[6].

The function of a partitioning algorithm is to detect natural subgroupings (clusters) within a large finite data set X of multidimensional vectors (patterns), relative to some given quantitative measure of pairwise distance (or similarity) between the elements of X. However, since the specification of a distance measure does not by itself impose a unique interpretation on the ambiguous phrase "natural grouping," it can happen that different algorithms working within the same metrical framework on X will nevertheless partition X in different ways; in this sense, the organization which an algorithm "sees" in X is dependent upon the structure of the data and the structure of the algorithm. Our particular concern in this paper is with algorithms that are sensitive to the existence of clusters in X which are "compact and well separated" (CWS) relative to a given metric on X (in a sense to be made precise in Sect. 2). Our objective is to devise an algorithm which signals the presence or absence of CWS clusters in X and, in the former case, identifies the characteristic functions of these clusters.

The graph theoretic techniques employed by Sneath [1], Johnson [7], Zahn [4], Wishart [8], and others, afford one possible avenue of approach to the detection of CWS clusters. However, here we follow a different line, which combines Zadeh's fuzzy set concept [9] with the criterion function approach to clustering. Ruspini appears to have been the first to suggest this general scheme and to propose specific fuzzy criterion functions [10] and associated algorithms [11] applicable to a very broad class of distance functions on X. More recently, Gitman and Levine [12] have also applied the theory of fuzzy sets to clustering problems. In the present investigation, we restrict ourselves to the case where X is a finite subset of a general inner product space V, and where the distance function on X is the inner product-induced metric. In this setting, we consider two of many possible differentiable

Reprinted with permission from *J. Cybernetics*, vol. 3, no. 3, pp. 32–57, 1973.

extensions of the k-means squared error criterion function[1] from the class of all "hard" (i.e. ordinary set theoretic) k-partitions of X to the class of all fuzzy k-partitions of X (Sect. 4), and derive corresponding properties of extremal points for these criteria (Sect. 4 and 5): in each case, the extrema are necessarily fixed points of certain operators T on the class of fuzzy k-partitions of X.

The first criterion function is of interest principally because simple iteration of the corresponding operators T is essentially the well-known ISODATA clustering algorithm [13]. Hence our development amounts to a formal derivation of this algorithm. However, in this case, the range of T consists for the most part of hard partitions irrespective of whether CWS clusters are present in X. Consequently, the first criterion function and the associated ISODATA process are unsuitable for our purposes. When CWS clusters are present, experience indicates that the ISODATA process converges rapidly to a partition consisting of these clusters. However, when CWS clusters are not present, the process still converges to some hard partition defined by "unequivocal" characteristic functions, and there is no way to tell from a simple inspection of this limiting partition that its component subsets are in fact not CWS.[2]

The situation is different for the second criterion function, where the range of the corresponding operators T consist essentually of fuzzy partitions. When CWS clusters are present in X, it appears that there is always an extremizing fuzzy partition whose membership functions closely approximate the characteristic functions of the clusters. Furthermore, numerical experiments indicate that simple iteration of T produces a sequence of fuzzy partitions which converge rapidly to the extremizing partition from virtually all starting guesses. On the other hand, when CWS clusters are not present, the iterates of T converge (more slowly) to some limiting partition which is truly fuzzy in the sense that the values of its component membership functions depart significantly from the hard limits 0 and 1. The results of several specific numerical experiments are offered in support of these contentions in Sect. 6. Of special interest are the results obtained for two planar CWS clusters embedded in a diffuse low density background of "strays," forming a connecting bridge and a halo (Fig. 3). The behavior of the algorithm in this case suggests that it may be quite effective when X is a sample drawn from a mixture of unimodal probability distributions. However, a further pursuit of this question and the related parameter estimation problem is not attempted here.

2. Compact Well-Separated Clusters

In this section, we introduce a parameter which provides a simple quantitative index of separation among the subsets of a partition of the data set X. This parameter has explicit theoretical significance for the k-means squared error criterion function approach to clustering, and is also meaningful for the fuzzy algorithm developed in Sect. 5.

For present purposes, we take X to be a non-empty finite subset of an arbitrary real vector space V, and let d denote an arbitrary metric on V. We define set diameters and set distances in the usual way relative to d, namely:

$$\begin{aligned} \operatorname{diam} A &= \sup_{x,y \in A} d(x,y) \\ \operatorname{dist}(A,B) &= \inf_{\substack{x \in A \\ y \in B}} d(x,y) . \end{aligned} \tag{1}$$

Finally $\mathcal{P}(k)$ will denote the class of all partitions $P = \{X_1, \ldots, X_k\}$ of X into k disjoint non-empty subsets X_i, i.e.,

$$\begin{aligned} X_i &\neq \phi \text{ (empty set)} \\ X_i \cap X_j &= \phi \quad i \neq j \\ \bigcup_{i=1}^{k} X_i &= X . \end{aligned} \tag{2}$$

Definition 1. The subsets X_i of a partition P in $\mathcal{P}(k)$ are said to be compact separated (CS) clusters relative to d if and only if they have the following property: for all p,q,r, with $q \neq r$, any pair of points x,y in X_p are closer together (as measured by d) than any pair of points u,v, with u in X_q and v in X_r.

[1] Neither extension belongs to Ruspini's scheme.

[2] This objection can be levelled at any algorithm whose output consists exclusively of hard partitions. In such cases it is often necessary to make very extensive secondary computations in order to determine whether or not the sought-after structural property actually is present in the limiting partition.

For each fixed k, the existence or non-existence of a k-partition consisting of CS clusters is an intrinsic property of the pair $\{X,d\}$. Furthermore, this property is readily quantified as follows. For each P in $\mathcal{P}(k)$ let,

$$\alpha(k,P) = \frac{\min\limits_{1\leq q\leq k}\ \min\limits_{\substack{1\leq r\leq k\\ r\neq q}} \operatorname{dist}(X_q, X_r)}{\max\limits_{1\leq p\leq k} \operatorname{diam}(X_p)}. \tag{3}$$

and let

$$\bar{\alpha}(k) = \max_{P\in P(k)} \alpha(k,P). \tag{4}$$

Then it is easily shown that X can be partitioned into k CS clusters relative to d if and only if $\bar{\alpha}(k) > 1$. The CS property is sometimes regarded as an indispensable feature of any intuitively acceptible concept of "cluster" based on metrics. Nevertheless, other apparently quite different definitions are possible and indeed, some of these appear to have greater operational significance for the prototypical cluster-detecting apparatus of the human visual system [4].

For example, we might agree that clusters should be recognized by the following fundamental "connectivity" property [7]: the subsets X_i of P are connected clusters relative to d if and only if for every x,y in X_p there exists a chain $\xi = \{x = \xi_1, \ldots, \xi_l = y\}$ of elements in X connecting x and y, such that the maximum edge length, $\max_{2\leq i\leq l} d(\xi_{i-1}, \xi_i)$, of ξ is less than the maximal edge length of any chain connecting u to v, with u in X_q, v in X_r and $r \neq q$. On the face of it, this concept of cluster is quite different from the CS definition; interestingly enough, however, it is not difficult to prove that while subsets X_i which satisfy this connectivity criterion relative to d are in general not CS relative to d, they are always CS relative to a certain (ultra) metric $\hat{d}$ induced by d, namely:

$$\hat{d}(x,y) = \min_{\xi}\left\{\max_{2\leq i\leq l} d(\xi_{i-1}, \xi_i)\right\}$$

where the min operation is taken over all chains ξ of arbitrary length l connecting x and y. In short, the intuitive notion of cohesiveness based upon connectivity relative to d has an alternative equivalent expression in terms of the CS concept relative to the induced metric $\hat{d}$. This example argues for the fundamental nature of Definition 1, while at the same time pointing up the fact that we have been talking about structural properties of the pair $\{X,d\}$ and not X alone.

We now limit ourselves to the class of metrics d induced by a norm on V, i.e., metrics of the form $d(x,y) = \|x-y\|$ where $\|\cdot\|$ is any positive definite real function on V satisfying $\|\alpha u\| = |\alpha|\,\|u\|$ for α real and u in V, as well as the triangle inequality $\|x+y\| \leq \|x\| + \|y\|$ [15].[3] In this narrower setting we introduce a more demanding separation index based upon the distance between X_i and the convex hull $\mathrm{Co}X_j$ of X_j in V, i.e., the smallest convex subset of V containing X_j. The related concept of cluster is significant for our purposes because it is directly linked to the fundamental CS definition and to the k-means least squared error approximation problems considered later.

Definition 2. The subsets X_i of a partition P in $\mathcal{P}(k)$ are compact well-separated (CWS) clusters relative to d if and only if they have the following property: for all p,q,r, with $q \neq r$, any pair x,y with x in X_p and y in $\mathrm{Co}X_p$ are closer together as measured by d than any pair u,v, with u in X_q and v in $\mathrm{Co}X_r$.

Once again, the existence or non-existence of a k-partition consisting of CWS clusters is an intrinsic property of $\{X,d\}$. Furthermore, when d is norm-induced, this property is readily quantified as follows. For each P in $\mathcal{P}(k)$ let

$$\beta(k,P) = \frac{\min\limits_{1\leq q\leq k}\ \min\limits_{\substack{1\leq r\leq k\\ r\neq q}} \operatorname{dist}(X_q, \mathrm{Co}X_r)}{\max\limits_{1\leq p\leq k} \operatorname{diam}(X_p)} \tag{5}$$

[3] Ultrametrics are excluded from this class (cf. [14]); in particular, the mini-max chain length metric $\hat{d}$ described above is not induced by any norm. Consequently, the methods described in the following sections are generally not applicable to the detection of "connected" clusters.

and let

$$\bar{\beta}(k) = \max_{P \in \mathcal{P}(k)} \beta(k,P) . \tag{6}$$

It is not difficult to prove that X can be partitioned into k CWS clusters relative to d if and only if

$$\bar{\beta}(k) > 1 . \tag{7}$$

The proof depends on the fact that norm-induced distances between any x in X_i and any y in CoX_i cannot exceed diam (X_i); details are omitted in the interest of brevity.

In view of Eqs. (3) and (5), and the fact that $X_i \subset CoX_i$, it follows that the subsets X_i of P are CWS clusters only if they are CS clusters; this justifies the terminology of Definitions 1 and 2. Moreover, since the centroid $\bar{x}_i$ of X_i lies in CoX_i, it readily follows that the X_i's in P are CWS clusters only if

$$d(x, \bar{x}_i) < d(x, \bar{x}_j) \tag{8}$$

for all x in X_i and for all i, j, with $i \neq j$. Finally, as a consequence of Eq. (8) it follows that the X_i's in P are CWS clusters only if P is a fixed point of the ISODATA process; this result establishes a link between CS and CWS clusters and the k-means least squared error approximation problems which we now consider.

3. The k-Means Least Square Approximation Problem and ISODATA

The presence of CWS clusters in X relative to some given metric d (or perhaps, any member of some general class of metrics d) will be assumed an "interesting" structural property. We then want algorithms which are capable of indicating the presence or absence of CWS clusters relative to d, and in the former case, of identifying the characteristic functions of the clusters. Since the class $\mathcal{P}(k)$ is finite when X is finite we can, in principal, use brute force exhaustion to find the "most" interesting partition in $\mathcal{P}(k)$, namely, the partition P' which solves

$$\beta(k,P') = \bar{\beta}(k) = \max_{P \in \mathcal{P}(k)} \beta(,P) . \tag{9}$$

Once P' and $\bar{\beta}(k)$ are known, the problem is effectively solved. However, even for moderately large sets X, the number of elements in $P(k)$ can be huge (being equal to $\frac{1}{k!} \sum_{i=1}^{k} \binom{k}{i} (-1)^{k-i} i^n$ for $1 \leqslant k \leqslant n$; (cf. [2]), consequently, exhaustion is not feasible in general. In fact, the mere calculation of $\beta(k,P)$ is a decidedly nontrivial task for all but the simplest problems. It follows that the separation parameter $\bar{\beta}(k)$ and the corresponding maximally separated partition P' which solves (9) are effectively inaccessible by a straightforward approach at this level of generality. On the other hand, an indirect heuristic approach based upon criterion functions and associated approximation problems may provide useful algorithms, especially when d is not simply an arbitrary metric but has some geometrical significance in $V \supset X$. Consequently, in the balance of this paper we make the further restriction that d is induced by a norm $\|\cdot\|$ on V which in turn is induced by an inner product $\langle \cdot | \cdot \rangle$ on V, i.e.,

$$d(x,y) \triangleq \|x - y\| \triangleq \langle x - y | x - y \rangle^{1/2} \tag{10}$$

where $\langle \cdot | \cdot \rangle$ is any symmetric positive-definite bi-linear function from the Cartesian product $V \times V$ into R^1 [15]. This abstract formulation includes as a special case,

$$\begin{aligned} V &= R^n \\ \langle x | y \rangle &= x^t M y \\ d(x,y) &= [(x-y)^t M (x-y)]^{1/2} \end{aligned} \tag{11}$$

where M is an arbitrary symmetric positive definite $n \times n$ matrix, and the superscript t signifies the transpose operation. From the standpoint of clustering problems, three sub-cases are worth mentioning here, namely:

a) $M = I$ = identity matrix,
b) $M^{-1} = \text{diag}\{\sigma_1, \ldots, \sigma_n\}$, σ_i = sample variance of the ith component of vectors $x \in X$,
c) M^{-1} = sample covariance matrix for vectors $x \in X$.

In case *a*, the corresponding metric d in (11) is simply the prototypical Euclidean metric which is invariant under the sub-group of orthogonal transformations on $R^n \supset X$; in case *b* the metric in (11) is a weighted Euclidean metric invariant under the sub-group of scale transformations on R^n (i.e., non-singular linear transformations whose matrices are diagonal, relative to the natural basis in R^n); in case c the metric in (11) is a weighted Euclidean metric invariant under the full linear group on R^n. For a further discussion of invariance considerations for clustering problems see [2], [16], and [17].[4]

When d is inner product-induced and when $\overline{\beta}(k)$ is sufficiently large, it seems clear that the maximally separated partition P' solving (7) should also solve the following generalized problem.

k-Means Least Square Approximation (LSA) Problem

Let $\mathfrak{L}$ denote the linear hull of X in V, i.e., $\mathfrak{L}$ is the (finite dimensional) linear subspace spanned by the elements of X. Let $v = \{v_1, \ldots, v_k\}$ denote an ordered k-tuple of vectors in $\mathfrak{L}$, i.e., v is a general element in the k-fold Cartesian product $\mathfrak{L}^k$ of $\mathfrak{L}$ with itself. For each $P = \{X_1, \ldots, X_k\} \in \mathcal{P}(k)$ and each $v \in \mathfrak{L}^k$ put

$$J(P, v) = \sum_{i=1}^{k} \sum_{x \in X_i} d(x, v_i)^2 = \sum_{i=1}^{k} \sum_{x \in X_i} \|x - v_i\|^2 = \sum_{i=1}^{k} \sum_{x \in X} \langle x - v_i | x - v_i \rangle . \quad (12)$$

Find $P' \in \mathcal{P}(k)$ and $v' \in \mathfrak{L}^k$ such that

$$J(P', v') = \min_{P \in \mathcal{P}(k)} \min_{v \in \mathfrak{L}^k} J(P, v) . \quad (13)$$

Since d is inner product-induced, we always have $v_i' = \overline{x}_i$ = the unweighted mean, or centroid of X_i. Furthermore, when $\beta(k)$ is sufficiently large, computational experience suggests that the optimal partition P' in (13) can probably be found, and very efficiently, by the following ISODATA Process [13]:

step 1) Choose $P \in \mathcal{P}(k)$;
step 2) Compute the centroids $\overline{x}_i$ of $X_i \in P$;
step 3) Construct a new partition $\hat{P}$ according to the rule:

$$x \in \hat{X}_i \leftrightarrow d(x, \overline{x}_i) = \min_{1 \leq j \leq k} d(x, \overline{x}_j);$$

step 4) If $\hat{P} = P$, stop. Otherwise put $P = \hat{P}$ and go to step 2.

We note that step 3 is ambiguous if $d(x, \overline{x}_j)$ does not have a proper minimum over $1 \leq j \leq k$. Furthermore, it is possible (although not likely) that one or more of the sets $\hat{X}_i$ may be empty at the conclusion of step 3, in which event difficulties will arise after the loop back to step 2. For these reasons, working versions of ISODATA must incorporate "tie-breaking" rules which assign "centroids" to empty subsets X_i in step 2, and resolve ambiguities in step 3 (a common procedure is to take i to be the smallest index satisfying $d(x, \overline{x}_i) = \min_{1 \leq j \leq k} d(x, \overline{x}_j)$). Regardless of which tie-breaker rule is used, it can be shown that the sequence of partitions $P^{(n)}$ and the corresponding sequence of centroids $\{\overline{x}^{(n)}\} = \{\overline{x}_1^{(n)}, \ldots, \overline{x}_h^{(n)}\}$ has the descent property relatively to J, i.e., $J(P^{(n+1)}, \overline{x}^{(n+1)}) \leq J(P^{(n)}, \overline{x}^{(n)})$, for all n (see Theorem 2).

A partition $P \in \mathcal{P}(k)$ is called a fixed point of ISODATA if and only if the derived partition $\hat{P}$ in step 3 is identical to P. In the next section, we explore the relationship between extremal points for the k-means LSA problem and the fixed points of ISODATA. Here we observe that every partition P consisting of CWS clusters is necessarily a fixed point of ISODATA, in view of Eq. (8). As we have noted elsewhere, these considerations motivate Definition 2 and provide explicit links between the k-means LSA problem, the ISODATA process, and the general notion of separated clusters in X.

Unfortunately, it is not difficult to produce simple examples in R^1 and R^2 where ISODATA has many attracting fixed points which are not solutions of (9) and/or of (13) (see Sect. 6). Experience also indicates that the domains of attraction of these spurious fixed points can become quite large as $\overline{\beta}(k)$ decreases, leading to the so called "cluster-splitting" tendency of ISODATA [2]. In short, as $\overline{\beta}(k)$ decreases, the desired relationship between the maximally separated solution of (9) and the attracting fixed points of ISODATA tends to disintegrate. Furthermore, as noted in the introduction, one cannot tell whether this is actually happening from an inspection of the hard partitions generated

[4] The clustering algorithm proposed in [17] is essentially the ISODATA process applied to the metric in (11), corresponding to case c above.

by ISODATA. Experience indicates that ISODATA converges to some hard partition, irrespective of the value of $\overline{\beta}(k)$. However, since $\overline{\beta}(k)$ is effectively not computable for non-trivial X, we have no way of knowing the true relationship between this limiting partition and the maximally separated solution of (9). For this reason, ISODATA is an effective technique for identifying CWS clusters in X only if one knows in advance that such clusters are actually present; without such *a priori* knowledge, inferences drawn from ISODATA partitions can be very dangerous.

To avoid this difficulty, we shall base our approach to the detection of CWS clusters upon the following mathematical device. We embed the class $\mathcal{P}(k)$ of hard k-partitions in the larger class $\mathcal{P}_f(k)$ of fuzzy k-partitions. Among the class of all possible extensions of the LSA criterion function J from $\mathcal{P}(k)$ to $\mathcal{P}_f(k)$, we then seek one such extension which meets the following conditions:

a) As $\overline{\beta}(k)$ increases beyond 1 the membership functions of the fuzzy partition which minimizes J over $\mathcal{P}_f(k)$ should closely approximate the characteristic functions of the solution of (9).

b) As $\overline{\beta}(k)$ decreases below 1 the extremizing partitions for J should become increasingly fuzzy in the sense that the values of their membership functions depart significantly from 0 or 1, on certain subsets of X.

c) There should exist a simple and efficient algorithm for computing the extremizing fuzzy partitions for J.

In the following sections we consider two of the infinitely many possible fuzzy extensions of J. The first and most obvious extension leads directly back to a formal derivation of the ISODATA process, and consequently does not advance our purposes. However, the second extension apparently does satisfy conditions *a* through *c* above.

4. Fuzzy Embedding I

In carrying out the embedding described in the previous section, we note that by virtue of condition (2) $\mathcal{P}(k)$ is isomorphically represented by the class of all functions $u(\cdot) = \{u_1(\cdot), \ldots, u_k(\cdot)\} : X \to R^k$ such that

$$\begin{aligned}&1)\ \text{for all } i,\ 1 \leq i \leq k, \text{ there is some } x \in X \text{ such that } u_i(x) \neq 0,\\ &2)\ \text{for all } i,\ 1 \leq i \leq k, \text{ and for all } x \in X,\ u_i(x) = 0 \text{ or } 1,\\ &3)\ \text{for all } x \in X,\ \sum_{i=1}^{k} u_i(x) = 1.\end{aligned} \tag{14}$$

The isomophic correspondence is obtained by simply identifying $u_i(\cdot)$ with the characteristic function of the ith subset X_i of a given partition $P \in \mathcal{P}(k)$. From now on, we will therefore say that any function $u(\cdot): X \to R^k$ satisfying (14) is a (hard) k-partition of X and we denote the class of all such functions by the same symbol $\mathcal{P}(k)$ used previously with a set theoretic connotation, i.e.,

$$\mathcal{P}(k) = \{u(\cdot): X \to R^k \mid u(\cdot) \text{ satisfies (14)}\}. \tag{15}$$

The larger class of all fuzzy k-partitions of X is now defined as follows:

$$\begin{aligned}\mathcal{P}_f(k) &= \{u(\cdot): X \to U_f \subset R^k\}\\ U_f &= \left\{u \in R^k \mid 0 \leq u_i \leq 1,\ 1 \leq i \leq k;\ \sum_{i=1}^{k} u_i = 1\right\}.\end{aligned} \tag{16}$$

The component functions $u_i(\cdot)$ of a fuzzy partition $u(\cdot)$ are called the membership functions of the partition (see [9] for the origins of fuzzy set theory).

Evidently, $\mathcal{P}_f(k) \supset \mathcal{P}(k)$. In fact, since condition 1) of (14) is not carried out in (16), $\mathcal{P}_f(k)$ includes degenerate k-partitions containing one or more empty subsets X_i; for technical reasons, this is a convenience in the development of Theorems 1 and 2 to follow. If $\overline{\mathcal{P}}(k)$ denotes $P(k)$ + all degenerate hard k-partitions (condition 1 omitted), then $\mathcal{P}_f(k)$ is simply the convex hull of $\overline{\mathcal{P}}(k)$ in the linear space of functions $u(\cdot)$: $X \to R^k$. We now obtain our first extension of the criterion function J from $\mathcal{P}(k)$ to $\mathcal{P}_f(k)$.

Let $u_i(\cdot)$ denote the characteristic functions of $X_i \in P$. Then in view of Eq. (12), we have

$$\begin{aligned}J(P, v) = J_1(u(\cdot), v) &= \sum_{i=1}^{k} \sum_{x \in X} u_i(x) \|x - v_i\|^2\\ &= \sum_{i=1}^{k} \sum_{x \in X} u_i(x) \langle x - v_i \mid x - v_i \rangle .\end{aligned} \tag{17}$$

If $u(\cdot)$ is now permitted to range over all of $\mathcal{P}_f(k) \supset \mathcal{P}(k)$, formula (17) defines a continuous and differentiable extension J_1 of J from $\mathcal{P}(k) \times \mathcal{L}^k$ to $\mathcal{P}_f(k) \times \mathcal{L}^k$. Corresponding to this extension we have the following problem.

Relaxed k-Means Least Square Approximation Problem I

Find $u'(\cdot) \in \mathcal{P}_f(k)$ and $v' \in \mathcal{L}^k$ such that

$$J_1(u'(\cdot), v') = \min_{u(\cdot) \in \mathcal{P}_f(k)} \min_{v \in \mathcal{L}^k} J_1(u(\cdot), v) . \tag{18}$$

The optimal solutions of this problem are characterized in the following theorem.

Theorem 1. If $u'(\cdot) \in \mathcal{P}_f(k)$ and $v' \in \mathcal{L}^k$ solve (18), then the following conditions must hold:

a. For each fixed $x \in X$, let

$$\xi = \min_{1 \leq j \leq k} ||x - v_j'||$$

$$I = \{1 \leq i \leq k \mid ||x - v_i'|| = \xi\}$$

$$I^c = \{1 \leq i \leq k \mid ||x - v_i'|| > \xi\} = \text{complement of } I \text{ in } 1 \leq i \leq k.$$

Then

$$i \in I^c \Rightarrow u_i'(x) = 0$$

and

$$\sum_{i \in I} u_i'(x) = 1.$$

In particular, if $\| x - v_j' \|$ has a proper minimum over $1 \leq j \leq k$, then I consists of a single integer i and we must have

$$u_i'(x) = \begin{cases} 0 & i \neq i \\ 1 & i = i \end{cases} .$$

b. For all i, $1 \leq i \leq k$, there is some $x \in X$ such that $u_i'(x) \neq 0$, i.e., the optimal k-partition $u'(\cdot) \in \mathcal{P}_f(k)$ always consists of k non-empty fuzzy sets.

c.
$$v_i' = \frac{\sum_{x \in X} u_i'(x) \cdot x}{\sum_{x \in X} u_i'(x)} .$$

Proof.

a) If $u'(\cdot)$ and v' satisfy (18) then in particular,

$$J_1(u'(\cdot), v') \leq J_1(u(\cdot), v') \tag{19}$$

for all $u(\cdot) \in \mathcal{P}_f(k)$. In view of (16) and (17), condition (19) holds if and only if

$$\sum_{i=1}^{k} u_i'(x) ||x - v_i'||^2 \leq \sum_{i=1}^{k} u_i(x) ||x - v_i'||^2 \tag{20}$$

for all $x \in X$, or equivalently.

$$\sum_{i=1}^{k} u_i'(x) ||x - v_i'||^2 = \min_{w \in U_f} \sum_{i=1}^{k} w_i ||x - v_i'||^2 \tag{21}$$

for all $x \in X$. With reference to (16) we have

$$w \in U_f \Rightarrow \sum_{i=1}^{k} w_i ||x - v_i'||^2 = \left(\sum_{i \in I} w_i\right)\xi^2 + \sum_{i \in I^c} w_i ||x - v_i'||^2 \geq \left(\sum_{i=1}^{k} w_i\right)\xi^2 = \xi^2 \tag{22}$$

where the strict inequality holds if and only if $w_i > 0$ for some $i \in I^c$. It follows from (22) that $u(\cdot)$ satisfies (20) if and only if $u_i'(x) = 0$, for $i \in I^c$, and $\sum_{i \in I} u_i'(x) = 1$.

b) Suppose that

$$u_l'(x) = 0 \quad \text{all } x \in X . \tag{23}$$

Since there are k vectors v_i' and since $1 \leq k \leq N$ = number of elements in X, there is at least one element of X, say $\hat{x}$, such that

$$\|\hat{x} - v_i'\| > 0 \quad \text{all } i \neq l . \tag{24}$$

Put $v'' = (v_1'', \ldots, v_k'')$, with

$$v_i'' = \begin{cases} v_i' & i \neq l \\ \hat{x} & i = l \end{cases} . \tag{25}$$

We have $v'' \in \mathfrak{L}^k$ and, in view of (17), (23), and (25)

$$J_1(u'(\cdot), v'') = J_1(u'(\cdot), v')$$

Thus $(u'(\cdot), v'')$ is also an optimal solution of (18) and consequently must satisfy condition a of this theorem. since $\| \hat{x} - v_j'' \|$ has a proper minimum over $1 \leqslant j \leqslant k$ at $j = l$, because of (24) and (25), we must have $u_l'(\hat{x}) = 1$, which contradicts (23).

c) If $(u'(\cdot), v')$ satisfies (18), then, in particular,

$$J_1(u'(\cdot), v') \leq J_1(u'(\cdot), v) \quad \text{all } v \in \mathfrak{L}^k \tag{26}$$

i.e., v' must minimize the quadratic function

$$g(v) \triangleq J_1(u'(x), v) = \sum_{i=1}^{k} \sum_{x \in X} u_i'(x) \|x - v_i\|^2 = \sum_{i=1}^{k} \sum_{x \in X} u_i'(x) \langle x - v_i \mid x - v_i \rangle$$

on the linear space $\mathfrak{L}^k$. Furthermore, since $u_i'(x) \geqslant 0$, g is positive semidefinite. Consequently, v' minimizes g if and only if g is stationary at v', i.e. if and only if the directional derivative $Dg(v', w)$ vanishes for all $w \in \mathfrak{L}^k$. By definition, we have

$$\begin{aligned} Dg(v', w) &\triangleq \frac{d}{dh} g(v' + hw)\Big|_{h=0} \\ &= \sum_{i=1}^{k} \sum_{x \in X} u_i'(x) \frac{d}{dh} \langle x - v_i' - hw_i \mid x - v_i' - hw_i \rangle \Big|_{h=0} \\ &= -2 \sum_{i=1}^{k} \sum_{x \in X} u_i'(x) \langle x - v_i' \mid w_i \rangle \\ &= -2 \sum_{i=1}^{k} \Big\langle \sum_{x \in X} u_i'(x)(x - v_i') \mid w_i \Big\rangle . \end{aligned}$$

Thus v' satisfies (26) if and only if

$$\Big\langle \sum_{x \in X} u_i'(x)(x - v_i') \mid w_i \Big\rangle = 0 \quad \text{for all } w \in \mathfrak{L}^k . \tag{27}$$

But (27) holds for arbitrary $w \in \mathfrak{L}^k$ if and only if

$$\sum_{x \in X} u_i'(x)(x - v_i') = 0 \quad 1 \leq i \leq k$$

i.e. v' satisfies (26) if and only if

$$\Big(\sum_{x \in X} u_i'(x)\Big) v_i' = \sum_{x \in X} u_i'(x)\, x .$$

Finally, with reference to part *b* of this theorem, we therefore obtain

$$v_i' = \frac{\sum_{x \in X} u_i'(x) x}{\sum_{x \in X} u_i'(x)} . \qquad \text{QED}$$

Corollary 1. Suppose that $(u'(\cdot), v')$ is an optimal solution of the relaxed k-means LSA problem (18) and also satisfies condition (α): for all $x \in X$, $\| x - v_j' \|$ has a proper minimum over $1 \leqslant j \leqslant k$. Then $u'(\cdot)$ is a hard partition (i.e., $u'(\cdot) \in \mathcal{P}(k) \subset \mathcal{P}_f(k)$, v_i' = centroid of the subset $X_i' \subset X$ with characteristic function $u_i'(\cdot)$, and $(u'(\cdot), v')$ is an optimal solution of the original k-means LSA problem (13) over $\mathcal{P}(k) \times \mathfrak{L}^k$.

Corollary 2. The following condition defines a non-empty class $\mathcal{T}_1$ of operators T: $\mathcal{P}_f(k) \to \mathcal{P}_f(k)$.

If $\hat{u}(\cdot)$ denotes $T(u(\cdot))$ = image of $u(\cdot)$ under T, then for some $v \in \mathfrak{L}^k$ satisfying condition (β):

$$\left(\sum_{x \in X} u_i(x)\right) v_i = \sum_{x \in X} u_i(x)x \quad 1 \leq i \leq k$$

$\hat{u}(\cdot)$ must satisfy

$$\hat{u}_i(x) = 0 \quad ||x - v_i|| \neq \min_{1 \leq j \leq k} ||x - v_j|| .$$

A fuzzy partition $u'(\cdot)$ is part of an optimal solution $(u'(\cdot), v')$ of (18) only if $u'(\cdot)$ is a fixed point of some $T \in \mathcal{T}_1$, i.e.,

$$u'(\cdot) = T(u'(\cdot)) \text{ for some } T \in \mathcal{T}_1 . \quad (28)$$

In addition, $u'(\cdot)$ must also satisfy

$$u_i'(\cdot) \neq 0 \quad 1 \leq i \leq k. \quad (29)$$

Corollary 1 suggests that the characteristic functions of an optimal hard partition for the original k-means LSA problem are likely to differ from the membership functions of an optimal partition for the relaxed problem only on relatively "small" subsets of X, and in many cases, the two solutions will coincide everywhere on X. Furthermore, condition (β) of Corollary 2 suggests that we may be able to approximate optimal solutions of the relaxed problem by iterating some operator in $\mathcal{T}_1$, i.e. by implementing the recursion

$$u^{(m+1)}(\cdot) = T(u)^{(m)}(\cdot) \quad 0 \leq m < \infty \quad T \in \mathcal{T}_1 \quad (30)$$

for some T in $\mathcal{T}_1$ and for some initial guess $u^{\circ}(\cdot)$ in $\mathcal{P}_f(k)$. Indeed, we can now see that the ISODATA process described in Sec. 3 is essentially equivalent to (30). In general, the class $\mathcal{T}_1$ contains infinitely many operators T. However, all of these operators coincide on the subclass of fuzzy partitions $u(\cdot)$ satisfying (29) and condition (α) of Corollary 1. In this subclass, $T(u(\cdot))$ is always a hard partition uniquely prescribed by condition (β) of Corollary 2. Outside this subclass, Theorem 1 does not suggest a unique value for $T(u(\cdot))$,[5] and the tie-breaking rules employed in working versions of ISODATA (cf. Sect. 3) are merely *ad hoc* conventions for keeping $T(u(\cdot))$ in the class $\mathcal{P}(k)$ of hard partitions with k non-empty subsets, and for resolving ambiguities in condition (β). However, regardless of which tie-breaking rule is employed, the following result shows that ISODATA always has the descent property relative to J_1.

Theorem 2. For arbitrary fixed $T \in \mathcal{T}_1$ let $\{u^m(\cdot)\}$ denote the sequence of partitions in $\mathcal{P}_f(k)$ generated by (30), and let $\{v^{(m)}\}$ denote the corresponding sequence in $\mathfrak{L}^k$ associated with T and $u^m(\cdot)$ via condition (β). Then for all $m \geqslant 0$,

$$J_1(u^{(m+1)}(\cdot), v^{(m+1)}) \leq J_1(u^{(m)}(\cdot), v^{(m)}) .$$

Proof. As an immediate consequence of the reasoning employed in parts a and c in the proof of Theorem 1, we have

$$J_1(u^{(m+1)}(\cdot), v^m) = \min_{u(\cdot) \in \mathcal{P}_f(k)} J_1(u(\cdot), v^m)$$

and

$$J_1(u^{(m+1)}(\cdot), v^{(m+1)}) = \min_{v \in \mathfrak{L}^k} J_1(u^{(m+1)}(\cdot), v).$$

Thus

$$J_1(u^m(\cdot), v^m) \geq J_1(u^{(m+1)}(\cdot), v^m) \geq J_1(u^{(m+1)}(\cdot), v^{(m+1)}).$$

QED

In conclusion, we observe that the conditions of Theorem 1 are necessary, but in general not sufficient for (global) optimality. Thus, the operators in $\mathcal{T}_1$ may have many non-optimal fixed points and some of these may have substantial zones of attraction for the iterates of (30). This is indeed the case. As noted elsewhere, the ISODATA versions of (30) apparently always converge to some hard partition. However, this limiting partition may vary with the starting guess $u^{\circ}(\cdot)$, and need not be globally optimal. Behavior of this sort is apparently exacerbated by the absence of CWS clusters in X.

5. Fuzzy Embedding II

We now consider a second extension of the criterion function J which apparently does satisfy the condition set forth at the end of Sect. 3.

[5] In analogy with a situation which arises for "singular" extremals in optimal control theory.

Let $u_i(\cdot)$ denote the characteristic functions of $X_i \in P$; then in view of Eq. (12) we have

$$J(P, v) = J_2(u(\cdot), v) \triangleq \sum_{i=1}^{k} \sum_{x \in X} u_i^2(x) \|x - v_i\|^2$$
$$= \sum_{i=1}^{k} \sum_{x \in X} u_i^2(x) \langle x - v_i | x - v_i \rangle . \tag{31}$$

If $u(\cdot)$ is once again permitted to range over all of $\mathcal{P}_f(k) \supset \mathcal{P}(k)$, formula (31) defines another continuous and differentiable extension J_2 of J from $\mathcal{P}(k) \times \mathcal{L}^k$ to $\mathcal{P}_f(k) \times \mathcal{L}^k$. Corresponding to this extension we have the following problem.

Relaxed k-Means Least Square Approximation Problem II

Find $u'(\cdot) \in \mathcal{P}_f(k)$ and $v' \in \mathcal{L}^k$ such that

$$J_2(u'(\cdot), v') = \min_{u(\cdot) \in \mathcal{P}_f(k)} \min_{v \in \mathcal{L}^k} J_2(u(\cdot), v) . \tag{32}$$

The optimal solutions of this problem are characterized in the following theorem.

Theorem 3. If $u'(\cdot) \in \mathcal{P}_f(k)$ and $v' \in \mathcal{L}^k$ solve (32), then the following conditions must hold:

a. For each fixed $x \in X$, let

$$I = \{1 \le i \le k \,|\, v_i' = x\}$$
$$I^c = \{1 \le i \le k \,|\, v_i' \ne x\} = \text{complement of } I \text{ in } 1 \le i \le k .$$

case 1) Suppose $I = \phi$ = empty set. Then

$$u_i'(x) = \frac{1/\|x - v_i'\|^2}{\sum_{j=1}^{k} (1/\|x - v_j\|^2)} \qquad 1 \le i \le k$$

case 2) Suppose $I \neq \phi$. Then

$$i \in I^c \Rightarrow u_i'(x) = 0$$

and

$$\sum_{i \in I} u_i'(x) = 1 .$$

In particular, if I consists of a single integer i, then

$$u_i'(x) = \begin{cases} 1 & i = \text{i} \\ 0 & i \neq \text{i} \end{cases} .$$

b. For all i, $1 \leqslant i \leqslant k$, there is some $x \in X$ such that $u_i'(x) \neq 0$, i.e., the optimal k-partition $u'(\cdot) \in \mathcal{P}_f(k)$ always consists of k non-empty fuzzy sets.

c.
$$v_i' = \frac{\sum_{x \in X} (u_i'(x))^2 x}{\sum_{x \in X} (u_i'(x))^2} .$$

Proof.

a) If $(u'(\cdot), v')$ satisfies (32), then in particular,

$$J_2(u'(\cdot), v') \le J_2(u(\cdot), v') \tag{33}$$

for all $u(\cdot) \in \mathcal{P}_f(k)$. In view of (16) and (17), $u'(\cdot)$ satisfies (33) if and only if:

$$\sum_{i=1}^{k} (u_i'(x))^2 \|x - v_i'\|^2 \le \sum_{i=1}^{k} (u_i(x))^2 \|x - v_i\|^2$$

for all $x \in X$, or equivalently,

$$\sum_{i=1}^{k} (u_i'(x))^2 \|x - v_i'\|^2 = \min_{w \in U_f} \sum_{i=1}^{k} w_i^2 \|x - v_i'\|^2 \tag{34}$$

for all $x \in X$.

case 1 ($I = \phi$): Let $\overline{U}_f$ denote the set $\left\{u \in R^k \,\middle|\, \sum_{i=1}^{k} u_i = 1\right\} \supset U_f$, obtained by relaxing the inequality constraints in the definition of U_f (Eq. (16)). Consider the corresponding relaxed version of (34), namely

$$\min_{w \in \overline{U}_f} \sum_{i=1}^{k} w_i^2 \|x - v_i'\|^2 . \tag{35}$$

This quadratic minimization problem always has a solution. Furthermore, since no inequality constraints are present, the classical Lagrange multiplier rule can be applied here and yields the following results: $w' \in \overline{U}_f$ is an optimal solution of (35) only if for some real λ, the augmented function $\sum_{i=1}^{k} w_i^2\|x - v_i'\|^2 + \lambda \sum_{i=1}^{k} w_i$ is stationary at w'. This condition, together with the constraint $\sum_{i=1}^{k} w_i = 1$ and the fact that $I = \phi$, insure that the solution of (35) is unique and is given by

$$w_i' = \frac{1/\|x - v_i'\|^2}{\sum_{j=1}^{k} (1/\|x - v_j'\|^2)} .$$

Evidently $0 < w_i' < 1$ for $1 \leqslant i \leqslant k$. Consequently, the optimal solution of (35) lies in $U_f \subset \overline{U}_f$ after all, and is therefore also the unique solution of (34). It follows that $u'(\cdot)$ satisfies (33) if and only if $u'(x) = w'$ for all $x \in X$.

Case 2 ($I \neq \phi$): If $I \neq \phi$ then $\|x - v_i'\|^2 = 0$ for some i and it readily follows that

$$\min_{w \in U_f} \sum_{i=1}^{k} w_i^2 \|x - v_i'\|^2 = 0 .$$

Suppose $u_j'(x) \neq 0$ for some $j \in I^c$. Then $(u_j'(x))^2 \|x - v_j\|^2 > 0$ and it follows that

$$\sum_{i=1}^{k} (u'(x))^2 \|x - v_i'\|^2 > 0 = \min_{w \in U_f} \sum_{i=1}^{k} w_i^2 \|x - v_i'\|^2$$

which contradicts (34). Thus $u'(\cdot)$ satisfies (33) only if:

$$u_i'(x) = 0 \quad i \in I^c$$

and

$$\sum_{i \in I} u_i'(x) = 1 . \tag{36}$$

Conversely if $u'(x)$ satisfies (36) then

$$\sum_{i=1}^{k} (u_i'(x))^2 \|x - v_i'\|^2 = 0 = \min_{w \in U_f} \sum_{i=1}^{k} w_i^2\|x - v_i'\|^2 .$$

b) Suppose that

$$u_l'(x) = 0 \quad \text{all } x \in X . \tag{37}$$

Since there are k vectors, v_i', and since $1 \leqslant k \leqslant N$ = number of elements in X, there is at least one element of X, say $\hat{x}$, such that

$$v_i' \neq \hat{x} \quad i \neq l . \tag{38}$$

Put $v'' = \{v_1'', \ldots, v_k''\}$ with

$$v_i'' = \begin{cases} v_i' & i \neq l \\ \hat{x} & i = l \end{cases} . \tag{39}$$

We have $v'' \in \mathfrak{L}^k$, and in view of (31), (37), and (39)

$$J_2(u'(\cdot), v'') = J_2(u'(\cdot), v') .$$

Thus $(u'(\cdot), v'')$ is also an optimal solution of (32) and consequently must satisfy condition *a* of Theorem 3. With reference to (38) and (39), we have $\hat{x} = v_i'' \Leftrightarrow i = l$, hence $u_l'(\hat{x})$ must equal 1, which contradicts (37).

c) Proof is obtained by replacing J_1 with J_2 and $u_i'(x)$ with $(u_i'(x))^2$ in part c of the proof of Theorem 1. QED

Corollary 1. If $(u'(\cdot), v')$ is an optimal solution of (32), then v_i' is a weighted mean of X and consequently falls in $Co(X)$ for $1 \leqslant i \leqslant k$. Furthermore, for at least $n - k$ elements $x \in X$,

$$0 < u_i'(x) < 1 \quad 1 \leq i \leq k . \tag{40}$$

Corollary 2. The following condition defines a non-empty class $\mathcal{T}_2$ of operators T: $\mathcal{P}_f(k) \to \mathcal{P}_f(k)$. Let $\hat{u}(\cdot) = T(u(\cdot))$ = image of $u(\cdot)$ under T. For some $v \in L^k$ satisfying

$$\left(\sum_{x \in X} (u_i(x))^2\right) v_i = \sum_{x \in X} (u_i(x))^2 x \quad 1 \leq i \leq k, \tag{41}$$

Condition (γ): $\hat{u}(\cdot)$ must satisfy the following constraint: for each fixed $x \in X$, let

$$I = \{1 \leq i \leq k \mid v_i = x\}$$

$$I^c = \{1 \leq i \leq k \mid v_i \neq x\} .$$

If $I = \phi$ then

$$\hat{u}_i(x) = \frac{1/\|x - v_i\|^2}{\sum_{j=1}^{k} (1/\|x - v_j\|^2)} .$$

If $I \neq \phi$ then

$$u_i(x) = 0 \quad i \in I_c$$

and

$$\sum_{i \in I} u_i(x) = 1 .$$

A fuzzy partition $u'(\cdot)$ is part of an optimal solution $(u'(\cdot), v')$ of (32) only if $u'(\cdot)$ is a fixed point of some operator $T \in \mathcal{T}_2$, i.e.,

$$u'(\cdot) = T(u'(\cdot)) \quad \text{for some } T \in \mathcal{T}_2 . \tag{42}$$

In addition, $u'(\cdot)$ must also satisfy

$$u_i'(x) \neq 0 \quad 1 \leq i \leq k. \tag{43}$$

As in the previous sections, Corollary 2 of Theorem 3 suggests an iterative approach to the relaxed problem (32); specifically, it suggests that for some $T \in \mathcal{T}_2$ we implement

$$u^{(m+1)}(\cdot) = T(u^{(m)}(\cdot)) \quad 0 \leq m < \infty \quad T \in \mathcal{T}_2 . \tag{44}$$

Once again, the class $\mathcal{T}_2$ contains infinitely many operators. In general however, all of these operators coincide on the subclass of fuzzy partitions $u(\cdot)$ satisfying (43) and condition (δ): For each $x \in X$, I contains at most one element; i.e., $T(u(\cdot))$ is uniquely prescribed by conditions (43), (γ), and (δ). Furthermore, in contrast to the development of the previous section, we also have the following useful result.[6]

Theorem 4. Let $\mathcal{P}_f(k)$ denote the subclass of non-degenerate fuzzy k-partitions satisfying

$$u_i(\cdot) \neq 0 \quad 1 \leq i \leq k . \tag{45}$$

Then for all $T \in \mathcal{T}_2$, T maps $\mathcal{P}_f(k)$ into $\underline{\mathcal{P}}_f(k)$.

Proof. Since there are k vectors v_i and N elements $x \in X$ ($k \leqslant N$), either (i) there is at least one $x \in X$ such that $I = \phi$, or (ii) $k = N$ and for each $x \in X$, I contains precisely one element. In either case, condition (γ) insures that $\hat{u}(\cdot) = T(u(\cdot)) \in \underline{\mathcal{P}}_f(k)$. QED

In view of this result, the first step of (44) always places $u^{(1)}(\cdot)$ in $\underline{\mathcal{P}}_f(k)$ where condition (41) uniquely prescribes the vectors v_i. Thus, the only significant ambiguity in (γ) occurs when $u(\cdot)$ fails to satisfy (δ); in such cases (which appear to be very rare) a supplementary tie-breaking rule is required to make (44) a completely well-posed algorithm. For example if I contains c elements, we might put $u_i(x) = 1/c$ for $i \in I$; or, we might put $u_i(x) = 1$, where i is the smallest integer in I. The first order analysis of Theorem 3 makes no distinction between such rules. However, regardless of which rule is selected, the following result shows that the algorithm (44) always has the descent property relative to J_2.

Theorem 5. For arbitrary fixed $T \in \mathcal{T}_2$, let $\{u^{(m)}(\cdot)\}$ denote the sequence of partitions in $\mathcal{P}_f(k)$ generated by (44) and let $\{v^{(m)}\}$ denote the corresponding sequence in $\mathcal{L}^k$ associated with T and $u^m(\cdot)$ via condition (β). Then for all $m \geqslant 0$,

$$J_2(u^{(m+1)}(\cdot), v^{(m+1)}) \leq J_2(u^{(m)}(\cdot), v^{(m)}) .$$

[6] This result is generally false for operators $T \in \mathfrak{T}_1$. The more restrictive result, T: $\mathcal{P}_f(k) \to \mathcal{P}_f(k)$ also fails on $\mathfrak{T}_1$.

Proof. As an immediate consequence of the reasoning employed in parts *a* and *c* in the proof of Theorem 3, we have

$$J_2(u^{(m+1)}(\cdot), v^{(m)}) = \min_{u(\cdot) \in \mathcal{P}_f(k)} J_2(u(\cdot), v^{(m)})$$

and

$$J_2(u^{(m+1)}(\cdot), v^{(m)}) = \min_{v \in \mathcal{L}^k} J_2(u^{(m+1)}(\cdot), v)$$

thus

$$J_2(u^{(m)}(\cdot), v^{(m)}) \geq J_2(u^{(m+1)}(\cdot), v^{(m)}) \geq J_2(u^{(m+1)}(\cdot), v^{(m+1)}) \qquad \text{QED}$$

Several important questions remain. First, we would like to know whether the process (44) actually does converge to a fixed point of T, i.e., to a partition $u(\cdot)$ satisfying the necessary conditions of Theorem 3. In view of Corollary 1 we can see that such a limiting partition is typically fuzzy, however, when $\bar{\beta}(k) > 1$ we would like to know whether the membership functions of the limiting partition closely approximate the characteristic functions of the subsets X_i' in the maximally separated partition P' solving (9). Finally, when $\bar{\beta}(k)$ decreases below 1 we would like to know whether the limiting partition(s) produced by (44) is always genuinely fuzzy in the sense that $u_i(x)$ differs from 0 or 1 over a substantial subset of X. At present, these questions have not been decided rigorously. However, the numerical experiments presented in the next section suggest that the process (44) does behave the way we would like it to behave.

6. Numerical Results

The following version of (44) was programmed for the IBM 360 digital computer:

Step 1. Choose a partition $u(\cdot)$ in $\underline{\mathcal{P}}_f(k)$ = class of non-degenerate fuzzy partitions.
Step 2. Compute the weighted mean vectors

$$v_i = \frac{\sum_{x \in X} (u_i(x))^2 x}{\sum_{x \in X} u_i^2(x)} \qquad 1 \leq i \leq k. \tag{46}$$

Step 3. Construct a new partition $\hat{u}(\cdot) \in \underline{\mathcal{P}}_f(k)$ according to the following rule: for each $x \in X$, Let $I = \left\{1 \leqslant i \leqslant k \mid v_i = x\right\}$. If I is empty put

$$\hat{u}_i(x) = \frac{1/\langle x - v_i | x - v_i \rangle}{\sum_{j=1}^{k} (1/\langle x - v_j | x - v_j \rangle)} \qquad 1 \leq i \leq k.$$

If I is not empty, let i = smallest integer in I and put

$$\hat{u}_i(x) = \begin{cases} 1 & i = \mathrm{i} \\ 0 & i \neq \mathrm{i} \end{cases}.$$

Step 4. Compute new weighted mean vectors $\hat{v}_i$ corresponding to $\hat{u}(\cdot)$ via (46) and compute the corresponding maximum norm defect

$$\delta = \max_{1 \leqslant i \leqslant k} \max_{1 \leqslant j \leqslant d} |v_{i,j} - \hat{v}_{i,j}|$$

where d = dimension of $\mathcal{L}(X)$ = linear hull of X and $v_{i,j}$ = jth component of the vector v_i relative to some specified basis for $\mathcal{L}(X)$.

Step 5. If δ is less than some specified threshold ϵ, stop. Otherwise put $v = \hat{v}$ and go to Step 3.

We tried this algorithm on a variety of planar point sets $X \subset R^2$ using the ordinary Euclidean metric as the measure of distance, i.e.,

$$d^2(x_1, x_2) = \langle x_1 - x_2 | x_1 - x_2 \rangle = (x_{1,1} - x_{2,1})^2 + (x_{1,2} - x_{2,2})^2$$

where $x_{i,j}$ = jth entry of the 2-tuple $x_i \in R^2$. In all cases considered, we were able to achieve $\delta < \epsilon^* = 10^{-5}$ by performing a sufficiently large number N^* of iterations. As might be expected, the values of N^* required varied with the structure of X and, to a lesser extent, with the choice of initial partition; these values are quoted for each of the cases reported below, along with descriptions of the limiting fuzzy partition. For purposes of comparison, hard ISODATA partitions were also generated for each example, via the algorithm described in Sect. 3.

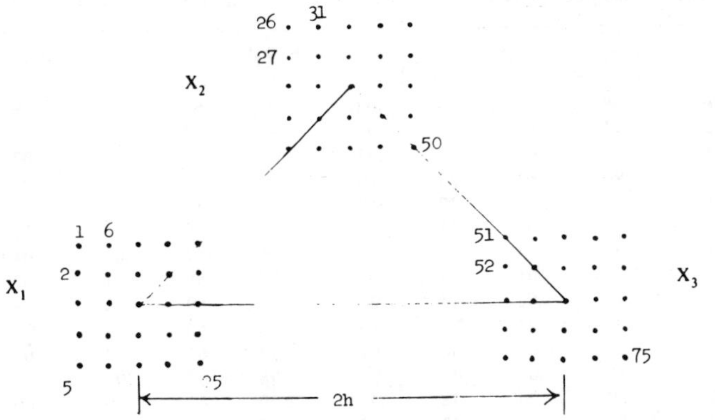

Fig. 1. Three Clusters with centroids on the vertices of an isosceles triangle with altitude h. Clusters are CWS for $h > 8\Delta$, where Δ = bilateral spacing within each lattice.

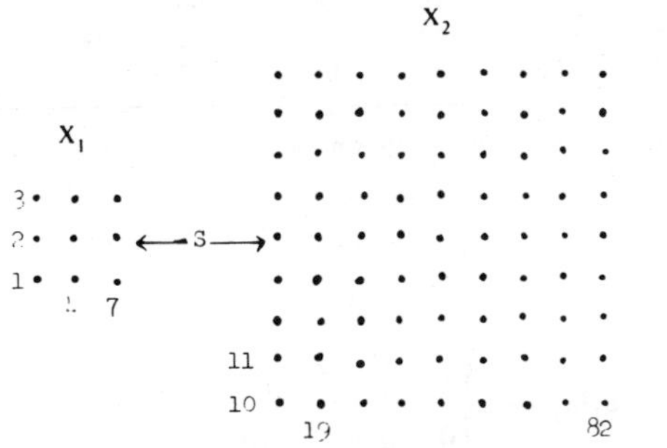

FIG. 2. One large and one small cluster. Clusters are CWS for $s > 8\sqrt{2}\Delta$, where Δ = bilateral spacing within each lattice.

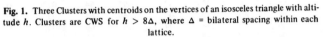

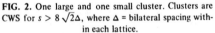

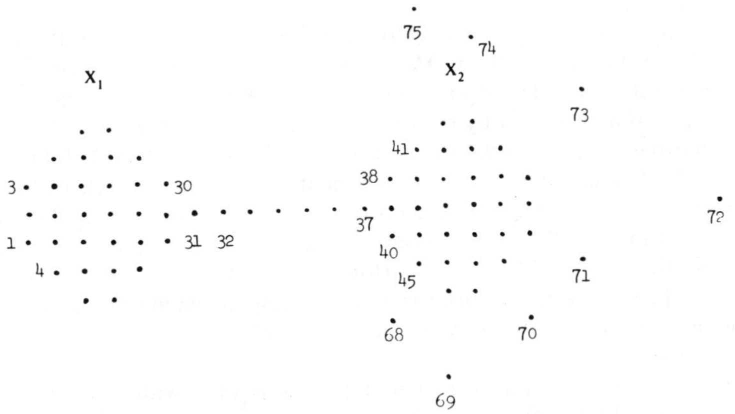

FIG. 3. Two CWS Clusters embedded in a background of strays forming a bridge and a halo.

The point sets considered are shown in Figs. 1, 2, and 3. In Fig. 1, X consists of three identical square lattices X_1, X_2, X_3 each containing 25 points with uniform bilateral internal spacing $\Delta = 1$, with centroids at the vertices of an isosceles triangle with altitude h and base $2h$, and with elements x_i, $1 \leqslant i \leqslant 75$, labeled as indicated. For $h > 5$, the component lattices X_i are "natural" clusters relative to the connectivity criterion discussed in Sect. 2. Furthermore we have $\bar{\alpha}(3) = \bar{\beta}(3) = h/4 - 1$ for $h > 5$. In particular $\{X_1, X_2, X_3\}$ consists of CWS clusters for $h > 8$. The initial partitions employed at the start of all calculations were always hard partitions of the following kind: $P = \{u_1(\cdot), u_2(\cdot),$

TABLE 1. Limiting Fuzzy Partition for the data set in Fig. 1, with $h = 6$ and $k = 3$[a]

i	$u_1(x_i)$	$u_2(x_i)$	i	$u_1(x_i)$	$u_2(x_i)$	i	$u_1(x_i)$	$u_2(x_i)$
1	.88	.09	26	.08	.86	51	.06	.19
2	.93	.05	27	.07	.89	52	.04	.11
3	.95	.04	28	.07	.90	53	.04	.07
4	.94	.04	29	.10	.84	54	.04	.07
5	.91	.06	30	.19	.74	55	.07	.09
6	.90	.07	31	.05	.91	56	.04	.11
7	.96	.03	32	.03	.96	57	.02	.04
8	.98	.01	33	.02	.97	58	.01	.02
9	.97	.02	34	.04	.94	59	.02	.03
10	.93	.04	35	.10	.83	60	.04	.05
11	.90	.07	36	.04	.93	61	.03	.07
12	.98	.02	37	.01	.98	62	.01	.02
13	1.00	.00	38	.00	1.00	63	.00	.00
14	.98	.01	39	.02	.97	64	.01	.01
15	.94	.04	40	.07	.86	65	.03	.04
16	.86	.11	41	.04	.91	66	.03	.07
17	.94	.04	42	.02	.96	67	.01	.03
18	.97	.02	43	.01	.97	68	.01	.01
19	.96	.03	44	.03	.94	69	.01	.02
20	.91	.05	45	.07	.83	70	.03	.04
21	.75	.19	46	.05	.86	71	.04	.09
22	.85	.11	47	.04	.89	72	.02	.05
23	.89	.07	48	.04	.90	73	.02	.04
24	.89	.07	49	.05	.85	74	.02	.04
25	.85	.09	50	.08	.74	75	.04	.06

[a]In Tables 1-3, $u_3(\cdot)$ is not shown, but may be obtained from the relation $\sum_{i=1}^{3} u_i(x) = 1$.

$u_3(\cdot)\}$, with

$$u_1(x_i) = \begin{cases} 1 & 1 \le i \le p \\ 0 & p < i \le 75 \end{cases}$$
$$u_2(x_i) = \begin{cases} 1 & p < i \le q \\ 0 & 1 \le i \le p \text{ or } q < i \le 75 \end{cases} \qquad (47)$$
$$u_3(x_i) = \begin{cases} 1 & q < i \le 75 \\ 0 & 1 \le i \le q \end{cases}$$

where $1 < p < q < 75$.

These partitions are completely characterized by the integer pair (p,q). Runs were made with the fuzzy algorithm and with ISODATA for a variety of different initial partitions (47) and for different values of h (i.e. $\bar{\beta}(3)$). Tables 1-3 give the first two decimal places of the limiting fuzzy partition produced by the fuzzy algorithm for $h = 6, 8,$ and 12 ($\bar{\beta}(3) = \frac{1}{2}, 1, 2$) respectively, starting from the initial partition (47) with $(p,q) = (30,55)$; Table 4 gives the corresponding absolute deviations of the components of the limiting weighted mean vector v_i in (46) from the corresponding components of the centroid vector for X_i. The numbers of iterations required to reach the 8-place versions of the limiting partitions displayed in Tables 1-3 were, respectively, $N^* = 14, 10$, and 8. However, the partitions obtained after only $N = 5, 4$, and 3 iterations, respectively, differ from the corresponding limiting partitions only by at most one or two units in the second place. Thus, $\epsilon^* = 10^{-5}$ is a conservatively small threshold for the present example.

Runs were also made starting from initial partitions (47) with $(p,q) = (51,61)$ and $(60,70)$; for each fixed value of h, the iterates generated by the fuzzy algorithm led always to the same limiting partition (up to 6 places) obtained for $(p,q) = (30,55)$, with little or no change in N^*. For instance, with $h = 6$, $N^* = 15$ iterations were required to reach the partition displayed in Table 1 from $(p,q) = (51,61)$. As anticipated, the limiting fuzzy partitions become increasingly fuzzy, and N^* becomes increasingly large, as $\bar{\beta}(3)$ decreases.

The behavior exhibited by ISODATA for this example is interesting. As one might expect, ISODATA does very well from the initial partition (47) with $(p,q) = (30,55)$; for all three values of h, just one iteration of ISODATA maps $(p,q) = (30,55)$ into $(p,q) = (25,50)$. However, in marked contrast to the fuzzy algorithm, ISODATA produces some rather surprising and dramatic splittings of the natural clusters X_i when different starting partitions are employed. For example, a simple calculation shows that the partitions (47) with $(p,q) =$

TABLE 2. Limiting fuzzy partition for the data set in Fig. 1, with $h = 8$, and $k = 3$

i	$u_1(x_i)$	$u_2(x_i)$	i	$u_1(x_i)$	$u_2(x_i)$	i	$u_1(x_i)$	$u_2(x_i)$
1	.92	.05	26	.05	.91	51	.04	.10
2	.95	.03	27	.04	.93	52	.02	.06
3	.97	.02	28	.04	.94	53	.02	.04
4	.96	.03	29	.05	.92	54	.02	.04
5	.94	.04	30	.10	.85	55	.04	.05
6	.94	.04	31	.03	.94	56	.02	.06
7	.98	.02	32	.02	.97	57	.01	.02
8	.99	.01	33	.01	.98	58	.00	.01
9	.98	.01	34	.02	.96	59	.01	.02
10	.96	.03	35	.05	.91	60	.02	.03
11	.95	.04	36	.02	.95	61	.02	.04
12	.99	.01	37	.01	.99	62	.00	.01
13	1.00	.00	38	.00	1.00	63	.00	.00
14	.99	.01	39	.01	.98	64	.00	.01
15	.96	.02	40	.04	.92	65	.02	.02
16	.92	.06	41	.03	.94	66	.02	.04
17	.97	.02	42	.01	.97	67	.01	.02
18	.99	.01	43	.01	.98	68	.00	.01
19	.98	.02	44	.02	.96	69	.01	.01
20	.95	.03	45	.04	.91	70	.02	.03
21	.87	.10	46	.04	.91	71	.02	.05
22	.92	.06	47	.03	.93	72	.02	.03
23	.94	.04	48	.02	.94	73	.01	.02
24	.94	.04	49	.03	.92	74	.02	.03
25	.91	.05	50	.05	.85	75	.02	.04

(50,60) and (50,65) are fixed points of the ISODATA algorithm. Furthermore, it turns out that many nearby partitions are either also fixed points or else get mapped quickly into such fixed points. Thus, for $h = 8$, $(p,q) = (60,70)$ maps into (50,65) after four iterations, and $(p,q) = (51,61)$ maps into (50,61) after 3 iterations. Therefore, for this example at least, it appears that the fuzzy algorithm is far superior to ISODATA in the sense that its convergence to the "correct" limiting partition is not disrupted by a multitude of spurious attracting fixed points corresponding to uninteresting local minimum of J. What seems to be happening here is that hard partitions which provide local minima of the extended payoff J_1 on the continuum $\mathcal{P}_f(3)$ are no longer local minima for the extended payoff J_2; as a consequence, these partitions are not stationary points of J_2, and therefore are not fixed points of the fuzzy algorithm. Furthermore, if spurious fuzzy local minima of J_2 do exist for this data set, their zones of influence were too small to deflect the iterates of the fuzzy algorithm in any of the experiments peformed.

The data set of X in Fig. 2 consists of two square lattices X_1 and X_2 containing 9 and 81

TABLE 3. Limiting fuzzy partition for the data set in Fig. 1, with $h = 12$ and $k = 3$

i	$u_1(x_i)$	$u_2(x_i)$	i	$u_1(x_i)$	$u_2(x_i)$	i	$u_1(x_i)$	$u_2(x_i)$
1	.96	.03	26	.03	.95	51	.02	.04
2	.98	.02	27	.02	.97	52	.01	.02
3	.98	.01	28	.02	.97	53	.01	.02
4	.98	.01	29	.02	.96	54	.01	.02
5	.97	.02	30	.04	.94	55	.02	.03
6	.97	.02	31	.02	.97	56	.01	.02
7	.99	.01	32	.01	.99	57	.00	.01
8	1.00	.00	33	.00	.99	58	.00	.00
9	.99	.01	34	.01	.98	59	.00	.01
10	.98	.01	35	.02	.96	60	.01	.02
11	.98	.02	36	.01	.98	61	.01	.02
12	.99	.00	37	.00	.99	62	.00	.00
13	1.00	.00	38	.00	1.00	63	.00	.00
14	1.00	.00	39	.00	.99	64	.00	.00
15	.98	.01	40	.02	.97	65	.01	.01
16	.97	.02	41	.01	.97	66	.01	.02
17	.99	.01	42	.01	.99	67	.00	.01
18	.99	.00	43	.00	.99	68	.00	.00
19	.99	.01	44	.01	.98	69	.00	.01
20	98	.02	45	.02	.96	70	.01	.01
21	.95	.04	46	.02	.95	71	.01	.03
22	.97	.02	47	.01	.97	72	.01	.02
23	.98	.02	48	.01	.97	73	.01	.01
24	.97	.02	49	.02	.96	74	.01	.01
25	.96	.03	50	.03	.94	75	.01	.02

TABLE 4. Absolute deviations of the limiting fuzzy mean vector components from centroid vector components for the data set in Fig. 1

h	$\lvert v_{1,1} - \bar{x}_{1,1} \rvert$	$\lvert v_{1,2} - \bar{x}_{1,2} \rvert$	$\lvert v_{2,1} - \bar{x}_{2,1} \rvert$	$\lvert v_{2,2} - \bar{x}_{2,2} \rvert$	$\lvert v_{3,1} - \bar{x}_{3,1} \rvert$	$\lvert v_{3,2} - \bar{x}_{3,2} \rvert$
6	.032712	.022391	.000111	.035244	.032750	.022422
8	.014845	.010167	.000110	.018010	.014840	.010191
12	.004565	.003089	.000020	.005900	.004570	.003107

TABLE 5. Limiting fuzzy partition for the data set in Fig. 2, with $s = 5$ and $k = 2$[a]

i	$u_1(x)$	i	$u_1(x)$	i	$u_1(x)$	i	$u_1(x)$	i	$u_1(x)$	i	$u_1(x)$
1	.79	16	.89	31	.63	46	.33	61	.11	76	.06
2	.79	17	.81	32	.65	47	.27	62	.19	77	.04
3	.79	18	.74	33	.63	48	.20	63	.26	78	.04
4	.81	19	.66	34	.60	49	.13	64	.22	79	.09
5	.82	20	.72	35	.57	50	.09	65	.15	80	.15
6	.81	21	.79	36	.55	51	.13	66	.08	81	.20
7	.84	22	.86	37	.43	52	.20	67	.03	82	.20
8	.85	23	.89	38	.41	53	.27	68	.01	83	.16
9	.84	24	.86	39	.38	54	.33	69	.03	84	.12
10	.74	25	.79	40	.34	55	.26	70	.08	85	.09
11	.81	26	.72	41	.32	56	.19	71	.15	86	.08
12	.89	27	.66	42	.34	57	.11	72	.22	87	.09
13	.96	28	.55	43	.38	58	.04	73	.20	88	.12
14	.99	29	.57	44	.41	59	.01	74	.15	89	.16
15	.96	30	.60	45	.43	60	.04	75	.09	90	.20

[a] In Tables 5–8, the value of $u_2(x)$ may be obtained from the relation $\sum_{i=1}^{2} u_i(x) = 1$.

TABLE 6. Limiting fuzzy partition for the data set in Fig. 2, with $s = 7$ and $k = 2$

i	$u_1(x_i)$	i	$u_1(x_i)$	i	$u_1(x_i)$	i	$u_1(x_i)$	i	$u_1(x_i)$	i	$u_1(x_i)$
1	.95	16	.38	31	.10	46	.12	61	.03	76	.04
2	.95	17	.39	32	.09	47	.08	62	.07	77	.04
3	.95	18	.41	33	.10	48	.04	63	.11	78	.04
4	.97	19	.30	34	.13	49	.01	64	.10	79	.06
5	.97	20	.27	35	.17	50	.00	65	.07	80	.08
6	.97	21	.23	36	.22	51	.01	66	.04	81	.11
7	.98	22	.21	37	.16	52	.04	67	.02	82	.12
8	.99	23	.20	38	.11	53	.08	68	.02	83	.10
9	.98	24	.21	39	.07	54	.12	69	.02	84	.08
10	.41	25	.23	40	.04	55	.11	70	.04	85	.07
11	.39	26	.27	41	.03	56	.07	71	.07	86	.06
12	.38	27	.30	42	.04	57	.03	72	.10	87	.07
13	.36	28	.22	43	.07	58	.01	73	.11	88	.08
14	.36	29	.17	44	.11	59	.00	74	.08	89	.10
15	.36	30	.13	45	.16	60	.01	75	.06	90	.12

elements respectively, with uniform bilateral internal spacing $\Delta = 1$, and labels as indicated. X_1 and X_2 are natural clusters relative to the connectivity criterion when the distance s between X_1 and X_2 exceeds 1. Furthermore, we have diam $X_2 = 8\sqrt{2}$, and $\bar{\alpha}(2) = \bar{\beta}(2) = s/8\sqrt{2}$; hence, $\{X_1, X_2\}$ consists of CWS clusters when $s > 8\sqrt{2} \approx 11.3$. The starting partitions used for this example were always of the form

$$u_1(x_i) = \begin{cases} 1 & 1 \le i \le p \\ 0 & p < i \le 90 \end{cases}$$
$$u_2(x_i) = \begin{cases} 1 & p < i \le 90 \\ 0 & 1 \le i \le p \end{cases} \tag{48}$$

with $p = 54$. Runs were made with the fuzzy algorithm and ISODATA for values of s ranging from 5 to 16 ($\bar{\beta}(2)$ ranging from $\approx .44$ to 1.41). Tables 5–8 give the first two decimal places of the limiting fuzzy partitions produced by the fuzzy algorithm for $s = 5, 7, 9$ and 16 ($\bar{\beta}(2) \approx .44, .62, .79$ and 1.4); the numbers of iterations required to obtain these partitions were, respectively, $N^* = 28, 73, 24$, and 12, although in each case substantially fewer iterations would suffice to reach partitions essentially like the limiting partitions.

TABLE 7. Limiting fuzzy partition for the data set in Fig. 2, with $s = 9$ and $k = 2$

i	$u_1(x_i)$	i	$u_1(x_i)$	i	$u_1(x_i)$	i	$u_1(x_i)$	i	$u_1(x_i)$	i	$u_1(x_i)$
1	.98	16	.20	31	.05	46	.08	61	.02	76	.03
2	.98	17	.23	32	.04	47	.05	62	.04	77	.03
3	.98	18	.26	33	.05	48	.02	63	.07	78	.03
4	.99	19	.18	34	.07	49	.01	64	.07	79	.04
5	1.00	20	.15	35	.10	50	.00	65	.05	80	.06
6	.99	21	.12	36	.13	51	.01	66	.03	81	.08
7	.99	22	.10	37	.10	52	.02	67	.02	82	.09
8	1.00	23	.09	38	.06	53	.05	68	.01	83	.07
9	.99	24	.10	39	.04	54	.08	69	.02	84	.06
10	.26	25	.12	40	.02	55	.07	70	.03	85	.05
11	.23	26	.15	41	.01	56	.04	71	.05	86	.05
12	.20	27	.18	42	.02	57	.02	72	.07	87	.05
13	.19	28	.13	43	.04	58	.01	73	.08	88	.06
14	.18	29	.10	44	.06	59	.00	74	.06	89	.07
15	.19	30	.07	45	.10	60	.01	75	.04	90	.09

TABLE 8. Limiting fuzzy partition for the data set in Fig. 2, with $s = 16$ and $k = 2$

i	$u_1(x_i)$	i	$u_1(x_i)$	i	$u_1(x_i)$	i	$u_1(x_i)$	i	$u_1(x_i)$	i	$u_1(x_i)$
1	.99	16	.07	31	.02	46	.04	61	.01	76	.02
2	1.00	17	.08	32	.01	47	.02	62	.02	77	.02
3	.99	18	.10	33	.02	48	.01	63	.03	78	.02
4	1.00	19	.07	34	.02	49	.00	64	.04	79	.02
5	1.00	20	.05	35	.04	50	.00	65	.02	80	.03
6	1.00	21	.04	36	.05	51	.00	66	.02	81	.04
7	1.00	22	.03	37	.04	52	.01	67	.01	82	.05
8	1.00	23	.03	38	.03	53	.02	68	.01	83	.04
9	1.00	24	.03	39	.01	54	.04	69	.01	84	.03
10	.10	25	.04	40	.01	55	.03	70	.02	85	.03
11	.08	26	.05	41	.00	56	.02	71	.02	86	.03
12	.07	27	.07	42	.01	57	.01	72	.04	87	.03
13	.06	28	.05	43	.01	58	.00	73	.04	88	.03
14	.06	29	.04	44	.03	59	.00	74	.03	89	.04
15	.06	30	.02	45	.04	60	.00	75	.02	90	.05

TABLE 9. Limiting fuzzy partition for the data set in Fig. 3, with $k = 2$[a]

i	$u_1(x_i)$	i	$u_1(x_i)$	i	$u_1(x_i)$
1	.96	26	.99	51	.03
2	.96	27	.97	52	.06
3	.96	28	.96	53	.05
4	.96	29	.97	54	.02
5	.98	30	.96	55	.01
6	.98	31	.91	56	.00
7	.98	32	.82	57	.01
8	.96	33	.70	58	.02
9	.95	34	.55	59	.05
10	.97	35	.39	60	.03
11	.99	36	.25	61	.01
12	.99	37	.14	62	.01
13	.99	38	.07	63	.01
14	.97	39	.06	64	.03
15	.95	40	.07	65	.03
16	.95	41	.05	66	.02
17	.98	42	.03	67	.03
18	.99	43	.02	68	.16
19	1.00	44	.03	69	.17
20	.99	45	.05	70	.08
21	.98	46	.06	71	.07
22	.95	47	.03	72	.15
23	.97	48	.01	73	.10
24	.99	49	.00	74	.15
25	.99	50	.01	75	.23

[a] $u_2(\cdot)$ may be obtained from the relation $\sum_{i=1}^{2} u_i(x) = 1$.

Once again, the limiting fuzzy partitions become increasingly fuzzy, and N^* tends to increase in general ($s = 5$ is the obvious exception) as $\overline{\beta}(2)$ decreases.

Again, the behavior of ISODATA is interesting. When $s > 3$, a simple calculation reveals that the "natural" partition (48) corresponding to $p = 9$ is indeed a fixed point of ISODATA, however the partitions corresponding to $p = 18, 27, 36$, and 45 are also fixed points when $8 \geqslant s > 4$, $9 > s > 3$, $8 \geqslant s > 1$, and $5 \geqslant s > 1$ respectively. Furthermore calculations for $s = 9, 8, 7, 6$, and 5 show that ISODATA quickly maps the initial partition corresponding to $p = 54$ into $p = 27, 36, 36, 36$, and 45 respectively. For $s = 7, 8$, and 9, the fuzzy algorithm generates substantially better approximations to the "natural" partition (48) with $p = 9$; for $s = 16$, ISODATA converges to the natural partition, and the fuzzy algorithm also generates a very good approximation to this partition.

Finally, the data set X in Fig. 3 contains two octagonal lattices X_1 and X_2, each comprised of 30 elements with uniform bilateral internal spacing $\Delta = 1$. The remaining elements of X form a six element bridge joining X_1 and X_2 (points 31-36) and a halo of eight elements about X_2 (points 68-75).[7] This data set differs from the previous examples in a significant way: Although $\overline{\beta}(2) << 1$ for X, we have $X = Y \cup Z$ where $\overline{\beta}(2) > 1$ for Y and where the "average density" of points in Z is much less than in Y (e.g., take Y = union of X_1 and X_2, and Z as the remaining bridge and halo elements.) In this sense X differs negligibly from a set consisting of two CWS clusters. Although we have not attempted a precise quantitative characterization of this kind of structure, it is clearly important in applications, especially where X is a sample drawn from a mixture of unimodal probability distributions. Zahn [4] and Wishart [8] describe pruning techniques for dealing with precisely this problem of extracting dense nuclear clusters from a noisy background. The general idea behind their methods is to first isolate and remove the "negligible" subset of X and then submit the remainder set to an algorithm capable to identifying clusters relative to the metric of interest. In the present investigation, we were curious to see how the fuzzy algorithm would behave on the unaltered set X of Fig. 3, for $k = 2$. Accordingly, calculations were made for initial partitions of the form

$$u_1(x_i) = \begin{cases} 1 & 1 \le i \le p \\ 0 & p < i \le 75 \end{cases} \qquad u_2(x_i) = \begin{cases} 1 & p < i \le 75 \\ 0 & 1 \le i \le p \end{cases} \tag{49}$$

In all cases considered, the fuzzy algorithm converged rapidly to the same limiting partition, which is given to 2 decimal places in Table 9 (the number of iterations required being $N^* = 10$). Since $\overline{\beta}(2) << 1$ for X, we expect fuzziness in this partition. However, it can be seen that divided membership is most pronounced on the bridge and halo elements. For x in the lattice X_1, $u_1(\cdot)$ is essentially equal to the characteristic function of X_1; similarly, for x in X_2, $u_2(\cdot)$ closely approximates the characteristic function of X_2. Thus, the limiting partition generated by the fuzzy algorithm provides insight into the structure of X. In contrast, ISODATA converges rapidly ($N^* \approx 3$) to the limiting hard partition (49) with $p = 34$ for all initial partitions considered; while this limiting partition does separate the nuclear clusters X_1 and X_2, it gives no clue to the structure of X.

References

[1] P. H. A. Sneath, "The application of computers to taxonomy," *J. Gen. Microbiology*, vol. 17, p. 201-226, 1957.
[2] R. O. Duda and P. E. Hart, *Pattern Classification and Scene Analysis*. New York: Academic Press, 1972.
[3] G. Nagy, "State of the art in pattern recognition," *IEEE Proc.*, vol. 56, no. 5, pp. 836-862, 1968.
[4] C. T. Zahn, "Graph theoretical methods for detecting and describing gestalt clusters," *IEEE Trans. on Comp.*, vol. C-20, no. 1, pp. 68-86, 1971.
[5] R. G. Casey and G. Nagy, "An autonomous reading machine," *IEEE Trans. on Comp.*, vol. C-17, no. 5, pp. 492-503, 1968.
[6] R. G. Casey and G. Nagy, "Recognition of printed chinese characters," *IEEE Trans. on Comp.*, vol. C-15, pp. 91-101, 1966.
[7] S. C. Johnson, "Hierarchical clustering schemes," *Psychometrika*, vol. 32, pp. 241-254, 1967.
[8] D. Wishart, "Mode analysis: A generalization of nearest neighbor which reduces chaining effects," in *Numerical Taxonomy*, A. J. Cole, Ed. New York: Academic Press, 1969.
[9] L. Zadeh, "Fuzzy sets," *Inform. and Control*, vol. 8, no. 3, pp. 338-353, 1965.
[10] E. H. Ruspini, "A new approach to clustering," *Inform. and Control*, vol. 15, pp. 22-32, 1969.

[7] Figure 3 is drawn to scale.

[11] E. H. Ruspini, "Numerical methods for fuzzy clustering," *Inf. Science,* vol. 2, p. 319, 1970.
[12] I. Gitman and M. D. Levine, "An algorithm for detecting unimodal fuzzy sets and its application as a clustering technique," *IEEE Trans. on Comp.*, vol. C-19, no. 7, pp. 583–593, 1970.
[13] G. H. Ball and D. J. Hall, "ISODATA, an iterative method of multivariate analysis and pattern classification," *Behavioral Science,* vol. 12, pp. 153–155, 1967.
[14] J. Dieudonne, *Foundations of Modern Analysis.* New York: Academic Press, 1960.
[15] C. W. Curtis, *Linear Algebra.* Boston: Allyn & Bacon, 1963.
[16] H. P. Friedman and J. Rubin, "On some invariant criteria for grouping data," *Amer. Stat. Assoc. J.*, vol. 62, no. 320, pp. 1159–1178, 1967.
[17] K. Fukunaga and W. L. G. Koontz, "A criterion and an algorithm for grouping data," *IEEE Trans. on Comp.*, vol. C-19, no. 10, pp. 917–923, 1970.

Received September 17, 1973

PATTERN CLASSIFICATION PROBLEMS AND FUZZY SETS

Marc ROUBENS
Faculté Polytechnique de Mons, B. 7000 Mons, Belgium

Received 24 June 1977

A unified presentation of classical clustering algorithms is proposed both for the hard and fuzzy pattern classification problems. Based on two types of objective functions, a new method is presented and compared with the procedures of Dunn and Ruspini. In order to determine the best, or more natural number of fuzzy clusters, two coefficients that measure the "degree of non-fuzziness" of the partition are proposed. Numerous computational results are shown.

Key Words: Clustering, Data structure analysis, Numerical taxonomy, Pattern recognition, Fuzzy sets.

1. Introduction

Suppose M points $\{x\}=E$ belong to a p-space. Some a priori weight $u(x)$ is assigned to each point $x \in E$ (eventually equal to $1/M$), $\sum_{x \in E} u(x)=1$.

The problem of *fuzzy clustering* is partitioning the M points in k fuzzy subsets, k being fixed, by determining for each point x a membership function $\mu_k(x)$:

$$0 \leqq \mu_k(x) \leqq 1.$$

If $\mu_k(x) \in \{0,1\}$, $\forall k$, one will recognize the classical clustering problem of partitioning a given set into a pre-assigned number of homogeneous and well separated non overlapping subsets (clusters).

Most of the methods proposed in the present state of cluster analysis are metric: a convenient distance measure being chosen (Euclidean, diagonal, Mahalanobis, L_1, L_2 norms) in p-space, some concept of homogeneity yields an objective function (minimal variance criterion) to be optimized.

Some more recent algorithms are non metric. Dissimilarity between entities is defined for each pair of entities (x, y) belonging to E. The dissimilarity index $d(x, y)$ satisfies: $d(x, y) \geq 0$, $d(x, y)=d(y, x)$, x, $y \in E$.

The concept of homogeneity is introduced in different ways using either

- The *diameter of a partition* as the maximum dissimilarity. between any pair of entities in the same cluster [14].

Reprinted with permission from *Fuzzy Sets and Systems*, vol. 1, pp. 239–253, 1978.

– A *fuzzy objective function*

$$\operatorname*{MIN}_{(\mu,\eta)} \sum_k \sum_x \sum_y f[u(x), \eta_k(x)] g[u(y), \mu_k(y)] d(x, y) \quad \text{under constraints}$$

relative to μ and η,

f and g being given functionals and μ, η membership functions [8, 37].

The problem of clustering can be handled in many ways using:

- Aggregative algorithms which merge the closest unclustered point to a moving centroid. Numerous procedures of this type are proposed [24, 26].
- Aggregative and separative procedures such as ISODATA [1] and IPHIGENIE [3].
- Techniques based on objective functions such as the iterated minimal distance partition [32], the exchange method [39], the dynamic clusters method [15].
- Algorithms based on dynamic programming [28], integer programs [43], branch and bound [30]. These programs are unfortunately not manageable in practical cases.
- Algorithms based on graph theory concepts: minimal spanning tree search [50], coloring [14].
- Algorithms based on fuzzy sets concepts such as fuzzy objective functions [5, 8, 17, 37] or fuzzy graphs [34, 45, 47].

Following the ideas of Dunn [17] and Ruspini [38] we propose a non metric and fuzzy method called MND 2. It is based on the objective function

$$\operatorname*{MIN}_{\mu_k} \sum_k \sum_x \sum_y \mu_k^2(x) \mu_k^2(y) d(x, y), \qquad d\text{: dissimilarity measure}$$

$$\mu_k \geqq 0, \qquad \sum_k \mu_k(x) = 1.$$

The global minimum of this non linear program is computationally impracticable for moderate or large M. A commonly used, feasible heuristic suits the minimum iteratively.

2. Fuzzy criteria

Let $d(x, y)$ be a dissimilarity index and $u(x)$ the a priori weights for all $x, y \in E$.

The membership function $\mu_k(x)$ is determined by optimizing one of the two following fuzzy criteria:

CR1:

$$\operatorname*{MIN}_{y_k, \mu_k} \sum_{y_k, \mu_k} \sum_k \sum_x g[u(x), \mu_k(x)] d(x, y_k) \quad \text{subject to constraints}$$

CR2:

$$\underset{\mu_k,\eta_k}{\text{MIN}} \sum_k \sum_x \sum_y f[u(x), \eta_k(x)] g[u(y), \mu_k(y)] d(x, y) \quad \text{subject to constraints.}$$

In CR2, $\eta_k(x)$ represents an auxiliary membership function ($0 \leqq \eta_k(x) \leqq 1$).

CR2 only needs the dissimilarity matrix d to be known for each pair of the pattern E. CR1 implies $d(x, a)$ being calculable for $x \in E$, $a \notin E$. This can be easily done if $E: \{x_1, \ldots, x_M\}$ is a finite subset of p-dimensional Euclidean space R^p; each $x_j = (x_{j1}, \ldots, x_{jp})$ is a feature vector of pattern E, x_{jk} being the jth observation of the kth characteristic.

If $d(x, y)$ is defined as $\|x - y\|^2$, $\|.\|$ being any inner product induced norm on R^p (Euclidean, diagonal, Mahalanobis norms) defined as $(x-y)' A (x-y)$, A being symmetric, definite positive, it can be easily shown for CR1 that

$$\underset{y_k}{\text{MIN}} \sum_k \sum_x g u(x), \mu_k(x) \|x - y_k\|^2$$

yields the *fuzzy centroids* CG(g, k):

$$\text{CG}(g, k) = [\text{G}(k)]^{-1} \sum_x g[u(x), \mu_k(x)] x$$

$$\text{G}(k) = \sum_x g[u(x), \mu_k(x)].$$

Moreover using the total sum of squares partition theorem:

$$\sum_x g[u(x), \mu_k(x)] \|x - y\|^2 = \sum_x g[u(x), \mu_k(x)] \|x - CG(g, k)\|^2 + G(k) \|CG(g, k) - y\|^2$$

and the "within group sum of squares" of the fuzzy K-partition being defined as

$$\text{VAR}(g, k) = \sum_x g[u(x), \mu_k(x)] \|x - CG(g, k)\|^2$$

the fuzzy criteria may be rewritten as follows:

CR1:

$$\underset{\mu}{\text{MIN}} \sum_k \text{VAR}(g; k) \quad \text{subject to constraints regarding } \mu$$

CR2:

$$\underset{(\mu,\eta)}{\mathrm{MIN}} \sum_{k} \{G(k)\,\mathrm{VAR}\,(f,k)+F(k)\,\mathrm{VAR}\,(g,k)+F(k)G(k)\|CG(f,k)$$

$$-CG(g,k)\|^2\} \quad \text{subject to constraints regarding } \eta \text{ and } \mu.$$

F(k), CG(f, k) and VAR (f, k) are obviously defined as

$$\mathrm{F}(k)=\sum_{y} f[u(y)\eta_k(y)]$$

$$\mathrm{CG}(f,k)=F(k)^{-1}\sum_{y} f(u(y),\eta_k(y))y$$

$$\mathrm{VAR}\,(f,k)=\sum_{y} f[u(y),\eta_k(y)]\|y-\mathrm{CG}(f,k)\|^2$$

When $f=g$,

CR2:

$$\underset{\mu}{\mathrm{MIN}} \quad \sum_{k} G(k)\,\mathrm{VAR}\,(g,k) \quad \text{subject to constraints regarding } \mu.$$

3. Some particular cases

3.1.

Let $g[u(x),\mu_k(x)]=\mu_k(x)/M$ and consider

CR1:

$$\underset{\mu}{\mathrm{MIN}} \sum_{k}\sum_{x} \mu_k(x)\|x-\mathrm{CG}(k)\|^2$$

$$\mu_k(x)\geqq 0, \qquad \sum_{k} \mu_k(x)=1, \qquad k=1,\ldots,K,$$

where

$$\mathrm{CG}(k)=\frac{\sum_{x} \mu_k(x)x}{\sum_{k} \mu_k(x)}.$$

It can be easily seen that

$$\mu_k(x)=\begin{cases}1 & \text{if } \|x-\mathrm{CG}(k)\| \leqq \|x-\mathrm{CG}(j)\|, \quad j\neq k,\\ 0 & \text{otherwise.}\end{cases}$$

The hard K-partition is denoted $E_1,\ldots,E_K$.

A widely used iterative hard procedure of "hill-climbing" type, reported in [1], [32], yields *local solutions* that depend on initial guesses:

Step 1: choose an initial $(E_1^0,\ldots,E_K^0)$;

Step 2: compute CG(k);

Step 3: update $(E_1,\ldots,E_K)$ with the nearest neighbor rule;

Step 4: go to 2 or stop.

3.2.

Let $g[u(x),\ \mu_k(x)]=\mu_k^m(x)/M$ and consider Bezdek's criterion [8] which generate the infinite family of fuzzy ISODATA clustering algorithms $(1\leqq m\leqq\infty)$,

CR1:

$$\underset{\mu}{\mathrm{MIN}}\sum_k\sum_x \mu_k^m(x)\|x-\mathrm{CG}(k)\|^2$$

$$\mu_k(x)\geqq 0, \qquad \sum_k \mu_k(x)=1, \qquad k=1,\ldots,K,$$

where

$$\mathrm{CG}(k)=\frac{\sum_x \mu_k^m(x)x}{\sum_x \mu_k^m(x)}.$$

The quadratic program CR1 leads to the fuzzy K-partition [4]

$$\mu_k^{-1}(x)=\sum_l\left(\frac{\|x-\mathrm{CG}(k)\|}{\|x-\mathrm{CG}(l)\|}\right)^{2/m-1}.$$

A metric fuzzy procedure similar to the "hill climbing" algorithm proposed in 3.1. can be easily implemented. The method proposed by Dunn [17] corresponds to $m=2$.

3.3.

Let $f[u(x),\ \eta_k(x)]=\eta_k(x)/M$, $g[u(x),\ \mu_k(x)]=\mu_k(x)/M$ and consider Diday's criterion [15]:

CR2:

$$\underset{(\mu,\eta)}{\mathrm{MIN}} \sum_k \sum_x \sum_y \eta_k(x)\mu_k(y)d(x,y)$$

$$\mu_k(x) \geqq 0, \qquad \sum_k \mu_k(x) = 1$$

$$\eta_k(x) \geqq 0, \qquad \sum_x \eta_k(x) = N_k,$$

where N_k is the number of points in cluster k.

A non metric hard procedure, which generalizes the "iteration relocation" procedure presented in 3.1., called "dynamic clusters method" is described in [15]:

Step 1: choose initial kernels $\{\eta_k^o(x_1), \ldots, \eta_k^o(x_M)\}$;

Step 2: aggregate points around kernels with the nearest neighbor rule. This defines a K-partition $E_1, \ldots, E_K$;

Step 3: update the kernels using the K-partition by taking for "kernel k" elements the N_k first lowest values of the sequence $\{\sum_{y \in E_k} d(x,y)\}$, $x \in E$;

Step 4: go to 2 or stop.

Under certain conditions, it is proved that the procedure converges to a local optimum depending on the initial choice of kernels.

3.4.

Let $\mu_k(x) = \eta_k(x)$ and

$$f[u(x), \mu_k(x)]g[u(y), \mu_k(y)] = u(x)\mu_k(x)u(y)\mu_k(y)\frac{\sum_z u(z)\mu_k(z)}{\sum_z u(z)d(x,z)}.$$

As reported by Ruspini [37] the components of the objective function CR2 may be rewritten in the following way:

$u(x)$: a priori probability $P(x)$

$\mu_k(x)$: conditional probability $P(k \mid x)$

$\sum_z u(z)\mu_k(z)$: a priori probability $P(k)$

$\dfrac{u(y)\mu_k(y)}{\sum_z u(z)\mu_k(z)}$: conditional probability $P(y \mid k)$

$$\frac{\sum_y u(y)\mu_k(y)d(x,y)}{\sum_z u(z)\mu_k(z)}: \quad \text{mean density of the fuzzy subset } k \text{ around } x,\ M_k(x)$$

$$\sum_z u(z)d(x,z): \quad \text{mean density of the pattern around } x, M(x),$$

CR2:

$$\mathrm{MIN} \sum_x P(x) \sum_k P(k) \left[\frac{P(k)M_k(x)}{M(x)} \right] P(k \mid x)$$

i.e. the objective function of Clustering II which tries "to minimize, in the average, the products $P(k \mid x)M_k(x)$ so that large mean densities will correspond to small degrees of belongingness and vice versa" (quoted from [37]). The method used to solve this program is a gradient process.

4. A new fuzzy non metric method

Our purpose is to follow Bezdek and Dunn in defining a fuzzy objective function. However, the method proposed should be useful if the data is given in a dissimilarity matrix form. This is the case for the criterion

CR2:

$$\mathrm{MIN}_{\mu} \sum_k \sum_x \sum_y \mu_k^2(x)\mu_k^2(y)d(x,y)$$

$$\mu_k(x) \geqq 0, \qquad \sum_k \mu_k(x) = 1.$$

Local solutions of this program may be obtained with the following algorithm, called MND2:

Step 1: choose an initial membership matrix $\{\mu_k^o(x)\}$

Step 2: calculate $D(x,k) = \sum_y \mu_k^2(y)d(x,y)$.

Step 3: optimize the quadratic program

$$\mathrm{MIN}_{\mu_k} \sum_k \sum_k \mu_k^2(x)D(x,k)$$

$$\mu_k(x) \geqq 0, \qquad \sum_k \mu_k(x) = 1$$

Step 4: go to 2 or stop.

The optimum of the quadratic program defined in step 3 can be readily obtained with the use of Lagrange multipliers.

$$\underset{\mu_k}{\mathrm{MIN}} \sum_k \sum_x \mu_k^2(x) D(x,k) + \sum_x \lambda(x) \left[\sum_k \mu_k(x) - 1 \right]$$

leads to

$$\frac{\partial}{\partial \mu_k(x)} = 0: \quad 2\,\mu_k(x) D(x,k) + \lambda(x) = 0$$

$$\frac{\partial}{\partial \lambda(x)} = 0: \quad \sum_k \mu_k(x) = 1$$

$$\mu_k(x) = \{D(x,k) \sum_l D^{-1}(x,l)\}^{-1} \qquad (\mu_k(x) \geqq 0).$$

It can be proved, with the arguments used by Diday in [15], that the procedure converges to a local optimum for CR2.

In order to determine the best, or most natural number of fuzzy subsets we propose the following coefficients that provide a measure of how fuzzy a K-partition is $(K > 1)$:

(a)

$$\mathrm{NFI}(K) = \frac{K\left[\sum_{k=1}^{K} \sum_x \mu_k^2(x) \right] - M}{M(K-1)}$$

$$\begin{aligned} \mathrm{NFI} &= 0 \quad \text{iff } \mu_k(x) = 1/K, \qquad \forall x \in E \\ &= 1 \quad \text{iff } \mu_k(x) \in \{0,1\}, \quad \forall x \in E \text{ (hard partition),} \end{aligned}$$

(b)

$$\mathrm{NFIP}(K) = \frac{\sum_{k > k'} \delta(k,k')}{\binom{K}{2}},$$

where $\delta(k,k')$ represents a dissimilarity index of the pair (k,k'):

$$\delta(k,k') = 1 - \frac{\sum_x \mathrm{MIN}\,\{\mu_k(x), \mu_{k'}(x)\}}{\sum_x \mathrm{MAX}\,\{\mu_k(x), \mu_{k'}(x)\}}$$

$$\begin{aligned} \text{NFIP} &= 0 \quad \text{iff } \mu_k(x) = 1/K, \quad \forall k, \forall x \in E \\ &= 1 \quad \text{iff } \mu_k(x) \in \{0, 1\}. \end{aligned}$$

The problem of chosing among partitions is solved by maximizing NFI or NFIP corresponding to a higher number of well determined (high belongingness) points.

5. Numerical experiments

Figs. 1.1–1.6 show several fuzzy classification in an increasing number of clusters using MND2 for data of "nonspherical clusters" type. This was done to appreciate the effect of K on NFI and NFIP.

Figs. 2.1–2.3 indicate the incidence of modifying the density (locally and globally) on the fuzziness of the classification for the same data and the effect on NFI and NFIP.

Figs. 3.1–3.4 show results obtained with MND2 and Dunn's procedure for data of "bridge between two clusters" and "unequal cluster population" types.

Fig. 4 shows the classification obtained with MND2 for the 75 points Ruspini's data [37] when $K=4$. Note that NFI(3)=0.16, NFI(4)=0.66, NFI(5)=0.49.

The lines appearing in the different figures settle boundaries of equal belongingness for each cluster.

From the study of these examples and from the fact that they are representative of some well known typical (or pathological!) cases [39, 50], we can conclude that MND2 associated with the non-fuzzy index NFI is free of the choice of the number of clusters and seems to be a good strategy to segment or structure objects in a fuzzy way which reflects proximity based on some global dissimilarity measure.

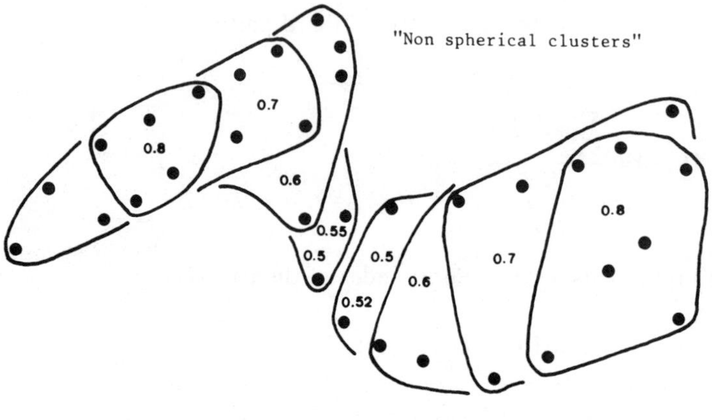

Fig. 1.1. MND2, $K=2$.

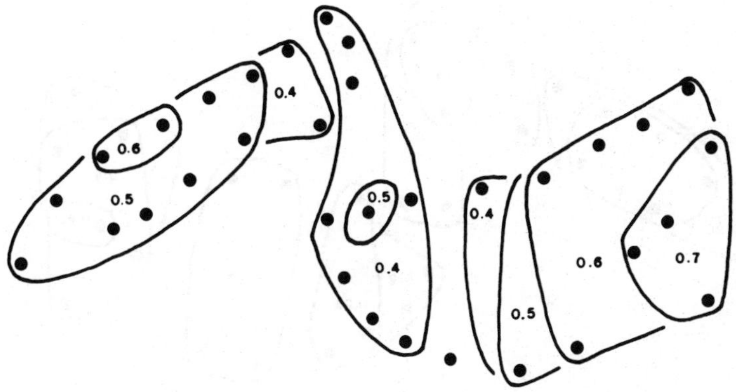

Fig. 1.2. MND2, $K = 3$.

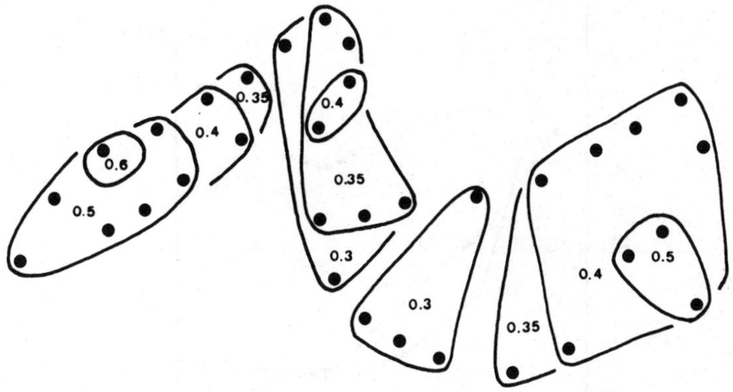

Fig. 1.3. MND2, $K = 4$.

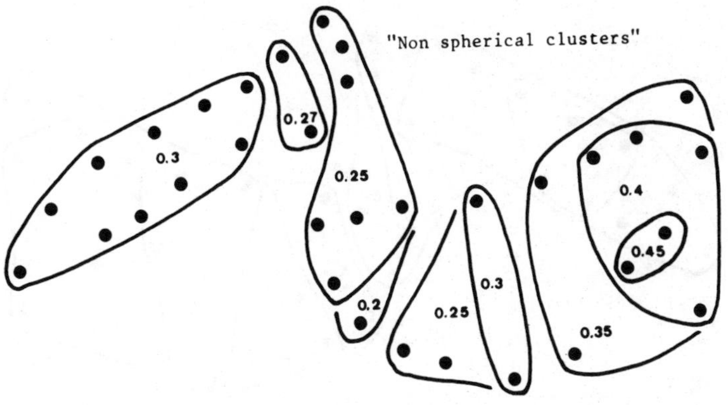

Fig. 1.4. MND2, $K = 5$.

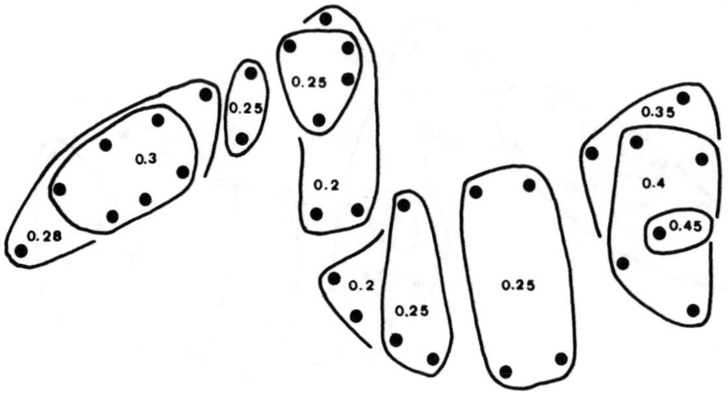

Fig. 1.5. MND2, $K=6$.

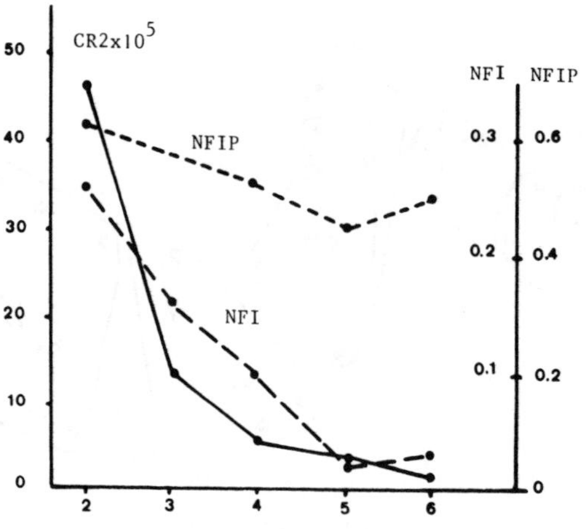

Fig. 1.6. MND2.

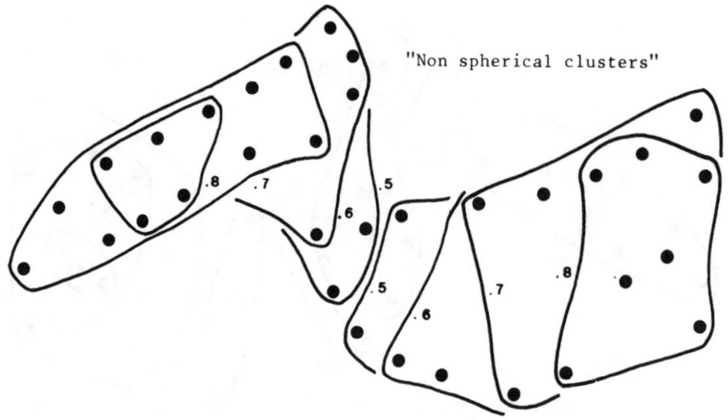

Fig. 2.1. MND2, $K=2$, $N=33$, NFIP $=0.60$, NFI $=0.25$.

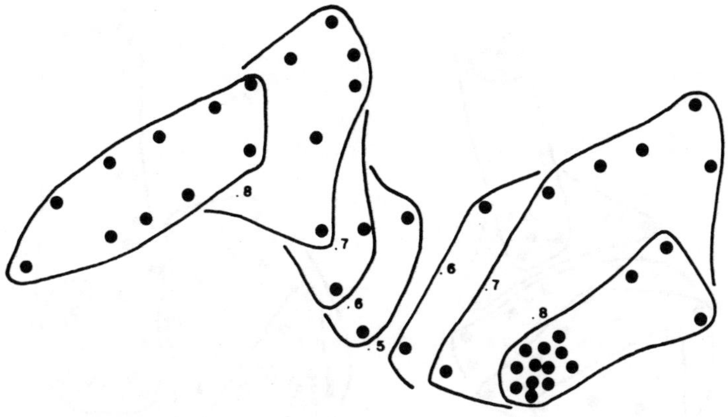

Fig. 2.2. MND2, $K=2$, $N=43$, NFIP = 0.71, NFI = 0.34.

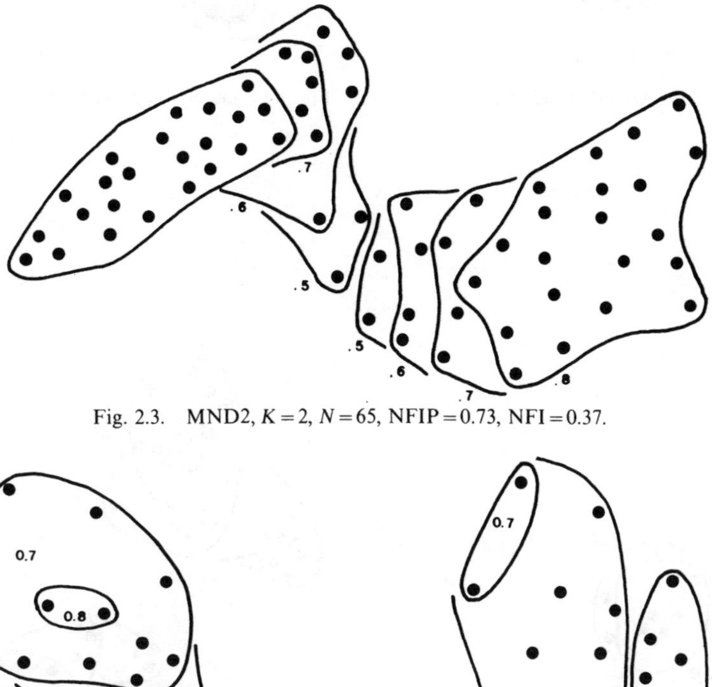

Fig. 2.3. MND2, $K=2$, $N=65$, NFIP = 0.73, NFI = 0.37.

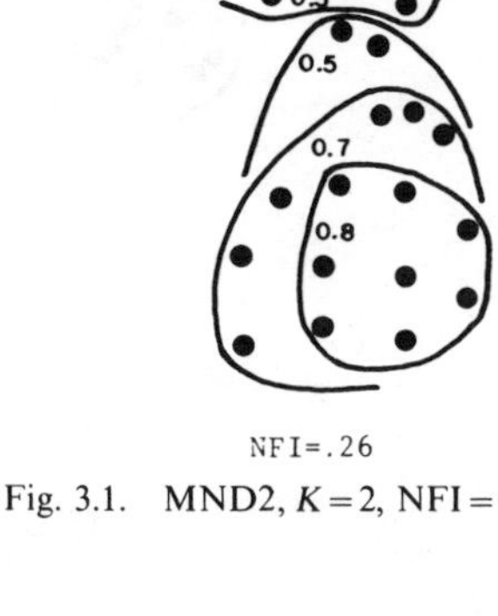

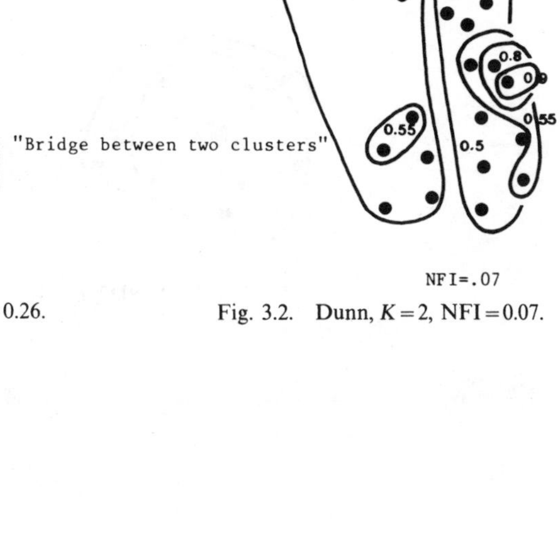

NFI=.26

Fig. 3.1. MND2, $K=2$, NFI = 0.26.

NFI=.07

Fig. 3.2. Dunn, $K=2$, NFI = 0.07.

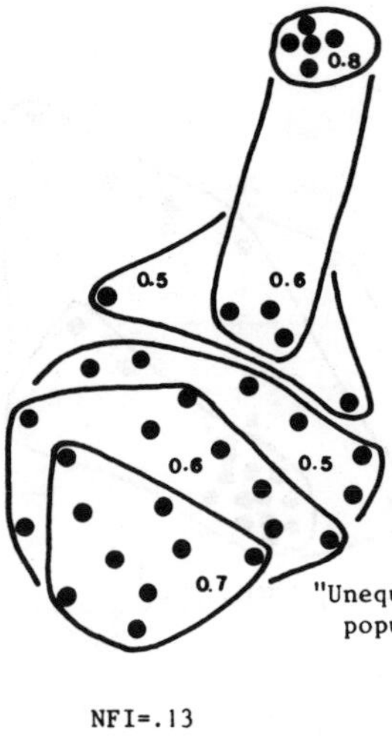

Fig. 3.3. MND2, $K=2$, NF $=0.13$.

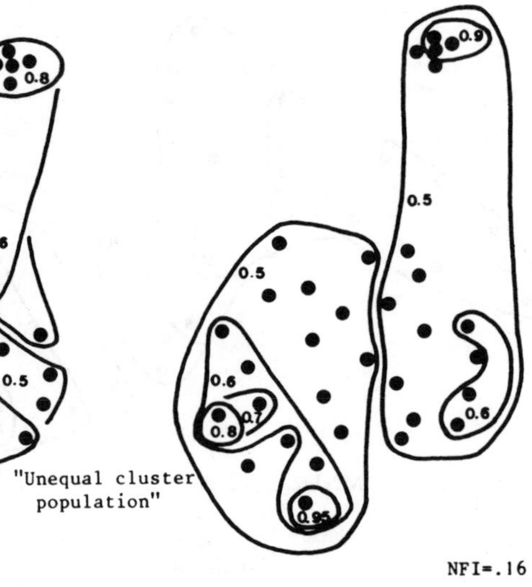

Fig. 3.4. Dunn, $K=2$, NFI $=0.16$.

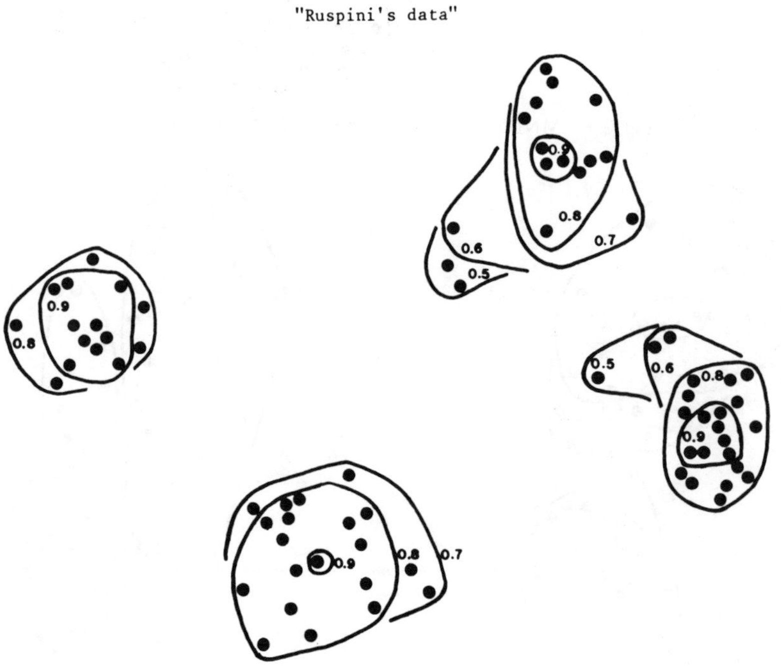

Fig. 4. MND2, $K=4$.

References

[1] G. Ball and D. Hall, A clustering technique for summarizing multivariate data, Behavioral Sci. 12 (1967) 153–155.
[2] R. Bellman, R. Kalaba and L. Zadeh, Abstraction and pattern classification, J. Math. Anal. Appl. 13 (1966) 1–7.
[3] G. Bernard and M. Besson, Douze méthodes d'analyse multicritère, Rev. Française Automat. Informat. Recherche Opérationnelle, 3 (1971) 19–66.
[4] J. Bezdek, Fuzzy mathematics in pattern classification, Ph.D. Thesis, Cornell University, Ithaca, NY (1973).
[5] J. Bezdek, Numerical taxonomy with fuzzy sets, (1974) J. Math. Biol. 1 57–71.
[6] J. Bezdek, Cluster validity with fuzzy sets, J. Cybernet. 3 (1974) 58–73.
[7] J. Bezdek, Mathematical models for systematics and taxonomy, in: G. Estabrook (ed.), Proc. Eighth Int. Conf. on Numerical Taxonomy (Freeman, San Francisco, 1975) 145–166.
[8] J. Bezdek, A physical interpretation of fuzzy ISODATA, IEEE Trans. Syst. Man Cybernet. (May 1976) 387–389.
[9] J. Bezdek, Feature selection for binary data: Medical diagnosis with fuzzy sets in: S. Winkler (ed.). National Computer Conference, AFIPS Proceedings 45 (AFIPS Press, Montvale, NJ, 1976) 1057–1068.
[10] J. Bezdek and P. Castelaz, Prototype classification and feature selection with fuzzy sets, IEEE Trans. Syst. Man Cybernet. (to appear).
[11] J. Bezdek and J. Dunn, Optimal fuzzy partitions: A heuristic for estimating the parameters in a mixture of normal distributions, IEEE Trans. Comput. (August 1975) 835–838.
[12] J. Bezdek and J. Harris, Convex decompositions of fuzzy partitions, Information Sci. (1977).
[13] J. Bezdek and J. Harris, Fuzzy partitions and relations: An axiomatic basis for clustering, J. Math. Anal. Appl. (in review).
[14] M. Delattre and P. Hansen, Bicriterion cluster analysis with a utility function, Proc. 8th IFORS Int. Conf. (to appear).
[15] E. Diday, Classification automatique séquentielle pour grands tableaux, Rev. Française Automat. Informat. Recherche Opérationnelle, (1975) 29–61.
[16] P. Duda and P. Hart, Pattern Classification and Scene Analysis (Wiley, New York, 1973).
[17] J. Dunn, A fuzzy relative of the ISODATA process and its use in detecting compact well-separated clusters, J. Cybernet. 3 (1974) 32–57.
[18] J. Dunn, Well separated clusters and optimal fuzzy partitions, J. Cybernet. 4 (1974) 95–104.
[19] J. Dunn, A graph-theoretic analysis of pattern classification via Tamura's fuzzy relation, IEEE Trans. Syst. Man Cybernet. (April 1974) 310–313.
[20] J. Dunn, Some recent investigations of a new fuzzy partitioning algorithm and its application to pattern classification problems, J. Cybernet. 4 (1974) 1–15.
[21] J. Dunn. Canonical forms of Tamura's fuzzy relation: A scheme for visualizing cluster hierarchies, Proc. Computer Graphics, Pattern Recognition and Data Structure Conf., Beverly Hills (May 1975).
[22] R. Flake and B. Turner, Numerical classification for taxonomic problems, J. Theoret. Biol. 20 (1968) 260–270.
[23] W. Fordon and K.S. Fu, Computer-aided differential diagnosis of hypertension, Technical Report, Electrical Engineering 76–27, Purdue University, Lafayette, IN (August 1976) 110–123.
[24] M. Fortin, Sur un algorithme pour l'analyse des données et la reconnaissance des formes, Rev. Statist. Appli. 23 (1975) 37–45.
[25] I. Gitman and M. Levine, An algorithm for detecting unimodal fuzzy sets and its application as a clustering technique, IEEE Trans. Comput. C (1970) 583–593.
[26] P. Green, R.E. Frank and P. J. Robinson, Cluster analysis in test market selection M. Sci. 13 (1967) 387–400.
[27] J. Hartigan, Clustering Algorithms (Wiley, New York, 1975).
[28] R.E. Jensen, A dynamic programming algorithm for cluster analysis, J.ORSA 17 (1969) 1034–1057.
[29] A. Kandel and L. Yelowitz, Fuzzy chains, IEEE Trans. Syst. Man and Cybernet. S-4 (1974) 472–475.

[30] W.L.G. Koonth, P.M. Narenda and K. Fukunaga, A branch and bound clustering algorithm, IEEE Trans. Comp. C24 (1975) 908–915.
[31] L. Larsen, E. Ruspini, J. McNew, D. Walter and W. Adey, A test of sleep staging systems in the unrestrained chimpanzee, Brain Res. 40 (1972) 319–343.
[32] J. MacQueen, Some methods for classification and analysis of multivariate observations, Proc. 5th Berkeley Symp. Mathematics, Statistics and Probability (1967) 281–297.
[33] D. Matula, Cluster analysis via graph theoretic techniques, Proc. Louisiana Conf. on Combinatorics, Graph-Theory and Computing (1970) 199–212.
[34] A. Rosenfeld, Fuzzy graphs, in L.A. Zadeh et al. (eds.), Fuzzy Sets and their Applications to Cognitive and Decision Processes (Academic Press, New York, 1975).
[35] L. Rossini, F. Martorana and P. Periti, Clustering cholinergic receptors by muscarine and muscarone analogs, Proc. Second Int. Meeting of Medical Advisors in the Pharmaceutical Industry, Firenze, Italy (October 1975).
[36] E. Ruspini, A new approach to fuzzy clustering, Information and Control 15 (1969) 22–32.
[37] E. Ruspini, Numerical methods for fuzzy clustering Information Sci. 2 (1970) 319–350.
[38] E. Ruspini, Optimization in sample descriptions: Data reduction and pattern recognition using fuzzy clustering, IEEE Trans. Syst. Man Cybernet. 2 (1972) 541.
[39 E. Ruspini, New experimental results in fuzzy clustering, Information Sci. 6 (1973) 273–284.
[40] H. Späth, Computational experiences with the exchange method, Europ. J. Opnl. Res. 1 (1977) 23–31.
[41] S. Tamura, S. Higuchi and K. Tanaka, Pattern classification based on fuzzy relations, IEEE Trans. Syst. Man Cybernet. 1 (1971) 61–66.
[42] J. Tou and R. Gonzales, Pattern Recognition Principles (Addison-Wesley, Reading, 1974).
[43] H.D. Vinod, Integer programming and theory of grouping, J. Amer. Stat. Assoc. 64 (1969) 506–519.
[44] W. Wee, On generalizations of adaptive algorithms and applications of the fuzzy sets concept to pattern classification, Ph.D. Thesis, Purdue University, Lafayette, IN (1967).
[45] M. Woodburry and J. Clive, Clinical pure types as a fuzzy partition, J. Cybernet. 4 (1974) 111–121.
[46] M. Woodbury, J. Clive and A. Garson, A generalized ditto algorithm for initial fuzzy clusters, J. Cybernet. (in review).
[47] R. Yeh and S. Bang, Fuzzy relations, fuzzy graphs and their applications to clustering analysis, in: L.A. Zadeh et al. (eds.) Fuzzy Sets and Their Applications to Cognitive and Decision Processes (Academic Press, New York, 1975).
[48] L.A. Zadeh, Fuzzy sets, Information and Control 8 (1965) 338–353.
[49] L.A. Zadeh, Similarity relations and fuzzy orderings, Information Sci. (1971) 177–200.
[50] C. Zahn, Graph theoretical methods for detecting and describing gestalt clusters, IEEE Trans. Comput. 20 (1971) 68–86.

FUZZY CLUSTERING WITH A FUZZY COVARIANCE MATRIX

Donald E. Gustafson and William C. Kessel
Scientific Systems, Inc.
186 Alewife Brook Parkway
Cambridge, Massachusetts 02138

Abstract

A class of fuzzy ISODATA clustering algorithms has been developed previously which includes fuzzy means. This class of algorithms is generalized to include fuzzy covariances. The resulting algorithm closely resembles maximum likelihood estimation of mixture densities. It is argued that use of fuzzy covariances is a natural approach to fuzzy clustering. Experimental results are presented which indicate that more accurate clustering may be obtained by using fuzzy covariances.

1. Introduction

The notion of fuzzy sets, first put forth by Zadeh [1], is an attempt to modify the basic conception of a space--that is, the set on which the given problem is defined. By introducing the concept of a fuzzy--i.e., an unsharply defined set, a different perspective is provided for certain problems in systems analysis, including pattern recognition.

One of the significant difficulties in development of a systematic approach to pattern recognition is that the phenomena of interest are modeled by equations which contain functions and operators which may appear simple and natural, but which yield some solutions which could be regarded as pathological. The difficulty stems from our desire to differentiate between classes in a manner which is simple and easy to visualize. In doing so, we restrict the solutions in an unknown way. The use of fuzzy sets is an attempt to ameliorate this problem.

Pattern classification problems have provided impetus for the development of fuzzy set theory. Recently, fuzzy sets have provided a theoretical basis for cluster analysis with the introduction of fuzzy clustering. The use of fuzzy sets in clustering was first proposed in [2] and several classification schemes were developed [3]. The first fuzzy clustering algorithm was developed in 1969 by Ruspini [4], and used by several workers [5]. Following this, Dunn [6] developed the first fuzzy extension of the least-squares approach to clustering and this was generalized by Bezdek [7] to an infinite family of algorithms.

Several problems in medical diagnosis have been attacked using fuzzy clustering algorithms. Adey [8] achieved promising results in interpreting EEG patterns in cerebral systems. Bezdek [9] has studied its use in differentiating hiatal hernia and gallstones. It appears that medical diagnosis may be an especially fruitful area of application for fuzzy clustering, since biological systems are extremely complex and the boundaries between "distinct" medical diagnostic classes are not sharply defined. This has been suggested for cardiovascular investigations [10].

In a "hard" clustering algorithm, each pattern vector must be assigned to a single cluster. This "all or none" membership restriction is not a realistic one, since many pattern vectors may have the characteristics of several classes. It is more natural to assign to each pattern vector a set of memberships, one for each class. The implication of this is that the class boundaries are not "hard" but rather are "fuzzy". Another problem is that the set of all partitions resulting from a "hard" clustering algorithm is extremely large, making an exhaustive search extremely complicated and expensive. Fuzzy clustering will generally lead to more computational tractability [11]. Another advantage of fuzzy clustering is that troublesome or outlying members of the data set are more easily recognized than with hard clustering, since the degree of membership is continuous rather than "all-or-none." Bezdek and Dunn [12] have noted the relationship of fuzzy clustering to estimating mixture distributions, but retained the Euclidean metric. Here, a generalization to a metric which appears more natural is made, through the use of a fuzzy covariance matrix.

2. Problem Formulation

The definition of a fuzzy partition used here agrees with that of Ruspini [4], Dunn [6] and Bezdek [13] and is a natural extension of the conventional partitioning definition. An ordinary, or "hard" partition is a k-tuple of Boolean functions $w(\cdot) = \{w_1, w_2, \ldots, w_k\}$ on the feature space $\Gamma \subset R^n$ which satisfy

$$w_j(x) = 0 \text{ or } 1,\ \forall\, x \in \Gamma,\ 1 \leq j \leq k \qquad (1)$$

$$\sum_{j=1}^{k} w_j(x) = 1 \quad \forall\, x \in \Gamma \qquad (2)$$

If Γ_j represents the j-th class, with $\Gamma_i \cap \Gamma_j = \Phi\ \forall\, i \neq j$ and $\cup_{j=1}^{k} \Gamma_j = \Gamma$, then $w_m(x) = 1$ means that $x \in \Gamma_m$ and (2) insures that x is a member of

Reprinted from *Proc. IEEE CDC*, San Diego, CA, pp. 761-766, Jan. 10-12, 1979.

precisely one class. It is possible to pass from this definition to a corresponding fuzzy partition by retaining (2) but replacing (1) with the relaxed condition $0 \leq w_j \leq 1$. Thus, a fuzzy partition is a k-tuple of membership functions $w(\cdot) = \{w_1(x), w_2(x), \ldots, w_k(x)\}$ which satisfy

$$0 \leq w_j(x) \leq 1, \ \forall x \epsilon \Gamma, \ 1 \leq j \leq k \tag{3}$$

$$\sum_{j=1}^{k} w_j(x) = 1, \ \ \forall x \in \Gamma \tag{4}$$

Equation (3) suggests a probabilistic interpretation for the membership functions, as discussed by Ruspini [4]. However, this may or may not be a correct interpretation.

In devising a conventional clustering algorithm, one typically looks for a scalar performance index which attains its minimum for a partition which maximally separates the naturally-occurring clusters. There should exist a feasible algorithm for minimizing the performance index. The weighted within-class squared error is a useful performance measure.

Denote the distance from a point x to the j-th class by $d_j(x) = d(x,\theta_j)$; $d_j(x) > 0$, where the j-th class is parametrized by θ_j. For an indexed set of samples $x_1, x_2, x_3, \ldots, x_N$ we denote the distance measure and membership function by $d_j(x_i) = d_{ij}$, $w_j(x_i) = w_{ij}$. We are interested in minimizing the following cost:

$$J(w,\theta) = \sum_{i=1}^{N} \sum_{j=1}^{k} w_{ij}^{\alpha} d_{ij} \ ; \ \alpha \geq 1 \tag{5}$$

where $\theta = \{\theta_j\}$, $w = \{w_{ij}\}$, k is the number of classes, and α is a smoothing parameter which controls the "fuzziness" of the clusters. For $\alpha = 1$, the clusters are separated by hard partitions and $w_{ij} = 0$ or 1. As α increases, the partitions become more fuzzy.

3. Determination of Fuzzy Clusters

3.1 Determination of Optimal Membership Functions

Now consider the problem of minimizing J with respect to (fuzzy)w, subject to $\alpha>1$ and the constraints (3) and (4). We defer for later the determination of the optimal parameters by minimizing J over θ. Constraint (3) may be eliminated by setting $w_{ij} = S_{ij}^2$ with S_{ij} real. We adjoin the constraints (3) and (4) to J with a set of Lagrange multipliers $\{\lambda_i\}$ to give

$$\bar{J}(S,\theta,\lambda) = \sum_{i=1}^{N} \sum_{j=1}^{k} S_{ij}^{2\alpha} d_{ij} + \sum_{i=1}^{N} \lambda_i \left(\sum_{j=1}^{k} S_{ij}^{2} - 1 \right) \tag{6}$$

The first-order necessary conditions for optimality are found by setting the gradients of $\bar{J}$ with respect to S to zero. Now,

$$\frac{\partial \bar{J}}{\partial S_{ij}} = 2\alpha \, S_{ij}^{2\alpha-1} d_{ij} + 2S_{ij} \lambda_i \tag{7}$$

By setting $\frac{\partial \bar{J}}{\partial S}$ to zero we obtain the following first-order necessary conditions:

$$S^*_{ij} (\alpha S^{*\,2(\alpha-1)}_{ij} d_{ij} + \lambda^*_i) = 0; \ \forall \ i,j \tag{8}$$

$$\sum_{j=1}^{k} S^{*\,2}_{ij} = 1 \qquad ; \ \forall \ i \tag{9}$$

where the asterik denotes association with optimality.

Equations (8) - (9) comprise a set of NK + N equations which can be solved for the Nk + N unknowns $W^* = \{w_{ij}^*\}$, and $\lambda^* = \{\lambda^*_i\}$. We proceed by first assuming that $S^*_{ij} \neq 0 \ \forall i, j$. This is consistent with the assumption that $\alpha>1$. With this assumption we have

$$w^*_{ij} = (-\lambda^*_i / \alpha d_{ij})^{1/(\alpha-1)} \tag{10}$$

By summing over j and using (4)

$$(-\lambda^*_i)^{\frac{1}{\alpha-1}} = \frac{1}{\sum_{j=1}^{k} \left(\frac{1}{\alpha d_{ij}}\right)^{1/(\alpha-1)}} \tag{11}$$

and (10) becomes

$$w^*_{ij} = \frac{1}{\sum_{\ell=1}^{k} (d_{ij}/d_{i\ell})^{1/(\alpha-1)}} \tag{12}$$

Then, from (5), <u>for any θ</u>, the associated extremum of $J(w,\theta)$ is

$$J^*(\theta) = \min_{w} J(w,\theta)$$

$$= \sum_{i=1}^{N} \left[\sum_{j=1}^{k} (d_{ij})^{1/(1-\alpha)} \right]^{1-\alpha} \tag{13}$$

<u>Limiting Case When $\alpha \to 1$</u>

If $\alpha \to 1$,

$$J \to \sum_{i=1}^{N} \sum_{j=1}^{k} w_{ij} \, d_{ij} \tag{14}$$

and the argument given by Dunn [6] will establish that $\forall$ i,k

$$w^*_{ik} \to \begin{cases} 1; \ d_{ik} = \min_{j} (d_{jk}) \\ 0; \ \text{otherwise} \end{cases} \tag{15}$$

provided $\min_j(d_{jk})$ is unique $\forall$k. Otherwise, W* is a hard k-partition which is unique up to arrangements caused by tie-breaking rules.

3.2 Determination of Optimal Parameters

We now turn to the problem of finding the optimal parameter set $\theta^* = \{\theta^*_1, \theta^*_2, \ldots, \theta^*_k\}$. From (5) we have

$$\frac{\partial}{\partial \theta_j} \bar{J}(w,\theta,\lambda) = \sum_{i=1}^{N} w_{ij}^{\alpha} \frac{\partial}{\partial \theta j} d_{ij} \tag{16}$$

The first-order necessary conditions for a local minimum of J are (8), (9) and

$$\sum_{i=1}^{N} w^{*\,\alpha}_{ij} \frac{\partial}{\partial \theta j} d_{ij} \Big|_{*} = 0 \ \forall j \tag{17}$$

To proceed we need to specify the parametrization of d_{ij}.

<u>Fuzzy ISODATA</u>. Let $d_{ij} = (x_i-\theta_j)^T A (x_i-\theta_j)$; $A>0$ (18)

Then (17) gives

$$\sum_{i=1}^{N} w^{*\,\alpha}_{ij} (x_i - \theta^*_j) = 0 \ \forall j \tag{19}$$

This is equivalent to

$$\theta_j^* = \frac{\sum_{i=1}^{N} w_{ij}^{*\,\alpha} x_i}{\sum_{i=1}^{N} w_{ij}^{*\,\alpha}} \triangleq m_{fj};\ k=1,\ldots,k \quad (20)$$

We will call m_{fj} the <u>fuzzy mean</u> of class j in recognition of its limiting property under hard partitioning. This case comprises fuzzy ISODATA [14].

<u>Hard ISODATA</u>. As $\alpha\to 1$ and the partitioning becomes hard:

$$w_{ij}^{*\,\alpha} \begin{cases} 1 \ ; \ j=m \\ 0 \ ; \ j\neq m \end{cases} \quad (21)$$

where

$$d_{im} = \min_j d_{ij} \quad (22)$$

That is, under the one-nearest-neighbor rule, $w_{ij}^{*\,\alpha}\big|_{\alpha=1} = 1$ for all pattern vectors x_i assigned to class j and is zero otherwise. Thus, for hard partitioning

$$\sum_{i=1}^{N} w_{ij}^* = N_j \quad (23)$$

where N_j is the number of pattern vectors assigned to Γ_j and

$$\theta_j^*\Big|_{\alpha\to 1} \to \frac{1}{N_j} \sum_{x_i\in\Gamma_j} x_i = \hat{m}_j \quad (24)$$

where $\hat{m}_j$ is the sample mean of Γ_j. This is the hard k-means algorithm: it constitutes the basic idea underlying hard ISODATA [15].

3.3 <u>Generalization to Include Fuzzy Covariance</u>

Now consider replacing (18) by an inner product induced norm metric of the form

$$d_{ij}(\theta_j) = (x_i - v_j)^T M_j (x_i - v_j),\ 1\le j\le k \quad (25)$$

with M_j symmetric and positive-definite. If $\theta_j = v_j$, equation (20) for θ_j^* still holds [14]. If, however, we take $\theta_j = \{v_j, M_j\}$, a class of algorithms more general than fuzzy ISODATA will ensue. Note that J is now linear in M_j, giving a singular problem. The cost J may be made as small as desired by simply making M_j less positive definite. To get a feasible solution, we must constrain M_j in some manner. Ideally we would like the metric to handle different scalings along each direction in feature space. That is, we would like to allow variations in the shape of each class induced by the metric but not let the metric grow without bound. A way of accomplishing this by using only one parameter is to constrain the determinant $|M_j|$ of the matrix M_j. This induces a volume constraint.

Consider the set of constraints

$$|M_j| = \rho_j \ ,\ \rho_j > 0 \quad (26)$$

with ρ_j fixed for each j. The augmented cost is now

$$J(w,\theta,\lambda,\beta) = \sum_{i=1}^{N}\sum_{j=1}^{k} w_{ij}^{\alpha} d_{ij}(\theta_j) + \sum_{i=1}^{N} \lambda_i \left(\sum_{j=1}^{k} w_{ij} - 1\right) + \sum_{j=1}^{k} \beta_j \left(|M_j| - \rho_j\right) \quad (27)$$

where $\{\beta_j\}$ is a set of Lagrange multipliers.

The partial derivatives with respect to θ_j now change. From (27), the necessary conditions are

$$\frac{\partial J}{\partial v_j}\Big|_* = -2\sum_{i=1}^{N} w_{ij}^{\alpha} M_j (x_i - v_j^*) = 0\ ;\ j=1,2,\ldots,k \quad (28)$$

which is identical to (19) and

$$\frac{\partial J}{\partial M_j}\Big|_* = 0 = \sum_{i=1}^{N} w_{ij}^{\alpha} (x_i - v_j)(x_i - v_j)^T + \beta_j |M_j^*| M_j^{*-1} \quad (29)$$

To get (29), we have used the identities

$$\frac{\partial}{\partial A}(x^T A x) = x x^T \ ,\ \frac{\partial}{\partial A}|A| = |A| A^{-1}$$

which hold for a non-singular matrix A and any compatible vector x. Eq. (28) gives (20) again:

$$v_j^* = \frac{\sum_{i=1}^{N} w_{ij}^{\alpha} x_i}{\sum_{i=1}^{N} w_{ij}^{\alpha}} \quad (30)$$

For the optimal membership functions ($w_{ij} = w_{ij}^*$), v_j^* is the fuzzy mean of Γ_j. Eq. (29) gives, for $v_j = v_j^*$,

$$M_j^{*-1} = \frac{1}{\beta_j |M_j^*|} \sum_{i=1}^{N} w_{ij}^{\alpha} (x_i - v_j^*)(x_i - v_j^*)^T \quad (31)$$

Now define the <u>fuzzy covariance</u> matrix for Γ_j by

$$P_{fj} = \frac{\sum_{i=1}^{N} w_{ij}^{\alpha} (x_i - m_{fj})(x_i - m_{fj})^T}{\sum_{i=1}^{N} w_{ij}^{\alpha}} \ ;\ \alpha > 1 \quad (32)$$

Then, using (32) and (26) in (31) gives

$$M_j^{*-1} = \left(\frac{1}{\rho_j |P_{fj}|}\right)^{1/n} P_{fj} \quad (33)$$

where n is the feature space dimension. In the sequel, a <u>hard covariance</u> matrix refers to P_{fj} of (32) evaluated at α=1. In view of (21), a <u>hard covariance</u> matrix is simply the sample class covariance matrix under the cluster assignment rule (22).

The previous discussion suggests the following iterative algorithm for finding stationary points of $J(w,\theta)$. Given data $\{x_i\}$ and an initial guess $\theta_j^{(o)} = \{m_{fj}^{(o)}, P_{fj}^{(o)}\}$, we proceed as follows:

for k=1,2,... :

(i) compute $\{d_i(\theta_j^{(k)})\}$ using (25).

(ii) compute $\{w_{ij}^{(k)}\}$ using (12). If d_{ik}=0 for some k, set w_{ik}=1, $w_{i\ell}$=0 $\forall \ell\neq k$.

(iii) compute new estimates $\theta_j^{(k+1)}$ using (30), (32) and (33). Recycle to (i) until a specified convergence criterion is satisfied.

4. Relation to Maximum Likelihood Estimation

There is an intimate relationship between fuzzy ISODATA algorithms and maximum likelihood algorithms designed to estimate mixture density parameters under the Gaussian assumption. Maximum likelihood estimation of parameters has been studied for a long time (see, e.g., Rao, 1952[16]), and the theory is quite well understood. The problem in applications is developing numerical techniques which can efficiently solve, or approximately solve, the problem. The development here follows the work of Wolfe [17].

Let $p(x|\Gamma_j)$ be the probability density for the random vector $x \epsilon R^n$, conditioned on x being a member of the j-th class $(x \epsilon \Gamma_j)$, and let P_j be the a priori probability associated with Γ_j. We assume that Γ_j is parametrized by a set of parameters $\theta_j \epsilon R^s$ and that $p(x|\Gamma_j)$ is a twice differentiable function of θ_j. Since x can be associated with more than one class, it has a mixture density function which is, for k classes,

$$p(x) = \sum_{j=1}^{k} P_j p(x,\theta_j) \ , \ \sum_{j=1}^{k} P_j = 1 \qquad (34)$$

where $p(x,\theta_j) = p(x|\Gamma_j)$. The "probability of membership" of x in class j can be found by using Bayes' Rule:

$$p(\Gamma_j|x) = \frac{P_j p(x,\theta_j)}{p(x)} \qquad (35)$$

Now suppose a sample of N random vectors is drawn from the mixture and denote these by $x_1, x_2, x_3, \ldots x_N$. Then, assuming independent sampling, the log probability is $\log p(x_1,x_2,\ldots,x_N) = \sum_{i=1}^{N} \log p(x_i)$. The maximum likelihood estimate of the parameters $\theta = \theta_1, \theta_2, \ldots, \theta_k$ is found by solving $\max_{\theta}[\log p(x_1,x_2,\ldots,x_N)]$ subject to the constraint in (34). The first order necessary conditions are

$$P_j^* = \frac{1}{N} \sum_{i=1}^{N} p^*(\Gamma_j|x_i) \qquad (36)$$

$$\sum_{i=1}^{N} p^*(\Gamma_j|x_i) \frac{\partial}{\partial \theta_j} \log p^*(x_i,\theta_j^*) = 0 \qquad (37)$$

Now consider the special case where x is conditionally Gaussian distrubuted. Then

$$\log p(x,\theta_j) = -\frac{n}{2}\log 2\pi + \tfrac{1}{2}\log|E_j^{-1}| - \tfrac{1}{2}(x-m_j)^T E_j^{-1}(x-m_j) \qquad (38)$$

where $\theta_j = \{m_j, E_j\}$ and E_j is assumed nonsingular. Taking the indicated partial derivatives in (37), we obtain the following three equations which describe the necessary conditions to be satisfied for the maximum likelihood estimates

$$m_j^* = \frac{1}{NP_j^*} \sum_{i=1}^{N} p(x_i,\theta_j^*)x_i \ , \ P_j^* = \frac{1}{N} \sum_{i=1}^{N} p(x_i,\theta_j^*) \qquad (39)$$

$$E_j^* = \frac{1}{NP_j^*} \sum_{i=1}^{N} p(x_i,\theta_j^*)(x_i - m_j^*)(x_i - m_j^*)^T \qquad (40)$$

The first order necessary conditions for fuzzy clustering and maximum likelihood estimation possess similarities which can be studied by imbedding both solutions in a larger class of solutions. Consider the following set of algebraic relations:

$$Q_j = \frac{1}{N} \sum_{i=1}^{N} q_{ij} \ , \ \eta_j = \frac{1}{NQ_j} \sum_{i=1}^{N} q_{ij} x_i \ ; \ 0 \le q_{ij} \le 1$$

$$M_j = \frac{\gamma_j}{NQ_j} \sum_{i=1}^{N} q_{ij} r_{ij} r_{ij}^T \ , \ r_{ij} = x_i - \eta_j \text{ with } x_i \epsilon R^n,$$

$\eta_j \epsilon R^n$, N a positive integer, and γ_j a positive scalar. The parameter q_{ij} is the membership function of x_i relative to class j and Q_j is the average membership for class j. Thus, q_{ij} increases as x_i comes closer to class j and relatively large values of Q_j are associated with the largest or most dense classes. The parameter η_j can be regarded as the nucleus point of class j and M_j is a matrix which describes the shape and size of the class. The parameter r_{ij} is the vector from x_i to the class j nucleus. The parameters r_{ij}, M_j are combined into a measure d_{ij} which is used to evaluate the distance x_i to class j: $d_{ij} = r_{ij}^T M_j^{-1} r_{ij}$

The values of q_{ij} and the associated constraints for fuzzy clustering and maximum likelihood estimation are summarized in Table 1. The parameter D_i is a normalization constant for x_i and C_j is a normalization constant for Γ_j. Note that q_{ij} decreases monotonically with increasing d_{ij} for both cases. It is also interesting to note that membership functions are normalized differently. With fuzzy clustering, normalization is done over the classes to get D_i, whereas normalization under maximum likelihood estimation is done over the whole space R^n to obtain C_j. Thus, q_{ij} is given a slightly different interpretation in the two methods. The constraints are quite different: a class volume constraint is used under fuzzy clustering whereas a total probability constraint is used under maximum likelihood estimation.

Even with these differences, there is a striking similarity between the two methods. Note in particular that the fuzzy covariance matrix appears naturally in the problem and appears to be more appropriate than a hard covariance matrix.

We now consider how to build a classifier using the q_{ij}'s from either maximum likelihood or fuzzy ISODATA. The decision rule by which x_i is assigned to a class is as follows:

Assign x_i to class m if $q_{im} \ge q_{ij}$; $j=1,2,\ldots,k$

In case of ties, assign x_i to the least-numbered class.

5. Fuzzy Clustering Experiments

The fuzzy clustering algorithm has been implemented and tested using two stylized classes which had some degree of overlap. The two classes are depicted in Figure 1 and consist of two long and narrow regions at right angles to one another in a cross pattern. The two cluster centroids coincide exactly so that the discrimination must be based on cluster shape information. In order to test the algorithms, a total of ten points in each class were chosen randomly, using a uniform distribution over each class. These points are depicted in Figure 1, with points labeled x selected from Class 1 and points labeled o selected from Class 2. All tests were run assuming two classes apriori. Updating of the covariance matrices was done using either: (a) full updating (use (32) directly in (25)), (b) no updating (use initial guess at all steps, (c) $|M_j|$ = constant (i.e., invoke (26)). The iterations were stopped when the change in each membership function was less than 0.001 in magnitude.

A test was run using hard ISODATA (α=1,A=I) seeded with the sample means. The resulting assignments are shown in Figure 2 and are poor since class shape is not accounted for. The algorithm converged after only two passes. The next test used fuzzy IDODATA, in which the means were fuzzy but A=I. The resulting clusters are shown in Figure 3 and are considerably different from the desired result.

Cluster 1 is very large and Cluster 2 is very small, encompassing only three peripheral points of Class 1. Convergence was obtained in 4 passes.

A test was next run using fuzzy clustering with $\alpha=2$ and using fuzzy covariance matrices, with initial guesses $M_{f1}^{(o)} = M_{f2}^{(o)} = I$. The clusters were seeded at the sample class means. The class assignments are shown in Figure 5 and are seen to be correct for all points, although the results for #5 and #11 would appear fortuitous. The difficulty in classifying these two points is apparent from the values of their membership functions. Thirteen passes were required to meet the convergence criterion.

The next run was similar to the previous run except that the cluster seeds were set at $S_1=(0.001, 0)$, $S_2=(0,0)$ which were used in the fuzzy ISODATA run, in order to make the discrimination more difficult. The discrimination was, in fact, more difficult. However, after 20 passes, the algorithm did converge to the configuration of Figure 6. As before, all of the assignments were correct. However, the way in which the clusters were formed was quite interesting. The histories of the membership functions for several critical points are given in Table 2 and demonstrate the nature of the iterative process. Note that $w_{3,1}$, $w_{4,1}$, $w_{10,1}$, $w_{13,2}$, and $w_{19,2}$ increase monotonically and approach a value of unity. This is the desired behavior and is expected for points which lie much closer to one class than the other. Note that the response of $w_{13,2}$ is relatively slow, staying close to 0.5 until the 15th pass and then increasing monotonically. Thus, for the first 14 passes point #13 is about equally distant from both clusters. Point #11 is strongly associated with Cluster 1 on the 11th through 15th passes. However, once point #10 is correctly assigned to Cluster 1, $w_{11,2}$ increases monotonically to its final value. Note that points #5 and #11 are both strongly associated with Cluster 1 from the 11th through 15th pass, indicating that Cluster 2 does not start to form correctly until the 16th pass.

The effect of using a fuzzy covariance matrix was studied by running a case differing from the previous one only in the way the covariance matrix was calculated. A hard covariance matrix was used instead of a fuzzy one. The solution is shown in Figure 8 and was obtained after eight passes. Note that points #4 and #11 are incorrectly classified. The failure to correctly assign #11 is hardly surprising but the misassignment of #4 is judged to be a clustering error. This result suggests that the use of fuzzy covariances can enhance clustering performance. Further numerical testing is required to verify this behavior in general.

It is interesting to note that the configuration of Figure 8 is relatively insensitive to the distance measure used. A run was made in which the distance measure $1 - \exp(-d_{ij}/2)$ was used rather than d_{ij} and the same cluster assignments were obtained. It should also be noted that no problems of convergence were encountered in any runs.

REFERENCES

1. L.A. Zadeh, "Fuzzy Sets", Information and Control, Vol. 8, pp. 338-353, 1965.
2. R.E. Bellman, R.A. Kalaba and L.A. Zadeh, "Abstraction and Pattern Classification", J. Math. Anal. Appl., Vol. 13, pp. 1-7, 1966.
3. I. Gitman and M. Levine, "An Algorithm for Detecting Unimodal Fuzzy Sets and Its Application as a Clustering Technique", IEEE Trans. Computers, Vol. C-19, pp. 917-923, 1970.
4. E.H. Ruspini, "A New Approach to Clustering", Information and Control, Vol.15, pp.22-32, 1969.
5. L. Larsen, E. Ruspini, J. McDew, D. Walter and W. Adey, "A Test of Sleep Staging Systems in the Unrestrained Chimpanzee", Brain Research, Vol. 40, pp. 319-343, 1972.
6. J. Dunn, "A Fuzzy Relative of the ISODATA Process and Its Use in Detecting Compact Well-Separated Clusters", J. Cybernetics, Vol. 3, pp. 32-57, 1974.
7. J. Bezdek, "Fuzzy Mathematics in Pattern Classification", Ph.D. Thesis, Cornell University, Ithaca, New York, 1973.
8. W. Adey, "Organization of Brain Tissue: Is the Brain a Noisy Processor?", Int. J. Neuroscience, Vol. 3, pp. 271-284, 1972.
9. J.C. Bezdek, "Feature Selection for Binary Data-Medical Diagnosis with Fuzzy Sets", National Computer Conference, 1976.
10. D. Kalmanson, H.F. Stegall, "Cardiovascular Investigations and Fuzzy Sets Theory", Amer. J. of Cardiology, Vol. 35, pp. 30-34, 1975.
11. J. Bezdek, "Cluster Validity with Fuzzy Sets", J. Cybernetics, Vol. 3, pp. 58-73, 1974.
12. J.C. Bezdek and J.C. Dunn, "Optimal Fuzzy Partitions: A Heuristic for Estimating the Parameters in a Mixture of Normal Distributions", IEEE Trans. Comp. Vol C-24, pp. 835-838, 1975.
13. J.C. Bezdek, "Numerical Taxonomy with Fuzzy Sets", J. Math. Biology, Vol. 1, pp.57-71, 1974.
14. J.C. Bezdek and P.F. Castelaz, "Prototype Classification and Feature Selection with Fuzzy Sets", IEEE Trans. on Systems, Man and Cybernetics, Vol. SMC-7, No. 2, February, 1971, pp. 87-92.
15. G.H. Ball, "Classification Analysis", Stanford Res. Inst. Rept. AD-716-482, November, 1970.
16. C.R. Rao, Advanced Statistical Methods in Biometric Research, New York: Wiley and Sons, 1952.
17. J.H. Wolfe, "Pattern Clustering by Multivariate Mixture Analysis", Multivariable Behavioral Research, July, 1970, pp. 329-350.

Fuzzy Clustering	parameter or condition	Maximum Likelihood
w_{ij}^{α} $(\alpha \geq 1)$	$q_{ij}=q_j(x_i)$	P_{ij}
$w_{ij}=d_{ij}^{1/(1-\alpha)}/D_i$		$P_{ij}=C_j \exp[-d_{ij}/2]$
$\sum_{j=1}^{k} w_{ij}=1 \Rightarrow D_i \ \forall i$	normalization	$\int_{X \in R^n} p(x)dx=1 \Rightarrow C_j \ \forall j$
$\|M_j\|=\rho_j \Rightarrow \gamma_j$	constraints	$\sum_{j=1}^{k} Q_j=1$

Table 1 Comparison of Fuzzy Clustering and Maximum Likelihood Solutions

Pass	$w_{3,1}$	$w_{4,1}$	$w_{5,1}$	$w_{10,1}$	$w_{11,2}$	$w_{13,2}$	$w_{14,2}$	$w_{19,2}$
1	.5001	.5004	.5015	.5001	.4993	.5000	.5000	.5000
7	.5029	.5001	.5153	.5002	.4907	.4996	.5119	.5022
10	.5218	.5495	.7047	.5085	.3676	.4934	.6599	.5341
15	.8690	.9574	.8664	.8757	.0104	.6992	.9353	.9373
17	.9905	.9521	.7921	.9899	.2424	.9680	.9808	.9905
18	.9972	.9509	.6850	.9968	.6268	.9911	.9794	.9965
20	.9988	.9606	.6836	.9985	.7403	.9949	.9715	.9975

Table 2 Membership Function Histories for Case Shown in Figure 5.

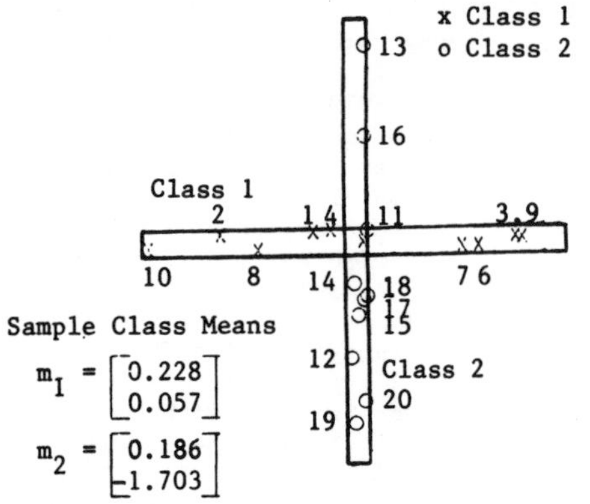

Figure 1: Two-Class Configuration

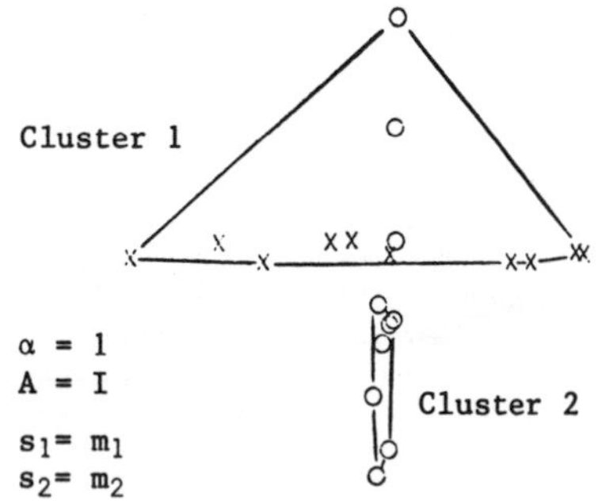

Figure 2: Cluster Assignments Using Hard ISODATA Seeded With Class Sample Means

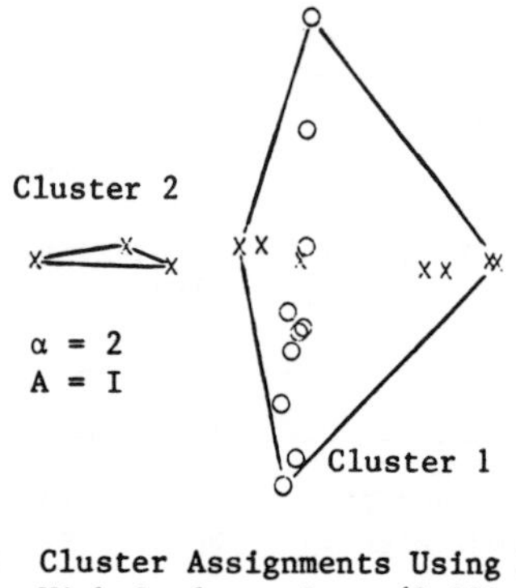

Figure 3: Cluster Assignments Using Fuzzy ISODATA With Seeds $S_1 = (0.001,0)$, $S_2 = (0,0)$

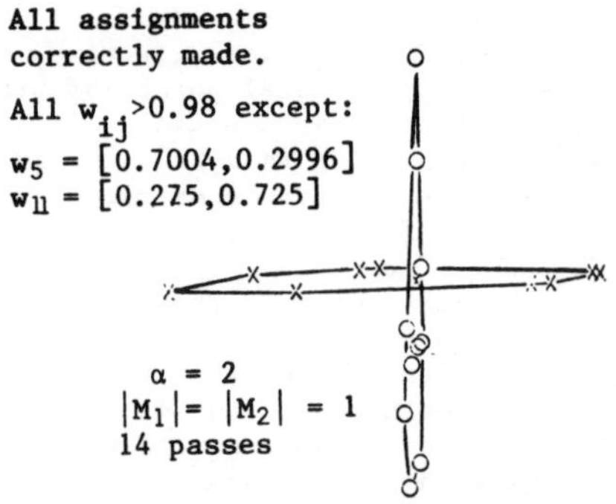

Figure 4: Cluster Assignments Using Fuzzy Covariance Seeded at Class Means

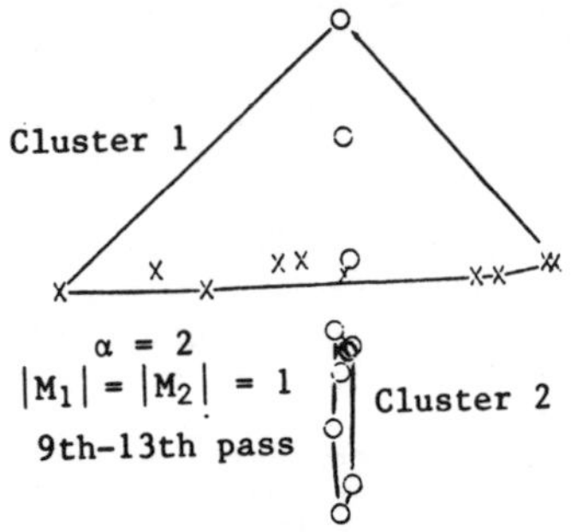

Figure 5(a): Cluster Assignments Using Fuzzy Covariance With Seeds $S_1 = (0.002,0)$, $S_2 = (0,0)$

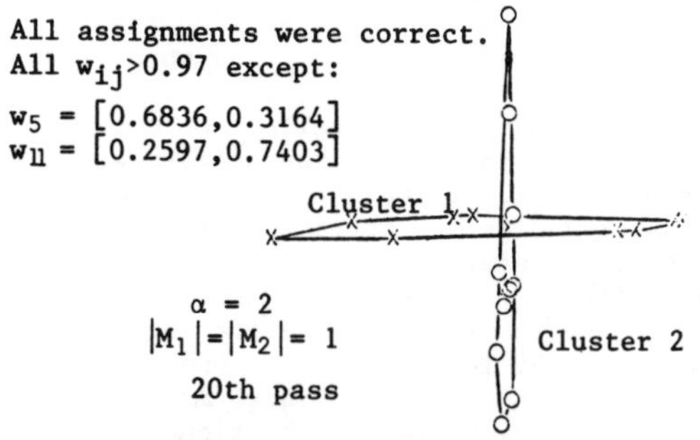

Figure 5(b): Cluster Assignments Using Fuzzy Covariances With Seeds $S_1 = (0.001,0)$, $S_2 = (0,0)$ After Convergence

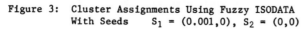

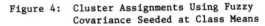

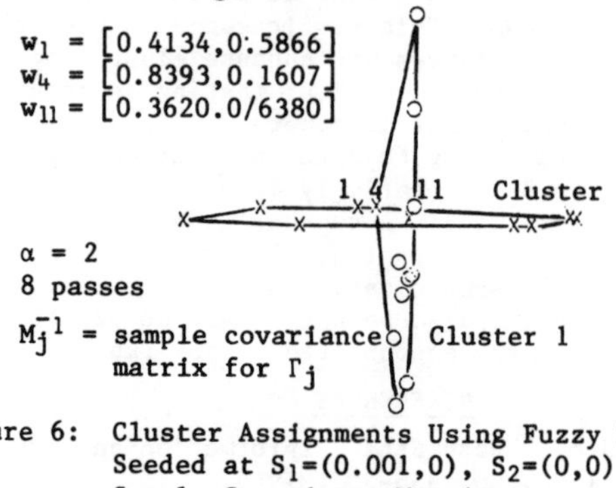

Figure 6: Cluster Assignments Using Fuzzy ISODATA Seeded at $S_1 = (0.001,0)$, $S_2 = (0,0)$ and Sample Covariance Matrices

GEOMETRICAL FUZZY CLUSTERING ALGORITHMS

Michael P. WINDHAM

Department of Mathematics, Utah State University, UMC 41, Logan, UT 84322, USA

Received February 1982
Revised July 1982

Fuzzy clustering algorithms are a basic tool for cluster analysis. Among these, the geometrical fuzzy clustering algorithms are used when the clustering problem can be viewed as trying to find linear or ellipsoidal concentrations in data. This paper provides a theoretical framework in which currently used geometrical fuzzy clustering algorithms become special cases. Also, a family of functions called feasible are defined which can be used to construct such algorithms and convergence results are obtained.

Keywords: Cluster analysis, Fuzzy clustering, Geometrical fuzzy clustering algorithms, Feasible functions.

Cluster analysis is one of the basic tools for identifying structure in data. Among the recent developments in cluster analysis, geometrical fuzzy clustering algorithms are proving to be quite useful in a wide variety of applications. (A comprehensive survey of these appear in [4].) There are several families of these algorithms which have been developed with different applications in mind. However, they all have common properties which suggest that they are special cases of a general structure. It is the purpose of this work to provide this structure. In doing so, a general scheme will be provided for constructing algorithms.

1. Fuzzy clusters and clustering algorithms

By a clustering, one usually means a partitioning of a collection of objects into disjoint subsets or clusters, the objects in a cluster having common properties which distinguish them from the members of the other clusters. A fuzzy clustering is a generalization of this in that the clusters are not subsets of the collection, but are instead fuzzy subsets as introduced by Zadeh [14]. That is, the 'clusters' are functions assigning to each object a number between zero and one which is called the *membership* of the object in the cluster. Objects which are similar to each other are identified by the fact that they have high memberships in the same cluster. It is also assumed that the memberships are chosen so that their sum for each object is one; so, the fuzzy clustering is, in this sense, also a partition of the set of objects.

A fuzzy clustering algorithm is a receipe for producing a fuzzy clustering. A quantitative measure of similarity between objects and criteria for relating similarity to the choice of membership usually constitute the basis for constructing these algorithms. The criteria are often specified as a function of the memberships whose minima or maxima define 'good' clustering (see, for example, [12] and [11]). The algorithm then becomes a numerical procedure for finding memberships which optimize the objective function.

The family of algorithms discussed here will be called geometrical fuzzy clustering algorithms, in that, for these the problem, the solution process, and the solution can all be visualized geometrically. In particular, it is assumed that the objects to be clustered are represented by vectors in some d-dimensional euclidean space, that is, we have a set $X=\{x_1, \ldots, x_N\} \subset \mathbb{R}^d$ where the components of each vector are measurements of one of d features of a particular object. Furthermore, it is assumed that the measure of similarity between objects can be characterized by a differentiable measure of distance between their corresponding

Reprinted with permission from *Fuzzy Sets and Systems*, vol. 10, pp. 271–279, 1983.

data vectors, i.e. $|x_k - x_l|_M^2 = (x_k - x_l)^T M(x_k - v_l)$, for some positive semidefinite matrix, M. Under these assumptions a cluster can be viewed geometrically as a region where the data points are highly concentrated or close together as determined by the metric.

A clustering of X into c clusters is described by a $c \times N$ matrix, U, whose i, kth entry, u_{ik}, is the membership of the kth object in the ith cluster. Therefore, the entries of U are numbers between zero and one and the sum of the entries in each column is one. A clustering can also be interpreted geometrically, in that the memberships can be used to identify the location and, to some extent, the shape of the concentrations of data identified by the clustering. The location of cluster i is given, for $m \geqslant 1$, by a vector

$$v_i = \sum_k (u_{ik})^m x_k \Big/ \sum_k (u_{ik})^m,$$

called the ith *cluster center*. This is simply a mean of the data, weighted by the membership so that those data points with high memberships in the ith cluster have greater influence on the determination of the mean. So, if data with high memberships in a particular cluster are concentrated together then the corresponding vector, v_i, should identify the location of these points. The *exponent weight*, m, can be used to adjust the weights, and hence the centers. For example, the larger m is chosen to be, the less influence points with uniformly low memberships will have on determining the centers. That v_i is an appropriate choice for the center is further justified by the fact that for any $v \in \mathbb{R}^d$,

$$\sum_k (u_{ik})^m \, |x_k - v|_M^2 = \sum_k (u_{ik})^m \, |x_k - v_i|_M^2 + \left(\sum_k (u_{ik})^m\right) |v_i - v|_M^2$$

so that

$$\sum_k (u_{ik})^m \, |x_k - v|_M^2 | \geqslant | \sum_k (u_{ik})^m \, |x_k - v_i|_M^2. \tag{1.1}$$

This result was, in fact, used as a basis for constructing the first geometrical fuzzy clustering algorithm, Fuzzy ISODATA, or Fuzzy c-Means [7, 1, 2], which is essentially an iterative procedure for choosing memberships to minimize

$$\sum_i \sum_k (u_{ik})^m \, |x_k - v_i|_M^2.$$

The shape of the ith cluster can be described, to some extent, by the *scatter matrix*,

$$S_i = \sum_k (u_{ik})^m (M^{1/2}(x_k - v_i))(M^{1/2}(x_k - v_i))^T.$$

The trace of S_i,

$$\mathrm{tr}(S_i) = \sum_k (u_{ik})^m \, |x_k - v_i|_M^2,$$

measures the distribution or scatter of the data about the cluster center, again emphasizing those data with high memberships in the cluster. The diagonal entries, themselves, measure the scatter in each feature. In fact, the scatter matrix is analogous to a within-cluster variance–covariance matrix and provides similar information. In particular, if the data concentrated around the center form an ellipsoidally shaped cluster, then the principal axes of the ellipsoid will be given approximately by the eigenvectors of S_i and the relative lengths of the axes by the corresponding eigenvalues, just as in principal component analysis.

Therefore, if a clustering can be visualized as identifying ellipsoidal concentrations of data, then the cluster centers and scatter matrices will provide a geometrical picture of this cluster. More importantly, if for a clustering problem, the kind of cluster structure that one would like to identify can be characterized in this manner, then centers and scatter matrices should be the objects on which to base the construction of an algorithm to do so. It is this assumption that provides a unification of the theory of geometrical clustering algorithms and guidelines for the construction of them. Before showing how this is done it would be worthwhile to review the algorithms of this kind that are currently in use.

The first and most widely used gometrical fuzzy clustering algorithm is the Fuzzy ISODATA or Fuzzy c-Means algorithm mentioned above. It is an iterative procedure for attempting to find a membership matrix, U, and vectors $v_1, \ldots, v_c \in \mathbb{R}^d$, which minimize the objective function,

$$J(U, v_1, \ldots, v_c) = \sum_{ik} (u_{ik})^m \, |x_k - v_i|_M^2,$$

where m is a fixed exponent weight strictly greater than one. By minimizing J, one should obtain high memberships in cluster i for data which are close to the vector, v_i. It follows from (1.1), that once the memberships are known the vectors $v_1, \ldots, v_c$ should be the cluster centers. Furthermore, the clusters represent concentration in the data about the centers, whose shape is determined by M. For example, if $M = I$, the clusters identified tend to be spherical.

Thinking of this algorithm as identifying concentrations of data about points prompted the development of algorithms which attempt to identify concentrations about other geometrical objects. For example, the Fuzzy r-Varieties algorithm [5, 6] attempts to find memberships and r-dimensional linear varieties which minimize an objective function like J, except that the distance to the vector v_i is replaced by the distance to the r-dimensional plane V_i. For such algorithms the shape of the clusters desired is specified by the choice of a geometrical object.

Other algorithms have been developed to detect rather than impose shapes in the data. For example, the Adaptive Norm algorithm [6, 8] treats not only the memberships and centers as variables, but also the metric, in fact, within each cluster. In other words, the algorithm attempts to choose $U, v_1, \ldots, v_c$, and positive semidefinite matrices $M_1, \ldots, M_c$ which minimize

$$\sum_{ik} (u_{ik})^m (x_k - v_i)^{\mathrm{T}} M_i (x_k - v_i).$$

The algorithm identifies ellipsoidally shaped clusters, but hopefully does not restrict the shape of the ellipsoids. In order to obtain non-trivial results it is necessary to further restrict the metric matrices. The restriction that is usually imposed is that the determinant of M_i, $\det(M_i) = 1$. Without this or some other constraint the minimum would be given by $M_i = 0$. The choice of this particular constraint appears somewhat arbitrary and has been criticized for that reason. However, as will be seen below, this choice produces an effect which is quite natural.

These examples indicate the nature and variety of most of the fuzzy clustering algorithms. Although they were designed for different applications, it is readily apparent that they have common characteristics. First, they are based on a desire to identify linear or ellipsoidally shaped concentrations of data. Furthermore, these algorithms are based on objective functions whose minima appear to identify the desired structure.

2. Theory of geometrical fuzzy clustering algorithms

Since the scatter matrices describe the ellipsoidal nature of the shape of the data associated to a cluster, it is reasonable to suspect that functions of the scatter matrices should suffice for constructing algorithms which identify such structure. For example, if we define $J(U) = \sum_i \det(S_i)$, then an algorithm which minimizes J could be thought of as identifying a clustering which minimizes the 'volumes' of the clusters. In general, one could choose a real-valued function, Φ, defined on the set of positive semidefinite, symmetric matrices, $\mathcal{S}$, then construct an algorithm to optimize the objective function $J(U) = \sum_i \Phi(S_i)$. The problem now becomes one of constructing the desired algorithm. If the function Φ is also chosen to satisfy the following conditions, then an algorithm for seeking the minimums of the associated objective function can be constructed.

Definition 2.1. $\Phi : \mathcal{S} \to \mathbb{R}$ is *feasible* if

(A) Φ is continuous and non-negative on $\mathcal{S}$ and differentiable on the subset of positive definite, symmetric matrices.

(B) Φ is positive homogeneous of degree one, i.e.

$$\Phi(tS) = t\Phi(s) \quad \text{for } t > 0.$$

(C) Φ is concave, i.e.

$$\Phi(tS_1 + (1-t)S_2) \geqslant t\Phi(S_1) + (1-t)\Phi(S_2) \quad \text{for } 0 \leqslant t \leqslant 1.$$

It is assumed, of course, that the membership matrices which minimize $J(U) = \sum_i \Phi(S_i)$ describe clusterings which are desirable in some sense which has been captured by the choice of Φ. In order to be able to construct the algorithm, it is also assumed that the exponent weight used to compute cluster centers and scatter matrices is strictly greater than one. Furthermore, it is assumed that the euclidean metric, $|x| = (\sum x_i^2)^{1/2}$ is used in $\mathbb{R}^d$. This assumption is simply a matter of convenience since the data can be transformed so that the euclidean metric on the transformed data is equivalent to the original metric on the original data.

It follows from the homogeneity of a feasible center function that

$$\Phi(S) = \sum_{pq} \partial\Phi/\partial S_{pq} S_{pq} = \text{tr}(F(S)S)$$

where $F(S)$ is the $d \times d$ matric $[\partial\Phi/\partial S_{pq}]$. Also, concavity can be characterized by

$$\Phi(S_1) \leqslant \text{tr}(F(S_2)S_1) \tag{2.2}$$

for all $S_1, S_2 \in \mathcal{S}$. It follows from these two facts and that $\Phi \geqslant 0$, that the matrix $F(S)$ will be positive semi-definite, since, for any $y \in \mathbb{R}^d$,

$$y^T F(S) y = \text{tr}(F(S) yy^T) \geqslant \Phi(yy)^T \geqslant 0.$$

The algorithm which seeks the minima of J is based on the function $A(U) = W$, where U and W are membership matrices with

$$w_{ik} = (1/D_{ik})^{1/(m-1)} \Big/ \sum_j 1/(D_{jk})^{1/(m-1)}$$

and $D_{ik} = (x_k - v_i)^T F(S_i)(x_k - v_i)$. The algorithm is given by:

Step 1: Choose $\varepsilon > 0$ and a membership matrix U^0.
Step 2: Construct a sequence of matrices U^n by $A(U^{n-1}) = U^n$.
Step 3: When $\max_{ik} |(U^n)_{ik} - (U^{n-1})_{ik}| < \varepsilon$, stop.

That this algorithm will tend to produce clusterings which have the properties determined by the choice of Φ is based on two facts. First, local minima of J occur at membership matrices, U, satisfying $A(U) = U$, and second, $J(A(U)) < J(U)$ unless $A(U) = U$. Therefore, the algorithm produces a sequence of membership matrices which decreases the objective function at each iteration. Since local minima occur at fixed points, the process is stopped when the change in memberships between successive iterations is sufficiently small.

Before verifying these facts, it is worth noting that each of the algorithms mentioned previously can be obtained from this procedure by an appropriate choice of feasible function. Fuzzy c-Means is obtained from $\Phi(S) = \text{tr}(S)$, Adaptive Norm from $\Phi(S) = (\det S)^{1/d}$, and Fuzzy r-Varieties from $\Phi(S) =$ sum of the $d - r$ smallest eigenvalues of S. That this last function is feasible is not obvious, but will follow from subsequent discussion. It should be noted, that the objective functions obtained from these feasible functions are not those that were used to generate the algorithms, but the resulting numerical procedures are identical. Also, it was mentioned above that $\det(S)$ might be used to construct an objective function, but this function is clearly not feasible. However, the function $(\det S)^{1/d}$ accomplishes the same purpose and is feasible.

Theorem 2.1. *If $J(U)$ is a local minimum for J and $A(U)$ exists, then $A(U) = U$.*

Proof. Local minima of J occur at the critical points of the problem: optimize J subject to the constraints, $\sum_i u_{ik} = 1$ for $k = 1, \ldots, N$. Using Lagrange multipliers yields that critical points satisfy $\partial J/\partial u_{ik} = \partial J/\partial u_{jk}$ for $i, j = 1, \ldots, c$. The theorem then follows from the fact that

$$\partial J/\partial u_{ik} = m(u_{ik})^{m-1}(x_k - v_i)^T F(S_i)(x_k - v_i) = m(u_{ik})^{m-1} D_{ik}.$$

Unfortunately, this theorem does not say that fixed points of A provide local minima, but rather the converse. The next result, however, shows that the iterations decrease the objective function unless the current membership matrix is a fixed point of A.

Theorem 2.2. *If $A(U)$ exists, then $J(A(U)) < J(U)$ unless $A(U) = U$.*

Proof. In order to facilitate the proof, quantities computed from a particular membership matrix will be denoted as functions of the matrix.

Letting $W = A(U)$ the proof consists of verifying the following inequalities

$$J(U) > \sum_{ik} (w_{ik})^m D_{ik}(U) \quad \text{unless } W = U \tag{2.3}$$

$$\geqslant \sum_{ik} (w_{ik})^m (x_k - v_i(W))^T F(S_i(U))(x_k - v_i(W)) \tag{2.4}$$

$$\geqslant J(W). \tag{2.5}$$

First of all, observe that

$$J(U) = \sum_i \operatorname{tr}(F(S_i)S_i) = \sum_{ik} (u_{ik})^m D_{ik}.$$

Inequality (2.3) is a basic result and has appeared often in the literature. It was proven by Bezdek [3] and Bock [6] in the context of the Fuzzy c-Means algorithm. Bezdek's proof used Lagrange multipliers essentially as in Theorem 2.1. Bock's proof avoids the use of calculus and is presented here in the form of the following lemma from which inequality (2.3) follows.

Lemma 2.3. *If $f: \mathbb{R}^c \to \mathbb{R}$ is defined by $f(u) = \sum (u_i)^m d_i$ where $d_i > 0$ for all i, and $m > 1$; and*

$$w_i = (1/d_i)^{1/(m-1)} \Big/ \sum_j (1/d_j)^{1/(m-1)},$$

then $f(w) < f(u)$ for all u satisfying $\sum u_i = 1$ and $u_i \geqslant 0$, unless $w = u$.

Proof. Let Y be a random variable which assumes the value $(u_i)^{m-1} d_i$ with probability u_i, then $E(Y) = f(u)$. Moreover, since $g(y) = y^{-1/(m-1)}$ is convex, by Jensen's inequality $g(E(Y)) \leqslant E(g(Y))$, with equality only if Y is constant with probability one. But,

$$E(g(Y)) = \sum u_i u_i^{-1} d_i^{-1/(m-1)} = \sum d_i^{-1/(m-1)} = g(f(w)).$$

Therefore, $g(f(u)) \leqslant g(f(w))$ and since g is decreasing this implies $f(w) \leqslant f(u)$. Equality implies that Y is constant with probability one, but this means $(u_i)^{m-1} d_i = (u_j)^{m-1} d_j$ and $\sum u_i = 1$, that is, $u = w$.

Since $F(S_i)$ is positive semidefinite, inequality (2.4) follows from (1.1). Finally,

$$\sum_{ik} (w_{ik})^m (x_k - v_i(W))^T F(S_i(U))(x_k - v_i(W))$$

$$= \sum_i \operatorname{tr}(F(S_i(U)) S_i(W))$$

so the last step follows from inequality (2.2).

This results shows that the objective function decreases at each iteration, and is sufficient to allow the application of Zangwill's Global Convergence Theorem [9] to show that a subsequence of the membership matrices converges to a critical point of J. It is not known whether or not the sequence, itself, converges; so, it is possible that the algorithm will not stop. However, the results of Windham [13] can be extended to show that if there is a $\delta > 0$ so that $u_{ik}D_{ik}(U) > \delta$ for all i, k, and iterates, U, then the distance between successive iterates converges to zero. Therefore, for any stopping criteria, ε, the algorithm will stop after a finite number of iterations.

Although the problem of convergence or even termination has not been completely solved, the results presented here in the context of the general construction scheme are the best that have been obtained for any of the particular geometrical fuzzy clustering algorithms. It is hoped that by being able to see the situation from the more general point of view given here, that more insight into these questions can be obtained.

3. Feasible functions

In theory at least, all that is needed for constructing a geometrical fuzzy clustering algorithm is a feasible function. The choice of such a function is determined by the nature of the clustering desired, but some discussion of general properties and examples of feasible functions will illustrate the wide range of possible choices.

The critical condition for feasibility is concavity; since, if Ψ is only differentiable, non-negative, and concave, then $\Phi(S) = \mathrm{tr}(S)\Psi(S/\mathrm{tr}(S))$ defines a feasible function, Φ. On the other hand, if Φ is homogeneous of degree one, then Φ is concave if $\Phi(S_1 + S_2) \geq \Phi(S_1) + \Phi(S_2)$. Feasible functions can also be built from feasible functions. For example, if $\Phi_1, \ldots, \Phi_L$ are feasible, then so are $\sum_l c_l \Phi_l$ for $c_l \geq 0$ and $\Phi_1^{\alpha_1}\Phi_2^{\alpha_2} \cdots \Phi_L^{\alpha_L}$ for $\alpha_l \geq 0$ and $\sum \alpha_l = 1$.

If a feasible function, Φ, is invariant under orthogonal transformations, that is $\Phi(B^{\mathrm{T}}SB) = \Phi(S)$ for $BB^{\mathrm{T}} = I$, then its values are determined entirely by the eigenvalues of S. If such a function is used, then the clusters will be identified by their shape independent of their orientation. Furthermore, such a function determines a unique function $\phi : L \to \mathbb{R}$ where $L = \{y \in \mathbb{R}^d : y_1 \geq y_2 \geq \cdots \geq y_d \geq 0\}$ by defining $\phi(\lambda) = \Phi(S)$ where S is any matrix in $\mathcal{S}$ with eigenvalues $\lambda = (\lambda_1, \ldots, \lambda_d)$ arranged in descending order. Since Φ is feasible, the function, ϕ, will also be non-negative, homogeneous of degree one, concave, and satisfy $\partial\phi/\partial\lambda_1 \leq \cdots \leq \partial\phi/\partial\lambda_d$. Conversely, any function, ϕ, satisfying these properties determines a unique Φ which is invariant under orthogonal transformations, so either will be referred to as feasible. This immediately leads to several examples of feasible functions. (See [10] for details on concavity.)

(1) Power mean of order p, are defined by

$$\phi_p(\lambda) = \begin{cases} (\lambda_1 \cdots \lambda_d)^{1/d} (= (\det(S))^{1/d}) & p = 0, \\ \left(\sum (\lambda_j)^p/d\right)^{1/p} (= (\mathrm{tr}(S^p)/d)^{1/d}) & p \neq 0. \end{cases}$$

These functions are feasible for $p \leq 1$.

(2) Let E_r be the elementary symmetric function of degree r and $E_0 = 1$ then for $1 \leq p \leq r \leq d$

$$\Phi_{r,p} = (E_r/E_{r-p})^{1/p}$$

is feasible.

(3) For $1 \leq r \leq d$, let

$$\phi_r(\lambda) = \sum_{j>r} \lambda_j.$$

This feasible function produces the Fuzzy r-Varieties algorithm.

There are, then, a wide variety of functions available for constructing algorithms, however, in selecting a function there are some practical considerations which should be made. In order to implement the algorithm, it is necessary to compute $F(S)$ for each cluster and each iteration. Therefore, this matrix should be as simple and as well-conditioned as possible. For example, for the power mean of order p the corresponding $F(S)=\Phi(S)^{1-p}S^{p-1}$. Except for a few cases it will be necessary to diagonalize the scatter matrix for each cluster at each iteration to obtain $F(S)$, a possibly expensive and dangerous numerical procedure.

Furthermore, it may be that $F(S)$ does not exist at some iteration. For example, this occurs when S is singular in the above example. For the function

$$\Phi(S)=(E_2(S))^{1/2}=(\mathrm{tr}(S)^2-\mathrm{tr}(S^2))^{1/2}$$

the corresponding

$$F(S)=(\mathrm{tr}(S)I-S)/\Phi(S).$$

This matrix will fail to exist if the scatter matrix has rank one. However, as is often the case, the function Φ can be modified to avoid this difficulty. Letting

$$\Phi_\alpha(S)=(\mathrm{tr}(S)^2-\alpha\ \mathrm{tr}(S^2))^{1/2} \quad \text{for } 0\leqslant\alpha\leqslant 1,$$

this agrees with Φ for $\alpha=1$ but $F(S)$ will always be non-singular for $\alpha<1$. Therefore, by using an α close to one, rather than equal to it, it would be hoped that essentially the same results could be obtained without the danger of failure of the algorithm.

4. Conclusion

Using this procedure it is now possible to produce a wide variety of clustering algorithms with the assurance that they will be computationally well-behaved. It is also possible to use this framework to better understand existing algorithms. For example, the Adaptive Norm algorithm was designed to allow the data to determine the shape of the clusters, but it can now be seen that it does so by minimizing the volume of the clusters. It is also possible that this framework will serve to focus attention on the essential characteristics of this family of algorithms and by doing so simplify problems such as the question of convergence, which have not yet been solved.

References

[1] J.C. Bezdek, Fuzzy mathematics in pattern classification, Ph.D. Thesis, Cornell University, Ithaca, NY (1973).
[2] J.C. Bezdek, Cluster validity with fuzzy sets, J. Cybernet. 3 (1974) 58–73.
[3] J.C. Bezdek, A convergence theorem for the Fuzzy ISODATA clustering algorithm, IEEE PAMI-2 (1) (1980) 1–8.
[4] J.C. Bezdek, Pattern Recognition with Fuzzy Objective Function Algorithms (Plenum, New York, 1980).
[5] J.C. Bezdek, C. Coray, R. Gunderson and J. Watson, Detection and characterization of cluster substructure, SIAM J. Appl. Math. 40 (2) (1981) 339–372.
[6] H.H. Bock, Clusteranalyse mit unscharfen Partitionen, in: H.H. Bock, Ed., Klassification und Erkenntnis III: Numerische Klassification (Gesellschaft für Klassification, Frankfurt a.M., 1979) pp. 137–163.
[7] J.C. Dunn, A fuzzy relative of the ISODATA process and its use in detecting compact, well-separated clusters, J. Cybernet. 3 (1974) 32–57.
[8] D.E. Gustafson and W. Kessel, Fuzzy clustering with a fuzzy covariance matrix, in: K.S. Fu, Ed., Proc. IEEE-CDC 2 (IEEE Press, Pisataway, NJ, 1979) pp. 761–766.
[9] D.L. Luenberger, An Introduction to Linear and Non-Linear Programming (Addison-Wesley, Reading, MA, 1973).
[10] M. Marcus and H. Minc, A Survey of Matrix Theory and Matrix Inequalities (Allyn and Bacon, Boston, IL, 1964).
[11] M. Roubens, Pattern classification problems and fuzzy sets, Fuzzy Sets and Systems 1 (1978) 239–253.
[12] E. Ruspini, Numerical methods for fuzzy clustering, Information Sci. 2 (1970) 319–350.
[13] M. Windham, Termination of fuzzy clustering algorithms, USU Mathematics Research Report 1981/2, Utah State University, Logan, UT (1981).
[14] L.A. Zadeh, Fuzzy sets, Information and Control 8 (1965) 338–353.

A Convergence Theorem for the Fuzzy ISODATA Clustering Algorithms

JAMES C. BEZDEK

Abstract—In this paper the convergence of a class of clustering procedures, popularly known as the fuzzy ISODATA algorithms, is established. The theory of Zangwill is used to prove that arbitrary sequences generated by these (Picard iteration) procedures always terminates at a local minimum, or at worst, always contains a subsequence which converges to a local minimum of the generalized least squares objective functional which defines the problem.

Index Terms—Cluster analysis, convergence of fuzzy ISODATA, fuzzy sets, generalized least squares, iterative optimization.

I. Introduction

In 1973 Dunn [1] defined the first fuzzy generalization of the conventional minimum-variance partitioning problem, and derived necessary conditions for minimizing the functional $J_2(U, v)$ defined below. He used these conditions to develop a Picard iteration scheme for iterative optimization of J_2 and called it fuzzy ISODATA, in deference to its relation to the hard ISODATA process of Ball and Hall [2] (hard "c-means" or "basic ISODATA" more accurately describes its historical predecessor, as it contains none of the decision-oriented embellishments of Ball and Hall). Numerical examples given in [1] suggested empirically that the algorithm was at least locally convergent, but no proof of convergence was formulated therein.

A generalization of $J_2(U, v)$ to an infinite family of objective functions—$\{J_m(U, v)\colon 1 \leqslant m < \infty\}$ defined below—also appeared in 1973 [3]; and for $m > 1$, a similar algorithm for iterative optimization of J_m was formulated. Numerical experiments with real data in various applications have subsequently established the usefulness of these fuzzy ISODATA partitioning algorithms [4]-[8], and no difficulty has ever been reported concerning the attainment (computationally) of convergence. Nevertheless, their theoretical convergence properties have remained an open question. In this paper we formulate a convergence theorem using the method of Zangwill, which applies to the fuzzy ISODATA algorithms for every $m > 1$.

In Section II we fix notation and establish the problem. Section III briefly reviews the form of Zangwill's theorem used in the sequel. Section IV contains the main result: fuzzy ISODATA terminates at a local minimum of J_m; or at worst, always generates a sequence containing a subsequence convergent to a local minimum. In Section V we observe that the proof *cannot* be extended directly to the conventional c-means algorithm for the iterative minimization of J_1; and Section VI concludes with a short discussion of how the present theory might extend to more general classes of fuzzy clustering algorithms.

Manuscript received August 10, 1978; revised March 23, 1979. This work was supported by the National Science Foundation under Grant MCS77-00855.

The author is with the Department of Mathematics, Utah State University, Logan, UT 84322.

II. The Fuzzy ISODATA Algorithms

Let $X = \{x_1, x_2, \cdots, x_n\} \subset \mathbb{R}^s$ be a finite data set in feature space $\mathbb{R}^s$; let c be an integer $2 \leqslant c < n$; and let V_{cn} denote the vector space of all real $(c \times n)$ matrices over $\mathbb{R}$, equipped with the usual scalar multiplication and vector addition. A conventional ("hard," or nonfuzzy) c-partition of X is conveniently represented by a matrix $U = [u_{ik}] \in V_{cn}$, the entries of which satisfy

$$u_{ik} \in \{0, 1\}; \quad 1 \leqslant i \leqslant c; \quad 1 \leqslant k \leqslant n, \tag{1a}$$

$$\sum_{i=1}^{c} u_{ik} = 1; \quad 1 \leqslant k \leqslant n, \tag{1b}$$

$$\sum_{k=1}^{n} u_{ik} > 0; \quad 1 \leqslant i \leqslant c. \tag{1c}$$

We denote the set of all such matrices by M_c:

$$M_c \doteq \{U \in V_{cn}\colon u_{ik} \text{ satisfies (1) } \forall\, i, k\}, \tag{2}$$

and by M_{co}, the superset of M_c obtained in relaxing (1c) by allowing zero rows in U. To interpret $U \in M_c$ as a hard c-partition of X, regard the ith row of U, say $U_{(i)} = (u_{i1}, u_{i2}, \cdots, u_{in})$, as exhibiting (the values of) the characteristic function $u_i\colon X \to \{0, 1\}$ defined by

$$u_i(x_k) \doteq u_{ik} = \left\{ \begin{array}{ll} 1; & x_k \in i\text{th subset } Y_i \text{ partitioning } X \\ 0; & \text{otherwise} \end{array} \right\}. \tag{3}$$

The subsets $\{Y_i\}$ in (3) are the set-theoretic realization of the characteristic functions $\{u_i\}$, and because they are isomorphic descriptions we may call either Y_i or u_i the ith hard *cluster*, or subset of X, in the c-partition U.

Next, let $v = (v_1, v_2, \cdots, v_c)$, where $v_i \in \mathbb{R}^s$ for $1 \leqslant i \leqslant c$; let $\|\cdot\|_E$ be the Euclidean norm on $\mathbb{R}^s$; and define the functional $J_1\colon (M_c \times \mathbb{R}^{cs}) \to \mathbb{R}$ by

Reprinted from *IEEE Trans. Pattern Anal. Machine Intell.*, vol. PAMI-2, no. 1, pp. 1-8, January 1980.

$$J_1(U, v) = \sum_{k=1}^{n} \sum_{i=1}^{c} (u_{ik}) \|x_k - v_i\|_E^2. \tag{4}$$

J_1 is the classical *within-group sum of squared (WGSS) errors objective function.* Its value is a measure of the total squared error (in the Euclidean sense) incurred by the representation of the c clusters defined by $U \in M_c$ by the c prototypes $\{v_i\}$. The use of $\|\cdot\|_E$ renders J_1 a measure of the total within-group scatter, or variance of the $\{x_{kj}\}$ from the $\{v_{ij}\}$ in the statistical sense of Wilks [9]. For these reasons, J_1 is a popular criterion for identifying optimal (defined as minimums of J_1) pairs (U^*, v^*), where U^* is assumed to be a clustering of X which exhibits inherent data substructure. J_1 performs well for certain kinds of data, but its failure at detection of, e.g., linear substructure, is well documented [1], [3]-[5], [9]. Nonetheless, it is an often-used clustering criterion; one of the most popular methods for approximating local minima of J_1 is iterative optimization, using the necessary conditions

$$u_{ik}^* = \begin{Bmatrix} 1: \; d_{ik}^* = \min_j \{d_{jk}^*\} \\ 0: \; \text{otherwise} \end{Bmatrix}; \quad \begin{matrix} 1 \leqslant i \leqslant c \\ 1 \leqslant k \leqslant n \end{matrix} \tag{5a}$$

$$v_i^* = \sum_{k=1}^{n} (u_{ik}^*) x_k \Big/ \sum_{k=1}^{n} u_{ik}^*; \qquad 1 \leqslant i \leqslant c. \tag{5b}$$

(U^*, v^*) must satisfy for minimums of J_1. In (5a) $d_{ik}^* \doteq \|x_k - v_i^*\|_E^2$, and we have assumed the existence of a unique $d_{ik}^* > 0 \; \forall k$. If this assumption fails, $U^* \in M_c$ is nonunique [1]. The necessity of (5b) follows easily by differentiation, that of (5a) by one of several arguments (cf. [1]). The hard c-means algorithm is, loosely speaking, iteration through (5) by an operator T_1: $(M_c) \to (M_c)$ defined by

$$(U^{(k)}) = T_1(U^{(k-1)}) = \cdots = (T_1)^{(k)}(U^{(0)}); \qquad k = 1, 2, \cdots \tag{6}$$

where $(U^{(0)})$ is an initial guess, T_1 is a composition of the two operations defined by (5a) and (5b), and superscripts in parentheses indicate the iteration number. Conditions (5) are not known to be sufficient, and no proof of convergence of the Picard iterates $\{T^{(k)}(U^{(0)})\} \to (U^*)$ is known (cf. Section V).

The disadvantages of $U^* \in M_c$ as a solution to the clustering problem are argued elsewhere at some length [1], [3]-[8]. Specifically, it is impossible for such a partition to exhibit partial relationships between x_k's in X as occurs, for example, in a mixture of hybrids and their progenitors. For this reason, Ruspini first suggested in 1969 [10] that the fuzzy set of Zadeh [11] could be used to improve the model of the substructure imposed upon X by M_c. His idea was to alter conditions (1) to

$$u_{ik} \in [0, 1]; \quad 1 \leqslant i \leqslant c; \quad 1 \leqslant k \leqslant n \tag{7a}$$

$$\sum_{i=1}^{c} u_{ik} = 1; \quad 1 \leqslant k \leqslant n \tag{7b}$$

$$\sum_{k=1}^{n} u_{ik} > 0; \quad 1 \leqslant i \leqslant c \tag{7c}$$

and call the set $M_{fc} \supset M_c$ defined thereby

$$M_{fc} = \{U \in V_{cn}: \; u_{ik} \text{ satisfies (7) } \forall i, k\}, \tag{8}$$

the set of *fuzzy c-partitions of X.* This terminology arises by regarding the ith row of $U \in M_{fc}$ as (the values of) membership function u_i: $X \to [0, 1]$ such that

$$u_i(x_k) \doteq u_{ik}; \quad 1 \leqslant i \leqslant c; \quad 1 \leqslant k \leqslant n. \tag{9}$$

For $U \in M_c$, (9) and (7) reduce to (3) and (1), respectively. Otherwise, u_i is called a *fuzzy subset (cluster) of X*; and u_{ik} is the *grade of membership* of x_k in u_i; (7b) requires each $x_k \in X$ to have unit membership over all of X, but (7a) allows this membership to be *distributed* among the c fuzzy clusters of X in U. U may, of course, be a mixture of hard and fuzzy clusters, just as each u_i may exhibit a mixture of hard and fuzzy memberships. Dunn suggested in [1] that optimal U^*'s in M_{fc} might be part of optimal pairs for the functional J_2: $(M_{fc} \times \mathbb{R}^{cs}) \to \mathbb{R}$ defined by

$$J_2(U, v) = \sum_{k=1}^{n} \sum_{k=1}^{c} (u_{ik})^2 \|x_k - v_i\|^2 \tag{10}$$

where $\|\cdot\|$ was allowed to be any inner product induced norm on $\mathbb{R}^s$. This was subsequently extended by Bezdek [3] to the family J_m: $(M_{fc} \times \mathbb{R}^{cs}) \to \mathbb{R}$ defined by

$$J_m(U, v) = \sum_{k=1}^{n} \sum_{i=1}^{c} (u_{ik})^m \|x_k - v_i\|^2; \quad 1 \leqslant m < \infty \tag{11}$$

where $\|\cdot\|$ was again any inner product induced norm on $\mathbb{R}^s$. It is shown in [3], under the assumption that $d_{ik}^* \doteq \|x_k - v_i^*\|^2 > 0 \; \forall i, k$, that (U^*, v^*) might be a local minimum of J_m only if, for any $m > 1$, there holds

$$u_{ik}^* = \frac{1}{\sum_{j=1}^{c} \left(\frac{d_{ik}^*}{d_{jk}^*}\right)^{1/(m-1)}}; \quad 1 \leqslant i \leqslant c; \; 1 \leqslant k \leqslant n \tag{12a}$$

$$v_i^* = \sum_{k=1}^{n} (u_{ik}^*)^m \, x_k \Big/ \sum_{k=1}^{n} (u_{ik}^*)^m; \quad 1 \leqslant i \leqslant c. \tag{12b}$$

About conditions (12) we make several observations.

1) Equation (12) is necessary, but not sufficient for (U^*, v^*) to be a local minimum of J_m.

2) As m approaches 1 from above ($m \overset{+}{\to} 1$), (12) converges to (5), the necessary conditions for (U^*, v^*) minimizing J_1, and $J_m \to J_1$, under the assumption that $0 < d_{ik}^* = \min_j \{d_{jk}^*\}$, $1 \leqslant k \leqslant n$.

3) The fuzzy ISODATA clustering algorithms are Picard iteration through the loop defined by (12). Thus we define a composite operator T_m: $(M_{fc}) \to (M_{fc})$ analgous to T_1 with conditions (12) by

$$U^{(k)} = T_m(U^{(k-1)}) = \cdots = (T_m)^{(k)}(U^{(o)}); \qquad k = 1, 2, \cdots. \tag{13}$$

The question we seek to resolve below is whether or not the iterate sequence $\{(T_m)^{(k)}(U^{(o)})\}$ converges to (U^*) so that (U^*, v^*) is a local minimum of J_m. In order to do this, it is necessary to specify the operator T_m more precisely. Accordingly, let

$$F: \mathbb{R}^{cs} \to M_{fc}, \quad F(v) = F(v_1, v_2, \cdots, v_c) = U = [u_{ik}] \tag{14a}$$

where the entries of $U = [u_{ik}] = F(v)$ are calculated via (12a) with

$$d_{ik} = \|x_k - v_i\|^2 \quad \text{for } 1 \leq i \leq c; \ 1 \leq k \leq n, \text{ and let}$$

$$G: M_{fc} \to \mathbb{R}^{cs}, \quad G(U) = v = (v_1, v_2, \cdots, v_c) \tag{14b}$$

where the vectors $v_i \in \mathbb{R}^s$ are calculated via (12b) for $1 \leq i \leq c$. In (14) we assume $X = \{x_1, x_2, \cdots, x_n\}$ fixed in $\mathbb{R}^s$. Using F and G, fuzzy ISODATA can be specified in several equivalent forms:

$$U^{(k)} = (F \circ G)(U^{(k-1)}) = \cdots = (F \circ G)^{(k)}(U^{(0)}); \quad k = 1, 2, \cdots, \tag{E1}$$

$$v^{(k)} = (G \circ F)(v^{(k-1)}) = \cdots = (G \circ F)^{(k)}(v^{(0)}); \quad k = 1, 2, \cdots. \tag{E2}$$

The only difference between (E1) and (E2) is whether one chooses to initialize the algorithm with $U^{(0)} \in M_{fc}$ or $v^{(0)} \in \mathbb{R}^{cs}$; either form constitutes the computational technique used to (hopefully) optimize $J_m(U, v)$. Our goal below is to prove that this strategy is theoretically sound. In order to proceed, we must modify T_m so that it generates Picard sequences in both U and v simultaneously. We define the (fuzzy ISODATA) operator $\mathcal{T}_m$: $(M_{fc} \times \mathbb{R}^{cs}) \to (M_{fc} \times \mathbb{R}^{cs})$ as follows:

$$\mathcal{T}_m = A_2 \circ A_1 \tag{15a}$$

where

$$A_1: M_{fc} \times \mathbb{R}^{cs} \to \mathbb{R}^{cs}; \quad A_1(U, v) = G(U); \tag{15b}$$

$$A_2: \mathbb{R}^{cs} \to M_{fc} \times \mathbb{R}^{sc}; \quad A_2(v) = (F(v), v). \tag{15c}$$

Writing out the action of $\mathcal{T}_m$ on (U, v) explicitly, we let $(\hat{U}, \hat{v})$ denote $\mathcal{T}_m(U, v)$; then

$$\begin{aligned}(\hat{U}, \hat{v}) &= \mathcal{T}_m(U, v) = (A_2 \circ A_1)(U, v) \\ &= A_2(A_1(U, v)) \\ &= A_2(G(U)) \\ &= (F(G(U)), G(U)) \\ &= (F \circ G(U), G(U)).\end{aligned}$$

In particular, properties of iterative algorithm $\mathcal{T}_m$ rest with the composition $A_2 \circ A_1$, which in turn reside in $F \circ G$ and G, and hence ultimately in F and G, defined at (14a), (14b) via (12a), (12b), respectively. We emphasize this here as the analysis below depends precisely upon this decomposition. Our strategy will be to apply Zangwill's theorem to the operator $\mathcal{T}_m$ of (15a). Towards this end, we give a brief review of the results we intend to use.

III. Zangwill's Convergence Theorem

The usual means for resolving convergence of Picard sequences is by fixed-point theorems, the contraction mapping theorem being the classical case. Picard sequences based on (12) have thus far resisted efforts along these lines, due mainly to the two-part compositional nature of one iteration, which prevents verification of the contractive property. Although $\mathcal{T}_m$ is probably at least a local contraction, there is with this approach the further difficulty of establishing local zones of convergence. The approach taken below, due mainly to Zangwill [12], avoids these difficulties. We state without proof the specific results we need, referring interested readers to [12] or [13] for details of generalizations not needed in the sequel.

Let f: $D_f \subset \mathbb{R}^m \to \mathbb{R}$ be a real functional, with D_f its domain, and let

$$S = \{x^* \in D_f: f(x^*) < f(y) \ \forall \ y \in B^0(x^*, r)\} \tag{16}$$

where

$$B^0(x^*, r) = \{y \in \mathbb{R}^m: \|x^* - y\| < r; \ \|\cdot\| \text{ any norm on } \mathbb{R}^m\}. \tag{16}$$

We may refer to S as the *solution set* of the optimization problem

$$\min_{D_f} \{f(x)\}. \tag{17}$$

Zangwill defined an iterative algorithm for solving (17) as any *point to set* mapping A: $D_f \to P(D_f)$, where $P(D_f)$ is the power set of D_f. The algorithm of interest here is a *point to point* map, viz., $\mathcal{T}_m = A$, so we are interested in the special case A: $D_f \to D_f$ defined as

$$x_{k+1} = A(x_k); \quad k = 0, 1, \cdots. \tag{18}$$

Any sequence $\{x_k = A^{(k)}(x_0)\}$ we call an iterative sequence generated by A.

Next, we attach to algorithm A a descent functional g.

Definition: g: $D_f \to \mathbb{R}$ is a *descent function for* $\{A, S\}$ if

$$g \text{ is continuous on } D_f \tag{19a}$$

$$x^* \notin S \Rightarrow g(A(x^*)) < g(x^*), \tag{19b}$$

$$x^* \in S \Rightarrow g(A(x^*)) \leq g(x^*). \tag{19c}$$

Loosely speaking, g is attached to sequences of iterates generated by A to monitor the progress of A in seeking a solution $x^* \in S$. Although g is commonly f itself, this is not necessarily the case. Note especially the strict inequality at (19b), which is essential for the proof of Theorem C below.

Finally, Zangwill generalized the ideas of continuity and composition for A: $D_f \to P(D_f)$. While the general convergence theorem for point-to-set algorithms requires the definition of a *closed* algorithmic map; this property reduces to ordinary continuity for the case at hand. Thus, our situation merely requires that A be continuous on $D_f \backslash S$. With these notions, the convergence theorem can be stated.

Theorem C (Zangwill [12]): Let

$$f: D_f \subset \mathbb{R}^m \to \mathbb{R}:$$

$$S = \{x^* \in D_f: f(x^*) < f(y) \ \forall \ y \in B^0(x^*, r)\}$$

$$A: D_f \to D_f \text{ be an iterative algorithm}, x_{k+1} = A(x_k); \quad k = 0, 1, \cdots.$$

If the following conditions hold,

g is a descent function for $\{A,S\}$ (20a)

A is continuous on $D_f \backslash S$ (20b)

the iterate sequences

$$\{A(x_k):\ k=0,1,2,\cdots; x_o \in D_f\} \subset K$$

are contained in a compact set

$K \subseteq D_f$ for arbitrary $x_o \in D_f$, (20c)

then for each iterative sequence $\{x_k\}$ generated by A, we have either

$\{x_k\}$ terminates at a solution $x^* \in S$ (20d)

or

$\exists$ a subsequence $\{x_{k_j}\} \subset \{x_k\}$ so that $\{x_{k_j}\} \to x^* \in S$. (20e)

Theorem C and its generalizations can be used to secure convergence proofs for almost all of the classical iterative optimization algorithms, e.g., steepest descent, Newton's method, etc., by using this approach as an alternative to more conventional arguments. Note especially that solution points $x^* \in S$ are strict *local* minima of f, while the theorem itself asserts *global* convergence for the iterates of A, that is, convergence to an $x^* \in S$ starting from an arbitrary $x_0 \in D_f$. In Section IV we show that Theorem 1 applies to the fuzzy ISODATA algorithms described above.

IV. Convergence of Fuzzy ISODATA

We assume in this section that $m > 1$, that the cn distances $d_{ik} = \|x_k - v_i\|^2$ are always positive, and that the norm in (11) is any inner product induced norm. First, we establish that J_m serves as its own descent functional. It was shown in ([3]) that J_m descends *weakly* on the iterates generated by fuzzy ISODATA, i.e., that

$$J_m(\mathcal{T}_m(U^{(k)}, v^{(k)})) = J_m(U^{(k+1)}, v^{(k+1)}) \leq J_m(U^{(k)}, v^{(k)});$$
$$k = 0, 1, 2, \cdots,$$

but in order to apply Theorem 1, we need *strict* descendance as in (19b). This can be established most conveniently in several stages, the first of which is contained in the following.

Proposition 1: Let φ: $M_{fc} \to \mathbb{R}$, $\varphi(U) \doteq J_m(U, v)$, where $v \in \mathbb{R}^{cs}$ is fixed. Then $U^* \in M_{fc}$ is a *strict* local minimum of φ *if and only if* U^* is calculated via (12a), $U^* = F(v)$.

Proof: Minimization of φ over M_{fc} is a Kuhn-Tucker problem carrying the $c(n+1)$ inequality constraints (7a), (7c), and the (n) equality constraints (7b). By letting $u_{ik} = (w_{ik})^2$ $\forall$ i, k, (7a) and (7b) are collectively represented by the n constraints $\Sigma_{i=1}^{c} (w_{ik})^2 = 1$; $1 \leq k \leq n$. Letting W represent $[w_{ik}^2]$, we consider the relaxed minimization of $\varphi(U)$ via Lagrange multipliers obtained by ignoring constraints (7c). Let $\alpha = (\alpha_1, \alpha_2, \cdots, \alpha_n)$ be the multipliers, and $\Phi(W, \alpha)$ be the Lagrangian

$$\Phi(W, \alpha) = \sum_{k=1}^{n} \sum_{i=1}^{c} (w_{ik})^{2m} d_{ik} + \sum_{k=1}^{n} \alpha_k \left(\sum_{i=1}^{c} w_{ik}^2 - 1 \right).$$

If (W^*, α^*) is to minimize Φ, its gradient in both sets of variables must vanish. Thus,

$$\text{a)}\quad \frac{\partial(W^*, \alpha^*)}{\partial \alpha_j} = \sum_{i=1}^{c} (w_{ij}^*)^2 - 1 = 0; \qquad 1 \leq j \leq n,$$

$$\text{b)}\quad \frac{\partial(W^*, \alpha^*)}{\partial w_{lp}} = 2m(w_{lp}^*)^{2m-1} d_{lp} + 2(w_{lp}^*)\, \alpha_p^* = 0,$$
$$1 \leq l \leq c:\ 1 \leq p \leq n.$$

From b) we find that

$$\text{c)}\quad (w_{lp}^*)^2 = u_{lp}^* = \left(\frac{-\alpha_p^*}{m d_{lp}} \right)^{1/(m-1)}$$

Summing c) over l and applying a) yields

$$\text{d)}\quad (-\alpha_p^*)^{1/(m-1)} = \frac{1}{\sum_{l=1}^{c} \left(\frac{1}{m d_{lp}} \right)^{1/(m-1)}}.$$

Substitution of d) into c) now admits the necessity of (12a) for U^*. To show sufficiency, we examine $H_\Phi(U^*)$, the $(cn \times cn)$ Hessian of the Lagrangian of φ as a function of U, evaluated at $U = U^*$. To this end, we take for each of the (cn) lp's in b) second partials with respect to all of the $\{w_{st}\}$

$$\frac{\partial}{\partial w_{st}} \left(\frac{\partial(w^*, \alpha^*)}{\partial w_{lp}} \right)$$
$$= \begin{Bmatrix} 2m(2m-1)(w_{lp}^*)\, d_{lp} + 2\alpha_p^*:\ s = l, t = p \\ 0;\ \text{otherwise} \end{Bmatrix}.$$

Using the first-order necessary values of (W^*, α^*) calculated above, we have for the nonzero entries of $H_\Phi(U^*)$—which are its diagonal elements—the values

$$2m(2m-1)(u_{lp}^*)^{m-1} d_{lp} + 2\alpha_p^*$$

$$= 2m(2m-1)\, d_{lp} \left\{ \frac{1}{\sum_{j=1}^{c} \left(\frac{d_{lp}}{d_{jp}} \right)^{1/(m-1)}} \right\}^{m-1}$$

$$- 2 \left\{ \frac{1}{\sum_{j=1}^{c} \left(\frac{1}{m d_{jp}} \right)^{1/(m-1)}} \right\}^{m-1}$$

$$= \frac{2m(2m-1) - 2m}{\left(\sum_{j=1}^{c} \left(\frac{1}{d_{jp}} \right)^{1/(m-1)} \right)^{m-1}}$$

$$= 4m(m-1) \left(\sum_{j=1}^{c} (d_{jp})^{1/(1-m)} \right)^{1-m}.$$

Letting

$$a_p = \left(\sum_{j=1}^{c} (d_{jp})^{1/(1-m)} \right)^{1-m}; \quad 1 \leqslant p \leqslant n, \text{ and}$$

e) $\lambda_p = 4m(m-1)\, a_p; \quad 1 \leqslant p \leqslant n,$

we have at e) the n distinct eigenvalues of $H_\Phi(U^*)$, each of multiplicity c, so the Hessian of Φ at U^* is a diagonal matrix of the form

$$H_\Phi(U^*) = \left[\begin{array}{c|c|c|c} \begin{matrix}\lambda_1 & & O \\ & \lambda_1 & \\ & & \ddots \\ O & & \lambda_1\end{matrix} & O & \cdots & O \\ \hline c \times c \quad O & \begin{matrix}\lambda_2 & & O \\ & \lambda_2 & \\ & & \ddots \\ O & & \lambda_2\end{matrix} & \cdots & O \\ \hline \vdots & c \times c \quad \vdots & \ddots & \vdots \\ \hline O & O & \cdots & \begin{matrix}\lambda_n & & O \\ & \lambda_n & \\ & & \ddots \\ O & & \lambda_n\end{matrix} \\ & & & c \times c \end{array}\right]_{cn \times cn.}$$

Recalling our assumption that $m > 1$ and $d_{jp} > 0 \; \forall j$ and p, we see that $\lambda_p > 0 \; \forall p$, so $H_\Phi(U^*)$ is positive definite at U^*, not only on the tangent subspace defined by equality constraints (7b), but over all of V_{cn}. Thus, (12a) is sufficient, and U^* is a strict local minimum of φ. Finally, note that $0 < u_{ik}^* < 1 \; \forall i, k$ in (12a), so the constraints (7c) are satisfied by solutions of the relaxed problem, and hence of the original problem as well. Q.E.D.

Next, we fix $U \in M_{fc}$ and consider minimization of $J_m(U, \boldsymbol{v})$ in the variables $\{\boldsymbol{v}_i\}$.

Proposition 2: Let ψ: $\mathbb{R}^{cs} \rightarrow \mathbb{R}$, $\psi(\boldsymbol{v}) \doteq J_m(U, \boldsymbol{v})$, where $U \in M_{fc}$ is fixed. Then $\boldsymbol{v}^*$ is a *strict* local minimum of ψ if and only if $\boldsymbol{v}_i^*$, $1 \leqslant i \leqslant c$, is calculated via (12b), $\boldsymbol{v}^* = G(U)$.

Proof: Since minimization of ψ over $\mathbb{R}^{cs}$ is an unconstrained problem, the necessity of (12b) follows by requiring $\nabla_{\boldsymbol{v}_i} \psi(\boldsymbol{v}^*)$ to vanish for every i. Equivalently, the directional derivatives $\psi'(\boldsymbol{v}_i^*, \boldsymbol{y})$ of ψ with respect to $\boldsymbol{v}_i$ vanish at $\boldsymbol{v}_i^*$ in arbitrary directions $\boldsymbol{y} \in \mathbb{R}^S$, $\boldsymbol{y} \neq \boldsymbol{\theta}$. Let $t \in \mathbb{R}$, and define $\forall i$

$$h_i(t) = \psi(\boldsymbol{v}_i^* + t\boldsymbol{y}) = \sum_{k=1}^{n} (u_{ik})^m \, \|\boldsymbol{x}_k - (\boldsymbol{v}_i^* + t\boldsymbol{y})\|^2$$

$$h_i(t) = \sum_{k=1}^{n} (u_{ik})^m \, \langle \boldsymbol{x}_k - \boldsymbol{v}_i^* - t\boldsymbol{y}, \boldsymbol{x}_k - \boldsymbol{v}_i^* - t\boldsymbol{y} \rangle$$

where $\langle \boldsymbol{z}, \boldsymbol{z} \rangle \doteq \|\boldsymbol{z}\|^2$ is the inner product on $\mathbb{R}^s$.

$$\frac{dh_i(t)}{dt} = \sum_{k=1}^{n} (u_{ik})^m \, \langle -\boldsymbol{y}, \boldsymbol{x}_k - \boldsymbol{v}_i^* - t\boldsymbol{y} \rangle + \langle \boldsymbol{x}_k - \boldsymbol{v}_i^* - t\boldsymbol{y}, -\boldsymbol{y} \rangle$$

$$= -2 \left(\sum_{k=1}^{n} (u_{ik})^m \, \langle \boldsymbol{y}, \boldsymbol{x}_k - \boldsymbol{v}_i^* - t\boldsymbol{y} \rangle \right)$$

$$\frac{dh_i(0)}{dt} = \psi'(\boldsymbol{v}_i^*, \boldsymbol{y}) = -2 \left(\sum_{k=1}^{n} (u_{ik})^m \, \langle \boldsymbol{y}, \boldsymbol{x}_k - \boldsymbol{v}_i^* \rangle \right) = 0, \quad 1 \leqslant i \leqslant c.$$

Thus, it is necessary for every i that

$$\text{a)} \quad \left\langle \boldsymbol{y}, \sum_{k=1}^{n} (u_{ik})^m (\boldsymbol{x}_k - \boldsymbol{v}_i^*) \right\rangle = 0 \qquad \forall \boldsymbol{y} \in \mathbb{R}^s, \; \boldsymbol{y} \neq \boldsymbol{\theta}.$$

Since a) can be zero for arbitrary $\boldsymbol{y} \neq \boldsymbol{\theta}$ if and only if its second argument is the zero vector, condition (12b) follows and necessity is established. While sufficiency of (12b) can be established by calculating the eigenvalues of $H_\psi(\boldsymbol{v}^*)$, the $(cs \times cs)$ Hessian of ψ at $\boldsymbol{v}^*$, it is instructive to give a different proof. Let $\boldsymbol{y} = (\boldsymbol{y}_1, \boldsymbol{y}_2, \cdots, \boldsymbol{y}_c)$, $\boldsymbol{y}_i \in \mathbb{R}^s \; \forall i$, and $t \in \mathbb{R}$. Then define

$$h(t) = \psi(\boldsymbol{v}^* + t\boldsymbol{y}) = \sum_{k=1}^{n} \sum_{i=1}^{c} (u_{ik})^m \, \|\boldsymbol{x}_k - \boldsymbol{v}_i^* - t\boldsymbol{y}_i\|^2.$$

Then

$$h'(t) = \sum_{k=1}^{n} \sum_{i=1}^{c} -2(u_{ik})^m \, \langle \boldsymbol{y}_i, \boldsymbol{x}_k - \boldsymbol{v}_i^* - t\boldsymbol{y}_i \rangle$$

and

$$h''(t) = \boldsymbol{y}^T [H_\psi(\boldsymbol{v}^* + t\boldsymbol{y})] \, \boldsymbol{y} = \sum_{k=1}^{n} \sum_{i=1}^{c} 2(u_{ik})^m \langle \boldsymbol{y}_i, \boldsymbol{y}_i \rangle.$$

Thus, at $t = 0$ we find that $\forall \boldsymbol{y} \neq \boldsymbol{\theta} \in \mathbb{R}^{cs}$,

$$\text{b)} \quad h''(0) = \boldsymbol{y}^T [H_\psi(\boldsymbol{v}^*)] \, \boldsymbol{y} = 2 \left(\sum_{i=1}^{c} \|\boldsymbol{y}_i\|^2 \left(\sum_{k=1}^{n} (u_{ik})^m \right) \right).$$

For $\boldsymbol{y} \neq \boldsymbol{\theta}$, we have from b) and constraints (7c), that $h''(0) > 0$, i.e., $H_\psi(\boldsymbol{v}^*)$ is positive definite. Thus, (12b) is sufficient, and $\boldsymbol{v}^*$ is a strict local minimum of ψ. Q.E.D.

Next, consider minimization of J_m over $(M_{fc} \times \mathbb{R}^{cs})$ jointly in the variables $(U, \boldsymbol{v})$. The U variables are of the Kuhn-Tucker variety due to (7), while $\boldsymbol{v}$ is unconstrained. Using the substitution $u_{ik} = w_{ik}^2$ and relaxation as in Proposition 1, it is easy to verify that $(U^*, \boldsymbol{v}^*)$ may minimize J_m locally only if $(U^*, \boldsymbol{v}^*) = (F(\boldsymbol{v}^*), G(u^*)) = ((F \circ G)(U^*), G(U^*)) = \mathcal{T}_m(U^*, \boldsymbol{v}^*)$, i.e., only if $(U^*, \boldsymbol{v}^*)$ is a fixed point of $\mathcal{T}_m$. In other words, (12) are *jointly* necessary: this follows by setting the gradient of the Lagrangian of J_m equal to zero. Since the multipliers $\{\alpha_i^*\}$ for constraints (7b) are not coupled to the $\{\boldsymbol{v}_i\}$, exactly the same conditions will follow.

The joint *sufficiency* of (12a) and (12b) is not so easy to establish. If $H_\Phi(U^*)$ and $H_\psi(\boldsymbol{v}^*)$ denote the same Hessian matrices as in Propositions 1 and 2, respectively, the Hessian of the Lagrangian L of J_m at $(U^*, \boldsymbol{v}^*)$ is the $(cn \times cs) \times$

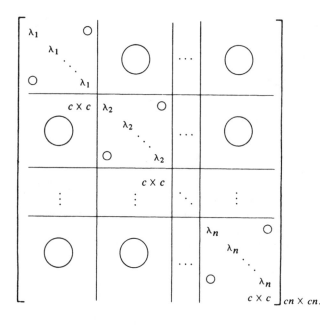

$(cn \times cs)$ matrix with partitioned form

$$H_L(U^*, v^*) = \left[\begin{array}{c|c} H_\Phi(u^*) \quad cn \times cn & M \quad cn \times cs \\ \hline M^T \quad cs \times cn & H_\psi(v^*) \quad cs \times cs \end{array}\right].$$

We know from Proposition 1 that $H_\Phi(U^*)$ is a diagonal matrix with n distinct eigenvalues each of multiplicity c, viz.,

$$\lambda_k = 4m(m-1) \cdot \left(\sum_{i=1}^{c} (d_{ik})^{1/(1-m)}\right)^{1-m}; \qquad 1 \leqslant k \leqslant n.$$

Proposition 2 shows that all the eigenvalues of $H_\psi(v^*)$ are positive: in fact, this matrix has c distinct eigenvalues each of multiplicity s, namely $\gamma_i = 2(\sum_{k=1}^{n} (u_{ik}^*)^m)$; $1 \leqslant i \leqslant c$; and $H_\psi(v^*)$ is also diagonal. Unfortunately, the matrix M in $H_L(U^*, v^*)$ is *not* the zero matrix; it contains $n(c \times s)$ blocks involving entries of the form $(w_{ik})^{2m-1}(x_k - v_i)$, and so the structure of $H_L(u^*, v^*)$ is not immediately obvious. To establish that conditions (12) are *jointly* sufficient, it would be enough to show that $H_L(U^*, v^*)$ was positive definite on *at least* the subspace of $M_{fc} \times \mathbb{R}^{cs}$ tangent to (U^*, v^*), i.e., that $H_L(U^*, v^*)$ restricted to the solution space of the linear system defined by applying the Jacobian of the *constraints* to (U, v) and equating it to zero was positive definite. Since this is an ambitious undertaking, we are content to conjecture here that (12a) and (12b) *are* jointly sufficient, and defer this question to a future investigation. We are, however, now in a position to establish that $\mathfrak{T}_m$ descends *strictly* on the iterates of J_m. This is the content of the following.

Theorem 1: Let

$$S = \{(U^*, v^*): J_m(U^*, v^*) < J_m(U, v), \quad \forall (U, v) \in B^0((U^*, v^*), r)\}.$$

Then J_m is a descent function for $\{\mathfrak{T}_m, S\}$.

Proof: $\{y \to \|y\|^2\}$ and $\{y \to y^m\}$ are continuous. J_m is the sum of products of such functions, so is continuous on $M_{fc} \times \mathbb{R}^{cs}$. Next, suppose $(U, v) \notin S$. Then

$$\begin{aligned} J_m(\mathfrak{T}_m(U, v)) &= J_m(A_2 \circ A_1(U, v)) \\ &= J_m(F(G(U)), G(U)) \\ &< J_m(U, G(U)) \text{ by Proposition 1} \\ &< J_m(U, v) \text{ by Proposition 2.} \end{aligned}$$

Finally, if $(U, v) \in S$, equality prevails throughout in the above argument. Q.E.D.

The second requirement of Theorem C is that algorithm $\mathfrak{T}_m$ be continuous on the domain of J_m with S deleted. $\mathfrak{T}_m$ is in fact continuous on all of $M_{fc} \times \mathbb{R}^{cs}$, as we show in the following.

Theorem 2: $\mathfrak{T}_m$ is continuous on $(M_{fc} \times \mathbb{R}^{cs})$.

Proof: Since $\mathfrak{T}_m = A_2 \circ A_1$, and the composition of continuous functions is again continuous, it suffices to show that A_1 and A_2 are each continuous. Since $A_1(U, v) = G(U)$, A_1 is continuous if G is. To see that G is continuous in the (cn) variables $\{u_{ik}\}$, note that G is a vector field, with the resolution by (cs) scalar field, say

$$G = (G_{11}, G_{12}, \cdots, G_{cs}): \mathbb{R}^{cn} \to \mathbb{R}^{cs}$$

where $G_{ij}: \mathbb{R}^{cn} \to \mathbb{R}$ is defined via (12b) as

$$G_{ij}(U) = \sum_{k=1}^{n} (u_{ik})^m x_{kj} \Big/ \sum_{k=1}^{n} (u_{ik})^m = v_{ij} \qquad \forall i, j.$$

Now $\{u_{ik} \to (u_{ik})^m\}$ is continuous, $\{(u_{ik})^m \to (u_{ik})^m \cdot x_{kj}\}$ is continuous, and the sum of continuous functions is continuous; thus,

$$G_{ij}(U) = \frac{B_{ij}(U)}{C_{ij}(U)}$$

is the quotient of two continuous scalar fields for all $1 \leqslant i \leqslant c$; $1 \leqslant j \leqslant n$. In view of constraint (7c), $C_{ij}(U)$ never vanishes, so G_{ij} is also continuous $\forall i, j$. Therefore, G, and in turn A_1, are continuous on their entire domains. Since $A_2(v) = (F(v), v)$, it suffices to show that F is a continuous function of the (cs) variables $\{v_{ij}\}$. F is a vector field with the resolution by (cn) scalar fields,

$$F = (F_{11}, F_{12}, \cdots, F_{cn}): \mathbb{R}^{cs} \to \mathbb{R}^{cn}$$

where $F_{ij}: \mathbb{R}^{cs} \to \mathbb{R}$ is defined via (12a) as

$$F_{ij}(v) = \frac{\|x_j - v_i\|^{-2/(m-1)}}{\sum_{l=1}^{c} \|x_j - v_l\|^{-2/(m-1)}} = u_{ij}.$$

Since any norm function is (uniformly) continuous, we have

$$\{v_i \to \|x_j - v_i\|\} \text{ is continuous} \qquad \forall i;$$

$$\{\|x_j - v_l\| \to \|x_j - v_l\|^{-2/(m-1)}\} \text{ is continuous;}$$

and the sum of continuous functions is continuous; thus,

$$F_{ij}(v) = \frac{D_{ij}(v)}{E_{ij}(v)}$$

is the quotient of two continuous scalar fields for all $1 \leqslant i \leqslant c$; $1 \leqslant j \leqslant n$. In view of our general hypothesis that $d_{jk} = \|x_k - v_j\| > 0$ $\forall j$ and k, F_{ij} is continuous for all i, j. Therefore, F, and in turn A_2, are continuous on their entire domains. Thus, $\mathfrak{T}_m = A_2 \circ A_1$ is continuous on $M_{fc} \times \mathbb{R}^{cs}$. Q.E.D.

The final condition needed for Theorem C is compactness of a subset of $(M_{fc} \times \mathbb{R}^{cs})$ which contains all of the possible iterate sequences generated by $\mathfrak{T}_m$. Note first that an initial guess for such a sequence consists of either $U^{(0)}$, for then $v^{(0)} = G(U^{(0)})$; or $v^{(0)}$, in which case $U^{(0)} = F(v^{(0)})$. If $U^{(0)}$ is the initial guess, then the *entire* Picard sequence $\{(T)^{(k)}(U^{(0)}, v^{(0)})\}$ always lies in a compact set; while if $v^{(0)}$ is the beginning point, all terms except $(U^{(0)}, v^{(0)})$ do. The result of Theorem 3 is valid in either instance.

Theorem 3: Let $[\text{conv}(X)]^c$ be the c-fold Cartesian product of the convex hull of X, and let $(U^{(0)}, G(U^{(0)}))$ be the starting point of iteration with $\mathfrak{T}_m$, with $U^{(0)} \in M_{fc}$ and $v^{(0)} = G(U^{(0)})$. Then

$$(\mathcal{T}_m)^{(k)}(U^{(0)}, v^{(0)}) \in M_{fc} \times [\mathrm{conv}(X)]^c, \quad k = 1, 2, \cdots \tag{21a}$$

$$M_{fc} \times [\mathrm{conv}(X)]^c \text{ is compact in } M_{fc} \times \mathbb{R}^{cs}. \tag{21b}$$

Proof: Let $U^{(0)} \in M_{fc}$ be chosen. Then $v^{(0)} = G(U^{(0)})$ is calculated using (12a) so that

$$v_i^{(0)} = \sum_{k=1}^{n} (u_{ik}^{(0)})^m x_k \Big/ \sum_{k=1}^{n} (u_{ik}^{(0)})^m; \quad 1 \leq i \leq c.$$

Let

$$\rho_{ik} = \frac{(u_{ik}^{(0)})^m}{\sum_{l=1}^{n} (u_{il}^{(0)})^m}, \quad 1 \leq k \leq n.$$

In view of constraints (7a) and (7c), it must be that $0 < \rho_{ik} < 1 \ \forall i, k$ and so $\forall i$

$$v_i^{(0)} = \sum_{k=1}^{n} \rho_{ik} x_k$$

with

$$\sum_{k=1}^{n} \rho_{ik} = \sum_{k=1}^{n} \left(\frac{u_{ik}^{(0)m}}{\sum_{l=1}^{n} (u_{il}^{(0)})^m} \right) = \frac{\sum_{k=1}^{n} (u_{ik}^{(0)})^m}{\sum_{l=1}^{n} (u_{il}^{(0)})^m} = 1.$$

Thus, $\forall i$, $v_i^{(0)} \in \mathrm{conv}(X)$, and therefore $v^{(0)} \in [\mathrm{conv}(X)]^c$. Continuing recursively, we know that $U^{(1)} = F(v^{(0)}) \in M_{fc}$ by (12b), and then $v^{(1)} = G(U^{(1)}) \in [\mathrm{conv}(X)]^c$ by the same argument as above. Thus, every iterate of $\mathcal{T}_m$ belongs to $M_{fc} x [\mathrm{conv}(X)]^c$. Note that if $v^{(0)}$ is the initialization of $\mathcal{T}_m$, we may choose $v^{(0)} \in \mathbb{R}^{cs} \backslash [\mathrm{conv}(X)]^c$, but $U^{(0)} = F(v^{(0)}) \in M_{fc}$, so that $v^{(k)} = G(U^{(k)}) \in [\mathrm{conv}(X)]^c \ \forall k \geq 1$.

To see that $M_{fc} \times [\mathrm{conv}(X)]^c$ is compact, we note that X is finite, each $x_k \in X$ has finite components, so the diameter of X = diameter (conv (X)) is bounded. Since conv (X) is the convex hull of finitely many generators (the x_k's), it is closed. Thus, conv (X) is closed and bounded in $\mathbb{R}^s \Rightarrow$ conv (X) is compact, by the generalized Heine-Borel theorem, and so $[\mathrm{conv}(X)]^c$ is also compact. An argument similar in every respect ($M_{fc} = \mathrm{conv}(M_{co})$) given in [2] establishes compactness of M_{fc}. Thus, $M_{fc} \times [\mathrm{conv}(X)]^c$ is compact.

We now assemble the hypotheses and results of the above theorems into a formal statement for convergence of fuzzy ISODATA.

Theorem 4: Let $X = \{x_1, x_2, \cdots, x_n\}$ be bounded in $\mathbb{R}^s$. Let

$$J_m(U, v) = \sum_{k=1}^{n} \sum_{i=1}^{c} (u_{ik})^m \|x_k - v_i\|^2; \quad 1 < m < \infty$$

where U satisfies (7), $v = (v_1, v_2, \cdots, v_c)$ with $v_i \in \mathbb{R}^s \ \forall i$. If $\mathcal{T}_m$: $(M_{fc} \times \mathbb{R}^{cs}) \to (M_{fc} \times \mathbb{R}^{cs})$ is the fuzzy ISODATA (Picard) iterative operator at (15), and for every i, j, k, $d_{ik}^{(j)} = \|x_k - v_i^{(j)}\|^2 > 0$, then for any $(U^{(0)}, G(U^{(0)})) \in M_{fc} \times [\mathrm{conv}(X)]^c$, either

$$\{(\mathcal{T}_m)^{(j)}(U^{(0)}, v^{(0)})\} \tag{22a}$$

terminates at a local minimum (U^*, v^*) of J_m; or

$$\{(\mathcal{T}_m)^{(j)}(U^{(0)}, v^{(0)})\} \tag{22b}$$

contains a subsequence such that

$$\{(\mathcal{T}_m)^{(j_k)}(U^{(0)}, v^{(0)})\} \to (U^*, v^*),$$

a local minimum of J_m as $j_k \to \infty$.

Proof: Taking J_m as g in Theorem C, Theorem 1 shows that J_m is a Zangwill descent functional for $\{\mathcal{T}_m, S\}$, where S is the set of strict local minima of J_m. Theorem 2 asserts that iterative descent algorithm $\mathcal{T}_m$ is continuous on $M_{fc} \times [\mathrm{conv}(X)]^c$; and by Theorem 3, the iterate sequences of fuzzy ISODATA operator $\mathcal{T}_m$ are always in a compact subset of the domain of J_m. Applying Theorem C secures (22a) and (22b). Q.E.D.

Theorem 4 is somewhat weaker that the type of convergence usually established by fixed-point theorems, in that (22b) asserts the convergence to (U^*, v^*) of a *subsequence* of Picard iterates of $\mathcal{T}_m$. Nonetheless, we are assured by this result that the fuzzy ISODATA algorithms *always* (i.e., from arbitrary initializations of $U^{(0)}$) generate sequences among which there is a subsequence which gets arbitrarily close to a local minimum of J_m. Due to the complexity of operator $\mathcal{T}_m$, this type of result may be best one can expect. We remark that *in practice*, the assumption that $d_{ik}^{(j)} > 0 \ \forall i, k, j$ is *not* restrictive, since the roundoff error alone will in all probability preclude this eventuality. Moreover, the *empirically* observed behavior of fuzzy ISODATA over some 20-25 different data sets indicates that (21a), termination *at* a local minimum of J_m, almost always occurs (whether such a (U^*, v^*) is a "good" solution in the contexts of clustering and classifier design is an entirely different matter! cf. [5]).

V. The Limiting Case: $m = 1$

It is natural to conjecture that by defining F and G in (14) with necessary conditions (5) for $J_1(U, v)$, and putting $\mathcal{T}_1$ as in (15), one might be able to extend Theorem 4 to the case $m = 1$, i.e., to establish "convergence" for the hard c-means algorithm. However, Proposition 1 is nonsensical at $m = 1$, because M_c is finite, so the notion of local minima for φ (and hence for J_1) is undefined. Thus, convergence of hard c-means as such is itself an undefined consideration.

VI. Other Fuzzy Extensions

It is entirely conceivable that the fuzzy ISODATA algorithms are themselves a subfamily of a more general set of procedures designed to minimize functionals such as

$$J_m(U, p) \doteq \sum_{k=1}^{n} \sum_{i=1}^{c} (u_{ik})^m d_{ik}; \quad 1 \leq m < \infty \tag{23}$$

where $U \in M_{fc}$; and p is a *parameterization* of the (cn) "distances" between the $n x_k$'s and the c fuzzy subsets $\{u_i\}$ in U involving variables other than v_i. Proposition 1 will hold with necessary conditions (12a) as long as the d_{ik} are all positive. Proposition 2 will be replaced by whatever necessary conditions emanate in place of (12b) for parameterization p of the $\{d_{ik}\}$. Independent of this change, $J_m(U, p)$

will descend strictly on iterates of the operator involved because of Proposition 1, so Theorem 1 should hold. Theorem 2 will hold with respect to G, but continuity in the variables other than U arising from parameterization $\boldsymbol{p}$ will have to be established. The validity of Theorem 3 will depend on being able to confine the necessary form of the $\boldsymbol{p}$-derived variables to a compact set. Although the method of Zangwill fails to establish convergence of J_m at $m = 1$, it may very well apply to generalizations of fuzzy ISODATA in the other direction.

References

[1] J. C. Dunn, "A fuzzy relative of the ISODATA process and its use in detecting compact well-separated clusters," *J. Cybern.*, vol. 3, no. 3, pp. 32-57, 1974.

[2] G. Ball and D. Hall, "A clustering technique for summarizing multivariate data," *Behav. Sci.*, vol. 12, pp. 153-155, 1967.

[3] J. C. Bezdek, "Fuzzy mathematics in pattern classification," Ph.D. dissertation, Appl. Math., Cornell Univ., Ithaca, NY, 1973.

[4] —, "Numerical taxonomy with fuzzy sets," *J. Math. Bio.*, vol. 1, pp. 57-71, 1974.

[5] —, "Cluster validity with fuzzy sets," *J. Cybern.*, vol. 3, no. 3, pp. 58-72, 1974.

[6] J. C. Bezdek and P. Castelaz, "Prototype classification and feature selection with fuzzy sets," *IEEE Trans. Syst., Man, Cybern.*, vol. SMC-7, no. 2, pp. 87-92, 1977.

[7] R. Gunderson, "Application of fuzzy ISODATA algorithms to star tracker pointing systems," in *Proc. 7th Triennial IFAC World Congr.*, Helsinki, 1978.

[8] J. C. Bezdek and W. A. Fordon, "Analysis of hypertensive patients by the use of the fuzzy ISODATA algorithms," in *Proc. Joint Automat. Contr. Conf.*, Philadelphia, PA, 1978.

[9] R. Duda and P. Hart, *Pattern Classification and Scene Analysis.* New York: Wiley-Interscience, 1974.

[10] E. Ruspini, "A new approach to clustering," *Inform. Contr.*, vol. 15, pp. 22-32, 1969.

[11] L. Zadeh, "Fuzzy sets," *Inform. Contr.*, vol. 8, pp. 338-353, 1965.

[12] W. Zangwill, *Nonlinear Programming: A Unified Approach.* Englewood Cliffs, NJ: Prentice-Hall, 1969, ch. 4.

[13] D. L. Luenberger, *Introduction to Linear and Non-Linear Programming.* Reading, MA: Addison-Wesley, 1973, pp. 120-127.

[14] J. MacQueen, "Some methods for classification and analysis of multivariate observations," in *Proc. 5th Berkeley Symp. on Math. Statist., and Prob.*, Le Cam and Neyman, Eds., 1967, pp. 281-297.

Convergence Theory for Fuzzy *c*-Means: Counterexamples and Repairs

JAMES C. BEZDEK, MEMBER, IEEE, RICHARD J. HATHAWAY, MICHAEL J. SABIN, MEMBER, IEEE, AND WILLIAM T. TUCKER

Abstract—First, a new counterexample to the original incorrect convergence theorem for the fuzzy *c*-means (FCM) clustering algorithms which was published in 1980 is provided. The importance of this counterexample is that it establishes the existence of saddle points of the FCM objective function at locations *other than* the geometric centroid of fuzzy *c*-partition space. The presentation is augmented by a summary of the counterexamples previously discussed by Tucker. Second, the correct theorem is stated without proof: every FCM iterate sequence converges, at least along a subsequence, to either a local minimum or saddle point of the FCM objective function. Tucker's counterexamples and the corrected theory appear elsewhere. The purpose in restating them here is to caution interested readers not to further propogate the original incorrect convergence statement.

I. Introduction

The fuzzy *c*-means (FCM) clustering algorithm is a set-partitioning method based on Picard iteration through necessary conditions for optimizing a weighted sum of squared errors objective function (J_m). The number m is a parameter ranging from 1 to ∞; J_1 is the well-known classical WGSS objective function which serves to define the hard (or crisp) *c*-means (HCM) and hard ISODATA algorithms [1]. Dunn first extended J_1 to J_2 in [2], and Bezdek then generalized J_2 to J_m for $1 < m < \infty$ in [3]. These algorithms (defined at length in the following) have been applied successfully to a number of problems involving feature analysis, clustering, and classifier design. A recent survey of related literature includes applications in agricultural engineering, astronomy, chemistry, geology, image analysis, medical diagnosis, shape analysis, and target recognition [4].

Concurrent with the growing body of literature on applications of FCM is an interest in theoretical issues connected with its mathematical structure. Much of the early work in both areas is summarized in Bezdek [5]. Included there, and the object of interest here, is the theory of convergence of the iterate sequence used to (approximately) minimize J_m through Picard iteration in the first-order necessary conditions on J_m. In 1980 Bezdek presented in [6] an application of Zangwill's theory [7] to FCM iteration that purported to show that every iterate sequence (or at worst, a subsequence thereof) of FCM converged to a local minimizer of J_m. The 1980 result was subsequently quoted and used in extensions of J_m to the fuzzy *c*-varieties (FCV) algorithms by Bezdek *et al.* [8], and the results of [6], [8] were reproduced in [5] before Tucker discovered a class of counterexamples to the supposed theorems that clearly established a flaw in the original argument. To record due credit, we note that Windham [12] opined that this was probably the case in a personal communication to Bezdek in early 1981. Tucker's example (example 2 to follow) was discussed at the first workshop of the North American Fuzzy Information Processing Society in Logan, UT, May, 1982, and in [9] Tucker extended his work to the quite general set of examples contained in Theorem T in Section II. More recently, Sabin discovered a second counterexample (example 1 to follow) that is interesting in that it occurs at a different location in the objective function's domain than any of Tucker's points. The purpose of this correspondence is to present these counterexamples in a unified way and to set the record straight regarding [5], [6], and [8] by exhibiting (without proof) the correct result. We begin with some notation and a description of FCM.

Let $c \geqslant 2$ be an integer; let $X = \{x_1, \cdots, x_n\} \subset R^s$ be a finite data set containing at least $c < n$ distinct points; and let R^{cn} denote the set of all real $c \times n$ matrices. A nondegenerate fuzzy *c*-partition of X is conveniently represented by a matrix $U = [u_{ik}] \in R^{cn}$, the entries of which satisfy

$$u_{ik} \in [0,1], \qquad 1 \leqslant i \leqslant c, 1 \leqslant k \leqslant n \tag{1a}$$

$$\sum_{i=1}^{c} u_{ik} = 1, \qquad 1 \leqslant k \leqslant n \tag{1b}$$

$$\sum_{k=1}^{n} u_{ik} > 0, \qquad 1 \leqslant i \leqslant c. \tag{1c}$$

The set of all matrices in R^{cn} satisfying (1) is denoted by M_{fcn}. A matrix $U \in M_{fcn}$ can be used to describe the cluster structure of X by interpreting u_{ik} as the grade of membership of x_k in the ith cluster: $u_{ik} = 0.95$ represents a strong association of x_k to cluster i, while $u_{ik} = 0.01$ represents a very weak one. Other useful information about cluster substructure can be conveyed by identifying prototypes (or cluster centers) $v = (v_1, \cdots, v_c)^T \in R^{cs}$, where v_i is the prototype for class i, $1 \leqslant i \leqslant c$, $v_i \in R^s$. "Good" partitions U of X and representatives (v_i for class i) may be defined by considering minimization of the *c*-means objective function J_m: $(M_{fcn} \times R^{cs}) \to R$ defined by

$$J_m(U, v) = \sum_{k=1}^{n} \sum_{i=1}^{c} (u_{ik})^m |x_k - v_i|^2 \tag{2}$$

where $1 \leqslant m < \infty$ and $|\cdot|$ is any inner product induced norm on R^s. For $m > 1$, Bezdek [2] gave the following necessary conditions

Manuscript received March 3, 1987; revised May 18, 1987. This work was supported in part by NSF Grants IST-8407860 and ECS-8451544. This correspondence was presented in part at the Third Workshop of the North American Fuzzy Information Processing Society, Kauai, HI, 1984.

J. C. Bezdek is with the Boeing Electronics Company, PO Box 2496, Seattle, WA 98124.

R. J. Hathaway is with the Department of Mathematics, Georgia Southern College, Statesboro, GA 30460.

M. J. Sabin is with Cylink Corporation, 920 W. Fremont Avenue, Sunnyvale, CA 94087.

W. T. Tucker is with the Statistics Program, Corporate Research and Development, General Electric Company, Schenectady, NY 12345.

IEEE Log Number 8716033.

Reprinted from *IEEE Trans. Syst., Man, Cybern.*, vol. SMC-17, no. 5, pp. 873-877, September/October 1987.

for a minimizer (U^*, v^*) of $J_m(U, v)$ over $M_{fcn} \times R^{cs}$:

$$v_i^* = \frac{\sum_{k=1}^{n} (u_{ik}^*)^m x_k}{\sum_{k=1}^{n} (u_{ik}^*)^m}, \quad \text{for all } i \tag{3a}$$

and for each k such that $d_{ik}^* = |x_k - v_i^*|^2 > 0$ for all i, then

$$u_{ik}^* = \left(\sum_{j=1}^{c} \left(\frac{d_{ik}^*}{d_{jk}^*} \right)^{1/(m-1)} \right)^{-1}, \quad \text{for all } i. \tag{3b}$$

However, if k is such that $d_{ik}^* = |x_k - v_i^*|^2 = 0$ for some i, then u_{ik}^* for all i are any nonnegative numbers satisfying

$$\sum_{i=1}^{c} u_{ik}^* = 1 \quad \text{and} \quad u_{ik}^* = 0, \quad \text{if } d_{ik}^* \neq 0. \tag{3c}$$

The FCM algorithms are iteration through the equations in (3). Note that (3c) may not *uniquely* specify U from v in case singularity ($d_{ik}^* = 0$) occurs. That is, (3c) specifies u_{ik}^* for $1 \leqslant i \leqslant c$ uniquely only if exactly one $d_{ik}^* = 0$. When multiple singularities exist for some k, the corresponding column in U^* has an infinite number of satisfactory forms. For this reason it is more convenient when applying Zangwill's results to leave the iteration loosely specified per (3c), although a particular choice for the resolution of singularities at (3c) must, of course, be made when implementing FCM.

The following notation is given to further describe FCM iteration. Let G: $M_{fcn} \to R^{cs}$ be the function defined by $G(U) = v = (v_1, \cdots, v_c)^T$, where the vectors $v_i \in R^s$ are calculated via (3a) for $1 \leqslant i \leqslant c$ using U, and let F: $R^{cs} \to P(M_{fcn})$ denote the point-to-set mapping defined by $F(v) = \{U \in M_{fcn} | (U, v)$ satisfies (3b) and 3(c)$\}$. $P(*)$ denotes the power set of $*$. The FCM iteration can be expressed using the point-to-set mapping T_m: $M_{fcn} \times R^{cs} \to P(M_{fcn} \times R^{cs})$ defined by the composition

$$T_m = A_2 \circ A_1 \tag{4a}$$

where

$$A_1: M_{fcn} \times R^{cs} \to R^{cs} \qquad A_1(U, v) = G(U) \tag{4b}$$

and

$$A_2: R^{cs} \to P(M_{fcn} \times R^{cs}) \qquad A_2(v) = \{(U, v) | U \in F(v)\}. \tag{4c}$$

Therefore, $T_m(U, v) = \{(\hat{U}, \hat{v}) | \hat{v} = G(U), \hat{U} \in F(\hat{v})\}$, and we say that $\{(U^{(k)}, v^{(k)})\}$, $k = 0,1,2, \cdots$ is an FCM iteration sequence if $(U^{(0)}, v^{(0)}) \in M_{fcn} \times R^{cs}$ and $(U^{(k)}, v^{(k)}) \in T_m(U^{(k-1)}, v^{(k-1)})$ for $k = 1,2, \cdots$.

II. Counterexamples and Repairs

The original theory concerns limits of iterate sequences of the form $\{(U^{(k)}, v^{(k)} | k = 0,1,2, \cdots\}$ with $(U^{(0)}, v^{(0)}) \in M_{fcn} \times R^{cs}$. The main result claimed in [6] was that every such sequence converged to a local minimizer of J_m or, at worst, had a subsequence which did. Tucker first exhibited fixed points of T_m (a limit of such a sequence) that were saddle points for J_m in [9]. However, Sabin's example is in some sense more elementary and will be presented first.

Counterexample 1

Let $s = 1$, $n = 4$, $\{x_1, x_2, x_3, x_4\} = \{-3, -1, 1, 3\}$, $c = 3$, $v^{(0)} = (-1, 0, 1)^T$, and $m = 2$. Let $U^{(0)} \in F(v^{(0)})$ and $(U^{(k)}, v^{(k)}) \in T_2(U^{(k-1)}, v^{(k-1)})$ for $k \geqslant 1$. For this example the iteration sequence is uniquely determined by $v^{(0)}$. Attention is first focused on the asymptotic behavior of $\{v^{(k)}\}$, with $U^{(k)}$ for $k \geqslant 1$ given by (3b).

Table I lists an initial segment of the sequence $\{v^{(k)}\}$, computed on a VAX computer using double-precision (64-bit) floating-point arithmetic. The table suggests that the sequence converges to $v^* = (-a, 0, a)$, where $a \approx 2.9$. The corresponding U^* is obtained by applying (3b) with v^* after noting that the right side of (3b) is continuous in v whenever all $d_{ik} \neq 0$, which is the case for v^*. However, (U^*, v^*) is not a local minimizer of J_2. To see this, let $\epsilon \in R$, and define $v_\epsilon = (-a, \epsilon, a)$. Let U_ϵ be the corresponding partition given by (3b) using v_ϵ. Trace a) of Fig. 1 plots $J_2(U_\epsilon, v_\epsilon)$ as a function of ϵ for small values of $|\epsilon|$. The plot indicates that $\epsilon = 0$ is a local maximizer of the function; i.e., $J_2(U_\epsilon, v_\epsilon) < J_2(U^*, v^*)$ for small nonzero ϵ. By the continuity of (3b) at v^*, (U_ϵ, v_ϵ) approaches (U^*, v^*) as ϵ tends to 0. Hence (U^*, v^*) is not a local minimizer of J_2.

To verify that trace a) of Fig. 1 accurately illustrates the behavior of $J_2(U_\epsilon, v_\epsilon)$ in the vicinity of $\epsilon = 0$, a Taylor expansion of the function about 0 is derived in Appendix. The expansion is

$$J_2(U_\epsilon, v_\epsilon) = c_0 + c_2\epsilon^2 + 0(\epsilon^2)$$

where $c_0 \cong 1.6$ and $c_2 \cong -0.015$. The fact that c_2 is negative verifies that $\in = 0$ is a local maximizer of $J_2(U_\epsilon, v_\epsilon)$. Trace (b) of Fig. 1 plots the value of $c_0 + c_2\epsilon^2$ versus ϵ.

Admittedly, this is a fairly contrived situation. Nevertheless, this counterexample illustrates again that it is incorrect to claim that iterative applications of T_m to any initial $(U^{(0)}, v^{(0)})$ will produce a sequence that converges along some subsequence to a local minimum of J_m. Finally, we compute the *approximate* values of (U^*, v^*). Using $v^* \approx (-2.91054, \cdots, 0, 2.91054, \cdots)^T$ with (3b) results in an approximate U^* as follows:

$$U^* \approx \begin{bmatrix} 0.9989\cdots & 0.2045\cdots & 0.0489\cdots & 0.0002\cdots \\ 0.0009\cdots & 0.7466\cdots & 0.7466\cdots & 0.0009\cdots \\ 0.0002\cdots & 0.0489\cdots & 0.2045\cdots & 0.9989\cdots \end{bmatrix}.$$

The point of exhibiting U^* for counterexample 1 is that it is well-distanced from $U_0 = [1/c]$ ($= [1/3]$ here), the geometric centroid of M_{f34}. Tucker's counterexamples all occur at U_0. Thus counterexample 1 establishes an important heretofore unknown fact: it is possible for J_m to have saddle points at locations other than U_0.

Counterexample 2 (after Tucker [9])

Counterexample 2 is actually an infinite set of counterexamples contained in the following theorem, which is proved in [9]. Let $2 \leqslant c < n$, and define

$$U^* = \begin{bmatrix} \frac{1}{c} & \frac{1}{c} & \cdots & \frac{1}{c} \\ \frac{1}{c} & \frac{1}{c} & \cdots & \frac{1}{c} \\ \vdots & \vdots & & \vdots \\ \frac{1}{c} & \frac{1}{c} & \cdots & \frac{1}{c} \end{bmatrix} \qquad D_1 = \begin{bmatrix} 1 & 0 & \cdots & 0 \\ -1 & 0 & \cdots & 0 \\ 0 & 0 & \cdots & 0 \\ \vdots & \vdots & & \vdots \\ 0 & 0 & \cdots & 0 \end{bmatrix}.$$

Then for $|\epsilon| < 1/c$ set $U_\epsilon = U^* + \epsilon D_1$. After suitably manipulating J_m, Tucker arrives at the following result using the notation $G(U)$ from (4b).

Theorem T (Tucker [9]): If $d_{ik}^* > 0$ for all i, k and $v^* = \bar{x}$, then for $n = 2$, $0 < |\epsilon| < 1/c$ and for any $m > 1$, $J_m(U_\epsilon, G(U_\epsilon)) < J_m(U^*, v^*)$. For $n > 2$ the inequality for J_m holds for every $\epsilon > 0$ sufficiently small if and only if $m < n/(n-2)$.

Theorem T tells us that for $n \geqslant 2$ an $m > 1$ exists at which

TABLE I
INITIAL SEGMENT OF $v^{(k)}$ FOR COUNTEREXAMPLE 1

k	$v_1^{(k)}$	$v_2^{(k)}$	$v_3^{(k)}$
0	−1.0000000000000000	0.0000000000000000	1.0000000000000000
1	−1.4448803452334249	0.0000000000000000	1.4448803452334249
2	−1.8447191880922269	0.0000000000000000	1.8447191880922269
3	−2.3617140462242804	0.0000000000000000	2.3617140462242804
4	−2.7684652456027995	0.0000000000000000	2.7684652456027995
5	−2.8884344120569064	0.0000000000000000	2.8884344120569064
6	−2.9075296476870907	0.0000000000000000	2.9075296476870907
7	−2.9101401891449808	0.0000000000000000	2.9101401891449808
8	−2.9104889298087584	0.0000000000000000	2.9104889298087584
9	−2.9105353719960641	0.0000000000000000	2.9105353719960641
10	−2.9105415541665939	0.0000000000000000	2.9105415541665939
11	−2.9105423770628628	0.0000000000000000	2.9105423770628628
12	−2.9105424865961154	0.0000000000000000	2.9105424865961154
13	−2.9105425011757435	0.0000000000000000	2.9105425011757435
14	−2.9105425031163918	0.0000000000000000	2.9105425031163918
15	−2.9105425033747054	0.0000000000000000	2.9105425033747054
16	−2.9105425034090888	0.0000000000000000	2.9105425034090888
17	−2.9105425034136654	0.0000000000000000	2.9105425034136654
18	−2.9105425034142746	0.0000000000000000	2.9105425034142746
19	−2.9105425034143557	0.0000000000000000	2.9105425034143557
20	−2.9105425034143665	0.0000000000000000	2.9105425034143665
21	−2.9105425034143679	0.0000000000000000	2.9105425034143679
22	−2.9105425034143682	0.0000000000000000	2.9105425034143682
23	−2.9105425034143682	0.0000000000000000	2.9105425034143682
24	−2.9105425034143682	0.0000000000000000	2.9105425034143682
25	−2.9105425034143682	0.0000000000000000	2.9105425034143682

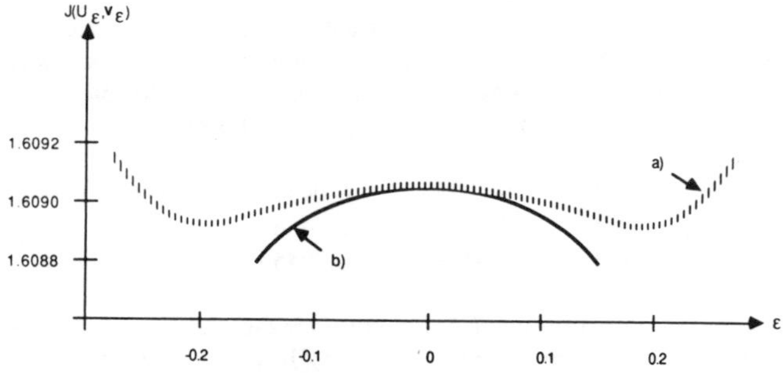

Fig. 1. Trace a) is $J_2(U_\epsilon, v_\epsilon)$. Trace b) is $c_0 + c_2\epsilon^2$.

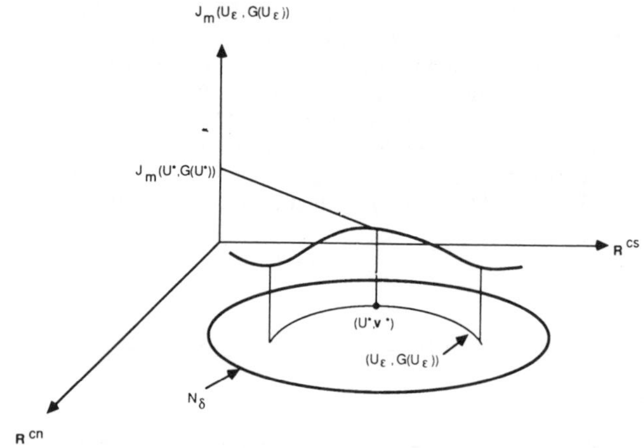

Fig. 2. Geometric idea for counterexample 2. Note: U^* in diagram is centroid of M_{fcn}: $U^* = U_0 = [1/c]$.

(U^*, v^*) is a saddle point. Tucker observes in [9] that Theorem T provides a general contradiction to the original convergence readers will see that Figs. 1 and 2 depict the "same" geometric situation at different locations in M_{fcn}.

The Repair

The following, proved in [10], is the corrected version of the original FCM convergence theorem presented in [6].

Theorem 1: Let $\{x_1, \cdots, x_n\}$ contain at least $c < n$ distinct points, and let

$$J_m(U, v) = \sum_{k=1}^{n} \sum_{i=1}^{c} (u_{ik})^m |x_k - v_i|^2$$

where $1 < m < \infty$, $U \in M_{fcn}$, and $v = (v_1, \cdots, v_c)^T$ with $v_i \in R^s$ for all i. Let $(U^{(0)}, G(v^{(0)}))$ be the starting point of iteration with T_m, with $U^{(0)} \in M_{fcn}$ and $v^{(0)} = G(U^{(0)})$. Then the iterate sequence $\{(U^{(r)}, v^{(r)})\}$, $r = 1, \cdots$ either terminates at a point (U^*, v^*) in the solution set Ω, or a subsequence exists convergent to a point in Ω, where

$$\Omega = \Big\{ (U^*, v^*) \in M_{fcn} \times R^{cs} \big| J_m(U^*, v^*) \leqslant J_m(U, v^*), \quad \text{for all } U \in M_{fcn}, \text{ and} \quad (5a)$$

$$J_m(U^*, v^*) < J_m(U^*, v), \quad v \neq v^* \Big\}. \quad (5b)$$

In [6] it was erroneously concluded that convergence could only occur to minimizers of J_m, but noting the form of Ω in (5) we see that the correct solution set may also contain points $(\hat{U}, \hat{v})$ such that $\hat{U}$ minimizes (uniquely, if all $\hat{d}_{ik} > 0$) $J_m(U, \hat{v})$ over M_{fcn}, and $\hat{v}$ uniquely minimizes $J_m(\hat{U}, v)$ over R^{cs}. However, $(\hat{U}, \hat{v})$ is *jointly* a saddle point for J_m. Note that Ω contains minimizers and saddle points only; it does *not* contain maximizers of J_m. It is worth noting here that in the case of convergence by a subsequence to a point where all the $\hat{d}_{ik}$ are positive, then we easily get the same result by patching up the original theorem for the nonsingular case. That result would guarantee convergence by the subsequence to a point in $\hat{\Omega}$ where $\hat{\Omega}$ is obtained from Ω by replacing $\leqslant$ in (5a) with $<$.

We conclude by noting that any tie-breaking strategy consistent with (3b) and (3c) for determining a unique U can be imposed with no change in the corresponding convergence results.

For convenience we used a general point-to-set mapping, but any point-to-point iteration consistent with (3) has all of the same convergence properties since an iteration sequence generated by it is also an iteration sequence of the original mapping.

The primary question arising from the modified convergence theory is this: does the addition of saddle points to the set Ω alter the usefulness or reliability of FCM for exploratory data analysis (clustering) and classifier design? Computational experience with FCM by a number of investigators over a decade of applied research [4] indicates that FCM almost always *terminates*. That is, the difference in successive estimates of U^* as measured by $|U^{(k+1)} - U^{(k)}| < \epsilon$, where $U^{(k+1)}$ is calculated via looping in (3), can usually be achieved for ϵ's in the 10^{-5} to 10^{-6} range at $k = 50$ or less iterations. At termination $(U^{(k+1)}, v^{(k+1)})$ is merely an *estimate* of (U^*, v^*); we put aside this further complication and assume that whenever FCM terminates, it has attained a point in Ω. In view of Theorem 1, U^* may be (part of) either a local minimizer or saddle point for J_m. The validity of U^* as an explanation of substructure in X is based on the belief that the clustering criterion J_m will be minimized when data points in X pack "tightly" around their prototypes $\{v_i^*\}$. In other words, the *mathematical* rationale for accepting U^* as a satisfactory explanation of X does indeed favor local minimizers. However, it is a well-documented fact that even the *global* minimizer of J_m can suggest visually unappealing (i.e., wrong!) clusters in X due to the tendency of least-squared-error functionals to favor equal subpopulations [3], [9]. This tendency toward cluster-splitting points up the fact that it is always advisable - to the extent possible—to assess the result for any n and sequence where $d_{ik}^* > 0$ for all i, k for some m with $1 < m < \infty$. In fact, however, an even stronger statement can be made: since the sequence $\{n/(n-2)\}$ decreases monotonically and is bounded below by 1, it follows that for $n > 2$ Theorem T provides a saddle point for $m \in (1,2)$ as $n \to \infty$, $m \to 1$. An interesting question left unresolved by Theorem T is this: do saddle points exist for $m > 2$ when $n > 2$? From a practical standpoint our observation suggests a rule of thumb: given n, choose $m \geqslant n/(n-2)$. Then (at least) the saddle points guaranteed by Theorem T will be avoided. The choice of m has always been relegated to an investigator's judgment. Theorem T contains the first *theoretical* rationale for *avoiding* distinguished values of m. Thus, e.g., when processing the IRIS data, $n = 150$, Tucker's theorem suggests choosing $m \geqslant 1.013$. On the other hand, experience with FCM suggests that m should be taken greater than about 1.05, corresponding roughly to $n = 42$. Since most data sets are larger than this, the foregoing rule of thumb seems to have limited practical value. The geometric idea of counterexample 2 is illustrated graphically in Fig. 2. Thoughtful results of clustering using whatever additional information an investigator may have about the process generating the data.

$U_0 = [1/c]$ is usually an undesirable extrema, although one can contrive cases wherein U_0 is at least as plausible as any other solution (e.g., $c = 2$ with $n = 3$, the data being the vertices of any equilateral triangle in $\mathbf{R}^2$ with $v_1 = v_2$ the centroid of the triangle). Neither the extent or relative numbers of the two types of fixed points of T_m in Ω are known. It would be useful to pursue this issue. Among the saddle points *other than* $U_0 = [1/c]$, do any circumstances exist under which this is known in advance (e.g., as functions of c, m, n, etc.)? Further, are saddle points other than U_0 necessarily undesirable (as explanations of data substructure)?

Finally, we observe that the convergence theory for the fuzzy c-varieties (FCV) algorithms developed in [6] and replicated in [5] must at the very least be modified to agree with the foregoing results. That is, the set of limits of FCV almost certainly includes $U_0 = [1/c]$ as a saddle point. However, this theory is complex and deserves a much more thorough investigation than can be given in this correspondence; its delineation will be the subject of a future report.

APPENDIX
DERIVATION OF TAYLOR SERIES FOR COUNTEREXAMPLE 1

After some manipulation (see [11]) we arrive at the equation

$$\begin{aligned} J_2(U_\epsilon, v_\epsilon) = &\left[(-3+a)^{-2} + (-3+\epsilon)^{-2} + (-3-a)^{-2}\right]^{-1} \\ &+\left[(3+a)^{-2} + (3+\epsilon)^{-2} + (3-a)^{-2}\right]^{-1} \\ &+\left[(-1+a)^{-2} + (-1+\epsilon)^{-2} + (-1-a)^{-2}\right]^{-1} \\ &+\left[(1+a)^{-2} + (1+\epsilon)^{-2} + (1-a)^{-2}\right]^{-1}. \end{aligned}$$

Letting $\alpha = [(3+a)^{-2} + (3-a)^{-2}]^{-1}$ and $\beta = [(1+a)^{-2} + (1-a)^{-2}]^{-1}$, we have

$$\begin{aligned} J_2(U_\epsilon, v_\epsilon) = &\left[\alpha^{-1} + (9-6\epsilon+\epsilon^2)^{-1}\right]^{-1} \\ &+\left[\alpha^{-1} + (9+6\epsilon+\epsilon^2)^{-1}\right]^{-1} \\ &+\left[\beta^{-1} + (1-2\epsilon+\epsilon^2)^{-1}\right]^{-1} \\ &+\left[\beta^{-1} + (1+2\epsilon+\epsilon^2)^{-1}\right]^{-1}. \end{aligned} \quad (6)$$

Observe that

$$\begin{aligned} &\left[x^{-1} + (y+\eta)^{-1}\right]^{-1} \\ &= (x^{-1}+y^{-1})^{-1} + x^2(x+y)^{-1}\left[\eta(x+y+\eta)^{-1}\right] \\ &= (x^{-1}+y^{-1})^{-1} - x^2(x+y)^{-1}\sum_{k=1}^{\infty}(-1)^k\eta^k(x+y)^{-k}. \end{aligned}$$

Substituting this expansion for each of the four bracketed terms in (6), we obtain

$$\begin{aligned} &J_2(U_\epsilon, v_\epsilon) \\ &= (\alpha^{-1}+9^{-1})^{-1} - \alpha^2(\alpha+9)^{-1}\sum_{k=1}^{\infty}(-1)^k \\ &\quad \times(\epsilon^2-6\epsilon)^k(\alpha+9)^{-k} + (\alpha^{-1}+9^{-1})^{-1} \\ &\quad - \alpha^2(\alpha+9)^{-1}\sum_{k=1}^{\infty}(-1)^k(\epsilon^2+6\epsilon)^k(\alpha+9)^{-k} \\ &\quad + (\beta^{-1}+1)^{-1} - \beta^2(\beta+1)^{-1}\sum_{k=1}^{\infty}(-1)^k \\ &\quad \times(\varepsilon^2-2\epsilon)^k(\beta+1)^{-k} + (\beta^{-1}+1)^{-1} \\ &\quad - \beta^2(\beta+1)^{-1}\sum_{k=1}^{\infty}(-1)^k(\epsilon^2+2\epsilon)^k(\beta+1)^{-k} \\ &= c_0 + c_2\epsilon^2 + o(\epsilon^2) \end{aligned}$$

where

$$\begin{aligned} c_0 &= 2(\alpha^{-1}+9^{-1})^{-1} + 2(\beta^{-1}+1)^{-1} \\ c_2 &= 2\alpha^2(\alpha+9)^{-2} + 2\beta^2(\beta+1)^{-2} \\ &\quad - 72\alpha^2(\alpha+9)^{-3} - 8\beta^2(\beta+1)^{-3} \end{aligned}$$

Numerically substituting $\alpha = 2.9105425034143682$ yields

$$\begin{aligned} \alpha &= 0.0080008109049835 \\ \beta &= 2.9467940300943870 \\ c_0 &= 1.5092612181431027 \\ c_2 &= -0.0150346430398501. \end{aligned}$$

REFERENCES

[1] R. Duda and P. Hart, *Pattern Classification and Scene Analysis*. New York: Wiley, 1973.

[2] J. C. Dunn, "A fuzzy relative of the ISODATA process and its use in

detecting compact, well-separated clusters," *J. Cybern.* vol. 3, no. 3, pp. 32–57, 1973.
[3] J. C. Bezdek, "Fuzzy mathematics in pattern classification," Ph.D. dissertation, Cornell Univ., Ithaca, NY, 1973.
[4] ___, "Partition structures: A tutorial," in *The Analysis of Fuzzy Information*, J. C. Bezdek, Ed. Boca Raton, FL: CRC Press, 1987, vol. 3, ch. 6.
[5] ___, *Pattern Recognition with Fuzzy Objective Function Algorithms.* New York: Plenum, 1981.
[6] ___, "A convergence theorem for the fuzzy ISODATA clustering algorithms," *IEEE Trans. Pattern Anal. Mach. Intell.*, vol. PAMI-2, pp. 1–8, 1980.
[7] W. Zangwill, *Non-Linear Programming: A Unified Approach.* Englewood Cliffs, NJ: Prentice-Hall, 1969.
[8] J. C. Bezdek, C. Coray, R. Gunderson, and J. Watson, "Detection and characterization of cluster substructure," *SIAM J. Appl. Math.*, vol. 40, no. 2, pp. 339–372, 1981.
[9] W. T. Tucker, "Counterexamples to the convergence theorem for fuzzy ISODATA clustering algorithms," in *The Analysis of Fuzzy Information*, J. C. Bezdek, Ed. Boca Raton, FL: CRC Press, 1987, vol. 3, ch. 7.
[10] R. Hathaway, J. C. Bezdek, and W. Tucker, "An improved convergence theorem for the fuzzy c-means clustering algorithms," in *The Analysis of Fuzzy Information*, J. C. Bezdek, Ed. Boca Raton, FL: CRC Press, 1987, vol. 3, ch. 8.
[11] J. C. Bezdek, "A physical interpretation of fuzzy ISODATA," *IEEE Trans. Syst., Man, Cybern.*, vol. SMC-6, pp. 387–390, May 1976.
[12] M. P. Windham, personal communication, 1981.

Convergence and Consistency of Fuzzy c-means/ISODATA Algorithms

MICHAEL J. SABIN

Abstract—The fuzzy c-means/ISODATA algorithm is usually described in terms of clustering a finite data set. An equivalent point of view is that the algorithm clusters the support points of a finite-support probability distribution. Motivated by recent work on the hard version of the algorithm, this paper extends the definition to arbitrary distributions and considers asymptotic properties. It is shown that fixed points of the algorithm are stationary points of the fuzzy objective functional, and vice versa. When the algorithm is iteratively applied to an initial prototype set, the sequence of prototype sets produced approaches the set of fixed points. If an unknown distribution is approximated by the empirical distribution of stationary, ergodic observations, then as the number of observations grows large, fixed points of the algorithm based on the empirical distribution approach fixed points of the algorithm based on the true distribution. Furthermore, with respect to minimizing the fuzzy objective functional, the algorithm based on the empirical distribution is asymptotically at least as good as the algorithm based on the true distribution.

Index Terms—c-means, consistency, convergence, fixed point, fuzzy clustering, ISODATA, k-means, stationary point.

I. Introduction

Let $Q = \{x_1, x_2, \cdots, x_n\}$ be a finite set of points in s-dimensional Euclidean space R^s. Let M_c be the subset of c-dimensional Euclidean space R^c defined by

$$M_c = \left\{(\lambda_1, \lambda_2, \cdots, \lambda_c) \in R^c : \lambda_i \geq 0, \sum_{i=1}^{c} \lambda_i = 1\right\}.$$

A mapping $U: Q \rightarrow M_c$ describes a c-cell fuzzy partition of Q. Denoting $U(x_k) = (u_1(x_k), u_2(x_k), \cdots, u_c(x_k))$, then $u_i(x_k)$ is the degree of membership of the point x_k in the ith cell of the fuzzy partition. Note that this definition includes degenerate partitions which have one or more empty cells, i.e., partitions in which, for some i, $u_i(x_k) = 0$ for all values of k. Denote by $(R^s)^c$ the set of ordered c-tuples of points in R^s; a point $V = (v_1, v_2, \cdots, v_c) \in (R^s)^c$ (i.e., each $v_i \in R^s$) describes a set of c prototypes. Let $m > 1$ be a given degree of fuzziness; throughout this paper, we take m fixed. Define the objective function

$$J_Q(U, V) = \frac{1}{n} \sum_{k=1}^{n} \sum_{i=1}^{c} u_i^m(x_k)\, d(x_k, v_i)$$

where $d(x, v)$ is an inner-product norm. The fuzzy c-means algorithm [2] seeks a partition U and a set of prototypes V that minimize J_Q. The algorithm is motivated by the following conditions that are necessarily satisfied if (U, V) minimizes J_Q:

$$\frac{1}{n} \sum_{k=1}^{n} u_i^m(x_k)\, d(x_k, v_i) = \min_{v \in R^s} \frac{1}{n} \sum_{k=1}^{n} u_i^m(x_k)\, d(x_k, v), \qquad 1 \leq i \leq c; \quad (1)$$

$$\frac{1}{n} \sum_{k=1}^{n} u_i^m(x_k)\, d(x_k, v_i) = \min_{\Lambda \in M_c} \frac{1}{n} \sum_{k=1}^{n} \lambda_i^m d(x_k, v_i), \qquad 1 \leq k \leq n \quad (2)$$

where $\Lambda = (\lambda_1, \lambda_2, \cdots, \lambda_c)$. Given an initial pair $(U^{(0)}, V^{(0)})$, the algorithm iteratively generates a sequence $\{(U^{(l)}, V^{(l)})\}$ by selecting $U^{(l+1)}$ to satisfy (2) with respect to $V^{(l)}$ and by selecting $V^{(l+1)}$ to satisfy (1) with respect to $U^{(l+1)}$. The motivation is that each new $V^{(l)}$ or $U^{(l)}$ decreases J_Q. Practically, the algorithm is useful because the steps implied by (1) and (2) are readily computed [2, p. 65ff]. Theoretically, it was shown in [3] that $\{(U^{(l)}, V^{(l)})\}$ converges, at least along a subsequence, to a pair (U^*, V^*) that satisfies necessary derivative conditions (i.e., Kuhn–Tucker conditions) for minimizing J_Q.

One application of the fuzzy c-means algorithm is to design a nearest prototype classifier for an unknown distribution function F on R^s using a training set of observations of F. In such a case, Q is taken to be the training set, and the algorithm is run on Q in the usual way. The algorithm generates a fuzzy partition and a set of prototypes that, hopefully, give good results when applied to observations of F not necessarily in Q, i.e., when applied outside the training set. It is important to note that the fuzzy c-means algorithm itself makes no explicit assumptions about F; it is driven only by the training set Q. This is, of course, of practical importance, because it allows the design of a classifier without further assumptions on F.

The descriptor "good" when applied outside the training set can be quantified by a straightforward generalization of J_Q: first, extend the domain of U to R^s so that $U: R^s \rightarrow M_c$ describes a c-cell fuzzy partition of R^s; then define the objective function J_F by

$$J_F(U, V) = \sum_{i=1}^{c} \int u_i^m(x)\, d(x, v_i)\, dF(x).$$

Manuscript received February 26, 1986; revised March 16, 1987. Recommended for acceptance by J. Kittler. This work was supported in part by the National Science Foundation under Grant ECS-8451544.

The author was with the Department of Electrical Engineering and Computer Science, University of California, Berkeley, CA 94720. He is now with the Cylink Corporation, Sunnyvale, CA 94087.

IEEE Log Number 8715812.

Reprinted from *IEEE Trans. Pattern Anal. Machine Intell.*, vol. PAMI-9, no. 5, pp. 661–668, September 1987.

Necessary conditions for minimizing J_F are

$$\int u_i^m(x)\, d(x, v_i)\, dF(x) = \min_{v \in R^s} \int u_i^m(x)\, d(x, v)\, dF(x), \qquad 1 \le i \le c; \tag{3}$$

$$\sum_{i=1}^{c} u_i^m(\cdot)\, d(\cdot, v_i) = \min_{\Lambda \in M_c} \sum_{i=1}^{c} \lambda_i^m(\cdot)\, d(\cdot, v_i), \qquad F\text{-a.e.} \tag{4}$$

Let F_n denote the distribution function that puts mass on value x_k according to its relative frequency of occurrence in Q. Then $J_{F_n} = J_Q$, and (3) and (4), respectively, yield (1) and (2) when F is replaced by F_n.

It was pointed out that the fuzzy c-means algorithm, when run on the training set Q, makes no assumptions about the underlying distribution F. Nevertheless, conditions (3) and (4) suggest that the fuzzy c-means algorithm could be applied directly to F if it were known. That is, starting with some initial $(U^{(0)}, V^{(0)})$, the algorithm would produce a sequence $\{(U^{(l)}, V^{(l)})\}$, where $U^{(l+1)}$ satisfies (4) with respect to $V^{(l)}$ and $V^{(l+1)}$ satisfies (3) with respect to $U^{(l+1)}$. The motivation is a decrease in J_F at each step, i.e., $J_F(U^{(l+1)}, V^{(l+1)}) \le J_F(U^{(l+1)}, V^{(l)}) \le J_F(U^{(l)}, V^{(l)})$. Since F is unknown, such a procedure is impossible, and the practical approach is to apply the algorithm to the training set Q. In doing so, the unknown distribution F is implicitly approximated by the empirical distribution F_n.

The preceding paragraph raises two fundamental questions. First, if F were known and the algorithm were applied to it, would a limiting (U^*, V^*) emerge, and if so, would it be good in the sense of J_F? Second, if the number of observations in Q is large, does the algorithm applied to Q yield results which are good in the sense of J_F and consistent with what would be obtained by applying the algorithm to F? These questions were studied in [5] and [7] for the hard c-means algorithm, i.e., the case that $m = 1$. In particular, the two questions were addressed simultaneously in [7] by generalizing the theory of descent algorithms and applying the theory to the hard c-means algorithm. In this paper, the descent algorithm approach is applied to the fuzzy c-means algorithm, yielding results similar to those in [7]. This approach also yields results when the fuzzy c-means algorithm is modified to include heuristic techniques for splitting and merging clusters at each iteration. We will refer to the modified algorithm as the fuzzy ISODATA algorithm. (We point out that "fuzzy ISODATA" is often used to name the algorithm called fuzzy c-means here, i.e., the algorithm without splitting/merging. The nomenclature used here is that used with hard versions of the algorithms.) For either algorithm, it is not necessary to restrict the dissimilarity function d to be an inner-product metric, or even to be a metric at all; instead, d need only satisfy relatively mild convexity properties (see Section II). This is of practical significance because it means the results are valid for a class of distortion functions used in speech processing (see [4], [5], [8]).

Section II discusses some preliminaries and formally defines the fuzzy c-means and ISODATA algorithms. Sections III and IV present and prove the main results.

II. Preliminaries

In order to get the desired results, it is necessary to restrict the class of allowed dissimilarity functions. We make the following assumptions.

(d.1) $d: R^s \times R^s \to [0, \infty)$ is continuous.

(d.2) $d(x, v)$ is a convex function of v for fixed x.

(d.3) For each x, $d(\tilde{x}, \tilde{v}) \to \infty$ as $\tilde{x} \to x$ and $\|\tilde{v}\| \to \infty$.

(d.4) $\int d(x, v)\, dF(x) < \infty$ for each v.

(d.5) For each v, $d(x, v) = 0$ on, at most, a finite set of x.

Conditions (d.1)–(d.4) are identical to the corresponding ones in [7]. Condition (d.5) here replaces the assumption there that nearest neighbor regions with respect to d have boundaries of zero volume. Also, it will not be necessary to assume here that F has no singular-continuous part.

In keeping with the terminology of [7], we will call any v_i satisfying (3) a centroid of the partition cell u_i. Existence of a centroid is easily shown: if $u_i = 0$ F-a.e., then the integral on the right in (3) equals zero, so that any v is a centroid; otherwise, the integral is lower semi-continuous in v (by Fatou's lemma) and tends to ∞ as $\|v\| \to \infty$, so that the minimum in (3) is achieved. Uniqueness is a condition that is usually observed in practice, but in theory it can be troublesome to guarantee.

Also in keeping with the terminology of [7], we will call any partition satisfying (4) a (fuzzy) Voronoi partition for V. It is evident that, for each x, an element of M_c achieving the minimum in (4) exists, since $(\cdot)^m$ is continuous and M_c is compact. Hence, a Voronoi partition always exists. When $d(x, v_j)$ is nonzero for $1 \le j \le c$, the minimizing element of M_c is unique and is given by

$$\lambda_i = \left[\sum_{j=1}^{c} \left(d(x, v_i)/d(x, v_j) \right)^{1/(m-1)} \right]^{-1} \tag{5}$$

for $1 \le i \le c$ [2, p. 66]. If one or more of the $d(x, v_j)$ is zero, then any element of M_c with zero components corresponding to the nonzero values of $d(x, v_j)$ achieves the minimum. Notice that if more than one of the $d(x, v_j)$ is zero, then the choice from M_c is not unique; hence, a Voronoi partition need not be unique. This is a technicality that does not seem to be of practical concern, but it is hard to exclude in theory.

Frequently it is convenient to specify only a set V of prototypes and to imply that the accompanying partition is a Voronoi partition for V. In such a case, the value of the objective function is found by integrating the right-hand side of (4). Denote the value by $J_F(V)$, i.e.,

$$J_F(V) = \int \min_{\Lambda \in M_c} \sum_{i=1}^{c} \lambda_i^m d(x, v_i)\, dF(x). \tag{6}$$

What we have actually done is redefine J_F to have domain $(R^s)^c$. This abuse of notation will be convenient.

Once it is understood that only a prototype set need be specified, then the algorithm can be defined in terms of prototypes only. That is, given a prototype set, first construct a Voronoi partition for it, then replace each prototype by the centroid of the corresponding cell. Since Voronoi partitions and centroids are not always unique, we need to apply a tie-breaking rule to select a particular prototype set from the collection of possible replacements. Formally, we accommodate this by defining the algorithm as a point-to-set mapping: the input *point* to the algorithm is a prototype set V; the output *set* of the algorithm is the collection of prototype sets that can be generated by first forming a Voronoi partition for V and then computing centroids. Each time we apply the algorithm, we select one of the possible prototype sets from the output set of the algorithm, i.e., we apply a tie-breaking rule.

As in [7], in the formal definition of the algorithm, prototypes are allowed to be drawn from the one-point compactification of R^s, denoted by $\overline{R}^s$, with infinite element $\underline{\infty}$ [1, p. 388]. A set of c prototypes is a point in $(\overline{R}^s)^c$. The domains of d and J_F are extended to $R^s \times \overline{R}^s$ and $(\overline{R}^s)^c$, respectively, by defining $d(x, \underline{\infty}) = \infty$ for each x. If a point in $(\overline{R}^s)^c$ has some components of value $\underline{\infty}$, the practical interpretation is to discard those components, leaving a set of (less than c) real-valued prototypes. Theoretically, we simply pretend that $\underline{\infty}$-valued prototypes are allowed. Convergence results are stated in the compactified topology, resulting in a much less cumbersome theory. We denote the metric on $(\overline{R}^s)^c$ by ν and the distance between a point V and a set S in $(\overline{R}^s)^c$ by $\nu(V, S) = \inf_{A \in S} \nu(V, A)$.

In [7], the algorithm considered was the hard c-means algorithm, i.e., $m = 1$. Special care was required in defining the algorithm in the case of repeated prototypes, i.e., points in $(\overline{R}^s)^c$ with repeated components. For the fuzzy version here ($m > 1$), no such considerations are needed, and we straightforwardly present a formal definition.

Definition: Let $A \in (\overline{R}^s)^c$. The fuzzy c-means algorithm T_F sends A into subset $T_F(A)$ of $(\overline{R}^s)^c$ as follows: $B = (b_1, b_2, \cdots, b_c)$ is an element of $T_F(A)$ if there is some Voronoi partition $(u_1, u_2, \cdots, u_c)$ for A such that, for $1 \le i \le c$,

$$\int u_i^m(x)\, d(x, b_i)\, dF(x) = \min_{v \in R^s} \int u_i^m(x)\, d(x, v)\, dF(x). \tag{7}$$

Given an initial set $A^{(0)}$ of prototypes, the algorithm is iteratively applied to form a sequence $\{A^{(l)}\}$, where $A^{(l)} \in T_F(A^{(l-1)})$ for $l \ge 1$. When $T_F(A^{(l-1)})$ consists of more than one point, selection of a particular $A^{(l)}$ represents the application of a tie-breaking rule. A set of prototypes A is called a fixed point of T_F if $A \in T_F(A)$.

In practice, the c-means algorithm is sometimes modified to include heuristic rules that change the partition from which centroids are computed. These heuristics are easily accommodated by the point-to-set approach, provided they result in a value of J_F that is no worse than would otherwise be obtained. Specifically, we define the fuzzy ISODATA algorithm as follows.

Definition: Let $A \in (\overline{R}^s)^c$. The fuzzy ISODATA algorithm T_F sends A into a subset $T_F(A)$ of $(\overline{R}^s)^c$ as follows: B is an element of $T_F(A)$ if there is some Voronoi partition $(u_1, u_2, \cdots, u_c)$ for A such that, for $1 \le i \le c$,

$$J_F(B) \le \sum_{i=1}^{c} \min_{v \in R^s} \int u_i^m(x)\, d(x, v)\, dF(x). \tag{8}$$

Here the flexibility of the point-to-set approach is obvious, as the choice of B satisfying (8) is clearly not unique unless A is a global minimum of J_F. A little thought will reveal that fixed points of the fuzzy c-means algorithm are identical to fixed points of the fuzzy ISODATA algorithm.

III. Stationary Versus Fixed Points

In this section, T_F can be taken to be either the c-means or the ISODATA algorithm defined above. We address the relationship of fixed points of T_F to stationary points of J_F, i.e., points which satisfy first-order necessary differential conditions (FONDC) for locally minimizing J_F. For a point $A \in (R^s)^c$, FONDC are

$$\liminf_{\tilde{A} \to A} \frac{J_F(\tilde{A}) - J_F(A)}{\|\tilde{A} - A\|} \ge 0 \tag{9}$$

If J_F is differentiable at A, then (9) implies that the derivative is zero. Even if J_F is not differentiable at A, which is possible since we do not require that d be differentiable, condition (9) reflects the requirement that $J_F(\tilde{A}) \ge J_F(A)$ when A is a local minimizer of J_F and $\|\tilde{A} - A\|$ is small. Thus (9) is the appropriate choice of FONDC for the application here. The following theorem establishes the relationship.

Theorem 1: Let $A \in (R^s)^c$. Then A is a fixed point of T_F if and only if A satisfies FONDC for minimizing J_F.

Proof: For convenience, define the difference quantity

$$\Delta_F(A, B) = \frac{J_F(A) - J_F(B)}{\|A - B\|}.$$

"If": Suppose $A = (v_1, v_2, \cdots, v_c)$ is not a fixed point of T_F. We will show that A does not satisfy FONDC. Let $U = (u_1, u_2, \cdots, u_c)$ be a Voronoi partition for A and let $A^* = (v_1^*, v_2^*, \cdots, v_c^*)$ be a set of centroids for U. Let $\tilde{A} = (\tilde{v}_1, \tilde{v}_2, \cdots, \tilde{v}_c) = \alpha A^* + (1 - \alpha) A$, with $0 < \alpha < 1$, and let $\tilde{U} = (\tilde{u}_1, \tilde{u}_2, \cdots, \tilde{u}_c)$ be a Voronoi

partition for $\tilde{A}$. Then

$$\alpha^{-1}[J_F(\tilde{A}) - J_F(A)]$$
$$= \sum_{i=1}^{c} \int \alpha^{-1}[\tilde{u}_i^m(x) d(x, \tilde{v}_i) - u_i^m(x)\, d(x, v_i)]\, dF(x)$$
$$\leq \sum_{i=1}^{c} \int u_i^m(x)\, \alpha^{-1}[d(x, \tilde{v}_i) - d(x, v_i)]\, dF(x)$$
$$\leq \sum_{i=1}^{c} u_i^m(x)[d(x, v_i^*) - d(x, v_i)]\, dF(x),$$

where the first inequality follows by properties of Voronoi partitions and the second by convexity of $d(x, \cdot)$ [6, p. 108]. Denote the last quantity by K; since A is not a fixed point of T_F, $K < 0$. Since $\alpha(A^* - A) = \tilde{A} - A$, the inequality yields

$$\Delta_F(\tilde{A}, A) \leq \frac{K}{\|A^* - A\|} < 0.$$

As $\alpha \to 0$, $\tilde{A} \to A$, and so A does not satisfy FONDC for minimizing J_F.

"Only if": Let $A = (v_1, v_2, \cdots, v_c)$ be a fixed point of T_F. Let $U = (u_1, u_2, \cdots, u_c)$ be a Voronoi partition for A for which each v_i is a centroid of u_i. Let $\tilde{A} = (\tilde{v}_1, \tilde{v}_2, \cdots, \tilde{v}_c)$ be such that $\tilde{A} \to A$. We want to show

$$\liminf_{\tilde{A} \to A} \Delta_F(\tilde{A}, A) \geq 0. \tag{10}$$

Let $\tilde{U} = (\tilde{u}_1, \tilde{u}_2, \cdots, \tilde{u}_c)$ be a Voronoi partition for $\tilde{A}$. Let E be the set of x for which $d(x, v_i) = 0$ for some $1 \leq i \leq c$.

First assume that E has zero F probability. For $x \notin$ E, $u_i(x)$ is given by (5), and continuity of d implies $\tilde{u}_i(x) \to u_i(x)$. Thus, $\tilde{U} \to U$ F-a.e. We have

$$J_F(\tilde{A}) - J_F(A) = \sum_{i=1}^{c} \int [\tilde{u}_i^m(x)\, d(x, \tilde{v}_i) - u_i^m(x)\, d(x, v_i)]\, dF(x)$$
$$\geq \sum_{i=1}^{c} \int \tilde{u}_i^m(x)[d(x, \tilde{v}_i) - d(x, v_i)] \cdot dF(x),$$

the inequality following by properties of Voronoi partitions. By applying elementary properties of absolute value,

$$J_F(\tilde{A}) - J_F(A) \geq \sum_{i=1}^{c} \int u_i^m(x)[d(x, \tilde{v}_i) - d(x, v_i)] \cdot dF(x) - \sum_{i=1}^{c} \int \left|\tilde{u}_i^m(x) - u_i^m(x)\right| \cdot \left|d(x, \tilde{v}_i) - d(x, v_i)\right| dF(x).$$

The first term on the right is nonnegative, since v_i is a centroid of u_i^m. Hence, to finish the argument in this case, we need only show that

$$\int \left|\tilde{u}_i^m(x) - \tilde{u}_i(x)\right| \frac{\left|d(x, \tilde{v}_i) - d(x, v_i)\right|}{\|\tilde{A} - A\|}\, dF(x) \to 0. \tag{11}$$

The first term in the integrand is bounded by 2 and tends to 0 F-a.e. If we can show that the second term is dominated by an integrable function for $\tilde{A}$ in some neighborhood of A, then, by dominated convergence, we establish that the integral tends to 0 as desired.

We will now show that the second term is dominated by an integrable function for $\|\tilde{A} - A\| < 1$. We are only concerned with the case that $\tilde{v}_i \neq v_i$ since otherwise the second term is 0. So we have $0 < \|\tilde{v}_i - v_i\| < 1$. Let H be a hypercube in R^s, with vertices $\{y_1, y_2, \cdots, y_L\}$ enclosing the sphere of radius 1 with center v_i. Define $u = (\tilde{v}_i - v_i)/\|\tilde{v}_i - v_i\|$. For fixed x, $d(x, v_i + tu)$ is a convex function of t. By properties of chords of convex functions [6, p. 108],

$$d(x, v_i) - d(x, v_i - u) \leq \frac{d(x, \tilde{v}_i) - d(x, v_i)}{\|\tilde{v}_i - v_i\|}$$
$$\leq d(x, v_i + u) - d(x, v_i).$$

Since d is nonnegative, we have the upper bound:

$$\frac{\left|d(x, \tilde{v}_i) - d(x, v_i)\right|}{\|\tilde{v}_i - v_i\|}$$
$$\leq \max\left\{d(x, v_i), d(x, v_i + u), d(x, v_i - u)\right\}.$$

Now, v_i, $v_i + u$, and $v_i - u$ are each convex combinations of the vertices of H. Hence, by convexity, each value of d on the right-hand side is bound above by $\Sigma_{i=1}^{L} d(x, y_i)$. Finally, since $\|\tilde{v}_i - v_i\| \leq \|\tilde{A} - A\|$,

$$\frac{\left|d(x, \tilde{v}_i) - d(x, v_i)\right|}{\|\tilde{A} - A\|} \leq \sum_{i=1}^{L} d(x, y_i).$$

The right side is an integrable function, by assumption (d.4). This completes the argument for the case that E has zero F probability.

To remove the condition that E has zero F probability, first write $F = \alpha F_1 + (1 - \alpha) F_2$, $0 \leq \alpha \leq 1$, where F_1 and F_2 are distribution functions placing all their mass on E and E^c, respectively. Since $d(x, v_i) = 0$ for $x \in E$, then $J_{F_1}(A) = 0$, so that $\Delta_{F_1}(\tilde{A}, A) \geq 0$. By the previous argument, (10) holds when F is replaced by F_2. Since $\Delta_F = \alpha \Delta_{F_1} + (1 - \alpha)\, \Delta_{F_2}$, we conclude that (10) holds for F as well. □

Discussion: The theorem is significant because fixed points of T_F are the solutions that T_F will yield, as will be seen. Thus, these solutions are the same as would be arrived at by a variational technique.

We remark that the "if" portion of the theorem still holds for the hard version of the algorithm. To see this, one need only review the proof to see that it still holds for $m = 1$. This appears to be a new result for the hard algorithm, i.e., that a stationary point of J_F is a fixed point of T_F. Unfortunately, the "only if" portion of the theorem does not hold for the hard case, i.e., a fixed point is not necessarily a stationary point. The argument fails because, for $m = 1$, it does not follow in (11) that $|\tilde{u}_i^m(x) - \tilde{u}_i(x)| \to 0$ for those x that are equally close, in the sense of d, to more than one of the v_i's. This was observed in [5]. So Theorem 1 is a stronger and more satisfying statement than can be made for the hard version of the algorithm.

To extend Theorem 1 to the case that $A \in (\bar{R}^s)^c$, first form A' by discarding the $\underline{\infty}$-valued components of A, then apply the theorem to $A' \in (R^s)^{c'}$, where c' is the number of real-valued components of A. Formally, we can define $J_F^{(k)}$ with domain $(R^s)^k$ by setting c equal to k in (6). Then, by the theorem, the set of fixed points of T_F represents the set of stationary points of $J_F^{(k)}$ for $1 \le k \le c$. (Note that $(\underline{\infty}, \underline{\infty}, \cdots, \underline{\infty})$ cannot be a fixed point, since that point yields a value of ∞ for J_F while any other point yields a finite value of J_F.)

IV. Descent Algorithm Properties

In this section, T_F can be taken to be either the c-means or the ISODATA algorithm defined above.

The three lemmas in [7, sect. II] present convergence and consistency properties of descent algorithms in a general setting. These lemmas are obtained via simple analytical arguments and are valid for algorithms that possess certain technical properties. This section proves that the fuzzy c-means and ISODATA algorithms possess these required properties. This establishes the remaining results of the paper, contained in Theorems 2–4 below. The theorem statements are self-contained and easily understood; the proofs are technical in nature and make use of arguments contained in [7]. Therefore, this section presents and discusses the theorems first, deferring the proofs to the latter half.

A. Statement of Results

Theorem 2: Let $A^{(0)} \in (\bar{R}^s)^c$ and $A^{(l)} \in T_F(A^{(l-1)})$ for $l \le 1$. Let Γ be the set of fixed points of T_F. Then $\nu(A^{(l)}, \Gamma) \to 0$. If A^* is an accumulation point of $\{A^{(l)}\}$, then $A^* \in \Gamma$, and $J_F(A^{(l)}) \to J_F(A^*)$.

This is an extension of the convergence result of [3] to the general setting here. It states that iterative applications of the algorithm to an arbitrary initial set of prototypes produce a sequence of prototypes that approaches the set of fixed points of the algorithm. Compactness of $(\bar{R}^s)^c$ ensures a convergent subsequence, and the theorem asserts that the limit of the subsequence is a fixed point. The significance of the theorem is its generality: it is valid whenever (d.1)–(d.5) are met, for either the c-means or the ISODATA definition, for any tie-breaking rule, for any distribution F, with no further qualifying assumptions. Furthermore, since Γ is the same for both algorithms, the asymptotic properties claimed by the theorem are the same for either. This does *not* imply that both algorithms will give equal performance; indeed, the limiting value of $J_F(A^{(l)})$ may very much depend on choice of tie-breakers. However, the limiting value is always that of some fixed point.

Under the claims of Theorem 2, it is possible for some of the components of $A^{(l)}$ to grow without bound in Euclidean norm. (Since $(\underline{\infty}, \underline{\infty}, \cdots, \underline{\infty})$ is not a fixed point, not all prototypes can grow without bound.) This is apparently a shortcoming of the result, as we are aware of no example in which this behavior is observed. In [3], it was pointed out that boundedness of $\{\|A^{(l)}\|\}$ can be guaranteed in the case that F is of finite support and $d(x, y)$ is the square of an inner-product norm; it is easy to verify that the reasoning there extends to the weaker assumption that F is of bounded support. We conjecture that assumptions (d.1)–(d.5) are sufficient to ensure the boundedness of $\{\|A^{(l)}\|\}$, but we have not been able to prove this. Whenever boundedness can be assured, then the subset of Γ approached by $A^{(l)}$ is in $(R^s)^c$ (as opposed to $(\bar{R}^s)^c$). However, Theorem 2 demonstrates that convergence does not depend on such boundedness.

Theorem 3: Let F_n be the empirical distribution of the first n members of a sequence of stationary, ergodic observations of F. Let Γ be the set of fixed points of T_F. Let A_n be a fixed point of T_{F_n}. Then, with probability one, $\nu(A_n, \Gamma) \to 0$.

T_{F_n} is the version of the algorithm that operates on a training set of observations described by an empirical distribution F_n; T_F is the ideal version, i.e., the one we would run if we knew the true distribution F. The theorem states that fixed points of T_{F_n} becomes arbitrarily close, as the number of observations gets large, to fixed points of T_F. Since J_F is continuous (see Lemma 2 below), it is easy to verify that, by compactness, there are fixed points A^* and A_* of T_F such that $\limsup J_F(A_n) = A^*$ and $\liminf J_F(A_n) = A_*$. Thus, from the point of view of minimizing J_F, a fixed point of T_{F_n} is asymptotically no worse (nor better) than a fixed point of T_F.

Theorem 2 can be applied to T_{F_n} to conclude that iterative applications of T_{F_n} will asymptotically yield a fixed point of T_{F_n}. Theorem 3 implies that, if n is large, the fixed point will nearly equal some fixed point of T_F. Thus, iterative applications of T_{F_n} are consistent with the goal of finding a fixed point of T_F. The following theorem provides a sharper statement of consistency.

Theorem 4: Let F_n be as in Theorem 3. Fix $A^{(0)} \in (\bar{R}^s)^c$. For each $n = 1, 2, \cdots$, let $\{A_n^{(l)}\}$ be a sequence such that $A_n^{(0)} = A^{(0)}$ and $A_n^{(l)} \in T_{F_n}(A_n^{(l-1)})$ for $l \ge 1$. Let A_n^* be an accumulation point of $\{A_n^{(l)}\}$. Then there is a sequence $\{A^{(l)}\}$ such that $A^{(l)} \in T_F(A^{(l-1)})$ for $l \ge 1$, and

$$\limsup_n J_F(A_n^*) \le \lim_l J_F(A^{(l)}). \tag{12}$$

The theorem implies that the fixed point derived by iteratively applying T_{F_n} is no worse, in the limit for large n, than a fixed point derived by iterative applications of T_F with *some* tie-breaking rule. Here, the choice of c-means versus ISODATA has significance in interpreting the claim.

With the c-means definition, it is often the case that $T_F(\cdot)$ contains a single point, i.e., no tie-breaking rule is needed. In such a case, $\{A^{(l)}\}$ satisfying $A^{(l)} \in T_F(A^{(l-1)})$ is uniquely determined by $A^{(0)}$. Thus, T_{F_n} will asymptotically perform as well as T_F when applied to $A^{(0)}$, regardless of any tie-breaking rule used with T_{F_n}. It is even possible that the inequality in (12) can be strict (see the Appendix).

On the other hand, the ISODATA definition always requires application of a tie-breaking rule (except on the rare occasion that is applied to a globally optimum set of prototypes) so that $\{A^{(l)}\}$ is not unique. Hence, the real interpretation of the theorem for ISODATA is the *existence* of some tie-breaking rule for T_F which results in a sequence $\{A^{(l)}\}$ satisfying (12). It can be shown that there is always a choice of tie-breaking rule for T_F by which (12) holds with equality.

B. Proof of Results

For this section, familiarity with the arguments in [7] is assumed.

In order to apply the results on descent algorithms in [7, sect. II], we need to establish continuity properties of J_F and sequential accumulation properties of T_F. We follow the same strategy as in [7, sect. III] where "setwise-weak" convergence of empirical distributions is first shown, and then the needed properties of J_F and T_F are proved for distributions that converge setwise-weakly. In [7], setwise-weak convergence was defined for limiting distributions with no singular-continuous part. Such a restriction is unneeded and undesired here. Instead, we define it as follows.

Definition: Let F be a mixture of a discrete distribution function F^d and a continuous distribution function F^c. Let D be the atoms of F^d. A sequence of distribution functions $\{F_n\}$ converges setwise-weakly to F, written as $F_n \overset{s,w}{\rightarrow} F$, if each F_n is a mixture of two distribution functions F_n^d and F_n^c such that F_n^d converges setwise to F^d, F_n^c converges weakly to F^c, and $\int_D dF_n \rightarrow \int_D dF$.

With this definition, the following result is still valid, by the same argument as in [7].

Lemma 1: Let $\{\xi_j\}$ be a sequence of stationary, ergodic observations of F. Let F_n be the empirical distribution function of the first n observations. Then, with probability one,

(c.1) $F_n \overset{s,w}{\rightarrow} F$,

(c.2) $\lim_n \int d(x, v)\, dF_n(x) = \int d(x, v)\, dF(x)$ for every $v \in R^s$.

The objective function J_F, with domain $(\overline{R}^s)^c$ and range $[0, \infty]$, has the same continuity and convergence properties as the function D in [7]:

Lemma 2: The function J_F is continuous. If (c.1) and (c.2) are met, J_{F_n} converges uniformly to J_F.

Proof: Nearly the same as for [7, Lemma 3.2]. For $A = (a_1, a_2, \cdots, a_c)$, define

$$h(x, A) = \min_{\Lambda \in M_c} \sum_{i=1}^{c} \lambda_i^m d(x, a_i).$$

Continuity of d implies continuity of h, and so the argument of [7] applies.

We remark that the lemma implies the following result, which is analogous to Theorem 3.

Corollary: Let F_n, F be as in Lemma 2. If O is the set of global minimizers for J_F, and if A_n globally minimizes J_{F_n}, then $v(A_n, O) \rightarrow 0$.

We also point out that Lemma 2 and its corollary are valid when setwise-weak convergence in (c.1) is replaced by weak convergence.

The key property to establish is sequential accumulation. This is done in the following lemma. The proof of the lemma is similar in strategy to the one in [7], but the details differ significantly. In [7], the delicate part is dealing with atoms of F that occur on boundaries of Voronoi cells. Here, the delicate part is dealing with the possibility that atoms of F occur on points that have zero cost, in the sense of d, to some limiting prototype.

Lemma 3: If (c.1) and (c.2) are met, then $\{T_{F_n}\}^- \subset T_F$.

Proof: Let $A_n = (a_{1n}, a_{2n}, \cdots, a_{cn})$, $A = (a_1, a_2, \cdots, a_c)$, with $A_n \rightarrow A$. Let $B_n = (b_{1n}, b_{2n}, \cdots, b_{cn}) \in T_{F_n}(A_n)$. Let $B = (b_1, b_2, \cdots, b_c)$ be the limit of a convergent subsequence $\{B_k\}_{K'}$. Let $U_n = (u_{1n}, u_{2n}, \cdots, u_{cn})$ be the Voronoi partition for A_n from which B_n is formed.

Let $E \subset R^s$ be the set of x for which $d(x, a_i) = 0$ for some $1 \leq i \leq c$. By (d.4), E is finite, and so by the compactness of M_c, there is a subsequence $\{U_k\}_K$ of $\{U_k\}_{K'}$ (i.e., $K \subset K'$) along which $U_n(x)$ converges for each $x \in E$. For $x \notin E$, $d(x, a_{in}) > 0$ for large n, and $U_n(x)$ is determined by (5); since the right-hand side of (5) is continuous in V, $U_n(x)$ converges. Thus, $\{U_k\}_K$ converges to some $U(x) = (u_1(x), u_2(x), \cdots, u_c(x))$ for each $x \in R^s$. It is a straightforward exercise to verify that the continuity of d implies that U is a Voronoi partition for A.

C-Means Algorithm: The following chain of equations and inequalities, subsequently justified, establishes each b_i as a centroid of the corresponding u_i:

$$\int u_i^m(x)\, d(x, b_i)\, dF(x)$$

$$\leq \liminf_{k \in K} \int u_{ik}^m(x)\, d(x, b_{ik})\, dF_k(x) \tag{13}$$

$$= \liminf_{k \in K} \inf_{v} \int u_{ik}^m(x)\, d(x, v)\, dF_k(x) \tag{14}$$

$$\leq \inf_{v} \limsup_{k \in K} \int u_{ik}^m(x)\, d(x, v)\, dF_k(x) \tag{15}$$

$$= \inf_{v} \int u_i^m(x)\, d(x, v)\, dF(x). \tag{16}$$

Justification: Let F be a mixture of a discrete distribution F^d and a continuous distribution F^c.

(13): First note that by continuity of d, for any x,

$\{u_{ik}^m(x)\, d(x, b_{ik})\}_K$ converges to $u_i^m(x)\, d(x, b_i)$. A stronger situation exists for $x \notin E$. If $x_n \to x \notin E$, then $d(x, a_i) > 0$ and $d(x_n, a_{in}) > 0$ for large n. Equation (5) and continuity of d yield $U_n(x_n) \to U(x)$. Thus, $u_{in}^m(x_n)\, d(x_n, b_i)$ converges to $u_i(x)\, d(x, b_i)$.

Now, [7, Proposition A.3] is still valid under the definition of setwise-weak convergence used here when F^a in the hypothesis is replaced by F^c. Since E is finite, it has zero F^c-probability, and claim (a) of the proposition establishes the inequality.

(14): Follows by definition of algorithm.

(15): Follows by elementary properties of sequences.

(16): By the same argument as for (13), $\{u_{ik}^m(x)\, d(x, b_{ik})\}_K$ converges to $u_i^m(x)\, d(x, b_i)$ for each x, and $u_{in}^m(x_n)\, d(x_n, b_i)$ converges to $u_i(x)\, d(x, b_i)$ whenever $x_n \to x \notin E$. Since $u_{ik}^m(x)\, d(x, v) \le d(x, v)$, we can apply part (b) of [7, Proposition A.3] to get the inequality.

ISODATA Algorithm: Define h as in the proof of Lemma 2. The following chain of equations and inequalities, subsequently justified, identifies B as an element of $T_F(A)$:

$$J_F(B) = \int h(x, B)\, dF(x) \tag{17}$$

$$\le \liminf_{k \in K} \int h(x, B_k)\, dF_k(x) \tag{18}$$

$$= \text{lin inf}_{k \in K} J_{F_k}(B_k) \tag{19}$$

$$\le \liminf_{k \in K} \sum_{i=1}^{c} \inf_{v} \int u_{ik}^m(x)\, d(x, v)\, dF_k(x) \tag{20}$$

$$\le \sum_{i=1}^{c} \inf_{v} \limsup_{k \in K} \int u_{ik}^m(x)\, d(x, v)\, dF_k(x) \tag{21}$$

$$= \sum_{i=1}^{c} \inf_{v} \int u_i^m(x)\, d(x, v)\, dF(x). \tag{22}$$

Justification:

(17) and (19): Follow by definition of J_F.

(18): Pick any $x \in R^s$ and let $x_n \to x$. By continuity, $\{h(x_k, B_k)\}_K \to h(x, B)$. Hence, the inequality follows by part (a) of [7, Proposition A.3].

(20), (21), (22): Same arguments as for (14), (15), and (16), respectively.

Appendix

Let $s = 1$, $c = 3$, and $d(x, v) = (x - v)^2$. Pick T_F to be the fuzzy c-means definition. Choose F to be the distribution function placing probability $1/4$ on each of the points $\{-3, -1, 1, 3\}$. Let $A^0 = (-1, 0, 1)$ and $A^{m+1} \in T_F(A^m)$. It was shown in [3] that $A^m \to A^*$ where A^* is approximately $(-2.91, 0, 2.91)$; $J_F(A^*)$ is approximately 1.509. A key observation in [3] is that A^* is a saddle point of J_F, not a local minimum. Convergence to A^* requires the exact symmetry of A^0 and F; in fact, when A° is perturbed slightly and the iterations are recomputed, the limiting value of A^m is $\pm(v_1, v_2, v_3)$ where v_1, v_2, and v_3 are approximately -2.68, 0.57, and 2.97, respectively. Either of these prototypes sets results in a value of J_F of about 1.491.

Now let F_n be the empirical distribution function formed from n independent observations of F. When n is large, F_n will place probability nearly equal to $1/4$ on each of the points $\{-3, -1, 1, 3\}$. But with high probability, F_n will *not* place probability *exactly* equal to $1/4$ on each of those points. It is easy to see that in such a case, when T_{F_n} is iteratively applied to A^0, the sequence produced will converge to a value A_n^* nearly equal to $\pm(v_1, v_2, v_3)$. Thus, $J_F(A_n^*) \cong 1.491 < 1.509 = J_F(A^*)$. This shows that T_{F_n} can yield a lower value of J_F than does T_F when applied to the same initial codebook.

In the preceding paragraph, we exploited the fact that for any particular choice of large n, the probability is high that mass is not equally placed on the four support points. However, it is also true that, with probability one, there are arbitrarily large values of n for which F_n places equal mass on the points. For such F_n, T_{F_n} and T_F are identical, so $A_n^* = A^*$. Thus, for this example, the inequality in Theorem 4 holds with equality.

In order to find an example where the inequality of Theorem 4 is strict, we need to pick F of infinite support. Let F be absolutely continuous with density function taking on value $1/4$ on the intervals $(-3, -1)$ and $(1, 3)$, as in [7, Appendix 1]. Computing T_F is difficult because the required centroid calculation [i.e., computing the minimizer in (3)] requires evaluating the expression

$$\frac{\int_{-3}^{-1} x\, u_i^2(x)\, dx + \int_{1}^{3} x\, u_i^2(x)\, dx}{\int_{-3}^{-1} u_i^2(x)\, dx + \int_{1}^{3} u_i^2(x)\, dx}$$

where $u_i(x)$ is as specified in (5). We did this using the VAXIMA symbolic manipulation program. The resulting expression is cumbersome, but easily evaluated numerically. Using A^0 as above, and $A^{m+1} \in T_F(A^m)$, A^m was of the form $(-a_m, 0, a_m)$, with a_m as listed in Table I.

The limiting value $A^* = (-a, 0, a)$ can be shown to be a saddle point of J_F by computing the first three terms of a Taylor series for $J_F((-a, \delta, a))$ about $\delta = 0$. This is done by observing that [2, p. 70ff]

$$J_F((-a, \delta, a)) = \int [(x + a)^{-2} + (x - \delta)^{-2} + (x - a)^{-2}]^{-1}\, dF(x).$$

The integrand straightforwardly expands into a Taylor series about $\delta = 0$, allowing each coefficient to be integrated with respect to $F(x)$. We did this using VAXIMA and evaluated the result numerically for a as indicated in Table I, yielding the approximation $0.258 - 0.0460\delta^2$. The fact that this expression is negative quadratic verifies that A^* is not a local minimum of J_F. Since Table I shows that it is not a local maximum, it must be a saddle point.

As in the previous example, convergence to A^* depends

TABLE I
NUMERICAL EVALUATION OF a^m IN EXAMPLE WHERE INEQUALITY OF THEOREM 4 IS STRICT

m	a^m
0	3.0
1	2.335191
2	2.184626
3	2.140937
4	2.127639
5	2.123537
6	2.122268
7	2.121874
8	2.121752
9	2.121714
10	2.121702
11	2.121699
12	2.121698
13	2.121697
14	2.121697
15	2.121697

on the exact symmetry of F and A^0. The slightest asymmetry will force the sequence away from A^* to a limiting value of J_F strictly less than $J_F(A^*)$. Without the symmetry, the resulting expressions for centroids and J_F become too nasty for even the VAXIMA program to evaluate. Instead, we used a numerical technique (i.e., approximating F by a distribution function of finite support) to compute a limiting prototype set of approximately $\pm(-2.03, 1.45, 2.51)$, with a corresponding value of J_F of about 0.187.

Now, when F_n is formed as the empirical distribution of n independent observations of F, then with probability one, F_n will not be exactly symmetric. For large n, this results in T_F producing a sequence converging to a value A_n^* near $\pm(-2.03, 1.45, 2.51)$. Thus, we get

$$\limsup_n J_F(A_n^*) = 0.187 < 0.258 = J_F(A^*).$$

REFERENCES

[1] R. B. Ash, *Real Analysis and Probability*. New York: Academic, 1972.

[2] J. C. Bezdek, *Pattern Recognition with Fuzzy Objective Function Algorithms*. New York: Plenum, 1981.

[3] J. C. Bezdek, R. J. Hathaway, M. J. Sabin, and W. T. Tucker, "Convergence theory for fuzzy c-means: Counterexamples and repairs," *IEEE Trans. Syst., Man., Cybern.*, 1987, to be published.

[4] A. Buzo, A. H. Gray, R. M. Gray, and J. D. Markel, "Speech coding based upon vector quantization," *IEEE Trans. Acoust., Speech, Signal Processing*, vol. ASSP-28, pp. 562–574, Oct. 1980.

[5] R. M. Gray, J. C. Kieffer, and Y. Linde, "Locally optimal block quantizer design," *Inform. Contr.*, vol. 45, pp. 178–198, May 1980.

[6] H. L. Royden, *Real Analysis*. New York: Macmillan, 1968.

[7] M. J. Sabin and R. M. Gray, "Global convergence and empirical consistency of the generalized Lloyd algorithm," *IEEE Trans. Inform. Theory*, vol. IT-32, pp. 148–165, Mar. 1986.

[8] H.-P. Tseng, M. J. Sabin, and E. A. Lee, "Fuzzy vector quantization applied to hidden Markov modeling," in *Proc. 1987 IEEE Int. Conf. Acoust., Speech, Signal Processing*, vol. 2, pp. 641–644, Apr. 1987.

Similarity Relations and Fuzzy Orderings†

L. A. ZADEH
Department of Electrical Engineering and Computer Sciences and Electronics Research Laboratory, University of California, Berkeley, California

ABSTRACT

The notion of "similarity" as defined in this paper is essentially a generalization of the notion of equivalence. In the same vein, a fuzzy ordering is a generalization of the concept of ordering. For example, the relation $x \gg y$ (x is much larger than y) is a fuzzy linear ordering in the set of real numbers.

More concretely, a *similarity relation*, S, is a fuzzy relation which is reflexive, symmetric, and transitive. Thus, let x, y be elements of a set X and $\mu_S(x,y)$ denote the grade of membership of the ordered pair (x,y) in S. Then S is a similarity relation in X if and only if, for all x, y, z in X, $\mu_S(x,x) = 1$ (reflexivity), $\mu_S(x,y) = \mu_S(y,x)$ (symmetry), and $\mu_S(x,z) \geqslant \bigvee_y (\mu_S(x,y) \wedge \mu_S(y,z))$ (transitivity), where $\vee$ and $\wedge$ denote max and min, respectively.

A *fuzzy ordering* is a fuzzy relation which is transitive. In particular, a *fuzzy partial ordering*, P, is a fuzzy ordering which is reflexive and antisymmetric, that is, $(\mu_P(x,y) > 0$ and $x \neq y) \Rightarrow \mu_P(y,x) = 0$. A *fuzzy linear ordering* is a fuzzy partial ordering in which $x \neq y \Rightarrow \mu_S(x,y) > 0$ or $\mu_S(y,x) > 0$. A *fuzzy preordering* is a fuzzy ordering which is reflexive. A *fuzzy weak ordering* is a fuzzy preordering in which $x \neq y \Rightarrow \mu_S(x,y) > 0$ or $\mu_S(y,x) > 0$.

Various properties of similarity relations and fuzzy orderings are investigated and, as an illustration, an extended version of Szpilrajn's theorem is proved.

1. INTRODUCTION

The concepts of equivalence, similarity, partial ordering, and linear ordering play basic roles in many fields of pure and applied science. The classical theory of relations has much to say about equivalence relations and various types of orderings [1]. The notion of a distance, $d(x,y)$, between objects x and y has long been used in many contexts as a measure of similarity or dissimilarity between elements of a set. Numerical taxonomy [2], factor analysis [3], pattern classification [4–7], and analysis of proximities [8–10] provide a number of concepts and techniques for categorization and clustering. Preference orderings have been the object of extensive study in econometrics and other fields [11, 12]. Thus, in sum, there exists a wide variety of techniques for dealing with problems involving equivalence, similarity, clustering, preference patterns, etc. Furthermore, many of these techniques are quite effective in dealing with the particular classes of problems which motivated their development.

The present paper is not intended to add still another technique to the vast armamentarium which is already available. Rather, its purpose is to introduce a unifying point of view based on the theory of fuzzy sets [13] and, more particularly, fuzzy relations. This is accomplished by extending the notions of equivalence relation and ordering to fuzzy sets, thereby making it possible to adapt the well-developed theory of relations to situations in which the classes involved do not have sharply defined boundaries.[1] Thus, the main contribution

† This work was supported in part by a grant from the National Science Foundation, NSF GK-10656X, to the Electronics Research Laboratory, University of California, Berkeley, California.

[1] In an independent work which came to this writer's attention [14], S. Tamura, S. Higuchi, and K. Tanaka have applied fuzzy relations to pattern classification, obtaining some of the results described in Section 3.

of our approach consists in providing a unified conceptual framework for the study of fuzzy equivalence relations and fuzzy orderings, thereby facilitating the derivation of known results in various applied areas and, possibly, stimulating the discovery of new ones.

In what follows, our attention will be focused primarily on defining some of the basic notions within this conceptual framework and exploring some of their elementary implications. Although our approach might be of use in areas such as cluster analysis, pattern recognition, decision processes, taxonomy, artificial intelligence, linguistics, information retrieval, system modeling, and approximation, we shall make no attempt in the present paper to discuss its possible applications in these or related problem areas.

2. NOTATION, TERMINOLOGY, AND PRELIMINARY DEFINITIONS

In [13], a fuzzy (binary) relation R was defined as a fuzzy collection of ordered pairs. Thus, if $X = \{x\}$ and $Y = \{y\}$ are collections of objects denoted generically by x and y, then a *fuzzy relation* from X to Y or, equivalently, a fuzzy relation in $X \cup Y$, is a fuzzy subset of $X \times Y$ characterized by a membership (characteristic) function μ_R which associates with each pair (x,y) its "grade of membership," $\mu_R(x,y)$, in R. We shall assume for simplicity that the range of μ_R is the interval $[0,1]$ and will refer to the number $\mu_R(x,y)$ as the *strength* of the relation between x and y.

In the following definitions, the symbols $\vee$ and $\wedge$ stand for max and min, respectively.

The *domain* of a fuzzy relation R is denoted by dom R and is a fuzzy set defined by

$$\mu_{\text{dom } R}(x) = \bigvee_y \mu_R(x,y), \qquad x \in X, \tag{1}$$

where the supremum, $\bigvee_y$, is taken over all y in Y. Similarly, the *range* of R is denoted by ran R and is defined by

$$\mu_{\text{ran } R}(y) = \bigvee_x \mu_R(x,y), \qquad x \in X, y \in Y. \tag{2}$$

The *height* of R is denoted by $h(R)$ and is defined by

$$h(R) = \bigvee_x \bigvee_y \mu_R(x,y). \tag{3}$$

A fuzzy relation is *subnormal* if $h(R) < 1$ and *normal* if $h(R) = 1$.

The *support* of R is denoted by $S(R)$ and is defined to be the non-fuzzy subset of $X \times Y$ over which $\mu_R(x,y) > 0$.

The *containment* of a fuzzy relation R in a fuzzy relation Q is denoted by $R \subset Q$ and is defined by $\mu_R \leqslant \mu_Q$, which means, more explicitly, that $\mu_R(x,y) \leqslant \mu_Q(x,y)$ for all (x,y) in $X \times Y$.

The *union* of R and Q is denoted by $R + Q$ (rather than $R \cup Q$) and is defined by $\mu_{R+Q} = \mu_R \vee \mu_Q$, that is

$$\mu_{R+Q}(x,y) = \max(\mu_R(x,y), \mu_Q(x,y)), \qquad x \in X, y \in Y. \tag{4}$$

Consistent with this notation, if $\{R_\alpha\}$ is a family of fuzzy (or non-fuzzy) sets, we shall write $\Sigma_\alpha R_\alpha$ to denote the union $\cup_\alpha R_\alpha$.

The *intersection* of R and Q is denoted by $R \cap Q$ and is defined by $\mu_{R \cap Q} = \mu_R \wedge \mu_Q$.

The *product* of R and Q is denoted by RQ and is defined by $\mu_{RQ} = \mu_R \mu_Q$. Note that, if R, Q, and T are any fuzzy relations from X to Y, then

$$R(Q+T) = RQ + RT.$$

The *complement* of R is denoted by R' and is defined by $\mu_R{}' = 1 - \mu_R$.

If $R \subset X \times Y$ and $Q \subset Y \times Z$, then the *composition*, or, more specifically, the *max-min composition*, of R and Q is denoted by $R \circ Q$ and is defined by

$$\mu_{R \circ Q}(x, z) = \bigvee_y (\mu_R(x, y) \wedge \mu_Q(y, z)), \qquad x \in X, z \in Z. \tag{5}$$

The n-fold composition $R \circ R \ldots \circ R$ is denoted by R^n.

From the above definitions of the composition, union, and containment it follows at once that, for any fuzzy relations $R \subset X \times Y$, $Q, T \subset Y \times Z$, and $S \subset Z \times W$, we have

$$R \circ (Q \circ S) = (R \circ Q) \circ S, \tag{6}$$

$$R \circ (Q + T) = R \circ Q + R \circ T, \tag{7}$$

and

$$Q \subset T \Rightarrow R \circ Q \subset R \circ T. \tag{8}$$

Note. On occasion it may be desirable to employ an operation $*$ other than $\wedge$ in the definition of the composition of fuzzy relations. Then (5) becomes

$$\mu_{R * Q}(x, z) = \bigvee_y (\mu_R(x, y) * \mu_Q(y, z)) \tag{9}$$

with $R * Q$ called the *max-star* composition of R and Q.

In order that (6), (7), and (8) remain valid when $\wedge$ is replaced by $*$, it is sufficient that $*$ be associative and monotone non-decreasing in each of its arguments, which assures the distributivity of $*$ over $+$.[2] A simple example of an operation satisfying these conditions and having the interval $[0, 1]$ as its range is the product. In this case, the definition of the composition assumes the form

$$\mu_{R \cdot Q}(x, z) = \bigvee_y (\mu_R(x, y) \cdot \mu_Q(y, z)), \tag{10}$$

where we use the sumbol $\cdot$ in place of $\wedge$ to differentiate between the max-min and max-product compositions. In what follows, in order to avoid a confusing multiplicity of definitions, we shall be using (5) for the most part as our definition of the composition, with the understanding that, in all but a few cases, an assertion which is established with (5) as the definition of the composition holds true also for (10) and, more generally, (9) (provided (6), (7), and (8) are satisfied).

Note also that, when X and Y are finite sets, μ_R may be represented by a relation matrix whose (x,y)th element is $\mu_R(x,y)$. In this case, the defining equation (5) implies that the relation matrix for the composition of R and Q is given by the max-min product[3] of the relation matrices for R and Q.

Level Sets and the Resolution Identity

For α in $[0, 1]$, an *α-level-set* of a fuzzy relation R is denoted by R_α and is a non-fuzzy set in $X \times Y$ defined by

$$R_\alpha = \{(x, y) | \mu_R(x, y) \geqslant \alpha\}. \tag{11}$$

Thus, the R_α form a nested sequence of non-fuzzy relations, with

$$\alpha_1 \geqslant \alpha_2 \Rightarrow R_{\alpha_1} \subset R_{\alpha_2}. \tag{12}$$

An immediate and yet important consequence of the definition of a level set is stated in the following proposition:

PROPOSITION 1. *Any fuzzy relation from X to Y admits of the resolution*

$$R = \sum_\alpha \alpha R_\alpha, \qquad 0 < \alpha \leqslant 1, \tag{13}$$

[2] An exhaustive discussion of operations having properties of this type can be found in [15].

[3] In the max-min (or quasi-Boolean) product of matrices with real-valued elements, $\wedge$ and $\vee$ play the roles of product and addition, respectively [16, 17].

where Σ stands for the union (see (4)) *and αR_α denotes a subnormal non-fuzzy set defined by*

$$\mu_{\alpha R_\alpha}(x,y) = \alpha\mu_{R_\alpha}(x,y), \qquad (x,y) \in X \times Y. \tag{14}$$

or equivalently

$$\begin{aligned}\mu_{\alpha R_\alpha}(x,y) &= \alpha, \qquad \textit{for } (x,y) \in R_\alpha, \\ &= 0, \qquad \textit{elsewhere.}\end{aligned}$$

Proof. Let $\mu_{R_\alpha}(x,y)$ denote the membership function of the non-fuzzy set R_α in $X \times Y$ defined by (11). Then (11) implies that

$$\begin{aligned}\mu_{R_\alpha}(x,y) &= 1, \qquad \text{for } \mu_R(x,y) \geqslant \alpha, \\ &= 0, \qquad \text{for } \mu_R(x,y) < \alpha,\end{aligned} \tag{15}$$

and consequently the membership function of $\Sigma_\alpha \alpha R_\alpha$ may be written as

$$\begin{aligned}\mu_{\Sigma_\alpha \alpha R_\alpha}(x,y) &= \bigvee_\alpha \alpha\mu_{R_\alpha}(x,y) \\ &= \bigvee_{\alpha \leqslant \mu_R(x,y)} \alpha \\ &= \mu_R(x,y),\end{aligned}$$

which in turn implies (13).

Note. It is understood that in (13) to each R_α corresponds a unique α. If this is not the case, e.g., $\alpha_1 \neq \alpha_2$ and $R_{\alpha_1} = R_{\alpha_2}$, then the two terms are combined by forming their union, yielding $(\alpha_1 \vee \alpha_2)R_{\alpha_1}$. In this way, a summation of the form (13) may be converted into one in which to each R_α corresponds a unique α. Furthermore, if X and Y are finite sets and the distinct entries in the relation matrix of R are denoted by α_k, $k = 1, 2, \ldots, K$, where K is a finite number, then (13) assumes the form

$$R = \sum_k \alpha_k R_{\alpha_k}, \qquad 1 \leqslant k \leqslant K. \tag{16}$$

As a simple illustration of (13), assume $X = Y = \{x_1, x_2, x_3\}$, with the relation matrix μ_R given by

$$\mu_R = \begin{bmatrix} 1 & 0.8 & 0 \\ 0.6 & 1 & 0.9 \\ 0.8 & 0 & 1 \end{bmatrix}.$$

In this case, the resolution of R reads

$$\begin{aligned}R = {} & 0.6\{(x_1,x_1),(x_1,x_2),(x_2,x_1),(x_2,x_2),(x_2,x_3),(x_3,x_1),(x_3,x_3)\} \\ & + 0.8\{(x_1,x_1),(x_1,x_2),(x_2,x_2),(x_2,x_3),(x_3,x_1),(x_3,x_3)\} \\ & + 0.9\{(x_1,x_1),(x_2,x_2),(x_2,x_3),(x_3,x_3)\} \\ & + 1\{(x_1,x_1),(x_2,x_2),(x_3,x_3)\}.\end{aligned} \tag{17}$$

In what follows, we assume that $X = Y$. Furthermore, we shall assume for simplicity that X is a finite set, $X = \{x_1, x_2, \ldots, x_n\}$.

3. SIMILARITY RELATIONS

The concept of a *similarity* relation is essentially a generalization of the concept of an equivalence relation. More specifically:

Definition. A *similarity* relation, S, in X is a fuzzy relation in X which is (a) *reflexive*, i.e.,

$$\mu_S(x,x) = 1, \qquad \text{for all } x \text{ in dom } S, \tag{18}$$

$$\mu_S = \begin{bmatrix} 1 & 0.2 & 1 & 0.6 & 0.2 & 0.6 \\ 0.2 & 1 & 0.2 & 0.2 & 0.8 & 0.2 \\ 1 & 0.2 & 1 & 0.6 & 0.2 & 0.6 \\ 0.6 & 0.2 & 0.6 & 1 & 0.2 & 0.8 \\ 0.2 & 0.8 & 0.2 & 0.2 & 1 & 0.2 \\ 0.6 & 0.2 & 0.6 & 0.8 & 0.2 & 1 \end{bmatrix}$$

FIGURE 1. Relation matrix of a similarity relation.

(b) *symmetric* i.e.,

$$\mu_S(x, y) = \mu_S(y, x), \qquad \text{for all } x, y \text{ in dom } S, \tag{19}$$

and (c) *transitive*, i.e.,

$$S \supset S \circ S, \tag{20}$$

or, more explicitly,

$$\mu_S(x, z) \geqslant \bigvee_y (\mu_S(x, y) \wedge \mu_S(y, z)).$$

Note. If $*$ is employed in place of $\circ$ in the definition of the composition, the corresponding definition of transitivity becomes

$$S \supset S * S \tag{21}$$

or, more explicitly

$$\mu_S(x, z) \geqslant \bigvee_y (\mu_S(x, y) * \mu_S(y, z)).$$

When there is a need to distinguish between the transitivity defined by (20) and the more general form defined by (21), we shall refer to them as *max-min* and *max-star* transitivity, respectively.

An example of the relation matrix of a similarity relation S is shown in Figure 1. It is readily verified that $S = S \circ S$ and also that $S = S \cdot S$.

Transitivity

There are several aspects of the transitivity of a similarity relation which are in need of discussion. First, note that, in consequence of (18), we have

$$S \supset S^2 \Rightarrow S \supset S^k, \qquad k = 3, 4, \ldots \tag{22}$$

and hence

$$S \supset S^2 \Leftrightarrow S = \bar{S}, \tag{23}$$

where

$$\bar{S} = S + S^2 + S^3 + \ldots \tag{24}$$

is the *transitive* closure of S. Thus, as in the case of equivalence relations, the condition that S be transitive is equivalent to

$$S = \bar{S} = S + S^2 + S^3 + \ldots . \tag{25}$$

An immediate consequence of (25) is that the transitive closure of any fuzzy relation is transitive. Note also that for any S

$$S = S^2 \Rightarrow S = \bar{S}$$

and, if S is reflexive, then

$$S = S^2 \Leftrightarrow S = \bar{S}.$$

The significance of (25) is made clearer by the following observation. Let $x_{i_1}, \ldots, x_{i_k}$ be k points in X such that $\mu(x_{i_1}, x_{i_2}), \ldots, \mu(x_{i_{k-1}}, x_{i_k})$ are all > 0. Then the sequence $C = (x_{i_1}, \ldots, x_{i_k})$ will be said to be a *chain* from x_{i_1} to x_{i_k}, with the strength of this chain defined as the strength of its weakest link, that is,

$$\text{strength of } (x_{i_1}, \ldots, x_{i_k}) = \mu(x_{i_1}, x_{i_2}) \wedge \ldots \wedge \mu(x_{i_{k-1}}, x_{i_k}). \tag{26}$$

From the definition of the composition (equation (5)), it follows that the (i,j)th element of S^l, $l = 1, 2, 3, \ldots$, is the strength of the strongest chain of length l from x_i to x_j. Thus, the transitivity condition (25) may be stated in words as: for all x_i, x_j in X,

$$\text{strength of } S \text{ between } x_i \text{ and } x_j = \text{strength of the strongest chain from } x_i \text{ to } x_j. \quad (27)$$

Second, if X has n elements, then any chain C of length $k \geqslant n+1$ from x_{i_1} to x_{i_k} must necessarily have cycles, that is, one or more elements of X must occur more than once in the chain $C = (x_{i_1}, \ldots, x_{i_k})$. If these cycles are removed, the resulting chain, $\tilde{C}$, of length $\leqslant n$, will have at least the same strength as C, by virtue of (26). Consequently, for any elements x_i, x_j in X we can assert that

$$\text{strength of the strongest chain from } x_i \text{ to } x_j = \text{strength of the strongest chain of length } \leqslant n \text{ from } x_i \text{ to } x_j. \quad (28)$$

Since the (i,j)th element of $\hat{S}$ is the strength of the strongest chain from x_i to x_j, (28) implies the following proposition [18], which is well known for Boolean matrices [16]:

PROPOSITION 2. *If S is a fuzzy relation characterized by a relation matrix of order n, then*

$$\hat{S} = S + S^2 + S^3 + \ldots = S + S^2 + \ldots + S^n. \quad (29)$$

Note. Observe that (29) remains valid when in the definition of the composition and the strength of a chain $\wedge$ is replaced by the product, i.e., S^k, $k = 2, 3, \ldots$ is replaced by the k-fold composition $S \cdot S \cdot \ldots \cdot S$, with $\cdot$ defined by (10), and (26) is replaced by

$$\text{strength of } (x_i, \ldots, x_{i_k}) = \mu(x_{i_1}, x_{i_2})\,\mu(x_{i_2}, x_{i_3}) \ldots \mu(x_{i_{k-1}}, x_{i_k}). \quad (30)$$

Since $ab \leqslant a \wedge b$ for $a, b \in [0,1]$, it follows that

$$S \supset S \circ S \Rightarrow S \supset S \cdot S, \quad (31)$$

that is, max-min transitivity implies max-product transitivity. This observation is useful in situations in which the strength of a chain is more naturally expressed by (30) than by (26).

A case in point is provided by the criticisms [19–21] leveled at the assumption of transitivity in the case of weak ordering. Thus, suppose that X is a finite interval $[a,b]$ and that we wish to define a non-fuzzy preference ordering on X in terms of two relations $>$ and $\approx$ such that

(a) for every x,y in X, exactly one of $x > y$, $y > x$, or $x \approx y$ is true,
(b) $\approx$ is an equivalence relation,
(c) $>$ is transitive.

In many cases, it would be reasonable to assume that

$$x \approx y \Leftrightarrow |x - y| \leqslant \epsilon > 0,$$

where ϵ is a small number (in relation to $b - a$) representing an "indifference" interval. But then, by transitivity of $\approx$, $x \approx y$ for all x,y in X, which is inconsistent with our intuitive expectation that when the difference between x and y is sufficiently large, either $x > y$ or $y > x$ must hold.

This difficulty is not resolved by making $\approx$ a similarity relation in X so long as we employ the max-min transitivity in the definition of $\approx$. For, if we make the reasonable assumption that $\mu_{\approx}(x,y)$ is continuous at $x = y$, then (20) implies that $\mu_{\approx}(x,y) = 1$ for all x,y in X.

The difficulty may be resolved by making $\approx$ a similarity relation and employing the max-product transitivity in its definition. As an illustration, suppose that

$$\mu_{\approx}(x,y) = e^{-\beta|x-y|}, \qquad x, y \in X, \tag{32}$$

where β is any positive number. In this case, $\approx$ may be interpreted as "is not much different from."

Let x, y, $z \in [a,b]$, with $x < z$. Then, substituting (32) in

$$\mu_{\approx^2}(x,z) = \bigvee_y \mu_{\approx}(x,y)\mu_{\approx}(y,z),$$

we have

$$\begin{aligned}\mu_{\approx^2}(x,z) &= \bigvee_y e^{-\beta|y-x|}e^{-\beta|z-y|}\\ &= \bigvee_{y\in[x,z]} e^{-\beta(y-x)}e^{-\beta(z-y)}\\ &= e^{-\beta(z-x)}\\ &= \mu_{\approx}(x,z),\end{aligned} \tag{33}$$

which establishes that $\approx^2 = \approx$ and hence that (32) defines a similarity relation which is continuous at $x = y$ and yet is not constant over X.

Finally, it should be noted that the transitivity condition (20) implies and is implied by the ultrameric inequality [22] for distance functions. Specifically, let the complement of a similarity relation S be a *dissimilarity* relation D, with

$$\mu_D(x,y) = 1 - \mu_S(x,y), \qquad x, y \in X. \tag{34}$$

If $\mu_D(x,y)$ is interpreted as a distance function, $d(x,y)$, then (20) yields

$$1 - d(x,z) \geqslant \bigvee_y ((1 - d(x,y)) \wedge (1 - d(y,z)),$$

and since

$$(1 - d(x,y)) \wedge (1 - d(y,z)) = 1 - (d(x,y) \vee (d(y,z)) \tag{35}$$

we can conclude that, for all x, y, z in X,

$$d(x,z) \leqslant d(x,y) \vee d(y,z), \qquad y \in X, \tag{36}$$

which is the ultrameric inequality satisfied by $d(x,y)$. Clearly, (36) implies the triangle inequality

$$d(x,z) \leqslant d(x,y) + d(y,z). \tag{37}$$

Thus, (20) implies (36) and (37), and is implied by (36).

Returning to our discussion of similarity relations, we note that one of their basic properties is an immediate consequence of the resolution identity (13) for fuzzy relations. Specifically,

PROPOSITION 3. *Let*

$$S = \sum_\alpha \alpha S_\alpha, \qquad 0 < \alpha \leqslant 1, \tag{38}$$

be the resolution of a similarity relation in X. Then each S_α in (38) is an equivalence relation in X. Conversely, if the S_α, $0 < \alpha \leqslant 1$, are a nested sequence of distinct equivalence relations in X, with $\alpha_1 > \alpha_2 \Leftrightarrow S_{\alpha_1} \subset S_{\alpha_2}$, S_1 non-empty and $\operatorname{dom} S_\alpha = \operatorname{dom} S_1$, *then, for any choice of α's in* (0, 1] *which includes $\alpha = 1$, S is a similarity relation in X.*

Proof. $\Rightarrow$ First, since $\mu_S(x,x) = 1$ for all x in the domain of S, it follows that $(x,x) \in S_\alpha$ for all α in (0, 1] and hence that S_α is reflexive for all α in (0, 1].

Second, for each α in (0, 1], let $(x,y) \in S_\alpha$, which implies that $\mu_S(x,y) \geqslant \alpha$ and hence, by symmetry of S, that $\mu_S(y,x) \geqslant \alpha$. Consequently, $(y,x) \in S_\alpha$ and thus S_α is symmetric for each α in (0, 1].

Third, for each α in $(0,1]$, suppose that $(x_1,x_2) \in S_\alpha$ and $(x_2,x_3) \in S_\alpha$. Then $\mu_S(x_1,x_2) \geqslant \alpha$ and $\mu_S(x_2,x_3) \geqslant \alpha$ and hence, by the transitivity of S, $\mu_S(x_1,x_3) \geqslant \alpha$. This implies that $(x_1,x_3) \in S_\alpha$ and hence that S_α is transitive for each α in $(0,1]$.

$\Leftarrow$ First, since S_1 is non-empty, $(x,x) \in S_1$ and hence $\mu_S(x,x) = 1$ for all x in the domain of S_1.

Second, expressed in terms of the membership functions of S and S_α, (38) reads

$$\mu_S(x,y) = \bigvee_\alpha \alpha \mu_{S_\alpha}(x,y), \qquad x,y \in \operatorname{dom} S.$$

It is obvious from this expression for $\mu_S(x,y)$ that the symmetry of S_α for each α in $(0,1]$ implies the symmetry of S.

Third, let x_1, x_2, x_3 be some arbitrarily chosen elements of X. Suppose that

$$\mu_S(x_1,x_2) = \alpha \qquad \text{and} \qquad \mu_S(x_2,x_3) = \beta.$$

Then, $(x_1,x_2) \in S_{\alpha \cdot \beta}$ and $(x_2,x_3) \in S_{\alpha \cdot \beta}$, and consequently $(x_1,x_3) \in S_{\alpha \cdot \beta}$ by the transitivity of $S_{\alpha \cdot \beta}$.

From this it follows that, for all x_1, x_2, x_3 in X, we have

$$\mu_S(x_1,x_3) \geqslant \alpha \wedge \beta$$

and hence

$$\mu_S(x_1,x_3) \geqslant \bigvee_{x_2} (\mu_S(x_1,x_2) \wedge \mu_S(x_2,x_3)),$$

which establishes the transitivity of S.

Partition Tree

Let π_α denote the partition induced on X by S_α, $0 < \alpha \leqslant 1$. Clearly, $\pi_{\alpha'}$ is a refinement of π_α if $\alpha' \geqslant \alpha$. For, by the definition of $\pi_{\alpha'}$, two elements of X, say x and y, are in the same block of $\pi_{\alpha'}$ iff $\mu_S(x,y) \geqslant \alpha'$. This implies that $\mu_S(x,y) \geqslant \alpha$ and hence that x and y are in the same block of π_α.

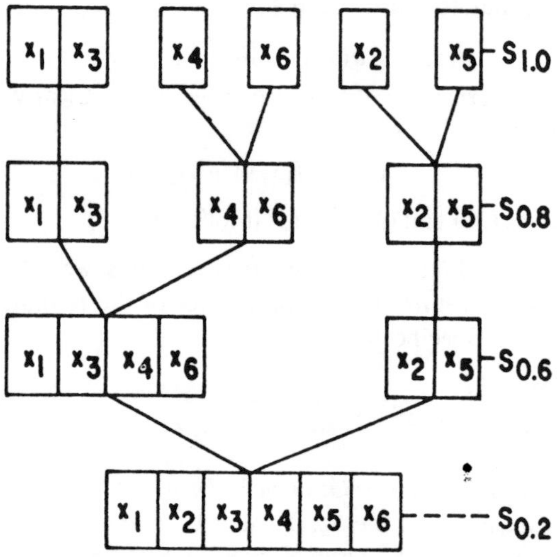

FIGURE 2. Partition tree for the similarity relation defined in Figure 1.

A nested sequence of partitions $\pi_{\alpha_1}, \pi_{\alpha_2}, \ldots, \pi_{\alpha_k}$ may be represented diagrammatically in the form of a *partition tree*,[4] as shown in Figure 2. It

[4] The notion of a partition tree and its properties are closely related to the concept of the hierarchic clustering scheme described in [22].

should be noted that the concept of a partition tree plays the same role with respect to a similarity relation as the concept of a quotient does with respect to an equivalence relation.

The partition tree of a similarity relation S is related to the relation matrix of S by the rule: x_i and x_j belong to the same block of π_α iff $\mu_S(x_i, x_j) \geq \alpha$. This rule implies that, given a partition tree of S, one can readily determine $\mu_S(x_i, x_j)$ by observing that

$$\mu_S(x_i, x_j) = \text{largest value of } \alpha \text{ for which } x_i \text{ and } x_j \text{ are in the same block of } \pi_\alpha. \tag{39}$$

An alternative to the diagrammatic representation of a partition tree is provided by a slightly modified form of the phrase-marker notation which is commonly used in linguistics [23]. Specifically, if we allow recursion and use the notation $\alpha(A, B)$ to represent a partition π_α whose blocks are A and B, then the partition tree shown in Figure 2 may be expressed in the form of a string:

$$0.2(0.6(0.8(1(x_1, x_3)), 0.8(1(x_4), 1(x_6))), 0.6(0.8(1(x_2), 1(x_5)))). \tag{40}$$

This string signifies that the highest partition, π_1, comprises the blocks (x_1, x_3), (x_4), (x_6), (x_2), and (x_5). The next partition, $\pi_{0.8}$, comprises the blocks $((x_1, x_3))$, $((x_4), (x_6))$, and $((x_2), (x_5))$. And so on. Needless to say, the profusion of parentheses in the phrase-marker representation of a partition tree makes it difficult to visualize the structure of a similarity relation from an inspection of (40).

Similarity Classes

Similarity classes play the same role with respect to a similarity relation as do equivalence classes in the case of an equivalence relation. Specifically, let S be a similarity relation in $X = \{x_1, \ldots, x_n\}$ characterized by a membership function $\mu_S(x_i, x_j)$. With each $x_i \in X$, we associate a *similarity class* denoted by $S[x_i]$ or simply $[x_i]$. This class is a fuzzy set in X which is characterized by the membership function

$$\mu_{S[x_i]}(x_j) = \mu_S(x_i, x_j). \tag{41}$$

Thus, $S[x_i]$ is identical with S conditioned on x_i, that is, with x_i held constant in the membership function of S.

To illustrate, the similarity classes associated with x_1 and x_2 in the case of the similarity relation defined in Figure 1 are

$$S[x_1] = \{(x_1, 1), (x_2, 0.2), (x_3, 1), (x_4, 0.6), (x_5, 0.2), (x_6, 0.6)\}$$

$$S[x_2] = \{(x_1, 0.2), (x_2, 1),)x_3, 0.2), (x_4, 0.2), (x_5, 0.8), (x_6, 0.2)\}.$$

By conditioning both sides of the resolution (38) on x_i we obtain at once the following proposition:

PROPOSITION 4. *The similarity class of x_i, $x_i \in X$, admits of the resolution*

$$S[x_i] = \sum_\alpha \alpha S_\alpha[x_i], \tag{42}$$

where $S_\alpha[x_i]$ denotes the block of S_α which contains x_i, and $\alpha S_\alpha[x_i]$ is a subnormal non-fuzzy set whose membership function is equal to α on $S_\alpha[x_i]$ and vanishes elsewhere.

For example, in the case of $S[x_1]$, with S defined in Figure 1, we have

$$S[x_1] = 0.2\{x_1, x_2, x_3, x_4, x_5, x_6\} + 0.6\{x_1, x_3, x_4, x_6\} + 1\{x_1, x_3\}$$

and similarly

$$S[x_2] = 0.2\{x_1, x_2, x_3, x_4, x_5, x_6\} + 0.8\{x_2, x_5\} + 1\{x_2\}.$$

The similarity classes of a similarity relation are not, in general, disjoint—

as they are in the case of an equivalence relation. Thus, the counterpart of disjointness is a more general property which is asserted in the following proposition:

PROPOSITION 5. *Let $S[x_i]$ and $S[x_j]$ be arbitrary similarity classes of S. Then, the height (see (3)) of the intersection of $S[x_i]$ and $S[x_j]$ is bounded from above by $\mu_S(x_i, x_j)$, that is,*

$$h(S[x_i] \cap S[x_j]) \leqslant \mu_S(x_i, x_j). \tag{43}$$

Proof. By definition of h we have

$$h(S[x_i] \cap S[x_j]) = \bigvee_{x_k} (\mu_S(x_i, x_k) \wedge \mu_S(x_j, x_k)),$$

which in view of the symmetry of S may be rewritten as

$$h(S[x_i] \cap S[x_j]) = \bigvee_{x_k} (\mu_S(x_i, x_k) \wedge \mu_S(x_k, x_j)). \tag{44}$$

Now the right-hand member of (44) is identical with the grade of membership of (x_i, x_j) in the composition of S with S. Thus

$$h(S[x_i] \cap S[x_j]) = \mu_{S \circ S}(x_i, x_j),$$

which, in virtue of the transitivity of S, implies that

$$h(S[x_i] \cap S[x_j]) \leqslant \mu_S(x_i, x_j). \tag{45}$$

Note that, if S is reflexive, then $S^2 = S$ and (45) is satisfied with the equality sign. Thus, for the example of Proposition 4, we have

$$h(\dot{S}[x_1] \cap S[x_2]) = 0.2 = \mu_S(x_1, x_2),$$

since S is reflexive.

The following corollary follows at once from Proposition 5:

COROLLARY 6. *The height of the intersection of all similarity classes of X is bounded by the infimum of $\mu_S(x_i, x_j)$ over X. Thus*

$$h(S[x_1] \cap \ldots \cap S[x_n]) \leqslant \bigwedge_{x_i} \bigwedge_{x_j} \mu_S(x_i, x_j). \tag{46}$$

We turn next to the consideration of fuzzy ordering relations.

4. FUZZY ORDERINGS

A *fuzzy ordering* is a fuzzy transitive relation.[5] In what follows we shall define several basic types of fuzzy orderings and dwell briefly upon some of their properties.

A fuzzy relation P in X is a *fuzzy partial ordering* iff it is reflexive, transitive, and antisymmetric. By antisymmetry of P is meant that

$$\mu_P(x, y) > 0 \quad \text{and}\ \mu_P(y, x) > 0 \Rightarrow x = y, \qquad x, y \in X. \tag{47}$$

(On occasion, we may use the notation $x \leqslant y$ to signify that $\mu_P(x, y) > 0$.)

$$\mu_P = \begin{bmatrix} 1 & 0.8 & 0.2 & 0.6 & 0.6 & 0.4 \\ 0 & 1 & 0 & 0 & 0.6 & 0 \\ 0 & 0 & 1 & 0 & 0.5 & 0 \\ 0 & 0 & 0 & 1 & 0.6 & 0.4 \\ 0 & 0 & 0 & 0 & 1 & 0 \\ 0 & 0 & 0 & 0 & 0 & 1 \end{bmatrix}$$

FIGURE 3. Relation matrix for a fuzzy partial ordering.

An example of a relation matrix for a fuzzy partial ordering is shown in Figure 3. The corresponding fuzzy Hasse diagram for this ordering is shown in

[5] Alternatively, a fuzzy ordering may be viewed as a metrized ordering in which the metric satisfies the ultrametric inequality.

Figure 4. In this diagram, the number associated with the arc joining x_i to x_j is $\mu_P(x_i, x_j)$, with the understanding that x_j is a *cover* for x_i, that is, there is no x_k

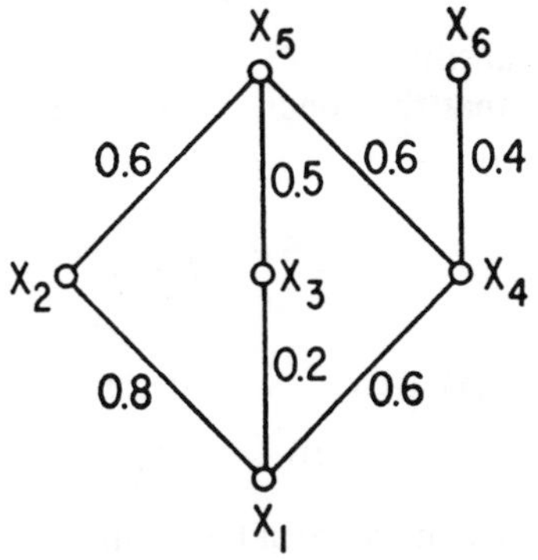

FIGURE 4. Fuzzy Hasse diagram for the fuzzy partial ordering defined in Figure 3.

in X such that $\mu_P(x_i, x_k) > 0$ and $\mu_P(x_k, x_j) > 0$. Note that the numbers associated with the arcs define the relation matrix by virtue of the transitivity identity $P = P^2$.

As in the case of a similarity relation, a fuzzy partial ordering may be resolved into non-fuzzy partial orderings. This basic property of fuzzy partial orderings is expressed by

PROPOSITION 7. *Let*

$$P = \sum_\alpha \alpha P_\alpha, \qquad 0 < \alpha \leqslant 1, \tag{48}$$

be the resolution of a fuzzy partial ordering in X. Then each P_α in (48) is a partial ordering in X. Conversely, if the P_α, $0 < \alpha \leqslant 1$, are a nested sequence of distinct partial orderings in X, with $\alpha_1 > \alpha_2 \Leftrightarrow P_{\alpha_1} \subset P_{\alpha_2}$, P_1 non-empty, and $\operatorname{dom} P_\alpha = \operatorname{dom} P_1$, *then, for any choice of α's in (0, 1] which includes α = 1, P is a fuzzy partial ordering in X.*

Proof. Reflexivity and transitivity are established as in Proposition 3. As for antisymmetry, suppose that $(x, y) \in P_\alpha$ and $(y, x) \in P_\alpha$. Then $\mu_P(x, y) \geqslant \alpha$, $\mu_P(y, x) \geqslant \alpha$ and hence by antisymmetry of P, $x = y$. Conversely, suppose that $\mu_P(x, y) = \alpha > 0$ and $\mu_P(y, x) = \beta > 0$. Let $\gamma = \alpha \wedge \beta$. Then $(x, y) \in P_\gamma$ and $(y, x) \in P_\gamma$, and from the antisymmetry of P_γ it follows that $x = y$.

In many applications of the concept of a fuzzy partial ordering, the condition of reflexivity is not a natural one to impose. If we allow $\mu_P(x, x)$, $x \in X$, to take any value in [0, 1], the ordering will be referred to as irreflexive.

To illustrate the point, assume that X is an interval $[a, b]$, and $\mu_P(x, y) = f(y - x)$, with $f(y - x) = 0$ for $y < x$ and $f(0) = 1$. Then, as was noted in Section 2 ((31) *et seq.*), if $f(x)$ is right-continuous at $x = 0$, the max-min transitivity of μ_P requires that $f(x) = 1$ for $x > 0$. However, if we drop the requirement of reflexivity, then it is sufficient that f be monotone non-decreasing in order to satisfy the condition of transitivity. For, assume that f is monotone non-decreasing and $x \leqslant y \leqslant z$, $x, y, z, \in [a, b]$. Then

$$\begin{aligned} \mu_P(x, z) &= f(z - x) \\ &= f((z - y) + (y - x)), \end{aligned} \tag{49}$$

and, since

$$f((z - y) + (y - x)) \geqslant f(z - y),$$

$$f((z - y) + (y - x)) \geqslant f(y - x),$$

we have

$$f((z - y) + (y - x)) \geqslant f(z - y) \wedge f(y - x),$$

and therefore

$$\mu_P(x,z) \geqslant \bigvee_y (\mu_P(x,y) \wedge \mu_P(y,z)),$$

which establishes the transitivity of P.

It should be noted that the condition is not necessary. For example, it is easy to verify that for any

$$\frac{1}{b-a} \leqslant \beta \leqslant \frac{2}{b-a},$$

the function

$$\begin{aligned} f(x) &= \beta x, \qquad & 0 \leqslant x \leqslant 1/\beta, \\ &= 2 - \beta x, \qquad & 1/\beta \leqslant x \leqslant b-a, \end{aligned}$$

corresponds to a transitive fuzzy partial ordering if $\beta(b-a) \leqslant \frac{4}{3}$.

With each $x_i \in X$, we associate two fuzzy sets: the *dominating* class, denoted by $P_{\geqslant}[x_i]$ and defined by

$$\mu_{P\geqslant[x_i]}(x_j) = \mu_P(x_i, x_j), \qquad x_j \in X, \tag{50}$$

and the *dominated* class, denoted by $P_{\leqslant}[x_i]$ and defined by

$$\mu_{P\leqslant[x_i]}(x_j) = \mu_P(x_j, x_i), \qquad x_j \in X. \tag{51}$$

In terms of these classes, x_i is *undominated* iff

$$\mu_P(x_i, x_j) = 0, \qquad \text{for all } x_j \neq x_i, \tag{52}$$

and x_i is *undominating* iff

$$\mu_P(x_j, x_i) = 0, \quad \text{for all } x_j \neq x_i. \tag{53}$$

It is evident that, if P is any fuzzy partial ordering in $X = \{x_1, \ldots, x_n\}$, the sets of undominated and undominating elements of X are non-empty.

Another related concept is that of a fuzzy upper-bound for a non-fuzzy subset of X. Specifically, let A be a non-fuzzy subset of X. Then the *upper-bound* for A is a fuzzy set denoted by $U(A)$ and defined by

$$U(A) = \bigcap_{x_i \in A} P_{\geqslant}[x_i]. \tag{54}$$

For a non-fuzzy partial ordering, this reduces to the conventional definition of an upper-bound. Note that, if the *least* element of $U(A)$ is defined as an x_i (if it exists) such that

$$\mu_{U(A)}(x_i) > 0 \quad \text{and} \quad \mu_P(x_i, x_j) > 0 \quad \text{for all } x_j \text{ in the support of } U(A), \tag{55}$$

then the *least upper-bound* of A is the least element of $U(A)$ and is unique by virtue of the antisymmetry of P.

In a similar vein, one can readily generalize to fuzzy orderings many of the well-known concepts relating to other types of non-fuzzy orderings. Some of these are briefly stated in the sequel.

Preordering

A fuzzy *preordering* R is a fuzzy relation in X which is reflexive and transitive. As in the case of a fuzzy partial ordering, R admits of the resolution

$$R = \sum_\alpha \alpha R_\alpha, \qquad 0 < \alpha \leqslant 1, \tag{56}$$

where the α-level-sets R_α are non-fuzzy preorderings.

For each α, the non-fuzzy preordering R_α induces an equivalence relation, E_α, in X and a partial ordering, P_α, on the quotient X/E_α. Specifically,

$$(x_i, x_j) \in E_\alpha \Leftrightarrow \mu_{R_\alpha}(x_i, x_j) = \mu_{R_\alpha}(x_j, x_i) = 1 \tag{57}$$

and

$$([x_i],[x_j]) \in P_\alpha \Leftrightarrow \mu_{R\alpha}(x_i,x_j)=1 \quad \text{and} \quad \mu_{R\alpha}(x_j,x_i)=0, \tag{58}$$

where $[x_i]$ and $[x_j]$ are the equivalence classes of x_i and x_j, respectively.

As an illustration, consider the fuzzy preordering characterized by the relation matrix shown in Figure 5. The corresponding relation matrices for $R_{0\cdot2}$, $R_{0\cdot6}$, $R_{0\cdot8}$, $R_{0\cdot9}$, and R_1 read as in Figure 6.

$$\mu_R = \begin{bmatrix} 1 & 0.8 & 1 & 0.8 & 0.8 & 0.8 \\ 0.2 & 1 & 0.2 & 0.2 & 0.8 & 0.2 \\ 1 & 0.8 & 1 & 0.8 & 0.8 & 0.8 \\ 0.6 & 0.9 & 0.6 & 1 & 0.9 & 1 \\ 0.2 & 0.8 & 0.2 & 0.2 & 1 & 0.2 \\ 0.6 & 0.9 & 0.6 & 0.9 & 0.9 & 1 \end{bmatrix}$$

FIGURE 5. Relation matrix of a fuzzy preordering.

The preordering in question may be represented in diagrammatic form as shown in Figure 7. In this figure, the broken lines in each level (identified by R_α) represent the arcs (edges) of the Hasse diagram of the partial ordering P_α, rotated clockwise by 90°. The nodes of this diagram are the equivalence classes of the equivalence relation, E_α, induced by R_α. Thus, the diagram as a whole is the partition tree of the similarity relation

$$S = 0.2E_{0\cdot2} + 0.6E_{0\cdot6} + 0.8E_{0\cdot8} + 0.9E_{0\cdot9} + 1E_1,$$

with the blocks in each level of the tree forming the elements of a partial ordering P_α which is represented by a rotated Hasse diagram.

Linear Ordering

A fuzzy *linear ordering* L is a fuzzy antisymmetric ordering in X in which for every $x \neq y$ in X either $\mu_L(x,y) > 0$ or $\mu_L(y,x) > 0$. A fuzzy linear ordering admits of the resolution

$$L = \sum_\alpha \alpha L_\alpha, \qquad 0 < \alpha \leqslant 1, \tag{59}$$

which is a special case of (48) and in which the L_α are non-fuzzy linear orderings.

A simple example of an irreflexive fuzzy linear ordering is the relation

$$R_{0\cdot2}: \begin{bmatrix} 1&1&1&1&1&1 \\ 1&1&1&1&1&1 \\ 1&1&1&1&1&1 \\ 1&1&1&1&1&1 \\ 1&1&1&1&1&1 \\ 1&1&1&1&1&1 \end{bmatrix} \quad R_{0\cdot6}: \begin{bmatrix} 1&1&1&1&1&1 \\ 0&1&0&0&1&0 \\ 1&1&1&1&1&1 \\ 1&1&1&1&1&1 \\ 0&1&0&0&1&0 \\ 1&1&1&1&1&1 \end{bmatrix} \quad R_{0\cdot8}: \begin{bmatrix} 1&1&1&1&1&1 \\ 0&1&0&0&1&0 \\ 1&1&1&1&1&1 \\ 0&1&0&1&1&1 \\ 0&1&0&0&1&0 \\ 0&1&0&1&1&1 \end{bmatrix}$$

$$R_{0\cdot9}: \begin{bmatrix} 1&0&1&0&0&0 \\ 0&1&0&0&0&0 \\ 1&0&1&0&0&0 \\ 0&1&0&1&1&1 \\ 0&0&0&0&1&0 \\ 0&1&0&1&1&1 \end{bmatrix} \quad R_1: \begin{bmatrix} 1&0&1&0&0&0 \\ 0&1&0&0&0&0 \\ 1&0&1&0&0&0 \\ 0&0&0&1&0&1 \\ 0&0&0&0&1&0 \\ 0&0&0&0&0&1 \end{bmatrix}$$

FIGURE 6. Relation matrices for the level sets of the preordering defined in Figure 5.

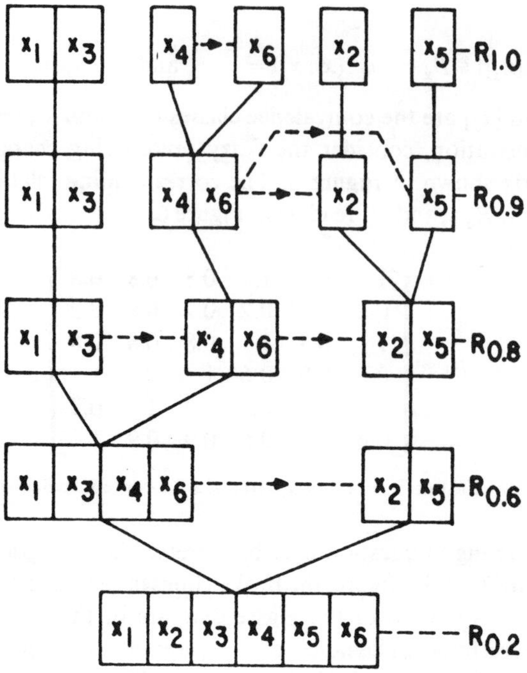

FIGURE 7. Structure of the preordering defined in Figure 5.

$y \gg x$ in $X = (-\infty, \infty)$. If we define $\mu_L(x, y)$ by

$$\mu_L(x,y) = (1 + (y - x)^{-2})^{-1}, \qquad \text{for } y - x \geq 0,$$
$$= 0, \quad \text{for } y - x < 0,$$

then L is transitive (in virtue of (49)), antisymmetric, and $\mu_L(x,y) > 0$ or $\mu_L(y,x) > 0$ for every $x \neq y$ in $(-\infty, \infty)$. Hence L is a fuzzy linear ordering.

Weak Ordering

If we remove the condition of antisymmetry, then a fuzzy linear ordering becomes a *weak ordering*. Equivalently, a weak ordering, W, may be regarded as a special case of a preordering in which for every $x \neq y$ in X either $\mu_W(x,y) > 0$ or $\mu_W(y,x) > 0$.

Szpilrajn's Theorem

A useful example of a well-known result which can readily be extended to fuzzy orderings is provided by the Szpilrajn theorem [24], which may be stated as follows: Let P be a partial ordering in X. Then, there exists a linear ordering L in a set Y, of the same cardinality as X, and a one-to-one mapping σ from X onto Y (called the Szpilrajn mapping) such that for all x, y in X

$$(x, y) \in P \Rightarrow (\sigma(x), \sigma(y)) \in L.$$

In its extended form, the statement of the theorem becomes:

THEOREM 8. *Let P be a fuzzy partial ordering in X. Then, there exist a fuzzy linear ordering L in a set Y, of the same cardinality as X, and a one-to-one mapping σ from X onto Y such that*

$$\mu_P(x,y) > 0 \Rightarrow \mu_L(\sigma(x), \sigma(y)) = \mu_P(x,y), \qquad x, y \in X. \tag{60}$$

Proof. The theorem can readily be established by the following construction for L and σ: Assume that a fuzzy partial ordering P in $X = \{x_1, \ldots, x_n\}$ is characterized by its relation matrix, which for simplicity will also be referred to as P. In what follows, the relation matrix shown in Figure 3 and the Hasse diagram corresponding to it (Fig. 4) will be used to illustrate the construction for L and σ.

First, we shall show that the antisymmetry and transitivity of P make it possible to relabel the elements of X in such a way that the corresponding relabeled relation matrix P is upper-triangular.

To this end, let C_0 denote the set of undominating elements of X (i.e., $x_i \in C_0 \Leftrightarrow$ column corresponding to x_i contains a single positive element (unity) lying on the main diagonal). The transitivity of P implies that C_0 is non-empty. For the relation matrix of Figure 3, $C_0 = \{x_1\}$.

Referring to the Hasse diagram of P (Fig. 4), it will be convenient to associate with each x_j in X a positive integer $\rho(x_j; C_0)$ representing the *level* of x_j above C_0. By definition

$$\rho(x_j; C_0) = \max_{x_i \in C_0} d(x_i, x_j), \tag{61}$$

where $d(x_i,x_j)$ is the length of the longest upward path between x_i and x_j in the Hasse diagram. For example, in Figure 4, $C_0 = \{x_1\}$ and $d(x_1,x_2) = 1$, $d(x_1,x_3) = 1$, $d(x_1,x_4) = 1$, $d(x_1,x_5) = 2$, $d(x_1,x_6) = 2$.

Now, let C_m, $m = 0, 1, \ldots, M$, denote the subset of X consisting of those elements whose level is m, that is,

$$C_m = \{x_j | \rho(x_j; C_0) = m\}, \tag{62}$$

with the understanding that, if x_j is not reachable (via an upward path) from some element in C_0, then $x_j \in C_0$. For the example of Figure 4, we have $C_0 = \{x_1\}$, $C_1 = \{x_2,x_3,x_4\}$, $C_2 = \{x_5,x_6\}$, $C_3 = \theta$ (empty set). In words,

$x_j \in C_m \Leftrightarrow$ (i) there exists an element of C_0 from which x_j is reachable via a path of length m, and

(ii) there does not exist an element of C_0 from which x_j is reachable via a path of length $> m$. (63)

From (61) and (62) it follows that $C_0, \ldots, C_M$ have the following properties:

(a) Every x_j in X belongs to some C_m, $m = 0, \ldots, M$. (64)

Reason. Either x_j is not reachable from any x_i in X, in which case $x_j \in C_0$, or it is reachable from some x_i in X, say x_{i_1} (i.e., $\mu_P(x_{i_1},x_j) > 0$). Now x_{i_1}, like x_j, either is not reachable from any x_i in X, in which case $x_{i_1} \in C_0$ and hence x_j is reachable from C_0, or is reachable from some x_i in X, say x_{i_2}. Continuing this argument and making use of the antisymmetry of P and the finiteness of X, we arrive at the conclusion that the chain $(x_{i_k}, x_{i_{k-1}}, \ldots, x_i, x_j)$ must eventually originate at some x_{i_k} in C_0. This establishes that every x_j in X which is not in C_0 is reachable from C_0 and hence that $\rho(x_j; C_0) > 0$ and $x_j \in C_{\rho(x_j; C_0)}$.

(b) $C_0, C_1, \ldots, C_M$ are disjoint. Thus, (a) and (b) imply that the collection $\{C_0, \ldots, C_M\}$ is a partition of X.

Reason. Single-valuedness of $\rho(x_j; C_0)$ implies that $x_j \in C_k$ and $x_j \in C_l$ cannot both be true if $k \neq l$. Hence the disjointness of $C_0, \ldots, C_M$.

(c) $$x_i, x_j \in C_m \Rightarrow \mu_P(x_i,x_j) = \mu_P(x_j,x_i) = 0. \tag{65}$$

Reason. Assume x_i, $x_j \in C_m$ and $\mu_P(x_i,x_j) > 0$. Then

$$\rho(x_j; C_0) > \rho(x_i; C_0),$$

which contradicts the assumption that x_i, $x_j \in C_m$. Similarly, $\mu_P(x_j,x_i) > 0$ contradicts x_i, $x_j \in C_m$.

(d) $x_j \in C_l$ and $k < l \Rightarrow x_j$ is reachable from some x_i in C_k.

Reason. If $x_j \in C_l$, then there exists a path T of length l via which x_j is reachable from some x_r in C_0, and there does not exist a longer path via which x_j is reachable from any element of C_0. Now let x_i be the kth node of T (counting in the direction of C_l), with $k < l$. Then $x_i \in C_k$, since there exists a path of length k from x_r to x_i and there does not exist a longer path via which x_i is reachable from any element of C_0. (For, if such a path existed, then x_j would be reachable via a path longer than l from some element of C_0). Thus x_j is reachable from some x_i in C_k.

An immediate consequence of (d) is that the C_m may be defined recursively by

$$C_{m+1} = \{x_j | \rho(x_j; C_m) = 1\}, \qquad m = 0, 1, \ldots, M, \tag{66}$$

with the understanding that $C_M \neq \theta$ and $C_{M+1} = \theta$. More explicitly,

$x_j \in C_{m+1} \Leftrightarrow \mu_P(x_i, x_j) > 0$ for some x_i in C_m, and there does not exist an x_i in C_m and an x_k in X distinct from x_i such that $\mu_P(x_i, x_k) > 0$ and $\mu_P(x_k, x_j) > 0$.

(e) $\quad x_i \in C_k \quad$ and $\quad x_j \in C_l \quad$ and $\quad k < l \Rightarrow \mu_P(x_j, x_i) = 0. \qquad (67)$

Reason. Suppose $\mu_P(x_j, x_i) > 0$. By (d), x_j is reachable from some element of C_k, say x_r. If $x_r = x_i$, then $\mu_P(x_i, x_j) > 0$, which contradicts the antisymmetry of P. If $x_r \neq x_i$, then by transitivity of P, $\mu_P(x_r, x_i) > 0$, which contradicts (c) since $x_r, x_i \in C_k$.

(f) $\quad x_i \in C_k \quad$ and $\quad x_j \in C_l \quad$ and $\quad \mu_P(x_i, x_j) > 0 \Rightarrow l > k. \qquad (68)$

Reason. By negation of (e) and (c).

The partition $\{C_0, \ldots, C_m\}$, which can be constructed from the relation matrix P or by inspection of the Hasse diagram of P, can be put to use in various ways. In particular, it can be employed to obtain the Hasse diagram of P from its relation matrix in cases in which this is difficult to do by inspection. Another application, which motivated our discussion of $\{C_0, \ldots, C_M\}$, relates to the possibility of relabeling the elements of X in such a way as to result in an upper-triangular relation matrix. By employing the properties of $\{C_0, \ldots, C_M\}$ stated above, this can readily be accomplished as follows:

Let n_m denote the number of elements in C_m, $m = 0, \ldots, M$. Let the elements of C_0 be relabeled, in some arbitrary order, as $y_1, \ldots, y_{n_0}$, then the elements of C_1 be relabeled as $y_{n_0+1}, \ldots, y_{n_0+n_1}$, then the elements of C_2 be relabeled as $y_{n_0+n_1+1}, \ldots, y_{n_0+n_1+n_2}$, and so on, until all the elements of X are relabeled in this manner. If the new label for x_i is y_j, we write

$$y_j = \sigma(x_i), \tag{69}$$

where σ is a one-to-one mapping from $X = \{x_1, \ldots, x_n\}$ to $Y = \{y_1, \ldots, y_n\}$. Furthermore, we order the y_j linearly by $y_j > y_i \Leftrightarrow j > i$, $i, j = 1, \ldots, n$.

The above relabeling transforms the relation matrix P into the relation matrix P_r defined by

$$\mu_{P_r}(\sigma(x_i), \sigma(x_j)) = \mu_P(x_i, x_j), \qquad x_i, x_j \in X. \tag{70}$$

To verify that P_r is upper-triangular, it is sufficient to note that, if $\mu_P(x_i, x_j) > 0$, for $x_i \neq x_j$, then by (f) $\sigma(x_j) > \sigma(x_i)$.

It is now a simple matter to construct a linear ordering L in Y which satisfies (60). Specifically, for $x_i \neq x_j$, let

$$\begin{aligned}
\mu_L(\sigma(x_i), \sigma(x_j)) &= \mu_P(x_i, x_j), \text{ if } \mu_P(x_i, x_j) > 0, \\
&= 0, \text{ if } \mu_P(x_i, x_j) = 0 \text{ and } \mu_P(x_j, x_i) > 0, \\
&= \epsilon, \text{ if } \mu_P(x_i, x_j) = \mu_P(x_j, x_i) = 0 \text{ and } \sigma(x_j) > \sigma(x_i), \\
&= 0, \text{ if } \mu_P(x_i, x_j) = \mu_P(x_j, x_i) = 0 \text{ and } \sigma(x_j) < \sigma(x_i),
\end{aligned} \tag{71}$$

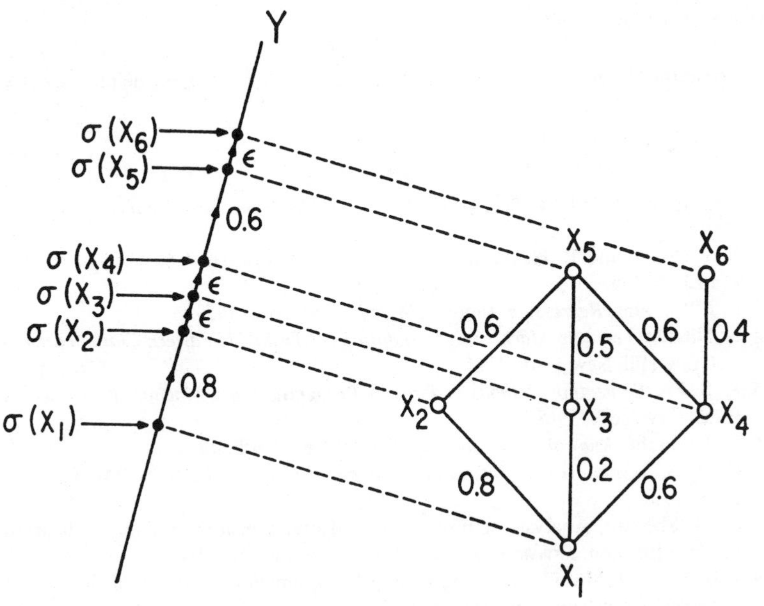

FIGURE 8. Graphic construction of L and σ.

where $\in$ is any positive constant which is smaller than or equal to the smallest positive entry in the relation matrix P.

Note. It is helpful to observe that this construction of L may be visualized as a projection of the Hasse diagram of P on a slightly inclined vertical line Y (Figure 8). The purpose of the inclination is to avoid the possibility that two or more nodes of the Hasse diagram may be taken by the projection into the same point of Y.

All that remains to be demonstrated at this stage is that L, as defined by (71), is transitive. This is insured by our choice of $\in$, for, so long as $\in$ is smaller than or equal to the smallest entry in P, the transitivity of P implies the transitivity of L, as is demonstrated by the following lemma:

LEMMA 9. *Let P_r be an upper-triangular matrix such that $P_r = P_r^2$. Let Q denote an upper-triangular matrix all of whose elements are equal to $\in$, where $0 < \in \leqslant$ smallest positive entry in P_r. Then*

$$P_r \vee Q = (P_r \vee Q)^2. \tag{72}$$

In other words, if P_r and Q are transitive, so is $P_r \vee Q$.

Proof. We can rewrite (72) as

$$(P_r \vee Q)^2 = P_r^2 \vee P_r \circ Q \vee Q \circ P_r \vee Q^2. \tag{73}$$

Now $P_r^2 = P_r$ and, since Q is upper-triangular, $Q = Q^2$. Furthermore, $P_r \circ Q = Q \circ P_r = Q$. Hence (72).

To apply this lemma, we note that L, as defined by (71), may be expressed as

$$L = P_r \vee Q, \tag{74}$$

where P_r and Q satisfy the conditions of the lemma. Consequently, L is transitive and thus is a linear ordering satisfying (60). This completes the proof of our extension of Szpilrajn's theorem.

CONCLUDING REMARK

As the foregoing analysis demonstrates, it is a relatively simple matter to extend some of the well-known results in the theory of relations to fuzzy sets. It appears that such extension may be of use in various applied areas, particularly those in which fuzziness and/or randomness play a significant role in the analysis or control of system behavior.

ACKNOWLEDGMENT

The author is indebted to P. Varaiya, E. T. Lee, and J. Yang for helpful criticisms.

REFERENCES

1 A. Kaufmann and M. Précigout, *Cours de Mathématiques Nouvelles*, Dunod, Paris, 1966.
2 R. R. Sokal and P. H. A. Sneath, *Principles of Numerical Taxonomy*, Freeman, San Francisco, 1963.
3 E. J. Williams, *Regression Analysis*, Wiley, New York, 1959.
4 N. Nilsson, *Learning Machines—Foundations of Trainable Pattern Classification Systems*, McGraw-Hill, New York, 1965.
5 K. S. Fu, *Sequential Methods in Pattern Recognition and Machine Learning*, Academic Press, New York, 1968.
6 S. Watanabe, *Knowing and Guessing*, Wiley, New York, 1969.
7 E. M. Braverman (Ed.), *Automatic Analysis of Complex Patterns*, Mir Press, Moscow, 1969.
8 R. N. Shepard, Analysis of proximities: Multidimensional scaling with an unknown distance function, *Psychometrica* **27** (1962), 125–140, 219–246.
9 J. B. Kruskal, Multidimensional scaling by optimizing goodness of fit to a nonmetric hypothesis, *Psychometrica* **29** (1964), 1–27.
10 J. H. Ward, Jr., Hierarchical grouping to optimize an objective function, *Amer. Statist. Assoc.* **58** (1963), 236–244.
11 G. Debreu, *Theory of Value* (Cowles Commission Monograph 17), Wiley, New York, 1959.
12 R. D. Luce and H. Raiffa, *Games and Decisions*, Wiley, New York, 1958.
13 L. A. Zadeh, Fuzzy sets, *Information and Control* **8** (June, 1965), 338–353.
14 S. Tamura, S. Higuchi, and K. Tanaka, Pattern classification based on fuzzy relations, Osaka University, Osaka, Japan, 1970. To be published in System Science and Cybernetics.
15 J. Aczél, *Lectures on Functional Equations and Their Applications*, Academic Press, New York, 1966.
16 P. L. Hammer (Ivănescu) and S. Rudeanu, *Boolean Methods in Operations Research and Related Areas*, Springer-Verlag, Berlin, New York, 1968.
17 E. G. Santos, Maximin automata, *Information and Control* **13** (Oct. 1968), 363–377.
18 R. E. Bellman and L. A. Zadeh, Decision-making in a fuzzy environment, Electronics Res. Lab. Rept. 69-8, University of California, Berkeley, Nov. 1969 (to appear in *Management Science*).
19 W. E. Armstrong, Uncertainty and the utility function, *Economic J.* **58** (1948), 1–10.
20 K. O. May, Intransitivity, utility and the aggregation of preference patterns, *Econometrica* **22** (Jan. 1954), 1–13.
21 R. D. Luce, Semiorders and a theory of utility discrimination, *Econometrica* **24** (1956), 178–191.
22 S. C. Johnson, Hierarchical clustering schemes, *Psychometrica* **32** (Sept. 1967), 241–254.
23 J. Lyons, *Introduction to Theoretical Linguistics*, Cambridge Univ. Press, Cambridge/New York, 1968.
24 R. M. Baer and O. Osterby, Algorithms over partially ordered sets, *BIT* **9** (1969), 97–118.

Pattern Classification Based on Fuzzy Relations

SHINICHI TAMURA, STUDENT MEMBER, IEEE, SEIHAKU HIGUCHI, AND KOKICHI TANAKA, SENIOR MEMBER, IEEE

***Abstract*—A method of classifying patterns using fuzzy relations is described. To start with, we give a suitable value of the measure of subjective similarity to each pair of patterns that is taken from the population of patterns to be classified. Then a similitude between any two patterns is calculated by using the composition of a fuzzy relation. The similitude induces an equivalence relation. Consequently, we can classify the present population of the patterns into some classes by the equivalence relation. An experiment of the classification of portraits has been performed to test the method proposed here.**

I. Introduction

SINCE Zadeh published the fuzzy set theory [1]–[6], it has been applied to some fields such as automata, learning, and control [7]–[10]. We introduce a concept of the fuzzy relation [1] to measure the subjective similarity as follows.

In the classification of smells and the classification of pictures, etc., subjective information plays an important role. This subjective information may be represented by the fuzzy relation that corresponds to the subjective similarity. However, since such a primary fuzzy relation is made on the basis of a personal subject, it does not satisfy the axioms of distance. Hence in this paper we construct an n-step fuzzy relation by the composition of the fuzzy relation, and define a similitude as a limit value of the n-step fuzzy relation in order to satisfy the axioms of distance. The similitude defined in such a way induces an equivalence relation. Thus we can classify patterns by the equivalence relation.

II. Fuzzy Relation

Let X be a set of patterns. The fuzzy relation A on X is characterized by $f_A(x,y) \in [0,1]$, for all $x,y \in X$. In this paper, we first consider a one-step fuzzy relation $f_1(x,y)$ satisfying the two conditions

$$f_1(x,x) = 1, \qquad \forall x \in X \tag{1}$$

$$f_1(x,y) = f_1(y,x), \qquad \forall x,y \in X. \tag{2}$$

Condition (1) means that x is perfectly the same with x. Condition (2) means that the fuzzy relation considered here is symmetric. Assume that the value of this one-step fuzzy relation $f_1(x,y)$ is given to each of the pairs of patterns in X. Any $f_1(x,y)$ will do if it satisfies conditions (1) and (2); for example, subjective similarities, normalized correlations, or potential functions, etc., may be conceived.

Now, we define the n-step fuzzy relation $f_n(x,y)$ by

$$f_n(x,y) = \sup_{x_1,x_2,\cdots,x_{n-1}\in X} \min [f_1(x,x_1),f_1(x_1,x_2), \cdots, f_1(x_{n-1},y)], \qquad n = 2,3,\cdots.$$

Then

$$\begin{aligned} f_{n+1}(x,y) &= \sup_{x_1,\cdots,x_{n-1},x_n\in X} \min [f_1(x,x_1), \cdots, f_1(x_{n-1},x_n),f_1(x_n,y)] \\ &\geq \sup_{x_1,\cdots,x_{n-2},x_{n-1}\in X} \min [f_1(x,x_1), \cdots, f_1(x_{n-1},y),f_1(y,y)] \\ &= f_n(x,y). \end{aligned}$$

Therefore, we see

$$0 \leq f_1(x,y) \leq f_2(x,y) \leq \cdots \leq f_n(x,y) \leq f_{n+1}(x,y) \leq \cdots \leq 1 \tag{3}$$

and we have the similitude $f(x,y)$ in $[0,1]$ such that

$$f(x,y) = \lim_{n\to\infty} f_n(x,y).$$

We will show some important properties of $f(x,y)$ in the following.

Definition 1: Let x and y be two elements of X. Then x and y are said to have a stronger relation than λ, written $xR_\lambda y$, iff $f(x,y) \geq \lambda$. Symbolically this is expressed as

$$xR_\lambda y \Leftrightarrow f(x,y) \geq \lambda.$$

Lemma 1: For all $x,y,z \in X$,

$$f(x,z) \geq \min [f(x,y),f(y,z)].$$

Proof: See Appendix I.

Theorem 1: R_λ is an equivalence relation on X.

Proof:

1) From (3) and the assumptions, we have

$$1 = f_1(x,x) \leq f(x,x) \leq 1.$$

Then $f(x,x) = 1$, or $xR_\lambda x$, for all $\lambda \in [0,1]$.

2) By the assumption, $f_1(x,y) = f_1(y,x)$. Then $f_n(x,y) = f_n(y,x)$, and we can conclude that $f(x,y) = f(y,x)$. This means that $xR_\lambda y \Leftrightarrow yR_\lambda x$.

Manuscript received March 12, 1970; revised September 1, 1970.
The authors are with the Department of Information and Computer Sciences, Faculty of Engineering Science, Osaka University, Toyonaka, Japan 560.

Reprinted from *IEEE Trans. Syst., Man, Cybern.*, vol. SMC-1, no. 1, pp. 61–66, January 1971.

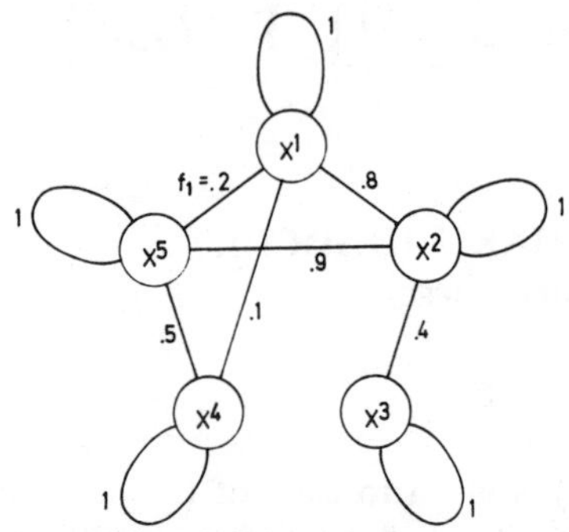

Fig. 1. One-step fuzzy relation $f_1(x,y)$ of Example 1.

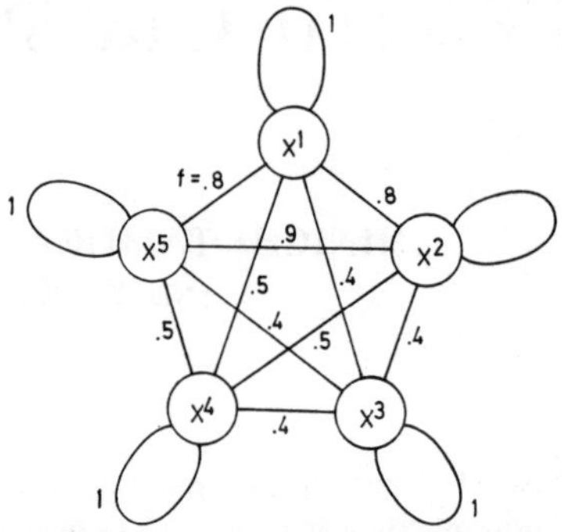

Fig. 2. $f(x,y)$ of Example 1.

3) From Lemma 1, we have

$$f(x,z) \geq \min\,[f(x,y),f(y,z)].$$

Therefore, we can conclude that

$$xR_\lambda y, yR_\lambda z \Rightarrow xR_\lambda z. \qquad \text{Q.E.D.}$$

Thus, by Theorem 1, we see that we can classify the patterns using the partition induced by the equivalence relation R_λ with the appropriate threshold λ.

Example 1. Let $X = \{x^1,x^2,\cdots,x^5\}$ and $f_1(x,y)$ be as follows.

	x^1	x^2	x^3	x^4	x^5
x^1	1				
x^2	0.8	1			
x^3	0	0.4	1		
x^4	0.1	0	0	1	
x^5	0.2	0.9	0	0.5	1

This table is illustrated in Fig. 1. Then we have $f(x,y) = f_3(x,y)$ as follows.

	x^1	x^2	x^3	x^4	x^5
x^1	1				
x^2	0.8	1			
x^3	0.4	0.4	1		
x^4	0.5	0.5	0.4	1	
x^5	0.8	0.9	0.4	0.5	1

This table is illustrated in Fig. 2. We have the partitions (see, e.g., Harrison [11])

$$R_0 = R_{0.3} = \{[x^1,x^2,x^3,x^4,x^5]\}$$
$$R_{0.45} = \{[x^1,x^2,x^4,x^5],[x^3]\}$$
$$R_{0.55} = \{[x^1,x^2,x^5],[x^4],[x^3]\}$$
$$R_{0.85} = \{[x^1],[x^2,x^5],[x^4],[x^3]\}$$
$$R_1 = \{[x^1],[x^2],[x^5],[x^4],[x^3]\}.$$

Thus the patterns are classified by the partition induced by R_λ.

Theorem 2: Let $\lambda \geq \mu$. Then R_λ refines R_μ.

Proof: It is sufficient to show that $xR_\lambda y \Rightarrow xR_\mu y$. Assume that $xR_\lambda y$, then $f(x,y) \geq \lambda \geq \mu$. Therefore, $xR_\mu y$. Q.E.D.

Conversely, if $f_1(x,y)$ is changed, we have the following theorem.

Theorem 3: Assume $f_1(x,y) \leq f_1'(x,y)$, for all $x,y \in X$, let R_λ be an equivalence relation induced by $f_1(x,y)$, and let R_λ' be one by $f_1'(x,y)$. Then R_λ refines R_λ'.

Proof: The proof is obvious.

Theorem 4: If $f(x,y) \neq 1$, for all $x,y \in X$ such that $x \neq y$, then $\rho(x,y) = 1 - f(x,y)$ satisfies the axioms of distance.

Proof:

1) Since by the assumptions $0 \leq f(x,y) < 1$, for $x \neq y$, and $f(x,x) = 1$, we have $\rho(x,y) > 0$, for $x \neq y$, and $\rho(x,x) = 0$.
2) Since $f(x,y) = f(y,x)$, then $\rho(x,y) = \rho(y,x)$.
3) By Lemma 1,

$$f(x,z) \geq \min\,[f(x,y),f(y,z)] \geq f(x,y) + f(y,z) - 1.$$

Then

$$\rho(x,z) \leq \rho(x,y) + \rho(y,z). \qquad \text{Q.E.D.}$$

When $f(x,y) = 1$ holds for some $x \neq y$, the assumption of Theorem 4 is not satisfied. In such a case, the following theorem can be easily demonstrated.

Theorem 5: Let R_1 be a set of the equivalence classes induced by R_1 on X, and $\bar{x}$ and $\bar{y}$ be two elements of R_1. Let x and y be arbitrary elements in $\bar{x}$ and $\bar{y}$, respectively. Then $\rho(\bar{x},\bar{y}) = 1 - f(x,y)$ satisfies the axioms of distance.

Note that if we make changes such as $f \leftrightarrow \rho$, $\geq \leftrightarrow \leq$, sup $\leftrightarrow$ inf, and max $\leftrightarrow$ min, our approach will be changed into the complementary one (see Mizumoto *et al.* [10]).

When the threshold λ is not changed, we may memorize only whether each $f_1(x,y)$ is greater than λ or not, instead of memorizing the values of $f_1(x,y)$. For such a case, let us consider the transitive closure (see Harrison [11]). The transitive closure of Q_λ, written $\hat{Q}_\lambda$, is defined as

$$\hat{Q}_\lambda = \bigcup_{i=1}^{\infty} Q_\lambda^{\,i} = Q_\lambda \cup (Q_\lambda Q_\lambda) \cup (Q_\lambda Q_\lambda Q_\lambda) \cup \cdots$$

where Q_λ is a relation on X. Let

$$xQ_\lambda y \Leftrightarrow f_1(x,y) \geq \lambda.$$

Then, since $xQ_\lambda x$ and $xQ_\lambda y \Leftrightarrow yQ_\lambda x$, for all $\lambda \in [0,1]$, $\hat{Q}_\lambda$ is the equivalence relation on X. Roughly speaking, the classification by $\hat{Q}_\lambda$ is based on whether there is a path connecting two patterns or not.

Theorem 6: For all λ in $[0,1]$, $\hat{Q}_\lambda$ refines R_λ.

Proof: It is sufficient to show that $x\hat{Q}_\lambda y \Rightarrow xR_\lambda y$. Assume $x\hat{Q}_\lambda y$, then, for some integer n, $xQ_\lambda{}^n y$. Then there exist $x_1,x_2,\cdots,x_{n-1}$ in X such that

$$f_1(x,x_1) \geq \lambda, f_1(x_1,x_2) \geq \lambda,\cdots,f_1(x_{n-1},y) \geq \lambda.$$

That is,

$$f_n(x,y) \geq \min\,[f_1(x,x_1),f_1(x_1,x_2),\cdots,f_1(x_{n-1},y)] \geq \lambda.$$

Then

$$f(x,y) \geq f_n(x,y) \geq \lambda$$

or

$$xR_\lambda y. \qquad \text{Q.E.D.}$$

In Section IV we will show that if X is finite, $\hat{Q}_\lambda$ becomes equal to R_λ. Furthermore, we can easily obtain the same theorems as Theorems 2 and 3 for $\hat{Q}_\lambda$.

III. Abbreviation Form

We show an abbreviation form of $f_n(x,y)$ as a preliminary step to discussing the properties when the pattern set X is finite. Let

$$g_n(x,x_1,x_2,\cdots,x_{n-1},y) = \min\,[f_1(x,x_1),f_1(x_1,x_2), \cdots, f_1(x_{n-1},y)].$$

Then

$$f_n(x,y) = \sup_{x_1,\cdots,x_{n-1}\in X} g_n(x,x_1,\cdots,x_{n-1},y).$$

Generally speaking, if $x_i = x_j$, then

$$g_n(x,x_1,\cdots,x_i,x_{i+1},\cdots,x_j,x_{j+1},\cdots,x_{n-1},y) \leq g_{n-j+i}(x,x_1,\cdots,x_i,x_{j+1},\cdots,x_{n-1},y).$$

This implies that we can remove the loop $(x_i,x_{i+1},\cdots,x_j)$ in the string $(x,x_1,\cdots,x_{n-1},y)$ when we calculate $f_n(x,y)$. Therefore, we have the abbreviation form

$$f_n(x,y) = \max_{k\in K} g_{nk}'(x,y)$$

where

$$g_{nk}'(x,y) = \begin{cases} \sup\limits_{(x_1,\cdots,x_k)\in X_k} g_n(x,x_1,\cdots,x_k,y,y,\cdots,y), & k = 1,2,\cdots,p \\ f_1(x,y), & k = 0 \end{cases}$$

$$X_k = \{(x_1,\cdots,x_k) \mid x_1 \in X - \{x,y\}, x_2 \in X - \{x,x_1,y\}, \cdots, x_k \in X - \{x,x_1,\cdots,x_{k-1},y\}\}$$

$$p = \min\,(n-1, N-2)$$

$$K = \{0,1,\cdots,p\}.$$

In our case, since $f_1(x,x) = 1$, when X is finite, we can easily show that (see Wee *et al.* [9], Mizumoto *et al.* [10])

$$f_{N-1}(x,y) = f_N(x,y) = \cdots = f(x,y)$$

where N is the number of elements in X.

Theorem 7: Let $x \neq y$ and $X' = X - \{x\}$. Then

$$f_n(x,y) \leq \sup_{x_1\in X'} f_j(x,x_1), \qquad j = 1,2,\cdots,n.$$

Proof: See Appendix II.

IV. Finite Sets

In actual cases, we usually deal with only the finite number of the patterns. Let us consider the equivalence relations on such a finite set.

Theorem 8: If the number N of elements in X is finite, then

$$R_\lambda = \hat{Q}_\lambda = Q_\lambda{}^{N-1}.$$

Proof: The latter half of the theorem is obvious (see Harrison [11]). Let us show that R_λ is equal to $\hat{Q}_\lambda$. Since we have shown that $\hat{Q}_\lambda$ refines R_λ in Theorem 6, it is sufficient to show that R_λ refines $\hat{Q}_\lambda$. Assume that $xR_\lambda y$. Then

$$f(x,y) = f_{N-1}(x,y) = \max_{x_1,\cdots,x_{N-2}\in X} \min\,[f_1(x,x_1), f_1(x_1,x_2),\cdots,f_1(x_{N-2},y)] \geq \lambda.$$

This means that there exist $x_1,\cdots,x_{N-2} \in X$ such that

$$f_1(x,x_1) \geq \lambda, f_1(x_1,x_2) \geq \lambda,\cdots,f_1(x_{N-2},y) \geq \lambda$$

so that

$$xQ_\lambda x_1, x_1Q_\lambda x_2,\cdots,x_{N-2}Q_\lambda y.$$

We see $xQ_\lambda{}^{N-1}y$ or $x\hat{Q}_\lambda y$. Q.E.D.

When X is finite, it is sometimes convenient to use the fuzzy matrix representation. We represent the fuzzy matrix as

$$F = \|f_1(x^i,x^j)\|, \qquad i,j = 1,2,\cdots,N.$$

Let us show some fundamental properties of our fuzzy matrix. We denote by a_{ij} the (i,j)th entry of a fuzzy matrix A, where $0 \leq a_{ij} \leq 1$. We define

$$A \prec B \Leftrightarrow a_{ij} \leq b_{ij}$$

$$I = \|m_{ij}\|$$

where

$$m_{ij} = \begin{cases} 1, & \text{if } i = j \\ 0, & \text{if } i \neq j \end{cases}$$

$$C = A \circ B \Leftrightarrow c_{ij} = \max_k \min\,(a_{ik},b_{kj})$$

$$A^{m+1} = A^m \circ A$$

$$A^0 = I$$

$$C = \max\,(A,B) \Leftrightarrow c_{ij} = \begin{cases} a_{ij}, & \text{if } a_{ij} \geq b_{ij} \\ b_{ij}, & \text{otherwise.} \end{cases}$$

Then, since all the diagonal elements of F are now equal to unity, we have (see Mizumoto *et al.* [10])

$$I \prec F \prec F^2 \prec \cdots \prec F^{N-1} = F^N = \cdots = F^\infty.$$

The (i,j)th entry of F^k is $f_k(x^i,x^j)$. Hence we can calculate $f(x^i,x^j)$ easily and rather quickly by using $F^k \circ F^k = F^{2k}$.

As in Example 1, we have

$$F = \begin{bmatrix} 1 & 0.8 & 0 & 0.1 & 0.2 \\ 0.8 & 1 & 0.4 & 0 & 0.9 \\ 0 & 0.4 & 1 & 0 & 0 \\ 0.1 & 0 & 0 & 1 & 0.5 \\ 0.2 & 0.9 & 0 & 0.5 & 1 \end{bmatrix}$$

$$F^2 = F \circ F = \begin{bmatrix} 1 & 0.8 & 0.4 & 0.2 & 0.8 \\ 0.8 & 1 & 0.4 & 0.5 & 0.9 \\ 0.4 & 0.4 & 1 & 0 & 0.4 \\ 0.2 & 0.5 & 0 & 1 & 0.5 \\ 0.8 & 0.9 & 0.4 & 0.5 & 1 \end{bmatrix}$$

$$F^3 = \begin{bmatrix} 1 & 0.8 & 0.4 & 0.5 & 0.8 \\ 0.8 & 1 & 0.4 & 0.5 & 0.9 \\ 0.4 & 0.4 & 1 & 0.4 & 0.4 \\ 0.5 & 0.5 & 0.4 & 1 & 0.5 \\ 0.8 & 0.9 & 0.4 & 0.5 & 1 \end{bmatrix} = F^4 = F^5 = \cdots = F^\infty$$

Thus

$$I \prec F \prec F^2 \prec F^3 = F^4 = \cdots = F^\infty.$$

Next, we show a divided calculation method of a fuzzy matrix. If $C = A \circ B$, then

$$c_{ij} = \max_{1 \le k \le N} \min (a_{ik}, b_{kj})$$
$$= \max [\max_{1 \le k \le \beta} \min (a_{ik}, b_{kj}), \max_{\beta+1 \le k \le N} \min (a_{ik}, b_{kj})].$$

We can then obtain the following results. If A and B are divided as

$$A = \begin{bmatrix} D & E \\ F & G \end{bmatrix} \quad \text{and} \quad B = \begin{bmatrix} H & J \\ K & L \end{bmatrix}$$

then

$$A \circ B = \begin{bmatrix} \max (D \circ H, E \circ K) & \max (D \circ J, E \circ L) \\ \max (F \circ H, G \circ K) & \max (F \circ J, G \circ L) \end{bmatrix}$$
$$= \max \left(\begin{bmatrix} D \circ H & D \circ J \\ F \circ H & F \circ J \end{bmatrix}, \begin{bmatrix} E \circ K & E \circ L \\ G \circ K & G \circ L \end{bmatrix} \right)$$

This is the same form as that of the nonfuzzy matrix.

Let us consider the case when a new pattern x^{N+1} comes into X. The pattern set X becomes $X + \{x^{N+1}\}$. We denote a new n-step fuzzy relation on $X + \{x^{N+1}\}$ by $f_n'(x,y)$. Generally speaking, $f_n'(x,y)$ becomes different from $f_n(x,y)$. After some manipulations, we obtain

$$f_n'(x^i,x^j) = \max [f_n(x^i,x^j), \min \{f_{n-1}'(x^i,x^{N+1}), f_1'(x^{N+1},x^j)\}, \min \{f_{n-2}'(x^i,x^{N+1}), f_2'(x^{N+1},x^j)\}, \cdots, \min \{f_1'(x^i,x^{N+1}), f_{n-1}'(x^{N+1},x^j)\}], \quad x^i,x^j \in X$$

$$f_n'(x^{N+1},x^{N+1}) = 1$$

$$f_n'(x^{N+1},x^i) = f_n'(x^i,x^{N+1}) = \max_{x_1 \in X} \min [f_1'(x^{N+1},x_1), f_{n-1}(x_1,x^i)], \quad x^i \in X.$$

However, in almost all cases it is easier to recompute the F^n than to calculate by these formulas.

V. Experimental Result

Portraits obtained from 60 families were used in our experiment, each of which is composed of between four and seven members. The reason why we chose the portraits is that we had conceived that even if parents do not resemble each other in face, they may be connected through their children, and consequently we could classify the portraits into families. First, we divided the 60 families into 20 groups, each of which was composed of 3 families. Each group was, on the average, composed of 15 members. The portraits of each group were presented to a different student to give the values of the subjective similarity $f_1(x,y)$ by 5 rank representation to all pairs between them. The reason why we used the 5 rank representation instead of continuous value representation is that it had been proved that the human being cannot distinguish into more than 5 ranks in the end. Twenty students joined in this experiment. Two examples of the experiment are shown in Table I, Table II, Fig. 3, and Fig. 4. In Table I, the 5 rank representations are converted to the values in [0,1]. In our case, the number of patterns is not so many that we can classify by inspection without calculating $f_n(x,y)$.

Since the levels of the subjective values are different according to individuals, the threshold was determined in each group as follows. As we bring down the threshold, the number of classes decrease. Hence, under the assumption that the number of classes c to be classified was known to be 3, bringing down the threshold we stopped at the value which divided the patterns into 3 classes (collection of the patterns composed of more than 2 patterns that have a stronger relation than λ with each other) and some nonconnected patterns. However, as in the present case, when some $f_1(x,y)$ take the same value, sometimes there is no threshold by which the patterns are divided into just c given classes. In such a case, we made it possible to divide them into just c classes by stopping the threshold at the value where the patterns are divided into less than c classes and separating some connections randomly that have a minimum $f_1(x,y)$ of connections that have the stronger relation than the threshold.

The correctly classified rates, the misclassified rates, and the rejected rates of 20 groups were within the range of 50–94 percent, 0–33 percent, and 0–33 percent, respectively, and we obtained the correctly classified rate 75 percent, the misclassified rate 13 percent, and the rejected rate 12 percent as the averages of the 20 groups. Here, since the classes made in this experiment have no label, we calculated these rates by making a one-to-one correspondence between 3 families and 3 classes, so as to have the largest number of correctly classified patterns.

VI. Conclusion

We have studied pattern classification using subjective information and performed experiments involving classification of portraits. The method of classification proposed here is based on the procedure of finding a path connecting 2

TABLE I

SUBJECTIVE SIMILARITIES OF FIG. 3

Portrait Number	1	2	3	4	5	6	7	8	9	10	11	12	13	14	15	16
1	1															
2	0	1														
3	0	0	1													
4	0	0	0.4	1												
5	0	0.8	0	0	1											
6	0.5[a]	0	0.2	0.2	0	1										
7	0	0.8	0	0	0.4	0	1									
8	0.4	0.2	0.2	0.5[a]	0	0.8	0	1								
9	0	0.4	0	0.8	0.4	0.2	0.4	0	1							
10	0	0	0.2	0.2	0	0	0.2	0	0.2	1						
11	0	0.5[a]	0.2	0.2	0	0	0.8	0	0.4	0.2	1					
12	0	0	0.2	0.8	0	0	0	0	0.4	0.8	0	1				
13	0.8	0	0.2	0.4	0	0.4	0	0.4	0	0	0	0	1			
14	0	0.8	0	0.2	0.4	0	0.8	0	0.2	0.2	0.6	0	0	1		
15	0	0	0.4	0.8	0	0.2	0	0	0.2	0	0	0.2	0.2	0	1	
16	0.6	0	0	0.2	0.2	0.8	0	0.4	0	0	0	0	0.4	0.2	0	1

[a] This value was converted from 0.6 to 0.5 for division into just three classes.

TABLE II

THE $f(x,y)$ $(= f_6(x,y) = f_7(x,y) = \cdots)$ OF TABLE I

Portrait Number	1	2	3	4	5	6	7	8	9	10	11	12	13	14	15	16
1	1															
2	0.4	1														
3	0.4	0.4	1													
4	0.5	0.4	0.4	1												
5	0.4	0.8	0.4	0.4	1											
6	0.6	0.4	0.4	0.5	0.4	1										
7	0.4	0.8	0.4	0.4	0.8	0.4	1									
8	0.6	0.4	0.4	0.5	0.4	0.8	0.4	1								
9	0.5	0.4	0.4	0.8	0.4	0.5	0.4	0.5	1							
10	0.5	0.4	0.4	0.8	0.4	0.5	0.4	0.5	0.8	1						
11	0.4	0.8	0.4	0.4	0.8	0.4	0.8	0.4	0.4	0.4	1					
12	0.5	0.4	0.4	0.8	0.4	0.5	0.4	0.5	0.8	0.8	0.4	1				
13	0.8	0.4	0.4	0.5	0.4	0.6	0.4	0.6	0.5	0.5	0.4	0.5	1			
14	0.4	0.8	0.4	0.4	0.8	0.4	0.8	0.4	0.4	0.4	0.8	0.4	0.4	1		
15	0.5	0.4	0.4	0.8	0.4	0.5	0.4	0.5	0.8	0.8	0.4	0.8	0.5	0.4	1	
16	0.6	0.4	0.4	0.5	0.4	0.8	0.4	0.8	0.5	0.5	0.4	0.5	0.6	0.4	0.5	1

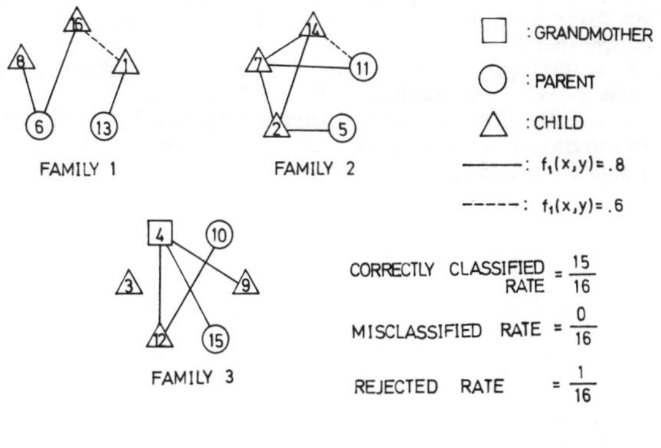

Fig. 3. Portrait classification of Table I.

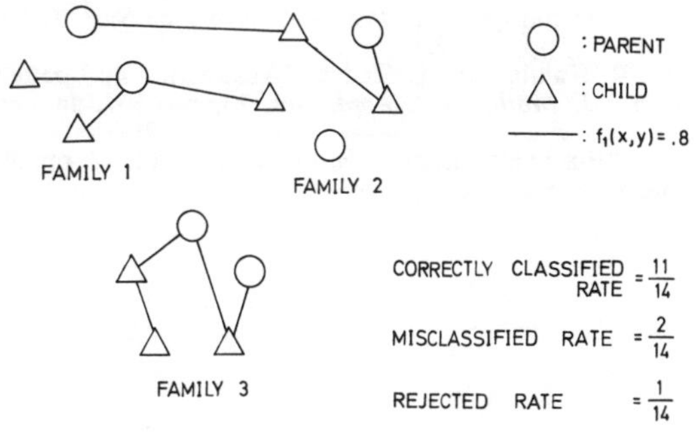

Fig. 4. Example of portrait classification.

patterns. Therefore, this method may be combined with nonsupervised learning and may also be applicable to information retrieval [12] and path detection.

Appendix I

Proof of Lemma 1

$$
\begin{aligned}
f_{m+n}(x,z) &= \sup_{x_1,\cdots,x_{m+n-1}} \min\,[f_1(x,x_1),\cdots,f_1(x_{m+n-1},z)] \\
&\geq \sup_{x_1,\cdots,x_{m-1}} \sup_{x_{m+1},\cdots,x_{m+n-1}} \min\,[f_1(x,x_1),\cdots, f_1(x_{m-1},y),f_1(y,x_{m+1}),\cdots,f_1(x_{m+n-1},z)] \\
&= \sup_{x_1,\cdots,x_{m-1}} \sup_{x_{m+1},\cdots,x_{m+n-1}} \min\,[\min\{f_1(x,x_1),\cdots,f_1(x_{m-1},y)\}, \min\{f_1(y,x_{m+1}),\cdots,f_1(x_{m+n-1},z)\}] \\
&= \min\,[\sup_{x_1,\cdots,x_{m-1}} \min\{f_1(x,x_1),\cdots,f_1(x_{m-1},y)\}, \sup_{x_{m+1},\cdots,x_{m+n-1}} \min\{f_1(y,x_{m+1}),\cdots,f_1(x_{m+n-1},z)\}] \\
&= \min\,[f_m(x,y),f_n(y,z)].
\end{aligned}
$$

We obtain the following inequality as $m \to \infty$ and $n \to \infty$:

$$f(x,z) \geq \min\,[f(x,y),f(y,z)].$$

Appendix II

Proof of Theorem 7

$$
\begin{aligned}
f_n(x,y) &= \sup_{x_j,\cdots,x_{n-1}\in X'} \sup_{x_1,\cdots,x_{j-1}\in X'} \min\,[\min\{f_1(x,x_1),\cdots,f_1(x_{j-1},x_j)\}, \min\{f_1(x_j,x_{j+1}),\cdots,f_1(x_{n-1},y)\}] \\
&= \sup_{x_j,\cdots,x_{n-1}\in X'} \min\left[\sup_{x_1,\cdots,x_{j-1}\in X'} \min\{f_1(x,x_1),\cdots,f_1(x_{j-1},x_j)\}, \min\{f_1(x_j,x_{j+1}),\cdots,f_1(x_{n-1},y)\}\right] \\
&= \sup_{x_j,\cdots,x_{n-1}\in X'} \min\,[f_j(x,x_j), \min\{f_1(x_j,x_{j+1}),\cdots, f_1(x_{n-1},y)\}] \leq \sup_{x_j,\cdots,x_{n-1}\in X'} f_j(x,x_j) \\
&= \sup_{x_j\in X'} f_j(x,x_j).
\end{aligned}
$$

Acknowledgment

The authors wish to thank M. Mizumoto, J. Toyoda, and other members of Prof. Tanaka's laboratory for their helpful suggestions and discussions.

References

[1] L. A. Zadeh, "Fuzzy sets," *Inform. Contr.*, vol. 8, pp. 338–353, June 1965.

[2] ——, "Fuzzy sets and systems," *Proc. 1965 Symp. on Syst. Theory* (Brooklyn, N.Y.), pp. 29–39.

[3] R. Bellman, R. Kalaba, and L. Zadeh, "Abstraction and pattern classification," *J. Math. Anal. Appl.*, vol. 13, pp. 1–7, January 1966.

[4] L. A. Zadeh, "Fuzzy algorithms," *Inform. Contr.*, vol. 12, pp. 99–102, February 1968.

[5] ——, "Probability measures of fuzzy events," *J. Math. Anal. Appl.*, vol. 23, pp. 421–427, August 1968.

[6] ——, "Toward a theory of fuzzy systems," Electron. Res. Lab., College of Engineering, University of California, Berkeley, Rep. ERL-69-2, June 1969.

[7] J. A. Goguen, "*L*-fuzzy sets," *J. Math. Anal. Appl.*, vol. 18, pp. 145–174, April 1967.

[8] E. S. Santos and W. G. Wee, "General formulation of sequential machines," *Inform. Contr.*, vol. 12, pp. 5–10, January 1968.

[9] W. G. Wee and K. S. Fu, "A formulation of fuzzy automata and its application as a model of learning systems," *IEEE Trans. Syst. Sci. Cybern.*, vol. SSC-5, pp. 215–223, July 1969.

[10] M. Mizumoto, J. Toyoda, and K. Tanaka, "Some considerations on fuzzy automata," *J. Comput. Syst. Sci.*, vol. 3, pp. 409–422, November 1969.

[11] M. A. Harrison, *Introduction to Switching and Automata Theory*. New York: McGraw-Hill, 1965, pp. 9–12, 296.

[12] G. Salton, "Associative document retrieval techniques using bibliographic information," *J. Ass. Comput. Mach.*, vol. 10, pp. 440–457, 1963.

A Graph Theoretic Analysis of Pattern Classification via Tamura's Fuzzy Relation

J. C. DUNN

Abstract—Graph theoretical arguments are used to show that the hierarchical clustering scheme induced by Tamura's N-step fuzzy relation f is contained in the maximal single linkage hierarchy. A method of computing f is proposed, based upon Prim's algorithm for generating maximal spanning trees and a result reported by Hu on maximal capacity routes in maximal spanning trees. It is shown that this procedure is superior to Tamura's generalized matrix multiplication algorithm with regard to both computing time and storage requirements.

I. Introduction

Tamura *et al.* [1] describe a hierarchical clustering scheme generated by a one parameter family of equivalence relations $xR_\lambda y$ on a data set X, obtained from an arbitrary symmetric fuzzy relation $f_1: X \times X \to [0,1]$ satisfying

$$f(x,x) = 1 \qquad f_1(x,y) = f_1(y,x) \tag{1}$$

for all $x,y \in X$. The equivalence relations R_λ are constructed in the following way.

For $x,y \in X$ and $\xi = \{\xi_1,\cdots,\xi_{n-1}\} \in X^{n-1}$ (($n-1$)-fold Cartesian product of X with itself), put

$$f_n(x,y) \triangleq \sup_{\xi \in X^{n-1}} \{\min [f(x_1,\xi_1),f(\xi_1,\xi_2),\cdots,f(\xi_{n-1},y)]\}. \tag{2}$$

Then for all $x,y \in X$ and all $n > 0$

$$0 \le f_n(x,y) \le f_{n+1}(x,y) \le 1. \tag{3}$$

Consequently

$$\lim_{n\to\infty} f_n(x,y) \triangleq f(x,y) \tag{4}$$

exists by the monotone convergence principle. For each $\lambda \in [0,1]$ define R_λ by the rule

$$xR_\lambda y \Leftrightarrow f(x,y) \ge \lambda. \tag{5}$$

The reflexive and symmetric properties for R_λ are immediate consequences of (1), and transitivity follows from the inequality

$$f(x,z) \ge \min [f(x,y),f(y,z)], \qquad x,y,z \in X \tag{6}$$

established in [1]. Furthermore, for $1 \ge \lambda \ge \mu \ge 0$, R_λ refines R_μ, consequently, for every monotone decreasing finite sequence of "thresholds" $1 \ge \lambda_1 \ge \lambda_2 \ge \cdots \ge \lambda_k \ge 0$, one obtains a corresponding k-level *hierarchy of clusters*

$$\mathscr{C}_i = \{\text{equivalence classes of } R_{\lambda_i} \text{ in } X\}, \qquad 1 \le i \le k. \tag{7}$$

For each i, $\mathscr{C}_i$ is a partition of X and every S in $\mathscr{C}_{i+1}$ is the union of some nonempty class of subsets in $\mathscr{C}_i$.

Manuscript received May 21, 1973; revised December 3, 1973.
The author is with the Department of Theoretical and Applied Mechanics, Cornell University, Ithaca, N.Y. 14850.

When X is a finite set $\{x_1,\cdots,x_N\}$, it is shown in [1] that

$$f_1(x,y) \le f_2(x,y) \le \cdots \le f_{N-1}(x,y) = f_N(x,y) = \cdots = f(x,y) \tag{8}$$

i.e., $f_k(x,y) = f(x,y)$, for $k \ge N-1$ (at most). Furthermore, if $[F]$ denotes the $N \times N$ matrix $[f_1(x_i,x_j)]$ and if "$\circ$" signifies a generalized matrix multiplication defined by the rule

$$[A] \circ [B] = [C] \qquad C_{ij} = \max_{1\le k\le N} \{\min [a_{ik},b_{kj}]\} \tag{9}$$

then the kth power of $[F]$ is given by

$$[F]^k = [f_k(x_i,x_j)]. \tag{10}$$

These results support the following algorithm proposed in [1] for constructing $f(x,y)$ and the related hierarchy (7). Put

$$[G_{n+1}] = [G_n]^2 \qquad [G_1] = [F]. \tag{11}$$

By induction, one then obtains

$$[G_k] = [F]^{2^k}. \tag{12}$$

In view of (8) and (10), this gives

$$k \ge \log_2 (N-1) \Rightarrow [G_k] = [f(x_i,x_j)]. \tag{13}$$

For certain data sets X, the equality on the right side of (13) may obtain for $k < \log_2 (N-1)$.

Having given this brief summary of the results presented in [1], we now observe that when X is a finite set the hierarchy of clusters (7) is precisely the sort of classification one obtains from the widely used single linkage approach to cluster analysis. The basis for this not immediately obvious assertion can be found in certain results published by Johnson [2]. In fact, with the exception of the algorithm (11), Tamura's results are essentially duals of Johnson's results under the exchange $\{\sup,\inf,\max,\min,\le,\ge,1,0\} \to \{\inf,\sup,\min,\max,\ge,\le,0,\infty\}$, when X is finite. In particular, Johnson obtains the crucial relation (6) in the form

$$f(x,z) \le \max [f(x,y),f(y,z)] \tag{14}$$

where f is obtained from the dual of the process described by (1)–(4); (14) is known as the ultrametric inequality.

Tamura's scheme for generating the hierarchy (7) via (11) is not contained in Johnson's results, nor is it like any of the other standard agglomerative or devisive single linkage algorithms; rather, it can be interpreted as an application of the method of successive approximations to a certain functional equation satisfied by f when X is finite, namely,

$$f(x,z) = \max_{y\in X} \{\min [f(x,y),f_1(y,z)]\}. \tag{15}$$

Reprinted from *IEEE Trans. Syst., Man, Cybern.*, vol. SMC-4, no. 3, pp. 310–313, May 1974.

This viewpoint is of interest mainly for historical reasons, e.g., Kalaba [3] has indicated how dynamic programming arguments produce an analog of (15) for a mini-max stress trajectory problem which turns out to be the dual of Tamura's problem. However, Kalaba was aware of the inherent advantages in a graph theoretic treatment of his problem and explicitly made note of the important relationship between optimal mini-max stress trajectories and routes in a minimal spanning tree for X.

The relationship between Tamura's hierarchies (7) and single linkage hierarchies can also be derived from graph theoretic considerations. In Section II, we will show that the equivalance relations (5) can be generated from a family of nested graphs $\mathscr{G}_\mu(X)$ obtained by deleting edges in a maximal spanning tree for X relative to the edge weighting function f_1. This viewpoint is particularity fruitful since there is a simple and efficient algorithm due to Prim [4] for generating maximal spanning trees. Within the past five years, several workers, notably Zahn [5] and Gower and Ross [6] have proposed efficient devisive clustering algorithms based upon the construction of maximal (or minimal)[1] spanning trees. In particular, Gower and Ross give a detailed description of a devisive procedure for generating single linkage hierarchies based on Prim's algorithm. In Section II, we show how Prim's algorithm, in conjunction with certain results given by Hu [7] on maximal capacity routes in maximal spanning trees, produces a method of generating the N-step fuzzy relation f, which is substantially more efficient than the algorithm (11) from the standpoint of operation counts and storage requirements when N is large. Specifically, (11) requires somewhere between $\sim N^3$ and $N^3 \log_2 N$ pairwise comparison operations, whereas the algorithm proposed in Section II requires only $\sim 3/2N^2$ comparisons. Furthermore, (11) requires storage for the upper triangular part of the symmetric $N \times N$ matrices $[G_k]$ and $[G_{k+1}]$ at each stage of the calculation and requires the upper triangular part of $[f_1(x,y)]$ as initial input. In contrast, the proposed algorithm utilizes each entry of $[f_1(x,y)]$ exactly once and requires at each stage k no more than N entries of $[F]$, N entries of $[f(x_i,x_j)]$ (computed in preceding stages), and three additional work space vectors of $\leq N$ components each.

As a final historical note, we mention that in 1957 Sneath [8] reported on one of the earliest large scale computer implemented applications of an agglomerative single linkage algorithm (to a problem in bacteriological taxonomy). Since then, many articles and several books published in this country have described variants of Sneath's algorithm and argued pro and con for the associated hierarchical classification scheme. Useful discussions can be found in Sokal and Sneath [9], Duda and Hart [10], Lance and Williams [11], Fisher and Van Ness [12], Wishart [13], and the previously cited work of Zahn, and Gower and Ross.

II. A Graph Theoretic Approach to Computing the N-step Fuzzy Relation

Any class $\mathscr{G}(X)$ of two element subsets $E = \{x,y\} \subset X$, $x \neq y$, is an undirected graph with edges E and vertices $x,y,\cdots$.[2] Let the graph $\hat{\mathscr{G}}(X)$ be a *maximal spanning tree* relative to the edge weights induced by f_1, let N = number of vertices in X, and let $E_\mu, \mu = 1,\cdots,N-1$ denote the $N-1$ edges of $\hat{\mathscr{G}}(X)$ arranged so that $0 \leq f_1(E_\mu) \leq f_1(E_{\mu+1}) \leq 1$, for $1 \leq \mu \leq N-2$. Furthermore, let $\hat{\mathscr{G}}_\mu(X)$ denote the graph obtained by deleting the edges $E_l, 1 \leq l \leq \mu - 1$, from $\hat{\mathscr{G}}(X)$; then $\hat{\mathscr{G}}(X) = \hat{\mathscr{G}}_1(X) \supset \hat{\mathscr{G}}_2(X) \supset \cdots \supset \hat{\mathscr{G}}_N(X) = \phi$ (the null graph). Each of the nested graphs $\hat{\mathscr{G}}_\mu(X)$ induces an equivalence relation $\hat{R}_\mu$ on X in the following way.

$$x\hat{R}_\mu y \Leftrightarrow x = y, \text{ or } x \text{ and } y \text{ are endpoints on a path of contiguous edges in } \hat{\mathscr{G}}_\mu(X). \quad (16)$$

The equivalence classes of $\hat{R}_\mu$ are either vertex sets of maximal connected subgraphs of $\hat{\mathscr{G}}_\mu$ or singletons excluded from the vertices of $\hat{\mathscr{G}}_\mu(X)$. Therefore, since $\hat{\mathscr{G}}_{\mu+1}(X)$ is obtained by deleting an edge from $\hat{\mathscr{G}}_\mu(X)$, it follows that $\hat{R}_{\mu+1}$ refines $\hat{R}_\mu$, for $1 \leq \mu \leq N-1$, and that

$$\mathscr{C}_\mu = \{\text{equivalence classes } R_{N-\mu+1}\} \qquad 1 \leq \mu \leq N \quad (17)$$

is a hierarchy of clusters in X. In fact, it turns out that (17) contains *every* hierarchy (7). To see this, we need the following version of a result reported by Hu [7].

For arbitrary $x,y \in X$, let $S(x,y)$ denote the *unique* path joining x and y with contiguous edges E from the maximal spanning tree $\hat{\mathscr{G}}(X)$. Let $\xi = \{\xi_1,\cdots,\xi_l\}$ denote an arbitrary finite sequence of vertices in X. Then

$$\min_{E \in S(x,y)} f_1(E) = \max_{\xi} \{\min [f_1(x,\xi_1),\cdots,f_1(\xi_l,y)]\}.$$

In Hu's terminology, the maximal spanning tree provides maximum capacity routes between every pair of distinct vertices in X. In the present context this means that the value of Tamura's N-step fuzzy relation $f(x,y)$ is given by the smallest edge weight in the path $S(x,y)$. It follows that the distinct values of $f(x,y)$ for $x \neq y$ are in one-to-one correspondence with the distinct edge weights $f_1(E), E \in \hat{\mathscr{G}}(X)$. Furthermore, we can now see that every equivalence relation R_λ in (5) coincides with one of the equivalence relations $\hat{R}_\mu$, e.g., for every λ in the interval $0 \leq \lambda \leq 1$ exactly one of the following mutually exclusive alternatives holds: a) $0 \leq \lambda \leq f_1(E_1)$, or b) there is a unique integer l such that $2 \leq l \leq N-1$ and $f_1(E_{l-1}) < \lambda \leq f_1(E_l)$, or c) $f_1(E_{N-1}) < \lambda \leq 1$. In case a) we have $xR_\lambda y \Leftrightarrow f(x,y) \geq \lambda \Leftrightarrow f(x,y) \geq f_1(E_1) \Leftrightarrow x\hat{R}_1 y$. Similarly, in case b) we have $xR_\lambda y \Leftrightarrow f(x,y) \geq f_1(E_l) \Leftrightarrow x\hat{R}_l y$, for some integer l satisfying b). Finally in case c), we have $xR_\lambda y \Leftrightarrow f(x,y) > f_1(E_{N-1}) \Leftrightarrow f(x,y) = 1 \Leftrightarrow x\hat{R}_N y$. It follows that (7) is a subhierarchy of the hierarchy (17) derived from $\hat{\mathscr{G}}(X)$. We now show how Prim's algorithm and Hu's result provide an efficient recursive method for computing $\hat{\mathscr{G}}(X)$ and the N-step fuzzy relation f.

Prim's algorithm for generating a maximal spanning tree on X relative to f_1 proceeds in the following way. Arbitrarily select a starting vertex x_1 in X. Find that vertex $x_2 \in X - \{x_1\}$ which is most similar to x_1 in the sense that x_2 maximizes $f_1(x_1,x)$ over $x \in X - \{x_1\}$. Put $E_1 = (x_1,x_2)$. Find that vertex $x_3 \in X - \{x_1,x_2\}$ which is most similar to the set $\{x_1,x_2\}$ in the sense that x_3 maximizes max $\{f_1(x_1,x),f_1(x_2,x)\}$ over $x \in X - \{x_1,x_2\}$. Put $Q(X_3)$ = vertex in $\{x_1,x_2\}$ most similar to x_3, i.e., the vertex which satisfies $f_1(Q(x_3),x_3) = \max \{f_1(x_1,x_3),f_1(x_2,x_3)\}$. Put $E_2 = (Q(x_3),x_3)$, etc. A continuation of this process eventually generates $N-1$ edges E_i in a maximal spanning tree $\hat{\mathscr{G}}(X)$ for f_1. As a by product, we also obtain maximum capacity routes $S(x,y)$ for each vertex pair $x,y \in X$ and a corresponding value for $f(x,y)$, which equals the smallest edge weight in $S(x,y)$. Moreover the entire process has a simple recursive structure which renders it substantially more efficient than (11) for computing $f(x,y)$. For example, at stage k in Prim's algorithm, we have the following quantities:

[1] The decision concerning maximal or minimal depends upon whether X is equipped with a "similarity" function such as the symmetric fuzzy relation (1) or a "dissimilarity" function, such as a metric.

[2] The terminology employed in this section conforms to Ore [14].

a) a nonempty vertex set A_k,
b) the corresponding vertex set $B_k = X - A_k$,
c) for each x in B_k, a corresponding number

$$\rho(x,A_k) \triangleq \max_{y \in A_k} f_1(x,y)$$

which measures the similarity of x to the set A_k,
d) for each x in B_k a corresponding vertex $Q_k(x)$ in A_k for which

$$f_1(x,Q_k(x)) = \rho(x,A_k)$$

e) a vertex x_{k+1} in B_k for which

$$\rho(x_{k+1},A_k) = \max_{x \in B_k} \rho(x,A_k) = \max_{x \in B_k} \max_{y \in A_k} f_1(x,y)$$

f) the edge $E_k = (Q(x_{k+1}),x_k)$.

The quantities a), c), and d) at stage k are obtained from the output of stage $k - 1$ via the recursion.

$$A_k = A_{k-1} \cup \{x_k\}$$

$$\rho(x,A_k) = \max \{\rho(x,A_{k-1}),f_1(x,x_k)\}, \qquad x \in B_k$$

$$Q_k(x) = \begin{cases} Q_{k-1}(x), & \text{if } \rho(x,A_{k-1}) \geq f_1(x,x_k) \\ x_k, & \text{if } \rho(x,A_{k-1}) < f_1(x,x_k), \end{cases} \qquad x \in B_k \tag{18}$$

Initially, for $k = 1$, we have

$$A_1 = \{x_1\}, \qquad x_1 = \text{arbitrary vertex in } X.$$

$$B_1 = X - \{x_1\}.$$

$$\rho(x,A_1) = f_1(x,x_1), \qquad x \in B_1.$$

$$Q_1(x) = x_1, \qquad x \in B_1.$$

$$x_2 \in B_1, \qquad \text{where } \rho(x_2,A_1) = \max_{x \in B_1} \rho(x,A_1) = \max_{x \in B_1} f_1(x,x_1).$$

$$E_1 = (x_1,x_2).$$

We can now see that there are $N - k$ vertices in B_k, and that $N - k$ pairwise comparisons are required to compute both $\rho(x,A_k)$ and $Q_k(x)$ on B_k via (18), given $\rho(x,A_{k-1}),Q_{k-1}(x)$, and x_k from stage $k - 1$. An additional $N - k - 1$ pairwise comparison is required to find a solution x_{k+1} of $\rho(x_{k+1},A_k) = \max_{x \in B_k} \rho(x,A_k)$. Finally, for $k = 1$, $\rho(x,A_1)$ and $Q_1(x)$ are input data, so that this stage requires only $N - 2$ pairwise comparisons (to compute x_2). Thus the total number of pairwise comparisons required to generate all $N - 1$ edges E_i in a maximal spanning tree is

$$\nu = N - 2 + \sum_{k=2}^{N-1} (N - k) + \sum_{k=2}^{N-1} (N - k - 1)$$

$$= (N - 2)(N - 1).$$

Furthermore, the scheme for computing $f(x,y)$ is equally efficient. For $1 \leq i \leq k - 1$, $E_{k-1} = (Q_{k-1}(x_k),x_k)$ is the terminal edge in the unique maximal capacity route lying in the maximal spanning tree and joining x_i to x_k. Moreover, every subpath of this maximum capacity route is also a maximum capacity route; in particular, this holds for the subpath joining x_i and $Q_{k-1}(x_k)$ so that we have

$$f(x_i,x_k) = \min \{f(x_i,Q_{k-1}(x_k)),f_1(Q_{k-1}(x_k),x_k)\},$$

$$1 \leq i \leq k - 1. \tag{19}$$

Since $Q_{k-1}(x_k)$ is one of the vertices x_i, $1 \leq i \leq k - 1$, it follows that (19) and the initial conditions $f(x_1,x_2) = f_1(x_1,x_2)$ recursively generate the columns of the upper triangular part of the symmetric $N \times N$ matrix $[f(x_i,x_j)]$. Evidently, stage k of this process involves only $k - 1$ pairwise comparisons (19), so that the total number of comparison operations required to generate f is

$$\nu_{\text{TOT}} = \nu + \sum_{k=3}^{N} (k - 1)$$

$$= \frac{(3N - 1)(N - 2)}{2} \sim \frac{3}{2} N^2.$$

In contrast, each stage of algorithm (11) entails the computation of $N(N - 1)/2$ elements in the upper triangular part of the symmetric matrix $[G_n]^2$. Furthermore, with reference to (9), each of these computations requires $N + (N - 1) = (2N - 1)$ pairwise comparison operations, so that $N(N - 1)(2N - 1)/2 \approx N^3$. Such operations are required at each stage of (15). In view of (13), this means that anywhere between $\sim N^3$ and $\sim N^3 \log_2 N$ pairwise comparisons are necessary in order to compute f from (11).

Finally, we note that the fast access storage requirements for a computer implemented version of (18) are quite modest. Since each stage of the algorithm requires only portions of one column from each of the $N \times N$ matrices $[f_1(x,y)]$ and $[f(x,y)]$ as input and produces a portion of one column of $[f(x,y)]$ as output, it is feasible to store f_1 and f out of core when N is large. In this case, fast access storage for five N-vectors is sufficient to hold the values of f_1, f, ρ, and Q required at any given stage of the calculation, and to record the relationship between the identifying indices attached to the elements of X and the subsequent relabeling imposed by the algorithm. In contrast, each stage of (11) requires the *entire* upper triangular portion of the $N \times N$ matrix $[G_k]$ as input, and produces the *entire* upper triangular portion of $[G_{k+1}]$ as output. Consequently, overall computing time (including I/0) will increase rapidly with N for this algorithm if $[G_k]$ and $[G_{k+1}]$ are held out of core.

References

[1] S. Tamura, S. Higuchi, and K. Tanaka, "Pattern classification based on fuzzy relations," *IEEE Trans. Syst., Man, Cybern.*, vol. SCM-1, pp. 61–66, Jan. 1971.
[2] S. C. Johnson, "Hierarchical clustering schemes," *Psychometrika*, vol. 32, pp. 247–254, Sept. 1967.
[3] R. Kalaba, "Graph theory and automatic control," in *Applied Combinatorial Mathematics*. New York: Wiley, 1964, ch. 8.
[4] R. C. Prim, "Shortest connection matrix network and some generalizations," *Bell Syst. Tech. J.*, vol. 36, pp. 1389–1401, 1957.
[5] C. T. Zahn, "Graph-theoretical methods for detecting and describing gestalt clusters," *IEEE Trans. Comput.*, vol. C-20, pp. 68–86, Jan. 1971.
[6] J. C. Gower and G. J. S. Ross, "Minimum spanning trees and single linkage cluster analysis," *Appl. Stat.*, vol. 18, pp. 54–110, 1969.
[7] T. C. Hu, "The maximum capacity route problem," *Oper. Res.*, vol. 9, pp. 898–900, 1961.
[8] P. H. A. Sneath, "Computers in taxonomy," *J. Gen. Microbiol.*, vol. 17, pp. 201–226, 1957.
[9] R. R. Sokal and P. H. A. Sneath, *Principles of Numerical Taxonomy*. San Francisco: Freeman, 1963.
[10] R. O. Duda and P. Hart, *Pattern Classification and Scene Analysis*. New York: Academic, 1972.
[11] G. N. Lance and W. T. Williams, "A general theory of classificatory sorting strategies; I. hierarchical systems," *Comput. J.*, vol. 9, pp. 373–380, 1966.
[12] L. Fisher and J. W. Van Ness, "Admissible clustering procedures," *Biometrika*, vol. 58, pp. 91–104, 1971.
[13] D. Wishart, "Mode analysis: a generalization of nearest neighbor which reduces chaining effects," in *Numerical Taxonomy*, A. J. Cole, Ed. New York: Academic, 1969.
[14] O. Ore, "Theory of graphs," *Amer. Math. Soc. Colloquium Publications*, vol. 38, Providence, R.I., 1962.

Fuzzy Chains

ABRAHAM KANDEL AND LAWRENCE YELOWITZ

Abstract—**Motivated by the ineffectiveness of classical mathematical techniques in dealing with imprecision in some real life systems, an investigation is made of fuzzy chains from x_1 to x_t, which are simply sequences of elements of the fuzzy set X. A suitable notation is used to represent a primitive connection matrix, and a procedure is given to convert this matrix to the fuzzy transmission matrix for the system. This procedure is a generalization to fuzzy algebra of a procedure to compute the transitive closure of a binary matrix, and it is very efficient, involving only a single scan over the matrix. A proof of correctness of the procedure is given. It should be noted that the imprecision involved stems not from randomness but from a lack of sharp transition from membership in a class to nonmembership in it. Various properties of the matrices involved in such representations are investigated and illustrated.**

I. Introduction

Ever since Zadeh [1] introduced the idea of fuzzy set theory by utilizing the concept of membership grade, a number of researchers have been concerned with the properties and applications of fuzzy sets, [2]–[26].

Essentially, fuzziness is a representation of imprecision that stems from a grouping of elements into classes that do not have sharply defined boundaries. Since certain aspects of reality always escape most mathematical models, the strictly binary approach to the treatment of physical phenomena is not always adequate to describe systems in the real world. Real world constraints, such as complexity, ill defined situations, and transition states are reflected upon the various attributes of our models.

Because of these constraints the attributes of the system variables often emerge from an elusive fuzziness, a readjustment to context, or an effect of human imprecision, as usually appears in modeling of "soft" sciences, such as sociology, psychology, natural languages, and pattern description.

Since systems that are either ill-defined or describe transitional behavior do not have a precise quantitative analysis, some graphical approach to represent these systems is needed. It is in this sense that fuzzy logic analysis, through the use of fuzzy chains, might enable us to process decision relevant information by using approximate relations to a primary set of precise data. This approach might be of use in areas such as decision processes linguistics, sequential systems analysis, system modeling approximation, and many more. Some problem oriented examples, which we made no attempt in the present correspondence to investigate are 1) graph representation of combinational and sequential systems during transition, namely, investigation of hazards by means of fuzzy chains; 2) classification of patterns and cluster analysis through the description of fuzzy matrices and graphs; 3) approximation of ill-defined transport networks and maximal matching systems by means of fuzzy representations of chains.

Manuscript received October 13, 1973; revised April 10, 1974.
The authors are with the Department of Computer Science, New Mexico Institute of Mining and Technology, Socorro, N.Mex. 87801.

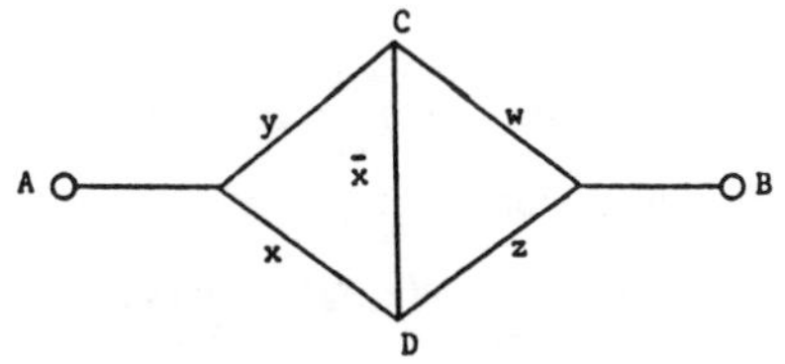

Fig. 1. Graph G_f corresponding to fuzzy system.

II. Fuzzy Chains

Fuzzy algebra completely specifies the performance of a fuzzy system with n-input terminals $x_1,\cdots,x_n$ and a single output terminal, where the fuzzy function f is represented by

$$f(x_1,\cdots,x_n) = \xi.$$

Consider, for example, the two-terminal fuzzy system of Fig. 1. The grade membership of the edges of this system are considered as fuzzy functions. It is quite clear that the set of fuzzy n-variable functions is closed under the operations of union, intersection, and complement and that this set forms a distributive lattice. Thus the fuzzy system may be considered an undirected finite graph, the edges of which are designated by the generators of the distributive lattice.

Definition 1: If Φ is a two-terminal fuzzy system constructed from edge-type elements $x_1,x_2,\cdots,x_n$, then the *fuzzy transmission function* (FTF) of Φ, F_Φ, is defined as the union of the closed chains between the terminals of the network. For the system of Fig. 1, the FTF of Φ is given by

$$F_\Phi = xz + x\bar{x}w + yw + \bar{x}yz$$

when concatenation represents min and $+$ represents max operations. Formally, the FTF of a two-terminal fuzzy chain network is obtained as follows.

1) Determine all irredundant input–output chains.
2) For each chain in 1) form the intersection of the corresponding edge grade-memberships in order to obtain the grade-membership of the chain.
3) Form the union of all chain grade-memberships obtained in 2).

Definition 2: The dual of a fuzzy function F, written F^D, is inductively defined as follows.

1) If $F = f_j$, then $F^D = f_j$, for $j = 1,2,\cdots,n$.
2) If A, B, and C are fuzzy functions and $A = B + C$, then $A^D = B^D C^D$.
3) If A, B, and C are fuzzy functions and $A = BC$, then $A^D = B^D + C^D$.
4) If A and B are fuzzy functions and $A = \bar{B}$, then $A^D = (\overline{B^D})$.

The relation between a fuzzy function F and its dual F^D is given by the following theorem.

Theorem 1 [23]*:* If F is a fuzzy function constructed from

Reprinted from *IEEE Trans. Syst., Man, Cybern.*, vol. SMC-4, no. 5, pp. 472–475, September 1974.

$$\rho = \begin{matrix} & A & B & C & D \\ A & 1 & 0 & y & x \\ B & 0 & 1 & w & z \\ C & y & w & 1 & \bar{x} \\ D & x & z & \bar{x} & 1 \end{matrix}$$

Fig. 2. Primitive connection matrix of Fig. 1.

x_i, for $i = 1,\cdots,n$, and F^D is its dual written as $F^D(x_1,\cdots,x_n)$, then $F^D(x_1,\cdots,x_n) = \bar{F}(\bar{x}_1,\cdots,\bar{x}_n)$.

Corollary 1: If F_1 and F_2 are fuzzy functions, and $F_1 \equiv F_2$, then $F_1{}^D \equiv F_2{}^D$.

We say that a fuzzy function F_A is self-dual if and only if $F_A = F_A{}^D$. Thus a self-dual expression for the FTF of Φ can be obtained as follows.

1) Determine all minimal cut-sets separating the two terminals.
2) For each cut-set in 1), form the union of the corresponding edge grade-memberships to obtain the grade membership of the cut-set.
3) Form the intersection of all cut-set grade-membership obtained in 2).

The self-dual expression for Fig. 1 is, therefore, $F_\Phi = (x + y)\cdot(\bar{x} + y + z)(x + \bar{x} + w)(z + w)$. This expression can be derived from the previous one by the absorption law and the distributive law.

We can also derive the FTF of Φ by a suitable fuzzy matrix theory. Fig. 2 shows the primitive connection matrix ρ corresponding to Fig. 1. To completely analyze the fuzzy system, one would desire a $k \times k$ matrix of which the ij entry is the fuzzy transmission function of the system with terminals i and j. This suggests the definition of a fuzzy transmission matrix and the examination of some properties of fuzzy matrices.

In [5] and [26], relation matrices have been discussed and several examples of the relation matrices of some similarity relations have been demonstrated. It is clear that the graph representation of a fuzzy system bears a similarity to the relation matrix discussed by Zadeh and applied by him to the investigation of fuzzy algorithms. It is claimed that the conceptual framework developed in [26] best describes the systems that are too complex or too ill-defined to admit of precise quantitative analysis. It should be noted, however, that there exists a very important source of imprecision in systems, and this is *transition behavior*. Transition of a system or of a specific element in a system can be best described and analyzed by means of a fuzzy description. This is true for hazard detection in combinational systems [24] or for transition models in such fields as economics, management sciences, artificial intellegence, physics, and linguistics. The fuzzy transition is best represented by a fuzzy chain or a fuzzy path on the graph representing the system.

Let $x_1,x_2,\cdots,x_k$ be k points in the fuzzy set X with $\mu(x_i,x_j)$ being the grade-membership describing the transition from x_i to x_j, $1 \le i, j \le k$. A sequence $S = (x_r,\cdots,x_t)$ will be said to be a fuzzy chain from x_r to x_t, where $1 \le r, t \le k$, and it is said to have the strength of its weakest link.

For any primitive connection matrix ρ we define the characteristic fuzzy matrix or fuzzy transmission matrix $\psi(\rho) = [x_{ij}]$ such that x_{ij} is the fuzzy transmission function of the two-terminal system connecting vertex i to j. It is clear that $\psi(\rho)$ is a symmetric matrix, since the graph is an undirected one, and thus $x_{ij} = x_{ji}$, for all i,j and $x_{ii} = 1$, for all i.

Theorem 2: Let ρ be a square fuzzy transmission matrix of order n. Then there exists an integer $q \le n - 1$ such that $\rho^q = \rho^{q+1} = \cdots = \psi(\rho)$.

Proof: Let $\rho = [p_{ij}]$. The ij entry of ρ^2 is

$$\sum_{k=1}^{n} p_{ik}p_{kj}$$

and this term has the grade-membership of

$$\max_k \,[\min(p_{ik},p_{kj})]$$

iff there is a direct path between vertices i and j, or there is a path from i to j through one intermediate vertex. Extending this argument to ρ^i it is clear that no path requires more than $n - 2$ intermediate vertices, since there are only n vertices, and internal loops are excluded. Hence, the ij entry of ρ^{n-1} has the grade-membership of

$$\max_{\text{subterms}} \{ij \text{ terms of } \rho^{n-1}\}$$

iff i and j are connected, namely, $\rho^{n-1} = \psi(\rho)$. Q.E.D.

Based on these results $\psi(\rho)$ can be computed by successive multiplication of ρ.

The repeated matrix multiplication makes it unattractive from an efficiency viewpoint. Algorithm 1 achieves the same result and requires only a single scan over the matrix. In fact, Algorithm 1 works correctly on a wider range of input, since it is not required that the diagonal elements of the input matrix equal one. Algorithm 1 is an extension to fuzzy logic of an algorithm of Warshall [28] to compute the transitive closure of a binary matrix.

Algorithm 1:

1) Label all vertices by the integers $1,\cdots,N$.
2) Construct the primitive connection matrix ρ the ij entry of which denotes the fuzzy transmission function of the two-terminal fuzzy system connecting vertices i and j through a direct chain.
3) DO $K = 1$ TO N
4) DO $I = 1$ TO N
5) IF $\rho(I,K) \neq 0$ THEN
6) DO $J = 1$ TO N
7) $\rho(I,J) = \max(\rho(I,J), \min(\rho(I,K), \rho(K,J)))$
8) END
9) END
10) END

The basic idea is to scan down *column K*, and for each nonzero element encountered (e.g., in row I), each element in *row I* (e.g., element $\rho(I,J)$) is possibly improved by comparing $\rho(I,J)$ to $\min(\rho(I,K), \rho(K,J))$. A rigorous proof of correctness is achieved by attaching the following inductive assertion A [27] between statements 7) and 8):

$$\rho(I,J) = M(I,J,K)$$

where $M(I,J,K) \triangleq \max\{\min(\text{all chains from } I \text{ to } J \text{ such that each } \textit{intermediate} \text{ element has a label} \le K)\}$.

Before proving that assertion A is true whenever control leaves step 7), it is noted that the relation $\rho(I,J) = M(I,J,N)$ is the desired relation at the termination of the algorithm, since $M(I,J,N) = \max\{\min(\text{all chains from } I \text{ to } J)\}$. Assertion A is proved by induction on K.

1) $K = 1$. The first time A is reached, K has the value one, and path analysis [27] shows that $\rho(I,J) = \max(\rho_0(I,J), \min(\rho_0(I,1), \rho_0(1,K)))$, where ρ_0 represents the original matrix and the right side of the equation equals $M(I,J,1)$.

2) Assume $\rho(I,J) = M(I,J,K)$, $1 \leq K < N$. Show $\rho(I,J) = M(I, J, K + 1)$.

There are two subcases to consider. If $M(I, J, K + 1)$ does not involve element $K + 1$, then no change is made to the matrix and the desired result is true. If $M(I, J, K + 1)$ does involve element $K + 1$, then we can guarantee that element $K + 1$ appears only once, since loops do not increase the max of any chain.

Thus we can break the optimal chain into two subchains $\rho(I, K + 1)$ and $\rho(K + 1, J)$. Since both subchains involve intermediate elements numbered $\leq K$, the inductive hypothesis applies to each subchain and the desired result follows.

It is interesting to note that during the process of computing the characteristic fuzzy matrix, minimization of the fuzzy structures are possible. In general, one can not apply the identities $x \cdot \bar{x} = 0$ and $x + \bar{x} = 1$ to fuzzy expressions, and thus binary techniques of minimization are insufficient. Therefore, more specific methods, directed toward the minimization of fuzzy functions, should be used.

The first author has presented [25] a novel method for the minimization of fuzzy functions by extending the concepts of prime implicants and consensus to fuzzy logic. In [25] an algorithm that generates all the fuzzy prime implicants is introduced, and a proof of completeness of the algorithm is given. The minimization technique takes into consideration the refinement of the classical map approach and the properties of fuzzy consensus in the context of fuzzy logic. It is recommended to implement the technique described in [25] for the derivation of the simplified characteristic fuzzy matrix $\psi(\rho)$.

The characteristic fuzzy matrix represents a mean by which the analysis of any finite fuzzy system can be obtained. The analysis technique that has been given is quite general, and the use of matrix techniques leads to efficient computations, particularly in the description of fuzzy sequential procedures such as decision-making and procedures involving sequences of imprecise operations, which can be best represented by graphs and fuzzy chains.

III. Conclusion

The applicability of fuzzy algebra to the study of fuzzy chains has been introduced. Program correctness techniques were used to certify the main algorithm.

The main contribution of this note consists of two parts. First, a new conceptual framework for the study of fuzzy systems is provided, facilitating the derivation and stimulating the discovery of various results in applied areas. Second, a proof of correctness of the main algorithm is given. This technique for certifying algorithms shows conclusively that no errors exist, in contrast to the usual technique of testing, which can only show that no errors have been found in a certain number of trial runs [27].

Several problem-oriented examples have been mentioned in the introduction, and it is our hope that the interested reader will be able to find many more applications in his field of interest.

Acknowledgment

The authors express sincere thanks to the referees of this paper for their excellent remarks and criticism, the effect of which on this work has been profound.

References

[1] L. A. Zadeh, "Fuzzy sets," *Inform. Contr.*, vol. 8, pp. 338–353, 1965.
[2] ——, "Fuzzy algorithms," *Inform. Contr.*, vol. 12, pp. 94–102, 1968.
[3] ——, "Fuzzy sets and systems," in *1965 Proc. Symp. on Systems Theory*, Polytechnic Institute of Brooklyn, Brooklyn, N.Y., 1965.
[4] ——, "Quantitative fuzzy semantics," Electron. Res. Lab., Univ. Calif., Berkeley, Memo no. ERL-M281, Aug. 1970.
[5] ——, "Similarity relations and fuzzy ordering," Electron. Res. Lab. Univ. Calif., Berkely, Memo no. ERL-M277, 1970.
[6] ——, "Toward a theory of fuzzy systems," Electron. Res. Lab., Univ. Calif., Berkeley, Rep. no. ERL-69-2, June 1969.
[7] ——, "Fuzzy languages and their relation to human and machine intelligence," in *Proc. Conf. Man and Computer*, 1970; also Electron. Res. Lab., Univ. Calif., Berkeley, Memo M302, 1971.
[8] ——, "Probability measures of fuzzy events," *J. Math. Anal. Appl.*, vol. 10, pp. 421–427, Aug. 1968.
[9] S. K. Chang, "On the execution of fuzzy programs using finite-state machines," *IEEE Trans. Comput.*, vol. C-21, pp. 241–253, Mar. 1972.
[10] S. S. L. Chang and L. A. Zadeh, "On fuzzy mapping and control," *IEEE Trans. Syst., Man, Cybern.*, vol. SMC-2, pp. 30–34, Jan. 1972.
[11] R. E. Bellman and L. A. Zadeh, "Decision-making in a fuzzy environment," *Management Sci.*, vol. 17, pp. B-141–B-164, 1970.
[12] E. T. Lee and L. A. Zadeh, "Note on fuzzy languages," Electron. Res. Lab., Univ. Calif., Berkeley, ERL Rep. 69-7, Nov. 1969.
[13] P. N. Marinos, "Fuzzy logic and its application to switching systems," *IEEE Trans. Comput.*, vol. C-18, pp. 343–348, Apr. 1969.
[14] R. C. T. Lee and C. L. Chang, "Some properties of fuzzy logic," *Inform. Contr.*, vol. 19, pp. 417–431, 1971.
[15] P. Siy and C. S. Chen, "Minimization of fuzzy functions," *IEEE Trans. Comput.*, vol. C-21, pp. 100–102, Jan. 1972.
[16] A. De Luca and S. Termini, "A definition of a non-probalistic entropy in the setting of fuzzy sets theory," *Inform. Contr.*, vol. 20, pp. 301–312, 1972.
[17] R. C. T. Lee, "Fuzzy logic and the resolution principle," *J. Assoc. Comput. Mach.*, vol. 19, pp. 109–119, 1972.
[18] C. L. Chang, "Fuzzy algebras, fuzzy functions and their application to function approximation," Division of Computer Research and Technology, *National Institutes of Health*, Bethesda, Md., 1971.
[19] P. P. Preparata and R. T. Yeh, "Continuously valued logic," *J. Comput. Syst. Sci.*, pp. 397–418, 1972.
[20] A. De Luca and S. Termini, "Algebraic properties of fuzzy sets," to be published.
[21] A. Kandel, "Comment on the minimization of fuzzy functions," *IEEE Trans. Comput.*, vol. C-22, p. 217, Feb. 1973.
[22] ——, "Comment on an algorithm that generates fuzzy prime implicants, by Lee and Chang," *Inform. Contr.*, pp. 279–282, Apr. 1973.
[23] ——, "On the analysis of fuzzy logic," in *Proc. Sixth Int. Conf. on System Sciences*, Honolulu, Hawaii, Jan. 1973.
[24] ——, "Application of fuzzy logic to the detection of static hazards in combinational switching systems," New Mexico Inst. of Mining & Technology, Socorro, N. M. Comput. Sci. Rep. 122, Apr. 1973.
[25] ——, "On minimization of fuzzy functions," *IEEE Trans. Comput*, vol. C-22, pp. 826–832, Sept. 1973.
[26] L. A. Zadeh, "Outline of a new approach to the analysis of complex systems and decision processes," *IEEE Trans. Syst., Man, Cybern.*, vol. SMC-3, pp. 28–44, Jan. 1973.
[27] R. L. London, "Proving programs correct: Some techniques and examples," *BIT*, vol. 10, pp. 168–182, 1970.
[28] S. Warshall, "A theorem on Boolean matrices," *J. Ass. Comput. Mach.*, vol. 9, pp. 11–12, Jan. 1962.

FUZZY PARTITIONS AND RELATIONS; AN AXIOMATIC BASIS FOR CLUSTERING*

James C. BEZDEK
Mathematics Department, Utah State University, Logan, UT 84322, U.S.A.

J. Douglas HARRIS
Mathematics Department, Marquette University, Milwaukee, WI 53233, U.S.A.

Received 25 May 1977
Revised September 1977

In this paper some connections between fuzzy partitions and similarity relations are explored. A new definition of transitivity for fuzzy relations yields a relation-theoretic characterization of the class of all psuedo-metrics on a fixed (finite) data set into the closed unit interval. This notion of transitivity also links the triangle inequality to convex decompositions of fuzzy similarity relations in a manner which may generate new techniques for fuzzy clustering. Finally, we show that every fuzzy c-partition of a finite data set induces a psuedo-metric of the type described above on the data.

Key Words: Convex decompositions, Cluster analysis, Fuzzy relations, Pseudo-metrics, Transitivity.

1. Introduction

The extant theory and applications of fuzzy relations are contained in the papers of Zadeh [1]; Tamura *et al.* [2]; Kandel and Yelowitz [3]; and Dunn [4]. In particular, the transitive closure of [0, 1], reflexive, symmetric fuzzy relations is discussed as a basis for constructing hierarchical clusters in finite data sets. Dunn showed in [4] that this methodology yielded essentially the same results as the well-known graph-theoretic technique called the single linkage method (c.f. Duda and Hart [5]). The basis for this observation was that the notion of transitivity used in [1–3] for fuzzy relations is equivalent to the ultra-metric inequality. One of our main goals in the present work is to enlarge this theory by redefining fuzzy transitivity so that it becomes equivalent to the triangle inequality. The class of fuzzy similarity relations characterized in this way appears to be an important space for applications in clustering.

In Section 2 we review *hard* (i.e., non-fuzzy) partitions and equivalence relations for finite sets. Section 3 extends these ideas to fuzzy partitions and similarity relations, and introduces Max-$\triangle$ transitivity. In Section 4 we discuss convex decompositions of fuzzy similarity relations. Section 5 presents an application of the preceding ideas, defining a new method for clustering via convex decomposition of similarity relation matrices. In Section 6 the work of Bezdek and Harris [6] is continued by connecting fuzzy partitions with fuzzy similarity relations. We show that *every* fuzzy c-partition of a finite data set induces a pseudo-metric on the data. In this way individual fuzzy relationships can be obtained from fuzzy class memberships.

2. Hard partitions and relations

Let $X=\{x_1, x_2, \ldots x_n\}$ be a finite data set. If, for a positive integer c, $2 \leqq c < n$, it is known (or assumed) that X contains representatives from c subclasses, then cluster analysis with respect to X is the problem of identifying the subclass labels, i.e., of partitioning X into c subsets (clusters).

A hard c-partition of X has three equivalent characterizations: sets, functions; and matrices. In what follows the description most convenient for us is in terms of matrices. Towards this end let V_{cn} be the usual vector space of real $c \times n$ matrices over V. Let u_{ik}

*This research supported by NSF Grant Number DCR75-05014.

Reprinted with permission from *Fuzzy Sets and Systems*, vol. 1, pp. 111–127, 1978.

be the ik^{th} element of $U \in V_{cn}$, and define

$$\mathscr{P}_c = \left\{ U \in V_{cn} | u_{ik} \in \{0,1\} \forall i,k;\ \sum_{i=1}^{c} u_{ik} = 1 \,\forall k;\ \sum_{k=1}^{n} u_{ik} > 0 \,\forall i \right\}. \tag{1}$$

Here u_{ik} is the membership of x_k in class i; $\mathscr{P}_c$ is exactly *non-degenerate hard c-partition space* for X, and the superset $\mathscr{P}_{co} \supset \mathscr{P}_c$ of matrices obtained by relaxing the last condition in (1) to $\sum_{k=1}^{n} u_{ik} \geqq 0 \,\forall i$ is the corresponding degenerate space.

To each $U \in \mathscr{P}_c$ there corresponds a unique hard equivalence relation in the Cartesian product $X \times X$. Loosely speaking, we have, given $U \in \mathscr{P}_c$, the relation matrix $R = [r_{ij}]$ in V_{nn} defined by:

$$r_{ij} = \begin{cases} 1; & u_{ki} = u_{kj} = 1 \,\exists k, \\ 0; & \text{otherwise.} \end{cases}$$

Since R is an equivalence relation, it satisfies three requirements:

$$r_{ii} = 1 \quad \forall i, \qquad \text{(reflexivity)} \tag{2a}$$

$$r_{ij} = r_{ji} \quad \forall i \neq j, \qquad \text{(symmetry)} \tag{2b}$$

$$\left. \begin{matrix} r_{ik} = 1 \\ r_{kj} = 1 \end{matrix} \right\} \Rightarrow r_{ij} = 1 \quad \forall i, j. \qquad \text{(transitivity)} \tag{2c}$$

Let S and R be two equivalence relations. The composition of R followed by S will be denoted as $S \circ R$. In particular, $\circ$ denotes generalized matrix multiplication when S and R are relation matrices. Thus if $P = S \circ R \in V_{nn}$, then

$$p_{ij} = \mathop{\square}_{l=1}^{n} (s_{il} * r_{lj}), \tag{3}$$

where $(\square, *)$ is the pair of operations defining $\circ$. In the sequel our interest lies with four matrix products:

$$\circ = (\textstyle\sum . \bullet) \sim \text{Sum-Product}, \tag{4a}$$

$$\circ = (\textstyle\sum . \wedge) \sim \text{Sum-Min}, \tag{4b}$$

$$\circ = (\vee . \bullet) \sim \text{Max-Product}, \tag{4c}$$

$$\circ = (\vee . \wedge) \sim \text{Max-Min}. \tag{4d}$$

Let I_n denote the $n \times n$ identity matrix, and define the ordering $A \leqq B \Leftrightarrow a_{ij} \leqq b_{ij} \forall i, j$; $A, B \in V_{nn}$. With these conventions and (3), (4), conditions (2) may be restated compactly as

$$I_n \leqq R, \qquad \text{(reflexivity)} \tag{2a$'$}$$

$$R = R^{\mathrm{T}}, \qquad \text{(symmetry)} \tag{2b$'$}$$

$$R = R(\vee . \bullet)R = R(\vee . \wedge)R = R^2. \qquad \text{(transitivity)} \tag{2c$'$}$$

The set of all *hard equivalence relations* on n data points we denote by

$$\mathscr{R}_n = \{ R \in V_{nn} | r_{ij} \in \{0,1\} \forall i, j;\ I_n \leqq R;\ R = R^{\mathrm{T}} = R(V . \wedge)R \}. \tag{5}$$

Another characterization (not used below) is in terms of graphs. We mention that the work of Rosenfeld [7] and Yeh and Bang [8] on fuzzy graphs might be substantially enriched by adopting for its basis the fuzzy relation structure described below.

3. Fuzzy relations and partitions

Physical and mathematical objections to $\mathscr{P}_c$(or $\mathscr{R}_n$) as a basis for pattern recognition models are discussed at length in [9]. For the present work our interest centers on the fact that each $U \in \mathscr{P}_c$ requires every $x_k \in X$ to belong unequivocally to precisely one partitioning subset of U; and the relation $R \in \mathscr{R}_n$ induced on $X \times X$ by U renders all x_k's in each equivalence class *indistinguishable* (from one another) to data in other classes, that is, totally related to one another and completely unrelated to members of other classes. Transitivity (2c) is particularly difficult to justify in many applications (c.f. Crowson [10]) and turns out to be the most subtle of properties (2) to generalize.

Zadeh in [11] originated the idea of allowing sets to have "fuzzy" boundaries. Following [11], we call a *membership function* $u_i : X \to [0, 1]$ a *fuzzy subset* of $X : u_i(x_k) \doteq u_{ik}$ is the *grade of membership* of x_k in u_i. For example, $u_A(8.98) = 0.96$ would imply for $r = 8.98$ a strong agreement with the properties characterizing the fuzzy subset $A = \{r \in R \mid r$ is "slightly less" than $9\}$. Fuzzy imbeddings for $\mathscr{P}_c$ and $\mathscr{R}_n$ can be constructed in a variety of ways. The most widely used imbedding for $\mathscr{P}_c$ is *non-degenerate fuzzy c-partition space:*

$$\mathscr{P}_{fc} = \left\{ U \in V_{cn} \middle| u_{ik} \in [0, 1] \,\forall i, k; \sum_{i=1}^{c} u_{ik} = 1 \,\forall k; \sum_{k=1}^{n} u_{ik} > 0 \,\forall i \right\}. \tag{6}$$

At least three algorithms for generating fuzzy c-partitions of X are now known: those of Ruspini [12]; Woodbury [13]; and the fuzzy ISODATA algorithm discussed in [9]. More recently, the nature of the embeddings $\mathscr{P}_c \subseteq \mathscr{P}_{co} \subseteq \mathscr{P}_{fc}$ have been explored in [6] to exploit the fact that $\mathscr{P}_{fc}$ is the convex hull of $\mathscr{P}_{co} : \mathscr{P}_{fc} = \text{conv}(\mathscr{P}_{co})$.

A matrix $U \in \mathscr{P}_{fc}$ of membership functions for points in X conveys the relationship each x_k bears to the c fuzzy subclasses partitioning X, but says nothing about relationships between individuals. To realize information of this kind we consider fuzzy relations in $X \times X$. A fuzzy relation in $X \times X$ is a membership function $\rho : X \times X \to [0, 1]$ whose values $\rho(x_i, x_j)$ denote the *strength of relationship* $\forall i$ and j between x_i and x_j. In a manner entirely analogous to the hard case above, ρ can be represented by an $n \times n$ relation matrix $R = [r_{ij}] = [\rho(x_i, x_j)]$. To generalize (2a) and (2b) we call a fuzzy relation R

$$\text{reflexive} \Leftrightarrow r_{ii} = 1 \,\forall i; \quad \text{and} \quad \text{symmetric} \Leftrightarrow r_{ij} = r_{ji} \,\forall i \neq j. \tag{7a)–(7b}$$

Again compactly expressed as $I_n \leqq R$ and $R = R^{\mathrm{T}}$ respectively.

The extensions given in (7a) and (7b) are quite natural. Extending transitivity to fuzzy relations requires more thought. In [1] Zadeh proposed the following definition: a fuzzy relation R is

$$\max - *\textit{transitive} \Leftrightarrow r_{ij} \geqq \bigvee_{l=1}^{n} (r_{il} * r_{lj}) \,\forall i, j \tag{7c}$$

or equivalently, if and only if $R \geqq R(\vee \,.\, *)R \doteq R^2$, where $*$ could be either min ($\vee$) or ordinary product ($\bullet$). Following Zadeh we call

$$\mathscr{R}* = \{R \in V_{nn} | r_{ij} \in [0, 1] \,\forall i, j; I_n \leqq R : R = R^{\mathrm{T}} \geqq R(\vee \,.\, *)R\} \tag{8}$$

sets of *fuzzy similarity relations* in $X \times X$. Since $ab \leqq a \wedge b$ for $a, b \in [0, 1]$, max–min transitivity implies max–prod transitivity, i.e., $\mathscr{R}_{\wedge} \subseteq \mathscr{R}_{\bullet}$.

There is a more general operation $*$ with natural physical meaning which extends $\mathscr{R}_n$ to a maximal set of fuzzy similarity relations. Let us define a fuzzy similarity relation R to be

$$\text{max-}\triangle \textit{ transitive} \Leftrightarrow r_{ij} \geqq \bigvee_{l=1}^{n} ((r_{il} + r_{lj} - 1) \vee 0) \,\forall i, j. \tag{9}$$

To see that max-$\triangle$ transitivity is implied by max–prod transitivity, note that $(a+b-1)\vee 0 \leqq ab$ for $a, b \in [0,1]$, so

$$r_{ij} \geqq \bigvee_{l=1}^{n} (r_{il} \cdot r_{lj}) \geqq \bigvee_{l=1}^{n} (r_{il}+r_{lj}-1)\vee 0.$$

In fact, if we define on $[0,1)\times[0,1]$ the operations

$$a \triangle b = (a+b-1)\vee 0, \tag{10a}$$

$$a \square b = \frac{a+b}{2}, \tag{10b}$$

$$a \oplus b = a+b-ab, \tag{10c}$$

then the inequalities

$$(a+b-1)\vee 0 \leqq ab \leqq a \wedge b \leqq \frac{a+b}{2} \leqq a \vee b \leqq a+b-ab \leqq 1 \tag{11}$$

result in the following hierarchy of similarity relation spaces upon substitution of the appropriate operation for $*$ in (8).

$$\mathcal{R}_n \subseteq \mathcal{R}_\oplus \subseteq \mathcal{R}_\vee \subseteq \mathcal{R}_\square \subseteq \mathcal{R}_\wedge \subseteq \mathcal{R}_\bullet \subseteq \mathcal{R}_\triangle. \tag{12}$$

The type of transitivity employed will presumably be dictated by the application at hand. We contend that max-$\triangle$ transitivity is the most interesting type on both physical and mathematical grounds. To see how restrictive max–min transitivity is, for example, note that any m numbers $a_1 \leqq a_2 \leqq \ldots \leqq a_m$ can satisfy the requirement $a_i \geqq a_j \wedge a_k$, $\forall i, j, k$ distinct, if and only if $a_1 = a_2 = \ldots = a_{m-1} \leqq a_m$, because $a_1 \geqq (a_{m-1} \wedge a_m)$. Indeed, for the matrix

$$R(\lambda) = \begin{bmatrix} 1 & 0.8 & 0.7 \\ 0.8 & 1 & \lambda \\ 0.7 & \lambda & 1 \end{bmatrix} \text{with } \lambda \in [0,1], \tag{13}$$

it is easy to check that $R(\lambda) \in \mathcal{R}_\wedge \Leftrightarrow \lambda = 0.7$; whereas $R(\lambda) \in \mathcal{R}_\triangle \, \forall \lambda \in [0.5, 0.9]$. This illustrates how sparse the relations $\mathcal{R}_\wedge$ are among the relations $\mathcal{R}_\triangle$.

A physical interpretation of max-$\triangle$ transitivity can be made using (13) and a graphical representation of the relationships involved. Consider first $R(0.7)$ with $r_{12} = r_{21} = 0.8$; $r_{13} = r_{31} = 0.7$; and $r_{23} = r_{32} = 0.7$. Since $R(\lambda)$ is max–min transitive iff $\lambda = 0.7$, only one possibility is allowed for the mutual bonding provided by x_1 in linking x_2 to x_3: namely, that *all* of the relatives of x_3 responsible for the relationships $r_{31} = 0.7$ are shared through with x_2 (Fig. 1).

In other words, max–min transitivity calls for the optimal "alignment" of mutual relatives. An alternative way to think of this follows by answering the question:

(If $x\,R\,y = 0.7$, what should $y\,R\,z = (?)$ to imply that $x\,R\,z \geqq 0.7$?)

It is our contention that (?) should be 1: x should be related to z by at least $x\,R\,y \Leftrightarrow y$ and z are indistinguishable to outside observers $\Leftrightarrow y\,R\,z = 1$. For $y\,R\,z < 1$, y and z are *not* fully equivalent to each other, and the mathematical restrictiveness manifested by max–min transitivity amounts to assuming the optimal alignment displayed in Fig. 1.

On the other hand, max-$\triangle$ transitivity for the matrix $R(\lambda)$ allows for the "worst" alignment, as illustrated in Fig. 2.

The max-$\triangle$ alignment in Fig. 2 assumes that x_2 and x_3 must be coupled by only 50 of each 100 relatives shared with x_1, the most *unoptimistic* alignment of mutual bonds is used, instead of all 70 as in Fig. 1.

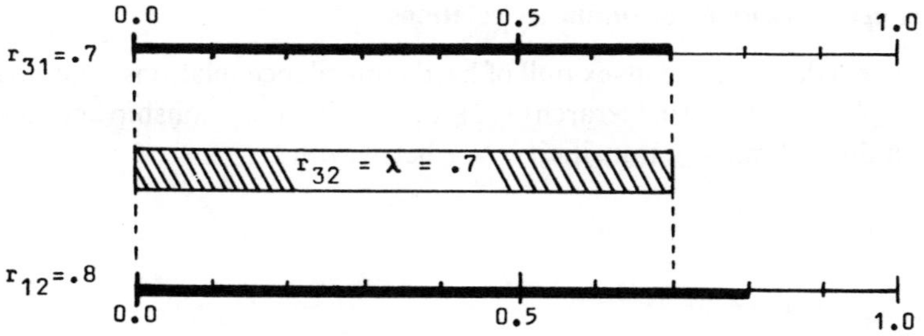

Fig. 1. Graphical illustration of max-$\wedge$ transitivity.

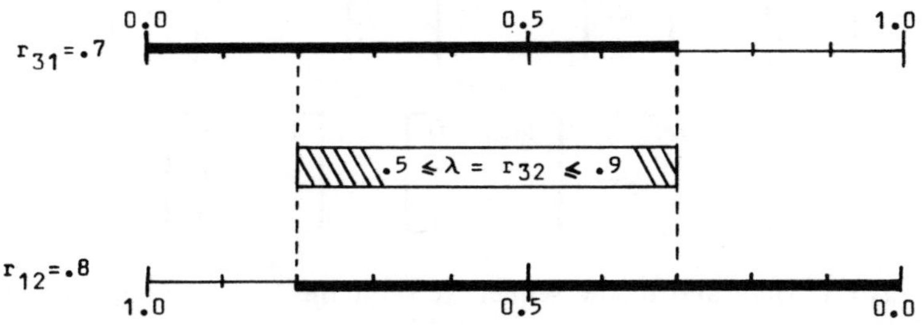

Fig. 2. Graphical illustration of max-$\triangle$ transitivity.

There is an interesting mathematical property of $R_{\triangle}$ which also argues for its use. Zadeh demonstrated in [1] that max–min transitivity was equivalent to the ultra-metric inequality for the function $d(x_i, x_j) = 1 - r_{ij}$, where $R = [r_{ij}] \in \mathscr{R}_{\wedge}$. Since $\mathscr{R}_{\wedge} \subseteq \mathscr{R}_{\triangle}$ and the ultra-metric inequality implies the triangle inequality, one might suspect that max-$\triangle$ transitivity is equivalent to the triangle inequality. This is precisely the case:

Theorem 3.1.

$$R \in \mathscr{R}_{\triangle} \Leftrightarrow \left\{ \begin{array}{l} \textit{The function } d: X \times X \to [0,1] \textit{ defined} \\ \textit{by } d(x_i, x_j) = 1 - r_{ij} \textit{ is a pseudo-metric.} \end{array} \right\} \tag{14}$$

Proof. Let $R = [r_{ij}] = [1 - d_{ij}]$, where we put $d_{ij} \doteq d(x_i, x_j)\, \forall i, j$

(i) $r_{ij} \in [0,1]\, \forall i, j \Leftrightarrow d_{ij} \in [0,1]\, \forall i, j$.

(ii) Suppose $i = j$: $r_{ii} = 1 \Leftrightarrow d_{ii} = 0$; thus $I_n \leqq R \Rightarrow d_{ii} = 0\, \forall i$, and conversely, $d_{ii} = 0\, \forall i \Rightarrow I_n \leqq R$.

Note, however, that $r_{ij} = 1$ with $i \neq j \Rightarrow d_{ij} = 0$ with $x_i \neq x_j$, so d is a pseudo-metric at best.

(iii) Symmetry for d follows from $R = R^{\mathrm{T}}$; symmetry for R from $d_{ij} = d_{ji}\, \forall_{i,j}$.

(iv) Finally, we show that max-$\triangle$ transitivity is equivalent to the triangle inequality:

$$0 \vee (r_{ij} + r_{jk} - 1) \leqq r_{ik}\ \forall \text{ distinct } i, j, k \quad \Leftrightarrow$$

$$r_{ij} + r_{jk} \leqq 1 \leqq 1 + r_{ik} \quad \Leftrightarrow$$

$$(1 - d_{ij}) + (1 - d_{jk}) \leqq 1 + (1 - d_{ik}) \quad \Leftrightarrow$$

$$-(d_{ij} + d_{jk}) \leqq -d_{ik} \quad \Leftrightarrow$$

$$d_{ik} \leqq d_{ij} + d_{jk}. \ \square$$

Theorem 3.1 shows that $\mathscr{R}_{\triangle}$ is the set of fuzzy similarity relations which induce pseudo-metrics on $X \times X$ in exactly the same way that $\mathscr{R}_{\wedge}$ induces pseudo ultra-metrics on $X \times X$, and substantiates our supposition that it is the maximal set in the hierarchy (12).

4. Convex decompositions of similarity relations

Let conv($\mathscr{R}_n$) denote the convex hull of hard equivalence relations. Our goal in this section is to place conv($\mathscr{R}_n$) in hierarchy (12), and exhibit a relationship between convex decomposition and max-$\triangle$ transitivity. We begin with:

Theorem 4.1. *For $n=3$ we have*

$$\text{conv}(\mathscr{R}_3)=\mathscr{R}_\triangle. \tag{15}$$

Proof. $R\in\text{conv}(\mathscr{R}_3)\Leftrightarrow\exists$ scalars $\{c_1, c_2, c_3, c_4, c_5)\subset[0,1]$ so that

$$R=\begin{bmatrix}1 & y_1 & y_2\\ & 1 & y_3\\ & & 1\end{bmatrix}=c_1\begin{bmatrix}1 & 1 & 1\\ & 1 & 1\\ & & 1\end{bmatrix}+c_2\begin{bmatrix}1 & 1 & 1\\ & 1 & 0\\ & & 1\end{bmatrix}+c_3\begin{bmatrix}1 & 0 & 1\\ & 1 & 0\\ & & 1\end{bmatrix}+$$

$$+c_4\begin{bmatrix}1 & 0 & 0\\ & 1 & 1\\ & & 1\end{bmatrix}+c_5\begin{bmatrix}1 & 0 & 0\\ & 1 & 0\\ & & 1\end{bmatrix} \tag{16}$$

with $\sum_{k=1}^5 c_k=1$. Here and in the sequel we omit the lower triangular portion of symmetric relation matrices. We use y_1, y_2, y_3 for r_{12}, r_{13}, and r_{23} in R to shorten the notation.

From (2a) and (2b) it follows that $I\leq R$ and $R=R^{\mathrm{T}}$; further, every entry of R is a partial sum of c_k's, so $0\leq r_{ij}\leq 1\,\forall i, j$. It remains to be seen that R is max-$\triangle$ transitive. We are to show that $1+y_i\geq y_j+y_k\;\forall$ distinct i, j, k. Towards this end we have from (16) the equations

$$y_1=c_1+c_2, \tag{17a}$$

$$y_2=c_1+c_3, \tag{17b}$$

$$y_3=c_1+c_4. \tag{17c}$$

Adding these and using $\sum_{k=1}^5 c_k=1$ yields

$$y_1+y_2+y_3=2c_1+1-c_5. \tag{18}$$

Using (17) and (18), the convex coefficients c_1, c_2, c_3, and c_4 can be written in terms of c_5 and the entries of R as

$$c_1=1/2(y_1+y_2+y_3+c_5-1), \tag{19a}$$

$$c_2=1/2(1+y_1-(y_2+y_3+c_5)), \tag{19b}$$

$$c_3=1/2(1+y_2-(y_1+y_3+c_5)), \tag{19c}$$

$$c_4=1/2(1+y_3-(y_1+y_2+c_5)). \tag{19d}$$

Now consider, for example, (19b): since $0\leq c_2\leq 1$ it is necessary that $1+y_1-(y_2+y_3+c_5)\geq 0$, or equivalently that $1+y_1-(y_2+y_3)\geq c_5$. But $0\leq c_5\leq 1$, so $1+y_1-(y_2+y_3)\geq c_5\geq 0\Rightarrow 1+y_1\geq(y_2+y_3)$. Similar arguments with (19c) and (19d) establish the required inequalities, so R is max-$\triangle$ transitive, and hence conv$(\mathscr{R}_3)\subseteq\mathscr{R}_\triangle$.

Conversely, suppose $R\in\mathscr{R}_\triangle$. We must prove that R can be decomposed as in (16). From $r_{ij}\in[0,1]\,\forall\, i, k$ and $I_n\leq R$ it follows that $\sum_{k=1}^5 c_k=1$ with $c_k\in[0,1]\,\forall\, k$. If we can choose the c_k's to satisfy these constraints and equations (19), then $R=R^{\mathrm{T}}$ guarantees that $R=\sum_{k=1}^5 c_kR_k$ with $R_k\in\text{conv}(\mathscr{R}_3)$ as exhibited at (16).

For c_2, c_3, and c_4 to be non-negative it is necessary from (19b), (19c), and (19d) that c_5

$\leqq 1+y_i-(y_j+y_k)$: for c_1 to be non-negative, that $c_5 \geqq 1-(y_1+y_2+y_3)$. Thus

$$1-(y_1+y_2+y_3) \leqq c_5 \leqq (1+y_2)-(y_j+y_k)\ \forall i, j, k \text{ distinct.} \tag{20}$$

But $R \in \mathscr{R}_\triangle \Rightarrow (1+y_i)-(y_j+y_k) \geqq 0\ \forall i, j, k$ distinct, so we can *always* choose convex coefficients as follows: assuming without loss that $y_3 = y_1 \wedge y_2 \wedge y_3$, we choose

$$c_1 = y_3 \qquad \text{(largest possible } c_1\text{)} \tag{21a}$$

$$c_2 = y_1 - y_3 \qquad \text{(least possible } c_2\text{)} \tag{21b}$$

$$c_3 = y_2 - y_3 \qquad \text{(least possible } c_3\text{)} \tag{21c}$$

$$c_4 = 0 \qquad \text{(least possible } c_4\text{)} \tag{21d}$$

$$c_5 = (1+y_3)-(y_1+y_2) \qquad \text{(largest possible } c_5\text{)} \tag{21e}$$

For this choice of c_k's we have a convex decomposition of R, so

$$\mathscr{R}_\triangle \subseteq \text{conv}(\mathscr{R}_3). \square$$

Before proceeding to the general case, we elaborate the possibilities for all convex decompositions with $n=3$. First, the coefficients (21) can always be chosen, yielding the largest c_1 and c_5 with least c_2, c_3, c_4. There are several cases for coefficients, depending on the relationship of $(y_1+y_2+y_3)$ to 1: again assuming $y_3 = y_1 \wedge y_2 \wedge y_3$, we find using the constraints $0 \leqq c_i \leqq 1\ \forall i$, that

Case 1. If $y_1+y_2+y_3 \geqq 1$, then $c_5 = 0$ and $c_1 = 1/2((y_1+y_2+y_3)-1)$ are minimum, while c_2, c_3, c_4 from equations (21) become largest.

Case 2. If $y_1+y_2+y_3 \leqq 1$, then $c_5 = 1-(y_1+y_2+y_3)$ and $c_1 = 0$ are minimum, whereas $c_2 = y_1$, $c_3 = y_2$, $c_4 = y_3$ are again largest.

Case 3. If $1+y_3 = y_1+y_2$, $c_5 = 0$, and the decomposition (16) is unique.

Case 4. If $y_3 = 0$, $y_1+y_2 \leqq 1$, then $c_5 = 1-(y_1+y_2)$, and the decomposition (16) is unique.

For $n>3$ we find that max-$\triangle$ transitivity is necessary but not sufficient for R to be in conv($\mathscr{R}_n$). If $\subset$ indicates *proper* subset, we have

Theorem 4.2. *For* $n>3$,

$$\text{conv}(\mathscr{R}_n) \subset \mathscr{R}_\triangle.$$

Proof. Let $R \in \text{conv}(\mathscr{R}_n)$, say $R = \sum_{k=1}^{p} c_k R_k$ with $\sum_{k=1}^{p} c_k = 1$; $0 \leqq c_k \leqq 1\ \forall k$, and each $R_k \in \mathscr{R}_n$. Let R_{ijk} be any 3×3 principal submatrix of R, i.e.,

$$R = \begin{bmatrix} 1 & & & \\ & \begin{bmatrix} 1 & y_i & y_j \\ & 1 & y_k \\ & & 1 \end{bmatrix} = R_{ijk} & & \\ & & \ddots & \\ & & & 1 \end{bmatrix}.$$

The decomposition of R also effects a convex decomposition of $R_{ijk} \in \text{conv}(\mathscr{R}_3) = \mathscr{R}_\triangle$ by

Theorem 4.1. Thus $1+y_i \geqq y_j + y_k \forall i, j, k$ distinct and for every principal (3×3) submatrix in R. Therefore $R \in \mathscr{R}_{\triangle} \forall n$.

To see that (22) is *proper* for $n>3$, we note that the matrix

$$R(\beta)=\begin{bmatrix} 1 & 0.3 & 0.6 & 0 \\ & 1 & 0.7 & 0 \\ & & 1 & \beta \\ & & & 1 \end{bmatrix}; \qquad \beta \in [0,1],$$

is in $\mathrm{conv}(\mathscr{R}_4) \Leftrightarrow \beta = 0$, but lies in $\mathscr{R}_{\triangle}$ for all $\beta \in [0, 0.30]$. □

To place $\mathrm{conv}(\mathscr{R}_n)$ in the hierarchy (12), we note that Zadeh exhibits in [1] a nested, non-convex decomposition of every $R \in \mathscr{R}_{\wedge}$ by hard relations in $\mathscr{R}_n$, viz., $R = \bigcup_k d_k R_k$, with $0 < d_k \leqq 1$, $R_1 \leqq R_2 \leqq \ldots \forall k$. Defining $c_{k+1} = d_{k+1} - d_k$, $k = 0, 1, 2, \ldots$ and replacing $\bigcup_k$ by $\sum_k$ yields convex decomposition $R = \sum_k c_k R_k$, hence we have

Theorem 4.3. *For* $n>2$

$$\mathscr{R}_{\wedge} \subset \mathrm{conv}(\mathscr{R}_n). \tag{23}$$

To see that containment in (23) is proper for $n>2$, recall that $R(\lambda)$ at (13) lies in $\mathscr{R}_{\wedge} \Leftrightarrow \lambda = 0.7$, whereas $R(\lambda) \in \mathscr{R}_{\triangle}$ for $\lambda \in [0.5, 0.9]$, and by Theorem 4.1 $\mathscr{R}_{\triangle} = \mathrm{conv}(\mathscr{R}_3)$. Accordingly, the placement of $\mathrm{conv}(\mathscr{R}_n)$ in (12) is

$$\mathscr{R}_{\wedge} \subset \mathrm{conv}(\mathscr{R}_n) \subset \mathscr{R}_{\triangle} \forall n > 3. \tag{24}$$

The position of $\mathrm{conv}(\mathscr{R}_n)$ with respect to $\mathscr{R}_{\bullet}$—not yet known—seems relatively unimportant, since the sets exhibited in (24) are the ones most useful in the applications.

Theorems 3.1, 4.1, and 4.3 combine to exhibit a rather interesting inter-relationship between the triangle inequality, max-△ transitivity, and convexity. Before proceeding we summarize the relationships between $\mathscr{R}_n$, $\mathscr{R}_{\wedge}$, $(\mathrm{conv}(\mathscr{R}_n)$, and $\mathscr{R}_{\triangle})$:

If $n=1: \mathscr{R}_n = \mathscr{R}_{\wedge} = \mathrm{conv}(\mathscr{R}_n) = \mathscr{R}_{\triangle}$,
If $n=2: \mathscr{R}_n \subset \mathscr{R}_{\wedge} = \mathrm{conv}(\mathscr{R}_n) = \mathscr{R}_{\triangle}$,
If $n=3: \mathscr{R}_n \subset \mathscr{R}_{\wedge} \subset \mathrm{conv}(\mathscr{R}_n) = \mathscr{R}_{\triangle}$,
If $n>3: \mathscr{R}_n \subset \mathscr{R}_{\wedge} \subset \mathrm{conv}(\mathscr{R}_n) \subset \mathscr{R}_{\triangle}$.

In each case, the proper imbeddings are *nowhere dense* in the indicated superset, illustrating how sparse each set of similarity relations is in the next larger set for $n>3$.

5. Clustering by convex decomposition

At present the only clustering procedure based on fuzzy relations appears to be the one described in [1–4]. A concise summary of this method follows: beginning with a reflexive, symmetric fuzzy relation matrix R, its *transitive closure* $\bar{R}$ is obtained by any of three algorithms: $(\vee . \wedge)$ composition iteration, $R \leqq R^2 \leqq R^3 \ldots \leqq R^q = \bar{R} = R^k \in \mathscr{R}_{\wedge} \forall k \geqq q \leqq n-1$, Zadeh [1], or Tamura *et al.* [2]; a column-row scanning algorithm, Kandel and Yelowitz [3]; or Prim's minimal spanning tree algorithm, Dunn [4].

Once $\bar{R}$ is obtained, its entries are used to define a nested sequence of hard relations $R_{ij} \in \mathscr{R}_n$ by thresholding at levels in-between successive values of $\bar{r}_{ij}$. Thus one might have from the entry $\bar{r}_{ij}$ the hard relation $x_p R_{ij} x_q \Leftrightarrow \bar{r}_{pq} \geqq \bar{r}_{ij} \forall p, q$. In this fashion one may construct a nested sequence of hard equivalence relations (therefore hard c-partitions of X) in $X \times X$, which ultimately yield a partition tree or dendogram. While this method appeared at first to be quite novel, it was shown by Dunn in [4] that because max–min transitivity is equivalent to the ultra-metric inequality, the resultant hierarchies of hard clusters were in fact a subset of *single-linkage* hierarchies, from a well known graph-theoretic method for hard clustering [5]. Thus, no apparent advantage was gained, and further, the density of $\mathscr{R}_\wedge$ in $\mathscr{R}_\triangle$ is so slight that hierarchies generated this way are severely limited.

As an alternative, if $R \in \text{conv}(\mathscr{R}_n)$, we can use its convex decomposition for clustering as follows: suppose $R = \sum_{k=1}^{p} c_k R_k$. Each $R_k \in \mathscr{R}_n$ is isomorphic to a hard c-partition of X, say $U_k \in \mathscr{P}_c$. Note that c, the number of clusters in X, is in general a function of k, so there will be no hope that $\sum_{k=1}^{p} c_k U_k$ is well-defined, although when it is, the resultant U lies in $\mathscr{P}_{fc}$. Thus from $R = \sum_{k=1}^{p} c_k R_k$ there follows the sequence

$$\left\{(c_k, U_k) \middle| U_k \in \mathscr{P}_c \,\forall 1 \leqq k \leqq p;\ \sum_{k=1}^{p} c_k = 1\right\}.$$

Since the decomposition $\sum c_k R_k$ exhibits the "percentage" of each R_k needed to build up fuzzy relation R, we interpret c_k as an indicator of the relative merit of the associated U_k as a c-partitioning of X. Note that this also provides a method for choosing c, the number of clusters most likely to exhibit substructure in X; and finally, observe that the partitions $\{U_k\}$ generated this way are *not* nested hierarchically. We exemplify both methods using the matrix $R(\beta)$ appearing above with $\beta = 0$.

Example.

$$R = \begin{bmatrix} 1 & 0.3 & 0.6 & 0 \\ & 1 & 0.7 & 0 \\ & & 1 & 0 \\ & & & 1 \end{bmatrix} \tag{25}$$

Composing R with itself using $\circ = (\vee \,.\, \wedge)$, we find

$$R^2 = \begin{bmatrix} 1 & 0.6 & 0.6 & 0 \\ & 1 & 0.7 & 0 \\ & & 1 & 0 \\ & & & 1 \end{bmatrix}; \quad R^3 = \begin{bmatrix} 1 & 0.6 & 0.6 & 0 \\ & 1 & 0.7 & 0 \\ & & 1 & 0 \\ & & & 1 \end{bmatrix} = R^2 = \bar{R}.$$

Hence the transitive closure of R is $\bar{R} = R^2 = R^3 \ldots$. A typical hierarchy of hard clusters derived from $\bar{R}$ using the $\bar{r}_{ij}$'s as thresholds is

$$\begin{pmatrix} x_i\, R_{0.59}\, x_j \Leftrightarrow \bar{r}_{ij} \geqq 0.59 \Rightarrow \{1,2,3\} \cup \{4\} \\ x_i\, R_{0.65}\, x_j \Leftrightarrow \bar{r}_{ij} \geqq 0.65 \Rightarrow \{1\} \cup \{2,3\} \cup \{4\} \\ x_2\, R_{0.71}\, x_j \Leftrightarrow \bar{r}_{ij} \geqq 0.71 \Rightarrow \{1\} \cup \{2\} \cup \{3\} \cup \{4\} \end{pmatrix} \tag{26}$$

In (26) we represent hard partition

$$\begin{bmatrix} 1 & 1 & 1 & 0 \\ 0 & 0 & 0 & 1 \end{bmatrix}$$

more compactly, for example, as $\{1, 2, 3\} \cup \{4\}$, etc. Another way to represent (26) is by a dendogram, as in Fig. 3 below.

If we define $v(c)$, $c = 2, 3, 4$, as the *jump in relation strength* between levels of clusters, we find that $v(2) = 0.6$; $v(3) = 0.10$; and $v(4) = 0.30$. One commonly assumes that the order of the values $\{v(c)\}$ indicates the relative attractiveness of choices for c: in the present instance we infer from (26) that single-linkage hierarchies will manifest a strong

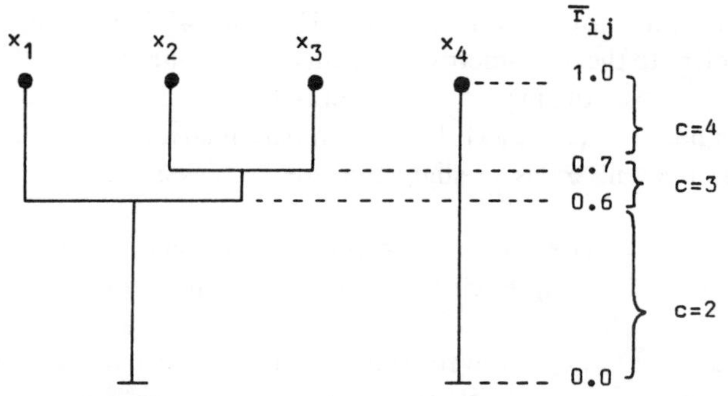

Fig. 3. Dendogram for clustering by transitive closure.

preference for $c=2$, $\{1,2,3\} \cup \{4\}$; and for a second choice, $c=4$, $\{1\} \cup \{2\} \cup \{3\} \cup \{4\}$. Returning to (25), we agree that $\{x_4\}$ should always be isolated from $\{x_1, x_2, x_3\}$, but whether total segregation ($c=4$) is preferable to 3-partitions of X on the basis of the relationships shown in R is questionable.

Because column 4 of R is special, R in (25) has the unique convex decomposition

$$R = 0.3\underbrace{\begin{bmatrix} 1 & 1 & 1 & 0 \\ & 1 & 1 & 0 \\ & & 1 & 0 \\ & & & 1 \end{bmatrix}}_{R_1} + 0.4\underbrace{\begin{bmatrix} 1 & 0 & 0 & 0 \\ & 1 & 1 & 0 \\ & & 1 & 0 \\ & & & 1 \end{bmatrix}}_{R_2} + 0.3\underbrace{\begin{bmatrix} 1 & 0 & 1 & 0 \\ & 1 & 0 & 0 \\ & & 1 & 0 \\ & & & 1 \end{bmatrix}}_{R_3}. \tag{27}$$

From (27) we obtain the sequence of clusterings

$$\begin{pmatrix} c_1 = 0.3; & c=2; & \{1,2,3\} \cup 4 \\ c_2 = 0.4; & c=3; & \{1\} \cup \{2,3\} \cup \{4\} \\ c_3 = 0.3; & c=3; & \{1,3\} \cup \{2\} \cup \{4\} \end{pmatrix}. \tag{28}$$

System (28) conveys a strikingly different portrait of substructure in X suggested by R than (26). From (28) and $c_2 = 0.4$ we infer that $c=3$; $\{1\} \cup \{2,3\} \cup \{4\}$ is the optimal clustering of X; and that $c=2$ or 3 with $c_2 = c_3 = 0.3$ are equally likely as second choices. Note that the clusters obtained in this way *never* admit $c=4$, a fact we find more consistent with our intuitive understanding of relationships in R. Moreover, the closeness of c_1, c_2, and c_3 indicates that R is fuzzier than the tree in Fig. 3 might imply.

A precise characterization of conv$(\mathscr{R}_n)$ is needed to make this technique applicable in general; Theorem 4.2 shows that max-$\triangle$ transitivity is necessary but not sufficient. Furthermore, an efficient algorithm, such as those described for convex decomposition of $U \in \mathscr{P}_{fc}$ in [6] has yet to be found. Nonetheless, our example seems to justify further efforts in this direction.

6. A connection between $\mathscr{P}_{fc}$ and $\mathscr{R}_\triangle$

As noted above, it is not generally possible to recover a $U \in \mathscr{P}_{fc} = \text{conv}(\mathscr{P}_{co})$ from an $R \in \text{conv}(\mathscr{R}_n)$. The difficulty lies with degeneracy in $\mathscr{P}_{co}$. In other words, the diagram in Fig. 4 is impossible (conv$(\mathscr{P}_{c0})$ cannot be isomorphic to conv$(\mathscr{R}_n)$).
Nonetheless, there is a mapping from $\mathscr{P}_{fc} \to \mathscr{R}_\triangle$ which provides a very nice method for deducing individual relationships in $X \times X$ from class membership in $U \in \mathscr{P}_{fc}$. To begin, we define the mapping $T_\circ : \mathscr{P}_{fc} \to V_{nn}$ by

$$T(U) = U^{\mathrm{T}} \circ U: \qquad (\circ) = \text{matrix multiplication as in (4).} \tag{29}$$

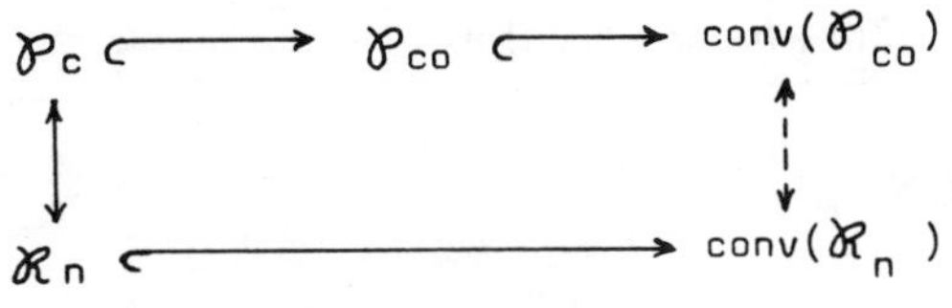

Fig. 4.

First, we prove that $T_\circ[\mathscr{P}_c]$, the image of hard c-partition space in V_{cn}, lies in hard equivalence relation space in V_{nn}:

Theorem 6.1. *For $T_\circ(U)$ defined in (29), we have for every $c=1,2,3,\ldots n$ with n fixed.*

$$T_\circ[\mathscr{P}_c]\subset\mathscr{R}_n. \tag{30}$$

Proof. Let $\sim$ denote the equivalence relation in $X\times X$ induced by $U\in\mathscr{P}_c$. Thus $x_i\sim x_j\Leftrightarrow x_i$ and x_j are in the same subset of U in $\mathscr{P}_c$. We verify (30) for $(\circ)=(\sum_\bullet\wedge)$: the other products are similar. If $r_{ij}=\sum_{l=1}^{c}(u_{li}\wedge u_{lj})$, we have $\forall i,j$

$$r_{ij}=1\Leftrightarrow \quad (u_{li}\wedge u_{lj})=1 \quad \exists l,$$

$$\Leftrightarrow \quad u_{li}=u_{lj}=1 \quad \exists l,$$

$$\Leftrightarrow x_i\sim x_j.$$

Otherwise, $r_{ij}=0$. Thus $R=U^{\mathrm{T}}(\sum_\bullet\wedge)U$ is equivalence relation $\sim$.

Corollary. *For fixed $n\in\mathbf{N}$, we have*

$$\bigcup_{i=1}^{n} T_\circ[\mathscr{P}_i]=\mathscr{R}_n. \tag{31}$$

It is clear from (31) that $T_\circ$ is not usually invertible. In fact, one may throw any number of degenerate images $T_\circ[\mathscr{P}_{io}]$ into the union (31) without altering its size. All one can assert when passing from $\mathscr{R}_n$ back to $\mathscr{P}_{co}$ is that there is a largest c, $1\leqq c\leqq n$, so that some

$$U\in\mathscr{P}_c\overset{T}{\rightarrow}R\in\mathscr{R}_n.$$

It is interesting that among the class of maps specified in (29) *only one* carries fuzzy c-partitions into similarity relations:

Theorem 6.2. *For $\circ=(\sum_\bullet\wedge)$ we have for $c=1,2,\ldots,n$ and n fixed,*

$$T_{\sum_\bullet\wedge}[\mathscr{P}_{fc}]\subseteq\mathscr{R}_\triangle. \tag{32}$$

Proof. Let $U\in\mathscr{P}_{fc}$, first, we note from (3) that in general

$$r_{ij}=\mathop{\square}_{l=1}^{c}(u_{li}*u_{lj}) \qquad \forall i,j.$$

Considering any of the products (4), we find that $R=U^T(\square_\bullet *)U$ is not reflexive (that is, that $r_{ii}<1\ \forall i$) unless $\square_\bullet *=\sum_\bullet\wedge$. To verify that $U^T(\sum_\bullet\wedge)U\in\mathscr{R}_\triangle$, we rewrite r_{ij} using the identity $a \wedge b = 1/2(a+b-|a-b|)$: thus

$$r_{ij} = \sum_{l=1}^{c} (u_{li} \wedge u_{lj})$$

$$= \sum_{l=1}^{c} \{1/2(u_{li} + u_{lj} - |u_{li} - u_{lj}|)\}$$

$$r_{ij} = 1 - 1/2 \sum_{l=1}^{c} |u_{li} - u_{lj}|. \tag{33}$$

Now $u_{li} \in [0,1]\ \forall l$ and i, and since $\sum_{l=1}^{c} u_{li} = 1\ \forall i$, $\sum_{l=1}^{c} |u_{li} - u_{lj}| \in [0,2]$. Thus

(i) $0 \leqq r_{ij} \leqq 1\ \forall i, j$.
(ii) $r_{ii} = 1\ \forall i$ follows directly from (33).
(iii) $r_{ij} = r_{ji}\ \forall i \neq j$ because $u_{li} \wedge u_{lj} = u_{lj} \wedge u_{li}\ \forall i, j$.
(iv) Finally we check max-$\triangle$ transitivity: $\forall i, j, k$ we have

$$r_{ij} + r_{jk} - 1 \leqq r_{ik} \quad \Leftrightarrow$$

$$\sum_{l=1}^{c} \{(u_{li} \wedge u_{lj}) + (u_{lj} \wedge u_{lk}) - (u_{lj} \wedge u_{lj})\} \leqq \sum_{l=1}^{c} (u_{li} \wedge u_{lk}). \tag{34}$$

To verify (34) it suffices to see that for each term

$$(u_{li} \wedge u_{lj}) + (u_{lj} \wedge u_{lk}) - (u_{lj} \wedge u_{lj}) \leqq (u_{li} \wedge u_{lk}). \tag{35}$$

Let $a = u_{li}$, $b = u_{lk}$, and $c = u_{lj}$. Then (35) becomes $(a \wedge c) + (b \wedge c) - (a \wedge b) \leqq c$. Equivalently,

$$1/2\{(a+c-|a-c|) + (b+c-|b-c|) - (a+b-|a-b|)\} \leqq c \quad \Leftrightarrow$$

$$c + 1/2\{|a-b| - |a-c| - |b-c|\} \leqq c \quad \Leftrightarrow$$

$$1/2\{|a-b| - |a-c| - |b-c|\} \leqq 0 \quad \Leftrightarrow$$

$$-|a-b| + |a-c| + |b-c| \geqq 0 \quad \Leftrightarrow$$

$$|a-c| + |c-b| \geqq |a-b|. \tag{37}$$

Since (37) is just the triangle inequality $\forall$ real a, b, c, it follows that (34) holds, i.e. R is max-$\triangle$-transitive. □

Combining Theorems 3.1 and 6.2, we have a way to induce from every fuzzy c-partition of X a pseudo-metric on the data:

$$U \xrightarrow{T_{\Sigma,\wedge}} R = U^T(\textstyle\sum . \wedge)U \rightarrow d_{ij} = 1 - r_{ij}. \tag{38}$$

As an example, suppose we find from the clustering algorithm fuzzy ISODATA [9] that an optimal 3-partitioning of X is

$$U = \begin{array}{c} \begin{matrix} x_1 & x_2 & x_3 & x_4 & x_5 \end{matrix} \\ \begin{bmatrix} 0.3 & 0.9 & 0.85 & 0.10 & 0.11 \\ 0.5 & 0.05 & 0 & 0.25 & 0.78 \\ 0.2 & 0.05 & 0.15 & 0.65 & 0.11 \end{bmatrix} \end{array} \in \mathscr{P}_{f3}. \tag{39}$$

Aside from the information conveyed by (39) about the membership of each x_i in the 3 fuzzy clusters of X, one may wonder about individual relationships suggested by this partitioning. Applying $T_{\Sigma.\wedge}$ to U, we have the fuzzy similarity relation

$$T_{\Sigma.\wedge}(U)=U^T(\Sigma.\wedge)U=R=\begin{bmatrix} 1 & 0.40 & 0.45 & 0.55 & 0.72 \\ & 1 & 0.90 & 0.20 & 0.21 \\ & & 1 & 0.25 & 0.22. \\ & & & 1 & 0.44 \\ & & & & 1 \end{bmatrix} \tag{40}$$

From (40) we infer that x_2 and x_3 are most strongly related, $r_{23}=0.90$; that the bond between x_2 and x_4 is weakest, $r_{24}=0.20$. These conclusions seem corroborated by an application of intuition to the memberships exhibited in (39). Moreover, we have by Theorem 3.1 that

$$D=1-R=\begin{bmatrix} 0 & 0.60 & 0.55 & 0.45 & 0.18 \\ & 0 & 0.10 & 0.80 & 0.79 \\ & & 0 & 0.75 & 0.78 \\ & & & 0 & 0.56 \\ & & & & 0 \end{bmatrix} \tag{41}$$

is a pseudo-metric in $X \times X$ which ostensibly provides a natural measure of distance or dissimilarity in $X \times X$ induced by fuzzy partition (39).

Finally, note that we find in the proof of Theorem 6.2 a natural interpretation for the relation induced on $X \times X$ by $T_{\Sigma.\wedge}$. To discuss it, let $\|\cdot\|_1$ denote the l_1 norm of $\mathbf{y} \in \mathbf{R}^c$, viz., $\|\mathbf{y}\|_1 = \sum_{l=1}^{c} |y_l|$. Then if $\mathbf{U}^{(i)}$ denotes the ith column of $U \in \mathscr{P}_{fc}$, we have for r_{ij} the expression

$$r_{ij}=1-1/2\left(\sum_{l=1}^{c} |u_{li}-u_{lj}|\right)=1-1/2(\|\mathbf{U}^{(i)}-\mathbf{U}^{(j)}\|_1). \tag{42}$$

Thus the pseudo-metric induced on $X \times X$ by $U^T(\Sigma.\wedge)U$, $d_{ij}=1-r_{ij}$, is just half of the l_1 distance between membership columns of U:

$$d(x_i, x_j)=1/2(\|\mathbf{U}^{(i)}-\mathbf{U}^{(j)}\|_1). \tag{43}$$

In (43) it is evident why d is necessarily a pseudo-metric: $d_{ij}=0 \Leftrightarrow \mathbf{U}^{(i)}=\mathbf{U}^{(j)}$, but clearly this can happen when x_i and x_j may be distinct. Since $d_{ij}=0 \Leftrightarrow r_{ij}=1$, we have for $i \neq j$ that $x_i R x_j = 1 \Leftrightarrow x_i$ and x_j have identical *membership vectors* in the c fuzzy clusters of U. This is a very appealing generalization of the physical and mathematical meanings of $x_i R x_j = 1$ for $R \in \mathscr{R}_n$. Conversely, from (42) it follows that $r_{ij}=0$ for $i \neq j \Leftrightarrow \|\mathbf{U}^{(i)}-\mathbf{U}^{(j)}\|_1 = 2 \Leftrightarrow \mathbf{U}^{(i)}$ and $\mathbf{U}^{(j)}$ are *disjoint*: wherever x_i has membership in a fuzzy cluster in U, x_j cannot, and vice-versa. This also extends the meaning of $x_i R x_j = 0$ for $R \in \mathscr{R}_n$ quite naturally.

7. Conclusions

Our imbedding of hard equivalence relations yields a new type of transitivity with very interesting properties. Max-$\triangle$ transitivity is equivalent to the triangle inequality, and is necessary for fuzzy similarity relations admitting a convex decomposition by equivalence relations. Furthermore, each similarity relation of this type induces a pseudo-metric in $X \times X$. For relations constructed from fuzzy c-partitions of X via $U^T(\sum.\wedge)U$, this pseudo-metric is half of the l_1 distance between membership vectors (for points in the data) for the fuzzy partition used. Examples of applications to cluster analysis and cluster validity seem to support our contention that the space of similarity relations characterized by max-$\triangle$ transitivity is an important one for applications in pattern recognition. A complete characterization of the convex hull of hard equivalence relation space together with an implementable decomposition algorithm will provide a new clustering method based on fuzzy similarity relations which seems to hold great promise: we hope to make this the subject of a future investigation.

References

[1] L.A. Zadeh, Similarity relations and fuzzy orderings, Inf. Sci. 3 (1971) 177–200.
[2] S. Tamura, S. Higuchi and K. Tanaka, Pattern classification based on fuzzy relations, IEEE Trans. SMC (1971) 61–66.
[3] A. Kandel and L. Yelowitz, Fuzzy chains, IEEE Trans. SMC (1971) 61–66.
[4] J. Dunn, A graph theoretic analysis of pattern classification via Tamura's fuzzy relation, IEEE Trans. SMC (1974) 310–313.
[5] R. Duda and P. Hart, Pattern Classification and Scene Analysis (Wiley-Interscience, New York, 1973).
[6] J. Bezdek and D. Harris, Convex decompositions of fuzzy partitions (in review) Inf. Sci. (1977).
[7] A. Rosenfeld, Fuzzy graphs, in: L.A. Zadeh et al., eds., Fuzzy Sets and their Applications to Cognitive and Decision Processes (Academic Press, New York, 1975) 77–96.
[8] R. Yeh and S. Bang, Fuzzy relations, fuzzy graphs, and their applications to clustering analysis, in: L.A. Zadeh et al., eds., Fuzzy Sets and Their Applications to Cognitive and Decision Processes (Academic Press, New York, 1975) 125–170.
[9] J. Bezdek, Mathematical models for systematics and taxonomy, in: G. Estabrock, ed., Proc. Eighth Int. Conf. Numerical Taxonomy (Freeman, SF, 1975) 143–166.
[10] R. Crowson, Classification and Biology (Atherton Press, New York, 1970).
[11] L.A. Zadeh, Fuzzy sets, Inf. Cont. (1965) 338–353.
[12] E. Ruspini, A new approach to clustering, Inf. Cont. (1969) 22–32.
[13] M. Woodbury and J. Clive, Clinical pure types as a fuzzy partition, J. Cybernetics (1974) 111–121.

Cluster Validity for the Fuzzy c-Means Clustering Algorithm

MICHAEL P. WINDHAM

Abstract—The uniform data function is a function which assigns to the output of the fuzzy c-means (Fc-M) or fuzzy isodata algorithm a number which measures the quality or validity of the clustering produced by the algorithm.

For the preselected number of cluster c, the Fc-M algorithm produces c vectors in the space in which the data lie, called cluster centers, which represent points about which the data are concentrated. It also produces for each data point c-membership values, numbers between zero and one which measure the similarity of the data points to each of the cluster centers. It is these membership values which indicate how the point is classified. They also indicate how well the point has been classified, in that values close to one indicate that the point is close to a particular center, but uniformly low memberships indicate that the point has not been classified clearly. The uniform data functional (UDF) combines the memberships in such a way as to indicate how well the data have been classified and is computed as follows. For each data point compute the ratio of its smallest membership to its largest and then compute the probability that one could obtain a smaller ratio (indicating better classification) from a clustering of a standard data set in which there is no cluster structure. These probabilities are then averaged over the data set to obtain the values of the UDF. By constructing the functional in this way one obtains a measure which is insensitive to parameters used to initialize and implement the Fc-M algorithm and respond only to differences in the quality of the clustering produced by the algorithm.

Index Terms—Cluster validity functional, fuzzy clustering algorithms, fuzzy c-means (Fc-M), fuzzy sets, uniform data functional (UDF).

I. Introduction

FUZZY CLUSTERING algorithms are mathematical tools for detecting similarities between members of a collection of objects. Perhaps the best known and most widely used member of the family is the fuzzy isodata or fuzzy c-means (Fc-M) algorithm developed by Dunn [1] and extended by Bezdek [2]. Information about the objects to be analyzed is input to the algorithm in the form of d-dimensional vectors. The vector used to represent a particular object has as its components the measurements of d features of the object which have been chosen as a basis for comparing it to other objects. The output of the algorithm can then be used to classify the data into subsets or clusters. Data vectors assigned to the same cluster are in some sense similar to each other, more so than they are to other data vectors not assigned to that cluster.

The primary concern with the use of this algorithm, as with any clustering algorithm, is how well has it identified the structure that is present in the data. This is the "cluster validity problem." We define here a function, the *uniform data functional* (UDF), which assigns to the output of the Fc-M algorithm a number, which measures the effectiveness with which the cluster structure has been properly identified, and show how it can be used to obtain the best clustering of the data.

Manuscript received April 9, 1981; revised January 11, 1982.

The author is with the Department of Mathematics, Utah State University, Logan, UT 84322.

II. Fuzzy Clustering Algorithms

We begin by describing what a fuzzy clustering is and how it is obtained using the Fc-M algorithm. A fuzzy clustering is best understood by contrasting it with the more common hard clustering of a data set. Let $X = \{x_1, \cdots, x_n\}$ be a set of n vectors in R^d, representing the data. For an integer $c \geqslant 2$, a *hard clustering* of X into c clusters consists of c disjoint subsets of X, $S_1, \cdots, S_c$ whose union is X. For example, if the data set consists of the measurement of d features of n flowers of the same species, a cluster S_i might contain those flowers of the same subspecies. Such a situation is considered in the examples presented below. An equivalent way of defining the clusters is obtained using functions. Namely, for each $i = 1, \cdots, c$ define u_i: $X \rightarrow \{0, 1\}$ by $u_i(x) = 1$ if $x \in S_i$ and $u_i(x) = 0$ if $x \notin S_i$. These functions are called membership functions, since they describe in which cluster each data point belongs. The hard clustering could then be described by these membership functions. A fuzzy clustering is a generalization of this point of view.

A *fuzzy clustering* of X into c clusters consist of functions $u_1, \cdots, u_c$ where u_i: $X \rightarrow [0, 1]$ and $\Sigma_i u_i(x) = 1$, for all $x \in X$. These functions are also called *membership functions*; however, they do not define subsets in the usual sense, but are, in fact, examples of fuzzy set as introduced by Zadeh [3]. The value of a fuzzy membership function can be any number between 0 and 1, and is meant to be a mathematical characterization of a "set" which may not be precisely defined. For example, consider the set of all people almost six feet tall. How does one determine membership in this set? Certainly, a person whose height is 5 ft 8 in would be more likely to be included in the set than a person who is only 5 ft tall. Zadeh proposed that rather than describe the set by its membership to describe it by a membership function, but allow the function to have values strictly between 0 and 1, if necessary, to indicate ambiguity which might be present in the concept which the set is to represent. So, the person who is 5 ft 8 in might be assigned a membership of 0.8 in the "set" of people almost 6 ft tall, whereas the 5 ft tall person might have a membership of 0.3.

Reprinted from *IEEE Trans. Pattern Anal. Machine Intell.*, vol. PAMI-4, no. 4, pp. 357-363, July 1982.

So, the "clusters" of a fuzzy clustering are the membership functions themselves. They indicate the substructure of the data in the following sense. If two data points have membership values close to one for the same membership function than they are to be considered similar to each other. The condition $\Sigma_i u_i = 1$ corresponds to the membership of each data point in X. One can use a fuzzy clustering as the basis for a hard clustering by defining for $i = 1, \cdots, c$, $S_i = \{x \in X: u_i(x) \geqslant u_j(x) \text{ for } j = 1, \cdots, c\}$. It should be noted that these sets may not be disjoint. If a data point attains its maximum membership with more than one membership function it will be in more than one of these sets. Moreover, this "hard" clustering does not provide as much information about the structure in the data set as does the fuzzy clustering. Although two points may have their maximum membership for the same membership function, if one has a higher membership than the other, it is better classified by the clustering.

III. The Fuzzy c-Means Algorithm

The Fc-M algorithm is designed to produce a fuzzy clustering of a data set. Again, the Fc-M algorithm is best understood by contrasting it with an algorithm designed to produce hard clusters, the classical c-means algorithm. For a given integer $c \geqslant 2$, this algorithm chooses subsets $S_1, \cdots, S_c$ of the data set X, which minimize

$$\Sigma_i \Sigma_{x \in S_i} |x - v_i|^2$$

where $v_i \in R^d$ is the mean of the data vectors in S_i and $|x|$ denotes the Euclidean norm of a vector x, $(\Sigma_j x_j^2)^{1/2}$. In other words, it chooses the clusters to minimize the distances of the points in the clusters to the "center" of the cluster as represented by the mean. The assumption that is made in using this algorithm is that similarity between objects is measured by the distance between their corresponding data vectors. So, if the distances to the mean of a cluster are small the points in the cluster are also close to each other

The Fc-M algorithm produces a fuzzy clustering in much the same way. For $c \geqslant 2$ and m any real number greater than 1, the algorithm chooses u_i: $X \rightarrow [0, 1]$ so that $\Sigma_i u_i = 1$ and $v_i \in R^d$ for $i = 1, \cdots, c$ to minimize the objective function

$$\Sigma_i \Sigma_k (u_{ik})^m \, |x_k - v_i|^2$$

where u_{ik} is the value of the ith membership function on the kth data point x_k. Here again, the assumption is made that similarity of objects is measured by distance between data vectors. The vectors $v_1, \cdots, v_c$ can be interpreted as prototypes for the clusters represented by the membership functions, and are called *cluster centers*. In order to minimize the objective function, the cluster centers and membership functions are chosen so that high memberships occur for points close to the corresponding cluster centers. The number m is called the *exponent weight*. It can be chosen to "tune out" noise in the data. The higher the value of m used, the less those data points whose memberships are uniformly low contribute to the objective function. Consequently, such points tend to be ignored in determining the centers and membership functions.

The actual construction of the Fc-M algorithm is based on the following set of equations which are a necessary condition for $u_1, \cdots, u_c$ and $v_1, \cdots, v_c$ to produce a local minimum:

$$v_i = \Sigma_k (u_{ik})^m \, x_k / \Sigma_k (u_{ik})^m \tag{1}$$

$$u_{ik} = (1/|x_k - v_i|^2)^{1/(m-1)} / \Sigma_j (1/|x_k - v_j|^2)^{1/(m-1)}. \tag{2}$$

The necessity is obtained by differentiating the objective function with respect to the components of v_i and u_{ik} for $i = 1, \cdots, c$ and $k = 1, \cdots, n$ subject to the constraint that $\Sigma_i u_{ik} = 1$. If these equations could be solved in closed form, the solution would provide the fuzzy clustering directly. However, no closed form solution has been found, but these equations are the basis for an iterative procedure which converges to a local minimum for the objective function. One chooses a value for c and m and a $c \times n$ matrix U which is an initial guess for the values of the memberships. Using these memberships and (1), one computes cluster centers, then using these cluster centers and (2) recomputes memberships and so forth, iterating back and forth between (1) and (2) until the memberships or cluster centers for successive iteration differ by more than some prescribed value. That this will occur for at least a subsequence of the iterations and that the result will provide approximately a local minimum for the object function has been shown by Bezdek [4]. This iterative procedure is the Fc-M algorithm.

IV. Cluster Validity

A *validity functional* is a function which assigns to the output of Fc-M a number which is intended to measure the quality of the clustering provided by the output. By evaluating the functional on the output for a variety of choices of c and m, one hopes to be able to determine the values of these parameters for which the corresponding clustering best identifies the structure in the data.

The quality of a clustering is indicated by how closely the data points are associated to the cluster centers, and it is the membership functions which measure the level of association or classification. If the value of one of the memberships is significantly larger than the others for a particular data point, then that point is identified as being a part of the subset of the data represented by the corresponding cluster center. But, each data point has c memberships; so, it is desirable to summarize the information contained in the memberships by a single number which indicates how well the data point is classified by the clustering. This can be done in a variety of ways; for example, for the data point x_k with memberships $u_{ik}, \cdots, u_{ck}$, one could use any of the following:

$$\Sigma_i (u_{ik})^2$$

$$-\Sigma_i u_{ik} \log u_{ik}$$

$$\max_i u_{ik}$$

$$\min_i u_{ik} / \max_i u_{ik}.$$

In fact, the first three of these have been used as a measure of the quality of clustering and are the basis for the validity functionals *partition coefficient* [5], *classification entropy* [6], and *proportion exponent* [7], respectively.

To illustrate the use of a validity functional, we focus on the partition coefficient. It is based on using $s_k = \Sigma_i (u_{ik})^2$ as a measure of how well the kth data point has been classified. This is a reasonable indicator because the closer a data point is to a cluster center, the closer s_k is to 1, the maximum value it could have. Conversely, the further away the kth point is from all the cluster centers the closer the value of s_k is to $1/c$, the minimum possible value. The partition coefficient is then the average over the data set of the s_k's. In particular, for a data set $X = \{x_1, \cdots, x_k\}$ and a specific choice of c and m one obtains the output of Fc-M and computes the *partition coefficient* (PC) by $PC = \Sigma_k (\Sigma_i (u_{ik})^2)/n$. The closer this value is to one the better the data are classified. So, in theory, one computes PC for the outputs of a variety of values of c and m and selects the best clustering as the one corresponding to the highest partition coefficient.

In practice, however, this approach has not worked. The reason for this is that the values of PC are sensitive to the values of c and m independent of any structure in the data. This can be seen by comparing the partition coefficients for different clusterings of the data set pictured in Fig. 1. This is a two-dimensional set consisting of points uniformly distributed over the unit disk. This data set clearly does not have any substructure of the kind identified by Fc-M, but the values of PC vary significantly, as is indicated by Table I. This variation is due entirely to the values of the parameters. Consequently, one cannot select the best clustering by finding the highest partition coefficient.

The classification entropy, which averages $-\Sigma_i u_{ik} \log u_{ik}$ over the data suffers from the same kind of sensitivity to parameters. The proportion exponent attempted to overcome this difficulty by looking not at the values of the measure of quality directly, but by looking at how they compared to a standard. It was constructed using the $\max_i u_{ik}$. The higher the maximum is the better the point is classified. The maximum value itself was not used as an indicator of quality but rather the probability that one could do better by selecting memberships for the data at random. By obtaining such a probability for each of the data points and multiplying them together one obtains the probability that one could have produced a better clustering of the data by simply drawing the memberships "out of a hat." The lower the probability, the better the classification should be. The rationale behind this approach is that if the memberships are selected at random, this probability is expected to be $1/2^n$, no matter what values of c and m are involved. Unfortunately, this measure of validity also fails to be effective in practice. The reason for this is quite simple, in a data set in which there is no structure it is the data points which are randomly or uniformly distributed not the memberships. If one constructs a table of values of the proportion exponent for the data set in Fig. 1, the same kind of variation that occurs for the partition coefficient is present.

Although the proportion exponent failed to provide an effective validity functional, an appropriate modification of the procedure does produce, in theory at least, a functional which should not be sensitive to any of the parameters involved in the Fc-M algorithm. What is meant by a functional not being sensitive to parameters is precisely the following. If one applies the Fc-M algorithm to a data set in which there are no clusters, then computes the value of the validity functional on the output, this value is the same no matter what values of c and m were used. If this functional is then used on any other data set, any deviation of its value away from the constant obtained above would of necessity be due to cluster structure in the data. Furthermore, the amount of deviation should indicate the quality of the clustering. Before attempting to construct a functional it is worthwhile to ask if there is a data set with which to test it. In other words, is there a data set in which there is no cluster structure. The identification of this data set is, in fact, the first step in the construction of the UDF.

A data set in which there is no cluster substructure is one which consists of exactly one cluster of uniformly distributed points. Furthermore, since the Fc-M algorithm tends to identify spherically shaped clusters the entire data set should be spherically shaped. The natural set to choose, then, would be $B^d = \{x \in R^d: |x| \leqslant 1\}$, the unit ball. Of course, this set is infinite and the Fc-M algorithm cannot be used with it. Rather than give up B^d, we construct an extension of the algorithm which can be used for infinite sets. Namely, by an *Fc-M clustering of* B^d, we mean vectors $v_1, \cdots, v_c \in B^d$ and

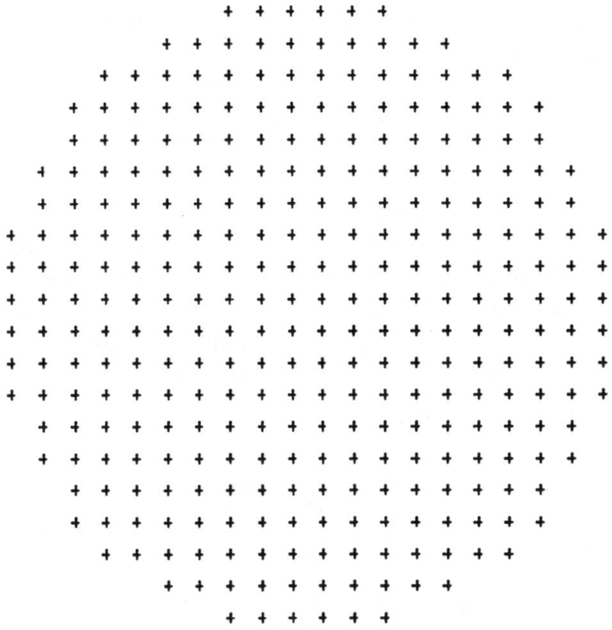

Fig. 1. Two-dimensional uniformly distributed data.

TABLE I
PARTITION COEFFICIENT FOR UNIFORM DATA

	Exponent Weight			
Clusters	1.5	2	3	4
2	.82	.68	.56	.53
3	.81	.61	.43	.37
4	.79	.56	.35	.29
5	.77	.53	.30	.23
6	.75	.49	.26	.20

functions u_i: $B^d \to [0, 1]$ for $i = 1, \cdots, c$ so that $\Sigma_i u_i = 1$ which minimize

$$\phi(v_1, \cdots, v_c, u_1, \cdots, u_c) = \int_{B^d} \Sigma_i (u_i(x))^m \, |x - v_i|^2 \, dx.$$

All we have done is replace summation over the data set in the objective function by integration over the set. Furthermore, by differentiating ϕ with respect to the components of $v_1, \cdots, v_c$ and taking variations with respect to $u_1, \cdots, u_c$ subject to the constraint that $\Sigma u_i = 1$, we obtain the following necessary condition for a local minimum. For $i = 1, \cdots, c$ and $j = 1, \cdots, d$

$$v_{ij} = \int_{B^d} (u_i(x))^m \, x_j dx \Big/ \int_{B^d} (u_i(x))^m \, dx \tag{3}$$

and

$$u_i(x) = (1/|x - v_i|^2)^{1/(m-1)} / \Sigma_j (1/|x - v_j|^2)^{1/m-1}. \tag{4}$$

These equations provide, in theory at least, an iterative procedure for obtaining a clustering of B^d and this procedure is what we mean by the extended Fc-M algorithm.

If such a clustering can be obtained for any choice of d, c, and m, then it can be used to construct a validity function which is not sensitive to these parameters. This can be done as follows. First select a measure of quality, for example, any of the four mentioned in the previous section, except that it should be constructed so that it decreases with increase in the quality of classification. So, one should use, for example, $1 - \Sigma_i (u_i(x))^2$ rather than $\Sigma_i (u_i(x))^2$. Then define ρ: $B^d \to R$ by $\rho(x)$ = the measure of quality of the classification of the point x. Next for each r in the range of ρ define $S_r \subset B^d$ by $S_r = \{x \in B^d: \rho(x) \leqslant r\}$. The set S_r then consists of all points in B^d which have a better quality of classification than the number r. Finally, define Φ: $R \to [0, 1]$ by

$$\Phi(r) = \text{volume of } S_r / \text{volume of } B^d.$$

The function Φ provides a measure of the degree of classification of a point in that $\Phi(\rho(x))$ is the proportion of the data set, B^d, which is better classified than x itself. This function also has the property that

$$\int_{B^d} \Phi(\rho(x)) \, dx \Big/ \text{volume of } B^d = \tfrac{1}{2}. \tag{5}$$

That is, the average value of $\Phi \cdot \rho$ over B^d is $\frac{1}{2}$ independent of the clustering obtained or the function ρ which is used. This fact can be seen easily as follows. Suppose we let X be a random vector with values in B^d which is uniformly distributed in B^d, then $R = \rho(X)$ is a random variable and $\Phi(r)$ is the probability that $R \leqslant r$. In other words, the function Φ we have defined is the cumulative distribution function of R. So the random variable $\Phi(R)$ is uniformly distributed on the interval $[0, 1]$ and has expected value $\frac{1}{2}$, but this expected value is also given by the expression on the left in (5).

We have, in fact, a family of functions Φ, one for each choice of ρ, c, m, and d. Using these functions we define a UDF as follows. If $X = \{x_1, \cdots, x_n\}$ is a set of d-dimensional vectors and U is a $c \times n$ matrix of memberships obtained by applying the Fc-M algorithm with parameters c and m, then

$$\text{UDF}(U) = \Sigma_k \Phi(\rho(x_k))/n$$

where ρ is a measure of classification and is the function obtained above for this ρ and the same values of c, m, and d. This is just the average over the data set of $\Phi \cdot \rho$ and, consequently, if the value of UDF is close to $\frac{1}{2}$ it can be inferred that the Fc-M has found no cluster structure in the data set. Furthermore, the UDF can be interpreted as the average of the probabilities that the data points would have been better clustered than they were had they been selected at random from the unit ball. Consequently, the closer the value of the UDF is to zero the better the clustering is.

As Dubes and Jains [8] have indicated an effective cluster validity analysis should be able to determine whether or not there is any structure in the data, that is, whether or not the data are random; and whether or not the clusters identified by the algorithm are "real," that is, whether they represent relationships among the data or artifacts of the mathematical procedure. The UDF certainly deals with the first problem in that it compares the clustering output for the data set with the clustering of a set with no structure. As to the second problem, the user has by choosing to use the Fc-M algorithm, determined mathematically what he means by a "real" cluster, in that the algorithm identifies compact, well-separated, spherically shaped clusters. The UDF cannot determine whether or not the Fc-M algorithm is the appropriate one to use, but does indicate how well the clusters meet the three criteria for being "real" as determined by the use of the algorithm. This is the case, because these three properties are all essentially functions of the relationships among distances of the data points to the cluster centers. These relationships are summarized in the membership functions which, in turn, are summarized in the UDF.

As we have previously stated this procedure, in theory at least, produces a validity functional which is not sensitive to parameters. The reason the phrase "in theory" must be used is that there are two difficult, if not impossible, steps in the construction of a working UDF. First, one must know all clusterings of the unit ball, namely, the solutions to (3) and (4). Next one must compute the volumes of the sets S_r. If the cluster centers are known then the membership functions are easy to obtain using (4). Also, although the computation of the volumes is greatly facilitated by the proper choice of ρ, the geometrical relationships among the centers are significant factors in being able to make these computations. So, everything hinges on being able to determine the cluster centers.

In the case $d = 2$, it is possible to guess at least the orientation of the centers. Because of the symmetry of the disk it is reasonable to expect that the centers would form the vertices a regular c-sided polygon centered at the origin. That this happens can be verified by clustering a data set such as the one in Fig. 1. In this case, all that remains is to determine the distance from a cluster center to the origin. Here again, approximation can be obtained empirically, but all that one finds is that this distance increases as c increases and decreases as m

increases. The exact relationship between these values is not known. For dimensions greater than 2, even the orientations of the centers is difficult to predict and empirical results are difficult to obtain. The data set in Fig. 1 contains 316 points; to approximate the three-dimensional ball with the same density requires 4224 points, for the four-dimensional ball, 49 648 points are required, so it rapidly becomes impractical to investigate empirically.

Until further information is obtained, the only way to construct a usable UDF is to assume the location of the cluster centers in a reasonable if not accurate way, then proceed with the remainder of the construction as described above. This is done as follows. For given $d \geqslant 2$ and $c \geqslant 2$ let for $k = 1, \cdots, c$, $v_k = D(\cos(2\pi k/c), \sin(2\pi k/c), 0, \cdots, 0)$ where

$$D = c \sin(\pi/c)\, \Gamma(d/2 + 1)/(2\pi^{1/2}\Gamma((d+1)/2 + 1).$$

These points are the centers of gravity of the c congruent sets

$$\Omega_k = \{(r\cos\Theta, r\sin\Theta, x_3, \cdots, x_d)\, B^d\colon\ 0 \leqslant r \leqslant 1 \text{ and } (2k-1)\,\pi/c \leqslant \Theta \leqslant (2k+1)\,\pi/c\}.$$

The case $d = 2$ is just a pie sliced into c equal pieces and for $d = 3$ these sets are analogous to the sections of an orange. The membership functions are then determined by (4) and all that remains is to choose ρ and describe the computation of the volumes of the sets S_r.

The function ρ is chosen to be $\rho(x) = \min_i u_i(x)/\max_i u_i(x)$.

First of all, the value $\rho(x) = |x - v_j|^{2/(m-1)}/|x - v_i|^{2/(m-1)}$ where the jth cluster center is the one closest to x and the ith center is the one furthest from x. Consequently, the closer x is to a cluster center the smaller the value of ρ is. Because of this and the symmetry in the location of the cluster centers, the volume of S_r is equal to c times the volume of the intersection of S_r with any one of the Ω_k's, in particular Ω_c. So, it suffices to consider the values of ρ on Ω_c and to compute the volume of $S_r \cap \Omega_c$. If c is even then for $x \in \Omega_c$ the cluster center closest to x is $v_c = (D, 0, \cdots, 0)$ and the one furthest from x is $v_* = (-D, 0, \cdots, 0)$. It follows from the nature of ρ that $S_r \cap \Omega_c$ is the intersection of Ω_c with a ball centered at $t(v_c - v_*) + v_c$ and radius $(t(t+1))^{1/2}|v_c - v_*|$ where $t = r^{m-1}/(1 - r^{m-1})$. If c is odd then for $x \in \Omega_c$ the closest center is, again, v_c, but the center furthest from x depends on which half of Ω_c x is in. That is, for $x = (r\cos\Theta, r\sin\Theta, x_3, \cdots, x_d)$, x is furthest from $v_{(c+1)/2}$ if $0 \leqslant \Theta \leqslant \pi/c$ and furthest from $v_{(c-1)/2}$ if $-\pi/c \leqslant \Theta \leqslant 0$. However, again because of symmetry, the volume of $S_r \cap \Omega_c$ is twice the volume of $S_r \cap \Omega_{c,+}$ where $\Omega_{c,+}$ is the set of points in Ω_c with $\Theta \geqslant 0$. Letting $v_* = v_{(c+1)/2}$, the set $S_r \cap \Omega_{c,+}$ is the intersection of $\Omega_{c,+}$ and a ball with the center and radius given above. So, the geometry of the sets S_r is such that their volume can be computed by integration. The necessary integration is tedious but possible, so the function Φ can be obtained and its computation implemented by a subroutine attached to the Fc-M algorithm program.

The uniform data functional can then be computed as described above:

$$\text{UDF} = \Sigma_k\, \Phi(\min_i u_{ik}/\max_i u_{ik})/n.$$

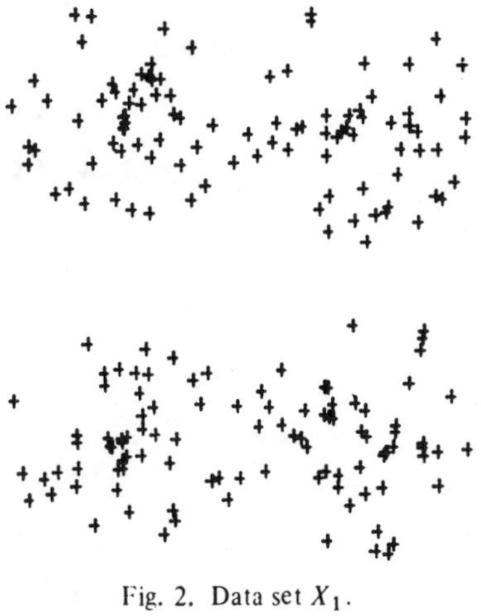

Fig. 2. Data set X_1.

However, it may be convenient and even necessary to transform the values of Φ before averaging. For example, if the values of Φ are spread over a wide range, roundoff error may produce inaccuracies in the average. One way to avoid this is to average the values of $-\log\Phi$ (using the natural logarithm). High values of the corresponding UDF indicate good clustering and one expects to see a value of one on an unstructured data set. It should be noted that if a data point coincides with a cluster center, this transformation is undefined since Φ has value zero.

So it is possible to construct a usable UDF based on the choice of centers given above. It is not the most desirable UDF, since it is not based on an actual fuzzy clustering of the standard data set, but it does provide a validity functional whose effectiveness is illustrated by the examples which follow.

V. Examples

Cluster validity functionals are often used to determine the number of clusters present in a data set. The Fc-M algorithm is applied for various values of c and the best clustering, as indicated by the value of the functional, serves to identify the number of clusters present. In order to illustrate the effectiveness of the UDF, we use it in this way to identify the number of clusters present in data sets where the answer is known.

The UDF was evaluated on clusterings of three data sets. Two of the data sets were artifically generated and the third is the famous Iris data of Anderson [9].

The first data set X_1 consists of the two-dimensional data pictured in Fig. 2. It was obtained by choosing 50 points at random in each of the disks of radius one centered at the points (2, 1), (2, -1), (-2, 1), and (-2, -1), respectively. As the figure indicates, it would be reasonable to expect that a clustering algorithm would identify the presence of four clusters. The second data set X_2 was obtained in exactly the same way, except that the radii of the disks were 1.5 rather than 1. As can be seen in Fig. 3, because of the overlap of the disks, this data set appears to have two clusters rather than four. Finally, the Iris data consists of 150 four-dimensional vectors. The components of a vector are the measurements of the petal length, petal width, sepal length, and sepal width of a particular Iris plant. There are 50 flowers in each of

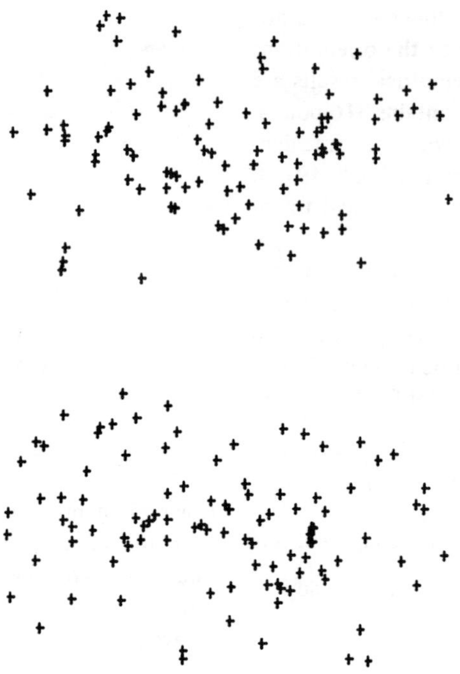

Fig. 3. Data set X_2.

TABLE II
UNIFORM DATA FUNCTIONAL AND PARTITION COEFFICIENT
(EXPONENT WEIGHT = 2)

Data set	X_1		X_2		Iris	
Clusters	PC	UDF	PC	UDF	PC	UDF
2	.87	2.4	.84	2.2	.89	7.4
3	.79	2.5	.74	2.0	.78	7.8
4	.80	2.8	.69	2.0	.70	7.2
5	.72	2.7	.63	2.0	.59	7.0
6	.66	2.6	.58	2.0	.44	6.8

three subspecies of Iris represented in the data, so it was assumed that an effective validity functional should indicate the presence of three clusters.

The results of the analysis are shown in Table II. The Fc-M was applied for the indicated values of c and m; and the UDF (using - log transformation) and the partition coefficient (PC) were evaluated for each of the outputs. Both of these functionals should indicate the best clustering by their highest value. As can be seen the UDF correctly identified the number of clusters in each case.

A closer examination of the values of the UDF for data set X_1 indicates results which appear to be counterintuitive. The UDF assumes its lowest value for two clusters, but the human observer may consider two clusters as a natural preference over three or perhaps even four clusters. In order to resolve this dilemma one must recall that the Fc-M algorithm tends to identify compact, well-separated, spherically shaped clusters, and the UDF measures how well this has been done. Although the two clusters are well-separated they are not compact, in that there are large concentrations of data away from the cluster center, and are not spherically shaped. So, the UDF has properly evaluated this clustering relative to all three criteria, but the preference of the human observer is influenced more by separation than by the density and shape of the individual clusters. So the dilemma has been produced by the choice of algorithms rather than the results obtained.

VI. SUMMARY

The uniform data functional is based on comparing the fuzzy clustering of a data set with an analogous clustering of a data set with no cluster substructure, in a way that is not sensitive to the parameters of the Fc-M algorithm. Consequently, variations in the value of the UDF are due to variations in the quality of the fuzzy clustering. Used in conjunction with Fc-M, it promises to make this fuzzy clustering algorithm an even more powerful tool for the analysis of data.

References

[1] J. C. Dunn, "A fuzzy relative of the ISODATA process and its use in detecting compact well-separated clusters," *J. Cybern.*, vol. 3, pp. 32–57, 1974.

[2] J. C. Bezdek, "Fuzzy mathematics in pattern classification," Ph.D. dissertation, Appl. Math., Cornell Univ., Ithaca, NY, 1973.

[3] L. A. Zadeh, "Fuzzy sets," *Inform. Contr.*, vol. 8, pp. 338–353, 1965.

[4] J. B. Bezdek, "A convergence theorem for the fuzzy ISODATA clustering algorithms," *IEEE Trans. Pattern Anal. Machine Intell.*, vol. PAMI-2, pp. 1–8, 1980.

[5] —, "Cluster validity with fuzzy sets," *J. Cybern.*, vol. 3, pp. 58–73, 1973.

[6] —, "Mathematical models for systematics and taxonomy," in *Proc. 8th Int. Conf. on Numerical Taxonomy*, G. Estabrook, Ed. San Francisco, CA: Freeman, 1975, pp. 143–166.

[7] M. P. Windham, "Cluster validity for fuzzy clustering algorithms," *Fuzzy Sets Syst.*, vol. 5, pp. 177–185, 1981.

[8] R. Dubes and A. Jain, "Validity studies in clustering methodologies," *Pattern Recognition*, vol. 11, pp. 235–253, 1979.

[9] E. Anderson, "The iris of the Gaspe peninsula," *Bull. Amer. Iris Soc.*, vol. 59, pp. 2–5, 1935.

A Clustering Performance Measure Based on Fuzzy Set Decomposition

ERIC BACKER, MEMBER, IEEE, AND ANIL K. JAIN, MEMBER, IEEE

Abstract—Clustering is primarily used to uncover the true underlying structure of a given data set and, for this purpose, it is desirable to subject the same data to several different clustering algorithms.

This paper attempts to put an order on the various partitions of a data set obtained from different clustering algorithms. The goodness of each partition is expressed by means of a performance measure based on a fuzzy set decomposition of the data set under consideration. Several experiments reported in here show that the proposed performance measure puts an order on different partitions of the same data which is consistent with the error rate of a classifier designed on the basis of the obtained cluster labelings.

Index Terms—Clustering performance measures, clustering tendency, clustering validity, fuzzy clustering.

I. INTRODUCTION

IN cluster analysis, a group of objects is split up into a number of more or less homogeneous subgroups on the basis of an often subjectively chosen measure of similarity, such that the similarity between objects within a subgroup is larger than the similarity between objects belonging to different subgroups. Both the diversity of clustering techniques and methods, and the number of different scientific disciplines in which they have been applied are striking [1], [2].

The subjective nature of the clustering problem precludes a realistic mathematical comparison of all clustering techniques [3]. Dubes and Jain [3] compared different clustering programs from several points of view. Their objective was not to choose a "best" clustering technique or program (such a task would be fruitless and contrary to the very nature of clustering) but rather to present the peculiarities of the techniques and programs, emphasizing those aspects most important to the user. Recently, Dubes and Jain [4] advocated the need and presented a framework for more rigorous and systematic research in the area of cluster validity.

In this paper we restrict ourselves to comparing different clustering programs by attempting to put an order on the performance of the partitions obtained from them. For this reason we introduce a performance measure which expresses the utility of each clustering result and enables us to rank the clustering results obtained from different clustering programs applied to the same database. In order to uncover the true structure of a data set, it should be presented to several different clustering algorithms. Thus, the performance measure which we propose can be used to rank various competing partitions of the given data set. However, it should be noted that we are not proposing a universal measure to evaluate clustering algorithms, neither that we are dealing with arbitrary data structures. Two additional questions related to cluster validity are not dealt here, namely,

1) whether a clustering algorithm should be applied at all (is the data random?) and

2) the adequacy of the structure imposed by the clustering technique (e.g., should a mean-squared error algorithm, which always generates hyperellipsoidal clusters, be used for the given data set?).

Irrespective of the program, the final result is usually given in the form of a collection of object-subsets (partition). In this context an object-subset is considered as a classical set which means that an object either belongs to the set or not. With respect to both the structural properties among objects in a certain representation space, and the way of assigning them to subsets, the above description of the group of objects is rather lacking in nuances. This justifies using the fuzzy set theory to achieve a much more nuanced and numerically interpretable description of object clusterings. In contrast to the classical set, an object can be assigned to a fuzzy set with a varying degree of membership from 0 up to and including 1. In [5], a clustering model is described which tries to achieve an optimal decomposition of the group of objects into a collection of fuzzy sets, where optimality does have a restrictive meaning in the sense that a performance measure based on the intersection of the induced collection of fuzzy sets is extremized.

Then a comparative analysis of different clustering results (partitions) simply means the following. Each clustering result induces its own collection of fuzzy sets and is (uniquely) characterized by the value of the performance measure. These values are to be ranked and consequently they put an order on the utility of the different clustering results.

However, the subjective nature of "utility" demands for a realistic goal-directed relationship to the application domain. Therefore, empirical evidence is given that the ranking of the values of the performance measure obtained from different clustering results fits with the ranking of the classification error rate of nearest-neighbor (NN) classifier. The NN classifier is designed on the basis of the obtained cluster labels for each of the clustering results considered and is tested with independent samples drawn from the same underlying distribution. Thus, when obtaining a set of design samples for a classifier is the stated goal of the clustering procedure, and obviously a direct measure like the classification error rate cannot be used as a measure of suitability, then the performance measure which has

Manuscript received September 18, 1978; revised May 8, 1979. The work of A. K. Jain was supported in part by the National Science Foundation under Grant 76-11936.

E. Backer is with the Information Theory Group, Delft University of Technology, Delft, The Netherlands.

A. K. Jain is with the Department of Computer Science, Michigan State University, East Lansing, MI 48823.

Reprinted from *IEEE Trans. Pattern Anal. Machine Intell.*, vol. PAMI-3, no. 1, pp. 66–75, January 1981.

been proposed becomes useful, since this measure is experimentally shown to be somehow related with the classification error probability.

II. Definitions

Reference is made in this paper to the results of five different clustering programs. Four of them exemplify the class of so-called squared-error programs. They differ both in computational details and in the approach taken to minimize the squared error [1], [3]. The fifth clustering program is the induced fuzzy set iterative optimization algorithm described in [5] which for a particular choice of the cluster-membership-value assignment is similar to the squared-error approach.

No data-scaling options have been used and since Euclidean distance is familiar and is invariant under translations of the origin and rotations of the representation space, it is adopted for this study.

A. Squared-Error Clustering Programs

Let the data set be given in the form of an object-property table (pattern matrix) denoted by

$$C = \{u_v\}_{v=1}^{N}$$

where

$$u_v = (u_v^{(1)}, u_v^{(2)}, \cdots, u_v^{(k)})^T \text{ is the } v\text{th object.}$$

The number of objects N is assumed significantly larger than the number of properties k. A clustering is an m-partition

$$\{C_i\}_{i=1}^{m}$$

of the integers $[1, 2, \cdots, N]$ that assigns each object to a single cluster label.

The objects corresponding to the integers in C_i form the ith cluster, whose center is

$$\mu_i = (\mu_i^{(1)}, \mu_i^{(2)}, \cdots, \mu_i^{(k)})^T$$

where

$$\mu_i^{(j)} = (1/N_i) \sum_{v \in C_i} u_v^{(j)}$$

where N_i is the number of objects in cluster i.

The squared error for cluster i is

$$e_i^2 = \sum_{v \in C_i} (u_v - \mu_i)^T (u_v - \mu_i)$$

and the squared error for the clustering is

$$E_m^2 = \sum_{i=1}^{m} e_i^2.$$

All programs try to find a local minimum of E_m^2 and the user hopes that the local minimum coincides with the global minimum.

The four squared-error programs used in this study are the following [3]. Details of these algorithms are available in [1].

FORGY: Given a set of cluster centers, the cluster label of the closest cluster center is assigned to each object. The cluster centers are then recomputed as sample means of all objects having the same cluster label. A new cluster is created when an object is found that is sufficiently removed from the existing structure.

ISODATA: Clusters are updated as in FORGY. The method is unique in the heuristics employed to create new clusters while trying to achieve the number of clusters requested by the user.

WISH: Cluster centers are updated in a "dispose" box immediately after a cluster label is assigned to each object. (The program processes one object at a time.)

CLUSTER: This program is based on the "hill-climbing" technique and has two phases. Phase 1 creates a sequence of clusterings containing $2, 3, \cdots, m$ clusters where m is specified by the user. Phase 2 merges clusters two at a time to produce a sequence of clusterings containing $m-1, m-2, \cdots, 2$ clusters. Phases 1 and 2 are alternated until a pass through both decreases the squared error of none of the clusterings. The best clustering ever achieved for each number of clusters ($\leqslant m$) is retained.

B. Induced Fuzzy Set Iterative Optimization Program

Basically, the program consists of an algorithm relationship between an inducing object partition $\{C_i\}_{i=1}^{m}$ on the one hand and a collection of induced fuzzy sets $\{(f_i, u), \forall\, u \in C\}_{i=1}^{m}$ on the other hand, where

$$f_i: C \to [0, 1], \quad i = 1, 2, \cdots, m$$

and

$$\sum_{i=1}^{m} f_i(u) = 1, \quad \forall\, u \in C.$$

Usually, the initial inducing object partition $\{C_i\}_{i=1}^{m}$ stems from a best guess and is subject to iterative optimization. A collection of fuzzy sets is induced by means of a point-to-subset affinity concept on the basis of the structural properties among objects in the representation space. This has been called affinity decomposition and performs in the same way as the Bayes theorem from probability theory. The appropriateness of the induced collection of fuzzy sets is made explicit by applying some performance measure. The collection of induced fuzzy sets may cause a repartition due to a reclassification function. Then, a new inducing step follows, so we get an iterative procedure.

Definition 1: The affinity decomposition of each object $u \in C$ is given by $\{r(u, C_i)\}_{i=1}^{m}$ in such a way that

$$r(u, C_i) \geqslant 0, \quad \forall\, u \in C \tag{1}$$

and

$$r(u, C) = \sum_{i=1}^{m} P_i r(u, C_i), \quad \forall\, u \in C \tag{2}$$

where

P_i denotes the relative size of the ith subset

given by

$$P_i = \frac{N_i}{N}. \tag{3}$$

The (user's intuitive) notion of point-to-(sub)set affinity should be such that

1) the affinity between an object and a group of objects is not smaller when the object itself is contained in the group

than if the object is not a member of the group, thus

$$r(u, C_i^+) \geqslant r(u, C_i)$$

where

$$C_i^+ = \{C_i, u\};$$

2) the affinity between an object and a group of objects is approximately zero when the object is distant from the group or is out of the region of interest; and

3) the affinity between an object and a group of objects is equal to an absolute maximum if the group consists of just one element having the same location as the object under consideration.

Then, the values of the cluster membership functions for the induced fuzzy sets related to the inducing m-partition $\{C_i\}_{i=1}^m$ are determined by the following definition.

Definition 2: Given an m-partition $\{C_i\}_{i=1}^m$ and some affinity measure $r(u, C)$, the cluster membership value $f_i(u)$ of object $u \in C$ induced by $C_i \in \{C_j\}_{j=1}^m$ is given by

$$f_i(u) = P_i \frac{r(u, C_i)}{r(u, C)}, \quad \forall\, u \in C. \tag{4}$$

Many different affinity concepts are discussed in [5], among them, the distance oriented concept appeared to be appropriate for this paper.

Let the subset affinity be given by

$$r(u, C_i) = 1 - \frac{1}{N_i} \sum_{v \in C_i} h^\beta[\partial(u, v)] \tag{5}$$

where $h^\beta[\partial(u, v)]$ is a nondecreasing distance function on the interval [0, 1], controlled by a certain parameter β, and $\partial(u, v)$ is a distance measure satisfying reflexive and symmetric properties.

Combining (2), (3), and (5), we get

$$r(u, C) = \sum_{i=1}^m \frac{N_i}{N}\left(1 - \frac{1}{N_i} \sum_{v \in C_i} h^\beta[\partial(u, v)]\right)$$

$$= 1 - \frac{1}{N} \sum_{v \in C} h^\beta[\partial(u, v)]. \tag{6}$$

Substituting (5) and (6) into (4) we get

$$f_i(u) = \frac{N_i - \sum_{v \in C_i} h^\beta[\partial(u, v)]}{N - \sum_{v \in C} h^\beta[\partial(u, v)]}. \tag{7}$$

In what follows we use

$$\partial(u, v) = \left(\sum_k (u^{(k)} - v^{(k)})^2\right)^{1/2}$$

and

$$h^\beta[\partial(u, v)] = \partial(u, v)^2/\beta \quad \text{for } \partial(u, v) \leqslant \beta^{1/2}$$

$$= 1 \quad \text{for } \partial(u, v) > \beta^{1/2}.$$

Note that for

$$\max_{u, v \in C} \partial(u, v) \leqslant \beta^{1/2}$$

we find

$$f_i(u) = P_i \frac{1 - \frac{1}{\beta}\left(\partial(u, \mu_i)^2 + \frac{1}{2} D_i^2\right)}{1 - \frac{1}{\beta}\left(\partial(u, \mu)^2 + \frac{1}{2} D^2\right)}, \quad \forall\, u \in C$$

where D_i^2 is the mean square intracluster distance of the ith cluster

$$D_i^2 = \frac{1}{N_i^2} \sum_{u \in C_i} \sum_{v \in C_i} \partial(u, v)^2$$

and μ_i is the mean vector of the ith cluster.

Likewise, D^2 is given by

$$D^2 = \frac{1}{N^2} \sum_{u \in C} \sum_{v \in C} \partial(u, v)^2$$

and μ is the mean vector of the entire set where its elements are given by

$$\mu^{(j)} = (1/N) \sum_{v=1}^N u_v^{(j)}, \quad j = 1, 2, \cdots, k$$

which is proportional to the ratio of the contribution of object u to e_i^w and E_m^2. So there is a strong relation between the squared-error and the induced fuzzy set approaches.

If we represent C_i only by its sample mean μ_i we obtain

$$D_i^2 = 0$$

$$P_i = \frac{1}{m}$$

and thus

$$f_i(u) = \frac{1}{m} \frac{1 - \frac{1}{\beta} \partial(u, \mu_i)^2}{1 - \frac{1}{\beta}\left(\partial(u, \mu)^2 + \frac{1}{2} D^2\right)}$$

which is equivalent to

$$f_i(u) = \frac{1 - \frac{1}{\beta} \partial(u, \mu_i)^2}{m - \frac{1}{\beta} \sum_{i=1}^m \partial(u, \mu_i)^2}$$

which measures the ratio of the contribution of object u to e_i^2 and E_m^2. So there is a strong relation between the squared-error and the induced fuzzy set approaches.

Once we have established an m-collection of induced fuzzy sets

$$\{(f_i, u), \forall\, u \in C\}_{i=1}^m$$

we may informally characterize the partitioning as follows. If the amount of induced fuzziness is low it means that the m-collection of induced fuzzy sets is reasonably separable and that the inducing partition reflects the real data structure reasonably well. On the other hand, if the amount of induced fuzziness is high, it means that the inter-fuzzy set separability is low and that either the inducing partition does not reflect the real structure well, or that almost no structure is present in the data. Consequently, our performance measure should measure the fuzziness in the gaps between fuzzy sets (along the fuzzy boundaries) and, therefore, should be based on the notion of intersection of fuzzy sets.

The intersection of two fuzzy sets f_i and f_j can be defined either by

$$f_{i \cap_1 j}(u) = \min\,[f_i(u) \cdot f_j(u)], \qquad \forall\, u \in C$$

or by

$$f_{i \cap_2 j}(u) = f_i(u) \cdot f_j(u), \qquad \forall\, u \in C.$$

In this paper we shall adopt the second type of intersection because of the mathematical and computational attractiveness.

Then, the clustering performance measure can be defined as follows.

Definition 3: Given an m-collection of fuzzy sets $\{(f_i, u), \forall\, u \in C\}_{i=1}^{m}$ satisfying $\Sigma_{i=1}^{m} f_i(u) = 1$, $\forall\, u \in C$, the clustering performance measure is given by

$$\psi = 1 - \frac{2m}{m-1} \sum_{i=1}^{m-1} \sum_{j=i+1}^{m} \frac{1}{N} \sum_{u \in C} f_i(u) \cdot f_j(u). \tag{8}$$

It is easy to show that

$$0 \leqslant \psi \leqslant 1$$

where $\psi = 0$ corresponds to maximum fuzziness and $\psi = 1$ corresponds to nonfuzziness.

It is also easy to show that

$$\psi = \frac{1}{m-1} \sum_{i=1}^{m-1} \sum_{j=i+1}^{m} \frac{1}{N} \sum_{u \in C} |f_i(u) - f_j(u)|^2 \tag{9}$$

which shows that the performance measure can be looked upon as a cluster membership distance measure. In [6], a coupling coefficient

$$w_{ij} = \frac{1}{N} \sum_{u \in C} f_i(u) \cdot f_j(u)$$

was suggested in order to characterize the performance of his fuzzy ISODATA program. Bezdek [6] defines a partition coefficient as

$$W = \frac{\sum_{i=1}^{m} \text{coupling "within" cluster } i}{\text{total coupling}}$$

$$= \frac{\sum_{i=1}^{m} w_{ii}}{\sum_{i=1}^{m} \sum_{j=1}^{m} w_{ij}}$$

which results in

$$W = 1 - \frac{m-1}{m}(1 - \psi)$$

or

$$\psi = 1 - \frac{m}{m-1}(1 - W).$$

As a result, the range of variation of W becomes $[1/m, 1]$ which is less attractive for comparison of different clustering results since the range of variation depends on the number of clusters.

Based on this performance measure the iterative optimization is controlled by the following reclassification function.

If an object $w \in C_i$ is reclassified into C_j, $j \neq i$, then the change in the value of the performance measure ψ is given by

$$\xi(w, C_i) = \psi(\{C_i\}_{i=1}^{m}, \{f_i\}_{i=1}^{m}) - \psi(\{C_i'\}_{i=1}^{m}, \{f_i\}_{i=1}^{m})$$
$$\xi(w, C_j) = \psi(\{C_i'\}_{i=1}^{m}, \{f_i\}_{i=1}^{m}) - \psi(\{C_i\}_{i=1}^{m}, \{f_i\}_{i=1}^{m}$$
$$j = 1, 2, \cdots, m, j \neq i \tag{10}$$

where

$$\{C_i'\}_{i=1}^{m} = \{C_1, \cdots, C_i^-, \cdots, C_j^+, \cdots, C_m\}$$

with

$$C_i = \{C_i^-, w\} \quad \text{and} \quad C_j^+ = \{C_j, w\}.$$

Substituting the value of ψ from (8) into (10) yields the reclassification functions

$$\xi(w, C_i) = \frac{1}{N_i}\left[f_i^2(w) - \frac{1}{N_i - 1} \sum_{u \in C_i^-} f_i^2(u)\right]$$

and

$$\xi(w, C_j) = \frac{1}{N_j}\left[f_j^2(w) - \frac{1}{N_j + 1} \sum_{u \in C_j^+} f_j^2(u)\right],$$
$$j = 1, 2, \cdots, m, j \neq i.$$

Let

$$\xi(w, C_M) = \max_j\,[\xi(w, C_j)].$$

Then the reclassification rule is if $\xi(u, C_M) > \xi(w, C_i)$ add object w to C_M and delete w from C_i else w remains classified in C_i.

In [5] all convergence properties of this iterative procedure are discussed in detail. After all reclassifications (with respect to ψ) have taken place, a new set of cluster membership values are calculated.

A simplified flowchart of this procedure is shown in Fig. 1.

III. Methods of Comparison and Experimental Results

The intuitive appeal of the fuzzy set approach lies in the fact that the data analyst is now equipped with a value of the performance measure as well as the identification of bridging (overlapping) points. This appeal is balanced by the fact that a single performance measure cannot summarize all the information that can be gleaned from a clustering [3]. In [3] different points of view in comparing clustering techniques and clustering results have been discussed. Consequently, no general answer can be given to questions like "which of the programs is best?" or "what is the 'true' structure?"

The method of comparison we are dealing with is to establish a ranking of the utility of clustering results obtained from different clustering programs with respect to a certain application domain where utility can be measured uniquely. So, we may call this a goal-directed comparison.

To make this point of view clear we conducted four different experiments.

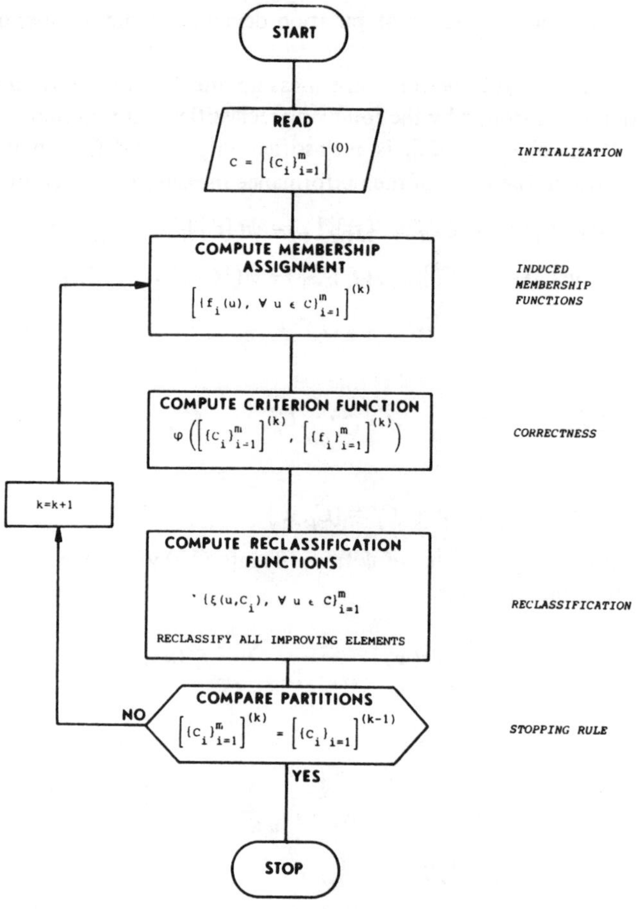

Fig. 1. Flowchart of the induced fuzzy set iterative optimization program.

Experiment 1: The difficulties inherent in the comparison problem can be appreciated somewhat by considering the set of two-property objects in Fig. 2, taken from [3].

Clusterings achieved by the five programs given in Section II are shown. Choosing the "best" clustering is a difficult task because no goal-directed realistic criterion exists (like the number of errors related to the "true" categories). Fig. 2 also shows the value of the clustering performance measure obtained for each of the individual clustering programs. These values were obtained by using each clustering result (with different m) as the inducing partitions $\{C_i\}_{i=1}^m$ for FUZZ. Thereby, only one iteration is observed providing us with the ψ-value as indicated attached to each of the $\{C_i\}_{i=1}^m$.

Clearly, the ranking based on ψ value is visually appealing to human understanding of the problem but no formal judgment can be made.

Experiment 2: In the second experiment the five clustering programs were applied to a particular data set, derived from the Munson handprinted Fortran character set. Four characters were selected, namely I, M, O, and X, for a total of 192 characters. Each character is represented by an eight-dimensional property vector. The same data set was also used in [3].

Fig. 3 shows a projection of the data on the two eigenvectors corresponding to the two largest eigenvalues. Clearly, the characters are not well clustered, although they are reasonably separable.

Since the true categories are known the number of errors ob-

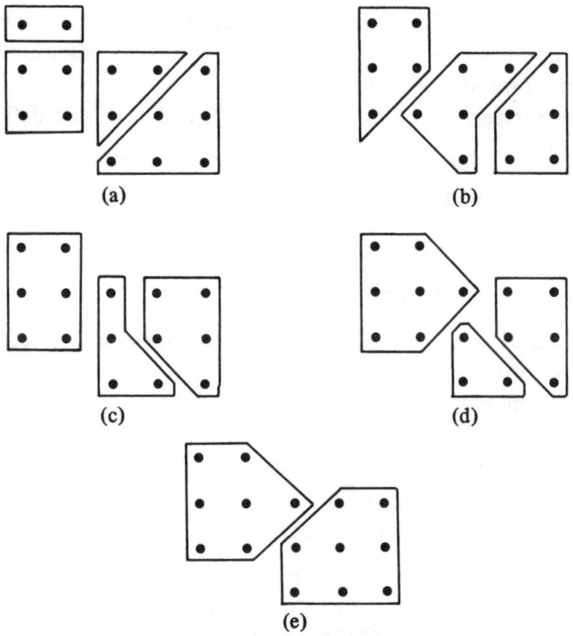

Fig. 2. Five clusterings of 15 two-property objects [3] with ψ values (for $\beta = 3$) shown. (a) FORGY–ψ = 0.267. (b) ISODATA–ψ = 0.274. (c) WISH–ψ = 0.303. (d) CLUSTER–ψ = 0.357. (e) FUZZ–ψ = 0.474.

tained by comparing the true categories and the clustering result may guide us in interpreting the values of the performance measure. These results are given in Table I.

Here, it is seen that the ranking based on the ψ-value meets the ranking based on the number of errors. The ψ-value obtained from the true categories yielding zero errors forms an obvious exception. Any true partition always yields zero errors. However, the true partition or structure of these data does not compare well with the hyperellipsoidal shaped clusters generated by these five squared-error type clustering algorithms. It is also interesting to note that while there are four categories in this data, all the squared-error algorithms preferred five clusters.

In most clustering problems, one does not know the true structure of the data. Even if the true structure is known, clustering algorithms are available to uncover only a few types of them (e.g., hyperellipsoidal and straggly or line-like).

A few aspects appearing in Table I require some explanation. The values of the squared error are taken from the case reported in [3]. The ranking of these values seems nicely correlated with the ranking of the ψ-values. However, this is generally only true when comparing results with an equal number of clusters. Evidently, ψ does not suffer from incompatability to unequal number of clusters. Results of Table I also show that one can generally improve a partition which is optimal in the mean-squared sense, by iterating with respect to ψ. The main reason being that the FUZZ algorithm is influenced more by the objects in the overlapping region whereas mean-squared algorithms treat all objects equally. As has been pointed out before, the performance measure ψ depends on a free parameter β. Results are reported here for only one value of β. However, a reasonable range of the free parameter β was tested and it showed no changes in the ranking. The absolute value of the performance measure is obviously effected by changing β. In fact, an ad hoc rule was adopted for choosing an appropriate value for β (to induce sufficient fuzziness). The maxi-

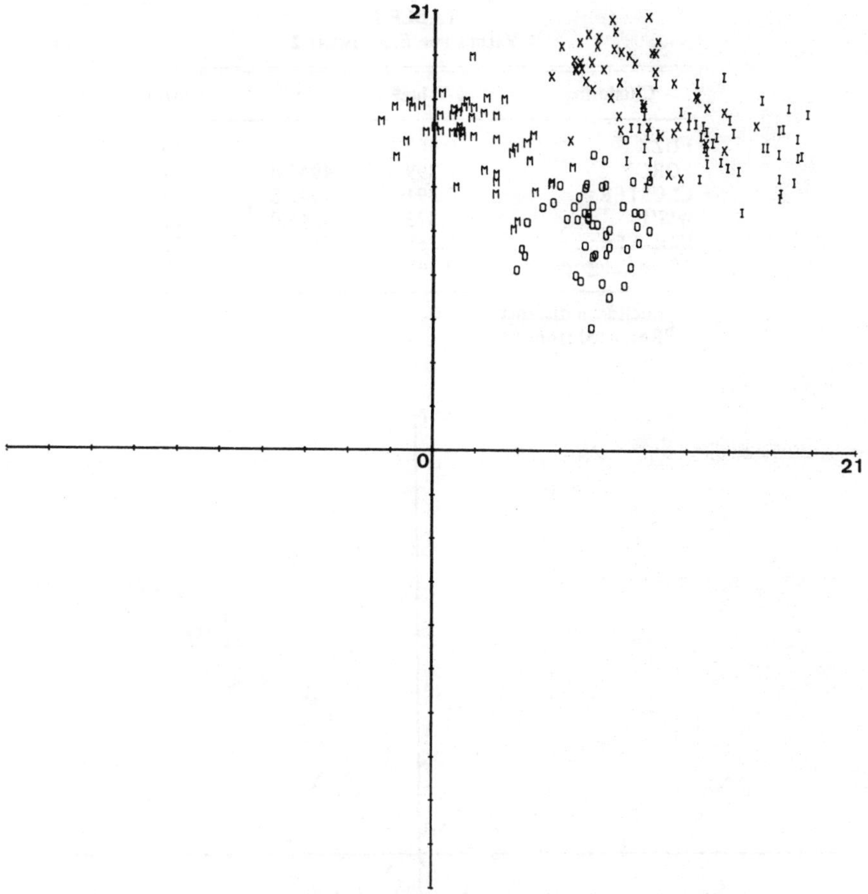

Fig. 3. Plot of the IMOX data on the two eigenvectors corresponding to the two largest eigenvalues.

mum distance between present cluster means was used to determine β, so

$$\beta_0 = \max_{i,j} [\partial(\mu_i, \mu_j)].$$

Another possibility for choosing an appropriate value of β might be the mean interpoint distance less the standard deviation of interpoint distances. This rule has the advantage of not being dependent of the initialization of the clustering procedure. The rule shows promising results and is subject of further investigation.

The results reported in Table I suggest that if a classifier should be designed on the basis of the resulting clustering, the utility of this approach is made explicit by the number of errors when testing this classifier. This leads to the next experiment.

Experiment 3: Two clustering programs, FUZZ and ISODATA, were applied to a particular data set which has been generated artificially. The data are two-dimensional; this enables the data to be plotted and examined visually, thus making the results obtained easily understood. The data contain two categories; achieved by sampling from two bivariate normal distributions with the following characteristics:

Category 1: mean vector μ_1

$$= (0, 0) \text{ and covariance matrix } \Sigma_1 = \begin{bmatrix} 1 & 1 \\ 0 & 0 \end{bmatrix};$$

Category 2: mean vector μ_2

$$= (3, 3) \text{ and covariance matrix } \Sigma_2 = \begin{bmatrix} 1 & 0.9 \\ 0.9 & 1 \end{bmatrix}.$$

Fifty observations were sampled from each population and the 100 bivariate observations presented to both FUZZ and ISODATA.

A plot of the data is given in Fig. 4.

Each of the clustering results, given in Fig. 5(a) and (b), forms the set of design labels for a 1-NN classifier. Each 1-NN classifier is then tested with another 200 samples (100 samples per class)—but the same 200 samples for each classifier—sampled from the above populations.

Clearly, ψ values show the utility of the clustering result obtained by FUZZ over the clustering result given by ISODATA. The goal-directed comparison yields 5 against 11 errors, respectively, in the testing phase. So, choosing the "best" clustering becomes meaningful if a goal (classification) is defined. In fact, when classification is the goal, the existence of a "gap" between clusters has to be estimated rather than the compactness of the cluster. In essense, the fuzzy set approach given in Section II-B, estimates the overlap of the fuzzy sets and gives an estimate of the fuzzy cluster separability [5]. For these data the maximum value of the clustering performance measure ψ is 0.701. It has been pointed out before that the absolute value has no significant meaning in how well clusters are separated. The absolute value is very dependent on the shape of the gaps between the clusters and the choice of the parame-

TABLE I
ψ-VALUES FOR EXPERIMENT 2

Clustering	ψ-value[a]	E_m^2 [b]	# errors
FUZZ	0.402	–	19
FORGY	0.399	4942.8	21
CLUSTER	0.391	4942.8	22
WISH	0.373	5046.0	27
ISODATA	0.365	5149.6	36
"True Categories"	0.348	–	0

[a]Euclidean distance, $\beta = 10$.
[b]Reported from [3].

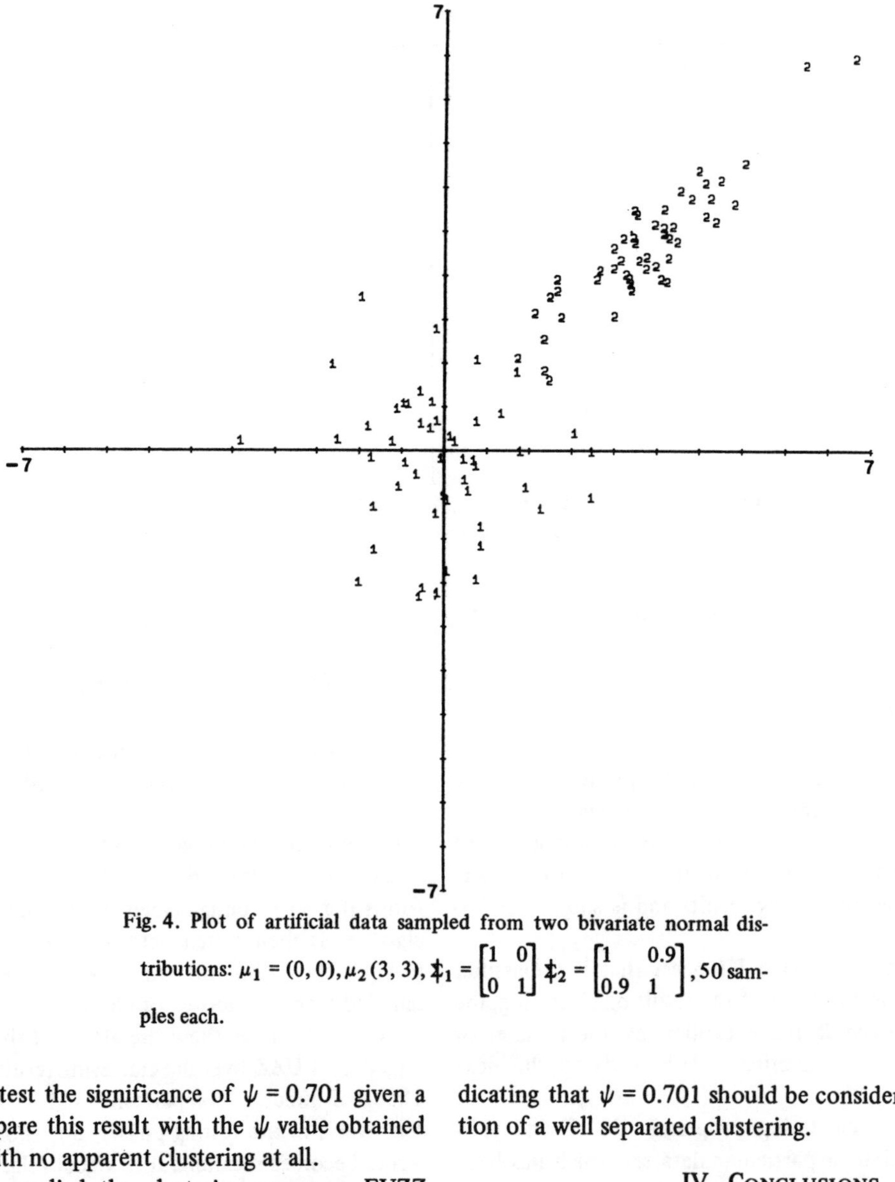

Fig. 4. Plot of artificial data sampled from two bivariate normal distributions: $\mu_1 = (0, 0), \mu_2 (3, 3), \Sigma_1 = \begin{bmatrix} 1 & 0 \\ 0 & 1 \end{bmatrix} \Sigma_2 = \begin{bmatrix} 1 & 0.9 \\ 0.9 & 1 \end{bmatrix}$, 50 samples each.

ter β. One way to test the significance of $\psi = 0.701$ given a certain β_0 is to compare this result with the ψ value obtained from random data with no apparent clustering at all.

Experiment 4: We applied the clustering programs FUZZ and ISODATA to a data set generated from a single bivariate normal distribution. We changed the scaling of this data set so that β_0 remains unchanged as shown in Fig. 6.

If, for a given β_0, the resulting ψ is also high it simply means that $\psi = 0.701$ does not indicate well separated clusters. On the contrary, if the resulting ψ for the random data is very low it signifies the result $\psi = 0.701$ as representing a well separated clustering.

Table II provides the ψ-values for the no-clustering case, indicating that $\psi = 0.701$ should be considered as a characterization of a well separated clustering.

IV. CONCLUSIONS

Following questions can be posed when a data set is to be analyzed using clustering methodology.

1) Which clustering algorithm(s) is best suited for a given data set?

2) Once it has been determined which algorithms are suitable for a data set, how do we determine which one of these algorithms gives more valid or useful results?

While no answer is yet available to the first question because one does not have sufficient knowledge (in most applications

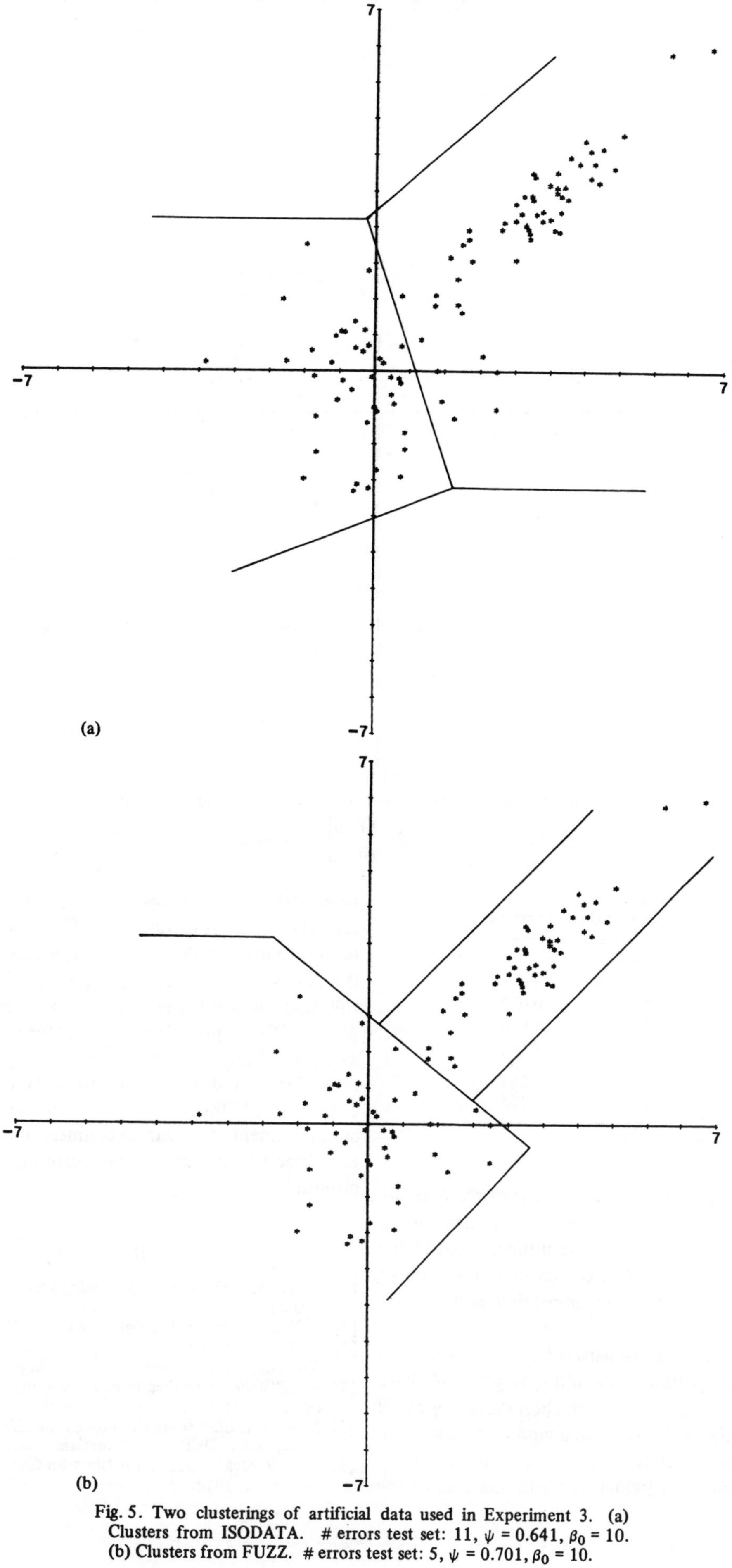

Fig. 5. Two clusterings of artificial data used in Experiment 3. (a) Clusters from ISODATA. # errors test set: 11, $\psi = 0.641$, $\beta_0 = 10$. (b) Clusters from FUZZ. # errors test set: 5, $\psi = 0.701$, $\beta_0 = 10$.

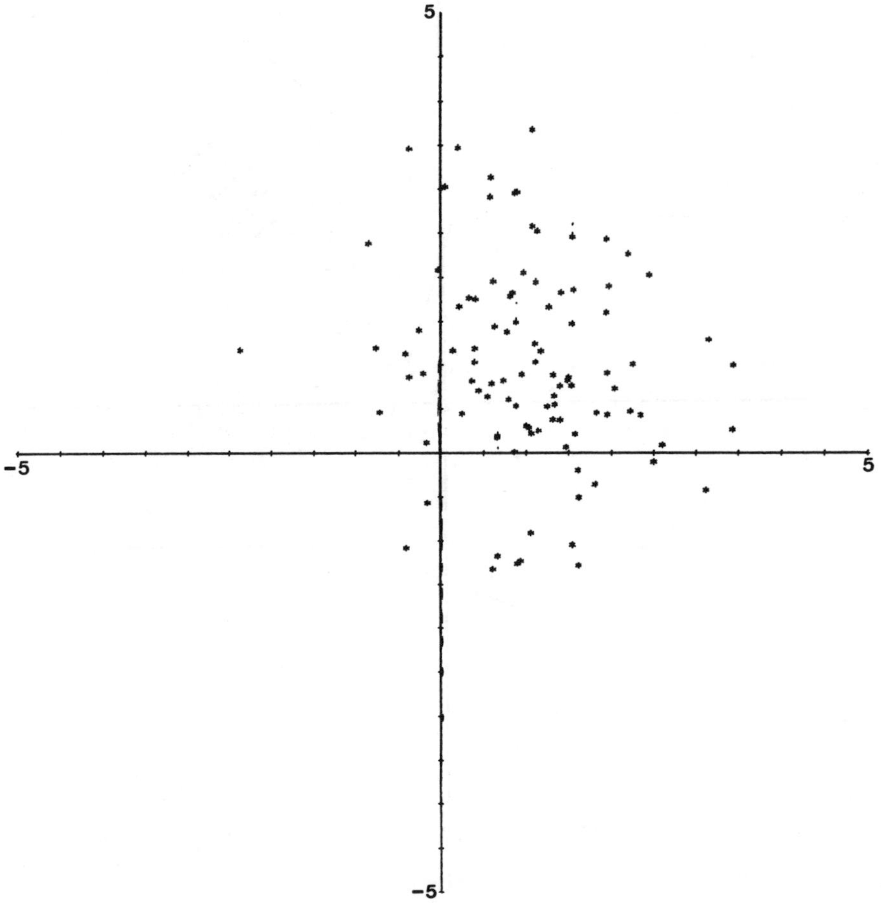

Fig. 6. Plot of artificial data sampled from the bivariate normal distribution: $\mu = (1, 1)$, $\Sigma = \begin{bmatrix} 1 & 0 \\ 0 & 1 \end{bmatrix}$, 100 samples.

TABLE II
ψ-VALUES FOR THE NO-CLUSTERING CASE, EXPERIMENT 4

Clustering	# of clusters	ψ-values[a]
ISODATA	2	0.077
	3	0.083
	4	0.101
	5	0.097
FUZZ	2	0.087
	4	0.105

[a]Euclidean distance, $\beta_0 = 10$.

there is no knowledge) about the true structure of the data, we have made an attempt here to answer the second question. In fact, whenever one is able to define the ultimate goal of the cluster analysis more specifically, a comparison of clustering techniques may become fruitful if an appropriate performance measure is adopted.

It is our belief that a measure of gaps between fuzzy clusters may serve well if classification is the ultimate goal. We have given empirical evidence that selecting the best clustering result on the basis of the value of ψ meets the lowest error rate when testing a 1-NN classifier which is designed based on the clustering result. The parameter β (which controls the size of the neighborhood around each object) needed to compute the performance measure ψ does not affect the ordering of the clustering results. It does, however, affect the absolute value of the performance measure ψ (choosing a very small value of β will lead to $\psi = 1$ and a very large value of β will result in $\psi = 0$). We do provide a heuristic for choosing β which works well. Further, one can evaluate the significance of the value of ψ (for a fixed β) obtained for a data set by comparing the ψ value (with the same β) for a random data set as we did in Experiment 4. Our experimental results indicate that a goal-directed comparison of clustering results appears to be promising.

REFERENCES

[1] M. R. Anderberg, *Cluster Analysis for Applications.* New York: Academic, 1973.
[2] B. Everitt, *Cluster Analysis.* New York: Wiley, 1974.
[3] R. C. Dubes and A. K. Jain, "Clustering techniques: The user's dilemma," *Pattern Recognition*, vol. 8, pp. 247–260, 1970.
[4] ——, "Validity studies in clustering methodologies," *Pattern Recognition*, vol. 11, pp. 235–254, 1979.
[5] E. Backer, *Cluster Analysis by Optimal Decomposition of Induced Fuzzy Sets.* Delft, The Netherlands: Delft Univ. Press, 1978.
[6] J. C. Bezdek, "Cluster validity with fuzzy sets," *J. Cybern.*, vol. 3, pp. 58–73, 1974.

Unsupervised Optimal Fuzzy Clustering

I. GATH AND A. B. GEVA

Abstract—**Many algorithms for fuzzy clustering depend on initial guesses of cluster prototypes, and on assumptions made as to the number of subgroups present in the data. This study reports on a method for carrying out fuzzy classification without *a priori* assumptions on the number of clusters in the data set. Assessment of cluster validity is based on performance measures using hypervolume and density criteria. The new algorithm is derived from a combination of the fuzzy *K*-means algorithm and the fuzzy maximum likelihood estimation (FMLE). The UFP-ONC (unsupervised fuzzy partition-optimal number of classes) algorithm performs well in situations of large variability of cluster shapes, densities, and number of data points in each cluster. It has been tested on a number of simulated and real data sets.**

Index Terms—**Clustering of sleep EEG, fuzzy clustering, hyperellipsoidal clusters, performance measures for cluster validity, unequally variable features, unsupervised tracking of cluster prototype.**

I. INTRODUCTION

Cluster analysis is based on partitioning a collection of data points into a number of subgroups, where the objects inside a cluster (a subgroup) show a certain degree of closeness or similarity. Hard clustering assigns each data point (feature vector) to one and only one of the clusters, with a degree of membership equal to one, assuming well defined boundaries between the clusters. This model often does not reflect the description of real data, where boundaries between subgroups might be fuzzy, and where a more nuanced description of the object's affinity to the specific cluster is required. Thus, numerous problems in the life sciences are better tackled by decision making in a fuzzy environment [1]–[4]. Bezdek [5] developed a family of clustering algorithms, based on fuzzy extension of the least-square error criterion, and proved the convergence of the algorithms to a local minimum [6]. Related algorithms, taking into account differences in cluster shapes have been proposed by Bezdek and Dunn [7], Bezdek *et al.* [8], [9], and Gustafson and Kessel [10].

There are three major difficulties encountered during fuzzy clustering of real data: 1) The number of clusters can not always be defined apriori, and one has to find a cluster validity criterion [11], in order to determine the optimal number of clusters present in the data. 2) The character and location of cluster centroids is not necessarily known *a priori*, and initial guesses have to be made. 3) The presence of large variability in cluster shapes, variations in cluster densities, and variability in the number of data points in each cluster. A good example which demonstrates the complexity of handling real data is classification of EEG recordings [12], [13]. Fuzzy clustering of sleep EEG in order to classify the signal into various sleep stages is reported in [1], [4], [14].

In the present study an algorithm for fuzzy classification into optimal number of clusters will be described. Optimality is restricted here to the notion of optimizing new performance measures, based on cluster hypervolume and density criteria. The algorithm accounts for variability in cluster shapes, cluster densities, and the number of data points in each of the subsets. Classification prototypes for initiation of the iterative process are generated through a process of unsupervised learning. The new algorithm will be tested on different classes of simulated data, and on a real data set derived from sleep EEG signal.

Manuscript received June 26, 1987; revised May 5, 1988. Recommended for acceptance by A. K. Jain. This work was supported by the Kennedy-Leigh fund for Biomedical Engineering Research.

The authors are with the Department of Biomedical Engineering, Technion, Haifa 32000, Israel.

IEEE Log Number 8927500.

II. UNSUPERVISED FUZZY PARTITION

In order to obtain satisfactory solution to the problem of large variability in cluster shapes and densities, and to the problem of unsupervised tracking of classification prototypes, a two-layer clustering strategy has been developed. During the first step, a modification of the fuzzy *K*-means algorithm [5] is carried out. There are no initial conditions on the location of cluster centroids, and classification prototypes are identified during a process of unsupervised learning. Using these prototypes, the second step involves the utilization of a second clustering algorithm in order to achieve optimal fuzzy partition. This scheme is iterated for increasing number of clusters in the data set, computing performance measures in each run, until partition into optimal number of subgroups is obtained:

1) Cluster with fuzzy *K*-means (Section II-A), using unsupervised tracking of initial classification prototypes (Section II-B).

2) Cluster with the fuzzy modification of the maximum likelihood estimation (refinement of step 1, Section II-A).

3) Compute-performance measures (Section II-C).

4) Increase K (number of subgroups) and repeat steps 1–3 until optimum value of performance measure is obtained.

A. The Fuzzy K-Means Algorithm and Its Derivatives

The fuzzy *K*-means algorithm [5] is based on minimization of the following objective function, with respect to U, a fuzzy K-partition of the data set, and to V, a set of K prototypes:

$$J_q(U, V) = \sum_{j=1}^{N} \sum_{i=1}^{K} (u_{ij})^q d^2(X_j, V_i); \qquad K \leq N \tag{1}$$

where q is any real number greater than 1, X_j is the jth m-dimensional feature vector, V_i is the centroid of the ith cluster, u_{ij} is the degree of membership of X_j in the ith cluster, $d^2(X_j, V_i)$ is any inner product metric (distance between X_j and V_i), N is the number of data points, K is number of clusters. The parameter q is the weighting exponent for u_{ij} and controls the "fuzziness" of the resulting clusters [11].

Fuzzy partition is carried out through an iterative optimization of (1) according to [5]:

1) Choose primary centroids V_i (prototypes).

2) Compute the degree of membership of all feature vectors in all the clusters:

$$u_{ij} = \frac{\left[\dfrac{1}{d^2(X_j, V_i)}\right]^{1/(q-1)}}{\sum_{k=1}^{K} \left[\dfrac{1}{d^2(X_j, V_k)}\right]^{1/(q-1)}}. \tag{2}$$

Reprinted from *IEEE Trans. Pattern Anal. Machine Intell.*, vol. PAMI-11, no. 7, pp. 773–781, July 1989.

3) Compute new centroids $\hat{V}_i$:

$$\hat{V}_i = \frac{\sum_{j=1}^{N} (u_{ij})^q X_j}{\sum_{j=1}^{N} (u_{ij})^q} \tag{3}$$

and update the degree of memberships, u_{ij} to $\hat{u}_{ij}$, according to (2).

4)

$$\text{if } \max_{ij} \left[\left| u_{ij} - \hat{u}_{ij} \right| \right] < \epsilon \text{ stop, otherwise goto step 3} \tag{4}$$

where ϵ is a termination criterion between 0 and 1.

Computation of the degree of membership u_{ij} depends on the definition of the distance measure, $d^2(X_j, V_i)$, [11]:

$$d^2(X_j, V_i) = (X_j - V_i)^T A (X_j - V_i). \tag{5}$$

The inclusion of A (an $m \times m$ positive-definite matrix) in the distance measure results in weighting according to the statistical properties of the features [10]. In the following, two different distance measures will be defined, to be used in the two different layers of the clustering process:

1) For the case where A equals the identity matrix the distance is Euclidean. The resulting algorithm is the fuzzy K-means.

2) For hyperellipsoidal clusters, as well as in the presence of variable cluster densities and unequal numbers of data points in each cluster, an "exponential" distance measure, $d_e^2(X_j, V_i)$, based on maximum likelihood estimation [7], [11], [15] is defined. This distance will be used in calculation of $h(i \mid X_j)$, the posterior probability (the probability of selecting the ith cluster given the jth feature vector):

$$h(i \mid X_j) = \frac{1/d_e^2(X_j, V_i)}{\sum_{k=1}^{K} 1/d_e^2(X_j, V_k)} \tag{6}$$

$$d_e^2(X_j, V_i) = \frac{\left[\det(F_i)\right]^{1/2}}{P_i} \exp\left[(X_j - V_i)^T F_i^{-1} (X_j - V_i)/2\right] \tag{7}$$

where F_i is the fuzzy covariance matrix of the ith cluster, and P_i, the *a priori* probability of selecting the ith cluster.

Comparison of (6) and (2) shows that for $q = 2$ $h(i \mid X_j)$ is similar to u_{ij}. Thus, substituting (6) instead of (2) in step 2 of the fuzzy K-means algorithm results in the fuzzy modification of the maximum likelihood estimation (FMLE). Step 3 of the FMLE algorithm includes, in addition to computation of the new centroid, calculation of P_i, the *a priori* probability of selecting the ith cluster:

$$P_i = \frac{1}{N} \sum_{j=1}^{N} h(i \mid X_j) \tag{8}$$

and of F_i, the fuzzy covariance matrix of the ith cluster:

$$F_i = \frac{\sum_{j=1}^{N} h(i \mid X_j)(X_j - V_i)(X_j - V_i)^T}{\sum_{j=1}^{N} h(i \mid X_j)}. \tag{9}$$

Due to the "exponential" distance function incorporated in the FMLE algorithm it seeks an optimum in a narrow local region. It therefore does not perform well, and might be even unstable during unsupervised identification of classification prototypes described in Section II-C. Its major advantage is obtaining good partition results in cases of unequally variable features and densities, but only when starting from "good" classification prototypes. The first layer of the algorithm (unsupervised tracking of initial centroids) is therefore based on the fuzzy K-means algorithm, whereas in the next phase optimal fuzzy partition is being carried out with the FMLE algorithm.

B. Unsupervised Tracking of Cluster Prototypes

The algorithms described in the previous section start with initial guesses of classification prototypes, and the iterative process results in convergence of the cluster centroids to a local optimum. Different choices of classification prototypes may lead to convergence to different local optima, i.e., to different partitions. In many practical situations *a priori* knowledge of the approximate locations of the initial centroids does not exist, and in order to achieve optimal partition unsupervised tracking of classification prototypes is required.

Given a partition into k clusters, the basic idea is to place the $(k + 1)$st cluster center in a region where data points have low degree of membership in the existing k clusters. The following scheme describes the steps for the selection of initial cluster centers, incorporated in the fuzzy K-means algorithm:

1) Compute average and standard deviation of the whole data set.

2) Choose the first initial cluster prototype at the average location of all feature vectors.

3) Choose an additional classification prototype equally distant (with a given number of standard deviations) from all data points (a nonphysical location).

4) Calculate a new partition of the data set according to steps 1 and 2 of the scheme outlined in Section II.

5) If k, the number of clusters is less than a given maximum, goto 3, otherwise stop.

C. Performance Measures for Cluster Validity

During clustering of real data one usually has to make assumptions as to the number of underlying subgroups present in the data set. When no *a priori* information exists as to the internal structure of the data, or in case of conflicting evidence about the optimal number of subgroups, performance measures for comparison between the goodness of partitions with different numbers of clusters need to be formulated.

A goal-directed approach [16] to the cluster validity problem can be chosen, where the goal is classification, in the sense of minimization of the classification error rate. Hence, one may accept the basic heuristic that "good" clusters are actually not very fuzzy [11]. Therefore, the criteria for the definition of "optimal partition" of the data into subgroups were based on three requirements:

1) Clear separation between the resulting clusters.

2) Minimal volume of the clusters.

3) Maximal number of data points concentrated in the vicinity of the cluster centroid.

Thus, although the environment is fuzzy, the aim of the classification is generation of well-defined subgroups, and hence these requirements lead to a "harder" partitioning of the data set.

The performance measures were based on criteria for hypervolume and density. Fuzzy hypervolume, F_{HV}, is defined by:

$$F_{HV} = \sum_{i=1}^{K} \left[\det(F_i)\right]^{1/2} \tag{10}$$

where F_i is given by (9).

Average partition density D_{PA} is calculated from:

$$D_{PA} = \frac{1}{K} \sum_{i=1}^{K} \frac{S_i}{\left[\det(F_i)\right]^{1/2}} \tag{11}$$

where S_i, the "sum of central members," is given by:

$$S_i = \sum_{j=1}^{N} u_{ij}$$

$$\forall X_j \in \left\{X_j : (X_j - V_i) F_i^{-1} (X_j - V_i)\right] < 1\right\} \tag{12}$$

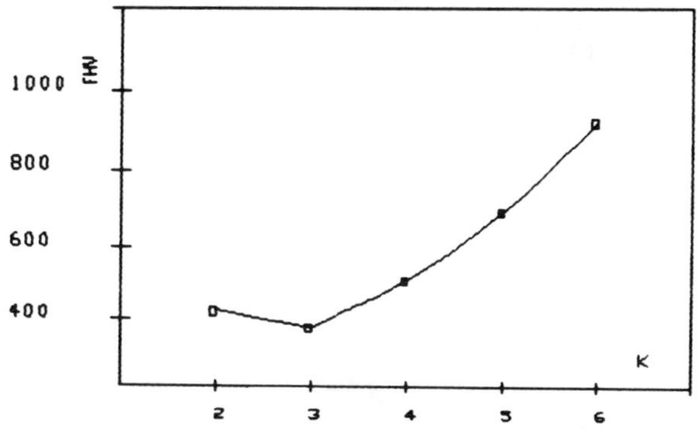

(a)

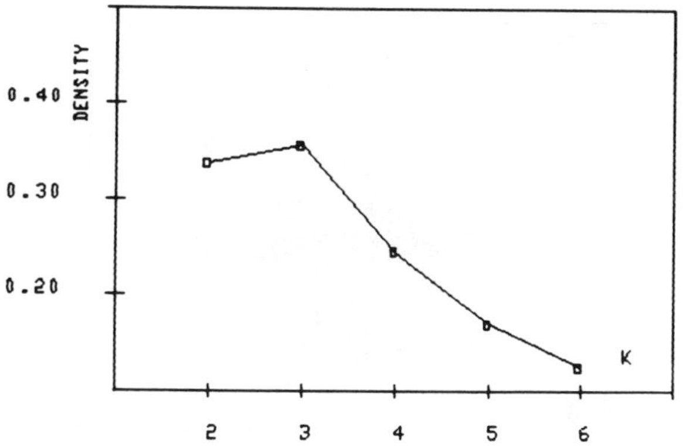

(b)

Fig. 1. Performance criteria for the Iris data. (a) FHV—Fuzzy hypervolume as a function of the number of subgroups in the data. (b) Partition density as a function of number of subgroups. Extrema are seen for $k = 3$.

taking into account only those members within the hyperellipsoid, whose radii are the standard deviations of the cluster features.

The partition density P_D is calculated from

$$P_D = \frac{S}{F_{HV}} \tag{13}$$

where

$$S = \sum_{i=1}^{K} \sum_{j=1}^{N} u_{ij}$$

$$\forall X_j \in \left\{X_j : (X_j - V_i) F_i^{-1} (X_j - V_i) < 1\right\}. \tag{14}$$

An example for estimating the optimal number of subsets in a data set, using the performance measures, is demonstrated in Fig. 1. The data set is the 150 patterns describing three iris subspecies [17], [18]. Plotting the performance measures F_{HV} and P_D as a function of the number of subgroups in the data set shows points of extremum at $k = 3$, in accordance with the botanically correct number of classes.

The F_{HV} criterion shows a clear extremum in most of the cases. However, the density criteria will be more sensitive as performance measures when there are substantial overlapping between the clusters and when large variability in compactness of the clusters exists. The D_{PA} criterion reflects the presence of single dense clusters (the fuzzy density is calculated for each cluster and then averaged over all clusters), and thus, partition resulting in both dense and loose clusters is considered a "good" partition because of the dense substructures. The P_D criterion expresses the general partition density according to the physical definition of density.

III. Sample Runs

In order to test the performance of the algorithm a simulation program was written, generating N artificial m-dimensional feature vectors from a multivariate normal distribution. The input to the program consisted of: 1) N, the number of data points. 2) m, dimension of feature space. 3) K, the number of required subsets in the data. 4) The required m-dimensional cluster prototypes. 5) The variance of each feature in each of the clusters. 6) The relative number of data points in each subset. By choosing the distances between cluster prototypes to be near each other, and controlling the variance of the features, overlapping between clusters could be obtained, resulting in a fuzzy environment. The features had unequal variance generating hyperellipsoidal clusters. The number of subgroups in the data, their density, and number of data points in each subgroup were subject to variation. Another artificial data set was taken from Gustafson and Kessel [10], and the algorithm was also tested on the iris data of Anderson [17] and Fisher [18], and feature vectors derived from sleep EEG. As to the algorithmic parameter q, a theoretical basis for an optimal choice of the weighting exponent is so far not available [11], [19], [20]. A value of $q = 2$ [7], [10], [11], [21] was chosen for the UFP-ONC algorithm.

Example 1: This example demonstrates optimal partition of touching clusters with large variability in cluster densities and number of data points in each cluster. In Fig. 2(a), an artificial data set with two-dimensional feature vectors drawn from a bivariate normal distribution is demonstrated. One of the subgroups in the data is large and loose, while the other is small and shows a much higher density of the data points. There is no clear border between the subgroups.

Using the fuzzy K-means algorithm alone results in misclassification of boundary data points, Fig. 2(b). Peripheral data points generated by the loose cluster will be misclassified as belonging to the high density cluster. Application of the UFP-ONC algorithm classifies correctly all 200 data points, Fig. 2(c).

Example 2: This example demonstrates successful partition of

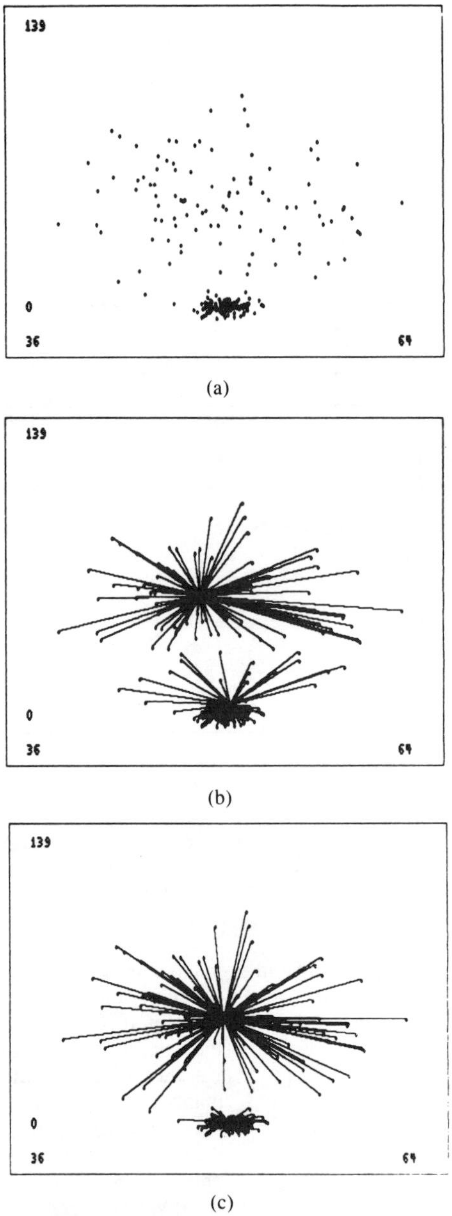

Fig. 2. Partition of simulated data with unequally variable features. (a) Two hundred data points generated from a bivariate Gaussian distribution. There are two subgroups in the data, one large and loose and the other small and dense. (b) Partition using the fuzzy K-means algorithm. Peripheral points generated by the loose cluster are misclassified as belonging to the smaller cluster. (c) The UFP-ONC algorithm classifies correctly all 200 data points.

linear substructures. Fig. 3(a) demonstrates two linear clusters, generated from a uniform distribution by Gustafson and Kessel [10]. The two subsets consist of two long and narrow formations, at right angle to each other. The cluster centers were generated to coincide exactly with each other. Running the UFP-ONC algorithm gives the two clusters, Fig. 3(b), with no misclassification of any of the points.

Example 3: This example shows optimal partition of a data set with multiple substructures. Twelve different clusters are generated from a multivariate normal distribution, Fig. 4(a). The feature space is five-dimensional. There is a significant variability of shapes, densities, and number of patterns in each cluster. The performance measures for estimating the number of subgroups in the data set are depicted in Figs. 4(b) and (c). A minimum for $k = 12$ is clearly seen for the F_{HV} criterion, as well as a maximum for $k = 12$ for the partition density criterion. The partition, running the UFP-ONC algorithm is shown in Fig. 4(d). All the patterns have been correctly classified.

Example 4: The iris data set of Anderson [17] and Fisher [18] has three subgroups, two of which are overlapping. Estimation of the optimal number of substructures in the data set (whether it is 2 or 3) is the crucial point here. The patterns are depicted in Fig. 5(a), and the F_{HV} and P_D curves in Fig. 1. The optimal number of subgroups in the data set is given by the minimum of the F_{HV} curve and the maximum of the P_D curve at $k = 3$ clusters. Partition into the three clusters is shown in Fig. 5(b). There are 4 misclassifications within the 150 patterns (an error of 2.7 percent). Three plants of Iris Versicolor have been classified as Iris Virginica, whereas only one plant of Iris Virginica has been attributed to Iris Versicolor. All 50 Iris Setosa plants have been correctly classified.

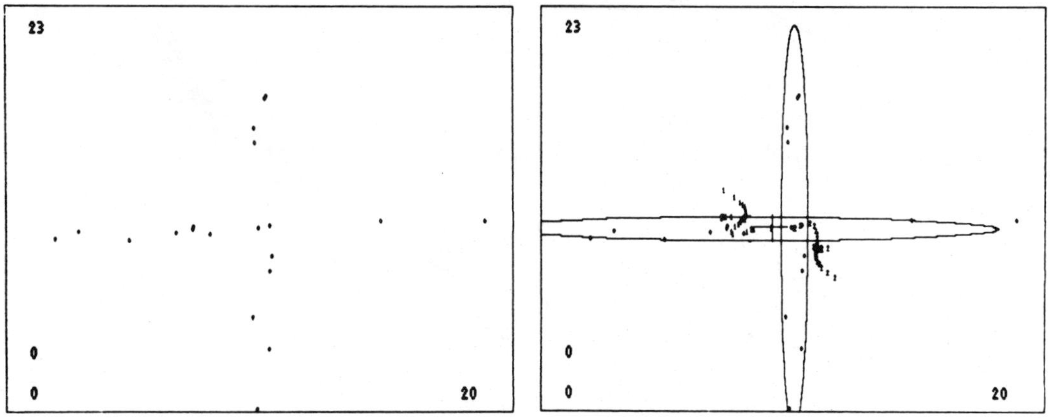

(a) (b)

Fig. 3. Partition of linear clusters, data of Gustafson and Kessel [10]. (a) Twenty data points drawn from a uniform distribution. The two subsets consist of two long and narrow formations, at right angle to each other. (b) Convergence of the two centroids to their final locations running the UFP-ONC algorithm. The trajectories of the two centroids during the iterations can be followed by the points denoted by small numerals 1 and 2. Two standard deviations are drawn around the final centroids. All data points have been correctly classified.

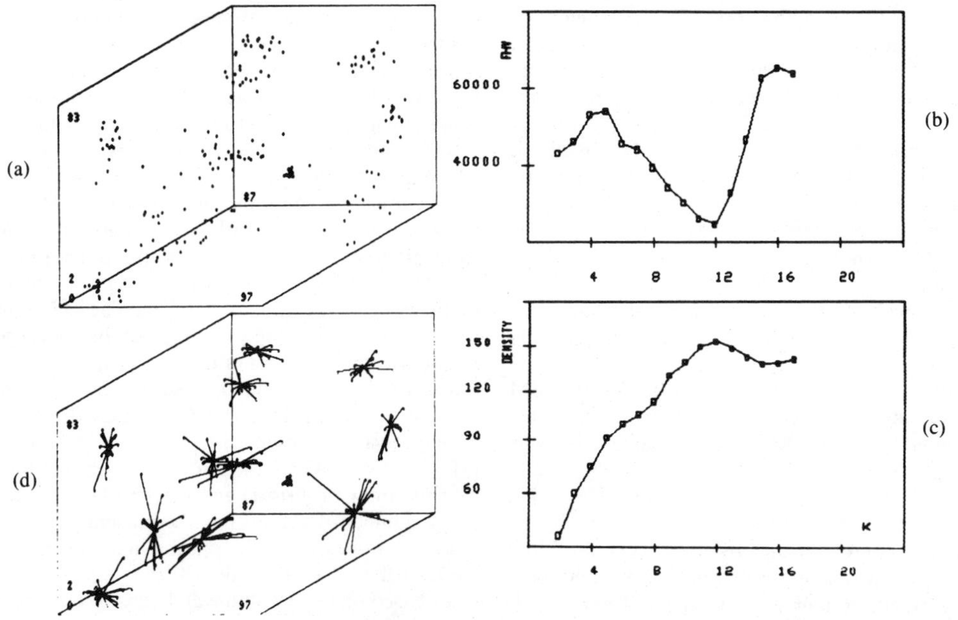

Fig. 4. Partition of 12 clusters generated from five-dimensional multivariate Gaussian distribution with unequally variable features, variable densities and variable number of data points in each cluster. (a) Data points before partition. Only three of the features are displayed. (b), (c) Fuzzy hypervolume (FHV) and partition density, as a function of the number of subgroups in the data. Extrema for $k = 12$ can be seen. (d) Partition of 12 subgroups using the UFP-ONC algorithm. All data points have been correctly classified.

Example 5: Computerized scoring of sleep EEG into various stages [1], [4], [14], [22] represents a typical example of handling real data by fuzzy clustering. The patterns characterizing sleep EEG segments generate a fuzzy environment, with some traits complicating any process of classification:

1) Physiologically, there are continuous transitions between the sleep stages, i.e., the subgroups *are not well separated.*

2) There is a great deal of intersubject variability of the spectral features of the various sleep stages, and *the features have unequal variance* (large variability in cluster shapes).

3) The number of stationary EEG segments and the variability of their features differ for the various sleep stages (variability in cluster densities and number of data points in each cluster).

4) The number of sleep stages might vary between subjects (depends on age, pathological conditions, etc.), i.e., the number of subgroups in the data *is not known a priori.*

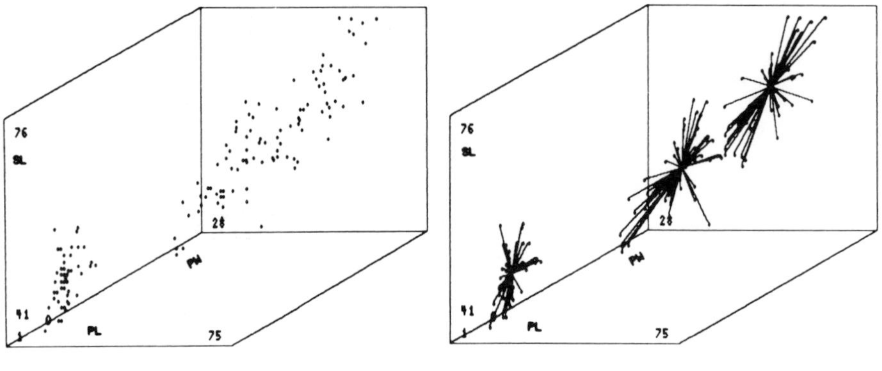

Fig. 5. Classification of the Iris data of Anderson and Fisher using the UFP-ONC algorithm. (a) 150 four-dimensional feature vectors. Only three of the features are displayed here: PL—Petal length. PW—Petal width. SL—Sepal length. (b) Fuzzy partition to three subgroups. There are a total of four errors, three items of Iris Versicolor have been misclassified as Iris Virginica whereas one Iris Virginica has been misclassified as Iris Versicolor.

Thus, even if one fixes the number of subgroups in the data set, fuzzy clustering of sleep EEG using either of the algorithms described in [5], [10], [19] does not guarantee optimal partition.

Patterns representing a whole night's sleep EEG segments from a 30 year old female are shown in Fig. 6(a). The five features, derived by adaptive segmentation and time-dependent clustering of the signal [4], are the relative power in the physiological frequency bands, delta, theta, alpha, sigma, and beta. One of the criteria for estimating the optimal number of classes in the data F_{HV} is plotted in Fig. 6(b). From the minimum in the curve it can be concluded that there are five subgroups. The partition and classification histogram (hypnogram) are depicted in Figs. 6(c) and (d), respectively. For comparison, a hypnogram scored manually by a physician is given in Fig. 6(e). There is a clear similarity between the two classification histograms. Due to the scanty number of EEG segments belonging to sleep stage I, sleep stage wake and sleep stage I have been classified by the UFP-ONC algorithm as being one class.

The CPU requirements of the UFP-ONC algorithm on the IBM AT personal computer, analyzing four-dimensional 150 patterns (iris data), with K, the maximal number of clusters equal to 6, was 14 min.

IV. Conclusions

Implementing the strategy of unsupervised tracking of initial cluster centroids, the most flexible algorithm has been found to be the fuzzy K-means, although it does not give optimal partition in cases of variable cluster shapes and densities. On the other hand, using an "exponential" distance measure including the fuzzy covariance matrix (the FMLE algorithm [7], [11], [15]) results in optimal partition even when a great variability of cluster shapes and densities is present. An optimal performance of the FMLE algorithm requires starting from "good" seed points, because due to the "exponential" distance this algorithm converges to a local optimum in a rather narrow region. Taking this limitation into account, the FMLE algorithm is superior to Gustafson and Kessel's [10] fuzzy covariance algorithm, in that it does not require an extra volume constraint (the ρ_j of Gustafson and Kessel), limitation on the hypervolume being achieved through the exponent.

The new algorithm described in the present study combines the favorable features of both the fuzzy K-means algorithm and the FMLE, together with unsupervised tracking of classification prototypes. Optimal partition has been achieved with the UFP-ONC algorithm for several synthetic data sets, as well as for sleep EEG classification, omitting the need for initial guesses on cluster prototypes. The iris data set [17], [18] is a well known example of overlapping substructures. The results of applying the UFP-ONC algorithm in this case were optimal, both from the point of view of estimating the number of underlying substructures, and that of classification error rate [23]–[25]. Extending the notion of hyperellipsoidal clusters to the extreme, by letting one feature vary much less than the others, gives rise to line-like clusters. Graph-theoretic methods have been proven to be successful in detecting linear substructures [26], but in general these methods fail on hyperellipsoidal clusters [8]. Due to the inclusion of the FMLE in the UFP-ONC algorithm, the new algorithm is also able to detect line-like clusters, as demonstrated on the data of Gustafson and Kessel [10].

Performance measures for assessing cluster validity have been proposed in the framework of ranking various partitions obtained from different clustering algorithms. Such a cluster validity strategy was implemented in [16], using performance measures based on fuzzy decomposition of the data. The search for a proper cluster validity criterion in the present study has been goal-oriented, with relation to the application domain [16], [27]. The aim was to estimate the optimal number of substructures in the data set for the purpose of classification (minimum classification error rate). It has been motivated by studies of automatic classification of sleep stages [4], [14], [22], where the number of subsets in the data is not necessarily known *a priori*, and where a large intersubject variability of the number of classes may be present.

In order to estimate the optimal number of subgroups present in the data the UFP-ONC algorithm incorporates performance measures based on hypervolume and density criteria. The hypervolume criterion is related to the within-cluster scatter, but due to its fuzzy characteristics the F_{HV}, unlike the square error criterion, is not a monotone function of k. These performance measures (and in particular the hypervolume criterion) plotted as a function of the number of clusters k show a clear extremum, from which conclusions as to the optimal number of substructures in the data can be drawn. This has been demonstrated for the iris data, where the botanically correct number of clusters was detected by the new algorithm.

Other performance measures, aimed at delineating the number of subgroups in the data set, are either monotone functions of k [11], [28], or show a very slight preference for a certain value of k, as is the case with Windham's proportional exponent and the UDF criterion [24], [21] applied to the iris data. The cluster separation measure of Davis and Bouldin [29] failed to uncover the botanically correct number of classes for the iris data, in addition to exhibiting two extra local minima, botanically meaningless. Jain and Moreau [30] developed a method for cluster validity based on the bootstrap technique, that could be used with any clustering algorithm. Using a criterion based on Davis and Bouldin's [29] clus-

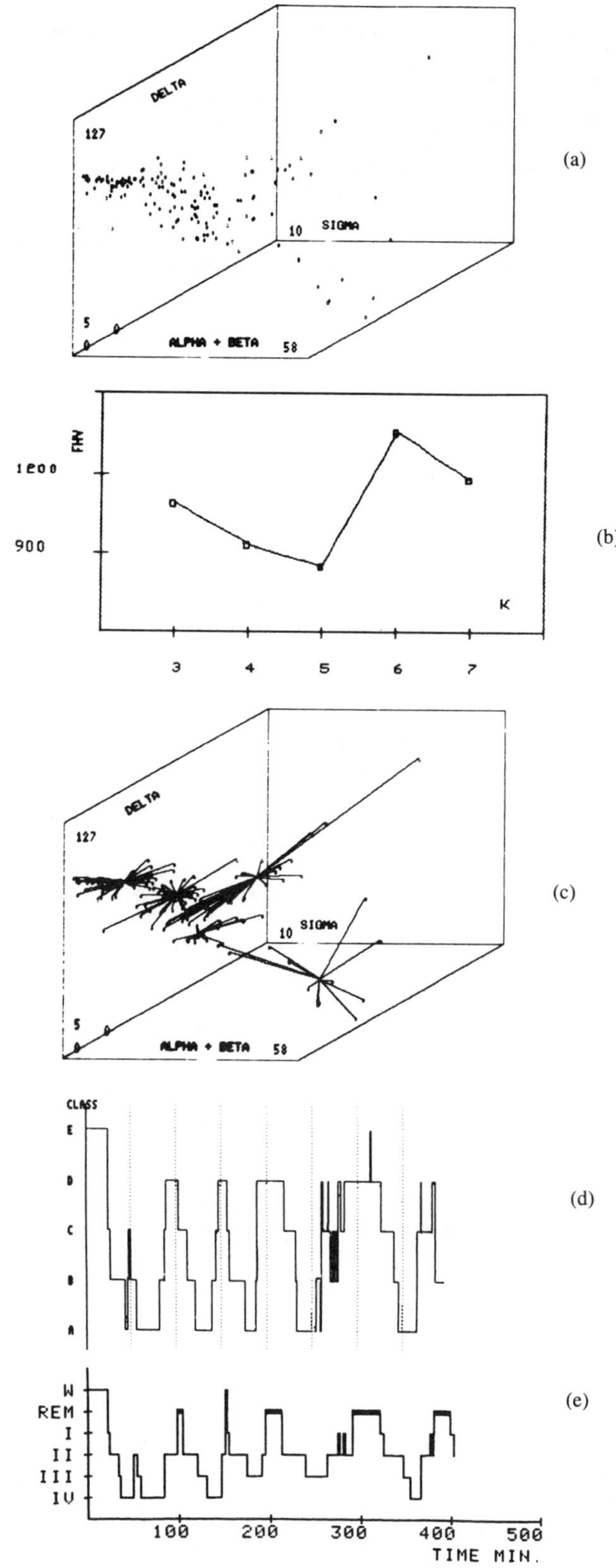

Fig. 6. Fuzzy classification of sleep EEG segments derived from adaptive segmentation of a whole nights sleep EEG. The five-dimensional feature vectors include the relative power in the physiological frequency bands delta, theta, alpha, beta, and sigma. (a) Data points before partition. (b) Performance measures. Fuzzy hypervolume as a function of k, the number of subgroups in the data. A minimum for $k = 5$ can be seen. (c) Partition using the UFP-ONC algorithm. (d) Classification histogram. (a)-(e) are the various classes. (e) Manual scoring of the same EEG as in (a)-(d) by a physician into sleep stages. W—waking. REM—rapid eye movement sleep. I, II, III, IV—non-REM sleep stages.

ter separation measure, and on cluster compactness measure (within-cluster scatter), both the K-means and Ward clustering algorithms succeeded in detecting the botanically correct number of classes for the iris data set.

Acknowledgment

The authors wish to thank Dr. E. Bar-On for valuable discussions, and to Prof. A. K. Jain for reading the manuscript and providing many useful suggestions. The research was supported by the Kennedy-Leigh fund for Biomedical Engineering Research.

References

[1] L. Larsen, E. Ruspini, J. McDew, D. Walter, and W. Adey, "A test of sleep staging system in the unrestrained chimpanzee," *Brain Res.*, vol. 40, pp. 319-343, 1972.

[2] J. C. Bezdek, "Feature selection for binary data: Medical diagnosis with fuzzy sets," in *Proc. 25th Nat. Computer Conf.*, 1976, pp. 1057-1068.

[3] J. C. Bezdek and W. A. Fordon, "Analysis of hypertensive patients by the use of fuzzy ISODATA algorithm," in *Proc. JACC*, vol. 3, 1978, pp. 349-356.

[4] I. Gath and E. Bar-On, "Computerized method for scoring of polygraphic sleep recordings," *Comput. Progr. Biomed.*, vol. 11, pp. 217-223, 1980.

[5] J. C. Bezdek, "Fuzzy mathematics in pattern classification," Ph.D. dissertation, Cornell Univ., Ithaca, NY, 1973.

[6] —, "A convergence theorem for the fuzzy ISODATA clustering algorithms," *IEEE Trans. Pattern Anal. Machine Intell.*, vol. PAMI-2, no. 1, pp. 1-8, 1980.

[7] J. C. Bezdek and J. C. Dunn, "Optimal fuzzy partition: A heuristic for estimating the parameters in a mixture of normal distributions," *IEEE Trans. Comput.*, vol. C-24, pp. 835-838, 1975.

[8] J. C. Bezdek, C. Coray, R. Gunderson, and J. Watson, "Detection and characterization of cluster substructure. I. Linear structure: Fuzzy c-lines," *SIAM J. Appl. Math.*, vol. 40, pp. 339-357, 1981.

[9] J. J. C. Bezdek, C. Coray, R. Gunderson, and J. Watson, "Detection and characterization of cluster substructure. II. Fuzzy c-varieties and convex combinations thereof," *SIAM J. Appl. Math.*, vol. 40, pp. 358-372, 1981.

[10] E. E. Gustafson and W. C. Kessel, "Fuzzy clustering with a fuzzy covariance matrix," in *Proc. IEEE CDC*, San Diego, CA, 1979, pp. 761-766.

[11] J. C. Bezdek, *Pattern Recognition with Fuzzy Objective Function Algorithms.* New York: Plenum, 1981.

[12] A. S. Gevins, "Pattern recognition of human brain electrical potentials," *IEEE Trans. Pattern Anal. Machine Intell.*, vol. PAMI-2, no. 5, pp. 383-404, 1980.

[13] B. H. Jansen and W. K. Cheng, "Classification of sleep patterns by means of markov modeling and correspondence analysis," *IEEE Trans. Pattern Anal. Machine Intell.*, vol. PAMI-9, no. 5, pp. 707-710, 1987.

[14] I. Gath and E. Bar-On, "Classical sleep stages and the spectral content of the EEG signal," *Int. J. Neurosci.*, vol. 22, pp. 147-155, 1983.

[15] N. E. Day, "Estimating the components of a mixture of normal distributions," *Biometrika*, vol. 56, pp. 463-474, 1969.

[16] E. Backer and A. K. Jain, "A clustering performance measure based on fuzzy set decomposition," *IEEE Trans. Pattern Anal. Machine Intell.*, vol. PAMI-3, no. 1, pp. 66-74, 1981.

[17] E. Anderson, "The irises of the Gaspe peninsula," *Bull. Amer. Iris Soc.*, vol. 59, pp. 2-5, 1935.

[18] R. A. Fisher, "The use of multiple measurements in taxonomic problems," *Ann. Eugenics*, vol. 7, pp. 179-188, 1936.

[19] K. Leszczynski, P. Penczek, and W. Grochulski, "Sugeno's fuzzy measure and fuzzy clustering," *Fuzzy Sets Syst.*, vol. 15, pp. 147-158, 1985.

[20] R. L. Cannon, J. V. Dave, and J. C. Bezdek, "Efficient implementation of the fuzzy c-means clustering algorithms," *IEEE Trans. Pattern Anal. Machine Intell.*, vol. PAMI-8, no. 2, pp. 248-255, 1986.

[21] M. P. Windham, "Cluster validity for the fuzzy c-means clustering algorithm," *IEEE Trans. Pattern Anal. Machine Intell.*, vol. PAMI-4, no. 4, pp. 357-363, 1982.

[22] I. Gath and E. Bar-On, "Sequential fuzzy clustering of sleep EEG recordings," in *Methods of Sleep Research*, S. Kubicki and W. Herrmann, Eds. Jena, Germany: Gustav Fischer, 1985, pp. 55-64.
[23] J. C. Bezdek, "Numerical taxonomy with fuzzy sets," *J. Math. Biol.*, vol. 1-1, pp. 57-71, 1974.
[24] M. P. Windham, "Cluster validity for fuzzy clustering algorithms," *Fuzzy Sets Syst.*, vol. 3, pp. 1-9, 1980.
[25] T. Gou and B. Dubuisson, "A loose-pattern process approach to clustering fuzzy data sets," *IEEE Trans. Pattern Anal. Machine Intell.*, vol. PAMI-7, no. 3, pp. 366-372, 1985.
[26] C. T. Zahn, "Graph-theoretical methods for detecting and describing gestalt clusters," *IEEE Trans. Comput.*, vol. C-20, no. 1, pp. 68-86, 1971.
[27] R. Dubes and A. K. Jain, "Validity studies in clustering methodologies," *Pattern Recognition*, vol. 11, pp. 235-254, 1979.
[28] P. H. A. Sneath and R. Sokal, *Numerical Taxonomy*. San Francisco, CA: Freeman, 1973.
[29] D. L. Davis and D. W. Bouldin, "A cluster separation measure," *IEEE Trans. Pattern Anal. Machine Intell.*, vol. PAMI-1, no. 2, pp. 224-227, 1979.
[30] A. K. Jain and J. V. Moreau, "Bootstrap technique in cluster analysis," *Pattern Recognition*, vol. 20, no. 5, pp. 547-568, 1987.

A Validity Measure for Fuzzy Clustering

XUANLI LISA XIE AND GERARDO BENI

Abstract—**Cluster analysis has been playing an important role in solving many problems in pattern recognition and image processing. This correspondence presents a fuzzy validity criterion based on a validity function which identifies overall compact and separate fuzzy c-partitions without assumptions as to the number of substructures inherent in the data. This function depends on the data set, geometric distance measure, distance between cluster centroids, and more importantly on the fuzzy partition generated by any fuzzy algorithm used. The function is mathematically justified via its relationship to a well-defined hard clustering validity function: the separation index, for which the condition of uniqueness has already been established. The performance evaluation of this validity function compares favorably to that of several others. Finally, we have applied this validity function to color image segmentation in a computer color vision system for recognition of IC wafer defects which are otherwise impossible to detect using gray-scale image processing.**

Index Terms—**Cluster validity, color vision, fuzzy clustering, IC wafer defect detection, image segmentation, pattern recognition, separate and compact clusters.**

I. INTRODUCTION

The engineering literature has paid very little attention to cluster validity issues [1], limiting the effort to present new clustering algorithms which perform reasonably well on a few data sets. In particular, the issue of validity for clustering of fuzzy data sets has been neglected (with few notable exceptions [2],[3]). On the other hand, if fuzzy cluster analysis is to make a significant contribution to engineering applications, much more attention must be paid to fundamental questions of cluster tendency. Recently, validity of fuzzy clustering has been discussed in applications to mixtures of normal distributions [4]. Also applications to distributed perception [5] have been proposed which rely in an essential way on good validity criteria for fuzzy clustering.

In the latter applications, separated sensors observe a common set of objects. They communicate to a central processor and not (perceptual) data (which, due to their size, cannot be transmitted in real time) [6] but decisions (which, due to their smaller bit size, can be transmitted in real time). In such cases, a fundamental decision is often the determination of the number of "objects" observed, i.e., the validity of the clustering procedure. Since higher level decisions by the central processor are based on the validity of these separated clustering procedures, it is essential that an efficient method is developed for fuzzy clustering validity.

Generally, the issue of cluster validity is a broad one and involves many questions. In view of the applications to distributed perception, in this correspondence, we focus on the validity of a partition. The answer is sought, as is generally accepted [1],[3], in measures of separation among clusters and cohesion within clusters.

The correspondence is organized as follows. In Section II, we review the fuzzy c-means clustering algorithm and some validity criteria related to our work for both fuzzy and hard clustering. Section III presents our new fuzzy validity function and its implementation strategy. Section IV contains the mathematical justification of the fuction and numerical comparisons to other validity fuctions. In Section V, we describe an application of our validity fuction to color image segmentation for recognition of defects in integrated circuit (IC) wafers.

Manuscript received August 15, 1989; revised December 21, 1990. This work was supported in part by the National Science Foundation under Grant 08421415.

The authors are with the Center for Robotic Systems, University of California, Santa Barbara, CA 93106.

IEEE Log Number 9142752.

II. CLUSTERING ALGORITHM AND VALIDITY CRITERIA

Clustering is a tool that attempts to assess the relationships among patterns of the data set by organizing the patterns into groups or clusters such that patterns within a cluster are more similar to each other than are patterns belonging to different clusters. Many algorithms [2],[3],[7] for both hard and fuzzy clustering have been developed to accomplish this. An intimately related important issue is the "cluster validity" which deals with the significance of the structure imposed by a clustering method. Performance of many existing clustering algorithms are studied in [8]. Here we briefly review the fuzzy c-means clustering algorithm for later reference.

A. Fuzzy c-Means Clustering Algorithm

The fuzzy c-means (FCM) clustering algorithm (Bezdek [2]) is the fuzzy equivalent of the nearest mean "hard" clustering algorithm (Duda and Hart [9]), which minimizes the following objective function with respect to fuzzy membership μ_{ij} and cluster centroid V_i.

$$J_m = \sum_{i=1}^{c}\sum_{j=1}^{n}(\mu_{ij})^m d^2(X_j, V_i), \tag{1}$$

where

$$d^2(X_j, V_i) = (X_j - V_i)^T A(X_j - V_i). \tag{2}$$

A is a $p \times p$ positive definite matrix, p is the dimension of the vectors $X_j (j = 1, 2, \cdots, n)$, c is the number of clusters, n is the number of vectors (or data points), and $m > 1$ is the fuzziness index [2]. The FCM algorithm is executed in the following steps [2].

1) Initialize memberships μ_{ij} of X_j belonging to cluster i such that

$$\sum_{i=1}^{c}\mu_{ij} = 1. \tag{3}$$

2) Compute the fuzzy centroid V_i for $i = 1, 2, \cdots, c$ using

$$V_i = \frac{\sum_{j=1}^{n}(\mu_{ij})^m X_j}{\sum_{j=1}^{n}(\mu_{ij})^m}. \tag{4}$$

Reprinted from *IEEE Trans. Pattern Anal. Machine Intell.*, vol. PAMI-13, no. 8, pp. 841–847, August 1991.

3) Update the fuzzy membership μ_{ij} using

$$\mu_{ij} = \frac{\left(\frac{1}{d^2(X_j,V_i)}\right)^{\frac{1}{(m-1)}}}{\sum_{i=1}^{c}\left(\frac{1}{d^2(X_j,V_i)}\right)^{\frac{1}{(m-1)}}}. \tag{5}$$

4) Repeat steps 2) and 3) until the value of J_m is no longer decreasing.

The FCM algorithm always converges to strict local minima of J_m [2, p. 80] starting from an initial guess of μ_{ij}, but different choices of initial μ_{ij} might lead to different local minima.

B. Validity Criteria for Hard and Fuzzy Clustering

A well-established hard cluster validity criterion is the separation index D_1 (Dunn [12]) which identifies "compact, separate" (CS) clusters and is defined by

$$D_1 = \min_{1\le i\le c}\left\{\min_{i+1\le j\le c-1}\left\{\frac{\text{dis}\,(u_i,u_j)}{\max\limits_{1\le k\le c}\{\text{dia}\,(u_k)\}}\right\}\right\}, \tag{6}$$

where

$$\text{dia}\,(u_k) = \max_{X_i,X_j\in u_k} d(X_i,X_j), \tag{7}$$

$$\text{dis}\,(u_i,u_j) = \min_{X_i\in u_i, X_j\in u_j} d(X_i,X_j). \tag{8}$$

d is any metric induced by an inner product on R^p. The CS clustering of X is to be found by solving $\max\limits_{2\le c\le n}\left\{\max\limits_{\Omega_c} D_1\right\}$, where Ω_c denotes the optimality candidates at fixed c. It is proved [12] that a hard c-partition of X contains c compact, separate (CS) clusters if $D_1 > 1$. Furthermore, there is at most one CS partition of X if $D_1 > 1$. The main drawback with direct implementation of this validity measure is computational since calculating D_1 becomes computationally very expensive as c and n increase. Another validity criterion which also measures compact and separate clusters is introduced by Davies and Bouldin [13]. Its major difference from D_1 is that it considers the average case by using the average error of each class. Jain and Moreau [14] also defined a method for cluster validity by using a bootstrap technique, that could be used with any clustering algorithm.

As a fuzzy clustering validity function Bezdek [15] designed the partition coefficient F to measure the amount of "overlap" between clusters.

$$F = \frac{1}{n}\sum_{i=1}^{c}\sum_{j=1}^{n}(\mu_{ij})^2. \tag{9}$$

In this form F is inversely proportional to the overall average overlap between pairs of fuzzy subsets. In particular, there is no membership sharing between any pairs of fuzzy clusters if $F = 1$. Solving $\max\limits_{c}\left\{\max\limits_{\Omega_c}\{F\}\right\}$ $(c = 2, 3 \ldots n-1)$ is assumed to produce valid clustering of the data set X. Disadvantages of the partition coefficient are the lack of direct connection to a geometrical property and its monotonic decreasing tendency with c. There are several other criteria in the literature which also measure the amount of fuzziness, such as classification entropy [16], proportion exponent [17], uniform data functional [18], nonfuzziness index [19], and information ratio [20]. Those criteria share a similar drawback with F, that is the lack of direct connection to the geometrical property of data set.

Gunderson [21] introduced a separation coefficient which takes into account geometrical properties. This validity criterion is designed to identify compact and separated clusters (which is similar to our goal). However, this method cannot be directly applied. It works on fuzzy clustering outputs by first converting them to hard ones. Since there are many ways one can convert fuzzy partitions to hard ones, this method shares the shortcomings of nonuniqueness of transferring from fuzzy partitions to hard partitions.

III. A Compact and Separate Fuzzy Validity Criterion

In this section, we define S as a fuzzy clustering validity function which measures the overall average compactness and separation of a fuzzy c-partition. We also present an implementation strategy for the use of this function.

A. Definition of a New Fuzzy Clustering Validity Function S

Consider a fuzzy c-partition of the data set $X = \{X_j; j = 1, 2, \cdots, n\}$ with $V_i (i = 1, 2, \cdots, c)$ the centroid of each cluster and $\mu_{ij} (i = 1, 2, \cdots, c, j = 1, 2, \cdots, n)$ as the fuzzy membership of data point j (also called vector j) belonging to class i.

Definition 1: $d_{ij} = \mu_{ij}\|X_j - V_i\|$, is called the *fuzzy deviation* of X_j from class i.

Note that $\|\cdot\|$ is the usual Euclidean norm. Thus d_{ij} is just the Euclidean distance between X_j and V_i weighted by the fuzzy membership of data point j belonging to class i.

Definition 2: $n_i = \sum_{x}{}_j\mu_{ij}$ is the *fuzzy number* of vectors in or fuzzy cardinality of class i.

Note that $\sum_{x}{}_i n_i = n$, where n is a "hard" number, e.g., the total number of data points in X. In the extreme case, when the partition is hard, n_i becomes exactly the number of vectors in class i.

Definition 3: For each class i, the summation of the squares of fuzzy deviation of each data point, denoted by σ_i, is called the *variation* of class i, that is: $\sigma_i = \sum_{x}{}_j(d_{ij})^2 = (d_{i1})^2 + (d_{i2})^2 + \cdots + (d_{in})^2$. The summation of the variations of all classes, denoted by σ, is called the *total variation* of data set X with respect to the fuzzy c-partition, i.e., $\sigma = \sum_{x}{}_i\sigma_i = \sum_{x}{}_i\sum_{x}{}_j(d_{ij})^2$.

Note that σ_i and σ depend on the data set, but more importantly they depend on the fuzzy c-partition, i.e., μ_{ij}'s and V_i's. A better c-partition should result in smaller σ. These values are not normalized, and they depend on how we choose our coordinate system. For example, if the fuzzy c-partition is obtained by using the fuzzy c-means algorithm with $m = 2$, the value of σ will be equal to the c-means objective function J_2 in (1).

Definition 4: The ratio, denoted by π, of the total variation to the size of the data set, that is, $\pi = (\sigma/n)$, is called the *compactness* of the fuzzy c-partition of the data set.

The value π measures how compact each and every class is. The more compact the classes are, the smaller π is. π is a function of the distribution characteristics of the data set itself, and more importantly a function of how we divide the data points into clusters. But it is independent of the number of data points. For a given data set, a smaller π indicates that we have reached a partition with more compact clusters, thus indicating a better partition. Gath and Geva [4] introduced fuzzy hypervolume which is the probability weighted total variation. This validity measure can identify ellipsoidal clusters and overlapped clusters. By incorporating covariance into the distance matrix A in (2), π can also identify ellipsoidal clusters.

Definition 5: The quantity $\pi_i = (\sigma_i/n_i)$ is called the *compactness of class* i.

Since n_i is the number of vectors in class i, σ_i/n_i is the average variation in class i. We have defined the compactness of fuzzy c-partition in terms of total variation and number of vectors. After defining π_i, we have some alternative ways to define the compactness of the fuzzy c-partition, such as: $\pi = (\sum_x {}_i\pi_i)/c$, i.e., the average compactness of each class; or $\pi = \max \pi_i$, i.e., the worst case. It can be shown that both ways have similar effect to Definition 4.

Definition 6: $s = (d_{\min})^2$ is called the *separation* of the fuzzy c-partition, where $d_{\min}$ is the minimum distance between cluster centroids, i.e.,

$$d_{\min} = \min_{i,j} \|V_i - V_j\|.$$

A larger s indicates that all the clusters are separated.

Definition 7: The *compactness and separation validity function* S is defined as the ratio of compactness π to the separation s, i.e., $S = \pi/s$.

After substituting for π and s, we get $S = (\sigma/n)/(d_{\min})^2$. A smaller S indicates a partition in which all the clusters are overall compact, and separate to each other. Thus, our goal is to find the fuzzy c-partition with the smallest S.

S can be explicitly written as

$$S = \frac{\sum_{i=1}^{c}\sum_{j=1}^{n} \mu_{ij}^2 \|V_i - X_j\|^2}{n \min_{i,j} \|V_i - V_j\|^2}. \tag{10}$$

We note that the definition of S is independent of the algorithm used to obtain μ_{ij}. Thus it is not internal to the clustering algorithm. For the FCM algorithm with $m = 2$, S can be shown to be

$$S = \frac{J_2}{n * (d_{\min})^2} \tag{11}$$

which is very easy to calculate. More importantly, minimizing S corresponds to minimizing J_2, which is the goal of FCM. The additional factor in S is $(d_{\min})^2$, which is the separation measurement. The more separate the clusters, the larger $(d_{\min})^2$, and the smaller S. Thus, the smallest S indeed indicates a valid optimal partition. If the fuzzy clustering algorithm used is to optimize some very different J, one may wish to modify the compactness measure so that minimizing S is compatible with minimizing J. For example, in (1) $m \neq 2$; then we can substitute ${\mu_{ij}}^2$ by ${\mu_{ij}}^m$ in (10).

We note, however, that S is still monotonically decreasing when c gets very large and close to n. One thing we can do is to impose an *ad hoc* punishing function [22] to eliminate this decreasing tendency. How to choose this function is not discussed here. Nevertheless, we shall see that even without a punishing function the validity function S provides a well defined method to solve the validity problem.

There are some existing validity criteria in the literature which measure compact and separate clustering. The separation coefficient in [21] considers the worst case, whereas S considers the total average case. Furthermore, the separation coefficient cannot be directly applied to fuzzy clustering as mentioned before. In [13], Davies and Bouldin introduce a hard partition validity criterion R. It is roughly related to S by $R = S/c$ if S is used for hard partitions. However, from our experience, S/c has a strong decreasing tendency as c increases.

B. Minimization of S and Implementation Strategy

Since smaller S means a more compact and separate c-partition, we assume that the minimum S partition is the most valid. Thus, a heuristic strategy to use S as a validity function is as follows. Using any fuzzy clustering algorithm, find one or more optimal c-partitions of the data set X for each $c = 2, 3, \cdots, n-1$. Let Ω_c denote the optimality candidates at each c; then the solution of

$$\min_{2 \le c \le n-1} \left\{ \min_{\Omega_c} S \right\}$$

is assumed to yield the most valid fuzzy clustering of the data set X.

Once we have defined the validity function S, our implementing strategy can be summarized into the following pseudo algorithm.

1) Initialize $c \leftarrow 2, S^* \leftarrow \infty, c^* \leftarrow 1$;
2) Initialize fuzzy membership μ_{ij};
3) Use any stable fuzzy clustering algorithm to update centroids V_i and μ_{ij};
4) Do convergence test; if negative goto 3;
5) Compute function S;
6) If $S < S^*, S* \leftarrow S, c^* \leftarrow c$;
7) If optimal candidate not found, goto 2;
8) $c \leftarrow c + 1$, if c =stop-value, stop;
9) Goto 2;

Steps 2–4 are the fuzzy c-partition algorithm. For FCM, (4) and (5) can be used. The convergence test can be $(J_m)_{q+1} - (J_m)_q \epsilon$ (e.g., 0.001), where q is an iteration index and J_m is as in (1). With $m = 2$, the S can be easily calculated as in (11). In step 2, the initial values of μ_{ij} can be assigned randomly and then normalized to satisfy $\sum_i \mu_{ij} = 1$ for all j. There is another way to initialize μ_{ij} for $c > 2$ in [23]: we do not discuss it here.

A problem of implementation is that S will have a tendency to eventually decrease when c is very large. So, the value of S is meaningless when c gets close to n. Fortunately, this is not a serious problem since in practice the feasible number of clusters c is much smaller than the number of data points n. Thus we can use the following three heuristic methods to determine the stop-value of step 8.

First, as mentioned in Section III-A, we can use a punishing function which imposes on S to counter this decreasing tendency. In Dunn [22], the "normalization and standardization of a validity function" is a simple example of the idea of punishing function.

The second method is that of plotting the optimal value of S for $c = 2$ to $n - 1$, then selecting the starting point of monotonically decreasing tendency as the maximum c to be considered. Let $c_{\max}$ denote such a c; then, we find c by solving $\min_{2 \le C \le C_{\max}} \left\{ \min_{\Omega_c} s \right\}$.

The third way is application dependent. For most applications we do not need to compute S for very large c. It is almost always the case that c at the stop-value is $\ll n$. In this instance, we can either choose the maximum c according to preknowledge or, e.g., let $c_{\max} = n/3$ which very likely would not reach the starting point of the decreasing tendency.

IV. Mathematical and Numerical Justifications

We have already defined the new validity function and given an implementation strategy to use this function. In this section, we will mathematically justify this new fuzzy validity function via its relationship to a well-established hard partition validity measure and give a numerical example.

A. Uniqueness and Global Optimality of the c-Partition

The separation index D_1 (proposed by Dunn [12]) is a hard c-partition clustering validity criterion. If $D_1 > 1$, unique compact and separated hard clusters have been found. This result turns out to be useful also for fuzzy clustering validity. In fact, we may expect that if the data set X really has distinct substructure, i.e., hard clusters, a fuzzy partitioning algorithm should produce relatively hard memberships μ_{ij} and small total variations. We can prove that if the optimal solution D_1 becomes sufficiently large, the optimal validity function S will be very small, which means that a unique c-partition has been found. The proof of this is as follows.

Definition 8: Let $\mu_{ij}(i = 1,\cdots,c; j = 1,\cdots,n)$ be the membership of any fuzzy c-partition. The corresponding hard c partition of μ_{ij} is defined as ω_{ij}: for $j = 1,2,\cdots,n$: $\omega_{ij} = 1$ if $i = \text{argmax}_i\{\mu_{ij}\}$; $\omega_{ij} = 0$ otherwise.

Theorem 1: For any $c = 2,\cdots,n-1$, let S be the overall compact and separated validity function of any fuzzy partition, and D_1 be the separation index of the corresponding hard partition; then we have

$$S \leq \frac{1}{(D_1)^2}.$$

Proof: Let the fuzzy c-partition be an optimal partition of the data set $X = \{X_j; j = 1,2,\cdots,n\}$ with $V_i(i = 1,2,\cdots c)$ the centroids of each class u_i, and μ_{ij} the fuzzy membership of the data points X_j belonging to class u_i. The total variation σ_{opt} of the optimal fuzzy c-partition is defined in Definition 3. Thus, the total variation σ_h of the corresponding hard c partition is

$$\sigma_h = \sum_i \sum_{X_j \in u_i} \|X_j - V_i\|^2.$$

From the definitions of σ_{opt} and σ_h above, we can get

$$\sigma_{\text{opt}} \leq \sum_i \sum_{X_j \in u_i} \|X_j - V_i\|^2.$$

Suppose that the centroid V_i is inside the boundary of cluster i for $i = 1$ to c. Then

$$\|X_j - V_i\|^2 \leq \text{dia}^2(u_i)$$

for $X_j \in u_i$, where dia(u_i) is defined in (7) . We thus have

$$\begin{aligned}\sigma_{\text{opt}} &\leq \sum_i \sum_{X_j \in u_i} \text{dia}^2(u_i)\\ &\leq \sum_i n_i\, \text{dia}^2(u_i)\\ &\leq n \max\{\text{dia}^2(u_i)\}.\end{aligned}$$

We also have that $(d_{\min})^2 \geq \min\{\text{dis}^2(u_i, u_j)\}$, where dis($u_i, u_j$) was defined in (8); thus

$$\frac{\sigma_{\text{opt}}}{n * (d_{\min})^2} \leq \frac{\max\limits_i\{\text{dia}^2(u_i)\}}{\min\limits_{i,j}\{\text{dis}^2(u_i, u_j)\}}.$$

Using (6) and (10), we get

$$S \leq \frac{1}{(D_1)^2}.$$

Evidently, S becomes arbitrarily small as D_1 grows without bound. As mentioned, it has been proved by Dunn [12] that if $D_1 > 1$ the hard c-partition is unique. Thus, if the data set has a distinct substructure and the fuzzy partition algorithm has found it, then the corresponding $S < 1$.

There are some standard data sets in the literature that have been widely used to verify validity criteria. In Section IV-B, we apply our validity function S to one of this data sets, and compare its performance to existing validity criteria.

B. Clustering Validity Function S and Partition Coefficient F

Both the validity function S and the partition coefficient F are fuzzy validity criteria. Thus we can use the functions directly for

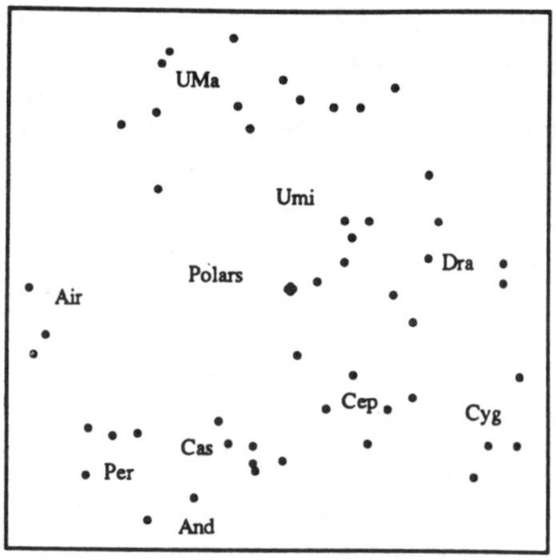

Fig. 1. Nine visually apparent starfield clusters classified by astronomers for fifty-one bright stars near Polaris.

fuzzy cluster validity. But there are differences between the two. F is inversely proportional to the overall average overlap between any pairs of fuzzy subsets, whereas S is proportional to the overall average compactness and separation. F lacks a direct connection to some property of the data themselves. On the other hand, S is directly related to the geometric properties of the data set X, the distance measure on R^p and the locations of cluster centroid. We give an example to compare the results obtained from F and S.

Example 1: Fig. 1 depicts a well-known set data X of 51 points corresponding to 51 bright stars near Polaris projected onto the plane of the Celestial Equator [21]. Considering position and light intensity, astronomers have grouped those stars into nine visual clusters as shown in Fig. 1. This data set has caused difficulty for fuzzy clustering algorithms based on position alone since it has chain-like and unequal population substructure. For example, the graph-theoretic method [24] could be successfully applied to a 60-points superset of X using only (x, y)-coordinates on the equatorial plane. In contrast, the fuzzy c-means did quite poorly with a 48-point subset of X [2].

Several validity methods have been applied to X, such as the partition entropy H [2], the separation coefficient G [21] and the partition coefficient F [2]. However, by directly using these methods, F and H yield $c^* = 2, G$, which measures hard partitions, yields $c^* = 3$. Gunderson in [21] has used a second application of G and obtained $c^* = 10$.

We processed the data set X (x-y coordinates only) using the FCM algorithm with $m = 2, \epsilon = 0.0001$, $\|\cdot\|$ = Euclidean, and $c = 2,3,\cdots 17$. The values of S and F for each c are listed in Table I.

The minimum of S in Table I is $c^* = 8$, the second smallest values yield $c^* = 9$, and $c^* = 10$; all results are close to the number of visual clusters. In contrast the maximum of F is at $c^* = 2$. F decreases to a minimum at $c = 7$, then progresses to $c = 17$ at a nearly constant low value. For the partition of $c^* = 8$ indicated by S, observe (Fig. 2) from the cluster centroids (indicated by symbol '+') that five of them are located in the visual clusters; and for $c^* = 9$ and $c^* = 10$, seven are located in the visual clusters. The fuzzy partition $c^* = 9$ is shown in Fig. 3.

We notice that the star cluster "And" is not an independent cluster according to our results in the partition of either $c^* = 8$ or $c^* = 9$. Also the "UMa" is split into two different clusters. This is expected since considering only the x-y geometric location of X, the distance of two stars of "And" is not close enough and well separated to form an independent cluster while "UMa" has the geometric property

TABLE I
VALUES OF VALIDITY FUNCTION F AND S FOR EXAMPLE 1

No. of Clusters c	Partition Coefficient F	CS Function S
2	0.72*	0.26
3	0.68	0.12
4	0.63	0.18
5	0.62	0.13
6	0.61	0.12
7	0.60	0.20
8	0.62	0.10*
9	0.63	0.11*
10	0.63	0.11*
11	0.62	0.16
12	0.63	0.13
13	0.63	0.14
14	0.63	0.13
15	0.62	0.12
16	0.63	0.27
17	0.63	0.17

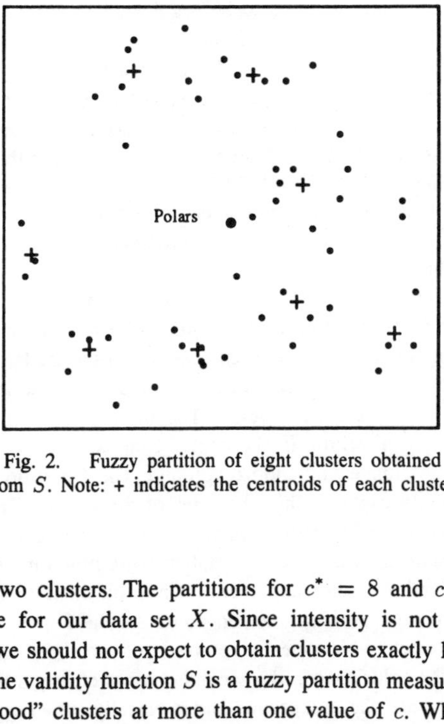

Fig. 2. Fuzzy partition of eight clusters obtained from S. Note: + indicates the centroids of each cluster.

to form two clusters. The partitions for $c^* = 8$ and $c^* = 9$ are reasonable for our data set X. Since intensity is not taken into account, we should not expect to obtain clusters exactly like Fig. 1.

Since the validity function S is a fuzzy partition measurement, we expect "good" clusters at more than one value of c. Which one is more suitable should be determined from prior knowledge about the data [1]. In our case, the visual clusters (Fig. 1) could be a reference, but not necessarily the best one to use.

Thus, the validity function S has suggested a substructure reasonable for our data set. In contrast, the partition coefficient F, which yields $c^* = 2$, does not correspond well with the actual substructure. Even if we take into account that for fuzzy functional (such as F and S) we do not need to identify the very best solution but we can choose (depending on prior knowledge and/or application) among the best few, F still yields unsatisfactory results [1) $c^* = 2$, 2) $c^* = 3$; see Table I]. In contrast, S yields [1) $c^* = 8$, 2) $c^* = 9, 10$] which are all close to the actual substructure. It is also worth noting that effective dynamic range for S is very wide.

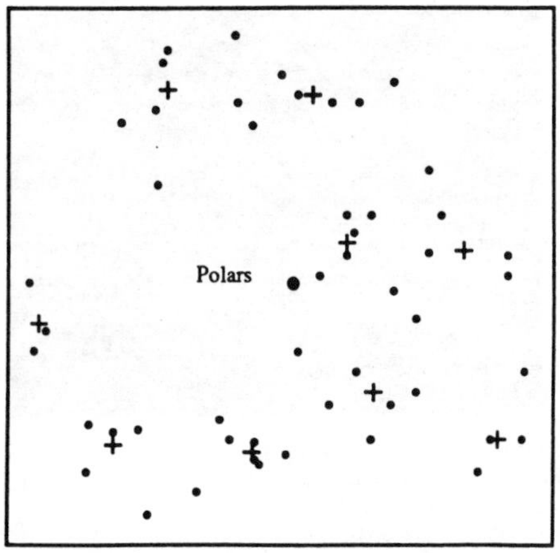

Fig. 3. The fuzzy partition of nine clusters obtained from S. Note: + indicates the centroids of each cluster.

V. APPLICATION TO COMPUTER COLOR VISION

Cluster analysis has been playing an important role in solving many problems in pattern recognition and image processing. For example, it is used for feature selection in Jain and Dubes [25] and for image segmentation for range image in Hoffman and Jain [26]. Image segmentation is a very critical step in image processing because errors at this stage influence feature extraction, classification, and interpretation at later stages.

In this section, we describe an application of our clustering criterion to color image segmentation for recognition of defects in integrated circuit (IC) wafers. The features of IC wafers are inherently colorful because of the interference effects taking place on the thin films which make up the IC structures [27]. Certain classes of IC defects can be detected by the use of colors which are otherwise not possible to detect in gray-scale image processing [27]. Various IC patterns manifest different colors due to the varying thicknesses in their structure.

In particular, we are interested in color ring defect recognition. A color ring defect is formed by a particle on the IC wafer causing a nonuniform thin film thickness surrounding the particle. The interference of different light wave lengths forms several cocentered color rings. The maximum number of rings among the colors reflects the size of the defect. Our task is to segment the color ring defect image and find the number of colors in the image and number of rings strongly formed in each color.

Ideally, one would expect an image to have regions of distinct colors separated by well-defined boundaries. However, in practice there is always some source of fluctuation or noise which imparts some uncertainty to the image. The noise in the image could be due to the degradations occurring in the process of image capture (sensor noise, variation of intensity of the light, error due to digitization, etc.). In any case, the actual image is quite complicated and it is not possible to label distinct regions in the image without using the segmentation.

In a color image, intensity of each pixel is represented by RGB, the three primary colors, and each pixel is viewed as a point in this three-dimensional color space. The image segmentation of a color image is to partition the image into regions or segments such that pixels belonging to a region are more similar to each other than pixels belonging to different regions. This can be done by using clustering methods to group the pixels in the color space into clusters. Consequently, a clustering criterion is used and it directly affects segmentation results.

For the color ring defect problem, Barth [28] used a clustering

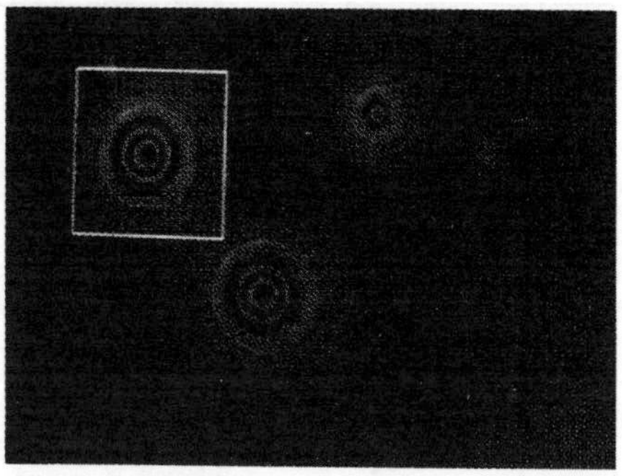

Fig. 4. Picture of color ring image for Example 2.

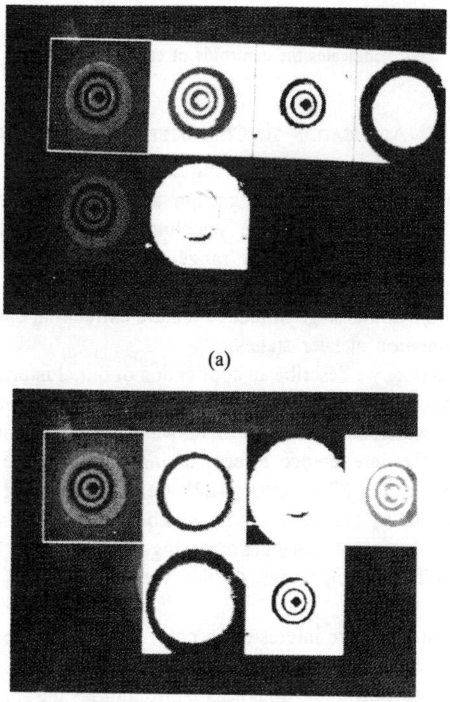

(a)

(b)

Fig. 5. Segmented image of 4–5 partitions for Example 2.

method together with an appropriate distance threshold to successfully detect some defects. However, the performance of the method depends very much on the choice of the distance threshold. An improper choice of the threshold may lead to erroneous partitions. Furthermore, the right choice of such a threshold is unknown *a priori*. Another concern is the potential of the method to give a very large number of partitions which may not be very useful for solving problems such as the "ring" defect problem.

Here, we describe the use of our clustering validity criterion to the segmentation of a color ring defect image taken from real sample (showing in Fig. 4). The image is of 512×480 pixels. Since each defect occupies a very small part of the image, a focusing-of-attention strategy [28] is employed, that is, we only segment a small part of the image which contains one color ring defect. In such a way, the size of data to be processed can be largely reduced and computing time saved. Notice that there are some noises in the image. To reduce the noise effect, a threshold for pixel density in color space is used. Only those colors with density larger than the threshold are processed by using the clustering algorithm. The choice of this threshold does not essentially affects the results. The remaining data points are assigned

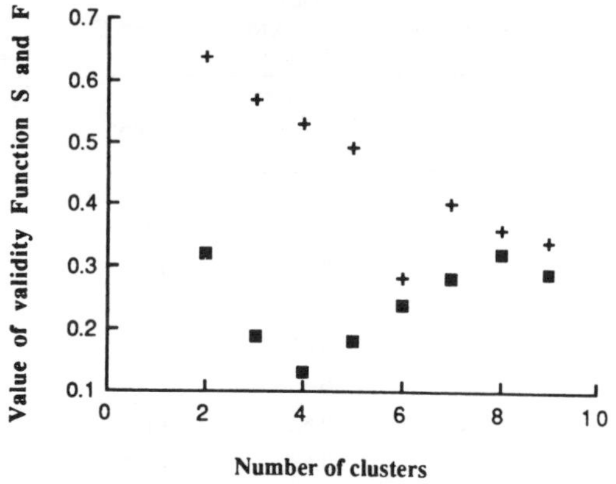

Fig. 6. Validity value of S and F for the segmented image in Example 2. *Note:* • indicates validity value of S; + indicates validity value of F.

to the nearest cluster. After segmentation, all pixels in each cluster are assigned the color value of the centroid of that cluster.

Example 2: Fig. 4 shows an image with three color ring defects. The color structure in this image is not so obvious to human eyes, which is usually the case for most color images (which makes computerized cluster analysis necessary). We focus our attention on the left defect inside window, whose color structure is relatively clear. This part of the image needs to be segmented in order to find the number of colors existing in this defect as well as the number of color rings formed in each color. In the area inside the window in Fig. 4, the human guesses that the number of distinct color rings could be four, five, or six. Two-hundred and sixty-seven distinct data points in the color space are obtained from the image in the attention window, using a density threshold of 6. Fig. 5 shows the results of 4 to 5 partitions with each segmented color displayed in a separate window. In Fig. 5(a), the lower left window shows the segmented image for the window above it.

Although the image in the attention area does not seem to have a very clear color structure at first glance, the results from validity function S in Fig. 6 indicate four cluster partitions as the best partition by quite a clear margin. A careful re-examination of the image tells us that this result is quite rational. The three rings of dark green and three rings of yellow in the center contrast quite clearly with the outer large orange ring and background. The 4-partition result in Fig. 5(a) clearly captured this character of the image. The second-best partition is the 5 partition, in which the orange color of the 4 partition is split in two: the inner smaller one a little bit close to the yellow end and the outer larger one a little bit close to the brown end. Although the three segmented colors of the 3–partition result are quite distinct (which means centroids of the three clusters are separate in the color space), the second color is clearly a mixture of the dark green and the background and is visually not a correct color. This means that the corresponding cluster is not compact, leading to a validity value larger than that of the 4 partitions. In the 2 partition, the orange color and the yellow color are further mixed, yielding another incompact cluster and even larger validity value. On the other hand, in the 6–9 positions, some colors (at least one) are split into two or more quite similar colors, resulting in nonseparate clusters, hence, larger validity value.

In addition, we give the partition results by using F shown in Fig. 6. F identifies the 2–partition as the best solution, and the validity value keeps decreasing until $c = 7$. It is clear that the best and second-best solutions indicated by F do not correctly reflect the actual color structure in the image. We also note that F has a very monotonically decreasing tendency as c increases.

VI. Conclusion

The issue of fuzzy cluster validity is still an open problem. More developments are expected before it can be effectivly used in applications. Any new validity function needs to satisfy the following requirements: 1) It has intuitive meaning; 2) it is easy to compute; 3) it is mathmaticaly justifiable. The fuzzy validity function S introduced in this correspondence has the above three features. In addition, its numerical performance compares well with existing validity functions. We also specifically applied this validity function to color image segmentation for IC ring defect detection. However, more numerical tests are needed, and this validity function only measures compact and separate clusters, as defined.

Acknowledgment

The authors wish to thank D. Chen for many valuable discussions and suggestions and Dr. M. Barth and Y. Xu for useful comments on clustering in color vision. We also thank B. Anderson and Prof. S. Hackwood for making the color vision system available and Prof. A. K. Jain for providing many useful suggestions.

References

[1] A. K. Jain, *Handbook of Pattern Recognition and Image Processing.* New York: Academic, 1988.

[2] J. C. Bezdek, *Pattern Recognition with Fuzzy Objective Function Algorithms,* Plenum, New York, 1981.

[3] A. K. Jain and R. C. Dubes, *Algorithms for Clustering Data.*Englewood Cliffs, NJ: Prentice-Hall, 1988.

[4] I. Gath and A. B. Geva, "Unsupervised optimal fuzzy clustering," *IEEE Trans. Patt. Anal. Machine Intell.,* vol. 11, no 7, July 1989.

[5] X. L. Xie and G. Beni, "Distributed hierarchical decision fusion with cluster validity," in *Proc. IEEE Int. Conf. Syst. Man Cybern.* (Los Angeles, CA), 1990, p. 515.

[6] A. M. Al-Bassiouni, "Optimal signal processing in distributed sensor systems," Ph.D. dissertation, Naval Postgraduate School, Monterey, CA, 1987.

[7] A. Kandel, *Fuzzy Techniques in Pattern Recognition.* New York: Wiley, 1982.

[8] E. Backer and A. K. Jain, "A clustering performance measure based on fuzzy set decomposition," *IEEE Trans. Patt. Anal. Machine Intell.,* vol. PAMI-3, no 1, Jan. 1981.

[9] R. O. Duda and P. E. Hart, *Pattern Classification and Scene Analysis.* New York: Wiley, 1973.

[10] N. E. Day, "Estimating the components of a mixture of normal distributions," *Biometrika* vol. 56, pp. 463–474, 1969.

[11] J. H. Wolfe, "Pattern clustering by multivariate mixture analysis," *Multivar. Behav. Res.,* vol. 5, pp. 329–350, 1970.

[12] J. C. Dunn, "Well separated clusters and optimal fuzzy partitions," *J. Cybern.,* vol. 4, pp. 95–104, 1974.

[13] D. I. Davies and D. W. Bouldin, "A cluster seperation measure," *IEEE Trans. Patt. Anal. Machine Intell.,* vol. PAMI-1, no. 2, Apr. 1979.

[14] A. K. Jain and J. V. Moreau, "Bootstrap technique in cluster analysis," *Patt. Recog.,* vol. 20, no. 5, pp. 547–568, 1987.

[15] J. C. Bezdek, "Numerical taxonomy with fuzzy sets," *J. Math. Biol.,* vol. 1, pp. 57–71, 1974.

[16] J. B. Bezdek, "Mathematical models for systematics and taxonomy," in *Proc. 8th Int. Conf. Numerical Taxonomy,* G. Estabrook, Ed. San Francisco, CA: Freeman, 1975, pp. 143–166.

[17] M. P. Windham, "Cluster validity for fuzzy clustering algorithms," *Fuzzy Sets Syst.,* pp. 177–185, 1981.

[18] ——, "Cluster validity for fuzzy c-means clustering algorithm," *IEEE Trans. Patt. Anal. Machine Intell.,* vol. PAMI-4, no 4, July 1982.

[19] G. Libert and M. Roubens, "New experimental results in cluster validity of fuzzy clustering algorithms," in *New Trends in Data Analysis and Applications,* J. Janssen, J.-F. Macrotorchino, and J.-M. Proth, Eds. Amsterdam, The Netherlands: North-Holland, 1983, pp. 205–218.

[20] M. P. Windham, H. Bock, and H. F. Walker, "Clustering information from convergence rate," in *Proc. 2nd Conf. Int. Federation Classification Soc.* (Washington, DC), 1989, p. 143.

[21] R. Gunderson, "Application of fuzzy ISODATA algorithms to star tracker pointing systems," in *Proc. 7th Triennial World IFAC Cong.* (Helsinki, Finland), 1978, pp. 1319–1323.

[22] J. C. Dunn, "Indices of partition fuzziness and detection of clusters in large data sets," in *Fuzzy Automata and Decision Processes.* New York: Elsevier, 1977.

[23] X. Xie and G. Beni, "A new fuzzy clustering validity criterion and its application to color image segmentation," to be presented at the *IEEE int. Symp. Intell. Contr.* (Arlington, VA), Aug. 13–15, 1991.

[24] R. F. Ling, "Cluster analysis," Ph.D. dissertation, Yale Univ., New Haven, CT, 1971.

[25] A. K. Jain and R. Dubes, "Feature definition in pattern recognition with small sample size," *Patt. Recog.,* vol. 10, pp. 85–97, 1978.

[26] R. Hoffman and A. K. Jain, "Segmentation and Classification of range images," *IEEE Trans. Patt. Anal. Machine Intell.,* vol. PAMI-9, pp. 608–620, 1987.

[27] S. Parthasarathy, D. Wolfe, E. Hu, S. Hackwood, and G. Beni, "A color vision system for film thickness determination," in *Proc. IEEE Conf. Robotics Automat.* (Raleigh, NC), 1987, p. 515.

[28] M. Barth, "Robotic attentive sensing and its application to integrated circuit wafer inspection," Ph.D. dissertation, Univ. California, Santa Barbara, Aug. 1989.

Chapter 3
Classifier Design and Feature Analysis

3.0 Introduction

IN Section 1.3 of Chapter 1, we mentioned that the concepts of fuzzy sets and membership functions can be incorporated at both the feature analysis and classification levels. The twelve papers reprinted here demonstrate these characteristics for different types of classifiers and their applications to various real life data. The previous chapter dealt with the application of fuzzy sets in unsupervised pattern classification problems. Classifier design, on the other hand, can be performed with labeled or unlabeled data. When the computer is given a set of objects with known classifications (i.e., labels) and is asked to classify an unknown object based on the information acquired by it during training, we call the design scheme supervised learning; otherwise, learning (the function $\underline{\mathbf{D}}$) is unsupervised. Many of the clustering algorithms exhibited in the papers of Chapter 2 can be used as precursors to the design of a classifier when the only data available are unlabeled data. The so-called counter-propagation neural network (see Chapter 5) is of this type; there is a clustering layer (often a Kohonen type network) followed by a feed-forward, back-propagation (FFBP) type of learning network. Several of the papers reprinted in this chapter use clustering as a means toward the end of classifier design; others require labeled data.

Supervised pattern recognition in its various forms is treated in a unified way in the seminal note of Bellman, Kalaba, and Zadeh (Paper 3.1) in terms of two basic operations, *abstraction* and *generalization*, using the framework of fuzzy set theory. Abstraction in fuzzy set theory means estimation of a membership function m of a fuzzy class from the training samples. Having obtained the estimate, generalization is performed when this estimate is used to compute the values of m for unknown objects not contained in the training set. Consideration of linguistic features and fuzzy relations in representing a class has also been suggested by Zadeh [1]. Papers 3.2–3.6 describe various classification approaches.

Paper 3.2 outlines an early application of fuzzy sets for decision theoretic classification, where a pattern is considered as an array of linguistically phrased features denoting certain properties and where each of these features is a fuzzy set. Instead of computing a distance from an unlabeled pattern to a class prototype, the concept-of-similarity vector is used to measure similarity with respect to each fuzzy property and to provide class-membership information of each pattern. For speech and speaker recognition problems, these fuzzy feature properties are defined in the domain of acoustic measurements (formant frequencies). Besides showing how the pattern descriptions in terms of membership functions can be processed, the work also shows another approach that is based on the computation of class memberships of a pattern as a decreasing function of its Euclidean distance from the prototypes in the measurement space. The variation of the recognition score with the change of fuzziness in the linguistically phrased features values (i.e., with the successive uses of the fuzzy hedges *dilation*, *concentration*, and *contrast intensification* operators [2]) has subsequently been reported [3]. These classifiers have also been used for designing a self-supervised recognition system [4–6].

Paper 3.3 proposes a classification model applicable in the soft sciences (including medical diagnostics) where enough a priori knowledge about the classifier is available from experts in linguistic form. The design procedure is primarily based on expert experiences followed by a refinement stage, which uses labeled samples. The algorithm involves the theory of approximate reasoning [7–13] and fuzzy relations between fuzzy statements. Some properties of the classifier have subsequently been described [14]. The reader can also refer, in this context, to the articles [15–17] which explain how the imprecise information in a pattern can be encoded for processing.

Paper 3.4 deals with the well known k-nearest neighbor (k-nn) classifier, and provides a fuzzy version of the algorithm. In the conventional approach [18–19] each of the labeled samples is given equal importance in deciding the class membership of an unknown pattern; this frequently causes problems in places where the labeled samples overlap. This is tackled in Paper 3.4 by providing fuzzy label vectors in N_{fc} for the samples as an indication of their class representativeness and subsequently leads to a fuzzy classification rule. The algorithm results in lower error rates than the crisp version for the data discussed in the paper. In work by Bezdek et al. [20], generalized fuzzy k-nn rules based on several other ideas are formulated and compared with their hard counterparts; again, the fuzzy versions seem to offer better performance (lower error rates) than crisp rules. There has been a recent attempt [21] to formulate a decision theoretic multivalued linguistic recognition system that involves the concept of fuzziness at both the feature and classification levels. The feature space is decomposed into a few overlapping subregions depending on the geometric complexity of the classes found in the training samples. The uncertainty arising from incompleteness of the training samples in representing a class is managed by extracting multivalued shapes [22] during training. The system uses Zadeh's compositional rule of inference [9], accepts linguistic input in various forms, and provides linguistic output associated with a confidence factor. Its merit over the Bayes classifier in certain cases has been demonstrated. A theoretical framework of the performance has also been reported [23].

Paper 3.5 deals with the concept of fuzzy decision trees in

developing an efficient algorithm for making decisions in pattern recognition problems. The paper explains the relation between such trees and linear classifiers and presents an example (on hand written numeral recognition) showing the advantage of the former over 0-1 decision trees.

Fuzzy tree automata are defined in Paper 3.6 for processing fuzzy tree representations of patterns using syntactic recognition. This work shows how membership functions for structural patterns can be defined and how a fuzzy language can be used for handling imprecision in structural pattern recognition. There are several sources for a good introduction to fuzzy languages and fuzzy grammars [24–28]. (Some important applications of fuzzy grammars and syntactic recognition are contained in Papers 3.10 and 3.11.)

An adaptive system can be viewed as a learning machine in which systemic decisions gradually approach optimal decisions by acquiring the necessary information from observed patterns. System performance can be improved as a result of this approach. The recognition methods described in Papers 3.2–3.6 use a specified set of labeled data for training (i.e., for estimating or learning class parameters, membership functions, etc.) of a classifier $\underline{\mathbf{D}}$ before it is used for classifying unknown patterns. In some adaptive recognition systems, on the other hand, the tasks of learning from the labeled data and classification of unlabeled samples occur simultaneously. This approach is especially useful when very few labeled samples are available. In this case, the algorithm makes an initial estimation of the class parameters and then it updates the parameters as new incoming samples are presented to it, based on previous decisions of the classifier and an updating or learning strategy (i.e., decision-directed learning). Decision-directed learning sometimes enables a system not only to learn more about the classes than otherwise, but also about the classification scheme itself. The learning strategy can be supervised (e.g., using an extra source of knowledge, usually of a higher order, for checking the classifier decisions), self-supervised (e.g., using the same parameters as used by the classifier for checking classifier decisions) and unsupervised (e.g., the classifier's decision is final) in order to facilitate the updating program. On the down side, the performance of the system depends on the sequence in which the samples are presented to it, a characteristic that is never desirable in pattern recognition schemes. Details of some of these techniques, including fully supervised, unsupervised, and self-supervised learning; Bayesian estimation; stochastic estimation; nonlinear thresholding; generalized guard zone algorithms; convergence properties; Bayes classifiers; and fuzzy classifiers are available [29–38].

Paper 3.7 discusses one method for eliminating or discarding doubtful or unreliable samples from the training procedure (i.e., restricted updating to good samples). This work describes an adaptive algorithm using a fuzzy approximation to the gradient descent technique for training a classifier sequentially. An exponential membership function is assumed for each class and the parameters of the functions are estimated recursively using the method of gradient descent. The objective function of the fuzzy c-means model (described in Chapter 2 and Paper 3.8) has been used here as the loss function for computing the gradient.

As mentioned in Section 1.3.B of Chapter 1, the task of feature selection plays an important role in designing a pattern recognition system. However, research in this area using fuzzy set theory has not been as extensive as it is on either clustering or classification. We have selected two articles (Papers 3.8 and 3.9) wherein the problem of dimensionality reduction of the feature space has been tackled both with and without performing simultaneous classification of the data. Paper 3.8 shows an application of the fuzzy c-means clustering algorithm to select an optimum feature subset from a set of eleven binary features representing six stomach diseases so that there is no appreciable loss of classifier performance with the reduced set of features. Additionally, this report also shows that a fuzzy 1-nearest prototype classifier (the prototypes being the cluster centers generated by the fuzzy c-means algorithm) increases the expected probability of correct classification to a higher level than all k-nn classifiers can achieve (it is important to remember that this is a finite sample based statistic—the asymptotic optimality of k-nn rules via Cover and Hart's famous theorem [18] is well known). Cluster analysis has also been used together with possibility theory for selecting the most significant variables from electron spin resonance spectroscopy measurements on patients with a brain injury [39].

Feature selection based on possibility functions takes into account the morphological nature of the sample points. Paper 3.9 explains, on the other hand, an application of fuzziness measures, for example, the index of fuzziness, entropy, and π-ness of a set in doing this task without going through classification. Fuzzy measures are computed with various S- and π-type functions to define an index for feature evaluation in terms of interset and intraset ambiguities (which are analogous to the concepts of interset and intraset distances, respectively, in classical pattern recognition). In a subsequent article [40], this work has been extended to evaluate the importance of any subset of features, to provide an average quantitative index of goodness, and to provide a comparison of the algorithm with statistical measures like divergence, J-M distance, and Mahalanobis distance [18–19, 41]. The application of this algorithm has also been demonstrated on six class, three feature vowel data, four class, five feature consonant data, and three class, fifteen feature mango leaf data. The problem of extracting features and primitives from a gray image pattern is addressed in Chapter 4.

Papers 3.10 and 3.11 demonstrate two typical applications of fuzzy set theoretic approaches to real recognition problems, namely phonetic and phonemic labeling of continuous speech signals and identification of skeletal maturity of a child from x-rays of the hand and wrist. Speech is biological in origin and transmits, over and above the semantic content of the message, information regarding the mood, health, age and sex of the speaker as well as various other physiological and psychological states. The resulting pattern, therefore, manifests a considerable amount of fuzziness (or vagueness). The vagueness may result in ill-defined boundaries among pattern classes, affect the features extracted from the acoustic data, and result in a degree of imprecision in relationships between acoustic features and their phonetic or phonemic interpretation. The use of fuzzy sets for measuring similarity or closeness between patterns in terms of their fuzzy properties, along with an application for recognition of vowel and speaker from speech sounds in consonant-vowel nucleus-constant (CNC) combination are described in Paper 3.2. In Paper 3.10, a method consisting of fuzzy restriction for extracting features, fuzzy relations for relating these features with phonetic and phonemic interpretation, and their use for interpretation of a speech pattern in terms of possibility theory has been described. The intuitive logic used by a phonetician for interpreting a spectrogram has been formalized in the development of rules and approach. The knowledge source is a series of syntactic rules whose syntactic categories are phonetic and phonemic features detected by a precategorical and a categorical classification of speech sounds. The reader can further refer to references [42, 43].

Paper 3.11 demonstrates an application of fuzzy and fractionally fuzzy grammars (its merits over nonfuzzy approaches are reported elsewhere [44]) in syntactic recognition of ages of different bones by identifying nine stages from x-ray image patterns. The ultimate aim is to be able to make a computer diagnosis of diseases and the effects of malnutrition on the skeletal growth of a child. The features of the structural development (e.g., the contours, shape, and orientation of the metaphysis and epiphysis [45]) and the physical relation among them do not lend themselves to precise definition. It is shown that incorporation of the concept of fuzziness in defining sharp, fair, and gentle curves and the production rules used enable one to work with a smaller number of primitives and to use the same set of rules and nonterminals at each stage. Therefore, one needs to parse an input string with only one grammar at each stage, unlike the case in the nonfuzzy approach, where one may have to parse each string by more than one grammar, in general, at each stage. However, this has to be balanced against the fact that the fuzzy grammars are not as simple as the corresponding nonfuzzy grammars. Furthermore, these grammars need not be unambiguous, whereas nonambiguity is an absolutely necessary requirement for the nonfuzzy approach.

Automatic recognition of a handwritten character is another area where ambiguity occurs because of imprecision in writing rather than from randomness, and the fuzzy set theory has been used quite extensively both in feature extraction and in classification. Paper 3.12 reports earlier work on handwritten character recognition. The research reported in [43, 46-51] is representative of the development in this area. For some other applications readers can refer to references [52-62].

References

[1] L. A. Zadeh, "Fuzzy sets and their application to pattern classification and cluster analysis," *Memo UCB/ERL. M-607*, University of California, Berkeley, 1976.

[2] L. A. Zadeh, "An outline of a new approach to the analysis of complex systems and decision processes," *IEEE Trans. Syst., Man, Cybern.*, vol. SMC-3, pp. 28-44, 1973.

[3] S. K. Pal and D. Dutta Majumder, "On automatic plosive identification using fuzziness in property sets," *IEEE Trans. Syst., Man, Cybern.*, vol. SMC-8, pp. 302-308, 1978.

[4] S. K. Pal, A. K. Dutta, and D. Datta Majumder, "A self-supervised vowel recognition system," *Pattern Recognition*, vol. 12, no. 1, pp. 27-34, 1980.

[5] S. K. Pal, "Optimum guard zone for self-supervised learning," *IEE Proceedings-E*, vol. 129, no. 1, pp. 9-14, 1982.

[6] A. Pathak and S. K. Pal, "On the convergence of a self-supervised vowel recognition system," *Pattern Recognition*, vol. 20, no. 2, pp. 237-244, 1987.

[7] L. A. Zadeh, "The concept of linguistic variable and its application to approximate reasoning—II," *Inform. Sci.*, vol. 8, pp. 301-357, 1975.

[8] L. A. Zadeh, "A fuzzy set theoretic interpretation of linguistic hedges," *J. Cybern.*, vol. 2, pp. 4-34, 1972.

[9] L. A. Zadeh, "Fuzzy logic and approximate reasoning," *Synthese*, vol. 30, pp. 407-428, 1977.

[10] R. R. Yager, "Multiple objective decision making using fuzzy subsets," *Int. J. Man-Machine Studies*, vol. 9, pp. 375-382, 1977.

[11] R. R. Yager, "Validation of fuzzy linguistic models," *J. Cybern.*, vol. 8, pp. 17-30, 1978.

[12] R. R. Yager, "Approximate reasoning and possibility model in classification," *Int. J. Comp. Inf. Sci.*, vol. 10, pp. 141-175, 1981.

[13] M. M. Gupta, A. Kandel, W. Bandler, and J. B. Kiszka (Eds.), *Approximate Reasoning in Expert Systems*, New York: North Holland, 1985.

[14] A. K. Nath, S. W. Liu and, T. T. Lee, "On some properties of a linguistic classifier," *Fuzzy Sets and Syst.*, vol. 17, pp. 297-311, 1985.

[15] M. Schneider and A. Kandel, "Properties of the fuzzy expected value and the fuzzy expected interval," *Fuzzy Sets and Syst.*, vol. 26, pp. 373-385, 1988.

[16] M. Schneider and A. Kandel, "Properties of the fuzzy expected value and the fuzzy expected interval in fuzzy environment," *Fuzzy Sets and Syst.*, vol. 28, pp. 55-68, 1988.

[17] S. K. Pal and D. P. Mandal, "Linguistic recognition system based on approximate reasoning," *Inform. Sci.*, vol. 61, no. 2, pp. 135-161, 1992.

[18] K. Fukunaga, *Introduction to Statistical Pattern Recognition*, New York: Academic Press, 1972.

[19] R. Duda and P. Hart, *Pattern Classification and Scene Analysis*, New York: Wiley Interscience, 1973.

[20] J. Bezdek, S. Chuah, and D. Leep, "Generalized k-nearest neighbor rules," *Fuzzy Sets and Syst.*, vol. 18, no. 3, pp. 237-256, 1986.

[21] D. P. Mandal, C. A. Murthy, and S. K. Pal, "Formulation of a multivalued recognition system," *IEEE Trans. Syst., Man, Cybern.*, vol. 22, no. 3, 1992 (in press).

[22] D. P. Mandal, C. A. Murthy, and S. K. Pal, "Determining the shape of a pattern class from sampled points in R^2," *Int. J. General Syst.*, vol. 20, no. 2 or 4, 1992 (in press).

[23] D. P. Mandal, C. A. Murthy, and S. K. Pal, "Theoretical performance of a multivalued recognition system," *IEEE Trans. Syst., Man, Cybern.*, 1992 (in press).

[24] E. T. Lee and L. A. Zadeh, "Note on fuzzy languages," *Inform. Sci.*, vol. 1, pp. 421-434, 1969.

[25] N. Honda and M. Nasu, "Recognition of fuzzy languages," in L. A. Zadeh, K. S. Fu, K. Tanaka, and M. Shimura, Eds., *Fuzzy Sets and Their Applications to Cognitive and Decision Processes*, London: Academic Press, 1975, pp. 279-299.

[26] A. K. Majumder, A. K. Ray, and B. Chatterjee, "Inference of fuzzy regular language using formal power series representation," *Proc.*

Indian Statistical Institute Golden Jubilee Conference on Advances in Information Sciences and Technology, Calcutta, January 1982, vol. 1, pp. 155-165.

[27] G. F. DePalma and S. S. Yau, "Fractionally fuzzy grammars with applications to pattern recognition," in L. A. Zadeh, K. S. Fu, K. Tanaka, and M. Shimura, Eds., *Fuzzy Sets and Their Applications to Cognitive and Decision Processes*, London: Academic Press, 1975, pp. 329-351.

[28] M. G. Thomason, "Finite fuzzy automata, regular fuzzy language and pattern recognition," *Pattern Recognition*, vol. 5, pp. 383-390, 1973.

[29] K. S. Fu, *Sequential Methods in Pattern Recognition and Machine Learning*, London: Academic Press, 1968.

[30] J. M. Mendel and K. S. Fu (Eds.), *Adaptive Learning and Pattern Recognition Systems—Theory and Applications*, New York: Academic Press, 1970.

[31] Y. T. Chien, "The threshold effect of a nonlinear learning algorithm for pattern recognition," *Inform. Sci.*, vol. 2, pp. 351-358, 1970.

[32] W. S. Meisel, *Computer Oriented Approaches to Pattern Recognition*, New York: Academic Press, 1972.

[33] S. K. Pal, A. K. Datta, and D. Dutta Majumder, "Adaptive learning algorithm in classification of fuzzy patterns: An application to vowels in CNC context," *Int. J. Syst. Sci.*, vol. 9, no. 8, pp. 887-897, 1978.

[34] A. Pathak and S. K. Pal, "A generalized learning algorithm based on guard zones," *Pattern Recognition Letters*, vol. 4, no. 2, pp. 63-69, 1986.

[35] A. Pathak-Pal and S. K. Pal, "Learning with mislabelled training samples using stochastic approximation," *IEEE Trans. Syst., Man, Cybern.*, vol. SMC-17, no. 6, pp. 1072-1077, 1987.

[36] S. K. Pal, A. Pathak, and C. Basu, "Dynamic guard zone for self-supervised learning," *Pattern Recognition Letters*, vol. 7, no. 3, pp. 135-144, 1988.

[37] A. Pal (Pathak) and S. K. Pal, "Generalised guard zone algorithm (GGA) for learning: Automatic selection of threshold," *Pattern Recognition*, vol. 23, no. 3/4, pp. 325-335, 1990.

[38] A. Pal (Pathak) and S. K. Pal, "Effect of wrong samples on the convergence of learning processes—II: A remedy," *Inform. Sci.*, vol. 60, no. 1/2, pp. 77-105, 1992.

[39] V. Di Gesu and M. C. Maccarone, "Feature selection and 'possibility theory,'" *Pattern Recognition*, vol. 19, pp. 63-72, 1986.

[40] S. K. Pal, "Fuzzy set theoretic measure for automatic feature evaluation—II," *Inform. Sci.*, 1992 (in press).

[41] P. Devijver and J. Kittler, *Pattern Recognition: A Statistical Approach*, Englewood Cliffs, NJ: Prentice-Hall, 1982.

[42] R. Di Mori, *Computerized Models of Speech Using Fuzzy Algorithms*, New York: Plenum Press, 1983.

[43] S. K. Pal and D. K. Dutta Majumder, *Fuzzy Mathematical Approach to Pattern Recognition*, New York: Wiley, 1986.

[44] A. Pathak, S. K. Pal, and R. A. King, "Syntactic recognition of skeletal maturity," *Pattern Recognition Letters*, vol. 2, pp. 193-197, 1984.

[45] J. M. Tanner, R. H. Whitehouse, W. A. Marshall, M. J. R. Healy, and H. Goldstein, *Assessment of Skeletal Maturity and Prediction of Adult Height (TW2 Method)*, New York: Academic Press, 1975.

[46] W. Pedrycz, "Algorithms of fuzzy clustering with partial supervision," *Pattern Recognition Letters*, vol. 3, pp. 13-20, 1985.

[47] W. J. M. Kickert and H. Koppelaar, "Application of fuzzy set theory to syntactic pattern recognition of handwritten capitals," *IEEE Trans. Syst., Man, Cyberns.*, vol. SMC-6, pp. 148-151, 1976.

[48] S. K. Pal, D. Dutta Majumder, and B. B. Chaudhuri, "Fuzzy sets in handwritten character recognition," *Proc. All India Interdisciplinary Symp. on Digital Technology and Pattern Recognition*, February 1977, Indian Statistical Institute, Calcutta, pp. 63-71.

[49] P. Biswas and A. K. Majumder, "A multistage fuzzy classifier for recognition of handprinted characters," *IEEE Trans. Syst., Man, Cybern.*, vol. SMC-11, pp. 834-838, 1981.

[50] K. Hirota and W. Pedrycz, "Subjective entropy of probabilistic sets and fuzzy cluster analysis," *IEEE Trans. Syst., Man, Cybern.*, vol. SMC-16, pp. 173-179, 1986.

[51] A. Meisels, A. Kandel, and G. Gecht, "Entropy, and the recognition of fuzzy letters," *Fuzzy Sets and Syst.*, vol. 31, pp. 297-309, 1989.

[52] L. A. Zadeh, K. S. Fu, K. Tanaka, and M. Shimura (Eds.), *Fuzzy Sets and Their Applications to Cognitive and Decision Processes*, London: Academic Press, 1975.

[53] P. P. Wang and S. K. Chang (Eds.), *Fuzzy Sets: Theory and Applications to Policy Analysis and Information Systems*, New York: Plenum Press, 1980.

[54] J. R. Key, J. A. Maslanik, and R. G. Barry, "Cloud classification from satellite data using a fuzzy-sets algorithm-a polar example," *Int. J. Remote Sensing*, vol. 10, pp. 1823-1842, 1989.

[55] M. A. Woodbury and J. Clive, "Clinical pure types as a fuzzy partition," *J. Cybernetics*, vol. 3, pp. 111-121, 1974.

[56] E. T. Lee, "Shape-oriented chromosome classification," *IEEE Trans. Syst., Man, Cybern.*, vol. SMC-5, pp. 629-632, 1975.

[57] A. Kumar, "A real-time system for pattern recognition of human sleep stages by fuzzy systems analysis," *Pattern Recognition*, vol. 9, pp. 43-46, 1977.

[58] A. Kandel, "Fuzzy statistics and forecast evaluation," *IEEE Trans. Syst., Man, Cybern.*, vol. SMC-8, pp. 396-401, 1978.

[59] L. Saitta and P. Torasso, "Fuzzy characteristics of coronary disease," *Fuzzy Sets and Syst.*, vol. 5, pp. 245-258, 1981.

[60] R. Degani and G. Bortolan, "Computerized electrocardiogram diagnosis: Fuzzy approach," *Encyclopedia of Systems and Control*, Oxford, England: Pergamon Press, 1987.

[61] S. K. Pal and A. Bhattacharyya, "Pattern recognition techniques in analysing the effect of thiourea on brain neurosecretory cells," *Pattern Recognition Letters*, vol. 11, pp. 443-452, 1990.

[62] S. K. Pal, "Uncertainty management in space station autonomous research: pattern recognition perspective," *Inform. Sci.*, 1992 (in press).

[63] J. C. Bezdek, "Feature selection for binary data: medical diagnosis with fuzzy sets," *Proc. 1976 NCC*, AFIPS vol. 45, pp. 1057-1068, AFIPS Press, Montvale, NJ, 1976.

[64] W. Dong, A. Boissonade, H. C. Shah, and F. Wong, "Fuzzy classification of seismic intensity," *Proc. ISFMER*, pp. 129-148, Beijing: Seismological Press, 1985.

[65] K. Fukunaga and W. Koontz, "Application of the Karhunen-Loeve expansion to feature selection and ordering," *IEEE Trans. Comput.*, vol. C-19, pp. 311-318, 1970.

[66] A. Jozwik, "A learning scheme for a fuzzy k-nn rule," *Pattern Recognition Letters*, vol. 1, pp. 287-289, 1983.

[67] P. M. Narendra and K. Fukunaga, "A branch and bound algorithm for feature subset selection," *IEEE Trans. Comput.*, vol. C-26, pp. 917-922, 1977.

[68] A. K. Jain and B. Chandrasekaran, "Dimensionality and sample size consideration in pattern recognition practice," in *Handbook of Statistics, Vol. 2*, P. R. Krishnaiah and L. N. Kanal, Eds., Amsterdam, The Netherlands: North Holland, 1982, pp. 835-855.

[69] K. Peeva, "Fuzzy acceptors for syntactic pattern recognition," *Int. J. Approx. Reasoning*, vol. 5, no. 3, pp. 291-306, 1991.

Abstraction and Pattern Classification

R. Bellman, R. Kalaba, and L. Zadeh

The RAND Corporation, Santa Monica, California

1. Introduction

This note deals in a preliminary way with several concepts and ideas which have a bearing on the problem of pattern classification—a problem which plays an important role in communication and control theories.

There are two basic operations: abstraction and generalization, which appear under various guises is most of the schemes employed for classifying patterns into a finite number of categories. Although abstraction and generalization can be defined in terms of operations on sets of patterns, a more natural as well as more general framework for dealing with these concepts can be constructed around the notion of a "fuzzy" set—a notion which extends the concept of membership in a set to situations in which there are many, possibly a continuum of, grades of membership.

To be more specific, a *fuzzy set* A in a space $\Omega = \{x\}$ is represented by a characteristic function f which is defined on Ω and takes values in the interval $[0, 1]$, with the value of f at x, $f(x)$, representing the "grade of membership" of x in A. Thus, if A is a set in the usual sense, $f(x)$ is 1 or 0 according as x belongs or does not belong to A. When A is a fuzzy set, then the nearer the value of $f(x)$ to 0, the more tenuous is the membership of x in A, with the "degree of belonging" increasing with increase in $f(x)$. In some cases it may be convenient to concretize the belonging of a point to a fuzzy set A by selecting two levels ϵ_1 and ϵ_2 ($\epsilon_1, \epsilon_2 \in [0, 1]$) and agreeing that (a) a point x "*belongs*" to A if $f(x) < 1 < \epsilon_1$; (b) *does not belong* to A if $f(x) \leqslant \epsilon_2$; and (c) x is *indeterminate relative to* A if $\epsilon_2 < f(x) < 1 - \epsilon_1$. In effect, this amounts to using a three-valued characteristic function, with $f(x) = 1$ if $x \in A$; $f(x) = 1/2$, say, if x is indeterminate relative to A; and $f(x) = 0$ if $x \notin A$.

Let A and B be two fuzzy sets in the sense defined above, with f_A and f_B denoting their respective characteristic functions. The *union* of A and B will be denoted in the usual way as

$$C = A \cup B, \tag{1}$$

with the characteristic function of C defined by

$$f_C(x) = \mathrm{Max}(f_A(x), f_B(x)). \tag{2}$$

For brevity, the relation expressed by (2) will be written as

$$f_C = f_A \vee f_B. \tag{3}$$

Note that when A and B are sets, (2) reduces to the definition of "or."

In a similar fashion, the *intersection* of two fuzzy sets A and B will be denoted by

$$C = A \cap B \tag{4}$$

with the characteristic function of C defined by

$$f_C(x) = \mathrm{Min}(f_A(x), f_B(x)), \tag{5}$$

Reprinted with permission from *J. Math. Anal. Appl.*, vol. 13, pp. 1–7, 1966. (Copyright © 1966 by Academic Press, Inc.)

which for brevity will be written as

$$f_C = f_A \wedge f_B. \tag{6}$$

In the case of the intersection, when A and B are sets (5) reduces to the definition of "and." When the characteristic functions are three-valued, (2) and (5) lead to the three-valued logic of Kleene [1].

2. ABSTRACTION AND GENERALIZATION

Let $x^1, ..., x^n$ be given members of a set A in Ω. In informal terms, by abstraction on $x^1, ..., x^n$ is meant the identification of those properties of $x^1, ..., x^n$ which they have in common and which, in aggregate, define the set A.

The notion of a fuzzy set provides a natural as well as convenient way of giving a more concrete meaning to the notion of *abstraction*. Specifically, let f^i denote the value of the characteristic function, f, of a fuzzy set A at a point x^i in Ω. A collection of pairs $\{(x^1, f^1), ..., (x^n, f^n)\}$ or, for short $\{(x^i, f^i)\}^n$, will be called a collection of *samples* or *observations* from A. By an abstraction on the collection $\{(x^i, f^i)\}^n$, we mean the estimation of the characteristic function of A from the samples $(x^1, f^1), ..., (x^n, f^n)$. Once an estimate of f has been constructed, we perform a *generalization* on the collection $\{(x^i, f^i)\}^n$ when we use the estimate in question to compute the values of f at points other than $x^1, ..., x^n$.

An estimate of f employing the given samples $(x^1, f^1), ..., (x^n, f^n)$ will be denoted by $\tilde{f}$ or, more explicitly, by $\tilde{f}(x; \{x^i, f^i)\}^n)$, and will be referred to as an abstracting function. Clearly, the problem of determining an abstracting function is essentially one of reconstructing a function from the knowledge of its values over a finite set of points. To make this problem meaningful, one must have some a priori information about the class of functions to which f belongs, such that this information in combination with the samples from A would be sufficient to enable one to construct a "good" estimate of f. As in interpolation theory, this approach involves choosing—usually on purely heuristic grounds—a class of estimates of f: $\tilde{F} = \{\tilde{f}(x; \lambda) \mid \lambda \in R^l\}$ and finding that member of this family which fits, or fits "best" (in some specified sense of "best"), the given samples $(x^1, f^1), ..., (x^n, f^n)$. A special case of this procedure which applies to ordinary rather than fuzzy sets is the widely used technique for distinguishing between two sets of patterns via a separating hyperplane. Stated in terms of a single set of patterns, the problem in question is essentially that of finding, if it exists, a hyperplane L passing through the origin of $R^l(\Omega = R^l$, by assumption) such that the given points $x^1, ..., x^n$ belonging to a set A are all on the same side of the hyperplane. (Note that, since A is a set, $f^1 = f^2 = \cdots = f^n = 1$.) In effect, in this case $\tilde{f}(x; \lambda)$ is of the form

$$\tilde{f}(x; \lambda) = 1 \quad \text{for} \quad \langle x, \lambda \rangle \geq 0,$$
$$\tilde{f}(x; \lambda) = 0 \quad \text{for} \quad \langle x, \lambda \rangle < 0, \tag{7}$$

where $\langle x, \lambda \rangle$ denotes the scalar product of x and λ, and the problem is to find a λ in R^l such that

$$\langle x^i, \lambda \rangle \geq 0 \quad \text{for} \quad i = 1, ..., n.$$

Any $\tilde{f}(x; \lambda)$ whose λ satisfies (8) will qualify as an abstracting function, and the corresponding generalization on $(x^1, 1), ..., (x^n, 1)$ will take the form of the statement "Any x satisfying $\langle x, \lambda \rangle \geq 0$ belongs to the same set as the samples $x^1, ..., x^n$." If one is not content with just satisfying (8) but wishes, in addition, to maximize the distance between L and the set of points $x^1, ..., x^n$

(in the sense of maximizing $\text{Min}\langle x^i, \lambda\rangle$), $\|\lambda\| = 1$, then the determination of the corresponding abstracting function requires the solution of a quadratic program, as was shown by Rosen [2] in connection with a related problem in pattern recognition.

In most practical situations, the a priori information about the characteristic function of a fuzzy set is not sufficient to construct an estimate of $f(x)$ which is "optimal" in a meaningful sense. Thus, in most instances one is forced to resort to a heuristic rule for estimating $f(x)$, with the only means of judging the "goodness" of the estimate yielded by such a rule lying in experimentation. In the sequel, we shall describe one such rule for pattern classification and show that a special case of it is equivalent to the "minimum-distance" principle which is frequently employed in signal discrimination and pattern recognition.

3. Pattern Classification

For purposes of our discussion, a *pattern* is merely another name for a point in Ω, and a *category of patterns* is a (possibly fuzzy) set in Ω. When we speak of *pattern classification*, we have in mind a class of problems which can be subsumed under the following formulation and its variants.

Let A and B denote two[1] disjoint sets in Ω representing two categories of patterns. Suppose that we are given n points (patterns) $\alpha^1, ..., \alpha^n$ which are known to belong to A, and m points $\beta^1, ..., \beta^m$ which are known to belong to B. The problem is to construct estimates of the characteristic functions of A and B based on the knowledge of the samples $\alpha^1, ..., \alpha^n$ from A and $\beta^1, ..., \beta^m$ from B.

Clearly, one can attempt to estimate f_A without making any use of the β^j, $j = 1, ..., m$. However, in general, such an estimate would not be as good as one employing both α's and β's. This is a consequence of an implied or explicit dependence between A and B (e.g., the disjointness of A and B), through which the knowledge of β's contributes some information about f_A. The same applies to the estimation of f_B.

The heuristic rule suggested in the sequel is merely a way of constructing estimates of f_A and f_B, given $\alpha^1, ..., \alpha^n$, and $\beta^1, ..., \beta^m$, in terms of estimates of f_A and f_B, given a single pair of samples α^i and β^j. Specifically, suppose that with every $\alpha \in A$ and every $\beta \in B$ are associated two sets $\tilde{A}(\alpha; \beta)$ and $\tilde{B}(\beta; \alpha)$ representing the estimates of A and B, given α and β. (In effect, $\tilde{A}(\alpha; \beta)$ defines the set of points in Ω over which the estimate $\tilde{f}_A(\alpha; \beta)$ of f_A is unity, and likewise for $\tilde{f}_B(\beta; \alpha)$ and $\tilde{B}(\beta; \alpha)$. Points in Ω which are neither in $\tilde{A}(\alpha; \beta)$ nor in $\tilde{B}(\beta; \alpha)$ have indeterminate status relative to these sets.)

In terms of the sets in question, the estimates of A and B (or, equivalently, f_A and f_B), given $\alpha^1, ..., \alpha^n$ and $\beta^1, ..., \beta^m$, are constructed as follows

$$\tilde{A} = \bigcap_{j=1}^{m} \bigcup_{i=1}^{n} \tilde{A}(\alpha^i; \beta^j), \tag{9}$$

$$\tilde{B} = \bigcap_{i=1}^{n} \bigcup_{j=1}^{m} \tilde{B}(\beta^j; \alpha^i). \tag{10}$$

Thus, under the rule expressed by (9) and (10), we generalize on $\alpha^1, ..., \alpha^n$ and $\beta^1, ..., \beta^m$ by identifying A with $\tilde{A}$ and B with $\tilde{B}$. Note that this rule is consistent in the sense that if α is known to belong to A then $\alpha \in \tilde{A}$, and likewise for a point belonging to B. However, the consistency of this rule does not extend to fuzzy sets. Thus, if (9) and (10) were applied to the estimation of f_A and f_B when A and B are fuzzy sets, it would not necessarily be true that $f_A(\alpha) = \tilde{f}_A(\alpha)$ for all given α in A.

[1] The restriction to two sets serves merely to simplify the analysis and does not entail any essential loss in generality.

In essence, the rule expressed by (9) and (10) implies that a point x is classified as a member of A if and only if for all β^j there exists an α^i such that x lies in $\tilde{A}(\alpha^i, \beta^j)$. For this reason, the rule in question will be referred to as the "rule of complete dominance."

To illustrate the rule of complete dominance and indicate its connection with the "minimum-distance" principle which is frequently employed in signal discrimination, consider the simple case where Ω is R^l and $\tilde{A}(\alpha; \beta)$ and $\tilde{B}(\beta; \alpha)$ are defined as follows:

$$\tilde{A}(\alpha; \beta) = \left\{x \,\middle|\, \left\langle x - \frac{(\alpha + \beta)}{2}, \alpha - \beta \right\rangle \geqslant 0 \right\}, \tag{11}$$

$$\tilde{B}(\beta; \alpha) = \left\{x \,\middle|\, \left\langle x - \frac{(\alpha + \beta)}{2}, \alpha - \beta \right\rangle < 0 \right\}. \tag{12}$$

In effect, $\tilde{A}(\alpha; \beta)$ is the set of all points which are nearer to α than to β or are equidistant from α and β, while $\tilde{B}(\beta; \alpha)$ is the complement of this set with respect to R^l.

Now consider the following "minimum-distance" decision rule. Let A^* and B^* denote the sets of samples $\alpha^1, \ldots, \alpha^n$ and $\beta^1, \ldots, \beta^m$, respectively. Define the distance of a point x in Ω from A^* to be $\mathrm{Min}_i \| x - \alpha^i \|$, where $\| \;\|$ denotes the Euclidean norm and $i = 1, \ldots, n$; do likewise for B^*. Then, given a point x in Ω, decide that $x \in A$ if and only if the distance of x from A^* is less than or equal to the distance of x from B^*.

It is easy to show that this decision rule is a special case of (9) and (10). Specifically, with $\tilde{A}(\alpha; \beta)$ and $\tilde{B}(\beta; \alpha)$ defined by (11) and (12), respectively, the decision rule in question can be expressed as follows:

$$x \in \tilde{A} \Leftrightarrow \forall \beta^j \, \exists \, \alpha^i \{\| x - \alpha^i \| \leqslant \| x - \beta^j \|\}, \qquad \begin{array}{l} i = 1, \ldots, n, \\ j = 1, \ldots, m. \end{array} \tag{13}$$

Now

$$\tilde{A}(\alpha^i; \beta^j) = \{x \mid \| x - \alpha^i \| \leqslant \| x - \beta^j \|\} \tag{14}$$

and consequently (13) defines the set

$$\tilde{A} = \{x \mid \forall \beta^j \, \exists \, \alpha^i (x \in \tilde{A}(\alpha^i; \beta^j))\}. \tag{15}$$

Clearly, (15) is equivalent to

$$\tilde{A} = \bigcap_{j=1}^{m} \bigcup_{i=1}^{n} \tilde{A}(\alpha^i; \beta^j), \tag{16}$$

and similarly for B. Q.E.D.

In the foregoing discussion of the minimum-distance decision rule, we identified Ω with R^l and used the Euclidean metric in R^l to measure the distance between two patterns in Ω. However, in many cases of practical interest, Ω is a set of line patterns in R^2 such as letters, numerals, etc., to which the Euclidean metric is not applicable. In this case, the distance between two line patterns in R^2, say L_0 and L_1, can be defined by

$$d(L_0, L_1) = \underset{y_0 \in L_0}{\mathrm{Max}} \; \underset{y_1 \in L_1}{\mathrm{Min}} \| y_0 - y_1 \|, \tag{17}$$

where $\| \;\|$ is the Euclidean norm in R^2, and y_0 and y_1 are points in R^2 belonging to L_0 and L_1, respectively.

Now suppose that we agree to regard two patterns L_0 and L_1 as equivalent if one can be obtained from the other through translation, rotation, contraction (or dilation) or any combination of these operations. Thus, let T_δ denote the translation $y \to y + \delta$, where $y, \delta \in R^2$; let T_θ denote the rotation through an angle θ around the origin of R^2; and let T_ρ denote the contraction (or dilation) $x \rightarrow \rho x$ where $\rho \in R^1$. Then, we define the ***reduced*** distance of L_1 from L_0 by the relation

$$d^* (L_1 ; L_0) = \underset{T_\delta}{\text{Min}} \underset{T_\theta}{\text{Min}} \underset{T_\rho}{\text{Min}} d(L_0 , T_\delta T_\theta T_\rho L_1), \tag{18}$$

where $T_\delta T_\theta T_\rho L_1$ denotes the image of L_1 under the operation $T_\delta T_\theta T_\rho$, and $d(L_0 , T_\delta T_\theta T_\rho L_1)$ is the distance between L_0 and $T_\delta T_\theta T_\rho L_1$ in the sense of (17). Clearly, it is the reduced distance in the sense of (18) rather than the distance in the sense of (17) that should be used in applying the minimum-distance decision rule to the case where Ω is a set of line patterns in R^2.

To conclude our discussion of pattern classification, we shall indicate how the formulation given in the beginning of this section can be extended to fuzzy sets. Thus, let A and B denote two such sets in Ω, with f_A and f_B denoting their respective characteristic functions. Suppose that we are given n sample triplets $(x^1, f_A{}^1, f_B{}^1), ..., (x^n, f_A{}^n, f_B{}^n)$, with $(x^i, f_A{}^i, f_B{}^i)$ representing a sample consisting of x^i and the values of f_A and f_B at x^i. The problem of pattern classification in this context is essentially that of estimating the characteristic functions f_A and f_B from the given collection of samples. Clearly, this formulation of the problem includes as a special case the pattern-classification problem stated earlier for the case where A and B are sets in Ω.

REFERENCES

1. S. C. Kleene, "Introduction to Metamathematics," p. 334. D. Van Nostrand Co., Inc., New York, 1952.
2. J. B. Rosen, "Pattern Recognition by Convex Programming," Tech. Rept. No. 30 (Stanford University, June 1963).

Fuzzy Sets and Decisionmaking Approaches in Vowel and Speaker Recognition

SANKAR K. PAL AND DWIJESH DUTTA MAJUMDER

Abstract—**Some applications based on the theory of fuzzy sets in problems of computer recognition of vowels and identifying the person from his spoken words using only the first three formants (F_1, F_2, and F_3) of the unknown utterance are presented. Two decision algorithmic methods using weighted-distance functions and property sets are developed and implemented with the optimum size of the training set on a large number of Telugu (an important Indian language) speech sounds with a recognition score of 82 percent for vowels and 97 percent for the speaker.**

I. Introduction

The problem of pattern recognition in general and that of speech recognition in particular are increasingly drawing the attention of scientific workers because of the potentiality for man-machine communication. The concept of pattern classification may be viewed as a partition of feature space or a mapping from feature space to decision space. There are various mathematical tools suggested by different authors [1]–[3] leading to the machine recognition of patterns. But more often than not, situations in the field of natural and social sciences are too complex for precise mathematical analysis. Classes of objects in that field do not have well-defined criteria of membership. To demonstrate such complexly behaved systems, the concepts of fuzzy sets and the subsequent developments in decision process [4]–[6] could be applied to a reasonable extent. This concept is approximate but provides an effective and more flexible basis for analysis of systems which are not precisely defined.

The problem of speech recognition has been dealt with by several researchers [7]–[12], [26] using time, frequency, or time-frequency (spectrograph) domain analysis. Use of computers in the speech recognition problem was first made by Forgie and Forgie [8] who recognized ten vowels with 93 percent accuracy. Denis and Mathews [12] indicated the advantages of computers for solving many of the problems encountered in speech research. The feasibility of automatic speaker identification has been demonstrated by many authors using various speech characteristics such as spectral data from filter banks [13], nasals [14], pitch contours [15], pitch intensity and formants [16], linear predictor coefficient (LPC) analysis [17], and zero crossings and amplitude measurement [18]. The method of formant analysis for speaker recognition was first adopted by Doddington [16] who had used Schafer and Rabiner's technique [11] to convert speech into pitch, intensity, and formant values. It has been found that higher order formants (4th and 5th) are more speaker dependent, but it is generally difficult to extract them. In spite of measurement difficulty and larger processing time, formants have potential application in speech and speaker recognition because of their remarkable inter-repetition stability [19] and their close relation to the phonetic concepts of segmentation and equivalence.

The present correspondence shows an application of fuzzy set theory in the field of artificial intelligence for machine recognition of speech and informants using the first three formants only. The problem has a far-reaching significance in man–machine communication problems where simultaneous identification of speaker and speech sound is important. This is a part of the investigations [20]–[25] on man–machine communication research, a program under development in the ECS Laboratory, Indian Statistical Institute. Two methods for classification analysis on the basis of fuzzy algorithms are, first of all, described in this correspondence, and these are implemented to develop an automatic system to answer sequentially, with a minimum number of errors, the question, "What is the vowel contained in and who is the informant of an unknown utterance in a large number of spoken CNC (consonant–vowel nucleus–consonant) words?" The first part of the question requires the computation of weighted distance functions used in estimating the membership value for each vowel class. Second, a recognition method based on evaluating property sets and finding the similarity vectors corresponding to different classes were considered for identifying speakers. The Honeywell-400 electronic computer was used as the data processing system.

This program was carried out on a set of Telugu (one of the major Indian languages) words containing about 900 commonly used speech units for 10 vowels in CNC combination and uttered by three informants in the age group of 28–30 years. It is expected that variations in sex and age will lead to a better recognition score. As it is believed that formants have potential application in speech and speaker recognition because of their remarkable inter-repetition stability and their close relation to the phonetic concepts of segmentation and equivalence, the first three formants F_1, F_2, and F_3 only were considered as characterizing features from a spectrum analysis made on a Kay Sonagraph (model no. 7029A). It is to be noted that higher formants (4th and 5th) and fundamental voice frequency F_0 are found to be very speaker dependent and are not considered essential as recognition criteria. Since F_3 is more speaker dependent as compared to F_1 and F_2, parameters selected for informant recognition are (F_3/F_1) or $(F_3 - F_1)$, (F_3/F_2) or $(F_3 - F_2)$, and F_3. Since each of these is a function of F_3, the inverse of standard deviation of the F_3 features is used as the weighting coefficient. The second part of the experiment consists in the study of the variation of the machine's performance in identifying a speaker with different sizes of training samples used in learning. Results are described in tabular form, where each score mentioned is the average value of three observations performed on a specified training set.

Manuscript received May 3, 1976; revised September 20, 1976, and March 8, 1977. This work was supported in part by the Council of Scientific and Industrial Research, Government of India.

The authors are with the Department of Electronics and Communication Sciences, Indian Statistical Institute, Calcutta 700 035, India.

Reprinted from *IEEE Trans. Syst., Man, Cybern.*, pp. 625–629, August 1977.

II. Classification Analysis Using Fuzzy Sets

A. Fuzzy Sets

A fuzzy set (A) in space of points $X = \{x\}$ is a class of events with a continuum of grades of membership and is characterized by a membership function $\mu_A(x)$ which associates with each point in X a real number in the interval [0,1] with the value of $\mu_A(x)$ at x representing the grade of membership of x in A. Formally, a fuzzy set A with its finite number of supports $x_1, x_2, \cdots, x_n$ is defined as

$$A = \{(\mu_A(x_i),x_i)\} \tag{1}$$

or

$$A = \bigcup_i \mu_i/x_i, \qquad i = 1, 2, \cdots, n. \tag{2}$$

The characteristic function denotes the degree to which an event x_i may be a member of A, and as it approaches unity, the grade of membership of x_i in A becomes higher.

B. Decisional Algorithms

Consider an unknown pattern

$$X = \begin{bmatrix} x_1 \\ x_2 \\ \vdots \\ x_n \\ \vdots \\ x_N \end{bmatrix}$$

where x_n denotes the measured nth feature of the event, represented by a point in the multidimensional vector space Ω_X, consisting of m ill-defined pattern classes $C_1, C_2, \cdots, C_j, \cdots, C_m$. Let $R_1, R_2, \cdots, R_j, \cdots, R_m$ be the reference vectors where R_j associated with C_j contains h_j number of prototypes such that

$$R_j \ni R_j^{(l)}, \qquad l = 1, 2, \cdots, h_j$$

The pattern X can then be assigned to be a member of that class to which it shows maximum similarity as measured by the algorithms described below.

Method I: We define a membership function $\mu_j(X)$ associated with pattern X for the jth class as

$$\mu_j(X) = [1 + (d(X,R_j)/E)^F]^{-1.0} \tag{3}$$

where E is an arbitrary positive constant, F is any integer, $d(X,R_j)$ is the distance between X and R_j, and

$$d(X,R_j) = \bigwedge_l \left[\sum_n (W_{jn}^{(l)}(x_n - R_{jn}^{(l)}))^2\right]^{0.5} \tag{4}$$

where $\wedge$ denotes minimum. The above expression represents the minimum value of the weighted distances of an unknown pattern X from all its expected values in class C_j and $W_{jn}^{(l)}$ ($|W_{jn}^{(l)}| \leq 1$) corresponds to the lth prototype in C_j and denotes the magnitude of the weighting coefficient along the nth coordinate.

Constants E and F in (3) have the effect of altering the fuzziness of a set [5], [6], [22], [23]. The μ-value defining the grade of membership of X in C_j as shown by this equation is unity for $d(X,R_j) = 0$, zero for $d(X,R_j) = \infty$, and increases with decreasing the value of $d(X,R_j)$. Thus an unknown pattern X is recognized to be a member of the kth class if

$$\mu_k(X) = \bigvee_j \{\mu_j(X)\}$$

where $\vee$ denotes maximum and $j, k = 1, 2, \cdots, m$.

Method II: Let $p_1, p_2, \cdots, p_n, \cdots, p_N$ be the N properties each of which represents some aspects of the unknown pattern X and has value only in the interval [0,1] such that

$$X = \{p_1, p_2, \cdots, p_n, \cdots, p_N\} \tag{5}$$

where

$$p_n = \left(1 + \left|\frac{\bar{x}_n - x_n}{E}\right|^F\right)^{-1.0} \tag{6}$$

and $\bar{x}_n$ is nth reference constant determined from representative events of all the classes. Constants E and F have the same effect as in the previous method in affecting the fuzziness of a set.

If there are h number of prototypes in a class C_j, each reference point may then be represented as

$$R_j^{(l)} = \{p_{1j}^{(l)}, p_{2j}^{(l)}, \cdots, p_{nj}^{(l)}, \cdots, p_{Nj}^{(l)}\} \tag{7}$$

where $p_{nj}^{(l)}$ denotes the degree to which property p_n is possessed by the lth prototype in C_j. Then the similarity vector $S_j(X)$ for the pattern X with respect to the jth class has the form

$$S_j(X) = \{s_{1j}, s_{2j}, \cdots, s_{nj}, \cdots, s_{Nj}\} \tag{8}$$

$$s_{nj} = \frac{1}{h}\sum_l s_{nj}^{(l)} \tag{9}$$

$$s_{nj}^{(l)} = (1 + W|1 - (p_n/p_{nj}^{(l)})|)^{-2Z} \tag{10}$$

where the numerical value of s_{nj} denotes the grade of similarity of the nth property with that of C_j. W is any positive constant dependent on each of the properties, and Z is an arbitrary integer. With the knowledge of all the similarity vectors one can decide $X \in C_k$ if

$$|S_j(X)| < |S_k(X)|, \qquad k, j = 1, 2, \cdots, m; k \neq j.$$

III. Method of Segmentation and Feature Extraction

A number of discrete phonetically balanced (PB) speech samples for all the vowels in CNC form were selected from the Telugu vocabulary. CNC combination is taken because the form of consonants connected to a vowel is responsible for influencing the role and quality of vowels. These speech units were recorded by five informants on an AKAI tape recorder. By listening experiments among ten listeners, only 871 samples uttered by three male informants in the age group of 28–30 years were chosen. Spectrum analyses were carried through a very standard audio frequency spectrum analyzer, Kay Sonagraph (model no. 7029A), which yields a permanent record of the formant frequencies F_1, F_2, and F_3 in the range 5 Hz–16 kHz. Sonagraph was operated in the normal mode in the band 80 Hz–8 kHz with a wide BPF (bandwidth 300 Hz).

A. Segmentation Procedure

The segmentation procedure should satisfactorily solve the problems of determination of vowel boundary in relation to stops, fricatives, affricates, laterals in voiced/unvoiced, aspirated/unaspirated as well as their combined manners. The boundaries in these different situations need to be defined first.

1) For the stop consonants in the final position the start of occlusion period of the consonant will indicate the termination of the vowel. In some particular cases the vowel formants extend to a certain limit into the occluded part of the stop consonant, and for these cases the terminal point of the vowel includes this extended part. For unaspirated stops in the initial position, a gap very often separates the energy of plosion and the adjacent vowel formants. The starting point of the formants excludes this gap. For aspirated

TABLE I
VOWEL SPEAKER MATRIX SHOWING NUMBER OF EVENTS IN EACH CLASS

	X	Y	Z
/i/	43	61	68
/e/	60	68	79
/∂/	20	24	28
/a:/	29	19	41
/o/	39	35	56
/u/	41	59	51

stops in the initial position, the onset of F_0 is taken to be the boundary.

2) The fricatives with a wide-band continuous energy spectrum of low intensity can be easily separated from the narrow band of much stronger intensity of vowel formants. The line separating these two distinctly separate spectral distributions is the vowel boundary for fricatives in the initial and also in final position. The line of demarcation for affricates in initial and final position is same as in fricative and stop consonants, respectively.

3) The segmentation problem becomes more complex for the liquid and vowel combinations. The liquids possess a formant-like structure very similar to vowel formants and thus create real confusion. But careful observation will reveal that the formant structure of liquids is less intense with a much lesser degree of transition. These characteristic differences are used for determining the vowel boundary in this case.

B. Measurement Procedure

Formants F_1, F_2, and F_3 were obtained manually at the steady state of the vowels. The steady state of the vowel is that part on the record in which all formants lie parallel to the time axis. The transition is depicted by the inclined formant patterns. The exact point of inflection is difficult to locate in the records. This can be done very satisfactorily by tracing the central line for each formant band. Once these points are located for all available formants, the steady state of the vowel is taken to be the shortest horizontal span for all the formants.

In view of the large amount of data to be handled, the formant frequencies have been measured from the base line with a specially constructed scale. A rechecking on 5 percent of the samples revealed that formant frequencies have been recorded within an accuracy of 10 Hz. In a few cases, for particularly fast informants, it has been noticed that the vowel hardly reaches a stable state. In such cases the congruences of the on- and off-glides have been taken as the steady state.

In order to make the method of segmentation and formant extraction automatic, the maxima in the rate of change of spectral composition determined by a running summation of the absolute values of the rate of intensity change in a number of successive bands may be used, in general, as the criteria for the automatic method of determining segment boundaries. The method for automatic formant frequency extraction has been reported in a previous communication [20].

The respective features thus constitute a three-dimensional feature vector space Ω_F where each utterance of a speaker may be treated as an event from a population and each dimension represents an invariant characteristic of that event. Ten Telugu vowels (/∂/, /a:/, /i⊢/, /i:/, /u⊣/, /u:/, /e⊢/, /e:/, /o⊣/, and /o:/) including shorter and longer categories were divided into six groups which contain vowels differing only in phonetic feature. Therefore, the multidimensional vector space is partitioned into 18 pattern classes (6 vowels × 3 speakers), and each point in Ω_F thus associates three measured features corresponding to a vowel uttered by one of the three informants. The number of samples belonging to each group is tabulated through a vowel-speaker (X, Y, and Z, let us say) matrix (Table I).

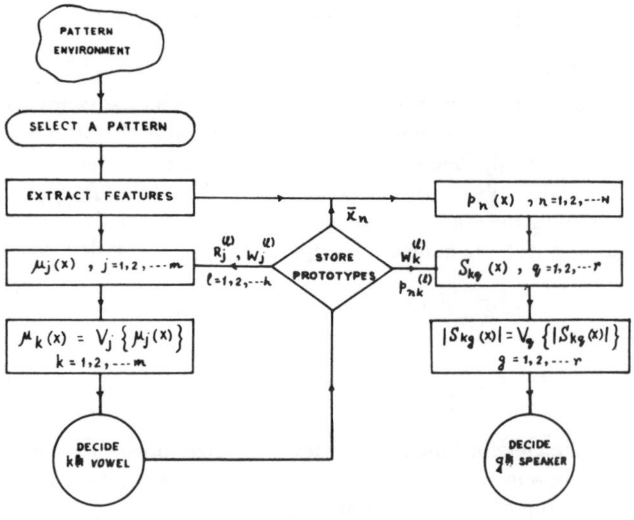

Fig. 1. Sequential recognition of vowel and its informant.

IV. RECOGNITION PROCEDURE

The block diagram of the recognition program based on the automatic spoken word recognition model [20] developed at ISI is shown in Fig. 1, in which an appropriate serial answer of the question, "What is the vowel and who is its speaker?" is given. The system first of all searches for the vowel class irrespective of speakers, and then with the information of the vowel uttered, the specific informant is identified.

Prototype points chosen for vowel identification are the average of the coordinate values corresponding to the entire set of samples in a particular class. The features with increasing variance have been weighted with decreasing values of the weighting coefficients, and the inverse of the standard deviation of the formants as weighting coefficients were studied. Although shorter and longer types of vowels /i/, /u/, /e/, and /o/ are treated as the same group, they were given individual reference vectors and weighting coefficients computed over their respective set of events. Thus in our experiment of vowel sound recognition, $m = 6$, $N = 3$, $h = 1$, for /∂/, and /a:/, and $h = 2$ for /i/, /o/, /e/, and /u/. Computing membership values with respect to all the vowel classes using (3), an unknown vowel speech pattern is assigned to the kth class ($k = 1, 2, \cdots, 6$) associated with maximum μ-value.

Whenever a vowel class of the unknown utterance is determined, then the system is engaged in finding its informants with the knowledge of stored prototypes for three speaker subclasses ($r = 3$) in that recognized vowel region. Since F_3 as compared to F_1 and F_2 bears more significant information about the speaker, the recognition features selected are (F_3/F_1), (F_3/F_2), and F_3. Experiments were also done replacing the first two parameters by $(F_3 - F_1)$ and $(F_3 - F_2)$, respectively. Properties corresponding to each of the features were computed with $E = 100$, $F = 2$, and using (11):

$$\bar{x}_n = \bigvee_q \frac{1}{h} \sum_l x_n^{(l)}, \qquad n,q = 1,2,3. \tag{11}$$

Similarity of the pattern with all the classes of informants was

SPOKEN \ RECOGNISED AS	/i/	/e/	/ə/	/a:/	/o/	/u/
/i/	155	17				
/e/	25	154	20	8		
/ə/		9	52	8	2	1
/a:/			17	70	2	
/o/		1	7		138	34
/u/			1		6	144

CORRECT RATE = 82%

Fig. 2. Confusion matrix illustrating machine's performance on vowel recognition.

measured for $Z = 1$ by (9) and (10). Constant W was considered to be the inverse of the standard deviation of the recognition parameters, and in a part of the experiment (only for vowel /i/), similarity vectors were measured with $W = 1$ to investigate the influence of phase weights attached with the features. A subregion C_g ($g = 1,2,3$) possessing maximum closeness as measured by the magnitude of the similarity vectors is decided by the machine to be the corresponding speaker of the utterance.

To study the effect of training sets used in learning on a classified set, the above method of speaker identification was repeated thrice for each of the different sample sizes, viz., 1, 3, 5, 7, 10, and 15. This part of the experiment was carried out only with formants of the vowel /i/. Here samples were randomly drawn from each group of informants by which reference constants $\bar{x}_n$ and W corresponding to the size of training samples were estimated. In a few cases, where the standard deviation of the magnitudes of a coordinate in a training set was zero, the corresponding W value was set at unity. Although it does not satisfy (4), it is still logical in the sense that an attribute occurring with identical magnitude in all members of a training set is an all-important feature of the set, and hence its contribution in the discriminant function needs not be reduced.

V. Experimental Results

The results of vowel recognition are explained by a confusion matrix in Fig. 2, where the figure in a cell represents the number of instances in which the same decision was made by the machine, and the diagonal elements thus indicate the number of utterances correctly identified. Overall recognition is about 82 percent, and it was found that the second maximum membership for classes /i/, /e/, /ə/, /a:/, /o/, and /u/, as expected from their phonetical order, correspond to vowel regions /e/, /i/, /a:/, /ə/, /u/, and /o/, respectively. In Fig. 2, confusion in machine recognition of a vowel is seen to be limited only to neighboring classes constituting a vowel triangle. This is in agreement with other experiments [22]–[24], [26].

Typical formant frequencies for the vowel /i/ uttered by three male informants in the age group of 28–30 years are shown in Table II. Table III illustrates the correct rate of decision rendered by the machine in identifying formants for each of the vowel speech sounds.

Scores shown are the average value of three observations only

TABLE II
Typical Formants for Telugu Vowel /i/ Uttered by Three Speakers

Informant	F_1 (Hz)	F_2 (Hz)	F_3 (Hz)
X	350	2350	2800
Y	350	2250	2700
Z	300	2350	3000

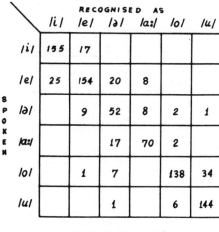

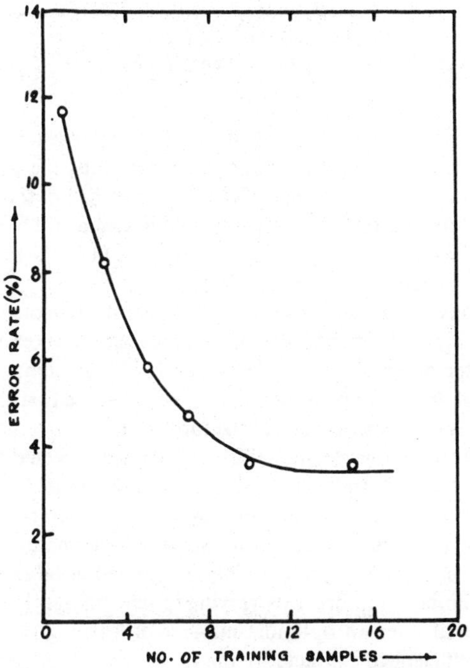

Fig. 3. Effect of training set on speaker identification score.

when the machine was trained by a set of five utterances for each speaker. With the fixation of appropriate phase weights which ensure the correct representation of feature-importance in classification, overall recognition accuracy is much improved (≈ 12 percent) compared to the case of no coefficients ($W = 1$). Whether parameters $(F_3 - F_1)$ and $(F_3 - F_2)$ are taken instead of (F_3/F_1) and (F_3/F_2), respectively, the computer decision is altered very little.

Finally, variations of error rate (percent) with the set of training samples is graphically shown in Fig. 3, which demonstrates improvement in the machine's performance as the number of known labeled samples is increased. The curve is drawn using only the patterns of the vowel /i/. Sample sizes containing more than 8–10 utterances used in learning do not reduce the percentage error significantly. It could therefore be stated that after an optimum size of training patterns is achieved to provide good representation and weighting coefficients which characterize the classes, variation of recognition scores with training sets becomes insignificant.

VI. Conclusions

Classification analysis using the concept of fuzzy sets is studied for machine recognition of informant and speech sounds for a large number of utterances. Accuracy of vowel sound recognition is about 82 percent when the decision of the machine was based only on the highest membership values. By incorporating a

TABLE III
ACCURACY RATE (PERCENT) (AVERAGED OVER THREE OBSERVATIONS) OF SPEAKER IDENTIFICATION FOR EACH VOWEL FORMANT

Speaker	Recognition Score (percent) for $h = 5$							
	/i/	/i/*	/i/**	/e/	/ə/	/a:/	/o/	/u/
X	89.47	73.69	84.21	92.60	100.00	82.76	95.84	91.30
Y	90.90	69.67	93.94	90.63	83.40	78.95	94.45	90.63
Z	100.00	100.00	100.00	100.00	96.43	95.13	83.34	92.00
TOTAL:	94.12	82.36	94.12	94.85	93.06	87.64	90.63	91.25

* Without weighting coefficient.
** Replacing (F_3/F_1) and (F_3/F_2) by (F_3-F_1) and (F_3-F_2), respectively.

second choice under the control of a supervisory learning scheme, supposed to be based on linguistic constraints, the above score can be improved by 15 percent [21]. Knowledge of the weighting coefficients and reference vectors used is also available from any size of the training samples containing more than 12-16 utterance, without affecting the overall score [21].

Although it is well known that the fundamental voice frequency F_0 and higher formants (F_4 and F_5) are more speaker dependent, computer decision on the identification of informants in the age group of 28-30 years using property sets and the first three formants only is found to be satisfactory. It may be remarked that informants widely varying in age and sex are expected to result in a large discrimination in F_3, leading to a better identification. At best, for 97 percent of the speech sounds, the machine was seen to render correct recognition of the speaker by comparing the magnitudes of similarity vectors. This is expected to be extended to a large number of informants varying in sex and age. It can be also stated that after an optimum number of learning samples (8-10 only) sufficient to characterize the representative points of a class, the size of the sample space can be extended enormously without disturbing the overall recognition score.

The paper therefore shows the possibility of recognizing both vowels and speakers with the help of the same features measured on a CNC word. Results of speaker identification were tabulated with the assumption that the vowel in the utterance is correctly recognized. If the immediate knowledge of the vowel is used (for sequential processing) then some but not all of the 18 percent error for vowel recognition will pass to speaker identification, since some samples were found to have error both in identifying the vowel and the speaker. However, our decision algorithm does not preclude the possibility of correct speaker identification from the misrecognized vowel features.

ACKNOWLEDGMENT

The authors wish to express their appreciation to Prof. C. R. Rao, F.R.S., Director, Indian Statistical Institute, for his interest in the work and acknowledge with thanks the help rendered by A. K. Datta, N. R. Ganguli, and B. Mukherjee in processing the spectrographic data. S. K. Pal, one of the authors, is also indebted to the Council of Scientific and Industrial Research, Government of India, for the award of a fellowship for this project.

REFERENCES

[1] G. S. Sebestyen, *Decision Making Processes in Pattern Recognition.* New York: Macmillan, 1962.
[2] K. S. Fu, *Sequential Methods in Pattern Recognition and Machine Learning.* London: Academic, 1968.
[3] ——, *Syntactic Methods in Pattern Recognition.* London: Academic, 1974.
[4] L. A. Zadeh, "Fuzzy sets," *Inform. Control*, vol. 8, pp. 338-353, 1963.
[5] ——, "Outline of a new approach to the analysis of complex systems and decision processes," *IEEE Trans. Syst., Man, Cybern.*, vol. SMC-3, pp. 28-44, Jan. 1973.
[6] L. A. Zadeh, K. S. Fu, K. Tanaka, and M. Shimura, *Fuzzy Sets and Their Application to Cognitive and Decision Processes.* London: Academic, 1975.
[7] T. Sakai and S. Doshita, "The automatic speech recognition system for conversational sound," *IEEE Trans. Electronic Computers*, vol. EC-12, pp. 835-846, Dec. 1963.
[8] J. W. Forgie and C. D. Forgie, "Results obtained from a vowel recognition computer program," *J. Acoust. Soc. Am.*, vol. 31, pp. 1480-1489, 1959.
[9] D. R. Reddy, "Segmentation of speech sounds," *J. Acoust. Soc. Am.*, vol. 40, pp. 307-312, 1966.
[10] R. Jacobson, C. G. N. Fant, and M. Halle, "Preliminaries to speech analysis," MIT Acoust. Lab. Rep., no. 13, May 1952.
[11] R. W. Shaffer and L. R. Rabiner, "System for automatic formant analysis of voiced speech," *J. Acoust. Soc. Am.*, vol. 47, pp. 634-648, 1970.
[12] P. B. Denes and M. V. Mathews, "Spoken digit recognition using time-frequency pattern matching," *J. Acoust. Soc. Am.*, vol. 32, pp. 1450-1455, 1960.
[13] S. Pruzensky, "Pattern matching procedure for automatic talker recognition," *J. Acoust. Soc. Am.*, vol. 35, pp. 354-358, 1963.
[14] J. W. Glenn and N. Kleiner, "Speaker identification based on nasal phonation," *J. Acoust. Soc. Am.*, vol. 43, pp. 368-372, 1968.
[15] B. S. Atal, "Automatic speaker recognition based on pitch contours," *J. Acoust. Soc. Am.*, vol. 52, pp. 1687-1697, 1972.
[16] G. R. Doddington, "A method of speaker verification," *J. Acoust. Soc. Am.*, vol. 49, pp. 139, 1971.
[17] A. E. Rosenberg and M. R. Sambur, "New technique for automatic speaker verification," *IEEE Trans. Acoust. Speech and Sig. Processing*, vol. ASSP-23, p. 169, Apr. 1975.
[18] D. A. Wasson and R. W. Donaldson, "Speech amplitude and zero crossing for automated identification of human speakers," *IEEE Trans. Acoust. Speech and Sig. Processing*, vol. ASSP-23, pp. 390-392, Aug. 1975.
[19] D. J. Broad, "Formants in automatic speech recognition," *Int. J. Man-Machine Studies*, vol. 4, p. 411, 1972.
[20] D. D. Majumder and A. K. Datta, "A model for spoken word recognition," *Proc. Automazione Estrumentazione*, Milan, Italy, pp. 249-259, 1968.
[21] D. D. Majumder, A. K. Datta, and S. K. Pal, "Computer recognition of vowel speech sounds using three-dimensional weighted discriminant function," IEEE Computer Group Repository, 1976.
[22] D. D. Majumder and S. K. Pal, "The concept of fuzzy sets and its application in pattern recognition problems," *Proc. CSI*, 76 Convention, Hyderabad, India, no. SD 02, Jan. 1976.
[23] ——, "On some applications of fuzzy algorithm in man-machine communication research," *J. Inst. Telecom. Electron. Eng.*, vol. 23, pp. 117-120, Mar. 1977.
[24] D. D. Majumder, S. K. Pal, and B. B. Chaudhuri, "Some experiments on computer recognition of speech pattern," *Proc. Int. Conf. Inform. Sc. Syst.*, Patras, Greece, August 1976, Hemisphere Publishing, USA (to appear).
[25] A. K. Datta, "An experimental procedure for handwritten character recognition," *IEEE Trans. Comput.*, vol. C-23, pp. 536-545, May 1974.
[26] K. K. Paliwal and P. V. S. Rao, "Computer recognition of isolated phonemes," *Proc. CSI*, 76 Convention, Hyderabad, India, no. SR 04, Jan. 1976.

ON THE DESIGN OF A CLASSIFIER WITH LINGUISTIC VARIABLES AS INPUTS*

A.K. NATH and T.T. LEE

Institute of Control Engineering National Chiao Tung University, Hsinchu, Taiwan, Republic of China

Received March 1982
Revised July 1982

The paper proposes a design method for a classifier with linguistic variables as inputs. The method consists of two distinct parts. In the first part, the classifier is designed utilizing the expertise of an expert. In the second part, the classifier is refined through experimentation utilizing labeled samples. An algorithm has been developed for this refinement. It appears that the classifier may have potential applications in the areas of 'soft' sciences, including such fields as medicine and medical diagnostics.

Keywords: Classifier, Linguistic variable, Refinement, Medical Diagnostics, Fuzzy sets.

1. Introduction

In general, the pattern classifiers are developed through a process of learning [1]. In the learning phase, sets of labeled patterns of all classes are utilized for the formation of the classification algorithms. The nature and an a priori knowledge of the patterns along with the nature of the given classification problem dictate the selection of a particular technique, either statistical or syntactic, for the construction of the classifier [2]. More or less, these techniques are quantitative in nature and are used for the 'mechanistic' type of problems. Other than these, there are classfication problems, e.g. in the fields of 'soft' sciences, where enough a priori knowledge about the classifier itself is available from human beings, called experts. The primary aim in solving such classification problems should be in utilizing the expert's knowledge to the fullest extent. So, the technique for the development of classifiers for these problems should be compatible with the thought and communication processes of the expert. Such a technique, thus, becomes 'human-centered'. For these classifiers, the input patterns are in the linguistic form, or in a mixed form where part of the pattern is quantitative and part linguistic. Two different approaches may be adopted for the solution of these classification problems. In the first approach, the linguistic part of the input pattern is converted into quantitative form and then any of the techniques, either syntactic or statistical, can be used. But this approach is incompatible with these classification problems. First, it is difficult, if not impossible, to convert the linguistic data into a quantitative form. Linguistic data contain summarized information; they are approximate and fuzzy in nature. To assign meaningful quantitative values to them is very difficult. Secondly, since the human thought processes are basically fuzzy in nature, the quantitative technique is incompatible with these classification problems. According to Zadeh [3], the conventional quantitative techniques of system analysis are intrinsically unsuited for dealing with humanistic systems, or for that matter, any system whose complexity is comparable to that of humanistic systems. In the second approach, the quantitative part of the input patterns is converted into the linguistic form and then a compatible technique, e.g. a technique based on fuzzy subset theory [4], is used. Since the linguistic representation is a summarized form of information, it is easier to convert any quantitative data into the linguistic forms.

Consider an example for clarifying the above ideas, viz. the problem of

* This work was supported in part by the National Science Council of the Republic of China.

Reprinted with permission from *Fuzzy Sets Syst.*, vol. 11, pp. 265–286, 1983.

classifying chest pain into two classes, i.e. cardiac and noncardiac. The doctors (experts) are doing this classification for a long time and in the process have acquired an expertise. Although their technique may be heuristic, fuzzy, or may be simply their 'feel', still any method for the development of this classifier should utilize this expertise. Further, the input pattern in this problem will consist of, say, severity of pain, its location, frequency, spreading, past history, etc., which are generally in the linguistic form, along with the quantitative data like age, bloodpressure, build, etc. Now, if one wants to express the severity of pain in quantitative form, one will face a real difficult task. Even if he is successful, it will be very complex to be meaningful. In that matter, the spreading of pain can be represented very accurately in spatial and temporal domains. But it will make the pattern very complex. On the other hand, perhaps an approximate linguistic description about the spreading may serve the purpose. Similar is the case with the data, say, age. The very accurate quantitative information about age may not be needed for this classification problem. An approximate and summarized version, like 'old' or 'very old' or 'young' or 'not so young' may be adequate. It is thus evident that in this example of mixed patterns, it will be easier to convert the quantitative data into linguistic form and use a compatible technique for the development of the classifier.

In essence, the human thinking is fuzzy in nature, and the human communication is in natural language which is approximate and summarized and so fuzzy. Hence, a 'human-centered' classifier must be a fuzzy one and should have the capability of manipulating information in the linguistic variable form. Such a classifier will be easier to develop by utilizing the fullest expertise of the human expert.

The method of expressing the strategy of human operators of complex control processes using fuzzy subset theory has already been proposed. These are expert-knowledge-based systems. Since the original papers on fuzzy logic controllers appeared [5, 6], considerable interest has been shown in the application of similarly structured fuzzy logic controllers to simulated systems [7, 8, 9], to pilot plants [10, 11, 12], and even to an industrial process [13, 14]. Zadeh [15] has developed a theory of approximate reasoning based on fuzzy subset theory. This theory has the capability to handle both soft and hard data as well as various types of uncertainty. Many aspects of this development can be incorporated into a general classifier. Sanchez has used this methodology for medical diagnostics [16, 17]. Yager has used this theory in formulating solutions to multicriterion decision problems [18]. Yager has also shown how the ideas from the theory of approximate reasoning and from possibility theory can form the basis for building classification models which enable one to use imprecise information in their construction [19].

In this paper, a technique for the development of the 'human-centered' classifier has been proposed, where the input pattern is assumed to be in the linguistic variable form. Primarily, the technique is based on the expert's experience. Subsequent refinement of the classifier can be achieved by using class-labeled samples. An algorithm for the refinement has been proposed. In Section 2 of the paper pertinent information about linguistic variables is provided. In Section 3, the technique for the development of the 'human-centered' classifier based on the expert's knowledge is given. Section 4 describes the technique of the refinement of the classifier using class-labeled samples, while Section 5 records the conclusions.

2. Linguistic patterns and their representation

In this section, we will introduce the concept of linguistic patterns and show how they can be mathematically represented.

Definition 1. A linguistic pattern consists of linguistic variables.

Definition 2. A linguistic variable is characterized by a quintuple $(H, T(H), U, G, M)$ in which H is the name of the variable; $T(H)$ denotes the term-set of H, that is, the set of names of linguistic values of H, with each value being a fuzzy variable denoted generically by X and ranging over a universe of discourse U which is associated with the base variable u; G is a syntactic rule for generating the names, X, of values of H; and M is a semantic rule for associating with each X its meaning, $M(X)$ which is a fuzzy subset of U. A particular X, that is, a name generated by G, is called a *term*. A term consisting of a word or words which function as a unit is called an *atomic term*. A term which contains one or more atomic terms is a *composite term*. A concatenation of components of a composite term is a *subterm* [20].

Example 1. Consider the linguistic variable named H = Temperature. Here the name of the linguistic variable is Temperature. The term-set, T (Temperature) = {HIGH, VERY HIGH, NOT VERY HIGH, LOW, NOT VERY LOW, VERY LOW, NORMAL, ABOVE NORMAL, . . .}. Each of the term-set denotes some value (in a fuzzy sense) to the linguistic variable, Temperature, and each of them is a fuzzy variable having the universe of discourse, say, 0°C to 100°C. The base variable here is t°C. All the components of the term-set can be generated by a syntactic rule, G. The meaning of HIGH, i.e. M(HIGH), is a fuzzy subset over the universe of discourse 0°C to 100°C and its membership function may be given in terms of the base variable t as

$$\mu_{M(\text{HIGH})}(t) = f(t) \tag{1}$$

where $f(t)$ is a suitable function of t. Thus, "Temperature is High" is a linguistic variable whose value is high which is a fuzzy variable whose meaning is a fuzzy subset whose membership function is given in (1). Here, HIGH, LOW, NORMAL are atomic terms, and VERY HIGH, VERY LOW, ABOVE NORMAL, etc. are composite terms.

It is apparent from the above definition that a linguistic variable may be words or a sentence in a natural or artificial language, and its value is not a number but is a word (words) which is a fuzzy variable whose meaning is a fuzzy subset in a universe of discourse. In general, the linguistic variables are composites of atomic terms concatenated in the form, $X = X_1X_2X_3 \cdots X_n$, where X is the composite linguistic variable, and X_i, $i = 1, \ldots, n$, are atomic terms. Generally, the atomic terms can be divided into four categories, viz.,

(i) Primary terms, e.g. OLD, YOUNG, BIG, SMALL, etc.

(ii) The negation 'not', and the connectives 'and', 'or', e.g. not SMALL, BIG and YOUNG, MEDIUM or BIG, etc.

(iii) Linguistic hedges, e.g. VERY, MUCH, SLIGHTLY.

(iv) Markers such as parentheses, e.g. not (VERY OLD).

The meaning of the composite term can be obtained if the meaning of each of the atomic terms comprising it is known. Consider, $X = hp$, where p is a primary term and h is a hedge. The linguistic function of the hedge may be explained as that of an operator which transforms the meaning $M(P)$ into the meaning $M(hp)$ [both of them are fuzzy subsets].

Example 2. Consider, X = VERY OLD, where OLD is the primary term and VERY is the hedge. The linguistic function of the hedge, VERY can be considered as an intensifier which intensify the meaning of the primary term, OLD. Mathematically, this intensification can be achieved as follows. If $\mu_{\text{OLD}}(y)$ is the membership function of the fuzzy subset M(OLD) (the meaning of OLD where y is the base variable years in the universe of discourse 0 to 100 years) then the membership function of the fuzzy subset M(VERY OLD), the meaning of VERY OLD, can be given as

$$\mu_{\text{VERY OLD}}(y) = [\mu_{\text{OLD}}(y)]^2. \tag{2}$$

The linguistic characteristics of other hedges can be utilized in the appropriate manner in finding the meaning of the composites involving them [21].

The meaning associated with the composite linguistic variables can be obtained by the application of the suitable fuzzy subset operations on the meaning associated with the component terms. The following example will shed some idea about the procedure involved.

Example 3. (i) The meaning associated with the linguistic variable, "*H* IS SMALL" ≡ Fuzzy subset of the meaning of SMALL to be suitably assigned.

(ii) The meaning associated with the linguistic variable, "*H* IS VERY SMALL" ≡ Fuzzy subset whose membership function is the square of the membership function of the meaning of 'SMALL' – characteristic hedge operation.

(iii) The meaning associated with the linguistic variable, "*H* IS NOT VERY SMALL" ≡ Fuzzy subset whose membership function is [1 – the membership function of the meaning associated with "*H* IS VERY SMALL"] – fuzzy not operation on relevant fuzzy subset.

(iv) The meaning associated with the linguistic variable, "*H* IS NOT VERY SMALL AND NOT VERY LARGE" ≡ Fuzzy subset whose membership function can be obtained by the intersection of the meaning associated with "*H* IS NOT VERY SMALL" and the meaning associated with "*H* IS NOT VERY LARGE" – intersection on the appropriate fuzzy subsets.

(v) The meaning associated with the linguistic variable, "*H* IS VERY SMALL OR *H* IS VERY LARGE" ≡ Fuzzy subset whose membership function can be obtained by the union of the meaning associated with "*H* IS VERY SMALL" and the meaning associated with "*H* IS VERY LARGE" – union on the appropriate fuzzy subsets.

The above examples show how the meaning of a linguistic variable can be obtained. In the sequel, whenever a linguistic variable will be involved in any fuzzy operation, we will use the meaning of the corresponding linguistic variable.

3. The classifier

The technique for the development of the classifier as proposed in this paper can be divided into two distinct parts. In the first stage, the classifier is designed utilizing only the expert's knowledge about the classification problem concerned, while in the second stage, the classifier is refined through experimentation. In this section, the first part of the technique will be elaborated.

The structure of the proposed classifier is given in Fig. 1. The input pattern to the classifier is denoted as the Essential Input Pattern (EIP). EIP is a vector of linguistic variables, i.e. each member of EIP is some sort of information given in natural language. If the original pattern is of mixed form, it is assumed that the quantitative part of the pattern has been converted into linguistic form before presenting to the classifier. The dimension of the EIP is not fixed. That is, the EIPs for the patterns to be classified may have different dimensions. This suggests

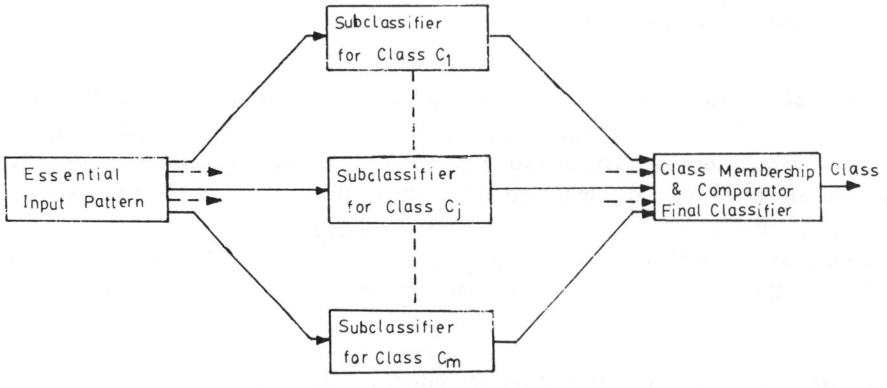

Fig. 1. Proposed classifier structure.

that sometimes the classifier is used to classify patterns with partial information or measurements. Apart from this, the input patterns for different classes may have different dimensions. For each class, there will be a subclassifier. Thus, if there are $C_1, C_2, \ldots, C_m$ classes, there will be m such subclassifiers. The input to each subclassifier will be a vector of linguistic variables. Each of these inputs will be a subset of the EIP. The output from each subclassifier will be a single linguistic variable. All the m outputs from the subclassifiers will be inputted to the final classifier. The final classifier will find the membership functions of the given pattern for all the classes, compare them and will give the final classification.

Let $MC_1, MC_2, \ldots, MC_m$ denote the membership functions corresponding to the classes $C_1, C_2, \ldots, C_m$, respectively. Since the term 'membership function' is a word in an artificial language and denotes some summarized but approximate information, we can treat it as the name of a linguistic variable and associate a fuzzy subset $M(X)$, the meaning to the value of it. Under the circumstances, we might have the linguistic variables involving the linguistic variable name, 'membership function', e.g. the membership function is low, the membership function is high, the membership function is medium, etc. As already explained in Section 2, we can find the meaning of the values of these linguistic variables. The following example will illustrate this.

Example 4. Consider MC_1, the membership function of class 1 which has the universe of discourse [0, 1]. Let us consider the linguistic variable, "MC_1 IS HIGH". The meaning associated with this linguistic variable is the fuzzy subset M_1(HIGH). The membership function of M_1(HIGH) can be obtained through the naming relation, say N_1. Thus, for illustration, we assign the naming relation N_1 as (say)

$$\mu_{N_1}(\text{HIGH}, y) = y, \quad y \in \text{Universe of discourse of } MC_1,$$

then

$$\mu_{M_1(\text{HIGH})}(y) = y.$$

It should be pointed out here that Zadeh has considered fuzzy sets with fuzzy membership function, which is denoted as fuzzy sets of type II. Here, we have considered the membership function as the name of a linguistic variable, as explained above. It is to be noted in this case that the name of the linguistic variable and the meaning associated with it have the similar universe of discourse.

The meaning associated with all the linguistic variables involving MC_i, $i = 1, \ldots, m$, can be obtained through the proper choice of the naming relations as done in Example 4. The outputs of the subclassifiers will be of this type of linguistic variables. As for example, the output of the pth subclassifier will be from the set, {"MC_p IS LOW", "MC_p IS MEDIUM", "MC_p IS HIGH"}. Here, only the three primary terms, viz., LOW, MEDIUM and HIGH have been used. If more primary terms and linguistic hedges, like VERY, VERY VERY, NEARLY, PLUS, MINUS etc. have been included, this set of the linguistic variables will be much larger. Obviously, this will increase the resolution of the description of the outputs of the subclassifiers. But this will, unfortunately, increase the complexity of the subclassifier demanding more memory space and more real time for classification. The designer has to decide upon the number of primary terms and the number of hedges to be included for the generation of the set of linguistic variables for the output description of the subclassifiers considering the amount of resolution needed and the degree of complexity to be allowed.

Question Matrix Table (QMT)

As already stated, the first stage of the classifier design will solely depend on the expert's experience. For this purpose, we form a *Question Matrix Table (QMT)*. We will explain this table with the help of an example. Let H_1 and H_2 be the names of two linguistic variables, and HIGH and LOW are two primary terms. Assume that they will form all the linguistic patterns for the EIP. Hence, all the possible linguistic patterns for the EIP, for this example will be:

(i) H_1 IS HIGH,

(ii) H_1 IS LOW,
(iii) H_2 IS HIGH,
(iv) H_2 IS LOW,
(v) H_1 IS HIGH, H_2 IS HIGH,
(vi) H_1 IS HIGH, H_2 IS LOW,
(vii) H_1 IS LOW, H_2 IS HIGH,
(viii) H_1 IS LOW, H_2 IS LOW.

Let there be two classes, C_1 and C_2. Suppose the output linguistic variables will be formed with the help of two primary terms LOW and HIGH and no hedges. Then the possible output linguistic variables for this example will be:

MC_1 IS HIGH, MC_1 IS LOW, MC_2 IS HIGH, MC_2 IS LOW.

Now we form the Question Matrix Table (QMT) for this example, as given in Table 1. If one reads any of the rows first and then any of the columns of the QMT, a question will be formed. The answer to this question has to be put in the corresponding elemental position of the matrix. If the answer is yes, we put a '+', if no, a '−' and if not answerable, a '~'. As for illustration, if we read the first

Table 1. Question matrix table

	WILL MC_1 BE		WILL MC_2 BE	
IF	HIGH	LOW	HIGH	LOW
H_1 IS LOW				
H_1 IS HIGH				
H_2 IS LOW				
H_2 IS HIGH				
H_1 IS HIGH, H_2 IS LOW				
H_1 IS LOW, H_2 IS HIGH				
H_1 IS HIGH, H_2 IS HIGH				
H_1 IS LOW, H_2 IS LOW				

row and then the third column, we will have the question: "IF H_1 IS LOW WILL MC_2 BE HIGH?" If the answer is yes, we put a '+' in (1, 3) position of the QMT.

It should be noted that we have put the linguistic patterns for EIP in the rows of QMT in such a way that simple questions will be formed at the beginning, provided one starts forming questions from the first row. As one proceeds downwards, gradually the questions will become harder and harder. The idea is, if one starts answering simpler questions, one would have a 'feel' of the problem and might be able to answer the harder questions later on.

In general, let the number of the names of the linguistic variables be n, i.e. $H_1, H_2, \ldots, H_n$, the number of primary terms be p, the number of hedges be q, number of connectives be r, and let there be the negativity. It is apparent that even for the moderate values of n, p, q, and r, the number of possible linguistic patterns for the EIP will be large. If one tries to form the QMT in such a situation, it turns out to be enormous and is unmanageable. In such cases, it is not needed to form the complete QMT. It is obvious by now that the filling-up of the QMT has to be done by the expert. In the case of an enormous QMT (if formed and presented to the expert), the latter rows where the stiffer questions are to be answered, will contain only '~'s, i.e. will remain unanswered. So, in general, a partial QMT containing the questions answerable by the expert will serve our purpose.

Let us introduce some terminologies now. Let l be the number of all possible output linguistic variables involving MC_i, $i = 1, 2, \ldots, m$. We denote the columns of QMT as COL$C_i(j)$ where $j = 1, 2, \ldots, l$, and $i = 1, 2, \ldots, m$, in which i is tracking the class and j the output linguistic variable. In Table 1, $l = 2$; COL$C_1(1)$ denotes the first column; COL$C_2(1)$ denotes the third column, and so on. In the following discussions, we denote a combination of any row with any column of the QMT as the input–output linguistic variable pair and use the symbol IOLVP(k, COL$C_i(j)$), where k indicates the row. In Table 1, IOLVP(3, COL$C_1(2)$) is the pair {H_2 IS LOW, MC_1 BE LOW}.

Table 2

IF	WILL MC_1 BE LOW	WILL MC_1 BE HIGH	WILL MC_2 BE LOW	WILL MC_2 BE HIGH
H_1 IS LOW	~	~	~	~
H_2 IS HIGH	−	+	+	−
H_1 IS MEDIUM, H_2 IS HIGH	−	+	−	+
H_1 IS HIGH, H_2 IS MEDIUM	+	−	−	+

The complete or partial QMT, as the case may be, is presented to the expert for filling up. This involves in forming the questions using rows and columns of the QMT and answering them with the experience and all the available knowledge. The filled-up QMT is utilized for the development of the classifier.

Different sets of IOLVPS are used for the construction of the different subclassifiers. We select these sets of IOLVPS from the filled-up QMT by using the following rules:

(i) If all the elements of a particular row of QMT are '~', no IOLVP involving that row is included in any of the sets.

(ii) If the element of the QMT corresponding to kth row and COL$C_i(j)$ is '+', the IOLVP(k, COL$C_i(j)$) will be included in the set corresponding to the ith subclassifier.

(iii) Step (ii) is repeated for $i = 1, 2, \ldots, m$, $k = 1, 2, \ldots,$ and $j = 1, 2, \ldots, l$.

Example 5. The filled-up QMT for a particular classification problem is given in Table 2. Then the set of IOLVPs for the first subclassifier is:

(i) IOLVP(2, COLC_1(2)), i.e. [H_2 IS HIGH, MC_2 IS HIGH].

(ii) IOLVP(3, COLC_1(2)), i.e. {[H_1 IS MEDIUM, H_2 IS HIGH], MC_1 IS HIGH}.

(iii) IOLVP(4, COLC_1(1)), i.e. {[H_1 IS HIGH, H_2 IS MEDIUM], MC_1 IS LOW}.

The set of IOLVPS for the second subclassifier is:

(i) IOLVP(2, COLC_2(1)), i.e. {H_2 IS HIGH, MC_2 IS LOW}.

(ii) IOLVP(3, COLC_2(2)), i.e. {[H_1 IS MEDIUM, H_2 IS HIGH], MC_2 IS HIGH}.

(iii) IOLVP(4, COLC_2(2)), i.e. {[H_1 IS HIGH, H_2 IS MEDIUM], MC_2 IS HIGH}.

Design of the subclassifiers

Let NSC_p be the number of elements in the set of IOLVPs for the pth subclassifier. Each of these IOLVPs, in fact, denotes a fuzzy conditional statement and can be realized by a fuzzy relation. Thus the pth subclassifier can be realized by NSC_p fuzzy relations.

Each of the IOLVPs is, functionally, in the form of "IF A THEN B", or "IF [A, C] THEN B", or "IF [A, C, D] THEN B", or. . . . where A, B, C, D are linguistic variables with the associated fuzzy subsets (meaning) with them. If A, B having the associated universe of discourses U and V, respectively, and $\mu_A(u)$ and $\mu_B(v)$, $u \in U$, $v \in V$, are the membership functions of the fuzzy subsets (meaning) of A and B, respectively, the membership function of the fuzzy relation of the ordered pair (u, v) in the product set of the universe of discourse $U \times V$ can be written as [22],

$$\mu_{R_{A\times B}}(u, v) = \mu_A(u) \wedge \mu_B(v) \tag{3}$$

where $\mu_{R_{A\times B}}(u, v)$ is the membership function of the fuzzy relation and Λ indicates the minimum operation.

Example 6. Find the fuzzy relation of the fuzzy condition statement "IF H_2 IS HIGH THEN MC_2 IS LOW".

Let the universe of discourse associated with "H_2 IS HIGH" be $U = [1, 2, 3, 4]$ and the corresponding membership function of the meaning be [0.1, 0.2, 0.4, 0.7].

Let the universe of discourse associated with "MC_2 IS LOW" be $V = [0.1, 0.4,$

0.6, 1] and the corresponding membership function of the meaning be

$$[0.9, 0.7, 0.2, 0.1].$$

Then the fuzzy relation of the above fuzzy conditional statement can be obtained in the matrix form as

	0.1	0.4	0.6	$1 \rightarrow V$
1	0.1	0.1	0.1	0.1
2	0.2	0.2	0.2	0.1
3	0.4	0.4	0.2	0.1
4	0.7	0.7	0.2	0.1
↓				
U				

We consider another example.

Example 7. Find the fuzzy relation of the fuzzy conditional statement "IF [H_1 IS HIGH, H_2 IS MEDIUM] THEN MC_2 IS HIGH".

Let the universe of discourse associated with the linguistic variable "H_1 IS HIGH" be $U_1 = [1, 2, 3, 4]$ and the corresponding membership function of the meaning be [0.1, 0.2, 0.4, 0.7].

Let the universe of discourse associated with the linguistic variable, "H_2 IS MEDIUM" be $U_2 = [6, 7, 8]$ and the corresponding membership function of the meaning be [0.6, 0.8, 0.6].

Assuming that the linguistic variables are noninteractive, the membership function of the fuzzy subset (meaning) of the linguistic vector [H_1 IS HIGH, H_2 IS MEDIUM] can be obtained by the intersection of fuzzy subsets (meanings) of the two linguistic variables and can be obtained in the matrix form as

	6	7	$8 \rightarrow U_2$
1	0.1	0.1	0.1
2	0.2	0.2	0.2
3	0.4	0.4	0.4
4	0.6	0.7	0.6
↓			
U_1			

We can write this membership function of the meaning of the linguistic vector in vector form by concatenating the columns of the above matrix one after another as

Universe of discourse $U_1 \times U_2$	(1, 6), (2, 6), (3, 6), (4, 6), (1, 7), (2, 7), (3, 7), (4, 7), (1, 8), (2, 8), (3, 8), (4, 8)
Membership function	0.1, 0.2, 0.4, 0.6, 0.1, 0.2, 0.4, 0.7, 0.1, 0.2, 0.4, 0.6

Let the universe of discourse of MC_2 be $V = [0.1, 0.4, 0.6, 1]$ and the membership function of the maning of the linguistic variable "MC_2 IS HIGH" be [0.1, 0.4, 0.6, 1].

Then the fuzzy relation of the conditional statement of this example can be given in the matrix form as in Table 3.

It is to be noted from this example that if the conditional statement contains n-ary linguistic vector and if n is large, the dimension of the fuzzy relation matrix would be very large. This might lead to the problem of memory space in implementing the classifier.

For the pth subclassifier, there will be NSC_p fuzzy relations, $R_p(s)$, $s = 1, 2, \ldots, \text{NSC}_p$. Each of them can be obtained by following the procedure as outlined in Examples 6 and 7.

Table 3

	0.1	0.4	0.6	$1 \to V$
(1, 6)	0.1	0.1	0.1	0.1
(2, 6)	0.1	0.2	0.2	0.2
(3, 6)	0.1	0.4	0.4	0.4
(4, 6)	0.1	0.4	0.6	0.6
(1, 7)	0.1	0.1	0.1	0.1
(2, 7)	0.1	0.2	0.2	0.2
(3, 7)	0.1	0.4	0.4	0.4
(4, 7)	0.1	0.4	0.6	0.7
(1, 8)	0.1	0.1	0.1	0.1
(2, 8)	0.1	0.2	0.2	0.2
(3, 8)	0.1	0.4	0.4	0.4
(4, 8)	0.1	0.4	0.6	0.6
$\downarrow$ $U_1 \times U_2$				

Let us now discuss the role of these fuzzy relations of the subclassifiers when the classifier is used for the classification of unknown patterns. If $R_p(s)$ is a fuzzy relation from H_1 to MC_p and A is the fuzzy subset (meaning) of any linguistic variable with the name H_1, then the fuzzy subset (meaning) B of MC_p which is induced by A is given by the composition rule of inference as [22],

$$B = A \circ R_p(s) \tag{4}$$

where $\circ$ denotes the max–min product operation.

Example 8. Let the fuzzy subset (meaning) A of the linguistic variable having name H_1 be $[0.05, 0.1, 0.2, 0.4]$ and the $R_p(s)$ be

$$R_p(s) = \begin{bmatrix} 0.1 & 0.1 & 0.1 \\ 0.2 & 0.2 & 0.2 \\ 0.4 & 0.4 & 0.4 \\ 0.6 & 0.7 & 0.6 \end{bmatrix}.$$

Then the fuzzy subset meaning B of MC_p induced by A will be

$$N = A \circ R_p(s) = [0.05, 0.1, 0.2, 0.4] \circ \begin{bmatrix} 0.1 & 0.1 & 0.1 \\ 0.2 & 0.2 & 0.2 \\ 0.4 & 0.4 & 0.4 \\ 0.6 & 0.7 & 0.6 \end{bmatrix}$$

$$= [0.4, 0.4, 0.4].$$

If, for the pth subclassifier, $A_p(s)$, $s = 1, 2, \ldots, NSC_p$, are the fuzzy subsets (meaning) corresponding to the input linguistic variables, and $R_p(s)$, $s = 1, 2, \ldots, NSC_p$, are the corresponding fuzzy relations, then $B_p(s)$, $s = 1, \ldots, NSC_p$, the induced fuzzy subsets (meaning) of MC_p can be obtained by the compositional rule of inference as

$$B_p(s) = A_p(s) \circ R_p(s), \quad s = 1, 2, \ldots, NSC_p. \tag{5}$$

The fuzzy subset (meaning) BC_p of MC_p which can be considered as the output of the pth subclassifier can be obtained by taking the union of the fuzzy subsets $B_p(s)$, $s = 1, 2, \ldots, NSC_p$. So,

$$BC_p = \bigcup_s B_p(s). \tag{6}$$

Thus, for a given EIP, we can generate the outputs of the subclassifiers using (5) and (6), as BC_p, $p = 1, 2, \ldots, m$.

Depening upon the given EIP or when a classification is desired with partial information, all the $A_p(s)$'s needed for (5) may not be available. In such cases, the membership function of the nonavailable $A_p(s)$'s are taken to be zero over the range of the corresponding universe of discourses and BC_p is obtained as usual using (5) and (6).

Final block of the classifier

We are now in a position to explain the function of the final block of the classifier. It performs two functions, viz.,

(i) finds the membership function of the given EIP to different classes, and

(ii) finds the maximum of these membership functons and assigns the given EIP to that class which corresponds to the maximum membership function.

One obvious way to find the class membership functions from the fuzzy set (meaning) BC_p, is to choose the value of MC_p which corresponds to the peak in BC_p, averaging when, as in the case, there are several peaks. Another obvious technique is to form average based on the shape of BC_p, center-of-area for example and choosing that value of MC_p which corresponds this center-of-area. We denote this value of MC_p corresponding to the peak or the center-of-area of BC_p is MC_p^*. There is no clear reason for making one or the other choices. But the different choices will result in different structures of the classifier. The maximum of the membership functions of different classes, i.e. $\{\text{Max}\, MC_p^*,\ p = 1, 2, \ldots, m\}$ for a particular *EIP* can be obtained by using a simple method of comparison. This, in effect, completes the first stage of the development of the classifier. We may now give the steps for this stage as follows:

(i) Form the QMT from all possible EIPs.

(ii) Fill up the QMT. This is done by expert utilizing his experience and expertise.

(iii) Select the sets of IOLVPs for the subclassifiers using the filled-up QMT.

(iv) Realize the fuzzy relations corresponding to each IOLVPs of the sets.

(v) For the classification of an unknown EIP, use the fuzzy relations in the compositional rule of inference for finding the outputs of the subclassifiers.

(vi) From the outputs of the subclassifier, obtain the membership functions of the given EIP to different classes by using either the average of the peak, or the center-of-area. The given EIP will be assigned to that class which will have the maximum membership function for the given EIP.

The classifier, thus designed, has the following important features:

(i) All the input variables of the classifier are linguistic variables.

(ii) The classifier is designed using solely the expert's experience and expertise.

(iii) The dimension of the given input linguistic pattern vector may not be fixed.

(iv) A classification can be enforced by imputing partial information.

4. Refinement of the classifier

The classifier obtained by the procedure of the preceding section can be refined for better performance. The refinement can be achieved through experimentation using class labeled EIPs. Suppose a set of class labeled EIPs is provided. The objective of the refinement of the classifier can then be stated as the proper tuning of the classifier so as to get correct classifications at least for the given labeled samples. The process of refinement involves the proper adjustment of the fuzzy relation subsets of the subclassifiers. These adjustments are performed utilizing the method of identification in fuzzy systems [23].

Consider the fuzzy system governed by the fuzzy equation,

$$Y_k = X_k \circ R, \tag{7}$$

where X_k is the input fuzzy subset, Y_k is the output fuzzy subset, R is the fuzzy relation, and $\circ$ indicates the max-min operation. The identification problem for fuzzy system in (7) involves estimation of the unknown fuzzy relation R by means of the appropriate sequences $\{Y_k\}$ and $\{X_k\}$, $k = 1, 2, \ldots$. This can be done using the α-operation.

Definition 3. For every $A \in E$, the α-operation can be defined as

$$\mu_A(x)\ \alpha\ \mu_A(y) = \begin{cases} 1 & \text{if } \mu_A(x) \leq \mu_A(y), \\ \mu_A(y) & \text{if } \mu_A(x) > \mu_A(y), \end{cases} \quad \text{for all } x, y \in E. \tag{8}$$

The α-composition of the fuzzy set and fuzzy relation can be defined in the following way:

$$B = A\, \alpha\, R, \tag{9}$$

where A is the fuzzy subset having the universe of discourse E_1, B is a fuzzy subset of the universe of discourse E_2, and R is the binary fuzzy relation in $E_1 \times E_2$. Then the membership function of B can be given as:

$$\mu_B(x) = \bigwedge_y [\mu_A(y)\ \alpha\ \mu_R(y, x)]. \tag{10}$$

Example 9. If A and R are given as:

A

1	2	3	4
0.1	0.4	0.3	0.6

R

	4	5	6
1	0.3	0.4	0.2
2	0.6	0.2	0.7
3	0.2	0.6	0.4
4	0.5	0.7	0.8

then $\mu_B(x)$ is

4	5	6
0.2	0.2	1

Similarly, the α-composition of two fuzzy sets can be defined as

$$G = A\, \alpha\, B, \tag{11}$$

where G is a fuzzy relation having the membership function

$$\mu_G(x, y) = \mu_A(x)\ \alpha\ \mu_B(y), \quad x \in E_1 \quad \text{and} \quad y \in E_2. \tag{12}$$

Example 10. If the universe of A is $U_A = [0.1, 0.2, 0.3, 0.4]$, the membership function of A is $[0.9, 0.4, 0.5, 0.6]$, the Universe of B is $U_B = [0.1, 0.2, 0.3, 0.4]$, and the membership function of $B = [0.1, 0.5, 0.6, 0.3]$, then G is

	0.1	0.2	0.3	0.4 → U_B
0.1	0.1	0.5	0.6	0.3
0.2	0.1	1	1	0.3
0.3	0.1	1	1	0.3
0.4	0.1	0.5	1	0.3
↓ U_A				

The identification problem in (7) can be solved as follows. For every pair of fuzzy sets X_k, Y_k, we calculate

$$\hat{R}_k = X_k\ \alpha\ Y_k, \tag{13}$$

and get the final fuzzy relation as

$$\hat{R} = \bigcap_k \hat{R}_k. \tag{14}$$

For the tuning of the classifier, the above result of the fuzzy system identification is used in the following manner.

Suppose the labeled sample belongs to the pth class, but the classifier has classified it wrongly to the qth class. Define

$$x_1 := \sigma_0, \qquad x_2 := \tfrac{1}{2}(MC_q^* - MC_p^*) + \delta_1,$$

where σ_0 and δ_1 are small positive numbers, and MC_q^* and MC_p^* are the belongingness of the labeled sample to the qth and pth classes, respectively. We modify the outputs of the pth and qth subclassifiers either as

$$\begin{aligned} \mu_{B'_p(s)}(x+x_1) &= \mu_{B_p(s)}(x), \quad s=1,2,\ldots,\mathrm{NSC}_p, \quad \text{for all values of } x,\\ \mu_{B'_q(s)}(x-x_1) &= \mu_{B_q(s)}(x), \quad s=1,2,\ldots,\mathrm{NSC}_q, \quad \text{for all values of } x, \end{aligned} \tag{15a}$$

or as

$$\begin{aligned} \mu_{B'_p(s)}(x+x_2) &= \mu_{B_p(s)}(x), \quad s=1,2,\ldots,\mathrm{NSC}_p, \quad \text{for all values of } x,\\ \mu_{B'_q}(s)(x-x_2) &= \mu_{B_q(s)}(x), \quad s=1,2,\ldots,\mathrm{NSC}_q, \quad \text{for all values of } x. \end{aligned} \tag{15b}$$

It should be noted that the above modifications of the outputs of the fuzzy relations are the shifts of the membership functions over the universe of discourse, in one direction for the pth subclassifier and in the opposite direction for the qth subclassifier. These shifts, in effect, are the manifestation of a correcting effort which tends to move the peaks and the center-of-area for the pth subclassifier to the right, and those for the qth subclassifier to the left so that the classifier tends towards more correct classification so far as the given labeled sample is concerned.

The fuzzy relations $R_p(s)$, $s=1,2,\ldots,\mathrm{NSC}_p$, and $R_q(s)$, $s=1,2,\ldots,\mathrm{NSC}_q$, are refined using $B'_p(s)$, $s=1,2,\ldots,\mathrm{NSC}_p$, and $B'_q(s)$, $s=1,2,\ldots,\mathrm{NSC}_q$, and utilizing (13) and (14). The refined fuzzy relations are

$$\begin{aligned} R'_p(s) &= R_p(s) \cap (A_p(s)\, \alpha\, B'_p(s)), \quad s=1,2,\ldots,\mathrm{NSC}_p,\\ R'_q(s) &= R_q(s) \cap (A_q(s)\, \alpha\, B'_q(s)), \quad s=1,2,\ldots,\mathrm{NSC}_q, \end{aligned} \tag{16}$$

where $A_p(s)$ and $A_q(s)$ are the corresponding inputs.

Now we give an algorithm for the tuning of the classifier. The labeled samples are stored along with their class indices. A run consists of testing of each of the stored samples by the classifier. Then the algorithm may be stated as:

1) START
2) RUN = 0
3) RUN = RUN + 1
4) SAMPLE NUMBER = 0
5) SAMPLE NUMBER = SAMPLE NUMBER + 1
5) CLASSIFY THE SAMPLE. IF CORRECT, GO TO 5, ELSE CONTINUE
7) REFINE THE FUZZY RELATIONS USING 15(a) [OR 15(b)] AND 16
8) ALL THE SAMPLES TESTED? IF YES, CONTINUE, ELSE GO TO 5
9) PERCENTAGE OF CORRECT CLASSIFICATIONS WITHIN ACCEPTABLE LIMIT? IF YES, CONTINUE, ELSE GO TO 3
10) STOP

We present an empirical proof of the convergence of this algorithm. Before that we consider the following example.

Example 11. Consider the following fuzzy relation R_1 in the universe of discourse $U \times V$ given in Table 4.

Let A and B be the fuzzy subsets defined over universe of discourses U and V, respectively. If

$$\mu_A(u) = [0.1, 0.1, 0.3, 0.3, 0.4, 0.6, 0.8, 0.8, 0.9, 0.9], \quad u \in U,$$

then

$$\mu_B(v) = [0.1, 0.2, 0.4, 0.6, 0.8, 0.9, 0.8, 0.4, 0.3, 0.2], \quad v \in V. \tag{17}$$

Table 4. R_1 of Example 11

	0.1	0.2	0.3	0.4	0.5	0.6	0.7	0.8	0.9	$1 \to V$
1	1	1	1	1	1	1	1	1	1	1
2	1	1	1	1	1	1	1	1	1	1
3	0.1	0.2	1	1	1	1	1	1	1	0.2
4	0.1	0.2	1	1	1	1	1	1	1	0.2
5	0.1	0.2	1	1	1	1	1	1	0.3	0.2
6	0.1	0.2	0.4	1	1	1	1	0.4	0.3	0.2
7	0.1	0.2	0.4	0.6	1	1	1	0.4	0.3	0.2
8	0.1	0.2	0.4	0.6	1	1	1	0.4	0.3	0.2
9	0.1	0.2	0.4	0.6	0.8	1	0.8	0.4	0.3	0.2
10	0.1	0.2	0.4	0.6	0.8	1	0.8	0.4	0.3	0.2
$\downarrow$ U										

If we shift $\mu_B(v)$ as $\mu_B(v-0.1) \leftarrow \mu_B(v)$, we will have

$$\mu_B(v) = [0.2, 0.4, 0.6, 0.8, 0.9, 0.8, 0.4, 0.3, 0.2, 0].$$

With this $\mu_B(v)$ and $\mu_A(u)$ as before, using (13), we get $\hat{R}_2$ as given in Table 5. Then $\hat{R}_1 \cap \hat{R}_2$ is as in Table 6.

With this new fuzzy relation, and using $\mu_A(u)$ as before, we get $\mu_B(v)$ as

$$\mu_B(v) = [0.1, 0.2, 0.4, 0.6, 0.8, 0.8, 0.4, 0.3, 0.2, 0] \tag{18}$$

If we again shift $\mu_B(v)$ as $\mu_B(v-0.1) \leftarrow \mu_B(v)$, we will have

$$\mu_B(v) = [0.2, 0.4, 0.6, 0.8, 0.8, 0.4, 0.3, 0.2, 0, 0].$$

Table 5. $\hat{R}_2$ of Example 11

	0.1	0.2	0.3	0.4	0.5	0.6	0.7	0.8	0.9	$1 \to V$
1	1	1	1	1	1	1	1	1	1	0
2	1	1	1	1	1	1	1	1	1	0
3	0.2	1	1	1	1	1	1	1	0.2	0
4	0.2	1	1	1	1	1	1	1	0.2	0
5	0.2	1	1	1	1	1	1	0.3	0.2	0
6	0.2	0.4	1	1	1	1	0.4	0.3	0.2	0
7	0.2	0.4	0.6	1	1	1	0.4	0.3	0.2	0
8	0.2	0.4	0.6	1	1	1	0.4	0.3	0.2	0
9	0.2	0.4	0.6	0.8	1	0.8	0.4	0.3	0.2	0
10	0.2	0.4	0.6	0.8	1	0.8	0.4	0.3	0.2	0
$\downarrow$ U										

Table 6. $\hat{R}_1 \cap \hat{R}_2$ of Example 11

	0.1	0.2	0.3	0.4	0.5	0.6	0.7	0.8	0.9	$1 \to V$
1	1	1	1	1	1	1	1	1	1	0
2	1	1	1	1	1	1	1	1	1	0
3	0.1	0.2	1	1	1	1	1	1	0.2	0
4	0.1	0.2	1	1	1	1	1	1	0.2	0
5	0.1	0.2	1	1	1	1	1	0.3	0.2	0
6	0.1	0.2	0.4	1	1	1	0.4	0.3	0.2	0
7	0.1	0.2	0.4	0.6	1	1	0.4	0.3	0.2	0
8	0.1	0.2	0.4	0.6	1	1	0.4	0.3	0.2	0
9	0.1	0.2	0.4	0.6	0.8	0.8	0.4	0.3	0.2	0
10	0.1	0.2	0.4	0.6	0.8	0.8	0.4	0.3	0.2	0
$\downarrow$ U										

Table 7. $\hat{R}_3$ of Example 11

	0.1	0.2	0.3	0.4	0.5	0.6	0.7	0.8	0.9	$1 \rightarrow V$
1	1	1	1	1	1	1	1	1	0	0
2	1	1	1	1	1	1	1	1	0	0
3	0.2	1	1	1	1	1	1	0.2	0	0
4	0.2	1	1	1	1	1	1	0.2	0	0
5	0.2	1	1	1	1	1	0.3	0.2	0	0
6	0.2	0.4	1	1	1	0.4	0.3	0.2	0	0
7	0.2	0.4	0.6	1	1	0.4	0.3	0.2	0	0
8	0.2	0.4	0.6	1	1	0.4	0.3	0.2	0	0
9	0.2	0.4	0.6	0.8	0.8	0.4	0.3	0.2	0	0
10	0.2	0.4	0.6	0.8	0.8	0.4	0.3	0.2	0	0
$\downarrow$ U										

With this $\mu_B(v)$ and $\mu_A(u)$ as before, using (13), we get $\hat{R}_3$ as in Table 7. Then $\hat{R}_1 \cap \hat{R}_2 \cap \hat{R}_3$ is as in Table 8.

With this new fuzzy relation and $\mu_A(u)$ as given before, we get $\mu_B(v)$ as

$$\mu_B(v) = [0.1, 0.2, 0.4, 0.6, 0.8, 0.4, 0.3, 0.2, 0, 0]. \tag{19}$$

If we again shift $\mu_B(v)$ as $\mu_B(v-0.1) \leftarrow \mu_B(v)$, we will have

$$\mu_B(v) = [0.2, 0.4, 0.6, 0.8, 0.4, 0.3, 0.2, 0, 0, 0].$$

Table 8. $\hat{R}_1 \cap \hat{R}_2 \cap \hat{R}_3$ of Example 11

	0.1	0.2	0.3	0.4	0.5	0.6	0.7	0.8	0.9	$1 \rightarrow V$
1	1	1	1	1	1	1	1	1	0	0
2	1	1	1	1	1	1	1	1	0	0
3	0.1	0.2	1	1	1	1	1	0.2	0	0
4	0.1	0.2	1	1	1	1	1	0.2	0	0
5	0.1	0.2	1	1	1	1	0.3	0.2	0	0
6	0.1	0.2	0.4	1	1	0.4	0.3	0.2	0	0
7	0.1	0.2	0.4	0.6	1	0.4	0.3	0.2	0	0
8	0.1	0.2	0.4	0.6	1	0.4	0.3	0.2	0	0
9	0.1	0.2	0.4	0.6	0.8	0.4	0.3	0.2	0	0
10	0.1	0.2	0.4	0.6	0.8	0.4	0.3	0.2	0	0
$\downarrow$ U										

Table 9. $\hat{R}_4$ of Example 11

	0.1	0.2	0.3	0.4	0.5	0.6	0.7	0.8	0.9	$1 \rightarrow V$
1	1	1	1	1	1	1	1	0	0	0
2	1	1	1	1	1	1	1	0	0	0
3	0.2	1	1	1	1	1	0.2	0	0	0
4	0.2	1	1	1	1	1	0.2	0	0	0
5	0.2	1	1	1	1	0.3	0.2	0	0	0
6	0.2	0.4	1	1	0.4	0.3	0.2	0	0	0
7	0.2	0.4	0.6	1	0.4	0.3	0.2	0	0	0
8	0.2	0.4	0.6	1	0.4	0.3	0.2	0	0	0
9	0.2	0.4	0.6	0.8	0.4	0.3	0.2	0	0	0
10	0.2	0.4	0.6	0.8	0.4	0.3	0.2	0	0	0
$\downarrow$ U										

Table 10. $\hat{R}_1 \cap \hat{R}_2 \cap \hat{R}_3 \cap \hat{R}_4$ of Example 11

	0.1	0.2	0.3	0.4	0.5	0.6	0.7	0.8	0.9	1→V
1	1	1	1	1	1	1	1	0	0	0
2	1	1	1	1	1	1	1	0	0	0
3	0.1	0.2	1	1	1	1	0.2	0	0	0
4	0.1	0.2	1	1	1	1	0.2	0	0	0
5	0.1	0.2	1	1	1	0.3	0.2	0	0	0
6	0.1	0.2	0.4	1	0.4	0.3	0.2	0	0	0
7	0.1	0.2	0.4	0.6	0.4	0.3	0.2	0	0	0
8	0.1	0.2	0.4	0.6	0.4	0.3	0.2	0	0	0
9	0.1	0.2	0.4	0.6	0.4	0.3	0.2	0	0	0
10	0.1	0.2	0.4	0.6	0.4	0.3	0.2	0	0	0
↓ U										

With this $\mu_B(v)$ and $\mu_A(u)$ as before, using Eq. 13, we get $\hat{R}_4$ as in Table 9 and then $\hat{R}_1 \cap \hat{R}_2 \cap \hat{R}_3 \cap \hat{R}_4$ is as in Table 10.

With this new fuzzy relation and $\mu_A(u)$ as before, we now get $\mu_B(v)$ as

$$\mu_B(v) = [0.1, 0.2, 0.4, 0.6, 0.4, 0.3, 0.2, 0, 0, 0]. \tag{20}$$

To visualize the effects of shifting the output and refining the fuzzy relation, we plot the outputs in (17)–(20) in Fig. (2a). It can be observed from the figure that this process of shifting (to the left) and refining shifts the peak and the center-of-area of the membership function to the left.

In a similar manner, if we shift the output to the right (every time by 0.1) and refine the fuzzy relation, we get the outputs as follows. The initial output is

$$[0.1, 0.2, 0.4, 0.6, 0.8, 0.9, 0.8, 0.4, 0.3, 0.2]. \tag{21}$$

After the first shift, we have the outputs

$$[0, 0.1, 0.2, 0.4, 0.6, 0.8, 0.8, 0.4, 0.3, 0.2]; \tag{22}$$

after the second shift,

$$[0, 0, 0.1, 0.2, 0.4, 0.6, 0.8, 0.4, 0.3, 0.2]; \tag{23}$$

and after the third shift,

$$[0, 0, 0, 0.1, 0.2, 0.4, 0.6, 0.4, 0.3, 0.2]. \tag{24}$$

Again to see the effect of this shifting and refining, we plot the outputs in (21)–(24) and find that this process shifts both the peak and the center-of-area to the right [Fig. (2b)].

From the consideration of (15) and (16) and from the above illustrative example, we come to the following important conclusions:

(i) For a given input fuzzy subset, if the output is gradually shifted towards the left (right) and the fuzzy relation is refined using (16), the peak and the center-of-area of the output fuzzy subset shift towards the left (right).

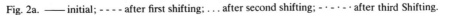

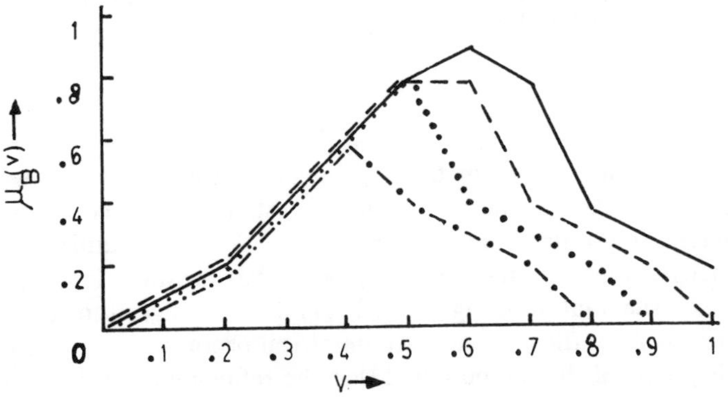

Fig. 2a. —— initial; - - - - after first shifting; . . . after second shifting; - · - · - · after third Shifting.

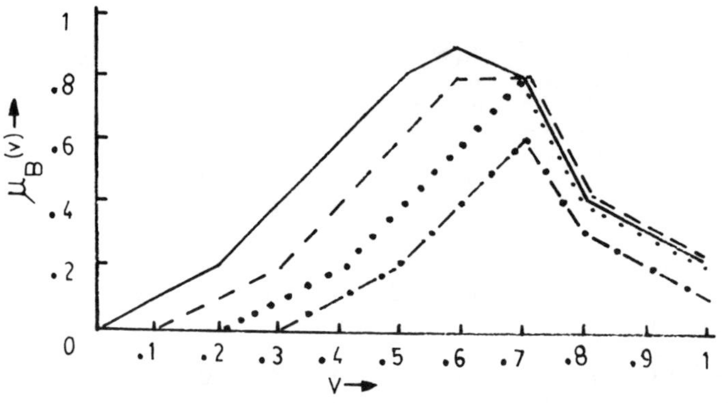

Fig. 2b. —— initial; ---- after first shifting; ··· after second shifting -·-·-· after third shifting.

(ii) By this process of shifting and refining, more modification in the membership function of the output fuzzy subset occurs in leading edge in comparison to the trailing edge, when the shifting is leftwards, and vice versa.

Now we give the empirical proof of the convergence of the algorithm. We make the following assumptions:

(i) For the given labeled samples, S_λ, $\lambda = 1, 2, \ldots, mn$, there exists a classifier with the structure in Fig. 1, which will classify all of them correctly.

(ii) The classifier, obtained after the first stage of the design, is nearly the same as the desired one which classified all the given samples correctly.

First assumption implies that there exist the fuzzy relations $R_p^c(s)$, $s = 1, 2, \ldots, NSC_p$; $p = 1, 2, \ldots, m$, which are the correct fuzzy relations of the subclassifiers, and by these, all the given labeled samples are correctly classified. $R_p^c(s)$'s may not be unique; in all possibilities, they are from a set of correct fuzzy relations. These correct fuzzy relations, for a given sample with class index p, must satisfy

$$MC_p^* > MC_q^*, \quad q = 1, 2, \ldots, m, \quad q \neq p. \tag{25}$$

In our algorithm, when a misclassification occurs, a correcting effort is introduced through (15a) or (15b). From the conclusions of Example 11, this correcting effort through the modification of fuzzy relations by (16) takes the fuzzy relations towards one of the correct values, $R_p^c(s)$, $s = 1, 2, \ldots, NSC_p$; $p = 1, 2, \ldots, m$. Since the algorithm will not terminate until all the given samples are correctly classified, and since by assumption (1), such a solution exists, and further, through (15) and (16), the correcting effort takes the fuzzy relations towards the desired ones, the algorithm will eventually converge, i.e. the fuzzy relations will terminate to one of the sets of correct fuzzy relations.

By the second assumption, since the initial fuzzy relations are quite close to the correct ones, the algorithm will converge rather rapidly. Obviously, the rate of convergence will depend upon the value of δ_0 chosen in (15a). If it is chosen very very small, the rate of convergence will be slow. On the otherhand, a choice of a larger value of δ_0 might give rise to oscillations and the algorithm will take a longer time to converge. Thus it is conjectured that there possibly exists an optimal range of values of δ_0 for which the convergence will be very rapid.

5. Conclusions

This paper proposes a method for the development of a classifier of which the inputs are linguistic variables. The technique suggested involves consideration of two distinct phases. In the first stage, the classifier is developed utilizing only the expert's experience, while in the second phase, the classifier is subjected to refinement by experimentation using labeled samples. An algorithm is suggested also for the refinement of the classifier. An empirical proof of the convergence of the algorithm is provided. It may be noted that the refinement can be carried out even when the classifier may be in actual use. In this sense the classifier has the adaptive potentiality. The classifier may be developed utilizing the expertise of more than one expert as well. Each expert has then to fill out the QMT separately, and the classifier can be developed utilizing the information of all the filled-up QMTs. It appears that the proposed classifier may have potential applications in various fields including such fields as medicine and medical diagnostics.

Acknowledgment

The authors would like to thank the anonymous referees for their constructive comments which greatly helped in revising the manuscript. The authors would like to take this opportunity of expressing their sincere indebtedness to Professor Sunil R. Das of the Institute of Computer Engineering of the National Chiao Tung University for his many helpful comments and suggestions that resulted in a substantial improvement of the overall quality of presentations, and also to Ms. Arine Liu for her help in the final preparation of the manuscript.

References

[1] N.J. Nilsson, Learning Machines-Foundations of Trainable Pattern-classifying systems (McGraw-Hill, New York, 1965).

[2] K.S. Fu, Syntactic Methods in Pattern Recognition (Academic Press, New York, 1974).

[3] L.A. Zadeh, Outline of a new approach to the analysis of complex systems and decision processes, IEEE Trans. Syst. Man Cybernet. (1973) 28–44.

[4] L.A. Zadeh, Fuzzy sets, Inf. Control 8 (1964) 338–353.

[5] S. Assilian, Artificial intelligence in the control of real dynamic systems, Ph.D. Thesis, Queen Mary College, London, (1974).

[6] E.H. Mamdani, Advances in the linguistic synthesis of fuzzy controllers, Int. J. Man–Machine Studies 8 (1976) 669–678.

[7] C.G. Bloore, A heuristic adaptive controller for a sinter plant, M. Sc. Dissertation, UMIST, Manchester (1974).

[8] E.H. Mamdani, and N. Baaklini, Prescriptive method for deriving control policy in a fuzzy-logic controller, Electronics Lett. 11 (1975) 625–626.

[9] R.M. Tong, Analysis of fuzzy control algorithms using the relation matrix, Cambridge University, Engineering Report, CUED/F-CAMS-TR133 (1976).

[10] W.J.M. Kickert, and H.R. Van Nauta Lemke, Application of a fuzzy controller to a warm water plant, Automatica 12 (1976) 301–308.

[11] J.J. Østergaard, Fuzzy logic control of a heat exchanger process. Publ. No. 7601, Elec. Power Engng. Dept., Techn. University of Denmark, Lyngby (1976).

[12] J.H. Jensen, Application for fuzzy logic control, No. 1., Publ. No. 7606, Elec. Power Engng. Dept., Techn. University of Denmark, Lyngby (1976).

[13] G.A. Carter and D.A. Rutherford, A heuristic adaptive controller for a sinter plant, IFAC Symp. on Automation in Mining, Met and Met Processing, Johannesburg (1976).

[14] G.A. Carter and M.J. Hague, Fuzzy control of raw mix permeability at a sinter plant, Proc. Fuzzy Workshop Conf., QMC, London (1976).

[15] L.A. Zadeh, A theory of approximate reasoning, Memo # UCB/ERL M 77/58, University of California, Berkeley (1977).

[16] E. Sanchez, J. Gouvernet and H. Joly, Medical diagnosis oriented linguistic approach to pattern classification, Proc. Medinfo, Tokyo. (1980).

[17] E. Sanchez, Medical diagnosis and composite fuzzy relations, in: M.M. Gupta, R.K. Ragade and R.R. Yager, Advances in fuzzy set theory and applications (North-Holland, Amsterdam, 1979).

[18] R.R. Yager, Multiple objective decision making using Fuzzy Subsets, Int. J. Man–Machine Studies 9 (1977) 375–382.

[19] R.R. Yager, Validation of fuzzy-linguistic models, J. Cybernet. 8 (1978) 17–30.

[20] L.A. Zadeh, The concept of a linguistic variable and its application to approximate reasoning – II, Information Sciences 8 (1975) 301–357.

[21] L.A. Zadeh, A fuzzy-set-theoretic interpretation of linguistic hedges, J. Cybern. 2 (1972) 4–34.

[22] A. Kaufman, Theory of Fuzzy Subsets (Academic Press, New York, 1975).

[23] E. Czogala and W. Pedrycz, On identification in fuzzy systems and its applications in control problems, Fuzzy Sets and Systems 6 (1981) 73–83.

A Fuzzy *K*-Nearest Neighbor Algorithm

JAMES M. KELLER, MICHAEL R. GRAY, AND JAMES A. GIVENS, JR.

***Abstract*—Classification of objects is an important area of research and application in a variety of fields. In the presence of full knowledge of the underlying probabilities, Bayes decision theory gives optimal error rates. In those cases where this information is not present, many algorithms make use of distance or similarity among samples as a means of classification. The *K*-nearest neighbor decision rule has often been used in these pattern recognition problems. One of the difficulties that arises when utilizing this technique is that each of the labeled samples is given equal importance in deciding the class memberships of the pattern to be classified, regardless of their "typicalness." The theory of fuzzy sets is introduced into the *K*-nearest neighbor technique to develop a fuzzy version of the algorithm. Three methods of assigning fuzzy memberships to the labeled samples are proposed, and experimental results and comparisons to the crisp version are presented. In fact, not only does the fuzzy algorithm dominate its counterpart in terms of a lower error rate, the resulting memberships give a confidence measure of the classification. The fuzzy *K*-NN rule is also shown to compare well against other standard, more-sophisticated pattern recognition procedures in these experiments. A fuzzy analog of the nearest prototype algorithm is also developed.**

I. Introduction

Classification of objects is an important area of research and of practical applications in a variety of fields, including pattern recognition and artificial intelligence, statistics, cognitive psychology, vision analysis, and medicine [1]–[10]. Considered as a pattern recognition problem, there have been numerous techniques investigated for classification. Clearly, the more *a priori* information that is known about the problem domain, the more the classification algorithm can be made to reflect the actual situation. For example, if the *a priori* probabilities and the state conditional densities of all classes are known, then Bayes decision theory produces optimal results in the sense that it minimizes the expected misclassification rate [3]. However, in many pattern recognition problems, the classification of an input pattern is based on data where the respective sample sizes of each class are small and possibly not representative of the actual probability distributions, even if they are known. In these cases, many techniques rely on some notion of similarity or distance in feature space, for instance, clustering and discriminant analysis [2], [3]. Under many circumstances, the *K*-nearest neighbor (*K*-NN) algorithm [3], [11] is used to perform the classification. This decision rule provides a simple nonparametric procedure for the assignment of a class label to the input pattern based on the class labels represented by the *K*-closest (say, for example, in the Euclidean sense) neighbors of the vector.

The *K*-NN rule is a suboptimal procedure. However, it has been shown that in the infinite sample situation, the error rate for the 1-NN rule is bounded above by no more than twice the optimal Bayes error rate and, that as *K* increases, this error rate approaches the optimal rate asymptotically [11], [12]. Since its introduction, the *K*-NN rule has been studied and improved upon by numerous researchers [13]–[18]. But it is not this asymptotic behavior in the limit that has maintained interest in this family of decision rules, but rather their computational simplicity and the perhaps surprising good results obtained by their use in many problems of small sample size [19]–[22]. It has been found for example that *K*-NN classification is well suited to those problem domains characterized by data that is only partially exposed to the system prior to employment [21], [22].

One of the problems encountered in using the *K*-NN classifier is that normally each of the sample vectors is considered equally important in the assignment of the class label to the input vector. This frequently causes difficulty in those places where the sample sets overlap. Atypical vectors are given as much weight as those that are truly representative of the clusters. Another difficulty is that once an input vector is assigned to a class, there is no indication of its "strength" of membership in that class. It is these two problems in the *K*-NN algorithm that we address by incorporating fuzzy set theory into the *K*-NN rule.

Fuzzy sets were introduced by Zadeh in 1965 [23]. Since that time researchers have found numerous ways to utilize this theory to generalize existing techniques and to develop new algorithms in pattern recognition and decision analysis [24]–[27]. In [24] Bezdek suggests that interesting and useful algorithms could result from the allocation of fuzzy class membership to the input vector, thus affording fuzzy decisions based on fuzzy labels. This work is concerned with incorporating fuzzy set methods into the classical *K*-NN decision rule. In particular, a "fuzzy *K*-NN" algorithm is developed utilizing fuzzy class memberships of the sample sets and thus producing a fuzzy classification rule. Three methods of assigning fuzzy membership for the training sets are proposed, and their advantages and disadvantages are discussed. Results of both the "crisp" (that based on traditional set theory) and fuzzy *K*-NN rule are compared on two data sets, and the fuzzy algorithm is shown to dominate its crisp counterpart by having lower error rates and by producing membership values that serve as a confidence measure in the classification.

Finally, a simple variant of the *K*-NN rule, the nearest prototype technique, is considered. In this decision scheme, a typical pattern of each class is chosen, and the unknown vector is assigned to the class of its closest prototype. A fuzzy analog to this procedure is developed and the results of the two versions are compared.

II. Fuzzy Sets

Given a universe U of objects, a conventional crisp subset A of U is commonly defined by specifying the objects of the universe that are members of A. An equivalent way of defining A is to specify the characteristic function of A, $u_A\colon U \rightarrow \{0,1\}$ where for all $x \in U$

$$u_A(x) = \begin{cases} 1, & x \in A \\ 0, & x \notin A. \end{cases}$$

Fuzzy sets are derived by generalizing the concept of a characteristic function to a membership function $u\colon U \rightarrow [0,1]$. An example of a fuzzy set is the set of real numbers much larger than zero, which can be defined with a membership function as

Manuscript received September 1, 1984; revised February 26, 1985.

J. Keller and J. Givens are with the Department of Electrical and Computer Engineering, University of Missouri, Columbia, MO 65211, USA.

M. Gray was in the Department of Electrical and Computer Engineering, University of Missouri. He is now with Wright-Patterson Air Force Base, OH 45433, USA.

Reprinted from *IEEE Trans. Syst., Man, Cybern.*, vol. SMC-15, no. 4, pp. 580–585, July/August 1985.

follows:

$$u(x) = \begin{cases} x^2/(x^2+1), & x \geqslant 0 \\ 0, & x < 0. \end{cases}$$

Numbers that are not at all larger than zero are not in the set ($u = 0$), while numbers which are larger than zero are partially in the set based on how much larger than zero they are. Thus the impetus behind the introduction of fuzzy set theory was to provide a means of defining categories that are inherently imprecise [24]. Since the introduction of fuzzy set theory the terms *hard* and *crisp* have been used to describe sets conforming to traditional set theory.

Most crisp set operations (such as union and intersection) and set properties have analogs in fuzzy set theory. (See [28] for a more detailed presentation of fuzzy set theory.)

The advantage provided by fuzzy sets is that the degree of membership in a set can be specified, rather than just the binary is or isn't a member. This can be especially advantageous in pattern recognition, where frequently objects are not clearly members of one class or another. Using crisp techniques an ambiguous object will be assigned to one class only, lending an aura of precision and definiteness to the assignment that is not warranted. On the other hand, fuzzy techniques will specify to what degree the object belongs to each class, which is information that frequently is useful.

Given a set of sample vectors, $\{x_1,\cdots,x_n\}$, a fuzzy c partition of these vectors specifies the degree of membership of each vector in each of c classes. It is denoted by the c by n matrix U, where $u_{ik} = u_i(x_k)$ for $i = 1,\cdots,c$, and $k = 1,\cdots,n$ is the degree of membership of x_k in class i. The following properties must be true for U to be a fuzzy c partition

$$\sum_{i=1}^{c} u_{ik} = 1,$$

$$0 < \sum_{k=1}^{m} u_{ik} < n,$$

$$u_{ik} \epsilon [0,1].$$

The fact that a vector's memberships in the c classes must sum to one is for mathematical tractability. In the two class case for example, memberships near 0.5 indicate that the vector has a high degree of membership in both classes; i.e., the "bounding region" separates one class from another.

III. The K-Nearest Neighbor Algorithms

The nearest neighbor classifiers require no preprocessing of the labeled sample set prior to their use. The crisp nearest-neighbor classification rule assigns an input sample vector y, which is of unknown classification, to the class of its nearest neighbor [11]. This idea can be extended to the K-nearest neighbors with the vector y being assigned to the class that is represented by a majority amongst the K-nearest neighbors. Of course, when more than one neighbor is considered, the possibility that there will be a tie among classes with a maximum number of neighbors in the group of K-nearest neighbor exists. One simple way of handling this problem is to restrict the possible values of K. For example, given a two-class problem, if we restrict K to odd values only no tie will be possible. Of course, when more than two classes are possible, this technique is not useful. A means of handling the occurrence of a tie is as follows. The sample vector is assigned to the class, of those classes that tied, for which the sum of distances from the sample to each neighbor in the class is a minimum. Of course, this could still lead to a tie, in which case the assignment is to the last class encountered amongst those which tied, an arbitrary assignment. Clearly, there will be cases where a vector's classification becomes an arbitrary assignment, no matter what additional procedures are included in the algorithm.

A. The Crisp K-NN Algorithm

Let $W = \{x_1, x_2,\cdots,x_n\}$ be a set of n labeled samples. The algorithm is as follows:

```
BEGIN
  Input y, of unknown classification.
  Set K, 1 ≤ K ≤ n.
  Initialize i = 1.
  DO UNTIL (K-nearest neighbors found)
    Compute distance from y to x_i.
    IF (i ≤ K) THEN
      Include x_i in the set of K-nearest neighbors
    ELSE IF (x_i is closer to y than any previous nearest
      neighbor) THEN
      Delete farthest in the set of K-nearest neighbors
      Include x_i in the set of K-nearest neighbors.
    END IF
    Increment i.
  END DO UNTIL
  Determine the majority class represented in the set of K-
  nearest neighbors.
  IF (a tie exists) THEN
    Compute sum of distances of neighbors in each class
    which tied.
    IF (no tie occurs) THEN
      Classify y in the class of minimum sum
    ELSE
      Classify y in the class of last minimum found.
    END IF
  ELSE
    Classify y in the majority class.
  END IF
END
```

B. Fuzzy K-NN Classifier

While the fuzzy K-nearest neighbor procedure is also a classification algorithm the form of its results differ from the crisp version. The fuzzy K-nearest neighbor algorithm assigns class membership to a sample vector rather than assigning the vector to a particular class. The advantage is that no arbitrary assignments are made by the algorithm. In addition, the vector's membership values should provide a level of assurance to accompany the resultant classification. For example, if a vector is assigned 0.9 membership in one class and 0.05 membership in two other classes we can be reasonably sure the class of 0.9 membership is the class to which the vector belongs. On the other hand, if a vector is assigned 0.55 membership in class one, 0.44 membership in class two, and 0.01 membership in class three, then we should be hesitant to assign the vector based on these results. Howevei, we can feel confident that it does not belong to class three. In such a case the vector might be examined further to determine its classification, because the vector exhibits a high degree of membership in both classes one and two. Clearly the membership assignments produced by the algorithm can be useful in the classification process.

The basis of the algorithm is to assign membership as a function of the vector's distance from its K-nearest neighbors and those neighbors' memberships in the possible classes. The fuzzy algorithm is similar to the crisp version in the sense that it must also search the labeled sample set for the K-nearest neighbors. Beyond obtaining these K samples, the procedures differ considerably.

Let $W = \{x_1, x_2,\cdots,x_n\}$ be the set of n labeled samples. Also let $u_i(x)$ be the assigned membership of the vector x (to be computed), and u_{ij} be the membership in the ith class of the jth vector of the labeled sample set. The algorithm is as follows:

```
BEGIN
  Input x, of unknown classification.
  Set K, 1 ≤ K ≤ n.
  Initialize i = 1.
  DO UNTIL (K-nearest neighbors to x found)
    Compute distance from x to x_i.
    IF (i ≤ K) THEN
      Include x_i in the set of K-nearest neighbors
    ELSE IF (x_i closer to x than any previous nearest neigh-
    bor) THEN
      Delete the farthest of the K-nearest neighbors
      Include x_i in the set of K-nearest neighbors.
    END IF
  END DO UNTIL
  Initialize i = 1.
  DO UNTIL (x assigned membership in all classes)
    Compute u_i(x) using (1).
    Increment i.
  END DO UNTIL
END
```

where

$$u_i(x) = \frac{\sum_{j=1}^{K} u_{ij}\left(1/\|x - x_j\|^{2/(m-1)}\right)}{\sum_{j=1}^{K}\left(1/\|x - x_j\|^{2/(m-1)}\right)}. \tag{1}$$

As seen by (1), the assigned memberships of x are influenced by the inverse of the distances from the nearest neighbors and their class memberships. The inverse distance serves to weight a vector's membership more if it is closer and less if it is farther from the vector under consideration. The labeled samples can be assigned class memberships in several ways. First, they can be given complete membership in their known class and nonmembership in all other classes. Other alternatives are to assign the samples' membership based on distance from their class mean or based on the distance from labeled samples of their own class and those of the other class or classes, and then to use the resulting memberships in the classifier. Both of these techniques have been used in this study and the results are reported. It is noted that in [29] an alternate scheme for assigning initial memberships based on a learning scheme was considered.

The variable m determines how heavily the distance is weighted when calculating each neighbor's contribution to the membership value. If m is two, then the contribution of each neighboring point is weighted by the reciprocal of its distance from the point being classified. As m increases, the neighbors are more evenly weighted, and their relative distances from the point being classified have less effect. As m approaches one, the closer neighbors are weighted far more heavily than those farther away, which has the effect of reducing the number of points that contribute to the membership value of the point being classified. In the results presented in Section V we used $m = 2$, but note that almost equal error rates have been obtained on these data over a wide range of values of m.

IV. Nearest Prototype Classifiers

These classifiers bear a marked resemblance to the one-nearest neighbor classifier. Actually, the only difference is that for the nearest prototype classifier the labeled samples are a set of class prototypes, whereas in the nearest neighbor classifier we use a set of labeled samples that are not necessarily prototypical. Of course, the nearest prototype classifier could be extended to multiple prototypes representing each class, similar to the K-nearest neighbor routine. Nevertheless, this study considers only the nearest prototype classifier in both a crisp and fuzzy version. The prototypes used for these routines are taken as the class means of the labeled sample set.

A. The Crisp Nearest Prototype Classifier

Let $W = \{Z_1, Z_2, \cdots, Z_c\}$ be the set of c prototype vectors representing the c classes. The algorithm is as follows:

```
BEGIN
  Input x, vector to be classified.
  Initialize i = 1
  DO UNTIL (distance from each prototype to x computed)
    Compute distance from Z_i to x.
    Increment i.
  END DO UNTIL
  Determine minimum distance to any class prototype.
  IF (tie exists) THEN
    Classify x as last class found of minimum distance
  ELSE
    Classify x as class of closest prototype.
  END IF
END
```

B. Fuzzy Nearest Prototype Algorithm

As above, let $W = \{Z_1, Z_2, \cdots, Z_c\}$ be the set of c prototypes representing the c classes. The algorithm is as follows:

```
BEGIN
  Input x, vector to be classified.
  Initialize i = 1.
  DO UNTIL (distance from each prototype to x computed)
    Compute distance from Z_i to x.
    Increment i.
  END DO UNTIL
  Initialize i = 1.
  DO UNTIL (x assigned membership in all classes)
    Compute u_i(x) using (2)
    Increment i
  END DO UNTIL
END
```

where

$$u_i(x) = \frac{1/\|x - Z_i\|^{2/(m-1)}}{\sum_{j=1}^{c}\left(1/\|x - Z_j\|^{2/(m-1)}\right)}. \tag{2}$$

The difference between (2) and (1) is that membership in each class is assigned based only on the distance from the prototype of the class. This is because the prototypes should naturally be assigned complete membership in the class that they represent.

V. Results

The results presented in this section were produced by software implementation of the algorithms described above. The software was developed using Fortran 77 on a Perkin-Elmer 3220 in the Image Analysis Laboratory at the University of Missouri-Columbia.

Three labeled data sets were utilized to test the algorithms. The data sets and their attributes are as follows:

Data Set Name	Number of Classes	Number of Vectors	Number of Features per Vector
IRIS	3	150	4
IRIS23	2	100	4
TWOCLASS	2	242	4

TABLE I
RESULTS OF K-NEAREST NEIGHBOR CLASSIFIERS
NUMBER OF MISCLASSIFIED VECTORS[1]

	Crisp			Fuzzy-(1)			Fuzzy-(2)		Fuzzy-(3)		
K	I	T	I'	I	T	I'	T	I'	I	T	I'
1	6	26	6	6	26	6	26	6	6	26	6
2	7	26	7	6	26	6	21	6	6	21	6
3	6	21	6	6	22	6	21	7	5	19	6
4	5	20	5	6	19	6	20	7	5	20	5
5	5	20	5	5	21	5	20	7	4	19	4
6	6	19	6	5	18	5	20	6	4	20	4
7	5	19	5	5	21	5	18	6	4	19	4
8	7	21	7	6	18	6	20	6	4	20	4
9	6	21	6	4	21	4	18	5	4	18	4
Average	5.9	21.4	5.9	5.4	21.3	5.4	20.4	6.2	4.7	20.2	4.8

[1] K number of neighbors used
I IRIS data (four features)
T TWOCLASS data (four features)
I' IRIS23 data (four features)
(1) crisp initialization
(2) exponential initialization
(3) fuzzy 3-nearest neighbor initialization.

The data set IRIS is that of Anderson. This particular data set has been utilized extensively by researchers in the area of cluster analysis since 1936, when R. A. Fisher first used it to illustrate the concept of linear discriminant analysis [30]. The data represents three subspecies of irises, with the four feature measurements being sepal length, sepal width, petal length, and petal width, all in centimeters. There are fifty vectors per class in this data set. The IRIS23 data set is a subset of the IRIS data. It includes classes two and three, the nonseparable classes, of the IRIS data.

The TWOCLASS data set is an artificially generated normally distributed set of vectors. This data set was included because classification results from a Bayes classifier were available to use in the comparison. This data set contains 121 samples per class.

The results of the fuzzy classifications are reported in terms of the simplest crisp partition, where a sample vector is assigned to the class of maximum membership. The classifications are obtained using the "leave one out" technique. The procedure is to leave one sample out of the data set and classify it using the remaining samples as the labeled data set. This technique is repeated until all samples in the data set have been classified. In addition, in order to evaluate one technique used to initialize memberships of the labeled samples used in the classifier the IRIS23 set was created by using only class two and three of the IRIS data set. This was necessary because the initialization technique will only work on two class classification problems.

Before comparing the results produced by the nearest neighbor algorithms, the types of labeling techniques used for the fuzzy classifier are explained. Three different techniques of membership assignment for the labeled data are considered. The first method, a crisp labeling, is to assign each labeled sample complete membership in its known class and zero membership in all other classes. The second technique assigns membership based on the procedure presented in [31]. This technique works only on two class data sets. The procedure assigns a sample membership in its known class based on its distance from the mean of the labeled sample class. These memberships range from one to one half with an exponential rate of change between these limits. The sample's membership in the other class is assigned such that the sum of the memberships of the vector equals one. A more detailed explanation of this technique is given in [31]. The third method assigns memberships to the labeled samples according to a K-nearest neighbor rule. The K (not K of the classifier)-nearest neighbors to each sample x (say x in class i) are found, and then membership in each class is assigned according to the following

TABLE II
COMPARISON OF CRISP AND FUZZY K-NN CLASSIFIERS ON TWOCLASS Data AND ON IRIS Data WITH FUZZY KINIT-NN INITIALIZATION

	Number of Misclassified Vectors (out of 242)					
		Fuzzy KINIT				
K	Crisp	1	3	5	7	9
	TWOCLASS Data					
1	26	26	26	26	26	26
2	26	23	21	23	22	22
3	21	20	19	21	21	23
4	20	17	20	19	19	19
5	20	16	19	19	20	19
6	19	20	20	20	21	20
7	19	17	19	20	20	20
8	21	17	20	20	20	20
9	21	18	21	21	21	21
Average Misclassification	21.4	19.3	20.6	21.0	21.1	21.1
	IRIS Data					
1	6	6	6	6	6	6
2	7	6	6	6	6	6
3	6	5	5	5	5	6
4	5	5	5	5	5	5
5	5	4	4	5	5	5
6	6	4	4	4	4	4
7	5	4	4	4	4	4
8	7	4	4	4	4	4
9	6	4	4	4	4	4
Average Misclassification	5.9	4.7	4.7	4.8	4.8	4.9

TABLE III
CONFUSION MATRICES FOR THE K-MEANS ALGORITHM

	IRIS[1]				TWOCLASS[2]	
	1	2	3		1	2
1	50	0	0	1	114	7
2	0	48	2	2	15	106
3	0	14	36			

[1] Terminated in three iterations.
[2] Terminated in ten iterations.

equation:

$$u_j(x) = \begin{cases} 0.51 + (n_j/K) * 0.49, & \text{if } j = i \\ (n_j/K) * 0.49, & \text{if } j \neq i. \end{cases}$$

The value n_j is the number of the neighbors found which belong to the jth class. This method attempts to "fuzzify" the memberships of the labeled samples, which are in the class regions intersecting in the sample space, and leaves the samples that are well away from this area with complete membership in the known class. As a result, an unknown sample lying in this intersecting region will be influenced to a lesser extent by the labeled samples that are in the "fuzzy" area of the class boundary.

Thus with these three initialization techniques, three sets of results of the fuzzy K-nearest neighbor classifier are produced. These results are presented in Tables I and II. Upon comparison of the results of the crisp classifier and the fuzzy classifier with crisp initialization, we can see that on the average the fuzzy classifier has slightly lower error rates. In addition, the fuzzy classifier, which uses the second initialization technique, produced nearly equal results. Although not reported in the tables, the results of this fuzzy classifier using the membership assignment rule described in [31] did not produce memberships for the

TABLE IV
CONFUSION MATRICES OF THE FIRST-NEAREST PROTOTYPE CLASSIFIER

IRIS Data

	Four Features						Features Three and Four					
	Crisp			Fuzzy			Crisp			Fuzzy		
	1	2	3	1	2	3	1	2	3	1	2	3
1	50	0	0	50	0	0	50	0	0	50	0	0
2	0	45	5	0	45	5	0	48	2	0	48	2
3	0	7	43	0	7	43	0	4	46	0	4	46

TWOCLASS Data

Four Features						Features Three and Four					
Crisp			Fuzzy			Crisp			Fuzzy		
	1	2		1	2		1	2		1	2
1	113	8	1	113	8	1	113	8	1	113	8
2	12	109	2	12	109	2	12	109	2	12	109

misclassified vectors that suggest that they actually belong to a different class. Instead this second initialization technique causes an overall reduction in the values of memberships assigned with most of the samples given majority memberships less than 0.7. But the nearest neighbor initialization technique does produce membership assignments that give an indication of degree of correctness of classification.

Examining the results given in Table II for the K-nearest neighbor classifier with nearest neighbor sample membership initialization, the following observations can be made. First of all, the results show a somewhat lower overall error rate. But, more importantly, the number of misclassified vectors with high assigned membership (greater than 0.8) in the wrong class is considerably less than half of the misclassified vectors for most choices of KINIT. In addition, the correctly classified samples were given relatively higher membership in their known class than in other classes. Therefore, more sophisticated classification schemes utilizing these memberships (other than just maximum membership) could be devised to increase the overall correct classification rate, and the final membership values produce a natural confidence measure.

While the main concern of this paper was to demonstrate that the fuzzy K-NN technique dominates the crisp version in both decreased error rates and information content of the results, our algorithm compares favorably to several other more complicated techniques on these data sets. In particular, we have run the K-means clustering procedure, two types of linear discriminant function algorithms, and a Bayes classifier on the data. For the K-means [3], we initialized the cluster centers to the sample mean and those vectors furthest from the mean. The results are shown in Table III. The fuzzy K-NN does at least as well as this procedure (better for the IRIS data) with the added information on class membership.

The perceptron is representative of a class of iterative schemes for finding linear decision boundaries between classes using the gradient descent approach. This procedure is guaranteed to converge to a solution if the data sets are linearly separable [3]. However, since neither of our data sets possess this property, the perceptron does not converge. Stopping it after a fixed number of iterations may or may not produce a reasonable decision boundary. For example, terminating it after two iterations on the TWOCLASS data, the linear discriminant result misclassified 62 of the 242 vectors; after 70 iterations, 107 vectors were misclassified; and after 150 iterations, the number of misclassified was down to 29 but by 200 iterations, it was back to 67. This of course demonstrates the erratic behavior of this algorithm on overlapping data. There have been approaches to modify this technique to produce reasonable boundaries even in the nonseparable case. One such method, using fuzzy sets, is reported in [31]. This technique converged in two iterations misclassifying 21 vectors, again comparable to the fuzzy K-NN. Similar results are obtained on the IRIS set.

TABLE V
FUZZY CLASSIFIER MEMBERSHIP ASSIGNMENTS[1]

	IRIS Data A	IRIS Data B	TWOCLASS Data A	TWOCLASS Data B
Misclassified samples (membership assigned > 0.7)	1	1	3	3
Classified samples (membership assigned > 0.5 and < 0.7)	15	15	36	36

[1]The intent here is to illustrate that there are very few correctly classified samples in the "fuzzy" region between 0.5 and 0.7. A denotes four feature and B denotes features three and four used.

While the primary use of the K-NN algorithms is in those situations where the *a priori* probabilities and class conditional densities are unknown, the TWOCLASS data was in fact generated with equal *a priori* probabilities and multivariate normal distributions. So as a final comparison, consider the results of the Bayes classifier for the TWOCLASS data. Running a ten-percent jacknife procedure[1] and assuming equal *a priori* probabilities for both classes, the Bayes classifier misclassified twenty of the samples. Clearly, depending on the value chosen for K, the fuzzy nearest neighbor classifier can perform as well as a Bayes classifier, but with much less restrictive assumptions. Certainly, the posterior probabilities in the Bayes classifier provide a measure of strength of classification; i.e., they represent the probability that the object is a member of each class. The fuzzy K-nearest neighbor classifier provides different form of this information. In this case, we obtain a measure of how "typical" this object is of each class.

The nearest prototype classifier in both the crisp and fuzzy versions is the quickest and simplest of the classifiers considered. The reason is that in both versions of the first-nearest prototype algorithm, an unknown sample is compared to one prototype per class as opposed to the K-nearest neighbor algorithms, where an entire set of labeled samples representing each class must be compared before the K nearest are obtained. The results reported in Table IV show that the fuzzy prototype classifier and the crisp nearest prototype classifier produced equivalent results. But, by looking at the memberships of the misclassified samples in terms of the number with membership greater than 0.7 in the wrong class, given in Table V, it is clear that these memberships do provide a useful level of confidence of classification. Further, the number of correctly classified samples with memberships in the range between 0.4 and 0.7 is small compared to the number of correctly classified samples that have membership in the correct class greater than 0.7. Thus, we can be assured, based on the memberships assigned, that the samples are correctly classified.

VI. CONCLUSION

A fuzzy K-NN decision rule and a fuzzy prototype decision rule have been developed along with three methods for assigning membership values to the sample sets.

The fuzzy K-nearest neighbor and fuzzy nearest prototype algorithms developed and investigated in this report show useful results. In particular, concerning the fuzzy K-nearest neighbor algorithm with fuzzy K-nearest neighbor initialization, the membership assignments produced for classified samples tend to

[1]This procedure involves taking ten percent of the samples as test data and the remaining as training data, classifying these, and then repeating the procedure until all samples have been used as test samples.

possess desirable qualities. That is, an incorrectly classified sample will not have a membership in any class close to one while a correctly classified sample does possess a membership in the correct class close to one. The fuzzy nearest prototype classifier, while not producing error rates as low as the fuzzy nearest neighbor classifier, is computationally attractive and also produces membership assignments that are desirable.

REFERENCES

[1] E. Hunt, *Artificial Intelligence*. New York: Academic, 1975.

[2] P. Winston, *Artificial Intelligence*. Reading, MA: Addison-Wesley, 1977.

[3] R. O. Duda and P. E. Hart, *Pattern Classification and Scene Analysis*. New York: Wiley, 1973.

[4] B. G. Batchelor, *Pattern Recognition*. New York: Plenum, 1978.

[5] R. Gnanadesikan, *Methods for Statistical Data Analysis of Multivariate Observations*. New York: Wiley, 1977.

[6] A. Reynolds and P. Flagg, *Cognitive Pyschology*. Cambridge, MA: Winthrop, 1977.

[7] P. Dodwell, *Visual Pattern Recognition* New York: Holt, Rinehart, and Winston, 1970.

[8] K. T. Spoehr, and S. W. Lehmkuhle, *Visual Information Processing*. San Francisco, CA: Freeman, 1982.

[9] *Computer Diagnosis and Diagnostic Methods*, J. A. Jacquez, Ed. Springfield, Ill.: Charles Thomas, 1972.

[10] A. Wardle and L. Wardle, "Computer aided diagnosis—a review of research," *Meth. Inform. Med.*, vol. 17, no. 1, pp. 15–28, 1978.

[11] T. M. Cover and P. E. Hart, "Nearest neighbor pattern classification," *IEEE Trans. Inform. Theory*, vol. IT-13, pp. 21–27, Jan. 1967.

[12] K. Fukunaga and L. D. Hostetler, "*K*-nearest neighbor Bayes risk estimation," *IEEE Trans. Inform. Theory*, vol. IT-21, no. 3, pp. 285–293, 1975.

[13] P. Hart, "The condensed nearest neighbor rule," *IEEE Trans. Inform. Theory*, vol. IT-14, pp. 515–516, 1968.

[14] T. M. Cover, "Estimates by the nearest neighbor rule," *IEEE Trans. Inform. Theory*, vol. IT-14, no. 1, pp. 50–55, 1968.

[15] M. E. Hellman, "The nearest neighbor classification rule with a reject option," *IEEE Trans. Syst. Sci. Cybern.*, vol. SSC-6, pp. 179–185, 1970.

[16] I. Tomek, "A generalization of the *k*-NN rule," *IEEE Trans. Syst. Man Cybern.*, vol. SMC-6, no. 2, pp. 121–126, 1976.

[17] B. V. Dasarathy, "Visiting nearest neighbor—A survey of nearest neighbor classification techniques," in *Proc. Int. Conf. Cybern. Soc.*, 1977, pp. 630–636.

[18] P. A. Devijver, "New error bounds with the nearest neighbor rule," *IEEE Trans. Inform. Theory*, vol. IT-25, pp. 749–753, 1979.

[19] P. Scheinok and J. Rinaldo, "Symptom diagnosis: optimal subsets for upper abdominal pain," *Comp. Bio Res.*, vol. 1, pp. 221–236, 1967.

[20] G. T. Toussaint and P. Sharpe, "An efficient method for estimating the probability of misclassification applied to a problem in medical diagnosis," *Comp. Biol. Med.*, vol. 4, pp. 269–278, 1975.

[21] A. Whitney and S. J. Dwyer, III, "Performance and implementations of *k*-nearest neighbor decision rule with incorrectly identified training samples," in *Proc. 4th Ann. Allerton Conf. on Circuits Band System Theory*, 1966.

[22] B. V. Dasarathy, "Nosing around the neighborhood: A new system structure and classification rule for recognition in partially exposed environments," *IEEE Trans. Pattern Anal. Machine Intell.*, vol. PAMI-2, no. 1, pp. 67–71, 1980.

[23] L. A. Zadeh, "Fuzzy Sets," *Inf. Control*, vol. 8, pp. 338–353, 1965.

[24] J. C. Bezdek, *Pattern Recognition with Fuzzy Objective Function Algorithms*, New York: Plenum Press, 1981.

[25] M. Gupta, R. Ragade, and P. Yager, Eds., *Advances in Fuzzy Set Theory and Applications*. Amsterdam: North-Holland, 1979.

[26] P. P. Wang and S. K. Chang, Eds., *Theory and Applications to Policy Analysis and Information Systems*. New York: Plenum, 1980.

[27] A. Kandel, *Fuzzy Techniques in Pattern Recognition*. New York, John Wiley, 1982.

[28] A. Kaufmann, *Introduction to the Theory of Fuzzy Subsets*, vol. I. New York: Academic, 1975.

[29] A. Jozwik, "A learning scheme for a fuzzy *K*-NN Rule," *Pattern Recognition Letters*, vol. 1, pp. 287–289, July 1983.

[30] R. A. Fisher, "The use of multiple measurements in taxonomic problems," *Ann. Eugenics*, vol. 7, pp. 179–188, 1936.

[31] J. Keller and D. Hunt, "Incorporating fuzzy membership functions into the perceptron algorithm," submitted to *IEEE Trans. Pattern Anal. Machine Intell.*

Fuzzy Decision Tree Algorithms

ROBIN L. P. CHANG, MEMBER, IEEE, AND THEODOSIOS PAVLIDIS, MEMBER, IEEE

***Abstract*—Certain theoretical aspects of fuzzy decision trees and their applications are discussed. The main result is a branch-bound-backtrack algorithm which, by means of pruning subtrees unlikely to be traversed and installing tree-traversal pointers, has an effective backtracking mechanism leading to the optimal solution while still requiring usually only $O(\log n)$ time, where n is the number of decision classes.**

I. Introduction

The DECISION tree is a well known technique for making classification decisions in pattern recognition. Its main virtue lies in the fact that we can maintain a large number of classes while at the same time minimize the time for making the final decision by a series of small local decisions. In fact, very often it takes only $O(\log n)$[1] time to reach one of the n possible classes, since a tree of n leaves usually has depth $\log n$.

To facilitate subsequent discussions, we first state a few frequently used definitions. However, we assume the definitions of tree, node, branch, son, father, descendant, ancestor, root, leaf, subtree, path, and path length to be known. (See [6, Section 2.3], for instance). The fuzzy algebra used is similar to those given in [2], [12], and other papers on fuzzy logic. For a systematic exposure we refer to [3].

Definition 1: A fuzzy decision function f_x at node x is a real-valued unary k-tuple function $k \geq 2$,

$$f_x: X \to [0,1]^k,$$

where X is the input (e.g., a digitized picture I, or a voice spectrograph S) and the k-tuple is the labels (decision values) $v(x_i)$ of the outgoing branches (x,x_i), $i = 1,\cdots,k$ where x_i is the ith son of node x. A 0–1 decision function f_x is a fuzzy decision function that can assume only integer values 0,1:

$$f_x: X \to \{0,1\}^k,$$

with exactly one element of the k-tuple equal to 1.

Definition 2: A decision tree T_r is a tree with root r such that each nonleaf node i has a corresponding k-tuple decision function f_i and k ordered sons $i_1,\cdots,i_k$. A fuzzy decision tree is one with fuzzy decision functions, and a 0–1 decision tree is one with 0–1 decision functions. A decision tree is binary if and only if all the decision functions are double functions. A complete (or, completely balanced) k-ary decision tree is a decision tree in which the decision function at each nonleaf node is k-ary and each path from the root to a leaf has the same length.

Definition 3: The decision path (x,y) is the path of the decision tree from node x to node y. The decision path x is the decision path (root, x). The decision path $(w,x,\cdots,y,z)$ is the path from node w via nodes $x,\cdots,y$ to node z.

A complicated decision represented by a decision tree is always made up of several simple decisions, each represented by a node in the tree.

We assume realistically that the time required for making a k-tuple decision (i.e., for evaluating a k-tuple decision function) is of $O(k)$.

Definition 4: The (decision) value $V(x)$ of a decision path x is the product of the decision values (labels) of the branches composing it. That is,

$$V(x) = \bigwedge_{y \in \text{path } x} v(y).$$

("Product" $\wedge$ is the real number product in the prob model or is the minimum function as defined in the max-min model.[2]

It can be shown [3] that given the same decision tree T with the same decision values, the 0–1, fuzzy max-min, and fuzzy prob criteria may lead to all different decisions.

Definition 5: Two decision trees are equivalent if and only if they give the same decisions.

It is interesting to note, however, that the max-min decision tree and the prob decision tree are mutually reducible to one another in $O(n)$ time, where n is, as usual, the number of decision classes.

Theorem 1: There exists a max-min decision tree T_1 if and only if there exists an equivalent prob decision tree of the same structure (but different labels). Furthermore, they are mutually reducible in linear time with respect to the number of decision classes.

Proof: The proof is quite straightforward and is omitted. The reader may refer to [3].

II. Various Decision Tree Algorithms

The naïve, yet efficient top-down decision algorithm for 0–1 decision trees is too straightforward to mention. The reader may refer to [1, section 2.4], for instance. The reader may also refer to [7] for more insight on the subject. The top-down algorithm looks very attractive since it

Manuscript received April 19, 1976; revised August 19, 1976. This work was supported by the National Science Foundation under Grant ENG72-04133.

R. L. P. Chang was with the Department of Electrical Engineering and Computer Science, Princeton University, Princeton, NJ. He is now with Rapistan, Inc., Grand Rapids, MI 49505.

T. Pavlidis is with the Department of Electrical Engineering and Computer Science, Princeton University, Princeton, NJ 08540.

[1] The notation $O(m)$ is read "order of m." When we say that x is $O(m)$ it means that x/m has a limit less than 1 when $m \to \infty$.

[2] A fuzzy algebra can be defined on any closed well-ordered set with at least two elements and two binary operators $\wedge$ and $\vee$ and a unary operator $|$ such that a proper set of postulates is satisfied. See [3] for further details and references to the literature. In the prob model $a \wedge b = ab$, while in the max-min model $a \wedge b = \min(a,b)$.

Reprinted from *IEEE Trans. Syst., Man, Cybern.*, vol. SMC-7, no. 1, pp. 28–35, January 1977.

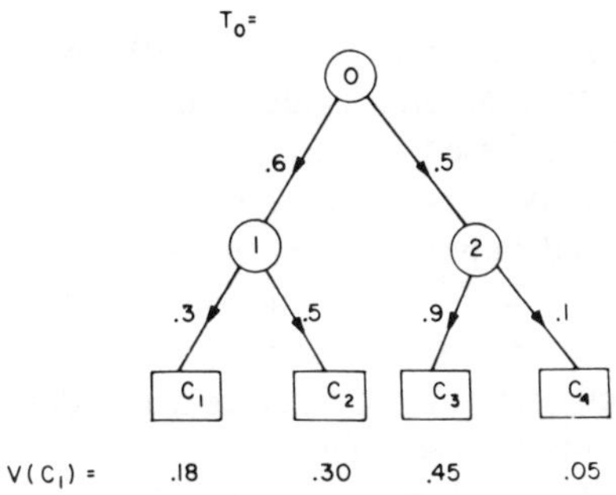

Fig. 1. Fuzzy decision tree.

has good time complexity $O(\log n)$. It is not, in general, applicable to any fuzzy decision tree, however.

Consider the example in Fig. 1. If at each decision node we pick the highest value branch, then we will end up with class C_2. Obviously, class C_3 is a better choice, since the path to class C_3 has decision value $0.45 > 0.24$ value of the path to class C_2. There is a guaranteed bottom-up algorithm for general fuzzy decision trees. The mechanism is essentially the same as the well-known tournament method for finding the maximum of n numbers, but it has a time complexity $O(n)$.

Least Upper Bound for Decision Tree Algorithms

Note that $O(n)$ is the theoretical least upper bound (LUB) of the time complexity of a perfectly general fuzzy decision tree decision algorithm. Consider a complete tree whose branches are all labeled 0.1 except one which is labeled 0.9 at the bottom. So the decision values of all paths are $(0.1)^d$ except for one which is $(0.1)^{d-1}(0.9) > (0.1)^d$. However, this 0.9 label may be at any of the n branches at the bottom, and hence all the n branches must be examined before the best decision can be found, taking $O(n)$ time.

The top-down algorithm, though efficient, may cause errors when applied to fuzzy decision trees. The bottom-up algorithm is general enough but not efficient. We will present now an algorithm for fuzzy decision trees whose complexity is usually $O(\log n)$, but still gives the optimal solution. We call it the branch-bound-backtrack algorithm (BBB), since it belongs to the family of branch-and-bound methods [8].

III. The Branch-Bound-Backtrack Algorithm

We link the sons $(x_1,\cdots,x_k)$ of each node x *from left to right* in descending order $(x_{i_1},\cdots,x_{i_k})$, where $i_1,\cdots,i_k$ is a sorting of $1,\cdots,k$, of their decision function values $f_x(I)$. Descendants of each node are linked downwards.

$L(x)$ is the label value of x designating the decision value of path bottom-up to this point. A node x on the right of, and having the same father as, node w is called a younger brother of w. The following theorem gives us the idea behind the new algorithm.

Theorem 2: Suppose node x is on the right side of the path from root r to node y in tree T_r. Then there exists some subtree T_x (by construction) such that there exists a path to the right of or below node x with decision value $> L(y)$ if and only if $L(x) > L(y)$.

Proof: Refer to Fig. 2. Since x is on the right of the

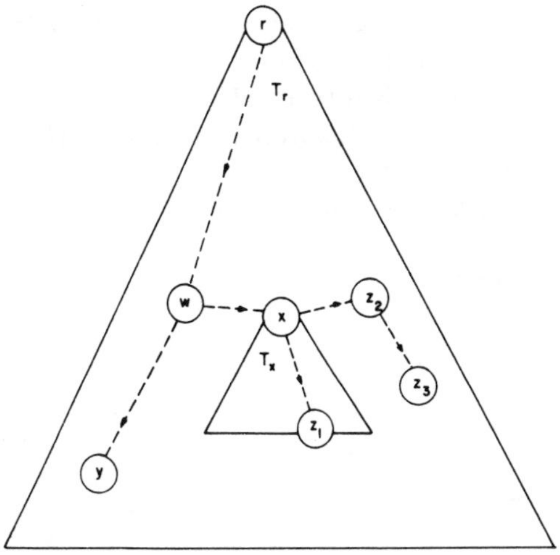

Fig. 2. T_r and T_x.

path defined by y, there must be some node w which is an elder brother of x and an ancestor of y.

($\Rightarrow$:) Let the path be defined by z, (may be r to z_1, z_2, or z_3) with z below or on the right of x.

Given $L(z) > L(y)$, but $L(z_1) = L(x) \cdot$ (value of path $(x,z_1)) \leq L(x)$. $L(z_2) \leq L(x)$ by convention, and $L(z_3) = L(z_2) \cdot$ (value of path $(z_2,z_3)) \leq L(z_2) \leq L(x)$. In any case, $L(z) \leq L(x)$. Therefore, $L(y) < L(x)$.

($\Leftarrow$:) Let T_x be the tree:

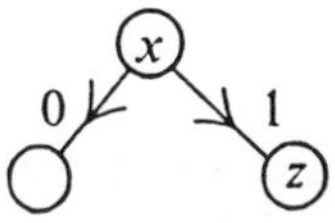

Then $L(z) = L(x) \cdot 1 = L(x)$. Therefore, $L(x) > L(y) \Rightarrow L(z) > L(y)$.

BBB Algorithm

Goal: To find the best decision path and its corresponding decision value for a given decision tree T_r (with unknown input).

Input: I, T_r.

Output: Node x defining the best decision path with the best decision value $L(x)$.

Data-structure: T_r is represented by an array of nodes, each node x of the tree consisting of four fields including one attribute and three links.

1) $L(x)$ is the label (decision value) of the branch from the father of x to x.
2) $F(x)$ points to the father of x.
3) $ES(x)$ points to the eldest son of x.
4) $YB(x)$ points to the next younger brother of x.

A null pointer is indicated by a 0. The root has $L(\text{root}) = 1'$, $F(\text{root}) = 0$, $YB(\text{root}) = 0$. Note also that the algorithm may terminate before the tree is completed.

Procedure:

$$L(r) \leftarrow 1;$$

$$x \leftarrow \text{BBB}(I,r,0).$$

Recursive Function BBB(I,r,d)

Goal: To give the leaf defining the best decision path for subtree T_r, with decision value $> d$. It returns 0 if no leaf has label (decision path value) $> d$. (It may label any r by 0 for useless subtree T_r to save time.)

1) If r is a leaf, then return BBB $\leftarrow r$, $x \leftarrow r$.
2) $(l_1,\cdots,l_k) \leftarrow f_x(I)$. Sort $(l_1,\cdots,l_k)$ to get $(l_i,\cdots,l_i)$ such that $l_i \geq \cdots \geq l_i$.
3) $l \leftarrow L(x)l_i$: if $l \leq d$ then do:

```
   L(x) ← 0;
   go to 5);
   end.
ES(x) ← x_i;
FT(x_i) ← x;
L(x_i) ← 1;
for j = 2,···,k, do;
   l ← L(x)·l_i;
   FT(x_i) ← x;
   if l ≤ d then do;
      YB(x_i) ← 0;
      go to 4);
      end;
   YB(x_i) ← x_i;
   L(x_i) ← l;
   end;
YB(x_i) ← 0.
```

4) $x \leftarrow ES(x)$; if x is not a leaf then go to 2).
5) $y \leftarrow x$; (x is a leaf here).
6) If $FT(x) = r$ then return BBB $\leftarrow y$; $x \leftarrow FT(x)$.
7) If $YB(x) = 0$ then go to 6); $x \leftarrow YB(x)$; if $L(x) \leq L(y)$ then go to 6).
8) $p \leftarrow$ BBB$(I,x,L(y))$; if $p \neq 0$ then $y \leftarrow$ p; go to 7).

Steps 1)–4) are for depth-first evaluation of the decision path. Steps 6)–8) are for backtracking.

IV. Analysis of the BBB Algorithm

A. Correctness

Theorem 3: The BBB algorithm given above is correct.

1) Termination: (Assume that T_r is finite.) The main procedure has a finite number of steps. BBB(I,r,d) terminates, since every decision function is evaluated at most once. (For details, see the complexity analysis section.)

2) Completeness: (i.e., every correct input yields an output.) By examining all the exits of BBB, some value is always returned when exiting.

3) Validity: (i.e., every output is the output intended.) BBB can exit only in steps 1) and 6). We prove validity by induction on the number of times BBB is recursively executed.

Basis: BBB exits in step 1). r is trivially the only possible node.

Induction step: We break up the proof into proofs of a few lemmas for clarity.

Lemma 3.1: For all x, $L(x) = 0$ if the decision value is $\leq d$, or undefined, or every son has a decision value $\leq d$; $=$ decision value if otherwise.

Proof: By induction on the length of path to x, which is previously x_i, some j. Step 3) gives $L(x_i) \leftarrow L(x) \cdot l_i$ whenever a decision function is evaluated with $L(x_i) > d$.

Lemma 3.2: $FT(x)$, $YB(x)$, $ES(x)$ are correct links.

Proof: Examine step 2). Whenever a decision function is evaluated, all connecting links to and among sons are set up correctly.

Lemma 3.3: Any path left of the path to y (the y in step 5)) must have a decision value $\leq$ that of the path to y. (Initial portions of these paths may coincide.)

Proof: Initially, y is the leftmost path. (See step 5).) y may be modified only in step 8), in which case we know $p =$ BBB$(I,x,L(y)) \neq 0$. By induction hypothesis of the main correctness theorem, we know that BBB$(I,x,L(y))$ is executed correctly since $T_x \leq T_r$ since x is a descendant of r. So $p \neq 0$ means $L(p) < L(y)$.

Lemma 3.4: Any path right of the path to y must have a decision value $\leq d$ or $\leq$ that of y, or else y will be modified subsequently.

Proof: Let these two paths be defined by nodes z and y, respectively. Since the path to z is on the right of the path to y there must be some node w in both paths such that $YB(w)$ is in the path to z but not in the path to y. $L(YB(w)) < L(w)$ by the sorting in step 2). Furthermore, by the property of fuzzy decision functions, $0 \leq l_i \leq 1, \forall j$, and hence the label of any descendant must be equal or smaller by multiplication. Therefore, $L(z) \leq L(w)$. So nothing is lost by pruning the tree in step 3). ($YB(x_i) \leftarrow 0$ prunes the tree.) All other nodes are eventually traversed and labeled by the backtracking in steps 6)–8) and recursion.

Now that the induction step of the proof of the main correctness theorem is completed, the theorem is proved.

B. Complexity

Space required is of $O(n)$ since it takes constant space for each node.

Time Required (Worst Case): The whole tree is traversed. The main procedure takes constant time. We prove BBB(I,r,d) takes $O(n)$ time by induction on number of nodes n of T_r.

Basis: Root r is a leaf. Constant time.

Induction step: Consider the procedure steps: step 1) takes constant time, and step 2) is reachable only from step 1) or step 4).

(Recursion in step 8) is considered separately.) It is reached only once from step 1). Thereafter step 2) is executed at most once for each new x (by $x \leftarrow ES(x)$, which makes x go downwards until the tree bottom). Each iteration takes constant time.

Step 3) takes at most constant time for each son x_{ij}. Each node can be such a son at most once. Each of steps 4) and 5) is traversed at most once for each node.

Now consider steps 6)–8). x either goes up by $x \leftarrow FT(x)$, or goes right by $x \leftarrow YB(x)$, or both after each iteration, and each iteration takes constant time. Therefore, total time is $O(n)$. By the induction hypothesis, BBB$(I,x,L(y))$ in step 8) takes O(number of nodes in T_x) time where T_x is a smaller tree, and all nodes in T_x have not been traversed yet. So we conclude that the whole algorithm takes $O(n)$ time.

Time Required (Best Case): T_r is a 0–1 decision tree, for example. Here the BBB algorithm reduces to the top-down 0–1 decision tree algorithm of time complexity $O(\log n)$ since only the depth-first evaluation part of the algorithm, and not the backtracking part, is executed, which is often the case in practice. In fact, this is the motivation behind the BBB algorithm to replace the BU algorithm.

The most interesting aspect of the BBB algorithm is that it gives the best possible time complexity for both the worst and best cases considered above.

V. Comparison with Other Decisionmaking Techniques

There are two very widely used classification techniques: the linear classifier [4] and the 0-1 decision tree. We will show that by the proper choice of parameters, our fuzzy decision tree method of classification is more general than both of them in a bounded Euclidean space, although more execution time is required.

It is not surprising that a 0-1 decision tree can be obtained as a limiting case of a fuzzy decision tree [3]. A more interesting result is that any two-dimensional linear classifier can be "simulated" by a fuzzy decision tree with trivial comparisons alone.

Definition 6: A trivial comparison is an elementary predicate in which a simple variable is compared with a constant with respect to a constant scale, e.g., $GT_r(x,a)$[3] where r, a are constants.

Observation: A trivial comparison is a unary function mapping into the interval $[0,1]$.

Definition 7: The corresponding fuzzy decision tree T' of a 0-1 decision tree T is the tree formed by replacing in T: $x > y$ by $GT_r(x,y)$, $x = y$ by $EQ_r(x,y)$[3] and so on, where each "yes" decision branch has the decision value of the fuzzy predicate $p(r,x,y)$ directly, while each "no" branch has the value $\neg p(r,x,y)$.

Conversely, in this case, T is the corresponding 0-1 decision tree of the fuzzy decision tree T'. Similarly, we have corresponding branches, nodes, paths, roots, and subtrees.

Lemma 4.1: Given an arbitrary binary 0-1 decision tree T using an arbitrary input set of m parameters in a given space, a corresponding fuzzy decision tree T can be designed such that the probability that T' gives the same outcome decision as T does is 1 with respect to the random input parameters.

Proof: Consider the m input parameters $(p_1,\cdots,p_m)$ and T', each node i of which has the comparison predicate $GT_r(p_j,c_i)$ or $LT_r(p_j,c_i)$. Either 1) the input parameter p_j is exactly equal to the value c_i in at least one mode i, or 2) none of these pairs is exactly equal.

The probability of 1) is 0 since the space occupied by the separation hyperplanes is 0 compared with the sample space. If we can prove the lemma by assuming 2), we have proved the lemma. So let us assume 2).

Let

$$d = \min_i \{|p_j - c_i|\}$$

and l = maximum length of the paths (number of branches). Pick some number $a > \Phi^{-1}(0.5^{1/l})$, which is well defined since $0.5^{1/l} \in (0,1)$ and Φ is a monotonic function. Choose $r = (d/a)$. Then we claim that T' will give the same decision as T.

For any given input, consider the consequent decision path p' in T' corresponding to the path p followed in T. Then each node i' on p' corresponding to i on p must have the branch decision value $\Phi(|(p_j - c_i)/r|)$ because of the following.

1) If in T the comparison is $p_j > c_i$, then in T' the corresponding comparison is $GT_r(p_j,c_i)$, and the "yes" branch from node i' has the decision value $\Phi((p_j - c_i)/r)$ by definition of GT, while the "no" branch has value $1 - \Phi((p_j - c_i)/r) = \Phi((c_i - p_j)/r)$. If the "yes" branch in T is followed, meaning $p_j > c_i$, then the corresponding branch in T' will have value

$$\Phi((p_j - c_i)/r) = \Phi(|(p_j - c_i)/r|).$$

If the "no" branch in T is followed, meaning $p_j < c_i$, then the corresponding branch in T' will have value

$$\Phi((c_i - p_j)/r) = \Phi(|(p_j - c_i)/r|).$$

With either branch, we have $\Phi(|(p_j - c_i)/r|)$.

2) If in T the comparison is $p_j < c_i$, then in T' the corresponding comparison is $LT_r(p_j,c_i)$, and we arrive at the same $\Phi(|(p_j - c_i)/r|)$ decision value by an analogous argument.

So the decision value of the path p' is given by

$$V(p') = \bigwedge_{i \in p_,} \Phi(|(p_j - c_i)/r|) = \prod_{i \in p_,} \Phi(|(p_j - c_i)/r|)$$

$$\geq \prod_{i \in p_,} \Phi(d/r), \text{ by definition of } d \text{ since } \Phi \text{ is monotonically increasing,}$$

$$\geq \Phi(d/r)^l, \text{ since } |p'| \leq l \text{ and } \Phi(d/r) \leq 1,$$

$$= \Phi(a)^l > 0.5, \text{ by definition of } a \text{ since } \Phi \text{ is monotonically increasing.}$$

Now consider in T' any other path q' different from p'. Starting from the root, let i' be the node where q' starts to deviate from p' (i' may be the root). (See Fig. 3.)

We have already shown that the branch p' from node i' has value $\Phi(|(p_j - c_i)/r|)$. Since T' is a binary tree, the branch b_0' on q' from node i' must have value

$$v(b_0') = \neg\Phi(|(p_j - c_i)/r|) = 1 - \Phi(|(p_j - c_i)/r|),$$

but

$$\Phi(|(p_j - c_i)/r|) \geq \Phi(d/r) = \Phi(a) > .05^{1/l} \geq 0.5.$$

Therefore, $v(b_0') < 0.5$. Therefore,

$$V(q') = \bigwedge_{b' \in q'} v(b') < 0.5$$

since $b_0' \in q'$, and $\forall b'$, $v(b') \leq 1$.

From (1), we have $V(p') > 0.5$. Therefore, $V(q') < V(p')$, indicating that the path p' in T' will be chosen corresponding to the path p chosen in T.

The theorem follows immediately from the lemma.

Theorem 4: Given any binary 0-1 decision tree T which

[3] $GT_r(a,b) = LT_r(b,a) = \Phi((a - b)/r) = 1/\sqrt{2\pi} \int_{-\infty}^{(a-b)/r} \exp(-u^2/2) \cdot du$; $EQ_r(a,b) = \exp((a - b)^2/2r^2)$.

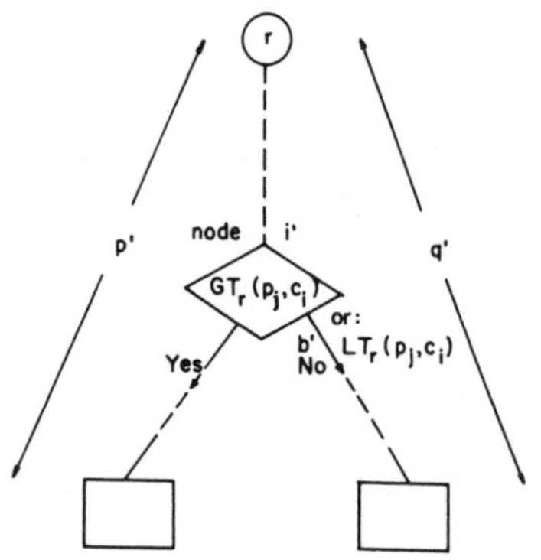

Fig. 3. Paths p' and q' in T'.

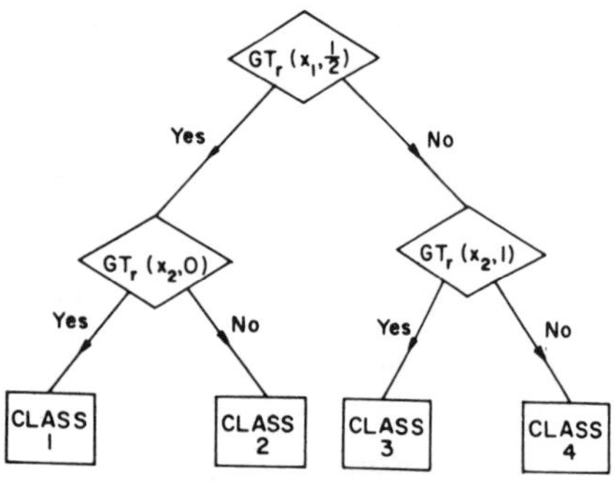

Fig. 4. Decision tree T of Lemma 5.2.

divides a bounded m-dimensional space into k subspaces, (i.e., classification into k classes with m parameters), we can always construct a corresponding fuzzy decision tree T' arbitrarily closely equivalent to T (by choice of the scale r). In other words, the classification hyperplanes induced by T' may be made as close to those induced by T as desired.

For the linear classifier-decision tree theorem, we need a few lemmas. The proofs are given elsewhere [3].

Lemma 5.1: For $|x - y| \leq 1$ and $r > 1$,

$$GT_r(x,y) = \frac{1}{2} + \frac{x - y}{2 - r} + O(r^{-3}),$$

and

$$\neg GT_r(x,y) = \frac{1}{2} - \frac{x - y}{2 - r} + O(r^{-3}).$$

Lemma 5.2: Let T be the decision tree in Fig. 4. Then r can be chosen such that $x_1 + x_2 > 1 \Leftrightarrow T$ decides Class 1, for $x_1,x_2 \in (0,1)$.[4]

Lemma 5.3: Let T be the decision tree in Fig. 5. Then r can be chosen such that for $x_1,x_2 \in (0,1)$, $x_1 - x_2 > 0 \Leftrightarrow T$ decides Class 1.

Theorem 5: For any general two-parameter two-class linear classifier, if $Ax_1 + Bx_2 > C$, then Class 1, and if $Ax_1 + Bx_2 < C$, then Class 2, where $C \geq 0$. For a bounded (open or closed) two-dimensional sample space S, there always exists an equivalent fuzzy decision tree T' using trivial comparisons alone. (Equivalent in the sense that T' always gives exactly the same classification as the linear classifier.)

[4] Alternatively we may use a simpler tree but with more complex nodes.

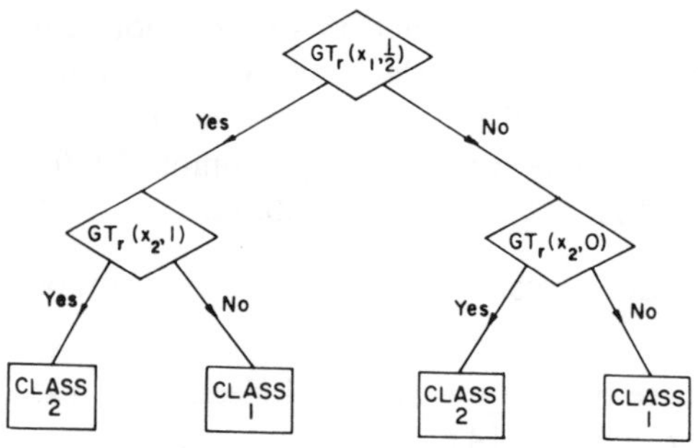

Fig. 5. Decision tree T of Lemma 5.3.

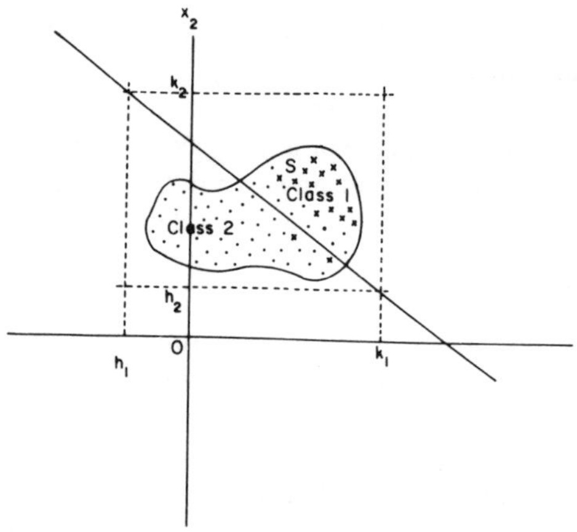

Fig. 6. Linear classifier.

Proof: Consider the slope of the classification line $Ax_1 + Bx_2 = C$. There are three cases.

Case I. Slope negative ($AB > 0$): Assume without loss of generality that $A > 0$, $B > 0$. It is always possible to find two points (h_1,k_2), (k_1,h_2) on the line $Ax_1 + Bx_2 = C$ such that $S \subseteq (h_1,k_1) \times (h_2,k_2)$, $h_1 < k_1$, $h_2 < k_2$ and $k_1 > 0$, $k_2 > 0$, as shown in Fig. 6. Let $y_1 = (x_1 - h_1)/(k_1 - h_1)$, $y_2 = (x_2 - h_2)/(k_2 - h_2)$, remembering $k_1 > h_1$, $k_2 > h_2$. We first want to show that $Ax_1 + Bx_2 > C$ for $h_1 < x_1 < k_1$, $k_2 < x_2 < k_2$ (in particular, for $(x_1,x_2) \in S$)

$$\Leftrightarrow y_1 + y_2 > 1, \qquad \text{for } 0 < y_1 < 1,\ 0 < y_2 < 1.$$

Case I.I. $C > 0$: By construction,

$$Ah_1 + Bk_2 = C \qquad Ak_1 + Bh_2 = C.$$

Therefore,

$$(k_1k_2 - h_1h_2)A = (k_2 - h_2)C$$

$$(k_1k_2 - h_1h_2)B = (k_1 - h_1)C$$

Therefore, for $h_1 < x_1 < k_1$, $h_2 < x_2 < k_2$,

$$Ax_1 + Bx_2 > C$$

$$\Leftrightarrow (k_1k_2 - h_1h_2)Ax_1 + (k_1k_2 - h_1h_2)Bx_2 > (k_1k_2 - h_1h_2)C$$

assuming without loss of generality that $k_1k_2 - h_1h_2 > 0$.

(If $k_1k_2 - h_1h_2 < 0$, then we obtain $<$ instead of $>$, and all we have to do is to exchange the outcome decisions Class 1 and Class 2 for one another in the linear classifier. By (2), $k_1k_2 - h_1h_2 \neq 0$ since $k_2 > h_2$ and $C > 0$).

$$\Leftrightarrow (k_2 - h_2)Cx_1 + (k_1 - h_1)Cx_2 > (k_1k_2 - h_1h_2)C$$

$$\Leftrightarrow (k_2 - h_2)x_1 + (k_1 - h_1)x_2 > k_1k_2 - h_1h_2$$

for $h_1 < x_1 < k_1$, $h_2 < x_2 < k_2$, since $C > 0$,

where $k_1k_2 - h_1h_2 = (k_1 - h_1)(k_2 - h_2) + h_1(k_2 - h_2) + h_2(k_1 - h_1)$

$$\Leftrightarrow (k_2 - h_2)x_1 + (k_1 - h_1)x_2 > (k_1 - h_1)(k_2 - h_2) + (k_2 - h_2)h_1 + (k_1 - h_1)h_2$$

for $0 < x_1 - h_1 < k_1 - h_1$, $0 < x_2 - h_2 < k_2 - h_2$

$$\Leftrightarrow (k_2 - h_2)(x_1 - h_1) + (k_1 - h_1)(x_2 - h_2) > (k_1 - h_1)(k_2 - h_2)$$

$$\Leftrightarrow (x_1 - h_1)/(k_1 - h_1) + (x_2 - h_2)/(k_2 - h_2) > 1$$

for $0 < (x_1 - h_1)/(k_1 - h_1) < 1$, $0 < (x_2 - h_2)/(k_2 - h_2) < 1$,

since $k_1 > h_1$, $k_2 > h_2$

$$\Leftrightarrow y_1 + y_2 > 1 \text{ for } 0 < y_1 < 1,\ 0 < y_2 < 1.$$

Case I.II. $C = 0$:

$$Ax_1 + Bx_2 > C \text{ for } h_1 < x_1 < k_1,\ h_2 < x_2 < k_2$$

$$\Leftrightarrow x_1 + Dx_2 > 0, \text{ where } D = \frac{B}{A} > 0,$$

where by construction, $h_1 + Dk_2 = 0$ and $k_1 + Dh_2 = 0$, i.e., $D = -h_1/k_2 = -k_1/h_2$, i.e., $k_1k_2 = h_1h_2$,

$$\Leftrightarrow (k_2 - h_2)x_1 + (k_2 - h_2)Dx_2 > 0$$

$$\Leftrightarrow (k_2 - h_2)x_1 + (k_1 - h_1)x_2 > 0 = k_1k_2 - h_1h_2$$

$$\Leftrightarrow (k_2 - h_2)x_1 + (k_1 - h_1)x_2 > (k_1 - h_1)(k_2 - h_2) + (k_2 - h_2)h_1 + (k_1 - h_1)h_2$$

$$\Leftrightarrow y_1 + y_2 > 1 \text{ for } 0 < y_1 < 1,\ 0 < y_2 < 1$$

(See Case I.I.)

Secondly, by Lemma 2, $y_1 + y_2 > 1$ for $0 < y_1 < 1$, $0 < y_2 < 1 \Leftrightarrow T$ decides Class 1 (with x_1,x_2 replaced by y_1,y_2) in Fig. 4. However,

$$GT_r(y_1,) = \Phi((y_1,-)/r)$$
$$= \Phi(((x_1 - h_1)/(k_1 - h_1) -)/r)$$
$$= \Phi((x_1 - (k_1 + h_1)/2)/(k_1 - h_1)r)$$
$$= GT_{(k-h)r}(x_1,(k_1 + h_1)/2);$$

and

$$GT_r(y_2,0) = GT_{(k-h)r}(x_2,h_2)$$

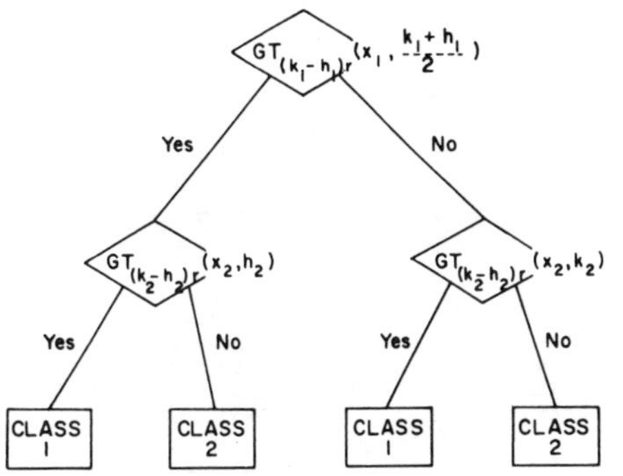

Fig. 7. Fuzzy decision tree T'.

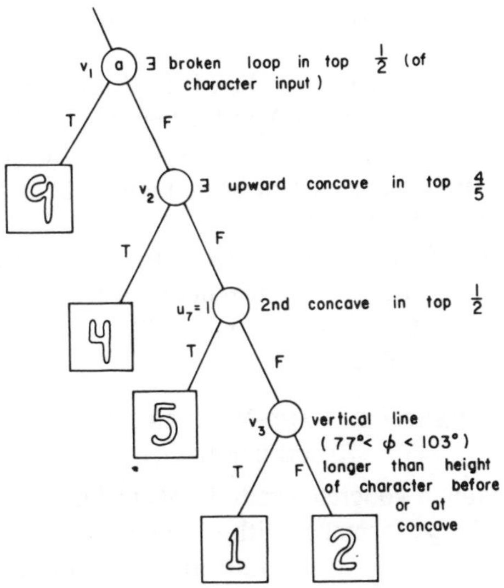

Fig. 8. Subtree of hand-written numeral decision tree.

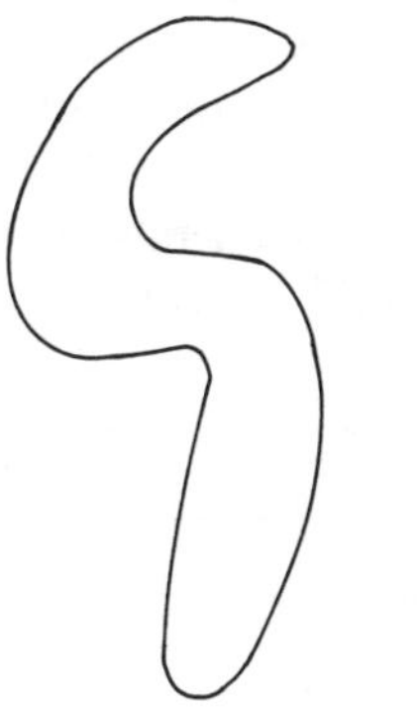

Fig. 9. Input for example discussed in text.

in a similar fashion; and

$$GT_r(y_2,1) = GT_{(k-h)r}(x_2,k_2).$$

Therefore, we have

$$Ax_1 + Bx_2 > C, \quad \text{for } h_1 < x_1 < k_1,\ h_2 < x_2 < k_2$$

$\Leftrightarrow T'$ decides Class 1 in Fig. 7.

Since T' involves only trivial comparisons, the theorem is justified.

Case II. Slope positive ($AB < 0$): Assume without loss of generality that $A > 0$, $E < 0$. (If $A < 0$, $B > 0$, change

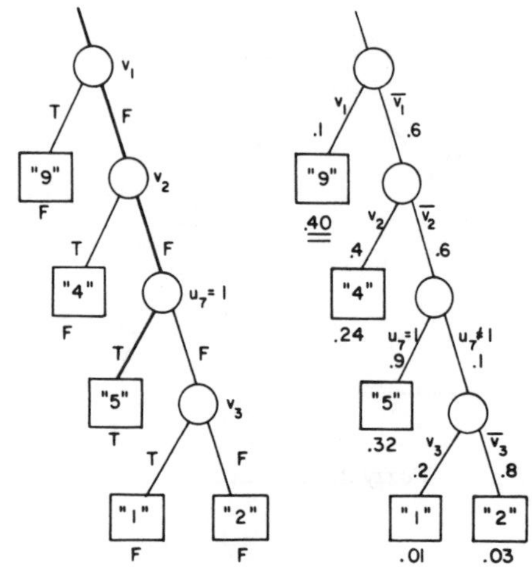

Fig. 10. Decision values for various numerals.

variables $x_1 \leftarrow x_2$, $x_2 \leftarrow x_1$.) Here it is always possible to find two points (h_1,h_2), (k_1,k_2) on the line $Ax_1 + Bx_2 = C$ such that $S \subseteq (h_1,k_1) \times (h_2,k_2)$. The rest of the proof is very similar to Case I, except with Lemma 3 in lieu of Lemma 2, and is hence omitted.

Case III. Slope 0 *or* ∞ ($A = 0$ *or* $B = 0$)*:* The problem becomes trivial since it reduces to the one-dimensional classifier ($x_1 > A'$ or $x_2 > B'$). The one-node decision tree will suffice.

VI. Example in Hand-Written Numeral Recognition

We will show a concrete example where fuzzy decisions do improve the performance with our favorite prob model.

Consider the hand-written numeral recognition[5] paper by Pavlidis and Ali [9]. In the decision tree in Fig. 4(a) in that paper, we have the following subtree as shown in Fig. 8. Suppose the input picture to be recognized looks like Fig. 9, and we have arrived at node a after some obvious decisions. Consider the most confusing part of the decision, the subtree rooted at a, by which we are to distinguish among the numerals 9, 4, 5, 1, and 2 (see Fig. 10). With 0–1 decisions, we will have the following decision values:

Predicate	Value
v_1	F
v_2	F
$u_7 = 1$	T

and will come up with the numeral 5. With fuzzy decisions, however, we will obtain values like the following.

[5] Other approaches by fuzzy logic to the same problem are possible. See [10], for instance.

Predicate	Value
v_1	0.4
v_2	0.4
$u_7 = 1$	0.9
v_3	0.2

Predicate	Value
$\bar{v}_1$	0.6
$\bar{v}_2$	0.6
$u_7 \neq 1$	0.1
$\bar{v}_3$	0.8

(These values may be justified intuitively by looking at the input picture; or more rigorously, by the method described in [3, ch. 2]). We will have the following decision values.

Numeral	Decision Value	(Max-Min)	(Prob)
9	0.4	(= 0.4)	(= 0.40)
4	$0.6 \wedge 0.4$	(= 0.4)	(= 0.24)
5	$0.6 \wedge 0.6 \wedge 0.9$	(= 0.6)	(= 0.32)
1	$0.6 \wedge 0.6 \wedge 0.1 \wedge 0.2$	(= 0.1)	(= 0.01)
2	$0.6 \wedge 0.6 \wedge 0.1 \wedge 0.8$	(= 0.1)	(= 0.03)

With the max-min model where $\wedge$ is interpreted as minimum, we will come up with the numeral 5 as in the 0–1 decision case. With the prob model, we will come up with the numeral 9 instead, since 0.40 is the best value among the five. Referring back to Fig. 10, obviously 9 is a better choice than 5.

VII. Conclusions

We have presented an efficient algorithm for fuzzy decision trees. We then have shown the relation between such trees and linear classifiers and presented an example showing the advantages of the former over 0–1 decision trees.

References

[1] A. V. Aho, J. E. Hopcroft, and J. D. Ullman, *The Design and Analysis of Computer Algorithms*. Reading, MA: Addison-Wesley, 1974.
[2] J. G. Brown, "A note on fuzzy sets," *Info. & Control*, vol. 18, pp. 32–39, 1971.
[3] R. L. P. Chang, "Application of fuzzy decision techniques to pattern recognition and curve fitting," Ph.D. Thesis, Dept. of EECS, Princeton Univ., 1976.
[4] R. O. Duda and P. E. Hart, *Pattern Classification and Scene Analysis*. New York: Wiley, 1973.
[5] F. Harary, *Graph Theory*. Reading, MA: Addison-Wesley, 1971.
[6] D. E. Knuth, *The Art of Computer Programming*, vol. 1. Reading, MA: Addison-Wesley, 1969.
[7] ——, "Optimum binary search trees," *Acta Informatica*, vol. 1, pp. 14–25, 1971.
[8] E. L. Lawler and D. E. Wood, "Branch-and-bound methods: A survey," *Operations Research*, vol. 14, no. 4, pp. 699–719, 1966.
[9] T. Pavlidis and F. Ali, "Computer recognition of handwritten numerals by polygonal approximations," *IEEE Trans. Systems, Man, Cybern.*, vol. SMC-5, pp. 610–614, 1975.
[10] P. Siy and C. S. Chen, "Fuzzy logic approach to handwritten character recognition problem," *Proc. IEEE Conf. Systems, Man, Cybern.*, Anaheim, Calif., 1971, pp. 113–117.
[11] L. A. Zadeh, "Outline of a new approach to the analysis of complex systems and decision processes," *IEEE Trans. Systems, Man, Cybern.*, vol. SMC-3, pp. 28–44, 1973.
[12] L. A. Zadeh, "A fuzzy-algorithmic approach to the definition of complex or imprecise concepts," Memorandum ERL-M474, Electronics Research Lab., College of Eng., U.C., Berkeley, 1974.

Fuzzy Tree Automata and Syntactic Pattern Recognition

EDWARD T. LEE

Abstract—An approach of representing patterns by trees and processing these trees by fuzzy tree automata is described. Fuzzy tree automata are defined and investigated. The results include that the class of fuzzy root-to-frontier recognizable Σ-trees is closed under intersection, union, and complementation. Thus, the class of fuzzy root-to-frontier recognizable Σ-trees forms a Boolean algebra. Fuzzy tree automata are applied to processing fuzzy tree representation of patterns based on syntactic pattern recognition. The grade of acceptance is defined and investigated.

Quantitative measures of "approximate isosceles triangle," "approximate elongated isosceles triangle," "approximate rectangle," and "approximate cross" are defined and used in the illustrative examples of this approach. By using these quantitative measures, a house, a house with high roof, and a church are also presented as illustrative examples.

In addition, three fuzzy tree automata are constructed which have the capability of processing the fuzzy tree representations of "fuzzy houses," "houses with high roofs," and "fuzzy churches," respectively. The results may have useful applications in pattern recognition, image processing, artificial intelligence, pattern database design and processing, image science, and pictorial information systems.

Index Terms—Fuzzy tree automata, grade of acceptance, syntactic pattern recognition.

I. Introduction

The pioneering work in the area of syntactic pattern recognition by Fu [1]-[4] and Pavlidis [5] has had a profound influence on the recent development of pattern recognition as well as artificial intelligence [6] and image science [7]. The syntactic approach is a new and powerful approach to pattern recognition.

During the past several years, linguisitic concepts and techniques have attracted growing attention as promising avenues of approach to problems in pattern recognition and image processing [1]-[11].

Linguistic techniques in pattern recognition serve the purpose of exploiting the structure or underlying relationships in a two-dimensional pattern. If such a structure exists, then a complex pattern can be described in terms of simpler pattern, and the problem of pattern recognition becomes similar to that of phrase recognition in a language.

The precision of formal languages contrasts rather sharply with the imprecision of patterns encountered in typical pattern recognition problems. To reduce the gap between them, it is natural to introduce randomness or fuzziness into the structure of formal languages. This leads to the concepts of stochastic languages [12] and fuzzy languages [13].

Language representation by strings was generalized to pattern description by trees in [14]. In this correspondence the concepts of fuzzy languages and tree systems are applied to pattern recognition through the use of fuzzy tree automata. Fuzzy root-to-frontier tree automata are defined and investigated in the following section. Detailed experiments of this approach and the relationships between fuzzy tree automata and fuzzy tree grammars will be presented in subsequent papers.

Manuscript received August 20, 1981; revised January 25, 1982.

The author is with the Department of Mathematical Sciences, Memphis State University, Memphis, TN 38152.

II. Fuzzy Root-to-Frontier Tree Automata

Definition 1: A fuzzy root-to-frontier tree automaton (FRFTA) over an alphabet Σ is a quintuple $(K, \Sigma, \delta, q_0, F)$, where K is a finite nonempty set of states, Σ is a finite input alphabet, $q_0 \in K$ is the initial state, and $F \subset K$ is a set of final states which may be a fuzzy set over K. The symbol δ denotes a fuzzy mapping from $K \times \Sigma$ to $K \times K$. This means that each pair (q_i, a) in $K \times \Sigma$ defines a pair of fuzzy "next states" in $K \times K$ which is characterized by the conditional membership functions $\mu_1(q_j|q_i, a)$ and $\mu_2(q_j|q_i, a)$ with arguments $q_j \in K$, $q_i \in K$ and $a \in \Sigma$.

The formation of the state tree is described inductively as follows.

1) The root of the state tree is labeled q_0.

2) Given that any node of the state tree is labeled Q which in general is a fuzzy set in K defined by a membership function $\mu(q_i)$ and the corresponding node of the input is labeled a, then the two successor nodes of the state tree are labeled with the pair $\langle Q_1, Q_2 \rangle$ whose membership function is given by

$$\mu_1(q_j) = \bigvee_{q_i} (\mu(q_i) \wedge \mu_1(q_j|q_i, a)) \tag{1}$$

$$\mu_2(q_j) = \bigvee_{q_i} (\mu(q_i) \wedge \mu_2(q_j|q_i, a)) \tag{2}$$

where $\vee_{q_i}$ denotes the supremum over $q_i \in K$. Note that when Q is a singleton $\{q_i\}$, the membership functions for next state reduces to $\mu_1(q_j|q_i, a)$ and $\mu_2(q_j|q_i, a)$.

The Grade of Acceptance

In what follows, fuzzy root-to-frontier tree automata will be used primarily as recognizers. For this purpose, we define the *grade of acceptance* of a Σ-tree by a fuzzy root-to-frontier tree automaton. The root of a tree is the top node of the tree and the phrase "frontier of the tree" will be used ambiguously to mean either the set of nodes at the bottom of the tree (the end opposite the root) or the string of symbols labeling the frontier nodes. For a tree t, $fr(t)$ will have the latter meaning.

Definition 2: Let $Q_1, Q_2, \cdots, Q_m$ denote the fuzzy sets of states labeling the frontier nodes of a Σ-tree, t. Let F be a designated set of final states, which may be a fuzzy subset of K. Then $\mu_A(t)$, the *grade of acceptance* of t by the FRFTA A, is given by the minimal grade in the set of maximal grade in $F \cap Q_1, F \cap Q_2, \cdots, F \cap Q_m$, the intersections of F and Q_1, F and $Q_2, \cdots, F$ and Q_m. More specifically,

$$\mu_A(t) = \min (\max_{q_j} \mu_{F \cap Q_1}(q_j), \max_{q_j} \mu_{F \cap Q_2}(q_j), \cdots, \max_{q_j} \mu_{F \cap Q_m}(q_j)) \tag{3}$$

Reprinted from *IEEE Trans. Pattern Anal. Machine Intell.*, vol. PAMI-4, no. 4, pp. 445-449, July 1982.

or

$$\mu_A(t) = \left(\bigvee_{q_j} (\mu_F(q_j) \wedge \mu_{Q_1}(q_j)) \right) \wedge \left(\bigvee_{q_j} (\mu_F(q_j) \wedge \mu_{Q_2}(q_j)) \right)$$
$$\wedge \cdots \wedge \left(\bigvee_{q_j} (\mu_F(q_j) \wedge \mu_{Q_m}(q_j)) \right) \tag{4}$$

where the supremum is taken over all states in K.

Definition 3: Let $A = (K, \Sigma, \delta, q_0, F)$ and $A' = (K', \Sigma, \delta', q_0', F')$ be two fuzzy root-to-frontier tree automata. The direct product $A \times A'$ is the fuzzy root-to-frontier tree automaton $A \times A' = (K \times K', \Sigma, \delta \times \delta', (q_0, q_0'), F \times F')$, where $K \times K'$ and $F \times F'$ are the Cartesian products of sets, (q_0, q_0') is the ordered pair of q_0 and q_0', and fuzzy mapping $\delta \times \delta'$, which is characterized by a conditional membership function, is defined by the formula

$$\mu_1((q_j, q_j')|(q_i, q_i'), a) = (\mu_1(q_j|q_i, a), \mu_1'(q_j|q_i, a)) \tag{5}$$

$$\mu_2((q_j, q_j')|(q_i, q_i'), a) = (\mu_2(q_j|q_i, a), \mu_2'(q_j|q_i, a)) \tag{6}$$

for all

$$q_j \in K, \quad q_i \in K, \quad q_j' \in K, \quad q_i' \in K \quad \text{and} \quad a \in \Sigma.$$

The fuzzy set of Σ-trees accepted by an FRFTA A is denoted $T(A)$, and a fuzzy set U of Σ-trees is *recognizable* if $U = T(A)$ for some fuzzy root-to-frontier automaton A.

Theorem 1: If A and A' are fuzzy root-to-frontier automata, then $T(A \times A') = T(A) \cap T(A')$, that is, $\mu_{A \times A'}(t) = \min(\mu_A(t), \mu_{A'}(t))$ t in T_Σ.

Corollary 1: The class of fuzzy root-to-frontier recognizable Σ-trees is closed under intersection.

As is very familiar, a direct product construction identical to that found in [15], [19], and [20] yields the following.

Theorem 2: The class of fuzzy root-to-frontier recognizable Σ-trees is closed under union.

Theorem 3: The class of fuzzy root-to-frontier recognizable Σ-trees is closed under complementation.

Theorem 4: The class of fuzzy root-to-frontier recognizable Σ-trees forms a Boolean algebra.

The proofs of these theorems may be obtained from the author.

A fuzzy tree automaton is just a fuzzy automaton [15] in which labeled trees replace strings as inputs. For illustrative purposes we only consider binary trees.

Taking the informal concept of a fuzzy finite automaton [15], we are led to the following definition of a generalized fuzzy finite automaton operating on fuzzy binary trees.

A fuzzy root-to-frontier tree automaton (FRFTA) consists of a finite set S of states; a fuzzy transition function

$$M: \Sigma \times S \rightarrow S \times S \tag{7}$$

with fuzzy transition membership functions m_L and m_R.

$$M[(a, f_a), S_i] = \langle (S_L, f_a \wedge m_{LS_ia}), (S_R, f_a \wedge m_{RS_ia}) \rangle \tag{8}$$

with a in Σ, and S_i, S_L, S_R in S. The initial state is denoted by S_o and a set of final states is denoted by F, where F is a subset of S.

The formation of the fuzzy state tree is described inductively as follows.

1) The root of the fuzzy state tree is labeled S_0.

2) Given that any node of the fuzzy state tree is labeled (S_i, m_i), and the corresponding node of the input is labeled (a, f_a), then the two successor nodes of the fuzzy state tree are labeled with the pair

$$M[(a, f_a), (S_i, m_i)]$$
$$= \langle (S_L, f_a \wedge m_i \wedge m_{LS_ia}), (S_R, f_a \wedge m_i \wedge m_{RS_ia}) \rangle. \tag{9}$$

The fuzzy binary input tree is accepted if every state labeling the frontier of the fuzzy state tree is a final state.

The grade of acceptance of the fuzzy binary input tree is equal to the minimum of the memberships of all the states labeling the frontier of the fuzzy state tree.

III. APPLICATION OF FUZZY TREE AUTOMATA TO SYNTACTIC PATTERN RECOGNITION

Having presented fuzzy tree automata, we turn to the application of these types of automata to syntactic pattern recognition. This approach is illustrated by the following examples.

A House: For illustration purposes, let us define a simplified version of a "house" to be an isosceles triangle vertically concatenated to a rectangle. Thus, a house may be represented by a tree as

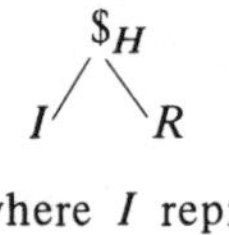

$$\overset{\$_H}{\underset{I \quad\quad R}{\diagup \quad \diagdown}} \tag{10}$$

where I represents an isosceles triangle, R represents a rectangle, and the syntactic relation between I and R is vertical concatenation.

By using the concept of a fuzzy language [13], an "approximate house" may be defined as an "approximate isosceles triangle" vertically concatenated to an "approximate rectangle." Therefore, the tree representation of a "fuzzy house" is denoted by

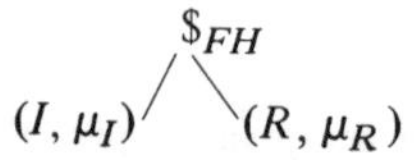

$$\overset{\$_{FH}}{\underset{(I, \mu_I) \quad\quad (R, \mu_R)}{\diagup \quad \diagdown}} \tag{11}$$

where μ_I and μ_R are grades of membership of "approximate isosceles triangle" and "approximate rectangle," respectively.

For a triangle $\triangle ABC$ with angles B and C as the base angles, a quantitative measure of the similarity of this triangle to isosceles triangles may be defined as

$$\mu_I(\triangle ABC) = 1 - \frac{|B - C|}{90^\circ}. \tag{12}$$

Example 1: For $A = 30^\circ$, $B = 90^\circ$, and $C = 60^\circ$ as shown in Fig. 1(b)

$$\mu_I(\triangle ABC) = \tfrac{2}{3}.$$

For $A' = 45^\circ$, $B' = 90^\circ$, and $C' = 45^\circ$ as shown in Fig. 1(c)

$$\mu_I(\triangle A'B'C') = \tfrac{1}{2}.$$

In [21] a quantitative measure of the similarity of a quadrangle with angles A, B, C, and D to rectangles was defined as

$$\mu_R = 1 - \frac{|A - 90^\circ| + |B - 90^\circ| + |C - 90^\circ| + |D - 90^\circ|}{360^\circ}. \tag{13}$$

Example 2: Generating a fuzzy root-to-frontier tree automaton which has the capability of processing the fuzzy tree representation of "fuzzy houses" denoted as $TR(\$_{FH})$ as shown in (11).

The generated fuzzy tree automaton is constructed as follows. The set of states is

$$S = \{S_0, S_1, S_2, S_3, S_4, S_5, S_6\}.$$

The fuzzy mapping $M: \Sigma \times S \rightarrow S \times S$ is defined as follows:

$$M[\$_{FH}, S_0] = \langle S_1, S_2 \rangle$$

$$M[(I, \mu_I), S_1] = \langle (S_3, \mu_I), (S_4, \mu_I) \rangle$$

$$M[(R, \mu_R), S_2] = \langle (S_5, \mu_R), (S_6, \mu_R) \rangle.$$

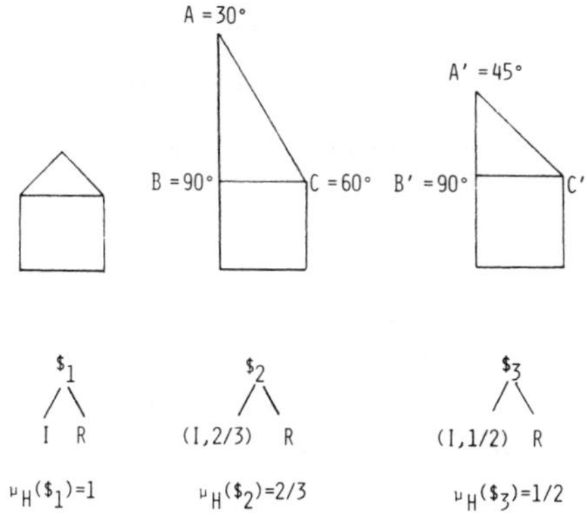

(a) (b) (c)

Fig. 1. The grade of membership of "approximate houses."

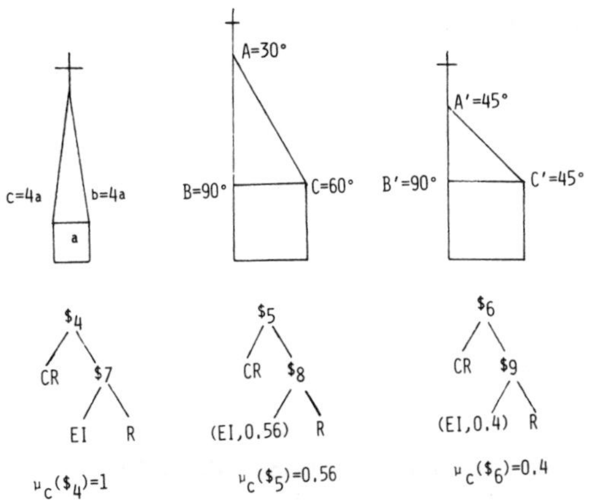

(a) (b) (c)

Fig. 2. The grade of membership of "approximate churches."

The set of final states is

$$F = \{S_3, S_4, S_5, S_6\}.$$

Example 3: The grades of membership of "approximate houses" for the three figures shown in Fig. 1 are

$$\mu_H(\$_1) = 1$$
$$\mu_H(\$_2) = \tfrac{2}{3}$$
$$\mu_H(\$_3) = \tfrac{1}{2}.$$

A House with High Roof: A simplified version of "a house with high roof" may be defined as "an elongated isosceles triangle" vertically concatenated to a rectangle.

For a triangle ΔABC with sides a, b, c and angles A, B, C, where B and C are the base angles, a quantitative measure of the similarity of this triangle to "elongated isosceles triangles" may be defined as

$$\mu_{EI}(\Delta ABC) = \frac{\mu_I(\Delta ABC) + \mu_E(\Delta ABC)}{2} \tag{14}$$

where

$$\mu_E(\Delta ABC) = \frac{\mu_{ab}(a, b) + \mu_{ac}(a, c)}{2} \tag{15}$$

and

$$\begin{aligned} \mu_{ab}(a, b) &= 1 && \text{if } b \geqslant 4a \\ &= b/4a && \text{if } b \leqslant 4a \end{aligned} \tag{16}$$

$$\begin{aligned} \mu_{ac}(a, c) &= 1 && \text{if } c \geqslant 4a \\ &= c/4a && \text{if } c \leqslant 4a. \end{aligned} \tag{17}$$

Depending on its prospective application, the constant used in defining μ_{EI}, μ_E, μ_{ab}, and μ_{ac} may take on different values.

The fuzzy tree representation of "a house with high roof" is denoted as

$$\begin{array}{ccc} & \$_{HHR} & \\ & / \quad \backslash & \\ (EI, \mu_{EI}) & & (R, \mu_R). \end{array} \tag{18}$$

Example 4: Generating a fuzzy root-to-frontier tree automaton which has the capability of processing the fuzzy tree representation of "houses with high roofs" denoted as $TR(\$_{HHR})$ as shown in (18).

The generated fuzzy tree automaton is constructed as follows. The set of states is

$$S = \{S_0, S_1, S_2, S_3, S_4, S_5, S_6\}.$$

The fuzzy mapping M: $\Sigma \times S \rightarrow S \times S$ is defined as follows:

$$M[\$_{HHR}, S_0] = \langle S_1, S_2 \rangle$$
$$M[(EI, \mu_{EI}), S_1] = \langle (S_3, \mu_{EI}), (S_4, \mu_{EI}) \rangle$$
$$M[(R, \mu_R), S_2] = \langle (S_5, \mu_R), (S_6, \mu_R) \rangle.$$

The set of final states is

$$F = \{S_3, S_4, S_5, S_6\}.$$

A Church: A simplified version of "a church" may be defined as a cross vertically cancatenated to "a house with high roof." The fuzzy tree representation of "a fuzzy church" is denoted as

$$\begin{array}{ccccc} & \$_C & & & \\ & / \quad \backslash & & & \\ (CR, \mu_{CR}) & & \$_{HHR} & & \\ & & / \quad \backslash & & \\ & (EI, \mu_{EI}) & & (R, \mu_R) & \end{array} \tag{19}$$

where CR represents a cross with intersection angles A and B and

$$\mu_{CR} = \frac{\min(A, B)}{90^\circ}. \tag{20}$$

Depending on its prospective application, μ_{CR} may take on different values.

Example 5: Generating a fuzzy root-to-frontier tree automaton which has the capability of processing the fuzzy tree representation of "fuzzy churches" denoted as $TR(\$_C)$ as shown in (19).

The generated fuzzy tree automaton is constructed as follows. The set of states is

$$S = \{S_0, S_1, S_2, S_3, S_4, S_5, S_6, S_7, S_8, S_9, S_{10}\}.$$

The fuzzy mapping M: $\Sigma \times S \rightarrow S \times S$ is defined as follows:

$$M[\$_C, S_0] = \langle S_1, S_2 \rangle$$
$$M[(CR, \mu_{CR}), S_1] = \langle (S_3, \mu_{CR}), (S_4, \mu_{CR}) \rangle$$
$$M[\$_{HHR}, S_2] = \langle S_5, S_6 \rangle$$
$$M[(EI, \mu_{EI}), S_5] = \langle (S_7, \mu_{EI}), (S_8, \mu_{EI}) \rangle$$
$$M[(R, \mu_R), S_6] = \langle (S_9, \mu_R), (S_{10}, \mu_R) \rangle.$$

The set of final states is

$$F = \{S_3, S_4, S_7, S_8, S_9, S_{10}\}.$$

Example 6: For Fig. 2(a)

$$\mu_{EI} = 1.$$

Hence, the tree representation of this figure is

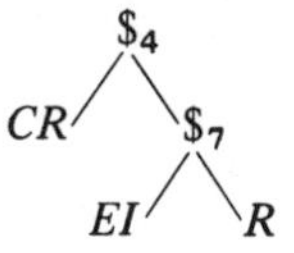

$$
\begin{array}{c}
\$_4 \\
CR \diagup \$_7 \\
 EI \diagup R
\end{array}
\qquad (21)
$$

and $\mu_C(\$_4) = 1$.
    For Fig. 2(b)

$$\mu_{EI} = 0.56.$$

Thus, the fuzzy tree representation of Fig. 2(b) is

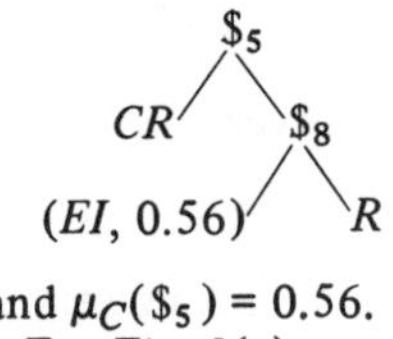

$$
\begin{array}{c}
\$_5 \\
CR \diagup \$_8 \\
(EI, 0.56) \diagup R
\end{array}
\qquad (22)
$$

and $\mu_C(\$_5) = 0.56$.
    For Fig. 2(c)

$$\mu_{EI} = 0.4.$$

Therefore, the fuzzy tree representation of Fig. 2(c) is

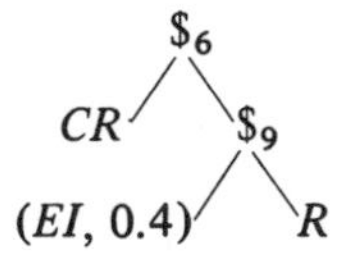

$$
\begin{array}{c}
\$_6 \\
CR \diagup \$_9 \\
(EI, 0.4) \diagup R
\end{array}
\qquad (23)
$$

and $\mu_C(\$_6) = 0.4$.

IV. Conclusion

The foregoing analysis has shown that the concept of a fuzzy tree automaton can be applied to syntactic pattern description and recognition. In addition, fuzzy tree automata may also be applied to processing chromosomes [22]–[24], leukocytes [25], or medical radiographs [26]. Much further work in these areas remains to be done. Nevertheless, even at this early stage of the development of this subject, this approach offers what appears to be a fertile field for further study. The results obtained in this correspondence may have useful applications in syntactic pattern recognition, image processing, shape-oriented image database study [27]–[29], pattern storage and retrieval, artificial intelligence, pattern database design and processing [30]–[31], image science, and pictorial information systems [32].

References

[1] K. S. Fu, *Syntactic Methods in Pattern Recognition.* New York: Academic, 1974.

[2] K. S. Fu, Ed., *Syntactic Pattern Recognition: Applications.* New York: Springer-Verlag, 1976.

[3] ——, *Digital Pattern Recognition.* New York: Springer-Verlag, 1975.

[4] K. S. Fu and S. K. Chang, Eds., *Pictorial Information Systems.* New York: Springer-Verlag, 1979.

[5] T. Pavlidis, *Structural Pattern Recognition.* New York: Springer-Verlag, 1977.

[6] C. H. Chen, Ed., *Pattern Recognition and Artificial Intelligence.* New York: Academic, 1976.

[7] *Proc. 1978 Pattern Recognition and Image Process. Conf.*, Chicago, IL, May 31–June 2, 1978.

[8] A. Rosenfeld and A. C. Kak, *Digital Picture Processing.* New York: Academic, 1976.

[9] A. Rosenfeld, "Picture processing: 1975," Univ. of Maryland, College Park, TR-433, Jan. 1976.

[10] A. Rosenfeld, Ed., *Digital Picture Analysis.* New York: Springer-Verlag, 1976.

[11] R. A. Kirsch, "Computer interpretation of English text and picture patterns," *IEEE Trans. Comput.*, vol. 13, pp. 363–376, Aug. 1964.

[12] K. S. Fu, "Stochastic automata, stochastic languages and pattern recognition," *J. Cybern.*, vol. 1, no. 3, pp. 31–49, 1971.

[13] E. T. Lee and L. A. Zadeh, "Note on fuzzy languages," *Inform. Sci.*, vol. 1, pp. 421–434, 1969.

[14] K. S. Fu and B. K. Bhargava, "Tree systems for syntactic pattern recognition," *IEEE Trans. Comput.*, vol. C-22, pp. 1087–1099, Dec. 1973.

[15] E. T. Lee, "Fuzzy languages and their relation to automata," Ph.D. dissertation, Univ. of California, Berkeley, Mar. 1972.

[16] L. A. Zadeh, "Fuzzy sets," *Inform. Contr.*, vol. 8, pp. 338–353, June 1965.

[17] L. A. Zadeh *et al.*, Eds., *Fuzzy Sets and Their Applications to Cognitive and Decision Processes.* New York: Academic, 1975.

[18] S. S. L. Chang and L. A. Zadeh, "On fuzzy mapping and control," *IEEE Trans. Syst., Man, Cybern.*, vol. SMC-2, pp. 30–34, 1972.

[19] M. O. Rabin and D. Scott, "Finite automata and their decision problems," *IBM J. Res. Develop.*, vol. 3, pp. 114–125, Apr. 1959.

[20] J. W. Thatcher, "There's a lot more to finite automata theory than you would have thought," in *Proc. Annu. Princeton Conf. on Inform. Sci. and Syst.*, 1970, pp. 263–270.

[21] E. T. Lee, "Proximity measures for the classification of geometric figures," *J. Cybern.*, vol. 2, pp. 43–59, 1972.

[22] ——, "The shape-oriented dissimilarity of polygons and its application to the classification of chromosome images," *Pattern Recognition*, vol. 6, pp. 47–60, 1974.

[23] ——, "Shape-oriented chromosome classification," *IEEE Trans. Syst., Man, Cybern.*, vol. SMC-5, pp. 629–632, 1975.

[24] ——, "Algorithms for finding most dissimilar images with possible applications to chromosome classification," *Bull. Math. Biol.*, vol. 38, pp. 505–516, 1976.

[25] ——, "Shape-oriented classification storage and retrieval of leukocytes," in *Proc. Int. Joint Conf. on Pattern Recognition*, Nov. 8–11, 1976.

[26] J. Sklansky, "Boundary detection in medical radiographs," Univ. of California, Irvine, TP-75-10, Nov. 1975.

[27] E. T. Lee, "A shape-oriented image data base," in *Proc. Symp. on Current Problems in Image Sci.*, sponsored by Office of Naval Res., Nov. 10–12, 1976.

[28] ——, "Similarity measures and their relation to fuzzy query languages," *Policy Anal. Inform. Syst.*, vol. 1, no. 1, pp. 127–152, 1977.

[29] E. T. Lee, "A similarity directed picture database," *Policy Anal. Inform. Syst.*, vol. 1, no. 2, pp. 113–125, 1977.

[30] D. Kroenke, *Database Processing: Fundamentals, Modeling, Applications.* Palo Alto, CA: Science Research Associates, Inc., 1977.

[31] G. Wiederhold, *Database Design.* New York: McGraw-Hill, 1977.

[32] E. T. Lee, "Similarity retrieval techniques," in *Pictorial Information Systems*, S. K. Chang and K. S. Fu, Eds. New York: Springer-Verlag, 1980, ch. 6, pp. 128–176.

A Fuzzy Approximation Scheme for Sequential Learning in Pattern Recognition

BHARATHI B. DEVI AND V. V. S. SARMA, SENIOR MEMBER, IEEE

Abstract—An adaptive learning scheme, based on a fuzzy approximation to the gradient descent method for training a pattern classifier using unlabeled samples, is described. The objective function defined for the fuzzy ISODATA clustering procedure is used as the loss function for computing the gradient. Learning is based on simultaneous fuzzy decisionmaking and estimation. It uses conditional fuzzy measures on unlabeled samples. An exponential membership function is assumed for each class, and the parameters constituting these membership functions are estimated, using the gradient, in a recursive fashion. The induced possibility of occurrence of each class is useful for estimation and is computed using 1) the membership of the new sample in that class and 2) the previously computed average possibility of occurrence of the same class. An inductive entropy measure is defined in terms of induced possibility distribution to measure the extent of learning. The method is illustrated with relevant examples.

I. Introduction

ELICITATION of natural structures in a set of unlabeled pattern samples is required for designing an automatic pattern recognition (PR) scheme. This process, called *unsupervised learning*, is usually carried out by one of the following two broad categories of procedures. The first requires the entire data set to group them into classes. This is usually referred to as *clustering*. Often, the final clusters are obtained after several iterations of clustering. All the variants of the ISODATA procedure belong to this category. In the second approach, any prior information is used to design an initial classifier and the decisions of this classifier are used to label the succeeding samples. The samples are fed sequentially, and the parameters of the classifier are updated each time a sample is classified. This procedure of updating the parameters depending on the previous decision is called the *decision-directed* approach to unsupervised learning. Some of the drawbacks of this procedure are 1) the initial structure fed to the learning scheme is crucial to the success of the final PR scheme, especially if learning is adaptive, 2) the sequence in which data samples arrive affects the final classifier, and thus when an unfavorable sequence is encountered, learning is led in a wrong way, and 3) more often than not, the results are suboptimal and the estimates are biased especially when the classes are overlapping.

When the training set is small and a procedure derived from the loss functions of the gradient descent method is used for adjusting the parameter vectors, the procedure is only *approximate*. It is more so when a very small subset (sometimes only one sample—as in the sequential learning already described) is used. Nevertheless, decision-directed and other learning schemes for pattern classification are attractive due to their simplicity and computational feasibility. This paper is concerned with the development of a decision-directed learning scheme and is based on fuzzy approximation to the descent technique.

The proposed method is tested in the context of two distinct applications. The first, in numerical taxonomy using the *iris* data, is now a standard textbook example. It consists of 150 individuals of *iris*. These data contain measurements on flowers of three species of iris, 1) Setosa (SE), 2) Versicolor (VC), and 3) Virginica (VG), each having 50 samples. Out of these classes, Setosa is well separated from the other two classes. The overlapping classes are from different plants, VC and VG. As the available data are not sequential, a uniform random number generator is used to select a training sample at any time instant. These data have been selected mainly because it is a standard example whose characteristics are well established. The second application reported here is on voiced-unvoiced-silence (V/U/S) classification in speech. V/U/S classification is an important problem in speech recognition and low bit rate communication. It also serves as a first level of classification in multilevel continuous speech recognition systems. Atal and Rabiner [1] first reported on pattern recognition approach for V/U/S classification. A speech segment is assigned to a particular class depending on the minimum distance rule. Features used by different investigators include zero-crossing rate (N_z), the speech energy (E_s), the correlation between adjacent speech samples (C_1), the predictor coefficients from linear predictive coding analysis (α_i), the energy in prediction error (E_p), spectral energy, etc. Speech data are inherently sequential, and sequential classification is ideally suited for on-line speech recognition systems.

In certain practical pattern recognition problems, it is possible to identify or infer the class labels of a few samples in the unsupervised design set. Peculiarities presented by certain practical data sets and problem-

Manuscript received December 23, 1984; revised August 28, 1985 and May 27, 1986.
B. B. Devi was with the Indian Institute of Science, Bangalore, India. She is now with the Department of Mathematics, Computer Science and Physics, Texas Woman's University, P. O. Box 22865, Denton, TX 76204.
V. V. S. Sarma is with the School of Automation Indian Institute of Science, Bangalore 560 012, India.
IEEE Log Number 8610216.

Reprinted from *IEEE Trans. Syst., Man, Cybern.*, vol. SMC-16, no. 5, pp. 668–679, September/October 1986.

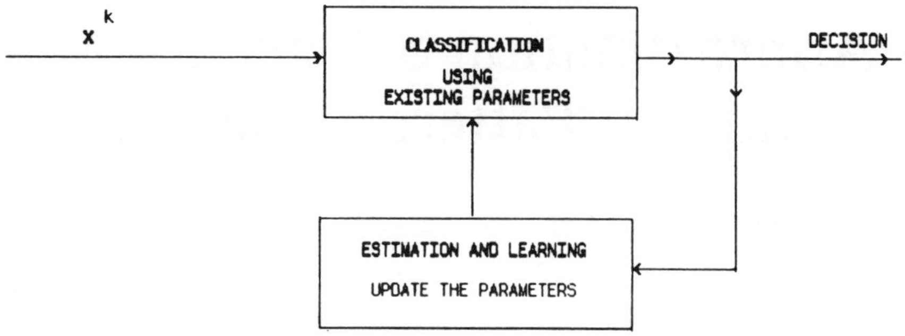

Fig. 1. Typical adaptive pattern classification and learning scheme.

specific *a priori* knowledge are not always easy to incorporate in the design of pattern classifiers. As an example, consider the V/U/S classification of speech segments. In this case, *a priori* knowledge from speech production mechanism can help us in improving the classification. For example, we can infer that the sample with the highest energy among all the samples is voiced. Such information can effect a considerable improvement in the learning mechanism. This type of knowledge is utilized in the presently proposed learning scheme. Here, in order to learn the characteristics of pattern data, these samples (whose classes have been inferred as explained earlier) are used as initial representatives (or knowledge). The rest of the samples in the set are used to correct the characteristic parameters. An advantage with such a scheme is that samples can arrive on-line, once the initial representatives have been chosen. Other applications of sequential learning include classification of biomedical signals, like EEG, ECG, VCG, etc. On-line classification of these signals is important in order to take necessary clinical actions in time.

Fig. 1 shows a typical adaptive pattern classification and learning scheme. The main ingredients are a decisionmaking scheme followed by an estimation scheme to feed back its results to the decision scheme. Each of these components may in general be realized by one of the several approaches such as Bayesian decisionmaking and estimation [7], [13], perceptron algorithms, stochastic approximation [15], fuzzy learning [9], [14], etc. The present method uses conditional fuzzy measures on the unlabeled samples. Thus the entire process may be termed *learning with a fuzzy teacher*. To initiate the learning process, one labeled sample from each class is required, as discussed earlier. That is, a selected sample should have a membership value of unity in one class and zero in others. Available knowledge about the class characteristics may be utilized to identify such samples. Parameters of the decision scheme, i.e., those of the membership functions of all the classes, are estimated by a fuzzy approximation to the gradient descent procedure. The objective function used in the fuzzy ISODATA [6] procedure is used for computing proportional increments in the estimates. Due to the complexity of the problem, no attempt has been made in this paper to prove the convergence of the estimates analytically. Instead, the extent of learning is measured by an entropy function defined in this study. The overall system being an adaptive learning scheme, samples can be simultaneously classified.

The general methodology of inductive learning is introduced in Section II. The estimation of the parameters is worked out in Section III. Section IV presents details of the adaptive learning scheme. It also includes discussion of the choice of the membership function, the initial parameter setting for the learning process, the classification method used, and the definition of the fuzzy entropy function to measure the extent of learning. Experimental results with discussions are in Section V.

II. The Learning Methodology

As depicted in Fig. 1, the components of many adaptive learning schemes are

1) a PR scheme with known parameters to update the class possibilities of a fresh pattern sample and make decisions, and
2) an estimation scheme to use the updated possibilities to refine the parameters of the same PR scheme.

Thus the second scheme feeds its new findings back to the first scheme. In this section, two cases of a generalized model for inductive learning are discussed to realize the first scheme mentioned. Estimation is worked out in Section III.

Inductive Learning

A sample is a vector x of dimension d and X is the set of samples. Each component of the sample is called a feature. We consider, for simplicity, scalar featured ($d = 1$) variables x. Let x^k be the value of that variable at kth instant of learning. Let $\Omega = \{\omega_1, \omega_2, \cdots, \omega_C\}$ be the set of C classes.

Let $\mu_i(x) \in [0, 1]$ be the membership of x in ω_i (or the conditional fuzzy measure $\pi(x|\omega_i)$ on x) and $\pi(\omega_i)$ be the prior information about the possibility of the class ω_i occurring, a fuzzy measure on Ω. $\pi(x|\omega_i)$ can be interpreted as the fuzziness of the statement "element x results because of class ω_i occurring," and $\pi(\omega_i)$, as the possibility measure of the statement, "the class is ω_i" [18].

Definition: Inductive learning is a modification of the possibility distribution function $\pi(\omega_i)$ due to new information in x through $\pi(x|\omega_i)$. The modified possibility distribution is referred as the *induced conditional possibility distribution* and is defined as follows:

$$\pi(\omega_i|x) \triangleq \alpha\{\pi(x|\omega_i) \wedge \pi(\omega_i)\}, \qquad \text{for } i = 1,2,\cdots,C \tag{1}$$

where α is a normalizing factor chosen such that

$$\pi(\omega_i|x) \in [0,1]; \tag{2}$$

$\wedge$ is an operator representing minimum. Two normalizations can be considered in the present context. Model 1:

$$\sup_{\omega_i \in \Omega} \pi(\omega_i|x) = 1. \tag{3}$$

Model 2:

$$\sum_{\omega_i \in \Omega} \pi(\omega_i|x) = 1. \tag{4}$$

The inductive inference at the kth instant of learning is

$$\pi(\omega_i|x^k) = \frac{\pi(x^k|\omega_i) \wedge \pi^{k-1}(\omega_i)}{\pi(x^k)} \tag{5}$$

where $\pi^k(\omega_i)$ is the possibility of the ith class occurring at the kth instant and $\pi(x^k)$ is the *marginal possibility distribution function* and may be defined as follows:

$$\pi(x^k) = \begin{cases} \bigvee_{\omega_j \in \Omega} \pi(x^k|\omega_j) \wedge \pi^{k-1}(\omega_j): \text{ model 1} \\ \sum_{\omega_j \in \Omega} \pi(x^k|\omega_j) \wedge \pi^{k-1}(\omega_j): \text{ model 2} \end{cases} \tag{6}$$

where the operator $\vee$ represents max function.

Definition: The estimated values of $\pi(\omega_i)$, represented as $\hat{\pi}^k_\omega(\omega_i)$, may be obtained by reinforcement. In this study, the following reinforcement rule is used:

$$\hat{\pi}^k_\omega(\omega_i) \triangleq \beta\hat{\pi}^{k-1}_\omega(\omega_i) + (1-\beta)\pi(\omega_i|x^k) \tag{7a}$$

with $0 < \beta < 1$. When $\beta = (k-1)/k$, (7a) is similar to the maximum likelihood estimate in statistical inference, and we will call it the *fuzzy maximum likelihood estimate* of $\pi(\omega_i)$.

Definition: Another reinforcement scheme may be obtained by the marginal possibility distribution function, which is defined as

$$\hat{\pi}^k_\omega(\omega_i) = \sup_{x \in \{x^1, x^2, \cdots, x^k\}} \{\pi(\omega_i|x), \hat{\pi}^0_\omega(\omega_i)\}$$
$$= \max\{\hat{\pi}^{k-1}_\omega(\omega_i), \pi(\omega_i|x^k)\}. \tag{7b}$$

However, this when used with (3) will soon lose the possibilistic information when a sample having maximum membership in a class or equal membership value in all the classes arrives.

From the foregoing discussion we are led to define a general model for learning in terms of an expression for the induced possibility as

$$\pi(\omega_i|x^k) = \frac{\pi(x^k|\omega_i) \oplus \hat{\pi}^{k-1}_\omega(\omega_i)}{\pi(x^k)}$$

where

$$\pi(x^k) = \oplus\{\pi(x^k|\omega_j) \circledast \hat{\pi}^{k-1}_\omega(\omega_i)\} \tag{8}$$

where the operators $\oplus$ and $\circledast$ are more general than that for any particular model. It is seen from (8) that when π's are probability density functions, the expression leads to the Bayesian model with $\circledast$ for multiplication and $\oplus$ for summation. Thus probabilistic learning is a particular case of this general fuzzy model with π's being the *sharpened* version, π^* [8].

The conditional possibility distribution functions $\pi(x^k|\omega_i)$, also called as membership functions, are characterized by the parameters representing the classes; i.e.,

$$\mu_{\omega_i}(x) = \pi(x^k|\omega_i) = \pi(x^k|\theta^k_i, \omega_i) \tag{9a}$$

where θ^k_i are the parameters of the membership function of the ω_ith class at the kth instant of learning, and

$$\theta^{k+1}_i = f(\theta^k_i, \pi(\omega_i|x^k), x^k). \tag{9b}$$

In the next section, we describe an adaptive updating technique for estimating the parameters using the inductive learning.

III. Estimation of Parameters

The induced possibilities obtained in the previous section are utilized to update the existing estimates as described later. The vector parameter θ characterizing the classes are updated with the occurrence of each pattern sample. Suppose a loss function $J(\theta)$ is defined over the scalar θ. Let $J'(\theta)$ and $J''(\theta)$ denote the first and second derivative of $J(\theta)$, respectively. Then θ can be estimated by minimizing an objective function or loss function using the Newton's recursive algorithm as follows. Making a first-order approximation to $J'(\theta)$ using Taylor's series,

$$J'(\theta+\delta) \approx J'(\theta) + \delta J''(\theta). \tag{10}$$

If $J'(\theta+\delta) = 0$, then

$$\delta \approx -\frac{J'(\theta)}{J''(\theta)}.$$

If this approximation is applied iteratively, the kth iteration of δ may be written as follows:

$$\delta^k = \theta^{k+1} - \theta^k = -\frac{J'[\theta^k]}{J''[\theta^k]}$$

which will result in the following recursive estimator.

$$\hat{\theta}^{k+1} = \hat{\theta}^k + \delta^k. \tag{11}$$

To derive an expression for δ^k (for recursive estimation), the loss function used in the fuzzy ISODATA method is studied first. In the fuzzy ISODATA method for clustering, the class representatives v_i are obtained in an iterative fashion. Each iteration uses the entire set of data. The parameters are updated to minimize the weighted average intracluster distance to get the fuzzy partitions:

$$J_w(F,v) = \sum_{i=1}^{C} \sum_{x \in X} [\mu_{F_i}(x)]^w d(x,v_i)^2 \tag{12}$$

where $w \in \boldsymbol{R}^+$, and $F = (F_1, \cdots, F_C)$ is the hard (i.e., nonfuzzy) partition of X; $d(x,v_i)^2$ is a distance measure of x from v_i. $\mu_{F_i}(x) \in [0,1]$, $i = 1, C$, and

$$\sum_{i=1}^{C} \mu_{F_i}(x) = 1, \qquad \forall x,$$

Bezdek [6] shows that J_w reaches a minimum (possibly only a local minimum), with $w \in]1, \infty)$ and $v_i \in X$, $i = 1, C$ only if

$$v_i = \frac{\sum_{x \in X} [\mu_{F_i}(x)]^w x}{\sum_{x \in X} [\mu_{f_i}(x)]^w}, \qquad i = 1, \cdots, C, \tag{13}$$

when $d(x, v_i)^2 = \|x - v_i\|^2$, and when an expression for μ_{F_i} is given.

When $w = 1$, F is necessarily a hard partition, becoming more fuzzy when w increases. $w = 2$ was found to be optimal, empirically, in the sense that the partitions obtained truly reflects the actual fuzziness of the clusters in the data X.

The expression for v_i, (13), which represents the central member of any class or cluster can be modified as follows for recursive learning. Rewriting (12), we have

$$J(v) = \sum_{i=1}^{C} \sum_{x \in X} \mu_{F_i}^2(x)(x - v_i)^2. \tag{14}$$

Assuming the first and the second derivatives of $J(v)$ with respect to v_i exist, we get

$$J'(v_i) = -2 \sum_{x \in X} \mu_{F_i}^2(x)(x - v_i)$$

$$J''(v_i) = 2 \sum_{x \in X} \mu_{F_i}^2(x)$$

$$\delta_i = \frac{\sum_{x \in X} \mu_{F_i}^2(x)(x - v_i)}{\sum_{x \in X} \mu_{F_i}^2(x)}, \qquad \text{for } i = 1, \cdots, C. \tag{15}$$

When the samples arrive in sequence, all the $x \in X$ are not available simultaneously for computing δ_i. The following approximation for (15) suits recursive updating of the parameters v:

$$\delta_i^k = \frac{\hat{\mu}_{F_i}^2(x^k)(x^k - \hat{v}_i^{k-1})}{f_i^k} \tag{16}$$

where $\hat{\mu}_{F_i}(x^k)$ is the membership of x^k in the cluster F_i and is a function of the previous estimate of the parameters $\hat{v}_i^{k-1}$ as

$$\hat{\mu}_{F_i}(x^k) = g(\hat{v}_i^{k-1}, x^k)$$

and

$$f_i^k = f_i^{k-1} + [\hat{\mu}_{F_i}(x^k)]^2.$$

Finally, we have

$$\hat{v}_i^k = \hat{v}_i^{k-1} + \rho_i^k \epsilon_i^k, \qquad i = 1, \cdots, C \tag{17}$$

where $\epsilon_i^k = x^k - \hat{v}_i^{k-1}$, $0 \leqslant \rho_i^k \leqslant 1$, and

$$\rho_i^k = \frac{[\hat{\mu}_{F_i}(x^k)]^2}{f_i^k}. \tag{18}$$

$\hat{\mu}_{F_i}(x^k)$ is nothing but the conditional fuzzy measure on x^k given the class is F_i. Therefore, we substitute

$$\mu_{F_i}(x^k) = \pi(\omega_i | x^k). \tag{19}$$

One can see the similarity between fuzzy learning of the central member v_i and the maximum likelihood learning of the mean of a random variable.

Suppose we have more than one parameter v_i to be learned for each class ω_i, say v_i and $E_i = \sigma_i^2$, where E_i represents the spread of class ω_i, then J can be modified to

$$J(v, E) = \sum_{i=1}^{C} \sum_{x \in X} \mu_{F_i}^2(x)[\|x - v_i\|^2 - E_i]^2.$$

Then we can easily show that an expression similar to the one derived in (17) will hold true (see the Appendix for details) for σ_i as well. For example, if the exponential membership to be given in (21a) is used, then the following expression gives an estimate of σ_i^2 at the kth instant of learning:

$$\sigma_i^{2^k} = \sigma_i^{2^{k-1}} + \rho_i^k \epsilon_i^k, \qquad i = 1, \cdots, C \tag{20}$$

where

$$\epsilon_i^k = \|x^k - \hat{v}_i^k\|^2 - \sigma_i^{2^{k-1}}.$$

IV. The Complete Classification and Learning Scheme

In this section, the earlier derived inductive learning schemes incorporating the foregoing, estimation procedures are used to arrive at an adaptive scheme for simultaneous decision making and learning. The specific membership function used is presented first. Then, a fuzzy entropy measure for possible use in stopping the learning procedure is defined. The classification and learning procedures follow these.

Membership Function

Equation (5) in Section II is a general form for computing the induced possibilities of classes from the feature information and the possibility of class occurrence. The exact parametric expressions for the class conditional possibilities were left as problem-dependent choices. In most of the studies involving fuzzy sets, the choice of an appropriate form for the membership function is usually a subjective decision. It is a mapping from the feature space to the real line in the range [0, 1]. Many statistical PR approaches assume normally distributed features in every class. Features may be class conditionally dependent or independent. The latter case is usually only a practical approximation. The fuzzy set approach is advantageous in many problems due to reasons such as 1) a sample having nonzero membership in more than one class, 2) subjective definition of classes, 3) very small training set, and 4) imprecise boundaries of classes. Then even the assumption of normal features is only approximate. An exponential expression for the membership function is an equally good approximation to many probability distribution functions. While retaining the desirable properties of the normal curve such as smooth tapering, smooth peak, and control of width, the fuzzy exponential function eliminates undue accentuation (or flattening) of the peak by not requiring the function to integrate to one. Considering these properties, the following membership function is used for the present learning scheme. It has also been successfully used by the present authors [2]–[5] in different PR problems:

$$\mu_{\omega_i}(x^k) = \pi(x^k|\omega_i) = \exp\left[-\gamma\left(\frac{x^k - v_i^{k-1}}{\sigma_i^{k-1}}\right)^2\right] \tag{21a}$$

where v_i^k and σ_i^k are given by (19) and (20), respectively, and $0 < \gamma \leqslant 1$. $\mu_{\omega_i}(x^k)$ can be normalized, such that $\sum_{i=1}^{C}\mu_{\omega_i}(x^k) = 1$ and $\mu_{\omega_i}(x^k) \in [0,1], \forall i$, especially when using model 2 given by (4). The expression for μ given by (21) satisfies the following conditions:

1) μ is a function from $(-\infty, \infty)$ on to $(0,1]$,
2) $\mu(x) = 1$ when $x = v_i$.

The second condition indicates that a central member exists much like a prototype of a class and a spread parameter σ which changes the shape of the membership function. A comparison of this function to the Gaussian density function is in order. In the fuzzy environment, if the spread of a fuzzy set decreases, the membership value of the central member should not peak. Thus $\mu_{\omega_i}(x = v_i) = 1$ irrespective of σ_i. On the other hand, in probability theory, a decrease in the standard deviation increases the density value of the mean resulting in the *peaking phenomenon* [7]. Thus it has the advantage of the normal density function, but without its high peaking nature. This results in a decision function which has a smooth transition from class to class.

The membership function, similar to the one given below, has been extensively used in fuzzy ISODATA procedures [6]:

$$\mu_{\omega_i}(x^k) = \frac{1}{\sum_{j=1}^{C}\frac{\|x^k - v_i^{k-1}\|^2}{\|x^k - v_j^{k-1}\|^2}}. \tag{21b}$$

It has the advantage of having to learn only one parameter vector for each class. It is useful to consider here the same membership function used in the fuzzy ISODATA procedure for comparison purposes. Then the fuzzy possibility distribution functions need be defined only for samples and not for each feature of a sample thus reducing the computational complexity.

Returning to the learning procedure, at any stage of learning, the extent of learning can be measured by using a suitable index. For this purpose, we define a fuzzy entropy function and discuss some of its properties.

Fuzzy Entropy as a Measure of Learning

For the fuzzy inductive learning problem discussed in Section II, define a fuzzy entropy function at the kth instant of learning as

$$H_F(x^k) = -K\sum_{i=1}^{C}\left\{\pi(\omega_i|x^k)\log\pi(\omega_i|x^k) + [1-\pi(\omega_i|x^k)]\log[1-\pi(\omega_i|x^k)]\right\} \tag{22}$$

where terms on the right-hand side of (22) have been defined earlier and K is some constant. Note that $H_F(x^k)$ is a function of all the pattern samples up to and inclusive of x^k.

Consider any probabilistic experiment in which one element of $X = \{x^1, x^2, \cdots, x^n\}$ occurs at each instant. If a fuzzy set Π is now defined on the total set X, there will be two kinds of uncertainties [8].

1) The uncertainty of a random nature, related to the occurrence of the element x_i.

2) The uncertainty of a fuzzy nature concerning the interpretation as one or zero while assigning labels.

There will be fluctuations in $H_F(x^k)$ due to fluctuations in $\pi(x^k|\omega_i)$. Therefore, an average entropy is defined at any instant k of learning as

$$\bar{H}_F^k = \gamma_k\bar{H}_F^{k-1} + (1-\gamma_k)H_F(x^k) \tag{23}$$

where

$$\gamma_k = \frac{k-1}{k}.$$

It is known (Watanabe [16]) in probabilistic learning that, for smaller values of k, the entropy increases up to a certain instant, say $k = k_0$, and then will decrease with k. This increase of entropy in the beginning is called the *unlearning period*, when the initial uncertainty is unlearned. The decrease in entropy beyond $k = k_0$ is proved in the *inverse-H theorem* by Watanabe [16]. Similar unlearning has been observed in our fuzzy inductive learning, when the vagueness in the initial knowledge is unlearned:

$$\bar{H}_F^{k-1} < \bar{H}_F^k \quad \text{when } k \leqslant k_0$$
$$\bar{H}_F^k > \bar{H}_F^{k+1} \quad \text{when } k > k_0. \tag{24}$$

However, note that a decrease in entropy does not necessarily imply learning, even though the entropy decreases due to learning.

Pattern Classification

Simultaneous with learning, arriving pattern samples can be classified. A sample is classified by maximizing the possibility of occurrence among classes. The max–min scheme for decisionmaking, to be described later, has been found suitable for classification in the fuzzy environment [2], [4], [5]. This is useful for the exponential membership function defined in (21a) when implemented for each feature. The decisionmaking is based on the notion of *noninteractiveness* [17] of the features and is achieved by the *rigid conjunction* [9] of the feature memberships in any class.

Definition: Two fuzzy variables x, y are *noninteractive* if

$$\pi(x,y) = \min\{\pi(x), \pi(y)\}.$$

Note that noninteractiveness is less stringent than *possibilistic independence* [12].

Thus the class membership for x^k in class ω_i is given by

$$\pi(\omega_i|x^k) = \min_j \pi(\omega_i|x_j^k) \qquad (25)$$

where $\pi(\omega_i|x_j^k)$ is obtained from (5) by substituting x_j^k in (5)–(21). The crisp classification can be arrived at by selecting that class for which the class membership value is maximum. A sample x^k is said to belong to class ω_m, if

$$\pi(\omega_m|x^k) = \max_i \pi(\omega_i|x^k). \qquad (26)$$

It can be observed that (26) can be used for decisionmaking even when the features are not assumed to be noninteractive. In such a case, one way to use the exponential membership function is as follows:

$$\mu_{\omega_i} = \exp\left[-\gamma \sum_{j=1}^{d}\left(\frac{x_j^k - v_j^{k-1}}{\sigma_j^{k-1}}\right)^2\right].$$

The advantages of max–min decisionmaking are 1) it alleviates the need to assume feature independence, 2) it avoids the necessity to specify feature correlations, 3) closely related features do not pose problems of doubly influencing the decision, and 4) it is easy to implement on a computer.

The total entropy, when features are assumed to be noninteractive, is obtained as follows:

$$H_F(x^k) \triangleq \sum_{j=1}^{d} H_F(x_j^k) \qquad (27)$$

where x_j^k is the jth feature value of the kth sample.

The Complete Adaptive Learning Scheme

Usually, in adaptive learning schemes the initial behavior is very crucial. The more information we can provide to the system, the better and faster its learning will be. In our case, the scheme is initialized as follows.

Initialization: To start with, there is *equal possibility* of all classes occurring. Thus

$$\pi^0(\omega_i) = \frac{1}{C}, \qquad i = 1,\cdots,C \text{ and } \forall \text{ features}.$$

It is also assumed that one sample from each class is available in the beginning. A sample is said to be from a particular class, if its membership in that class is more than its membership in other classes. Let $f_i^0 = (f_{i1}^0,\cdots,f_{id}^0)$ where $f_{ij}^0 = 1$, $\forall j$ and $i = 1, C$, and σ_i^0 be set approximately proportional to the range of the feature values in X. Thus

$$v_i^0 = x^0$$

where

$$x^0 \in \omega_i \text{ and}$$

$$\sigma_i^0 = \alpha \cdot \left[\max_{x\in X}\{x\} - \min_{x\in X}\{x\}\right] \qquad \forall i \qquad (28)$$

where $0 < \alpha \leqslant 1$. Usually, a limited set of data will be available for training. As with all approximate descent procedures [15], an approximate convergence of the estimated parameters is achieved by recycling the given data set.

Termination: The recycling procedure may be terminated when some convergence criterion is met. This may be expressed in terms of the average entropy or the correcting factor ρ as follows:

$$J_1 = \frac{\overline{H}_F^k}{\overline{H}_F^{k-1}} \leqslant 1 - \frac{\delta}{k}$$

or

$$J_2 = \max_i \|\rho_i\| \leqslant \rho_0 \qquad (29)$$

where $1 \leqslant \delta < k$ and $\rho_0 > 0$. We now describe the adaptive learning procedure.

Procedure:

Step 1: Set $k \leftarrow 0$. Initialize the learning scheme with initial estimates for v_i^k, σ_i^k, f_i^k, and $\pi^k(\omega_i)$, $i = 1,\cdots,C$.

Step 2: Set $k \leftarrow k+1$. For x^k, compute $\pi(x^k|\omega_i)$ for $i = 1,\cdots,C$ using (21). Normalize $\pi(x^k|\omega_i)$ such that $\Sigma_i \pi(x^k|\omega_i) = 1$, if model 2 is used. Compute and normalize $\pi(\omega_i|x^k)$, for $i = 1,\cdots,C$.

Step 3: Classify x^k by using (26).

Step 4: Update the estimates of v_i^k, σ_i^k, $\pi^k(\omega_i)$. Compute the entropy function; update the average entropy function.

Step 5: If the stopping criterion is met, stop. Otherwise, repeat steps 2–4 using the next sample. If samples are exhausted recycle the samples.

V. Experiments and Discussion

Experimental Results

Two distinct examples are considered to illustrate our methodology: 1) V/U/S classification and 2) the classical iris data of Fisher [11].

V / U / S Classification: The first example is from speech processing. Two utterances of each of eight phrases—1) Chester Bowles, 2) justice, 3) six chickens, 4) watch them, 5) hotch potch, 6) Miss King, 7) she sells, and 8) cross vote—of a single male speaker in a computer room with a Shure microphone placed at about 3 in from lips are directly entered into the signal processing facility with a sampling rate of 10 kHz. (Signal to noise ratio = 40 dB.) This is an interactive Hewlett Packard 5451 A/B Fourier Analyzer built around a HP 2100 computer. After visually deciding the appropriate class label of each frame of 128 samples, the features speech energy (E_s), zero-crossing rate (N_z), and the normalized correlation between adjacent speech samples (A_1) are extracted.

This V/U/S classification is a good example of

1) continuous class labels, as there is a smooth transition from one class to another,
2) mixture of classes, as a single frame may contain a transition from one class to another,
3) fuzzy classes due to multiple speakers, recording conditions, and use of a limited feature set for recognition.

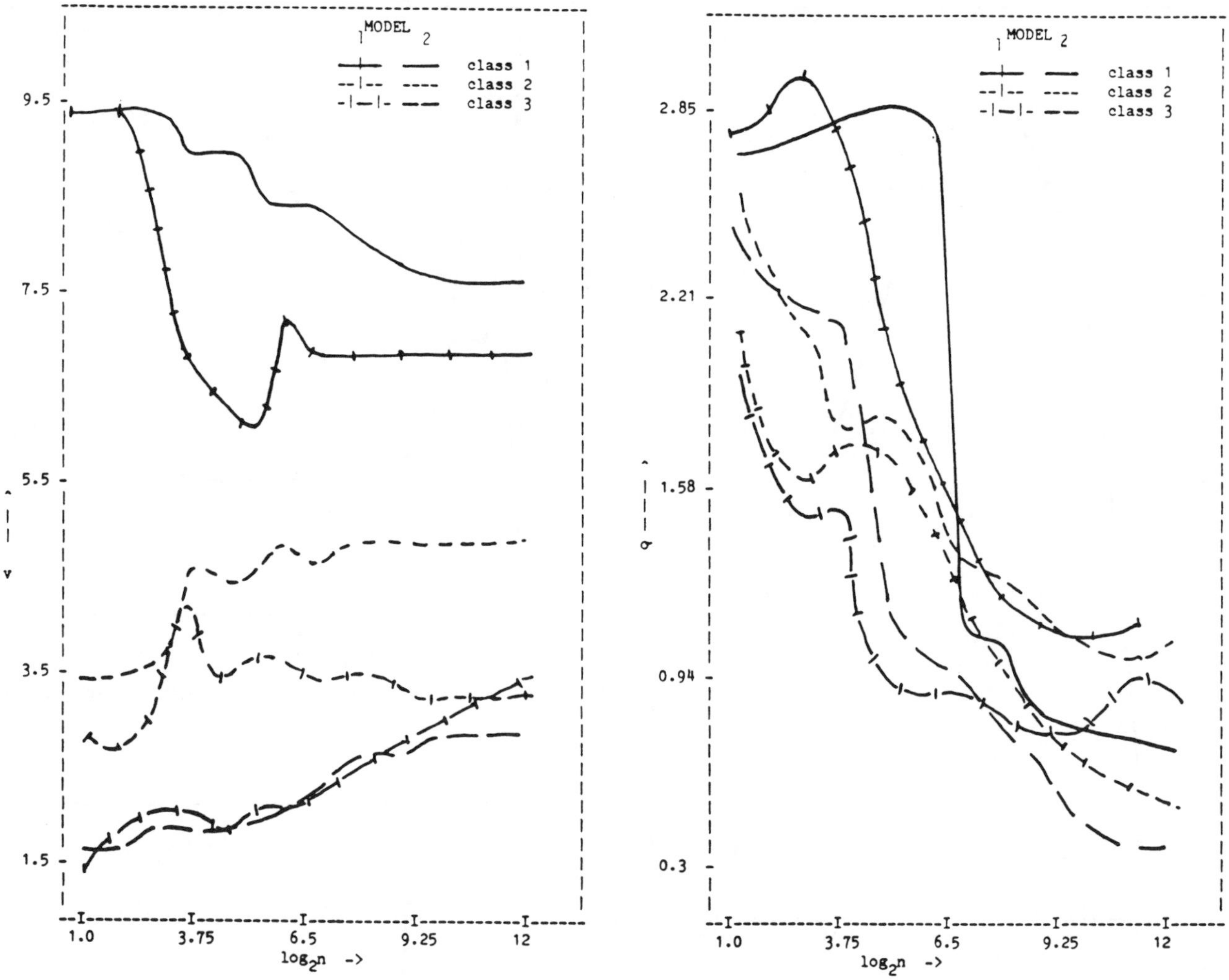

(a) (b)

Fig. 2. (a) Results for V/U/S data (I feature) showing convergence of v. (b) Convergence of spread parameter σ for same data.

Initial knowledge about the classes is obtained by the following information known about the classes: the speech segment with the highest energy corresponds to the voiced class; that with the highest zero crossing corresponds to the unvoiced part of the speech; the one with the lowest energy, to the silence class. Accordingly, a sample representative is picked from each class to initialize the learning. Features are assumed to be noninteractive; the exponential membership function is used for each feature. Hence steps 1–5 of the learning procedure are applicable to each feature of a sample, all of them running in parallel except while classifying a pattern sample.

Iris Data: With *iris* data, two problems are considered: 1) two overlapping classes, i.e., Virginica and Versicolor, and 2) all the three available classes.

In both experiments on *iris* data, one sample from each class is picked at random for the initial guess of the central member. The spread, which is another parameter to be estimated for each feature in each class, is set to a reasonably assumed proportion of the total spread of the feature space.

In both *iris* and speech examples, the available samples are fed to the learning scheme one at a time. When the samples are exhausted, the same data set is used again possibly in a different sequence selected by a random number generator. The features are assumed to be noninteractive. A sample is considered misclassified when the known label is different from the label assigned by the classifier. This contributes to the recognition error of the classifier. While updating the parameters, the samples are classified with the previous estimates according to the maximum membership value, and the running average of the recognition error is computed. The *iris* data are scrambled, to introduce randomness in the occurrence. Since speech data is a real-time signal, it is used in order of its occurrence.

Both the models discussed in Section II were used to study the efficacy of the schemes. Model 2 converges slowly, but convergence is steady, as can be seen in Fig. 2. Model 1 is rapid in convergence of parameters (as in Fig. 2). Its recognition rate therefore increases rapidly. For PR problems with limited samples, Sklansky [15] points out that asymptotic convergence is usually of less practical importance than good performance of the classifier on a limited training set. It is sometimes possible to obtain a nonconvergence training procedure that performs better

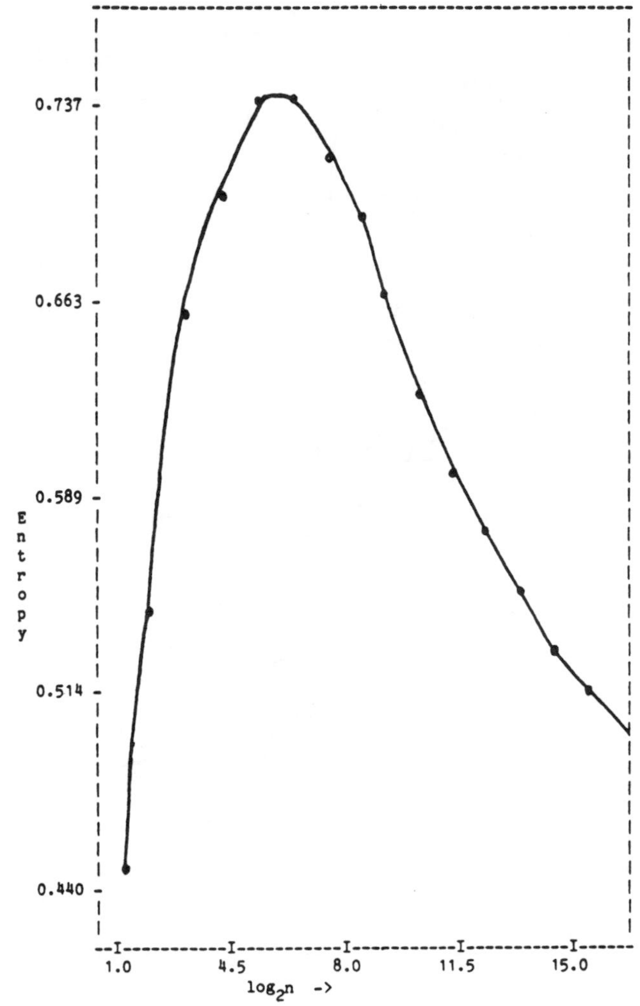

Fig. 3. Entropy trajectory for V/U/S data.

over a finite training period than a convergent training procedure on the same data. The mathematical complexity of our recursive learning scheme prohibits addressing questions of convergence as the number of samples increases to infinity. Requirement of on-line classification and learning for problems, such as V/U/S classification, and good performance on limited data justify our scheme. The experimental fuzzy entropy variation is depicted in Fig. 3. It shows a steady decrease beyond a certain learning instance. This is found to be true in both the models.

Separability of Classes and Prior Information

The effect of prior information on the convergence and the influence of the separation of classes are studied in another experiment. In this case also, the exponential membership function given by (21a) is used for each feature. *Iris* data have two overlapping classes and one well-separated class. When only the two overlapping classes are considered for the experiment, the recognition accuracy increased rapidly as compared to the three class problem. This is illustrated in Fig. 4. In the latter case, most of the errors occurred in the overlapping region: the well-separated class was recognized almost correctly. This

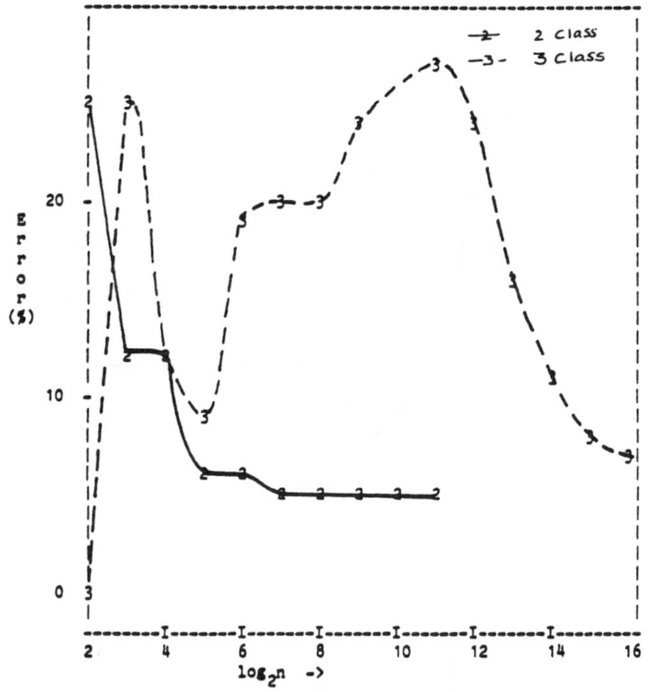

Fig. 4. Trajectory of recognition error for *iris* data: two and three class problems using model 2.

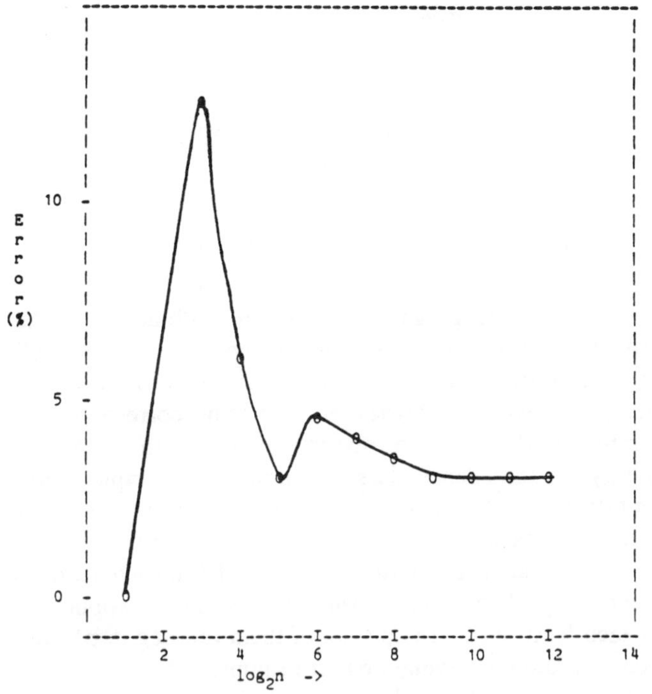

Fig. 5. Trajectory of recognition error with more *a priori* information: three class problem of *iris* data.

leads to a delay in convergence. However, with a sufficient number of samples for learning, most of the samples are classified correctly.

When the spread of each feature in each class is set proportional to the range corresponding to that particular class, instead of the whole sample set, learning is relatively fast and the error involved in recognition is far less than

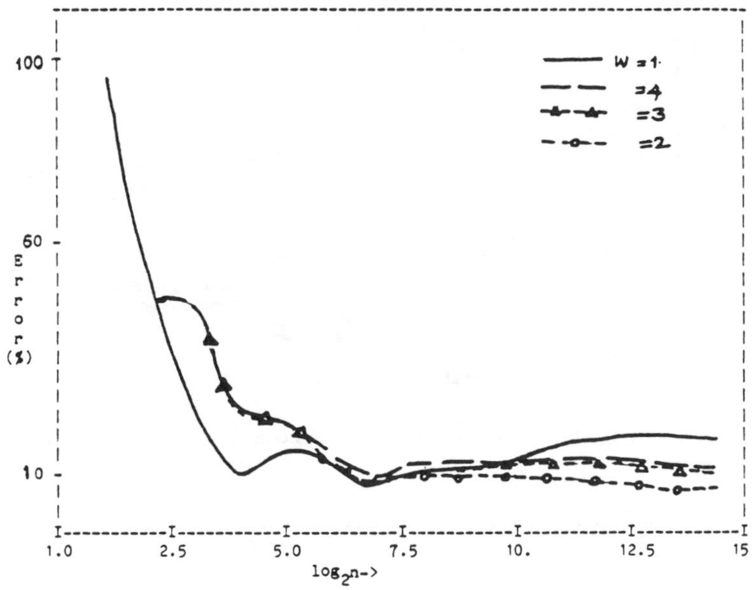

Fig. 6. Effect of w on convergence: V/U/S data with model 2.

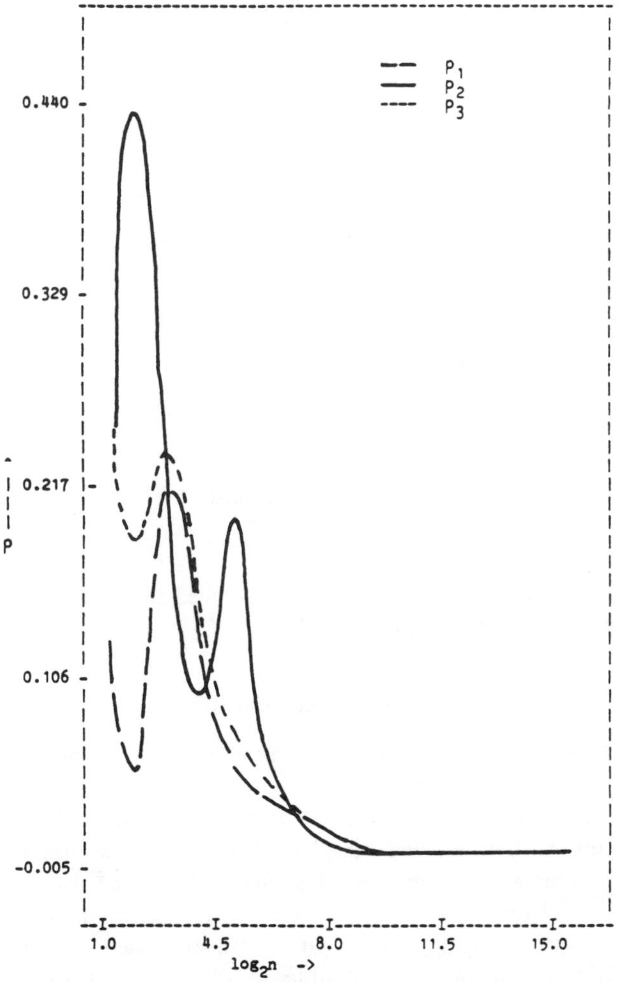

Fig. 7. Trajectory of $\|\rho\|$ for model 2 using V/U/S data. (Subscripts represent classes.)

when no such information is given. This can be seen from Fig. 5. In practice, partial information about classes may be available to guess reasonable approximations. For example, in V/U/S classification experiments, we know that the spread of the energy feature is in the decreasing order for the voiced, unvoiced, and silence classes.

Effect of Some Terms on Convergence

The effect of w in (13) on the convergence of the recognition error has been studied. $w = 2$ is found to be better than other values in our experiments (see Fig. 6). This confirms the observation of Dunn [10]. As learning progresses ρ's, contributing to the updating of parameters should converge to zero for the parameters to converge. Experimental results indicate this convergence, as illustrated in Fig. 7.

Discussion

It is appropriate to compare the present method with the fuzzy ISODATA. Fuzzy ISODATA requires all the samples to be available in every iteration. The iterations are repeated till the defined stopping criterion is met, to get the samples clustered. It basically belongs to the class of clustering for unsupervised learning. When a large number of samples are to be clustered or when the number of classes is very large, this iterative technique requires considerable computation and storage facilities. On the other hand, the method studied here belongs to the class of decision-directed approaches to learning and processes unlabeled pattern samples one by one, not only to learn more about the classes, but also to learn a classification scheme. This reduces the storage problem considerably.

An experiment conducted to compare the performances of the present learning scheme and the fuzzy ISODATA yielded interesting results. The membership function (21b), which is usually used in the fuzzy ISODATA procedures, is deployed for this purpose in the present learning scheme. An obvious computational gain in this case is that learning for individual features is unnecessary. Whereas the fuzzy ISODATA algorithm took a few iterations to converge, each iteration using all the available 150 samples, the

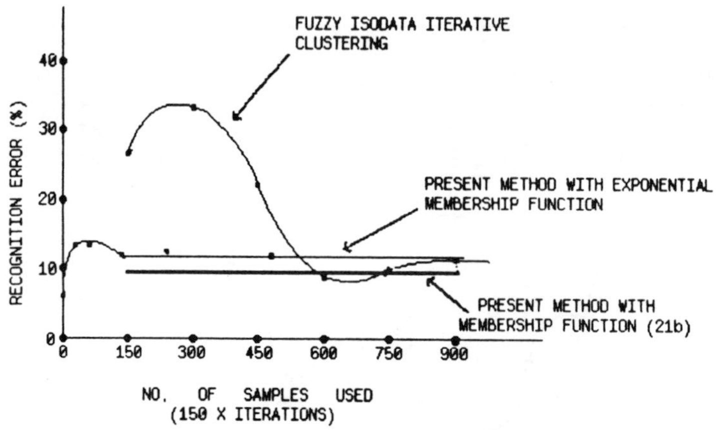

Fig. 8. Comparison of present learning scheme with fuzzy ISODATA clustering method using *iris* data: sample memberships used.

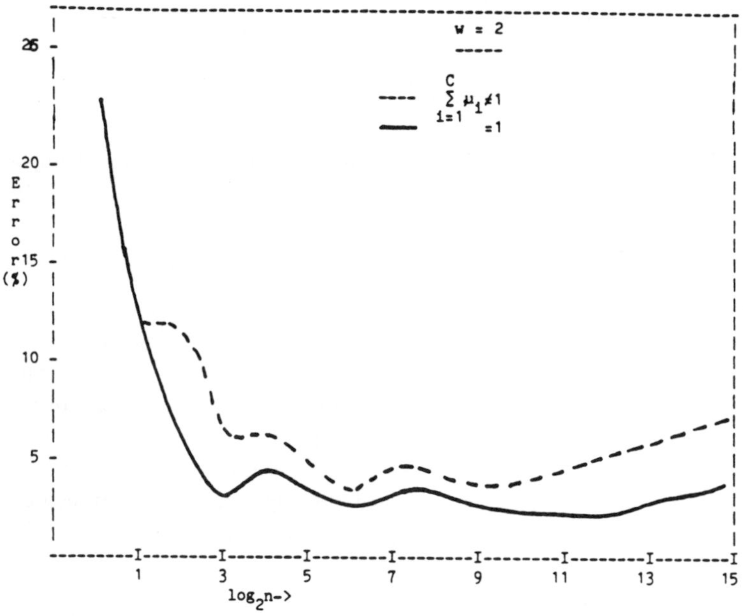

Fig. 9. Study of effect of normalization of membership values on recognition error: V/U/S data in model 2.

present sample by sample learning scheme almost converged around the one hundred fiftieth sample itself. The ISODATA procedure is defined to have converged when the maximum difference in the present and the previous membership value over all the sample set is below a prespecified constant. Even with the exponential membership function, when the samples are not assumed to be noninteractive, we observed a faster rate of convergence in our learning scheme. This is illustrated in Fig. 8. However, it is observed that convergence is slower, for these particular data, when features are assumed to be noninteractive and the exponential membership function is used as can be seen in Fig. 4. This calls for a proper assessment of the PR problem at hand and for deploying an appropriate learning model.

In model 2 ((5), Section II), the importance of normalizing μ has also been investigated. It is noted that, for this model, that π's will be normalized to add to one. If μ's are also in the same range, learning will be less biased and equal weightage will be given to the new information in the samples as well as to that in the induced possibility measures. This is illustrated in Fig. 9.

VI. Conclusion

Many PR algorithms deal with two extreme problems in classification and classifier design: 1) classification when labeled samples are available for training, and 2) classification with unlabeled samples. However, many practical problems are intermediate. Usually, only partial information will be available so that the learning environment is not purely supervised or purely unsupervised. In such situations, it may be possible to identify at least one sample from each class. This sample can be used as an initial estimate of the true prototype, to be adaptively updated with more samples using a learning strategy. Naturally, such a technique works only on certain data sets with desirable properties. In particular, a stream of pattern samples in which class labels of successive samples change slowly is a good candidate.

A fuzzy approximation to sequential estimation and learning is proposed for training such a pattern classifier, when it is possible to identify at least one sample from each class in the unlabeled sample set. This is similar to clustering and is suitable for situations in which data are obtained on-line. The model of learning is based on simultaneous fuzzy decisionmaking and estimation. It uses conditional fuzzy measures on the unlabeled set.Two models are proposed, depending on the type of normalization of the induced possibilities. They indicate the existence of a generalized family of models which, when used with other measures and operators, will yield different sets of parameters for pattern classification purposes. However, since the decisionmaking scheme is adaptively tuned by the learning scheme, the exact interpretation of the physical meaning of these parameters is not very important. Parameters tune themselves to the peculiarities of the recognition scheme. The overall experimental results indicate that an appropriate deployment of a learning model is essential for any effective pattern classifier design.

Appendix

The cluster size or the spread of the cluster plays an important role when the underlying clusters are not of equal sizes. In such a case, using only one parameter—for example, the central member—will result in an erroneous classification of the data. This is illustrated in Fig. 10, where cluster A is larger than cluster B. As a result, if only the central member is used as a parameter for classification, any sample like x will have higher membership in cluster B, even though it is well within the boundary of cluster A. A simple case of well-separated clusters is considered here for clarity. This is applicable to fuzzy clusters whose boundary is not so well defined.

The membership function defined in (21a) incorporates the spread parameter E_i or σ_i^2. The modified loss function, which incorporates the spread of each cluster E_i is given as follows:

$$J(v, E) = \sum_{i=1}^{C} \sum_{x \in X} \mu_i^2(x)\left[\|x - v_i\|^2 - E_i\right]^2. \quad \text{(A1)}$$

This ensures that the samples which are closer to the central member of the wrong class, because of the unevenness of the sizes, be pulled back to the right class.

The expression for updating the spread parameter E_i is derived as follows. Differentiating (A1) with respect to E_i, we get

$$\frac{\partial J}{\partial E_i} = -2 \sum_{x \in X} \mu_i^2(x)\left[\|x - v_i\|^2 - E_i\right],$$

and

$$\frac{\partial^2 J}{\partial E_i^2} = 2 \sum_{x \in X} \mu_i^2(x).$$

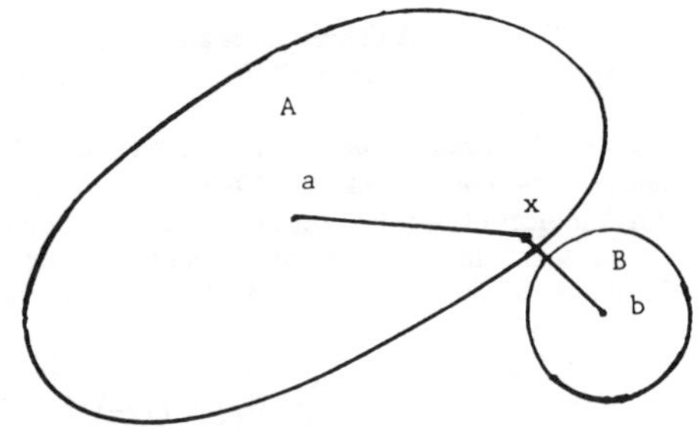

Fig. 10. Effect of cluster size on classification.

So,

$$\delta_i = \sum_{x \in X} \frac{\mu_i^2(x)\left[\|x - v_i\|^2 - E_i\right]}{\sum_{x \in X} \mu_i^2(x)}. \quad \text{(A2)}$$

The approximation for sequentially updating using a single sample is

$$\delta_i^k = \frac{\hat{\mu}_i^2(x^k)\left[\|x^k - \hat{v}_i^k\|^2 - \hat{E}_i^{k-1}\right]}{\sum_{j=1}^{k} \hat{\mu}_i(x^k)}. \quad \text{(A3)}$$

The recursive updating for the spread parameter thus becomes

$$\hat{E}_i^k = \hat{\sigma}_i^{2^k} = \sigma_i^{2^{k-1}} + \frac{\hat{\mu}_i^2(x^k)\left[\|x^k - \hat{v}_i^k\|^2 - \hat{E}_i^{k-1}\right]}{\sum_{j=1}^{k} \hat{\mu}_i^2(x^j)} \quad \text{(A4)}$$

or

$$\hat{E}_i^k = \hat{\sigma}_i^{2k} = \hat{\sigma}_i^{2k-1} + \rho_i^k\left[\|x^k - \hat{v}^k\|^2 - \hat{E}_i^{k-1}\right],$$

where ρ_i^k is given by (18) and $\mu_i(\cdot) = \mu_{f_i}(\cdot)$.

Acknowledgment

One of the authors, Bharathi Devi, wishes to thank Dr. L. N. Kanal, for his encouragement and his laboratory facilities at the University of Maryland.

References

[1] B. S. Atal and L. R. Rabiner, "A pattern recognition approach to voiced-unvoiced-silence classification with applications to speech recognition," *IEEE Trans. Acoust., Speech, Signal Proc.*, vol. ASSP-24, pp. 201–212, June 1976.

[2] B. B. Devi and V. V. S. Sarma, "Vowel recognition using fuzzy set concepts," *Acoust. Lett.*, vol. 4, pp. 44–48, Sept. 1980.

[3] ——, "A multistage evolutionary (FUME) clustering technique," *Pat. Recog. Lett.*, vol. 2, pp. 139–145, Mar. 1984.

[4] ——, "Estimation of fuzzy memberships from histogram," *Inform. Sci.*, vol. 35, pp. 43–59, 1985.

[5] B. B. Devi, "Pattern recognition via fuzzy set methods," Ph.D. dissertation, School of Automation, Indian Inst. Sci., Bangalore, India, Aug. 1984.

[6] J. C. Bezdek, *Pattern Recognition with Fuzzy Objective Function Algorithm*. New York: Plenum, 1981.

[7] C. H. Chen, "Learning in statistical pattern recognition," in *Proc. IEEE Conf. Cybern. and Soc.*, 1980, pp. 924–929.

[8] De Luca and S. Termini, "A definition of a non-parametric entropy in the setting of fuzzy sets theory," *Inform. Contr.*, vol. 20, pp. 301–312, May 1972.
[9] D. Dubois and H. Prade, *Fuzzy Sets and Systems: Theory and Applications*. New York: Academic, 1980.
[10] J. C. Dunn, "Indices of partition fuzziness and detection of clusters in large data sets," in *Fuzzy Automata and Decision Processes*, M. M. Gupta, R. K. Ragade, and R. R. Yager, Eds. New York: North-Holland, 1977.
[11] R. A. Fisher, "The use of multiple measurements in taxonomic problems," *Ann. Eugenics*, vol. 7, pt. II, pp. 179–188, 1936.
[12] E. Hisdal, "Possibilistically dependent variables and general theory of fuzzy sets," in *Fuzzy Automata and Decision Processes*, M. M. Gupta, R. K. Ragade, and R. R. Yager, Eds. New York: North-Holland, 1977.
[13] T. Imai and M. Shimura, "Learning with probabilistic labelling," *Pattern Recognition*, vol. 8, pp. 5–10, Jan. 1976.
[14] R. L. De Mantaras and J. Aguilar-Martin, "Self-learning pattern classification using a sequential clustering technique," in *Proc. IEEE Computer Soc. Conf. Pattern Recognition and Image Processing*, 1979, pp. 192–201.
[15] J. Sklansky and G. N. Wassel, *Pattern Classifiers and Trainable Machines*. New York: Springer-Verlag, 1981.
[16] S. Watanabe, "Creative learning and propensity automaton," *IEEE Trans. Syst., Man, Cybern.*, vol. SMC-5, pp. 603–609, Nov. 1975.
[17] L. H. Zadeh, "The concept of a linguistic variable and its application to approximate reasoning-II," *Inform. Sci.*, vol. 8, no. 4, pp. 301–357, 1975.
[18] L. H. Zadeh, "Fuzzy sets as a basis for a theory of possibility," *Fuzzy Sets Syst.*, vol. 1, no. 1, pp. 3–28, 1978.

Prototype Classification and Feature Selection with Fuzzy Sets

JAMES C. BEZDEK AND PATRICK F. CASTELAZ, STUDENT MEMBER, IEEE

Abstract—**The fuzzy ISODATA algorithms are used to address two problems: first, the question of feature selection for binary valued data sets is investigated; and second, the same method is applied to the design of a fuzzy one-nearest prototype classifier. The efficiency of this fuzzy classifier is compared to conventional *k*-NN classifiers by a computational example using the stomach disease data of Scheinok and Rupe, and Toussaint's method for estimation of the probability of misclassification: the fuzzy prototype classifier appears to decrease the error rate expected from all *k*-NN classifiers by roughly ten per cent.**

I. Introduction

FEATURE SELECTION is meant here to refer to the problem of dimensionality reduction of data which initially contain a high number of features (or characters): one hopes to choose "optimal" subsets of the original features which still contain the information essential for computer detection of substructure in the data, while reducing the computational burden imposed by using many features. Excellent introductions to many current techniques are to be found in the books of Duda and Hart [1], or Tou and Gonzalez [2]. Our interest is focused here on a method recently proposed in [3] for feature selection in two-class binary-valued data sets. The method is based on the fuzzy ISODATA clustering algorithms: our intention is to propose and exemplify an extension of this technique to binary data representing an arbitrary number of subclasses.

The second objective of our investigation concerns the efficacy of fuzzy ISODATA as a basis for *prototype classification*. In particular, we hope to show that the cluster centers generated by this algorithm provide a very competitive classifier, by comparing the performance of our fuzzy classifier to the family of *k*-nearest neighbor classifiers of the type defined in Cover and Hart [4].

In Section II the fuzzy ISODATA algorithms are briefly reviewed. Section III summarizes the feature selection method reported in [3] and defines a natural extension of this technique to an arbitrary number of classes. Section IV delineates the design of a fuzzy prototype classifier based on fuzzy ISODATA. In Section V several methods for empirically estimating the probability of misclassification are discussed. Section VI offers a numerical example to support the effectiveness of the proposed methods. The data set used is one which has been studied before, allowing comparison of our conclusions with those of previous authors.

Our principal results are these: first, the use of t.. ee features selected by our method from among the original 11 in the fuzzy classifier results in virtually identical average classifier performance; and secondly, our fuzzy classifier apparently lowers the expected error rate of any *k*-nearest neighbor classifier applied to the data used by roughly ten percent.

Manuscript received June 16, 1976; revised September 15, 1976. This work was supported by the National Science Foundation under Grant DCR75-05014.

J. C. Bezdek is with the Department of Mathematics, Utah State University, Logan, UT 84322.

P. F. Castelaz is with the Department of Electrical Engineering, Marquette University, Milwaukee, WI 53233

II. The ISODATA Algorithms

Let $X \doteq \{x_1, x_2, \cdots, x_n\} \subset R^s$; $x_i = (x_{i1}, x_{i2}, \cdots, x_{is}) \in R^s$ is a *feature vector*; $x_{ij} \in R$ is the jth *feature or characteristic* of individual x_i. We call X binary data in case $x_{ij} \in \{0,1\}\ \forall i,j$. For each integer c, $2 \le c < n$, let V_{cn} be the vector space of real $(c \times n)$ matrices, and let u_{ij} denote the ijth element of any $U \in V_{cn}$. Consider the following subset of V_{cn}:

$$M_c = \left\{ U \in V_{cn} \mid u_{ij} \in \{0,1\}\ \forall i,j; \sum_{i=1}^{c} u_{ij} = 1\ \forall j; \sum_{j=1}^{n} u_{ij} > 0\ \forall i \right\}. \quad (1)$$

For $U \in M_c$ we interpret the ith row of U, $U_{(i)} = (u_{i1}, u_{i2}, \cdots, u_{in})$, as values of a characteristic function, let us say $u_i: X \to \{0,1\}$ so that

$$u_{ij} = u_i(x_j) = \begin{Bmatrix} 1, & x_j \in Y_i \subset X \\ 0, & \text{otherwise.} \end{Bmatrix}. \quad (2)$$

The c rows of $U \in M_c$ define via (2) c *hard* (i.e., conventional or nonfuzzy) subsets of X, and because of the conditions in (1), these subsets $(Y_1, Y_2, \cdots, Y_c)$ form a conventional c-partition of X. For this reason, M_c can be shown isomorphic to the set of all hard c-partitions of X, hence we M_c *hard c-partition space*.

If the range of each u_i in (2) is extended to the closed interval $[0,1]$, the resultant function $u_i: X \to [0,1]$ becomes a *membership function* (after Zadeh [5]), and u_i is called a *fuzzy subset* or *fuzzy cluster* in X. Here $u_{ij} = u_i(x_j)$ is called the *grade of membership* of x_j in fuzzy set u_i. Generalizing (1) by this device produces the set

$$M_{fc} = \left\{ U \in V_{cn} \mid u_{ij} \in [0,1]\ \forall i,j; \sum_{i=1}^{c} u_{ij} = 1\ \forall j; \sum_{j=1}^{n} u_{ij} > 0\ \forall i \right\}. \quad (3)$$

Each $U \in M_{fc}$ is called a fuzzy c-partition of X; M_{fc} is *fuzzy c-partition space* associated with X. The salient mathematical properties of M_{fc} are discussed, for example, in [6],

Reprinted from *IEEE Trans. Syst., Man, Cybern.*, vol. SMC-7, no. 2, pp. 87–92, February 1977.

where it is shown that M_{fc} is the convex hull of a slightly enlarged superset of M_c. Physically, partitions of X which lie in M_{fc} enjoy the advantage of allowing each individual in the data the choice of belonging unequivocally to one and only one partitioning subset (e.g., a progenitor), or of sharing membership in several partitioning subsets (e.g., a hybrid). In either instance total membership of each subject in the data is restricted by the column sum condition to unity.

To generate c-partitions of X which are fuzzy in the above sense we proceed as follows: let L be the linear hull or span of the data, $L = \text{span}(X)$, and let L_c denote the c-fold Cartesian product of L with itself. For each real number $m \in [1,\infty)$ define the real-valued functional J_m: $M_{fc} \times L_c \to R$ by

$$J_m(U,v) = \sum_{k=1}^{n} \sum_{i=1}^{c} (u_{ik})^m \|x_k - v_i\|^2, \qquad 1 \le m < \infty. \tag{4}$$

In (4) we allow $\|\cdot\|$ to be any differentiable norm on R^s, and the vector $v = (v_1, v_2, \cdots, v_c)$ has as components the vectors $v_i \in L$. These v_i are interpreted as *cluster centers* or prototypes of the c fuzzy clusters defined by their companion U matrix, and play a fundamental role in our development. J_m is a weighted, least squares objective function: for $U \in M_c$, $J_m = J_1$ for all m, and J_1 is the classical within groups sum of squares objective function evident in much of the early literature on cluster analysis [1].

The fuzzy ISODATA clustering algorithms arise from necessary conditions for local minima of the constrained nonlinear programming problem associated with (4), viz.,

$$\text{minimize } \{J_m(U,v)\} \text{ over } M_{fc} \times L_c. \tag{5}$$

Local solutions of (5) were shown in [6] to fall into four cases: $m = 1$ versus $m > 1$; and singular ($x_k = v_i$ for some i,k) and nonsingular. In particular, for $m > 1$ and $x_k \ne v_i \; \forall i,k$, it was demonstrated that (U,v) may be a local minimum of J_m only if

$$u_{ik} = \frac{1}{\sum_{j=1}^{c} \left(\frac{\|x_k - v_i\|}{\|x_k - v_j\|} \right)^{(2/m-1)}}, \qquad \forall i,k \tag{6a}$$

$$v_i = \frac{\sum_{k=1}^{n} (u_{ik})^m x_k}{\sum_{k=1}^{n} (u_{ik})^m}, \qquad \forall i. \tag{6b}$$

Observe that for this case, $u_{ik} \in (0,1) \; \forall i,k$, and so the denominators in (6b) never vanish. For $m > 1$ it is the nonsingular case which almost always occurs in practice because roundoff errors are usually sufficient to preclude singularities. The fuzzy ISODATA algorithms are the infinite family (one for each $m \in [1,\infty)$] of iterative procedures defined by necessary conditions (6).

The Fuzzy ISODATA Algorithms

$$\text{Guess any } U \in M_c. \tag{7a}$$

$$\text{Calculate cluster centers } \{v_1, v_2, \cdots, v_c\} \text{ with (6b).} \tag{7b}$$

$$\text{Update } U \to U^* \text{ with (6a).} \tag{7c}$$

If $\max_{i,k} \{|u_{ik}^* - u_{ik}|\} \le \varepsilon$, stop. Otherwise, relabel

$$U^* \to U \text{ and return to (7b).} \tag{7d}$$

With an appropriate tie-breaking rule the loop in (7) provides an iterative descent algorithm which converges to local solutions of (5). We take as optimal fuzzy partitionings of X the U obtained in this fashion which are part of optimal pairs for J_m.

At $m = 1$, (5) is called the minimum variance partitioning problem. Ball and Hall proposed in [7] conditions for minimizing J_1 and called their iterative procedure hard ISODATA; their conditions, which replace (6a) by a nearest prototype rule and leave (6b) fixed, were shown by Dunn in [8] to be necessary. The theory of fuzzy ISODATA and some applications of it in clustering, taxonomy, and unsupervised learning are reported in [6], [8]–[12].

III. Feature Selection for Binary Data

If X is binary, the optimal cluster centers $\{v_i\}$ from (6b) are related to X in a very interesting and ostensibly useful way. We state the results, and refer interested readers to [3] for proofs.

Proposition: If X is binary, then the components of each v_i from (6b) satisfy:

$$0 \le v_{ij} \le 1, \qquad \forall i,j \tag{8a}$$

$$v_{ij} = 0 \Leftrightarrow x_{pj} = 0, p = 1,2,\cdots,n \Leftrightarrow v_{kj} = 0, \qquad \forall k \tag{8b}$$

$$v_{ij} = 1 \Leftrightarrow x_{pj} = 1, p = 1,2,\cdots,n \Leftrightarrow v_{kj} = 1, \qquad \forall k. \tag{8c}$$

In what follows we call the v_{ij} *feature centers* of cluster center v_i. The implications of (8) for feature selection are these: $v_{ij} = 0$, iff *none* of the data possesses feature j so it is uncharacteristic of the mixed populations, and is minimal as a subclass descriptor. On the other hand, $v_{ij} = 1$, iff *all* members of the data have feature j; in this instance j is a maximal descriptor of all subclasses. In either situation, feature j will be totally irrelevant to subclass discrimination. Note that one of the cluster centers v_i can have all its components in (0,1) if and only if all cs feature centers $v_{ij} \in (0,1)$; in this instance v_{ij} would appear to indicate the relative quality of feature j as a descriptor of class i. If $v_{ij} \to 0$, feature j becomes uncharacteristic of class i; conversely, as $v_{ij} \to 1$, we presume that feature j is strongly indicative of class i individuals.

To use the v_{ij} for identification of optimal features for subclass discrimination, we define the following measure of cluster center separation (see [23] for similar measures):

$$f_{ij} = (|v_{i1} - v_{j1}|, |v_{i2} - v_{j2}|, \cdots, |v_{is} - v_{js}|), \tag{9}$$

$1 \le i \le c$; $1 \le j \le c$. Since $f_{ij} = f_{ji}$ and $f_{ii} = \theta$ is the zero vector, our attention can be confined to the $c(c-1)/2$ f's with $1 \le i \le c - 1$ and $i + 1 \le j \le c$. Equations (8) yield for the components $f_{ij,k}$ of f_{ij}:

$$0 \le f_{ij,k} < 1, \qquad \forall i,j, \text{ and } k \tag{10a}$$

$$f_{ij,k} = 0 \Leftrightarrow \begin{cases} \text{(i) either all vectors in } X \text{ have feature } k, \text{ or} \\ \text{(ii) none of the vectors in } X \text{ has feature } k. \end{cases} \tag{10b}$$

When $f_{ij,k} = 0$, feature k is apparently useless as a measure of variability between subclasses i and j. Observe that $f_{ij,k}$ cannot attain the value 1 because v_{ik} and v_{jk} are simultaneously either 0 or 1. However, when $0 < v_{ij} < 1 \ \forall i$ and j, $f_{ij,k}$ can become arbitrarily close to 1 as more and more members of one class possess feature k while very few opposite subclass members have it. Accordingly, it seems plausible to infer from $f_{ij,k} \to 1$ that k is an optimal discriminator for subclasses i and j, and hence the numbers $\{f_{ij,k} \mid k = 1,2,\cdots,s\}$ rank—by their magnitudes—the relative utility of the s features as separators of classes i and j.

For $c = 2$ the components of f_{12} rank the features, and any number of features from 1 to s can be selected directly. For $c > 2$, the procedure is more complex, for then the best features for pairwise discrimination are generally a function of i and j. In this case, moreover, one cannot select less than M features, $c \leq 2^M$, for separation of binary valued data. A natural way to extend the method for c subclasses is to average the values of $f_{ij,k}$ over the $c(c-1)/2$ pairs (i,j) to obtain an *overall average efficiency* of feature k:

$$f_k = \left\{\frac{2}{(c)(c-1)}\right\} \sum_{j=i+1}^{c} \sum_{i=1}^{c-1} f_{ij,k}, \tag{11}$$

which indicates the relative ability of feature k to separate all distinct pairs of the c subclasses. Since $0 \leq f_k < 1 \ \forall k$, our procedure is to calculate the numbers $(f_1,f_2,\cdots,f_s)$ and order them in decreasing magnitude; the optimal features are those having the highest values.

Two observations about this procedure are worth mentioning: first, we note that fuzzy ISODATA and the prototype classifier to be described below are well defined and applicable for data subject only to the constraint $x_{ij} \in R$ for all i and j. The *feature selection* method described here, however, is explicitly dependent on binary data, for otherwise (8)–(10) are invalid. Second, this method of feature selection cannot work at $m = 1$, i.e., using hard ISODATA, because it is clear from (6b) with $m = 1$ that the crucial relations (8b) and (8c) between the data and the cluster centers will fail to hold.

IV. Prototype Classification

The basic idea in prototype classification is to use the n data points to generate c protypical representatives of the subclasses involved. In our case, the prototypes will be the fuzzy cluster centers $\{v_i\}$. Once the prototypes are found, they are used to define a rule which partitions R^s into c decision regions for classification of subsequent data. The mathematical properties of the classifier depend on the prototypes and the decision rule. Each v_i calculated as in (6b) is a convex combination of the data used to compute it, and is chosen to minimize the total weighted squared error measured by J_m. Although no direct statistical or geometrical interpretation of the objective function for $m > 1$ has yet been found, an analogy in [13] suggests that J_m assesses the total "equivalent variance" incurred by partial representation of each x_k by all c of the prototypes $\{v_i\}$. A simple decision rule based on this is the *one-nearest prototype* (1-NP) rule:

> Given $\{v_1,v_2,\cdots,v_c\}$ as in (6b), decide for $x_m \notin X$ that x_m belongs to class i if $\|x_m - v_i\| = \min_j \{\|x_m - v_j\|\}$. If there is no proper minimum, place x_m in the first class at which a common value is attained. (12)

The 1-*NP* classifier defined in (12) can be trained (i.e., optimal v_i can be calculated with fuzzy ISODATA) with any type of data set as long as $\|\cdot\|$ is a meaningful similarity measure and is differentiable. The rule in (12) could be extended to a k-NP classifier, $k > 1$, if classification using multiple prototypes is desired. Observe that (12) is actually a mixed fuzzy-hard model: fuzzy partitions of the data are generated during training; and then the fuzzy cluster centers are used to produce hard classifications of subsequent data.

For later comparisons we define the *one-nearest neighbor* (1-NN) classifier:

> For $x_m \notin X$, decide x_m belongs to class i if $\|x_m - x_k\| = \min_j \{\|x_m - x_j\|\}$, $x_j \in X$, and x_k bears label i. (13)

Ties in (13) are ordinarily resolved as in (12). The k-NN classifier (c.f., Fukunaga [14]) is defined in the obvious way if multiple nearest neighbors are to be used. Our numerical example below compares the performance of 1-NP and k-NN classification using some results published recently by Toussaint [15].

V. Estimation of Empirical Error Rates

Let $\tilde{P}_e$ denote the "actual" probability of error (misclassification) on all future samples when a given classifier is trained on half of an infinite data set, and let P_e denote our best estimate of $\tilde{P}_e$ when using a finite data set. Since $\tilde{P}_e$ and P_e are not directly available, there are in the literature a number of empirical methods devoted to estimation of P_e. Of these, we describe two, and refer interested readers to [15] for an excellent treatment of a more definitive nature concerning the others.

Method 1: Resubstitution (R-Method)

($r1$) Train the classifier on all of X.
($r2$) Test the classifier on all of X.
($r3$) Calculate the estimate $P_e(R)$ = number incorrect/n.

Method 2: Rotation Method of Toussaint [15] (π-Method)

($\pi1$) Choose an integer p so that $1 \leq p \ll n$, $p/n < \frac{1}{2}$, and n/p is an integer.
($\pi2$) Randomly partition X into a training set X_i^{tr} of cardinality $n - p$, and a test set $X_i^{ts} = X - X_i^{tr}$ of cardinality p, for indices $i = 1,2,\cdots,n/p$.
($\pi3$) For each i, train the classifier with X_i^{tr} and test it with X_i^{ts}.
($\pi4$) Calculate for each i the estimate $P_e(\pi_i)$ = number incorrect/p.
($\pi5$) After n/p rotations through the data using ($\pi2$)-($\pi4$), compute the average estimate

$$E(P_e(\pi)) = \sum_{i=1}^{n/p} P_e(\pi_i)/(n/p).$$

TABLE I
ATTRIBUTES OF 300 STOMACH DISEASE PATIENTS*

Symptom	Description or Type of Abdominal Pain
1	Male (=1); Female (=0)
2	Epigastric pain
3	Upper right quadrant pain
4	Back pain
5	Discomfort episodes of 1-4 weeks
6	Discomfort episodes of 0-1 days
7	Relief induced by food ingestion
8	Aggravation induced by food ingestion
9	Aggravation induced by position
10	Weight loss (at least 20 lbs. in 6 mos.)
11	Persistence (at least 1 month in length)

* Condensed from Scheinok and Rinaldo [20].

The rotation method generalizes several methods: at $p = 1$ it reduces to Lachenbruch's U-method (the "hold one out" method, [16]); at $p = n/2$ it is essentially two runs using the H-method (the "holdout" method studied by Highleyman [17] and others) with the roles of the test and training sets reversed. We denote the estimates generated by these methods as $E(P_e(U))$ and $E(P_e(H))$, respectively. The π-method was proposed to compromise the bias of the H-method with the computational burden imposed by the U-method. These estimates of P_e have often been conjectured to satisfy the following inequalities:

$$P_e(R) \leq P_e \leq E(P_e(U)) \leq E(P_e(\pi)) \leq E(P_e(H)). \quad (14)$$

Since (14) implies that the R-method is too optimistic, while the others are pessimistic, Toussaint reasoned that some convex combination of $P_e(R)$ and $E(P_e(\pi))$ should provide a more accurate estimate of P_e than either one alone; thus he proposed computing

$$P_e^*(\lambda) = \lambda P_e(R) + (1 - \lambda)E(P_e(\pi)), \qquad \lambda \in [0,1]. \quad (15)$$

$P_e^*(\lambda)$ incorporates the compromise embodied by the π-method, as well as an attempt to balance the inequalities in (14). In general, λ will be a function of n,p, and the number of parameters to be estimated. Lacking further theoretical evidence, we follow Toussaint in taking $\lambda = 1 - \lambda = \frac{1}{2}$. In what follows, we will actually report empirical estimates of the probability of *correct* classification, viz., $P_c = 1 - P_e$. Thus we compute $P_c(R)$, $E(P_c(\pi))$, and $P_c^*(\frac{1}{2})$ in the numerical example below. These estimates, obtained with fuzzy 1-NP classification with and without feature selection, will be compared to those given by Toussaint and Sharp in [18].

VI. A NUMERICAL EXAMPLE

The data used in our example was collected in 1963 by Rinaldo, Scheinok, and Rupe [19], and was passed along to us by Prof. Toussaint. It consists of 11 binary features ($1 \Rightarrow$ present, $0 \Rightarrow$ absent) representing symptoms of 300 patients suffering from one of six types of abdominal disorders: hiatal hernia, duodenal ulcer, gastric ulcer, cancer, gallstones, and functional disease. The symptoms are briefly described in Table I and appear in full detail in [20].

TABLE II
PROBABILITIES OF CORRECT CLASSIFICATION $P_c(\pi_i)$ AND OPTIMAL FEATURE TRIPLES FOR $m = 1.3$

Run No. (i)	$P_c(\pi_i)$ for all 11 Features	$P_c(\pi_i)$ for 3 Features Selected	Selected, Ordered Feature Triple
1	.644	.625	7,8,6
2	.532	.648	7,8,4
3	.699	.662	6,5,8
4	.502	.676	1,7,8
5	.574	.444	1,7,5
6	.731	.644	7,8,6
7	.602	.685	1,6,5
8	.639	.546	1,7,8
9	.657	.736	1,7,6
10	.620	.505	1,7,8
11	.699	.597	7,8,1
12	.745	.685	6,7,5
13	.514	.519	6,1,4
14	.574	.556	7,8,5
15	.620	.546	7,5,6
16	.537	.569	6,1,5
17	.500	.588	8,7,1
18	.583	.611	7,5,6
19	.532	.565	7,8,1
20	.481	.620	7,8,6

Our computer runs were made in single precision Fortran IV on a Xerox Sigma 9. The norm $\|\cdot\|$ in (4), (6a), and (12) was the Euclidean norm, a choice justified both by [3] and for compatibility of comparisons with previous studies. Two values of the weighting exponent in (4) were used: $m = 1.3$ and $m = 1.4$. A typical ith run with the rotation method required three minutes of CPU time to execute the following sequence of steps.

(i1) Randomly partition X into $X_i^{tr} \cup X_i^{ts}$, where training set X_i^{tr} contains 270 samples and test set X_i^{ts} the remaining 30.
(i2) Initiate fuzzy ISODATA at (7a) with the initial matrix denoted by U_0 in [3] operating on X_i^{tr}.
(i3) Terminate fuzzy ISODATA when (7d) is satisfied at $\varepsilon = 0.05$.
(i4) Test the fuzzy 1-NP classifier defined by the optimal cluster centers $\{v_i\}$ found in (i3) using rule (12) and test set X_i^{ts}. Compute $P_c(\pi_i)$.
(i5) Calculate the feature selection vector $(f_1,\cdots,f_s)$ via (11), and select the optimal feature triple it recommends.
(i6) Delete from X_i^{ts} and X_i^{tr} the eight nonoptimal features found in (i5), return to (i2), and repeat (i2)–(i4).

To effect comparisons with [18] we took $p = 30$, but varied from the procedure suggested at (π2) by rotating through the data $2n/p = 20$ times, instead of the recommended $n/p = 10$ times, feeling that this variation lends extra stability to the averaged estimate of P_c found with the rotation method. Tables II and III respectively list the results of 20 such runs for each choice of $m = 1.3, 1.4$. The results of these runs are summarized as row 1 of Table IV, where the estimates $E(P_c(\pi))$ are displayed. Table III indicates three points of interest: first, the expected accuracy

TABLE III
PROBABILITIES OF CORRECT CLASSIFICATION $P_c(\pi_i)$ AND OPTIMAL FEATURE TRIPLES FOR $m = 1.4$

Run No. (i)	$P_c(\pi_i)$ for all 11 Features	$P_c(\pi_i)$ for 3 Features Selected	Selected, Ordered Feature Triple
1	.602	.685	1,6,5
2	.639	.546	1,7,8
3	.574	.444	1,7,5
4	.731	.644	7,8,6
5	.565	.676	6,7,5
6	.644	.625	7,8,6
7	.699	.662	6,5,8
8	.602	.676	1,7,8
9	.657	.764	1,7,6
10	.644	.597	7,8,1
11	.745	.685	6,7,5
12	.551	.519	6,1,4
13	.574	.556	7,8,5
14	.620	.546	7,5,6
15	.537	.569	6,1,5
16	.458	.588	8,7,1
17	.560	.495	7,8,5
18	.532	.657	7,5,6
19	.481	.620	7,8,6
20	.583	.611	7,5,6

TABLE IV
ESTIMATED PROBABILITIES OF CORRECT CLASSIFICATION USING FUZZY 1-NP CLASSIFIER

Weighting Exponent	m=1.3		m=1.4	
Features Used	11	3	11	3
$E(P_c(\pi))$	.604	.601	.600	.608
$P_c(R)$	.675	.618	.675	.618
$P_c^*(\frac{1}{2})$	.639	.609	.637	.613

of the fuzzy 1-NP classifier seems remarkably stable to slight changes in weighting exponent m; secondly, the feature selection method apparently chooses optimal triples capable of yielding almost identical performance—on the average—as the classifications made with the original ones; and finally, that $E(P_c(\pi)) \approx 60\%$ with fuzzy 1-NP classification.

The data were also processed once for each m using the R-method of estimation for P_c. The second row of Table IV indicates identical error rates for both values of m. As predicted by (14), these estimates are somewhat more optimistic than those of $E(P_c(\pi))$. The fall off in accuracy when passing to the optimal triple selected (features 8,7,5 in that order for both runs) is probably due to the particular samples selected and would stabilize with more runs.

Taking $\lambda = \frac{1}{2}$ in (15), $P_c(R)$ and $E(P_c(\pi))$ combine to produce the values of $P_c^*(\frac{1}{2})$ listed in row 3 of Table IV. From these values we infer that the most reasonable estimate of fuzzy 1-NP classifier performance on all features is about 64%; and on optimal triples selected by our method about 61%. Combining these, we take 62% as the most meaningful estimate of average performance with this data using the

TABLE V
OCCURRENCE OF OPTIMAL FEATURES—WEIGHTED AND UNWEIGHTED

Feature or Symptom	Unweighted Frequency of Occurence*		Weighted Frequency of Occurence*	
	m=1.3	m=1.4	m=1.3	m=1.4
1	11	9	25	21
2	8	0	0	0
3	0	0	0	0
4	2	1	2	1
5	8	11	11	15
6	11	13	20	24
7	16	16	41	41
8	12	10	21	18
9	0	0	0	0
10	0	0	0	0
11	0	0	0	0

* In Tables II and III.

fuzzy 1-NP classifier. These values indicate that feature selection for the purposes described herein seems to uphold the level of accuracy attained with all features, while reducing the amount of calculation (in subsequent classification) quite a bit. Our figures should be compared with those given by Toussaint and Sharpe [18], who study all of the estimates listed in (14), and conclude that $P_c^*(\frac{1}{2}) \approx 52\%$ is the most credible estimate of the probability of correct classification using any k-NN classifier. We ascribe the approximate increase of 10% in expected classifier performance to the way in which memberships of the training vectors in partitioning subclasses are distributed by the fuzzy ISODATA algorithm; our classifier prototypes are designed using the advantage of membership sharing made possible by the use of fuzzy sets.

Tables II and III also list for each rotation through X the optimal features selected. As expected, the triple chosen is a function of the sample used for training. To gauge the relative usefulness of the various features, it is necessary to synthesize these results. Several ways to do this are shown in Table V. One obvious indication is the frequency of occurrence of feature k—without regard to order—in the triple selected. From Table V it will be seen that feature 7 appears most often for either m, while symptoms 2, 3, 9, 10, and 11 are never chosen. The same conclusions follow by considering weighted frequencies of occurrence. Thus by weighting each appearance of feature k in positions 1, 2, 3, respectively, by values 3, 2, 1, we again conclude that feature 7 is most important, while 2, 3, 9, 10, and 11 are irrelevant to (computer) detection of substructure in X. This result agrees with the findings of Lee [21], who analyzed this data using an information-theoretic method of feature selection, and also concluded that symptom 7—relief induced by food ingestion—is the most significant one of the 11 that were collected.

We observe that although Table V establishes 7 as the first choice, 4 as the sixth choice, and indicates no usefulness for 2, 3, 9, 10, and 11, no clear ordering of the remaining four features emerges. Our method of feature selection thus supports the following ordering for the relative efficacy of the features: 7 > {8,6,1,5} > 4 > {2,3,9,10,11}, where > indicates "more powerful for discrimination," and the subsets in brackets are not ordered. Based on this, it is our supposition that the quintet {7,8,6,1,5} would probably yield an average classifier performance of about 62% using fuzzy 1-NP classification for subsequent patients known to have one of the six stomach disorders under consideration.

VII. Conclusions

It has been demonstrated numerically that fuzzy 1-NP classification applied to a particular data set increases the expected probability of correct classification of all k-NN classifiers by a significant margin. Furthermore, feature selection with fuzzy ISODATA yielded optimal subsets of features which resulted in no appreciable loss of classifier performance and upheld results of other studies. These facts seem to recommend further study of the fuzzy techniques defined above.

References

[1] R. Duda and P. Hart. *Pattern Classification and Scene Analysis.* New York: Wiley-Interscience, 1973.

[2] J. Tou and R. Gonzalez, *Pattern Recognition Principles.* Reading: Addison-Wesley, 1974.

[3] J. Bezdek, "Feature selection for binary data; Medical diagnosis with fuzzy sets," *Proc. National Computer Conference*, S. Winkler, ed. Montvale: AFIPS, 1976, pp. 1057–1068.

[4] T. Cover and P. Hart. "Nearest neighbor pattern classification," *IEEE Trans. Inform. Theory*, vol. IT-13, pp. 21–27, 1967.

[5] L. Zadeh, "Fuzzy sets," *Inform. and Control*, vol. 8, pp. 338–353, 1965.

[6] J. Bezdek, "Fuzzy mathematics in pattern classification," Ph.D. dissertation, Cornell University, Ithaca, 1973.

[7] G. Ball and D. Hall, "A clustering technique for summarizing multivariate data," *Behav. Sci.*, vol. 12, pp. 153–155, 1967.

[8] J. Dunn, "A fuzzy relative of the ISODATA process and its use in detecting compact, well separated clusters," *J. Cybern.*, vol. 3, no. 3, pp. 32–57, 1974.

[9] J. Bezdek, "Cluster validity with fuzzy sets," *J. Cybern.*, vol. 3, no. 3, pp. 58–71, 1974.

[10] ——, "Numerical taxonomy with fuzzy sets," *J. Math. Biology*, vol. 1, no. 1, pp. 57–71, 1973.

[11] ——, "Mathematical models for systematics and taxonomy," *Proc. Eighth Int'l. Conf. on Numerical Taxonomy*, G. Estabrook, Ed. San Francisco: Freeman, pp. 143–164, 1975.

[12] J. Bezdek and J. Dunn. "Optimal fuzzy partitions: A heuristic for estimating the parameters in a mixture of normal distributions," *IEEE Trans. Comput.*, vol. C-24, pp. 835–838, 1975.

[13] J. Bezdek, "A physical interpretation of fuzzy ISODATA," *IEEE Trans. Systems, Man, Cybern.*, vol. SMC-6, pp. 387–390, 1976.

[14] K. Fukunaga, *Introduction to Statistical Pattern Recognition.* New York: Academic Press, 1972.

[15] G. Toussaint, "Machine recognition of independent and contextually constrained contour-traced handprinted characters," M.S. Thesis, Univ. of B.C., 1969.

[16] P. Lachenbruch, "Estimation of error rates in discriminant analysis," Ph.D. dissertation, USC, 1965.

[17] W. Highleyman, "Linear decision functions, with applications to pattern recognition," *Proc. IRE*, vol. 50, pp. 1501–1514, 1962.

[18] G. Toussaint and P. Sharpe, "An efficient method for estimating the probability of misclassification applied to a problem in medical diagnosis," *Comput. Biol. Med.*, vol. 4, pp. 269–278, 1975.

[19] J. Rinaldo, P. Scheinok, and C. Rupe, "Symptom diagnosis: A mathematical analysis of epigastric pain," *Annals Int. Medicine*, vol. 59, no. 2, pp. 145–154, 1963.

[20] P. Scheinok and J. Rinaldo, "Symptom diagnosis: Optimal subsets for upper abdominal pain," *Comp. and Bio. Res.*, vol. 1, pp. 221–236, 1967.

[21] R. C. T. Lee, "Application of information theory to select relevant variables," *Math. Biosciences*, vol. 11, pp. 153–161, 1971.

[22] L. Zadeh, K. S. Fu, K. Tanaka, and M. Shimura, *Fuzzy Sets and Their Applications to Cognitive and Decision Processes.* New York: Academic Press, 1975.

[23] E. T. Lee, "Shape oriented chromosome classification," *IEEE Trans. System, Man, Cybern.*, pp. 629–633, Nov. 1975.

Fuzzy Set Theoretic Measure for Automatic Feature Evaluation

SANKAR K. PAL, SENIOR MEMBER, IEEE, AND BASABI CHAKRABORTY, STUDENT MEMBER, IEEE

Abstract—**The terms *index of fuzziness, entropy,* and π-*ness*, which give measures of fuzziness in a set, are used to define an index of feature evaluation in pattern recognition problems in terms of their intraclass and interclass measures. The index value decreases as the reliability of a feature in characterizing and discriminating different classes increases. The algorithm developed has been implemented in cases of vowel and plosive identification problem using formant frequencies and different S and π membership functions.**

I. Introduction

The process of selecting the necessary information to present to the decision rule is called *feature selection*. Its main objective is to retain the optimum salient characteristics necessary for the recognition process and to reduce the dimensionality of the measurement space so that effective and easily computable algorithms can be devised for efficient classification.

The criterion of a good feature is that it should be unchanging with any other possible variation within a class, while emphasizing differences that are important in discriminating between patterns of different types. One of the useful techniques to achieve this is clustering transformation [1]–[3], which maximizes/minimizes the interset/intraset distance using a diagonal transformation, such that smaller weights are given to features having larger variance (less reliable). Other separability measures based on information theoretic approach include divergence, Bhattacharyya coefficient, and the Kolmogorov variational distance [1]–[7].

The present work demonstrates an application of the theory of fuzzy sets to the problem of evaluating feature quality. The terms *index of fuzziness* [8], *entropy* [9], and π-*ness* [10] provide measures of fuzziness in a set and are used here to define the measure of separability in terms of their interclass and intraclass measurements. These two types of measurements are found to reflect the concept of interset and intraset distances in classical set theory. An index of feature evaluation is then defined using these measures such that the lower the value of the index for a feature, the greater is the importance (quality) of the feature in recognizing and separating classes in the feature space.

It is also to be mentioned here that the above parameters provide algorithms for automatic segmentation [11] of grey tone image and measuring enhancement quality [12] of an image.

Effectiveness of the algorithm is demonstrated on vowel, plosive consonant, and speaker recognition problems using formant frequencies and their different combinations as feature set and S and π functions [13]–[15] as membership functions.

Manuscript received April 5, 1984; revised August 27, 1985 and April 21, 1986.

The authors are with the Electronics and Communication Science Unit, Indian Statistical Institute, 203 Barrackpore Trunk Road, Calcutta 700035, India.

IEEE Log Number 8609835.

II. Fuzzy Sets and Measurements of Fuzziness

A. Fuzzy Sets

A fuzzy set A with its finite number of supports $x_1, x_2, \cdots, x_n$ in the universe of discourse U is formally defined as

$$A = \{(\mu_A(x_i), x_i)\}, \qquad i = 1, 2, \cdots, n \tag{1}$$

where the characteristic function $\mu_A(x_i)$ known as membership function and having positive value in the interval $[0,1]$ denotes the degree to which an event x_i may be a member of A. A point x_i for which $\mu_A(x_i) = 0.5$ is said to be a crossover point of the fuzzy set A.

Let us now give some measures of fuzziness of a set A. These measures define, on a global sense, the degree of difficulty (ambiguity) in deciding whether an element x_i would be considered as a member of A.

B. Index of Fuzziness

The index of fuzziness γ of a fuzzy set A having n supporting points reflects the degree of ambiguity present in it by measuring the distance between A and its nearest ordinary set $\tilde{A}$ and is defined as [8]

$$\gamma(A) = \frac{2}{n^{1/k}} d(A, \tilde{A}) \tag{2}$$

where $d(A, \tilde{A})$ denotes the distance between A and its nearest ordinary set $\tilde{A}$. The set $\tilde{A}$ is such that

$$\mu_{\tilde{A}}(x_i) = 0, \qquad \text{if } \mu_A(x_i) \leqslant 0.5 \tag{3a}$$

and

$$\mu_{\tilde{A}}(x_i) = 1, \qquad \text{if } \mu_A(x_i) > 0.5. \tag{3b}$$

The positive constant k appears in order to make $\gamma(A)$ lie between zero and one, and its value depends on the type of distance function used. For example, $k = 1$ for a generalized Hamming distance, whereas $k = 2$ for a Euclidean distance. The corresponding indices of fuzziness are called the linear index of fuzziness $\gamma_l(A)$ and the quadratic index of fuzziness $\gamma_q(A)$. Considering d to be a generalized Hamming distance, we have

$$\begin{aligned} d_l(A, \tilde{A}) &= \sum_i |\mu_A(x_i) - \mu_{\tilde{A}}(x_i)| \\ &= \sum_i \mu_{A \cap \bar{A}}(x_i), \qquad i = 1, 2, \cdots, n \end{aligned} \tag{4}$$

and

$$\gamma_l(A) = \frac{2}{n} \sum_i \mu_{A \cap \bar{A}}(x_i), \qquad i = 1, 2, \cdots, n \tag{5}$$

where $\mu_{A \cap \bar{A}}(x_i)$ denotes the membership of x_i to a set which is the intersection of the fuzzy set A and its complement $\bar{A}$ and is

Reprinted from *IEEE Trans. Syst., Man, Cybern.*, vol. SMC-16, no. 5, pp. 754–760, September/October 1986.

defined as

$$\mu_{A\cap\bar{A}}(x_i) = \min\{\mu_A(x_i), (1-\mu_A(x_i))\}, \quad i = 1,2,\cdots,n.$$

Considering d to be an Euclidean distance, we have

$$\gamma_q(A) = \frac{2}{\sqrt{n}}\left[\sum_i (\mu_A(x_i) - \mu_{\bar{A}}(x_i))^2\right]^{1/2}, \quad i = 1,2,\cdots,n. \tag{6}$$

C. Entropy

The term entropy of a fuzzy set A is defined according to Deluca and Termini [9] as

$$H(A) = \frac{1}{n \ln 2}\sum_i S_n(\mu_A(x_i)), \quad i = 1,2,\cdots,n \tag{7}$$

with

$$S_n(\mu_A(x_i)) = -\mu_A(x_i)\ln(\mu_A(x_i)) - (1-\mu_A(x_i))\ln(1-\mu_A(x_i)). \tag{8}$$

In (7) and (8), ln stands for natural logarithm (i.e., base e). However, any other base would serve the purpose because of the normalization factor $\ln 2$ in (7).

$\gamma(A)$ and $H(A)$ are such that (from (5)–(7))

$$\gamma_{\min} = H_{\min} = 0(\min), \text{ for } \mu_A(x_i) = 0 \text{ or } 1 \quad \text{for all } i \tag{9a}$$

$$\gamma_{\max} = H_{\max} = 1(\max), \text{ for } \mu_A(x_i) = 0.5, \quad \text{for all } i. \tag{9b}$$

Suppose $\mu_A(x_i) = 0.5$, for all i. Then $\mu_{\bar{A}}(x_i) = 0$, for all i, and

$$\gamma_l(A) = \frac{2}{n}\sum_i\left(\frac{1}{2}\right) = \frac{2}{n}\cdot\frac{n}{2} = 1$$

$$\gamma_q(A) = \frac{2}{\sqrt{n}}\left(\sum_i\left(\frac{1}{2}\right)^2\right)^{1/2} = \frac{2}{\sqrt{n}}\cdot\frac{\sqrt{n}}{2} = 1$$

and

$$H(A) = \frac{1}{n \ln 2}\sum_i\left(-\ln\frac{1}{2}\right) = \frac{1}{n\ln 2}\cdot n\ln 2 = 1.$$

Therefore, γ and H increase monotonically in the interval $[0, 0.5]$ and decrease monotonically in $[0.5, 1]$ with a maximum of one at $\mu = 0.5$.

D. π-ness

The π-ness of A is defined as [10]

$$\pi(A) = \frac{1}{n}\sum_i G_\pi(x_i), \quad i = 1,2,\cdots,n \tag{10}$$

where G_π is any π function as explained in the Section III.

G_π $(0 \leqslant G_\pi \leqslant 1)$ increases monotonically in $[x_i = 0$ to $x_i = x_{\max}/2$, say$]$ and then decreases monotonically in $[x_{\max}/2, x_{\max}]$ with a maximum of unity at $x_{\max}/2$, where $x_{\max}$ denotes the maximum value of x_i.

III. Membership Functions

Let us now consider different S and π functions to obtain $\mu_A(x_i)$ from x_i. The standard S function as defined by Zadeh [13] has the form

$$\mu_{AS}(x_i; a, b, c)$$

$$= 0, \quad x_i \leqslant a \tag{11a}$$

$$= 2[(x_i - a)/(c-a)]^2, \quad a \leqslant x_i \leqslant b \tag{11b}$$

$$= 1 - 2[(x_i - c)/(c-a)]^2, \quad b \leqslant x_i \leqslant c \tag{11c}$$

$$= 1, \quad x_i \geqslant c \tag{11d}$$

in the interval $[a, c]$ with $b = (a+c)/2$. The parameter b is known as the crossover point for which $\mu_{AS}(b) = S(b; a, b, c) = 0.5$.

Similarly, the standard π function has the form

$$\mu_{A\pi}(x_i; a, c, a') = \mu_{AS}(x_i; a, b, c), \quad x_i \leqslant c \tag{12a}$$

$$= 1 - \mu_{AS}(x_i; c, b', a'), \quad x_i \geqslant c \tag{12b}$$

in the interval $[a, a']$ with $c = (a+a')/2$, $b = (a+c)/2$, and $b' = (a'+c)/2$. b and b' are the crossover points, i.e., $\mu_{A\pi}(b) = \mu_{A\pi}(b') = 0.5$, and c is the central point at which $\mu_{A\pi} = 1$.

Instead of using the standard S and π functions one can also consider the following equation as defined by Pal and Dutta Majumder [14], [15]

$$\mu_A(x_i) = G(x_i) = \left[1 + \left(\frac{|\hat{x}_n - x_i|}{F_d}\right)\right]^{-F_e} \tag{13}$$

which approximates the standard membership functions.

F_e and F_d (two positive constants) are known respectively as exponential and denominational fuzzy generators and control the crossover point, bandwidth, and hence the symmetry of the curve about the crossover point. $\hat{x}_n$ is the reference constant such that the function represents an S-type function G_S for $\hat{x}_n = x_{\max}$ and a π-type function G_π for $\hat{x}_n = x_l$, $0 < x_l < x_{\max}$, where $x_{\max}$ represents the maximum value of x_i.

IV. Feature Evaluation Index

Let $C_1, C_2, \cdots, C_j, \cdots, C_m$ be the m-pattern classes in an N-dimensional $(X_1, X_2, \cdots, X_q, \cdots, X_N)$ feature space Q_X. Also, let n_j $(j = 1,2,\cdots,m)$ be the number of samples available from class C_j. The algorithms for computing γ, H, and π-ness values of the classes in order to provide a quantitative index for feature evaluation are described in this section.

A. Computation of γ and H Using Standard π Function

Let us consider the standard π function (12) for computing γ and H of C_j along the qth component and take the parameters of the function as

$$c = (x_{qj})_{\text{av}} \tag{14a}$$

$$b' = c + \max\left\{\left|(x_{qj})_{\text{av}} - (x_{qj})_{\max}\right|, \left|(x_{qj})_{\text{av}} - (x_{qj})_{\min}\right|\right\} \tag{14b}$$

with

$$b = 2c - b' \tag{14c}$$

$$a = 2b - c \tag{14d}$$

$$a' = 2b' - c \tag{14e}$$

where $(x_{qj})_{\text{av}}$, $(x_{qj})_{\max}$, and $(x_{qj})_{\min}$ denote the mean, maximum, and minimum values respectively, computed along the qth coordinate axis, over all the n_j samples in C_j.

Since $\mu(c) = \mu((x_{qj})_{\text{av}}) = 1$, the values of γ and H are zero at $c = (x_{qj})_{\text{av}}$ and would tend to unity (9) as we move away from c towards either b or b' of the π function (i.e., from mean towards boundary of C_j). The lower the value of γ or H along the qth component in C_j, the greater would be the number of samples having $\mu(x) \simeq 1$ (or, the less would be the difficulty in deciding whether an element x can be considered, on the basis of its qth measurement, a member of C_j or not) and hence the greater would be the tendency of the samples to cluster around its mean value, resulting in less internal scatter or less intraset distance or more compactness of the samples along the qth axis within C_j. Therefore, the reliability (goodness) of a feature in characterizing a class increases as its corresponding γ or H value within the class (computed with π function) decreases.

The value of γ or H thus obtained along the qth coordinate axis in C_j may be denoted by γ_{qj}^{π} or H_{qj}^{π}.

Let us now pool together the classes C_j and C_k ($j, k = 1, 2, \cdots, m$, $j \neq k$) and compute the mean $(x_{qjk})_{av}$, maximum $(x_{qjk})_{max}$ and minimum $(x_{qjk})_{min}$ values of the qth component over all the samples (numbering $n_j + n_k$). The value of γ or H so computed with (14) would therefore increase as the goodness of the qth feature in discriminating pattern classes C_j and C_k increases, because there would be fewer samples around the mean $(x_{qjk})_{av}$ of the combined class, resulting in γ or $H \simeq 0$, and more samples far from the $(x_{qjk})_{av}$, giving γ or $H \simeq 1$. Let us denote the γ and H value so computed by γ_{qjk}^{π} and H_{qjk}^{π}, which increase as the separation between C_j and C_k (i.e., separation between b and b') along the qth dimension increases or, in other words, as the steepness of π function decreases.

It is to be mentioned here that one can also replace $(x_{qj})_{av}$, $(x_{qj})_{max}$ and $(x_{qj})_{min}$ of (14) by $(x_{qjk})_{av}$, $(x_{qj})_{av}$, and $(x_{qk})_{av}$, respectively, to compute γ_{qjk} or H_{qjk}. In this case, only their absolute values but not their behavior, as described previously, would be affected.

B. Computation of γ and H Using Standard S Function

For computing γ and H of C_j along the qth component let us now take the parameters of S function (11) as

$$b = (x_{qj})_{av} \tag{15a}$$

$$c = b + \max\left\{\left|(x_{qj})_{av} - (x_{qj})_{max}\right|, \left|(x_{qj})_{av} - (x_{qj})_{min}\right|\right\} \tag{15b}$$

where

$$a = 2b - c. \tag{15c}$$

Since $\mu(b) = \mu((x_{qj})_{av}) = 0.5$, the values of γ and H are 1 at $b = (x_{qj})_{av}$ and would tend to zero (9) as we move away from b towards either c or a of the S function. The higher the value of γ or H, the greater would be the number of samples having $\mu(x) \simeq 0.5$ and hence the greater would be the tendency of the samples to cluster around its mean value, resulting in less internal scatter within the class. Therefore, unlike the case with π function, the reliability (goodness) of a feature in characterizing a class C_j increases as its corresponding γ_{qj}^{s} or H_{qj}^{s} value within the class increases.

Similarly, if we now pool together the classes C_j and C_k ($j, k = 1, 2, \cdots, m$, $j \neq k$) and compute the mean, maximum and minimum values of the qth component over all the samples ($n_j + n_k$), then the value of γ_{qjk}^{s} or H_{qjk}^{s} so computed with (15) would therefore decrease as the goodness of the qth feature in discriminating pattern classes C_j and C_k increases; because there would be fewer samples around the mean of the classes C_j and C_k, resulting in γ or $H \simeq 1$, and more samples far from the mean, giving γ, or $H \simeq 0$.

It therefore appears that the γ_{qj} (or H_{qj}) and γ_{qjk} (or H_{qjk}) reflect the concept of intraset and interset distances, respectively, in a classical feature-selection problem. With decrease in intraset and interset distances along qth component in C_j the values of γ_{qj} (or H_{qj}) and γ_{qjk} (or H_{qjk}) are seen to decrease, or increase, when computed using the π, or S function.

C. Computation of π-ness

Similarly, for computing π_{qj} along the qth dimension in C_j, the parameters of the π function are set as follows:

$$c = (x_{qj})_{av} \tag{16a}$$

$$a' = c + \max\left\{\left|(x_{qj})_{av} - (x_{qj})_{max}\right|, \left|(x_{qj})_{av} - (x_{qj})_{min}\right|\right\} \tag{16b}$$

with

$$a = 2c - a', \qquad b = (a + c)/2, \qquad b' = (a' + c)/2. \tag{16c}$$

For computing π_{qjk}, the classes C_j and C_k are pooled together and these parameters are obtained from $(n_j + n_k)$ samples. Like the γ^s (or H^s) value obtained with S function, π_{qj} and π_{qjk} increase as intraset and interset distances in C_j decrease.

Considering these intraclass and interclass measures in each case, the problem of evaluating feature quality in Q_X therefore reduces to minimizing/maximizing the values of

$$\gamma_{qj}^{\pi} \text{ or } H_{qj}^{\pi}/\gamma_{qj}^{s} \text{ or } H_{qj}^{2} \text{ or } \pi_{qj}$$

while maximizing/minimizing the values of

$$\gamma_{qjk}^{\pi} \text{ or } H_{qjk}^{\pi}/\gamma_{qjk}^{s} \text{ or } H_{qjk}^{s} \text{ or } \pi_{qjk}.$$

The feature-evaluation index for the qth feature is accordingly defined as

$$(\text{FEI})_q = \frac{d_{qj} + d_{qk}}{d_{qjk}},$$

$$j, k = 1, 2, \cdots, m, \; j \neq k, \; q = 1, 2, \cdots, N \tag{17a}$$

where d stands for γ^{π} or H^{π} and

$$(\text{FEI})_q = \frac{d_{qjk}}{d_{qj} + d_{qk}} \tag{17b}$$

where d stands for γ^{s} or H^{s} or π-ness. The lower the value of $(\text{FEI})_q$, the higher is, therefore, the quality (importance) of the qth feature in characterizing and discriminating different classes in Q_X.

V. Implementation and Results

For implementation of the above algorithm, the test material is prepared from a set of nearly 600 discrete phonetically balanced speech units in consonant–vowel–consonant Telugu (a major Indian Language) vocabulary uttered by three male speakers in the age group of 30–35 years.

For vowel sounds of ten classes (δ, a, i, i:, u, u:, e, e:, o and o:) including shorter and longer categories, the first three formant frequencies at the steady state (F_1, F_2, and F_3) are obtained through spectrum analysis.

For consonants, eight unaspirated plosive sounds namely the velars /k, g/, the alveolars /$\dot{t}, \dot{d}$/, the dentals /t, d/, and the bilabials /p, b/ in combination with six vowel groups (δ, a, E, I, O, U) are selected. The formant frequencies are measured at the initial and the final state of the plosives. The details of processing and formant extraction are available in [14]–[16].

A. Vowel Recognition

A set of 496 vowel sounds of ten different classes are used here as the data set with F_1, F_2, and F_3 as the features. Fig. 1 shows the feature space of vowels corresponding to F_1 and F_2 when longer and shorter categories are treated separately.

Fig. 2 shows the order of importance of formants in recognizing and discriminating different vowels as obtained with intra-class measures (diagonal cells) and FEI values (off-diagonal cells). Results using only S function in computing γ_l and H values are shown here. Lower triangular part of the matrix corresponds to the results obtained with standard S and π functions ((11) and (12)) whereas, the upper triangular portion gives the results corresponding to their approximated versions (13). While using (13) we selected the parameters as follows.

For S-type Function:

$$\hat{x}_n = (x_{qj})_{max}, \quad \text{for computing } \gamma_{qj} \text{ or } H_{qj} \tag{18a}$$

$$= (x_{qjk})_{max}, \quad \text{for computing } \gamma_{qjk} \text{ or } H_{qjk}. \tag{18b}$$

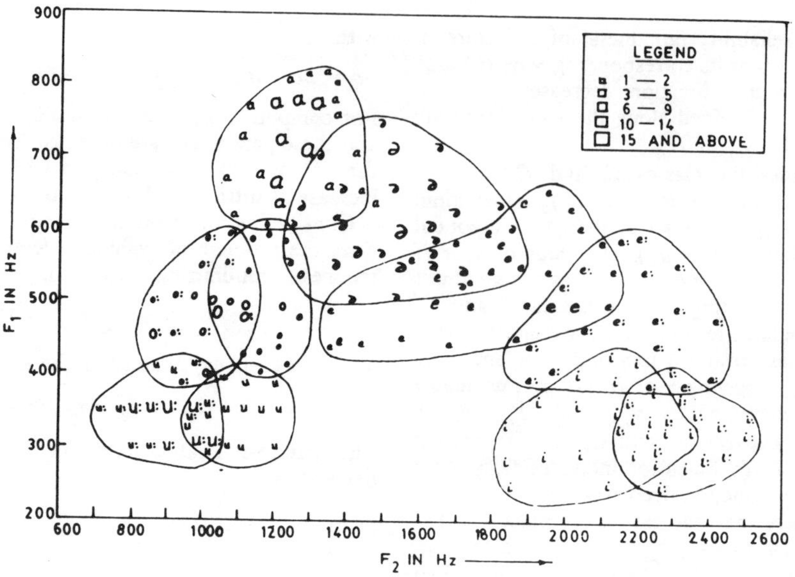

Fig. 1. Vowel diagram in F_1-F_2 plane.

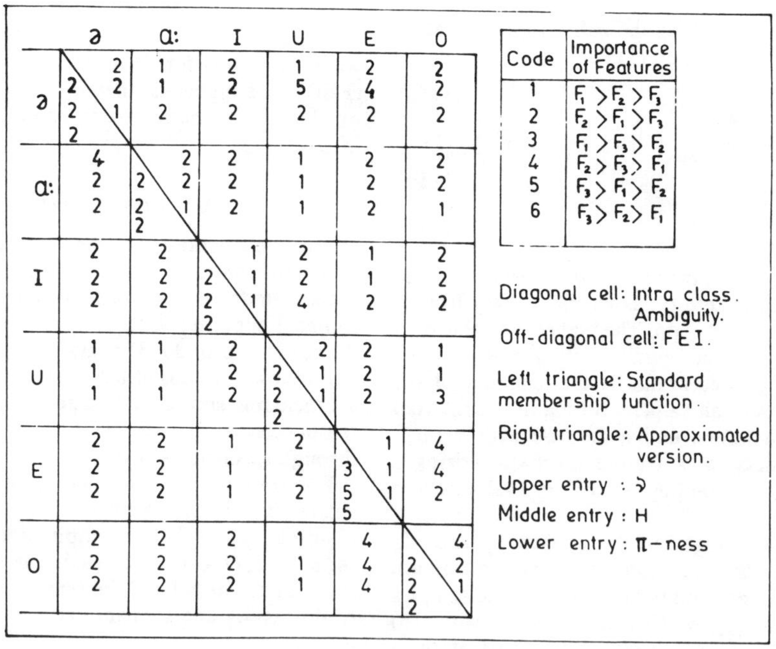

Fig. 2. Order of importance of features.

F_e and F_d were selected in such a way that $(x_q)_{av}$ corresponds to the crossover point, i.e., $G_S((x_q)_{av}) = 0.5$. To keep the crossover point fixed at $(x_q)_{av}$, different values of F_e and F_d may be used to result in various slopes of S function.

For π-type Function:

$$\hat{x}_n = (x_{qj})_{av}, \qquad \text{for computing } \pi_{qj} \tag{19a}$$

$$= (x_{qjk}), \qquad \text{for computing } \pi_{qjk}. \tag{19b}$$

As crossover points have no importance here in measuring π-ness, the selection of fuzzifiers is not crucial.

The results using (13) (as shown in the lower triangular part of Fig. 2) were obtained for $F_e = 1/16, 1/8, 1/4, 1/2$, and 1 with the crossover point at $(x_q)_{av}$. These values of F_e were also found

TABLE I
INTRACLASS AMBIGUITIES FOR SHORT AND LONG VOWEL CLASSES

Membership Function	Vowel Class							
	i	*i*:	*u*	*u*:	*e*	*e*:	*o*	*o*:
Standard	2	1	2	3	4	1	2	2
	2	1	2	6	6	1	2	2
	1	1	2	6	6	1	2	2
Approximated version	3	1	2	1	5	1	2	1
	3	1	2	1	5	1	2	1
	1	1	2	1	1	1	2	1

1: $F_1F_2F_3$ 2: $F_2F_1F_3$
3: $F_1F_3F_2$ 4: $F_2F_3F_1$
5: $F_3F_1F_2$ 6: $F_3F_2F_1$

TABLE II
TYPICAL FEI VALUES OF THE FORMANTS USING STANDARD MEMBERSHIP FUNCTIONS

Vowel Classes	FEI Values According to the Parameter: Index of Fuzziness F_1	F_2	F_3	Entropy F_1	F_2	F_3	π-ness F_1	F_2	F_3
δ, I	0.4521	0.3378	0.7142	0.4829	0.3874	0.6226	0.4828	0.3778	0.6402
a, U	0.2093	0.3649	0.5970	0.3038	0.4300	0.5860	0.2755	0.4253	0.5963
I, E	0.4503	0.4591	0.5894	0.4822	0.4841	0.5581	0.4795	0.4846	0.5649
I, O	0.3133	0.1018	0.6329	0.3994	0.1811	0.5586	0.3826	0.1483	0.5645
U, E	0.4538	0.2696	0.5635	0.4839	0.3289	0.5282	0.4822	0.3158	0.5286
U, O	0.3126	0.5196	0.5720	0.3948	0.4999	0.5547	0.3859	0.4994	0.5630

TABLE III
IMPORTANCE OF PLOSIVE FEATURES ACCORDING TO FEI

Membership Function	Position of Importance: First	Second	Third
Standard	$I_{36}, III_{34}, II_{20}$	V_{42}, III_{25}, I_{17}	IV_{36}, I_{22}, II_{21}
Approximate	IV_{61}, V_{28}, I_{13}	III_{46}, I_{24}, V_{20}	$III_{46}, I_{25}, II_{22}$
Standard	$I_{43}, III_{30}, II_{22}$	$III_{31}, II_{26}, I_{24}$	$II_{39}, III_{30}, V_{26}$
Approximate	IV_{62}, I_{17}, II_{12}	$III_{41}, I_{25}, IV_{17}$	$III4_{4}, I_{24}, V_{21}$

1) Suffixes indicate the number of times the feature has occurred in the position.

2)I, II, III, IV, V represent the features ΔF_1, ΔF_2, ΔT, $\Delta F_1/\Delta T$, $\Delta F_2/\Delta T$, respectively

to yield optimum recognition score in earlier investigations on vowel and plosive identification [14], [15]. For computing π_{qj} and π_{qjk}, F_d was selected to be 50 for $F_e = 1/16$.

Again, the order of importance as shown in Fig. 2 was obtained after pooling together the shorter and longer counterparts (differing mainly in duration) of a vowel. In a part of the experiment the shorter and longer categories were treated separately, and the order of importance of formants for the corresponding γ_{qj}, H_{qj}, and π_{qj} values (intraclass measures) is listed in Table I. This is included for comparison with the diagonal entries of Fig. 2.

For vowel recognition (except for /E/, as shown from Fig. 2) the first two formants are found to be much more important than F_3 (which is mainly responsible for speaker identification). Furthermore, better result has been obtained for the cases when the shorter and longer categories are pooled together than the cases when they are treated separately. The result agrees well with previous investigation [14]. From the FEI measures of different pair of classes (off-diagonal cells of Fig. 2), F_1 is seen to be more important than F_2 in discriminating the class combinations /U, O/, /I, E/, /a, U/, and /δ, U/, i.e., between /front and front/ or /back and back/vowels. For the other combinations, i.e., discriminating between /front and back/ vowels, F_2 is found to be the strongest feature. The above findings can readily be verified from Fig. 1.

Typical FEI values for F_1, F_2, and F_3 are shown in Table II to illustrate the relative difference in importance among the formants in characterizing a class.

Similar investigations have also been made in case of speaker identification problem using the same data set (Fig. 1) and $\{F_1 F_2, F_3, F_3 - F_2, F_3 - F_1, F_3/F_2, F_3/F_1\}$ as the feature set. FEI values have been computed for each of the three speakers individually for all the vowel classes. Contrary to the vowel recognition problem, F_3 and its combinations were found here to yield lower FEI values, i.e., more important than F_1 and F_2—resembling well the earlier report [14].

B. Plosive Recognition

A set of 588 unaspirated plosive consonants are used as the data set with $\Delta F_1, \Delta F_2$ (the difference of the initial and final values of the first and second formants), ΔT (duration), $\Delta F_1/\Delta T$, $\Delta F_2/\Delta T$ (the rates of transition) as the feature set.

The order of importance of the features for plosive recognition according to FEI values does not seem to be very regular as has been obtained in case of vowel recognition problem. Here all five features have more or less importance in determining the plosive classes, contrary to the case of vowel recognition, where F_3 has much less importance than F_1 and F_2 in defining the vowel classes. However, a qualitative assessment has been adopted here to formulate an idea about the quality of the features based on the measure of FEI.

Table III shows the number of times each feature has occupied a particular position of importance on the basis of FEI measure using γ, H, and π-ness values and different target vowels. Results corresponding to both standard membership functions and their approximated versions are included for comparison.

Let us now consider the case of unvoiced plosive sounds with the standard membership function. The features ΔF_1, ΔT, and ΔF_2 were first in order of importance 36, 34, and 20 times, respectively. They occupied the second position 42, 25, and 17 times, respectively, and the third 36, 22, and 21 times, respectively. Considering the first three number of occurrences in first two positions and the first two number of occurrences in first two positions, it is seen that the set $(\Delta F_1, \Delta T)$ is more effective than $(\Delta F_2/\Delta T, \Delta F_2)$, which is again more important than $\Delta F_1/\Delta T$ in discriminating unvoiced plosive sounds. Similarly, the features $(\Delta F_1$, ΔT, and $\Delta F_2)$ (particularly, $\Delta F_1, \Delta T$) are seen to be more reliable than the others in characterizing voiced plosives using the standard membership function.

Let us now consider the cases of using approximate version of the membership functions (13). To discriminate unvoiced plosives the set $(\Delta F_1/\Delta T, \Delta F_2/\Delta T)$ gives better characterizing feature than ΔF_1 and ΔT; whereas for the voiced counterparts $(\Delta F_1/\Delta T, \Delta F_1, \Delta T)$ came out to be the best feature set.

From these discussions, the features ΔF_1 and ΔT are overall found to be the most important in characterizing and discriminating different plosive sounds. The result conforms to the earlier findings [15], [16] obtained from the point of automatic plosive sound recognition.

VI. DISCUSSION AND CONCLUSION

An algorithm for automatic evaluation of feature quality in pattern recognition has been described using the terms *index of fuzziness*, *entropy*, and *π-ness* of a fuzzy set. These terms are used to define measures of separability between classes and compactness within a class when they are implemented with S and π membership functions. For example, when these measures are implemented with π function, d^{π}_{qj} (d stands for γ or H) then decreases as compactness within jth class along qth direction increases and d^{π}_{qjk} increases as separability between C_j and C_k increases in the qth direction. If the classes C_j and C_k do not differ in mean value but differ in second order moment, i.e., variances are different, then

$$\left[(x_{qj})_{\max} - (x_{qj})_{\min}\right] > \left[(x_{qk})_{\max} - (x_{qk})_{\min}\right]$$

(assuming C_j with larger variance than C_k). From (12) and (14) we have

$$d^{\pi}_{qj} > d^{\pi}_{qk},$$

i.e., the qth feature is more important in recognizing the kth class than the jth class. Value of the interset ambiguity d^{π}_{qjk} as expected, then decreases showing the deterioration in reliability (goodness) of the qth feature in discriminating C_j from C_k. Similar behavior would also be reflected for the third (representing skewness of a class) and higher order moments when they are different for C_j and C_k with the same mean value. The algorithm is found to provide satisfactory order of importance of the features in characterizing speech sounds, in discriminating different classes of speeches and also in identifying a speaker.

Since F_3 and its higher formants $(F_4, F_5, \cdots)$ are mostly responsible for identifying a speaker, we have considered in our experiment only F_3 in addition to F_1 and F_2 for evaluating feature quality in vowel recognition problem.

It is to be mentioned here that the well-known statistical measures of feature evaluation such as Bhattacharyya coefficient, divergence, Kolmogorov variational distance, etc., theoretically take into account the interdependence of feature variables. Their computation involves multivariate numerical integration and estimation of probability density functions [4]. In practice in their computation, the features are usually treated individually to avoid computational difficulty [17]. Our proposed measure also treats the features individually. In fact, the present algorithm attempts to rank individual features according to their importance in characterizing and discriminating classes. Combination of features in doing so is not of interest. Furthermore, even in the case of independent feature, the algorithm is computationally more efficient than the aforesaid statistical measures.

Acknowledgment

The authors gratefully acknowledge Prof. D. Dutta Majumder for his interest in this work and Mrs. S. De Bhowmik and Mr. S. Chakraborty for preparing the manuscript.

References

[1] K. Fukunaga, *Introduction to Statistical Pattern Recognition and Machine Learning*. New York: Academic, 1972.

[2] J. T. Tou and R. C. Gonzalez, *Pattern Recognition Principles*. Reading, MA: Addison-Wesley, 1974.

[3] G. S. Sebestyen, *Decision Making Process in Pattern Recognition*. New York: Macmillan, 1962.

[4] R. A. Devijver and J. Kittler, *Pattern Recognition—A Statistical Approach*. London: Prentice-Hall, 1982.

[5] S. K. Pal and D. Dutta Majumder, *Fuzzy Mathematical Approach to Pattern Recognition*. New York: Wiley (Halsted Press), 1986.

[6] A. Bhattacharyya, "On a measure of divergence between two multinomial populations," *Sankhya*, vol. 6, pp. 401–406, 1946.

[7] T. Kailath, "The divergence and Bhattacharyya distance measures in signal detection," *IEEE Trans. Commun. Tech.*, vol. CT-15, pp. 52–60, 1967.

[8] A. Kaufmann, *Introduction to the Theory of Fuzzy Subsets—Fundamental Theoretical Elements*, vol. 1. New York: Academic, 1975.

[9] A. Deluca and S. Termini, "A definition of a nonprobabilistic entropy in the setting of fuzzy set theory," *Inform. Contr.*, vol. 20, pp. 301–302, 1972.

[10] S. K. Pal, "Fuzzy set theoretic approach–A tool for speech and image recognition," in *Pattern Recognition Theory and Applications*. Amsterdam: D. Reidel, 1982, pp. 103–117.

[11] S. K. Pal, R. A. King, and A. A. Hashim, "Automatic grey level thresholding through index of fuzziness and entropy," *Patt. Recognition Lett.*, vol. 1, pp. 141–146, Mar. 1983.

[12] ——, "A note on the quantitative measure of image enhancement through fuzziness," *IEEE Trans. Patt. Anal. Mach. Intell.*, vol. PAMI-4, pp. 204–208, 1982.

[13] L. A. Zadeh, "Calculus of fuzzy restrictions," in *Fuzzy Sets and Their Application to Cognitive and Decision Process*. London: Academic, pp. 1–39, 1975.

[14] S. K. Pal and D. Dutta Majumder, "Fuzzy sets and decision making approaches in vowel and speaker recognition," *IEEE Trans. Syst., Man, Cybern.*, vol. SMC-7, pp. 625–629, 1977.

[15] ——, "On automatic plosive identification using fuzziness in property sets," *IEEE Trans. Syst., Man, Cybern.*, vol. SMC-8, pp. 302–308, Apr. 1978.

[16] A. K. Datta, N. R. Ganguli, and S. Ray, "Recognition of unaspirated plosives—A statistical approach," *IEEE Trans. Acoustics, Speech, Signal Processing*, vol. ASSP-28, pp. 85–91, Feb. 1980.

[17] S. Ray, "The effectiveness of features in pattern recognition," Ph.D. thesis, Imperial College, Univ. of London, 1984.

Use of Fuzzy Algorithms for Phonetic and Phonemic Labeling of Continuous Speech

RENATO DE MORI AND PIETRO LAFACE

Abstract—A model for assigning phonetic and phonemic labels to speech segments is presented. The system executes fuzzy algorithms that assign degrees of worthiness to structured interpretations of syllabic segments extracted from the signal of a spoken sentence. The knowledge source is a series of syntactic rules whose syntactic categories are phonetic and phonemic features detected by a precategorical and a categorical classification of speech sounds. Rules inferred from experiments and results for male and female voices are presented.

Index Terms—Application of branching questionnaires, application of fuzzy algorithms, phoneme labeling, precategorical classification, speech recognition, syntactic pattern recognition.

I. Introduction

CONSIDERABLE effort has been made in the last few years to develop systems capable of understanding connected speech. Recent reviews of the problems involved in designing such systems and of the solutions proposed have been made by Reddy [1], [2], Martin [3], Jelinek [4], Klatt [5], Wolf [6], Reddy *et al.* [7], Walker *et al.* [8], Woods *et al.* [9], and De Mori [10].

The purpose of this paper is to propose a method for the interpretation of speech patterns and to give some experimental results of its application. The interpretation of speech patterns involves the generation of hypotheses concerning possible phonemic transcriptions of syllable segments automatically extracted from a numerical representation of energy-frequency-time obtained by short-term spectral analysis of a spoken sentence. Each hypothesis is evaluated and a degree of trustworthiness is assigned to it in such a way that it can be further processed for generating and coherently evaluating hypotheses about the words [11], the syntactic structure, and the semantics of the spoken sentence [12].

The interpretation of speech patterns is difficult because any vagueness may affect the features extracted from the acoustic data and there is a degree of imprecision in the relations between acoustic features and their phonetic or phonemic interpretation.

For example, a sonorant intervocalic consonant may be characterized by a marked dip in the time evolutions of the signal energy, and in the energy in a frequency band from 3-5 kHz; furthermore, for such consonants, the low-frequency energy (roughly below 1 kHz) is much higher than the high-frequency energy (above 5 kHz). Given a specific acoustic pattern of an intervocalic consonant with its adjacent vowels, a speech understanding system trying to interpret the pattern needs to take into account the fact that the consonant may be sonorant. This possibility can be evaluated numerically following the theory of possibility proposed by Zadeh [13]. To evaluate this possibility the vagueness inherent in the terms "marked dip" and "much higher energy" has to be numerically represented by "degrees of compatibility" between the statements and the acoustic pattern. This can be done by applying Zadeh's theory of possibility. To get the interpretation it has to be established how to combine the degrees of plausibility (or membership) of a marked dip in signal energy, in the 3-5 kHz energy, and the degree of plausibility with which the low-frequency energy is much higher than the high-frequency energy in order to obtain the possibility of the interpretation: "the consonant is sonorant."

In a previous paper [14], a method for obtaining acoustic patterns was proposed, together with a language for their description and syntax-directed procedures for the recognition of the vowel positions and for the segmentation of continuous speech into pseudosyllable segments (PSS's). In this paper, a method based on fuzzy restrictions is proposed for extracting acoustic features (such as "marked dip") from the description of acoustic patterns. A method based on fuzzy relations is also proposed for relating acoustic features with phonetic and phonemic interpretations. Finally, the use of restrictions and relations to compute the possibility of a hypothesis (a phonetic or a phonemic interpretation of a speech pattern) is illustrated.

The concepts of fuzzy restrictions and fuzzy relations are due to Zadeh [15], [16] and will be briefly recalled in Section II of this paper. The algorithms used for evaluating the possibility of a hypothesis will be referred to as fuzzy algorithms.

Recently, fuzzy set theory has been applied for decision making in vowel and speaker recognition [17]. In such an approach, an unknown vowel is represented by a vector of spectral measurements $X = x_1, x_2, \cdots, x_n, \cdots, x_N$ and a membership function $\mu_j(X)$ is associated with pattern X for the jth class. $\mu_j(X)$ is defined as a decreasing function of the Euclidean distance $d(X, R_j)$ between X and R_j, the reference vector of the jth class. The decision is made by assigning X to the class j for which $\mu_j(X)$ is maximum. The application of fuzzy sets in such a case is just a way of evaluating the closeness of points in a Euclidean space.

The approach proposed in this paper and the rules described in Section II are an attempt to formalize the intuitive logic used by a phonetician. Membership functions are defined as a measure of the plausibility of an interpretation of a speech pattern.

Manuscript received August 4, 1977; revised May 25, 1979.
R. De Mori is with the Istituto de Scienze dell'Informazione, Università di Torino, Torino, Italy.
P. Laface is with the CENS IENGF Istituto di Elettrotecnica, Politecnico di Torino, Torino, Italy.

Reprinted from *IEEE Trans. Pattern Anal. Machine Intell.*, vol. PAMI-2, no. 2, pp. 136–148, March 1980.

The advantages of such an approach lie in its flexibility. Each relation and each restriction can be established to represent as closely as possible the knowledge attained in research on phonetics and to optimize the recognition performances. The qualifying experimental results presented in Section IV of this paper show the advantages of the use of the proposed fuzzy algorithms.

The results were limited to one type of PSS, namely vowel-consonant-vowel (VCV) pseudosyllables, but they refer to every possible coarticulation of such syllables in the Italian language; the syllables were extracted from continuous speech without any limitation and the results were obtained by applying the same rules for different (male and female) speakers.

The fuzzy algorithms presented in this paper are used in a speech understanding system (SUS) organized with several levels of knowledge sources (KS's). Each KS consists of syntactic rules relating an item of a given level, represented by a syntactic category, with items of lower levels. There are many levels between the acoustic and the lexical ones.

The first levels just above the acoustic level have phonetic features as syntactic categories. Features that will be introduced in Section II, like vocalic-nonvocalic, sonorant-nonsonorant, etc., are extracted by a precategorical classification with a procedure that does not require any knowledge of the context.

Other categories, like liquid and nasal, are introduced to generate phonetic transcriptions with procedures that are context-dependent. Finally, phonemes belonging to the hypothesized phonetic classes are attached to the corresponding speech intervals, using algorithms discussed in Section III.

Fuzzy algorithms are used whenever a KS is invoked to generate an interpretation (a hypothesis). The hypothesis is a syntactic category H related by rules to items previously hypothesized and belonging to lower levels of interpretation. Each rule used is associated with a fuzzy relation and each lower level item used by the rule has been previously associated with a possibility of being a correct interpretation of a speech pattern p. To use H as an interpretation of p it is necessary to evaluate the possibility that H represents p correctly. This possibility is computed by composing the fuzzy relation between H and its constituents using the possibility of the constituents themselves.

Details on the composition of fuzzy relations and restrictions can be found in papers by Zadeh [18], [22].

The possibilities of the hypotheses are used for scheduling the activation of the KS's following the system that controls the process of understanding. Problems of knowledge representation and control strategies would make this paper too long and diverse. Nonhomogeneous parts will be considered in other papers; a preliminary and concise presentation of them can be found in [32].

The reasons for using possibilities instead of probabilities or purely heuristic methods for scoring hypotheses can be summarized as follows.

The theory of possibility, in contrast with heuristic approaches, offers algorithms for composing hypothesis evaluations which are consistent with axioms in a well-developed theory; the theory of possibility, rather than the theory of probability, relates to the perception of degrees of evidence instead of degrees of likelihood or frequency. The aim of the approach proposed in this paper is to express the evidence of a hypothesis concerning a speech pattern with the possibility of having high evidence measurements for clearly interpretable patterns even if the patterns and the features considered are scarcely probable. In any case, using possibilities does not prevent us from using statistics in the estimation of membership functions. But this estimation does not necessarily require such a large number of experiments as the estimation of a probability density. The use of phonetic and phonemic features as syntactic categories of a fuzzy grammar is a new idea allowing one to incorporate in a knowledge source the vagueness with which the relations between acoustic and phonetic or phonemic features are known.

Using such rules, degrees of evidence of speech interpretations can be obtained and a change of a single rule may have the same effect of updating a large number of prototypes in a more conventional parametric approach.

II. Algorithms for Precategorical Classification

A. Generalities

Precategorical classification consists primarily of the assignment of phonetic features to nonvocalic segments. The main purpose of such a classification is for segmentation of continuous speech into pseudosyllable segments (PSS's) and for driving a context-dependent extraction of more detailed features.

Fig. 1 shows a schematic block diagram of the feature extraction algorithm. After sampling the signal at a rate of 20 kHz, a spectral analysis based on fast Fourier transformation (FFT) and linear prediction (LP) is performed. A special purpose computer like the one described in [19] could allow performance of these operations in real time.

The spectra are then processed in order to obtain some "gross spectral features":

S the total energy of a spectrum,
B the energy in the 200-900 Hz band,
F the energy in the 5-10 kHz band,
A the energy in the 3-5 kHz band,
R_v the ratio between B and F.

The gross features are described by a language presented in [14] and the description in terms of these features, denoted DGF, is used for precategorical classification, denoted PC; PC is then used for segmenting continuous speech into syllabic units by a syntactic recognition algorithm introduced in [14].

The results of the precategorical classification are used for driving the extraction of detailed spectral features such as formant evolutions, characteristics of frication noise, burst, etc. following an approach presented in [14]. Such features are then described by a language presented in [14] and a linguistic description DDF of the acoustic patterns is given.

Precategorical classification has also been postulated in human perception (see Stevens [20] for a discussion on this item).

The approach proposed in this paper is based on the detec-

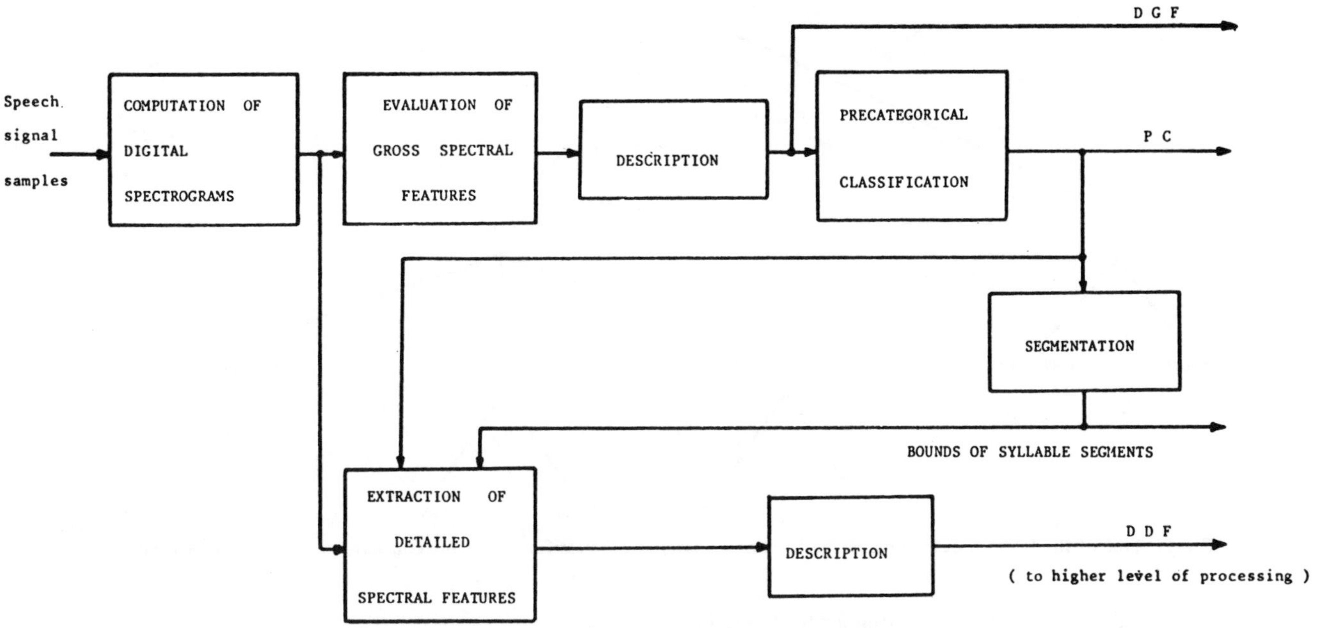

Fig. 1. General block diagram of the extraction and description of spectral features.

tion of phonetic categories related to some of the distinctive features proposed by Hughes and Hemdal [21]. The tree of Fig. 2 summarizes a scheme for precategorical classification that has been implemented, giving satisfactory results with few ambiguities. A node represents a feature that can be hypothesized only if the feature corresponding to the father has been previously hypothesized. Thus, for example, the feature "affricate" can be hypothesized only for nonsonorant consonants. Let us call such features "precategorical classification features" (PCF's).

The phonetic features shown in the tree in Fig. 2 are syntactic categories related to the lower level description DGF of the acoustic features by a "branching questionnaire" of the type proposed by Zadeh in a recent paper [22]. Thus, PCF is assigned to a speech segment after answering a composite classificational question $Q \triangleq B$, where the bodies of component questions Q_j $(j = 1, 2, \cdots, n)$ are fuzzy sets $B_1, B_2, \cdots, B_n$ involved in an analytic representation of B [22]. The fuzzy sets $B_1, B_2, \cdots, B_n$ are linguistic variables defined over the range of acoustic measurements that phoneticians have found useful for characterizing distinctive features.

Let Q_i $(i = 1, 2, \cdots, K)$ be the composite question related to the ith PCF to be hypothesized. The answers to component questions Q_{ij} of the composite question Q_i are fuzzy linguistic variables (e.g., high, medium, low, more or less high, more or less low) whose membership functions are computed from diagrams stored in the phonetic source of knowledge of the SUS and are defined over the universe of an acoustic measurement. The answers to the composite question Q_i are related by syntactic rules to the answers to the component questions Q_{ij}; thus, each answer to Q_i can be associated with a membership function whose value is computed under the control of semantic rules from the values of membership functions associated with each answer to the component questions.

This use of fuzzy algorithms models to some extent the fact that most of the acoustic-phonetic properties of speech sounds are only known with a degree of vagueness, e.g., the signal energy is high for vowels, nonsonorant consonants have high-frequency components, and in unvoiced stops there is an interval of silence followed by some noise.

A fuzzy linguistic variable, representing a judgment that can be expressed after the inspection of some acoustic parameters, is defined by a fuzzy restriction [15]

$$R(X, u)$$

where u is a generic value of an acoustic parameter and X is the subjective judgment. Abbreviating $R(X, u)$ to $R(X)$, the degree to which the assignment equation

$$X = u: \; R(X) \tag{1}$$

is satisfied, still has to be established. Denoting such a degree as the compatibility $C(u)$ of u with $R(X)$, by definition [15] it follows that

$$C(u) \triangleq \mu_{R(X)}(u) \tag{2}$$

where $\mu_{R(X)}(u)$ is a membership function defining $R(X)$ as a fuzzy subset of u.

For the sake of simplicity, the membership functions will be labeled by abbreviations of adjectives or phonetic features.

Fig. 3 shows the compatibility function of the fuzzy variable X:: = ⟨high consonant durations⟩ over the universe of the possible values of u which represents time in this example.

The fuzzy variables form a basis for a composite question Q. An answer to Q may be interpreted as a specification of the grade of evidence of a phonetic feature in a speech segment. This grade is a function of the grades of membership of the speech segment with every fuzzy variable.

The membership functions associated with each restriction were established subjectively after inspection of the distribution of acoustic measurements made on a large number of sound samples.

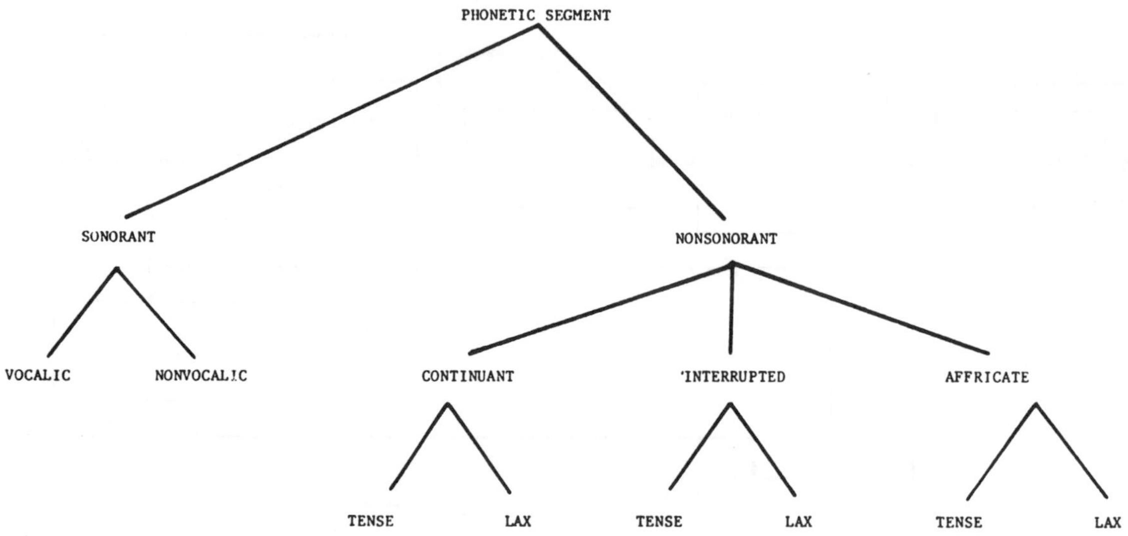

Fig. 2. Tree of the features detectable at the level of precategorical classification using context-independent algorithms.

Let Σ be the alphabet of the linguistic variables that may be answers to the component questions of the "questionnaire" used for characterizing the phonetic feature (FF). Obviously $X \in \Sigma$. Let p be an acoustic pattern represented by its description in terms of acoustic features. We are interested in the following possibility Poss $\{(FF)$ is in $p\}$. Let $D \in \Sigma^*$ be a string of linguistic variables; the string D identifies a composite fuzzy restriction $R_p(D)$ defined on some of the acoustic attributes of p. The KS invoked for generating or verifying the hypothesis that (FF) is in p contains a fuzzy naming relation $R(D, (FF))$.

Fuzzy naming relations have been introduced by Zadeh [23] and are represented in the approach proposed in this paper by simple fuzzy grammars. Fuzzy grammars, also introduced by Zadeh [23], are similar to stochastic grammars (see Fu [24] for details); their rewriting rules are associated with a degree of plausibility. In our case this degree of plausibility represents the imprecision of the knowledge. Examples of fuzzy grammars will be given below and in the successive sections. The possibility that a feature FF is present in a pattern p is obtained by the following composition ($\circ$ is the composition operator):

$$R_p(FF) = R_p(D) \circ R(D, (FF))$$

and is computed as follows:

$$\text{Poss } \{(FF) \text{ is in } p\} = \sup_{D \in \Sigma^*} \{\mu_p(D) \wedge \mu((FF), D)\} \qquad (3)$$

where $\wedge$ is the min operator, $\mu_p(D)$ is the compatibility of the string D with the pattern p and $\mu((FF), D)$ is the compatibility of the name (FF) with the string D. Equation (3) is obtained by applying the rules for evaluating the membership of the composition of a unary fuzzy relation and a binary fuzzy relation following Zadeh [15], [16], [18].

The conjunction of two fuzzy linguistic variables has a membership equal to minimum of the memberships of the variables. In this way the intersection is the largest fuzzy set which is contained in both the fuzzy linguistic variables because its membership is smaller than or equal to the memberships of the variables for every point of the space where the variables are defined.

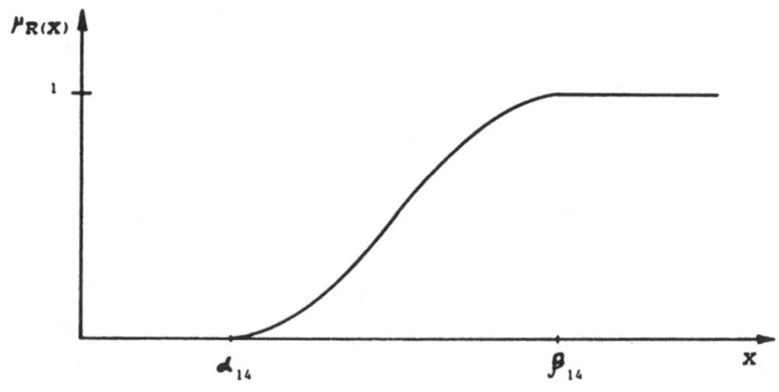

Fig. 3. Compatibility function of the fuzzy variable: x: :=⟨high consonant duration⟩.

The use of linguistic variables and fuzzy algorithms is an attempt to represent acoustic-phonetic knowledge, which is mostly expressed in a nonnumerical form, by a formalism suitable for computer systems. Acoustic-phonetic features are then processed in a logical, nonlinear, hierarchical system of concurrent processes; such a system is certainly more suitable for application in SUS than the crude mathematical approach of measuring distances in an N-dimensional space. Furthermore, the degrees of consistency of a hypothesis do not need to be known with great accuracy and should reflect a subjective, heuristic evaluation of the help the hypothesis can offer in grasping the meaning of the spoken sentence.

The hypothesis assignment consists basically of table look-up and the evaluation of min-max functions, making the program execution rapid; this aspect, together with flexibility in modifying the strategy as well as the sources of knowledge, adds motivations for using the proposed method in SUS design.

B. Sonorant-Nonsonorant Classification

The classification of a consonant as sonorant or nonsonorant is performed after the detection of vocalic intervals (see [14] for details) and is obtained as an answer to a composite question:

$Q_1 \triangleq$ is the interval corresponding to the acoustic pattern p

nonsonorant? The question Q_1 has six component questions:

$Q_{11} \triangleq$ how high is R_v?

$Q_{12} \triangleq$ how low is the minimum dip in R_v with respect to the values of R_v in the preceding and following vowels?

$Q_{13} \triangleq$ what is the minimum value of S with respect to the value assumed by S on the silences?

$Q_{14} \triangleq$ what is the duration of the consonant?

$Q_{15} \triangleq$ what is the minimum dip in the signal?

$Q_{16} \triangleq$ what is the maximum dip in R_v?

Each question admits two possible answers: low or high. These answers will be indicated as

$$l_{1i}, h_{1i}$$

where the subscripts $1i$ ($i = 1, 2, \cdots, 6$) refer to the answer of the $1i$th question; it is assumed that

$$l_{ji} = \bar{h}_{ji}. \tag{4}$$

The answer to such questions are fuzzy linguistic variables defined over the ranges in which the parameters they refer to may vary. Such paramcters are defined as follows:

$$u_{11} = R_v$$

$$u_{12} = \min (R_{vp} - R_{vc}; R_{vf} - R_{vc})$$

$$u_{13} = \min_{S \in \text{dip}} (S - S_{\text{sil}})$$

$$u_{14} = \text{consonant duration}$$

$$u_{15} = \min (S_p - S_c; S_f - S_c)$$

$$u_{16} = \max (R_{vp} - R_{vc}; R_{vf} - R_{vc})$$

where the subscript p refers to the detected vowel preceding the interval in which a nonsonorant feature is being sought; the subscript f refers to the detected vowel following the interval; the subscript c refers to the consonant interval and S_{sil} is the level of the signal energy in the silences.

The membership functions were defined after considering the range of the above parameters for each consonant in every context assigning values different from 1 to $\mu_{h_{1i}}$ and $\mu_{l_{1i}}$ ($i = 1, 2, \cdots, 6$) only in the range where sonorant and nonsonorant sounds may coexist.

Notice that $\mu_{l_{1i}}$ is for $\mu_{\text{low}}(u_{1i})$ and $\mu_{h_{1i}}$ is for $\mu_{\text{high}}(u_{1i})$; furthermore, $\mu_{l_{1i}} = 1 - \mu_{h_{1i}}$. (5)

The fuzzy restrictions obtained from the experiments and corresponding to the linguistic values *high* have the diagram shown in Fig. 3; the break points, indicated as α_{14} and β_{14} in Fig. 3 are the bounds of the interval where the memberships are neither 0 nor 1. In general, the break points for the variable h_{ji} will be indicated as α_{ji} and β_{ji}; these parameters assume different values depending on the questions, as listed in Table I.

The answers to atomic questions are related to the values of hypotheses about phonetic features by fuzzy rewriting rules [23]. These rules are the usual syntactic rules involved in the definition of phrase grammars. Furthermore, a degree of "grammaticality" and a semantic rule are associated with each syntactic rule. The grammaticality is an *a priori* evaluation of the plausibility of the syntactic rule. The semantic rule associated with a syntactic one is used for computing the value of the hypothesis expressed by the left-side member of the syntactic rule as a function of the membership functions of the right-side components.

TABLE I
BREAK POINTS OF THE MEMBERSHIP FUNCTIONS DEFINED OVER THE UNIVERSE OF ACOUSTIC PARAMETERS

Parameter	α_{ji}	β_{ji}	Dimension
u_{11}	-15	7	dB
u_{12}	-3	21	dB
u_{13}	2	20	dB
u_{14}	50	130	ms
u_{15}	6	23	dB
u_{16}	0	24	dB
u_{21}	10	16	dB
u_{22}	8	14	dB
u_{31}	-30	-20	dB
u_{32}	12	18	dB
u_{33}	80	130	ms
u_{34}	20	70	ms
u_{35}	20	30	dB

A set of fuzzy rules has been inferred for defining the syntactic categories sonorant and nonsonorant that correspond to the answers to Q_1. The inference methodology will be described in the next subsection; the inferred rules are given by the following:

π_1

$$\langle\text{nonsonorant}\rangle :: \overset{1}{=} \langle\text{dip in } S\rangle \tag{P11}$$

$$\langle\text{nonsonorant}\rangle :: \overset{1}{=} \langle\text{dip in } R_v\rangle \tag{P12}$$

$$\langle\text{dip in } S\rangle :: \overset{0.85}{=} l_{13} p_S \tag{P13}$$

$$\langle\text{dip in } S\rangle :: \overset{0.9}{=} h_{14} p_S \tag{P14}$$

$$\langle\text{dip in } S\rangle :: \overset{1}{=} h_{15} p_S \tag{P15}$$

$$\langle\text{dip in } S\rangle :: \overset{1}{=} h_{14} l_{13} p_S. \tag{P16}$$

The notation $\langle\text{dip in } S\rangle :: \overset{0.85}{=} l_{13}$ means that $l_{13} p_S$ (a low difference between the minimum of S and the silence level) allows us to generate the hypothesis that there is a dip in S with 0.85 plausibility provided that p_S is true.

The semantic rule associated with the syntactic definition of $\langle\text{dip in } S\rangle$ is derived from (3) as follows:

$$\mu_{\langle\text{dip in } S\rangle} = p_S \wedge \{(0.85 \wedge \mu_{l_{13}}) \vee (0.9 \wedge \mu_{h_{14}}) \vee \mu_{h_{15}} \vee (\mu_{l_{13}} \wedge \mu_{h_{14}})\}. \tag{6}$$

p_S is a Boolean variable defined as follows:

$$p_S = \begin{cases} 1 & \text{if } (S - S_{\text{sil}}) \leq 8 \text{ dB} \\ 0 & \text{if } (S - S_{\text{sil}}) > 8 \text{ dB}. \end{cases}$$

$$\langle\text{dip in } R_v\rangle :: \overset{0.6}{=} l_{11} \tag{P19}$$

$$\langle\text{dip in } R_v\rangle :: \overset{0.9}{=} h_{12} \tag{P110}$$

$$\langle \text{dip in } R_v \rangle ::\overset{0.9}{=} h_{16} \quad \text{(P111)}$$

$$\langle \text{dip in } R_v \rangle ::\overset{1}{=} l_{11} h_{12} \quad \text{(P112)}$$

$$\langle \text{dip in } R_v \rangle ::\overset{1}{=} l_{11} h_{16} \quad \text{(P113)}$$

$$\langle \text{dip in } R_v \rangle ::\overset{1}{=} h_{12} h_{16}. \quad \text{(P114)}$$

The semantic rule associated with the definition of ⟨dip in R_v⟩ is

$$\mu_{\langle \text{dip in } R_v \rangle} = (0.6 \wedge \mu_{l_{11}}) \vee (0.9 \wedge \mu_{h_{12}}) \vee (0.9 \wedge \mu_{h_{16}}) \vee (\mu_{l_{11}} \wedge \mu_{h_{12}}) \vee (\mu_{l_{11}} \wedge \mu_{h_{16}}) \vee (\mu_{h_{12}} \wedge \mu_{h_{16}}). \quad (7)$$

The symbols $\vee$ and $\wedge$ represent the *max* and the *min* operators, respectively.

The definition of the syntactic category ⟨sonorant⟩ could be simply established as: ⟨sonorant⟩ = $\overline{\langle\text{nonsonorant}\rangle}$.

Nevertheless, it has been found that this phonetic feature is better characterized in terms of fuzzy rules involving the answers to component questions that chiefly characterize the sonorant consonants. These elements are the complements of the elements appearing in the definition of nonsonorant,

π_2

$$\langle \text{sonorant} \rangle ::\overset{0.85}{=} \langle \text{SRV} \rangle \quad \text{(P21)}$$

$$\langle \text{sonorant} \rangle ::\overset{0.9}{=} \langle \text{SS} \rangle \quad \text{(P22)}$$

$$\langle \text{sonorant} \rangle ::\overset{1}{=} \langle \text{SRV} \rangle \langle \text{SS} \rangle \quad \text{(P23)}$$

$$\langle \text{SRV} \rangle ::\overset{0.9}{=} h_{11} \quad \text{(P24)}$$

$$\langle \text{SRV} \rangle ::\overset{0.9}{=} l_{12} \quad \text{(P25)}$$

$$\langle \text{SRV} \rangle ::\overset{1}{=} l_{16} \quad \text{(P26)}$$

$$\langle \text{SRV} \rangle ::\overset{1}{=} h_{11} \cdot l_{12} \quad \text{(P27)}$$

$$\langle \text{SS} \rangle ::\overset{1}{=} l_{14} \quad \text{(P28)}$$

$$\langle \text{SS} \rangle ::\overset{1}{=} l_{15} p_S. \quad \text{(P29)}$$

The semantic rules associated with the definitions of ⟨SRV⟩ and ⟨SS⟩ are given as follows:

$$\mu_{\langle \text{SRV} \rangle} = (0.9 \wedge \mu_{h_{11}}) \vee (0.9 \wedge \mu_{l_{12}}) \vee \mu_{l_{16}} \vee (\mu_{l_{12}} \wedge \mu_{h_{11}}) \quad (8)$$

$$\mu_{\langle \text{SS} \rangle} = \mu_{l_{14}} \vee (p_S \wedge \mu_{l_{15}}). \quad (9)$$

The measures of the hypotheses ⟨sonorant⟩ and ⟨nonsonorant⟩ are computed using the (3), considering ⟨dip in S⟩, ⟨dip in R_v⟩, ⟨SRV⟩, ⟨SS⟩ as descriptions of the acoustic pattern p and the grammaticalities of π_1 and π_2 as memberships of the fuzzy relations between the left side and the right side phrases of the rules. One gets

$$\text{Poss}\,\{\langle \text{nonsonorant} \rangle \text{ is in } p\} = \mu_{\langle \text{dip in } S \rangle} \vee \mu_{\langle \text{dip in } R_v \rangle} \quad (10)$$

$$\text{Poss}\,\{\langle \text{sonorant} \rangle \text{ is in } p\} = (\mu_{\langle \text{SRV} \rangle} \wedge 0.85) \vee (\mu_{\langle \text{SS} \rangle} \wedge 0.9) \vee (\mu_{\langle \text{SRV} \rangle} \wedge \mu_{\langle \text{SS} \rangle}). \quad (11)$$

Detailed examples are given in Appendix I.

C. Learning of the Knowledge Source for Precategorical Classification

All the possible vowel-consonant-vowel coarticulations of the Italian language have been considered. These pseudo-syllables were extracted by an automatic procedure, described in [14], from the pronounciation by a single male speaker of sentences made up of a VERB PHRASE and a NOUN PHRASE. The syllable under consideration was always in the same syntactic position and the second vowel was always stressed. The following vowels and consonants have been considered: a, e, i, o, u, n, m, l, r, ñ (as in Bologna), gl (as in Cagliari), p, t, k, b, d, g, v, s, r, f, s, z, tʃ, ʃ, d. All the consonants have been considered in every possible vocalic context, resulting in a total of 525 syllables analyzed. Other vowels appeared in the experiment as subclasses of the five vowels mentioned above but further distinctions were not considered significant for the experiment.

All the sentences were acquired through a 10 bit A/D converter at a sampling rate of 20 kHz. After data acquisition, the time-evolutions of the parameters introduced in Section II-A were obtained by fast Fourier transformation.

The time evolutions of S and A were described by a simple language introduced in [14], and the vowel positions were detected using a syntactic procedure described in [14].

Given a set of hypotheses about the positions of the vowels in each sentence, the time intervals between two vowels were considered and hypotheses about their classification as sonorant or nonsonorant were generated. Such operations may be viewed as the assignment of distinctive features. The cases of nonvocalic intervals that are to be further subdivided into subintervals belonging to different syntactic categories are under investigation and will be treated in a future paper.

For each nonvocalic interval, the parameters u_{11}-u_{16} were computed, and the fuzzy restrictions defining the meaning of h_{1i} $(i = 1, 2, \cdots, 6)$ were established subjectively according to the prototype curve shown in Fig. 3 and values of α_{ji} and β_{ji} defined by Table I. Furthermore, the variables h_{1i}, l_{1i} $(i = 1, 2, \cdots, 6)$, were combined into the rules π_1 and π_2 according to how far they can be acoustic renderings of the phonetic features sonorant and nonsonorant.

The "grammaticalities" of the rules in π_1 and π_2 have been inferred as follows. The set of available samples was subdivided into sample subsets $S_1, S_2, \cdots, S_t, \cdots, S_T$, each one containing 50 sonorant and 50 nonsonorant consonants.

Assuming

$$\text{Poss}\,[\langle \text{sonorant} \rangle \text{ is in } p] = \mu_{\langle \text{sonorant} \rangle} \text{ and}$$

$$\text{Poss}\,[\langle \text{nonsonorant} \rangle \text{ is in } p] = \mu_{\langle \text{nonsonorant} \rangle},$$

the following types of errors were considered:

1) type-1 error: $\mu_{\langle \text{sonorant} \rangle} = 1$ for a nonsonorant sound or $\mu_{\langle \text{nonsonorant} \rangle} = 1$ for a sonorant sound;

2) type-2 error: $\mu_{\langle \text{sonorant} \rangle} > \mu_{\langle \text{nonsonorant} \rangle}$ for a nonsonorant sound or $\mu_{\langle \text{nonsonorant} \rangle} > \mu_{\langle \text{sonorant} \rangle}$ for a sonorant sound.

Learning consists of varying the "grammaticalities" of the rules and selecting a set of rule memberships that ensure the absence of type-1 errors and minimizes the number of type-2 errors. This means that a wrong hypothesis never appears as certainly true and that the wrong hypothesis appears to be more plausible than the true hypothesis in a minimum number of situations.

Learning was performed by an interactive program that allows the operator to vary the grammaticalities of the rules in given intervals and with given steps. For each assignment of the grammaticalities, the program gives the number of type-1 errors and type-2 errors as well as the input samples for which an error has been found. The final assignment of the grammaticalities was done subjectively after experiments on all the above-mentioned VCV coarticulations, on the basis of the objective measurements of the number of type-1 and type-2 errors obtained with different assignments of grammaticalities.

Five sample sets $S_1, S_2, \cdots, S_t, \cdots, S_5$ were used for learning the grammaticalities of the rules defining the sonorant and nonsonorant classes. For each sample S_t $(t = 1, 2, \cdots, 5)$ a set Γ_t of grammaticality assignments was found for which the number of type-1 errors was zero and the number of type-2 errors appeared to be minimum after a large choice of assignments.

A solution was subjectively selected in the set of assignments given by

$$\Gamma = \Gamma_1 \cap \Gamma_2 \cap \cdots \cap \Gamma_t \cap \cdots \cap \Gamma_5. \tag{12}$$

The problem of learning grammaticalities was further investigated theoretically; the theoretical results have been applied to the cases treated in this paper leading to the assignments used in π_1 and π_2; a description of the algorithms is very long and is given in another paper [25].

The "grammaticalities" inferred using VCV syllables of a single talker were subsequently used for another experiment involving four talkers. The results of this experiment, reported in Section IV, do not show remarkable differences from talker to talker, thus suggesting that the rules, being related to basic acoustic realizations of phonetic features, are talker-independent.

D. Classification of the Other Features

Among the sonorant sounds, the feature "vocalic" is assigned with membership function $\mu_{\langle\text{vocalic}\rangle} = 1$ to the speech segments that are recognized as vowels by the syntactic procedure presented in [14].

Some other sounds exhibiting peaks in the signal amplitude and in the energies in the 3-5 kHz band may not be classified as vowels because the peaks are weak. In the latter case, if the peaks have a duration exceeding 50 ms, a membership function is assigned to the feature "vocalic" after answering a composite question Q_2 having the following component questions.

$Q_{21} \hat{=}$ what is the maximum of the signal energy with respect to the silence level?

$Q_{22} \hat{=}$ what is the maximum of the energy in the 3-5 kHz band with respect to the silence level?

The answers to these component questions are fuzzy sets h_{2i}, l_{2i} $(i = 1, 2)$ defined on the universe of the following variables:

$$u_{21} = S_v - S_{\text{sil}}$$

$$u_{22} = A_v - A_{\text{sil}}$$

where the subscript v stands for vowel.

The feature "vocalic" is defined as follows:

$$\pi_3 \quad \langle\text{vocalic}\rangle :: \overset{1}{=} h_{21} \cdot h_{22}, \tag{13}$$

the fuzzy restrictions of h_{21} and h_{22} have the behavior of Fig. 3, and their values of α_{2i} and β_{2i} are listed in Table I.

Using this procedure 10 percent of vowels (mostly u) not recognized with $\mu_{\langle\text{vocalic}\rangle} = 1$ are recognized with $\mu_{\langle\text{vocalic}\rangle} \geqslant 0.8$. For a further classification of nonsonorant sounds, a composite question Q_3 was introduced having the following components.

$Q_{31} \hat{=}$ how high is R_v?

$Q_{32} \hat{=}$ what is the maximum value of S in the interval where R_v is less than -12 dB?

$Q_{33} \hat{=}$ what is the duration of dip in the signal amplitude between the two vowels?

$Q_{34} \hat{=}$ what is the duration of the interval where R_v is less than -12 dB?

The answers to these questions are

$$l_{3i}, h_{3i} \quad (i = 1, 2, 3, 4).$$

The answers to Q_3 are linguistic variables defined on the following parameters:

$u_{31} = u_{11}$

$u_{32} = S_M$, maximum of the signal in the interval where R_v is less than -12 dB,

u_{33} = duration of dip in S,

u_{34} = duration of the interval for which R_v is less than -12 dB.

$u_{35} = u_{15}$.

The feature ⟨nonsonorant continuant⟩ is defined as follows:

$$\langle\text{nonsonorant continuant}\rangle = h_{32} \cdot h_{34} \cdot l_{33}.$$

Among the nonsonorants that are not continuant, a further subdivision between interrupted and affricate is made by considering the duration and the relative positions of the amplitude dip and the dip in R_v. A detailed definition of the questions pertaining to the features interrupted and affricate is omitted here for the sake of brevity.

A further specification of the nonsonorant sounds is made by assigning the feature "tense" or "lax" in accordance with the following rules:

$$\pi_4$$

$$\langle\text{tense}\rangle :: \overset{1}{=} l_{31} h_{34}$$

$$\langle\text{tense}\rangle :: \overset{1}{=} \langle\text{interrupted}\rangle \cdot l_{31}$$

$$\langle\text{tense}\rangle :: \overset{1}{=} \langle\text{interrupted}\rangle \cdot h_{33}$$

$$\langle\text{tense}\rangle :: \overset{1}{=} \langle\text{interrupted}\rangle \cdot h_{35}$$

$$\langle\text{lax}\rangle :: \overset{1}{=} \overline{\langle\text{tense}\rangle}$$

$$\mu_{\langle\text{tense}\rangle} = (\mu_{l_{31}} \wedge \mu_{h_{34}}) \vee \mu_{\langle\text{interrupted}\rangle}(\mu_{l_{31}} \vee \mu_{h_{33}} \vee \mu_{h_{35}});$$

$$\mu_{\langle\text{lax}\rangle} = 1 - \mu_{\langle\text{tense}\rangle}. \tag{14}$$

III. Phoneme Classification

Phoneme labeling of pseudosyllables is performed by a fuzzy algorithm consisting of a branching questionnaire. The generation of a hypothesis about the presence of a phoneme is the answer to a composite question associated with a membership function.

Phoneme classification is a context-dependent operation, except for nonreduced vowels that can be recognized with no knowledge of the context. Vowels belong to sonorant segments, for which formants are tracked. Emission of hypotheses about vowels is primarily based on the analysis of the plot of $F2$ (the second formant frequency) versus $F1$ (the first formant frequency) for the sonorant portion of the PSS. The graph drawn in the $F1$-$F2$ plane by the pronunciation of a syllable is described by a language whose detailed definition is given in [14].

Formant tracking (see [29] for details) is performed on a pseudosyllable segment by looking for formant arcs made by concatenation of spectral peaks having high energy. Particular care has been taken in order to guarantee as much as possible agreement between FFT and LPC spectra and to control formant tracking by transition rules.

The primitives of the language are basically stable zones (SZ's) and lines (LN's) (see [31] for definitions). Stable zones correspond to the stationary portions of the speech waveform. It is assumed that nonreduced vowels are always represented by stable zones, with a duration of more than 40 ms.

Vowel classification is based on the detection of stable zones in speech intervals that have been previously hypothesized as vocalic segments. Some SZ's in segments that have not been previously classified as "vocalic" may also cause this assignment if some conditions involving relations with gross spectral features are satisfied. This assignment is controlled by rules that are omitted here for the sake of brevity.

The vocalic SZ's are then labeled by one or more vowel symbols, and a membership function is assigned to each label. This operation uses a definition of vowel loci as fuzzy sets in the $F1$-$F2$ plane. Each SZ has the coordinates of its center of gravity as attributes. The coordinates identify a point in the $F1$-$F2$ plane that may belong to one or more vowel loci with certain membership functions.

Vowel loci, defined as fuzzy sets, have an assignment of membership functions that can be made by a subjective adjustment of probability densities estimated after a long period of learning. The resulting assignment is speaker-dependent.

In the approach presented in this paper, a vocalic hypothesis v_i is defined by the following rule:

$$\pi_5$$

$$v_i ::= \langle \text{vocalic} \rangle \langle SZ_v \rangle \langle v_i(F_1, F_2) \rangle$$

where ⟨vocalic⟩ is a phonetic feature attached during precategorical classification, $\langle SZ_v \rangle$ represents the fact that a vocalic stable zone has been found inside the vocalic segment and $v_i(F_1, F_2)$ represents the fact that the center of gravity of SZ_v is in the locus of the vowel v_i.

A semantic rule is associated with π_5 to evaluate the vocalic hypothesis v_i:

$$\mu_{\langle v_i \rangle} = \mu_{\langle \text{vocalic} \rangle} \wedge \mu_{\langle SZ_v \rangle} \wedge \mu_{\langle v_i(F_1, F_2) \rangle}. \tag{15}$$

$\mu_{\langle \text{vocalic} \rangle}$ is a result of the precategorical classification,

$$\mu_{\langle v_i(F_1, F_2) \rangle}$$

is the degree of membership of the center of gravity of SZ_v in the fuzzy set which is the locus of v_i in the $F1$-$F2$ plane, and $\mu_{\langle SZ_v \rangle}$ is a measure, defined by heuristic rules, of the "stationarity" of the spectra of the vocalic segment.

Classification of sonorant sounds into phonemes requires a preliminary recognition of the features liquid or nasal. This operation as well as the phonemic transcription is controlled by rules that may be context-dependent. Such rules are functions of answers to the questions of a branching questionnaire.

A discussion of the features that are extracted for classifying nasal sounds as well as the inference of a source of knowledge for controlling this classification requires a long description and has been presented in separate papers [26], [27]. The papers describe how the hypotheses

⟨liquid⟩, ⟨nasal⟩, ⟨m⟩, ⟨n⟩, ⟨ñ⟩, ⟨gl⟩, ⟨r⟩, ⟨l⟩

can be evaluated giving, for each sonorant sound, the values

$$\mu_{\langle \text{liquid} \rangle}, \mu_{\langle \text{nasal} \rangle}, \mu_{\langle m \rangle}, \mu_{\langle n \rangle}, \mu_{\langle \tilde{n} \rangle}, \mu_{\langle gl \rangle}, \mu_{\langle r \rangle}, \mu_{\langle l \rangle}.$$

These membership functions are used for evaluating the total hypotheses that, for example, a consonant sound is sonorant, nasal, and /m/. Let M be such a total hypothesis. Its value is computed as follows:

$$\mu_{\langle M \rangle} = \mu_{\langle \text{sonorant} \rangle} \wedge \mu_{\langle \text{nasal} \rangle} \wedge \mu_{\langle m \rangle}. \tag{16}$$

Finally, the classification of nonsonorant sounds is sufficiently detailed after precategorical classification. Hypotheses about possible phonemic labeling of speech intervals are obtained by asking questions about the frication noise spectra for continuant and affricate sounds. Recognition of interrupted sounds requires the analysis of formant transitions in the neighbor segments as is well shown by Öhman [28] at least for VCV utterances. Tracking formants in these syllables is a very delicate operation. An interesting algorithm for extracting a formant pattern considered as a fuzzy graph has recently been proposed by Laface [29]. Research on the recognition of nonsonorant phonemes is in progress.

IV. Experimental Results

Table II shows the experimental result of the generation of hypotheses about the features sonorant and nonsonorant for four talkers, three male and one female, using the syntactic rules π_1 and π_2 with all the grammaticalities set equal to one. The results refer to syllables extracted from spoken sentences of various and unconstrained syntactic structure. One hundred syllables were analyzed for each talker. Although it has been found that adapting some of the α_{1i} and β_{1i} to the talker and letting all the grammaticalities be equal to one, leads to some improvement, a better result has been obtained by leaving α_{1i} and β_{1i} unchanged and assigning grammaticalities lower than one to some rules. The assignment shown in the rules π_1

TABLE II
CONFUSION MATRIX FOR THE CLASSIFICATION SONORANT/NONSONORANT OF CONSONANTS

		Recognized	
		Sonorant	Nonsonorant
Pronounced	Sonorant	91 percent	9 percent
	Nonsonorant	7 percent	93 percent

TABLE III
ERROR RATES FOR THE CLASSIFICATIONS SONORANT/NONSONORANT USING FUZZY DATA

Speaker	Sex	Type-2 Error Rate
R.D.	M	7 percent
A.C.	M	5 percent
A.R.	F	4 percent
P.L.	M	3 percent

and π_2 gave an average error rate of 5 percent for about 400 samples pronounced by the four talkers. All the errors were type-2 errors.

The details of the error rates for each talker are reported in Table III. The distribution of the errors shows no marked differences among the talkers, suggesting that the features considered are talker-independent.

The improvements on the results of Table II show the advantages of assigning the grammaticalities to the rules. The consonants that gave most errors were /v/ and /b/, both in context of front vowels. Such errors may be recovered by tracking formants for the /v/ and /b/ consonants classified as sonorants and performing a quaternary classification (liquid/glide/nasal/bad-sonorant) based on the formants extracted for each pseudo-syllable segment. In any case, the fuzzy algorithms enhance the performance of phonetic classification with respect to recent works.

The DIP classification, performed by Weinstein *et al.* [30], is probably one of the best published works dealing with a type of problem comparable to that proposed in this paper. The confusion statistics on DIP classification reported by Weinstein *et al.* [30] show that 82 percent of the sonorant consonants were correctly classified using their approach while, even without weighted grammaticalities, the fuzzy algorithms resulted in 91 percent correct classifications of sonorants and this rate increased to 96 percent after weighting the grammaticalities. In [30], 26 out of 38 /v/ were labeled by the DIP classification as nasals. With the approach proposed in this paper, less than 30 percent of the /v/ reached a score as "sonorant" higher than the score as "nonsonorant" and never obtained a value of $\mu_{\langle\text{sonorant}\rangle}$ equal to one.

The principal reason for these improvements is that DIP classification is only one of the deterministic components of the rules used by the fuzzy algorithms.

The comparison between the approach proposed in this paper and the one followed in [30] may seem unfair. In [30], for example, a 10 kHz sampling rate was used and the information in the 5-10 kHz band was therefore neglected. Moreover, material from a different set of speakers speaking a different language with more complicated consonant clusters was used. A more convincing experiment was carried out using the data tabulated in [25] in order to compare the fuzzy decision algorithm strategies with more conventional weighted-Euclidean-distance strategy. The second approach gave 6 percent of errors on a corpus of 100 data while the fuzzy approach gave 4 percent of errors.

Similar results and a constant advantage of the fuzzy approach were observed on other three experiments with different sets of 100 samples each. The low error rates achieved even with the weighted-Euclidean-distance confirms that the set of features used is a good one.

Another interesting result emerged from the experiments; when

$$\mu_{\langle\text{nonsonorant}\rangle} > \mu_{\langle\text{sonorant}\rangle} + 0.05, \tag{17}$$

the consonant is certainly nonsonorant. This rule can be useful for the system strategy that does not have to execute the process of formant tracking when (17) is satisfied. When formants are tracked, if $\mu_{\langle\text{nonsonorant}\rangle} > 0.65$, the test of "bad sonorant" is performed to detect the few calls of /v/, /b/, and very rarely /d/ which exhibit marked sonorant features.

The results of the classification continuant/interrupted/affricate for nonsonorant sounds are shown in Table IV. Table V shows the results of the classification tense/lax. For the classification tense/lax the performance has been improved further by using more complex fuzzy rules; details concerning these are omitted here for the sake of brevity. By weighting the grammaticalities we can ensure that $\mu_{\langle\text{tense}\rangle} > \mu_{\langle\text{lax}\rangle}$ never occurs for the lax sounds without type-1 errors. In consequence, about 30 percent of the tense sounds are classified as lax; for these cases the first formant is tracked and the classification scores are improved by the analysis of the first formant. The details are omitted here for the sake of brevity.

For the recognition of vowels, better results than the ones recently presented by Pal and Majumder [17] have been obtained. This is probably due to the use of linear prediction coefficients for tracking formants and to the accuracy of the algorithm for extracting stable zones (see [31] for details). As in other SUS reports [9], the performances are measured giving the percentage of times that the correct phoneme is within the top N choices. Using a definition of vowel loci dependent on each talker, the percentage of N choices out of 5 shown in Table VI have been found. Table VI should be interpreted as follows. Among the five Italian vowels, the correct one appears with highest membership 97 percent of the time and either first or second 99 percent of the time.

The experimental results for the classification of nasals are reported and discussed in [27]. An overall error rate of 6 percent is achieved in the recognition of nasals obtained for 200 utterances by four male speakers. None of these errors corresponds to the assignment of unit degree of worthiness to a wrong hypothesis but only to the fact that a wrong interpretation obtained a degree of worthiness higher than the right one.

VI. CONCLUSIONS

A method for generating phonetic and phonemic hypotheses on a spoken message has been proposed. It is based on a

TABLE IV
CONFUSION MATRIX FOR THE CLASSIFICATION OF NONSONORANT SOUNDS INTO CONTINUANT, INTERRUPTED, AND AFFRICATE

		Recognized		
		Continuant	Interrupted	Affricate
Pronounced	Continuant	95 percent	–	5 percent
	Interrupted	–	100 percent	–
	Affricate	6 percent	–	94 percent

TABLE V
CONFUSION MATRIX FOR THE CLASSIFICATION TENSE/LAX OF NONSONORANT SOUNDS

		Recognized	
		Tense	Lax
Pronounced	Tense	76 percent	24 percent
	Lax	8 percent	92 percent

TABLE VI
PERCENTAGES OF N CHOICES OUT OF FIVE FOR VOWEL RECOGNITION

N	1	2
	97 percent	99 percent

hierarchy of concurrent processes or steps of fuzzy algorithms, whereby the acoustic rendering of phonetic and phonemic features are combined in a hierarchy of rules. To get the right hypothesis with the highest degree of confidence, the effectiveness of these rules is measured by their grammaticalities.

The rules and their grammaticalities represent the knowledge of a phonetician who interprets a spectrogram on the basis of his experience, which is subjective, but is based on objective facts and relations established by experiment. The experimental results obtained suggest that the rules used for precategorical classification depend neither on the talker nor the context.

Some other rules (for example those used for the classification of nasals) are context-dependent but give results that are talker-independent.

The use of phonetic and phonemic features as syntactic categories to acoustic features by "branching questionnaires" is a new development of work done by De Mori *et al.* [14], [31], [33]-[35] and Mermelstein [36] on the use of syntactic methods for automatic speech recognition. It is an attempt to use computer algorithms to perform some of the processes held to be involved in speech perception. This is not in disaccordance with Liberman [37] and Studdert-Kennedy [38], who have concluded, on the basis of valuable investigations, that complex coding, not simple matching, relates acoustic and phonemic features.

By the use of fuzzy algorithms we can account for the imprecision of the knowledge used in interpreting acoustic patterns and for the vagueness that may arise when a pattern is described in terms of acoustic features. Since the algorithms are flexible, advantage can be taken of the redundancy of features to get the best evidence assigned to the right hypothesis

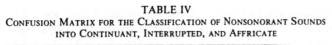

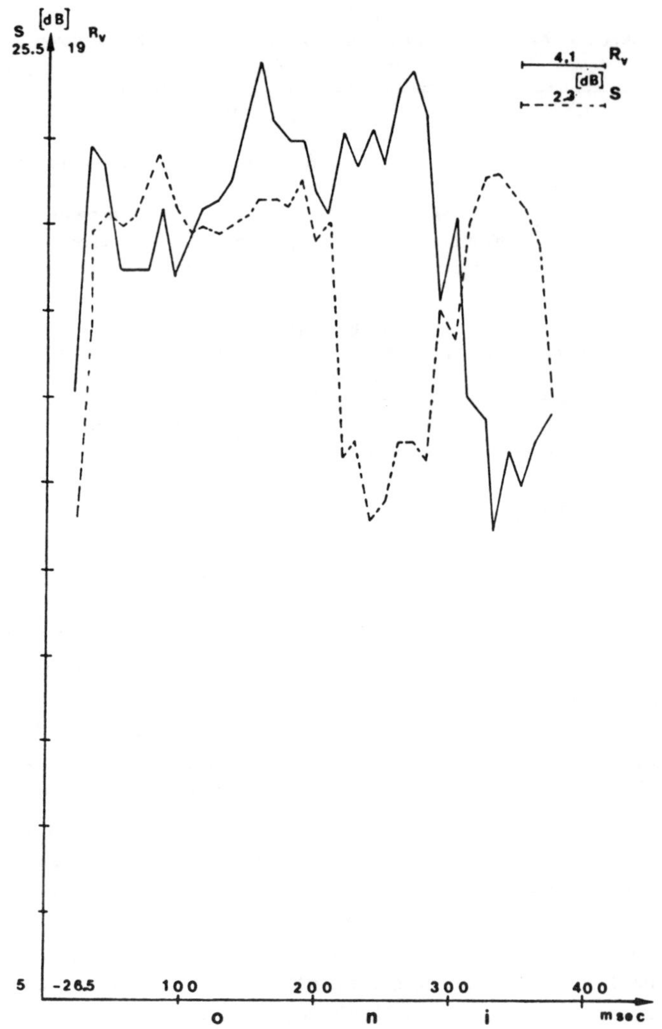

Fig. 4. Time evolutions of the parameters S and R_v for the syllable /oni/.

in spite of the vagueness and imprecision of the data and rules used to generate it. The success of the system clearly depends on the number of acoustic features used, their significance, detectability, and noninteraction.

Further work on the lines of this paper should enhance the performance of an acoustic classifier, which would be a worthwhile contribution to speech understanding systems.

APPENDIX

Example 1

Fig. 4 shows the plots versus time of the parameters S and R_v defined by (1). They refer to the syllable /oni/ extracted from continuous speech.

The values assumed by the parameters u_{1i} $(i = 1, 2, \cdots, 6)$ for the consonant /n/ are the following:

$u_{11} = 15.5$ dB
$u_{12} = -20$ dB
$u_{13} = 10.4$ dB
$u_{14} = 100$ ms
$u_{15} = 7.45$ dB
$u_{16} = 4.5$ dB.

Using the diagram of Fig. 3 with the break points given by Table I and remembering the definitions given by (4) and (5) one gets

$\mu_{h_{11}} = 1, \quad \mu_{l_{11}} = 0,$
$\mu_{h_{12}} = 0, \quad \mu_{l_{12}} = 1,$
$\mu_{h_{13}} = 0.55, \quad \mu_{l_{13}} = 0.45,$
$\mu_{h_{14}} = 0.7, \quad \mu_{l_{14}} = 0.3,$
$\mu_{h_{15}} = 0.1, \quad \mu_{l_{15}} = 0.9,$
$\mu_{h_{16}} = 0.2, \quad \mu_{l_{16}} = 0.8.$

Applying (6), (7), (8), (9) one gets

$$\mu_{\langle \text{dip in } S \rangle} = \min[0, \{\max(\min(0.85, 0.45), \min(0.9, 0.7), \min(0.45, 0.7), 0.1)\}] = 0$$

$$\mu_{\langle \text{dip in } R_v \rangle} = \max\{\min(0.6, 0), \min(0.9, 0), \min(0.9, 0.2), \min(0, 0), \min(0, 0.2), \min(0, 0.2)\} = \max(0, 0, 0.2, 0, 0, 0) = 0.2$$

$$\mu_{\langle \text{SRV} \rangle} = \max\{\min(0.9, 1), \min(0.9, 1), \min(1, 1), 0.8\} = \max(0.9, 0.9, 1, 0.8) = 1$$

$$\mu_{\langle \text{SS} \rangle} = \max(0, 3, 0.9) = 0.9.$$

Applying (10) and (11) one gets:

$$\text{Poss}\,[\langle\text{sonorant}\rangle \text{ is in } p] = \max\{\min(0.85, 1), \min(0.9, 0.9), \min(1, 0.9)\} = \max(0.85, 0.9, 0.9) = 0.9$$

$$\text{Poss}\,[\langle\text{nonsonorant}\rangle \text{ is in } p] = \max(0, 0.2) = 0.2.$$

Thus, the hypothesis that the consonant is sonorant is more consistent.

Example 2

Fig. 5 shows the plots of S and R_v for the syllable /edi/ extracted from continuous speech.

Using the same approach as for Example 1 one gets

$u_{11} = -13$ dB
$u_{12} = 0$ dB
$u_{13} = 0$ dB
$u_{14} = 100$ ms
$u_{15} = 16.7$ dB
$u_{16} = 5.6$ dB

$\mu_{h_{11}} = 0.1, \quad \mu_{l_{11}} = 0.9,$
$\mu_{h_{12}} = 0.8, \quad \mu_{l_{12}} = 0.2,$
$\mu_{h_{13}} = 0, \quad \mu_{l_{13}} = 1,$
$\mu_{h_{14}} = 0.7, \quad \mu_{l_{14}} = 0.3,$
$\mu_{h_{15}} = 0.6, \quad \mu_{l_{15}} = 0.4,$
$\mu_{h_{16}} = 0.4, \quad \mu_{l_{16}} = 0.6.$

$$\mu_{\langle \text{dip in } S \rangle} = \min[1, \{\max(\min(0.85, 1), \min(0.9, 0.7), \min(1, 0.7), 0.6)\}] = 0.85$$

$$\mu_{\langle \text{dip in } R_v \rangle} = \max\{\min(0.6, 0.9), \min(0.9, 0.8), \min(0.9, 0.4), \min(0.9, 0.8), \min(0.9, 0.4), \min(0.8, 0.4)\} = \max(0.6, 0.8, 0.4, 0.8, 0.4, 0.4) = 0.8$$

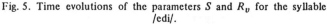

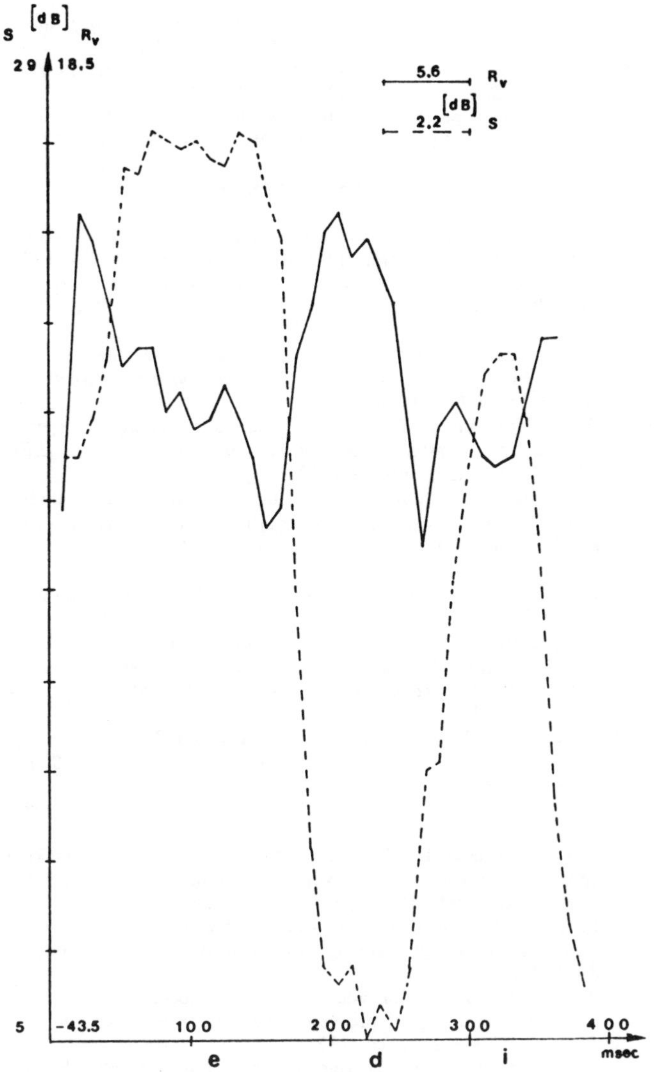

Fig. 5. Time evolutions of the parameters S and R_v for the syllable /edi/.

$$\mu_{\langle \text{SRV} \rangle} = \max\{\min(0.9, 0.1), \min(0.9, 0.2), \min(0.2, 0.1), 0.6\} = 0.6$$

$$\mu_{\langle \text{SS} \rangle} = \max(0.3, 0.4) = 0.4$$

$$\text{Poss}\,[\langle\text{nonsonorant}\rangle \text{ is in } p] = \max(0.85, 0.8) = 0.85$$

$$\text{Poss}\,[\langle\text{sonorant}\rangle \text{ is in } p] = \max\{\min(0.85, 0.6), \min(0.9, 0.4), \min(0.6, 0.4)\} = 0.6.$$

Thus, the most consistent hypothesis is that the consonant is nonsonorant.

References

[1] D. Raj Reddy, Ed., *Speech Recognition: Invited Papers of the IEEE Symp.* New York: Academic, 1975.
[2] —, "Speech recognition by machine: A review," *Proc. IEEE*, vol. 64, pp. 501–531, Apr. 1976.
[3] T. B. Martin, "Practical applications of voice input to machines," *Proc. IEEE*, vol. 64, pp. 487–501, Apr. 1976.

[4] F. Jelinek, "Continuous speech recognition by statistical methods," *Proc. IEEE*, vol. 64, pp. 532-556, Apr. 1976.

[5] D. H. Klatt, "Review of the ARPA speech understanding project," *J. Acoust. Soc. Amer.*, vol. 62, pp. 1345-1366, Dec. 1977.

[6] J. J. Wolf, "Speech recognition and understanding," in *Digital Pattern Recognition*, K. S. Fu, Ed. New York: Springer, 1976.

[7] D. Raj Reddy, Ed., "Speech understanding system–Summary of results of the five-year research effort at Carnegie Mellon University," Pittsburgh, PA, 1977.

[8] D. E. Walker, Ed., "SRI speech understanding systems–Final report, Stanford Research International," Menlo Park, CA, 1977.

[9] W. A. Woods *et al.*, "Speech understanding systems–Final report, Bolt, Beranek and Newman Inc.," Cambridge, MA, Rep. 3438, 1976.

[10] R. De Mori, "Recent advances in speech recognition" invited paper, in *Proc. 4th Int. Joint Conf. on Pattern Recognition*, Kyoto, Japan, Oct. 1978.

[11] R. D. Mori and P. Torasso, "Lexical classification in a speech understanding system using fuzzy relations," in *Proc. IEEE ASSP Conf.*, Philadelphia, PA, 1976, pp. 565-568.

[12] M. Coppo and L. Saitta, "Semantic support for a speech understanding system based on fuzzy relations," in *Proc. IEEE Conf. on Cybernetics and Society*, Washington, DC, 1976, pp. 520-525.

[13] L. A. Zadeh, "Fuzzy sets as a basis for a theory of possibility," *Fuzzy Sets and Systems*, vol. 1, p. 3-28, 1978.

[14] R. De Mori, P. Laface, and E. Piccolo, "Automatic detection and description of syllabic features in continuous speech," *IEEE Trans. Acoust., Speech, Signal Processing*, vol. ASSP-24, pp. 365-379, Oct. 1976.

[15] L. A. Zadeh, "The concept of a linguistic variable and its application to approximate reasoning–II," *Inform. Sci.*, vol. 8, pp. 301-357, 1975.

[16] —, "Similarity relations and fuzzy ordering," *Inform. Sci*, vol. 3, pp. 177-200, 1971.

[17] S. K. Pal and D. D. Majumder, "Fuzzy set and decisonmaking approaches in vowel and speaker recognition," *IEEE Trans. Syst., Man, Cybern.*, vol. SMC-7, pp. 625-629, Aug. 1977.

[18] L. A. Zadeh, "The concept of a linguistic variable and its application to approximate reasoning–III," *Inform. Sci.*, vol. 9, pp. 43-80, 1975.

[19] R. De Mori, S. Rivoira, and A. Serra, "A special purpose computer for digital signal processing," *IEEE Trans. Comput.*, vol. C-24, pp. 1202-1211, Dec. 1975.

[20] K. N. Stevens, "Potential role of property detectors in the perception of consonants," MIT-RLE, Quart. Progress Rep. 110, pp. 155-168, July 1973.

[21] G. W. Hughes and J. F. Hemdal, "Speech analysis," Purdue Univ., Rep. AFCRL-65-681 (P 13552), 1965.

[22] L. A. Zadeh, "A fuzzy algorithmic approach to the definition of complex or imprecise concepts," *Int. J. Man-Mach. Studies*, vol. 8, pp. 249-291, 1976.

[23] —, "Fuzzy languages and their relation to human and machine intelligence," in *Proc. Int. Conf. on Man Comput.*, Bordeaux, France, S. Kargle Basel, Ed. New York: Munchen, 1972, pp. 130-165.

[24] K. S. Fu, *Syntactic Methods in Pattern Recognition.* New York: Academic, 1974.

[25] R. De Mori and L. Saitta, "Automatic learning of fuzzy relations," *Inform. Sci.*, to be published.

[26] R. De Mori, P. Laface, and P. Torasso, "Automatic classification of liquids and nasals in continuous speech," in *Proc. IEEE ICASSP 77 Conf.*, Hartford, CT, 1977, pp. 644-647.

[27] R. De Mori, R. Gubrinowicz, and P. Laface, "Inference of a knowledge source for the recognition of nasals in continuous speech," *IEEE Trans. Acoust., Speech, Signal Processing*, vol. ASSP-27, pp. 538-549, Oct. 1979.

[28] S. E. G. Öhman, "Coarticulation in VCV utterances: Spectrographic measurements," *J. Acoust. Soc. Amer.*, vol. 39, no. 1, pp. 151-168, 1966.

[29] P. Laface, "Ambiguities in feature extraction from continuous speech," in *Proc. 4th Int. Joint Conf. on Pattern Recognition*, Kyoto, Japan, Nov. 1978.

[30] C. J. Weinstein, S. S. McCandless, L. F. Mondshein, and V. W. Zue, "A system for acoustic-phonetic analysis of continuous speech," *IEEE Trans. Acoust., Speech, Signal Processing*, vol. ASSP-23, pp. 54-67, Feb. 1975.

[31] R. De Mori, "A descriptive technique for automatic speech recognition," *IEEE Trans. Audio Electroacoust.*, vol. AU-21, pp. 89-100, Apr. 1973.

[32] R. De Mori and P. Laface, "Representation of phonetic and phonemic knowledge in a speech understanding system," in *Proc. AISB/GI Conf. Artificial Intelligence*, Hamburg, Germany, July 1978, pp. 201-203.

[33] R. De Mori, "Syntactic recognition of speech patterns," in *Syntactic Pattern Recognition, Applications*, K. S. Fu, Ed. New York: Springer-Verlag, 1977.

[34] —, "Design for a syntax-controlled acoustic classifier," *Information Processing 74*, J. L. Rosenfeld, Ed. Amsterdam, The Netherlands: North-Holland, 1974, pp. 753-757.

[35] R. De Mori, S. Rivoira, and A. Serra, "A speech understanding system with learning capability," in *Proc. 4th Int. Joint Conf. on Artificial Intelligence*, Tbilisi, USSR, Sept. 1975, pp. 468-475.

[36] P. Mermelstein, "A phonetic-context controlled strategy for segmentation and phonetic labeling of speech," *IEEE Trans. Acoust., Speech, Signal Processing*, vol. ASSP-23, pp. 79-82, Feb. 1975.

[37] A. M. Liberman, "The grammars of speech and language," *Cognitive Psychol.*, vol. 1, pp. 301-323, Oct. 1970.

[38] M. Studdert-Kennedy, "Speech perception," Haskins Lab., New Haven, CT, Status Rep. SR 39-40, pp. 1-52, July/Dec. 1974.

Fuzzy Grammars in Syntactic Recognition of Skeletal Maturity from X-Rays

AMITA PATHAK AND SANKAR K. PAL, SENIOR MEMBER, IEEE

Abstract—A hierarchical three-stage syntactic recognition algorithm using six-tuple fuzzy and seven-tuple fractionally fuzzy grammars is described for identifying different stages of maturity of bones from X-rays of hand and wrist. The primitives considered are "dot," "straight line," and "arc" as obtained elsewhere. For each arc, its memberships in the sets of "sharp," "fair," and "gentle" arcs have been considered in order to describe and interpret the structural development of epiphysis and metaphysis with growth of a child. The two algorithms are illustrated with the help of the radiograph of a 10–12-year old boy along with some "noisy" versions of the radiograph, which was artificially generated by taking into account possible variations in shape of the relevent contours in the radiograph. Relative merits of the two algorithms with respect to each other and as well as the existing nonfuzzy approach are also discussed.

I. Introduction

THE PRESENT WORK is a continuation of the previous correspondence on image description and primitive extraction using fuzzy sets [1] and is an attempt at syntactic recognition of different stages of maturity of bones from X-rays of hand and wrist using fuzzy grammar and the fuzzy primitives obtained from [1]. The ultimate aim is to be able to make computer-diagnosis of diseases and effects of malnutrition on the skeletal growth of a child.

During the growth of a child, each of the bones of the hand and wrist, as shown in Fig. 1, provides us with an invariant sequence of events that invariably occur in the same order in all individuals and cover the developmental age-span evenly and completely. These sequences therefore provide us with some basis for defining different stages of maturity (age) of the bones. The radius, ulna, metacarpals, and phalanges of the hand and wrist provide us with 28 such sequences, with events in one or another sequence occurring at almost all stages of development [2].

The problem of recognition therefore involves four major parts, namely,

1) study of the radiograph and detection of the specific bones and their location,
2) preprocessing of X-ray images with a view to extracting the edges of the different regions of bones and tissues,
3) primitive extraction of the edge-detected images, and
4) syntactic classification into one of the possible stages of skeletal maturity.

We are concerned here with the last part. The results of the previous parts have already been reported [1], [3]–[5].

Formal language theory has been applied to syntactic recognition of patterns which are rich in structural information i.e., the patterns contain most of their information in their structure rather than in numeric values [6]–[12]. To increase the generative power of a grammar for pattern recognition problems, the concept of phrase-structure grammars has been extended to stochastic grammars [7], [13] and fuzzy grammars, respectively [8], [11], [15]–[19] by randomizing and fuzzifying the use of the production rules. A fuzzy grammar produces a language that is a fuzzy set of strings with each string's membership value (lying in the interval [0, 1]), denoting the degree of belonging of the string in that language. These languages have shown some promise in dealing with patterns which possess ill-defined (fuzzy) boundaries [8], [11], [15], [16].

A three-stage hierarchical syntactic approach [9] is presented here for automatic recognition of the ages of different bone. The classifier accepts strings of primitives [1] defining approximated versions of contours in radiographs representing the epiphyses[1] and metaphyses[2] including palmar and dorsal[3] surfaces [2] as input. Two algorithms based on six-tuple fuzzy grammars and seven-tuple fractionally fuzzy grammars [14] have been used separately for classification at each stage. The primitives considered are a line segment of unit length, clockwise and counter-clockwise curves and a "dot." (By a curve here we mean a simple curve and not a curve obtained by the concatenation of simple curves.) For any such curve we have also defined its membership values corresponding to fuzzy sets of "sharp," "fair," and "gentle" curves.

The two algorithms are illustrated with the help of an X-ray image of the radius of a 10–12-year old boy. Some other distorted versions (artificially generated) of the input string are also considered for their implementation.

Manuscript received August 27, 1984; revised December 13, 1985 and June 1, 1986. This work was supported by the Medical Research Council, UK.
The authors are with the Electronics and Communication Sciences Unit, Indian Statistical Institute, Calcutta 700 035, India.
IEEE Log Number 8610217.

[1]An epiphysis, in some bones, is a separate terminal ossification which only becomes united with the main bone at the attainment of maturity.
[2]A metaphysis of a long bone is the end of the shaft where it joins the epiphysis.
[3]The palmar surface of any bone in the hand and wrist is that surface which is towards the palm of the hand. Likewise, the dorsal surface is the diametrically opposite one.

Reprinted from *IEEE Trans. Syst., Man, Cybern.*, vol. SMC-16, no. 5, pp. 657–667, September/October 1986.

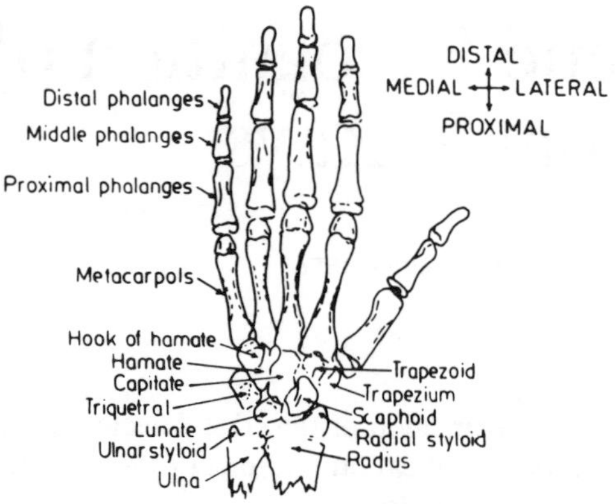

Fig. 1. Bones of hand and wrist [2].

II. Different Stages of Maturity

Fig. 2 shows different stages of skeletal maturity of radius of hand and wrist. This is considered as a typical illustration since radius contributes mostly in determining maturity score [2]. Its structural development with growth is explained below.

In the beginning, the epiphysis is totally absent (Stage A). It gradually appears above the metaphysis as a single (or, rarely, as multiple) deposit(s) of calcium with irregular outline (Stage B). After that, it gradually assumes a well-defined oval shape as seen in the radiograph (Stage C), its maximum diameter being less than half the width of the metaphysis. It continues to grow in size but becomes slightly tapering at its medial end, being more rounded at the lateral end (Stage D). Its maximum diameter now exceeds half the width of the metaphysis. In Stage E, its shape is more or less the same though it becomes larger, and a thickened white line representing the edge of the palmar surface appears within it at the distal border. In Stage F, the palmar surface of the proximal border also develops and becomes visible as a thickened white line at the proximal edge of the epiphysis. At Stage G, the palmar surface of the medial border also becomes apparent as a white line so that the three visible palmar surfaces combine to appear as a single continuous, thickened ⊂-shaped contour. The epiphysis continues to grow larger, and by Stage H it caps the metaphysis almost entirely (at one end or both). The styloid process is also much developed. Finally, at Stage I, fusion of the epiphysis and the metaphysis begins.

The features of the structural development of the radius therefore include the contour, shape, and orientation of the metaphysis and epiphysis including palmar and dorsal surfaces as appearing on the epiphysis and metaphysis with growth, and styloid process. A similar sequence of stages of structural development is also observed [2] in the other bones, namely, ulna, metacarpals, and phalanges (Fig. 1).

III. Definitions

Definition 1a): A fuzzy grammar (FG) is a six-tuple

$$\mathrm{FG} = (V_N, V_T, P, S, J, f)$$

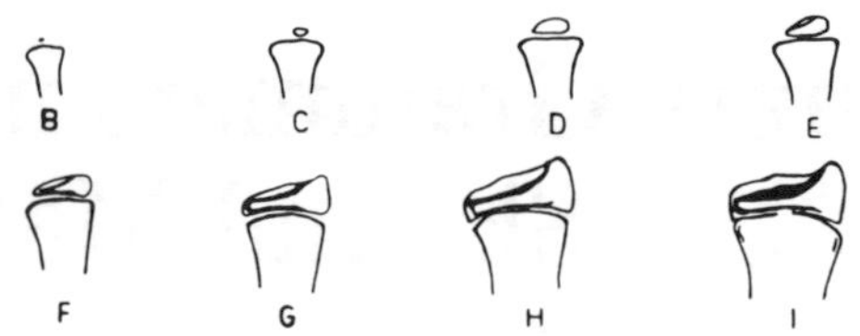

Fig. 2. Different stages of skeletal maturity of radius (Stage A, in which epiphysis is totally absent, is not shown here.)

where

- V_N set of nonterminals, i.e., labels of certain fuzzy sets on V_T^* called fuzzy syntactic categories,
- V_T set of terminals such that $V_N \cap V_T = \phi$,
- V_T^* set of finite strings constructed by concatenation of elements of V_T,
- P set of production rules,
- S starting symbol ($\in V_N$),
- J $\{r_i | i = 1, 2, \cdots, n, n = \#(P)\}$, a set of distinct labels for all productions in P, where $\#(P)$ is the number of elements in the set P,
- f mapping $f: J \to [0,1]$, $f(r_i)$ denoting the fuzzy membership in P of the rule labelled r_i.

Definition 1b): For any string x having m ($\geqslant 1$) derivation(s) in the language $L(\mathrm{FG})$ generated by FG, its membership in $L(\mathrm{FG})$ is given by

$$\mu_{L(\mathrm{FG})}(x) = \max_{1 \leqslant k \leqslant m} \left[\min_{1 \leqslant i \leqslant l_k} f(r_i^k) \right],$$

where

- k index of a derivation chain leading to x,
- l_k length of the kth derivation chain,
- r_i^k label of the ith production rule in the kth derivation.

Definition 2a): A fractionally fuzzy grammar (FFG) is a seven-tuple $\mathrm{FFG} = (V_N, V_T, P, S, J, g, h)$ where V_N, V_T, P, S are as above, and g and h are mappings from J into the set of nonnegative integers such that

$$g(r_k) \leqslant h(r_k), \qquad \forall r_k \in J.$$

Definition 2b): The membership of any string x having $m(\geqslant 1)$ derivation(s) in the language $L(\mathrm{FFG})$ generated by FFG is

$$\mu_{L(\mathrm{FFG})}(x) = \sup_{1 \leqslant k \leqslant m} \frac{\sum_{j=1}^{l_k} g(r_j^k)}{\sum_{j=1}^{l_k} h(r_j^k)}$$

where $0/0$ is taken to be zero by convention.

IV. Classification Algorithm

Remarks: In this section, G has been used to denote a specific type of grammar. For the fuzzy grammar approach, G denotes a fuzzy grammar, while for the fractionally fuzzy grammar approach it denotes a fractionally fuzzy grammar (FFG).

The symbol $\in_C$ used denotes "is classified into." (This binary relation is defined later on.)

We have defined $\mu_S(b)$, $\mu_F(b)$, and $\mu_G(b)$, the degrees of membership of a curve b in the set of sharp, fair, and gentle curves, respectively, as follows.

A. Determination of μ_S, μ_F, and μ_G Values

For any curve b, the degree of arcness $\mu_{\text{arc}}(b)$ has been defined in the primitive extraction algorithm [1] as

$$\mu_{\text{arc}}(b) = \left(1 - \frac{l}{p}\right)^{F_e}$$

where l is the length of the line segment joining the two extreme points of the arc b, p is the length of the arc b and F_e is a suitably chosen exponential fuzzifier with $F_e > 0$. Clearly, when the arc b is a line segment, we have $p = l$ so that $\mu_{\text{arc}}(b) = 0$, whatever F_e may be. Also, $\mu_{\text{arc}}(b)$ can never attain the value 1 although it does approach that value as the sharpness of b increases, so that $\mu_{\text{arc}} \in [0, 1)$.

For any curve b for which $\mu_{\text{arc}}(b) > 0$, its degrees of membership $\mu_S(b)$, $\mu_F(b)$, and $\mu_G(b)$ to the fuzzy sets of sharp, fair, and gentle curves, respectively, may be defined as

$$\mu_S(b) = f_S(\mu_{\text{arc}}(b)) \tag{2a}$$

$$\mu_F(b) = f_F\left(|\mu_{\text{arc}}(b) - \frac{1}{2}|\right) \tag{2b}$$

and

$$\mu_G(b) = f_G(\mu_{\text{arc}}(b)) \tag{2c}$$

such that

a) $f_G(\cdot)$ and $f_F(\cdot)$ are monotonically decreasing functions over [0, 1] and [0, 1/2], respectively;
b) $f_S(\cdot)$ is a monotonically increasing function over [0, 1]; and
c) $\mu_S(b)$, $\mu_F(b)$, and $\mu_G(b)$ all take values in [0, 1] only.

For example, we can take

$$\mu_S(b) = S\left(\mu_{\text{arc}}(b); 0, \frac{1}{2}, 1\right) \tag{3}$$

$$\mu_F(b) = \begin{cases} S\left(\mu_{\text{arc}}(b); 0, \frac{1}{4}, \frac{1}{2}\right), & \text{if } 0 \leq \mu_{\text{arc}}(b) \leq \frac{1}{2} \quad (4a) \\ 1 - S\left(\mu_{\text{arc}}(b); \frac{1}{2}, \frac{3}{4}, 1\right) & \text{if } \frac{1}{2} \leq \mu_{\text{arc}}(b) \leq 1 \quad (4b) \end{cases}$$

$$\mu_G(b) = 1 - S\left(\mu_{\text{arc}}(b); 0, \frac{1}{2}, 1\right) \qquad \mu_{\text{arc}}(b) \in (0, 1) \tag{5}$$

where S denotes standard S function [20] such that

$$S(x; \alpha, \beta, \gamma) = \begin{cases} 0, & x \leq \alpha \\ 2\left(\frac{x - \alpha}{\gamma - \alpha}\right)^2, & \alpha \leq x \leq \beta \\ 1 - 2\left(\frac{\gamma - x}{\gamma - \alpha}\right)^2, & \beta \leq x \leq \gamma \\ 1, & x \geq \gamma \end{cases} \tag{6}$$

with $\beta = (\alpha + \gamma)/2$.

As mentioned earlier, $\mu_{\text{arc}} = 0$ (which corresponds to a straight line) is not included in computing μ_S, μ_F, and μ_G values. However, even if we put $\mu_{\text{arc}} = 0$ in (3)–(5), the values we get namely, $\mu_G = 1$, $\mu_F = \mu_S = 0$ do not contradict our intuition, since a straight line can be looked upon as the *most* gentle curve. Again, since the boundaries among the fuzzy sets sharp, fair, and gentle are not hard, any curve may have nonzero membership values for all three sets.

As an example, we consider $\mu_{\text{arc}}(b) = 0.22$, 0.52, and 0.82. Then from the following table, the degree of membership of these b, as expected, is found to be maximum for the sets gentle, fair, and sharp, respectively.

	$\mu_{\text{arc}}(b)$ 0.22	0.52	0.82
μ_S	0.097	0.539	0.935
μ_F	0.387	0.997	0.181
μ_G	0.903	0.461	0.065

Besides using the standard functions (3)–(5), one can also use a function

$$f(\mu_{\text{arc}}) = \left[1 + \left(\frac{|\mu_{\text{arc}} - \mu|}{F_d}\right)^{F_e}\right]^{-1} \tag{7}$$

(where μ is some reference constant) that approximates the standard functions. For $\mu = 1$, 0.5, and 0, (7) represents the membership function corresponding to the sets sharp, fair, and gentle, respectively. Positive constants F_e and F_d are the fuzzifiers which control the amount of fuzziness in a set.

B. Algorithm

The structure of the three-stage hierarchical procedure is depicted in Fig. 3. At each stage context-free grammars with $V_T = \{a, b, \bar{b}, c\}$ have been used. The a, b, $\bar{b}$, and c denote a line segment of unit length, a clockwise curve, an anticlockwise curve, and a dot, respectively.

Let x denote the string representing the contour of the epiphysis and y the string representing the interior of the epiphysis contour, i.e., the boundaries of the image of the palmar surface of the epiphysis.

Stage 1 (primary classification): We define five classes C_i, $i = 1, 2, \cdots, 5$ as $C_1 = \{A\}$, $C_2 = \{B\}$, $C_3 = \{C, D, E\}$, $C_4 = \{F, G, H\}$, $C_5 = \{I\}$.

Let G_i denote the grammar corresponding to class C_i, $i = 1, 2, \cdots, 5$ and $L(G_i)$ the language generated by G_i.

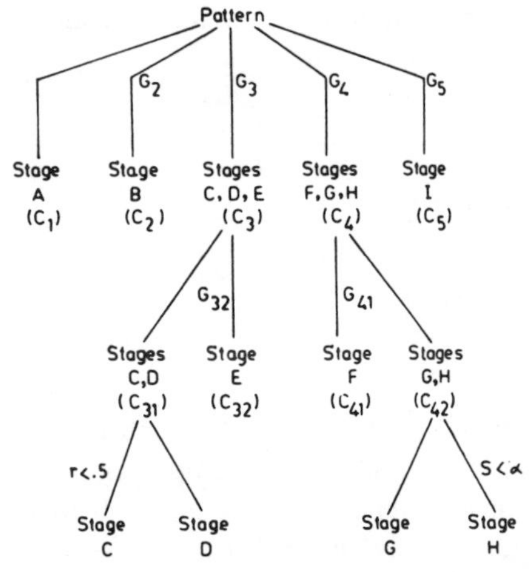

Fig. 3. Three-stage hierarchical classification scheme.

If x is found to be the empty string (λ), we infer the class C_1 (Stage A). If not, and if x is parsed by the first stage grammar, then

$$x \in_C L(G_k), \text{if } \mu_{L(G_k)}(x) = \max_{2 \leqslant i \leqslant 5} \mu_{L(G_i)}(x), \quad k = 2,3,4,5.$$

Ties, if present, can be dealt with in a number of ways. A statistical approach is to use randomization techniques whereby the final decision is based on the outcome of a random experiment, usually simulated with the help of random numbers.

The reasons for adopting this particular form of clustering of events A–I are rather obvious from Fig. 2. For example, each of the stages A, B, and I is unique in itself and hence is put in a separate class. Again, the forms of x in Stages C, D, and E bear greater similarity to each other than to strings from other classes. These are, therefore, put together in C_3. The same reasoning applies to F, G, and H. Of course, there is the possibility that C_3 and C_4 will overlap, mainly because of the similarities in E and F in respect to x. Provisions have been made at the next stage for minimizing the error resulting from this.

If $x \in_C L(G_i)$, $i = 1,2,5$, then stop; otherwise, go to the second stage.

Stage 2: We come here if in the first stage $x \in_C L(G_3)$ or $x \in_C L(G_4)$. We now bring y into the picture. If $x \in_C L(G_3)$, go to step 2.1, and if $x \in_C L(G_4)$, go to step 2.2.

Step 2.1: a) If y can be parsed by means of the second-stage grammar and if

$$\mu_{L(G_{32})}(y) = \max\left[\mu_{L(G_{32})}(y), \mu_{L(G_{41})}(y)\right],$$

i.e.,

$$y \in_C L(G_{32})$$

then decide on Stage E. If not, go to step 2.3. b) If y can not be parsed by means of the second stage grammar, go to step 3.1.

Step 2.2: a) If y can be parsed by means of the second stage grammar and

$$\mu_{L(G_{41})}(y) = \max\left[\mu_{L(G_{32})}(y), \mu_{L(G_{41})}(y)\right],$$

TABLE I
LIST OF STRINGS FROM EACH CLASS

Class	Strings
C_2	$X = c$
C_3	$X = a^m b a^n b$, $m, n \geqslant 0$ and b is fair or sharp
C_4	$X = P b a^q b Q$, b is sharp or fair, $q \geqslant 0$ with $P = a^r$ or $a^r b a^s$ (b 'gentle'); $Q = a^t R$ or $a^t R^2$; and $R = b$ (sharp or fair), $r, s, t > 0$.
C_5	$X = L' \bar{b} E \bar{b} L''$, b sharp or fair, with $L = a^x$, $a^x M a^y M a^z$ or $a^x M M a^z$ $M = b$ or $\bar{b}$ (gentle), $x, y, z > 0$ $L' = L$, Lb, or LbL $L'' = L$, bL, or LbL, b 'sharp' or 'fair' $E = GF$, G^2F, GFa^y or G^2Fa^y, $x, y > 0$ $F = LbLb$ $G = a^x b$
C_{32}	$Y = L^* b L^* b$, b 'not gentle' with $L^* = L$, ML, LM, $a^x M a^y$, $M a^x M a^y M$, $a^x M a^y M$ or $M a^x M a^y$; L, M are as above and $x, y > 0$
C_{41}	$Y = L^* b L^* \bar{b} L^* b L^* b L^* \bar{b} L^* b$, b 'not gentle'. L^* is as above.

i.e., if $y \in_C L(G_{41})$, decide on Stage F. If not, go to step 2.3. b) If y can not be parsed by the second stage grammar go to step 3.2.

Step 2.3: We come here if there are contradictory decisions in the first two stages, that is, either i) $x \in_C L(G_3)$ but $y \in_C L(G_{41})$ or ii) $x \in_C L(G_4)$ but $y \in_C L(G_{32})$. We can tackle this situation in either of two ways.

1) We can completely ignore the first-stage information and take the second-stage decision to be final. However, such decisionmaking is not sound.

2) We can combine the information obtained at both stages and then come to a final decision. This can be done in a number of ways. For instance, writing

$$a_3 = \mu_{L(G_3)}(x), \quad a_4 = \mu_{L(G_4)}(x),$$
$$b_3 = \mu_{L(G_{32})}(y), \quad b_4 = \mu_{L(G_{41})}(y),$$

we decide on the class C_{32} (Stage E), if $\phi_3 = \max[\phi_3, \phi_4]$ and on the class C_{41} (Stage F), otherwise, where ϕ_i, $i = 3,4$, can be defined in one of the following ways (using collective or connective property):

1) $\phi_i = (a_i + b_i)/2$
2) $\phi_i = (a_i^2 + b_i^2)^{1/2}$
3) $\phi_i = \min(a_i, b_i)$
4) $\phi_i = \max(a_i, b_i)$.

It can be observed from Fig. 2 that the interior of the epiphysis contour is empty in Classes C and D but not in classes E, F, G, and H. It is this additional information that we utilize at this stage. The forms of y in $C_{31} = \{C, D\}$, $C_{32} = \{E\}$, $C_{41} = \{F\}$, and $C_{42} = \{G, H\}$ are distinct enough to facilitate differentiation by syntactic means.

Stage 3:

Step 3.1: Determine D_E (the maximum diameter of the epiphysis) and W_M (the width of the metaphysis). If $r = D_E/W_M \leqslant 0.5$, decide on event C; otherwise, decide on D.

Step 3.2: Determine S_E (the slope of the proximal edge of the epiphysis at the medial end) and S_M (the slope of the distal edge of metaphysis at the medial end). There are numerous algorithms available in the literature for this purpose [21]. If $S = S_E - S_M$ is less than some predetermined α, suitably small, then decide on event H; otherwise, decide on event G.

In practice, S_E and S_M are reflected by the degree of arcness of the curve at the medial end of the epiphysis contour.

In this stage, the classification is not, strictly speaking, syntactic in nature. We have merely made use of some differences between C and D, and between G and H, as described before, to facilitate classification.

The sample strings from each class used for constructing the grammars is given in Table I. The grammars for the first stage are given in Table II while those for the second stage are given in Table III.

It is not difficult to verify that every one of the representatives of each class, given in Table I, has by our grammars, a maximum membership for the language corresponding to its own class, its membership in all other languages (at the same stage) being less or at most as large. The classification algorithm is described in the structured format of Listing 1.

Listing 1. Classification Algorithm.

```
Procedure CLASSIFY:
      BEGIN;
      IF x ∈ L(G1) THEN decide on A;
        ELSE IF x ∈ L(G2) THEN decide on B;
            ELSE IF x ∈ L(G3) THEN
                DO;
                  IF y can be parsed by second stage grammar THEN
                    DO;
                      IF μL(G32)(y) =
                         max[μL(G32)(y), μL(G41)(y)]
                         THEN decide on E;
                      ELSE DO;
                         a3 ← μL(G3)(x);
                         a4 ← μL(G4)(x);
                         b3 ← μL(G32)(y);
                         b4 ← μL(G41)(y);
                         compute φ3;
                         compute φ4;
                         /* Definitions of
                         φ3, φ4 given in
                         text */
                         IF φ3 = max(φ3, φ4)
                         THEN decide on E;
                         ELSE decide on F;
                         END;
                    END;
                      ELSE DO;
                         DE ← maximum diameter of the epiphysis;
                         WM ← width of the metaphysis;
                         r ← DE/WM;
                         IF r ≤ 0.5 THEN decide on C;
                         ELSE decide on D;
                         END;
                END;
                ELSE IF x ∈ L(G4) THEN
                  DO;
                      IF y can be parsed by second stage grammar
                         THEN
                           DO;
                             IF μL(G41)(y) = max[μL(G32)(y), μL(G41)(y)] THEN decide on F;
                              ELSE DO;
                                 a3 ← μL(G3)(x);
                                 a4 ← μL(G4)(x);
                                 b3 ← μL(G32)(y);
                                 b4 ← μL(G41)(y);
                                 compute φ3;
                                 compute φ4;
                                 IF φ4 = max (φ3, φ4) THEN decide on F; ELSE decide on E;
                                 END;
                           END;
                      ELSE DO;
                             SE ← slope of the proximal edge of the epiphysis at the medial end;
                             SM ← slope of the distal edge of the epiphysis at the medial end;
                             S ← SE − SM;
                             IF S < α/* α predetermined */ THEN decide on H;
                             ELSE decide on G;
                         END;
                  END;
                ELSE IF x ∈ L(G5) THEN decide on I;
      END.
```

TABLE II
PRODUCTION RULES FOR THE FIRST STAGE

Srl.	Production Rules	Membership Values $(FG)_3$	$(FG)_4$	$(FG)_5$	g_i/h_i Values $(FFG)_3$	$(FFG)_4$	$(FFG)_5$
1	$S \rightarrow AA$	1	0	0	10/10	0/10	0/10
2	$S \rightarrow AAA$	0	1	0	0/10	10/10	0/10
3	$S \rightarrow ACA$	0	1	0	0/10	10/10	0/10
4	$S \rightarrow DS$	0	1	0	0/5	5/5	0/5
5	$S \rightarrow SC$	0	1	0	0/5	5/5	0/5
6	$S \rightarrow LFM$	0	0	1	0/10	0/10	10/10
7	$A \rightarrow BC$	1	1	0	0/0	0/0	0/5
8	$A \rightarrow C$	1	0	0	1/1	0/1	0/1
9	$B \rightarrow aB$	1	1	1	0/0	0/0	0/0
10	$B \rightarrow a$	1	1	1	0/0	0/0	0/0
11	$C \rightarrow b$	$\mu_F(b)$	$\mu_F(b)$	1	$g_F(b)/5$	$g_F(b)/5$	0/5
12	$C \rightarrow b$	$\mu_S(b)$	$\mu_S(b)$	1	$g_S(b)/5$	$g_S(b)/5$	0/5
13	$D \rightarrow BE$	0	1	1	0/1	1/1	1/1
14	$E \rightarrow b$	0	$\mu_G(b)$	$\mu_G(b)$	0/5	$g_G(b)/5$	$g_G(b)/5$
15	$F \rightarrow \bar{b}G\bar{b}$	0	0	1	0/5	0/5	5/5
16	$G \rightarrow AHH$	0	0	1	0/1	0/1	1/1
17	$G \rightarrow AHHB$	0	0	1	0/1	0/1	1/1
18	$G \rightarrow AG$	0	0	1	0/1	0/1	1/1
19	$H \rightarrow IC$	0	0	1	0/1	0/1	1/1
20	$I \rightarrow B$	0	0	1	0/1	0/1	1/1
21	$I \rightarrow BKB$	0	0	1	0/1	0/1	1/1
22	$I \rightarrow KB$	0	0	1	0/1	0/1	1/1
23	$I \rightarrow BK$	0	0	1	0/1	0/1	1/1
24	$K \rightarrow \bar{b}$	0	0	$\mu_G(\bar{b})$	0/5	0/5	$g_G(\bar{b})/5$
25	$K \rightarrow b$	0	0	$\mu_G(b)$	0/5	0/5	$g_G(b)/5$
26	$L \rightarrow ICI$	0	0	1	0/2	0/2	2/2
27	$L \rightarrow IC$	0	0	1	0/2	0/2	2/2
28	$L \rightarrow I$	0	0	1	0/2	0/2	2/2
29	$M \rightarrow ICI$	0	0	1	0/2	0/2	2/2
30	$M \rightarrow CI$	0	0	1	0/2	0/2	2/2
31	$M \rightarrow I$	0	0	1	0/2	0/2	2/2

TABLE III
PRODUCTION RULES FOR THE SECOND STAGE

l.	Production Rules	Membership Values $(FG)_{32}$	$(FG)_{41}$	g_i/h_i Values $(FFG)_{32}$	$(FFG)_{41}$
1	$S \rightarrow A$	1	0	10/10	0/10
2	$S \rightarrow BB$	0	1	0/10	10/10
3	$A \rightarrow DD$	1	1	0/0	0/0
4	$B \rightarrow DFD$	0	1	0/2	2/2
5	$D \rightarrow Eb$	$1 - \mu_G(b)$	$1 - \mu_G(b)$	$\bar{g}_G(b)/2$	$\bar{g}_G(b)/2$
6	$D \rightarrow b$	0	$1 - \mu_G(b)$	0/2	$\bar{g}_G(b)/2$
7	$E \rightarrow H$	1	1	0/0	0/0
8	$E \rightarrow HJH$	1	1	0/0	0/0
9	$E \rightarrow JE$	1	1	0/0	0/0
10	$E \rightarrow HL$	1	1	0/0	0/0
11	$E \rightarrow HJHL$	1	1	0/0	0/0
12	$E \rightarrow JEL$	1	1	0/0	0/0
13	$E \rightarrow J$	0	1	0/0	0/0
14	$F \rightarrow \bar{b}$	0	$1 - \mu_G(\bar{b})$	0/2	$\bar{g}_G(\bar{b})/2$
15	$F \rightarrow E\bar{b}$	0	$1 - \mu_G(\bar{b})$	0/2	$\bar{g}_G(\bar{b})/2$
16	$H \rightarrow aH$	1	1	0/0	0/0
17	$H \rightarrow a$	1	1	0/0	0/0
18	$J \rightarrow K$	1	1	0/0	0/0
19	$J \rightarrow KK$	1	1	0/0	0/0
20	$J \rightarrow KHK$	1	1	0/0	0/0
21	$K \rightarrow \bar{b}$	$\mu_G(\bar{b})$	$\mu_G(\bar{b})$	$g_G(\bar{b})/2$	$g_G(\bar{b})/2$
22	$K \rightarrow b$	$\mu_G(b)$	$\mu_G(b)$	$g_G(b)/2$	$g_G(\bar{b})/2$
23	$L \rightarrow J$	1	1	0/0	0/0
24	$L \rightarrow JL$	1	1	0/0	0/0

C. Some Guidelines and Observations

It should be noted that for all the grammars used in the first stage (as also in the second stage), we have used the same production rules but of course, with different values of $\mu_i(g_i/h_i)$. This is because of the basic similarity between the patterns of the different classes in the first stage (second stage).

A brief discussion of the manner in which the weights of the production rules are assigned for the two approaches is in order.

The Fuzzy Grammar Approach: At either stage, some of the rules have weights of either zero or one for the different classes. The interpretation is obvious; a rule has membership 0 for the grammar of a class if it plays no part in the generation of the language corresponding to that class. On the other hand, if a rule plays with certainty, a role in the generation, it has membership 1 for that class. Some rules have weights of a third type—they depend on the values of μ_S, μ_F, or μ_G for the corresponding curves. For example, rule numbered 25 (Table II) has a weight $\mu_G(b)$ for the grammar $(FG)_5$. This means that its weight is dependent on the gentleness of the curve in the sense that the gentler the curve, the greater the weight of the rule.

Fractionally Fuzzy Grammar Approach: For assigning g_i/h_i values to different production rules we have been guided by the criteria laid down by DePalma and Yau [14] which are as follows:

First, a rule which cannot help to distinguish one class from another can be given the value 0/0, and would then have no effect on the final membership assuming some rule i, for which $h_i \neq 0$, is also applied.

Second, a rule for which h_i is small has little effect on the final membership of any string generated by that rule.

Third, any rule for which h_i is large has a large effect on the final membership of any string generated by using that rule.

Fourth, if rule i is used, the fuzzy membership of the string is changed in the direction towards the value g_i/h_i by the application of rule i. Thus if g_i/h_i is close to zero, it is decreased.

Finally, a rule which is used in all the strings can be given a membership value which could serve as a starting point from which we could subtract by rules with $g_i/h_i = 0$ and to which we could add by rules with $g_i/h_i = 1$.

For some of the rules, the g-values have been made dependent on μ_S or μ_F or μ_G-values by means of nondecreasing integer-valued functions $g_i(b)$ defined, for $i = S, F, G$ as

$$g_i(b) = \text{int}\left[h \times \mu_i(b)\right], \quad \text{if } h\mu_i(b) - \text{int}\left[h \times \mu_i(b)\right] \leqslant \frac{1}{2}$$
$$= 1 + \text{int}\left[h \times \mu_i(b)\right], \quad \text{otherwise} \tag{8}$$

where int$[x]$ = integer part of x, x being any real number, and h is the corresponding h_i-value.

Another issue of concern to us is whether the absolute dimensions of the subject and hence those of the epiphysis and the metaphysis may affect the results of the classification. The magnification or reduction of a given image of the epiphysis will cause two types of changes:

1) the straight line segments in the image will increase/decrease in length; and
2) the curves in the image will become gentler and sharper, or both.

The first is taken care of in the grammars by means of production rules of the type given by rules 9 and 10 for Stage 1 and 16 and 17 for Stage 2. Changes of the second type will, in general, change the weights of those rules which depend on μ_S, μ_F, or μ_G values. However, the relative values of the weights remain unchanged, and hence the final outcome is not affected.

Finally, we would also like to point out that although in Tables II and III the membership values of certain productions are taken to be zero and one, we consider this to be an oversimplification of the situation. It would be more realistic to have for such rules membership values which are close to zero or one. This entails that they be estimated with the help of a large number of samples with known classification, however. In other words, supervised learning is required.

D. Some Practical Considerations

The classification algorithm as described before has been developed on the basis of the description given in Section II [2] for the different stages. As far as possible, the minor variations in pattern that are quite likely to occur have been accounted for in the grammars.

However, in practice, due to the limitations of the pre-processing (digitization, thresholding, enhancement, and contour extraction) algorithms, it is quite likely that we may encounter situations in which the above algorithm will need some modification for machine identification of different stages. For instance, in the cases of C_3 and C_4 (though it is very unlikely for C_3), we may obtain an edge-detected image in which the contours representing the epiphysis and the metaphysis are partly joined. In such a case, we skip the method of primary classification in Step 1 and proceed from Step 2 for final classification.

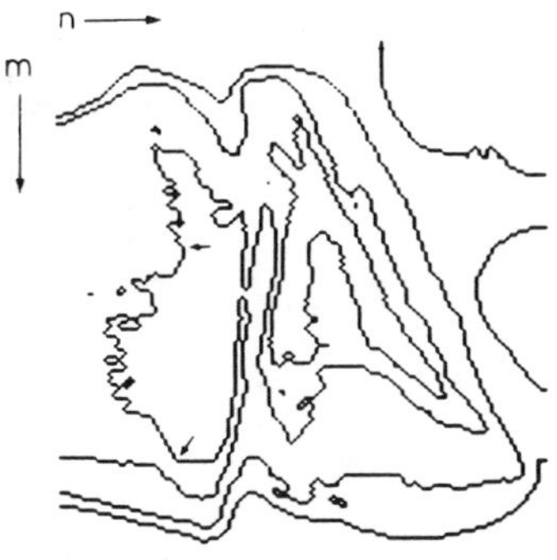

Fig. 4. Input image.

V. Implementation and Results

Fig. 4 shows an edge-detected version of an 128 × 145 dimensional image of radius of 10–12-year old boy [4]. These contours are extracted using contrast intensification operator along with S and π membership functions. The computer-based description of the relevant contours (with a 90° clockwise rotation of the image) after a) octal code representation, b) smoothing to remove the spurious wiggles, and c) segmentation [1], is as follows.

1) *Starting Point of Contour*; (22, 1)
   End of Contour: (129, 1)
   Description of the Contour:
   $L_3\ A_{0.465}\ L_2\ \bar{A}_{0.541}\ L\ A_{0.272}\ L\ A_{0.272}$
   $L_{15}\ A_{0.533}\ L_7\ A_{0.272}\ L_3\ \bar{A}_{0.465}\ L_2\ A_{0.541}$
   $\bar{A}_{0.272}\ L\ A_{0.272}$;
2) *Starting Point of Contour*: (24, 1)
   End of Contour: (119, 1)
   Description of the Contour:
   $\bar{A}_{0.272}\ L_2\ A_{0.377}\ L_3\ \bar{A}_{0.644}\ L_2\ A_{0.488}\ L_{12}$
   $A_{0.757}\ L_4\ \bar{A}_{0.348}\ L_4\ A_{0.644}\ \bar{A}_{0.272}\ A_{0.272}$
   $L_8\ \bar{A}_{0.702}\ L_3\ A_{0.816}\ L_2\ \bar{A}_{0.644}\ A_{0.541}\ L_4$
   $\bar{A}_{0.765}\ L_3\ A_{0.465}\ L\ \bar{A}_{0.541}\ A_{0.645}\ \bar{A}_{0.587}$
   $A_{0.559}\ \bar{A}_{0.816}\ A_{0.707}\ A_{0.272}\ \bar{A}_{0.47}\ L_3\ \bar{A}_{0.429}$
   $L_5\ \bar{A}_{0.816}\ L_6\ A_{0.272}\ L\ A_{0.377}\ L_2\ \bar{A}_{0.272}\ L_2$;
3) *Starting Point of Contour*: (22, 64)
   The Contour is Closed
   Description of the Contour:
   $L_{11}\ A_{0.86}\ L_4\ A_{0.272}\ L\ \bar{A}_{0.662}\ L_4\ A_{0.598}\ L_7$
   $\bar{A}_{0.272}\ A_{0.765}\ \bar{A}_{0.816}\ \bar{A}_{0.272}\ L\ A_{0.765}$.

Here, L, A, and $\bar{A}$ denote the straight line, clockwise arc, and counterclockwise arc, respectively. (This was the notation used in [1] to denote what we have called a, b, and $\bar{b}$ in this work.) Suffices of L and A represent the number of

TABLE IV
μ_{arc}- AND μ_G-VALUES OF ARCS IN STRINGS y, y_1, y_2, y_3, y_4

String		μ_{arc} AND μ_G-VALUES OF ARCS IN THE STRINGS								
y	μ_{arc}	0.860	0.272	0.662	0.598	0.272	0.765	0.816	0.272	0.765
	μ_G	0.039	0.852	0.228	0.323	0.852	0.110	0.068	0.852	0.110
y_1	μ_{arc}	0.272	0.816	0.765	0.662	0.272	0.765	0.860	0.816	
	μ_G	0.852	0.068	0.110	0.228	0.852	0.110	0.039	0.068	
y_2	μ_{arc}	0.860	0.765	0.662	0.662	0.816	0.860			
	μ_G	0.039	0.110	0.228	0.228	0.068	0.039			
y_3	μ_{arc}	0.816	0.598	0.598	0.272	0.272	0.765	0.272	0.765	0.816
	μ_G	0.068	0.323	0.323	0.852	0.852	0.110	0.852	0.110	0.068
y_4	μ_{arc}	0.272	0.765	0.598	0.662	0.816	0.765	0.765		
	μ_G	0.852	0.110	0.323	0.228	0.068	0.110	0.110		

TABLE V
LIST OF LEFT-MOST DERIVATIONS OF STRING y AND THEIR EVALUATIONS

Leftmost Derivation of String	Evaluation of Derivation $(FG)_{32}$	$(FG)_{41}$	$(FFG)_{32}$	$(FFG)_{41}$	Membership of String in $L(FG)_{32}$	$L(FG)_{41}$	$L(FFG)_{32}$	$L(FFG)_{41}$
a) (2)(4)(5)(7)(16)^{10}(17)(15)(8)(16)^{3}(17)(18)(22)(17)(5)(7)(16)^{3}(17)(4)(5)(10)(16)^{6}(17)(23)(18)(21)(14)(5)(9)(18)(21)(7)(17)	0	0.110	0.156	0.594				
b) (2)(4)(5)(7)(16)^{10}(17)(15)(8)(16)^{3}(17)(18)(22)(17)(5)(7)(16)^{3}(17)(4)(5)(10)(16)^{6}(17)(23)(18)(21)(15)(13)(18)(21)(5)(7)(17)	0	0.110	0.281	0.719				
c) (2)(4)(5)(8)(16)^{10}(17)(18)(22)(16)^{3}(17)(15)(7)(17)(5)(7)(16)^{3}(17)(4)(5)(10)(16)^{6}(17)(23)(18)(21)(14)(5)(9)(18)(21)(7)(17)	0	0.110	0.219	0.656	0	0.110	0.281	0.719
d) (2)(4)(5)(8)(16)^{10}(17)(18)(22)(16)^{3}(17)(15)(7)(17)(5)(7)(16)^{3}(17)(4)(5)(10)(16)^{6}(17)(23)(18)(21)(15)(13)(18)(21)(5)(7)(17)	0	0.110	0.281	0.719				

line units and the degree of arcness μ_{arc} of the arc A, respectively. To explain the meaning of the descriptions given above, let us consider for example, the contour number (3).

The starting point is given as (22, 64), which means that the location of the point at which the scan of the contour begins with respect to the coordinate (m, n)-axis shown in Fig. 4, is (22, 64). As the contour is closed, the end-point of the contour is the same, i.e., (22, 64). The contour starts with a line segment of eleven units followed by a clockwise curve whose degree of arcness is 0.86 and so on, and finally it terminates with a clockwise curve having $\mu_{arc} = 0.765$. Since we are interested only in the epiphysis and metaphysis, other contours of the image (Fig. 4) are not considered.

From this image pattern we find that the contours representing the epiphysis and the metaphysis are partly joined. So we proceed directly from Step 2 of the algorithm. Here we have the string corresponding to the palmar and dorsal surface

$$y = a^{11}ba^{4}ba\bar{b}a^{4}ba^{7}\bar{b}b\bar{b}\bar{b}ab. \tag{9}$$

The values of μ_{arc} and μ_G for the sequence of arcs in this string are given in Table IV. The values of μ_G and g_G for these arcs are computed, with (5) and (8).

The different derivations for the string y given in (9) as well as their corresponding evaluations are given in Table V. As is evident from the table, the string is classified into C_{41}; that is, the input image (Fig. 4) is identified by both approaches as being in stage F as far as maturity of the radius is concerned.

Let us consider again the contours of different regions in Fig. 4. These are seen to have some staircase lines, wiggles and minor arcs of two to three pixels which have been generated during its edge-detection process [4]. To extract primitives, four different smoothers were used before hand whose purpose was to make the contours as straight as

TABLE VI
EVALUATION OF DERIVATIONS OF y_1, y_2, y_3, y_4 AND THEIR MEMBERSHIP VALUES

		Evaluation of Derivation				Membership of String in			
String	Derivation	$(FG)_{32}$	$(FG)_{41}$	$(FFG)_{32}$	$(FFG)_{41}$	$L(FG)_{32}$	$L(FG)_{41}$	$L(FFG)_{32}$	$L(FFG)_{41}$
	1	0	0.110	0.267	0.733				
y_1						0	0.110	0.267	0.7 33
	2	0	0.068	0.267	0.733				
	1	0.039	0	0.636	0.182				
y_2						0.039	0.772	0.636	1
	2	0	0.772	0.462	1				
	1	0.068	0	0.714	0.357				
	2	0	0.068	0.188	0.625				
	3	0	0.068	0.313	0.750				
	4	0	0.110	0.250	0.688				
	5	0	0.148	0.375	0.813				
	6	0	0.110	0.250	0.688				
y_3	7	0	0.110	0.375	0.813	0.68	0.148	0.714	0.813
	8	0	0.110	0.375	0.813				
	9	0.068	0	0.607	0.250				
	10	0	0.110	0.375	0.813				
	11	0	0.068	0.250	0.688				
	12	0	0.068	0.250	0.688				
	13	0.068	0	0.643	0.286				
	1	0.068	0	0.458	0.042				
	y_4	2	0	0.110	0.346	0.885	0.068	0.110	0.4580.885
	3	0.068	0	0.458	0.042				

possible by eliminating such undesirable elements. The string y (9), in fact, corresponds to such a smoothed (approximated) version of the contour of the palmar–dorsal surface.

Therefore, if there is any such variation in contour pattern that might occur because of the inherent variability of the classes, these can either be removed or be reduced greatly leaving behind some gentle curves (i.e., some gentle curve may remain in the straighter part even after smoothing) during their primitive extraction operation. Such possibilities have also been accounted for in the grammars. For example, the string y may take one of the following typical forms (artificially generated), among others, for Stage F.

1) $y_1 = a^4ba^3ba^6\bar{b}a^5ba^8\bar{b}aba\bar{b}ab$
2) $y_2 = a^{11}ba^5\bar{b}a^5ba^9ba\bar{b}a^2b$
3) $y_3 = a^{11}ba^6\bar{b}a^4ba^2ba^2\bar{b}bba\bar{b}b$
4) $y_4 = a^8\bar{b}ba^4\bar{b}a^5ba^{10}b\bar{b}b.$

For these strings also, the values of μ_{arc} and μ_G for the sequence of arcs are given in Table IV. The evaluations of their different derivations as well as the corresponding memberships are shown in Table VI. To limit the size of the paper, the details of their parses are not shown. In each case, the string is identified as undergoing Stage F by both approaches.

VI. DISCUSSION

Two different syntactic recognition algorithms based on fuzzy and fractionally fuzzy grammars are developed here for identifying stages of bone maturity from X-ray images using the primitives extracted in the earlier work [1]. Of the two approaches, the fractionally fuzzy one has a slight edge over the other because of the following reasons [14].

With a parsing algorithm that requires backtracking, it is not just sufficient to keep track of the derivation tree alone when a fuzzy grammar is being used. The fuzzy value at each step must also be remembered at each node, so that the memory requirements are greatly increased for many practical problems. (This, incidentally, places a fuzzy grammar at a disadvantage with respect to a non-fuzzy grammar too.) With a fractionally fuzzy grammar, however, backtracking poses no problems, as we only need to subtract the g and h values for the rule being eliminated from the respective running totals.

A second drawback of fuzzy grammar in pattern recognition is the fact that all strings in L(FG) can be classified into a finite number of subsets by their membership in the language. The number of such subsets is strictly limited by the number of productions in the grammar. With a fractionally fuzzy grammar, this problem does not arise.

An algorithm for recognizing maturity using ordinary grammars had also been reported [22] by the authors. In that approach, the sets of sharp, fair, and gentle curves were sharply defined by means of thresholds on the μ_{arc} values. Separate grammars were defined for the different classes using the same three-stage hierarchical procedures. In the present algorithms, the sets of sharp, fair, and gentle curves have been treated as fuzzy subsets so that, in general, any arc can have nonzero (but not equal) memberships in all three. The incorporation of the element of fuzziness in defining sharp, fair, and gentle curves in the present algorithms has enabled us to work with a smaller number of primitives. By introducing fuzziness in the physical relations among the primitives, it has also been possible to use the same set of production rules and nonterminals at each stage.

However, for a given stage, the different production rules of the single grammar used therein are given different weights for the classes considered at that stage, to reflect the characteristics peculiar to that class. The grammars are, in general, ambiguous, but different parses of a single string may have distinct weights generally, depending upon the weights of the rules in the parse lists. The degree of belonging to the language corresponding to a given class is taken to be equal to the largest of the weights, for that class, of its different parses. The string is finally assigned to a class to which its degree of membership (belonging) is maximum. Therefore, we may need to parse an input string with only one grammar at each stage, unlike the case of the nonfuzzy approach [22] where we may have to parse each string by more than one grammar in general, at each stage. However, this has to be balanced against the fact that the grammars used here are not as simple as the corresponding nonfuzzy grammars [22]. Furthermore, these grammars need not be unambiguous, whereas non-ambiguity is an absolutely necessary requirement for the nonfuzzy approach.

In this connection mention must be made of the attributed grammars [23] to tackle similar situations where the patterns are having shapes slightly differing in details for different classes. The local shape information of the palmar and dorsal surfaces of X-ray image was used in extracting primitives [1] and in the present work the global structural information is incorporated by the weighted production rules. These two steps are combined into one in case of attributed grammar, i.e., the production rule is used to guide the primitive extraction. In attributed grammars, semantic information about the shape of a curve is borne by the attributes, namely direction, curve length, total angular change, and degree of declination. Since the information carried by primitives is of a high order, the production rules can be made simple. In our method, semantic information is carried in the μ_S, μ_F, and μ_G values of a curve and in the length of a line segment.

It is to be mentioned here that the descriptions of the different stages of maturity are standard and are taken from the book of Tanner *et al.* [2]. They have emphasized the point that samples from the same stage may exhibit a great deal of variation. In developing the grammars, we have taken into account all such variations. In fact, the noisy versions (Section V) of the input string generated artificially also takes into account those considerations. The robustness of the algorithm has been exhibited by the correct classification of the noisy inputs. Furthermore, the recognition ambiguity (as seen from Figs. 2 and 3) lies mostly between classes E and F, and we have considered patterns from Stage F to demonstrate the robustness of the algorithm.

Acknowledgment

The authors wish to acknowledge Professor D. Dutta Majumder and Dr. R. A. King for their interest in this work and Mrs. S. De Bhowmick and Mr. N. Chatterjee for typing the manuscript. Authors' thanks are also due to Dr. A. A. Hashim and Prof. J. M. Tanner for their assistance in initiating the project at Imperial College, London.

References

[1] S. K. Pal, R. A. King, and A. A. Hashim, "Image description and primitive extraction using fuzzy sets," *IEEE Trans. Syst., Man, Cybern.*, vol. SMC-13, no. 1, pp. 94–100, 1983.

[2] J. M. Tanner, R. H. Whitehouse, W. A. Marshall, M. J. R. Healy, and H. Goldstein, *Assessment of Skeletal Maturity and Prediction of Adult Height (TW2 Method)*. New York: Academic, 1975.

[3] S. A. Kwabwe, S. K. Pal, and R. A. King, "Recognition of bones from X-rays of the hand and wrist," *Int. J. Syst. Sci.*, vol. 16, no. 4, pp. 403–413, 1985.

[4] S. K. Pal and R. A. King, "On edge detection of X-ray images using fuzzy sets," *IEEE Trans. Patt. Anal. Machine Intell.*, vol. PAMI-5, no. 1, pp. 69–77, 1983.

[5] S. K. Pal, R. A. King, and A. A. Hashim, "Automatic grey level thresholding using index of fuzziness and entropy," *Patt. Recog. Lett.*, vol. 1, pp. 141–146, Mar. 1983.

[6] K. S. Fu and P. H. Swain, "On syntactic-pattern recognition," *Software Engineering*, J. T. Tou, Ed. New York, Academic, 1971, pp. 155–182.

[7] P. H. Swain and K. S. Fu, "Stochastic programmed grammars for syntactic pattern recognition," *Patt. Recog.*, vol. 4, pp. 83–100, 1972.

[8] W. G. Wee, "A formulation of fuzzy automata and its application as a model of learning systems," *IEEE Trans. Syst., Sci., Cybern.*, vol. SSC-5, pp. 215–223, July 1969.

[9] K. S. Fu, *Syntactic Pattern Recognition and Applications*. Englewood Cliffs, NJ: Prentice-Hall, 1982.

[10] E. T. Lee, "Proximity measures for the classification of geometric figures," *J. Cybern*, vol. 2, pp. 43–59, 1972.

[11] E. T. Lee and L. A. Zadeh, "Note on Fuzzy Languages," *Inform. Sci.*, vol. 1, pp. 421–434, 1969.

[12] T. G. Evans, "Grammatical inference technique in pattern analysis," in *Software Engineering*, vol. 2, J. T. Tou, Ed. New York: Academic, 1971.

[13] K. S. Fu and T. J. Li, "On stochastic automata and languages," *Inform. Sci.*, vol. 1, pp. 403–419, 1969.

[14] G. F. DePalma and S. S. Yau, "Fractionally fuzzy grammars with application to pattern recognition," in *Fuzzy Sets and their Applications to Cognitive and Decision Processes*, L. A. Zadeh, K. S. Fu, and M. Shimura, Eds. New York: Academic, 1975.

[15] M. G. Thomason, "Finite fuzzy automata, regular fuzzy languages and pattern recognition," *Patt. Recog.*, vol. 5, pp. 383–390, 1973.

[16] S. Tamura and K. Tanaka, "Learning of fuzzy formal language," *IEEE Trans. Syst., Man, Cybern.*, vol. SMC-3, pp. 98–102, 1973.

[17] D. D. Majumder and S. K. Pal, "On Fuzzification, fuzzy language and multicategory fuzzy classifier," in *Proc. IEEE Seventh Int. Conf. Cybern. Soc.*, 1977, pp. 591–595.

[18] A. Kandel, *Fuzzy Techniques in Pattern Recognition*. New York: Wiley Interscience, 1982.

[19] S. K. Pal and D. D. majumder, *fuzzy Mathematical Approach to Pattern Recognition*. New York: Wiley, 1986.

[20] L. A. Zadeh, "Calculus of fuzzy restrictions," in *Fuzzy Sets and Their Applications to Cognitive and Decision Processes*, L. A. Zadeh, K. S. Fu, K. Tanaka, and M. Shimura, Eds. New York: Academic, 1975, pp. 1–26.

[21] G. T. Toussaint, "Computational geometric problems in pattern recognition," in *Pattern Recognition Theory and Applications*, J. Kittler, K. S. Fu, and L. F. Pau, Eds. Dortrecht, FRG: D. Reidel, 1982, pp. 73–91.

[22] A. Pathak, S. K. Pal, and R. A. King, "Syntactic recognition of skeletal maturity," *Patt. Recogn. Lett.*, vol. 2, pp. 193–197, 1984.

[23] K. C. You and K. S. Fu, "A syntactic approach to shape recognition using attributed grammars," *IEEE Trans. Syst., Man, Cybern.*, vol. SMC-9, pp. 334–345, 1979.

Fuzzy Logic for Handwritten Numeral Character Recognition

PEPE SIY, MEMBER, IEEE, AND C. S. CHEN, MEMBER, IEEE

Abstract—A recognition system based on the concept of fuzzy logic for handwritten numeral character recognition is presented. A handwritten character is considered as a directed abstract graph, of which the node set consists of tips, corners, and junctions, and the branch set consists of line segments connecting pairs of adjacent nodes. The line segments (branches) are fuzzily classified to branch types (features) such as straight lines, circles or portions of circles. Since the features under consideration here are fuzzy in nature, the fuzzy set concept is utilized, and the features are treated as fuzzy variables. A fuzzy variable is characterized by a membership grade function the value of which ranges in the closed unit interval. The two extreme membership grades of zero and unity indicate nonmembership and full membership status of the branch under consideration. Handwritten characters are considered ill-defined objects. With the aid of fuzzy functions such objects can be objectively defined and studied. A handwritten character is represented by the fuzzy function, which relates its fuzzy variables, and by the node pair involved in each fuzzy variable. The process of recognition is accomplished in two steps. First, the unknown character is preprocessed to produce its representation and second, the classification of the unknown character is reduced to finding a character (previously learned) of which the representation is isomorphic to the representation of the unknown character. Experimental results using IEEE Pattern Recognition Data Base No. 1.2.1 Handprinted Numeric Characters are presented. A recognition accuracy of 98.4 percent has been attained.

I. Introduction

Pattern recognition is an area that requires interdisciplinary collaboration among engineers, physicists, physiologists, psychologists, logicians, mathematicians, and philosophers. Its objective is the mechanization of human perception and concept formation. It is known that the brain does not store a picture of the world, but some aspects of it [1]. Recognition of objects is then based on these aspects or features and not on hard copy. Neurologists have been trying to crack the neural codes to shed light on the inner workings of the brain. Hubel and Wiesel of Harvard University, Cambridge, Mass., have disclosed some of the features that are coded in the neurons, such as lines and edges of various orientations, junctions, end points, etc. [2], [10].

In this correspondence a handwritten character recognition system is proposed that incorporates: 1) the neurological findings of Hubel and Wiesel [2] as the natural feature set, 2) the psychological findings of Pavlov [1] on stimulus generalization as the means of features reduction, 3) the fuzzy set concept introduced by Zadeh [3] in 1965 as the tool to resolve the great distortion found in handwritten characters, and 4) the structural approach of pattern recognition as the tool to achieve size and position invariant properties.

Features that include elements of a node set and elements of a branch set, which are similar to those used by several researchers [11], [13] are selected. The lack of precision in the definitions of the elements of the feature set necessitates the use of the fuzzy set concept. The abstract graph concept is then used to characterize the network of fuzzy sets, which represent the handwritten character under consideration. This characterization is position, size, and distortion invariant.

The structure and operation of the character recognition system is presented in the next section. Preprocessing, membership assignment of each feature element, and the pattern classifier are discussed in detail. Section IV presents the results of testing the system using the IEEE Pattern Recognition Data Base No. 1.2.1. This standard data base was selected in order that different recognition systems may be compared.

II. Handwritten Character Recognition System

The system consists of two basic units: A) features extraction and the handwritten character representation, and B) the pattern classifier.

A. Handwritten Character Representation

Handwritten characters are a distorted variant of printed characters; therefore, any study of handwritten characters must start with printed characters. There are essentially three basic elements of alpha-numeric characters: 1) the straight line (vertical, horizontal, and slant), 2) the circle, and 3) a portion of a circle of various orientations [4].

In 1965, L. A. Zadeh [3] introduced the "fuzzy set" concept. A fuzzy set is a class of objects with a continuum of grades of membership. Such a set is characterized by a membership (characteristic) function, which assigns to each object a grade of membership ranging between zero and one. The class of hand-drawn lines, circles, or portions of circles are considered as fuzzy sets in this correspondence.

The following features are found sufficient for handwritten numerals, many of which have also been used by other authors [11].

1) Straight line features:
   - horizontal (H)
   - vertical (V)
   - positive slope (P)
   - negative slope (N)
2) Portion of a circle features:
   - C curve (C)
   - D curve (D)
   - A curve (A)
   - V curve (V)
   - S curve (S)
   - Z curve (Z)
3) Circles:
   - circle on the left of its node (OL)
   - circle on the right of its node (OR)

Manuscript received January 16, 1974; revised May 29, 1974.

P. Siy was with the Department of Electrical Engineering, University of Akron, Akron, Ohio 44235. He is now with the Burroughs Corp., Detroit, Mich.

C. S. Chen is with the Department of Electrical Engineering, University of Akron, Akron, Ohio 44325.

Reprinted from *IEEE Trans. Syst., Man, Cybern.*, pp. 570–575, November 1974.

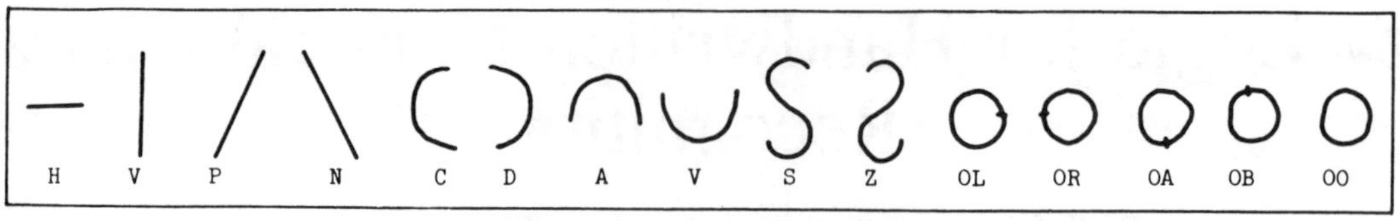

Fig. 1. The branch feature set.

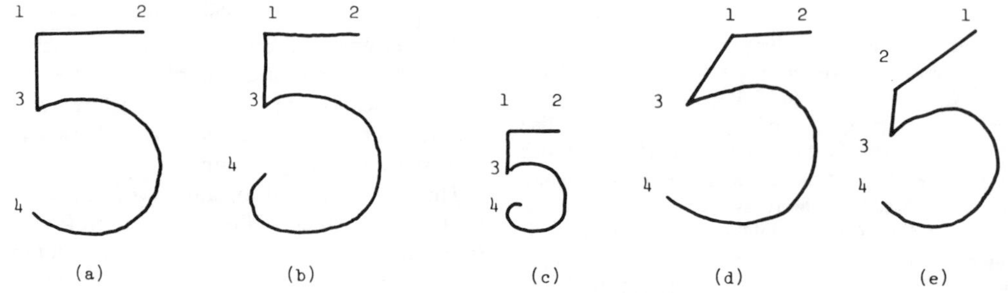

Fig. 2. Typical examples of character 5.

circle above its node	(OA)
circle below its node	(OB)
circle	(OO)

Let $B = \{H,V,P,N,C,D,A,V,S,Z,OL,OR,OA,OB,OO\}$ denote the branch feature set shown in Fig. 1.

The patterns in Fig. 2(a)–(c) are not exactly alike, however, their functional descriptions are the same, i.e., $F(5\text{a}) = F(5\text{b}) = F(5\text{c}) = H(1,2) \cdot V(1,3) \cdot D(3,4)$. Two patterns are said to be equivalent if their functional descriptions are the same. Thus $F(5) = H(1,2) \cdot V(1,3) \cdot D(3,4)$ defines an equivalent class in which the characters in Fig. 2(a)–(c) are typical members. This is the same as the idea of generalization, which means that one has only to learn one typical example of character 5 in order to recognize any equivalent variants. This definition of pattern (or stimulus) equivalence is both size and position invariant, which is compatible with visual perception in man. Other variants of the character 5 of which the functional descriptions are different are shown in Fig. 2(d) and (e). They are $F(5\text{d}) = H(1,2) \cdot P(1,3) \cdot D(3,4)$; $F(5\text{e}) = P(1,2) \cdot V(1,3) \cdot D(3,4)$. Using the fuzzy logical OR operation, one can combine the various descriptions of a character. For example, the character 5 in Fig. 2 can be represented by

$$\begin{aligned} F(5) &= F(5\text{a}) + F(5\text{b}) + F(5\text{c}) + F(5\text{d}) + F(5\text{e}) \\ &= H(5,2) \cdot V(1,3) \cdot D(3,4) \\ &\quad + H(1,2) \cdot P(1,3) \cdot D(3,4) \\ &\quad + P(1,2) \cdot V(1,3) \cdot D(3,4). \end{aligned}$$

B. Pattern Classifier

The decision criteria used for pattern classification are executed in two steps.

1) The branch features of the pattern to be classified and the branch features of the prototypes of each class are compared. Those prototypes that perfectly match the branch features of the pattern are retrieved.

2) The node pairs of the same branch type of the pattern to be classified and each retrieved prototype are compared. The fact that the numbering of the nodes in the pattern and prototypes may not be the same implies that an isomorphic mapping has to be found. This can be done as follows. Let $(n_\phi'(bi),n_\theta'(bi))$ and $(n_\phi(bi),n_\theta(bi))$ denote the node pair of branch type bi, $i = 1,\cdots,n$, of the pattern and prototype under consideration, respectively. The mapping

$$\Psi = \{(n_\phi'(bi),n_\phi(bi)),(n_\theta'(bi),n_\theta(bi) \mid k = 1,\cdots,n\}$$

is defined. When this is isomorphic, the prototype is accepted; when this is not, it is rejected.

III. The Recognition System

The block diagrams of the recognition system for the learning phase and the recognition phase are shown in Fig. 3(a) and 3(b), respectively. The main features of these diagrams consist of the following components: input pattern, thinning, labeling, coding, prototype memory, and pattern classifier. Each component is described in the following.

A. Input Pattern

The input pattern of the system must be digitized into a rectangular picture-frame array $P = \{p = (i,j) \mid 1 \leq i \leq n, 1 \leq j \leq m;\ n,m \in N\}$. The pattern is a binary picture; that is, the points on the pattern assume the value of one while the other points of the frame take the value of zero.

B. Thinning

The skeleton of a pattern is obtained by using Hilditch's thinning algorithm [6]. In this work the algorithm is restricted for binary patterns. Basically, the algorithm tests the boundary points of the pattern. Those points on the boundary the removal of which would not alter connectivity and those that do not lie on a tip of a line are deleted.

C. Labeling

1) Node Detection and Labeling: A node set in the skeleton of a pattern is defined as the collection of tips (points that have one neighbor), corners (points that have two neighbors and where an abrupt change of line direction occurs), and junctions (points that have three or more neighbors).

2) Branch Detection and Labeling: A branch is a line segment connecting a pair of adjacent nodes. For the degenerate case of a line pattern without nodes, the pattern is considered as a circular branch. A branch of which the length is less than

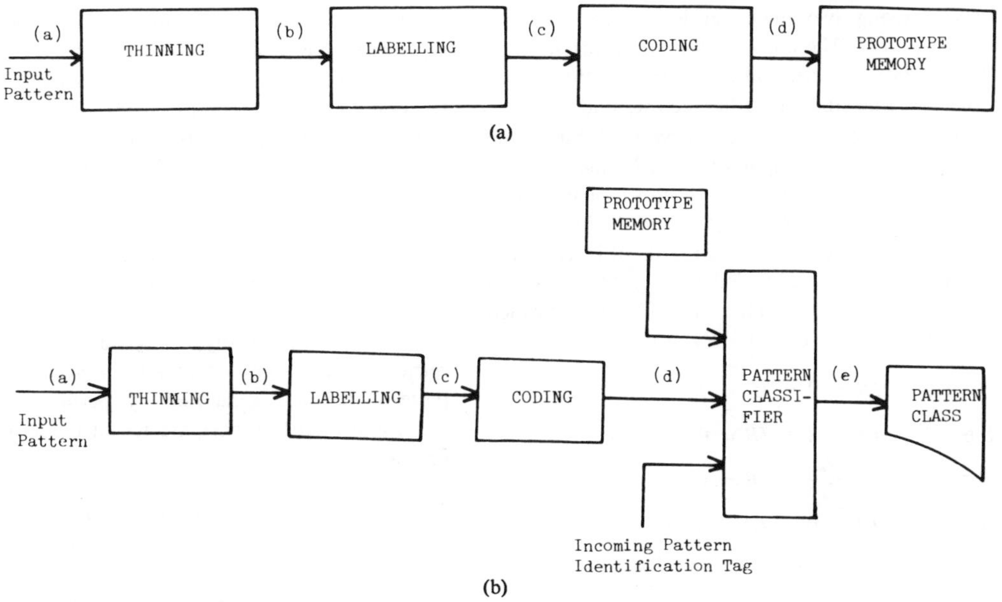

Fig. 3. Block diagram of recognition system. (a) Learning phase. (b) Recognition phase.

threshold S_B is considered extraneous and consequently removed by declaring its nodes equivalent.

In classifying branches, two sources of fuzziness are attributed to the measure of a) straightness and b) orientation. Both sources are present in noncircular branches and only the second source is present in circular branches with node.

a) Measure of straightness: The measure of straightness of a branch is determined by fitting a straight line with the minimum least squares error, and the branch is represented by the line with the least squares error.

A measure of straightness for a noncircular branch can be defined by

$$f_{SL} = 1 - S/S_T, \quad \text{if } S < S_T$$
$$= 0, \quad \text{if } S \leq S_T$$

where S_T is the threshold least squares error. A given branch is classified as a portion of a circle, if $0 \leq f_{SL} < 0.5$; a straight line, if $0.5 < f_{SL} \leq 1$; either, if $f_{SL} = 0.5$.

b) Measure of orientation: If the classification of a branch to the class of a straight line, a portion of a circle, or a circle with node is known, then the measure of orientation can be used to further characterize this branch.

Straight line class: This class contains the sets H,V,P,N. To classify a given branch into one of these sets, a measure of orientation based on the slope $\theta = \tan^{-1} m$ of the best fit line is required. With this slope the following membership grade functions for the sets H,V,P,N are defined as

$$FH(\theta) = 1 - \min\{\min[|\theta|, |180 - \theta|, |360 - \theta|]/45, 1\}$$

$$FV(\theta) = 1 - \min\{\min[|90 - \theta|, |270 - \theta|]/45, 1\}$$

$$FP(\theta) = 1 - \min\{\min[|45 - \theta|, |225 - \theta|]/45, 1\}$$

$$FN(\theta) = 1 - \min\{\min[|135 - \theta|, |315 - \theta|]/45, 1\}.$$

The branch is classified to the set with the highest membership grade assignment.

Portion of circle class: This class contains the sets C,D,A,V,S,Z. These sets can be further grouped as vertical (C,D), horizontal (A,V), or either (S,Z). To assign a given branch into one of the above groups in accordance with its measure of orientation, the slope $\theta = \tan^{-1}(y_n - y_1)/(x_n - x_1)$ of the line connecting the end points of the branch is considered. To accomplish this, two fuzzy sets are considered, namely, the horizontal curve (HC) and the vertical curve (VC). Based on the slope, the membership grade functions for HC, VC are defined as

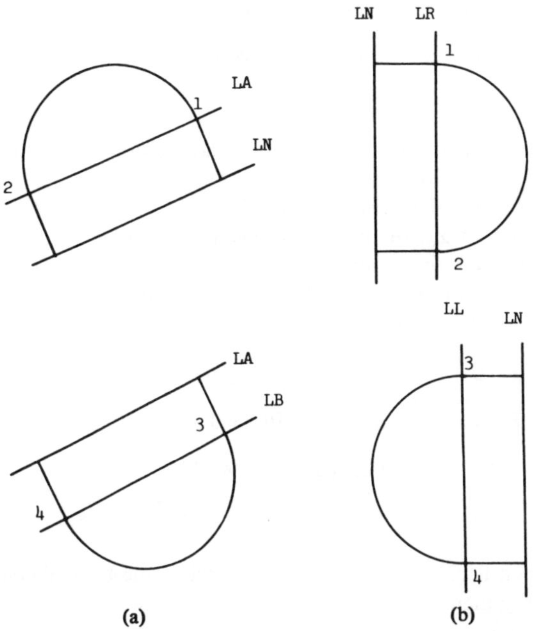

Fig. 4. Line construction for classifying given branch into class of portion of circle. (a) For horizontal curves. (b) For vertical curves.

$$FHC(\theta) = 1 - \min\{\min[|\theta|, |180 - \theta|, |360 - \theta|]/90, 1\}$$

$$FVC(\theta) = 1 - \min\{\min[|90 - \theta|, |270 - \theta|]/90, 1\}.$$

Consequently, the branch is classified to the set with the highest membership grade assignment. The group classified as either (S,Z) depending on its orientation is treated as HC or VC.

The branch is further characterized to one of the elements of each group by considering nonfuzzy information. This is accomplished by drawing two lines parallel to the LN line connecting the end points. The construction to be discussed is illustrated in Fig. 4. For a horizontal curve, one of the lines is drawn above the LN line and the other below, and they are denoted as LA and LB, respectively. For a vertical curve, the lines are drawn to the left and right of the LN line and are denoted as LL and LR, respectively. The number of points of intersection between the lines LA,LB,LR,LL, and the branch are denoted by IA,IB,IR,IL, respectively. The points of intersection of the branch with LA (or LR) are labeled as $(x_1,y_1),(x_2,y_2)$, and with LB (or LL) as $(x_3,y_3),(x_4,y_4)$. The conditions for a branch (b) to belong to one of the sets C,D,A,V,S,Z are

$$C = \{b \mid b \in VC \wedge IR = 0 \wedge IL = 2\}$$

$$D = \{b \mid b \in VC \wedge IA = 2 \wedge IB = 0\}$$

$$A = \{b \mid b \in HC \wedge IA = 2 \wedge IB = 0\}$$

$$V = \{b \mid b \in HC \wedge IA = 0 \wedge IB = 2\}$$

$$S = \{b \mid [b \in VC \wedge IR = 2 \wedge IL = 2 \wedge \min(y_1,y_2) < \max(y_3,y_4)] \, V \, [b \in HC \wedge IA = 2 \wedge IB = 2 \wedge \max(x_1,x_2) > \min(x_3,x_4)]\}$$

$$Z = \{b \mid [b \in VC \wedge IR = 2 \wedge IL = 2 \wedge \max(y_1,y_2) > \min(y_3,y_4)] \, V \, [b \in HC \wedge IA = 2 \wedge IB = 2 \min(x_1,x_2) < \max(x_3,x_4)]\}.$$

Circle with node class: This class contains the sets OL,OR,OA,OB. To classify a given branch into one of these sets, a measure of orientation based on the slope $\theta = \tan^{-1}(y_c - y_0)/(x_c - x_0)$ of the line connecting the node (x_0,y_0) of the branch and the centroid (x_c,y_c) of the inscribed area is considered. With this slope the following membership grade functions for the sets OL,OR,OA,OB are defined as

$$FOL = 1 - \min[|180 - \theta|/90, 1]$$

$$FOR = 1 - \min\{\min[\theta, |360 - \theta|]/90, 1\}$$

$$FOA = 1 - \min[|90 - \theta|/90, 1]$$

$$FOB = 1 - \min[|270 - \theta|/90, 1].$$

The branch is classified to the set with the highest membership grade assignment.

D. Computer Coding of Characters

The functional character representation as discussed in Section IIA consists of both alphabetic and numeric codes. For example, a functional representation of character 5 is $F(5) = H(1,2) \cdot V(1,3) \cdot D(3,4)$. In order to reduce labor, the elements $H,V,\cdots,OO$ of the branch feature set described in Fig. 1 are coded by $01,02,\cdots,15$, respectively. The computer coding then consists of three strings of numbers. The first string consists of the numeric codes of the branch features arranged in ascending order. The second string consists of the node pairs arranged in accordance with the branch features of the first string, and the third string is a one-digit identification tag.

E. Prototype Memory

The computer coding of a character generates an integer string that is too long to be stored in one computer memory location. To circumvent this difficulty a matrix array with 21 columns, and a variable number of rows is allocated. Each row represents a prototype. The first string code of the prototype occupies the first ten columns, the second string code the next ten columns, and the third string code (character represented) the last column. The computer coding of character 5 is stored in the memory as 010206000012133400005.

F. Pattern Classifier

The decision criteria, as discussed in Section IIB, are simplified by computer coding into the following form. Step 1 is now changed to an equality test between the first string code of the pattern and the prototypes, while in step 2 all the prototypes retrieved from step 1 and all the second string codes of the pattern that are generated by permuting the node pairs of the nondistinct branches are tested by setting up arrays of the following form:

$$\begin{pmatrix} \text{second string code of the pattern} \\ \text{second string code of the prototype} \end{pmatrix}$$

If at least one of the arrays tested is a permutation, the prototype is accepted; otherwise it is rejected.

IV. The System Operation and the Experimental Results

The operation of the recognition system consists of two phases: A) the learning phase and B) the recognition phase.

A. Learning Phase

The prototypes of each pattern class are learned and stored in the prototype memory. Each pattern is thinned, labeled, and coded. The code of the first pattern is stored in the prototype memory and starts a running code count of one, which means that there is one pattern classified to this code. If the succeeding code of a pattern is of the same form as the previous one, the running code count is incremented by one, while if the code is different it is stored in the prototype memory and starts a new code count. This process is repeated for the codes of all the incoming patterns, and they are accordingly allocated. Upon the end of the learning process, the memory contains all the prototype codes and their corresponding code counts. The code count represents the frequency of occurrence of each prototype code and, therefore, its relative importance compared to the other prototype codes. This can be utilized to speed up the recognition time by arranging the prototype codes in descending order according to their code counts.

B. Recognition Phase

The learned prototype codes are used to classify the unknown incoming patterns to the class of the matching prototype. The pattern code in the recognition phase in an actual system does not include an identification tag. However, for the purpose of generating misclassification statistics, the identification tag is required. Each incoming pattern is also thinned, labeled, and coded. Then the pattern classifier searches for the prototypes that match the pattern code. Three results can be obtained: classification, misclassification, and unclassification. Classification occurs when only one prototype is accepted and its identification tag matches that of the incoming pattern. Unclassification occurs when no prototype is accepted. Misclassification occurs when only one prototype is accepted and its identification tag is different from that of the incoming pattern.

TABLE I
LEARNING STATISTICS

Prototype Code	Identification Tag	Code Count
15000000000000000000	0	44
12000000001100000000	0	1
06000000001200000000	0	2
13000000001100000000	0	1
05000000001200000000	0	1
08000000001200000000	0	1
02000000001200000000	1	49
02020000012340000000	1	1
01060000023120000000	2	12
01010600003224120000	2	1
01010600002134130000	2	1
10000000001200000000	2	34
07100000002113000000	2	1
01061400002312220000	2	1
01060600002313340000	3	11
01070800002313430000	3	8
01060800002313430000	3	2
03060600002312240000	3	1
01060700003224120000	3	7
06070000002312000000	3	5
06000000001200000000	3	1
06060000001223000000	3	13
06080000001232000000	3	1
01060700004323120000	3	1
02020500001334230000	4	30
02020800001334230000	4	2
02050000002313000000	4	4
01020205003413352300	4	11
01020500003423130000	4	2
02030500003423130000	4	1
09000000001200000000	5	43
01020600001234450000	5	1
01090000002313000000	5	1
06000000001200000000	5	1
01060000001234000000	5	2
06070000002321000000	5	1
01061400002123220000	5	1
02140000001222000000	6	5
03140000001222000000	6	16
02020600001223230000	6	1
05120000001222000000	6	12
07120000002122000000	6	2
03120000001222000000	6	11
02120000001222000000	6	2
03141400001222220000	6	1
06000000001200000000	7	45
01030000002113000000	7	4
03070000003412000000	7	1
02030506003534132300	8	1
03050606003413352300	8	1
05050600001445460000	8	1
05061300001213110000	8	1
02050606003413352300	8	1
13140000001111000000	8	41
02051300001312110000	8	1
12140000001111000000	8	1
05061400001212220000	8	1
02061400002313330000	8	1
02130000001211000000	9	26
02020500002334130000	9	2
02110000001211000000	9	13
02030500002312120000	9	1
02030500003423130000	9	2
03130000001211000000	9	2
13000000001100000000	9	1
03030500002334130000	9	1
03110000001211000000	9	2

C. Experimental Results

The ideal situation occurs when the codes that characterize different pattern classes are distinct. However, in handwritten characters the ideal situation usually does not occur since different characters, because of the way a person writes, may look the same. This situation creates ambiguous characters, and a confusing code is produced. By confusing code is meant that a pattern code can be assigned to different character classes. These confusing codes must be resolved before recognition can proceed.

The data of 50 samples for each character class (totaling 500 samples) is fed into the system for learning. The results are presented in Table I. After a careful study it is seen that there are four confusing codes; these are shown in Table II. Column one of Table II indicates the confusing codes, column two represents the characters allocated to each confusing code, and column three indicates the number of times that a character is assigned to a confusing code. The confusion is resloved by attaching the dominant character to the code.

TABLE II
SUMMARY OF CONFUSING CODES

Confusing Code	Possible Character	No. of Character Classified
06000000001200000000	0	2
	3	1
	5	1
	7	45
02020500001334230000	4	30
02020500002334130000	9	2
02030500003423130000	4	1
	9	2
13000000001200000000	0	1
	9	1

In order to increase the recognition efficiency of the system, the prototypes are arranged in descending order according to their code counts. That is, the most frequently occurring prototypes appear first on the list. These prototypes are stored in the prototype memory of the system. The input to the system is the Honeywell 500 samples with their Honeywell classification disregarded. Three samples in nine-class, two in zero-class, and one in three-, four-, and five-classes were misclassified. The rest were all classified correctly. The percentage of correct classification of this experiment is 98.4 percent, and the processing time on IBM 370 computer is 5 min 14.32 s.

V. CONCLUSION

Fuzzy logic is applied to the feature extraction of handwritten numerical characters. Dominant prototypes that are functional representations of branch features and node features are learned and stored for each character. For pattern classification, the functional representation of the incoming pattern is compared with those of the prototypes. The recognition system proposed was successfully simulated on a digital computer using the IEEE pattern recognition data base.

REFERENCES

[1] K. Oatley, *Brain Mechanisms and Mind.* New York: Dutton, 1972.
[2] D. H. Hubel and T. N. Wiesel, "Receptive fields of single neurons in the cat's striate cortex," *J. Physiology*, vol. 148, pp. 574–591, 1959.
[3] L. A. Zadeh, "Fuzzy sets," *Inform. Contr.*, vol. 8, pp. 338–353, 1965.
[4] M. Dallmann, *Teaching the Language Arts in the Elementary School.* Dubuque, Ia.: Wm. C. Brown, 1966, p. 131.
[5] J. C. Hilditch, "An application of graph theory in pattern recognition," in *Machine Intelligence 3*, D. Michie, Ed. New York: American Elsevier, 1968, pp. 325–347.
[6] J. C. Hilditch, "Linear skeletons from square cupboards," in *Machine Intelligence 4*, B. Meltzer and D. Michie, Eds. New York: American Elsevier, 1969, pp. 403–420.
[7] M. A. Aiserman *et al.*, *Logic, Automata, and Algorithms.* New York: Academic, 1971, pp. 79–83.
[8] F. D. Parker, "Boolean matrices and logic," *Mathematics Magazine*, pp. 33–38, Jan.–Feb. 1964.
[9] Pepe Siy, "Fuzzy logic for handwritten character recognition," Ph.D. dissertation, Dep. Elec. Eng., Univ. Akron, Akron, Ohio, June 1973.
[10] H. B. Barlow, R. Narasimhan, and A. Rosenfeld, "Visual pattern analysis in machines and animals," *Science*, 18, vol. 177, Aug. 1972.
[11] J. T. Tou and R. C. Gonzalez, "Recognition of handwritten characters by topological feature extraction and multilevel categorization," *IEEE Trans. Comput.*, vol. C-21, pp. 776–785, July 1972.
[12] R. Narasimhan, "On the description, generation, and recognition of classes of pictures," in *Automatic Interpretation and Classification of Images*, A. Grasselli, Ed. New York: Academic, 1969, pp. 1–42.
[13] R. L. Grimsdale, F. H. Sumner, C. J. Turnis, and T. Kilburn, "A system for the automatic recognition of patterns," in *Proc. IEE*, vol. 106, Pt. B, no. 26, pp. 210–221, Mar. 1959.

Chapter 4
Image Processing and Machine Vision

4.0 Introduction

THIS chapter is devoted to the specialized area of pattern recognition called *image processing*. Although applications of fuzzy pattern recognition models for real problems are sprinkled throughout the papers in Chapters 2 and 3, those articles usually had a more general flavor than those reproduced in this chapter in that they considered methods for clustering, classifier design, and feature analysis that could often be applied, among other places, to digital image data. Images are, by their very nature, usually associated with "real" problems; for example, many control and decision systems with high degrees of complexity include one or more imaging sensors. Thus, the papers in this chapter are a well-developed and practical arena in which to demonstrate the power of fuzzy algorithms.

A gray tone image possesses ambiguity within each pixel because of the possible multivalued levels of brightness. If the gray levels are scaled to lie in the range [0, 1], we can regard the gray level of a pixel as its degree of membership in the set of high-valued "bright" pixels—thus a gray image can be viewed as a fuzzy set. Regions, features, primitives, properties, and relations among pixels that are not crisply defined can similarly be regarded as fuzzy subsets of images. In Section 1.3.E of Chapter 1, we explained the relevance of fuzzy set theory in weakening crisp decisions (as is done in the case of conventional techniques) in extracting them as ordinary subsets and in managing and/or representing the uncertainties in a recognition system. The ten papers included in this chapter describe the theory, algorithms, and applications of fuzzy set theoretic approaches to image processing and machine vision problems.

In the first two papers in this chapter, 4.1 and 4.2, Rosenfeld explains various concepts of fuzzy geometry in a gray image, many of which are generalizations of crisp properties of, and relationships between, regions in an image. These extensions include the topological concepts of connectedness, adjacency and surroundness, star-shapedness and convexity, area, perimeter, compactness, height, width, extent, diameter, etc. Further information on topics of this nature is available [1–11]. Other geometrical properties (e.g., length, breadth, index of area coverage, adjacency, major axis, minor axis, center of gravity, and density) have recently been defined [9, 10], and fast methods of computation of these parameters using co-occurrence matrices discussed [10]. Prewitt first noted that image subsets representing objects might be regarded as fuzzy [11].

It is possible to generalize and develop fuzzy approaches for many well-known imaging operations, such as shrinking and expanding, thinning, splitting and merging, dilation, concentration and intensification, all of which can be used effectively in processing an image pattern. Applications of these operations include image enhancement, filtering, edge detection, smoothing, skeleton extraction, and quantitative analysis. Papers 4.3 and 4.4 represent two of the earliest developments in this area. A gray scale thinning algorithm is described in Paper 4.3 based on the concept of fuzzy connectedness (cf. Paper 4.1) between two pixels; the dark regions in an image can be thinned without ever being explicitly segmented. Paper 4.4 demonstrates the formulation of a basic processing scheme involving fuzzification of the image space, performing various operations, and then defuzzification. This processing scheme has been implemented for the enhancement of an image (such as smoothing and contrast enhancement) using the max, min, and INT operators along with S and π functions [12]. It has also been shown that fuzziness in an image decreases with its enhancement and Paper 4.4 gives a means for quantitatively assessing fuzziness with fuzzy entropy and other indices of fuzziness. An extension of this concept to enhance the contrast among various ill-defined regions using multiple applications of π and $(1 - \pi)$ functions has been described [13, 14] for edge detection of x-ray images. The edge detection operators involve max and min operations. Paper 4.5 demonstrates, in this regard, a recent attempt to use a relaxation (iterative) algorithm for fast image enhancement utilizing various orders of fuzzy S functions; convergence has also been analyzed in this paper. Readers can consult numerous sources [15–37] for further references on fuzzy set theoretic image processing techniques, information measures (including color images), their applications, and quantitative indices for image analysis.

Another research area where fuzzy set theory finds significant applications [19–22, 30–34] is the problem of evaluation of image quality because of the fuzziness of the human senses. Paper 4.6 is reprinted in this context and describes an application of a relaxation-type pixel classification procedure using fuzzy measures and fuzzy integrals for subjective evaluation of printed color images.

The problem of image segmentation plays a key role in many areas of recognition, analysis, and description. Image segmentation can be performed in several ways, of which gray level (histogram) thresholding and pixel classification using global and/or local information of an image space are perhaps the most important. Papers 4.7 and 4.8 represent typical approaches to these two variants on fuzzy segmentation. In Paper 4.7, Pal and Rosenfeld describe a histogram thresholding technique that provides both fuzzy and nonfuzzy segmentations by minimizing the grayness ambiguity (global entropy, index of fuzziness, index of crispness) and geometrical ambiguity (fuzzy compactness) of an image. They use different S type membership functions to define fuzzy object regions and then select the one that is associated with a minimum value of some ambiguity measure. (Nonfuzzy thresholds, obtained automatically, can then be used in defining crossover points of S functions or π functions [cf. Paper 4.4] for enhancing contrast among various regions.) The mathematical framework of the algorithm, including the selection of S functions, its bandwidth, and its bounds is available [38]. Many other measures of image ambiguity (e.g., local and conditional entropy [28, 39], fuzzy correlation [40], index of area coverage [9], and adjacency [10] can also be used). If there is a difference in opinion in defining an S function, the concept of spectral fuzzy sets [41] can be used to provide a set of thresholds along with their certainty values. Use of grayness and spatial ambiguity measures has recently been made in automatic selection of an appropriate enhancement (nonlinear) function for an unknown image [33].

Paper 4.8, in contrast with Paper 4.7, shows an application of the fuzzy c-means clustering techniques (the theory of which is adequately described and represented in the papers in Chapter 2) for segmentation of a color image by pixel classification. Paper 4.8 involves coarse segmentation using thresholding techniques followed by a fine segmentation that uses the fuzzy c-means algorithm for labeling those pixels that remain unclassified after coarse segmentation. An evaluation criterion based on the probability of error is used as a basis for comparing fuzzy segmentations with other techniques. The coarse–fine strategy reduces the computational burden of the fuzzy c-means algorithm. Some recent results on image segmentation using the fuzzy c-means algorithm and the conventional c-means algorithm with fuzzy integrals and geometrical properties as features have been reported [10, 42–46].

As described in Section 1.3.E of Chapter 1, a vision system should provide for the representation of the uncertainties involved at every stage so that the system retains as much of the information content of the input image as possible for making a decision at the highest level. The ultimate output of the system will then be associated with the least uncertainty and, unlike conventional systems, it may not be biased or affected as much by lower level decisions. There have been several attempts along these lines to extract fuzzy primitives (or features) from fuzzy edge and segmented outputs of image regions for shape analysis, matching, and recognition. Paper 4.9 is a recent article that considers the fuzzy c-means algorithm for segmentation of color images, and shows methods of performing the tasks of edge detection and shape matching within the domain of fuzzy sets derived during the segmentation phase. An interpretation of the shape parameters of triangle, rectangle, and quadrangle in terms of membership for approximate isosceles triangles, approximate equilateral triangles, approximate right triangles, and so on has been made for classification. Other earlier attempts for extraction of fuzzy primitives (e.g., vertical, horizontal, and oblique lines; sharp, fair, and gentle curves; corner; cornerity; symmetry) or in providing similarity measures between triangle, rectangle, and quadrangle for shape analysis and syntactic classification have been made [22, 47–58]. Attempts have also been made in extracting the fuzzy skeleton of a region from its fuzzy segmented version [10, 59], which is obtained by a gray-level thresholding technique described in Paper 4.7. Here, the membership of a pixel for the subset skeleton can be computed with respect to the ϵ edge (edge points of an object for which its class membership value is less than or equal to ϵ, $0 < \epsilon < 1$) of the object region. The skeletons produced by these methods do not depend heavily on the boundary selection. A fuzzy medial axis transformation (FMAT) based on fuzzy disks has recently been formulated [60, 61] that provides fuzzy skeletons of the higher intensity regions (and also the exact representation of the image) without requiring any kind of segmentation or thresholding. (Note that the skeleton or MAT of a region in a binary picture is determined with respect to its boundary [62, 63].) The definition of the FMAT involves natural extensions (generalizations) of the concepts of maximal disk, union, inclusion, and symmetry for an ordinary set to a fuzzy set. Other papers on these topics include references [64–66].

Polygonal approximation, linear splining, curve fitting, or segmentation of plane curves constitutes another important area in machine vision [62, 67–70]. Paper 4.10 is an example of those in the field of contour analysis that demonstrates an application of the fuzzy c-varieties clustering algorithm for providing good polygonal approximations (in the mean-squared error sense) to subsets of planar data sets. The utility of this approach is demonstrated through several numerical examples. A companion paper [79] shows that this scheme can be used for corner detection in 2-D image data that is in either chain-coded or rectangular coordinate format. This paper compares this scheme with the two best-known corner detectors (i.e., the Freeman-Davis and Rosenfeld-Johnston algorithms). A number of workers have developed generalizations of this application by allowing cluster prototypes to be, for example, hyperquadric surfaces in the feature space. The use of fuzzy techniques for detecting ellipses or circles in two dimensional data has been reported [71, 72].

A large number of researchers are currently concentrating on fusing the merits of both fuzzy set theory and neural network theory for intellectual and material gain in the field of computer and system science. Readers can refer to articles [73–75] that demonstrate such an application for image segmentation, scene labeling, and object extraction problems. Use of Hopfield-type neural nets and self-organizing nets has also been made [76–78] for the object extraction problem. Further applications on the fusion of these two technologies in pattern recognition problems are shown in Chapter 5.

References

[1] A. Rosenfeld, "Fuzzy graphs," in *Fuzzy Sets and Their Applications to Cognitive and Decision Processes*, L. A. Zadeh, K. S. Fu, K. Tanaka, and M. Shimura (Eds.), New York: Academic Press, 1975, pp. 77–96.

[2] R. Lowen, "Convex fuzzy sets," *Fuzzy Sets and Syst.*, vol. 3, pp. 291–310, 1980.

[3] L. Janos and A. Rosenfeld, "Some results on fuzzy (digital) convexity," *Pattern Recognition*, vol. 15, no. 5, pp. 379–382, 1982.

[4] A. Rosenfeld, "On connectivity properties of grayscale pictures," *Pattern Recognition*, vol. 16, no. 1, pp. 47–50, 1983.

[5] A. Rosenfeld, "The diameter of a fuzzy set," *Fuzzy Sets and Syst.*, vol. 13, pp. 241–246, 1984.

[6] A. Rosenfeld and S. Haber, "The perimeter of a fuzzy set," *Pattern Recognition*, vol. 18, pp. 125–130, 1985.

[7] A. Rosenfeld, "Distance between fuzzy sets," *Pattern Recognition Letters*, vol. 3, pp. 229–233, 1985.

[8] A. Rosenfeld, "Fuzzy rectangles," *Pattern Recognition Letters*, vol. 11, pp. 677–679, 1990.

[9] S. K. Pal and A. Ghosh, "Index of area coverage of fuzzy image subsets and object extraction," *Pattern Recognition Letters*, vol. 11, pp. 831–841, 1990.

[10] S. K. Pal and A. Ghosh, "Fuzzy geometry in image analysis," *Fuzzy Sets and Syst.*, 1992 (in press).

[11] J. M. B. Prewitt, "Object enhancement and extraction," in *Picture Processing and Psychopictorics*, B. Lipkin and A. Rosenfeld (Eds.), New York: Academic Press, 1970, pp. 75–149.

[12] L. A. Zadeh, "Calculus of fuzzy restrictions," in *Fuzzy Sets and Their Applications to Cognitive and Decision Processes*, L. A. Zadeh, K. S. Fu, K. Tanaka and M. Shimura (Eds.), New York: Academic Press, 1975, pp. 1–39.

[13] S. K. Pal and R. A. King, "Histogram equalisation with S and π functions in detecting x-ray edges," *Electronics Letters*, vol. 17, no. 8, pp. 302–304, April 1981.

[14] S. K. Pal and R. A. King, "On edge detection of x-ray images using fuzzy set," *IEEE Trans. Pattern Anal. Machine Intell.*, vol. PAMI-5, no. 1, pp. 69–77, 1983.

[15] Y. Nakagowa and A. Rosenfeld, "A note on the use of local max and min operations in digital picture processing," *IEEE Trans. Syst., Man, Cybern.*, vol. SMC-8, pp. 632–635, 1978.

[16] R. Jain, "Application of fuzzy sets for the analysis of complex scenes," in *Advances in Fuzzy Set Theory and Applications*, M. M. Gupta (Ed.), Amsterdam, The Netherlands: North Holland, 1979, pp. 577–587.

[17] S. K. Pal and R. A. King, "Image enhancement using fuzzy set," *Electronics Letters*, vol. 16, no. 10, pp. 376–378, 1980.

[18] V. Goetcherian, "From binary to gray tone image processing using fuzzy logic concepts," *Pattern Recognition*, vol. 12, pp. 7–15, 1980.

[19] S. K. Pal, "A note on the quantitative measure of image enhancement through fuzziness," *IEEE Trans. Pattern Anal. Machine Intell.*, vol. PAMI-4, pp. 204–208, 1982.

[20] T. L. Huntsberger and M. F. Descalzi, "Color edge detection," *Pattern Recognition Letters*, vol. 3, pp. 205–209, 1984.

[21] S. K. Pal, "A measure of edge ambiguity using fuzzy sets," *Pattern Recognition Letters*, vol. 4, pp. 51–56, 1986.

[22] S. K. Pal and D. Dutta Majumder, *Fuzzy Mathematical Approach to Pattern Recognition*, New York: John Wiley & Sons, 1986.

[23] A. De Luca and S. Termini, "A definition of a nonprobabilistic entropy in the setting of fuzzy set theory," *Inform. Control*, vol. 20, pp. 301–312, 1972.

[24] R. Jain and S. Haynes, "Imprecision in computer vision," *Computer*, vol. 15, pp. 39–48, 1982.

[25] W. X. Xie and S. D. Bedrosian, "An information measure for fuzzy sets," *IEEE Trans. Syst., Man, Cybern.*, vol. SMC-14, pp. 151–156, 1984.

[26] J. Keller, G. Hobson, J. Wootton, A. Nafarieh, and K. Luetkemeyer, "Fuzzy confidence measures in midlevel vision," *IEEE Trans. Syst., Man, Cybern.*, vol. SMC-17, no. 4, pp. 676–683, 1987.

[27] W. X. Xie and S. D. Bedrosian, "Experimentally derived fuzzy membership function for gray level images," *J. Franklin Inst.*, vol. 325, pp. 154–164, 1988.

[28] N. R. Pal and S. K. Pal, "Entropy: A new definition and its applications," *IEEE Trans. Syst., Man, Cybern.*, vol. SMC-21, no. 5, 1991.

[29] N. R. Pal and S. K. Pal, "Higher order fuzzy entropy and hybrid entropy of a set," *Inform. Sci.*, vol. 61, no. 3, pp. 211–231, 1992.

[30] N. R. Pal, *On Image Information Measures and Object Extraction*, Ph.D. Thesis, Indian Statistical Institute, Calcutta, March 1990.

[31] W. X. Xie, "An information measure for a color space," *Fuzzy Sets and Syst.*, vol. 36, pp. 157–165, 1990.

[32] M. K. Kundu and S. K. Pal, "A note on gray level-intensity transformation: Effect on HVS thresholding," *Pattern Recognition Letters*, vol. 8, no. 4, pp. 257–269, 1988.

[33] M. K. Kundu and S. K. Pal, "Automatic selection of object enhancement operator with quantitative justification based on fuzzy set theoretic measure," *Pattern Recognition Letters*, vol. 11, pp. 811–829, 1990.

[34] S. K. Pal, "Fuzzy tools for the management of uncertainty in pattern recognition, image analysis, vision and expert system," *Int. J. Syst. Sci.*, vol. 22, no. 3, pp. 511–549, 1991.

[35] S. K. Pal and N. R. Pal, "Higher order entropy, hybrid entropy and their applications," *Spectrum Analysis in One and Two Dimensions*, S. Prasad and R. L. Kashyap (Eds.), New Delhi: Oxford and IBH Publ. Co., pp. 285–300, 1990.

[36] H. Tahani and J. Keller, "Information fusion in computer vision using the fuzzy integral," *IEEE Trans. Syst., Man, Cybern.*, vol. SMC-20, no. 3, pp. 733–741, 1990.

[37] A. Nafarieh and J. Keller, "A fuzzy logic rule-based automatic target recognizer," *Int. J. Intell. Syst.*, vol. 6, pp. 295–312, 1991.

[38] C. A. Murthy and S. K. Pal, "Fuzzy thresholding: Mathematical framework, bound functions and weighted moving average technique," *Pattern Recognition Letters*, vol. 11, pp. 197–206, 1990.

[39] N. R. Pal and S. K. Pal, "Object-background segmentation using new definitions of entropy," *Proc. IEEE*, vol. 136, pp. 284–295, 1989.

[40] S. K. Pal and A. Ghosh, "Image segmentation using fuzzy correlation," *Inform. Sci.*, vol. 62, 1992 (in press).

[41] S. K. Pal and A. Dasgupta, "Spectral fuzzy sets and soft thresholding," *Inform. Sci.* (to appear).

[42] T. L. Huntsberger, C. L. Jacobs, and R. L. Cannon, "Iterative fuzzy image segmentation," *Pattern Recognition*, vol. 18, pp. 131–138, 1985.

[43] R. Cannon, J. Dave, J. C. Bezdek, and M. Trivedi, "Segmentation of a thematic mapper image using the fuzzy *c*-means clustering algorithm," *IEEE Trans. Geographical Sci. and Remote Sensing*, vol. 24, no. 3, pp. 400–408, 1986.

[44] M. Trivedi and J. C. Bezdek, "Low level segmentation of aerial images with fuzzy clustering," *IEEE Trans. Syst., Man, Cybern.*, vol. SMC-16, no. 4, pp. 580–598, 1986.

[45] J. Keller, D. Subhangkasen, and K. Unklesbay, "Approximate reasoning for recognition in color image of beef steaks," *Int. J. General Syst.*, vol. 16, no. 4, pp. 331–342, 1990.

[46] B. Yan and J. Keller, "Conditional fuzzy measures and image segmentation," *Proc. NAFIPS 1991*, University of Missouri—Columbia, May 14–17, 1991, pp. 32–36.

[47] E. T. Lee, "Proximity measures for the classification of geometric figures," *J. Cybern.*, vol. 2, pp. 43–59, 1972.

[48] E. T. Lee, "Shape-oriented chromosome classification," *IEEE Trans. Syst., Man, Cybern.*, vol. SMC-5, pp. 629–632, 1975.

[49] M. G. Thomason, "Finite fuzzy automata, regular fuzzy language and pattern recognition," *Pattern Recognition*, vol. 5, pp. 383–390, 1973.

[50] E. T. Lee, "The shape oriented dissimilarity of polygons and its application to the classification of chromosome images," *Pattern Recognition*, vol. 6, pp. 47–60, 1974.

[51] D. Dutta Majumder and S. K. Pal, "On fuzzification, fuzzy language and fuzzy classifier," *Proc. IEEE 7th Int. Conf. Cybern. Soc.*, Washington, D.C., 1977, pp. 591–595.

[52] B. B. Chaudhuri and D. Dutta Majumder, "Recognition of fuzzy description of sides and symmetries of figures by computer," *Int. J. Syst. Sci.*, vol. 11, pp. 1435–1445, 1980.

[53] L. Vanderheydt, F. Dom, A. Oosterlinck, and H. Van den Berghe, "Two-dimensional shape decomposition using fuzzy set theory applied to automated chromosome analysis," *Pattern Recognition*, vol. 13, pp. 147-157, 1981.

[54] E. T. Lee, "Fuzzy tree automata and syntactic pattern recognition," *IEEE Trans. Pattern Anal. Machine Intell.*, vol. PAMI-4, no. 4, pp. 445-449, 1982.

[55] S. K. Pal, R. A. King, and A. A. Hashim, "Image description and primitive extraction using fuzzy set," *IEEE Trans. Syst., Man, Cybern.*, vol. SMC-13, pp. 94-100, 1983.

[56] S. A. Kwabwe, S. K. Pal, and R. A. King, "Recognition of bones from x-ray of the hand," *Int. J. Syst. Sci.*, vol. 16, no. 4, pp. 403-413, 1985.

[57] A. Pathak and S. K. Pal, "Fuzzy grammars in syntactic recognition of skeletal maturity from x-rays," *IEEE Trans. Syst., Man, Cybern.*, vol. SMC-16, pp. 657-667, 1986.

[58] S. K. Pal and A. Bhattacharyya, "Pattern recognition technique in analyzing the effect of thiourea on brain neurosecretory cells," *Pattern Recognition Letters*, vol. 11, pp. 443-452, 1990.

[59] S. K. Pal, "Fuzzy skeletonization of an image," *Pattern Recognition Letters*, vol. 10, pp. 17-23, 1989.

[60] S. K. Pal and A. Rosenfeld, "A fuzzy medial axis transformation based on fuzzy disks," *Pattern Recognition Letters*, vol. 12, no. 10, pp. 585-590, 1991.

[61] S. K. Pal and L. Wang, "Fuzzy medial axis transformation (FMAT): Practical feasibility," *Fuzzy Sets and Syst.*, (to appear).

[62] A. Rosenfeld and A. C. Kak, *Digital Picture Processing*, 2nd ed., New York: Academic Press, 1982.

[63] R. C. Gonzalez and P. Wintz, *Digital Image Processing*, 2nd ed., Reading, MA: Addison-Wesley, 1987.

[64] S. Peleg and A. Rosenfeld, "A min-max medial axis transformation," *IEEE Trans. Pattern Anal. Mach. Intell.*, vol. PAMI-3, pp. 208-210, 1981.

[65] E. Salari and P. Siy, "The ridge-seeking method for obtaining the skeleton of digital images," *IEEE Trans. Syst., Man, Cybern.*, vol. SMC-14, pp. 524-528, 1984.

[66] J. Serra, *Image Analysis and Mathematical Morphology*, London: Academic Press, 1982.

[67] E. L. Hall, *Computer Image Processing and Recognition*, New York: Academic Press, 1978.

[68] T. Pavlidis, *Structural Pattern Recognition*, New York: Springer-Verlag, 1977.

[69] D. Marr, *Vision*, San Francisco: W. H. Freeman, 1982.

[70] R. Duda and P. Hart, *Pattern Classification and Scene Analysis*, New York: Wiley Interscience, 1973.

[71] R. Dave, "Fuzzy shell-clustering and applications to circle detection in digital images," *Int. J. General Syst.*, vol. 16, no. 4, pp. 343-355, 1990.

[72] R. Dave and K. Bhaswan, "Adaptive fuzzy *c*-shells clustering," *Proc. NAFIPS 1991*, University of Missouri-Columbia, May 14-17, 1991, pp. 195-199.

[73] L. O. Hall, A. Bensaid, L. Clarke, R. Velthuisen, and J. C. Bezdek, "Segmentation of MR images with fuzzy and neural network techniques," *IEEE Trans. Neural Networks*, 1992 (in press).

[74] A. Ghosh, N. R. Pal, and S. K. Pal, "Self-organization for object extraction using multilayer neural network and fuzziness measures," *IEEE Trans. Fuzzy Systems*, 1992 (in press).

[75] R. Krishnapuram and J. Lee, "Fuzzy compensative—connected-based hierarchical networks and their applications to computer vision," *J. Neural Networks*, 1992 (in press).

[76] A. Ghosh, N. R. Pal and S. K. Pal, "Object background classification using Hopfield type neural network," *Int. J. Pattern Recog. Artificial Intell.* (communicated).

[77] A. Ghosh, N. R. Pal, and S. K. Pal, "Object extraction using a self-organizing neural network," *Proc. Int. Symp. Intell. Robotics (ISIR)*, Bangalore, India, January 1991, pp. 686-697.

[78] A. Ghosh, N. R. Pal, and S. K. Pal, "Image segmentation using neural networks," *Biological Cybernetics*, 1992 (in press).

[79] I. Anderson and J. C. Bezdek, "Curvature and tangential deflection of discrete arcs: A theory based on the commutator of scatter matrix pairs and its application to vertex detection in planar shape data," *IEEE Trans. Pattern Anal. Machine Intell.*, vol. PAMI-6, no. 1, pp. 27-40, 1984.

Fuzzy Digital Topology

AZRIEL ROSENFELD

Computer Science Center, University of Maryland, College Park, Maryland 20742

Topological relationships among parts of a digital picture, such as connectedness and surroundedness, play an important role in picture analysis and description. This paper generalizes these concepts to fuzzy subsets, and develops some of their basic properties.

1. INTRODUCTION

Geometrical properties of and relationships among parts of a digital picture play an important role in picture analysis and description (Rosenfeld and Kak, 1976, Chap. 9). Conventionally, these properties and relationships are defined for subsets of the picture, extracted from it by segmentation processes of various types (Rosenfeld and Kak, 1976, Chap. 8). However, segmentation of a picture into subsets represents a strong commitment; in many cases, it would be preferable to weaken this commitment by "extracting" fuzzy subsets (see Section 2), rather than ordinary subsets, from the picture. If this is done, it becomes desirable to extend the concepts of digital picture geometry to fuzzy subsets. This paper develops such an extension for the topological concepts of connectedness and surroundness (Rosenfeld and Kak, 1976, Section 9.1), and develops some of the basic properties of these generalized concepts.

2. BACKGROUND

In this section we briefly review some of the basic concepts of digital topology and of fuzzy sets.

Let Σ be a rectangular array of integer-coordinate points. Thus the point $P \equiv (x, y)$ of Σ has four horizontal and vertical neighbors, namely $(x \pm 1, y)$ and $(x, y \pm 1)$; and it also has four diagonal neighbors, namely $(x \pm 1, y \pm 1)$ and $(x \pm 1, y \mp 1)$. We say that former points are 4-adjacent to, or 4-neighbors of, P; and we say that both types of neighbors are 8-adjacent to, or 8-neighbors of, P. Note that if P is on the border of Σ, some of these neighbors may not exist.

For all points P, Q of Σ, by a *path* ρ from P to Q we mean a sequence of points $P = P_0, P_1, \ldots, P_n = Q$ such that P_i is adjacent to P_{i-1}, $1 \leqslant i \leqslant n$. Note that this is two definitions in one ("4-path" and "8-path"), depending on whether "adjacent" means "4-adjacent" or "8-adjacent." The same is true for many of the definitions that follow, but we usually do not mention this.

Let S be any subset of Σ. We say that the points P, Q of Σ are *connected* in S if there is a path from P to Q consisting entirely of points of S. Readily, "connected" is an equivalence relation: P is connected to P (by a path of length 0); if P is connected to Q, then Q is connected to P (the reversal of a path is a path); and if P is connected to Q and Q to R, then P is connected to R (the concatenation of two paths is a path). This relation partitions S into equivalence classes, which are maximal subsets S_i of S such that every P, Q belonging to a given S_i are connected. These classes are called the *(connected) components* of S.

Let $\bar{S} = \Sigma - S$ be the complement of S. We assume, for simplicity, that the border points of Σ are all in $\bar{S}$. Thus one component of $\bar{S}$ always contains

Reprinted with permission from *Inform. Control*, vol. 40, no. 1, pp. 76–87, January 1979.

the border B of Σ. The other components, if any, are called ***holes*** in S. [It turns out that opposite types of connectedness (4- and 8-, or 8- and 4-) should be used for S and for $\bar{S}$, in order for various algorithms to work properly; see Rosenfeld and Kak (1976, Section 9.1).] If S has no holes, it is called ***simply-connected.***

Let S and T be disjoint subsets of Σ. We say that S ***surrounds*** T if any path from T to the border of Σ must meet S. Readily, "surrounds" is a strict order relation: If S surrounds T, then T does not surround S; and if S surrounds T and T surrounds W, then S surrounds W. [More generally, for any subsets U, V, W of Σ, we say that V ***separates*** U from W if any path from U to W must meet V; thus S surrounds T if it separates T from the border B of Σ.]

In this paper we develop extensions of these concepts to fuzzy sets. We recall that a ***fuzzy subset*** of Σ is a function σ: $\Sigma \to [0, 1]$. For any $P \in \Sigma$, the value $\sigma(P)$ is called the degree of membership of P in σ. Note that an ordinary subset S of Σ can be regarded as a fuzzy subset for which the function takes on only the values 0 and 1, where points of S map into 1 and points of $\bar{S}$ into 0. [The function χ_S: $\Sigma \to \{0, 1\}$ that takes points of S into 1 and points of $\bar{S}$ into 0 is called the ***characteristic function*** of S.] The function $1 - \sigma$, which takes each $P \in \Sigma$ into $1 - \sigma(P)$, is called the ***complement*** of σ; evidently this is consistent with the nonfuzzy definition. We assume that for all points P on the border B of Σ we have $\sigma(P) = 0$.

3. Fuzzy Connectedness

Let σ be a fuzzy subset of Σ, and let ρ: $P = P_0, P_1, \ldots, P_n = Q$ be any path between two points of Σ. We define the ***strength*** $s_\sigma(\rho)$ of ρ (with respect to σ) as $\min_{0 \leqslant i \leqslant n} \sigma(P_i)$—"a path is as strong as its weakest link." We define the ***degree of connectedness*** of P and Q (with respect to σ) as $c_\sigma(P, Q) \equiv \max_\rho s_\sigma(\rho)$, where the max is taken over all paths from P to Q. Thus $0 \leqslant s_\sigma(\rho) \leqslant 1$ for all ρ, and $0 \leqslant c_\sigma(P, Q) \leqslant 1$ for all P, Q.

Proposition 3.1. *For all* P, Q *we have* $c_\sigma(P, P) = \sigma(P)$ *and* $c_\sigma(P, Q) = c_\sigma(Q, P)$.

Proof. P is on any path ρ from P to P; hence for any such path we have $s_\sigma(\rho) = \min \sigma(P_i) \leqslant \sigma(P)$. On the other hand, P itself is a path of length 0 from P to P, for which $s_\sigma(\rho) = \sigma(P)$; thus $\sigma(P) = \max_\rho s_\sigma(\rho) \equiv c_\sigma(P, P)$ The second part follows from the fact that the reversal of a path is a path, and reversal preserves path strength. ∎

If σ is into $\{0, 1\}$, let $S = \sigma^{-1}(1) \equiv \{P \mid P \in \Sigma \text{ and } \sigma(P) = 1\}$; then $s_\sigma(\rho) = 1$ iff ρ consists entirely of points of S, and $c_\sigma(P, Q) = 1$ iff P and Q are connected in S. Thus degree of connectedness generalizes the ordinary (nonfuzzy) concept of connectedness. Note that in general, $c_\sigma(P, Q) = 1$ iff there exists a path from P to Q all of whose points are mapped into 1 by σ (and in particular, $\sigma(P) = \sigma(Q) = 1$). For any set $T \subseteq \Sigma$, we can define the degree of connectedness of T (with respect to σ) as $c_\sigma(T) \equiv \min_{P, Q \in T} c_\sigma(P, Q)$.

Proposition 3.2. *For all* P, Q *we have* $c_\sigma(P, Q) \leqslant \min(\sigma(P), \sigma(Q))$.

Proof. For any path ρ: $P = P_0, P_1, \ldots, P_n = Q$ we have $s_\sigma(\rho) = \min_{0 \leqslant i \leqslant n} \sigma(P_i) \leqslant \min(\sigma(P_0), \sigma(P_n)) = \min(\sigma(P), \sigma(Q))$; hence the same is true for $\max_\rho s_\sigma(\rho)$. ∎

Corollary. *For all* T *we have* $c_\sigma(T) \leqslant \min_{P \in T} \sigma(P)$.

It also follows from Proposition 3.2 that $c_\sigma(P, Q)$, regarded as a fuzzy relation on Σ (i.e., as a fuzzy subset of $\Sigma \times \Sigma$), is a fuzzy relation on the fuzzy set σ in the sense defined in Rosenfeld (1975).

We say that P and Q are *connected* in σ if $c_\sigma(P, Q) = \min(\sigma(P), \sigma(Q))$, so that $c_\sigma(P, Q)$ takes on its maximum possible value. [This is analogous to the definition of convexity for fuzzy sets (Zadeh, 1965): σ is convex iff for all P, Q, and any point P' on the straight line segment from P to Q, we have $\sigma(P') \geqslant \min(\sigma(P), \sigma(Q))$; in our definition, P' is allowed to be on the strongest path from P to Q, rather than on the straight line segment.]

PROPOSITION 3.3. *P and Q are connected in σ iff there exists a path ρ': $P = P_0, P_1, ..., P_n = Q$ such that $\sigma(P_i) \geqslant \min(\sigma(P), \sigma(Q))$, $1 \leqslant i < n$.*

Proof. If there exists such a path ρ', we have $c_\sigma(P, Q) = \max_\rho s_\sigma(\rho) \geqslant s_\sigma(\rho') = \min_i \sigma(P_i) \geqslant \min_i(\sigma(P), \sigma(Q))$, so that $c_\sigma(P, Q) = \min(\sigma(P), \sigma(Q))$ by Proposition 3.2. Conversely, if P and Q are connected in σ, let ρ' be a path for which $s_\sigma(\rho') = \max_\rho s_\sigma(\rho) = c_\sigma(P, Q) = \min(\sigma(P), \sigma(Q))$; then for all P_i on ρ' we have $\sigma(P_i) \geqslant \min_i \sigma(P_i) = s_\sigma(\rho')$. ∎

Here again, if $\sigma(P) = \sigma(Q) = 1$, P and Q are connected iff there exists a path from P to Q such that, for any point P' of σ, we have $\sigma(P') = 1$. Thus if σ is into $\{0, 1\}$, and $S = \sigma^{-1}(1)$, two points P, Q of S are connected in σ iff they are connected in S. Note, however, that points can be connected in σ without being connected in S; in fact, if $\sigma(P) = 0$, P is connected in σ to *any* Q—though, of course, its degree of connectedness to Q is zero.

The remarks in the preceding paragraph indicate that "connected in σ" is a generalization of "connected in S" only in some respects, but not in others. In fact, $C_\sigma \equiv \{(P, Q) \mid P, Q \text{ are connected in } \sigma\}$ is not in general, an equivalence relation, as we see from

PROPOSITION 3.4. *C_σ is reflexive and symmetric, but not necessarily transitive.*

Proof. For all P we have $c_\sigma(P, P) = \sigma(P) = \min(\sigma(P), \sigma(P))$; and symmetry is clear, since c_σ and $\min(\sigma(P), \sigma(Q))$ are both symmetric. On the other hand, let Σ be the 1-by-3 array P, Q, R, and let $\sigma(P) = \sigma(R) = 1$, $\sigma(Q) < 1$; then (P, Q) and (Q, R) are connected in σ, but P and R are not. ∎

Nevertheless, C_σ is a useful relation on Σ, as we show in the next section. For any set $T \subseteq \Sigma$, we call T connected with respect to σ if all P, Q in T are connected in σ.

4. FUZZY COMPONENTS

Although C_σ is not an equivalence relation, we can still define a notion of "connected component" with respect to σ. Specifically, our definition is based on the concept of a "plateau" in σ. As we show, this definition has many properties in common with the standard one, even though the components do not constitute a partition.

4.1. *Plateaus, Tops, and Bottoms*

By a *plateau* in σ we mean a maximal connected subset of Σ on which σ has constant value. In other words, $\Pi \subseteq \Sigma$ is a plateau iff

(a) Π is connected;

(b) $\sigma(P) = \sigma(Q)$ for all P, Q in Π;

(c) $\sigma(P) \neq \sigma(Q)$ for all pairs of neighboring points $P \in \Pi$, $Q \notin \Pi$.

Clearly any $P \in \Sigma$ belongs to exactly one plateau.

We call the plateau Π a *top* if its σ value is a local maximum, i.e., if $\sigma(P) > \sigma(Q)$ for all pairs of neighboring points $P \in \Pi$, $Q \notin \Pi$. Similarly, we call Π a *bottom* if its value is a local minimum.

PROPOSITION 4.1. *Π is a plateau in σ iff it is a plateau in $1 - \sigma$. Π is a bottom in σ iff it is a top in $1 - \sigma$, and vice versa.* ▮

In the nonfuzzy case, the plateaus are just the connected components of S and of $\bar{S}$. In fact, if $S \neq \varnothing$, the tops are just the components of S, and the bottoms are the components of $\bar{S}$; every plateau is either a top or a bottom. Thus we can regard tops and bottoms as generalizations of connected components. In the remainder of this section, Π is a top, and we assume that the points $P \in \Pi$ have $\sigma(P) > 0$ (otherwise, Π must be all of Σ).

4.2. *Sets Associated with a Top*

With any top Π we can associate three sets of points, defined as follows:

$$A_\pi = \{P \in \Sigma \mid \text{There exists a path } P = P_0, P_1, ..., P_n = Q \in \Pi \text{ such that } \sigma(P_{i-1}) \leqslant \sigma(P_i),\ 1 \leqslant i \leqslant n\}.$$

$$B_\pi = \{P \in \Sigma \mid \text{There exists a path } P = P_0, P_1, ..., P_n = Q \in \Pi \text{ such that } \sigma(P) \leqslant \sigma(P_i) \leqslant \sigma(Q),\ 1 \leqslant i \leqslant n\}.$$

$$C_\pi = \{P \in \Sigma \mid \text{There exists a path } P = P_0, P_1, ..., P_n = Q \in \Pi \text{ such that } \sigma(P) \leqslant \sigma(P_i),\ 1 \leqslant i \leqslant n\}.$$

PROPOSITION 4.2. $\Pi \subseteq A_\pi \subseteq B_\pi \subseteq C_\pi$. ▮

By these definitions, P is in A_π iff there is a monotonically nondecreasing path from P to Π; thus there cannot be a local minimum between P and Π. Similarly, if P is in B_π, there cannot be a peak higher than Π between P and Π. The sets P_π, B_π, and C_π need not be connected in the ordinary sense (though C_π is connected in the σ sense; see Theorem 4.4). Note also that all points whose σ values are sufficiently low will be in C_π, e.g., if $\sigma(P) = 0$, P is in C_π for all Π. On the other hand, as we show next (Proposition 4.3), points whose values are higher than $\sigma(\Pi)$ (the common σ value of the points in Π) cannot be in C_π; indeed, if P is in C_π and $\sigma(P) \geqslant \sigma(\Pi)$, we must have $P \in \Pi$.

The points adjacent to a top Π are evidently in A_π. Note also that two tops can never be adjacent to one another. (Proof: If they have the same height, they are a single top; if they have different heights, the shorter one cannot be a top.)

4.3. *Tops and Connectedness*

PROPOSITION 4.3. *If $P \in C_\pi$ and $P \notin \Pi$, then $\sigma(P) < \sigma(\Pi)$.*

Proof. If $\sigma(P) \geqslant \sigma(\Pi)$, then $P \in C_\pi$ implies that there exists a path ρ from P to Π such that, for all P_i on ρ, we have $\sigma(P_i) \geqslant \sigma(P) \geqslant \sigma(\Pi)$. But if $P \notin \Pi$, ρ must pass through a point Q that is adjacent to Π but not in Π; and for any such Q we have $\sigma(Q) < \sigma(\Pi)$, contradiction. ▮

THEOREM 4.4. *C_π is the set of points of Σ that are connected to points of Π.*

Proof. Let P be connected to $Q \in \Pi$, so that by Proposition 3.3 there exists a path ρ from P to Q such that, for all P_i on ρ, we have $\sigma(P_i) \geqslant \min(\sigma(P), \sigma(Q))$. If $\sigma(P) > \sigma(Q)$, we have $P \notin \Pi$, and $\sigma(P_i) \geqslant \sigma(Q)$ for all P_i on ρ; but by the proof of Proposition 4.3, this is impossible, since ρ must pass through a point Q' adjacent to Π but not in Π, and for such a point we must have $\sigma(Q') < \sigma(\Pi)$. Hence $\sigma(P) \leqslant \sigma(Q)$, and $\sigma(P_i) \geqslant \sigma(P)$ for all P_i on ρ, so that $P \in C_\pi$.

Conversely, if $P \in C_\pi$, then $\sigma(P) \leqslant \sigma(\Pi)$ by Proposition 4.3. Hence there exists a path ρ from P to a point Q of Π such that, for all P_i on ρ, we have $\sigma(P_i) \geqslant \sigma(P) = \min(\sigma(P), \sigma(Q))$, which makes P connected to Q by Proposition 3.3. ▮

THEOREM 4.5. *For any P there exists a top Π such that $P \in A_\pi$.*

Proof. Let P be in the plateau Π_0; in other words, let Π_0 be the connected component of points having value $\sigma(P)$ that contains P. If Π_0 is a top, we have $P \in \Pi_0 \subseteq A_{\pi_0}$, and we are done. If not, let P_1 be a neighbor of Π_0 such that $\sigma(P_1) > \sigma(P_0)$; thus we have a monotonically nondecreasing path from P_0 to P_1 (going through Π_0 up to a neighbor of P_1). Repeat this argument with P_1 replacing P, and continue in this way to obtain $P_2, P_3, \ldots$. This process must terminate, say at P_n, since Σ is finite. Then Π_n is a top, and we have a monotonic nondecreasing path from P to P_n, so that $P \in A_{\pi_n}$. ▮

THEOREM 4.6. *For any two distinct tops Π, Π' we have $\Pi' \cap C_\pi = \varnothing$.*

Proof. Suppose we had $P \in \Pi' \cap C_\pi$; then there would exist a path ρ from P to Π such that, for any point P_i on ρ, we have $\sigma(P) \leqslant \sigma(P_i)$. But for a point P_i adjacent to Π' but not in Π we must have $\sigma(P_i) < \sigma(\Pi') = \sigma(P)$, contradiction. ▮

These two theorems show that the tops Π' and their connected "components" C_π (see Theorem 4.4) have partition-like properties: Any point belongs to some top in a strong sense ($P \in A_\pi$), and a fortiori in a weak sense ($A_\pi \subseteq C_\pi$); but no top can belong to another top even in a weak sense ($\Pi' \cap C_\pi = \varnothing$). These remarks are further supported by the following.

THEOREM 4.7. *P and Q are connected iff there exists a top Π such that P and Q are both in C_π.*

Proof. If P, Q are in C_π, there are paths ρ_1, ρ_2 from P and Q (respectively) to Π such that for all P_i on ρ_1 we have $\sigma(P_i) \geqslant \sigma(P)$, and for all Q_i on ρ_2 we have $\sigma(Q_i) \geqslant \sigma(Q)$. Thus we have a path $\rho_1\rho_2^{-1}$ from P to Q, and for all points R on this path we have $\sigma(R) \geqslant \min(\sigma(P), \sigma(Q))$, which makes P connected to Q by Proposition 3.3.

Conversely, let P and Q be connected, let $\sigma(P) \leqslant \sigma(Q)$ (say), and let ρ' be a monotonic nondecreasing path from Q to some top Π (see Theorem 4.5). Thus $Q \in A_\pi \subseteq C_\pi$. On the other hand, by Proposition 4.3 there is a path ρ from P to Q such that for all P_i on ρ we have $\sigma(P_i) \geqslant \min(\sigma(P), \sigma(Q)) = \sigma(P)$, and we already know that for all Q_i on ρ' we have $\sigma(Q_i) \geqslant \sigma(Q) \geqslant \sigma(P)$. Thus the path $\rho\rho'$ from P to Π guarantees that $P \in C_\pi$. ▮

COROLLARY. *Σ is connected with respect to σ iff there exists a unique top in σ.*

Proof. Theorems 4.6 and 4.7. ▮

Results analogous to those for tops also hold for bottoms, since they are just tops with respect to $1 - \sigma$. In particular, the connected component of points having $\sigma = 0$ that contains the border B of Σ is a bottom, which we can think of as the "background component" of $1 - \sigma$; while all other bottoms can be regarded as "holes in σ." If σ has no holes, we call it *simply-connected.*

4.4. *Membership in a Component*

For any top Π, we can define a fuzzy subset σ_π of Σ whose membership function is given by

$$\sigma_\pi(P) = \sigma(P)/\sigma(\Pi), \quad \text{if } P \in C_\pi,$$
$$= 0 \quad \text{otherwise.}$$

Note that by Proposition 4.3, $\sigma_\pi(P) = 1$ iff $P \in \Pi$.

An alternative method of defining membership in the component defined by Π is as follows[1]:

[1] In this definition, the notation $[x]^+$ means x if $x > 0$; 0 if $x \leqslant 0$.

$$\sigma'_\pi(P) = \left[1 - \min_\rho \sum_{i=1}^{n} | \sigma(P_i) - \sigma(P_{i-1})|/\sigma(\Pi)\right], \quad \text{if} \quad P \in C_\pi,$$
$$= 0 \quad \text{otherwise,}$$

where the minimum is taken over all paths ρ from P to a point of Π. It is not hard to show that if $\sigma(P) \leqslant \sigma(\Pi)$ (as is the case for $P \in C_\pi$), the sum is minimized by a monotonic path, for which it has the value $[\sigma(\Pi) - \sigma(P)]/\sigma(\Pi)$. Thus if $P \in A_\pi$, we have $\sigma'_\pi(P) = 1 - [\sigma(\Pi) - \sigma(P)]/\sigma(\Pi) = \sigma(P)/\sigma(\Pi) = \sigma_\pi(P)$. If no monotonic path exists, the minimum value of the sum must be greater than $[\sigma(\Pi) - \sigma(P)]/\sigma(\Pi)$, so that if $P \notin A_\pi$, we have $\sigma'_\pi(P) < \sigma_\pi(P)$. In any case, we still have $\sigma'_\pi(P) = 1$ iff $P \in \Pi$.

5. Fuzzy Surroundedness

Let σ, τ, v be fuzzy subsets of Σ. We say that τ *separates* σ from v if for all points P, R in Σ, and all paths ρ from P to R, there exists a point Q on ρ such that $\tau(Q) \geqslant \min(\sigma(P), v(R))$. In particular, we say that τ *surrounds* σ if it separates σ from the border B of Σ. [Since B is a nonfuzzy subset, this definition requires nothing if $R \notin B$, since $v(R)$ is then 0. Thus the definition of surroundedness reduces to: For all $P \in \Sigma$ and all paths ρ from P to B, there exists a point Q on ρ such that $\tau(Q) \geqslant \sigma(P)$. Note that $\sigma(P) = \min(\sigma(P), v(R))$, since $v(R) = 1$ for $R \in B$.]

If σ, τ, v are nonfuzzy subsets S, T, U, these definitions reduce to the ordinary ones given in Section 2. Indeed, we need only consider the case where $P \in S$ and $R \in U$, since otherwise the min is zero. The definition of separatedness thus reduces to: T separates S from U if for all $P \in S$ and $R \in U$, and all paths ρ from P to R, there exists a point Q on ρ such that $Q \in T$.

In Section 2 we defined "surrounds" only for disjoint sets, and pointed out that it is antisymmetric and transitive (and irreflexive, since no nonempty set is disjoint from itself). For nondisjoint sets, the situation is more complicated, since two sets can surround one another without being the same —e.g., in

xxx
xsx
xtx
xxx

if $s \in S$, $t \in T$, and the *x*s are in $S \cap T$, then S and T surround each other. However, it can be shown that if S and T surround each other, then $S \cap T$ must surround both of them (which is impossible for disjoint nonempty sets, since $\varnothing$ can only surround $\varnothing$). Analogously, in the fuzzy case we can prove

Theorem 5.1. *"Surrounds" is a weak partial order relation—in other words, for all σ, τ, v, we have*

(a) *Reflexivity: σ surrounds σ.*

(b) *"Antisymmetry": If σ and τ surround each other, then $\sigma \wedge \tau$ surrounds both of them (where $\wedge$ means* "min"*).*

(c) *Transitivity: If σ surrounds τ and τ surrounds v, then σ surrounds v.*

Proof. Reflexivity is obvious, since we can take $Q = P$. Transitivity is straightforward: Given any $P \in \Sigma$ and any path ρ from P to B, there is a point Q on ρ such that $\tau(Q) \geqslant v(P)$, since τ surrounds v. Moreover, on the part of ρ between Q and B there is a point R such that $\sigma(R) \geqslant \tau(Q)$, since σ surrounds τ.

To prove "antisymmetry," let ρ be any path from P to B, and let Q be the last point on ρ such that $\tau(Q) \geqslant \sigma(P)$. Since σ surrounds τ, there must be a point Q' on ρ beyond Q (or possibly Q itself) such that $\sigma(Q') \geqslant \tau(Q)$. Since τ surrounds σ, there must also be a point Q'' on ρ beyond (or equal to) Q' such that $\tau(Q'') \geqslant \sigma(Q') \geqslant \sigma(P)$. By our choice of Q, this implies that $Q = Q' = Q''$, so that $\sigma(Q) \wedge \tau(Q) \geqslant \sigma(P)$. Since P was arbitrary, we have thus proved that $\sigma \wedge \tau$ surrounds σ; and similarly it surrounds τ. [Note that we have $\sigma(Q) = \tau(Q)$, so that the fuzzy set "$\sigma \equiv \tau$," having value $\sigma(P)$ when $\sigma(P) = \tau(P)$, and 0 otherwise, actually surrounds σ and τ.] ▮

For any σ, and any $0 \leqslant t \leqslant 1$, let σ_t be the set $\{P \in \Sigma \mid \sigma(P) \geqslant t\}$.

PROPOSITION 5.2. *If σ surrounds τ, then for any t, σ_t surrounds τ_t.* ▮

6. COMPONENTS, HOLES, AND SURROUNDEDNESS

In ordinary digital topology, if a component of S and a component of $\bar{S}$ are adjacent, then one of them surrounds the other. This is certainly not true about the tops and bottoms of a fuzzy subset. For example, in the array of membership values

.5	.5	1	.5
1	0	0	.5
.5	0	0	1
.5	1	.5	.5

the 1s are all adjacent to the 0s, but the 0s are not surrounded by any one of these components.

Nevertheless, we can establish some relationships between surroundedness for tops or bottoms and surroundedness for the corresponding components. In fact, by Proposition 5.2, if σ_π surrounds $\sigma_{\pi'}$, then Π must surround Π', since $\Pi = (\sigma_\pi)_1$ is just the set of points for which σ_π has value $(\geqslant)1$, and similarly for Π'. Moreover, Π must even surround $A_{\pi'}$, since we cannot have a monotonic path from a point outside Π to a point (of Π') inside Π; the path must go both up and down when it enters and leaves Π. On the other hand, if Π is a top and Π' is a bottom (or vice versa), and P is outside Π, suppose that P were in both C_π and $C_{\pi'}$. Then we would have $\sigma(\Pi') < \sigma(P) < \sigma(\Pi)$, and there would be a path from P to Π' that had σ values below $\sigma(P)$; but this is impossible, since the path must cross Π. We have thus proved

THEOREM 6.1. *Let Π be a top, Π' a bottom, and let σ_π surround $\sigma_{\pi'}$. Then Π surrounds $A_{\pi'} \supseteq \Pi'$, while outside Π we have $C_\pi \cap C_{\pi'} = \varnothing$.* ▮

COROLLARY. *If Π is simply-connected, σ_π cannot surround any $\sigma_{\pi'}$.*

We have seen in the proof of Theorem 6.1 that if Π and Π' are tops, and Π surrounds Π', it also surrounds $A_{\pi'}$. Analogously, we can prove

THEOREM 6.2. *If Π and Π' are tops, and A_π surrounds Π', it also surrounds $A_{\pi'}$.*

Proof. Suppose $P \in A_{\pi'}$ were not surrounded by A_π, so that in particular $P \notin A_\pi$. Let ρ be a monotonic path from P to Π'; then ρ meets A_π, since otherwise we could get from Π' to B (first using ρ^{-1} to get to P) without crossing A_π. Let ρ meet A_π at the point Q; then there is a monotonic path from P to Π (use ρ up to Q, then take a monotonic path from Q to Π), so that $P \in A_\pi$, contradiction. ▮

We can also prove

THEOREM 6.3. *If a point P is surrounded by a union $\bigcup \Pi_i$ of tops, it is surrounded by one of them.*

Proof. If P is in one of the Π_i, that Π_i surrounds it; hence we may suppose that P is not in any of the Π_i. Each Π_i is a connected set, and P is contained in its complement $\overline{\Pi}_i$. This complement consists of a background component (containing the border B of Σ), and possibly other components which are holes in Π_i. If P is contained in a hole, then Π_i surrounds it, and we are done. Otherwise, P is in the background component of $\overline{\Pi}_i$. If a path ρ from P to B meet Π_i, we can divert ρ to pass through points adjacent to Π_i; and none of these points can be in any other Π_j, by the remarks at the end of Section 4.2. Hence points in Π_i can be eliminated from ρ, and this is true for any i, so that we can find a ρ that does not meet any of the Π_is, contradicting the assumption that $\bigcup \Pi_i$ surrounds P. ∎

More generally, suppose that a connected set C is surrounded by $\bigcup \Pi_i$. We can assume that without loss of generality that no two Π_is surround one another. Suppose C meets more than one of the Π_is, say Π_j and Π_k. Since Π_k is in the background component of $\overline{\Pi}_j$, and C is connected, there must exist a point $Q \in C$ adjacent to Π_j and in the background component of $\overline{\Pi}_j$. Q is not in any Π_i, since tops cannot be adjacent. Moreover, since no $\Pi_i \neq \Pi_j$ surrounds Π_j, there is a path from Q to B (through Π_j) that does not meet any $\Pi_i \neq \Pi_j$. Thus no Π_i surrounds Q, and neither does Π_j; it follows by Theorem 6.3 that $\bigcup \Pi_i$ does not surround Q, contradicting the fact that $Q \in C$. Thus C can meet at most one of the Π_is, say Π_j; and by the argument just given, no point of C can be in the background component of $\overline{\Pi}_j$ (since there would then be such a point Q adjacent to Π_j, which would lead to the same contradiction). Hence C is contained in the union of Π_j and its holes, so that Π_j surrounds it. We have thus proved

THEOREM 6.4. *If a connected set is surrounded by a union of tops, it is surrounded by one of them.* ∎

In particular, if a top or bottom is surrounded by a union of tops (or bottoms), it is surrounded by one of them. On the other hand, a union of tops *and* bottoms can nontrivially surround a point (without it being surrounded by any one of them), since tops and bottoms can be mutually adjacent.

7. Component Counting; the Genus

We can define the *number of components* of σ as simply the number of its tops. It is straightforward to define a "one-pass" algorithm that counts these tops. We scan Σ row by row and assign distinct labels to each plateau Π. At the same time, we note for each label the existence of neighbors (not in Π) that have higher and lower σ values. After the scan, we determine all the equivalence classes of neighbors that were found to belong to the same plateau. If all the labels in a given class had only neighbors with lower σ values, the corresponding plateau is a top; and similarly for bottoms.

We can also define the *genus* of σ as the number of its tops minus the number of its bottoms (excluding the border B of Σ). Evidently this too can be computed in a single pass, by counting both the tops and the bottoms. On the other hand, it is not clear whether, as in the nonfuzzy case, the genus can be computed by taking a linear combination of local property values summed over Σ.

8. Concluding Remarks

This paper has developed a collection of properties of "connectedness" and "surroundedness" with respect to fuzzy subsets of an array of lattice points. These results generalize some of the standard results about ordinary subsets, which makes them interesting from the standpoint of fuzzy set theory. At the same time, they should also be of some practical interest in connection with digital picture segmentation, for reasons that we now indicate.

Let f be a digital picture defined on the array Σ. If we normalize the grayscale of f to the interval [0, 1], then f defines a fuzzy subset σ_f of Σ, where the membership of P in σ_f is just $f(P)$. If f contains dark objects on a light background, or vice versa, we can attempt to segment it by thresholding, so that the objects become (say) connected components of above-threshold points. On the other hand, if we want to avoid commitment to a particular threshold, we can still talk about the objects in terms of peaks in σ_f. Note that for any top Π, there exists a threshold (namely, $\sigma_f(\Pi)$) which yields exactly Π as connected component of above-threshold points. Moreover, P is in C_π iff thresholding at $\sigma_f(P)$ puts P into the same connected component as Π. Thus our theory of fuzzy components can be regarded as a generalized theory of "thresholdable connected objects" in digital pictures that does not require choosing a specific threshold.

If the objects in f have smooth profiles, so that each object contains only one top, we can count objects by simply counting tops, as described in Section 7. If f is noisy, there will be many "local tops" that do not correspond to significant objects; but such tops would presumably be "dominated by" other tops (e.g., we might say that Π dominates Π' if A_π surrounds $A_{\pi'}$; see Theorem 6.2), or would be small and could be discarded on grounds of size.

The foregoing remarks indicate how the ideas in this paper should be useful in developing methods of defining and counting objects in unsegmented digital pictures. A top Π can be regarded as the "core" of an object, and the A, B, C sets associated with Π can be regarded as "belonging to" that object in various senses. In this paper we have established some interesting properties of these sets which should be conceptually helpful in working with them.

Acknowledgments

The support of the National Science Foundation under Grant MCS-76-23763 is gratefully acknowledged, as is the help of Mrs. Shelly Rowe in preparing this paper. The author also wishes to thank Dr. P. V. Sankar for many helpful discussions.

Received: October 28, 1977; revised: April 21, 1978

References

Rosenfeld, A. (1975), Fuzzy graphs, *in* "Fuzzy Sets and Their Applications to Cognitive and Decision Processes" (L. A. Zadeh *et al.*, Eds.), pp. 75–95, Academic Press, New York.

Rosenfeld, A., and Kak, A. C. (1976), "Digital Picture Processing," Academic Press, New York.

Zadeh, L. A. (1965), Fuzzy sets, *Inform. Contr.* **8**, 338.

The fuzzy geometry of image subsets

Azriel ROSENFELD
Center for Automation Research, University of Maryland, College Park, MD 20742, USA

Received 4 May 1984

Abstract: In pattern recognition we often want to measure geometric properties of regions in an image, but these regions are not always 'crisply' defined; it is sometimes more appropriate to regard them as fuzzy subsets of the image. Many of the basic geometric properties of and relationships among regions can be generalized to fuzzy sets; these include connectedness, adjacency and surroundedness, starshapedness and convexity, area and perimeter, extent and diameter. This paper summarizes past work on such fuzzy geometric concepts, and also includes some new results.

Key words: Fuzzy geometry, adjacency, segmentation.

1. Introduction

The standard approach to image analysis and recognition begins by segmenting the image into regions and computing various properties of and relationships among these regions. However, the regions are not always 'crisply' defined; it is sometimes more appropriate to regard them as fuzzy subsets of the image [1]. For example, when we segment an image by classifying its pixels, we may want to estimate their probabilities of belonging to the classes but not commit ourselves to the final classification step.

It is not always obvious how to measure geometrical properties of fuzzy sets, but definitions have been given and basic properties established for a variety of such properties and relationships, including connectedness and surroundedness [2,3], convexity [4–6], area, perimeter and compactness [7], extent and diameter [8]. This paper summarizes this work, and also includes some new material on fuzzy adjacency, starshapedness, and elongatedness. It also discusses geometrical operations on fuzzy sets, including shrinking and expanding [9,10], thinning [11,12], splitting and merging. Methods of representing fuzzy image subsets are also briefly discussed.

Now that most of the standard geometric properties of and relations among regions in images have been generalized to the fuzzy case, it becomes possible to use these definitions to construct image descriptions without the need to commit oneself to a specific segmentation of the image. By matching the resulting descriptions to models, one can then determine how the segmentation might be improved.

Of course, fuzzy subsets are more cumbersome to represent, and their properties are somewhat more expensive to compute. But as computer memory and computing power continue to become cheaper, the fuzzy approach to image description may begin to deserve more serious consideration.

The support of the National Science Foundation under Grant MCS-82-18408 is gratefully acknowledged, as is the help of Janet Salzman in preparing this paper.

2. Fuzzy subsets [2]

A *fuzzy subset* of a set S is a mapping μ from S

Reprinted with permission from *Pattern Recognition Letters*, vol. 2, pp. 311–317, September 1984.

into [0,1]. For any $P \in S$, $\mu(P)$ is called the *degree of membership* of P in μ. A crisp (i.e., ordinary, nonfuzzy) subset of S can be regarded as a special case of a fuzzy subset in which the mapping μ is into $\{0,1\}$; in fact, such a μ is the characteristic function of a subset, namely $\{P \in S | \mu(P) = 1\}$.

The standard set-theoretic relations and operations have natural generalizations to fuzzy subsets. We say that $\mu \subseteq \nu$ if $\mu(P) \leq \nu(P)$ for all $P \in S$; evidently this reduces to the ordinary definition of $\subseteq$ when μ and ν are crisp. We define *union, intersection, difference,* and *complement* by

$$(\mu \cup \nu)(P) \equiv \max[\mu(P), \nu(P)],$$

$$(\mu \cap \nu)(P) \equiv \min[\mu(P), \nu(P)],$$

$$(\mu - \nu)(P) \equiv \min[\mu(P) - \nu(P), 0],$$

$$\bar{\mu}(P) \equiv 1 - \mu(P),$$

for all $P \in S$; again, these reduce to the ordinary definitions when μ and ν are crisp, and the usual laws of set algebra still hold for them. The 'empty' fuzzy set is the constant function $\mu \equiv 0$, i.e., it is the same as the crisp empty set. We say that μ and ν are *disjoint* if $\mu \cap \nu \equiv 0$.

The *level sets* of μ are the sets

$$\mu_t \equiv \{P \in S | \mu(P) \geq t\},$$

where $0 \leq t \leq 1$.

From now on we will assume that S is the Euclidean plane, and that μ has bounded support, i.e., $\mu = 0$ outside a bounded region. Some of the concepts that we will discuss (such as those defined in this section) are defined for arbitrary fuzzy sets; others are defined only for fuzzy sets that satisfy certain analytical properties (e.g., integrability); still others will be defined only for 'piecewise constant' fuzzy sets (having constant value on each of a finite set of bounded regions that meet pairwise along rectifiable arcs). *Digital* fuzzy sets are a special case of this last class, where the regions are unit squares.

3. Connectedness and surroundedness [2,3]

Let $P, Q \in S$ and let μ be a fuzzy subset of S. By the *degree of connectedness* of P and Q with respect to μ we mean

$$C_\mu(P, Q) \equiv \max_{\varrho_{PQ}} \left[\min_{R \in \varrho_{PQ}} \mu(R) \right],$$

where the max is taken over all paths ϱ_{PQ} from P to Q, and the min is taken over all points R on the path. We say that P, Q are *connected* in μ if

$$C_\mu(P, Q) \geq \min[\mu(P), \mu(Q)],$$

and we say that μ is connected if any pair of points P, Q is connected in μ. Readily, if μ is crisp, these are the same as the standard definitions. Note that if $\mu(P) = 0$, P is trivially 'connected in μ' to *any* Q; the definition is a restriction only for points whose degrees of membership in μ are nonzero.

Proposition 3.1. *μ is connected (in the fuzzy sense) iff its level sets are all connected (in the ordinary sense).* □

'Connected in μ' is reflexive and symmetric, but not necessarily transitive, so it does not define a partition of S into 'connected components'. However, we can define a looser notion of 'component' by observing that if U, V are 'plateaus' (= connected level sets of μ whose values are local maxima), no point in U can be connected in μ to any point of V and vice versa; but every point is connected in μ to a point in some plateau. It follows that P and Q are connected in μ iff they are connected to points in the same plateau; and μ is connected iff it has a unique plateau. Plateaus in $1-\mu$ can be regarded, analogously, as defining 'holes' in μ. (As in the crisp case, we exclude the unbounded 'hole' that surrounds the region in which $\mu \neq 0$.) For a discussion of genus in the fuzzy (digital) case, see [3]; it is defined in terms of the differences in values between the adjacent level sets of μ, and can be computed by summing a set of local differences.

Let μ, ν, π be fuzzy subsets of S. We say that π *separates* μ from ν if for all points P, R in S and all paths ϱ from P to R, there exists a point $Q \in \varrho$ such that

$$\pi(Q) \geq \min[\mu(P), \nu(R)].$$

In particular, we say that ν *surrounds* μ if it

separates μ from the unbounded region O on which $\mu=0$. In other words, ν surrounds μ iff for all $P\in S$ and all $R\in O$, and any path ϱ from P to R, there exists $Q\in\varrho$ such that $\nu(Q)\geq\mu(P)$. Readily, these reduce to the standard definitions if μ, ν, and π are crisp. 'Surrounds' is reflexive and transitive, and also has a 'weak antisymmetry' property: If μ and ν surround each other, their $\cap$ surrounds both of them (which is impossible if they are nonempty and disjoint).

Proposition 3.2. *ν surrounds μ iff ν_t surrounds μ_t, for all t.* □

Some surroundedness properties of components are derived in [2].

4. Adjacency

In this section we define the *degree of adjacency* of two piecewise constant fuzzy sets. Our definition is a generalization of the 'degree of adjacency' of two disjoint crisp sets as defined by the length of their common border.

Let μ, ν be piecewise constant fuzzy subsets of S. Then we can partition S into a finite number of bounded regions B_i, meeting pairwise along rectifiable arcs, on each of which both μ and ν are constant, say having values μ_i, ν_i. Let μ and ν be disjoint; then on each B_i either $\mu=0$ or $\nu=0$. Let A_{ijk} be the kth arc along which B_i and B_j meet, and let its length be $|A_{ijk}|$. Then we define the degree of adjacency of μ and ν as

$$A(\mu,\nu)\equiv\sum_{\substack{i,j,k\\ i\neq j}}\mu_i\nu_j|A_{ijk}|.$$

Note that for any pair (i,j), if $\mu_i\nu_j\neq 0$ then $\mu_j=\nu_i=0$, so that (i,j) and (j,i) cannot both contribute to the sum. Evidently, if μ and ν are crisp, $A(\mu,\nu)$ is just the total length of their common border. In the fuzzy case, we weight each border arc length by the product $\mu_i\nu_j$; this quantity is 1 only when μ_i and ν_j are both 1 ('full' adjacency), and it is small when either of them is small (e.g., if ν is only weakly present on its side of the border, $\mu\nu$ is small even if μ is strongly present on its side).

Requiring perfect disjointness in defining $A(\mu,\nu)$ is rather restrictive; it would be desirable to extend the definition to μ, ν arbitrary. In the crisp case, if μ and ν overlap slightly, we might define their degree of adjacency as $\frac{1}{2}[A(\mu-\nu,\nu)+A(\mu,\nu-\mu)]$, i.e., the average of the common border lengths for the pairs of disjoint sets $(\mu-\nu,\nu)$ and $(\mu,\nu-\mu)$. We can use this definition in the fuzzy case too. There does not seem to be any natural way of defining $A(\mu,\nu)$ for nondisjoint sets so as to allow their area of overlap to contribute to their degree of adjacency; such a definition would be a mixture of area-based and arc-length-based terms, and so would be dimensionally ill-formed. It would also be of interest to extend the definition so that close approaches of μ and ν contribute something to their degree of adjacency, e.g., using their area of overlap when they are expanded, inversely weighted by the amount of expansion (on expansion of fuzzy sets see Section 8 below).

5. Convexity [4–6] and starshapedness

A fuzzy subset μ of S is called *convex* if for all $P,Q\in S$ and all R on the line segment $\overline{PQ}$ we have

$$\mu(R)\geq\min[\mu(P),\mu(Q)].$$

Evidently, if μ is crisp, this reduces to the standard definition.

Proposition 5.1. *μ is convex iff its level sets are all convex.* □

Proposition 5.2. *Any $\cap$ of convex μ's is convex.* □

Proposition 5.3. *If μ is convex, it is connected and has no holes.* □

The *convex hull* $\hat{\mu}$ of μ is the $\cap$ of all convex fuzzy sets $\supseteq\mu$ (hence it is the smallest such, in the sense of $\subseteq$, by Proposition 5.2). The *convex deficiency* of μ is the area of $\hat{\mu}-\mu$ (where area is defined by integration; see Section 6). If we normalize the convex deficiency, e.g., $\int(\hat{\mu}-\mu)/\int\hat{\mu}$, we can regard the result as a measure of the degree of concavity of μ.

If we define the *cross-section* of μ by a line l as the restriction of μ to l, then it is easily seen that μ is convex iff all its cross-sections are convex. (Thus convexity is closely related to the concept of convexity as usually defined for real functions.) We can also define the *projection* of μ on l as the function that maps each point P of l into the sup of the values of μ along the line perpendicular to l at P. It can be shown [6] that if μ is convex, so are all its projections, but the converse is not true.

More generally, we call μ *starshaped from P* if its cross-sections by lines through P are all convex. This too reduces to the standard definition if μ is crisp. Evidently, μ is convex iff it is starshaped from every P; μ is starshaped from P iff its level sets are all starshaped from P; and any $\cap$ of μ's that are starshaped from P is starshaped from P. It is easily seen that if μ is starshaped from any point P, it can have no holes; and if μ is starshaped from any point P that belongs to a plateau of μ, it can have no other plateaus, and so is connected. (Note that in this last case, every point of this plateau must be 'visible' from P.) All of these observations are generalizations of properties of crisp starshaped sets.

6. Area, perimeter, and compactness [7]

The *area* of μ is defined as $a(\mu) \equiv \int \mu$, where the integral is taken over the plane (or equivalently, over any region outside which $\mu = 0$). Evidently this generalizes the crisp definition. Note that if μ is piecewise constant, $a(\mu)$ is the weighted sum of the areas of the regions on which μ has constant values, weighted by these values.

If μ is piecewise constant, we define the *perimeter* of μ as

$$p(\mu) \equiv \sum_{\substack{i,j,k \\ i<j}} |\mu_i - \mu_j||A_{ijk}|;$$

this is just the weighted sum of the lengths of the arcs A_{ijk} along which the regions on which μ has constant value meet, weighted by the absolute differences of these values. (A definition of $p(\mu)$ for a more general class of μ's is given in [7]; it is shown there that for a 'smooth' μ we have $p(\mu) = \int |\nabla \mu|$, where $\nabla \mu$ is the gradient of μ.) Evidently, this too generalizes the crisp definition.

If μ is crisp, its perimeter is the same as its degree of adjacency to its complement. This property does not generalize to fuzzy μ's; in fact, if we define degree of adjacency only for disjoint fuzzy subsets, μ cannot be disjoint from its complement $1-\mu$ (i.e., we cannot have $\min(\mu(P), 1-\mu(P)) = 0$ for all P) unless μ is crisp.

If μ is convex and piecewise constant, its level sets are a nest of convex sets bounded by simple closed curves; thus its perimeter is just the weighted sum of the outer perimeters of its level sets (for levels >0), weighted by the drops in membership value from each level set to the one surrounding it.

Proposition 6.1. *Let μ, ν be piecewise constant and convex, and let $\mu \subseteq \nu$; then $p(\mu) \le p(\nu)$.* □

Note that for arbitrary fuzzy sets, $\mu \subseteq \nu$ implies $a(\mu) \le a(\nu)$.

We can define the 'compactness' of μ as $a(\mu)/p^2(\mu)$. For crisp sets, this is largest for a disk, where it is equal to $1/4\pi$; this is the well-known 'isoperimetric inequality'. In the fuzzy case, however, the situation is more complicated. For example, let μ be a 'fuzzy disk' in which the value of μ depends only on the distance from some point (which we take as the origin), i.e., $\mu(r, \theta)$ does not depend on θ. Then it can be shown [7] that $a(\mu)/p^2(\mu) \ge 1/4\pi$; in other words, of all possible fuzzy disks, the compactness is *smallest* for a crisp disk.

7. Extent and diameter [8]

The *height* of μ is defined as the integral of its projection on a vertical line, i.e.,

$$h(\mu) \equiv \int \left[\max_x \mu(x, y) \right] \mathrm{d}y,$$

and similarly the *width* of μ is

$$w(\mu) \equiv \int \left[\max_y \mu(x, y) \right] \mathrm{d}x.$$

It can be easily seen that $a(\mu^2) \le h(\mu) w(\mu)$. The *extrinsic diameter* of μ is defined as the sup of the integrals of its projections, i.e.,

$$e(\mu) \equiv \max_u \int \left[\max_v \mu(u, v) \right] du,$$

where u and v are any pair of orthogonal directions. Evidently we have $a(\mu^2) \leq e^2(\mu)$. These definitions and observations are natural generalizations of the corresponding crisp concepts (note that if μ is crisp, $\mu^2 = \mu$).

If μ is connected, we define the *intrinsic diameter* of μ as

$$i(\mu) \equiv \max_{P,Q} \left[\min_{\varrho_{PQ}} \int_{\varrho_{PQ}} \mu \right],$$

where the max is taken over all pairs of points P, Q in the plane, and the min is taken over all paths ϱ_{PQ} between P and Q such that, for any point R on ϱ_{PQ}, we have

$$\mu(R) \geq \min[\mu(P), \mu(Q)].$$

Note that such paths always exist, since μ is connected. If μ is crisp, and P or Q is not in μ, ϱ_{PQ} can be any path from P to Q, so that such a pair (P, Q) will not yield the max. On the other hand, if P, Q are both in μ, ϱ_{PQ} must lie entirely in μ, so that $\int_{\varrho_{PQ}} \mu = |\varrho_{PQ}|$, the length of ϱ_{PQ}; thus when μ is crisp, $i(\mu)$ reduces to the standard definition of intrinsic diameter (= the greatest possible distance between two points in μ, where only paths lying in μ are allowed).

If μ is crisp, it is easily shown that $e(\mu) \leq i(\mu)$, and if μ is also convex, $e(\mu) = i(\mu)$. In the fuzzy case, we can have $e(\mu) > i(\mu)$ (even if μ is convex, and even if it is a fuzzy disk); but we can prove:

Proposition 7.1. *If μ is convex, then $e(\mu) \geq i(\mu)$.* □

Proposition 7.2. *If μ is convex, then $i(\mu) \leq \frac{1}{2}p(\mu)$.* □

This last result (that the intrinsic diameter of a set is at most half the perimeter) is true in general for crisp sets, but for fuzzy sets it holds only in the convex case.

8. Shrinking and expanding, medial axes, elongatedness, and thinning

Many useful operations can be performed on a crisp image subset by shrinking or expanding it – i.e., deleting points from μ if they are within a given distance δ of the complement $\bar{\mu}$, or adding points to μ if they are within δ of μ. The fuzzy generalizations of shrinking and expanding are local min and local max operations – i.e., we replace $\mu(x, y)$ by the min (or max) of all μ's within distance δ of (x, y). Readily, in the crisp case these operations are the same as shrinking and expanding, respectively. We shall denote the results of these operations by $\mu_{-\delta}$ and μ_δ. For a discussion of these operations and some of their properties see [9]. In particular, we have for all integers a, b, $(\mu_a)_b = (\mu_b)_a = \mu_{a+b}$ if a and b both have the same sign, and $(\mu_{-a})_b \leq \mu_{b-a} \leq (\mu_b)_{-a}$ if a and b are positive, where $\mu_0 \equiv \mu$.

The 'medial axis' of a crisp subset μ of a digital picture, using an integer-valued δ, can be defined as

$$\bigcup_{\delta \geq 0} (\mu_{-\delta} - (\mu_{-\delta-1})_1);$$

this is the set of pixels of all $\mu_{-\delta}$ that disappear when $\mu_{-\delta}$ is shrunk by one unit $(\mu_{-\delta-1} = (\mu_{-\delta})_{-1})$ and do not reappear when it is reexpanded by one unit. For a fuzzy μ we can use exactly the same definition, where $\cup$ now denotes the sup and we use fuzzy set difference (which in this case is the same as subtraction, since $(\mu_{-\delta-1})_1 \leq \mu_\delta$). On this definition and its properties see [10]. An alternative method of defining the medial axis [11] is as the set of local maxima of the 'weighted distance' to the set of points B where $\mu = 0$ (i.e.,

$$d_\mu(P, B) \equiv \min_\varrho \int_\varrho \mu,$$

where the min is taken over all paths ϱ from P to a point of B); this too is a generalization of the crisp definition of the medial axis, but it seems less natural, since it gives the set B (on which $\mu = 0$) a very special role.

The *thickness* $t(\mu)$ of a crisp set μ can be defined as twice the smallest δ such that $\mu_{-\delta} = \emptyset$. The *elongatedness* of μ can then be defined as $\delta(\mu) \equiv a(\mu)/t^2(\mu)$. These concepts have no simple generalizations to the fuzzy case, but we can give a closely related definition of fuzzy elongatedness:

$$\bar{e}(\mu) = \max_{\delta > 0} \frac{a(\mu - \mu_{-\delta})}{(2\delta)^2}.$$

Here, as δ increases, $\mu_{-\delta}$ gets smaller, so $\mu-\mu_{\delta}$ gets larger; hence $a(\mu-\mu_{-\delta})$ reaches its max $(=a(\mu))$ when $\mu_{-\delta}\equiv 0$. Therefore the ratio $a(\mu-\mu_{-\delta})/(2\delta)^2$ cannot have its max for δ larger than this (the numerator remains constant while the denominator keeps increasing); but it may have its max for some smaller δ, even in the crisp case, if a large amount of μ disappears under a small amount of shrinking. (For example, this would be true if μ consisted of a large network of very thin lines, comprising most of its area, together with a small thicker piece.) It seems that our definition of $\bar{e}$ is more reasonable than the 'classical' definition.

We can also define other types of fuzzy shrinking operations that preserve fuzzy connectedness. For crisp subsets of a digital picture, such operations are defined by allowing the deletion of a pixel P from μ only if it has a neighbor in $\bar{\mu}$ and if its deletion does not change the connectedness of the pixels of μ in P's neighborhood. Analogously, in the fuzzy case, we can allow $\mu(P)$ to be replaced by the min of the μ's of its neighbors only if this does not reduce the degree of connectedness of these neighbors (considering only paths that lie in the neighborhood). A fuzzy thinning operation of this type was introduced in [12].

9. Gray-level-dependent properties; splitting and merging

The standard types of gray-level-dependent properties of image subsets can all be naturally extended to fuzzy subsets μ by simply weighting each pixel by its degree of membership in μ. For example, the moments of the image $f(x, y)$ over a fuzzy subset $\mu(x, y)$ are given by

$$\iint x^i y^j \mu f \,\mathrm{d}x\,\mathrm{d}y.$$

If we characterize textures by the values of a set of local properties $g(x, y)$ computed at each pixel and averaged over the given region, then for a fuzzy subset we need only compute

$$\iint \mu g \,\mathrm{d}x\,\mathrm{d}y / \iint \mu \,\mathrm{d}x\,\mathrm{d}y.$$

Thus many types of gray-level-dependent properties, as well as geometric properties, can be easily computed for fuzzy subsets.

Region splitting and merging techniques are often used to improve a given segmentation of an image. The criteria used for splitting and merging may depend on various region properties – e.g., we attempt to achieve greater textural homogeneity or greater shape compactness. We have shown in this paper how many of these properties can be computed for fuzzy subsets.

For fuzzy subsets, 'merging' μ' and μ'' means combining their membership functions into a new μ defined, e.g., by $\max(\mu'', \mu')$ or by $\mu'+\mu''-\mu'\mu''$. (The latter formula is appropriate if μ' and μ'' represented probabilities of membership in two classes C' and C'', since the probability of membership in $C' \cup C''$ is then $1-(1-\mu')(1-\mu'')=\mu'+\mu''-\mu'\mu''$.) Splitting is more complicated; the way we want to divide μ into μ' and μ'' will generally vary from place to place in the image, just as in the nonfuzzy case.

10. Representation of fuzzy subsets

An image subset μ can be represented by its characteristic function, i.e., by a two-valued 'overlay' image that has 1's at the points of μ and 0's elsewhere. More commonly, however, subsets are represented by various types of codes that are more compact than the overlay μ if the subset is geometrically simple. Fuzzy image subsets are generally much less compact than crisp subsets; in the fuzzy case, μ is real-valued rather than two-valued. However, compact encoding is possible here too, particularly if we are willing to accept approximations to μ. In the following paragraphs we briefly review some of the standard methods of representing image subsets and indicate how they can be extended to the fuzzy case. We assume in what follows that μ is piecewise constant (e.g., digital).

Any image subset is the union of the maximal blocks (e.g., upright squares) that are contained in it; thus a subset is determined by specifying the set of positions and sizes of these blocks. (The medial axis, defined in Section 8, is just the set of centers of the maximal blocks, if we define it using the 'chessboard' distance measure $\delta((u, v), (x, y)) \equiv |u-x|+|v-y|$.) We can determine a fuzzy subset μ exactly by representing each of its level sets μ_t in this way. Alternatively, we can approximate μ as a superposition of maximal blocks on each of which μ is approximately constant (e.g., its variance is below some threshold). A method of image approximation using this approach is described in [13].

Another way of using maximal blocks to represent subsets is to require the blocks to have standard sizes and positions; this allows the set of blocks to be specified very compactly. For example, if we require the sizes and positions to be powers of 2, we obtain the 'quadtree' representation, which is constructed as follows: Start with the entire image as an initial block, represented by the root node of the tree. If a block does not have constant value, split it into quadrants, and give its tree node four children; if a block has constant value, its node is a leaf of the tree. This method can be used to exactly represent (the level sets of) a fuzzy set μ. Alternatively, we can approximate μ by loosening the splitting criterion, so that a block is not split if its value is approximately constant; this is just the method of image segmentation by splitting described by Pavlidis [14].

Run length coding can be regarded as a maximal block representation in which the 'blocks' are $1 \times k$ rectangles; it too can be used to represent (the level sets of) μ exactly, or we can generalize it to allow runs of approximately constant value. Border coding (e.g., chain coding) can be used to exactly represent the level sets of μ; or more generally, we can approximate their borders, e.g., polygonally. In general, we can simplify μ by coarsely quantizing its values before encoding it.

11. Concluding remarks

When we segment an image, we can avoid committing ourselves to a specific segmentation by allowing the segments to be fuzzy subsets of the image. Fuzzy subsets are more complex to specify than crisp subsets, but it may be possible (and acceptable) to approximate them relatively compactly. We have seen in this paper that many (though not all) of the standard geometrical and gray-level-dependent properties of crisp subsets can be generalized to fuzzy subsets, and in many cases the cost of computing them is of the same order of magnitude. More important, the fuzzy properties are approximations of the crisp properties if the fuzzy set is approximately crisp; thus they allow an image to be meaningfully described in terms of its parts and relationships without the need to commit oneself to a crisp segmentation. It is hoped that this paper will stimulate increased interest in the fuzzy approach to image description.

References

[1] J.M.S. Prewitt. Object enhancement and extraction. In: B.S. Lipkin and A. Rosenfeld, Eds., *Picture Processing and Psychopictorics*. Academic Press, New York, 1970, p. 121.

[2] A. Rosenfeld. Fuzzy digital topology. *Inform. Control* 40 (1979), 76–87.

[3] A. Rosenfeld. On connectivity properties of grayscale pictures. *Pattern Recognition* 16 (1983), 47–50.

[4] L. Zadeh. Fuzzy sets. *Inform. Control* 8 (1965), 338–353.

[5] R. Lowen. Convex fuzzy sets. *Fuzzy Sets and Systems* 3 (1980), 291–310.

[6] L. Janos and A. Rosenfeld. Some results on fuzzy (digital) convexity. *Pattern Recognition* 15 (1982), 379–382.

[7] A. Rosenfeld and S. Haber. The perimeter of a fuzzy set. University of Maryland Center for Automation Research TR-8 (Computer Science TR-1286), May 1983.

[8] A. Rosenfeld. The diameter of a fuzzy set. *Fuzzy Sets and Systems* 13 (1984), 241–246.

[9] Y. Nakagawa and A. Rosenfeld. A note on local min and max operations on digital pictures, *IEEE Trans. Systems Man Cybernet.* 8 (1978), 632–635.

[10] S. Peleg and A. Rosenfeld. A min-max medial axis transformation. *IEEE Trans. Pattern. Anal. Mach. Intell.* 3 (1981), 208–210.

[11] G. Levi and U. Montanari. A grey-weighted skeleton. *Inform. Control* 17 (1970), 62–91.

[12] C.R. Dyer and A. Rosenfeld. Thinning operations on gray-scale pictures. *IEEE Trans. Pattern Anal. Mach. Intell.* 1 (1979) 88–89.

[13] N. Ahuja, L.S. Davis, D.L. Milgram, and A. Rosenfeld. Piecewise approximation of pictures using maximal neighborhoods. *IEEE Trans. Comput.* 27 (1978), 375–379.

[14] T. Pavlidis. *Structural Pattern Recognition*. Springer, New York, 1977.

Thinning Algorithms for Gray-Scale Pictures

CHARLES R. DYER AND AZRIEL ROSENFELD

Abstract—Elongated black objects in black-and-white pictures can be "thinned" to arcs and curves, without changing their connectedness, by (repeatedly) deleting black border points whose deletion does not locally disconnect the black points in their neighborhoods. This technique generalizes to gray-scale pictures if we use a weighted definition of connectedness: two points are "connected" if there is a path joining them on which no point is lighter than either of them. We can then "thin" dark objects by changing each point's gray level to the minimum of its neighbors' gray levels, provided this does not disconnect any pair of points in its neighborhood. Examples illustrating the performance of this technique are given.

Index Terms—Image processing, pattern recognition, thinning, skeletonization.

I. Introduction

Elongated black objects in black-and-white pictures can be "thinned" to arcs and curves, without changing their connectedness, by repeatedly deleting black border points whose deletion does not locally disconnect the black points in their neighborhoods. In order to prevent objects two points wide from vanishing completely, this deletion process should be performed from one side at a time—e.g., first delete north border points that satisfy the conditions, then south, then east, then west, and so on repeatedly. [In any case, the deletion should not be performed from two opposite sides at once, though it may be performed simultaneously from two adjacent sides (e.g., north and east, then south and west, and so on repeatedly), if a somewhat more complicated algorithm is used.] In order to prevent thin arcs from shrinking at their ends or isolated points from vanishing, black points that have fewer than two black neighbors should not be deleted. A number of such thinning algorithms have been described in the literature; see [1] for a review and [2] for a mathematical treatment of the simple algorithm described above. [1]

Thinning algorithms have been used extensively for processing thresholded images of printed or written characters and of nuclear bubble chamber particle tracks, as well as for "skeletonizing" chromosomes. (Detailed references will not be given here; see the review in [1].)

In [3] a generalization of the notion of connectedness to gray-scale pictures was proposed. In this "fuzzy" definition of connectedness, two points are called "connected" if there is a path joining them that contains no point lighter than both of them. Using this definition, we can formulate a gray-scale thinning algorithm in which a point is set equal to the lightest of its neighbors (including itself) if doing so does not disconnect any pair of its neighbors. The details of this algorithm are presented in Section II, and some examples are given and discussed in Section III.

Gray-scale thinning has the obvious advantage that it does not require commitment to a particular threshold; the dark regions in an image can be thinned without ever being explicitly segmented. Thus, the proposed algorithm deserves serious consideration as an alternative to conventional thinning schemes. As we shall see, it yields very acceptable results in a variety of cases (chromosomes, rivers, characters, edges).

No claim is made here that gray-scale thinning yields results superior to those of conventional thinning preceded by thresholding, nor that it is computationally cheaper. Its advantage is primarily a conceptual one: it permits thinning without requiring explicit segmentation. As will be seen in the examples, gray-scale thinning operates on all the dark regions in the image simultaneously, whether they have high or low contrast; the low-contrast regions would be difficult to extract by thresholding.

II. The Gray-Scale Thinning Algorithm

It is not trivial to define an exact analog of the black-and-white thinning algorithm in the gray-scale case. In particular, it is not immediately clear how to generalize the condition that a black point must have at least two black neighbors. Moreover, the requirement that no pair of neighbors be disconnected may be very strong, since it rules out changing the center point (to 1) in cases like

50	50	0
50	50	2
50	1	0

since this disconnects the 2 from the 50's.

The approach that we have adopted here is to define the neighbor count and disconnection conditions in terms of a threshold that is proportional to the gray level range in the neighborhood. Specifically, given the neighborhood

abc
def
ghi

let us define the gray level range in this neighborhood as

$$R = \max(b, d, e, f, h) - \min(b, d, e, f, h) + 1$$

and let R' be some fixed fraction of this range ($0 \leqslant R' \leqslant R$). We can then formulate two necessary conditions for changing the center point e of the neighborhood as follows.

1) At least two of b, d, f, h have values $\geqslant e - R'$ (this corresponds to the requirement that a black point e must have at least two black neighbors.)

2) For each pair of b, d, f, h, let m be the pair's minimum; then either $e < m - R'$, or there is a path joining the pair within the neighborhood, but not involving e (e.g., for the pair b, f, the path must contain either c or a, d, g, h, i) such that

Manuscript received December 21, 1977; revised February 21, 1978. This work was supported by the U.S. Army Night Vision Laboratory under Contract DAAG53-76C-0138 (ARPA Order 3206).

The authors are with the Computer Science Center, University of Maryland, College Park, MD 20742.

[1] There are two versions of these algorithms, depending on whether or not we regard diagonally adjacent points as neighbors. In this correspondence we regard only horizontal and vertical points as neighbors, but it is straightforward to define a version of our technique that allows diagonal neighbors as well. We assume here that dark points have higher values than light points.

Reprinted from *IEEE Trans. Pattern Anal. Machine Intell.*, vol. PAMI-1, no. 1, pp. 88–89, January 1979.

for every point p on the path we have $p \geqslant m - R'$. (This corresponds to the requirement that deleting e must not disconnect any pair of its black neighbors. In our case, "deletion" means setting e equal to the minimum of itself and its neighbors. If $e < m - R' < m$, then the pair of neighbors whose minimum is m has no effect on e, since e is smaller than their minimum. Otherwise, we must insure that these neighbors are still connected; we do this by requiring that there be a path joining them whose lightest point $\geqslant m - R'$. Note that this allows us to change the center point to 1 in the example

50	50	0
50	50	2
50	1	0

provided that R' is at least 4 percent of R, since in this case we have $R = 51$, $R' \geqslant 2$, and there is still a path from 2 to the 50's whose points satisfy $p \geqslant 2 - 2 = 0$.)

In order to apply this algorithm from one or two sides at a time (north, etc.), we would define e to be a north border point if $b < e - R'$, and so on. A simpler approach is to simply replace e by the minimum of itself and its north neighbor b, without regard to their relative values; if $b < e - R'$, this will change e significantly, but otherwise it will not. (By the same reasoning, we need never check whether e is a "border point" at all; if it is an "interior point," we can replace it by the minimum of its neighbors' values without changing it significantly.) We have chosen to apply the algorithm from two sides at a time; at alternate steps we replace e by the minimum of b, e, f or by the minimum of d, e, h, provided conditions 1) and 2) are satisfied. All points that satisfy these conditions are replaced simultaneously; the algorithm is "parallel." R' was taken to be 10 percent of R in our experiments, but the results are not sensitive to this choice.

III. Examples and Discussion

Fig. 1 shows the results of applying seven iterations of this algorithm to a picture of some chromosomes. (Each iteration consists of the two steps described in Section II, involving the minimum of b, e, f and of d, e, h, respectively.) We see that each chromosome is reduced to a thin, 4-connected "skeleton." Fig. 2 shows three iterations applied to pictures of characters and terrain. Fig. 3 shows an application of the algorithm to the output of an edge detector (based on differences of averages); the thick, fuzzy streaks of edge values are reduced to thin curves.

In these examples, connectedness appears to be preserved, but this is not absolutely guaranteed, since we have applied the algorithm from two sides at once rather than from one side at a time (see [2]). In fact our algorithm allows the connectedness between dark points to be weakened, e.g., in the case

0	12	0
0	10	0
0	12	0

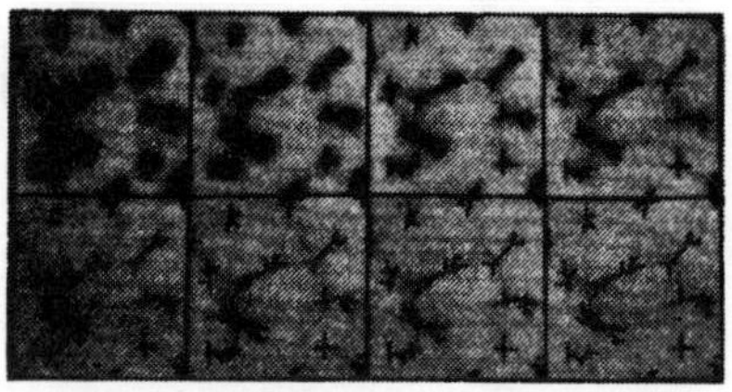

Fig. 1. Successive thinning steps for a picture of some chromosomes.

Fig. 2. Same for a portion of a Landsat picture showing fields and rivers, and for a picture of some printed characters.

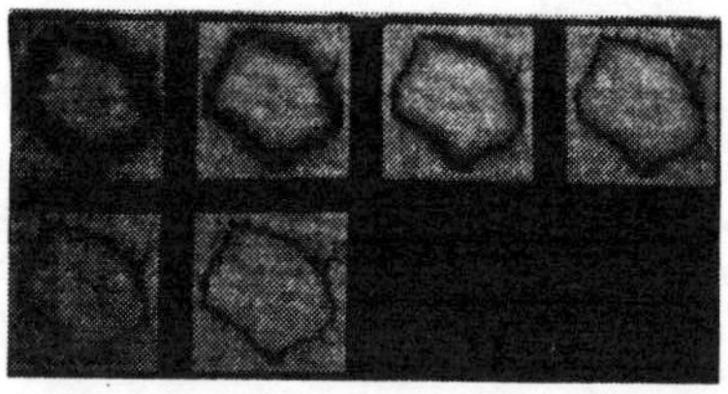

Fig. 3. Same for a picture of blurred edge detector output.

we can change the center 10 to 0. A more sophisticated version of the algorithm would define the degree of connectedness of two points as the gray level of the lightest point on the darkest path joining them, and would change a point only if doing so did not weaken the connectedness of any pair of its neighbors. In any event, the algorithm seems to be useful in a variety of cases, since it provides a thinning procedure that does not require prior thresholding, thus making it possible to avoid premature commitment to a threshold.

Acknowledgment

The authors wish to thank Mrs. S. Rowe for her assistance.

References

[1] R. Stefanelli and A. Rosenfeld, "Some parallel thinning algorithms for digital pictures," *J. Assoc. Comput. Mach.*, pp. 255-264, 1971.

[2] A. Rosenfeld, "A characterization of parallel thinning algorithms," *Inform. Contr.*, vol. 29, pp. 286-291, 1975.

[3] —, "Fuzzy digital topology," Computer Science Tech. Rep. 573, University of Maryland, College Park, MD, Sept. 1977.

Image Enhancement Using Smoothing with Fuzzy Sets

SANKAR K. PAL AND ROBERT A. KING

Abstract—**A model for grey-tone image enhancement using the concept of fuzzy sets is suggested. It involves primary enhancement, smoothing, and then final enhancement. The algorithm for both the primary and final enhancements includes the extraction of fuzzy properties corresponding to pixels and then successive applications of the fuzzy operator "contrast intensifier" on the property plane. The three different smoothing techniques considered in the experiment are defocussing, averaging, and max-min rule over the neighbors of a pixel. The reduction of the "index of fuzziness" and "entropy" for different enhanced outputs (corresponding to different values of fuzzifiers) is demonstrated for an English script input. Enhanced output as obtained by histogram modification technique is also presented for comparison.**

I. Introduction

The theory of fuzzy set [1], [2] provides a suitable algorithm in analyzing complex systems and decision processes when the pattern indeterminacy is due to inherent variability and/or vagueness (fuzziness) rather than randomness. Since a grey tone picture possesses some ambiguity within pixels due to the possible multivalued levels of brightness, it is justified to apply the concept and logic of fuzzy set rather than ordinary set theory to an image processing problem. Keeping this in mind, an image can be considered as an array of fuzzy singletons [1], [2] each with a membership function denoting the degree of having some brightness level.

The methods so far developed for image enhancement may be categorized into two broad classes [3]–[6], namely, frequency domain methods and spatial domain methods. The technique in the first category depends on modifying the Fourier transform of an image, whereas in spatial domain methods the direct manipulation of the pixel is adopted. Some fairly simple and yet powerful processing approaches are seen to be formulated in the spatial domain [3], [4]. It is to be mentioned here that all these techniques are problem oriented. When an image is processed for visual 'interpretation,' it is ultimately up to the viewers to judge its quality for a specific application. The process of evaluation of image quality therefore becomes a subjective one.

In this correspondence we present a model (Fig. 1) consisting of primary and final enhancement for a grey tone image using fuzzy algorithm along with smoothing operations. The procedure involves a primary enhancement of an image by the block E followed by a smoothing through S and a subsequent enhancement by a second use of block E. The fuzzy contrast intensification (INT) operator is taken as a tool for both the primary and final enhancements in the fuzzy property domain. This domain is extracted from the spatial domain using fuzzifiers [7], [8] which play the role of creating different amounts of ambiguity in the

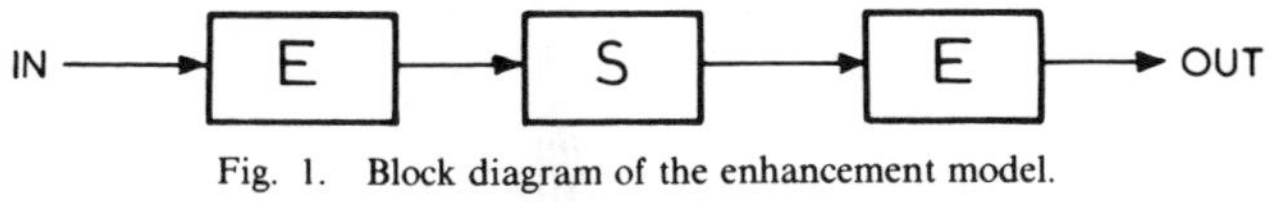

Fig. 1. Block diagram of the enhancement model.

property plane. The function of an image smoother (block S) as introduced after the primary enhancement is to blur the image and the blurred image is then reprocessed by another enhancement block E. The ultimate object of using a second E block is to have further improvement in image quality. The performance of the model for different values of the fuzzifiers is demonstrated on a picture of handwritten English recursive script when the defocussing, averaging, and max-min techniques are used separately in the smoothing algorithm. The results are compared with those obtained using histogram modification technique [4].

The "index of fuzziness" [9], [10] which reflects a kind of quantitative measure of an image quality is measured for each output and is compared with that of "entropy" [11]. The system CDC 6400/6500 was used for numerical analysis.

II. Fuzzy Set and the Concept of Enhancement

A fuzzy set (A) with its finite number of supports $x_1, x_2, \cdots, x_n$ in the inverse of discourse U is defined as

$$A = \{(\mu_A(x_i), \quad x_i)\} \tag{1a}$$

or, in union form,

$$A = \bigcup_i \mu_i/x_i, \quad i = 1, 2, \cdots, n \tag{1b}$$

where the membership function $\mu_A(x_i)$ having positive values in the interval (0, 1) denotes the degree to which an event x_i may be a member of A. This characteristic function can be viewed as a weighting coefficient which reflects the ambiguity (fuzziness) in A. A fuzzy singleton is a fuzzy set which has only one supporting point. If $\mu_A(x_i) = 0.5$, x_i is said to be the crossover point in A.

Similarly, the property p defined on an event x_i is a function $p(x_i)$ which can have values only in the interval (0, 1). A set of these functions which assigns the degree of possessing some property p by the event x_i constitutes what is called a property set [12].

A. Image Definition

With the concept of fuzzy set, an image X of $M \times N$ dimension and L levels can be considered as an array of fuzzy singletons, each with a value of membership function denoting the degree of having brightness relative to some brightness level l, $l = 0, 1, 2, \cdots, L-1$. In the notion of fuzzy set, we may therefore write

$$X = \bigcup_m \bigcup_n p_{mn}/x_{mn}, \qquad m = 1, 2, \cdots, M; \quad n = 1, 2, \cdots, N \tag{2}$$

where $p_{mn}/x_{mn'}$ $(0 \leqslant p_{mn} \leqslant 1)$ represents the grade of possessing some property p_{mn} by the (m, n)th pixel x_{mn}. This fuzzy property p_{mn} may be defined in a number of ways with respect to any brightness level depending on the problems at hand. In our experiment, we have defined (as shown in (6)) it with respect to the maximum level $L-1$.

Manuscript received November 17, 1980; revised March 31, 1981. This paper was supported in part by the Association of Commonwealth Universities in the United Kingdom and the Indian Statistical Institute, Calcutta.

S. K. Pal is with the Department of Electrical Engineering, Imperial College of Science and Technology, Exhibition Road, London, SW7 2BT, England, on leave from the Electronics and Communication Sciences Unit, Indian Statistical Institute, Calcutta 700035, India.

R. A. King is with the Department of Electrical Engineering, Imperial College of Science and Technology, Exhibition Road, London, SW7 2BT, England.

Reprinted from *IEEE Trans. Syst., Man, Cybern.*, vol. SMC-11, no. 7, pp. 494–501, July 1981.

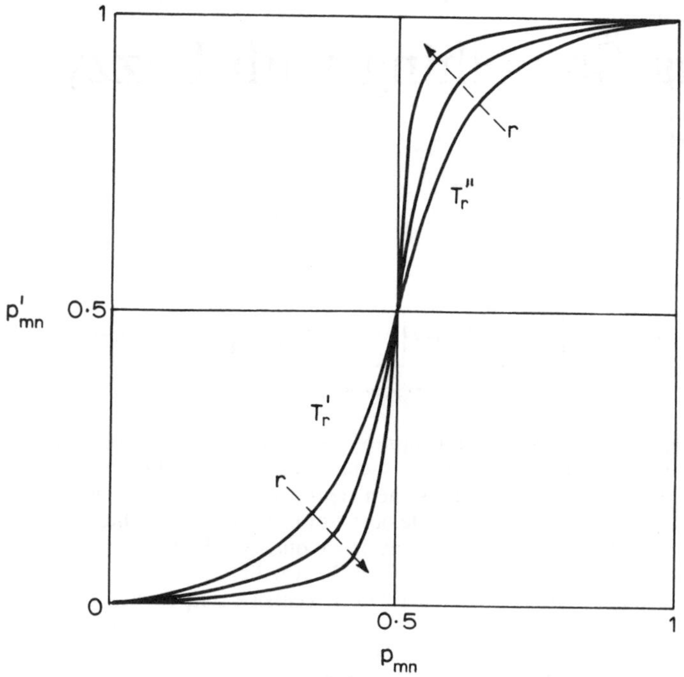

Fig. 2. INT transformation function for contrast enhancement in property plane.

B. Contrast Intensification and Enhancement in Property Plane

The contrast intensification operator (INT) on a fuzzy set A generates another fuzzy set $A' = \mathrm{INT}(A)$, the membership function of which is

$$\mu_{A'}(x) = \mu_{\mathrm{INT}(A)}(x)$$

$$= \begin{cases} 2[\mu_A(x)]^2, & 0 \leq \mu_A(x) \leq 0.5 \quad \text{(3a)} \\ [1 - 2(1 - \mu_A(x))^2], & 0.5 \leq \mu_A(x) \leq 1. \quad \text{(3b)} \end{cases}$$

This operation reduces the fuzziness of a set A by increasing the values of $\mu_A(x)$ which are above 0.5 and decreasing those which are below it. Let us now define operation (3) by a transformation T_1 of the membership function $\mu(x)$.

In general, each p_{mn} in X (2) may be modified to p'_{mn} to enhance the image X in the property domain by a transformation function T_r where

$$p'_{mn} = T_r(p_{mn}) = \begin{cases} T'_r(p_{mn}), & 0 \leq p_{mn} \leq 0.5 \quad \text{(4a)} \\ T''_r(p_{mn}), & 0.5 \leq p_{mn} \leq 1 \quad \text{(4b)} \end{cases}$$

$$r = 1, 2 \cdots.$$

The transformation function T_r is defined as successive applications of T_1 by the recursive relationship

$$T_s(p_{mn}) = T_1\{T_{s-1}(p_{mn})\}, \qquad s = 1, 2, \cdots \tag{5}$$

and $T_1(p_{mn})$ represents the operator INT defined in (3) in our problem.

This is shown graphically in Fig. 2. As r increases, the curve tends to be steeper because of the successive application of INT. In the limiting case, as $r \to \infty$, T_r produces a two-level (binary) image. It is to be noted here that corresponding to a particular operation of T' one can use any of the multiple operations of T'' and vice versa to attain a desired amount of enhancement.

C. Property Plane and Fuzzification

All the operations described above are restricted to the fuzzy property plane. To enter this domain from the spatial x_{mn} plane, we define an expression of form similar to that defined by one of the authors in speech recognition [7], [8]:

$$p_{mn} = G(x_{mn}) = \left[1 + \frac{(x_{\max} - x_{mn})}{F_d}\right]^{-F_e},$$

$$m = 1, 2, \cdots, M; \; n = 1, 2, \cdots, N \tag{6}$$

where $x_{\max}$ denotes the maximum grey level $(L - 1)$ desired, F_e and F_d denote the exponential and denominational fuzzifiers, respectively. These fuzzifiers have the effect of altering ambiguity in the p plane. As will be shown later, the values of these two positive constants are determined by the crossover point (x_c, for which $p_{x_c} = G(x_c) = 0.5$) in the enhancement operation.

Equation (6) shows that $p_{mn} \to 1$ as $(x_{\max} - x_{mn}) \to 0$ and decreases as $(x_{\max} - x_{mn})$ increases. In other words, the fuzzy property p_{mn} as defined here denotes the degree of possessing maximum brightness level $x_{\max}$ by the (m, n)th pixel $x_{mn} \cdot p_{mn} = 1$ denotes light and $p_{mn} = 0$ dark.

It is to be noted from (6) that for $x_{mn} = 0$, p_{mn} has a finite positive value α, say where

$$\alpha = \left(1 + \frac{x_{\max}}{F_d}\right)^{-F_e}. \tag{7}$$

So the p_{mn} plane becomes restricted in the interval $[\alpha, 1]$ instead of $[0, 1]$. After enhancement, the enhanced p'_{mn} plane may contain some regions where $p'_{mn} < \alpha$ due to the transformation T'. The algorithm includes a provision for constraining all the $p'_{mn} < \alpha$ values to α so that the inverse transformation

$$x'_{mn} = G^{-1}(p'_{mn}), \quad \alpha \leq p'_{mn} \leq 1 \tag{8}$$

will allow those corresponding x'_{mn} values to have zero grey level. Of course, one can change α to some other value depending on the contrast or background level desired.

Furthermore, since there are only $L(0, 1, 2, \cdots, L - 1)$ equally spaced allowed levels in an image, each of the transformed x'_{mn} values must be assigned to its closest valid level to result in an enhanced image X'.

D. Selection of F_e and F_d

From the enhancement operation it is noted that we have to select a suitable crossover point x_c from the image plane so that all the $x_{mn} \gtrless x_c$ in spatial domain would possess values $p_{mn} \gtrless 0.5$ in property domain. The successive use of INT operator would then intensify the contrast by increasing the values of $p_{mn} > 0.5$ and decreasing those $p_{mn} < 0.5$.

Suppose we want to put the threshold of enhancement operation between the levels l and $l + 1$ so that after the enhancement operation, all the $x_{mn} \geq (l + 1)/\leq l$ would possess increased/decreased levels. Then we consider,

$$x_c = l + 0.5$$

$$p_{x_c} = 0.5$$

and the value of F_d for a specific F_e can correspondingly be determined from (6). The higher the value of F_e, the greater will be the rate of increase/decrease of p_{mn} values after/before x_c and hence the lower is the value of r to attain a desired amount of enhancement.

For example, if $l = 9$ then $x_c = 9.5$ and with $x_{\max} = 31$, and for $F_e = 1$ and 2, we obtain from (6) that F_d is 21.5 and 52, respectively. The corresponding p_{mn} values corresponding to $x_{mn} = \cdots, 7, 8, 9, 10, 11, 12 \cdots$, are $\cdots$, 0.473, 0.483, 0.494, 0.506, 0.518, 0.531, $\cdots$ and $\cdots$, 0.468, 0.481, 0.494, 0.507, 0.522, 0.536, $\cdots$ for $F_e = 1$ and 2; respectively. The rate of increase/decrease of p_{mn} values after/before the crossover point is seen to be higher for values of $F_e = 2$ than 1. The enhancement of the contrast for a specific value of r would therefore be better for $F_e = 2$.

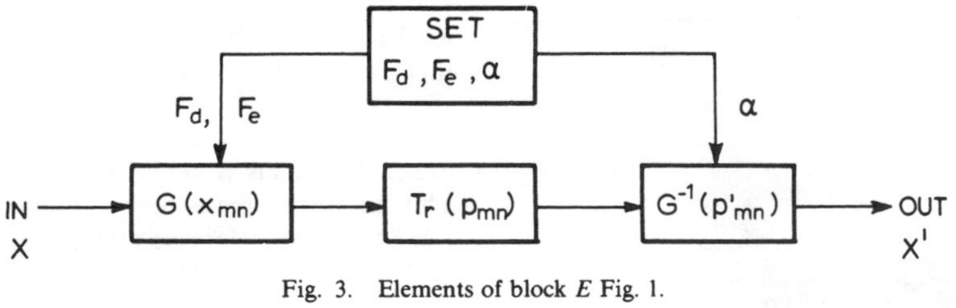

Fig. 3. Elements of block E Fig. 1.

E. Elements of the Enhancement Block 'E'

The elements constituting the primary and final enhancement blocks E (in Fig. 1) are shown in Fig. 3.

The function $G(x_{mn})$ as defined by (6) uses two fuzzifiers F_e and F_d to extract the fuzzy property p_{mn} for the (m, n)th pixel x_{mn} of an $M \times N$ input image array X. The transformation function $T_r(p_{mn})$ serves the role of enhancement in property plane using r successive use of the fuzzy INT operator. This is explained by (3) to (5). The enhanced p' domain after being inversely transformed by $G^{-1}(p'_{mn})$ (8) produces the corresponding enhancement image X' in spatial domain.

III. Index of Fuzziness and Entropy

The index of fuzziness of a set A having n supporting points is defined as [10]

$$\gamma(A) = \frac{2}{n^k} d(A, \tilde{A}) \tag{9}$$

where $d(A, \tilde{A})$ denotes the distance between fuzzy set A and its nearest ordinary set $\tilde{A}$. The set $\tilde{A}$ is such that $\mu_{\tilde{A}}(x_i) = 0$ if $\mu_A(x_i) \leqslant 0.5$ and 1 for $\mu_A(x_i) > 0.5$. The positive constant k appears in order to make $\gamma(A)$ lie between 0 and 1 and its value depends on the type of distance function used. For example, $k = 1$ for a generalized Hamming distance whereas $k = 0.5$ for an Euclidean distance. The corresponding indices of fuzziness are called the linear index of fuzziness $\gamma_l(A)$ and the quadratic index of fuzziness $\gamma_q(A)$. Considering 'd' to be a generalized Hamming distance we have

$$d(A, \tilde{A}) = \sum_i |\mu_A(x_i) - \mu_{\tilde{A}}(x_i)| = \sum_i \mu_{A \cap \bar{A}}(x_i) \tag{10}$$

and

$$\gamma_l(A) = \frac{2}{n} \sum_i \mu_{A \cap \bar{A}}(x_i), \qquad i = 1, 2, \cdots, n \tag{11a}$$

where $A \cap \bar{A}$ is the intersection between fuzzy set A and its complement $\bar{A}$. $\mu_{A \cap \bar{A}}(x_i)$ denotes the grade of membership of x_i to such a fuzzy set $A \cap \bar{A}$ and is defined as

$$\begin{aligned} \mu_{A \cap \bar{A}}(x_i) &= \min\{\mu_A(x_i), \mu_{\bar{A}}(x_i)\}, \qquad \text{for all } i \\ &= \min\{\mu_A(x_i), (1 - \mu_A(x_i))\}, \qquad \text{for all } i. \end{aligned} \tag{11b}$$

Extending (11) in a two-dimensional image plane we may write

$$\gamma_l(X) = \frac{2}{MN} \sum_m \sum_n \mu_{X \cap \bar{X}}(x_{mn}), \qquad m = 1, 2, \cdots M; n = 1, 2, \cdots, N. \tag{12a}$$

Equation (12a) defines the amount of fuzziness present in the property plane of an image X. μ corresponds to p_{mn}. $X \cap \bar{X}$ is the intersection between fuzzy image planes $X = \{p_{mn}/x_{mn}\}$ and $\bar{X} = \{(1 - p_{mn})/x_{mn}\}$, the complement of X. $\mu_{X \cap \bar{X}}(x_{mn})$ denotes the degree of membership of (m, n)th pixel x_{mn} to such a fuzzy property plane $X \cap \bar{X}$ so that

$$\begin{aligned} \mu_{X \cap \bar{X}}(x_{mn}) &= p_{mn} \cap \bar{p}_{mn} \\ &= \min\{p_{mn}, (1 - p_{mn})\}, \qquad \text{for all } (m, n). \end{aligned} \tag{12b}$$

The entropy of a fuzzy set A having n supporting points as defined by De Luca and Termini (11) is

$$H(A) = \frac{1}{n \ln 2} \sum_i \text{sn}(\mu_A(x_i)), \qquad i = 1, 2, \cdots, n \tag{13a}$$

with the Shannon's function

$$\text{sn}(\mu_A(x_i)) = -\mu_A(x_i) \ln \mu_A(x_i) - (1 - \mu_A(x_i)) \ln (1 - \mu_A(x_i)). \tag{13b}$$

Extending (13) in a two-dimensional image plane we have

$$H(X) = \frac{1}{MN \ln 2} \sum_m \sum_n \text{sn}(\mu_X(x_{mn})) \tag{14a}$$

where

$$\begin{aligned} \text{sn}(\mu_X(x_{mn})) &= -\mu_X(x_{mn}) \ln \mu_X(x_{mn}) - (1 - \mu_X(x_{mn})) \ln (1 - \mu_X(x_{mn})), \\ & m = 1, 2, \cdots, M; n = 1, 2, \cdots, N. \end{aligned} \tag{14b}$$

The term $H(X)$, $0 \leqslant H(X) \leqslant 1$, measures the ambiguity in X on the basis of the well-known property of Shannon's function sn (μ)—montonically increasing in the interval $(0, 0 \cdot 5)$ and monotonically decreasing in $(0 \cdot 5, 1)$ with a maximum (= unity) at $\mu = 0 \cdot 5$—in the fuzzy property plane of X.

IV. Smoothing Algorithm

The idea of the smoothing is based on the property that image points which are spatially close to each other tend to possess nearly equal grey levels. Let us now explain three smoothing algorithms which have been tested in S block of Fig. 1.

A. Defocussing

The (m, n)th smoothed pixel intensity in the first method is defined as

$$x'_{mn} = a_0 x_{mn} + a_1 \sum_{Q_1} x_{ij} + a_2 \sum_{Q_2} x_{ij} + \cdots + a_s \sum_{Q_s} x_{ij} \tag{15a}$$

where

$$\begin{aligned} & a_0 + N_1 a_1 + N_2 a_2 + \cdots + N_s a_s = 1, \qquad 1 > a_1 > a_2 \cdots a_s > 0, \\ & (i, j) \neq (m, n), \ m = 1, 2, \cdots, M \text{ and } n = 1, 2, \cdots, N \end{aligned} \tag{15b}$$

x_{mn} represents the (m, n)th pixel intensity of the primary enhanced image. Q_1 denotes a set of N_1 coordinates (i, j) which are on or within a circle of radius R_1 centered at (but excluding) the point (m, n). Q_s denotes a set of N_s coordinates (i, j) which are on or within a circle of radius R_s centered at (m, n)th point but which do not fall into Q_{s-1}. For example, $Q = \{(m, n + 1), (m, n - 1), (m + 1, n), (m - 1, n)\}$ is the set of coordinates which are on/within a circle of radius one unit from a point (m, n).

This smoothing algorithm is therefore a kind of defocussing technique using a linear nonrecursive filter, where a part of the intensity of a pixel is being distributed to its neighbors. The amount of energy transmitted to a neighbor decreases as its distance from the pixel in question increases. a_0 represents the fraction retained by a pixel after transmission of part of its energy to neighbors. The set $a = \{a_0, a_1, a_2, \cdots, a_s\}$ as seen from this algorithm, plays an important role in smoothing an image and the choice of its values is problem oriented.

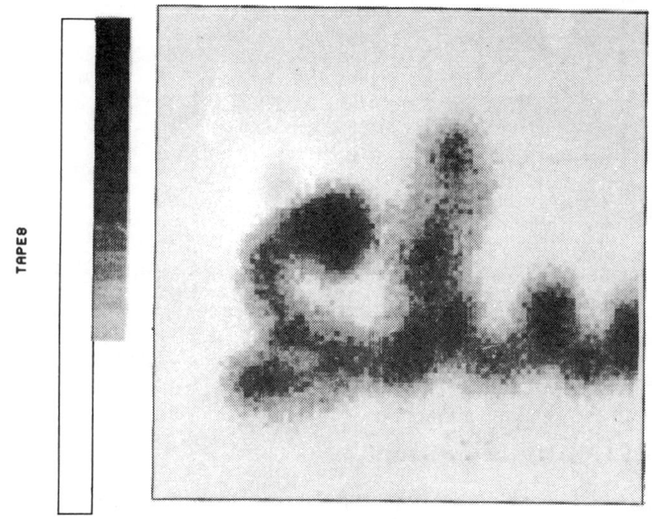

Fig. 4. Input picture.

B. Averaging

The second method is based on averaging the intensities within neighbors and is usually used to remove "pepper and salt" noise. The smoothed (m, n)th pixel intensity is

$$x'_{mn} = \frac{1}{N_1} \sum_{Q_1} x_{ij}, \qquad (i, j) \neq (m, n), \quad (i, j) \in Q_1. \quad (16)$$

This is a special case of defocussing technique (15) with $a_0 = a_2 = a_3 = \cdots = a_s = 0$. For a given radius, the blurring effect produced by neighborhood averaging can also be reduced by using a threshold procedure [3], [4] where the (m, n)th intensity is changed only if its difference from neighborhood values exceeds a specific nonnegative threshold.

C. Max–Min Rule

Equations (15) and (16) are formulated using collective properties of pixels. The third method on the other hand, uses q successive applications of "min" and then "max" operators [13] within neighbors such that the smoothed grey level value of (m, n)th pixel is

$$x'_{mn} = \max_{Q_1}{}^q \min_{Q_1}{}^q \{x_{ij}\},$$
$$(i, j) \neq (m, n), \ (i, j) \in Q_1, \ q = 1, 2, \cdots. \quad (17)$$

All the smoothing algorithms described above blur the image by attenuating the high spatial frequency components associated with edges and other abrupt changes in grey levels. The higher the values of Q_s, Q_1, and q, the greater is the degree of blurring.

V. Enhancement by Histogram Equalization

If s_l and n_l denote the value of lth gray level and the number of times the lth level has appeared in the image X and n_t is the total number $(M \times N)$ of pixels in X, then the probability of the lth level in X is

$$P(s_l) = \frac{n_l}{n_t}, \qquad l = 0, 1, 2, \cdots, L - 1. \quad (18)$$

Now we apply a transformation function [4]

$$s'_l = T(s_l) = (L - 1) \sum_j \frac{n_j}{n_t} = (L - 1) \sum_j P(s_j),$$
$$j = 0, 1, 2, \cdots, l \quad (19)$$

which is equal to the cumulative distribution of s_l and we will have the modified values s'_l which is mapped from an original level s_l. Since only L equally spaced discrete levels are allowed in this case, each of the transformed values s'_l was assigned to its closest valid level.

A plot of $P(s'_l)$, the probability of the lth level in enhanced image X', versus s'_l would give the resulting equalized histogram. This implies an increase in the dynamic range of the pixels which can have a considerable effect in the appearance of an image. A detailed discussion about histogram modification techniques is available in [4].

VI. Implementation and Results

Fig. 4 shows an input picture of handwritten script (Shu) which is to be processed with the enhancement model described above. The digitized version of the image of this picture is represented by a 96×99 array where each pixel can have one of the $32(0, 1, 2, \cdots, 9, A, B, \cdots, V)$ grey levels. Thus in our algorithm $M = 96$, $N = 99$, $x_{\max} = L - 1 = 31$.

Some primary enhanced pictures [9] obtained using the operator INT(INT) alone as an enhancement tool ($r = 2$) are demonstrated in Fig. 5. F_e was kept constant at a value of 2. The value of F_d was 45, 43, and 40 for the Figs. 5(a), 5(b), and 5(c), respectively so that the corresponding threshold lay between the grey level C and D, D and E, and E and F. The change in enhancement between Figs. 5(b) and 5(c) is seen to be insignificant. Use of $F_d = 40$ made the output overcorrected and thinner.

Consider the picture of Fig. 5(b) as an input to the smoother. The smoothing algorithm (15) included $R_1 = 1$ unit, i.e., $N_1 = 4$ and $a_0 = 0.4$ so that

$$N_1 a_1 = 0.6 \quad \text{or} \quad a_1 = 0.15.$$

The final enhanced outputs of this smoothed image are shown in Fig. 6 for three different sets of fuzzifiers. $T_2 \equiv$ INT(INT) was considered as an enhancement tool with $F_e = 2$ throughout. The threshold in T_2 operation was placed between the levels 8 and 9 (Fig. 6(a)), 9 and A (Fig. 6(b)), and A and B (Fig. 6(c)) and corresponding values of F_d were 55, 52, and 49.5. Thus the value of α becomes 0.4091, 0.3926, and 0.3782 in the respective cases.

Figs. 7 and 8 correspond to the final outputs when the averaging technique and max(min) rule (16) and (17) within four neighbors ($R_1 = 1$ unit and $q = 1$) were used in the smoother. The crossover points in T_2 operation and the values of the fuzzifiers were considered to be the same as in the three cases of Fig. 6.

The other parameters remaining constant, as in Fig. (6) the output corresponding to $T_3 \equiv$ INT(INT(INT)) operator is demonstrated in Fig. 9. These results (for $F_d = 52$ and $F_e = 2$, corresponding to each of the three smoothed images) are shown as an illustration of system performance resulting from the successive use of the fuzzy INT operator.

The edges in Figs. 6–9 as compared to Fig. 5 are seen to be more smoothed and some of the thinned or missing pixels (especially for S) are also found to be recovered. With the decrease in the value of F_d (i.e., increasing the crossover point) the output becomes more corrected and thin. Use of $r = 3$ (T_3 operation) as compared to $r = 2$ only makes an increase/decrease in intensity value of each of the pixels that is after/before the crossover point. The quality of picture is not altered.

Experiments were also conducted for some other values of a_0, a_s, and Q_s, but the output performance was not satisfactory. For example, for defocusing we considered $a_0 = 0.2$, 0.4, and 0.6 in (15) for each of the three different sets of radii namely, 1) $R_1 = \sqrt{2}$, 2) $R_1 = 1$ and $R_2 = 2$, and 3) $R_1 = \sqrt{2}$ and $R_2 = 2\sqrt{2}$. For averaging and max–min rule (16) and (17) we had used $R_1 = \sqrt{2}$ and 2 separately. The energy distribution corresponding to all these parameters was seen to make such a modification in pixel values that some relevant information (e.g., the white patches, which should exist in the lower whorl of S) got lost.

Fig. 10 shows an output obtained by histogram equalization technique. This is included for comparison of the performance of

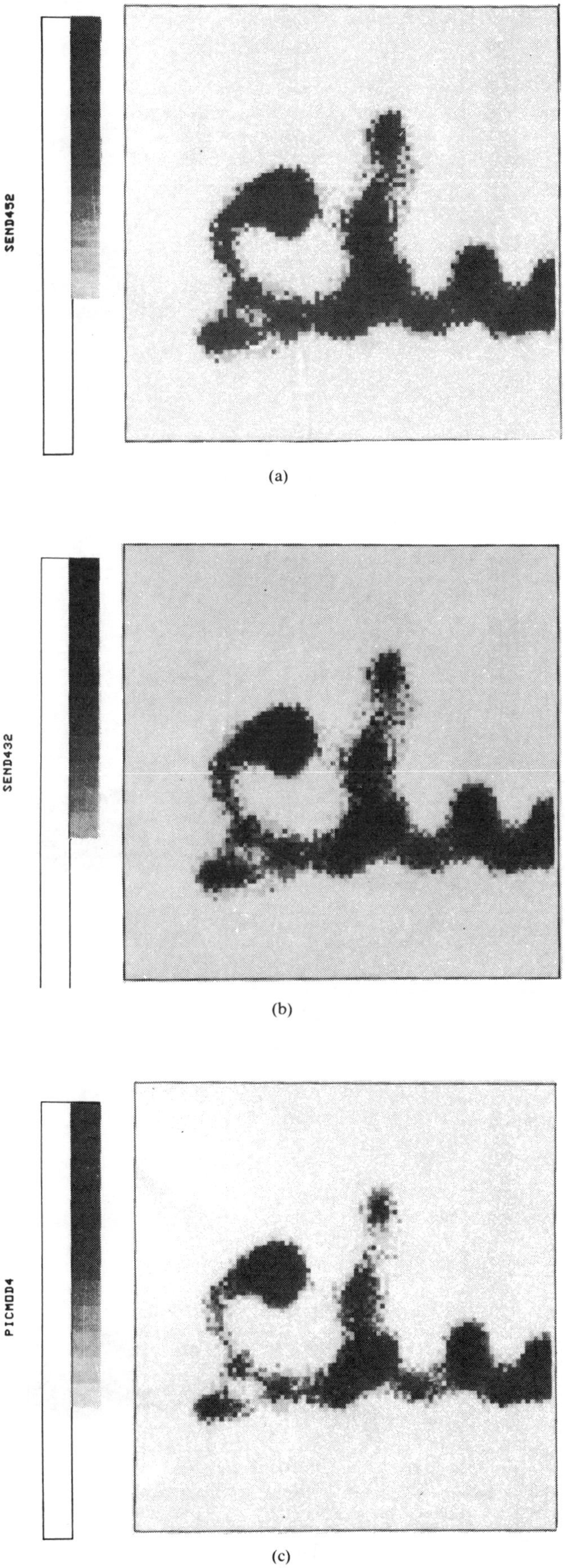

Fig. 5. Primary enhanced output. (a) $F_e = 2$, $F_d = 45$, $r = 2$. (b) $F_e = 2$, $F_d = 43$, $r = 2$. (c) $F_e = 2$, $F_d = 40$, $r = 2$.

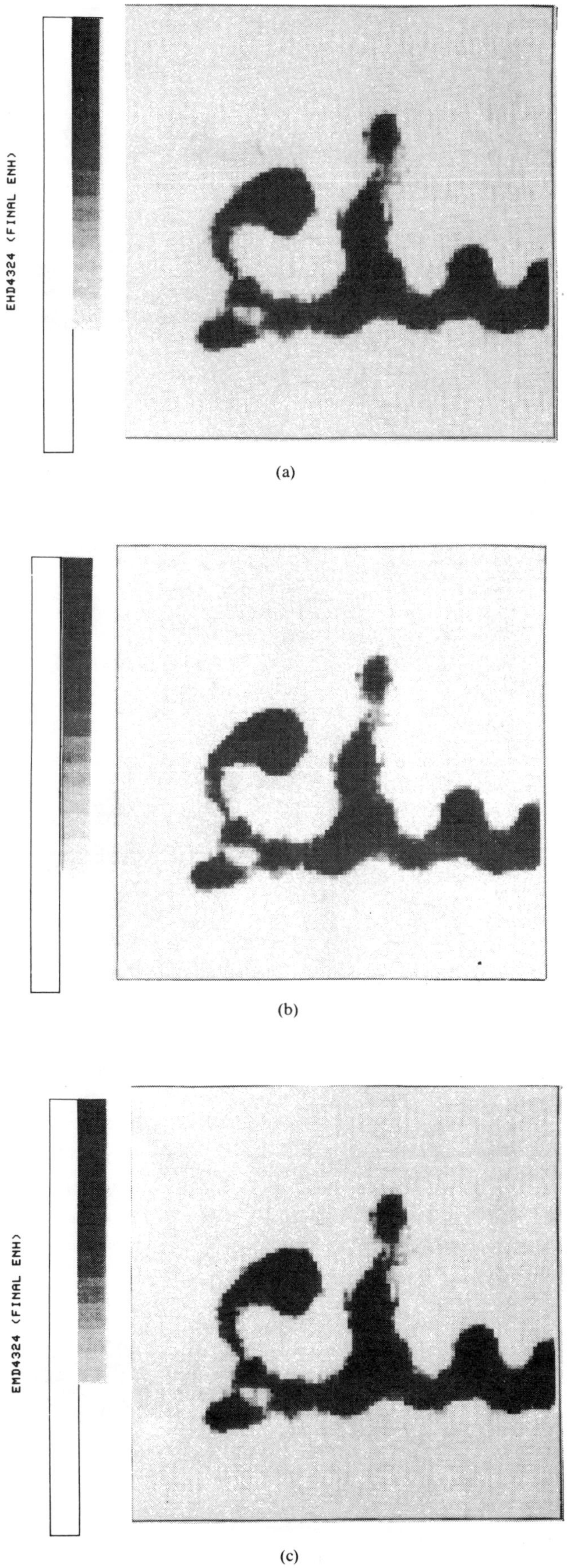

Fig. 6. Final enhanced output using (15). (a) $F_e = 2$, $F_d = 55$, $r = 2$. (b) $F_e = 2$, $F_d = 52$, $r = 2$. (c) $F_e = 2$, $F_d = 49.5$, $r = 2$.

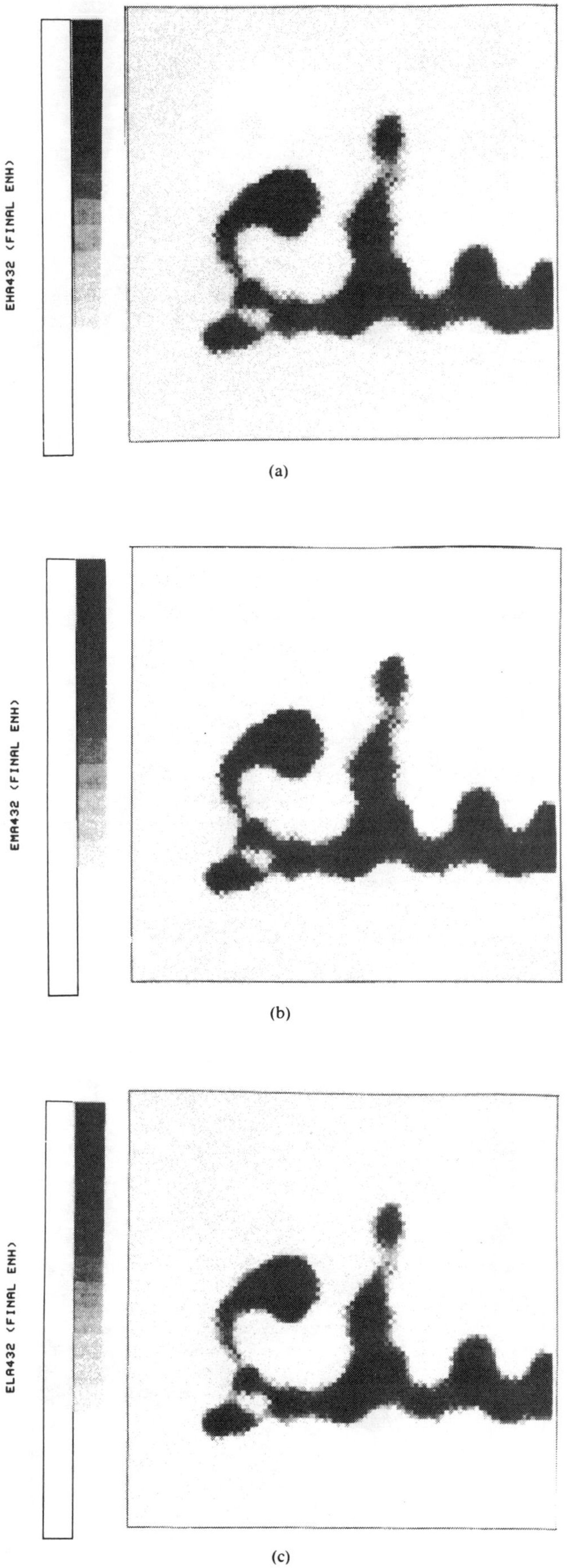

Fig. 7. Final enhanced output using (16). (a) $F_e = 2$, $F_d = 55$, $r = 2$. (b) $F_e = 2$, $F_d = 52$, $r = 2$. (c) $F_e = 2$, $F_d = 49.5$, $r = 2$.

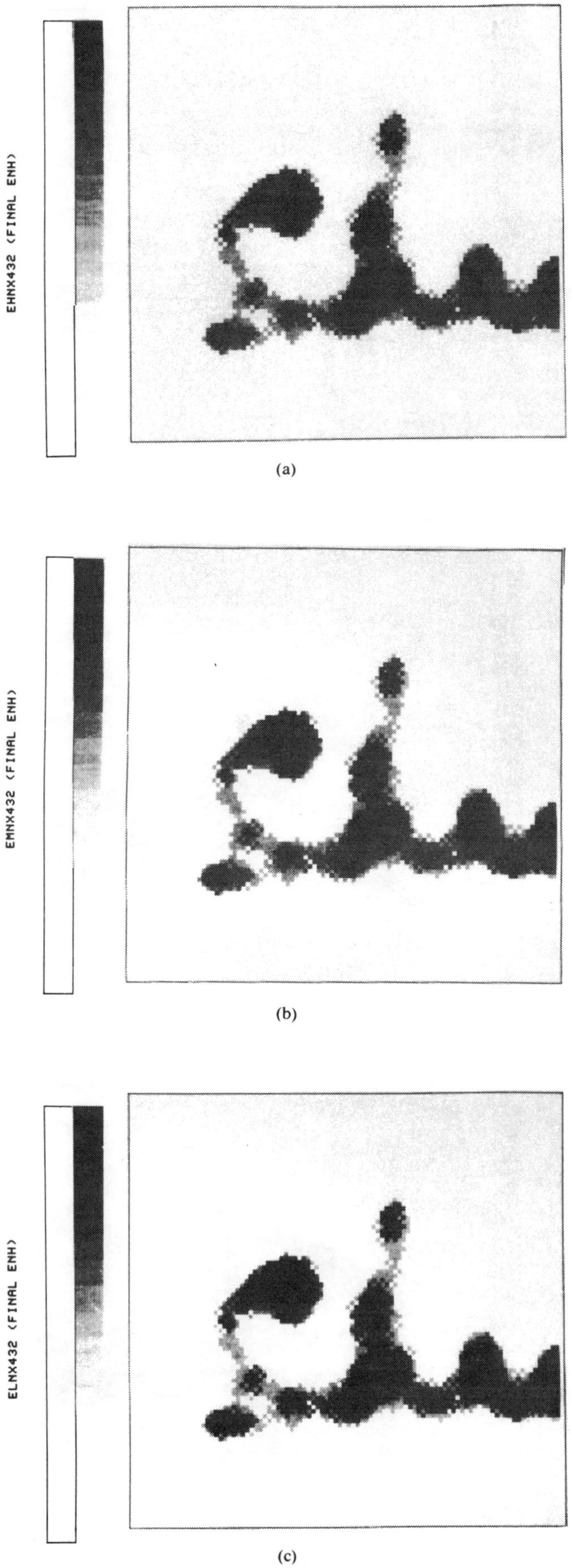

Fig. 8. Final enhanced output using (17). (a) $F_e = 2$, $F_d = 55$, $r = 2$. (b) $F_e = 2$, $F_d = 52$, $r = 2$. (c) $F_e = 2$, $F_d = 49.5$, $r = 2$.

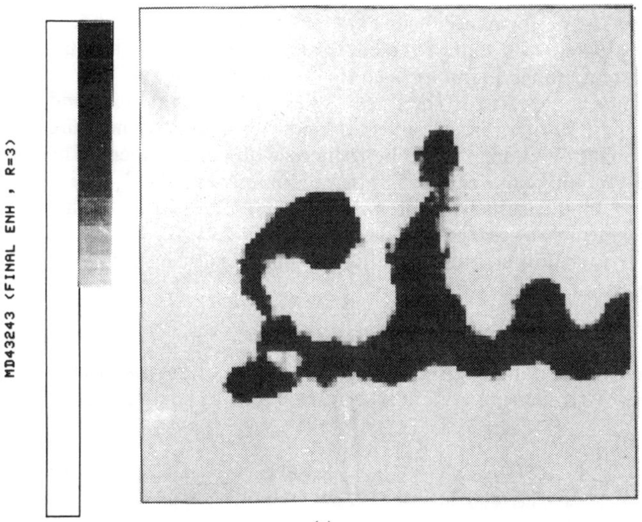

(a)

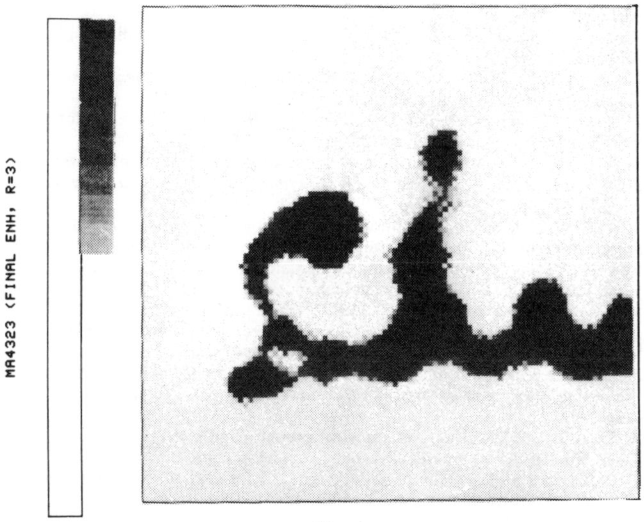

(b)

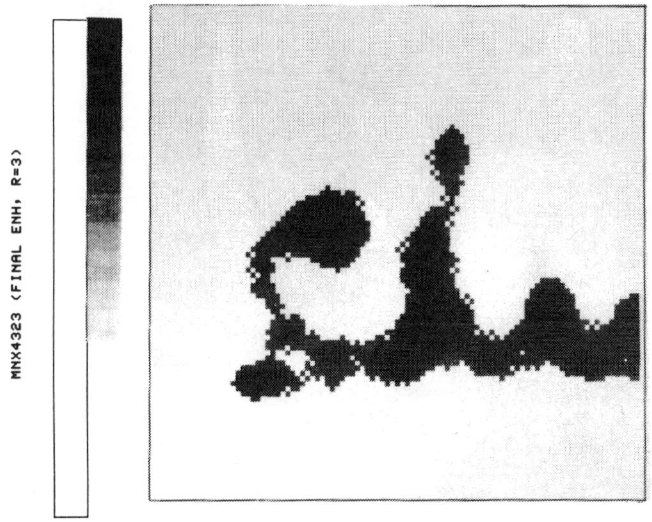

(c)

Fig. 9. Final enhanced output for $F_e = 2$, $F_d = 52$, and $r = 3$. (a) Using (15). (b) Using (16). (c) Using (17).

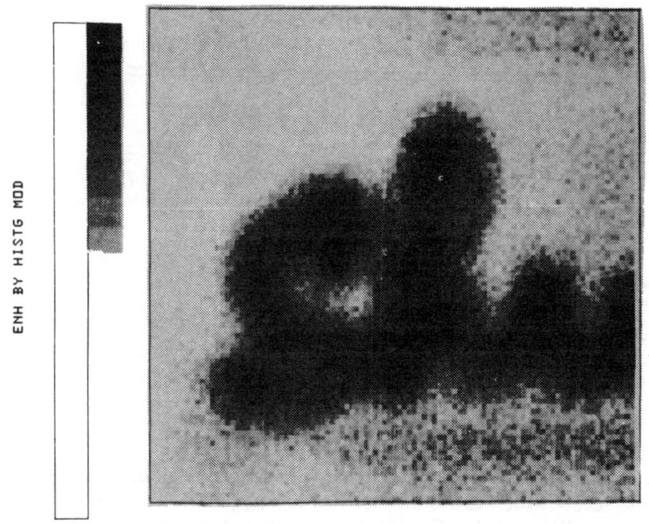

Fig. 10. Enhanced output using histogram modification technique.

TABLE I
LINEAR INDEX OF FUZZINESS OF PICTURES FOR DIFFERENT VALUES OF FUZZIFIERS

PICTURE X	LINEAR INDEX OF FUZZINESS $\gamma_1(X)$					
	$F_e=2$			$F_e=3$		
	$F_d=20$	$F_d=30$	$F_d=40$	$F_d=20$	$F_d=30$	$F_d=40$
Fig. 4	0.439	0.643	0.794	0.209	0.370	0.517
Fig. 5(a)	0.391	0.555	0.672	0.197	0.327	0.445
Fig. 5(b)	0.380	0.545	0.669	0.185	0.315	0.431
Fig. 5(c)	0.363	0.532	0.664	0.169	0.297	0.416
Fig. 6(a)	0.346	0.486	0.602	0.187	0.287	0.383
Fig. 6(b)	0.349	0.489	0.606	0.188	0.289	0.386
Fig. 6(c)	0.346	0.487	0.606	0.184	0.286	0.383
Fig. 7(a)	0.348	0.488	0.603	0.189	0.289	0.385
Fig. 7(b)	0.351	0.491	0.607	0.190	0.291	0.388
Fig. 7(c)	0.348	0.490	0.608	0.186	0.287	0.385
Fig. 8(a)	0.344	0.489	0.604	0.190	0.284	0.384
Fig. 8(b)	0.343	0.489	0.605	0.184	0.283	0.382
Fig. 8(c)	0.341	0.486	0.608	0.176	0.281	0.379
Fig. 9(a)	0.313	0.454	0.574	0.158	0.254	0.350
Fig. 9(b)	0.314	0.456	0.575	0.160	0.255	0.352
Fig. 9(c)	0.318	0.456	0.575	0.156	0.257	0.355
Fig. 10	0.586	0.668	0.681	0.430	0.545	0.622

the present system in enhancing an image with that of an existing technique.

Finally, the "linear index of fuzziness" $\gamma_1(X)$ reflecting the amount of ambiguity in a picture was measured for all these outputs by (12a). Table I illustrates the $\gamma_1(X)$ values of these pictures when F_d was considered to be 20, 30, and 40 separately with $F_e = 2$ and 3 in measuring p_{mn} values (μ in (12a)). With the increase in F_d or decrease in F_e, the index value of a picture is seen to be increased. This can be explained considering (6) and (12b). Since the p_{mn} value for a pixel increases as F_d increases or F_e decreases, its $(p_{mn} \cap \bar{p}_{mn})$ value (responsible for measuring $\gamma_1(X)$) would correspondingly increase/decrease for $p_{mn} < 0.5/> 0.5$. Now for all the pictures, it is found that the number of pixels having grey levels lower than the crossover point (as determined by those fuzzifiers) is much greater than those having levels higher than the crossover point. Therefore, there will be an overall increase in $(p_{mn} \cap \bar{p}_{mn})$ and hence $\gamma_1(X)$ with increase in F_d or decrease in F_e.

γ_1 values are seen to be reduced (except for Fig. 10) with enhancement. For Fig. 10, since the enhancement is done by histogram equalization technique, it possesses an almost uniform histogram. As a result, it contains, as compared with the input

TABLE II
ENTROPY OF PICTURES FOR DIFFERENT VALUES OF FUZZIFIERS

PICTURE X	ENTROPY H(X)					
	$F_e=2$			$F_e=3$		
	$F_d=20$	$F_d=30$	$F_d=40$	$F_d=20$	$F_d=30$	$F_d=40$
Fig.4	0.749	0.896	0.963	0.474	0.679	0.812
Fig.6(a)	0.639	0.778	0.854	0.398	0.561	0.682
Fig.6(b)	0.642	0.783	0.860	0.399	0.564	0.686
Fig.6(c)	0.640	0.783	0.862	0.395	0.562	0.685
Fig.7(b)	0.644	0.785	0.862	0.400	0.566	0.688
Fig.8(b)	0.639	0.782	0.861	0.393	0.560	0.683
Fig.10	0.825	0.867	0.864	0.681	0.793	0.842

(Fig. 4), a large number of levels near the crossover points and it is these levels which cause an increase in $(p_{mn} \cap \bar{p}_{mn})$ value. But the case is different for $F_e = 2$ and $F_d = 40$, where the crossover point becomes lower than all the others and the number of pixels having intensity below this point therefore becomes smaller than that in the input picture. The index value is thus decreased. Outputs in Fig. 9 do possess a minimum γ_1 value due to the T_3 operation, which reduces the ambiguity by further increasing/decreasing the property values which are greater/smaller than 0.5.

In a part of the experiment, these γ values were compared with those of "entropy" $H(X)$ (14) of the pictures. Table II shows the H values for some of the images (as typical cases for illustration) with the same values of F_e and F_d as used for $\gamma_1(X)$. The nature of variation of entropy with F_e and F_d is seen to conform to that of the linear index of fuzziness; only the effective values are larger.

VII. CONCLUSION

The concept of the fuzzy set is found to be applied successfully to the problems of grey-tone image enhancement. The addition of a smoothing algorithm between primary and final enhancement operations resulted in an improved performance. The three different smoothing techniques considered here are defocussing, averaging, and max–min rule over the neighbors of a pixel. All these techniques are seen to be almost equally effective (as measured by the amount of fuzziness present) in enhancing the image quality. The performance of this system in enhancing an image is also compared with that of the histogram equalization technique, an existing method and is seen to be much better as far as ambiguity is concerned. The linear index of fuzziness $\gamma_1(X)$ and entropy $H(X)$ of an image reflect a kind of quantitative measure of its quality and are seen to be reduced with enhancement. The amount of ambiguity is found to be minimum when the T_3 rule is adopted in the enhancement algorithm. $H(X)$ provides higher effective values of fuzziness as compared to $\gamma_1(X)$ but the nature of their variation among the different images with respect to F_e and F_d is identical.

ACKNOWLEDGMENT

Provision of data by Dr. P. Saraga and typing of the manuscript by Mrs. V. Kettle are gratefully acknowledged by the authors.

REFERENCES

[1] L. A. Zadeh, "Outline of a new approach to the analysis of complex systems and decision processes," *IEEE Trans. Syst., Man, Cybern.*, vol. SMC-3, pp. 28–44, Jan. 1973.
[2] L. A. Zadeh, K. S. Fu, K. Tanaka, and M. Shimura, Eds., *Fuzzy Sets and their Applications to Cognitive and Decision Processes.* London: Academic, 1975.
[3] A. Rosenfeld and A. C. Kak, *Digital Picture Processing.* New York: Academic, 1976.
[4] R. C. Gonzalez and P. Wintz, *Digital Image Processing.* Reading, MA: Addison-Wesley, 1977.
[5] J. K. Aggarwal, R. O. Duda, and A. Rosenfeld, Eds., *Computer Methods in Image Analysis.* New York: IEEE, 1977.
[6] *IEE Proc. Computer, Digital Techniques*, special issue on Image Restoration, Enhancement, vol. 127, no. 5, Sept. 1980.
[7] S. K. Pal and D. Dutta Majumder, "On automatic plosive identification using fuzziness in property sets," *IEEE Trans. Syst., Man, and Cybern.*, vol. SMC-8, pp. 302–308, Apr. 1978.
[8] S. K. Pal, "Studies on the application of fuzzy set theoretic approach in some problems of pattern recognition and man-machine communication by voice," Ph.D. dissertation, Univer. of Calcutta, Calcutta, India, 1978.
[9] S. K. Pal and R. A. King, "Image enhancement using fuzzy set," *Electron. Lett.*, vol. 16, pp. 376–378, May 9, 1980.
[10] A. Kaufmann, *Introduction to the Theory of Fuzzy Subsets—Fundamental Theoretical Elements*, vol. 1. New York: Academic, 1975.
[11] A. De Luca and S. Termini, "A definition of nonprobabilistic entropy in the setting of fuzzy sets theory," *Inform. and Contr.*, vol. 20, pp. 301–312, May 1972.
[12] A. D. Allen, "Measuring the empirical properties of sets," *IEEE Trans. Syst., Man, Cybern.*, vol. SMC-4, no. 1, pp. 66–73, 1974.
[13] Y. Nakagawa and A. Rosenfeld, "A note on the use of local min and max operations in digital picture processing," *IEEE Trans. Syst., Man, Cybern.*, vol. SMC-8, no. 8, pp. 632–635, 1978.

Fast and Reliable Image Enhancement Using Fuzzy Relaxation Technique

HUA LI AND HYUN S. YANG

Abstract—**A fast and reliable image enhancement technique based upon the fuzzy relaxation algorithm is proposed. Different orders of fuzzy membership functions and different rank statistics are attempted to improve the enhancement speed and quality, respectively. The proof of the convergence of our fuzzy relaxation algorithm and some experimental results are provided.**

I. Introduction

Since its emergence in 1965, fuzzy set theory has received a lot of attention from researchers in many different scientific fields; over 4,000 papers have been published in relation to both theoretical or applied aspects of fuzzy set theory [1]. Some of them deal with applications of fuzzy set theory for high and/or low level image analysis [2]–[8].

Fuzzy set theory could be distinguished from conventional mathematics in the sense that it has no well defined boundaries; the transition between full membership and no membership is gradual [1]. However since it is a generalization of set theory, definitions, theorems, and proofs for fuzzy set theory always hold for nonfuzzy set theory [9].

It is generally believed that image processing bears some fuzziness in nature due to the following factors:

1. Information being lost while three dimensional shape or scene is projected into two dimensional image;
2. Lack of the quantitative measurement of image quality (One of the annoying problems in image processing is how to define the quality of a given image. The judgement is subjective since it is based on visual perception.);
3. Ambiguity and vagueness in some definitions (For instance, there is no crisp boundary between edges and nonedges or between homogeneous regions and nonhomogeneous regions.);
4. Ambiguity and vagueness in interpreting the result generated by low level image processing.

Using the fuzzy set theory, we can handle these uncertainties effectively.

This paper is organized as follows: In Section II, we will briefly review the definition of an image in terms of a fuzzy set theory; in Section III, we will propose a fuzzy relaxation technique that exploits S fuzzy membership functions; we provide the proof of the convergence of the proposed relaxation algorithm; in Section IV, we will illustrate some experimental results on image enhancement based on the proposed technique; and in Section V, we will discuss some items related to the proposed scheme.

Manuscript received May 1, 1988; revised April 13, 1989.

H. Li is with the Dept. of Electrical and Computer Engineering, University of Iowa, Iowa City, IA 52242.

H. S. Yang was with the Dept. of Electrical and Computer Engineering, University of Iowa, Iowa City, IA 52242 and is now with the Dept. of Computer Science, the Korea Advanced Institute of Science and Technology (KAIST), P.O. Cheongryang 150, Seoul, Korea.

IEEE Log Number 8929622.

II. Definition of Image by Fuzzy Set Theory

As described in [3] and [6], an image can be defined in terms of a fuzzy set theory as follows: for an M by N image X with L number of gray levels ranging 0 to $L-1$, each pixel can be considered as a fuzzy singleton whose membership function ranges from 0 to 1. Thus

$$X = \bigcup_{i=1}^{M} \bigcup_{j=1}^{N} (P_{ij}|x_{ij})$$

where $(P_{ij}|x_{ij})$ is defined as a fuzzy membership function associated with the variable x_{ij}.

III. Fuzzy Relaxation Algorithm

Relaxation is a general computational technique where computations are iterated until certain parameter measurements converge to a set of values. In this section, we propose a relaxation algorithm that is based on a fuzzy membership function and exploits image histogram as a parameter; at each iteration, image histogram is modified by a fuzzy membership function. Image enhancement can be achieved with a few iterations, and the image could be finally binarized if the iteration continues until convergence. This technique provides a way to handle the uncertainty of image histogram, and enhances image faster and more reliably. In addition since we adopt a subregion process, it is possible to be executed in parallel.

First, a given image X is divided into subregions X_i, where $i = 1, 2, \cdots, N$. Each subregion of the image can then be characterized by the different rank statistics such as minimum, maximum, standard deviation, mean, mode, and median. We design this algorithm in such a way that it changes the pixel values into smaller ones if they are near the local minimum or changes them into larger ones if they are near the local maximum. To deal with noisy images, one might choose the local minimum and maximum differently. For example the gray levels of 10 percent and 90 percent of the local maximum can replace the local minimum and the local maximum, respectively; or gray levels of two times standard deviation smaller and greater than the mean might be used also. To accomplish this the S membership function, which is one of the two standard fuzzy membership functions [6], has been used as a transformation function (Fig. 1). Note that after transformation the gray levels closer to the parameter a become smaller, while the gray levels closer to the parameter c become larger due to the nonlinearity of the fuzzy membership function. Higher order functions can expedite this process since their slopes become steeper.

The entire procedure of the algorithm can be described as follows:

1) Partition the image into subregions;
2) Choose proper rank statistics according to the given image properties;
3) On each subregion compute the rank statistics; determine a, b, and c;

Reprinted from *IEEE Trans. Syst., Man, Cybern.*, vol. SMC-19, no. 5, pp. 1276–1281, September/October 1989.

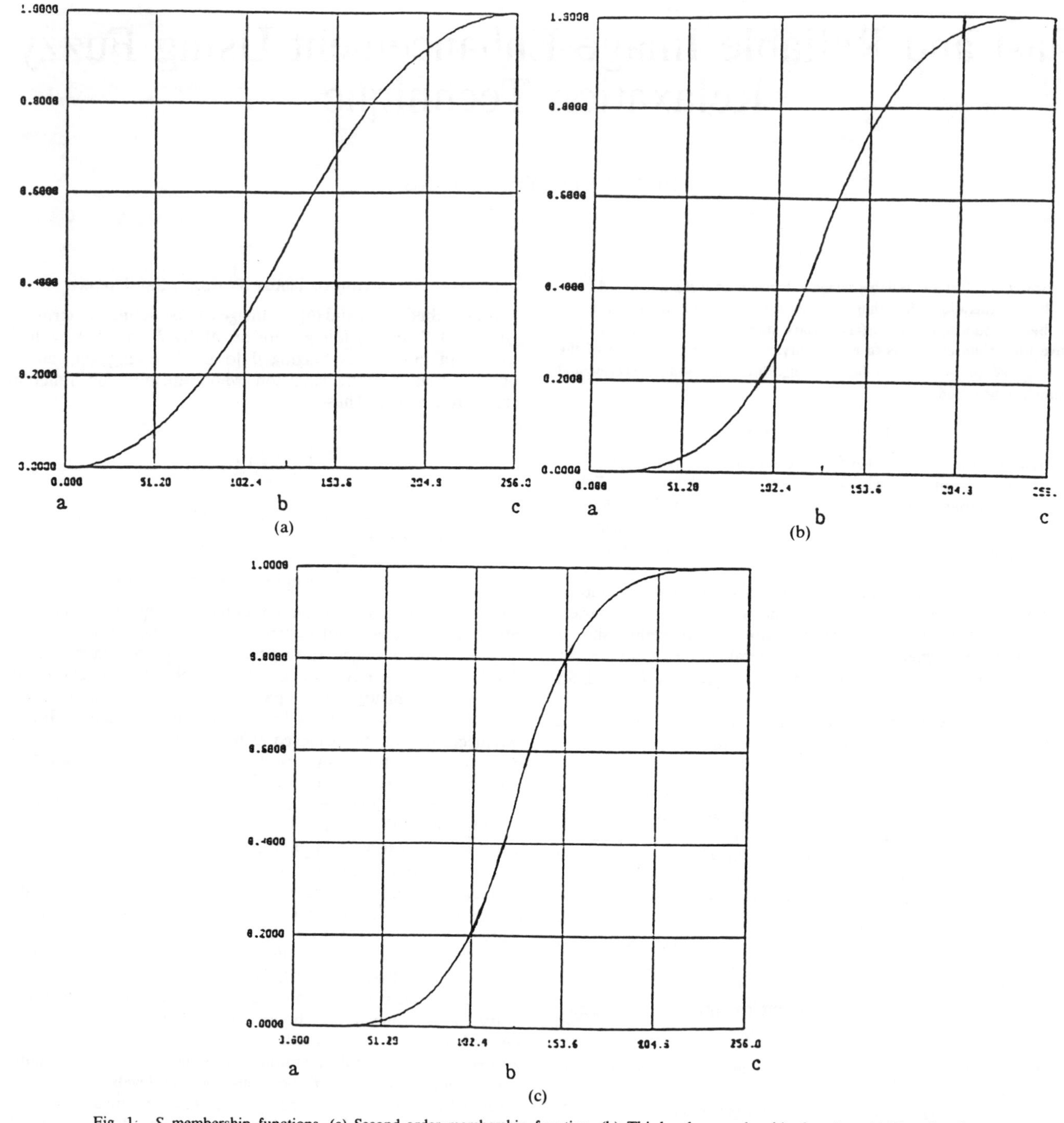

Fig. 1: *S* membership functions. (a) Second-order membership function. (b) Third-order membership function. (c) Fourth-order membership function.

4) Transform the gray levels using fuzzy membership function characterized by parameters determined in step 2;
5) Scale fuzzy membership into the gray levels;
6) Go back to step 3 and repeat until the image is sufficiently well enhanced.

We define the fuzzy membership function $S(x; a, b, c)$ in such a way that the parameter b can be any value between a and c:

$$S(x;a,b,c)=\begin{cases}0 & \text{if } x\leqslant a\\ S_1 & \text{if } a<x\leqslant b\\ S_2 & \text{if } b<x\leqslant c\\ 1 & x>c\end{cases}$$

where

$$S_1(x;a,b,c)=\frac{(x-a)^2}{K_1}$$

$$S_2(x;a,b,c)=1-\frac{(x-c)^2}{K_2}$$

$$K_1=(b-a)(c-a)$$

$$K_2=(c-b)(c-a).$$

iteration # 0

12	11	32
45	36	47
52	39	67

iteration # 1

0	0	20
47	28	51
58	35	67

iteration # 2

0	0	12
55	23	59
65	36	67

iteration # 3

0	0	4
62	15	65
67	37	67

iteration # 4

0	0	0
66	6	67
67	39	67

iteration # 5

0	0	0
67	1	67
67	43	67

iteration # 6

0	0	0
67	0	67
67	49	67

iteration # 7

0	0	0
67	0	67
67	57	67

iteration # 8

0	0	0
67	0	67
67	64	67

iteration # 9

0	0	0
67	0	67
67	67	67

(a)

iteration # 0

12	11	32
45	36	47
52	39	67

iteration # 1

0	0	15
52	26	56
62	36	67

iteration # 2

0	0	3
64	14	66
67	38	67

iteration # 3

0	0	0
66	2	67
67	43	67

iteration # 4

0	0	0
67	0	67
67	54	67

iteration # 5

0	0	0
67	0	67
67	65	67

iteration # 6

0	0	0
67	0	67
67	67	67

(b)

Fig. 2. Illustrated here are examples showing convergence of relaxation algorithm based on second-order function (a) and third-order function (b).

The parameters K_1 and K_2 are determined by solving the following equations:

$$\begin{cases} S_1(x;a,b,c)=0 & \text{if } x=a \\ \dfrac{d}{dx}S_1(x;a,b,c)=0 & \text{if } x=a \\ S_1(x;a,b,c)=S_2(x;a,b,c) & \text{if } x=b \\ \dfrac{d}{dx}S_1(x;a,b,c)=\dfrac{d}{dx}S_2(x;a,b,c) & \text{if } x=b \\ S_2(x;a,b,c)=1 & \text{if } x=c \\ \dfrac{d}{dx}S_2(x;a,b,c)=0 & \text{if } x=c. \end{cases}$$

These equations satisfy the following conditions: 1) the low part of S function (S_1) should pass through point a and also its first derivative at a should be zero; 2) The upper part of S function (S_2) should pass through the point c and also its first derivative at c should be zero; 3) S_1 and S_2 should meet at point b and their first derivatives at b should be equal.

This membership function has been chosen since it has a desirable nonlinear property for our purpose. Similarly, we can define the third order S fuzzy membership functions as

$$S_1(x;a,b,c)=\frac{(x-a)^3}{K_1}$$

$$S_2(x;a,b,c)=1+\frac{(x-c)^3}{K_2}$$

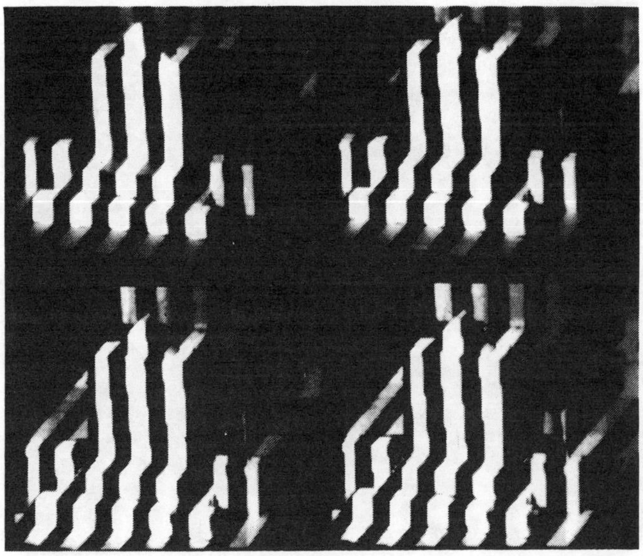

(a)

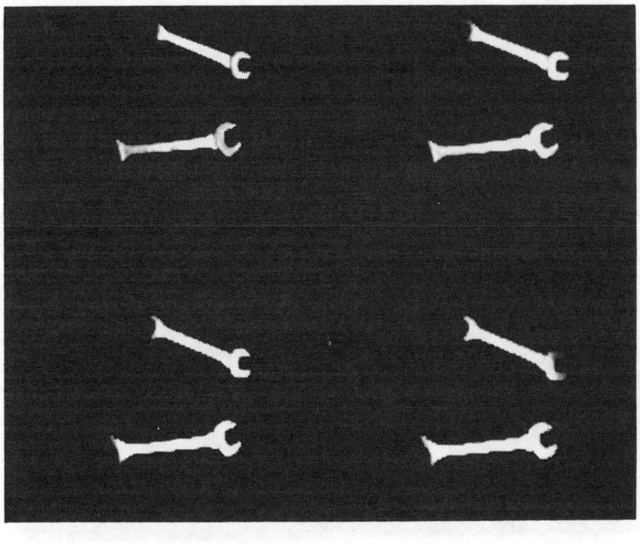

(b)

Fig. 3. Illustrated here are stripe images (a) and tool images (b) enhanced by fuzzy relaxation algorithm based on second-order S fuzzy membership function; upper left image is original, upper right, lower left and lower right are enhanced images after first, second, and third iterations respectively.

with

$$K_1=(b-a)^2(c-a)$$

$$K_2=(c-b)^2(c-a)$$

the parameter K's can be determined following the similar conditions used for the 2nd order function. Note that at a and c, the second derivatives must be zero, and at b, the 2nd order derivatives of S_1 and S_2 must be identical such as

$$\begin{cases} \dfrac{d^2}{dx^2}S_1(x;a,b,c)=0 & \text{if } x=a \\ \dfrac{d^2}{dx^2}S_1(x;a,b,c)=\dfrac{d^2}{dx^2}S_2(x;a,b,c) & \text{if } x=b \\ \dfrac{d^2}{dx^2}S_2(x;a,b,c)=0 & \text{if } x=c. \end{cases}$$

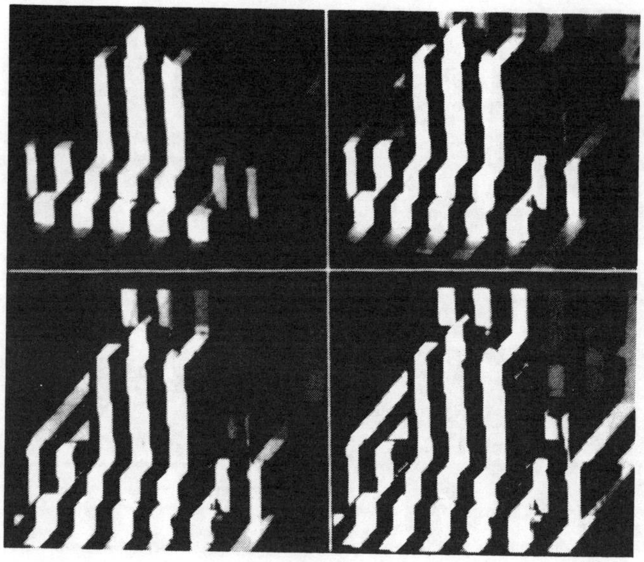

(a)

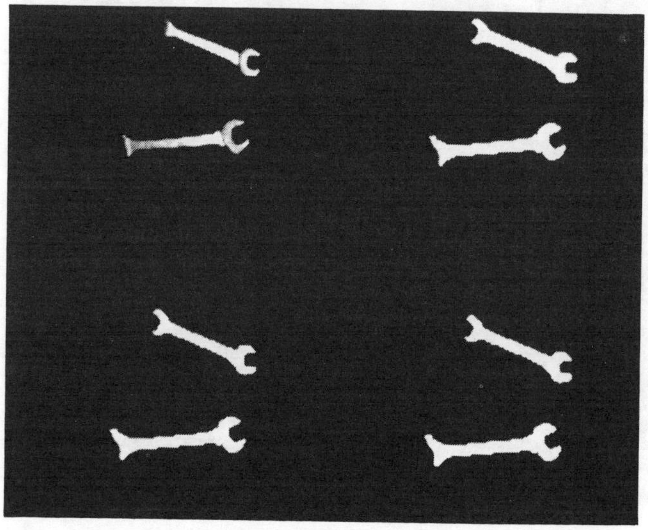

(b)

Fig. 4. Depicted here are stripe images (a) and tool images (b) enhanced by fuzzy relaxation algorithm based on third order S fuzzy membership function; upper left image is original, upper right, lower left and lower right are enhanced images after the first, second, and third iterations respectively.

and

$$0 \leqslant \mu_i(x_i) \leqslant 1$$

then after scaling, we have $c\mu_i(x_i)$, to show convergence, one needs to show:

$$x_{i+1} < x_i$$

or

$$\frac{c(x_i - a)^2}{(c-a)(b-a)} < x_i$$

or

$$F(x_i) = c(x_i - a)^2 - x_i(c-a)(b-a) < 0.$$

It is not difficult to show this parabolic function has the following properties:

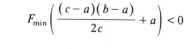

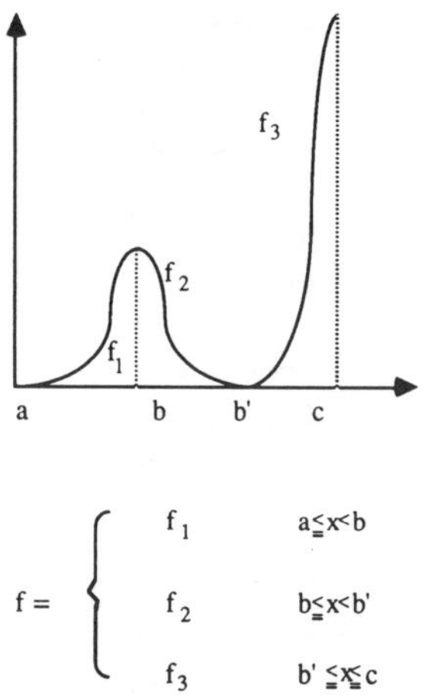

Fig. 5. Membership function that can be exploited for three-class problem.

$$F(a) < 0$$
$$F(b) < 0$$

and the extremum

$$F_{\min}\left(\frac{(c-a)(b-a)}{2c} + a\right) < 0$$

therefore

$$x_{i+1} < x_i.$$

Case 2: When the transformation is defined by the function S_2. Following the similar way as we did in Case 1, it can be shown that

$$x_{i+1} > x_i.$$

At each iteration, the fuzzy membership is modified as

$$P'_{ij} = \begin{cases} S_1(P_{ij}) & \text{if } a \leqslant cP_{ij} < b \\ S_2(P_{ij}) & \text{if } b \leqslant cP_{ij} < c. \end{cases}$$

New pixel values are computed using this function $S(x; a, b, c)$.

Convergence of histogram into bimodal using the 2nd order S fuzzy membership function can be proved as follows.

Case 1: When the transformation is defined by the function S_1. Given

$$\mu_i(x_i) = \frac{(x_i - a)^2}{K_{1i}}$$

$$x_{i+1} = \mu_i(x_i)c$$

where

$$a \leqslant x_i \leqslant b,$$

The proof of convergence for the higher order functions can be done similarly.

In Figs. 2(a) and (b) are shown examples of the convergence of pixel values in 3×3 regions using the second order and the third order membership functions. Note that pixel values converge faster by the third order function.

IV. Experimental Results

Two 128×128 gray tone images with 256 gray levels were chosen to test the algorithm. Each image was divided into 16 subregions of size 32×32 and each subregion overlaps 2 pixels with its neighboring subregions. In each subregion a fuzzy relaxation was performed to enhance the contrast. In Figs. 3(a) and (b) are shown enhanced images using the second order S fuzzy membership function; in Figs. 4(a) and (b) are illustrated enhanced images using the third order S fuzzy membership function. Note that dark part of the image becomes darker while bright part becomes brighter, implying that the contrast is well enhanced.

V. Discussion

The proposed technique has been developed mainly to enhance the contrast between the object region and the background region. However this fuzzy relaxation algorithm can be also applicable to those images with more than two regions (or classes) characterized by the different gray levels. An appropriate membership function may be defined according to the number of classes. For instance a different membership function (Fig. 5) from the one used for the two-class problem (Fig. 1) can be exploited to handle the three-class problem.

Iterative enhancement of the contrast can be also achieved by using the probabilistic relaxation technique. In applying the probabilistic relaxation technique, one generally considers only the relation between a point and one of its eight neighbors and does not consider feasible interrelationships among the multiple points in the neighbors; the pairwise constraint called *compatibility* is used for relaxation. In our method the rank statistics are computed on the pixels in each subregion and used for relaxation. Thus the neighboring points have influence on a point cooperatively via these rank statistics.

In our method we have not implemented the stopping criterion for the iteration. Most relaxation techniques terminate iteration in a subjective manner. Albeit computationally expensive, one might examine the characteristic of histogram after each iteration is completed to see if it sufficiently well represents the number of classes.

VI. Conclusion

In this paper a fuzzy relaxation algorithms based on the second and higher order S fuzzy membership functions have been proposed for the purpose of image enhancement. We also provided the proof of the convergence of this relaxation algorithm. In the future we would like to compare the performance of the fuzzy relaxation technique with that of the probabilistic relaxation technique in detail.

Acknowledgment

The authors thank the referees for their comments and suggestions.

References

[1] A. Kaufmann and M. Gupta, *Introduction to Fuzzy Arithmetic.* New York: Van Nostrand Co. Inc., 1985.

[2] V. Goetcherian, "From binary to gray tone image processing using fuzzy logic concepts," *Pattern Recognition*, vol. 12, pp. 7–15, 1980.

[3] T. L. Huntsberger *et al.*, "Interactive fuzzy image segmentation," *Pattern Recognition*, vol. 18, no. 2, pp. 131–138, 1985.

[4] Y. Nakagawa and A. Rosenfeld, "A note on the use of local min and max operations in digital picture processing," *IEEE Trans. Syst. Man and Cybern.*, vol. 11, pp. 632–635, 1978.

[5] Y. Nakagawa and A. Rosenfeld, "Some experiments on variable thresholding," *Pattern Recognition*, vol. 11, pp. 191–204, 1979.

[6] K. Pal and R. A. King, "On edge detection of X-ray images using fuzzy set," *IEEE Trans PAMI*, no. 1, pp. 69–77, 1983.

[7] A. Rosenfeld, "The fuzzy geometry of image subsets," *Pattern Recognition*, vol. 2, pp. 311–317, 1984.

[8] L. Vanderheydt *et al.*, "Two-dimensional shape decomposition using fuzzy set theory applied to automated chromosome analysis," *Pattern Recognition*, vol. 13, pp. 147–157, 1981.

[9] A. Kandel, *Fuzzy Mathematical Techniques with Applications.* Reading, MA: Addison-Wesley, 1986.

A Study on Subjective Evaluations of Printed Color Images

Kazuhiko Tanaka
Image & Information Research Institute, Dai Nippon Printing Co., Ltd., Tokyo, Japan
Michio Sugeno
Department of System Science, Tokyo Institute of Technology, Yokohama, Japan

ABSTRACT

Fuzzy measures and fuzzy integrals are applied to build an evaluation model of printed color images. First, subjective evaluation data of seven people are collected by pairwise comparisons. The subjects give 16 kinds of evaluations for each color proof. Then a two-layer evaluation model is proposed based on the result of factor analysis. In this study, the authors adopt Choquet's integral as a form of fuzzy integral because it has good properties compared with other forms of fuzzy integrals. A relaxation-method-like procedure has been devised to identify fuzzy measures of the two-layer model. After its effectiveness is confirmed with artificial data, the algorithm is applied to actual subjective evaluation data. This gives us results, revealing that the seven subjects are divided into two groups whose evaluation characteristics are structurally different from each other.

KEYWORDS: ***fuzzy measure, fuzzy integral, structure identification, subjective evaluation, color printing***

1. INTRODUCTION

Evaluations of color printing quality have rarely been the object of scientific research because of the fuzziness of the human senses. However, in the current situation of the publication of massive quantities of visual printed matter, a more reasonable and efficient evaluation method is desired in the graphic arts and relevant industries. As the first step toward achieving this aim, we tried to construct a model suitable for subjective evaluation.

In a rare work in this field, Mishina [1] derived an equation of color-printing image evaluation from subjectively evaluated data by multiple regression analysis, where representations of material, color balance, and feeling of roughness were selected as predictor variables. In this evaluation model, predictor variables (and their values) are assumed to be additive and independent.

However, the human evaluation process with respect to reproduced images in which an evaluator subjectively selects the most preferable reproduction can be considered essentially fuzzy. Because such evaluations can be influenced by particular colors such as skin color or sky blue, fidelity to the original is not always important to its reproduction. Therefore, we tried to build a model based on the idea of fuzzy measures, where we do not have to assume additivity and independence among predictor variables.

Address correspondence to K. Tanaka, Image & Information Research Institute, Dai Nippon Printing Co., Ltd., 1-1-1, Ichigaya-Kagacho Shinjuku-ku, Tokyo 162-01, Japan.

2. COLLECTING SUBJECTIVE EVALUATION DATA

First, we collected subjective evaluation data on printed color images in order to study the relationship between overall evaluation and evaluations specific to various viewpoints. The subjects were seven people who work for a printing company. For samples we made 20 proofs from four originals (color reversal films), five slightly different proofs from each original.

The test form is shown in Figure 1. The subevaluation items (attributes) were selected as typical words that people in the printing industry frequently use in expressing their evaluations of color proofs.

Each attribute score for each proof was calculated as follows:

With respect to attribute k,

- If proof A is distinctly more favorable than proof j, then $s(j) = +2$.
- If Proof A is slightly more favorable than proof j, then $s(j) = +1$.
- If Proof A is much the same as proof j, then $s(j) = 0$.
- If proof A is slightly less favorable than proof j, then $s(j) = -1$.
- If proof A is distinctly less favorable than proof j, then $s(j) = -2$.

The $s(j)$ values for all proofs other than proof A are summed, adding in the constant 8 to make the result nonnegative.

$$\text{SCORE}(A, k) = \sum_{j \neq A} s(j) + 8 \quad \geq 0$$

Comparison of Proof ___ (L) and Proof ___ (R)

Which proof . . .	(L)	(L) rather than (R)	Much the same	(R) rather than (L)	(R)
1. displays 3-dimensional feeling?					
2. displays transparent feeling?					
3. displays feeling of metallic surface?					
4. displays feeling of fine texture?					
5. displays feeling of volume?					
6. has more contrast?					
7. displays feeling of sharpness?					
8. is more bluish?					
9. is more reddish?					
10. is more yellowish?					
11. is vivid, fresh in color?					
12. displays details in lighter part?					
13. displays details in darker part?					
14. is away from muddiness?					
15. is bright as a whole?					
16. do you like better?					
	+2	+1	0	−1	−2

Figure 1. Test form for pairwise comparison.

	s(A)	s(B)	s(C)	s(D)	s(E)	$\Sigma s(j)$	Score
Proof A	*	1	1	2	−1	3	11
Proof B	−1	*	1	2	−2	0	8
Proof C	−1	−1	*	2	−1	−1	7
Proof D	−2	−2	−2	*	−2	−8	0
Proof E	1	2	1	2	*	6	14

Figure 2. How to determine proof scores.

Table 1. Factor Loadings and Cumulative Contribution Rates (CCR)

	F_1	F_2	F_3	F_4
1	0.74998	−0.51367	0.01859	−0.12555
2	0.21037	−0.83463	0.09731	−0.14157
3	−0.14265	−0.12086	0.83571	−0.12021
4	0.02056	−0.40787	0.75141	0.05090
5	0.87958	0.06078	−0.06407	−0.19624
6	0.82205	−0.38752	−0.12933	−0.14731
7	0.50481	−0.69627	0.13028	0.20734
8	−0.17877	0.24732	0.02073	0.86580
9	0.74076	0.44887	0.15436	−0.10562
10	0.58857	−0.03248	−0.00776	−0.71396
11	0.74629	−0.43571	0.17642	−0.15980
12	0.37875	0.15110	0.57723	0.25087
13	−0.11397	−0.50342	0.13149	−0.01098
14	0.23220	−0.79572	0.20052	−0.25179
15	0.01855	−0.78579	−0.09903	−0.46396
CCR	0.38632	0.56217	0.68225	0.75651

where SCORE(A, k) denotes the score of proof A with respect to attribute k. An example is illustrated in Figure 2.

3. FACTOR ANALYSIS AND THE RESULT

Factor analysis was performed to investigate latent factors concerning human subjective evaluations of printed color images. The results were as follows. Items having a high correlation with the principal factors are

1, 5, 6, 11	with the first factor
2, 7, 14, 15	with the second factor
3, 4, 12	with the third factor

(See Table 1.)

Then three factors are interpreted as follows:

- The first factor (P factor) concerns physical and space representation.
- The second factor (T factor) concerns transparency, sharpness, and clarity of appearance.
- The third factor (Q factor) concerns representation of material constituting the main object in a reproduced picture.

These results suggested a subjective evaluation model like that of Figure 3 incorporating the concepts of fuzzy measures and fuzzy integrals. The G_P, G_T, G_Q of Figure 3 are fuzzy measures that each give the evaluation score of the respective intermediate block (P, T, and Q) from subevaluation scores 1–15. G_x is the fuzzy measure that determines the overall evaluation of a picture with the scores of the P, T, and Q factors. Attributes having relatively small correlation with the principal factors were ignored.

Generally speaking, an evaluation model like that of Figure 3, which consists of two layers, with the upper one corresponding to the principal factors derived from factor analysis, can be considered more transparent than a one-layer model, which gives the overall evaluation directly from many attributes. This is so because a two-layer model can roughly explain evaluation results in terms of fewer principal factors.

In this study, we adopted Choquet's integral as a form of fuzzy integral, since Choquet's integral is an extension of the Lebesgue integral (Sugeno and Murofushi [2]) and easy to calculate as described in the next section.

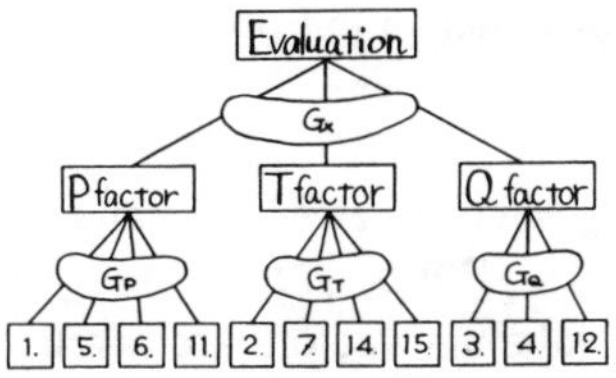

Figure 3. A subjective evaluation model for printed color images. The numbers in the lowest layer coincide with item numbers of Figures 1 and 2.

4. SUBJECTIVE EVALUATION MODEL USING CHOQUET'S INTEGRAL [2]

Suppose there are three evaluation items s_1, s_2, and s_3. Let $K = \{s_1, s_2, s_3\}$, h: K → [0, ∞), be a function giving the evaluation score for each item. In the case of $h(s_1) = a_1 \leqq h(s_2) = a_2 \leqq h(s_3) = a_3$, we have

$$(C)\int h\,d\mu = a_1\mu(K) + (a_2 - a_1)\mu(\{s_2, s_3\}) + (a_3 - a_2)\mu(\{s_3\})$$

$$= C$$

where μ represents the fuzzy measure.

The desired subjective evaluation model is obtained if we can determine the fuzzy meausure μ so that the result C is close enough to the actual overall evaluation E.

Let $\mathbf{x} = (x_1, \ldots, x_7) \in R^7$ denote the fuzzy measure μ, where $x_7 = \mu(K)$, $x_1 = \mu(\{s_1\}), \ldots, x_4 = (\{s_1, s_2\})$, $x_5 = \mu(\{s_2, s_3\})$, $x_6 = \mu(\{s_3, s_1\})$. The fuzzy measure we seek is the $\mathbf{x}$ minimizes

$$f(\mathbf{X}) = \sum_j (E_j - C_j)^2$$

under the following constraints:

$$x_1 \leqq x_4, \quad x_1 \leqq x_5, \quad x_2 \leqq x_4, \quad x_2 \leqq x_6, \quad x_3 \leqq x_5,$$
$$x_3 \leqq x_5, \quad x_4 \leqq x_7, \quad x_5 \leqq x_7, \quad x_6 \leqq x_7, \quad \text{and} \quad \theta \leqq x_1,$$

where θ is the zero vector.

We found this problem to be one of quadratic programming. It can be solved by applying the Lemke method (Kojima [3]).

IDENTIFYING AN ACTUAL EVALUATION MODEL

When we consider a two-layer model as in Figure 3, we cannot apply the result of the previous section unless we have all scores of the intermediate blocks. Therefore, we devised a relaxation-method-like procedure to identify fuzzy measure that infers scores of the intermediate blocks as well as the fuzzy measures, repetitively, eliminating incompatibilities among data. An outline of this algorithm is as follows. (For relaxation methods, refer to Rosenfeld et al. [4].)

Each block score of the ith sample ${}_iP$, ${}_iT$, or ${}_iQ$ is regarded as an object to be labeled, where the label is a kind of block score of the ith sample that can take only one discrete value, for instance, any one of $\Lambda = \{0, 1, 2, \ldots, 10\}$, according to a certain probability distribution.

To represent the above assumption for each ${}_iP$, ${}_iT$, or ${}_iQ$ labeling vector, we define ${}_iPP$, ${}_iTP$, or ${}_iQP$. ${}_iPP(\lambda)$, which denotes the λth component of

${}_iPP$, has the real number equal to the probability that ${}_iP$ takes λ as its block score.

STEP 1 Initialize labeling vectors ${}_iPP$, ${}_iTP$, and ${}_iQP$ for all i. Set the initial scores of temporary blocks ${}_iPtmp$, ${}_iTtmp$, and ${}_iQtmp$ based on the labeling vectors. Expectations of labeling vectors are taken.

Let $K = 1$.

STEP 2 By applying the Lemke method for these temporary block scores and the data obtained from subjective evaluations, obtain fuzzy measures Gp, Gt, Gq, and Gx. Let M^k denote the result.

STEP 3 Check the degree to which actual evaluations agree with calculated scores on M^k for all combinations of labeling of ${}_iP, {}_iT, {}_iQ$. This is called compatibility. The compatibility for ${}_iP = \lambda$, ${}_iT = \lambda'$ on model M^K, which is denoted ${}_i\mathrm{COM}_{PT}(\lambda, \lambda')$ is calculated as the residual of the ith sample over the P block,

$${}_i\mathrm{RES}_P = \left| \lambda - (C) \textstyle\int hd\mu \displaystyle\int_i (P_1, P_2, P_3)\, dG_P \right|$$

The second term on the right-hand side denotes Choquet's integral result with evaluation scores P_1, P_2, P_3 with respect to the fuzzy measure G_P.

$${}_i\mathrm{RES}_T = \left| \lambda' - (C) \textstyle\int hd\mu \displaystyle\int_i (T_1, T_2, T_3)\, dG_T \right|$$

$${}_i\mathrm{RES}_{XPT} = \left| {}_iE - (C) \textstyle\int hd\mu \displaystyle\int_i (\lambda, \lambda', iQtmp)\, dG_x \right|$$

where ${}_iE$ denotes the overall evaluation score of the ith sample.

$${}_i\mathrm{ORES}_{PT} = 0.5\,{}_i\mathrm{RES}_{XPT} + 0.25({}_i\mathrm{RES}_P + {}_i\mathrm{RES}_T)$$

(overall residual of the ith sample), and

$${}_i\mathrm{COM}_{PT}(\lambda, \lambda') = 1 - \frac{2\,{}_i\mathrm{ORES}_{PT}}{\max_j({}_j\mathrm{ORES}_{PT})}$$

${}_i\mathrm{COM}_{PQ}(\lambda, \lambda')$, ${}_i\mathrm{COM}_{TQ}(\lambda, \lambda')$ can be calculated in a similar manner.

STEP 4 If the compatibility of a label is big, then the probability assigned to the label is increased and if it is small, then the profitability is decreased. In this way, the modification quantity of each assigned probability is determined. For instance, the modification quantity of ${}_iPP(\lambda)$ is calculated from the equation

$$\begin{aligned}\Delta_i PP(\lambda) &= 0.5 \sum_k [{}_i\mathrm{COM}_{PT}(\lambda, k) * {}_iTP(k)] \\ &\quad + 0.5 \sum_k [{}_i\mathrm{COM}_{PQ}(\lambda, k) * {}_iQP(k)]\end{aligned}$$

STEP 5 Modify the labeling vectors. Calculate new temporary block values from the new labeling vectors.

Let $K = K + 1$. Go to step 2.

Figure 4 shows experimental results obtained with the above procedure. Three hundred artificial data sets, each consisting of P_1, P_2, P_3, T_1, T_2, T_3, Q_1, Q_2, Q_3, and E, were given to the test program. Each E was calculated through arbitrary fuzzy measures G_x, G_P, G_T, and G_Q.

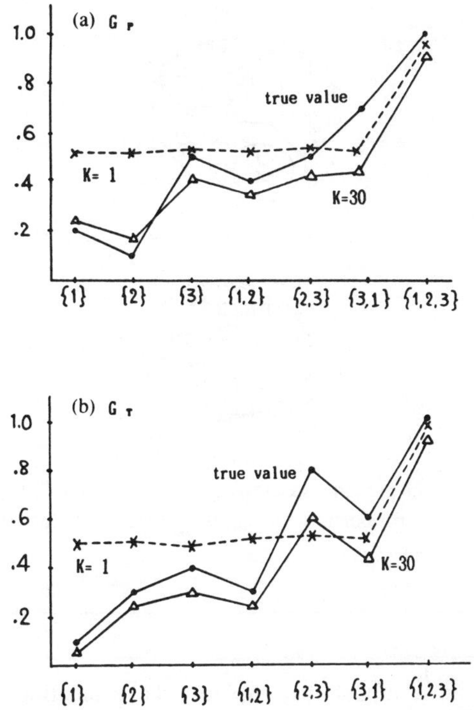

Figure 4. Experimental results with the relaxation-method-like procedure.

Since the algorithm does not guarantee convergence, we have to stop execution of the program at the most appropriate times of iteration. Experiments with several data sets show that the best identified result for G_x tends to be obtained after about 20 iterations, whereas those for G_P, G_T, and G_Q tend to be obtained after about 50 iterations. Thus, we conclude that 30 iterations is best for identifying the four sets of fuzzy measures.

Comparing the result of 30 iterations ($K = 30$) with that of $K = 1$, it is seen that the accuracy of the calculated overall evaluation of model M^K was improved approximately threefold. Furthermore, it is found that the fuzzy measure values of G_P, G_T, G_Q of $K = 30$ clearly show their characteristic tendencies, whereas those of $K = 1$ appear almost trivial.

6. IDENTIFIED RESULTS

Before devising the relaxation-method-like procedure described above, we had a prediction that the seven subjects could be divided into two groups whose approaches to evaluation of the color prints were distinctly different. This prediction was obtained by applying subjective evaluation data of each subject to a linear model and comparing the results.

Therefore, we applied the relaxation-method-like procedure for each of the two groups.

Figure 5 shows the identified results of the Figure 3 models. Only G_x's are illustrated. The four-person model reveals that when members of this group evaluate printed color images, they give almost equal importance to P, T, and Q factors. Results obtained with the other group (three-person model) reveal that they almost ignore the Q factor and that the P and T factors are interdependent in their evaluations.

Figure 5 not only shows the differences between corresponding fuzzy measures (which are often seen in linear models as differences between corresponding coefficients), but also reveals, so to speak, structural differences, which appear as differences in interdependency among the three factors.

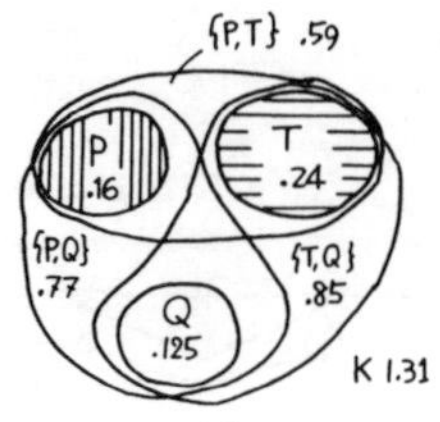

(a)

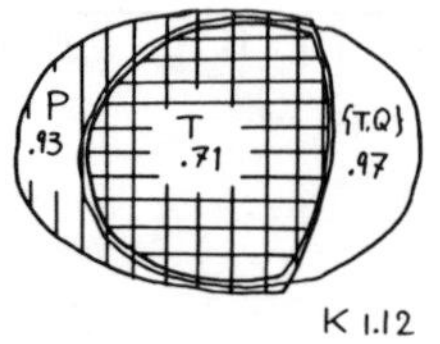

(b)

Figure 5. (a) G_x of four-person model. Any set $K = \{P, T, Q\}$ corresponds to a closed loop whose area is proportional to its fuzzy measure value. (b) G_x of three-person model.

CONCLUSION

In order to build a model that explains the evaluation mechanism more understandably, we used fuzzy measures rather than linear models. The reason we consider a two-layer model based on the result of factor analysis is that we hope to devise a still more transparent evaluation model.

We have shown a concrete procedure to construct those models. Differences in the ways in which pictures are evaluated are revealed that are not merely quantitative but also structural.

References

1. Mishina H., Ohno, Y., Niikura, M., Irie, H., Mikami, S., Ohtsuki, K., and Kominami, T., Evaluation of print quality, *Proceedings of the 72nd Spring Conference of Japanese Society of Printing Science and Technology*, 1-4, 1984 (in Japanese).

2. Sugeno, M., and Murofushi, T., Choquet's integral as an integral form for a general class of fuzzy measures, *Proceedings IFSA'87*, 408-411, 1987.

3. Kojima, M., *Souhosei to Hudouten*, Sangyou Tosyo, Tokyo, 1981 (in Japanese).

4. Rosenfeld, A., Hummel, R., and Zucker, S., Scene labeling by relaxation operations, *IEEE Trans. Syst., Man Cybern.* SMC-6(6), 420-433, 1976.

5. Onisawa, T., Sugeno, M., Nishiwaki, Y., Kawai, H., and Harima, Y., Fuzzy measure analysis of public attitude towards the use of nuclear energy, *Fuzzy Sets Syst.* 20, 259-289, 1986.

Image enhancement and thresholding by optimization of fuzzy compactness

Sankar K. PAL* and Azriel ROSENFELD
Center for Automation Research, University of Maryland, College Park, MD 20742, USA

Received 11 August 1987

Abstract: Algorithms based on minimization of compactness and of fuzziness are developed whereby it is possible to obtain both fuzzy and nonfuzzy (thresholded) versions of an ill-defined image. The incorporation of fuzziness in the spatial domain, i.e., in describing the geometry of regions, makes it possible to provide more meaningful results than by considering fuzziness in grey level alone. The effectiveness of the algorithms is demonstrated for different bandwidths of the membership function using a blurred chromosome image having a bimodal histogram and a noisy tank image having a unimodal histogram as input.

Key words: Image enhancement, tresholding, compactness, fuzzy sets, fuzziness, fuzzy compactness.

1. Introduction

The problem of grey level thresholding plays a key role in image processing and recognition. For example, in enhancing contrast in an image, we need to select proper threshold levels so that some suitable non-linear transformation can highlight a desirable set of pixel intensities compared to others. Similarly, in image segmentation one needs proper histogram thresholding whose objective is to establish boundaries in order to partition the image space (crisply) into meaningful regions.

When the regions in an image are ill-defined (i.e., fuzzy), it is natural and also appropriate to avoid committing ourselves to a specific segmentation by allowing the segments to be fuzzy subsets of the image. Fuzzy geometric properties (which are the generalization of those for ordinary regions) as defined by Rosenfeld [1–6] seem to provide a helpful tool for such analysis.

The present paper is an attempt to perform the above mentioned task automatically with the help of a compactness measure [4] which takes into account fuzziness in the spatial domain, i.e., in the geometry of the image regions. Besides this measure, we have also considered the ambiguity in grey level through the concepts of index of fuzziness [6], entropy [7] and index of nonfuzziness (crispness) [8]. These concepts were found by Pal [9–13] to provide objective measures for image enhancement, threshold selection, feature evaluation and seed point extraction.

The algorithms described here extract the fuzzy segmented version of an ill-defined image by minimizing the ambiguity in both the intensity and spatial domain. For making a nonfuzzy decision one may consider the cross-over point of the corresponding S function [14] as the threshold level. The nonfuzzy decisions corresponding to various algorithms are compared here when a blurred chromosome image and a noisy tank image are used as input.

The support of the National Science Foudation under Grant DCR-86-03723 is gratefully acknowledged, as is the help of Sandra German in preparing this paper.

*On leave from the Electronics and Communication Sciences Unit, Indian Statistical Institute, Calcutta 700035, India.

2. Measures of fuzziness in an image [8–10, 13]

An image X of size $M \times N$ and L levels can be considered as an array of fuzzy singletons, each

Reprinted with permission from *Pattern Recognition Letters*, vol. 7, pp. 77–86, February 1988.

having a value of membership denoting its degree of brightness relative to some brightness level l, $l = 0, 1, 2, \ldots, L-1$. In the notation of fuzzy sets, we may therefore write $X = \{\mu_X(x_{mn}) = \mu_{mn}/x_{mn};\ m = 1, 2, \ldots, M;\ n = 1, 2, \ldots, N\}$ where $\mu_X(x_{mn})$ or μ_{mn}/x_{mn} $(0 \le \mu_{mn} \le 1)$ denotes the grade of possessing some brightness property μ_{mn} (as defined in the next section) by the (m, n)th pixel intensity x_{mn}.

The index of fuzziness reflects the average amount of ambiguity (fuzziness) present in an image X by measuring the distance ('linear' and 'quadratic' corresponding to linear index of fuzziness and quadratic index of fuzziness) between its fuzzy property μ_X and the nearest two-level property $\mu_{\underline{X}}$; in other words, the distance between the gray tone image and its nearest two-tone version. The term 'entropy', on the other hand, uses Shannon's function but its meaning is quite different from classical entropy because no probabilistic concept is needed to define it. The index of nonfuzziness, as its name implies, measures the amount of nonfuzziness (crispness) in μ_X by computing its distance from its complement version. These quantities are defined below.

(a) Linear index of fuzziness

$$\nu_l(X) = \frac{2}{MN}\sum_m\sum_n |\mu_X(x_{mn}) - \mu_{\underline{X}}(x_{mn})| \quad (1a)$$

$$= \frac{2}{MN}\sum_m\sum_n \mu_{X \cap \overline{X}}(x_{mn}) \quad (1b)$$

$$= \frac{2}{MN}\sum_m\sum_n \min(\mu_X(x_{mn}), 1 - \mu_X(x_{mn})),$$

$$m = 1, 2, \ldots, M;\ n = 1, 2, \ldots, N,$$

where $\mu_{\underline{X}}(x_{mn})$ denotes the nearest two-level version of X such that

$$\mu_{\underline{X}}(x_{mn}) = 0 \quad \text{if } \mu_X(x_{mn}) \le 0.5, \quad (2a)$$

$$= 1 \quad \text{otherwise.} \quad (2b)$$

(b) Quadratic index of fuzziness

$$\nu_q(X) = \frac{2}{\sqrt{MN}}\left[\sum_m\sum_n [\mu_X(x_{mn}) - \mu_{\underline{X}}(x_{mn})]^2\right]^{0.5}, \quad (3)$$

$$m = 1, 2, \ldots, M;\ n = 1, 2, \ldots, N.$$

(c) Entropy

$$H(X) = \frac{1}{MN \ln 2}\sum_m\sum_n S_n(\mu_X(x_{mn})) \quad (4a)$$

with

$$S_n(\mu_X(x_{mn})) = -\mu_X(x_{mn})\ln \mu_X(x_{mn}) - (1 - \mu_X(x_{mn}))\ln(1 - \mu_X(x_{mn})),$$

$$m = 1, 2, \ldots, M;\ n = 1, 2, \ldots, N. \quad (4b)$$

(d) Index of nonfuzziness (crispness)

$$\eta(X) = \frac{1}{MN}\sum_m\sum_n |\mu_X(x_{mn}) - \mu_{\overline{X}}(x_{mn})|, \quad (5)$$

$\overline{X}$ is the complement of X,

$m = 1, 2, \ldots, M;\ n = 1, 2, \ldots, N.$

All these measures lie in [0, 1] and have the following properties

$$I(X) = 0 \text{ (min)} \quad \text{for } \mu_X(x_{mn}) = 0 \text{ or } 1,\ \forall(m, n), \quad (6a)$$

$$I(X) = 1 \text{ (max)} \quad \text{for } \mu_X(x_{mn}) = 0.5,\ \forall(m, n), \quad (6b)$$

$$I(X) \ge I(X^*), \quad (6c)$$

$$I(X) = I(\overline{X}), \quad (6d)$$

where I stands for $\nu(X)$, $H(X)$ and $1 - \eta(X)$. X^* is the 'sharpened' or 'intensified' version of X such that

$$\mu_{X^*}(x_{mn}) \ge \mu_X(x_{mn}) \quad \text{if } \mu_X(x_{mn}) \ge 0.5, \quad (7a)$$

$$\le \mu_X(x_{mn}) \quad \text{if } \le 0.5. \quad (7b)$$

3. Fuzzy geometry of image subsets [1–5, 13]

Rosenfeld [1–5] extended the concepts of digital picture geometry to fuzzy subsets and generalized some of the standard geometric properties of and relationships among regions to fuzzy subsets. Among the extensions of the various properties, we only discuss here the area, perimeter and compactness of a fuzzy image subset, characterized by $\mu_X(x_{mn})$, which will be used in the following section for developing threshold selection algorithms. In defining the above mentioned parameters we replace $\mu_X(x_{mn})$ by μ for simplicity.

The area of μ is defined as

$$a(\mu) \triangleq \int \mu \tag{8}$$

where the integral is taken over any region outside which $\mu = 0$.

If μ is piecewise constant (for example, in a digital image) $a(\mu)$ is the weighted sum of the areas of the regions on which μ has constant values, weighted by these values.

For the piecewise constant case, the perimeter of μ is defined as

$$p(\mu) \triangleq \sum_{i,j}\sum_{k} |\mu_i - \mu_j|\,|A_{ijk}| \tag{9}$$

$$i,j = 1, 2, \ldots, r;\ i < j;\ k = 1, 2, \ldots, r_{ij}.$$

This is just the weighted sum of the length of the arcs A_{ijk} along which the i-th and j-th regions having constant μ values μ_i and μ_j respectively meet, weighted by the absolute difference of these values.

The compactness of μ is defined as

$$\mathrm{comp}(\mu) \triangleq a(\mu)/p^2(\mu). \tag{10}$$

For crisp sets, this is largest for a disk, where it is equal to $1/4\pi$. For a fuzzy disk where μ depends only on the distance from the origin (center), it can be shown that

$$a(\mu)/p^2(\mu) \geq 1/4\pi. \tag{11}$$

In other words, of all possible fuzzy disks, the compactness is smallest for its crisp version. For this reason, in this paper we will use minimization (rather than maximization) of fuzzy compactness as a criterion for image enhancement and threshold selection.

4. Threshold selection

A. Minimizing fuzziness [10, 13]

Let us consider for example, the minimization of $v_1(X)$. It is seen from equations (2) that the nearest ordinary plane μ_X (which represents the closest two-tone version of the grey tone image X) is dependent on the position of the cross-over point, i.e., the 0.5 value of μ_X. Therefore a proper selection of the cross-over point may be made which will result in a minimum value of $v(X)$ only when the cross-over point corresponds to the appropriate boundary between regions (clusters) in X.

This can be explained further as follows. Suppose we consider the standard S-function (Figure 1) [14]

$$\begin{aligned}
\mu_X(x_{mn}) &= S(x_{mn}; a, b, c) \\
&= 0, && x_{mn} \leq a, && \text{(12a)} \\
&= 2[(x_{mn} - a)/(c - a)]^2, && a \leq x_{mn} \leq b, && \text{(12b)} \\
&= 1 - 2[(x_{mn} - c)/(c - a)]^2, && b \leq x_{mn} \leq c, && \text{(12c)} \\
&= 1, && x_{mn} \geq c, && \text{(12d)}
\end{aligned}$$

with cross-over point $b = (a + c)/2$ and bandwidth

$$\Delta b = b - a = c - b$$

for obtaining $\mu_X(x_{mn})$ or μ_{mn} (representing the degree of brightness of each pixel) from the given x_{mn} of the image X. Then for a cross-over point selected at, say, $b = l_i$ we have $\mu_X(l_i) = 0.5$ and μ_{mn} would take on values > 0.5 and < 0.5 corresponding to $x_{mn} > l_i$ and $< l_i$; which implies allocation of the grey levels into two ranges. The term $v(X)$ then measures the average ambiguity in X by computing $\mu_{X \cap \bar{X}}(x_{mn})$ in such a way that the contribution of the levels towards $v(X)$ comes mostly from those near l_i and decreases as we move away from l_i.

Therefore, modification of the cross-over point will result in different segmented images with vary-

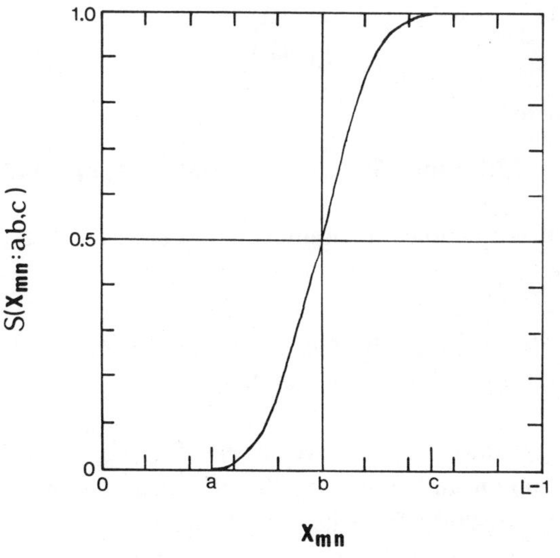

Figure 1. *S* function.

ing $\nu(X)$. When b corresponds to the appropriate boundary (threshold) between two regions, there will be a minimum number of pixel intensities in X having $\mu_{mn} \simeq 0.5$ (resulting in $\nu \simeq 1$) and a maximum number of pixel intensities having $\mu_{mn} \simeq 0$ or 1 (resulting in $\nu \simeq 0$) thus contributing least towards $\nu(X)$. This optimum (minimum) value of fuzziness would be greater for any other selection of the cross-over point.

Method of computation (Algorithm 1)

Given an $M \times N$ image with minimum and maximum grey levels $l_{\min}$ and $l_{\max}$:

Step 1. Construct the 'bright image' membership μ_X, where

$$\mu_X(l) = S(l; a, l_i, c), \quad l_{\min} \le l, l_i \le l_{\max}, \qquad (13)$$

using equation (12) with cross-over point $b = l_i$ and a particular bandwidth $\Delta b = c - l_i = l_i - a$.

Step 2. Compute the amount of fuzziness in μ_X corresponding to $b = l_i$ with

$$\nu(X) \mid l_i = \frac{2}{MN} \sum_l \min\{S(l; a, l_i, c), 1 - S(l; a, l_i, c)\} h(l) \qquad (14a)$$

$$= \frac{2}{MN} \sum_l T_i(l) h(l) \qquad (14b)$$

where

$$T_i(l) = \min\{S(l; a, l_i, c), 1 - S(l; a, l_i, c)\} \qquad (14c)$$

and $h(l)$ denotes the number of occurrences of the level l.

Step 3. Vary l_i from $l_{\min}$ to $l_{\max}$ and select $l_i = l_c$, say, for which $\nu(X)$ is a minimum.

l_c is thus the cross-over point of $\mu_X(x_{mn})$ having minimum ambiguity (i.e., for which μ_X has minimum distance from its closest two-tone version). μ_{mn} can be regarded as a *fuzzy segmented version* of the image, with $\mu_{mn} < 0.5$ and > 0.5 corresponding to regions $[l_{\min}, l_c - 1]$ and $[l_c, l_{\max}]$.

For the purpose of nonfuzzy segmentation, one can consider the level l_c as the threshold between background and object, or the boundary of the object region. This can further be verified from equation (14) which shows that the minimum value of $\nu(X)$ would always correspond to the valley region of the histogram having minimum number of occurrences.

Variation of bandwidth (Δb)

Let us call $T_i(l)$ (equation 14(c)) a Triangular Window function centered at l_i with bandwidth Δb. As Δb decreases, μ_X would have more intensified contrast around the cross-over point resulting in decrease of ambiguity in μ_X. As a result, the possibility of detecting some undesirable thresholds (spurious minima in the histogram) increases because of the smaller width of the $T_i(l)$ function.

On the other hand, increase of Δb results in a higher value of fuzziness and thus leads toward the possibility of losing some of the weak minima.

The application of this technique to both bimodal and multimodal images with various T_i functions based on $\nu_l(X)$, $\nu_q(X)$, $H(X)$ and $\eta(X)$ is demonstrated in [10, 13].

B. Minimizing compactness

In the previous discussion of threshold selection we considered fuzziness in the grey levels of an image. In this section we take fuzziness in the spatial domain into consideration by using the compactness measure for selecting nonfuzzy thresholds.

It is seen from Section 3 that both the perimeter and area of a fuzzy segmented image depend on the membership value, denoting the degree of brightness, say, of each region. It is further to be noted that the compactness of a fuzzy region decreases as its μ value increases and it is smallest for a crisp one. We will now define two algorithms to show how the above mentioned concept can be utilized for selecting a threshold between two regions (say, the background and a single object) in a bimodal image X.

As in the case of the previous algorithm, we construct μ_{mn} with different S functions having constant

Δb value and select the cross-over pointof the μ_X as the boundary of the object for which comp(μ) is a minimum.

Method of computation (Algorithm 2)

Given an $M \times N$ image with minimum and maximum grey levels $l_{\min}$ and $l_{\max}$:

Step 1. Construct 'bright' image μ_X as in Step 1 of Algorithm 1.

Step 2. Compute the area and perimeter of μ_X corresponding to $b = l_i$ with

$$a(\mu)\,|\,l_i = \sum_m\sum_n \mu_{mn} = \sum_l S(l;\, a,\, l_i,\, c)h(l), \qquad (15)$$

$$m = 1, 2, \ldots, M;\; n = 1, 2, \ldots, N;$$
$$l_{\min} \leq l,\, l_i \leq l_{\max}$$

and

$$p(\mu)\,|\,l_i = \sum_{m=1}^{M}\sum_{n=1}^{N-1}\left|\mu_{mn} - \mu_{m,n+1}\right| + \sum_{n=1}^{N}\sum_{m=1}^{M-1}\left|\mu_{mn} - \mu_{m+1,n}\right| \qquad (16)$$

(excluding the frame of the image).

For example, consider the 4×4 μ_{mn} array

$$\begin{matrix} 0 & 0 & 0 & 0 \\ 0 & \alpha & \beta & 0 \\ 0 & 0 & \beta & \gamma \\ 0 & \delta & 0 & 0 \end{matrix}, \quad 1 \geq \alpha, \beta, \gamma, \delta > 0.$$

Here, $a(\mu) = \alpha + 2\beta + \gamma + \delta$
and

$$p(\mu) = [\alpha + |\beta - \alpha| + \beta + \beta + |\gamma - \beta| + \delta + \delta] + [\alpha + \alpha + \delta + \beta + 0 + \beta + \gamma + \gamma].$$

Step 3. Compute the compactness of μ_X corresponding to $b = l_i$ with

$$\text{comp}(\mu)\,|\,l_i = \frac{a(\mu)\,|\,l_i}{p^2(\mu)\,|\,l_i}. \qquad (17)$$

Step 4. Vary l_i from $l_{\min}$ to $l_{\max}$ and select that $l_i = l_c$, say, for which comp(μ) is minimum

The level l_c therefore denotes the cross-over point of the fuzzy image plane μ_{mn} which is least compact (or most crisp). The μ_{mn} so obtained can therefore be viewed as a *fuzzy segmented version* of the image X.

Like the previous algorithm, one can consider l_c as the threshold for making a nonfuzzy decision on classifying/segmenting the image into regions.

Method of computation (Algorithm 3)

Here we approximate the definitions of area and compactness of μ_X by considering that μ_X has only two values corresponding to the background and object regions. The μ value for the background is assumed to be zero, whereas the μ-value of the object region is monotonically increasing with increase in threshold level. Therefore, by varying the threshold, one can have different segmented versions of the object region. Each segmented version thresholded at l_t has its area and perimeter computed as follows:

$$a(\mu_t) = a \cdot \mu_t \qquad (18a)$$

$$= \mu_t \sum_l h(l), \quad l_t \leq l \leq l_{\max}, \qquad (18b)$$

where a denotes the area of the region on which $\mu = \mu_t$ (constant), i.e., the number of pixels having grey level greater than or equal to l_t and

$$p(\mu_t) = \mu_t \cdot p \qquad (18c)$$

where p denotes the length of the arcs along which the regions having $\mu = \mu_t$ and $\mu = 0$ meet, or, in other words, the perimeter of the region on which $\mu = \mu_t$ (constant).

For the example considered in Algorithm 2, the values of $a(\mu_t)$ and $p(\mu_t)$ for $\alpha = \beta = \gamma = \delta = \mu_t$ will be $5\mu_t$ and $12\mu_t$ respectively.

The algorithm for selecting the boundary of a single-object region from an $M \times N$ dimensional image may therefore be stated as follows:

Step 1. Construct the 'bright' image μ_X using

$$\mu_X(l) = S(l;\, a,\, b,\, c) \qquad (19)$$

with $a = l_{\min}$, $c = l_{\max}$ and $b = (a + c)/2$.

Step 2. Generate a segmented version putting

$$\mu = 0 \quad \text{for } \mu < \mu_t, \tag{20a}$$

$$= \mu_t \quad \text{for } \mu \geq \mu_t, \tag{20b}$$

where μ_t is the value of $\mu_X(l_t)$ obtained in Step 1.

Step 3. Compute the compactness of the segmented version thresholded at l_t:

$$\text{comp}(\mu_t) = \frac{a \cdot \mu_t}{p^2 \cdot \mu_t^2} = \frac{a}{p^2 \cdot \mu_t}. \tag{21}$$

Step 4. Vary l_t in $(l_{\min}, l_{\max})$ and hence μ_t in $(0, 1)$ and select the level as boundary of the object for which equation (21) attains its minimum.

It should be noted here that after approximation of the area and perimeter of μ_{mn}, the compactness measure (equation (21)) reduces to $1/\mu_t$ times the crisp compactness of the object region. Unlike Algorithms 1 and 2, here μ_X is kept fixed throughout the process and the output of the algorithm is a nonfuzzy segemted version of X determined by l_t.

C. Minimizing the product ***(Algorithm 4)***

Algorithms 1–3 minimize either the amount of fuzziness or the compactness of an image X. We can combine these measures and compute the product of fuzziness and compactness, and determine the level for which the product becomes a minimum. In other words, we compute

$$\theta_{l_i} = v(X)\,|_{l_i} \cdot \text{comp}(\mu)\,|_{l_i} \tag{22}$$

(using equations (14) and (17))

$$\text{or } \theta_{l_t} = v(X)\,|_{l_t} \cdot \text{comp}(\mu_t) \tag{23}$$

(using equations (14) and (21))

at each value of l_i (or l_t), $l_{\min} < l_i, l_t < l_{\max}$, and select $l_i = l_c$, say, as threshold for which equation (22) (or (23)) is a minimum. The corresponding μ_{mn} represents the *fuzzy segmented version* of the image as far as minimization of its fuzziness in grey level and the spatial domain is concerned.

It should be mentioned here that although we considered the linear index of fuzziness in Algorithms 1 and 4, one can also consider the other measures, namely $v_q(X)$, $H(X)$ and $\eta(X)$, for computing the total amount of fuzziness in μ_{mn}.

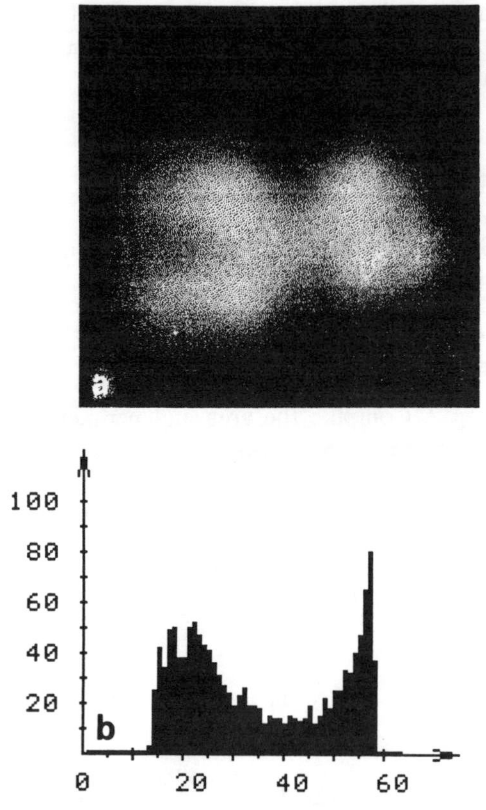

Figure 2. (a) Chromosome image; (b) Histogram.

5. Implementation and results

Figure 2a shows a 64 × 64, 64 level image of a blurred chromosome with $l_{\min} = 12$ and $l_{\max} = 59$. Figure 2b shows its bimodal histogram.

The different minima obtained using Algorithms 1–4 for $\Delta b = 2, 4, 8, 16$ are given in Table 1. The enhanced version of the chromosome corresponding to these thresholds (minima) are shown in Figures 3 to 8 only for $\Delta b = 4$, 8 and 16. In each of Figures 3–5, (a), (b) and (c) correspond to Algorithm 1, Algorithm 2 and equation (22) of Algorithm 4. Similarly, in Figures 6–7, (a), (b) and (c) correspond to Algorithm 1, Algorithm 3 and equation (23) of Algorithm 4.

It is seen that the compactness measure usually results in more minima as compared to index of fuzziness. The index of fuzziness (Algorithm 1) basically sharpens the histogram and it detects a single threshold in the valley region of the histogram for $\Delta b = 4$, 8 and 16. At $\Delta b = 2$, the algorithm as expected results in some undesirable thresholds cor-

Table 1
Minima for chromosome image

	$\Delta b=2$	$\Delta b=4$	$\Delta b=8$	$\Delta b=16$
$\nu(X)$ (Algorithm 1)	19, 30, 40*, 46	40	40	46
comp(μ) Algorithm 2)	18, 24, 31, 56*	29, 54*	31, 47*	34
comp(μ) (Algorithm 3)	33, 48*	33, 48*	33, 48*	33, 48*
Product (eqn. (22) of Algorithm 4)	19, 31, 40, 42*, 46	40	41	41
Product (eqn. (23) of Algorithm 4)	40, 42, 44, 46*, 53	42*, 45, 53	42*, 45, 48	33, 48*

* Denotes global minimum.
Algorithm 3 does not involve variation of Δb.

responding to weak minima of the histogram. This conforms to the earlier investigation [10]. Algorithms 2 and 3 based on the compactness measure, on the other hand, detect a higher-valued threshold (global minimum) which results in better segmentation (or enhancement) of the chromosome as far as its shape is concerned.

The advantage of the compactness measures over the index value is that they take fuzziness in the spa-

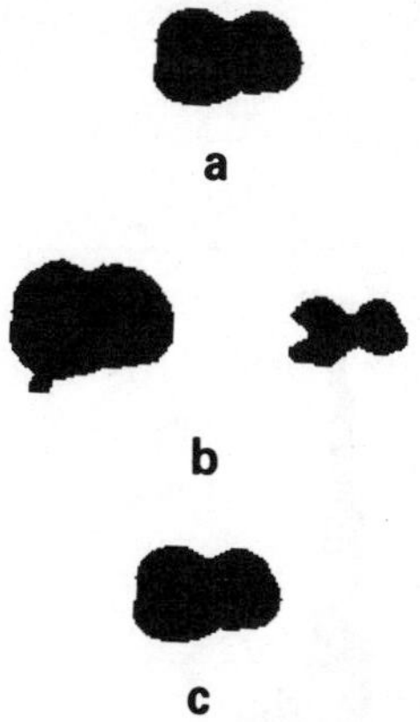

Figure 3. Enhanced/thresholded versions of chromosome for $\Delta b = 4$. (a) Algorithm 1 ($l_c = 40$); (b) Algorithm 2 ($l_c = 29, 54$); (c) Equation (22) ($l_c = 40$).

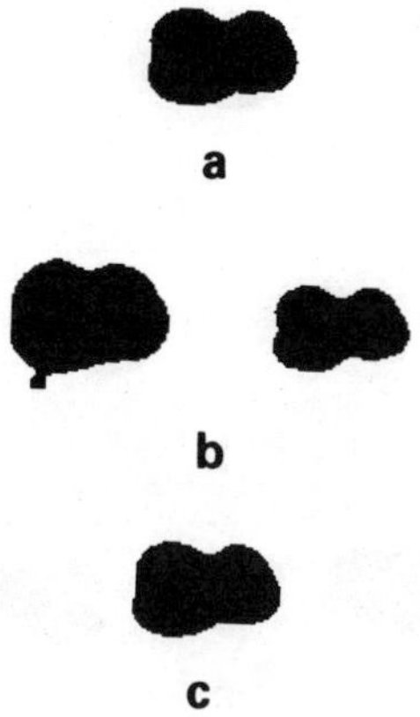

Figure 4. Enhanced/thresholded versions of chromosome for $\Delta b = 8$. (a) Algorithm 1 ($l_c = 40$); (b) Algorithm 2 ($l_c = 31, 47$); (c) Equation (22) ($l_c = 41$).

Figure 5. Enhanced/thresholded versions of chromosome for $\Delta b = 16$. (a) Algorithm 1 ($l_c = 46$); (b) Algorithm 2 ($l_c = 34$); (c) Equation (22) ($l_c = 41$).

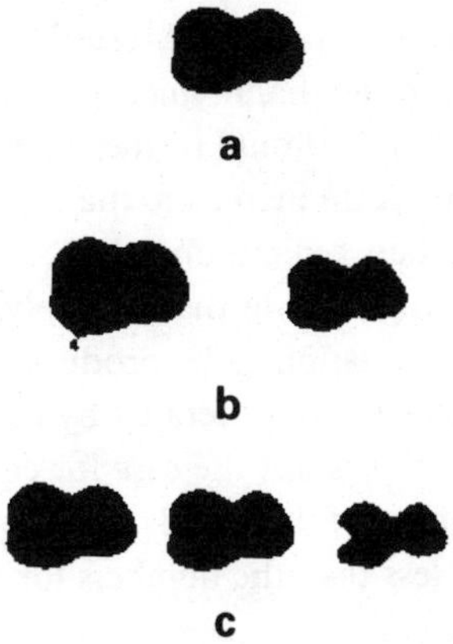

Figure 6. Enhanced/thresholded versions of chromosome for $\Delta b = 4$. (a) Algorithm 1 ($l_c = 40$); (b) Algorithm 3 ($l_c = 33, 48$); (c) Equation (23) ($l_c = 42, 45, 53$).

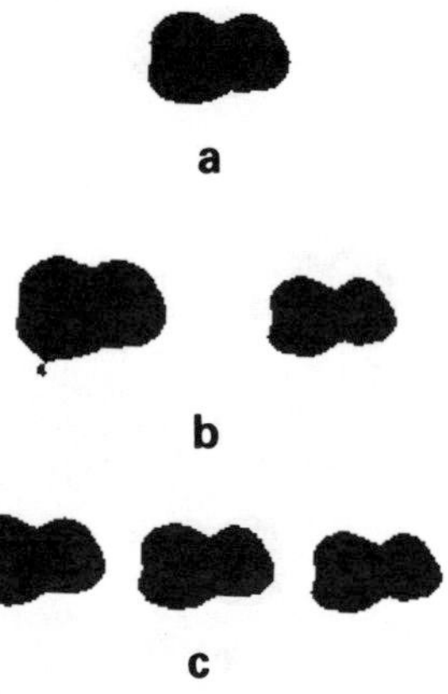

Figure 7. Enhanced/thresholded versions of chromosome for $\Delta b = 8$. (a) Algorithm 1 ($l_c = 40$); (b) Algorithm 3 ($l_c = 33, 48$); (c) Equation (23) ($l_c = 42, 45, 48$).

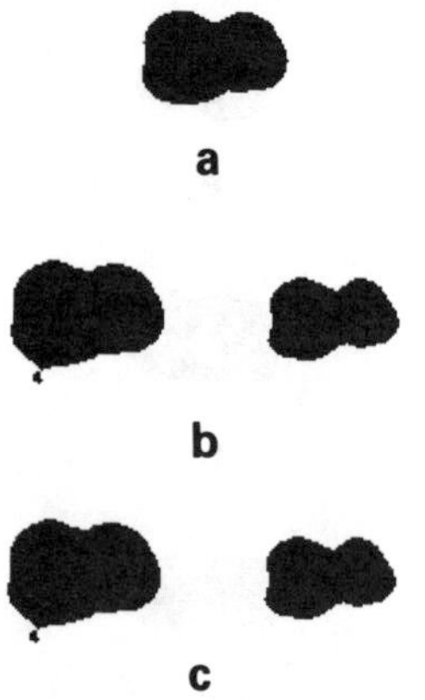

Figure 8. Enhanced/thresholded versions of chromosome for $\Delta b = 16$. (a) Algorithm 1 ($l_c = 46$); (b) Algorithm 3 ($l_c = 33, 48$); (c) Equation (23) ($l_c = 33, 48$).

tial domain (i.e., the geometry of the object) into consideration in extracting thresholds. The index value, on the other hand, incorporates fuzziness only in grey level. It should further be noted for Algorithm 2 that as Δb increases, the number of and the separation between minima also decrease.

It is interesting to note that multiplying $\nu(X)$ by comp(μ_t), i.e., equation (23), produces at least as many thresholds as are generated by the individual measures. But this is not the case for equation (22) where the number of thresholds is (except for $\Delta b = 2$) equal to or less than the numbers for the individual measures.

The above observations can be explained as follows. As mentioned before, $\nu(X)$ basically sharpens the histogram. Therefore as l_i increases, it first increases until it reaches a maximum, and then decreases until a minimum (threshold) is attained. After this it follows the same pattern for the other mode of the histogram. The compactness measure, on the other hand, first starts decreasing until it reaches a minimum, then increases for a while, and then starts decreasing again.

It is further seen from our results that the variation of compactness in Algorithm 3 plays a more dominant role than the variation of index value in Algorithm 1 in detecting minima. The case is reversed for the combination of Algorithm 1 and Algorithm 2, where the product is influenced more by the index value. As a result, the threshold obtained by equation (22) is found to be within the range of threshold values obtained by the individual measures. Equation (23), on the other hand, is able to create a higher-valued (or at least equal) threshold which results in better object enhancement than those of the individual measures.

Figures (9(a) and 9(b) show a noisy image of a tank and its unimodal histogram, having $l_{min} = 14$,

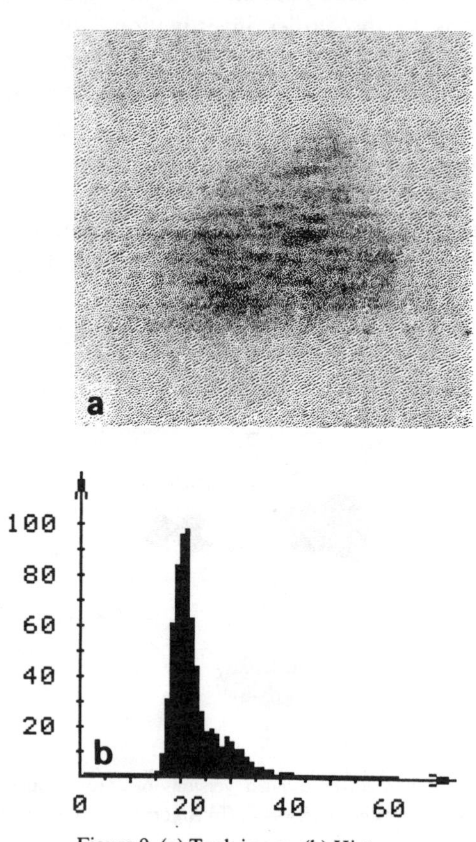

Figure 9. (a) Tank image; (b) Histogram.

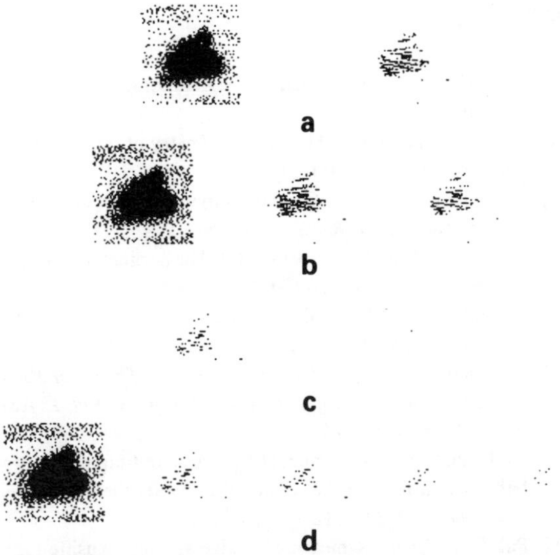

Figure 10. Enhanced/thresholded versions of tank for $\Delta b = 4$. (a) Algorithm 2 ($l_c = 23, 34$); (b) Algorithm 3 ($l_c = 22, 33, 36$); (c) Equation (22) ($l_c = 40, 49$); (d) Equation (23) ($l_c = 22, 40, 42, 44, 46$).

$l_{max} = 50$. The minima obtained by the different algorithms for $\Delta b = 2$, 4, 8 and 16 are given in Table 2. The corresponding enhanced versions for $\Delta b = 4$, 8 and 16 are shown in Figures 10–12 for various combinations of algorithms.

As expected, the index of fuzziness alone was not able to detect a threshold for the tank image because of its unimodal histogram. The compactness measure, on the other hand, does give good thresholds. As in the case of the chromosome image, equation (23) yields at least as many thresholds as

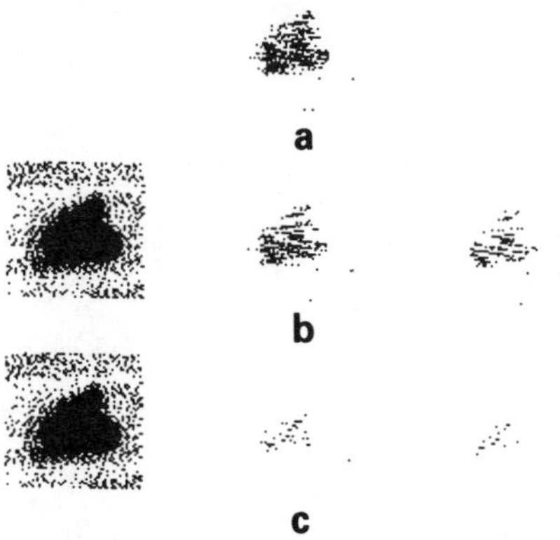

Figure 11. Enhanced/thresholded versions of tank for $\Delta b = 8$. (a) Algorithm 2 ($l_c = 31$); (b) Algorithm 3 ($l_c = 22, 33, 36$); (c) Equation (23) ($l_c = 22, 42, 44$).

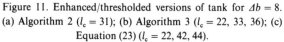

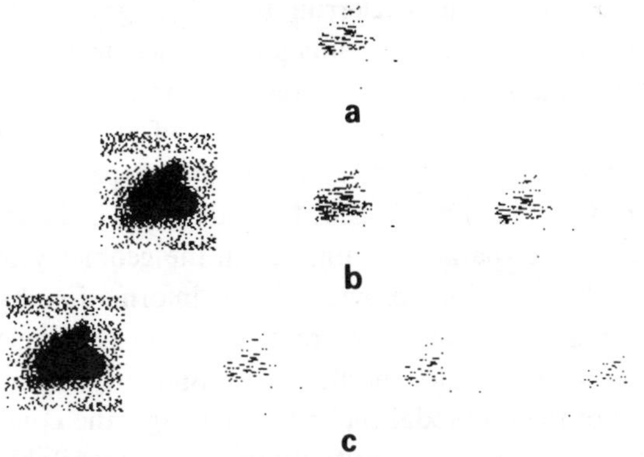

Figure 12. Enhanced/thresholded versions of tank for $\Delta b = 16$. (a) Algorithm 2 ($l_c = 36$); (b) Algorithm 3 ($l_c = 22, 33, 36$); (c) Equation (23) ($l_c = 22, 38, 40, 42$).

are generated by the compactness measure. Similarly (except for $\Delta b = 2$) equation (22) yields at most as many thresholds as the compactness measure.

6. Conclusions

Algorithms based on compactness measures of fuzzy sets are developed and used to determine thresholds (both fuzzy and nonfuzzy) of an ill-defined image (or the enhanced version of a fuzzy ob-

Table 2
Minima for tank image

	$\Delta b=2$	$\Delta b=4$	$\Delta b=8$	$\Delta b=16$
$\nu(X)$ (Algorithm 1)	–	–	–	–
comp(μ) (Algorithm 2)	21*, 33	23*, 34	31	36
comp(μ) (Algorithm 3)	22, 33*, 36	22, 33*, 36	22, 33*, 36	22, 33*, 36
Product (eqn. (22) of Algorithm 4)	24, 39*, 43, 46, 49	40, 49*	–	–
Product (eqn. (23) of Algorithm 4)	24, 40, 42, 46*	22, 40, 42*, 44, 46	22, 42*, 44	22, 38, 40, 42*

*Denotes global minimum.
Algorithm 3 does not involve variation of Δb.

ject region) without referring to its histogram. The enhanced chromosome images obtained from the global minima of the measures are found to be better than those obtained on the basis of minimizing fuzziness in grey level, as far as the shape of the chromosome is concerned. Consideration of fuzziness in the spatial domain, i.e., in the geometry of the object region, provides more information by making it possible to extract more than a single thresholded version of an object. Similarly in the case of the unimodal (noisy) tank image, the compactness measure is able to determine some suitable thresholds but the index parameter is not. Furthermore, optimization of both compactness and fuzziness usually allows better selection of thresholded/enhanced versions.

Acknowledgement

The authors wish to thank Mr. Shijie Wang for doing the computer programming, Mr. R. Sitaraman for his constructive criticism of the work, and Ms. Sandra German for typing the manuscript. One of the authors (S.K. Pal) is also grateful to the CIES, Washington, DC and the United States Educational Foundation in India for providing him a Fulbright Visiting Fellowship to work in the U.S.A.

References

[1] Rosenfeld, A. (1979). Fuzzy digital topology. *Inform. and Control* 40, 76–87.

[2] Rosenfeld, A. (1984). The fuzzy geometry of image subsets. *Patt. Recog. Lett.* 2, 311–317.

[3] Rosenfeld, A. (1983). On connectivity properties of grey-scale pictures. *Patt. Recog.* 16, 47–50.

[4] Rosenfeld, A. and S. Haber (1985). The perimeter of a fuzzy set. *Patt. Recog.* 18, 125–130.

[5] Rosenfeld, A. (1984). The diameter of a fuzzy set. *Fuzzy Sets and Systems* 13, 241–246.

[6] Kaufmann, A. (1975). *Introduction to The Theory of Fuzzy Subsets – Fundamental Theoretical Elements, Vol 1.* Academic Press, New York.

[7] De Luca, A. and S. Termini (1972). A definition of non-probabilistic entropy in the setting of fuzzy set theory. *Inform. and Control* 20, 301–312.

[8] Pal, S.K. (1986). A measure of edge ambiguity using fuzzy sets. *Patt. Recog. Lett.* 4, 51–56.

[9] Pal, S.K. (1982). A note on the quantitative measure of image enhancement through fuzziness. *IEEE Trans., PAMI* 4, 204–208.

[10] Pal, S.K., R.A. King and A.A. Hashim (1983). Automatic grey level thresholding through index of fuzziness and entropy. *Patt. Recog. Lett.* 1, 141–146.

[11] Pal, S.K. and B. Chakraborty (1986). Fuzzy set theoretic measure for automatic feature evaluation. *IEEE Trans. SMC* 16, 754–760.

[12] Pal, S.K. and P.K. Pramanik (1986). Fuzzy measures in determining seed points in clustering. *Patt. Recog. Lett.* 4, 159–164.

[13] Pal, S.K. and D. Dutta Majumder (1986). *Fuzzy Mathematical Approach to Pattern Recognition.* Wiley (Halsted Press), New York.

[14] Zadeh, L.A. (1975). Calculus of fuzzy restrictions. In: L.A. Zadeh et al., Eds., *Fuzzy Sets and Their Applications to Cognitive and Decision Processes.* Academic Press, London, 1–39.

ON THE COLOR IMAGE SEGMENTATION ALGORITHM BASED ON THE THRESHOLDING AND THE FUZZY c-MEANS TECHNIQUES

YOUNG WON LIM and SANG UK LEE*
Department of Control and Instrumentation Engineering, Seoul National University, Shinlim-Dong, Kwanak-Ku, Seoul, 151-742, Korea

(*Received* 3 *February* 1989; *in revised form* 25 *July* 1989; *received for publication* 18 *September* 1989)

Abstract—In this paper, a segmentation algorithm for color images based on the thresholding and the fuzzy c-means (FCM) techniques is presented. The scale-space filter is used as a tool for analyzing the histograms of three color components. The methodology uses a coarse-fine concept to reduce the computational burden required for the FCM. The coarse segmentation attempts to segment coarsely using the thresholding technique, while the fine segmentation assigns the pixels, which remain unclassified after the coarse segmentation, to the closest class using the FCM. Attempts also have been made to compare the performance of the proposed algorithm with other existing algorithms—Ohlander's, Rosenfeld's, and Bezdek's. Intensive computer simulation has been performed and the results are discussed in this paper. The simulation results indicate that the proposed algorithm yields the most accurate segmented image on the color coordinate proposed by Ohta *et al.*, while requiring a reasonable amount of computational effort.

Scale-space filter   Fuzzy c-means   Segmentation   Color image   Thresholding

1. INTRODUCTION

Segmentation is a process of grouping an image into units that are homogeneous with respect to one or more characteristics and it is an important task in image analysis.[1–5] However, most attention has been focused on the monochrome image segmentation whose goal is the initial separation of the individual objects in the perception of the scene. A common problem in segmentation of a monochrome image occurs when an image has a background of varying gray level such as gradually changing shades, or when collections we would like to call regions or classes assume some broad range of gray scales. This problem is inherent since intensity is the only available information from monochrome images. It has long been recognized that the human eye can detect only in the neighborhood of one or two dozen intensity levels at any one point in a complex image due to brightness adaptation, but can discern thousands of color shades and intensities.[2,6] Color is a perceptual phenomenon related to human response to different wavelengths in the visible electromagnetic spectrum.[6] Three psychological attributes, namely hue, saturation and intensity, are generally used to represent color. Compared to a monochrome image, a color image provides, in addition to intensity, additional information in the image. In fact, human beings intuitively feel that color is an important part of their visual experience, and color is useful or even necessary for powerful processing in computer vision. In computer vision researchers have attempted to utilize this additional information. Thus applications with color image are becoming increasingly prevalent nowadays.

Earlier work on color image segmentation views color as a random variable to be analyzed statistically and prior knowledge about characteristic object colors is used to classify pixels. This technique is called spectral signature analysis and has been used widely in remote sensing and biomedical image analysis. However, in a situation where specific object colors are not known in advance, clustering technique can be used instead.[7] The rationale of the clustering technique is that typically, the colors tend to form clusters in the histogram, one for each object in the image.[7] In clustering technique, a histogram is first obtained by the color values at all pixels and the shape of each cluster is found. Then, each pixel in the image is assigned to the cluster that is closest to the pixel color in space. Many clustering algorithms exist in the pattern recognition literature.[8,9] Among these, the fuzzy c-means (FCM) algorithm has received extensive attention.[10] Based upon fuzzy clustering principle, Bedzek *et al.*[11] developed a low-level segmentation methodology, in which the approach utilizes region growing concepts and pyramidal data structure (PDS) for the hierachical analysis of aerial image. Since in their approach a higher level image was acquired by averaging its four lower level images, block effects are observed in the segmentation result. The FCM is one of the best known

* To whom correspondence should be addressed.

clustering techniques. However, it is widely recognized that the clustering technique, including the FCM, suffers from problems related to (1) adjacent clusters frequently overlap in color space, causing incorrect pixel classification; and (2) clustering is more difficult when the number of clusters is unknown, as is typical for segmentation application. Especially, problem (2) is critical to the success of FCM (i.e. it requires prior knowledge of the number of regions existing in the image.) Otherwise false results are returned. Also this problem is at the heart of the cluster validity question, and as yet has no known general solution.[12,13] Moreover, the FCM has a problem of exhaustive computational burden. In conjunction with clustering, relaxation[14] and region splitting[15] has been proposed for color image segmentation. However both algorithms are computationally expensive and suffer from problems discussed above.

In this paper, a color image segmentation algorithm based upon the thresholding[16,17] and FCM[11] techniques in an image feature space is presented. The proposed segmentation strategy can be considered as a kind of coarse to fine technique, in the sense used by Spann and Wilson for texture image segmentation.[18] But it is worth stressing here that in our approach the main reason for adopting the coarse to fine strategy is to reduce the computational complexity required for the FCM. The coarse segmentation stage attempts to segment coarsely by using the thresholding technique. Various techniques for image segmentation have been developed so far.[19] However, in limited applications, histogram analysis for the setting of thresholds has also been successful in image segmentation. Of course, it is less appropriate in segmenting textured images. However, it still has various applications in situations where the object and background are homogeneous or smooth.[19] The thresholds and the number of regions to be searched are determined by the application of scale-space filtering to the histograms of the three color components. Those pixels which are not segmented by the coarse segmentation are further segmented using the FCM in the fine segmentation stage. The underlying assumption made in our approach is that the histograms are not unimodal. More specifically, it is assumed that measurement vectors corresponding to perceptually homogeneous regions cluster together in the measurement space; whereas those belonging to different classes lie farther apart from each other in the measurement space. Recently, Huntsberger *et al.* proposed an iterative algorithm for image segmentation in the feature space.[20] The difference between that algorithm and the work reported in this paper is an approach for finding the number of clusters. Our approach is to use the scale-space filter on the histograms, while their approach is to fix the number of clusters at four for each iteration of the algorithm.[20] The validity of the proposed approach is tested on the real images and the performance is compared with three existing algorithms, namely, Ohlander's,[15] Rosenfeld's,[14] and Bezdek's.[11] So far, very little formal evaluation and comparison among the different types of segmentation algorithms have been attempted. Since the usefulness of color image segmentation is dependent not only on the algorithm but also on the color coordinate, all algorithms are tested on the R–G–B, X–Y–Z, Y–I–Q, U–V–W and Ohta's coordinate.[21] Ohta *et al.* proposed the use of three components I1–I2–I3 that represent a simple linear transform from R–G–B: $I1 = (R + G + B)/3$; $I2 = R - B$; $I3 = (2G - R - B)/2$. During the rest of the paper, we shall call the Ohta's coordinate I1–I2–I3 for convenience. Performance comparison of these algorithms is made by computing the probability of error between the segmentation result and the ideally segmented image by hand.

The paper is organized as follows. Section 2 describes the proposed color image segmentation algorithm. Section 3 discusses the simulation results of the proposed algorithm and the other three algorithms. Finally, in Section 4, we present our conclusions.

2. PROPOSED ALGORITHM

When an image consists of object and background only (i.e. a two-class image), the best way to pick up a threshold is to search the histogram assuming it is bimodal, and find a gray level which separates the two peaks. If the histogram has two distinctly separated peaks, it is a trivial task to set a midgray threshold. Practical problem occurs, however, when the histogram is not bimodal and both object and background assume some broad range of gray levels as shown in Fig. 1. Specifically, it is ambiguous which class is assigned to the hatched area in Fig. 1 by the thresholding technique. Moreover, if an image contains more than one object (i.e. a multi-class image) it is necessary to determine the number of objects first, then pick up thresholds corresponding to the objects. In what follows next, the operation of the scale-space filter is described briefly for the sake of completeness. The scale-space filter is used as a tool for analyzing the histogram. We shall show how the number of regions can be automatically determined via the scale-space filtering technique. Subsequently, the methodology for coarse segmentation is given and a fine segmentation, in which it assigns the pixel that can not be grouped into any valid region after the coarse segmentation stage, to the closest one, is then described.

2.1. *Coarse segmentation*

It has been known that the derivatives, the extrema and the interval bounded by the extrema of a signal are very useful entities for a qualitative analysis of a physical signal. For this purpose, Witkin[22] defined

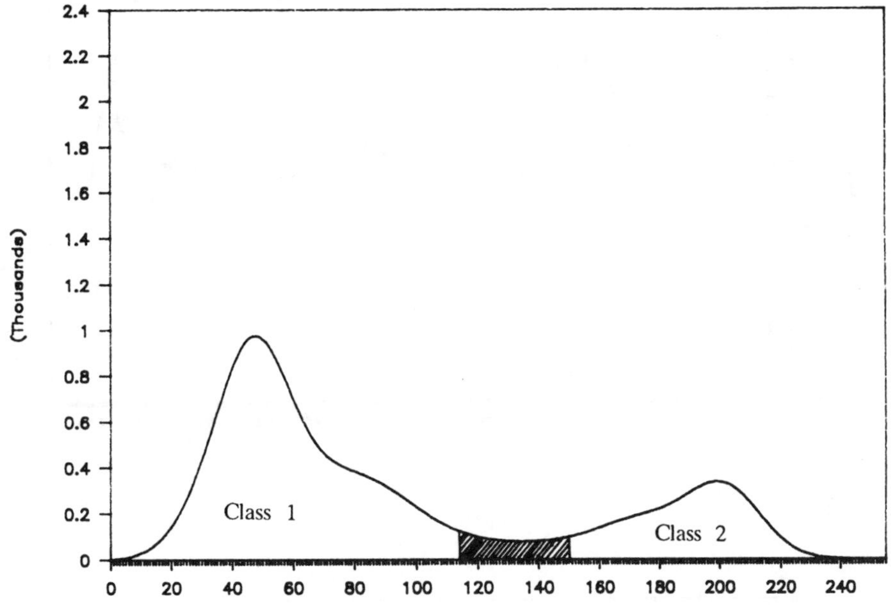

Fig. 1. A histogram assuming some broad range of gray values.

the Gaussian convolution of a 1-D signal $f(x)$ as the scale-space image of $f(x)$. The convolution is given by

$$F(x, \tau) = f(x) * g(x, \tau)$$
$$= \int_{-\infty}^{\infty} f(u) \frac{1}{(2\pi)^{1/2}\tau} \exp\left[-\frac{(x-u)^2}{2\tau^2}\right] du \quad (1)$$

where "*" implies a 1-D convolution. It depends both on the signals independent variable x and on the Gaussian deviation τ. Thus (x, τ) constitutes a surface and the (x, τ)-space is known to be a scale-space. The scale-space image of f is called F. It is well-known that the zero-crossing information of the derivatives of a signal is important to find the peaks and valleys of the histogram. Also the pairs of zero-crossings represent meaningful events such as peaks and valleys.[23] If we mark these zero-crossing locations of $F_{xx}(x, \tau)$ of (2) on the scale-space, this is the so called fingerprint.

$$F_{xx}(x, \tau) = \left[\frac{\partial^2}{\partial x^2} F(x, \tau)\right]. \quad (2)$$

As we decrease τ in the fingerprint, we can observe the new pairs of zero-crossings appearing. The parameter τ is called the scale constant, and it is very important to select a proper scale for a histogram analysis. The reason is that pairs of zero-crossings at lower scale could be meaningless local extrema and those at higher scale might not represent all the desired peaks and valleys. Based on these facts, Witkin[22] developed a multiscale representation based on tertiary trees and he proposed a method for extracting the perceptually salient features such as valleys and peaks of a signal. In fact, he defined the interval tree and found active nodes from fingerprints. The scale-space extrema at a certain scale τ partition the x-axis into several intervals. Each of these intervals defines a rectangle in the scale-space, bounded above by the scale at which the pair of zero-crossings emerges, bounded below by the scale at which the new different pair of zero-crossings appears, and bounded on either side by the x-locations of the pair of zero-crossings. Active nodes are the rectangles in the interval tree, of which the difference between the scale of bounding extrema and that of the largest extremum between them is large.[22] But it is noted that the x-axis locations of the properly found active nodes are associated with the meaningful peaks and valleys of a histogram. Therefore, if one finds the active nodes from the interval tree, one can easily determine the number of significant peaks which exist in the histogram. In addition, an optimum scale constant τ_{opt}, where only significant peaks remain, also can be determined by identifying the active nodes.

In our approach, the number of regions, which is essential to the success of FCM, corresponds to the number of significant peaks in the histogram. For the coarse segmentation, it is necessary to generate the fingerprint from the histogram of an image. After obtaining the interval tree from the fingerprint and marking the active nodes, one can determine the number of regions and the optimal scale τ_{opt}. The valley locations existing in the histogram can be possible candidates for the thresholds. However, it may be difficult to find the valid valleys between peaks of the histogram, unless the histogram is a smooth function. But this is no problem in our

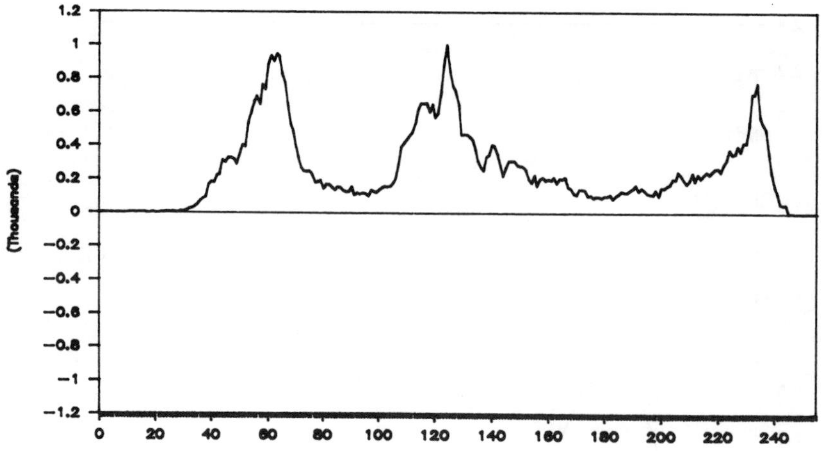
(Thousands)
1.2
1
0.8
0.6
0.4
0.2
0
−0.2
−0.4
−0.6
−0.8
−1
−1.2
0 20 40 60 80 100 120 140 160 180 200 220 240

(a)

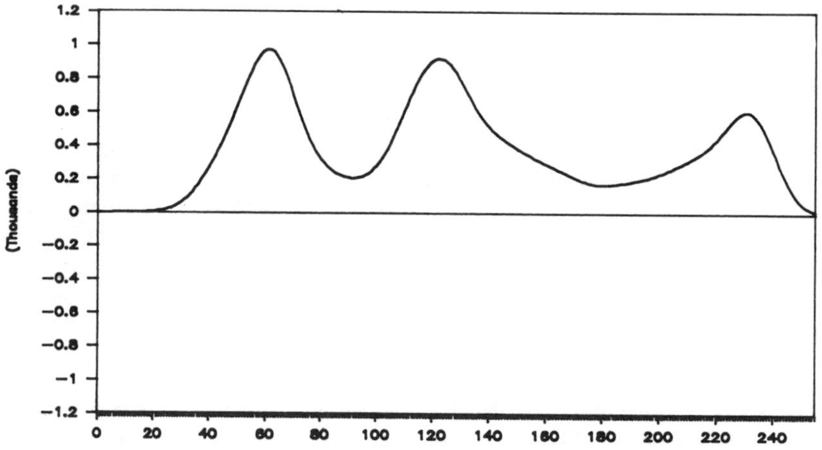
(Thousands)
1.2
1
0.8
0.6
0.4
0.2
0
−0.2
−0.4
−0.6
−0.8
−1
−1.2
0 20 40 60 80 100 120 140 160 180 200 220 240

(b)

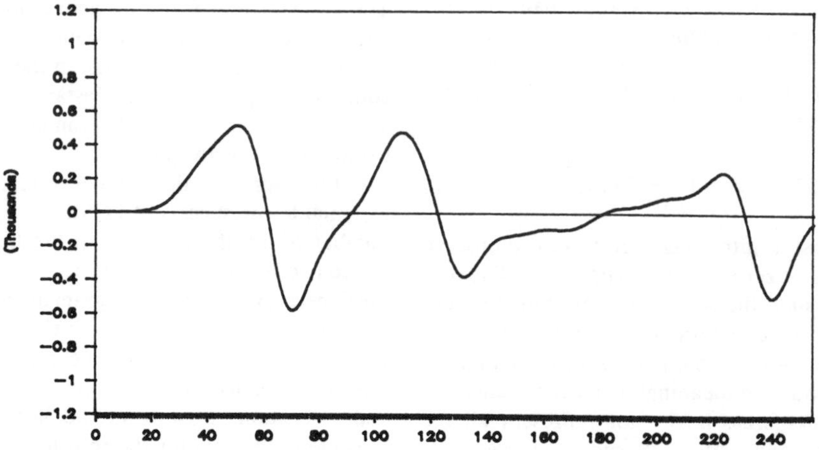
(Thousands)
1.2
1
0.8
0.6
0.4
0.2
0
−0.2
−0.4
−0.6
−0.8
−1
−1.2
0 20 40 60 80 100 120 140 160 180 200 220 240

(c)

Fig. 2 (a)–(c).

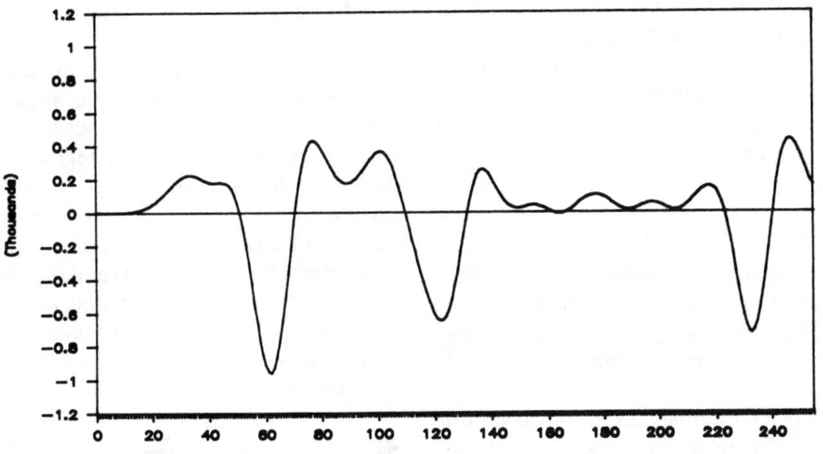

(d)

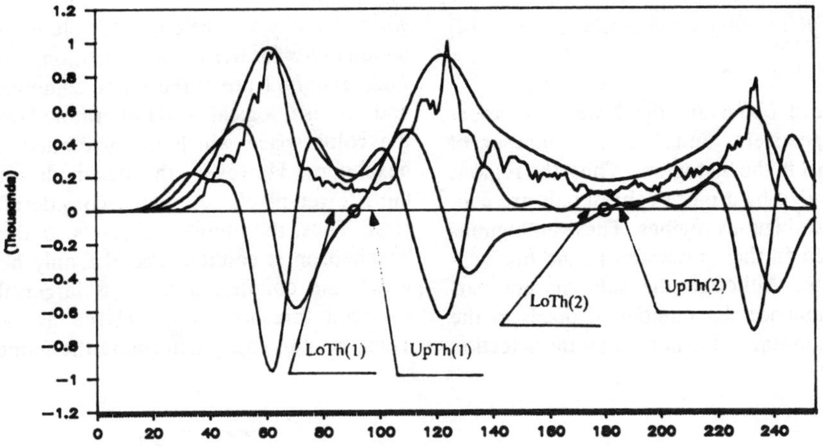

(e)

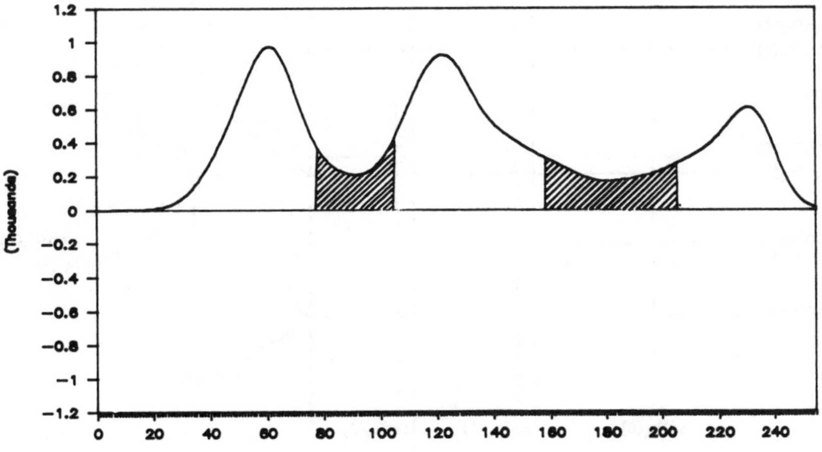

(f)

Fig. 2. A procedure of finding thresholds from a histogram. (a) Original histogram. (b) Smoothed histogram. (c) First derivative. (d) Second derivative. (e) Thresholds. (f) Ambiguous areas.

approach, because the histogram can be suitably smoothed by applying the scale-space filter to the histogram of each color component with τ_{opt}. Thus one can easily find the valleys by computing the first and second derivative of a histogram and finds locations satisfying (3).

$$\frac{\partial F}{\partial x} = f * \frac{\partial g}{\partial x} = 0, \frac{\partial^2 F}{\partial x^2} > 0. \qquad (3)$$

This is a unique feature of the scale-space filter. But the points obtained by differentiating the histogram do not match peaks and valleys if other smoothing techniques such as low pass filtering and moving average are used.

But it is noted that the ambiguous regions as shown in Fig. 1 still exist even if we properly select the thresholds. In order to resolve the ambiguous regions in the histogram, a pair of thresholds (the upper and the lower) for each valley location are defined as

$$LoTh(i) = m(i) - \text{safe\_margin},$$
$$UpTh(i) = m(i) + \text{safe\_margin}, \qquad (4)$$
$$i = 0, 1, \ldots, k$$

where $LoTh$ and $UpTh$ are the lower and upper threshold, respectively, and k is the number of regions that exist in the histogram. Thus, the regions which are bounded by a pair of thresholds are considered as the ambiguous regions. These ambiguous regions are then further processed in the fine segmentation stage. Although the safe_margin parameter may influence the number of pixels in the fine segmentation stage, it is noted that the selection of safe_margin does not affect the segmentation result significantly.

We shall show the described procedure in more detail by illustrating an example. Figure 2(a) is the histogram of an image. Obviously, this histogram must be segmented into three regions. Through the scale-space filtering the histogram in Fig. 2(a), we can obtain the smoothed histogram of Fig. 2(b). Figure 2(c) and Fig. 2(d) are the first and second derivative of Fig. 2(b). By (3) and (4), the thresholds for the histogram are computed as shown in Fig. 2(e). Finally, applying this procedure to each color component's histogram, we can partition the color space into several hexahedra by

$$\text{Class}(u) = \sum_{Im1 = LoTh_1(1)}^{UpTh_1(1)} Im1(x, y) \Lambda \sum_{Im2 = LoTh_2(m)}^{UpTh_2(m)} \times Im2(x, y) \Lambda \sum_{Im3 = LoTh_3(n)}^{UpTh_3(n)} Im3(x, y) \qquad (5)$$

where x and y are the row and column of an image, u is an index for hexahedral partitioned classes, $Im1$, $Im2$, and $Im3$ are three color component images, and "Λ" is a logical AND operator. Figure 3 shows the color space which is partitioned into several hexahedra. However, the hexahedron which contains fewer pixels cannot be considered as a valid class. Thus, the number of pixels contained in each hexahedron is counted and the only hexahedra of which the counted number is larger than a prespecified threshold are declared as valid classes. Thus, we can easily determine the number of valid

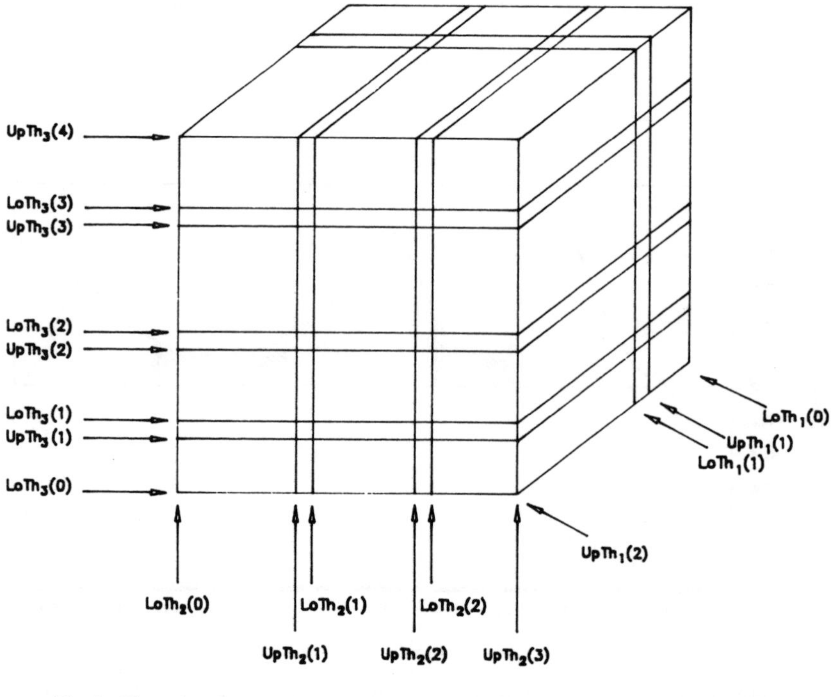

Fig. 3. The color space which is partitioned by the lower and upper thresholds.

classes and their mean vectors. These parameters will be used later in the fine segmentation stage. It is noted that the pixels belonging to the valid classes can be viewed as clustered around their mean vectors. Those pixels, which cannot be assigned to any valid class, are pixels in the hatched areas as shown in Fig. 2(f).

2.2. *Fine segmentation*

The FCM, which was proposed by Zadeh originally,[9,10] is a clustering algorithm. The FCM attempts to cluster the measurement vectors by finding local minima of the generalized within group sum of squared error objective function as shown in (6).

$$J_m(U, v) = \sum_{k=1}^{n} \sum_{i=1}^{c} (U_{ik})^m \|x_k - v_i\|_A^2, \quad 1 \leqq m < \infty \tag{6}$$

where $X = \{x_1, x_2, \ldots, x_n\}$ is a finite data set in R^d; $x_k \varepsilon R^d$, $1 \leqq k \leqq n$, is a d-dimensional measurement vector; $\|\cdot\|_A$ is any inner product norm, $\|Q\|_A = Q^T A Q$, A_{dxd} is a positive definite matrix; $v = \{v_1, v_2, \ldots, v_c\}$ is a set of class center, $v_i \varepsilon R^d$, $1 \leqq i \leqq c$, represents a d-dimensional ith class center; and $m \varepsilon [1, \infty)$ is the membership weighting exponent. Class center vector v_i is regarded as a prototype. It is known that for m greater than one under the assumption that $x_k \neq v_i$ local minimum can be found from (7) and (8).

$$U_{ik} = \left(\sum_{j=1}^{c} \left(\frac{\|x_k - v_i\|}{\|x_k - v_j\|} \right)^{2/(m-1)} \right)^{-1} \quad \forall_i, \forall_k. \tag{7}$$

$$v_i = \frac{\sum_{k=1}^{n} (U_{ik})^m \cdot x_k}{\sum_{k=1}^{n} (U_{ik})^m}. \tag{8}$$

In order to execute the FCM successfully, it is required to know the number of classes (regions) in advance. However, in our approach, during the coarse segmentation the number of classes and their center vectors have been determined. The pixels belonging to the valid class can be considered as clustered. Thus, it is not necessary to compute the center vector by (8). It can be replaced with the mean value of the valid class. Now, we can calculate the membership function of the pixels which have not yet assigned to any valid class in the coarse segmentation. Finally, by assigning those pixels to the closest class, of which the fuzzy membership of (7) has maximum value, the fine segmentation is completed.

Consequently, the proposed algorithm can decide the number of classes automatically as compared to the one proposed by Bezdek *et al.*[11] Since the most pixels are classified in the coarse segmentation stage, a significant computation time required for the FCM can be saved. In addition, because the proposed algorithm does not employ PDS,[11] the block effect can also be avoided. The following describes the proposed algorithm.

```
COARSE SEGMENTATION
  DO BEGIN
    Extract histograms of 3 color component
        images;
    Scale-space filtering the histograms;
    Find threshold values;
    Find valid classes (hexahedra);
    FOR x := 1 TO 256
      DO FOR y := 1 TO 256
        DO BEGIN
          IF a pixel P(x,y) belongs to any valid
              class
            THEN assign its class to P(x,y);
            ELSE tag P(x,y) as unclassified;
        END
      END
    Calculate the center of each valid class, v_i;
  END

FINE SEGMENTATION
  DO BEGIN
  FOR x := 1 to 256
      DO FOR y: = 1 to 256
      DO BEGIN
        Calculate fuzzy membership, U_ik
        for only unclassified pixels;
        Assign class of which membership value is
            max:
      END
    END
  END
```

3. SIMULATION RESULTS AND DISCUSSION

The test images used in the simulation are COLOR and HOUSE both of which are R–G–B images of size of 256 × 256. A conversion to other color coordinates is achieved by the conversion matrices.[3] Figure 4 shows the two test images and an ideally segmented image of COLOR. The ideally segmented image was obtained by a manual segmentation.

3.1. *The recursive region splitting method*

In this algorithm,[15] they used the precedence level to select the best peak on the R, G, B, I, H, S, Y, I, and Q. However, in our simulation, the modified precedence level was used on the R, G, B, X, Y, Z, I, Q, I1, I2, and I3.

In Ohlander's approach, all the possible peaks of the nine color components are found in order to compute the upper and lower thresholds. To do this, the precedence level is incremented from zero until there exists some valid peaks. Next, the best peak, which has definite left and right minima, is selected from the valid peaks. In this case, the important parameters are esp, weps and reps, which are computed from the maximum value, minimum and maximum range of the histogram. These parameters are somewhat subjective and should be adjusted in accordance with the shape of a histogram. In simulation, these parameters were adjusted as shown in (9).

$$\begin{aligned} &\text{eps} = \text{maximum\_histogram\_value[pic]}/10,\\ &\text{weps} = (\text{max\_his\_val[pic]} - \text{min\_pic\_val[pic]})/15,\\ &\text{reps} = 1.4. \end{aligned} \quad (9)$$

Figure 5 is the segmentation results for COLOR and HOUSE images. It is seen that the COLOR image yields a good segmented image. However, in the case of the HOUSE image, the roof and its shade are not segmented satisfactorily.

3.2. *The algorithm using the FCM and the PDS*

This algorithm also requires *a priori* knowledge of many parameters: the number of classes c, the membership weighting exponent m, the positive definite matrix A, and the initial level in the PDS, and the threshold T for the membership function.

In simulation, the following scheme was used in order to avoid the problem that the number of classes should be assigned at every level in the PDS. The region which was judged heterogeneous at the higher level is split further into four lower level subimages. After computing the membership function of these four newly split subimages, these subimages are appended to the measurement vectors which are to be clustered via the FCM. The homogeneity is decided by the threshold T of membership function. In other words, a region is split if the maximum value of membership function is less than the threshold T. But this threshold T affects the segmentation result significantly. Moreover, Bezdek *et al.* procured the higher level image by averaging its lower level images. As a result, once a region is declared as homogeneous at a certain level, it will never be split further even if it contains significant amount of edge pixels. This is the reason why the block effect occurs in the segmentation results.

Figure 6 is the result for COLOR and HOUSE images on the five color coordinates when $n = 2500$, $m = 2$, and $T = 0.9$. The actual number of classes c is seven in COLOR image, and four in HOUSE image, respectively. These results are poor compared to those obtained from other algorithms because of the block effect. In the result of COLOR image on I1–I2–I3, the region which should be separated is segmented into the same region, but the boundary of each region is similar to that of the hand segmented image. Also the results on X–Y–Z and U–V–W are worse that those obtained on the other coordinates.

In conclusion, whenever the FCM is applied to a single level image with properly selected parameters, a good segmentation is expected as pointed by Bezdek.[11] However, it is very difficult to decide the number of classes and all the necessary initial parameter values in advance.

3.3. *The relaxation approach*

In the relaxation approach, it is very important to select the number of classes and the initial probabilities correctly. Especially the initial probabilities are critical to the success of relaxation approach. In their approach,[14] these parameters were determined from the manually segmented image. The initial probabilities were computed from the mean vector and covariance matrix of each class. But in our approach, as explained previously, we can easily determine the number of classes in the coarse segmentation stage. In addition, since most pixels are assigned to the valid classes after the coarse segmentation, the mean and covariance matrices can be easily computed using the coarsely segmented pixels. Then the initial probabilities are finally obtained from these matrices. Thus we are able to execute the relaxation algorithm without requiring the manually segmented image.

Table 1 presents the mean vector and covariance matrices for COLOR image on the I1–I2–I3, which is segmented into seven classes. Also, the compatibility coefficients should be computed in order to use the probabilistic relaxation approach. The compatibility coefficients of $c \times c$ matrices are the combination of the probabilities of nine pixels as shown in Fig. 7. Figure 8 is the result for COLOR and HOUSE images on the five color coordinates. The results for COLOR on the R–G–B, Y–I–Q, and I1–I2–I3 are as good as the manually segmented image. The result for HOUSE is also good on all color coordinates. Thus, it is believed that with the correct initial probabilities the relaxation approach is insensitive to the particular choice of a color coordinate and it works reasonably well. However, this approach requires a considerable amount of memory and computation time. In fact, this approach requires the most computational effort among the algorithms considered in the paper. Furthermore it is found that the segmentation result is significantly affected by choice of the initial probabilities.

3.4. *Proposed algorithm*

As a first step for the proposed algorithm, it is necessary to pick up thresholds for the coarse segmentation. We shall show the method of determining thresholds in more detail. For example, Fig. 9(a) is a histogram of I1 component of COLOR on the I1–I2–I3 coordinate. In Fig. 9(a), it seems that gray value of 30, 50, 100, 150, 170, 210 are possible threshold candidates. However, it should be noted that we cannot obtain a good segmentation result using these thresholds. In fact, this histogram should

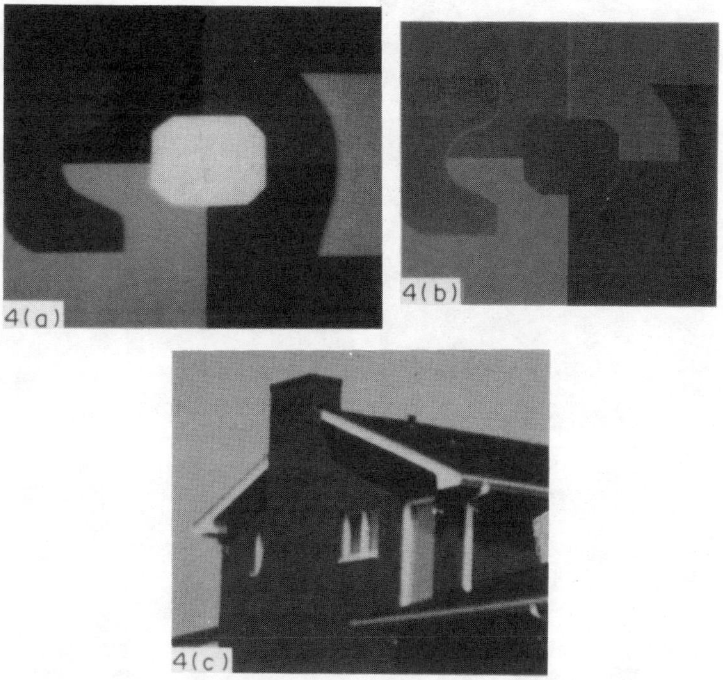

Fig. 4. Two test images. (a) COLOR. (b) The manually segmented image of COLOR. (c) HOUSE.

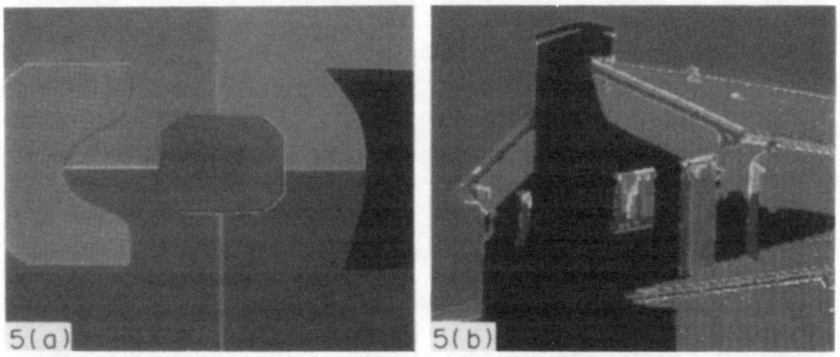

Fig. 5. The segmentation results for COLOR and HOUSE images by the recursive region splitting method. (a) The result for COLOR. (b) The result for HOUSE.

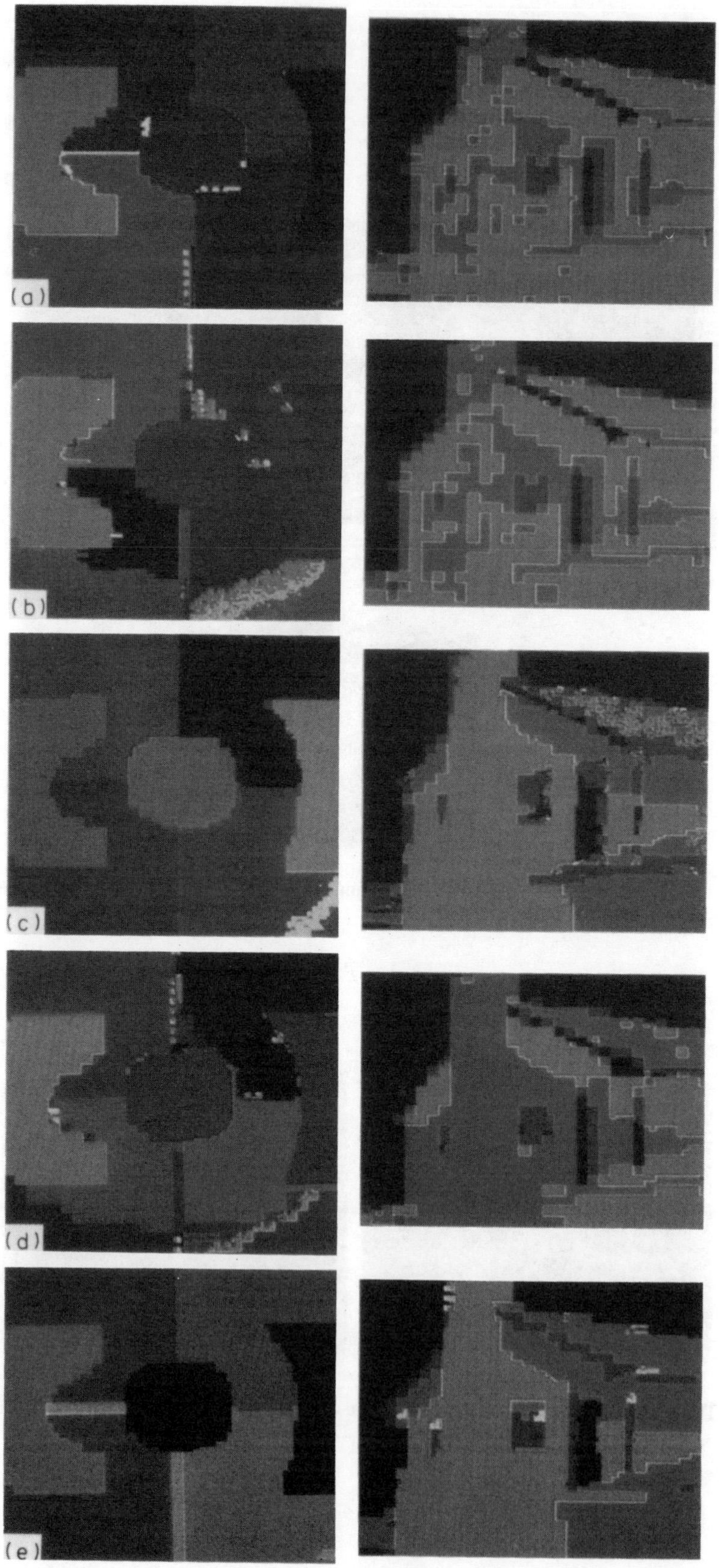

Fig. 6. The segmentation results for COLOR and HOUSE images by the algorithm using the FCM and PDS. (a) R–G–B. (b) X–Y–Z. (c) Y–I–Q. (d) U–V–W. (e) I1–I2–I3.

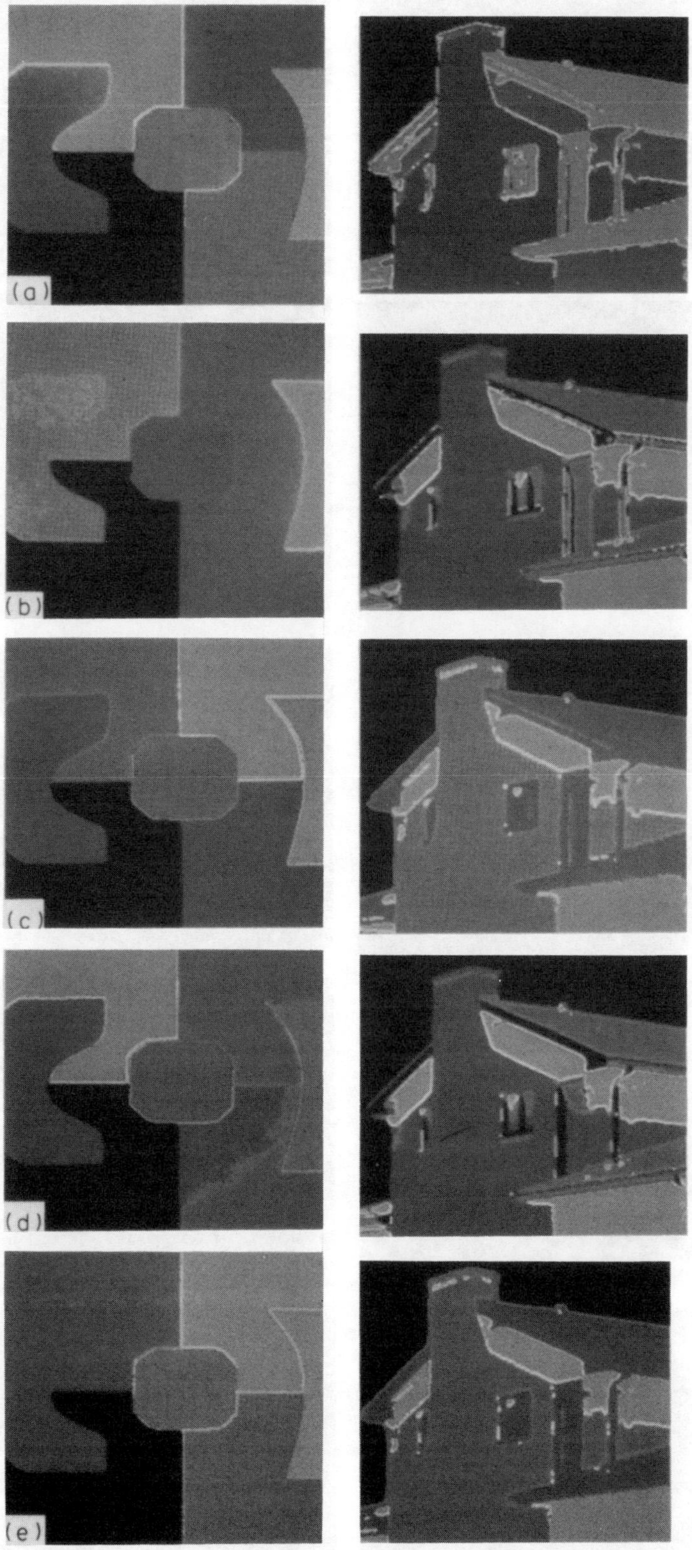

Fig. 8. The segmentation results for COLOR and HOUSE images by the relaxation algorithm. (a) R–G–B. (b) X–Y–Z. (c) Y–I–Q. (d) U–V–W. (e) I1–I2–I3.

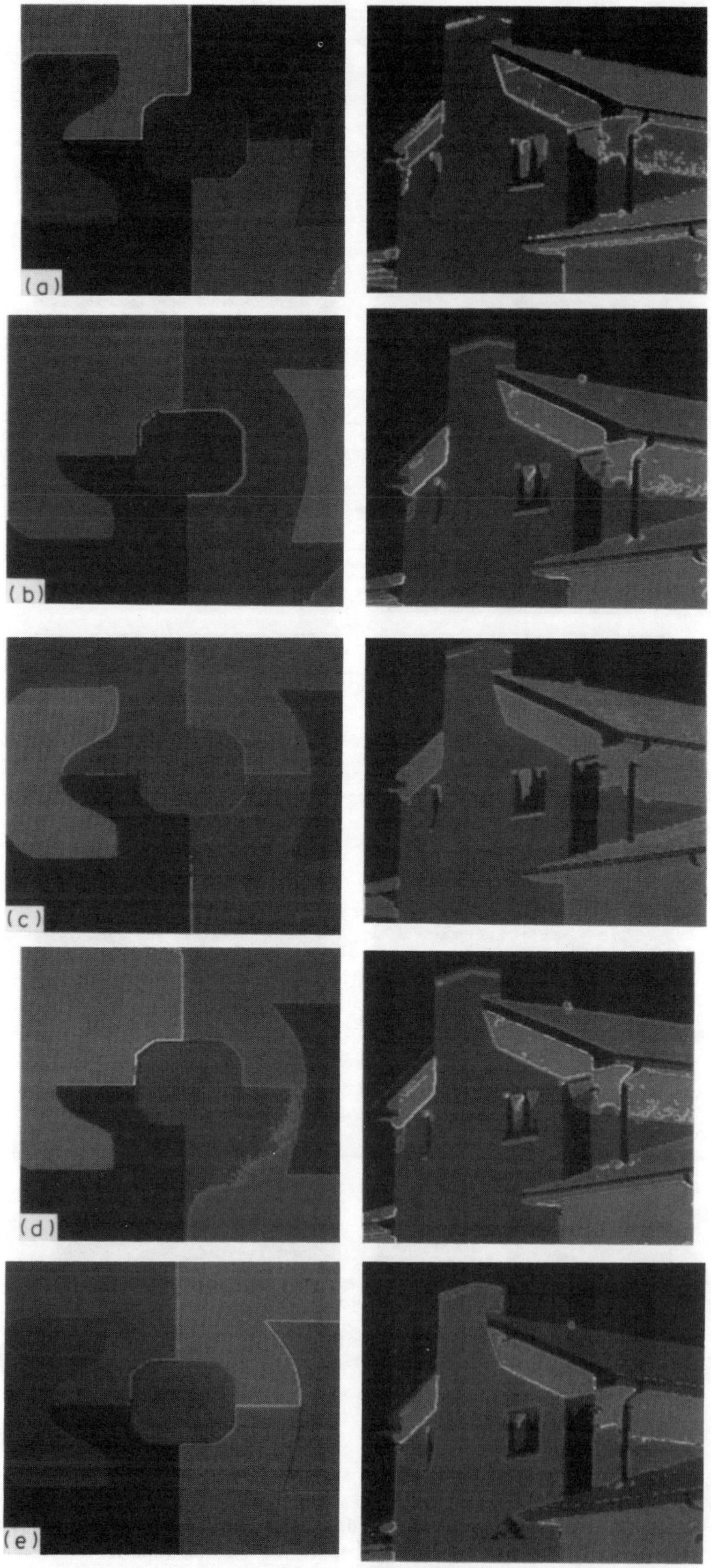

Fig. 10. The segmentation results for COLOR and HOUSE images by the proposed algorithm. (a) R–G–B. (b) X–Y–Z. (c) Y–I–Q. (d) U–V–W. (e) I1–I2–I3.

Table 1. The mean and covariance of seven classes for COLOR on I1–I2–I3

Class =	0			Class =	1		
Mean	137.692	20.321	228.698	Mean	20.472	115.567	89.646
Probability	0.183			Probability	0.167		
Covariance	0.015	0.025	−0.005	Covariance	0.017	−0.003	−0.007
	0.025	0.088	0.021		−0.003	0.049	0.023
	−0.005	0.021	0.033		−0.007	0.023	0.021
Class =	2			Class =	3		
Mean	55.982	171.568	112.765	Mean	67.825	234.909	25.113
Probability	0.191			Probability	0.167		
Covariance	0.008	−0.012	−0.013	Covariance	0.021	−0.030	−0.012
	−0.012	0.043	0.017		−0.030	0.065	0.036
	−0.013	0.017	0.037		−0.012	0.036	0.038
Class =	4			Class =	5		
Mean	39.731	69.357	224.028	Mean	183.211	179.418	218.107
Probability	0.133			Probability	0.093		
Covariance	0.018	−0.002	−0.010	Covariance	0.012	−0.010	−0.008
	−0.002	0.045	0.012		−0.010	0.033	0.008
	−0.010	0.012	0.026		−0.008	0.008	0.016
Class =	6						
Mean	239.644	148.194	122.922				
Probability	0.066						
Covariance	0.026	0.009	−0.014				
	0.009	0.064	−0.013				
	−0.014	−0.013	0.029				

be segmented into three classes by selecting 100 and 210 for correct thresholds. Figure 9(b) is the scale-space image, or fingerprint and Fig. 9(c) shows the interval tree obtained from the fingerprint. The interval tree, proposed by Witkin,[22] describes the division of intervals bounded by extrema into finer and finer sub-intervals, as the scale τ decreases. In other words, the scale-space extrema whose scales exceed a given threshold, τ_T, partition the x-axis into intervals. Each rectangle in the interval tree is a node, indicating an interval on the histogram, and the scale range over which the histogram interval exists. The hatched areas in Fig. 9(c) are active nodes and represent two valleys and three peaks which are existed in the histogram. Figure 9(c) also indicates that the scale should be larger than 17 in order to classify the histogram of I1 into three classes correctly. A detailed description on the interval tree can be found

X2	X3	X4
X1	X0	X5
X8	X7	X6

Fig. 7. A pixel and its 8 neighbors for compatibility coefficients.

elsewhere.[22] Figure 9(d) shows the smoothed histograms, with τ increasing from top to bottom. As can be seen from Fig. 9(d), there exist three peaks as long as τ is greater than or equal to 17. Otherwise, more than three peaks exist in the histogram. In Fig. 9(e) thresholds which are determined by the first and second derivative of the smoothed histogram at $\tau = 18$ are indicated by arrows. We can see that these thresholds are very close to the manually obtained thresholds of 100 and 210. After repeating the same procedure on the I2 and I3 components, we are able to obtain the correct 7 classes (see Fig. 4) finally. Thus it is seen that the number of classes can be correctly determined by applying the scale-space filtering to each histogram of three color components. In our simulation, every hexahedron which contains more than 3000 pixels are declared as a valid class.

Figure 10 presents the segmentation results for COLOR and HOUSE images. It is observed that the proposed algorithm yields the best segmentation result on I1–I2–I3. The results on Y–I–Q and R–G–B show several misclassified regions as shown in Fig. 10. The X–Y–Z and U–V–W coordinates produce the worst result. In the case of HOUSE image, all results except Y–I–Q are generally good as shown in Fig. 10. Finally, it is noted that if the histograms of the three color components are almost unimodal, the proposed algorithm cannot find proper

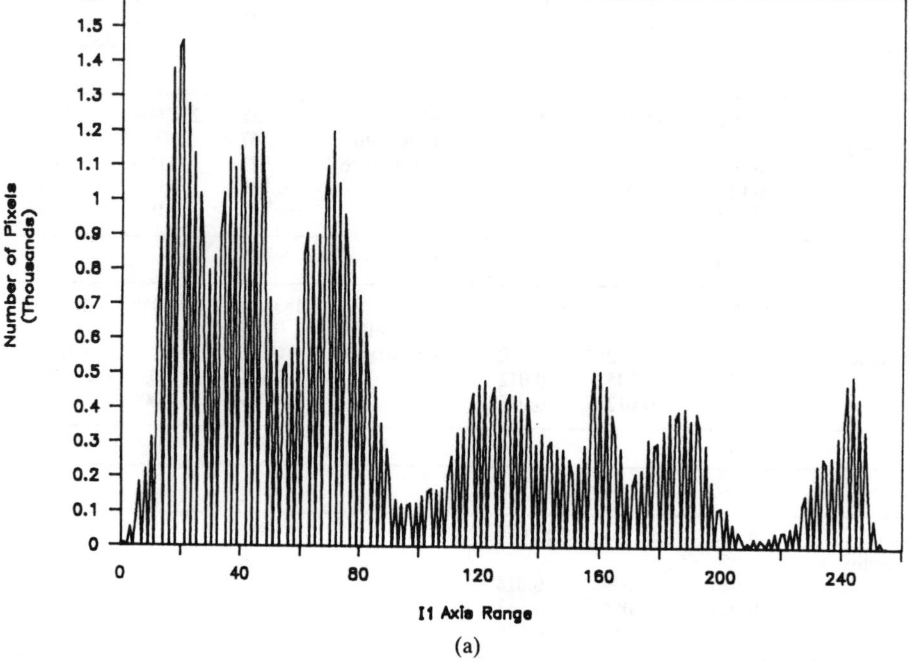

Number of Pixels (Thousands)
1.6
1.5
1.4
1.3
1.2
1.1
1
0.9
0.8
0.7
0.6
0.5
0.4
0.3
0.2
0.1
0
0
40
80
120
160
200
240
I1 Axis Range

(a)

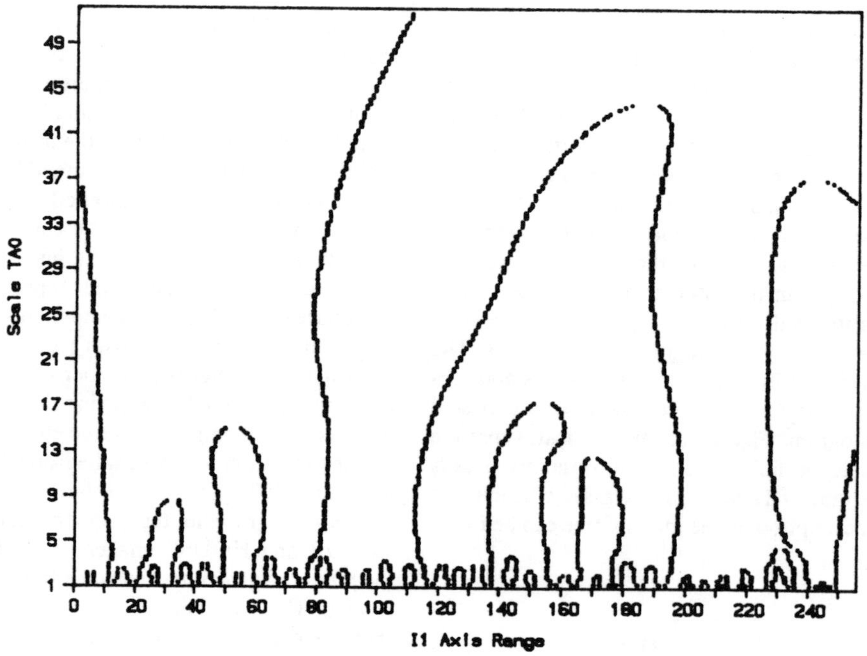

Scale TAO
49
45
41
37
33
29
25
21
17
13
9
5
1
0
20
40
60
80
100
120
140
160
180
200
220
240
I1 Axis Range

(b)

Fig. 9(a), (b).

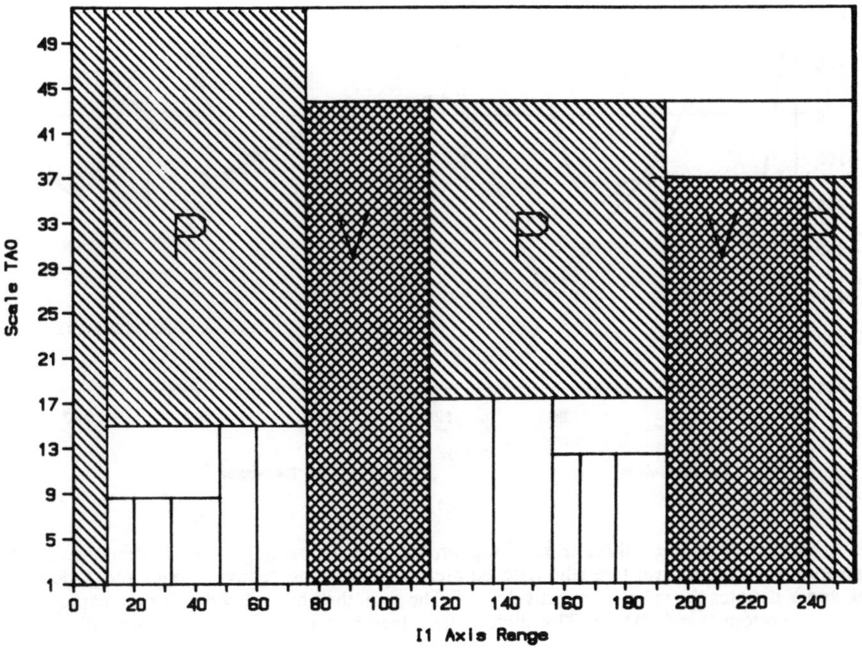

49
45
41
37
33
29
25
21
17
13
9
5
1
Scale TAO
P
V
P
V
P
0
20
40
60
80
100
120
140
160
180
200
220
240
I1 Axis Range

(c)

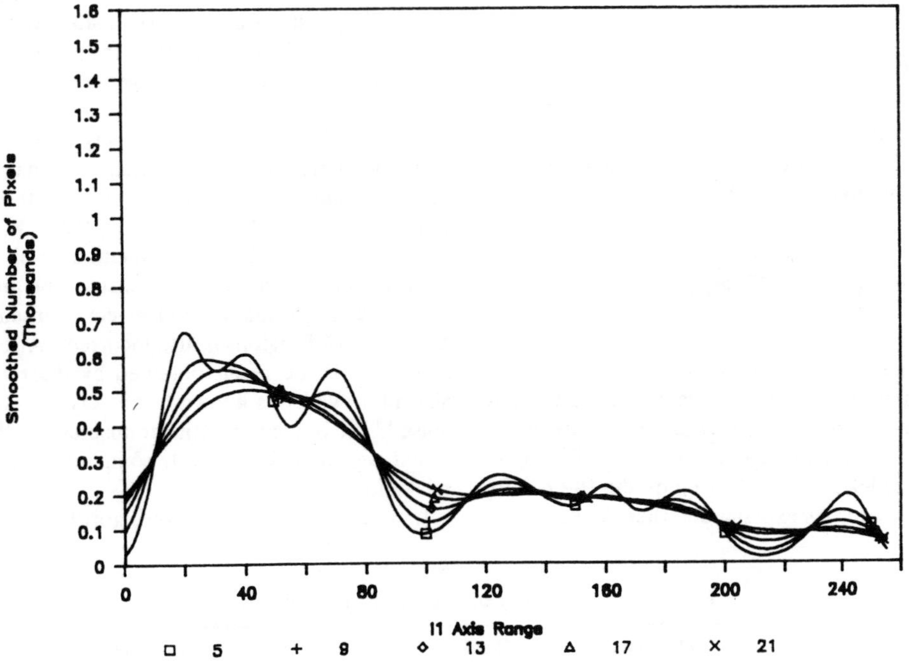

1.6
1.5
1.4
1.3
1.2
1.1
1
0.9
0.8
0.7
0.6
0.5
0.4
0.3
0.2
0.1
0
Smoothed Number of Pixels (Thousands)
0
40
80
120
160
200
240
I1 Axis Range
□ 5
+ 9
◇ 13
△ 17
× 21

(d)

Fig. 9(c), (d).

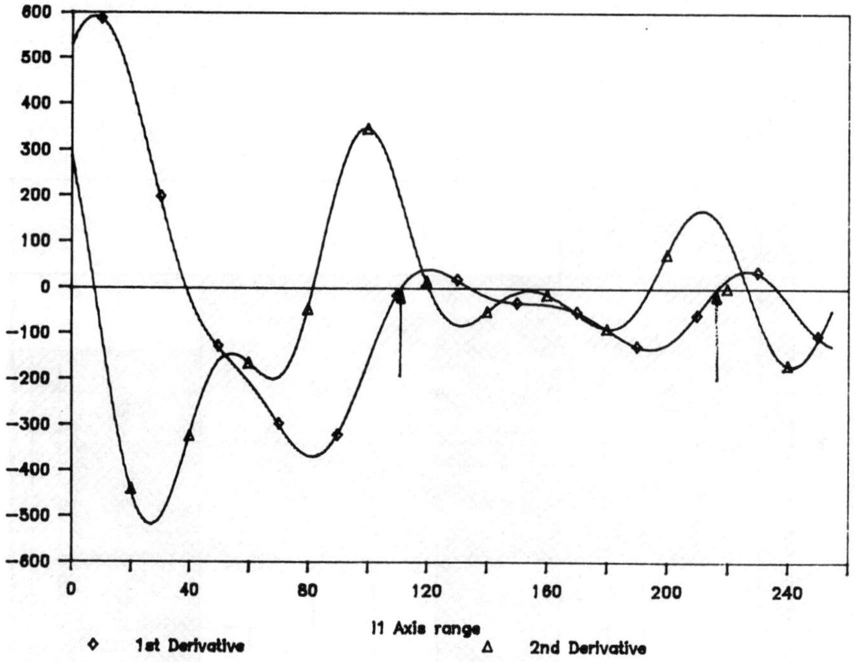

(e)

Fig. 9. Method of finding valleys from histogram. (a) The histogram of the I1 component. (b) The fingerprint. (c) The interval tree (the hatched areas represent the "active" nodes and P denotes the peak and V denotes the valley, respectively). (d) The smoothed histograms with τ increasing from top to bottom ($\tau = 5$–21). (e) Thresholds determined by the first and second derivatives.

thresholds like most other algorithms based on the thresholding technique.

3.5. *The performance evaluation*

In order to evaluate the performance of the proposed algorithms, the probability of error between the manually segmented image and the segmentation result is computed. The probability of error is defined as

$$P(\text{error}) = \sum_{j=1}^{c} \sum_{\substack{i=1 \\ i \neq j}}^{c} P(R_i|R_j) \cdot P(R_j) \qquad (10)$$

where R_i and R_j are the ith and jth regions among c regions in an image. The results in Table 2 indicate that X–Y–Z and Y–I–Q coordinates are inappropriate for a color image segmentation. The algorithm of Bezdek *et al.* works well on the R–G–B for COLOR image. As explained earlier, it seems that the relaxation algorithm is relatively insensitive to the chosen coordinates. The proposed algorithm shows the best results on I1–I2–I3. Also, in an attempt to test the robustness of the proposed algorithm, the noisy images were generated by adding Gaussian white noise to the I1–I2–I3 component image of COLOR. The test was made of segmentation performance as a function of image noise. Figure 11 shows that the proposed algorithm works well when the SNR is more than 19 dB. When the SNR is below 17 dB, the segmented result is very poor as shown in Fig. 11 because the obtained thresholds are found to be incorrect. Consequently, the number of regions is also incorrect. Also shown in Fig. 11 is the result obtained by the relaxation algorithm, which is known to be very robust to the noise.[20] It is seen that the robustness of the proposed algorithm is, at least, comparable to that of relaxation algorithm.

In conclusion, the relaxation algorithm yields good

Table 2. The probability of error for four algorithms

	Ohlander	Bezdek	Rosenfeld	Proposed
R–G–B		0.0622	0.0139	0.0287
X–Y–Z		0.3718	0.6526	0.6519
Y–I–Q	0.0222	0.0552	0.0164	0.3552
U–V–W		0.4171	0.3698	0.6563
O–K–S		0.2108	0.0133	0.0119

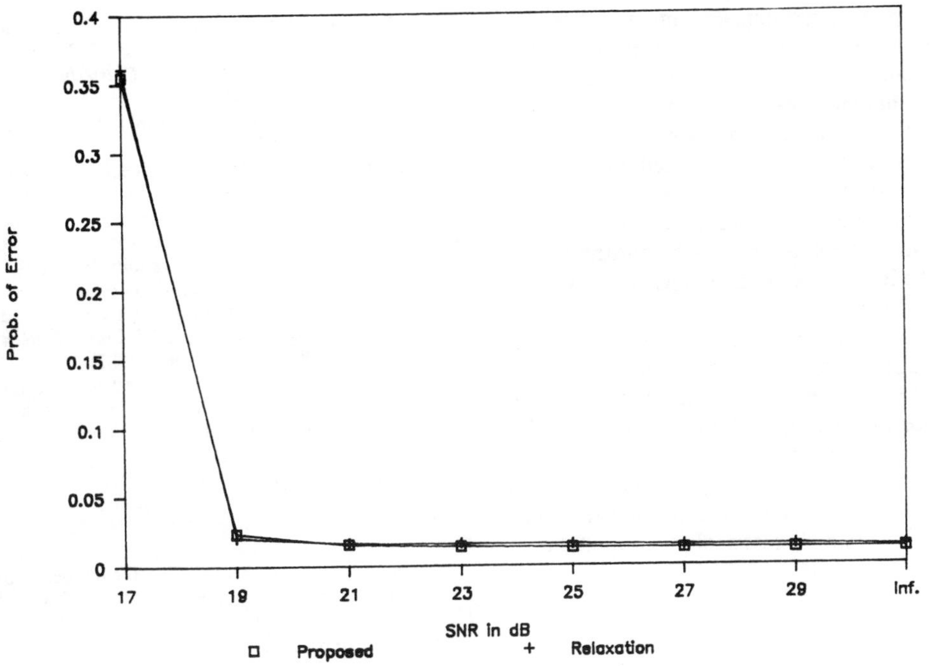

Fig. 11. The probability of error when white Gaussian noise is added to COLOR image on I1–I2–I3 coordinate.

results, but it requires the most computational effort. Since the proposed algorithm segments coarsely by thresholding and then performs the FCM to the pixels which can not be segmented in the coarse segmentation stage, it requires less computation time than the relaxation algorithm.[14]

4. CONCLUSIONS

In this paper a segmentation algorithm for color images based on the thresholding and the FCM technique was described. The methodology uses a "coarse-fine" concept to reduce the computational burden required for the FCM. The underlying assumption we made in the development of the proposed algorithm is that the histogram is not unimodal. The coarse segmentation stage attempts to segment coarsely by using the thresholding technique. The thresholds and the number of regions to be searched, which is essential to the success of the FCM, are determined automatically by the application of the scale-space filtering to the histograms of the three color components. Those pixels which are not segmented by a coarse segmentation are further segmented using the FCM in the fine segmentation stage. Because of the coarse-fine strategy, the enormous computational burden required for the FCM can be significantly saved. Two 256 × 256 test images were used to evaluate the feasibility of the proposed segmentation strategy. The proposed algorithm produced accurate segmentation of the test images. Attempts also have been made to compare the performance of proposed algorithm with other currently available algorithms in the literature and to evaluate the performance when noise exists in an image. The probability of error between the ideally segmented image obtained manually and the simulation result was chosen for the performance evaluation criterion. The results show that the proposed algorithm yields the lowest probability of error on the I1–I2–I3 coordinate while requiring a reasonable computational complexity.

5. SUMMARY

In this paper a new algorithm based on the thresholding and the Fuzzy c-Means Techniques was proposed for a color image segmentation. To verify the usefulness of this algorithm, the performance of the proposed algorithm has been evaluated and compared with those of commonly used algorithms.

The proposed algorithm can be considered as a kind of coarse to fine technique. The coarse segmentation stage attempts to segment coarsely by using the thresholding technique. The thresholds and the number of regions to be searched, which is essential to the success of the FCM, are determined automatically by applying scale-space filtering to the histograms of the three color components. Those pixels which are not segmented by a coarse segmentation are further segmented using the FCM in the fine segmentation stage. Because of the coarse-fine strategy, the enormous computational burden required for the FCM can be significantly saved.

Three existing algorithms, namely, Bezdek's algorithm[11] based on the fuzzy c-means and the pyramidal data structure, the recursive region splitting method of Ohlander *et al.*,[15] and the modified Rosenfeld's[14] have been chosen with which to compare the performance of the proposed algorithm.

Since the results of color image segmentation are dependent not only on the algorithm used but also on the chosen color coordinate, all algorithms were tested on the R–G–B, X–Y–Z, Y–I–Q, U–V–W, and Ohta's coordinate.[21]

The probability of error between the ideally segmented image and simulation result was employed for the performance evaluation criterion. Also, the performance of the proposed algorithm was evaluated on the noisy image.

The results indicate that the proposed algorithm yields the lowest probability of error on the Ohta's coordinate[21] with reasonable computational burden.

REFERENCES

1. A. Rosenfeld and A. C. Kak, *Digital Picture Processing*. Academic Press, New York (1982).
2. R. C. Gonzalez and P. Wintz, *Digital Image Processing*. Addison-Wesley, Reading, MA (1987).
3. W. K. Pratt, *Digital Image Processing*. Wiley, New York (1978).
4. P. H. Ballard and C. M. Brown, *Computer Vision*. Prentice-Hall, Englewood Cliffs, NJ (1982).
5. K. Price, Region-based segmentation, *Encyclopedia of Artificial Intelligence*, S. C. Shapiro and D. Eckroth, Eds, pp. 877–880. Wiley, New York (1987).
6. R. D. Overheim and D. L. Wagner, *Light and Color*. Wiley, New York (1982).
7. S. A. Shafer and T. Kanade, Color vision, *Encyclopedia of Artificial Intelligence*, S. C. Shapiro and D. Eckroth, Eds, pp. 124–131. Wiley, New York (1987).
8. R. O Duda and P. E. Hart, *Pattern Classification and Scene Analysis*. Wiley, New York (1973).
9. J. V. Ryzin, *Classification and Clustering*. Academic Press, New York (1977).
10. A. Kandel, *Fuzzy Techniques in Pattern Recognition*. Wiley, New York (1982).
11. J. C. Bezdek and M. M. Trivedi, Low level segmentation of aerial images with fuzzy clustering, *IEEE Trans. Syst. Man. Cyb.* **SMC-16**, 589–598 (1986).
12. J. C. Bezdek, M. P. Windham and R. Ehrlich, Statistical parameters of cluster validity functions, *Int. J. Comput. Inform. Sci.* **9**, 323–336 (1980).
13. M. P. Windham, Clustering validity for the fuzzy c-means clustering algorithm, *IEEE Trans. Pattern Anal. Mach. Intell.* **PAMI-4**, 357–363 (1982).
14. J. O. Eklundh, H. Yamamoto and A. Rosenfeld, A relaxation method for multispectral pixel classification, *IEEE Trans. Pattern Anal. Mach. Intell.* **PAMI-2**, 72–75 (1980).
15. R. Ohlander, K. Price and D. R. Reddy, Picture segmentation using a recursive region splitting method, *Comput. Graphics Image Process.* **8**, 313–333 (1978).
16. P. K. Sahoo, S. Soltani, A. K. C. Wong and Y. C. Chen, A survey of thresholding techniques, *Comput. Vision Graphics Image Process.* **41**, 233–260 (1988).
17. J. S. Weszka, A survey of threshold selection techniques, *Comput. Graphics Image Process.* **7**, 259–265 (1978).
18. M. Spann and R. Wilson, A quad-tree approach to image segmentation which combines statistical and spatial information, *Pattern Recognition* **18**, 257–269 (1985).
19. K. S. Fu and J. K. Mui, A survey on image segmentation, *Pattern Recognition* **13**, 3–16 (1981).
20. T. L. Huntsberger, C. L. Jacobs and R. L. Cannon, Iterative fuzzy image segmentation, *Pattern Recognition* **18**, 131–138 (1985).
21. Y. Ohta, T. Kanade and T. Sakai, Color information for region segmentation, *Comput. Graphics Image Process.* **13**, 224–241 (1980).
22. A. P. Witkin, Scale space filtering: a new approach to multi-scale description, *Image Understanding*, S. Ullman and W. Richards, Eds, pp. 79–95. Ablex Publishing, N.J. (1984).
23. M. J. Carlotto, Histogram analysis using a scale space approach, *IEEE Trans. Pattern. Anal. Mach. Intell.* **PAMI-9**, 121–129 (1987).

Representation of Uncertainty in Computer Vision Using Fuzzy Sets

TERRANCE L. HUNTSBERGER, CHANDRALEKA RANGARAJAN, AND SADALI N. JAYARAMAMURTHY, MEMBER, IEEE

Abstract — Uncertainty in computer vision can arise at various levels. It can occur in the low level in the raw sensor input, and extends all the way through intermediate and higher levels. Ideally, at any level where decisions are being made on the basis of previous processing steps, a computer vision system must have sufficient flexibility for representation of uncertainty in any of these levels.

The input cue representation portion of a computer vision system should maintain the information content of the original input images, while at the same time allowing for uncertainty in the identification of attributes required by other parts of the system for decision making. Processes such as edge detection, segmentation, and shape matching yield results which could bias higher level decision making, unless some framework is defined for the representation of uncertainty in all of these processes. This paper presents a method for representing uncertainty in the context of fuzzy set theory where membership values associated with the fuzzy sets contain a consistent but not necessarily complete description of image characteristics. We specifically address the representation of uncertainty in the segmentation process through the use of the fuzzy c-means clustering algorithm. Edge detection and shape matching are then performed within the domain of the fuzzy sets derived during the segmentation phase. Results for a number of color images are also presented.

Index Terms — Computer vision, edge detection, fuzzy clustering, segmentation, shape representation.

I. Introduction

COMPUTER vision represents one of the most difficult tasks undertaken within the framework of expert systems. Visual and nonvisual cues serve as input information to these types of systems, the output being a meaningful three-dimensional interpretation of the scene in front of the sensors. The quality of this interpretation is oftentimes limited by the lack of precision and uncertainty in the sensor input. Also, in a totally unknown environment, the search space of potential solutions can be quite large. Coupled with this are the variety of knowledge representations needed for a flexible system. These characteristics of the problem dictate the types of architectures that would be suitable designs for such a system.

In many ways, computer vision systems are faced with problems similar to those of speech understanding systems such as HEARSAY-II [9]. A recent system for computer vision uses the cooperating knowledge sources organization of HEARSAY-II for construction of a three-dimensional symbolic model of a natural scene [26]. Restrictions placed on the special schemata, which are the knowledge sources, limit the flexibility of the decision making capabilities of this system. Uncertainty is modeled by assigning probabilities to nodes in a graph representation of the problem domain. This probabilistic approach may lead to problems, due to lack of consistency in preconceived notions of attributes and possible nonconvergence during the graph search phase of the inference machine.

Another approach is that of the ACRONYM system, which uses generalized cylinders as three-dimensional symbolic models of aircraft scenes [4]. The viewpoint independence of this system is a prerequisite for any computer vision system to exhibit general vision capabilities. Purely edge-based segmentation as the input cues to the system probably account for its poor performance in the presence of noise in the image.

There are a number of other computer vision systems, all with varying degrees of flexibility and accuracy. Among these are the ARGOS system [30], an aerial photograph interpretation system [23], a system for outdoor scene interpretation [24], and an office scene system [31]. Binford gives a thorough review of the strengths and weaknesses of a number of computer vision systems [3].

There are a variety of approaches that can be taken for the representation of incomplete or uncertain input cues. The MYCIN system is perhaps one of the earliest expert systems to incorporate uncertainty in the reasoning process through the use of certainty factors [5], [32]. The approach taken in the MYCIN system was that of probabilistic certainty factors being given to all decisions rendered by the system. However, no attempt was made to model the imprecision present in the input cues to the system. Any robust computer vision system needs to include this notion of imprecision as well as the propagation of uncertainty in the decision making process.

Recently, a number of systems have used fuzzy set theory for computer vision and pattern recognition [10], [11], [17], [28]. Our system, is known as FLASH (fuzzy logic analysis system in hardware), treats uncertainty in the input cue representation in the context of Zadeh's fuzzy set theory [35]. Individual pixels in the input image or images in the case of time varying input are represented by their fuzzy membership values to clusters returned from an iterative segmentation technique.

The low-level portion of the FLASH system uses an iterative algorithm for image segmentation, based on clustering in an image color space. The clustering in color space is done with the fuzzy c-means algorithm generalized by Bezdek [2].

Manuscript received June 4, 1985; revised September 21, 1985.
The authors are with the Intelligent Systems Laboratory, Department of Computer Science, University of South Carolina, Columbia, SC 29208.
IEEE Log Number 8406760.

Reprinted from *IEEE Trans. Comput.*, vol. C-35, no. 2, pp. 145–156, February 1986.

Since the results of image segmentation at such a low level of analysis would not necessarily lead to meaningful regions without other supporting evidence, the fuzzy c-means algorithm allows uncertainty in the process to be modeled without the bias introduced by a hard segmentation. Image operations such as connectedness and adjacency can also be generalized to the multiple-valued case [29].

The next section reviews the image segmentation phase of the system, which treats regions with homogeneous color characteristics as fuzzy sets. Edge detection using these fuzzy sets is discussed next, followed by a description of a representation which can be used for primitive shape definition and matching. Of particular importance in the edge representation is the notion of edge strength, which is of use for the detection of candidates for shadow edges.

II. Color Image Segmentation

Similarities between pixels in a color image can be examined on either the local or global levels. Due to the multispectral nature of a color image, an efficient means must be devised for exhibiting these similarities. Optimization of an objective function which encodes this information gives the desired description of image color characteristics. The objective function is defined as

$$J_m(U, \mathbf{v}) = \sum_{k=1}^{n} \sum_{i=1}^{c} (\mu_{ik})^m (d_{ik})^2 \tag{1}$$

where μ_{ik} is the fuzzy membership value of pixel k in cluster center i, and d_{ik} is any inner product induced norm metric. The set of cluster centers $\mathbf{v}$ would be vectors in a color space, and as such represent the global color characteristics of an image. In contrast to hard clustering, the fuzzy membership value ranges from 0 to 1. The exponent m can be used to vary the nature of the clustering, ranging from absolute "hard" clustering at $m = 1$ to increasingly fuzzier clustering as m increases.

The fuzzy c-means algorithm relies on the appropriate choices of U and $\mathbf{v}$ to minimize the objective function given above. This can be accomplished using the algorithm given below [2]:

1) Fix the number of clusters c, $2 \leq c < n$ where n = number of data items. Fix m, $1 \leq m < \infty$. Choose any inner product induced norm metric $\|*\|$.

2) Initialize the fuzzy c partition, $U^{(O)}$.

3) At step b, $b = 0, 1, 2, \cdots$.

4) Calculate the c cluster centers $\{\mathbf{v}_i^{(b)}\}$ with $U^{(b)}$ and the formula: cluster center for cluster i equals

$$\mathbf{v}_i = \frac{\sum_{k=1}^{n} (\mu_{ik})^m \mathbf{x}_k}{\sum_{k=1}^{n} (\mu_{ik})^m}. \tag{2}$$

5) Update $U^{(b)}$: calculate the memberships in $U^{(b+1)}$ as follows:

a) Calculate I_k and T_k: $I_k = \{i \mid 1 \leq i \leq c; d_{ik} = \|\mathbf{x}_k - \mathbf{v}_i\| = 0\}$ $T_k = 1, 2, \cdots, c - I_k$.

b) For data item k, compute new membership values:

1) if $I_k = empty$,

$$\mu_{ik} = \frac{1}{\left[\sum_{j=1}^{c} \left(\frac{d_{ik}}{d_{jk}}\right)^{2/(m-1)}\right]} \tag{2'}$$

2) else, $\mu_{ik} = 0$ $\forall i$ member T_k,

and $\sum_{i \epsilon I_k} \mu_{ik} = 1$.

6) Compare $U^{(b)}$ and $U^{(b+1)}$ in a convenient matrix norm: if $\|U^{(b)} - U^{(b+1)}\| \leq \varepsilon_L$, stop; otherwise, set $b = b + 1$, and return to step 4.

The initial partition $U^{(O)}$ can be done randomly with relative independence from the membership values returned after convergence. Data values x_k used in the induced norm metric are the input color vectors. The fuzzy membership values μ_{ik} are used in the FLASH system to build a low-level representation of the pixels in the image which contains global information, while at the same time maintaining local information at the pixel level. Details of this phase of preprocessing were reported previously by Huntsberger *et al.* [12]. A comparison between fuzzy set-based and statistical segmentation methods was recently presented by Dubois and Jaulent [7].

A closed loop feedback mechanism can be used to direct parameter choices by low-level processes of the system [36]. The design of the interface of the feedback mechanism to the low-level portion of the computer vision system can have a great impact on the decisions that are made by higher level processes. Sufficient flexibility is automatically included in the low-level process described above in the fuzzy exponent m which varies the nature of the clustering. Thus, multiple views in cluster spaces with varying degrees of fuzziness can be used with combination of evidence techniques for higher level decisions.

The information returned from the segmentation phase of the FLASH system is insufficient by itself for general computer vision tasks. Since *RGB* color is the feature space that the segmentation was performed in, regions that are found are fuzzy sets in that space. Previous studies using color histogramming techniques have resulted in only 54 percent accuracy as far as meaningful region identification [26]. This is due in part to the lack of shape and texture information in the segmentation phase. Texture has been shown to be a very important cue for region identification in humans [3]. Unfortunately, there is no known texture measure that is robust enough or computationally efficient for general computer vision applications.

Since the FLASH system uses the fuzzy c-means algorithm for segmentation purposes, it relies on a distance metric. This is not necessarily a weak point, since the results of the color segmentation are not overly dependent on the choice of the type of metric, as was demonstrated in previous studies [13]. However, selection of a distance metric in a texture feature space has many difficulties associated with it. Even using normalized texture measures is not sufficient, since the distance between two texture measures may not even be in the same space. Segmentation results using statistical texture measures alone or in combination with color have been seen to be less meaningful due to severe fragmentation of the returned regions [15].

One of the parameters that can be varied in the image segmentation phase of the FLASH system is the fuzzy weighting exponent m in (1) above. The previous segmentation study indicated that for values of m around 2.0, segmentation was not sensitive to underlying texture in the regions. As m was increased, however, underlying texture characteristics manifested themselves as fragmentation in the resulting regions. This seems to indicate that m may be a good candidate for a texture index. A texture measure that incorporates these characteristics of the fuzzy set image representation for individual pixels is

$$\mathrm{TEX}_{ij} = \frac{d\mu_{ij}}{dm} \tag{3}$$

where cluster center j, and dm is the change in the fuzzy weighting exponent m. We are presently investigating the inclusion of this texture index into the FLASH system.

III. Color Edge Detection

Since the segmentation from the procedure above is represented in terms of fuzzy sets, the concept of an edge between these fuzzy sets needs to be defined for further processing steps such as shape matching. Underlying color characteristics of the image are maintained in the fuzzy membership values. The behavior of the fuzzy membership values in the transition between color regions will be an indication of the strength of the edge between the regions.

An edge detector that is independent of thresholds and uses combined luminance and chrominance information would be ideal for color images. In order to define such an operator, information about the relative homogeneity of colors within regions and mixing of colors across the discrete digitized transitions between regions must be included in the definition. The relative homogeneity of a color region given in terms of membership values to fuzzy sets in the segmentation can be written as

$$\mathrm{HOMOG}_k(\mu_i, \mu_j) = \mu_i - \mu_j \tag{4}$$

where μ_i and μ_j are the fuzzy membership values associated with pixel k to sets i and j in the lowest level representation. This operator is applied to each pixel in an image after a descending sort is performed on the membership values. Values of (4) close to 1.0 would indicate that class i is the dominant color characteristic for pixel k.

The location of a color edge can now be defined as the spatial location of the zero crossings of

$$\mathrm{EDGELOC}_{kl} = \mathrm{HOMOG}_k - \mathrm{HOMOG}_l \tag{5}$$

where k and l are two adjacent pixels in the horizontal or vertical direction. Since a descending sort is performed at each pixel, the set indexes across a transition between two color regions will switch places. This behavior will manifest itself as a change in the sign of the result returned from the HOMOG operator of (4). Zero crossings of the operator (5) will reveal where these points are located. Fig. 1 illustrates the zero crossing properties of (4) for two color classes. Details of an earlier study done with an outdoor image can be found elsewhere [13].

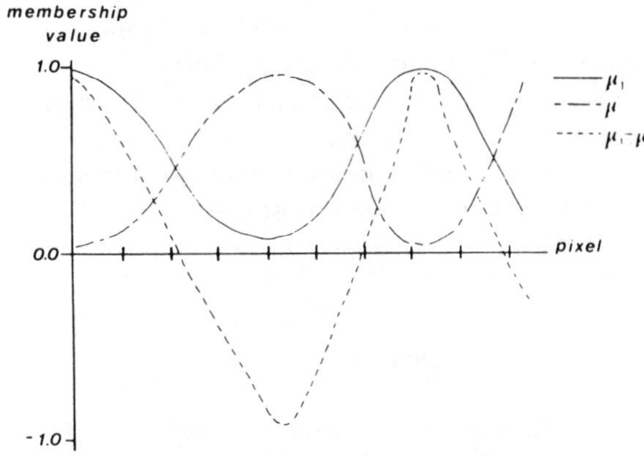

Fig. 1. Zero crossing properties of the HOMOG operator.

The strongest color step edge would be characterized by a value returned from (6) of 2.0. Pure homogeneous color regions with no mixture across a boundary would give rise to this value. The strength of a color edge in the FLASH system is defined as

$$\mu_E = |\mathrm{EDGELOC}_{kl}|/2 \tag{6}$$

where the normalization factor of 2 arises from the discussion above. The operator given in (6) is the membership value of the detected color edge to the class of color step edges. The operator is applied only at the points where evidence for an edge exists, i.e., at the zero crossings of the EDGELOC operator.

There are at least two types of region boundaries present in any natural image. These are sharp discontinuities which usually indicate abrupt changes in depth, and diffuse discontinuities which may indicate the presence of shadows or ramp edges. Values close to 0.25 and slightly above returned from (6) indicate diffuse edges, while sharp edges are characterized by values to 1.0. The membership value given by (6) is important in the identification of shadows, which can be used as a low-level input to three-dimensional models of the scene. Shadows are oftentimes characterized by a diffuse edge due to the penumbra.

IV. Shape Representation

Without some information about interrelationships between regions, image understanding is not possible. The generation of regions can be accomplished using edge linking or region growing techniques based on connectivity. This paper reports on an edge linking method. We alternately are developing an approach that uses both edge and membership value information for region formation [16]. Since FLASH is a model-based system, some model representation must be chosen. In the spirit of the overall design philosophy of the system, it is desirable that this representation be in terms of fuzzy set theory. Imprecision in the model attributes returned from the input image or images can be modeled and will not necessarily hamper pattern matching.

The lowest level of representation is the pixel, where each pixel has a set of membership values to the cluster centers returned from the iterative image segmentation modules. A data structure suitable for the lowest level is a modification of an ordered triple knowledge representation construct of the type [22]

$$(attribute, object, value).$$

Attribute in the lowest representation level of the FLASH system is a set of the color cluster centers, object is the individual pixel, and value is the set of fuzzy membership values to the set of cluster centers. Multiple representations of the image at the pixel level can be maintained if the fuzzy exponent m in (1) above serves as an index. However, as mentioned earlier, there is not enough information here for computer vision.

This problem was addressed by Marr in his computational theory of vision [21]. A symbolic representation called the raw primal sketch was used for the description of the image in this theory. The objects of the raw primal sketch are edges, bars, blobs and terminations. Attributes are orientation, contrast, length, width and position. Unfortunately, there is not enough shape information contained in the attributes of length and width for general computer vision. Also, the objects are defined in terms of predefined notions and no allowance is made for varying degrees of membership of these objects to the model base.

The objects of the raw primal sketch can still be used if suitable modifications are made to the attributes. It must be emphasized here that *objects* used in our system at this stage do not correspond to three-dimensional objects in a real sense, but instead are the unlabeled regions which may or may not be a two-dimensional view of the three-dimensional objects in the scene. This is most important in the handling of shadow regions, where a projection over a surface is actually occurring.

Spatial information can be maintained for pixel or region attributes using an associative memory structure for the representation base of the system. Since this type of a memory structure allows access by content, if its organization matches the original spatial organization of the input image or images in the case of time-varying imagery, operations needed for symbolic shape manipulations can be performed directly within the database. This type of memory organization has shown itself to be well suited for multiple-valued logic, encoded data representations, and operations [25].

The representation chosen in the FLASH system for regions or blobs was that of n-sided polygons [18], [19]. Another method which allows comparisons between approximate polygons and oval shaped regions was recently presented by Dubois and Jaulent [8]. Needed shape information for symbolic description and pattern matching is contained in the angles and sides of these polygons. These polygons are defined in terms of linking the edge elements given by the zero crossings of the operator defined above in (6) [27].

Connectivity of edges and position of corners for the edge representation used above are established using an algorithm developed by Anderson and Bezdek [1]. The basis for the commutator vertex detection (CVD) scheme is:

Let X, Y be the two sequential arcs in a discrete planar curve C. If the tangential deflection between X and Y is large then the location of a corner in C is between X and Y. The eigenvalue–eigenvector structure of the data sets X and Y minimizes in a least-square sense the orthogonal distance from the data set points to the eigenvector which is the major axis of the scatter matrix. Also, the shapes of the data points are assumed to be linear and elliptical because the shape of X is presumed to mimic the shape of the level sets of the probability density function of X. A data set which is more circular is labeled "noise." The principle angle between data sets X and Y is the angle between their principle eigenspaces which is given by the following equation:

$$\cos(2\Delta\vartheta) = \frac{(a_{22} - a_{11})(b_{22} - b_{11}) + 4a_{12}b_{12}}{\sqrt{(1 - 4detA)(1 - 4detB)}} \tag{7}$$

where $A = S_X/(\text{trace } S_X)$ and $B = S_Y/(\text{trace } S_Y)$. Here S_X and S_Y are the scatter matrices associated with X and Y, respectively.

For a fairly accurate results, we set the data set length of nine pixels points and a tangential deflection threshold $\vartheta_t = 20°$, empirically. The CVD algorithm gives the location of the vertices and the tangential deflection angle in the range $0° \leq \vartheta_t \leq 90°$.

The arc length and the arc direction for each of the vertices are also measured. With the directions of the base arc and successor arc, and the information that the vertex is a convex vertex or a nonconvex vertex, the approximate angle size is determined.

For a vertex v_i the midpoint m_p of the line joining the two points, one from each of the base arc v_i and the successor arc v_i are taken and a line is drawn from m_p in the direction of the v_i. If this line intersects the region boundary once then v_i is a convex vertex; otherwise it is a nonconvex vertex.

Approximate angle measure λ_{ap} using arc directions can be determined as

$$\lambda_{ap} = |dir_{ba} - dir_{sa}| = \delta = \begin{cases} \delta = 0; & \lambda_{ap} = 180° \\ 0 < \delta < 4; & \lambda_{ap} = \delta \times 45° \\ \delta = 4; & \lambda_{ap} = 0° \end{cases} \tag{8}$$

where dir_{ba} is the base arc direction and dir_{sa} is the successor arc direction. For a nonconvex vertex $\lambda_{ap} = 360° - \lambda_{ap}$. Using the tangential deflection ϑ_t we get an estimated angle size.

Interpretation of the Shape Parameters

Due to noise, occlusion and the degradation during digitization and other preprocessing of the image, there are irregularities and spurious contours in the region boundaries. These distorted edges contribute to the location of corners where there is none and missing those which ought to be there. We apply some general rules to detect possible spurious vertices. These rules are not influenced by the reason for the presence of irregularities in the region boundaries. Following are the criteria for considering a vertex spurious.

1) Angle size close to 180° for a convex vertex and 360° for a nonconvex vertex and the arc length is less than ⅓ of the average arc length.

2) When arc length is ¼ of the average length. In this case, we reassign the vertex at a location which is the current location +½ arc length. This case generally happens when a sharp corner gets flattened due to noise, occlusion, etc.

3) The angle size is close to 180° for a convex vertex and close to 360° for a nonconvex vertex and the arc directions of the base arc and the successor arc are the same.

We recompute the angle size, arc length and arc direction for all the vertices once again. This time the entire arc length is used as data set length so that the eigenspaces, for computing the tangential deflection angle for each of the vertices, are of the base arc and the successor arc. In other words, the entire base arc and the successor arc are approximated to a line here.

The final step in our interpretation is to determine whether the line between two consecutive vertices is a straight line or a curved line. This is done by measuring the tangential deflection ϑ_m at the midpoint of the line and finding the arc directions on either sides of this midpoint. If $\vartheta_m \leq \vartheta_t - \varepsilon$ (where $\varepsilon = 5°$) and the arc directions are the same then that side can be labeled as a straight line, otherwise as a curved line. If all lines between the vertices in the region are straight lines the region is a polygon, otherwise it is a curved region.

For curved regions the length of the major and minor axis are computed. Euclidean distance measure is used here. The center C, of the enclosing rectangle of the curved region, is taken and in each quadrant the shortest and the longest distances $d(C, I_s)$ and $d(C, I_l)$ where I_s and I_l are the points on the boundary, are measured. The lines (C, I_s) and (C, I_l) are extended to find the other intersection points I_s and I_l on the boundary. The distances $d(I_s, I_s)$ and $d(I_l, I_l)$ can be the shortest and the longest chords starting from each quadrant. We have four sets of possible major and minor axes. The shortest of these eight chords is the minor axis and the longest is the major axis.

Comparison to Models

Since the shapes of the regions actually found in a real image will very rarely match exactly those in the model base, fuzzy membership values to the polygonal sets in the model base can be defined in terms of angles and lengths of sides [18]. We have the regions marked as polygons or curved regions. A polygon with three angles and three sides is compared to the class of triangles; four angles and four sides to the class of quadrangles; more than four angles and four sides to n-sided regular polygon; and curved region to circle [27].

In the case of triangles, the angular measure of proximity is more sensitive than the dimensional measure. For example, if two angles of a triangle are more or less equal, this implies that the corresponding two sides are more or less equal. On the other hand, if two sides of a triangle are more or less equal, this does not necessarily mean that the corresponding angles are more or less equal.

A quantitative measure of an "approximate isosceles" triangle defined by the grade of membership μ_I is

$$\mu_I = 1 - \rho_I \frac{\min\{|A - B|, |B - C|, |C - A|\}}{180°} \tag{9}$$

where A, B, and C are the angles and the constant $\rho_I = 3$ is calculated using the triangle with angles most unlike an isosceles triangle.

For an "approximate equilateral triangle" the grade of membership is expressed as

$$\mu_E = 1 - \rho_E \frac{\max\{|A - B|, |B - C|, |C - A|\}}{180°} \tag{10}$$

For an "approximate right triangle" the grade of membership is expressed as

$$\mu_R = 1 - \rho_R \frac{\min\{|A - 90°|, |B - 90°|, |C - 90°|\}}{180°} \tag{11}$$

where A, B, and C are the angles and the constant $\rho_R = 2$ is calculated using the triangle with angles most unlike a right triangle.

Now the triangle is classified into one of the following five classes: "approximate right triangle," "approximate isosceles triangle," "approximate isosceles right triangle," "approximate equilateral triangle" or "ordinary triangle."

The $\cup \{\mu_I, \mu_E, \mu_R\}$ facilitates this classification.

If $\max\{\mu_I, \mu_E, \mu_R\} \geq \alpha$ (where $\alpha = 0.85$) then the two possibilities are:

a) If the maximum is unique, then we choose the class corresponding to the maximum value and classify the triangle accordingly.

b) If the maximum is not unique, e.g., if both μ_I and μ_E are maxima, then the triangle is classified as approximate equilateral triangle. If both μ_I and μ_R are maxima, then the triangle is classified as approximate isosceles right triangle.

If $\max\{\mu_I, \mu_E, \mu_R\} < \alpha$ it is an ordinary triangle.

For the classification of different classes of quadrangle we use information about either the angles or the sides or both. Euclidean distance is used to measure the length of the sides which is the distance between the vertices.

To classify a quadrangle in the "trapezoid-like" category we use the information only about its angles. The grade of membership of a trapezoid is defined as

$$\mu_T = 1 - \rho_T \frac{\min\{|A + B - 180°|, |B + C - 180°|\}}{180°}. \tag{12}$$

where A, B, C, and D are the angles and $\rho_T = 2$, a constant, which is calculated using the quadrangle with angles most unlike a trapezoid.

To classify a quadrangle in the "parallelogram-like" category the information about its angles or its sides can be used. We use the information only about its angles. The grade of membership of a parallelogram is defined as

$$\mu_P = 1 - \rho_P \frac{\max\{|A - C|, |B - D|\}}{180°} \tag{13}$$

where A, B, C and, D are the angles and $\rho_P = 1$, a constant, which is calculated using the quadrangle with angles most unlike a parallelogram.

To classify in the "approximate rectangle" category we use only the information about its angles. The grade of membership is defined as

$$\mu_{RE} = 1 - \rho_{RE} \frac{\{|A - 90°| + |B - 90°| + |C - 90°| + |D - 90°|\}}{90°} \quad (14)$$

where A, B, C, and D are the angles and the constant $\rho_{RE} = 1/4$ is calculated using the quadrangle with angles most unlike a rectangle.

To classify in the "approximate rhombus" category we use only the information about its sides as rhombus can not be distinguished, unlike a parallelogram, only in term of the information about its angles. The grade of membership for a rhombus is defined as

$$\mu_{RH} = 1 - \rho_{RH} \frac{\max\{|a - b|, |b - c|, |c - d|, |d - a|\}}{a + b + c + d} \quad (15)$$

where a, b, c, and d are the sides and the constant $\rho_{RH} = 2$ is calculated using the quadrangle with angles most unlike a rhombus.

For the classification in the "approximate square" category, we use the information on both its sides and angles. This is defined as

$$\mu_S = \mu_{RE} \times \mu_{RH}. \quad (16)$$

For the classification as an approximate n-sided regular polygon, the grade of membership is given by

$$\mu_{REG} = \mu_{SD} \times \mu_{AG} \quad (17)$$

where

$$\mu_{SD} = 1 - \rho_{SD} \frac{\max\{|a_1 - a_2|, |a_2 - a_3|, \cdots, |a_n - 1 - a_n|, |a_n - a_1|\}}{a_1 + a_2 + , \cdots, + a_n} \quad (17a)$$

$$\mu_{AG} = 1 - \rho_{AG} \cdot \frac{\max\{|A_1 - (n - 2)180°/n|, \cdots, |A_n - (n - 2)180°/n|\}}{180°} \quad (17b)$$

and $a_1, a_2, \cdots, a_n$ are the sides and $A_1, A_2, \cdots, A_n$ are the angles. The constants $\rho_{SD} = 1$ and $\rho_{AG} = 1$ are computed using the most unlike n-sided regular polygon.

For the classification of a curved region its major and minor axis are used [27]. The grade of membership is defined as

$$\mu_{CR} = 1 - \frac{|l_1 - l_2|}{l_1 + l_2} \quad (18)$$

where l_1 is the major axis and l_2 is the minor axis.

Once the shapes of the regions have been defined in terms of their fuzzy membership values to the polygonal sets in the model base, symbolic relationships between the regions and higher level models can be determined. This is in a two-dimensional sense only, since any of the algorithms which determine depth from a single static image are not usually robust enough for complicated scenes. Three-dimensional surface descriptions of the regions in most natural scenes can only be obtained with the introduction of explicit depth information or a sequence of images. Image sequence analysis capabilities in the FLASH system will be the subject of a forthcoming paper [14]. The low-level operations described above will be performed in parallel on each of the input images. Set theoretic operations between representations of the image sequence can then be used to derive motion information about the scene.

The next level two-dimensional model can be achieved with fuzzy tree grammars [20]. In its simplest form, a fuzzy tree grammar defines "approximate" models of more complicated objects such as houses, etc. The primitive shapes from the analysis above with their associated membership values are the nodes in the tree. Syntactic relations are used to define the arcs in the tree structure. In a complicated natural scene more information is needed concerning the arcs. A fuzzy adjacency measure is used in the FLASH system to weight the production rules of the grammar. This adjacency measure can be defined following Rosenfeld [29] as

$$ADJ_{ij} = \sum_k \mu_E \quad (19)$$

where i and j are the two regions and k is taken over the set of shared zero crossings of the operator given in (6) above. This is another operator that is well-suited for implementation in an associative memory framework, due to its dependence on local spatial characteristics of an input image.

The adjacency measure given in (19) above indicates diffuse versus sharp adjacency, and was defined as such to allow the description of shadow adjacency as well as surface adjacency. The inference machine portion of the computer vision system needs this information for matching in the model base, since it is impossible to model every possible shadow configuration. This approach controls the generation of false hypotheses as far as shadows being taken as solid regions.

Hypotheses about two-dimensional shape interpretations are put onto an agenda portion of a blackboard. The organization of the blackboard allows multiple images from an image sequence to be manipulated as far as three dimensional interpretation is concerned. Combination of evidence for existence of three dimensional objects will be one in the possibility/necessity framework of fuzzy pattern matching [22]. This phase of the system is presently under investigation.

V. Experimental Studies

We applied the techniques discussed above to a number of color images. Each image was digitized at a resolution of 240 rows × 256 columns with 24 bits of RGB color information. Figs. 2 and 3 show an office scene and a textured surface with a doorknob, respectively. The figures represent

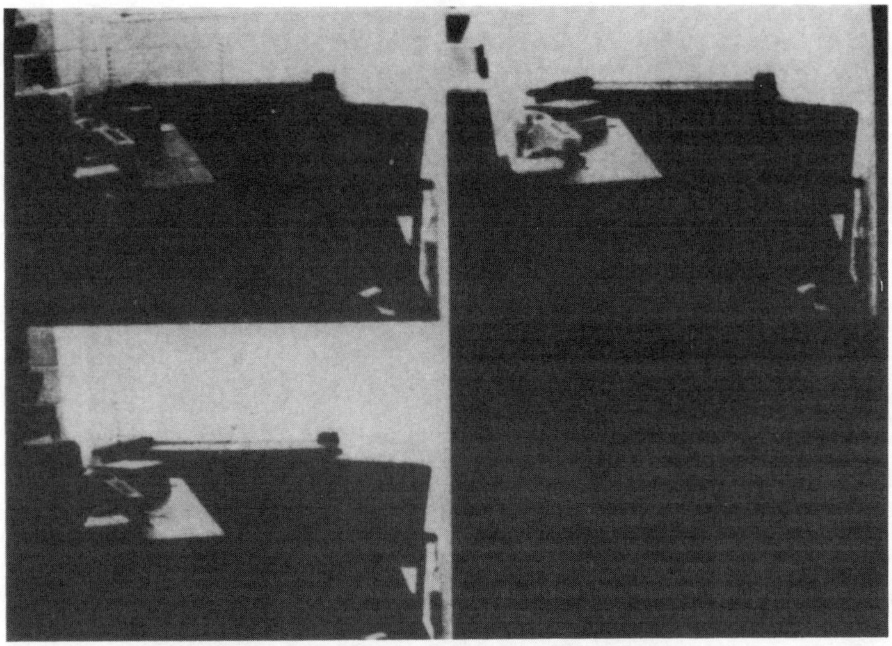

Fig. 2. Color image office scene. (Note: In this and other color images included in this paper, red, green and blue components of the image are shown in the NW, NE, and SW quadrants, respectively.)

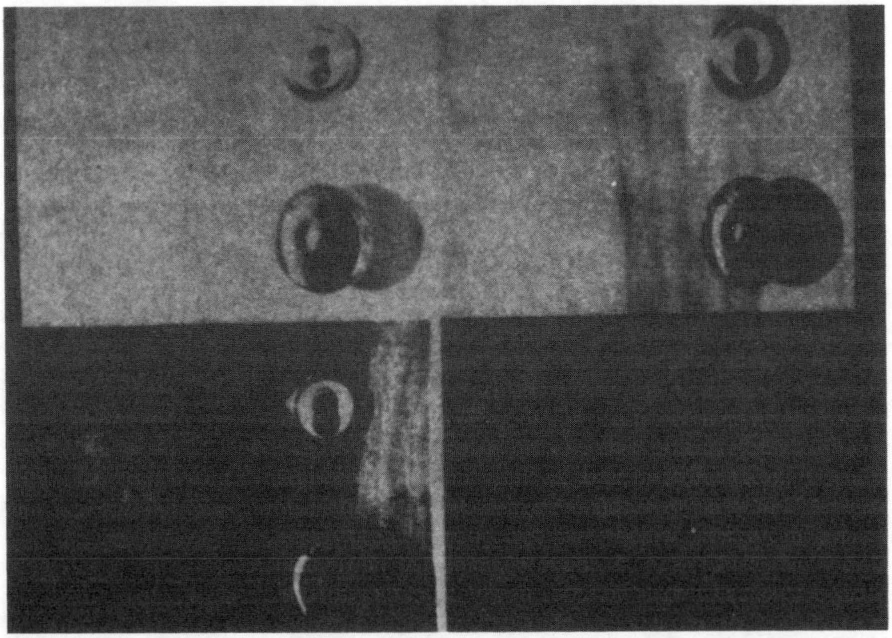

Fig. 3. Color image of textured surface with doorknob.

the red, green, and blue color planes. Membership values to the first four clusters returned from the iterative fuzzy image segmentation phase are shown for the same images in Figs. 4 and 5. These figures use a gray scale to represent the membership values, 0.0 being dark and varying shades of gray up to the brightest value for membership of 1.0. Homogeneous connected color regions such as the chair and doorknob in the two images are characterized by strong membership values. The background color texture of the door is shared among various classes.

Membership values to the first four classes for a natural color image (house) are shown in Fig. 6, where a gray scale is used once again for the range of the membership value. Application of the color edge detector to this image for a number of different color systems is shown in Fig. 7. The original image and details of the alternate color systems are described in Huntsberger *et al.* [13]. Most of the edges are very strong in this image, as can be seen from the sharpness of the region boundaries in Fig. 6. Each of the color systems investigated gave varying degrees of edge detail, and we are presently investigating the dependence of color edge detection on the color system and distance metrics that are used in the initial fuzzy segmentation stage.

Membership values for another color image (chair) are shown in Fig. 8. The edges that were detected for this image are shown in Fig. 9. Although the photograph does not have

Fig. 4. Membership values to the first four cluster centers for office scene in Fig. 2 (see text for gray-scale explanation).

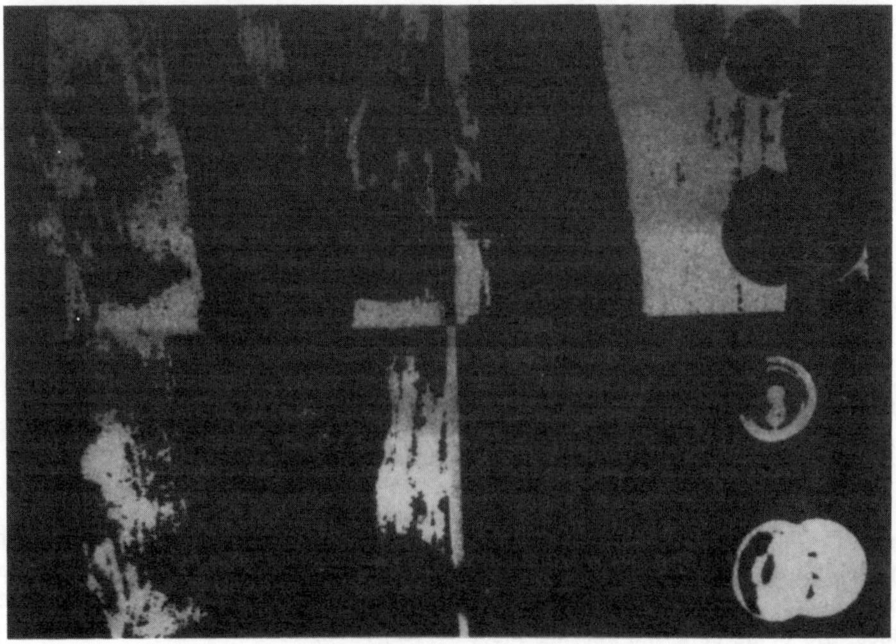

Fig. 5. Same as Fig. 4 for textured surface with doorknob.

Fig. 6. Same as Fig. 4 for natural color scene (house).

Fig. 7. Color edges for house image: (NW) RGB, (NE) OHTA [24], (SW) XYZ [33], (SE) Riemannian metric [32].

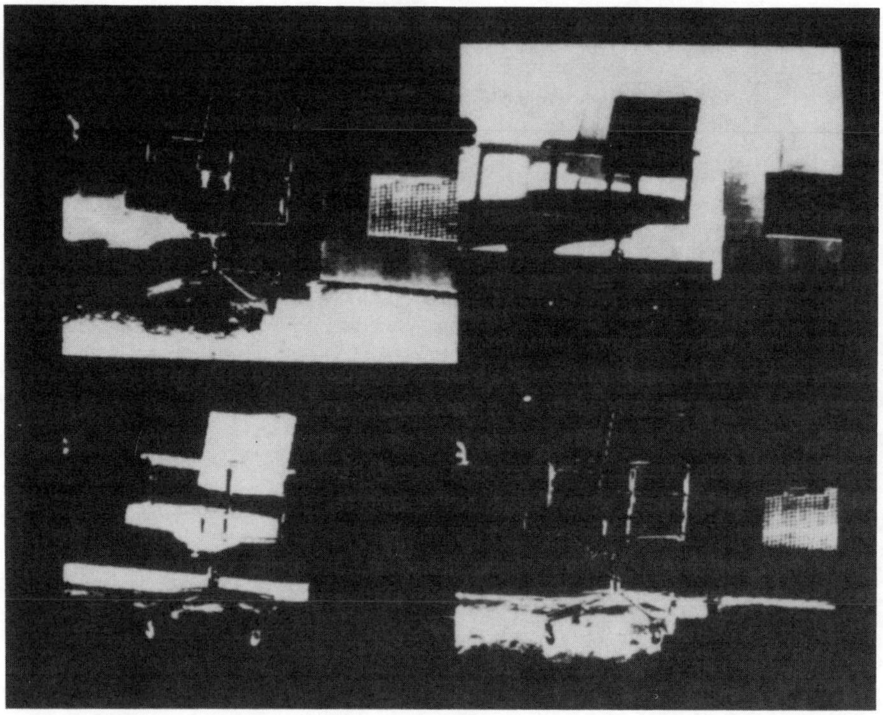

Fig. 8. Membership values to the first four cluster centers for natural color scene (chair).

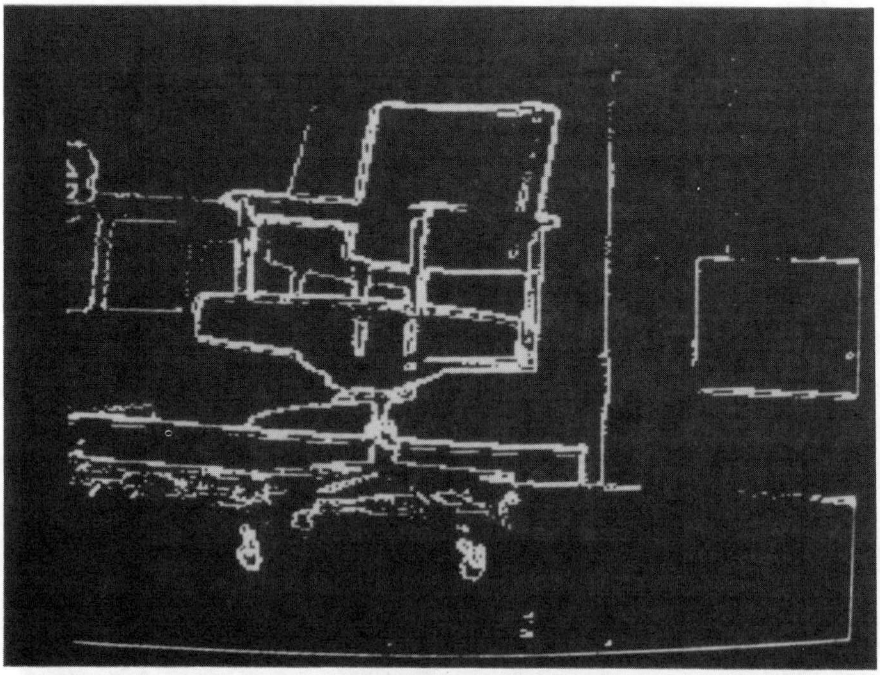

Fig. 9. Color edges for chair image.

the necessary contrast range to see the edge strength, the shadow of the chair was detected as a diffuse edge. This image was used for the shape modeling and matching operations described above. The results for some of the polygonal regions found in the image are shown in Table I. Further work incorporating concave regions is presently underway.

VI. Discussion

A computer vision system designed for flexibility in decision making, as well as representation allows the handling of uncertainty and incompleteness. The algebra and set operations of fuzzy sets seems to retain enough information about

TABLE I
SELECTED POLYGON MEMBERSHIP VALUES TO MODEL BASE FOR CHAIR IMAGE

Region #	Number of vertices	Models: Triangles: Isoscel.	Equilat.	Right tri.	Quadrangles: Parallell.	Rectangle	Trapizoid	Rhombus	Square	Regular polygon	Circle
23	4				.94	.86	.91	.69	.6		
26	3	.71	.8	.85							
35	4				.96	.96	.98	.43	.41		.49
88	4				.83	.85	.84	.35	.3		.09

Table 1. the fuzzy proximity measure for the regions in the picture of the chair to the models.

these factors, while at the same time not hampering decision making processes. Incorporation of fuzzy notions to shape descriptions allows enough information to be passed to higher levels of the system, without the need for exact quantitative matching. We have recently designed and simulated a parallel architecture module that is suitable for the operations defined above [6]. It is hoped that with the inclusion of time-varying image input cues to the system, effects such as motion blur can be detected and utilized for three-dimensional descriptions of the scene.

ACKNOWLEDGMENT

The authors would like to thank the reviewers for their thorough reading of the manuscript, and their many useful suggestions. We would also like to express our gratitude to J. Bezdek and other members of the Intelligent Systems Laboratory at the University of South Carolina for their encouragement.

REFERENCES

[1] I. M. Anderson and J. C. Bezdek, "Curvature and tangential deflection of discrete arcs: A theory based on the commutator of scatter matrix pairs and its application to vertex detection in planar shape data," *IEEE Trans. Pattern Anal. Machine Intell.*, vol. PAMI-6, pp. 27–40, Jan. 1984.
[2] J. C. Bezdek, *Pattern Recognition with Fuzzy Objective Function Algorithms*. New York: Plenum, 1981.
[3] T. O. Binford, "Survey of model-based image analysis systems," *Int. J. Robot. Res.*, vol. 1, pp. 18–64, 1982.
[4] R. Brooks, "Symbolic reasoning among 3-dimensional models and 2-dimensional images," *Artif. Intell.*, vol. 17, pp. 285–349, 1981.
[5] R. Davis, B. G. Buchanan, and E. Shortliffe, "Production rules as a representation for a knowledge-based consultation program," *Artif. Intell.*, vol. 8, pp. 15–45, 1977.
[6] M. Descalzi, "A modular architecture suitable for image processing applications," M.S. thesis, Univ. South Carolina, Columbia, 1983.
[7] D. Dubois and M. C. Jaulent, "Some techniques for extracting fuzzy regions," in *Proc. 1st I.F.S.A. Cong.*, vol. II, Mallorca, Spain, July 1–6, 1985.
[8] ——, "Shape understanding via fuzzy models," in *Proc. 2nd IFAC/IFIP/IFORS/IEA Conf. Anal., Design, Eval. Man–Machine Syst.*, Varse, Italy, 1985.
[9] L. D. Erman, F. Hayes-Roth, V. Lesser, and D. Reddy, "The HEARSAY-II speech-understanding system: Integrating knowledge to resolve uncertainty," *Comput. Surv.*, vol. 12, pp. 213–253, 1980.
[10] T. L. Huntsberger, "FLASH, a multivalued logic-based expert system suitable for computer vision," presented at NAFIPS II Workshop, Schenectady, NY, June 28–July 1, 1983.
[11] ——, "A multivalued logic-based computer vision system," in *Proc. 11th Ann. Meeting IEEE Syst. Man Cybern.*, Bombay, India, Dec. 28–Jan. 3, 1984, pp. 33–35.
[12] T. L. Huntsberger, C. L. Jacobs, and R. L. Cannon, "Iterative fuzzy image segmentation," *Pattern Recognition*, vol. 18, pp. 131–138, 1985.
[13] T. L. Huntsberger and M. F. Descalzi, "Color edge detection," *Pattern Recognition Lett.*, vol. 3, pp. 205–209, 1984.
[14] T. L. Huntsberger and S. N. Jayaramamurthy, "A framework for dynamic color scene analysis," in preparation.
[15] C. L. Jacobs, "Color image segmentation: texture and a fuzzy *c* means clustering implementation," M.S. thesis, Univ. South Carolina, Columbia, 1983.
[16] S. N. Jayaramamurthy and T. L. Huntsberger, "Edge and region analysis using fuzzy sets," in *Proc. 1985 IEEE Workshop Lang. Automat.*, Mallorca, Spain, June 28–29, 1985, pp. 71–75.
[17] R. Jain, "Applications of fuzzy sets for the analysis of complex scenes," in *Advances in Fuzzy Set Theory and Applications*, M. M. Gupta, Ed. Amsterdam, The Netherlands: North Holland, 1979, pp. 577–587.
[18] E. T. Lee, "Proximity measures for the classification of geometric figures," *J. Cybern.*, vol. 2, pp. 43–59, 1972.
[19] E. T. Lee, "The shape-oriented dissimilarity of polygons and its application to the classification of chromosome images," *Pattern Recognition*, vol. 6, pp. 47–60, 1974.
[20] ——, "Fuzzy tree automata and syntactic pattern recognition," *IEEE Trans. Pattern Anal. Machine Intell.*, vol. PAMI-4, pp. 445–449, 1982.
[21] D. Marr, *Vision*. San Francisco, CA: W. H. Freeman, 1982.
[22] R. Martin-Clouaire and H. Prade, "On the problem of representation and propagation of uncertainty in expert systems," *Int. J. Man–Machine Stud.*, vol. 22, 1985.
[23] M. Nagao and T. Matsuyama, *A Structural Analysis of Complex Aerial Photographs*. New York: Plenum, 1980.
[24] Y. Ohta, *et al.*, "Color information for region segmentation," *Comput. Graph. Image Processing*, vol. 13, pp. 222–241, 1980.
[25] C. A. Papachristou, "Content-addressable memory requirements for multivalued logic," in *Proc. 11th Int. Symp. Multiple-Valued Logic*, Norman, OK, 1981, pp. 62–72.
[26] C. C. Parma, A. M. Hanson, and E. M. Riseman, "Experiments in schema-driven interpretation of a natural scene," Univ. Massachusetts, Amherst, COINS Tech. Rep. 80-10, 1980.
[27] C. Rangarajan, "A recognition method for the shapes of the regions in images," M.S. thesis, Dep. Comput. Sci., Univ. South Carolina, Columbia, 1985.
[28] D. C. Rine, "Picture processing using multiple-valued logic," in *Proc. 11th Int. Symp. Multiple-Valued Logic*, Norman, OK, 1981, pp. 73–78.
[29] A. Rosenfeld, "The fuzzy geometry of image subsets," *Pattern Recognition Lett.*, in press.
[30] S. Rubin, "The ARGOS image understanding system," Ph.D. dissertation, Carnegie-Mellon Univ., Pittsburgh, PA, 1978.
[31] Y. Shirai, "Recognition of man-made objects using edge cues," in *Computer Vision Systems.*, A. Hanson and E. Riseman, Eds. New York: Academic, 1978.
[32] E. H. Shortliffe, *Computer-Based Medical Consultation: MYCIN*. New York: American Elsevier, 1976.
[33] W. S. Stiles, "A modified Helmholtz line-element in brightness-colour space," in *Proc. Roy. Soc. London*, vol. 58, pp. 41–65, 1946.

[34] G. Wyszecki and W. S. Stiles, *Color Science*. New York: Wiley, 1967.
[35] L. A. Zadeh, "Fuzzy sets," *Informat. Contr.*, vol. 8, pp. 338–353, 1965.
[36] S. W. Zucker, "Vertical and horizontal processes in low-level vision," in *Computer Vision Systems*, A. R. Hanson, E. M. Riseman, Eds. New York: Academic, 1978.

An Application of the *c*-Varieties Clustering Algorithms to Polygonal Curve Fitting

JAMES C. BEZDEK, MEMBER, IEEE, AND IAN M. ANDERSON

***Abstract*—An algorithm is described that fits boundary data of planar shapes in either rectangular coordinate or chain-coded format with a set of straight line segments. The algorithm combines a new vertex detection method, which locates initial vertices and segments in the data, with the *c*-elliptotype clustering algorithm, which iteratively adjusts the location of these initial segments, thereby obtaining a best polygonal fit for the data in the mean-squared error sense. Several numerical examples are given to exemplify the implementation and utility of this new approach.**

I. Introduction

Let $B = \{b_1, b_2, \ldots, b_N\}$ be N points in the plane ordered along the boundary of some planar shape. For such a data set, we present a new algorithm that finds a set of c line segments, which collectively provide a good polygonal fit to the points in B. This problem, variously referred to in the literature as segmentation of plane curves, curve fitting, linear splining or polygonal approximation, plays an important role in a wide variety of image-processing applications. Excellent surveys of many existing polygonal approximation routines, together with their many applications may be found in Duda and Hart [4], Hall [5], Pavlidis [7], and Rosenfeld and Kac [8].

Generally, polygonal approximation routines consist of three steps. The first step is one of initialization—vertices are tentatively located in the data that provide an initial polygonal approximation. In the second step, this initial polygon is iteratively adjusted, either by adding additional edges or by changing the slopes and centers of existing edges. This adjustment continues until some specific goodness of fit criteria is met. Finally, in step three the polygonal approximation may be "tidied up"—edges which are very nearly the same may be merged or concatenated, edges may be extended to form a connected polygonal approximation or, alternatively, edges supported by too few data points may be deleted altogether.

The algorithm described here, henceforth called boundary-fit, uses in step 1 the vertex detection method described in detail in Anderson and Bezdek [1]. This method is based upon a new geometric property of sample variance–covariance matrices; viz., that the matrix commutator of two such matrices constructed from successive arcs in the boundary data provides an analytical measure of the tangential deflection between these arcs. This leads to a highly reliable placement of the initial vertices (each vertex is a point in the data set B) and results in quicker convergence of the iterative process.

To adjust this initial polygonal approximation, the Boundaryfit program uses the fuzzy c-elliptotype (FCE) algorithm developed by Bezdek and Coray *et. al.* [3]. This algorithm is a sophisticated extension of the well-known "scatter matrix, eigenvalue–eigenvector" line-fitting method (see Duda and Hart [4] pp. 332–334),

Manuscript received October 6, 1984; revised May 13, 1985. This work was supported in part by the National Science Foundation under grants IST-84-07860 and MCS-80-02328.

J.C. Bezdek is with the Department of Computer Science, University of South Carolina, Columbia, SC 29208, USA. I. M. Anderson is with the Department of Mathematics, Utah State University, Logan, UT 84322, USA.

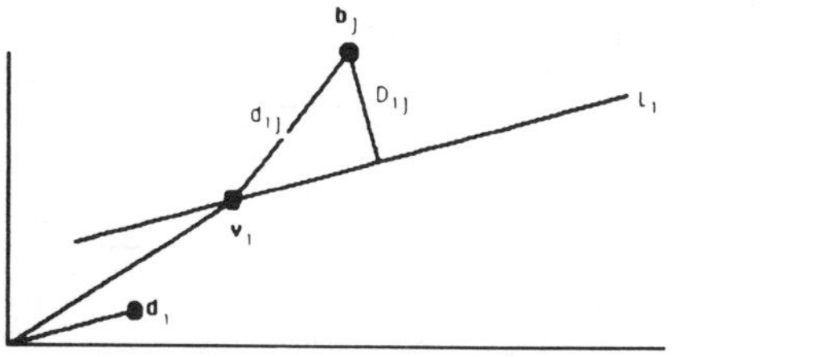

Fig. 1. Geometry of the FCE functional J. A is any positive definite (2×2) weight matrix. D_{ij} is the OG distance from b_j to L_i with respect to the inner product norm induced by matrix A and $d_{ij}^2 = \|b_j - v_i\|_A^2 = (b_j - v_i)^t A (b_j - v_i)$.

and it is designed specifically to accommodate data sets with many linear structures. It can be described briefly as follows.

First, the FCE algorithm assigns, during each iteration, to each point b_j, $j = 1, 2, \cdots N$ of the boundary, a membership value u_{ij} in each line segment L_i, $i = 1, 2, \cdots c$. These membership values are constrained by the conditions

$$0 \leqslant u_{ij} \leqslant 1$$

and

$$\sum_{i=1}^{c} u_{ij} = 1.$$

If the point b_j is very close to edge L_i, b_j has a membership value in L_i that is close to one; otherwise the membership value is small. Points near vertices in the polygonal approximation are assigned memberships of nearly 1/2 in the adjacent edges. This is in contrast to other line-fitting routines, where each data point must be associated with one and only one edge in the polygonal approximation.

The information contained in the $c \times N$ membership matrix $[u_{ij}]$ is used to define the goodness of fit criteria. Specifically, suppose the edges are described parametrically by $L_i = \{v_i + t\mathbf{d}_i | a_i \leqslant t \leqslant b_i\}$ where v_i is a point on the edge and d_i is a unit vector in the direction of L_i. Let D_{ij} be the othogonal distance from the point b_j to the edge L_i and let d_{ij} be the distance from b_j to v_i (Fig. 1). The FCE algorithm attempts to find a local minimum in the variables $\{(u_{ij}, \mathbf{v}_i, \mathbf{d}_i)\}$ of the functional

$$J = \sum_{i=1}^{c} \sum_{j=1}^{N} [u_{ij}]^m [\alpha D^2 ij + (1 - \alpha) d^2 ij]. \qquad (1)$$

Here α, $0 \leqslant \alpha \leqslant 1$, is viewed as a mixing coefficient. Loosely speaking, for example, with $\alpha = 0.8$ (the value used in the subsequent examples), 80 percent of J measures deviations from linear shape within each cluster or edge, while 20 percent of J assesses the central tendencies of these clusters. In ideal situations the memberships u_{ij} converge to zero or one, α may be assigned a value close to one, and J approximates the sum of the squared distances from the data points to their assigned lines.[1] Any inner

[1]A variable α scheme is described in [2]. This variation on the FCE routine is closely related to several algorithms discussed in [9].

Reprinted from *IEEE Trans. Syst., Man, Cybern.*, vol. SMC-15, no. 5, pp. 637–641, September/October 1985.

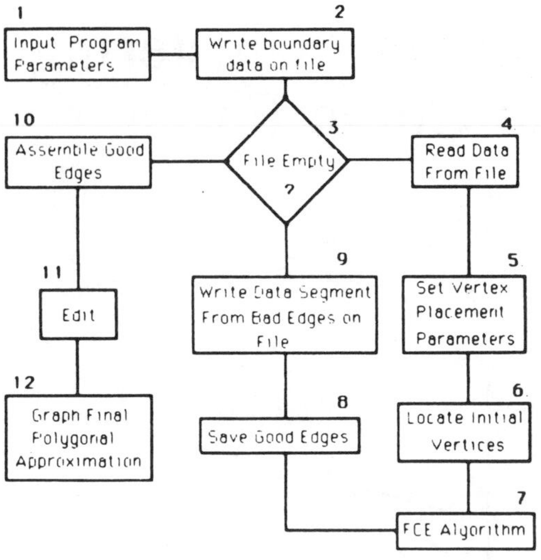

Fig. 2. The Boundaryfit program.

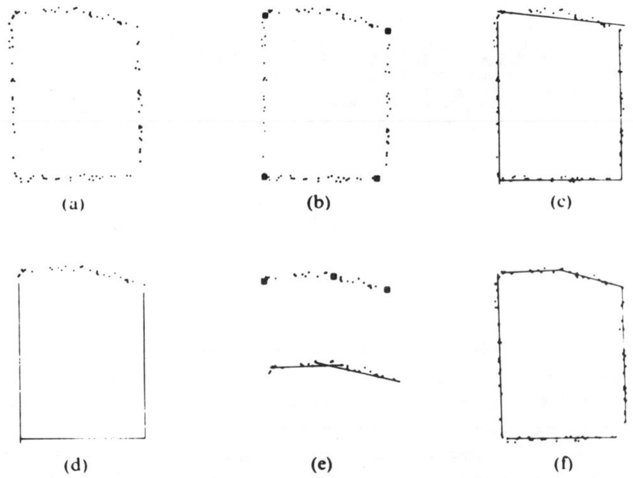

Fig. 3. A simple run of the Boundaryfit program. (a) The data set. (b) Initial placement of vertices. (c) FCE output. (d) Good edges saved and remaining data to be processed. (e) New vertices and FCE output. (f) Final output.

product induced norm can be used for d_{ij} and D_{ij}; in the sequel we take $A = I$, corresponding to choosing the Euclidean norm on $\mathbf{R}^2$

Another characteristic of the FCE algorithm is reflected by the presence of the user specified parameter m, $1 \leqslant m < \infty$. Spurious boundary points will typically have lower memberships in many lines so that with m large, their contribution to the functional J is minimal. Thus implicit in the FCE routine is a simple yet very effective means of suppressing noisy data points, which might otherwise result in unwanted or inaccurate edges. Front-end filtering or smoothing of the boundary is therefore unnecessary. The value $m = 2$ was used in the numerical examples that follow.

To minimize J, the edge centers $\{\boldsymbol{v}_i\}$, their directions $\{\boldsymbol{d}_i\}$ and the membership matrix $[u_{ij}]$ are iteratively adjusted as follows. Initially, the $\{\boldsymbol{v}_i\}$ and $\{\boldsymbol{d}_i\}$ are taken to be the midpoints and directions of the ith edge as constructed from the vertex detection routine. The initial membership matrix is a so-called "hard" membership matrix with

$$u_{ij} = \begin{cases} 1, & \textit{if } \mathbf{b}_i \textit{ is between the ith} \\ & \textit{and } (i+1)\textit{-th vertex} \\ 0, & \text{otherwise.} \end{cases}$$

These variables are updated in accordance with the theory developed in [3]. First the new points $\boldsymbol{v}_i^{(\text{new})}$ are computed from

$$\mathbf{v}_i^{(\text{new})} = \left\{ \sum_{k=1}^{N} \left[u_{ik}^{(\text{old})}\right]^m \mathbf{b}_k \right\} \Big/ \left\{ \sum_{k=1}^{N} \left[u_{ik}^{(\text{old})}\right]^m \right\}.$$

Then the fuzzy 2×2 scatter matrices S_i are found according to

$$S_i = \sum_{k=1}^{N} \left[u_{ik}^{(\text{old})}\right]^m \left(\mathbf{b}_k - \mathbf{v}_i^{(\text{new})}\right)\left(\mathbf{b}_k - \mathbf{v}_i^{(\text{new})}\right)^t$$

Let α_i and β_i be the maximum and minimum eigenvalues of S_i. Then we set $\boldsymbol{d}_i^{(\text{new})}$ equal to the unit eigenvector of S_i corresponding to α_i. Finally, the new memberships are given by

$$u_{ij}^{(\text{new})} = 1 \Big/ \left\{ \sum_{j=i}^{c} \left(\gamma_{ik}/\gamma_{jk}\right)^{1/(m-1)} \right\}$$

where

$$\gamma_{ik} = \|\mathbf{b}_k - \mathbf{v}_i^{(\text{new})}\|^2 - \epsilon_i \langle \mathbf{b}_k - \mathbf{v}_i^{(\text{new})}, \mathbf{d}_i^{(\text{new})} \rangle^2$$

and $\langle x, y \rangle = x^t y$ is the Euclidean inner product on $\mathbf{R}^2$ with

$$\epsilon_i = 1 - \beta_i/\alpha_i.$$

Once the FCE algorithm has converged (in the sense that successive differences in the values of the functional J are small) various elementary steps can be taken to aesthetically improve the final output. While these steps naturally reflect the specific application at hand, their implementation in general can be facilitated with the membership information provided by the FCE algorithm. In the routine illustrated subsequently, lines are extended to include all points within a certain minimum distance, overlapping lines are merged, and lines with too few points of sufficiently high membership are deleted. The endpoints of each line segment L_i are found from the othogonal projections onto L_i of the first and last point in the data set B assigned to L_i.

II. The Boundaryfit Program

A flowchart of the Boundaryfit program is presented in Fig. 2. The function of the various steps is as follows.

Step 1: The program parameters include a) the parameters for the vertex detection routine for steps 5 and 6 [1]; b) The parameters for the FCE algorithm for step 7 [3]; c) the goodness of fit criteria used in step 8—specifically, an edge is designated as "good" if the number of points in the boundary assigned to that edge by membership thresholding exceeds a certain minimum number and if the (unweighted) mean squared error for these points is within a certain tolerance; and d) the user-designed editing parameters used in step 11, which include criteria for extending edges to include nearby points and for merging edges which are nearly the same.

Steps 2–7(first pass): Initial vertices are located in the entire boundary data set using the scatter matrix commutator algorithm described in [1]. These vertices provide an initial polygonal approximation and an initial membership matrix as follows: points between the jth and $(j+1)$-th vertices are assigned a membership value of one in the jth edge and zero in all the other edges. This initial data is then used to initialize the FCE algorithm, which seeks a local minimum of the functional J via Picard iteration through the necessary conditions derived in [3].

Steps 8–9: Even when a local minimum of J has been approximately determined, there is no guarantee that the sum of the distances from the boundary points to their assigned line is within some specific tolerance. If each error is within acceptable limits, the edge is designed as a "good" edge and saved. If the edge is unacceptable, it is labeled a "bad" edge and the segment of the boundary data assigned to that edge is stored on file to be reprocessed.

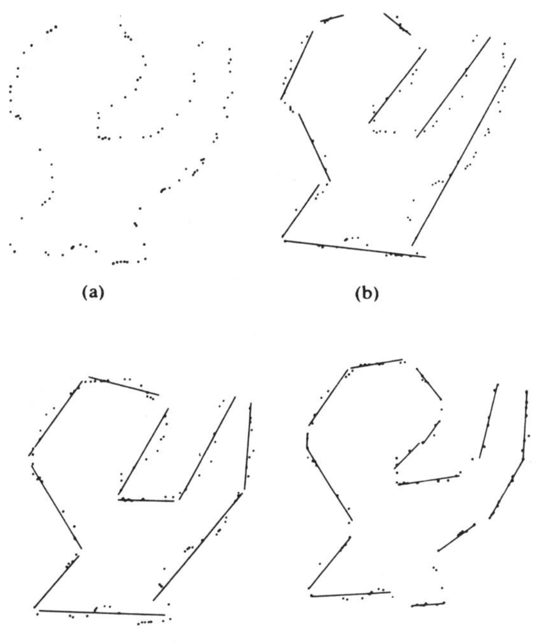

Fig. 4. (a) A cell outline. (b) Ramer's algorithm. (c) The Pavlidis–Horowitz split–merge method. (d) The Boundaryfit program.

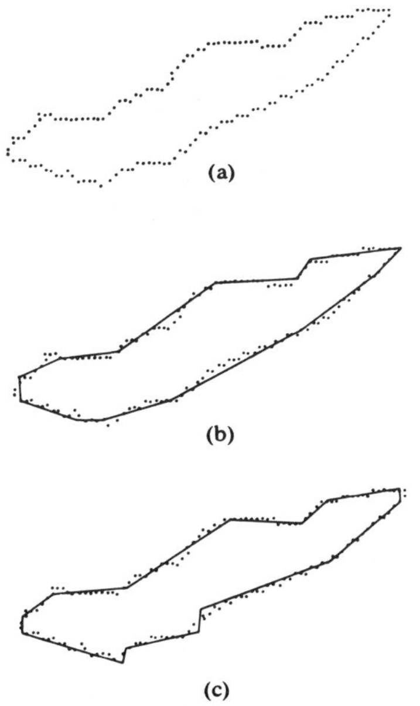

Fig. 5.(a) A digital boundary for Lake Erie. Fig. 5.(b) The minimum perimeter polygon of Kashyap and Oomen. Fig. 5.(c) A closed polygonal approximation from Boundaryfit.

Step 3(subsequent pass): Unsuccessfully fitted boundary data segments are filed. Thus, when the file is empty, all the boundary data has been successfully approximated by polygonal arcs. The totality of these good edges are then assembled together in step 10 and the final polygonal approximation edited in step 11.

Step 5(subsequent pass): Data for which an unacceptable polygonal approximation was produced by the FCE routine is reprocessed. To improve upon the polygonal approximation the parameters in the vertex placement routine are adjusted to generate additional vertices. With a larger number of edges to adjust the FCE algorithm will produce a better approximation. The loop in Fig. 2, which is comprised of steps 3–9, is repeated until the data is approximated entirely by good edges.

Further details of codification are available in a well-documented version of Boundaryfit available from the authors upon request.

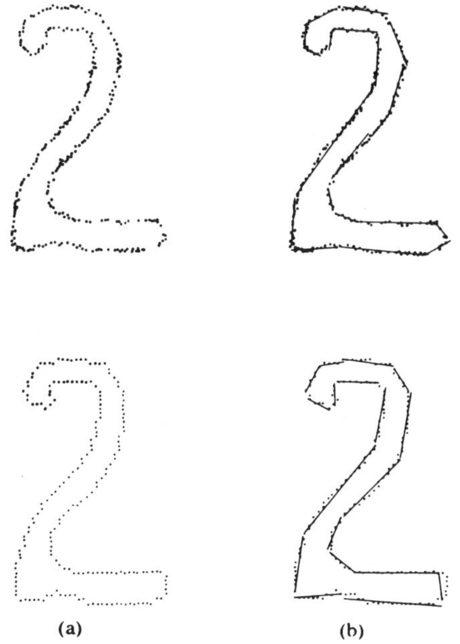

Fig. 6.(a) A polygonal approximation for the character "2" in Cartesian coordinates. (b) A polygonal approximation for the character TWO in chain coordinates.

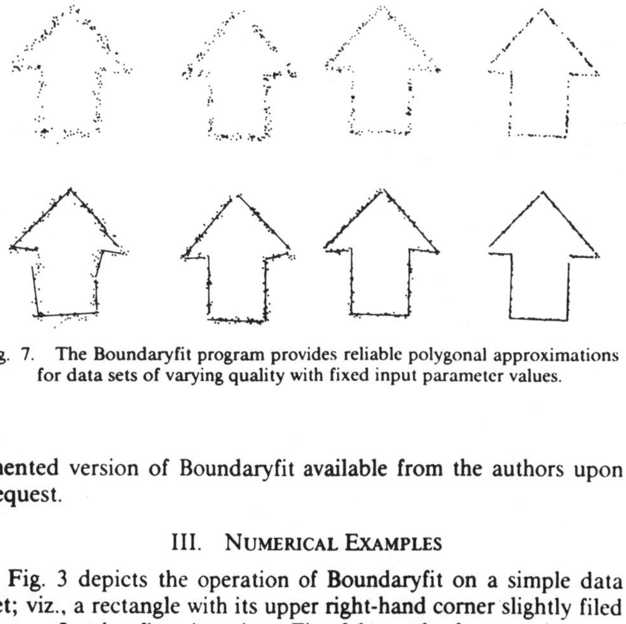

Fig. 7. The Boundaryfit program provides reliable polygonal approximations for data sets of varying quality with fixed input parameter values.

III. Numerical Examples

Fig. 3 depicts the operation of Boundaryfit on a simple data set; viz., a rectangle with its upper right-hand corner slightly filed down. In the first iteration, Fig. 3(b), only four vertices are detected. This leads to the quadrilateral approximation of Fig. 3c. The two sides and the bottom approximate the data sufficiently well, and these are labeled as good edges and are stored. However the data representing the top is not approximated accurately enough. An additional vertex in this data subset is located, and this leads to a better approximation (Figure 3(e)). Finally, the five good edges are assembled together in Fig. 3(f). The membership information provided by the FCE algorithm is used to eliminate the overlap between the top two edges and to truncate, owing to the absence of nearby data points, the right edge and the bottom edge near the lower right hand corner.

In order to compare the Boundaryfit program with existing polygonal approximation routines, a facsimile of the cell outline presented in Pavlidis [7] is reproduced in Fig. 4(a). The results of the Ramer algorithm, the Pavlidis–Horowitz split–merge algorithm, and the Boundaryfit program are displayed in Figs. 4(b), 4(c), and 4(d). The accuracy of the Boundaryfit polygon is due, in part, to the greater number of vertices initially used as determined by the commutator vertex detection routine.

To compare with the minimum-perimeter polygon method of Kashyap and Oomen [6], a digitalized boundary of Lake Erie is reproduced in Fig. 5(a). Figure 5(b) displays the minimum-perimeter polygon, while the output of Boundaryfit is shown in Fig. 5(c). Notice that because the minimum perimeter polygon is a closed polygon we modified, for purposes of comparison, the final steps of our program to produce closed polygons. Visually, the results are in fairly close agreement.

Fig. 6 shows that the Boundaryfit program produces comparable results for data sets in either Cartesian coordinate or chain-coded format.

Numerous other experiments have been performed that show that these algorithms can accurately capture fine structure in "clean" data sets, while at the same time they produce fairly consistent results on data of varying quality for fixed program parameter values. This last property of Boundaryfit is illustrated in Fig. 7.

IV. Conclusions

By using a corner detection routine to initialize the Fuzzy-c-elliptotype algorithm, we have created a program which produces good polygonal approximations for planar data sets. This algorithm has the following features.

1) It works well on either continuous (i.e. rectangular coordinates) or discrete (i.e. chain-coded) data sets.

2) It provides consistent results on data sets of varying quality.

3) It has intrinsic capabilities for suppressing noisy data points.

4) The minimized functional J provides an accurate and reliable measure of the success of the polygonal fit.

5) The introduction of the membership matrix avoids the problem of making hard membership assignments of points near vertices to one of the two adjacent edges.

6) The membership matrix provides useful information for refining the final polygonal approximation.

7) Exact quantitative comparison of the output of Boundaryfit with other algorithms is very difficult to construct. Since these algorithms automatically generate the number of edges that will be used in the polygonal approximation a simple tabulation of the othogonal least squares error is not particularly relevant. Obviously, the greater the number of edges used, the smaller the error will be. Also, any quantitative error analysis is very much dependent on certain design features of the algorithm. Is it, for example, to produce closed polygonals or are there to be gaps in the polygon wherever the data is sparse? In any event, extensive experimentation shows that the Boundaryfit program generates visually appealing polygonal fits on a wide variety of data sets. The FCE algorithm is also capable of generating polyhedra approximations to "surface-like" data sets in three-dimensional space. Thus with the development of an appropriate initialization technique essentially the same program as presented here will accommodate spatial data sets. We know of no other curve fitting algorithm with this potential.

References

[1] I. M. Anderson and J. C. Bezdek, "Curvature and tangential deflection of discrete arcs," *IEEE Trans. Patt. Anal. Mach. Intell.*, vol. PAMI-6, p. 27–40, 1984.

[2] I. M. Anderson, J. C. Bezdek, and R. Dave, "Polygonal shape description of plane boundaries," in *Systems Science and Science*, L. Troncale, Ed. Louisville, KY: SGSR, pp. 295–301, 1982.

[3] J. C. Bezdek, C. Coray, R. Gunderson, and J. Watson, "Detection and characterization of cluster substructure," *J. Appl. Math*, vol. 40, pp. 339–372, 1981.

[4] R. O. Duda and P. E. Hart, *Pattern Classification and Scene Analysis*. New York: Wiley, 1973.

[5] E. L. Hall, *Computer Image Processing and Recognition*, New York: Academic, 1978.

[6] R. L. Kashyap and B. J. Oomen, "Scale preserving smoothing of polygons," *IEEE Trans. Patt. Anal. Mach. Intell.*, vol. PAMI-5, pp. 667–671, 1983.

[7] T. Pavlidis, *Structural Pattern Recognition*. New York: Springer-Verlag, 1977.

[8] A. Rosenfeld and A. C. Kac, *Digital Picture Processing*. New York: Academic, 1976.

[9] M. P. Windham, "A Geometrical fuzzy clustering algorithm," *Fuzzy Sets and Systems*, vol. 10, pp. 271–279, 1983.

Chapter 5
Fuzzy Logic, Neural Networks, and Learning in Pattern Recognition

5.0 Introduction

THIS last chapter contains papers on the evolving interface between fuzzy logic and computational neural networks (CNNs). This field is so new that it is difficult to foresee what current research may or may not be significant in the long term. Although this volume is expressly devoted to the use of fuzzy models in pattern recognition, a large portion of the current research on synergistic connections between fuzzy models and CNNs is in the realm of control applications. Thus, several of the papers reproduced below are more properly classified as *fuzzy logic and CNNs for control systems*. We decided to include them anyway, on the premise that research in this latter area is really unequivocally linked to the use of fuzzy models with CNNs in pattern recognition. This premise is represented in Fig. 21, which purports to show that any control system with more than a trivial degree of complexity, such as the automatic target recognition problem shown on the lower right side of Fig. 21, requires a large, active, and reliable pattern recognition component. Thus, methods for constructing, handling, refining, and using, for example, linguistic control rule bases with CNN methods are important in the context of pattern recognition.

We chose to include one paper each on several topics that are typical of current interest in this area. Specifically, Papers 5.3–5.7 cover fuzzy automata for learning, fuzzy neurons, fuzzy perceptrons, relational modeling and CNNs, and fuzzy self-organizing networks. There are, at this writing, virtually hundreds of papers being submitted and published on the use of CNNs in fuzzy models and, conversely, on methods to fuzzify various CNN architectures for clustering and classifier design. Interested readers can certainly anticipate a future volume devoted entirely to the use of fuzzy models and CNNs for pattern recognition and control. We hope that the selections presented here will serve as a harbinger of future developments in this area.

Papers 5.1 and 5.2 contain no references to fuzzy sets at all. We decided to include these two papers because they provide readers with an excellent overview of the main areas of activity in CNNs with a strong emphasis on their application to problems in pattern recognition. It is our hope that these papers will enable the reader to enter the world of fuzzy CNNs with some confidence about nonfuzzy neuron-like network algorithms. Lippman does a nice job of tying CNNs to well known "conventional" algorithms from heuristic and statistical pattern recognition. Note, for example, his allusion to the relationship between Kohonen clustering networks and the hard *c*-means algorithms. In the short span of time since this paper was written, a fairly complete link has been developed between fuzzy *c*-means (cf. Chapter 2) and Kohonen-like networks. This is further discussed in conjunction with Paper 5.7. The reader can refer to reference [1] for a comprehensive survey of the state of the art (without fuzziness) as of 1988. Carpenter [2] provides a nice survey of CNNs, including some history, that is explicitly tied to pattern recognition. Other good general works are available [3, 4]. The first book to explicitly detail many of the exciting possibilities for the use of CNNs in fuzzy models (and vice versa) was Pao [5]; reference [6] is a more recent account of activity in this direction.

Paper 5.2 is a short, nonfuzzy technical article that has profound implications for users of CNNs in the context of pattern recognition. Specifically, Ruck and coworkers show that every fully connected feed-forward CNN that is driven by the performance goal of minimizing classifier errors on hard, labeled data from *c* classes (that is, trained as a hard classifier with crisply labeled data), is asymptotically equivalent to the well known optimal Bayes posterior probability design. This relationship was unknown when Lippman noted in Paper 5.1 that CNNs of this kind [multilayered perceptrons (MLPs)] were akin to k-nearest neighbor (k-nn) rule designs. The importance of this result is threefold. First, it explains why so many published papers on MLPs report little, if any, difference in error rates between CNN designs and the k-nn rule. Of course, the matter of convergence rate is open at this point, and because all approaches are, in the final analysis, data dependent, this result does not dictate that the much-easier-implemented k-nn rule is equivalent to MLPs. What it does indicate is that, in the limit, MLPs will approximate the Bayes posteriors arbitrarily well, just as the k-nn rule does. Second, this paper shows how CNN architectures often turn out to be different (perhaps better or more useful, perhaps not) implementations of well-known conventional designs. And third, this paper opens the way for extending this kind of relationship to fuzzy MLPs (such as the one in Paper 5.5). It may turn out that there is a clear, or at least identifiable, link between statistical pattern recognition and this more general class of fuzzy CNNs. Results of this kind always strengthen our understanding of algorithms and, hence, subsequently improve their utility in fielded systems.

Paper 5.3 is one of the earliest papers on fuzzy pattern recognition that is also related to the central idea of CNNs (learning). K. S. Fu was, from the very beginning of fuzzy models, one of its strongest advocates. (Indeed, we mention as a footnote that King Sun Fu was the founding president of the North American Fuzzy Information Processing Society.) As was the case in many other fields, Fu's vision was sharper than most; this paper is a precursor of much of the work that has followed. Readers may enjoy reading reference [3],

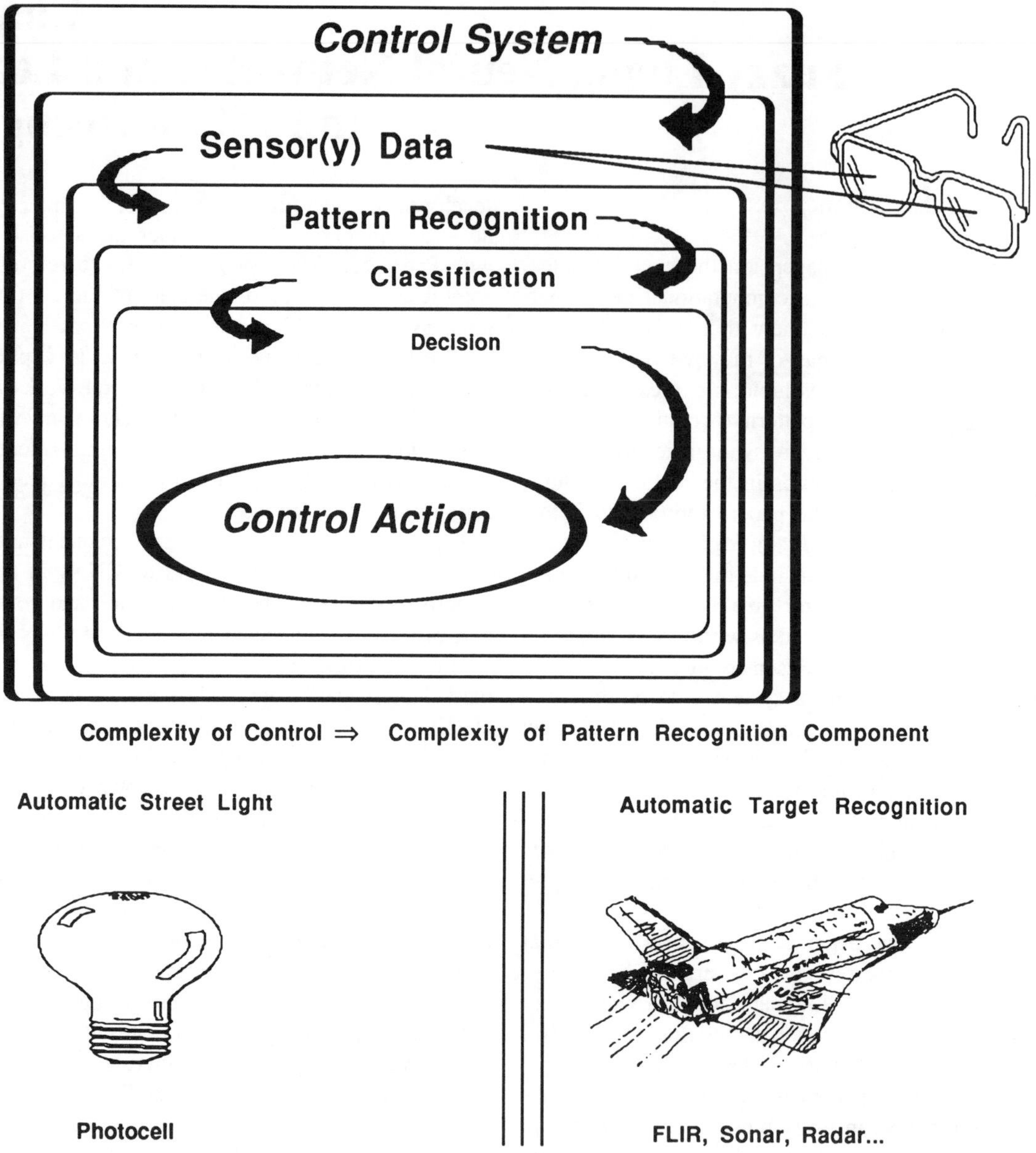

Fig. 21. The need for pattern recognition in control systems.

which was, like Paper 5.3, one of the early attempts to integrate ideas about learning into a computational setting. As an historical aside, we believe that Bill Wee was the first person to write a Ph.D. dissertation on fuzzy pattern recognition [7]—this work was performed under the direction of K. S. Fu.

Paper 5.4 is, to our knowledge, the first discussion of the extension of the classical McCulloch-Pitts neuron model (cf. Paper 5.2) to allow fuzzy activity (i.e., a fuzzy neuron). This paper gives a fairly detailed account of one way to erect a fuzzy neural network and relates well to the fuzzy automata concepts discussed in Paper 5.3. For example, Lee and Lee show that, under suitable circumstances, any n state fuzzy automata can be realized by a network of m fuzzy neurons. Although some of the particular results given in this paper have been subsumed by recent research, it remains, along with Paper 5.3, a true landmark in the evolution of the relationship between fuzzy models, pattern recognition, and computational neural networks. For additional reading on fuzzy neurons, readers may consult references [8–10].

In the decade between 1975 and 1985, activity in nonfuzzy CNNs was still largely latent; the groundswell surfaced shortly thereafter (e.g., formation of the INNS in 1987; the first IJCNN conference in 1989). Thus, Keller and Hunt's 1985 paper (Paper 5.5) on the incorporation of membership functions into the classical perceptron algorithm was clearly ahead of its time. In this article, the authors introduce two important ideas. First, they incorporate membership functions for the fuzzy clusters in the data into the usual perceptron criterion function and prove that this fuzzy generalization of the crisp version also converges if the training data are separable. Second, Keller and Hunt show a method for fuzzifying the labeled target data used for training (i.e., they convert the hard label in N_c of each training data vector to a fuzzy label in N_{fc} (cf. Fig. 14, Chapter 1) before training. This was one of the first papers to suggest incorporation of basic ideas from fuzzy pattern recognition into the domain of classifier design with perceptrons. Many authors have pursued this idea in various ways—for example, given the idea from Paper 5.5, it is an easy conceptual step to use the same idea in a full scale multilayered perceptron; many authors have done so. References [11–13] examine this area.

Paper 5.6 goes in an entirely different direction. Pedrycz introduces fuzzy relations (see Section 1.3.A of Chapter 1) into the CNN framework. The use of relational data, as mentioned in Chapter 1, is a much less developed idea in CNNs than is the use of feature vectors. Moreover, the use of fuzzy relations in this context is even more novel. Although Paper 5.6 is very new, we believe that it contains, like Keller and Hunt's work in Paper 5.5, seminal ideas in places where the synthesis between fuzzy sets, CNNs, and pattern recognition will occur. One of the main ideas in this paper is to connect the notions of fuzzy intersection and union operators with learning in neural networks. This idea has become pervasive in recent literature; the future holds many investigations that are oriented toward control applications that may rely on extensions of work such as that reported in Paper 5.6.

Paper 5.7 addresses the fuzzification of Kohonen's scheme for unsupervised learning (clustering). The important idea advanced in this paper is to replace the learning rate (α) usually found in Kohonen-type update rules for the weight vectors in the competitive layer with fuzzy memberships of the nodes in each class. If, for example, the update rule is written as $\mathbf{v}_{\text{new}, i} = \mathbf{v}_{\text{old}, i} + \alpha(\mathbf{x}_k - \mathbf{v}_{\text{old}, i})$, the authors of Paper 5.7 suggested instead the rule $\mathbf{v}_{\text{new}, i} = \mathbf{v}_{\text{old}, i} + u_{ik}(\mathbf{x}_k - \mathbf{v}_{\text{old}, i})$, where u_{ik} is the fuzzy membership of $\mathbf{x}_k$ in class i. The numerical results reported in Paper 5.7 showed that in many cases, Kohonen networks and fuzzy c-means produced very similar answers. This paper seems to have been the first attempt to link Kohonen clustering to fuzzy c-means; we believe that this connection has been extensively studied as a result of Huntsberger and Ajjimarangsee's work and that this link, first alluded to by Lippman, is very nearly complete. The reader may wish to consult references [14–19] for other work in this direction.

Another class of CNN clustering algorithms are based on Grossberg's Adaptive Resonance Theory (ART). Many papers have been written on ART but very few on fuzzy versions of ART. As of this writing, however, the authors are aware of several attempts to link ART to fuzzy models (and conversely) that will appear shortly. We offer the reader a glimpse of developments along these lines, as well as several other emergent fields, through references [20–27].

The last two papers in our collection approach problems in fuzzy control using CNN approaches. The inclusion of these two papers is simply to make readers aware of the type of work that is currently being done in this area; synthesis of fuzzy logic and CNNs is technologically sound, useful, and inevitable for applications in both control and pattern recognition. We did not develop in Chapter 1 the general ideas that are needed to understand the fine points of this topic. Indeed, so much has happened in the area of fuzzy control in the last five years that a decent presentation of this younger relative of fuzzy pattern recognition would require its own volume. We will circumvent our academic responsibilities in this regard by referring the reader to the excellent survey by C. C. Lee [28], which possesses 150 references on the topical area of fuzzy control. Suffice it to say here that commercial applications of fuzzy control technology developed in Japan have made this an exciting area for both scientific research as well as fielded applications. In particular, in Paper 5.8, Takagi and Hayashi discuss the use of CNNs to represent membership functions based on numerical input data and propose a scheme for partitioning a set of fuzzy control rules based on the use of CNNs. One of the obvious uses of CNNs in pattern recognition is to approximate membership functions based on finite training data sets, so this paper has relevance to the present volume. It is hard for us to make an accurate estimate of the number of variations on this scheme that are currently being investigated. In Paper 5.9, Keller and Tahani explore the representation and computation of aggregation operators (fuzzy unions and intersections) as used in fuzzy logic inferencing schemes. This is a central problem in the design of fuzzy controllers and is also of great utility in vision systems that rely on high-level reasoning methods to guide interpretation of image data using fuzzy models. Again, our motivation for presenting this last paper is to bring to readers the flavor of current efforts in integrating ideas from CNNs for fuzzy models. Approaches like the one presented in 5.9 will find their way into many pattern recognition systems in the next decade. Additional references to material related to the ideas in Papers 5.8 and 5.9 may be found in references [29–36].

References

[1] *DARPA Neural Network Study*, Fairfax, VA: AFCEA Press, 1988.

[2] G. Carpenter, "Neural network models for pattern recognition and associative memory," *Neural Networks*, vol. 2, pp. 243–257, 1989.

[3] N. J. Nilsson, *Learning Machines*, New York: McGraw-Hill, 1965.

[4] T. Kohonen, *Self-Organization and Associative Memory*, 3rd edition, Berlin: Springer-Verlag, 1989.

[5] Y. H. Pao, *Adaptive Pattern Recognition and Neural Networks*, Reading, MA: Addison-Wesley, 1989.

[6] B. Kosko, *Neural Networks and Fuzzy Systems: A Dynamical Approach to Machine Intelligence*, Englewood Cliffs, NJ: Prentice Hall, 1991.

[7] W. Wee, *On generalizations of adaptive algorithms and applications of the fuzzy sets concept to pattern classification*, Ph.D. thesis, Purdue University, W. Lafayette, IN, 1967.

[8] T. Yamakawa and S. Tomoda, "A fuzzy neuron and its application to pattern recognition," *Proc. 3rd IFSA Congress*, J. Bezdek (Ed.), Seattle, 1989, pp. 30-38.

[9] D. Kuncicky and A. Kandel, "A fuzzy interpretation of neural networks," *Proc. 3rd IFSA Congress*, J. Bezdek (Ed.), Seattle, 1989, pp. 113-116.

[10] T. Watanabe (Ed.), "A layered neural model using logic neurons," *Proc. Int. Conf. on Fuzzy Logic and Neural Networks*, T. Yamakawa (Ed.), Iizuka, Japan, 1990, pp. 675-679.

[11] H. Ishibuchi and H. Tanaka, "Identification of real-valued and interval-valued membership functions by neural networks," *Proc. Int. Conf. on Fuzzy Logic and Neural Networks*, T. Yamakawa (Ed.), Iizuka, Japan, 1990, pp. 179-183.

[12] J. Keller and H. Tahani, "Backpropagation neural networks for fuzzy logic," *Inf. Sci.*, 1991 (to appear).

[13] L. O. Hall, "Learning on fuzzy data with a backpropagation scheme," *Proc. NAFIPS 1991*, J. Keller and R. Krishnapuram (Eds.), Columbia (Missouri), 1991, pp. 329-332.

[14] J. Bezdek, "Self-organizing clustering algorithms," *Proc. NAFIPS '90*, I. B. Turksen (Ed.), University of Toronto, vol. VI, 1990, pp. 1-4.

[15] J. Bezdek, "A note on generalized self-organizing clustering algorithms," *Proc. SPIE*, vol. 1293, *Applications of AI (VIII)*, pp. 260-267, 1990.

[16] J. Bezdek, "Self-organization and clustering algorithms," in *Proc. 2nd Joint Tech. Workshop on Neural Networks and Fuzzy Logic*, R. Lea and J. Villereal (Eds.), NASA #CP 10061, vol. 1, pp. 143-158, 1991.

[17] J. Bezdek, E. C. K. Tsao, and N. Pal, "Kohonen clustering networks," *Proc. First IEEE Conf. on Fuzzy Systems*, San Diego, 1992 (in press).

[18] J. Bezdek, "Pattern recognition, neural networks, and artificial intelligence," *Proc. SPIE Applications of AI (9)*, M. Trivedi (Ed.), vol. 1468, 1991, pp. 924-935.

[19] S. Mitra and S. K. Pal, "Self-organizing neural network as a fuzzy classifier," *IEEE Trans. System, Man, Cybern.*, 1991 (in press).

[20] G. Carpenter and S. Grossberg, "A massively parallel architecture for a self-organizing neural pattern recognition machine," *Computer Vision, Graphics and Image Processing*, vol. 37, pp. 54-115, 1987.

[21] S. Mitra and S. C. Newton, "Leader clustering by unsupervised adaptive neural networks using a fuzzy learning rule," *Proc. SPIE Conference on Adaptive Signal Processing*, San Diego, CA, 1991.

[22] P. Simpson, "Fuzzy min-max classification with neural networks," *Heuristics, J. Knowledge Eng.*, vol. 4, no. 1, pp. 1-9, 1991.

[23] P. Simpson, "Fuzzy min-max neural networks I: Classification," *IEEE Trans. Neural Networks*, 1992 (in press).

[24] G. Carpenter, S. Grossberg, and D. Rosen, "Fuzzy ART: Fast stable learning and categorization of analog patterns by an adaptive resonance system," *Neural Networks*, vol. 4, pp. 759-771, 1992.

[25] G. Carpenter, S. Grossberg, and D. Rosen, "Fuzzy ART: An adaptive resonance algorithm for rapid stable classification of analog patterns," *Proc. IJCNN*, 1991, vol. II, pp. 411-420.

[26] L. Hall, A. Bensaid, L. Clarke, R. Velthuizen, M. Silbiger, and J. Bezdek, "A comparison of neural network and fuzzy clustering techniques in segmenting magnetic resonance images of the brain," *IEEE Trans. Neural Networks*, 1992 (in press).

[27] S. Mitra and S. K. Pal, "Multilayer perceptrons, fuzzy sets and classification," *IEEE Trans. Neural Networks*, 1992 (in press).

[28] C. C. Lee, "Fuzzy logic in control systems: Fuzzy logic controller, Parts I and II," *IEEE Trans. Syst., Man, Cybern.*, vol. 20, no. 2, pp. 404-435, 1990.

[29] E. Sanchez, "Fuzzy logic and neural networks in artificial intelligence and pattern recognition," *Proc. Int. Conf. Sto. and Neural Models*, SPIE, 1991.

[30] C. C. Lee, "Intelligent control based on fuzzy logic and neural net theory," *Proc. Int. Conf. on Fuzzy Logic and Neural Networks*, T. Yamakawa (Ed.), Iizuka, Japan, 1990, pp. 759-764.

[31] C. C. Lee, "A self-learning rule-based controller employing approximate reasoning and neural net concepts," *Int. J. Intelligent Systems*, vol. 6, pp. 71-93, 1991.

[32] E. Sanchez, "Fuzzy connectionist expert systems," *Proc. Int. Conf. on Fuzzy Logic and Neural Networks*, T. Yamakawa (Ed.), Iizuka, Japan, 1990, pp. 31-35.

[33] P. Werbos, "Neurocontrol and fuzzy logic—Connections and designs," *Int. J. Appr. Reas.*, 1991 (to appear).

[34] J. Yen, "Using fuzzy logic to integrate neural networks and knowledge-based systems, *Proc. 2nd NASA Workshop on Neural Networks and Fuzzy Logic*, J. Villereal and R. Lea (Eds.), NASA #CP 10061, vol. 1, pp. 217-233, 1991.

[35] J. Yen, "The role of fuzzy logic in the control of neural networks," *Proc. Int. Conf. on Fuzzy Logic and Neural Networks*, T. Yamakawa (Ed.), Iizuka, Japan, 1990, pp. 771-774.

An Introduction to Computing with Neural Nets

Richard P. Lippmann

Abstract

Artificial neural net models have been studied for many years in the hope of achieving human-like performance in the fields of speech and image recognition. These models are composed of many nonlinear computational elements operating in parallel and arranged in patterns reminiscent of biological neural nets. Computational elements or nodes are connected via weights that are typically adapted during use to improve performance. There has been a recent resurgence in the field of artificial neural nets caused by new net topologies and algorithms, analog VLSI implementation techniques, and the belief that massive parallelism is essential for high performance speech and image recognition. This paper provides an introduction to the field of artificial neural nets by reviewing six important neural net models that can be used for pattern classification. These nets are highly parallel building blocks that illustrate neural- net components and design principles and can be used to construct more complex systems. In addition to describing these nets, a major emphasis is placed on exploring how some existing classification and clustering algorithms can be performed using simple neuron-like components. Single-layer nets can implement algorithms required by Gaussian maximum-likelihood classifiers and optimum minimum-error classifiers for binary patterns corrupted by noise. More generally, the decision regions required by any classification algorithm can be generated in a straightforward manner by three-layer feed-forward nets.

INTRODUCTION

Artificial neural net models or simply "neural nets" go by many names such as connectionist models, parallel distributed processing models, and neuromorphic systems. Whatever the name, all these models attempt to achieve good performance via dense interconnection of simple computational elements. In this respect, artificial neural net structure is based on our present understanding of biological nervous systems. Neural net models have greatest potential in areas such as speech and image recognition where many hypotheses are pursued in parallel, high computation rates are required, and the current best systems are far from equaling human performance. Instead of performing a program of instructions sequentially as in a von Neumann computer, neural net models explore many competing hypotheses simultaneously using massively parallel nets composed of many computational elements connected by links with variable weights.

Computational elements or nodes used in neural net models are nonlinear, are typically analog, and may be slow compared to modern digital circuitry. The simplest node sums N weighted inputs and passes the result through a nonlinearity as shown in Fig. 1. The node is characterized by an internal threshold or offset θ and by the type of nonlinearity. Figure 1 illustrates three common types of nonlinearities; hard limiters, threshold logic elements, and sigmoidal nonlinearities. More complex nodes may include temporal integration or other types of time dependencies and more complex mathematical operations than summation.

Neural net models are specified by the net topology, node characteristics, and training or learning rules. These rules specify an initial set of weights and indicate how weights should be adapted during use to improve performance. Both design procedures and training rules are the topic of much current research.

The potential benefits of neural nets extend beyond the high computation rates provided by massive parallelism. Neural nets typically provide a greater degree of robustness or fault tolerance than von Neumann sequential computers because there are many more processing nodes, each with primarily local connections. Damage to a few nodes or links thus need not impair overall performance significantly. Most neural net algorithms also adapt connection weights in time to improve performance based on current results. Adaptation or learning is a major focus of neural net research. The ability to adapt and continue learning is essential in areas such as speech recognition where training data is limited and new talkers, new words, new dialects, new phrases, and new environments are continuously encountered. Adaptation also provides a degree of robustness by compensating for minor variabilities in characteristics of processing elements. Traditional statistical techniques are not adaptive but typically process all training data simultaneously before being used with new data. Neural net classifiers are also non-parametric and make weaker assumptions concerning the shapes of underlying distributions than traditional statistical classifiers. They may thus prove to be more robust when distributions are generated by nonlinear processes and are strongly non-Gaussian. Designing artificial neural nets to solve

Reprinted from *IEEE ASSP Mag.*, pp. 4–22, April 1987.

problems and studying real biological nets may also change the way we think about problems and lead to new insights and algorithmic improvements.

Work on artificial neural net models has a long history. Development of detailed mathematical models began more than 40 years ago with the work of McCulloch and Pitts [30], Hebb [17], Rosenblatt [39], Widrow [47] and others [38]. More recent work by Hopfield [18, 19, 20], Rumelhart and McClelland [40], Sejnowski [43], Feldman [9], Grossberg [15], and others has led to a new resurgence of the field. This new interest is due to the development of new net topologies and algorithms [18, 19, 20, 41, 9], new analog VLSI implementation techniques [31], and some intriguing demonstrations [43, 20] as well as by a growing fascination with the functioning of the human brain. Recent interest is also driven by the realization that human-like performance in the areas of speech and image recognition will require enormous amounts of processing. Neural nets provide one technique for obtaining the required processing capacity using large numbers of simple processing elements operating in parallel.

This paper provides an introduction to the field of neural nets by reviewing six important neural net models that can be used for pattern classification. These massively parallel nets are important building blocks which can be used to construct more complex systems. The main purpose of this review is to describe the purpose and design of each net in detail, to relate each net to existing pattern classification and clustering algorithms that are normally implemented on sequential von Neumann computers, and to illustrate design principles used to obtain parallelism using neural-like processing elements.

Neural net and traditional classifiers

Block diagrams of traditional and neural net classifiers are presented in Fig. 2. Both types of classifiers determine which of M classes is most representative of an unknown static input pattern containing N input elements. In a speech recognizer the inputs might be the output envelope values from a filter bank spectral analyzer sampled at one time instant and the classes might represent different vowels. In an image classifier the inputs might be the gray scale level of each pixel for a picture and the classes might represent different objects.

The traditional classifier in the top of Fig. 2 contains two stages. The first computes matching scores for each class and the second selects the class with the maximum score. Inputs to the first stage are symbols representing values of the N input elements. These symbols are entered sequentially and decoded from the external symbolic form into an internal representation useful for performing arithmetic and symbolic operations. An algorithm computes a matching score for each of the M classes which indicates how closely the input matches the exemplar pattern for each class. This exemplar pattern is that pattern which is most representative of each class. In many situations a probabilistic model is used to model the generation of input patterns from exemplars and the matching score represents the likelihood or probability that the input pattern was generated from each of the M possible exemplars. In those cases, strong assumptions are typically made concerning underlying distributions of the input elements. Parameters of distributions can then be estimated using a training data as shown in Fig. 2. Multivariate Gaussian distributions are often used leading to relatively simple algorithms for computing matching scores [7]. Matching scores are coded into symbolic representations and passed sequentially to the second stage of

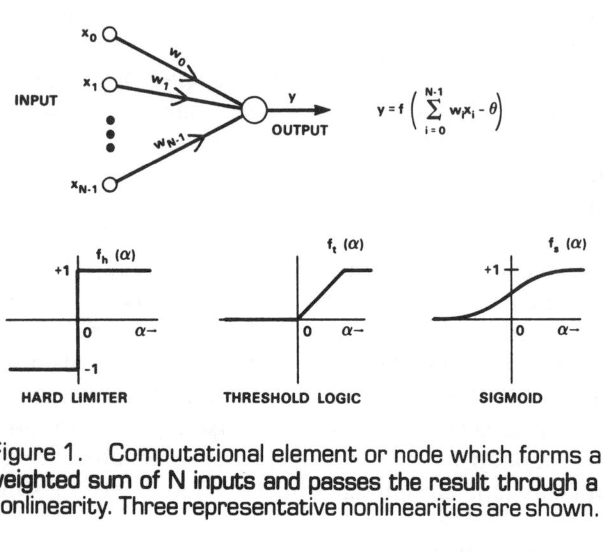

Figure 1. Computational element or node which forms a weighted sum of N inputs and passes the result through a nonlinearity. Three representative nonlinearities are shown.

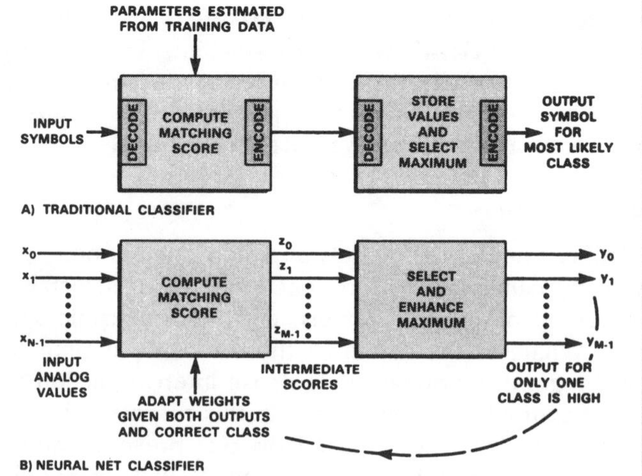

Figure 2. Block diagrams of traditional (A) and neural net (B) classifiers. Inputs and outputs of the traditional classifier are passed serially and internal computations are performed sequentially. In addition, parameters are typically estimated from training data and then held constant. Inputs and outputs to the neural net classifier are in parallel and internal computations are performed in parallel. Internal parameters or weights are typically adapted or trained during use using the output values and labels specifying the correct class.

the classifier. Here they are decoded and the class with the maximum score is selected. A symbol representing that class is then sent out to complete the classification task.

An adaptive neural net classifier is shown at the bottom of Fig. 2. Here input values are fed in parallel to the first stage via N input connections. Each connection carries an analog value which may take on two levels for binary inputs or may vary over a large range for continuous valued inputs. The first stage computes matching scores and outputs these scores in parallel to the next stage over M analog output lines. Here the maximum of these values is selected and enhanced. The second stage has one output for each of the M classes. After classification is complete, only that output corresponding to the most likely class will be on strongly or "high"; other outputs will be "low". Note that in this design, outputs exist for every class and that this multiplicity of outputs must be preserved in further processing stages as long as the classes are considered distinct. In the simplest classification system these output lines might go directly to lights with labels that specify class identities. In more complicated cases they may go to further stages of processing where inputs from other modalities or temporal dependencies are taken into consideration. If the correct class is provided, then this information and the classifier outputs can be fed back to the first stage of the classifier to adapt weights using a learning algorithm as shown in Fig. 2. Adaptation will make a correct response more likely for succeeding input patterns that are similar to the current pattern.

The parallel inputs required by neural net classifiers suggest that real-time hardware implementations should include special purpose pre-processors. One strategy for designing such processors is to build physiologically-based pre-processors modeled after human sensory systems. A pre-processor for image classification modeled after the retina and designed using analog VLSI circuitry is described in [31]. Pre-processor filter banks for speech recognition that are crude analogs of the cochlea have also been constructed [34, 29]. More recent physiologically-based pre-processor algorithms for speech recognition attempt to provide information similar to that available on the auditory nerve [11, 44, 27, 5]. Many of these algorithms include filter bank spectral analysis, automatic gain control, and processing which uses timing or synchrony information in addition to information from smoothed filter output envelopes.

Classifiers in Fig. 2 can perform three different tasks. First, as described above, they can identify which class best represents an input pattern, where it is assumed that inputs have been corrupted by noise or some other process. This is a classical decision theory problem. Second, the classifiers can be used as a content-addressable or associative memory, where the class exemplar is desired and the input pattern is used to determine which exemplar to produce. A content-addressable memory is useful when only part of an input pattern is available and the complete pattern is required, as in bibliographic retrieval of journal references from partial information. This normally requires the addition of a third stage in Fig. 2 to regenerate the exemplar for the most likely class. An additional stage is unnecessary for some neural nets such as the Hopfield net which are designed specifically as content-addressable memories. A third task these classifiers can perform is to vector quantize [28] or cluster [16, 7] the N inputs into M clusters. Vector quantizers are used in image and speech transmission systems to reduce the number of bits necessary to transmit analog data. In speech and image recognition applications they are used to compress the amount of data that must be processed without losing important information. In either application the number of clusters can be pre-specified or may be allowed to grow up to a limit determined by the number ber of nodes available in the first stage.

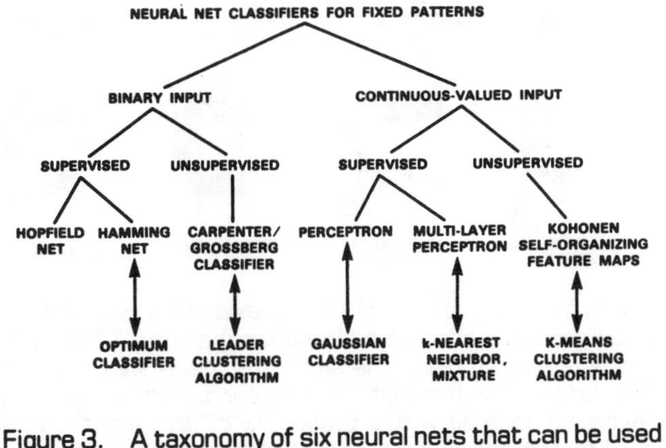

Figure 3. A taxonomy of six neural nets that can be used as classifiers. Classical algorithms which are most similar to the neural net models are listed along the bottom.

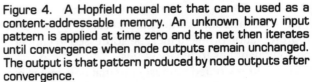

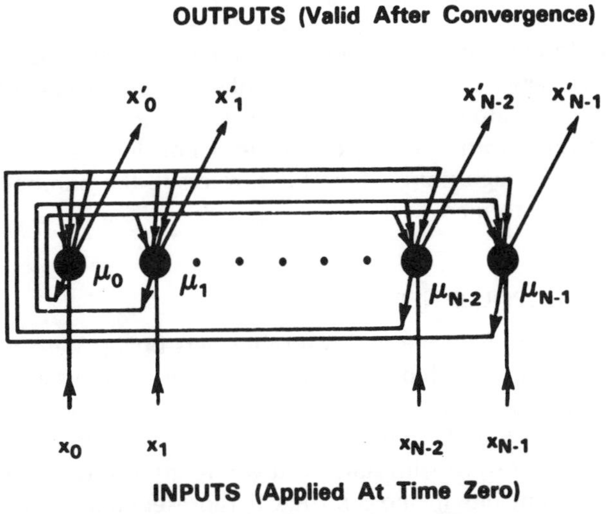

Figure 4. A Hopfield neural net that can be used as a content-addressable memory. An unknown binary input pattern is applied at time zero and the net then iterates until convergence when node outputs remain unchanged. The output is that pattern produced by node outputs after convergence.

A TAXONOMY OF NEURAL NETS

A taxonomy of six important neural nets that can be used for classification of static patterns is presented in Fig. 3. This taxonomy is first divided between nets with binary and continuous valued inputs. Below this, nets are divided between those trained with and without supervision. Nets trained with supervision such as the Hopfield net [18] and perceptrons [39] are used as associative memories or as classifiers. These nets are provided with side information or labels that specify the correct class for new input patterns during training. Most traditional statistical classifiers, such as Gaussian classifiers [7], are trained with supervision using labeled training data. Nets trained without supervision, such as the Kohonen's feature-map forming nets [22], are used as vector quantizers or to form clusters. No information concerning the correct class is provided to these nets during training. The classical K-means [7] and leader [16] clustering algorithms are trained without supervision. A further difference between nets, not indicated in Fig. 3, is whether adaptive training is supported. Although all the nets shown can be trained adaptively, the Hopfield net and the Hamming net are generally used with fixed weights.

The algorithms listed at the bottom of Fig. 3 are those classical algorithms which are most similar to or perform the same function as the corresponding neural net. In some cases a net implements a classical algorithm exactly. For example, the Hamming net [25] is a neural net implementation of the optimum classifier for binary patterns corrupted by random noise [10]. It can also be shown that the perceptron structure performs those calculations required by a Gaussian classifier [7] when weights and thresholds are selected appropriately. In other cases the neural net algorithms are different from the classical algorithms. For example, perceptrons trained with the perceptron convergence procedure [39] behave differently than Gaussian classifiers. Also, Kohonen's net [22] does not perform the iterative K-means training algorithm. Instead, each new pattern is presented only once and weights are modified after each presentation. The Kohonen net does, however, form a pre-specified number of clusters as in the K-means algorithm, where the K refers to the number of clusters formed.

THE HOPFIELD NET

The Hopfield net and two other nets in Fig. 3 are normally used with binary inputs. These nets are most appropriate when exact binary representations are possible as with black and white images where input elements are pixel values, or with ASCII text where input values could represent bits in the 8-bit ASCII representation of each character. These nets are less appropriate when input values are actually continuous, because a fundamental representation problem must be addressed to convert the analog quantities to binary values.

Hopfield rekindled interest in neural nets by his extensive work on different versions of the Hopfield net [18,19,20]. This net can be used as an associative memory or to solve optimization problems. One version of the original net [18] which can be used as a content addressable memory is described in this paper. This net, shown in Fig. 4, has N nodes containing hard limiting nonlinearities and binary inputs and outputs taking on the values +1 and −1. The output of each node is fed back to all other nodes via weights denoted t_{ij}. The operation of this net is described in Box 1. First, weights are set using the given recipe from exemplar patterns for all classes. Then an unknown pattern is imposed on the net at time zero by forcing the output of the net to match the unknown pattern. Following this initialization, the net iterates in discrete time steps using the given formula. The net is considered to have converged when outputs no longer change on successive iterations. The pattern specified by the node outputs after convergence is the net output.

Hopfield [18] and others [4] have proven that this net converges when the weights are symmetric ($t_{ij} = t_{ji}$) and

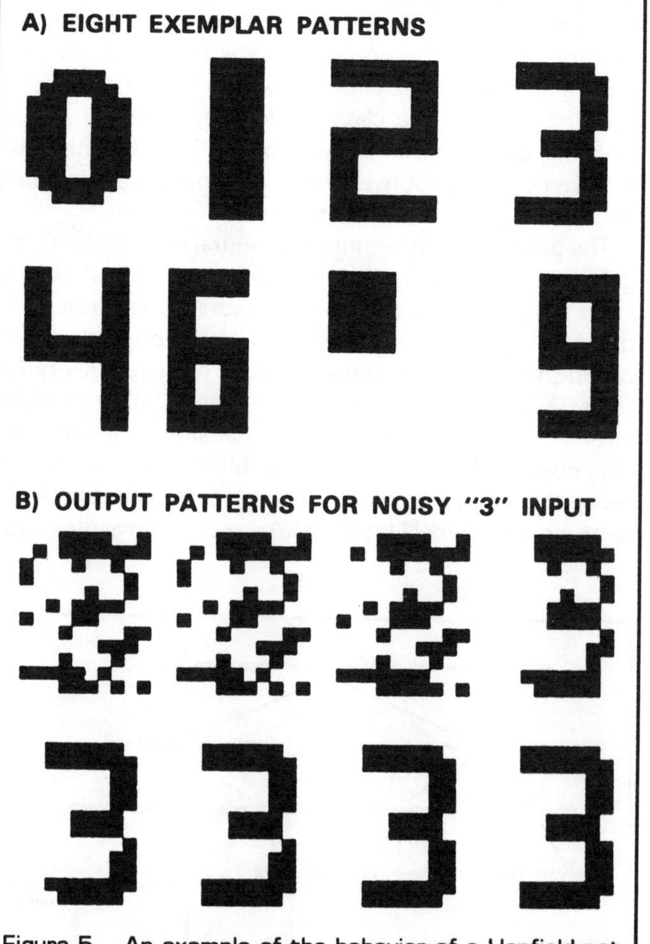

Figure 5. An example of the behavior of a Hopfield net when used as a content-addressable memory. A 120 node net was trained using the eight exemplars shown in (A). The pattern for the digit "3" was corrupted by randomly reversing each bit with a probability of .25, and then applied to the net at time zero. Outputs at time zero and after the first seven iterations are shown in (B).

node outputs are updated asynchronously using the equations in Box 1. Hopfield [19] also demonstrated that the net converges when graded nonlinearities similar to the sigmoid nonlinearity in Fig. 1 are used. When the Hopfield net is used as an associative memory, the net output after convergence is used directly as the complete restored memory. When the Hopfield net is used as a classifier, the output after convergence must be compared to the M exemplars to determine if it matches an exemplar exactly. If it does, the output is that class whose exemplar matched the output pattern. If it does not then a "no match" result occurs.

Box 1. Hopfield Net Algorithm

Step 1. Assign Connection Weights

$$t_{ij} = \begin{cases} \sum_{s=0}^{M-1} x_i^s x_j^s, & i \neq j \\ 0, \; i = j, \; 0 \leq i, \; j \leq M\text{-}1 \end{cases}$$

In this Formula t_{ij} is the connection weight from node i to node j and x_i^s which can be +1 or −1 is element i of the exemplar for class s.

Step 2. Initialize with Unknown Input Pattern

$$\mu_i(0) = x_i, \qquad 0 \leq i \leq N-1$$

In this Formula $\mu_i(t)$ is the output of node i at time t and x_i which can be +1 or −1 is element i of the input pattern.

Step 3. Iterate Until Convergence

$$\mu_j(t+1) = f_h\left[\sum_{i=0}^{N-1} t_{ij}\mu_i(t)\right], \quad 0 \leq j \leq M\text{-}1$$

The function f_h is the hard limiting nonlinearity from Fig. 1. The process is repeated until node outputs remain unchanged with further iterations. The node outputs then represent the exemplar pattern that best matches the unknown input.

Step 4. Repeat by Going to Step 2

The behavior of the Hopfield net is illustrated in Fig. 5. A Hopfield net with 120 nodes and thus 14,400 weights was trained to recall the eight exemplar patterns shown at the top of Fig. 5. These digit-like black and white patterns contain 120 pixels each and were hand crafted to provide good performance. Input elements to the net take on the value +1 for black pixels and −1 for white pixels. In the example presented, the pattern for the digit "3" was corrupted by randomly reversing each bit independently from +1 to −1 and vice versa with a probability of 0.25. This pattern was then applied to the net at time zero. Patterns produced at the output of the net on iterations zero to seven are presented at the bottom of Fig. 5. The corrupted input pattern is present unaltered at iteration zero. As the net iterates the output becomes more and more like the correct exemplar pattern until at iteration six the net has converged to the pattern for the digit three.

The Hopfield net has two major limitations when used as a content addressable memory. First, the number of patterns that can be stored and accurately recalled is severely limited. If too many patterns are stored, the net may converge to a novel spurious pattern different from all exemplar patterns. Such a spurious pattern will produce a "no match" output when the net is used as a classifier. Hopfield [18] showed that this occurs infrequently when exemplar patterns are generated randomly and the number of classes (M) is less than .15 times the number of input elements or nodes in the net (N). The number of classes is thus typically kept well below $.15N$. For example, a Hopfield net for only 10 classes might require more than 70 nodes and more than roughly 5,000 connection weights. A second limitation of the Hopfield net is that an exemplar pattern will be unstable if it shares many bits in common with another exemplar pattern. Here an exemplar is considered unstable if it is applied at time zero and the net converges to some other exemplar. This problem can be eliminated and performance can be improved by a number of orthogonalization procedures [14, 46].

THE HAMMING NET

The Hopfield net is often tested on problems where inputs are generated by selecting an exemplar and reversing bit values randomly and independently with a given probability [18, 12, 46]. This is a classic problem in communications theory that occurs when binary fixed-length signals are sent through a memoryless binary symmetric channel. The optimum minimum error classifier in this case calculates the Hamming distance to the exemplar for each class and selects that class with the minimum Hamming distance [10]. The Hamming distance is the number of bits in the input which do not match the corresponding exemplar bits. A net which will be called a Hamming net implements this algorithm using neural net components and is shown in Fig. 6.

The operation of the Hamming net is described in Box 2. Weights and thresholds are first set in the lower subnet such that the matching scores generated by the outputs of the middle nodes of Fig. 6 are equal to N minus the Hamming distances to the exemplar patterns. These matching scores will range from 0 to the number of elements in the input (N) and are highest for those nodes corresponding to classes with exemplars that best match the input. Thresholds and weights in the MAXNET subnet are fixed. All thresholds are set to zero and weights from each node to itself are 1. Weights between nodes are inhibitory with a value of $-\epsilon$ where $\epsilon < 1/M$.

After weights and thresholds have been set, a binary pattern with N elements is presented at the bottom of the Hamming net. It must be presented long enough to allow the matching score outputs of the lower subnet to settle and initialize the output values of the MAXNET. The input is then removed and the MAXNET iterates until the output of only one node is positive. Classification is then complete and the selected class is that corresponding to the node with a positive output.

The behavior of the Hamming net is illustrated in Fig. 7.

Box 2. Hamming Net Algorithm

Step 1. Assign Connection Weights and Offsets

In the lower subnet:

$$w_{ij} = \frac{x_i^j}{2}, \qquad \theta_j = \frac{N}{2},$$
$$0 \le i \le N-1, \qquad 0 \le j \le M-1$$

In the upper subnet:

$$t_{kl} = \begin{cases} 1, & k = l \\ -\varepsilon, & k \ne l, \quad \varepsilon < \dfrac{1}{M}, \end{cases}$$
$$0 \le k,l \le M-1$$

In these equations w_{ij} is the connection weight from input i to node j in the lower subnet and θ is the threshold in that node. The connection weight from node k to node l in the upper subnet is t_{kl} and all thresholds in this subnet are zero. x_i^j is element i of exemplar j as in Box 1.

Step 2. Initialize with Unknown Input Pattern

$$\mu_j(0) = f_t\left(\sum_{i=0}^{N-1} w_{ij}x_i - \theta_j\right)$$
$$0 \le j \le M-1$$

In this equation $\mu_j(t)$ is the output of node j in the upper subnet at time t, x_i is element i of the input as in Box 1, and f_t is the threshold logic nonlinearity from Fig. 1. Here and below it is assumed that the maximum input to this nonlinearity never causes the output to saturate.

Step 3. Iterate Until Convergence

$$\mu_j(t+1) = f_t\left(\mu_j(t) - \varepsilon\sum_{k \ne j} \mu_k(t)\right)$$
$$0 \le j,k \le M-1$$

This process is repeated until convergence after which the output of only one node remains positive.

Step 4. Repeat by Going to Step 2

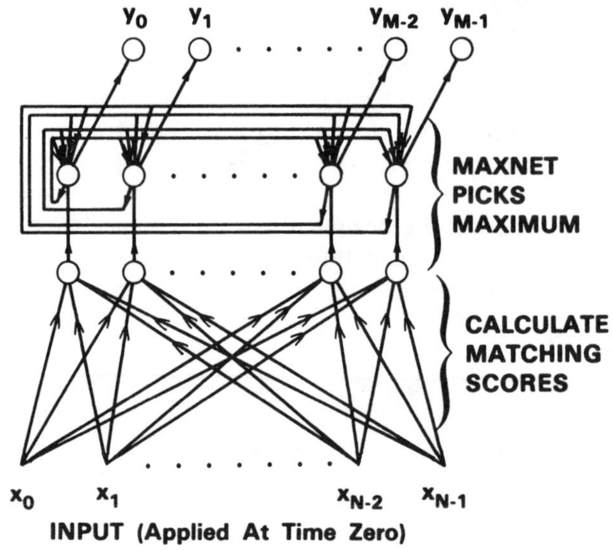

Figure 6. A feed-forward Hamming net maximum likelihood classifier for binary inputs corrupted by noise. The lower subnet calculates N minus the Hamming distance to M exemplar patterns. The upper net selects that node with the maximum output. All nodes use threshold-logic nonlinearities where it is assumed that the outputs of these nonlinearities never saturate.

The four plots in this figure show the outputs of nodes in a MAXNET with 100 nodes on iterations 0, 3, 6, and 9. These simulations were obtained using randomly selected exemplar patterns with 1000 elements each. The exemplar for class 50 was presented at time zero and then removed. The matching score at time zero is maximum (1000) for node 50 and has a random value near 500 for other nodes. After only 3 iterations, the outputs of all nodes except node 50 have been greatly reduced and after 9 iterations only the output for node 50 is non-zero. Simulations with different probabilities of reversing bits on input patterns and with different numbers of classes and elements in the input patterns have demonstrated that the MAXNET typically converges in less than 10 iterations in this application [25]. In addition, it can be proven that the MAXNET will always converge and find the node with the maximum value when $\varepsilon < 1/M$ [25].

The Hamming net has a number of obvious advantages over the Hopfield net. It implements the optimum minimum error classifier when bit errors are random and independent, and thus the performance of the Hopfield net must either be worse than or equivalent to that of the Hamming net in such situations. Comparisons between the two nets on problems such as character recognition, recognition of random patterns, and bibliographic retrieval have demonstrated this difference in performance [25]. The Hamming net also requires many fewer connections than the Hopfield net. For example, with 100 inputs and 10 classes the Hamming net requires

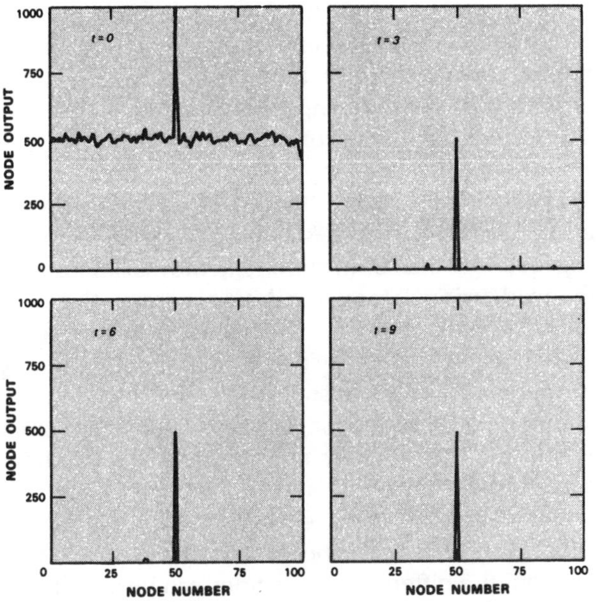

Figure 7. Node outputs for a Hamming net with 1,000 binary inputs and 100 output nodes or classes. Output values of all 100 nodes are presented at time zero and after 3, 6, and 9 iterations. The input was the exemplar pattern corresponding to output node 50.

only 1,100 connections while the Hopfield net requires almost 10,000. Furthermore, the difference in number of connections required increases as the number of inputs increases, because the number of connections in the Hopfield net grows as the square of the number of inputs while the number of connections in the Hamming net grows linearly. The Hamming net can also be modified to be a minimum error classifier when errors are generated by reversing input elements from +1 to −1 and from −1 to +1 asymmetrically with different probabilities [25] and when the values of specific input elements are unknown [2]. Finally, the Hamming net does not suffer from spurious output patterns which can produce a "no-match" result.

SELECTING OR ENHANCING THE MAXIMUM INPUT

The need to select or enhance the input with a maximum value occurs frequently in classification problems. Several different neural nets can perform this operation. The MAXNET described above uses heavy lateral inhibition similar to that used in other net designs where a maximum was desired [20, 22, 9]. These designs create a "winner-take-all" type of net whose design mimics the heavy use of lateral inhibition evident in the biological neural nets of the human brain [21]. Other techniques to pick a maximum are also possible [25]. One is illustrated in Fig. 8. This figure shows a comparator subnet which is described in [29]. It uses threshold logic nodes to pick the maximum of two inputs and then feeds this maximum value forward. This net is useful when the maximum value must be passed unaltered to the output. Comparator subnets can be layered into roughly $\log_2(M)$ layers to pick the maximum of M inputs. A net that uses these subnets to pick the maximum of 8 inputs is presented in Fig. 9.

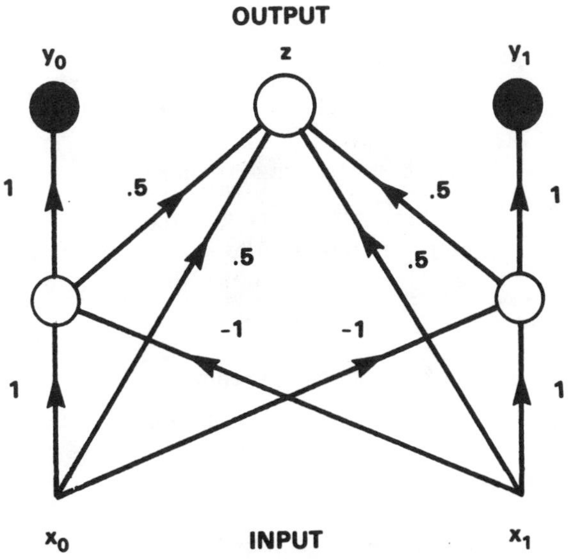

Figure 8. A comparator subnet that selects the maximum of two analog inputs. The output labeled z is the maximum value and the outputs labeled y_0 and y_1 indicate which input was maximum. Internal thresholds on threshold logic nodes (open circles) and hard limiting nodes (filled circles) are zero. Weights are as shown.

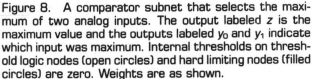

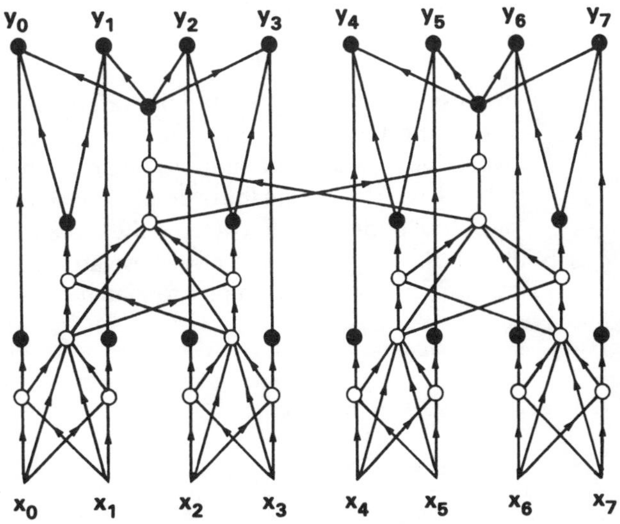

Figure 9. A feed-forward net that determines which of eight inputs is maximum using a binary tree and comparator subnets from Fig. 8. After an input vector is applied, only that output corresponding to the maximum input element will be high. Internal thresholds on threshold-logic nodes (open circles) and on hard limiting nodes (filled circles) are zero except for the output nodes. Thresholds in the output nodes are 2.5. Weights for the comparator subnets are as in Fig. 8 and all other weights are 1.

In some situations a maximum is not required and matching scores must instead be compared to a threshold. This can be done using an array of hard-limiting nodes with internal thresholds set to the desired threshold values. Outputs of these nodes will be −1 unless the inputs exceed the threshold values. Alternatively, thresholds could be set adaptively using a common inhibitory input fed to all nodes. This threshold could be ramped up or down until the output of only one node was positive.

THE CARPENTER/GROSSBERG CLASSIFIER

Carpenter and Grossberg [3], in the development of their Adaptive Resonance Theory have designed a net which forms clusters and is trained without supervision. This net implements a clustering algorithm that is very similar to the simple sequential leader clustering algorithm described in [16]. The leader algorithm selects the first input as the exemplar for the first cluster. The next input is compared to the first cluster exemplar. It "follows the leader" and is clustered with the first if the distance to the first is less than a threshold. Otherwise it is the exemplar for a new cluster. This process is repeated for all following inputs. The number of clusters thus grows with time and depends on both the threshold and the distance metric used to compare inputs to cluster exemplars.

The major components of a Carpenter/Grossberg classification net with three inputs and two output nodes is presented in Fig. 10. The structure of this net is similar to that of the Hamming net. Matching scores are computed using feed-forward connections and the maximum value is enhanced using lateral inhibition among the output nodes. This net differs from the Hamming net in that feedback connections are provided from the output nodes to the input nodes. Mechanisms are also provided to turn off that output node with a maximum value, and to compare exemplars to the input for the threshold test required by the leader algorithm. This net is completely described using nonlinear differential equations, includes extensive feedback, and has been shown to be stable [3]. In typical operation, the differential equations can be shown to implement the clustering algorithm presented in Box 3.

Box 3. Carpenter/Grossberg Net Algorithm

Step 1. Initialization

$$t_{ij}(0) = 1$$

$$b_{ij}(0) = \frac{1}{1 + N}$$

$$0 \le i \le N - 1,$$

$$0 \le j \le M - 1$$

$$\text{Set } \rho, \quad 0 \le \rho \le 1$$

In these equations $b_{ij}(t)$ is the bottom up and $t_{ij}(t)$ is the top down connection weight between input node i and output node j at time t. These weights define the exemplar specified by output node j. The fraction ρ is the vigilance threshold which indicates how close an input must be to a stored exemplar to match.

Step 2. Apply New Input

Step 3. Compute Matching Scores

$$\mu_j = \sum_{i=0}^{N-1} b_{ij}(t)x_i \qquad 0 \le j \le M - 1$$

In this equation μ_j is the output of output node j and x_i is element i of the input which can be 0 or 1.

Step 4. Select Best Matching Exemplar

$$\mu_j^* = \max_j \{\mu_j\}$$

This is performed using extensive lateral inhibition as in the maxnet.

Step 5. Vigilance Test

$$\|X\| = \sum_{i=0}^{N-1} x_i$$

$$\|T \cdot X\| = \sum_{i=0}^{N-1} t_{ij^*}x_i$$

$$\text{is } \frac{\|T \cdot X\|}{\|X\|} > \rho \text{ ?}$$

NO: GO TO STEP 6

YES: GO TO STEP 7

Step 6. Disable Best Matching Exemplar

The output of the best matching node selected in Step 4 is temporarily set to zero and no longer takes part in the maximization of Step 4. Then go to Step 3.

Step 7. Adapt Best Matching Exemplar

$$t_{ij^*}(t + 1) = t_{ij^*}(t)x_i$$

$$b_{ij^*}(t + 1) = \frac{t_{ij^*}(t)x_i}{.5 + \sum_{i=0}^{N-1} t_{ij^*}(t)x_i}$$

Step 8. Repeat by Going to Step 2

(First enable any nodes disabled in Step 6)

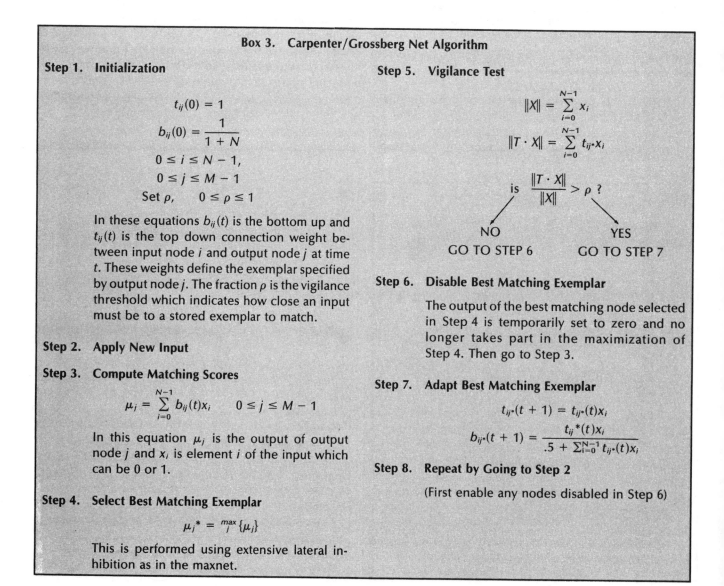

The algorithm presented in Box 3 assumes that "fast learning" is used as in the simulations presented in [3] and thus that elements of both inputs and stored exemplars take on only the values 0 and 1. The net is initialized by effectively setting all exemplars represented by connection weights to zero. In addition, a matching threshold called *vigilance* which ranges between 0.0 and 1.0 must be set. This threshold determines how close a new input pattern must be to a stored exemplar to be considered similar. A value near one requires a close match and smaller values accept a poorer match. New inputs are presented sequentially at the bottom of the net as in the Hamming net. After presentation, the input is compared to all stored exemplars in parallel as in the Hamming net to produce matching scores. The exemplar with the highest matching score is selected using lateral inhibition. It is then compared to the input by computing the ratio of the dot product of the input and the best matching exemplar (number of 1 bits in common) divided by the number of 1 bits in the input. If this ratio is greater than the vigilance threshold, then the input is considered to be similar to the best matching exemplar and that exemplar is updated by performing a logical AND operation between its bits and those in the input. If the ratio is less than the vigilance threshold, then the input is considered to be different from all exemplars and it is added as a new exemplar. Each additional new exemplar requires one node and 2N connections to compute matching scores.

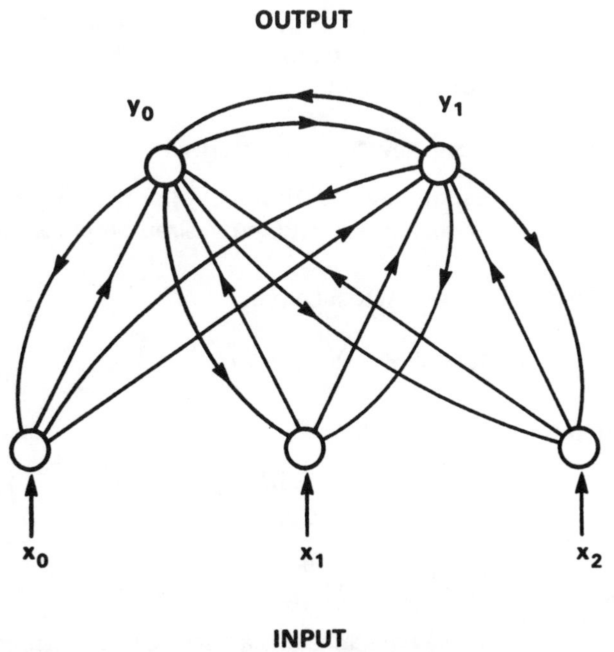

Figure 10. The major components of the Carpenter Grossberg Classification net. A binary input is presented at the bottom and when classification is complete only one output is high. Not shown are additional components required to perform the vigilance test and to disable the output node with the largest output.

The behavior of the Carpenter/Grossberg net is illustrated in Fig. 11. Here it is assumed that patterns to be recognized are the three patterns of the letters "*C*", "*E*", and "*F*" shown in the left side of this figure. These patterns have 64 pixels each that take on the value 1 when black and 0 when white. Results are presented when the vigilance threshold was set to 0.9. This forces separate exemplar patterns to be created for each letter.

The left side of Fig. 11 shows the input to the net on successive trials. The right side presents exemplar patterns formed after each pattern had been applied. In this example "C" was presented first followed by "E" followed by "F", etc. After the net is initialized and a "C" is applied, internal connection weights are altered to form an internal exemplar that is identical to the "C". After an "E" is then applied, a new "E" exemplar is added. Behavior is similar for a new "F" leading to three stored exemplars. If the vigilance threshold had been slightly lower, only two exemplars would have been present after the "F"; one for "F" and one for both "C" and "E" that would have been identical to "C" pattern. Now, when a noisy "F" is applied

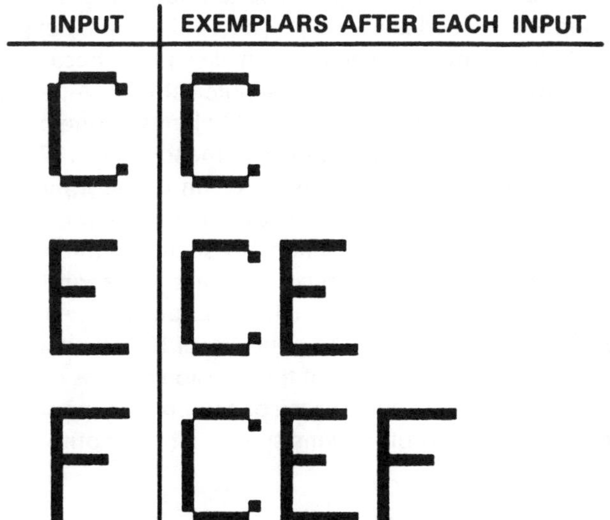

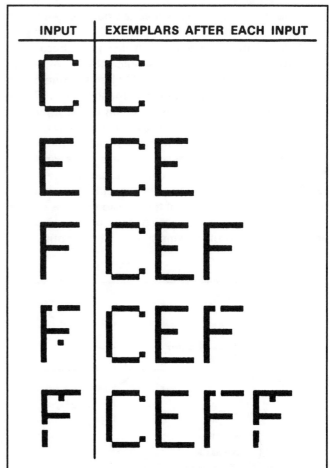

Figure 11. An example of the behavior of the Carpenter Grossberg net for letter patterns. Binary input patterns on the left were applied sequentially starting with the upper "C" pattern. Exemplars formed by top-down connection weights after each input was presented are shown at the right.

with a missing black pixel in the upper edge it is accepted as being similar to the "F" exemplar and degrades this exemplar due to the AND operation performed during updating. When another noisy "F" is applied again with only one black pixel missing, it is considered different from existing exemplars and a new noisy "F" exemplar is added. This will occur for further noisy "F" inputs leading to a growth of noisy "F" exemplars.

These results illustrate that the Carpenter/Grossberg algorithm can perform well with perfect input patterns but that even a small amount of noise can cause problems. With no noise, the vigilance threshold can be set such that the two patterns which are most similar are considered different. In noise, however, this level may be too high and the number of stored exemplars can rapidly grow until all available nodes are used up. Modifications are necessary to enhance the performance of this algorithm in noise. These could include adapting weights more slowly and changing the vigilance threshold during training and testing as suggested in [3].

SINGLE LAYER PERCEPTRON

The single layer perceptron [39] is the first of three nets from the taxonomy in Fig. 3 that can be used with both continuous valued and binary inputs. This simple net generated much interest when initially developed because of its ability to learn to recognize simple patterns. A perceptron that decides whether an input belongs to one of two classes (denoted A or B) is shown in the top of Fig. 12. The single node computes a weighted sum of the input elements, subtracts a threshold (θ) and passes the result through a hard limiting nonlinearity such that the output y is either +1 or −1. The decision rule is to respond class A if the output is +1 and class B if the output is −1. A useful technique for analyzing the behavior of nets such as the perceptron is to plot a map of the decision regions created in the multidimensional space spanned by the input variables. These decision regions specify which input values result in a class A and which result in a class B response. The perceptron forms two decision regions separated by a hyperplane. These regions are shown in the right side of Fig. 12 when there are only two inputs and the hyperplane is a line. In this case inputs above the boundary line lead to class A responses and inputs below the line lead to class B responses. As can be seen, the equation of the boundary line depends on the connection weights and the threshold.

Connection weights and the threshold in a perceptron can be fixed or adapted using a number of different algorithms. The original perceptron convergence procedure for adjusting weights was developed by Rosenblatt [39]. It is described in Box 4. First connection weights and the threshold value are initialized to small random non-zero values. Then a new input with N continuous valued elements is applied to the input and the output is computed as in Fig. 12. Connection weights are adapted only when an error occurs using the formula in step 4 of Box 4. This formula includes a gain term (η) that ranges from 0.0 to 1.0 and controls the adaptation rate. This gain term must be adjusted to satisfy the conflicting requirements of fast adaptation for real changes in the input distributions and averaging of past inputs to provide stable weight estimates.

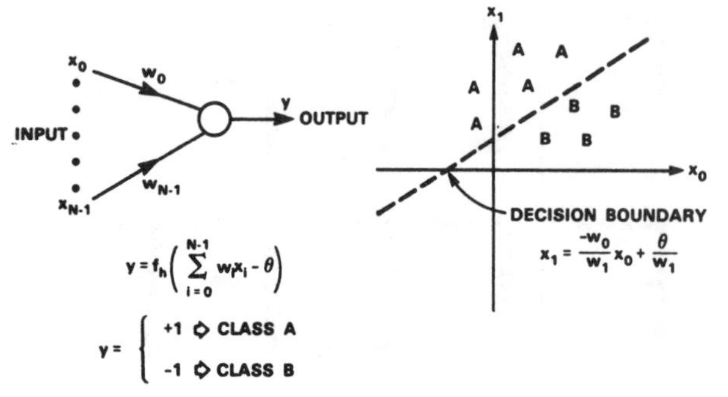

Figure 12. A single layer perceptron that classifies an analog input vector into two classes denoted A and B. This net divides the space spanned by the input into two regions separated by a hyperplane or a line in two dimensions as shown on the top right.

Box 4. The Perceptron Convergence Procedure

Step 1. Initialize Weights and Threshold

Set $w_i(0)$ $(0 \leq i \leq N-1)$ and θ to small random values. Here $w_i(t)$ is the weight from input i at time t and θ is the threshold in the output node.

Step 2. Present New Input and Desired Output

Present new continuous valued input $x_0, x_1 \ldots x_{N-1}$ along with the desired output $d(t)$.

Step 3. Calculate Actual Output

$$y(t) = f_h\left(\sum_{i=0}^{N-1} w_i(t)x_i(t) - \theta\right)$$

Step 4. Adapt Weights

$$w_i(t+1) = w_i(t) + \eta[d(t) - y(t)]x_i(t), \quad 0 \leq i \leq N-1$$

$$d(t) = \begin{cases} +1 \text{ if input from class A} \\ -1 \text{ if input from class B} \end{cases}$$

In these equations η is a positive gain fraction less than 1 and $d(t)$ is the desired correct output for the current input. Note that weights are unchanged if the correct decision is made by the net.

Step 5. Repeat by Going to Step 2

An example of the use of the perceptron convergence procedure is presented in Fig. 13. Samples from class A in this figure are represented by circles and samples from class B are represented by crosses. Samples from classes A and B were presented alternately until 80 inputs had been presented. The four lines show the four decision boundaries after weights had been adjusted following errors on trials 0, 2, 4, and 80. In this example the classes were well separated after only four trials and the gain term was .01.

Rosenblatt [39] proved that if the inputs presented from the two classes are separable (that is they fall on opposite sides of some hyperplane), then the perceptron convergence procedure converges and positions the decision hyperplane between those two classes. Such a hyperplane is illustrated in the upper right of Fig. 12. This decision boundary separates all samples from the A and B classes. One problem with the perceptron convergence procedure is that decision boundaries may oscillate continuously when inputs are not separable and distributions overlap. A modification to the perceptron convergence procedure can form the least mean square (LMS) solution in this case. This solution minimizes the mean square error between the desired output of a perceptron-like net and the actual output. The algorithm that forms the LMS solution is called the Widrow-Hoff or LMS algorithm [47,48,7].

The LMS algorithm is identical to the perceptron convergence procedure described in Box 4 except the hard limiting nonlinearity is made linear or replaced by a threshold-logic nonlinearity. Weights are thus corrected on every trial by an amount that depends on the difference between the desired and the actual input. A classifier that uses the LMS training algorithm could use desired outputs of 1 for class A and 0 for class B. During operation the input would then be assigned to class A only if the output was above 0.5.

The decision regions formed by perceptrons are similar to those formed by maximum likelihood Gaussian classifiers which assume inputs are uncorrelated and distributions for different classes differ only in mean values. This type of Gaussian classifier and the associated weighted Euclidean or straight Euclidean distance metric is often used in speech recognizers when there is limited training data and inputs have been orthogonalized by a suitable transformation [36]. Box 5 demonstrates how the weights and threshold in a perceptron can be selected such that the perceptron structure computes the difference between log likelihoods required by such a Gaussian classifier [7]. Perceptron-like structures can also be used to perform the linear computations required by a Karhunen Loeve transformation [36]. These computations can be used to transform a set of $N + K$ correlated Gaussian inputs into a reduced set of N uncorrelated inputs which can be used with the above Gaussian classifier.

It is straightforward to generalize the derivation of Box 5 to demonstrate how a Gaussian classifier for M classes can be constructed from M perceptron-like structures followed by a net that picks the maximum. The required net is identical in structure to the Hamming Net of Fig. 6. In this case, however, inputs are analog and the weights and node thresholds are calculated from terms II and III in likelihood equations similar to those for L_A in Box 5. It is likewise straightforward to generalize the Widrow-Hoff

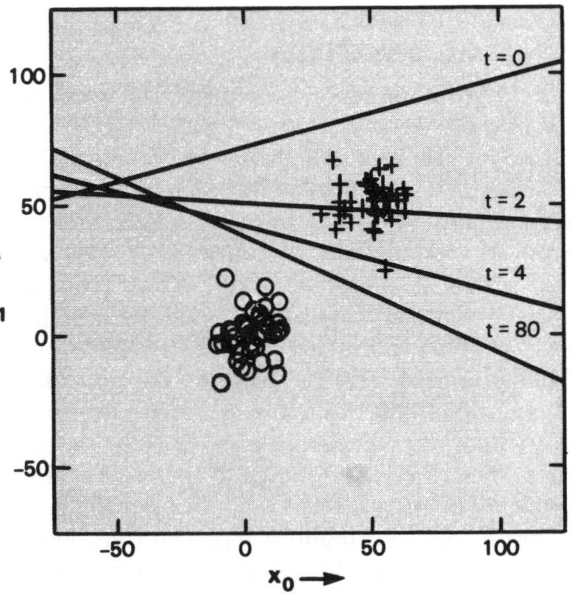

Figure 13. An example of the decision boundaries formed by the perceptron convergence procedure with two classes. Samples from class A are represented by circles and samples from class B by crosses. Lines represent decision boundaries after trials where errors occurred and weights were adapted.

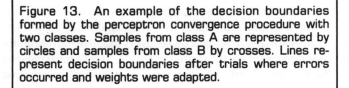

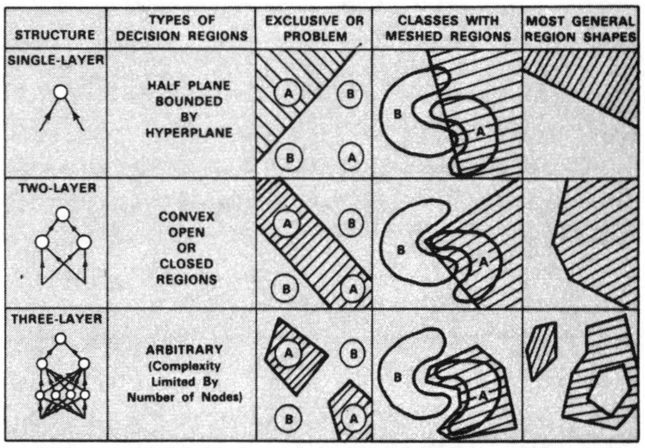

Figure 14. Types of decision regions that can be formed by single- and multi-layer perceptrons with one and two layers of hidden units and two inputs. Shading denotes decision regions for class A. Smooth closed contours bound input distributions for classes A and B. Nodes in all nets use hard limiting nonlinearities.

variant of the perceptron convergence procedure to apply for M classes. This requires a structure identical to the Hamming Net and a classification rule that selects the class corresponding to the node with the maximum output. During adaptation the desired output values can be set to 1 for the correct class and 0 for all others.

Box 5. A Gaussian Classifier Implemented Using the Perceptron Structure

If m_{Ai} and σ_{Ai}^2 are the mean and variance of input x_i when the input is from class A and M_{Bi} and σ_{Bi}^2 are the mean and variance of input x_i for class B and $\sigma_i^2 = \sigma_{Ai}^2 = \sigma_{Bi}^2$, then the likelihood values required by a maximum likelihood classifier are monotonically related to

$$L_A = -\sum_{i=0}^{N-1} \frac{(x_i - M_{Ai})^2}{\sigma_i^2}$$

$$= -\sum \frac{x_i^2}{\sigma_i^2} + 2\sum \frac{M_{Ai} x_i}{\sigma_i^2} - \sum \frac{M_{Ai}^2}{\sigma_i^2}$$

and

$$L_B = -\sum_{i=0}^{N-1} \frac{(x_i - M_{Bi})^2}{\sigma_i^2}$$

$$= -\sum \frac{x_i^2}{\sigma_i^2} + 2\sum \frac{M_{Bi} x_i}{\sigma_i^2} - \sum \frac{M_{Bi}^2}{\sigma_i^2}.$$

$$\uparrow \qquad\qquad \uparrow \qquad\qquad \uparrow$$

Term I Term II Term III

A maximum likelihood classifier must calculate L_A and L_B and select the class with the highest likelihood. Since Term I in these equations is identical for L_A and L_B, it can be dropped. Term II is a product of the input times weights and can be calculated by a perception and Term III is a constant which can be obtained from the threshold in a perceptron node. A Gaussian classifier for two classes can thus be formed by using the perceptron of Fig. 12 to calculate $L_A - L_B$ by setting

$$w_i = \frac{2(M_{Ai} - M_{Bi})}{\sigma_i^2},$$

and

$$\theta = \sum_{i=0}^{N-1} \frac{M_{Ai}^2 - M_{Bi}^2}{\sigma_i^2}.$$

The perceptron structure can be used to implement either a Gaussian maximum likelihood classifier or classifiers which use the perceptron training algorithm or one of its variants. The choice depends on the application. The perceptron training algorithm makes no assumptions concerning the shape of underlying distributions but focuses on errors that occur where distributions overlap. It may thus be more robust than classical techniques and work well when inputs are generated by nonlinear processes and are heavily skewed and non-Gaussian. The Gaussian classifier makes strong assumptions concerning underlying distributions and is more appropriate when distributions are known and match the Gaussian assumption. The adaptation algorithm defined by the perceptron convergence procedure is simple to implement and doesn't require storing any more information than is present in the weights and the threshold. The Gaussian classifier can be made adaptive [24], but extra information must be stored and the computations required are more complex.

Neither the perceptron convergence procedure nor the Gaussian classifier is appropriate when classes cannot be separated by a hyperplane. Two such situations are presented in the upper section of Fig. 14. The smooth closed contours labeled A and B in this figure are the input distributions for the two classes when there are two continuous valued inputs to the different nets. The shaded areas are the decision regions created by a single-layer perceptron and other feed-forward nets. Distributions for the two classes for the exclusive OR problem are disjoint and cannot be separated by a single straight line. This problem was used to illustrate the weakness of the perceptron by Minsky and Papert [32]. If the lower left B cluster is taken to be at the origin of this two dimensional space then the output of the classifier must be "high" only if one but not both of the inputs is "high". One possible decision region for class A which a perceptron might create is illustrated by the shaded region in the first row of Fig. 14. Input distributions for the second problem shown in this figure are meshed and also can not be separated by a single straight line. Situations similar to these may occur when parameters such as formant frequencies are used for speech recognition.

MULTI-LAYER PERCEPTRON

Multi-layer perceptrons are feed-forward nets with one or more layers of nodes between the input and output nodes. These additional layers contain hidden units or nodes that are not directly connected to both the input and output nodes. A three-layer perceptron with two layers of hidden units is shown in Fig. 15. Multi-layer perceptrons overcome many of the limitations of single-layer perceptrons, but were generally not used in the past because effective training algorithms were not available. This has recently changed with the development of new training algorithms [40]. Although it cannot be proven that these algorithms converge as with single layer perceptrons, they have been shown to be successful for many problems of interest [40].

The capabilities of multi-layer perceptrons stem from the nonlinearities used within nodes. If nodes were linear elements, then a single-layer net with appropriately chosen weights could exactly duplicate those calculations performed by any multi-layer net. The capabilities of perceptrons with one, two, and three layers that use hard-limiting nonlinearities are illustrated in Fig. 14. The second column in this figure indicates the types of decision regions that can be formed with different nets. The next two columns present examples of decision regions which could be formed for the exclusive OR problem and a problem with meshed regions. The rightmost column gives examples of the most general decision regions that can be formed.

As noted above, a single-layer perceptron forms half-plane decision regions. A two-layer perceptron can form any, possibly unbounded, convex region in the space spanned by the inputs. Such regions include convex polygons sometimes called convex hulls, and the unbounded convex regions shown in the middle row of Fig. 14. Here the term convex means that any line joining points on the border of a region goes only through points within that region. Convex regions are formed from intersections of the half-plane regions formed by each node in the first layer of the multi-layer perceptron. Each node in the first layer behaves like a single-layer perceptron and has a "high" output only for points on one side of the hyper-plane formed by its weights and offset. If weights to an output node from N_1 first-layer nodes are all 1.0, and the threshold in the output node is $N_1 - \varepsilon$ where $0 < \varepsilon < 1$, then the output node will be "high" only if the outputs of all first-layer nodes are "high". This corresponds to performing a logical AND operation in the output node and results in a final decision region that is the intersection of all the half-plane regions formed in the first layer. Intersections of such half planes form convex regions as described above. These convex regions have at the most as many sides as there are nodes in the first layer.

This analysis provides some insight into the problem of selecting the number of nodes to use in a two-layer perceptron. The number of nodes must be large enough to form a decision region that is as complex as is required by a given problem. It must not, however, be so large that the many weights required can not be reliably estimated from the available training data. For example, two nodes are sufficient to solve the exclusive OR problem as shown in the second row of Fig. 14. No number of nodes, however, can separate the meshed class regions in Fig. 14 with a two-layer perceptron.

A three-layer perceptron can form arbitrarily complex decision regions and can separate the meshed classes as shown in the bottom of Fig. 14. It can form regions as complex as those formed using mixture distributions and nearest-neighbor classifiers [7]. This can be proven by construction. The proof depends on partitioning the desired decision region into small hypercubes (squares when there are two inputs). Each hypercube requires $2N$ nodes in the first layer (four nodes when there are two inputs), one for each side of the hypercube, and one node in the second layer that takes the logical AND of the outputs from the first-layer nodes. The outputs of second-layer nodes will be "high" only for inputs within each hypercube. Hypercubes are assigned to the proper decision regions by connecting the output of each second-layer node only to the output node corresponding to the decision region that node's hypercube is in and performing a logical OR operation in each output node. A logical OR operation will be performed if these connection weights from the second hidden layer to the output layer are one and thresholds in the output nodes are 0.5. This construction procedure can be generalized to use arbitrarily shaped convex regions instead of small hypercubes and is capable of generating the disconnected and non-convex regions shown at the bottom of Fig. 14.

The above analysis demonstrates that no more than three layers are required in perceptron-like feed-forward nets because a three-layer net can generate arbitrarily complex decision regions. It also provides some insight into the problem of selecting the number of nodes to use in three-layer perceptrons. The number of nodes in the second layer must be greater than one when decision regions are disconnected or meshed and cannot be formed from one convex area. The number of second layer nodes required in the worst case is equal to the number of disconnected regions in input distributions. The number of nodes in the first layer must typically be sufficient to provide three or more edges for each convex area generated by every second-layer node. There should thus typically be more than three times as many nodes in the second as in the first layer.

The above discussion centered primarily on multi-layer perceptrons with one output when hard limiting nonlinearities are used. Similar behavior is exhibited by multi-layer perceptrons with multiple output nodes when sigmoidal nonlinearities are used and the decision rule is to select the class corresponding to the output node with the largest output. The behavior of these nets is more complex because decision regions are typically bounded by smooth curves instead of by straight line segments and analysis is thus more difficult. These nets, however, can be trained with the new back-propagation training algorithm [40].

$$y_\ell = f\left(\sum_{k=0}^{N_2-1} w''_{k\ell} x''_k - \theta''_\ell \right) \qquad 0 \leqslant \ell \leqslant M-1$$

$$x''_k = f\left(\sum_{j=0}^{N_1-1} w'_{jk} x'_j - \theta'_k \right) \qquad 0 \leqslant k \leqslant N_2-1$$

$$x'_j = f\left(\sum_{i=0}^{N-1} w_{ij} x_i - \theta_j \right) \qquad 0 \leqslant j \leqslant N_1-1$$

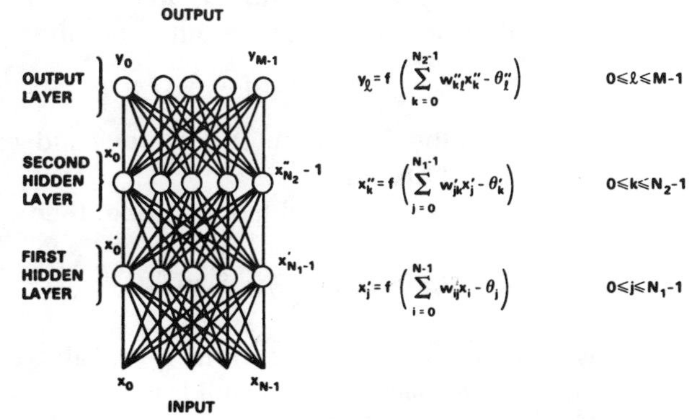

Figure 15. A three-layer perceptron with N continuous valued inputs, M outputs and two layers of hidden units. The nonlinearity can be any of those shown in Fig. 1. The decision rule is to select that class corresponding to the output node with the largest output. In the formulas, x'_j and x''_k are the outputs of nodes in the first and second hidden layers, θ'_k and θ''_l are internal offsets in those nodes, w_{ij} is the connection strength from the input to the first hidden layer, and w'_{ij} and w''_{ij} are the connection strengths between the first and second and between the second and the output layers respectively.

The back-propagation algorithm described in Box 6 is a generalization of the LMS algorithm. It uses a gradient search technique to minimize a cost function equal to the mean square difference between the desired and the actual net outputs. The desired output of all nodes is typically "low" (0 or <0.1) unless that node corresponds to the class the current input is from in which case it is "high" (1.0 or >0.9). The net is trained by initially selecting small random weights and internal thresholds and then presenting all training data repeatedly. Weights are adjusted after every trial using side information specifying the correct class until weights converge and the cost function is reduced to an acceptable value. An essential component of the algorithm is the iterative method described in Box 6 that propagates error terms required to adapt weights back from nodes in the output layer to nodes in lower layers.

An example of the behavior of the back propagation algorithm is presented in Fig. 16. This figure shows decision regions formed by a two-layer perceptron with two inputs, eight nodes in the hidden layer, and two output nodes corresponding to two classes. Sigmoid nonlinearities were used as in Box 6, the gain term η was 0.3, the momentum term α was 0.7, random samples from classes A and B were presented on alternate trials, and the desired outputs were either 1 or 0. Samples from class A were distributed uniformly over a circle of radius 1 centered at the origin. Samples from class B were distributed uniformly outside this circle up to a radius of 5. The initial decision region is a slightly curved hyperplane. This gradually changes to a circular region that encloses the circular distribution of class A after 200 trails (100 samples from each class). This decision region is near that optimal region that would be produced by a Maximum Likelihood classifier.

The back propagation algorithm has been tested with a number of deterministic problems such as the exclusive OR problem [40], on problems related to speech synthesis

Box 6. The Back-Propagation Training Algorithm

The back-propagation training algorithm is an iterative gradient algorithm designed to minimize the mean square error between the actual output of a multilayer feed-forward perceptron and the desired output. It requires continuous differentiable non-linearities. The following assumes a sigmoid logistic nonlinearity is used where the function $f(\alpha)$ in Fig. 1 is

$$f(\alpha) = \frac{1}{1 + e^{-(\alpha-\theta)}}$$

Step 1. Initialize Weights and Offsets

Set all weights and node offsets to small random values.

Step 2. Present Input and Desired Outputs

Present a continuous valued input vector $x_0, x_1, \ldots x_{N-1}$ and specify the desired outputs $d_0, d_1, \ldots d_{M-1}$. If the net is used as a classifier then all desired outputs are typically set to zero except for that corresponding to the class the input is from. That desired output is 1. The input could be new on each trial or samples from a training set could be presented cyclically until weights stabilize.

Step 3. Calculate Actual Outputs

Use the sigmoid nonlinearity from above and formulas as in Fig. 15 to calculate outputs $y_0, y_1 \ldots y_{M-1}$.

Step 4. Adapt Weights

Use a recursive algorithm starting at the output nodes and working back to the first hidden layer. Adjust weights by

$$w_{ij}(t+1) = w_{ij}(t) + \eta \delta_j x_i'$$

In this equation $w_{ij}(t)$ is the weight from hidden node i or from an input to node j at time t, x_i' is either the output of node i or is an input, η is a gain term, and δ_j is an error term for node j. If node j is an output node, then

$$\delta_j = y_j(1 - y_j)(d_j - y_j),$$

where d_j is the desired output of node j and y_j is the actual output.

If node j is an internal hidden node, then

$$\delta_j = x_j'(1 - x_j') \sum_k \delta_k w_{jk},$$

where k is over all nodes in the layers above node j. Internal node thresholds are adapted in a similar manner by assuming they are connection weights on links from auxiliary constant-valued inputs. Convergence is sometimes faster if a momentum term is added and weight changes are smoothed by

$$w_{ij}(t+1) = w_{ij}(t) + \eta \delta_j x_i' + \alpha(w_{ij}(t) - w_{ij}(t-1)),$$

where $0 < \alpha < 1$.

Step 5. Repeat by Going to Step 2

and recognition [43, 37, 8] and on problems related to visual pattern recognition [40]. It has been found to perform well in most cases and to find good solutions to the problems posed. A demonstration of the power of this algorithm was provided by Sejnowski [43]. He trained a two-layer perceptron with 120 hidden units and more than 20,000 weights to form letter to phoneme transcription rules. The input to this net was a binary code indicating those letters in a sliding window seven letters long that was moved over a written transcription of spoken text. The desired output was a binary code indicating the phonemic transcription of the letter at the center of the window. After 50 times through a dialog containing 1024 words, the transcription error rate was only 5%. This increased to 22% for a continuation of that dialog that was not used during training.

The generally good performance found for the back propagation algorithm is somewhat surprising considering that it is a gradient search technique that may find a local minimum in the LMS cost function instead of the desired global minimum. Suggestions to improve performance and reduce the occurrence of local minima include allowing extra hidden units, lowering the gain term used to adapt weights, and making many training runs starting with different sets of random weights. When used with classification problems, the number of nodes could be set using considerations described above. The problem of local minima in this case corresponds to clustering two or more disjoint class regions into one. This can be minimized by using multiple starts with different random weights and a low gain to adapt weights. One difficulty noted with the backward-propagation algorithm is that in many cases the number of presentations of training data required for convergence has been large (more than 100 passes through all the training data). Although a number of more complex adaptation algorithms have been proposed to speed convergence [35] it seems unlikely that the complex decision regions formed by multi-layer perceptrons can be generated in few trials when class regions are disconnected.

An interesting theorem that sheds some light on the capabilities of multi-layer perceptrons was proven by Kolmogorov and is described in [26]. This theorem states that any continuous function of N variables can be computed using only linear summations and nonlinear but continuously increasing functions of only one variable. It effectively states that a three layer perceptron with $N(2N + 1)$ nodes using continuously increasing nonlinearities can compute any continuous function of N variables. A three-layer perceptron could thus be used to create any continuous likelihood function required in a classifier. Unfortunately, the theorem does not indicate how weights or nonlinearities in the net should be selected or how sensitive the output function is to variations in the weights and internal functions.

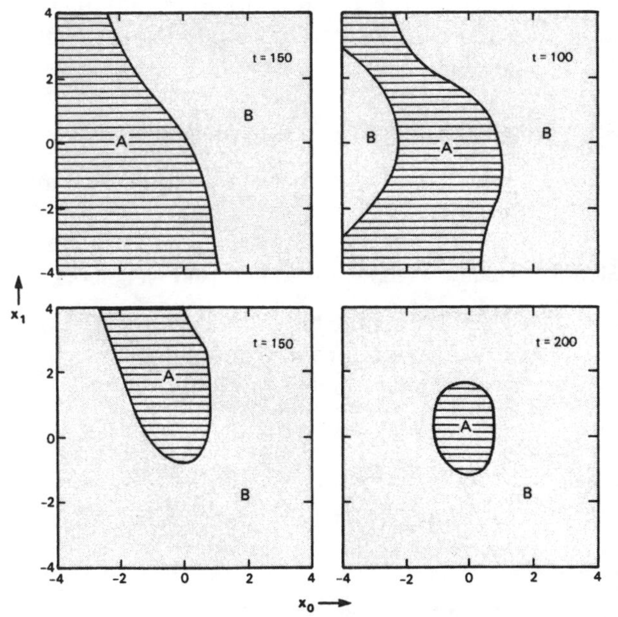

Figure 16. Decision regions after 50, 100, 150 and 200 trials generated by a two layer perceptron using the back-propagation training algorithm. Inputs from classes A and B were presented on alternate trials. Samples from class A were distributed uniformly over a circle of radius 1 centered at the origin. Samples from class B were distributed uniformly outside the circle. The shaded area denotes the decision region for class A.

KOHONEN'S SELF ORGANIZING FEATURE MAPS

One important organizing principle of sensory pathways in the brain is that the placement of neurons is orderly and often reflects some physical characteristic of the external stimulus being sensed [21]. For example, at each level of the auditory pathway, nerve cells and fibers are arranged anatomically in relation to the frequency which elicits the greatest response in each neuron. This tono-

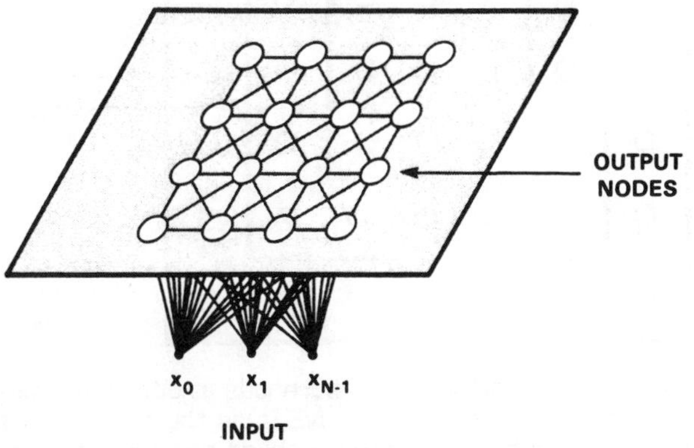

Figure 17. Two-dimensional array of output nodes used to form feature maps. Every input is connected to every output node via a variable connection weight.

topic organization in the auditory pathway extends up to the auditory cortex [33,21]. Although much of the low-level organization is genetically pre-determined, it is likely that some of the organization at higher levels is created during learning by algorithms which promote self-organization. Kohonen [22] presents one such algorithm which produces what he calls self-organizing feature maps similar to those that occur in the brain.

Kohonen's algorithm creates a vector quantizer by adjusting weights from common input nodes to M output nodes arranged in a two dimensional grid as shown in Fig. 17. Output nodes are extensively interconnected with many local connections. Continuous-valued input vectors are presented sequentially in time without specifying the desired output. After enough input vectors have been presented, weights will specify cluster or vector centers that sample the input space such that the point density function of the vector centers tends to approximate the probability density function of the input vectors [22]. In addition, the weights will be organized such that topologically close nodes are sensitive to inputs that are physically similar. Output nodes will thus be ordered in a natural manner. This may be important in complex systems with many layers of processing because it can reduce lengths of inter-layer connections.

The algorithm that forms feature maps requires a neighborhood to be defined around each node as shown in Fig. 18. This neighborhood slowly decreases in size with time as shown. Kohonen's algorithm is described in Box 7. Weights between input and output nodes are initially set to small random values and an input is presented. The distance between the input and all nodes is computed as shown. If the weight vectors are normalized to have constant length (the sum of the squared weights from all inputs to each output are identical) then the node with the minimum Euclidean distance can be found by using the net of Fig. 17 to form the dot product of the input and the weights. The selection required in step 4 then turns into a problem of finding the node with a maximum value. This node can be selected using extensive lateral inhibition as in the MAXNET in the top of Fig. 6. Once this node is selected, weights to it and to other nodes in its neighborhood are modified to make these nodes more responsive to the current input. This process is repeated for further inputs. Weights eventually converge and are fixed after the gain term in step 5 is reduced to zero.

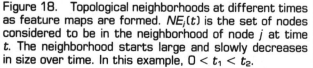

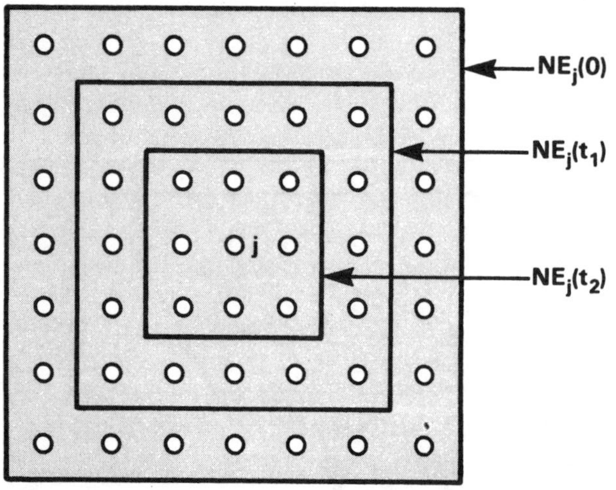

Figure 18. Topological neighborhoods at different times as feature maps are formed. $NE_j(t)$ is the set of nodes considered to be in the neighborhood of node j at time t. The neighborhood starts large and slowly decreases in size over time. In this example, $0 < t_1 < t_2$.

Box 7. An Algorithm to Produce Self-Organizing Feature Maps

Step 1. Initialize Weights

Initialize weights from N inputs to the M output nodes shown in Fig. 17 to small random values. Set the initial radius of the neighborhood shown in Fig. 18.

Step 2. Present New Input

Step 3. Compute Distance to All Nodes

Compute distances d_j between the input and each output node j using

$$d_j = \sum_{i=0}^{N-1} (x_i(t) - w_{ij}(t))^2$$

where $x_i(t)$ is the input to node i at time t and $w_{ij}(t)$ is the weight from input node i to output node j at time t.

Step 4. Select Output Node with Minimum Distance

Select node j^* as that output node with minimum d_j.

Step 5. Update Weights to Node j^* and Neighbors

Weights are updated for node j^* and all nodes in the neighborhood defined by $NE_{j^*}(t)$ as shown in Fig. 18. New weights are

$$w_{ij}(t+1) = w_{ij}(t) + \eta(t)(x_i(t) - w_{ij}(t))$$

For $j \in NE_{j^*}(t)$ $\quad 0 \le i \le N-1$

The term $\eta(t)$ is a gain term ($0 < \eta(t) < 1$) that decreases in time.

Step 6. Repeat by Going to Step 2

An example of the behavior of this algorithm is presented in Fig. 19. The weights for 100 output nodes are plotted in these six subplots when there are two random independent inputs uniformly distributed over the region enclosed by the boxed areas. Line intersections in these plots specify weights for one output node. Weights from

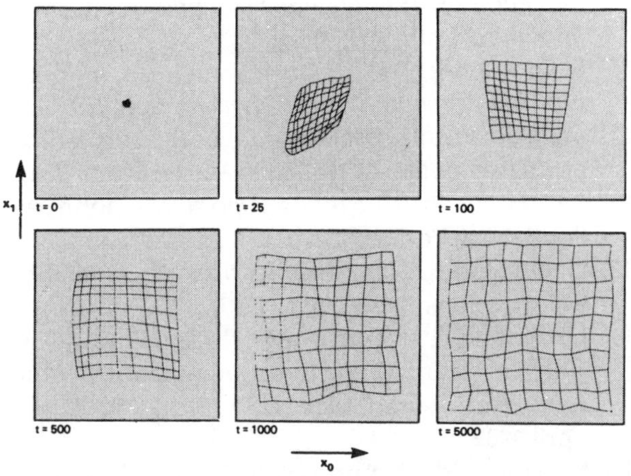

Figure 19. Weights to 100 output nodes from two input nodes as a feature map is being formed. The horizontal axis represents the value of the weight from input x_0 and the vertical axis represents the value of the weight from input x_1. Line intersections specify the two weights for each node. Lines connect weights for nodes that are nearest neighbors. An orderly grid indicates that topologically close nodes code inputs that are physically similar. Inputs were random, independent, and uniformly distributed over the area shown.

input x_0 are specified by the position along the horizontal axis and weights from input x_1 are specified by the position along the vertical axis. Lines connect weight values for nodes that are topological nearest neighbors. Weights start at time zero clustered at the center of the plot. Weights then gradually expand in an orderly way until their point density approximates the uniform distribution of the input samples. In this example, the gain term in step 5 of Box 7 was a Gaussian function of the distance to the node selected in step 4 with a width that decreased in time.

Kohonen [22] presents many other examples and proofs related to this algorithm. He also demonstrates how the algorithm can be used in a speech recognizer as a vector quantizer [23]. Unlike the Carpenter/Grossberg classifier, this algorithm can perform relatively well in noise because the number of classes is fixed, weights adapt slowly, and adaptation stops after training. This algorithm is thus a viable sequential vector quantizer when the number of clusters desired can be specified before use and the amount of training data is large relative to the number of clusters desired. It is similar to the *K*-means clustering algorithm in this respect. Results, however, may depend on the presentation order of input data for small amounts of training data.

INTRODUCTORY REFERENCES TO NEURAL NET LITERATURE

More detailed information concerning the six algorithms described above and other neural net algorithms can be found in [3,7,15,18,19,20,22,25,32,39,40]. Descriptions of many other algorithms including the Boltzmann machine and background historical information can be found in a recent book on parallel distributed processing edited by Rumelhart and McClelland [41]. Feldman [9] presents a good introduction to the connectionist philosophy that complements this book. Papers describing recent research efforts are available in the proceedings of the 1986 Conference on Neural Networks for Computing held in Snowbird, Utah [6]. Descriptions of how the Hopfield net can be used to solve a number of different optimization problems including the traveling salesman problem are presented in [20,45]. A discussion of how content-addressable memories can be implemented using optical techniques is available in [1] and an introduction to the field of neurobiology is available in [21] and other basic texts.

In addition to the above papers and books, there are a number of neural net conferences being held in 1987. These include the "1987 Snowbird Meeting on Neural Networks for Computing" in Snowbird, Utah, April 1–5, the "IEEE First Annual International Conference on Neural Networks" in San Diego, California, June 21–24, and the "IEEE Conference on Neural Information Processing Systems—Natural and Synthetic" in Boulder, Colorado, November 8–12. This last conference is cosponsored by the IEEE Acoustics, Speech, and Signal Processing Society.

CONCLUDING REMARKS

The above review provides an introduction to an interesting field that is immature and rapidly changing. The six nets described are common components in many more complex systems that are under development. Although there have been no practical applications of neural nets yet, preliminary results such as those of Sejnowski [43] have demonstrated the potential of the newer learning algorithms. The greatest potential of neural nets remains in the high-speed processing that could be provided through massively parallel VLSI implementations. Several groups are currently exploring different VLSI implementation strategies [31,13,42]. Demonstrations that existing algorithms for speech and image recognition can be performed using neural nets support the potential applicability of any neural-net VLSI hardware that is developed.

The current research effort in neural nets has attracted researchers trained in engineering, physics, mathematics, neuroscience, biology, computer sciences and psychology. Current research is aimed at analyzing learning and self-organization algorithms used in multi-layer nets, at developing design principles and techniques to solve dynamic range and sensitivity problems which become important for large analog systems, at building complete systems for image and speech and recognition and obtaining experience with these systems, and at determining which current algorithms can be implemented using neuron-like components. Advances in these areas and in VLSI implementation techniques could lead to practical real-time neural-net systems.

ACKNOWLEDGMENTS

I have constantly benefited from discussions with Ben Gold and Joe Tierney. I would also like to thank Don Johnson for his encouragement, Bill Huang for his simulation studies, and Carolyn for her patience.

REFERENCES

[1] Y. S. Abu-Mostafa and D. Pslatis, "Optical Neural Computers," *Scientific American*, 256, 88–95, March 1987.

[2] E. B. Baum, J. Moody, and F. Wilczek, "Internal Representations for Associative Memory," NSF-ITP-86-138 Institute for Theoretical Physics, University of California, Santa Barbara, California, 1986.

[3] G. A. Carpenter, and S. Grossberg, "Neural Dynamics of Category Learning and Recognition: Attention, Memory Consolidation, and Amnesia," in J. Davis, R. Newburgh, and E. Wegman (Eds.) *Brain Structure, Learning, and Memory*, AAAS Symposium Series, 1986.

[4] M. A. Cohen, and S. Grossberg, "Absolute Stability of Global Pattern Formation and Parallel Memory Storage by Competitive Neural Networks," *IEEE Trans. Syst. Man Cybern.* SMC-13, 815–826, 1983.

[5] B. Delgutte, "Speech Coding in the Auditory Nerve: II. Processing Schemes for Vowel-Like Sounds," *J. Acoust. Soc. Am.* 75, 879–886, 1984.

[6] J. S. Denker, *AIP Conference Proceedings 151, Neural Networks for Computing, Snowbird Utah, AIP*, 1986.

[7] R. O. Duda and P. E. Hart, *Pattern Classification and Scene Analysis*, John Wiley & Sons, New York (1973).

[8] J. L. Elman and D. Zipser, "Learning the Hidden Structure of Speech," Institute for Cognitive Science, University of California at San Diego, *ICS Report 8701*, Feb. 1987.

[9] J. A. Feldman and D. H. Ballard, "Connectionist Models and Their Properties," *Cognitive Science, Vol. 6*, 205–254, 1982.

[10] R. G. Gallager, *Information Theory and Reliable Communication*, John Wiley & Sons, New York (1968).

[11] O. Ghitza, "Robustness Against Noise: The Role of Timing-Synchrony Measurement," in *Proceedings International Conference on Acoustics Speech and Signal Processing*, ICASSP-87, Dallas, Texas, April 1987.

[12] B. Gold, "Hopfield Model Applied to Vowel and Consonant Discrimination," *MIT Lincoln Laboratory Technical Report, TR-747, AD-A169742*, June 1986.

[13] H. P. Graf, L. D. Jackel, R. E. Howard, B. Straughn, J. S. Denker, W. Hubbard, D. M. Tennant, and D. Schwartz, "VLSI Implementation of a Neural Network Memory With Several Hundreds of Neurons," in J. S. Denker (Ed.) *AIP Conference Proceedings 151, Neural Networks for Computing, Snowbird Utah, AIP*, 1986.

[14] P. M. Grant and J. P. Sage, "A Comparison of Neural Network and Matched Filter Processing for Detecting Lines in Images," in J. S. Denker (Ed.) *AIP Conference Proceedings 151, Neural Networks for Computing, Snowbird Utah, AIP*, 1986.

[15] S. Grossberg, *The Adaptive Brain I: Cognition, Learning, Reinforcement, and Rhythm*, and *The Adaptive Brain II: Vision, Speech, Language, and Motor Control*, Elsevier/North-Holland, Amsterdam (1986).

[16] J. A. Hartigan, *Clustering Algorithms*, John Wiley & Sons, New York (1975).

[17] D. O. Hebb, *The Organization of Behavior*, John Wiley & Sons, New York (1949).

[18] J. J. Hopfield, "Neural Networks and Physical Systems with Emergent Collective Computational Abilities," *Proc. Natl. Acad. Sci.* USA, Vol. 79, 2554–2558, April 1982.

[19] J. J. Hopfield, "Neurons with Graded Response Have Collective Computational Properties Like Those of Two-State Neurons," *Proc. Natl. Acad. Sci.* USA, Vol. 81, 3088–3092, May 1984.

[20] J. J. Hopfield, and D. W. Tank, "Computing with Neural Circuits: A Model," *Science*, Vol. 233, 625–633, August 1986.

[21] E. R. Kandel and J. H. Schwartz, *Principles of Neural Science*, Elsevier, New York (1985).

[22] T. Kohonen, *Self-Organization and Associative Memory*, Springer-Verlag, Berlin (1984).

[23] T. Kohonen, K. Masisara and T. Saramaki, "Phonotopic Maps—Insightful Representation of Phonological Features for Speech Representation," *Proceedings IEEE 7th Inter. Conf. on Pattern Recognition*, Montreal, Canada, 1984.

[24] F. L. Lewis, *Optimal Estimation*, John Wiley & Sons, New York (1986).

[25] R. P. Lippmann, B. Gold, and M. L. Malpass, "A Comparison of Hamming and Hopfield Neural Nets for Pattern Classification," *MIT Lincoln Laboratory Technical Report, TR-769*, to be published.

[26] G. G. Lorentz, "The 13th Problem of Hilbert," in F. E. Browder (Ed.), *Mathematical Developments Arising from Hilbert Problems*, American Mathematical Society, Providence, R.I. (1976).

[27] R. F. Lyon and E. P. Loeb, "Isolated Digit Recognition Experiments with a Cochlear Model," in *Proceedings International Conference on Acoustics Speech and Signal Processing, ICASSP-87*, Dallas, Texas, April 1987.

[28] J. Makhoul, S. Roucos, and H. Gish, "Vector Quantization in Speech Coding," *IEEE Proceedings, 73*, 1551–1588, Nov. 1985.

[29] T. Martin, *Acoustic Recognition of a Limited Vocabulary in Continuous Speech*, Ph.D. Thesis, Dept. Electrical Engineering Univ. Pennsylvania, 1970.

[30] W. S. McCulloch, and W. Pitts, "A Logical Calculus of the Ideas Imminent in Nervous Activity," *Bulletin of Mathematical Biophysics*, 5, 115–133, 1943.

[31] C. A. Mead, *Analog VLSI and Neural Systems*, Course Notes, Computer Science Dept., California Institute of Technology, 1986.

[32] M. Minsky, and S. Papert, *Perceptrons: An Intro-*

duction to Computational Geometry, MIT Press (1969).

[33] A. R. Moller, *Auditory Physiology,* Academic Press, New York (1983).

[34] P. Mueller, and J. Lazzaro, "A Machine for Neural Computation of Acoustical Patterns with Application to Real-Time Speech Recognition," in J. S. Denker (Ed.) *AIP Conference Proceedings 151, Neural Networks for Computing, Snowbird Utah, AIP,* 1986.

[35] D. B. Parker, "A Comparison of Algorithms for Neuron-Like Cells," in J. S. Denker (Ed.) *AIP Conference Proceedings 151, Neural Networks for Computing, Snowbird Utah, AIP,* 1986.

[36] T. Parsons, *Voice and Speech Processing,* McGraw-Hill, New York (1986).

[37] S. M. Peeling, R. K. Moore, and M. J. Tomlinson, "The Multi-Layer Perceptron as a Tool for Speech Pattern Processing Research," in *Proc. IoA Autumn Conf. on Speech and Hearing,* 1986.

[38] T. E. Posch, "Models of the Generation and Processing of Signals by Nerve Cells: A Categorically Indexed Abridged Bibliography," *USCEE Report 290,* August 1968.

[39] R. Rosenblatt, *Principles of Neurodynamics,* New York, Spartan Books (1959).

[40] D. E. Rumelhart, G. E. Hinton, and R. J. Williams, "Learning Internal Representations by Error Propagation" in D. E. Rumelhart & J. L. McClelland (Eds.), *Parallel Distributed Processing: Explorations in the Microstructure of Cognition. Vol. 1: Foundations.* MIT Press (1986).

[41] D. E. Rumelhart, and J. L. McClelland, *Parallel Distributed Processing: Explorations in the Microstructure of Cognition,* MIT Press (1986).

[42] J. P. Sage, K. Thompson, and R. S. Withers, "An Artificial Neural Network Integrated Circuit Based on MNOS/CD Principles," in J. S. Denker (Ed.) *AIP Conference Proceedings 151, Neural Networks for Computing, Snowbird Utah, AIP,* 1986.

[43] T. Sejnowski and C. R. Rosenberg, "NETtalk: A Parallel Network That Learns to Read Aloud," *Johns Hopkins Univ. Technical Report JHU/EECS-86/01,* 1986.

[44] S. Seneff, "A Computational Model for the Peripheral Auditory System: Application to Speech Recognition Research," in *Proceedings International Conference on Acoustics Speech and Signal Processing, ICASSP-86,* 4, 37.8.1-37.8.4, 1986.

[45] D. W. Tank and J. J. Hopfield, "Simple 'Neural' Optimization Networks: An A/D Converter, Signal Decision Circuit, and a Linear Programming Circuit," *IEEE Trans. Circuits Systems CAS-33,* 533–541, 1986.

[46] D. J. Wallace, "Memory and Learning in a Class of Neural Models," in B. Bunk and K. H. Mutter (Eds.) *Proceedings of the Workshop on Lattice Gauge Theory, Wuppertal, 1985,* Plenum (1986).

[47] B. Widrow, and M. E. Hoff, "Adaptive Switching Circuits," *1960 IRE WESCON Conv. Record, Part 4,* 96–104, August 1960.

[48] B. Widrow and S. D. Stearns, *Adaptive Signal Processing,* Prentice-Hall, New Jersey (1985).

The Multilayer Perceptron as an Approximation to a Bayes Optimal Discriminant Function

DENNIS W. RUCK, STEVEN K. ROGERS, MATTHEW KABRISKY, MARK E. OXLEY, AND BRUCE W. SUTER

Abstract—This letter proves that the popular multilayer perceptron, when trained as a classifier using backpropagation, approximates the Bayes optimal discriminant function. The result is demonstrated for both the two-class problem and multiple classes. It is shown that the outputs of the multilayer perceptron, in fact, are approximating the *a posteriori* probability functions of the classes being trained. The proof applies to any number of layers and any type of unit activation function, linear or nonlinear.

I. Introduction

Previous research into the area of pattern recognition has shown that multilayer perceptron classifiers and conventional nonparametric Bayesian classifiers yield the same classification accuracy, statistically speaking [1]–[3]. These results have been empirical and, hence, are dependent on the data sets used. However, the consistently similar performance has led us to investigate the theoretical connections. This letter will show how a multilayer perceptron approximates the Bayes optimal discriminant function when used for classification. This result shows conclusively that the multilayer perceptron is performing classification using the same rules as most traditional classifiers. The proof shown here was inspired by the work of R. O. Duda and P. E. Hart in their book, *Pattern Classification and Scene Analysis* [4].

The next section will show how a single output multilayer perceptron can be trained to approximate the Bayes optimal discriminant function. In Section III, the problem of multiple classes will be solved. The following section will discuss some of the implications of these results for neural network architecture and training criteria.

II. Two-Class Problem

In this section, we will consider the two-class discrimination problem and show that a multilayer perceptron can be trained to approximate, in a mean squared-error sense, the Bayes optimal discriminant function. Let us begin with some definitions.

Let x represent the feature vector which is to be classified. Define $F(x, w)$ to be the output of the multilayer perceptron where w is the weight vector. Let the two classes be denoted ω_1 and ω_2. Let $\mathcal{X}_i$ be the set of all possible feature vectors for class ω_i and $\mathcal{X}_1 \cup \mathcal{X}_2 = \mathcal{X}$. The set $\mathcal{X}$ represents the *ensemble* of all possible feature vectors that can be generated. Also suppose, for the two-class problem, the network is trained to produce 1 when the feature vector is from class ω_1 and -1 when the vector is from class ω_2. These outputs are commonly achieved using the $\tanh^{-1}(\cdot)$ function as the output nonlinearity for the network nodes. The Bayes optimal discriminant function, which minimizes the probability of error, can be written in many forms. For our purposes, let $g_0(x)$ be the Bayes optimal discriminant function given by

$$g_0(x) = P(\omega_1|x) - P(\omega_2|x) \tag{1}$$

Manuscript received April 13, 1990. This paper was supported in part by the Rome Air Development Center (RADC/COTC) and the Wright Research and Development Center (WRDC/AARA).

The authors are with the School of Engineering, Air Force Institute of Technology, Wright-Patterson AFB, OH 45433.

IEEE Log Number 9038748.

where $P(\omega_i|x)$ is the probability that x belongs to class ω_i. Hence, $g_0(x)$ is positive when x is most likely from class ω_1 and negative when x is most likely from class ω_2. The distribution of feature vectors is governed by

$$p(x) = p(x|\omega_1)P(\omega_1) + p(x|\omega_2)P(\omega_2)$$

where $P(\omega_i)$ is the *a priori* probability of class ω_i and $p(x|\omega_i)$ is the conditional probability density function of x given that x is from class ω_i, so that $p(x)$ is the probability density function governing x. In the following, a lower case $p(\cdot)$ always indicates a probability *density* function and an upper case $P(\cdot)$ represents a probability function.

We shall show that the following error criterion is minimized by backpropagation:

$$\epsilon^2(w) = \int_{\mathcal{X}} [F(x, w) - g_0(x)]^2 p(x)\, dx.$$

In other words, backpropagation finds a minimum mean squared-error approximation to the Bayes optimal discriminant function.

Suppose we have samples generated by $p(x)$ such that $X_1 = \{x_1, x_2, \cdots, x_{n_1}\} \subset \mathcal{X}_1$ and $X_2 = \{x_{n_1+1}, x_{n_1+2}, \cdots, x_{n_1+n_2}\} \subset \mathcal{X}_2$. Define the sample data error function $E_s(w)$ as shown below.

$$E_s(w) = \sum_{x \in X_1} (F(x, w) - 1)^2 + \sum_{x \in X_2} (F(x, w) + 1)^2$$

where X_i is the set of training vectors from class ω_i. It is well known that backpropagation approximately minimizes E_s with respect to w (see [5]–[7]). The sample data error function $E_s(w)$ describes a hyperdimensional surface which backpropagation traverses seeking a minimum; hence, $E_s(w)$ is often called the *sample data error surface*. Now let the average error $E_a(w)$ be defined as follows:

$$E_a(w) = \lim_{n \to \infty} \frac{1}{n} E_s(w)$$

where n is the total number of feature vectors for both classes. The average error $E_a(w)$ is the *ensemble error surface* for the pattern recognition problem, since it represents the error surface when all possible feature vectors are included in the computation. When we seek the minimum of the sample data error surface $E_s(w)$, we assume that $E_s(w)$ represents a reasonable approximation to the ensemble error surface $E_a(w)$. If, however, the sample data does not accurately represent the underlying probability density functions, then the minimum of $E_s(w)$ will not yield a classifier with comparable performance when tested with feature vectors not used in designing the classifier.

Now rewrite the expression for E_a using the number of vectors in each class.

$$E_a(w) = \lim_{n \to \infty} \left[\frac{n_1}{n} \cdot \frac{1}{n_1} \sum_{x \in X_1} (F(x, w) - 1)^2 + \frac{n_2}{n} \cdot \frac{1}{n_2} \sum_{x \in X_2} (F(x, w) + 1)^2 \right]$$

where n_i is the number of feature vectors from class ω_i. Since the

Reprinted from *IEEE Trans. Neural Networks*, vol. 1, no. 4, pp. 296–298, December 1990.

number of feature vectors drawn from $p(x)$ for any given class is proportional to the *a priori* probability of that class, as the total number of samples n increases without bound, so will the number of samples in each class n_i for all classes with nonzero *a priori* probability of occurrence (the only classes we are interested in satisfy this condition). By the Strong Law of Large Numbers [8],

$$E_a(w) = P(\omega_1) \int_{\mathfrak{X}} (F(x, w) - 1)^2 p(x|\omega_1)\, dx + P(\omega_2) \int_{\mathfrak{X}} (F(x, w) + 1)^2 p(x|\omega_2)\, dx.$$

Combining the integrals and gathering terms yields

$$E_a(w) = \int_{\mathfrak{X}} \{[F^2(x, w) + 1] \cdot [p(x|\omega_1)P(\omega_1) + p(x|\omega_2)P(\omega_2)] - 2F(x, w)[p(x|\omega_1)P(\omega_1) - p(x|\omega_2)P(\omega_2)]\}\, dx. \quad (2)$$

Using the Bayes Formula, we can simplify the above expression and introduce the optimal discriminant function given by (1). Note that

$$g_0(x)p(x) = p(x|\omega_1)P(\omega_1) - p(x|\omega_2)P(\omega_2)$$
$$p(x|\omega_1)P(\omega_1) + p(x|\omega_2)P(\omega_2) = p(x).$$

Thus, (2) becomes

$$\begin{aligned} E_a(w) &= \int_{\mathfrak{X}} [F^2(x, w)p(x) - 2F(x, w)g_0(x)p(x)]\, dx + 1 \\ &= \int_{\mathfrak{X}} [F(x, w) - g_0(x)]^2 p(x)\, dx + \left\{1 - \int_{\mathfrak{X}} g_0^2(x)p(x)\, dx\right\} \\ &= \epsilon^2(w) + \left\{1 - \int_{\mathfrak{X}} g_0^2(x)p(x)\, dx\right\}. \end{aligned} \quad (3)$$

Now since backpropagation is minimizing E_s with respect to w, it is also minimizing E_a with respect to w. Since the term in braces in (3) is independent of w, minimizing E_a with respect to w also minimizes ϵ^2. Hence, backpropagation yields a multilayer perceptron which is a minimum mean squared-error approximation to the Bayes optimal discriminant function. Note, however, that the accuracy of this approximation is limited by the architecture of the network being trained. If the network has too few nodes in the hidden layer(s), then the function approximating the Bayes optimal discriminant function will not provide a good match.

The next section will generalize this result to a multiclass discrimination problem and show that the outputs of the multilayer perceptron can be interpreted as probabilities.

III. Multiclass Problem

This section shows that the output functions of a multilayer perceptron approximate the Bayes optimal discriminant functions for a multiclass recognition problem. We begin with some definitions.

Let $F_i(x, w)$ be the ith output of a multilayer perceptron, $i = 1, \ldots, k$ (k-class problem). Also, let the desired output be one when $x \in \mathfrak{X}_i$ and zero otherwise. That is,

$$d_i(x) = \begin{cases} 1 & \text{if } x \in \mathfrak{X}_i \\ 0 & \text{otherwise} \end{cases}.$$

The Bayes optimal discriminant functions are given by

$$g_i(x) = P(\omega_i|x) \qquad \text{for all } i = 1, 2, \ldots, k$$

and the decision rule is: decide x is from class ω_i if $g_i(x) > g_j(x)$ for all $j \neq i$. The Bayes optimal discriminant functions are optimal in the sense that the probability of error is minimized by their use.

Define the sample data error function as before:

$$E_s(w) = \sum_{x\in X_1} \left[\sum_{j\neq 1} F_j^2(x, w) + (F_1(x, w) - 1)^2 \right] + \cdots + \sum_{x\in X_k} \left[\sum_{j\neq k} F_j^2(x, w) + (F_k(x, w) - 1)^2 \right].$$

The average error becomes

$$\begin{aligned} E_a(w) &= \lim_{n\to\infty} \frac{1}{n} E_s(w) \\ &= \lim_{n\to\infty} \left\{ \frac{n_1}{n} \cdot \frac{1}{n_1} \sum_{x\in X_1} \left[\sum_{j\neq 1} F_j^2(x, w) + (F_1(x, w) - 1)^2 \right] + \cdots \right\}. \end{aligned}$$

Applying the Strong Law of Large Numbers and simplifying yields the following:

$$\begin{aligned} E_a(w) &= P(\omega_1) \left[\int_{\mathfrak{X}} (F_1(x, w) - 1)^2 p(x|\omega_1)\, dx + \int_{\mathfrak{X}} F_2^2(x, w)p(x|\omega_1)\, dx + \cdots + \int_{\mathfrak{X}} F_k^2(x, w)p(x|\omega_1)\, dx \right] + \cdots + P(\omega_k)[\cdots] \\ &= \sum_{i=1}^{k} \left[\int_{\mathfrak{X}} (F_i(x, w) - 1)^2 p(x|\omega_i)P(\omega_i)\, dx + \sum_{j\neq i} \int_{\mathfrak{X}} F_i^2(x, w)p(x|\omega_j)P(\omega_j)\, dx \right] \\ &= \sum_{i=1}^{k} \int_{\mathfrak{X}} \left\{ F_i^2(x, w) \left[\sum_{j=1}^{k} p(x|\omega_j)P(\omega_j) \right] - [2F_i(x, w) - 1]p(x|\omega_i)P(\omega_i) \right\} dx. \end{aligned} \quad (4)$$

By the Bayes Law, the following identities hold:

$$\begin{aligned} \sum_{j=1}^{k} p(x|\omega_j)P(\omega_j) &= p(x) \\ p(x|\omega_i)P(\omega_i) &= p(x, \omega_i) \\ &= P(\omega_i|x)p(x) \\ &= g_i(x)p(x). \end{aligned}$$

Thus, (4) becomes

$$\begin{aligned} E_a(w) &= \sum_{i=1}^{k} \left[\int_{\mathfrak{X}} \{F_i^2(x, w)p(x) - [2F_i(x, w) - 1]g_i(x)p(x)\}\, dx \right] \\ &= \sum_{i=1}^{k} \left[\int_{\mathfrak{X}} [F_i(x, w) - g_i(x)]^2 p(x)\, dx + \left\{ \int_{\mathfrak{X}} g_i(x)(1 - g_i(x))p(x)\, dx \right\} \right]. \end{aligned} \quad (5)$$

Note that the term in braces is independent of w; hence, backpropagation minimizes the following error criterion:

$$\epsilon^2(w) = \sum_{i=1}^{k} \int_{\mathfrak{X}} [F_i(x, w) - g_i(x)]^2 p(x)\, dx.$$

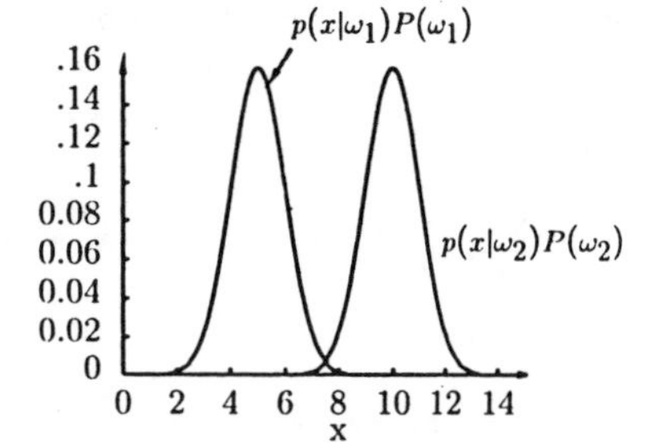

Fig. 1. Example showing that the decision boundaries do not necessarily occur where the density function is large. The decision boundary occurs where the weighted density functions cross over; yet the overall density function, $p(x) = p(x|\omega_1)P(\omega_1) + p(x|\omega_2)P(\omega_2)$, is greatest at the peaks of the individual density functions.

Thus, the output functions of a multilayer perceptron approximate the Bayes optimal discriminant functions in the minimum mean squared-error sense. The next section will discuss the implications of this result.

IV. Discussion

It has been shown that backpropagation provides a minimum mean squared-error approximation to the Bayes optimal discriminant functions for both the two-class problem and the multiclass problem. There are several implications of this result, which we will now discuss.

First, recall (3) and (5) for the two-class and multiclass problems, respectively. In both equations, the error between the Bayes optimal discriminant function and the multilayer perceptron's approximation is weighted by the probability density of the feature vector $p(x)$. Hence, the multilayer perceptron's output will more closely approximate the Bayes optimal discriminant function where $p(x)$ is large. If the goal is to minimize the probability of error, though, the fit between the multilayer perceptron and the Bayes optimal discriminant function should be better where $g_0(x) = 0$, in the two-class problem, and where $g_i(x) = g_j(x)$, in the multiclass case, since these conditions determine the decision boundaries of the classifier. In general, these conditions do not occur where $p(x)$ is large (see Fig. 1 for an example).

The second result of the foregoing is that this proof is not restricted to the multilayer perceptron trained with backpropagation. The architecture of the network was never used in the derivation. Hence, the result applies to any technique which attempts to minimize the mean squared-error and the desired outputs are 0 and 1 (for the multiclass problem).

Another important conclusion is that the outputs of the multilayer perceptron, when trained as previously described, represent *a posteriori* probabilities. That is,

$$F_i(x, w) \approx P(\omega_i|x).$$

This fact makes it possible to set sensible decision thresholds for the outputs of a multilayer perceptron. For example, a rejection criterion could be set that specifies that the input be rejected if the *a posteriori* probability of the indicated class is below 95%. Such criteria can be set not knowing what the outputs represent but, without a proper interpretation of the outputs, the criteria are at best *ad hoc*. Note, however, that how closely the multilayer perceptron approximates the *a posteriori* probabilities depends on the architecture of the network and the functional form of the underlying probability density functions. If there are insufficient units in the hidden layer of the multilayer perceptron to accurately model the *a posteriori* probability functions, then the network's outputs will be poor approximations to the actual probability functions.

V. Conclusion

This letter has shown that the multilayer perceptron trained using backpropagation approximates the Bayes optimal discriminant functions for both two-class and multiclass recognition problems. Most importantly, it has been shown that the outputs of the multilayer perceptron approximate the *a posteriori* functions when trained using backpropagation for the multiclass problem. In fact, the proof does not depend on the architecture of the network and is, hence, applicable to any network that minimizes the mean squared-error measure. The conclusion is that, contrary to popular opinion, these neural networks are simply another method for estimating the probability density function of the input feature vectors. There is really nothing magical or mysterious about these techniques. A multilayer perceptron simply provides a powerful architecture for function approximation. Recently, the work of Çybenko has shown that a multilayer perceptron with a single hidden layer can uniformly approximate any continuous function with support in the unit hypercube when sigmoidal activation functions are used in the hidden layer and the output units are linear [9]. Hence, these networks are reasonable architectures with which to attempt probability density function estimation. It should also be noted that the recently published paper by H. White [10] derives a similar result using a different, more generic approach. The work reported here was developed independently of his results.

The only question that remains is that of the rate of convergence of backpropagation. Given that a multilayer perceptron has the capacity to accurately approximate the Bayes optimal discriminant function, will the multilayer perceptron provide a better estimate of the *a posteriori* probabilities than conventional methods, such as the Parzen window technique, for density function estimation [4]? This question is being investigated.

References

[1] D. W. Ruck, S. K. Rogers, and M. Kabrisky, "Target recognition: Conventional and neural network approaches," in *Proc. IEEE/INNS Int. Joint Conf. Neural Networks*, 1989, Abstract.

[2] S. K. Rogers, D. W. Ruck, M. Kabrisky, and G. L. Tarr, "Artificial neural networks for automatic target recognition," in *Proc. SPIE Conf. Appl. Artif. Neural Networks*, Bellingham, WA, 1990.

[3] D. W. Ruck, S. K. Rogers, and M. Kabrisky, "Tactical target recognition: Conventional and neural network approaches," in *Proc. 5th Ann. Aerospace Appl. Artif. Intell. Conf.*, Oct. 1989.

[4] R. O. Duda and P. E. Hart, *Pattern Classification and Scene Analysis*. New York: Wiley, 1973.

[5] P. J. Werbos, "Beyond regression: New tools for prediction and analysis in the behavioral sciences," Ph.D. dissertation, Harvard Univ., Cambridge, MA, 1974.

[6] D. B. Parker, "Learning-logic," Stanford Univ., Stanford, CA, Invention Rep. 581-64, Oct. 1982.

[7] D. E. Rumelhart, J. L. McClelland, and the PDP Research Group, *Parallel Distributed Processing, Vol. 1: Foundations*. Cambridge, MA: M.I.T. Press, 1986.

[8] S. Ross, *A First Course in Probability*. New York: Macmillan, 1976.

[9] G. Cybenko, "Approximations by superpositions of sigmoidal functions," *Math. Contr., Signals, Syst.*, 1989.

[10] H. White, "Learning in artificial neural networks: A statistical perspective," *Neural Comput.*, vol. 1, pp. 425–464, 1989.

A Formulation of Fuzzy Automata and its Application as a Model of Learning Systems

WILLIAM G. WEE, MEMBER, IEEE, AND K. S. FU, MEMBER, IEEE

Abstract—Based on the concept of fuzzy sets defined by Zadeh, a class of fuzzy automata is formulated similar to Mealy's formulation of finite automata. A fuzzy automaton behaves in a deterministic fashion. However, it has many properties similar to that of stochastic automata. Its application as a model of learning systems is discussed. A nonsupervised learning scheme in automatic control and pattern recognition is proposed with computer simulation results presented. An advantage of employing fuzzy automaton as a learning model is its simplicity in design and computation.

I. Introduction

In the study of automaton formulation, Bruce and Fu [1] have formulated a class of stochastic automata on the basis of Mealy's [2] formulation of finite automata. Fu and McLaren [3] have employed stochastic automata as a model of learning systems operating in an unknown environment. The formulation of fuzzy automata used in this paper is based on the fuzzy relation defined by Zadeh [4]. The formulation of fuzzy automata is similar to that of the stochastic automata proposed by Bruce and Fu [1], and the fuzzy class of systems described by Zadeh [5]. The advantages of using fuzzy set concept in engineering systems has been discussed by Zadeh [4], [5]. In the recent paper by Santos and Wee [6] a general formulation has been given to cover both fuzzy and stochastic automata. The present paper deals with a specific formulation of fuzzy automata and its engineering applications.

II. Formulation of Fuzzy Automata

Definition: A (finite) fuzzy automaton is a quintuple (I,V,Q,f,g) where

- I nonempty finite set of objects (input states)
- V nonempty finite set of objects (output states)
- Q nonempty finite set of objects (internal states)
- f membership function of a fuzzy set in $Q \times I \times Q$; i.e., $f: Q \times I \times Q \rightarrow [0,1]$
- g membership function of a fuzzy set in $V \times I \times Q$; i.e., $g: V \times I \times Q \rightarrow [0,1]$.

It is important to note that I, V, and Q are ordinary sets of finite number of points, while f and g are membership functions of fuzzy sets of finite number of points.

Manuscript received December 20, 1967; revised February 18, 1969. This work was supported by NSF under Grants GK-696 and GK-1970.

W. G. Wee is with the Systems Research Division, Honeywell, Inc., St. Paul, Minn.
K. S. Fu is with the Department of Electrical Engineering, Purdue University, Lafayette, Ind. 47907.

f may be called the direct fuzzy transition function and g the direct fuzzy output function.

Let $I = \{i_1,i_2, \cdots, i_p\}$, $V = \{v_1,v_2, \cdots, v_r\}$, and $Q = \{q_1,q_2, \cdots, q_n\}$, then $f_A(q_l,i_j,q_m)$ is the grade of transition (class A) from state q_l or

$$q(k) = q_l \text{ to } q_m \text{ or } q(k+1) = q_m \tag{1}$$

when the input is i_j or $i(k) = i_j$, and where k denotes the discrete time element. Therefore,

$$f_A(q_l,i_j,q_m) = f\{q(k) = q_l,\ i(k) = i_j,\ q(k+1) = q_m\}.$$

A membership function of unity implies the definite existence of such a transition, and a zero implies no such transition exists. In order to decide the existence of the transition, a pair of thresholds may be introduced as follows: $\alpha > \beta$ where $0 < \alpha, \beta < 1$ which leads to a three-level logic as

1) x belongs to A, or "true" if $f_A(x) \geq \alpha$
2) x does not belong to A, or "false" if $f_A(x) \leq \beta$
3) x has an indeterminate status relative to A, or "undetermined" if $\beta < f_A(x) < \alpha$

where A is a fuzzy set defined as the establishment of the transition between states for a particular input; x denotes the 3-tuple (q_l,i_j,q_m) where $q_l, q_m \in Q$; $i_j \in I$; i.e., $f_A(x) = f_A(q_l, i_j, q_m)$ as defined in (1).

The function may be dependent or independent of k, the number of steps. If f is independent of k, it is called stationary fuzzy transition function. We will see later that nonstationary fuzzy transition functions are used to demonstrate learning behavior of a fuzzy automaton.

For the present, let f be independent of k with fuzzy transition matrix T_{i_j} for each $i_j \in I$. The T_{i_j} is of the following form.

i_j		
$q(k)$	$q(k+1)$ $q_1, q_2, \cdots, q_m, \cdots, q_s$	
q_1	$\cdot$	
$\cdot$	$\cdot$	
$\cdot$	$\cdot$	
$\cdot$		
q_l	$\cdots f_A(q_l,i_j,q_m)$	; $i_j \in I$.
$\cdot$		
$\cdot$		
$\cdot$		
q_n		

Reprinted from *IEEE Trans. Syst. Sci. & Cybern.*, vol. SSC-5, pp. 215-223, 1969.

The entries of T_{ij} are $f_A(q_l,i_j,q_m)$. The fuzzy transition table is as follows:

	$q(k+1)$			$v(k)$		
	$i(k)$			$i(k)$		
$q(k)$	a	b		a	b	
q_1						
q_2	$[A]$	$[B]$	$\cdots$	$[A_0]$	$[B_0]$	$\cdots$
.						
.						
.						
q_n						

where $[A]$ is a fuzzy matrix formed by $f_A(q_i,a,q_j)$, for all $q_i,q_j \in Q$, and $[A_0]$ is a fuzzy matrix formed by $g_A(v_j,a,q_i)$, for all $q_i \in Q$, $v_j \in V$.

The input sequence transition matrix for a particular n-input tape sequence is defined by an n-ary fuzzy relation in the product space $T_1 \times T_2 \times \cdots \times T_n$. The fuzzy transition function is as follows: Let $I_j(k)$ be an input sequence of length j, i.e., $i_1(k)$, $i_2(k+1)$, $\cdots$, $i_j-(k+j-1)$. Then $f_A(q_l,I_p(k),q_s) = f_A(q_l,i_j,i_o, \cdots, i_t,q_s) =$ the grade of transition (class A) from state q_l or $q(k) = q_l$ to q_s or $q(k+p) = q_s$ when the input sequence is $i(k) = i_j$, $i(k+1) = i_o$, $\cdots$, $i(k+p-1) = i_t$.

Therefore,

$$f_A(q_l,I_2(k),q_r) = f_A(q_l,i_j,i_o,q_r) = f_A(q_l,i_j,q_m;\ q_m,i_o,q_r), \quad \text{all } q_m \in Q$$

$$f_A(q_l,I_3(k),q_s) = f_A(q_l,i_j,i_o,i_p,q_s) = f_A(q_l,i_j,i_o,q_r;\ q_r,i_p,q_s)$$
$$= f_A(q_l,i_j,q_m;\ q_m,i_o,q_r;\ q_r,i_p,q_s), \quad \text{all } q_m,q_r \in Q.$$

In particular, for identical inputs i_s in a sequence of length j, $I_j(k)$ is denoted by $i_s{}^j(k)$.

The composition of two fuzzy relations A and B denoted by $B \circ A$ is defined as a fuzzy relation in X whose membership function is related to those of A and B by

1) $f_{B\circ A}(x,y) = \sup_v \min[f_A(x,v),f_B(v,y)]$

2) $f_{B\circ A}(x,y) = \inf_v \max[f_A(x,v),f_B(v,y)]$.

Definition 1) is given by Zadeh [4]. Definition 2) is introduced by the authors. Based on each definition, we have a particular kind of fuzzy automata. When these two kinds of automata operate together, we have a composite automaton similar to the structure of a zero-sum two-person game. This will be illustrated in a later section when a learning model is proposed. For the present we will concentrate on developing automata based on both definitions. In the case of a finite automaton, sup and inf can be replaced by max and min, respectively. In applying the preceding definition to automaton operation, fuzzy sets A and B are the same. Both denote the grade of transition from one state to another for a particular input.

Definitions 1) and 2) are similar, so only the first will be illustrated in detail. Applying definition 1) to $A \circ A$ we have

$$f_{A\circ A}(x,y) = \max_v \min[f_A(x,v), f_A(v,y)].$$

This relation serves an intuitive explanation; that is, the pessimistic case is being considered when the minimum f function is selected between $f_A(x,v)$ and $f_A(v,y)$ and the maximal grade of this minimum is being searched through v. Therefore,

$$f_A(q_l,I_2(k),q_r) = f_A(q_l,i_j,i_o,q_r)$$
$$= f_A(q_l,i_j,q_m;\ q_m,i_o,q_r)$$
$$= \max q_m \min[f_A(q_l,i_j,q_m), f_A(q_m,i_o,q_r)], \quad m = 1,2,\ldots,n;\ q_m \in Q$$

$$f_A(q_l,I_3(k),q_s) = f_A(q_l,i_j,i_o,i_p,q_s)$$
$$= f_A(q_l,i_j,i_o,q_r;\ q_r,i_p,q_s)$$
$$= f_A(q_l,i_j,q_m;\ q_m,i_o,q_r;\ q_r,i_p,q_s)$$
$$= \max q_r \min\{\max q_m \min[f_A(q_l,i_j,q_m), f_A(q_m,i_o,q_r)], f_A(q_r,i_p,q_s)\}, \quad r,m = 1,2,\cdots,n;$$
$$= \max q_m,q_r \min\{f_A(q_l,i_j,q_m), f_A(q_m,i_o,q_r), f_A(q_r,i_p,q_s)\}, \quad m,r = 1,2,\cdots,n.$$

The last extension follows directly from Lemma 1 given in Appendix I. In general,

$$f_A(q_l,I_j(k),q_m) = f_A(q_l,I_{j-1}(k)i_j(k+j-1), q_m)$$
$$= f_A(q_l,i_1(k)i_2(k+1)\cdots i_j(k+j-1), q_m)$$
$$= \max q_o,q_p,\cdots,q_s \min[f_A(q_l,i_1,q_o), f_A(q_o,i_2,q_p), \cdots, f_A(q_s,i_j,q_m)]$$

where $o,p,\cdots,s = 1,2,\cdots,n$; $q_o,q_p,\cdots,q_s \in Q$.

Example. Let T_{i_1} be as follows:

$q(k)$	$q(k+1)$: q_1	q_2	q_3	q_4
q_1	f_{11}	f_{12}	f_{13}	f_{14}
q_2	f_{21}	f_{22}	f_{23}	f_{24}
q_3	f_{31}	f_{32}	f_{33}	f_{34}
q_4	f_{41}	f_{42}	f_{43}	f_{44}

$$f_A(q_3,i_1,q_2) = f_{32}$$

$$f_A(q_3,i_1{}^2,q_2) = \max q_x \min[f_A(q_3,i_1,q_x), f_A(q_x,i_1,q_2)], \quad x = 1,2,3,4$$
$$= \max\{\min[f_{31}f_{12}], \min[f_{32}f_{22}], \min[f_{33}f_{32}], \min[f_{34}f_{42}]\}$$

$$f_A(q_3,i_1{}^3,q_2) = \max q_x,q_y \min[f_A(q_3,i_1,q_x), f_A(q_x,i_1,q_y), f_A(q_y,i_1,q_2)], \quad x,y = 1,2,3,4$$
$$= \max\{\min(f_{31}f_{11}f_{12}), \min(f_{31}f_{12}f_{22}), \min(f_{31}f_{13}f_{32}), \min(f_{31}f_{14}f_{42}), \min(f_{32}f_{21}f_{12}), \min(f_{32}f_{22}f_{22}), \min(f_{32}f_{23}f_{32}), \min(f_{32}f_{24}f_{42}), \min(f_{33}f_{31}f_{12}), \min(f_{33}f_{32}f_{22}), \min(f_{33}f_{33}f_{32}), \min(f_{33}f_{31}f_{42}), \min(f_{34}f_{41}f_{12}), \min(f_{34}f_{42}f_{22}), \min(f_{34}f_{43}f_{32}), \min(f_{34}f_{44}f_{42})\}.$$

Note,

$$f_A(q_3i_1{}^3,q_2) = \max q_x \min[f_A(q_3,i_1{}^2,q_x), f_A(q_x,i_1,q_2)], \quad x = 1,2,3,4$$
$$= \max\{\min[f(q_3,i_1{}^2,q_1), f_{12}], \min[f(q_3,i_1{}^2,q_2), f_{22}], \min[f(q_3,i_1{}^2,q_3),f_{32}], \min[f(q_3,i_1{}^2,q_4), f_{42}]\}.$$

This last relation serves as an iteration scheme for a particular sequence of input tape. Similar results for min max relation 2) can be derived with the aid of Lemma 2 given in Appendix I.

III. Special Cases of Fuzzy Automata

A. *Deterministic Automata*

In this case, the set A is no longer a fuzzy set; it is an ordinary set where f takes only two values, 0 and 1. Therefore, the entries for each row of matrices $[A]$, $[B]$, $[C]$, $\cdots$, $[A_o]$, $[B_o]$, $\cdots$ will have only one 1 and the rest 0. So the skeleton matrix $[D]$ of a deterministic automaton will be

$$[D] = [A] + [B] + [C] + \cdots + [H]$$

which is a reduction similar to that in the stochastic automata formulated by Bruce and Fu [1]. For a two-step transition chain, $f_A(q_l,i_j,i_o,q_r)$ will consist of finding the maximum of the minimum of pairs of value of four types as (0,0), (0,1), (1,0), (1,1). Certainly, in order to get a 1 for $f_A(q_l,i_j,i_o,q_r)$, if the path of length 2 exists for input sequence $I_2 = i_j,i_o$, it must have a pair (1,1). The total number of paths of length 2 from state q_l to state q_r will be equal to

$$\bar{d}_{lr} = \sum_{i_j,i_o} f_A(q_l,i_ji_o,q_r).$$

Similarly, for a path of length 3 to exist from q_l to q_r the same operation holds as

$$\bar{d}_{lr} = \sum_{i_j,i_o,i_p} f_A(q_{l,i_j,i_o,i_p,q_r})$$
$$= \sum_{i_j,i_o,i_p} \max q_xq_y \min[f_A(q_l,i_j,q_x), f_A(q_x,i_o,q_y), f_A(q_y,i_p,q_r)], \quad x,y = 1,2,\cdots,n.$$

It consists of terms as (1,1,1), (1,0,1), $\cdots$, (0,0,0); of course, only (1,1,1) defines the existence of the path.

B. *Nondeterministic Automata*

The following definition of a nondeterministic automaton has been used by Ginsburg [7]. A nondeterministic automaton is a quintuple $A = (K,\Sigma,\delta,S_o,F)$, where

- K nonempty finite set of objects (internal states)
- Σ nonempty finite set of objects (input states)
- δ function from $K \times \Sigma$ into 2^K (this includes the empty set ϕ)
- S_o,F subsets of K with S_o nonempty.

To fit this model from the fuzzy automata formulation, the set A is no longer a fuzzy set; it is an ordinary set where f takes only two values, 0 and 1. The entries for each row of the matrices $[A],[B],[C],\cdots$ have either 1 or 0. No restriction has been made to the number of 1 in each row of the matrices. If all the entries of a particular row are zero, then the transition maps the state into the empty set ϕ. If a particular row has more than one 1 then the transition may map the succeeding state into any one of the possible states $(q_i,q_j,\cdots)$. For example, if T_{i_1} is given as

$$T_{i_j} = \begin{bmatrix} 1 & 1 & 0 \\ 0 & 0 & 0 \\ 1 & 1 & 1 \end{bmatrix}$$

then the mapping is as

$i(k)$	
$q(k)$	$q(k+1)$
q_1	$\{q_1, q_2\}$
q_2	ϕ
q_3	$\{q_1, q_2, q_3\}$

C. *Normalized Fuzzy Automata and Its Relation to Stochastic Automata*

One important observation is that the membership function f (from its definition) does not reveal too much of the nature of the function itself except satisfying the following two conditions:

1) f is a "grade of membership" function defined for each $x \in X$;

2) f is in the close interval [0,1].

Thus it is felt that the f function is so general that extra constraints may be incorporated as long as the conditions 1) and 2) are fulfilled. A very special restriction will be the row sum of all transition matrices equal to unity similar to that in stochastic automata. In other words, $[A],[B],[C],\cdots$ have exactly the same structure as that of stochastic matrices. This type of automata can be called normalized fuzzy automata. There are many properties that can be explored for fuzzy automata similar to those for deterministic automata and stochastic automata [8]. They are given in Appendix II.

IV. Fuzzy Automata as Models of Learning Systems

A basic learning system is given in Fig. 1. The proposed model represents a nonsupervised learning system if a proper performance evaluator can be selected [9], [10]. The learning section primarily consists of a composite fuzzy automaton. The performance evaluator serves as an unreliable "teacher" who tries to teach the "student" (the learning section and the decision maker) to make right decisions.

The decision executed by the decision maker is deterministic. Since on-line operation is required, the decision will be based on the maximum grade of membership, i.e., to decide x being from h_i, or $x \sim \omega_i$, if

$$f_{\omega_i}(x) = \max_j f_{\omega_j}(x)$$

with

$$\omega_i,\omega_j \in \Omega, \quad i,j = 1,2,\cdots,R$$

where $\Omega = \{\omega_i : i = 1,2,\cdots,R\}$ denotes the set of pattern classes.

If the decision maker is allowed to stay undecided and defer its decision, especially at the beginning of the first few learning steps, then it will decide $x \sim \omega_i$ if

$$f_{\omega_i}(x) = \max_j f_{\omega_j}(x) \geq C$$

and be undecided if

$$f_{\omega_i}(x) = \max_j f_{\omega_j}(x) < C$$

where $0 < C \leq 1$. Under this condition, the decision maker is allowed to use a pure random strategy for making decisions until it can make a decision with a certain degree of confidence.

For an n-state fuzzy automaton, let $\hat{f}_j(k)$ be the grade of membership for the automaton to be at state q_j in step k. The entries of the fuzzy transition matrix are denoted by

$$f_{ij}^l(k) = f\{q(k) = q_i,\ i(k) = i_l,\ q(k+1) = q_j\}$$

then for input $i(k) = i_l$ and considering definition 1), we have

$$\hat{f}_j(k+1) = \max_m \min\{\hat{f}_m(k), f_{mj}^l(k)\}, \quad m = 1,2,\cdots,n$$

$$= \max\{\min[\hat{f}_m(k),f_{mj}^l(k)];\ \min[\hat{f}_j(k),f_{jj}^l(k)]\},$$

$$m = 1,2,\cdots,n \neq j.$$

Following similar development given by Fu and McLaren [3], the learning behavior is reflected by having nonstationary fuzzy transition matrices with convergent property. In order to simplify the problem, let

$$f_{mj}^l(k) = f_{jj}^l(k-1), \quad \text{for all } m \neq j$$

$$f_{jj}^l(k) = \alpha_j f_{jj}^l(k-1) + (1-\alpha_j)\lambda_j$$

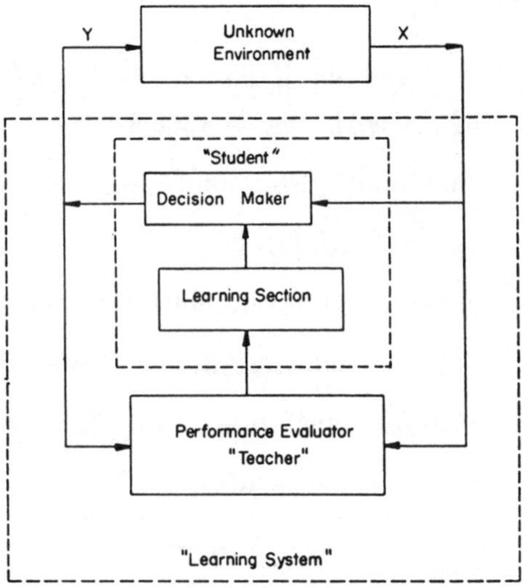

Fig. 1. Basic learning model.

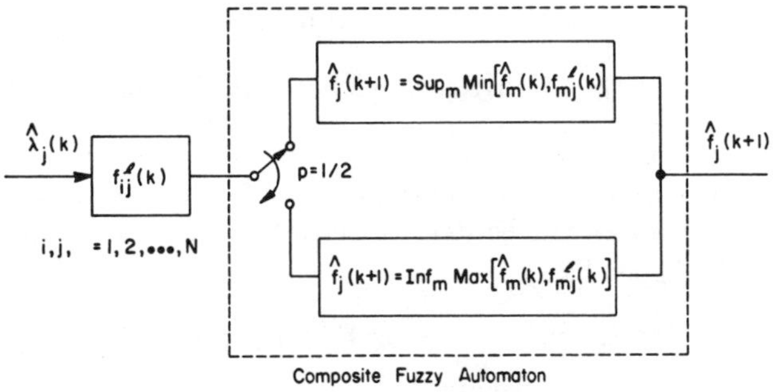

Fig. 2. Learning section.

where $0 < \alpha_j < 1$, $0 < \lambda_j \leq 1$, $j = 1,2,\cdots,n$. The structure of the learning section is illustrated in Fig. 2. The composite automaton switched by $p = 1/2$ constitutes the major part of the learning section; i.e., with $p = 1/2$, the composite fuzzy automaton operates between

1) $$\hat{f}_j(k+1) = \max_m \min[\hat{f}_m(k),f_{mj}^l(k)]$$

and

2) $$\hat{f}_j(k+1) = \min_m \max[\hat{f}_m(k),f_{mj}^l(k)].$$

The fuzzy automaton starts with no a priori information $\hat{f}_j(0) = 0$ or 1 for all j, or with a priori informations $\hat{f}_j(0) = \hat{\lambda}_j(0)$ for all j, $0 \leq \hat{\lambda}_j(0) \leq 1$. The convergence of the above algorithm can be shown as follows:

$$\hat{\lambda}_j(k) \rightarrow \hat{\lambda}_j \text{ as } k \rightarrow \infty.$$

Therefore, $f_{ij}^l(k) \rightarrow \hat{\lambda}_j$ as $k \rightarrow \infty$. The algorithm is said to converge when $\hat{f}_j(k) \rightarrow \hat{\lambda}_j$ as $k \rightarrow \infty$. Therefore, as $k \rightarrow \infty$, we have to show

$$\hat{\lambda}_j = \max_m \min[\hat{f}_m(k),\hat{\lambda}_j] = \min_m \max[\hat{f}_m(k),\hat{\lambda}_j] \quad (2)$$

so as to have the same output $\hat{f}_j(k+1)$. Applying the theorem in Appendix I we know that

$$\min\{\hat{f}_m(k)\} \leq \hat{\lambda}_j \leq \max\{\hat{f}_m(k)\} \quad (3)$$

must hold in order that (2) is true. But, $\hat{f}_j(k) \rightarrow \hat{\lambda}_j$ as $k \rightarrow \infty$. Therefore, (3) is true as $k \rightarrow \infty$. Notice $\hat{f}_j(k) \rightarrow \hat{\lambda}_j$ can be shown as follows. There exists at least one k such that

$$\hat{f}_j(k+1) = \max_m \min[\hat{f}_m(k),\hat{\lambda}_j]$$

followed by

$$\hat{f}_j(k+2) = \min_m \max[\hat{f}_m(k+1),\hat{\lambda}_j], \quad \text{for large } k.$$

Assume $\hat{\lambda}_j > \max_m \hat{f}_m(k)$ (for other value of $\hat{\lambda}_j$, we have $\hat{f}_j(k+1) = \hat{\lambda}_j$). We have $\hat{f}_j(k+1) = \max_m \hat{f}_m(k)$. But $\hat{f}_j(k+2) = \min\{\max[\hat{f}_1(k+1),\hat{\lambda}_j], \cdots, \max[\max_m \hat{f}_m(k), \hat{\lambda}_j] \cdots \max[\hat{f}_N(k+1),\hat{\lambda}_j]\}$. Therefore, $\hat{f}_j(k+2) = \hat{\lambda}_j$; i.e.,

$$\hat{f}_j(k) \rightarrow \hat{\lambda}_j \text{ as } k \rightarrow \infty.$$

V. Applications and Simulation Results

The learning model proposed above has been applied to engineering problems. Emphasis will be placed upon its applications to pattern classification and control systems. Let $Z(k)$ be the instantaneous performance evaluation at the kth step of learning [10]. The performance evaluator $M(Z,k)$ must be such that

$$0 < M(Z,k) \leq T < \infty, \quad k = 1,2, \cdots$$

and

$$\lim_{k \rightarrow \infty} M(Z,k) = M > 0.$$

The goal of the system is to maximize or minimize $M(Z,k)$. Thus $M(Z,k)$ is an estimator of $Z(k)$ at the kth step of learning. As an example,

$$\begin{aligned} M(Z,k) &= \frac{1}{k} \sum_{i=1}^{k} Z(i) \\ &= \frac{k-1}{k}\left[\frac{1}{k-1}\sum_{i=1}^{k-1} Z(i)\right] + \frac{Z(k)}{k} \\ &= \frac{k-1}{k} M(Z,k-1) + \frac{Z(k)}{k}, \quad k = 1,2, \cdots . \end{aligned}$$

In this particular case, $M(Z,k)$ is a sample average of $Z(k)$ estimated recursively at each step of learning.

A. Application to Pattern Classification

A pattern recognition system with nonsupervised learning is given in Fig. 3. The role of input and output can be briefly explained as follows. During each time interval, the pattern classifier receives a new sample X' from the unknown environment. After X' is processed through the receptor, the output is fed to both the decision maker for classification and the performance evaluator for performance evaluation. The performance criterion for the system must be selected so that its maximization or minimization reflects the clustering properties of the pattern classes, i.e., the unknown environment. Therefore, due to the natural distribution of the samples, the performance criterion can be incorporated into the system to serve as a teacher of the learning pattern recognizer.

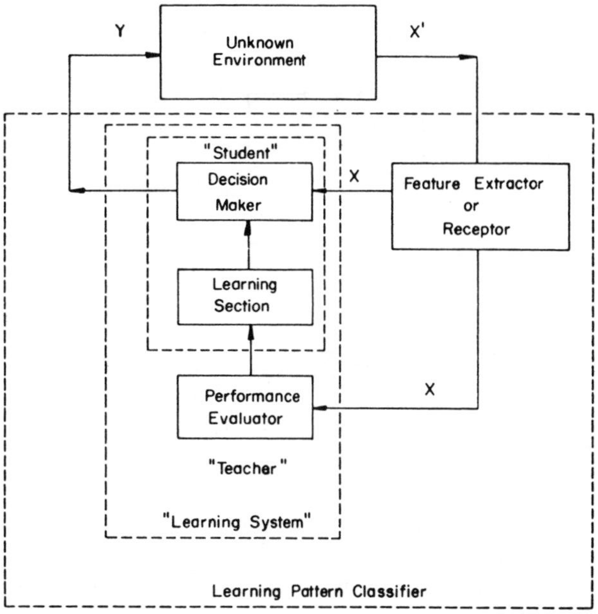

Fig. 3. Learning pattern classifier.

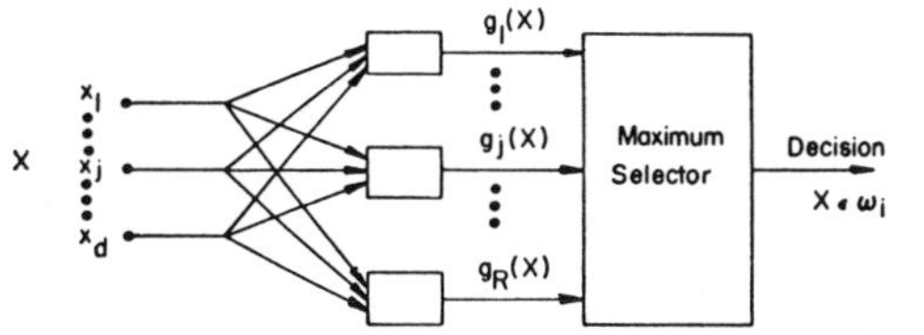

Fig. 4. Multiclass pattern categorizer.

The nonsupervised learning model as applied to the problems of pattern classification is formulated as follows. It is assumed that the classifier (the decision maker) has at its disposal sets of discriminant functions characterized by sets of parameters. With a proper specification of the performance evaluation and without any external supervision, the system adapts itself to the best solution. The best solution denotes the set of discriminant functions that gives the minimum misrecognition among the sets of discriminant functions for the given set of training samples. The criterion to be used in this particular case is based upon the sample averages and the average deviations from the sample averages of training patterns generated by each set of discriminant functions. The best set of discriminant functions must give the maximum total distance between its sample averages and the minimum total sample deviation (average of the squared deviation from the sample averages).

Let $\Omega = \{\omega_i: i = 1,2,\cdots,R\}$ be the set of pattern classes, and $X_1,X_2,\cdots$ be the sequence of incoming samples from the unknown environment in E^d. N sets of discriminant functions are given a priori. The decision maker may assume the structure as shown in Fig. 4.

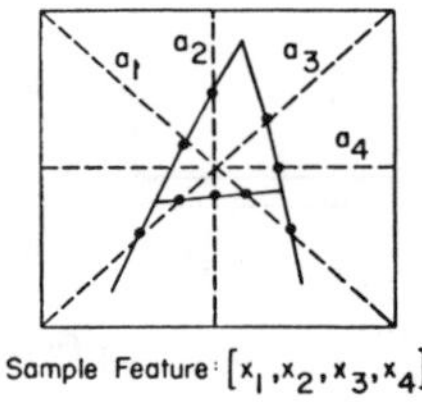

Fig. 5. Description of feature extraction.

Then

$$K_k{}^l = \left|w_1\left[\sum_{i=1}^{R} S_{ki}{}^l\right] - w_2\left[\sum_{i>j} (M_{ki}{}^l - M_{kj}{}^l)'(M_{ki}{}^l - M_{kj}{}^l)\right]\right|, \quad l = 1,2,\cdots,N$$

where

$K_k{}^l$ performance evaluation for lth set of discriminant functions at kth step of learning

$S_{ki}{}^l$ sample deviation for ith class of lth set of discriminant functions at kth step of learning

$M_{ki}{}^l$ sample average for ith class of lth set of discriminant functions at kth step of learning

and

$$0 \leq w_1, w_2 < \infty.$$

The values of the $K_k{}^l$, $S_{ki}{}^l$, and $M_{ki}{}^l$ can be estimated recursively as follows. For the lth set of discriminant functions, if

$$X_{k+1} \sim \omega_i, \quad i = 1,2,\cdots,R$$

then

$$M_{k+1,i} = \frac{N_{k,i}}{N_{k,i}+1} M_{ki} + \frac{X_{k+1}}{N_{k,i}+1}$$

$$S_{k+1,i} = \frac{1}{N_{k,i}+1} \sum_{j=1}^{N_{k,i}+1} (X_j - M_{k+1,i})'(X_j - M_{k+1,i}).$$

After expansion and simplification we have

$$S_{k+1,i} = \frac{N_{k,i}}{M_{k,i}+1} S_{ki} + \frac{N_{k,i}}{(N_{k,i}+1)^2} (X_{k+1} - M_{ki})'(X_{k+1} - M_{ki}).$$

Also,

$$M_{k+1,j} = M_{kj}, \quad \text{for } j \neq i$$

$$S_{k+1,j} = S_{kj}, \quad \text{for } j \neq i.$$

$N_{k,i}$ denotes the number of samples belonging to ω_i up to the kth step of learning. The minimum $K_k{}^l$, $l = 1,2,\cdots,N$, serves to indicate the best solution among the N sets of discriminant functions.

The patterns used in the computer simulations are the three English capital characters A, B, and C. From each character the four features x_1, x_2, x_3, x_4 are extracted. The extracted features correspond to the number of distinct intersections of the sample character with lines a_1, a_2, a_3, a_4 as indicated in Fig. 5. Specific computer simulations are conducted for 1) two equal numbers of training

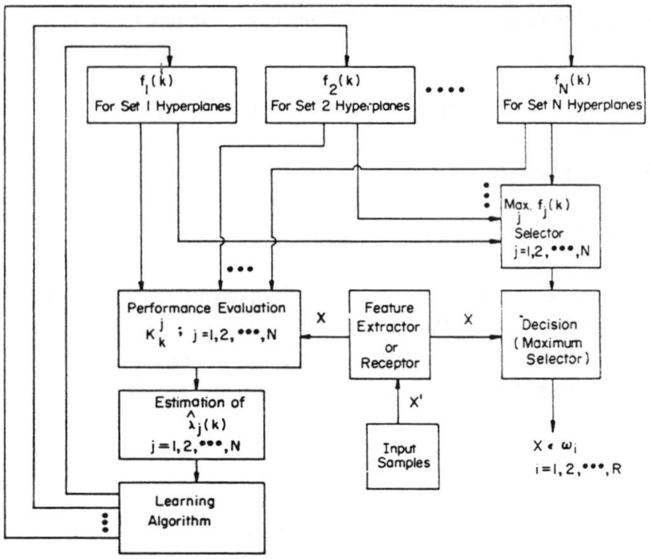

Fig. 6. Computer flow diagram for learning character classifier.

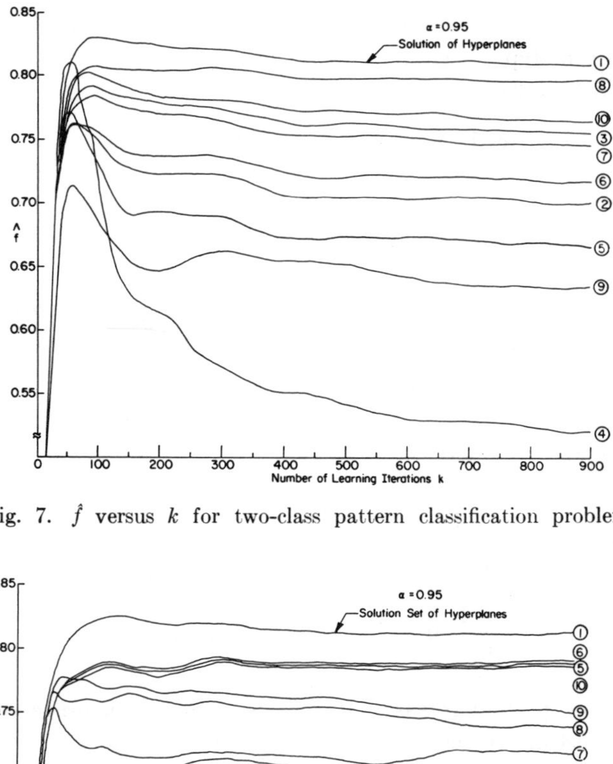

Fig. 7. $\hat{f}$ versus k for two-class pattern classification problem.

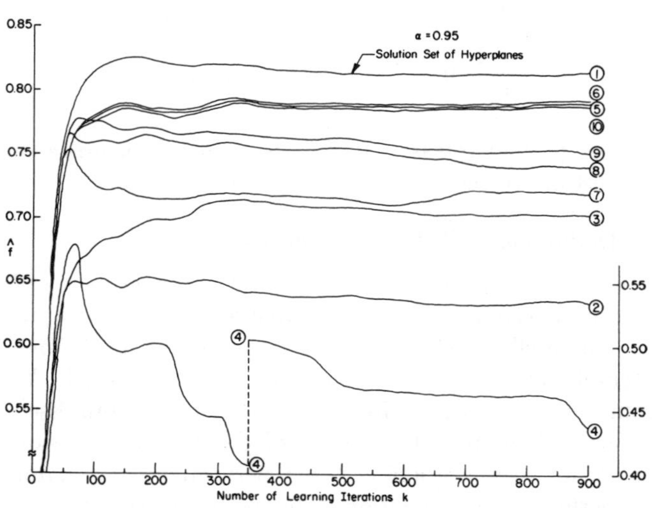

Fig. 8. $\hat{f}$ versus k for three-class pattern classification problem.

characters from A and B using one hyperplane, and 2) three equal numbers of training characters from A, B, and C using three hyperplanes.

The estimation of the N membership functions $\hat{\lambda}_j(k)$ at the kth step of learning is as follows:

$$\hat{\lambda}_j(k) = 1 - \frac{K_k^j}{C}, \quad j = 1,2,\cdots,N;\ k = 1,2,\cdots.$$

$$C \geq \max_{k,j} K_k^j$$

with

$$\lim_{k\to\infty} \hat{\lambda}_j(k) = \hat{\lambda}_j, \quad 0 \leq \hat{\lambda}_j \leq 1.$$

The details of the computer flow diagram are shown in Fig. 6. Ten sets of hyperplanes are used (predetermined) in both examples with 60 samples from each class. The incoming samples are introduced to the system in a random fashion. The results of the learning curves, $f_j(k)$ versus k for each example, are given in Figs. 7 and 8.

B. Application to Control System

The learning controller proposed here is similar to that proposed in [9]. It may be briefly explained as follows. A time-discrete plant may be described as

$$x(k+1) = \phi_{k+1}[x(k), u(k+1)]$$

where

$$x(k),\ x(k+1) \in \Omega_x = \{x_i: i = 1,2,\cdots,P;\ P < \infty\}$$

and

$$u(k) \in \Omega_u \triangleq \{u_i: i = 1,2,\cdots,P;\ P < \infty\}.$$

$x(k)$ is the observed response of the plant at the $(k+1)$th instant when the control action $u(k+1)$ is applied. It is assumed that ϕ_k is not known for $k = 1,2,\cdots$. The instantaneous performance evaluation of a control action $u(k)$ is given by

$$Z(k+1) = g(x(k), u(k+1), x(k+1))$$

with

$$0 < Z(k) < T < \infty, \quad k = 1,2,3,\cdots.$$

The goal of the control is to minimize $\hat{M}_{k+1}(Z|u(k), x(k), u(k+1))$, and the sample average of Z. The sample average for each control policy is estimated as follows. Let $+\ u(k+1) = u_l$ be applied after observing $u(k) = u_j$ and $x(k) = x_i$, then

$$\hat{M}_{k+1}[Z|u_j,x_i,u_l] = \frac{N}{N+1}\hat{M}_k[Z|u_j,x_i,u_l] + \frac{1}{N+1}\cdot Z(k+1)$$

$$\hat{M}_{k+1}[Z|u_j,x_i,u_h] = \hat{M}_k[Z|u_j,x_i,u_h], \quad h = 1,2,\cdots,P,\ h \neq l$$

where $N = N(j,i,l)$ denotes the number of occurrences of $u(k) = u_j$, $x(k) = x_i$, $u(k+1) = u_l$.

$$\hat{f}_{k+1}[u_l|u_j,x_i] = 1 - \frac{\hat{M}_{k+1}[Z|u_j,x_i,u_l]}{T}. \tag{4}$$

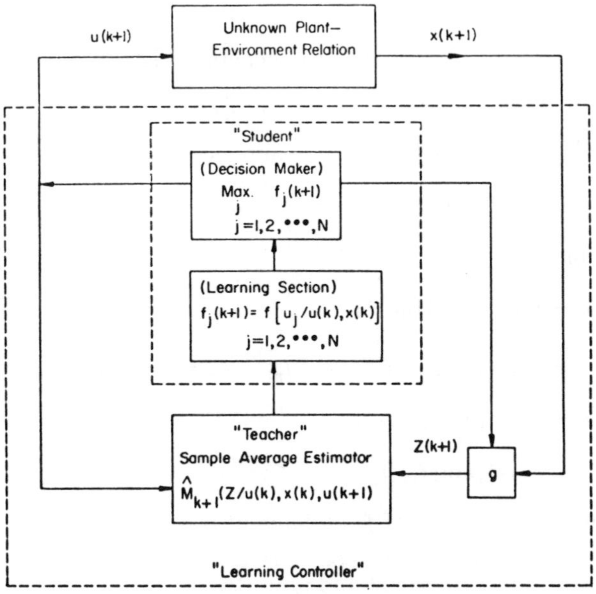

Fig. 9. Proposed learning controller.

Equation (4) enables the system to associate the control action with the maximum grade of membership with the minimum sample average of Z. Fig. 9 illustrates the learning controller.

VI. Conclusion

A class of fuzzy automata is formulated. Its application as a model of learning systems is proposed. A nonsupervised learning algorithm for a fuzzy automaton is presented, together with its application to pattern recognition and automatic control problems. Computer simulations of character recognition indicate satisfactory results.

Appendix I

Lemma 1

$$\min\{\max_j[\min_i f_{ji}], f_k\} = \max_j[\min_i(f_{ji},f_k)],$$

$$i = 1,2,\cdots,N < \infty;\ j = 1,2,\cdots,n < \infty.$$

Lemma 2

$$\max\{\min_j[\max_i f_{ji}],f_k\} = \min_j[\max_i(f_{ji},f_k)],$$

$$i = 1,2,\cdots,N < \infty;\ j = 1,2,\cdots,n < \infty.$$

Proof of Lemmas 1 and 2 is simple and therefore omitted.

Theorem

The necessary and sufficient condition for

$$\min_j[\max_i(f_{ji},f_k)] = \max_j[\min_i(f_{ji},f_k)] = f_k$$

is that

$$\min_j[\max_i f_{ji}] \leq f_k \leq \max_j[\min_i f_{ji}],$$

$$i = 1,2,\cdots,N < \infty;\ j = 1,2,\cdots,n < \infty.$$

Proof:

1) *Necessity:* Without loss of generality let

a) $f_{j1} = \max_i f_{jt} \geq f_{jN} = \min_i f_{jt}$

b) $f_{p1} = \max_j f_{j1} \geq f_{qN} = \min_j f_{jN}$

c) $f_{\delta N} = \max_j f_{jN}; f_{\alpha 1} = \min_j f_{j1}$.

We have

$$F_1 = \min_j [\max_i (f_{jt}, f_k)]$$
$$= \min\{\max(f_{11}, f_k), \cdots, f_{p1}, \cdots, \max(f_{n1}, f_k)\}$$
$$F_2 = \max_j [\min_i (f_{jt}, f_k)]$$
$$= \max\{\min(f_{1N}, f_k), \cdots, f_{qN}, \cdots, \min(f_{nN}, f_k)\}.$$

Assuming the value of f_k at different regions, one can show that if $F_1 = F_2 = f_k$, then $f_{\alpha 1} \leq f_k \leq f_{\delta N}$.

2) *Sufficiency:* Trivial and is omitted.

Appendix II
Properties of Fuzzy Automata

There are several parallel properties that can be explored from fuzzy automata similar to those of deterministic automata and the probabilitic automata. In this appendix only ergodic, stationary, periodic, and aperiodic fuzzy transiton matrices are discussed. The numerical illustrations are given not only to lay bare the specific property of fuzzy automata but also to furnish computational examples of the concepts discussed. In these examples definition 1) is used. Therefore, the computational procedure of Section II is followed.

There are instances that, after a certain number of iterations of identical inputs, the overall fuzzy transition matrix remains the same. For example, let

$$[T_{i_1}]^{(1)} = \begin{bmatrix} 0.9 & 0.5 & 0.3 \\ 0.2 & 0.4 & 0.95 \\ 0.8 & 0.1 & 0.25 \end{bmatrix}$$

then

$$[T_{i_1}]^{(2)} = \begin{bmatrix} 0.9 & 0.5 & 0.5 \\ 0.8 & 0.4 & 0.4 \\ 0.8 & 0.5 & 0.3 \end{bmatrix}$$

$$[T_{i_1}]^{(3)} = \begin{bmatrix} 0.9 & 0.5 & 0.5 \\ 0.8 & 0.5 & 0.4 \\ 0.8 & 0.5 & 0.5 \end{bmatrix}$$

$$[T_{i_1}]^{(4)} = \begin{bmatrix} 0.9 & 0.5 & 0.5 \\ 0.8 & 0.5 & 0.5 \\ 0.8 & 0.5 & 0.5 \end{bmatrix}$$
$$= [T_{i_1}]^{(5)} = \cdots = [T_{i_1}]^{(n)} = \cdots.$$

A stationary fuzzy transition matrix having the property $[T_{i_j}]^{(n)} \rightarrow T$ as $n \rightarrow \infty$ is called an ergodic fuzzy transition matrix. Certain stationary fuzzy transition matrices have no erodic property but have periodic property. This property is illustrated by the following examples.

Example 1

$$[T_i]^{(1)} = \begin{bmatrix} 0.3 & 1.0 \\ 0.8 & 0.1 \end{bmatrix}$$

$$[T_i]^{(2)} = \begin{bmatrix} 0.8 & 0.3 \\ 0.3 & 0.8 \end{bmatrix}$$

$$[T_i]^{(3)} = \begin{bmatrix} 0.3 & 0.8 \\ 0.8 & 0.3 \end{bmatrix}$$

$$[T_i]^{(4)} = \begin{bmatrix} 0.8 & 0.3 \\ 0.3 & 0.8 \end{bmatrix}$$

The matrix keeps oscillating between

$$\begin{bmatrix} 0.3 & 0.8 \\ 0.8 & 0.3 \end{bmatrix} \text{ and } \begin{bmatrix} 0.8 & 0.3 \\ 0.3 & 0.8 \end{bmatrix}$$

and the period of oscillation is 2.

Example 2

$$[T_i]^{(1)} = \begin{bmatrix} 0.3 & 0.4 & 0.7 \\ 0.9 & 0.1 & 0.6 \\ 0.5 & 0.8 & 0.2 \end{bmatrix}$$

$$[T_i]^{(2)} = \begin{bmatrix} 0.5 & 0.7 & 0.4 \\ 0.5 & 0.6 & 0.7 \\ 0.8 & 0.4 & 0.6 \end{bmatrix}$$

$$[T_i]^{(3)} = \begin{bmatrix} 0.7 & 0.4 & 0.6 \\ 0.6 & 0.7 & 0.6 \\ 0.5 & 0.6 & 0.7 \end{bmatrix}$$

$$[T_i]^{(4)} = \begin{bmatrix} 0.5 & 0.6 & 0.7 \\ 0.7 & 0.6 & 0.6 \\ 0.6 & 0.7 & 0.6 \end{bmatrix}$$

$$[T_i]^{(5)} = \begin{bmatrix} 0.6 & 0.7 & 0.6 \\ 0.6 & 0.6 & 0.7 \\ 0.7 & 0.6 & 0.6 \end{bmatrix}$$

$$[T_i]^{(6)} = \begin{bmatrix} 0.7 & 0.6 & 0.6 \\ 0.6 & 0.7 & 0.6 \\ 0.6 & 0.7 & 0.7 \end{bmatrix}$$

$$[T_i]^{(7)} = \begin{bmatrix} 0.6 & 0.7 & 0.7 \\ 0.7 & 0.6 & 0.6 \\ 0.6 & 0.7 & 0.6 \end{bmatrix}$$

$$[T_i]^{(8)} = \begin{bmatrix} 0.6 & 0.7 & 0.6 \\ 0.6 & 0.7 & 0.7 \\ 0.7 & 0.6 & 0.6 \end{bmatrix}$$

$$[T_i]^{(9)} = [T_i]^{(6)}; [T_i]^{(10)} = [T_i]^{(7)}; [T_i]^{(11)} = [T_i]^{(8)}, \cdots.$$

Example 2 has a period equal to 3. From these examples one can say that ergodicity has a period equal to 1. A fuzzy transition matrix having a period of length 1 is considered as an aperiodic fuzzy transition matrix.

References

[1] G. D. Bruce and K. S. Fu, "A model for finite-state probabilistic systems," *Proc. 1st Ann. Allerton Conf. Circuit and Systems Theory*, 1963.
[2] G. H. Mealy, "Method for synthesizing sequential circuits," *Bell Sys. Tech. J.*, vol. 34, 1955.
[3] K. S. Fu and R. W. McLaren, "An application of stochastic automata to the synthesis of learning systems," School of Elec. Engrg., Purdue University, Tech. Rept. TR-EE65-17, April 1965.
[4] L. A. Zadeh, "Fuzzy sets," *Information and Control*, vol. 8, pp. 338–353, June 1965.
[5] ——, "Fuzzy sets and systems," *Proc. 1965 Symp. on System Theory* (Brooklyn, N. Y.).
[6] E. S. Santos and W. G. Wee, "General formulation of sequential machines," *Information and Control*, vol. 12, pp. 5–10, January 1968.
[7] S. Ginsburg, *An Introduction to Mathematical Machine Theory*. Reading, Mass.: Addison-Wesley, 1962.
[8] W. G. Wee, "On generalizations of adaptive algorithm and application of the fuzzy sets concept to pattern classification," Ph.D. dissertation, Purdue University, Lafayette, Ind., June 1967.
[9] Z. J. Nikolic and K. S. Fu, "An algorithm for learning without external supervision and its applications to learning control systems," *IEEE Trans. Automatic Control*, vol. AC-11, pp. 414–422, July 1966.
[10] ——, "A mathematical model of learning in an unknown random environment," *Proc. 1966 NEC*, vol. 22, pp. 607–612.

Fuzzy Neural Networks

SAMUEL C. LEE
Department of Electrical Engineering,
University of Houston, Houston, Texas

AND

EDWARD T. LEE
Department of Electrical Sciences, State University of New York
at Stony Brook, Stony Brook, New York

Communicated by Lawrence Stark

ABSTRACT

In this paper, the McCulloch-Pitts model of a neuron is extended to a more general model which allows the activity of a neuron to be a "fuzzy" rather than an "all-or-none" process. The generalized model is called a *fuzzy neuron*. Some basic properties of fuzzy neural networks as well as their applications to the synthesis of fuzzy automata are investigated. It is shown that any n-state minimal fuzzy automaton can be realized by a network of m fuzzy neurons, where $\lceil \log_2 n \rceil < m < 2n$. Examples are given to illustrate the procedure. As an example of application, a realization of fuzzy language recognizer using a fuzzy neural network is presented. The techniques described in this paper may be of use in the study of neural networks as well as in language, pattern recognition, and learning.

1. INTRODUCTION

In the nearly three decades since its publication, the pioneering work of McCulloch and Pitts [1], has had a profound influence on the development of the theory of neural nets, in addition to stimulating much of the early work in automata theory and regular events [2–12].

Although the McCulloch-Pitts model of a neuron has contributed a great deal to the understanding of the behavior of neural-like systems, it fails to reflect the fact that the behavior of even the simplest type of nerve cell exhibits not only randomness but, more importantly, a type of imprecision which is associated with the lack of sharp transition from the occurrence of an event to its nonoccurrence.

It is possible that a better model for the behavior of a nerve cell may be provided by what might be called a *fuzzy* neuron, which is a generalization of the McCulloch-Pitts model. The concept of a fuzzy neuron employs some of the concepts and techniques of the theory of fuzzy sets which was introduced by Zadeh [13, 14] and applied to the theory of automata by Wee and Fu [15], Tanaka et al. [16], Santos [17] and others. In effect, the introduction of fuzziness into the model of a neuron makes it better adapted to the study of the behavior of systems which are imprecisely defined by virtue of their high degree of complexity. Many of the biological systems, economic systems, urban systems, and, more generally, large-scale systems fall into this category.

In what follows, we shall present a preliminary account of a theory of fuzzy neural networks stressing its relations to automata and languages. Biogically oriented applications of this theory will be presented in subsequent papers.

2. FUZZY SETS

Essentially, a fuzzy set is a class with unsharp boundaries in which the transition from membership to nonmembership is gradual rather than abrupt. For example, the class of *tall man* is a fuzzy set, as are the classes labeled *middle-aged, small, red,* etc..

A fuzzy set A in a space X is defined by its *membership function* μ_A which associates with each point x in X its *grade of membership* $\mu_A(x)$ in A. $\mu_A(x)$ is usually assume to be a number in the interval [0, 1], with 0 and 1 representing nonmembership and full membership respectively.

If X is a finite set $X=\{x_1,\ldots,x_n\}$, and is convenient to represent a fuzzy set A in X as a linear combination

$$A=\mu_1 x_1+\cdots+\mu_n x_n,$$

where μ_i is the grade of membership of x_i in A. For example, if X is a group of four men named John, Tom, Dick, and Jim, and A is the fuzzy set of tall men in X, then we can write symbolically

$$X=\text{John}+\text{Tom}+\text{Dick}+\text{Jim},$$

and

$$A=0.8\,\text{John}+0.6\,\text{Tom}+0.9\,\text{Dick}+0.4\,\text{Jim}. \tag{1}$$

A basic attribute of a nonfuzzy set A is its cardinality, $|A|$, that is, the number of elements belonging to A. Since the notion of belonging loses its meaning when A is a fuzzy set, it is not meaningful to speak of the number of elements in a fuzzy set. However, the notion of cardinality may be extended to fuzzy sets [24] by defining $|A|$ in a more general sense as

$$|A|=\sum_i \mu_i,$$

with the summation ranging over all elements in X which have a positive grade of membership in A. For example, in the case of (1), we have

$$|A|=0.8+0.6+0.9+0.4=2.7.$$

This notion of cardinality will be used in our definition of a fuzzy neuron.

3. FUZZY NEURONS

First, let us review the assumptions underlying the McCulloch and Pitts model of a cell (neuron) [1]. They are

(1) the activity of the cell is an "all-or-none" process;

(2) a certain fixed number of synapses must be excited within the period of latent addition in order to excite a cell at any time, and this number is independent of previous activity and position on the cell;

(3) the only significant delay within the cell is synaptic delay;

(4) the activity of any inhibitory synapse absolutely prevents excitation of the cell at that time;

(5) the structure of a neural network does not change with time.

Based on these five assumptions, McCulloch and Pitts [1] proposed the following model for modeling the logical aspect of a neuron.

DEFINITION 1.

A *McCulloch-Pitts neuron* is a multi-input and multi-output memory system:

(1) It has two types of inputs: excitatory and inhibitory. It is assumed that they can only take on values 0 and 1. The excitatory inputs and the inhibitory inputs of the neuron will be denoted by $e_j(k)$ and $i_j(k)$, which are symbollically represented by $\rightarrow$ and —• , respectively.

(2) The threshold of the neuron is a positive integer n.

(3) The firing rules of the neuron are:

(a) all the inhibitory inputs to the neuron must be 0;

(b) the sum of all e_j's to the neuron must be equal to or greater than the threshold n.

When both of these conditions are met at time k, the neuron will fire at time $k+1$.

(4) The outputs of the neuron are 1 when it is firing and are 0 when it is quiet.

A McCulloch-Pitts neuron is depicted in Fig. 1(a).

DEFINITION 2.

A *McCulloch-Pitts neural network* is a collection of interconnected McCulloch-Pitts neurons. Each neuron in the network receives one input from the input of the network which may be excitatory or inhibitory. In addition to this input from the network input, it may also receive other excitatory and inhibitory inputs which are the outputs of the neurons in the network including itself. An example of McCulloch-Pitts neural network is shown in Fig. 1(b). The analysis of McCulloch-Pitts neural networks may be found for example in Minsky [18].

Our model differs from the McCulloch-Pitts model mainly in the replacement of the first of the above assumptions with the less restrictive assumption.

(1′) The activity of the cell is a "fuzzy" process.[1]

This leads us to the following definition.

DEFINITION 3.

A *fuzzy neuron* is a McCulloch-Pitts neuron with the following modification:

(1) $0 \leqslant e_j(k), \quad i_j(k) \leqslant 1,$ (2)

$e_j(k)$ stands for the "degree" to which the jth excitatory input is excited at time k, where the excitatory input is denoted by an arrow $\rightarrow$. Thus, the input is assumed to be a fuzzy set

$$E = e_1(k)E_1 + e_2(k)E_2 + \cdots + e_m(k)E_m,$$

where E_i is a label for the ith excitatory input. $i_j(k)$ stands for the jth inhibitory input at time k, where the inhibitory input is denoted by a circle — o.

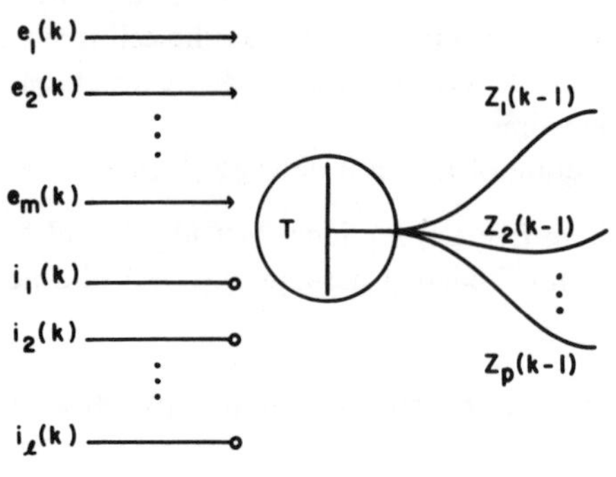

FIG. 1. A fuzzy neuron.

[1]Informally, a fuzzy process is a finite sequence of fuzzy operation. A formal definition of fuzzy process is given in Section 5.

(2) The threshold of the neuron is a positive *real* number.

(3) The outputs z_j's of the neuron are equal to some positive numbers μ_j's, $0 < \mu_j \leq 1$, if it is firing and are zero if it is quiet, i.e.,

$$z_j = \left\{ \begin{array}{ll} \mu_j & \text{if the neuron is firing} \\ 0 & \text{if the neuron is quiet} \end{array} \right\}$$

μ_j denotes the "degree" to which the jth output is fired. Thus, the output is assumed to be a fuzzy set Z

$$Z = \mu_1 Z_1 + \cdots + \mu_p Z_p,$$

where Z_j is a label for the jth output.

(4) The firing rules of the neurons are

(i) all the inhibitory inputs must be 0;

(ii) the sum of all e_i's must be equal to or greater than the threshold T of the neuron, i.e.,

$$\text{Neuron firing if } |E| \geq \text{threshold}, \tag{3}$$

when both of the above two firing rules are satisfied at time $t = k$, the neuron will fire at time $t = k+1$, otherwise the fuzzy neuron remains in the quiet state.

A fuzzy neuron is depicted in Fig. 2(a).

DEFINITION 4.

A fuzzy network is defined exactly the same way as a McCulloch-Pitts neural network except its components are fuzzy neurons. A fuzzy neural network is shown in Fig. 2(b).

Two remarks about the fuzzy neuron and the fuzzy neural network should be made here.

(1) The inhibition caused by a nonzero inhibitory input of a fuzzy neuron is assumed to be absolute, which means that if any one of the inhibitory inputs is nonzero, the neuron will cease to fire regardless of the status of its excitatory inputs. This is the same assumption made in the McCulloch-Pitts neuron.

(2) A fuzzy neuron is neither nondeterministic nor probabilistic. It is a fuzzy system [13, 14, 23], so is a fuzzy neural network.

In what follows, we shall present a general synthesis procedure for reasider the analysis of networks composed of fuzzy neurons, namely, the fuzzy neural networks.

4. ANALYSIS OF FUZZY NEURAL NETWORKS

It has been shown [18] that any (nonfuzzy) neural network is a finite state automaton. The state of a neural network is determined by the Cartesian product of the states (firing or quiet) of the neurons. The derivation of a state diagram from a fuzzy neural network is best illustrated by the use of an example.

Consider the network of Fig. 2(b). Assume that the initial state is the one where neuron A is firing (F) and neurons B and C are quiet (Q). In order to obtain the state transition diagram, we must first find the *fuzzy state transition tree* of the network which is described as follows:

(1) Apply the input symbol 0 to the initial state ($A = F, B = Q, C = Q$) and find the next states of the neurons A, B, and C by Definition 3. For example,

$$\left. \begin{array}{l} A = F \\ B = Q \\ C = Q \end{array} \right\} \xrightarrow{\text{input}=0} \left\{ \begin{array}{l} A = Q \\ B = Q \\ C = F \end{array} \right.$$

The next states of the neurons A, B, and C of the initial state with an input 1 applied are obtained similarly. Display them as shown in Fig. 2(c).

(2) Repeat (1). A branch b of level k will terminate if the k-level leaf associated with the branch b has appeared in the first k levels.

(3) The process ends when all the branches are terminated.

(4) The final step is to determine the grade of membership ρ of the state transition from the μ_i's, which is defined as follows:

DEFINITION 5.

Define the σ_i of a firing neuron as

$$\sigma_i = \max[\mu_1, \mu_2, \ldots, \mu_s], \tag{4}$$

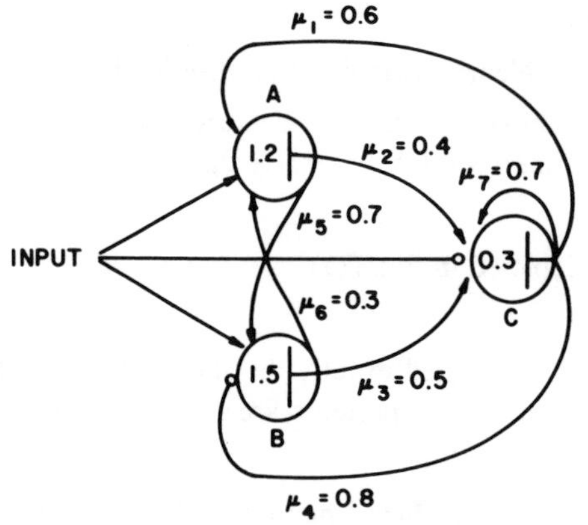

FIG. 2(a). A neural network.

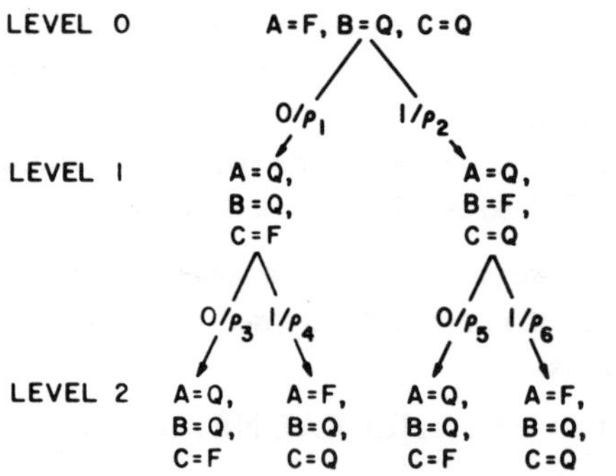

FIG. 2(b). The state transition tree of the network.

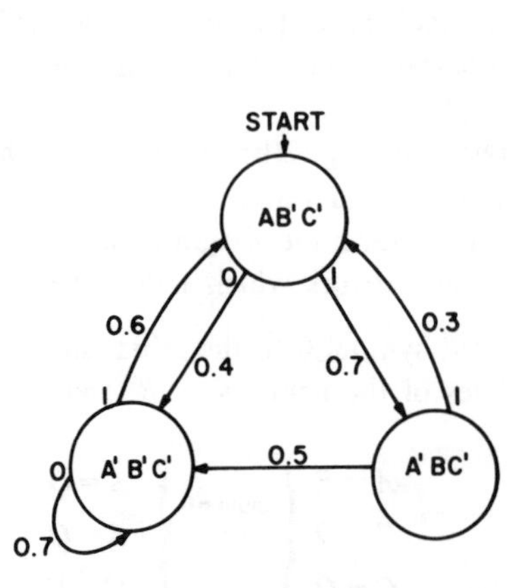

FIG. 2(c). The state diagram of the network.

and the σ_i of a quiet neuron to be zero, where μ_i are the inputs to the neuron at the time $t=k$, excluding the input of the network at time $t=k$.

We postulate that the membership ρ of the state transition from the state at time k to the state at time $k+1$ is given by

$$\rho=\min[\sigma_1,\ldots,\sigma_{m_f}], \tag{5}$$

where m_f is the number of firing neurons at time $t=k+1$. The ρ so defined implies that each firing neuron has at least one input whose value is greater than or equal to ρ.

The complete fuzzy state transition tree of the neural network of Fig. 2(b) is shown in Fig. 2(c) and the grades of membership ρ_i of the state transitions are tabulated in Table 1. For simplicity, we shall abbreviate a firing neuron and a quiet neuron by the capital letter with a prime. For instance, the initial state is abbreviated by $AB'C'$. Using the states, the state transition diagram of the network is given in Fig. 2(d).

It should be remarked here that the state transition tree of a neural network containing n neurons, can have *at most* 2^n levels, which, in this example is $2^3=8$.

5. SYNTHESIS OF FUZZY AUTOMATA BY FUZZY NEURONS

A fuzzy automaton is based on a fuzzy process which is formally defined as follows:

DEFINITION 6.

A (finite) process in discrete time with a discrete state space $K=(q_1,q_2,\ldots,q_n)$ is called a (finite) *fuzzy process* if it satisfies the following conditions:

(1) The matrix $\mathbf{F}$ which describes the state transition has the following form

$$\mathbf{F}=\begin{array}{c} \\ q_1\\ q_2\\ \vdots\\ q_n\end{array}\begin{array}{c}\begin{array}{cccc} q_1 & q_2 & \cdots & q_n\end{array}\\ \begin{bmatrix}\rho_{11} & \rho_{12} & \cdots & \rho_{1n}\\ \rho_{21} & \rho_{22} & \cdots & \rho_{2n}\\ \vdots & \vdots & & \vdots\\ \rho_{n1} & \rho_{n2} & \cdots & \rho_{nn}\end{bmatrix}\end{array},$$

where $0\leqslant\rho_{ij}\leqslant 1$, denotes the grade of membership of state transition from state q_i to state q_j. This matrix will be called *fuzzy state transition matrix* of the fuzzy process.

(2) Let M be a fuzzy set defined on K, and let

$$w_M^{(0)}=[\eta_{q_1}^{(0)},\eta_{q_2}^{(0)},\ldots,\eta_{q_n}^{(0)}]$$

be a row-vector, called *initial state designator of A*, where $\eta_{q_1}^{(0)}$ is the grade of membership of q_i with respect to M at time $t=0$. Then the state designator of M at $t=k$,

$$w_M^{(k)}=[\eta_{q_1}^{(k)},\eta_{q_2}^{(k)},\ldots,\eta_{q_n}^{(k)}]$$

is obtained by

$$w_M^{(k)}=w_M^{(0)}\circ\underbrace{(\mathbf{F}\circ\mathbf{F}\circ\cdots\circ\mathbf{F})}_{(k-1)\text{ operations}}$$

$$=w_M^{(0)}\circ\mathbf{F}^k=w_M^{(0)}\circ[\rho_{ij}^{(k)}], \tag{6}$$

TABLE 1
The Values of ρ_i of the State Transition of the Neural Network of Fig. 2(b)

ρ_1	0.4	ρ_4	0.6
ρ_2	0.7	ρ_5	0.5
ρ_3	0.7	ρ_6	0.3

where

$$\rho_{ij}^{(k)} = \max_{\substack{\text{overall parallel paths} \\ \text{from } q_i \text{ to } q_j \text{ with } (k-1) \\ \text{numbers of transitions}}} \left\{ \min_{\substack{\text{overall series paths} \\ \text{from } q_i \text{ to } q_j \text{ with } (k-1) \\ \text{numbers of transitions}}} \{\rho_{i_1}, \rho_{l_1 l_2}, \ldots, \rho l_{(k-1)} j\} \right\}. \quad (7)$$

COMMENTS

(1) The fuzzy state transition matrix **F** of a fuzzy process resembles somewhat to stochastic matrix of a Markov chain for $0 \leqslant \rho_{ij} \leqslant 1$; however, in general $\sum_{k=1}^{n} \rho_{ik} = 1$, for all i.

(2) The reason we use the max min (7) rule in defining $\rho_{ij}^{(k)}$ is that the state transition from q_i to q_j in a fuzzy process may be considered as water (gas, electricity, traffic flow, etc.) flow through a water supply system of which the water pipes are series-parallel interconnected.

(3) When ρ_{ij} takes only two values 0 and 1, the process becomes a *nondeterministic process*. In addition, if only any one element of each row of matrix F is 1 and the remaining elements of each row are equal to 0, then the process is a *deterministic process*.

A Fuzzy Finite Automaton (FFA)' and the grade of acceptance are defined in Definition A.1 and Definition A.2.

Let Σ^* denote the set of all input sequences (tapes) including the empty word ϵ over a finite set of alphabets Σ, then the domain of **F** is ex empty word and I_n is $n \times n$ identity matrix:

$$\mathbf{F}(\sigma_{i_1}\sigma_{i_2}\cdots\sigma_{i_k}) = \mathbf{F}(\sigma_{i_1}) \circ \mathbf{F}(\sigma_{i_2}) \circ \cdots \circ \mathbf{F}(\sigma_{i_k}),$$

$$= [\rho_{ij}^{(k)}],$$

$$k \geqslant 2 \quad \text{and} \quad \sigma_{i_j} \in \Sigma, \qquad j = 1, 2, \ldots, k, \quad (8)$$

The symbol $\circ$ denotes the max min, operation, and $\rho_{ij}^{(k)}$ is defined as in (7).

In the previous section, it has been shown that a fuzzy neural network is a fuzzy finite state automaton (FFSA) or automaton (FFA). Then it is natural to ask the question: For a given fuzzy automaton transition diagram, can we always find a fuzzy neural network realizing it? The answer is yes. We shall begin this discussion by introducing the following definitions.

DEFINITION 7.

Let M be a FFA and q be a state of M. State q is said to be *homogeneous* if all the state transition lines of the state diagram of M incident to q are driven by the same input; otherwise we call it a *nonhomogeneous state*. If the input space is (0, 1), the homogeneous state driven by 1 and 0, are, called *1-state* and *0-state*, respectively.

For example, in Fig. 2(d), the states $AB'C'$ and $A'BC'$ are 1-states, and the states $A'B'C$ is a 0-states.

DEFINITION 8.

A FFA M is *homogeneous* if all its states are homogeneous, otherwise it is *nonhomogeneous*.

For example, the automaton of Fig. 2(d) is a homogeneous automaton.

PART A. SYNTHESIS OF STATE TRANSITION DIAGRAM

Part A-1. Synthesis of Homogeneous FFA

The synthesis procedure is illustrated by the following example.

Example 1. Consider the automaton M_1, described by the state diagram of Fig. 3(a).

(1) For a homogeneous automaton M with n states $A, B, C, \ldots$, use n neurons. Each of the neurons is labeled by $A, B, C, \ldots$.

(2) Classify the 1-states and 0-states of the automaton A: 1-state and B, C, D: 0-states.

(3) Define the identity mapping ϕ from the set of n states onto the set of n neurons as $\phi(X) = X$, $X = A, B, C, \ldots$.

(4) Start with the input node, and draw a line to $\phi(X)$ with an excitatory input if X is a 1-state and with an inhibitory input if X is a 0-state. We shall call the neuron $\phi(X)$ a 1-neuron and 0-neuron if X is a 1-state and 0-state, respectively.

(5) Draw additional lines with excitatory inputs from the output of $\phi(X)$ to the input of $\phi(Y)$ for all state transitions from state X to state Y.

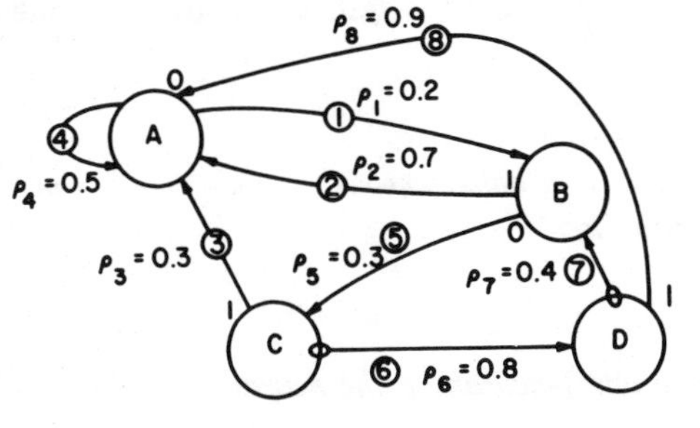

FIG. 3(a). The state diagram of automaton M_1.

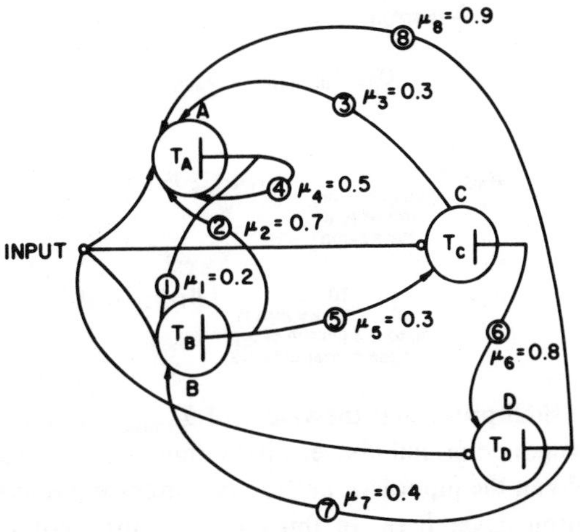

FIG. 3(b). Its fuzzy neural network realization.

(6) Define a one-to-one mapping ϕ from the n states of the automaton into the states of the n neurons as follows:

the n states of the automaton		the states of the n neurons
A	$\xrightarrow{\phi}$	$AB'C'\cdots$
B	$\xrightarrow{\phi}$	$A'BC'\cdots$
C	$\xrightarrow{\phi}$	$A'B'C\cdots$

....

(7) Determine the threshold values of the neurons. The way of determining the threshold values of the neurons is to construct the state transition table of the neural network of Fig. 4.3(b) according to the state transition diagram of M_1.

If state X to state Y is by an input a (either 0 or 1), then the state of the n neurons $\phi(X)$ to $\phi(Y)$ is by the same input a. This is shown in Table 2.

We find that the ranges of the threshold values of the fuzzy neurons are

$$0.9 < T_A \leqslant 1.3,$$

$$0 < T_B \leqslant 0.2,$$

$$0 < T_C \leqslant 0.3,$$

$$0 < T_D \leqslant 0.8.$$

The fuzzy neural network realization of automaton M_1 is shown in Fig. 3(b).

The way of determining the threshold values of the neurons described in step 7 of the above procedure is rather tedious. We shall prove that it is unnecessary.

THEOREM 1.

In the realization of a homogeneous automaton, the range of the threshold values of a 1*-neuron is*

$$\mu_{\max} < T_{1\text{-neuron}} \leqslant 1 + \mu_{\min}, \tag{9}$$

when there is only one 1*-neuron, in the neural network and*

$$1 < T_{1\text{-neuron}} \leqslant 1 + \mu_{\min}, \tag{10}$$

when there are more than one 1*-neuron in the neural network and the range of the threshold values a* 0*-neuron is*

$$0 < T_{0\text{-neuron}} \leqslant \mu_{\min}, \tag{11}$$

where

$$\mu_{\min} = \min_{\substack{\text{all excitatory} \\ \text{inputs } \mu_i \text{ to} \\ \text{the neuron}}} [\mu_1, \mu_2, \ldots, \mu_v], \tag{12}$$

$$\mu_{\max} = \max_{\substack{\text{all excitatory inputs} \\ \mu_i \text{ to the neuron except} \\ \text{to the neural network}}} [\mu_1, \mu_2, \ldots, \mu_r]. \tag{13}$$

Proof. We shall prove that the values of $T_{1\text{-neuron}}$ and $T_{0\text{-neuron}}$ cannot be outside the ranges described above. First consider the 0-neuron case shown in Fig. 4(a). When the input is 1, i.e., the inhibitory input having input value of 1, the neuron never fires. In this case, no information is provided in determining the threshold value of the neuron. Consider the case where the

TABLE 2
The State Transition Table and the Requirement on the Threshold Values of the Neurons of the Neural Network of Fig. 3(b).

	INPUT 0		INPUT 1	
Present State	Next State	Requirement on the Value T of the Threshold	Next State	Requirement on the Value T of the Threshold
A	A'	$T_A>0.5$	A	$T_A<1.5$
B'	B	$T_B<0.2$	B'	no information[a]
C'	C'	$T_C>0$	C'	no information
D'	D'	$T_D>0$	D'	no information
A'	A'	$T_A>0.7$	A	$T_A<1.7$
B	B'	$T_B>0$	B'	no information
C'	C	$T_C<0.3$	C'	no information
D'	D'	$T_D>0$	D'	no information
A'	A'	$T_A>0.3$	A	$T_A<1.3$
B'	B'	$T_B>0$	B'	no information
C	C'	$T_C>0$	C'	no information
D'	D	$T_D<0.8$	D'	no information
A'	A'	$T_A>0.9$	A	$T_A<1.9$
B'	B	$T_B<0.4$	B'	no information
C'	C'	$T_C>0$	C'	no information
D	D'	$T_D>0$	D'	no information

[a]No information about the requirement of the value of the neuron is provided when it has an input with input value 1.

input of the neural network is 0. There is at most one input to the 0-neuron with input value other than 0, because at each moment one and only one neuron of the neural network can be in the firing state. The threshold value of the 0-neuron cannot be 0, because otherwise it fires all the time. This implies that the automaton always remains in the same state, since at each moment one and only one neuron can be in the firing state. An automaton corresponding to a neural network containing such a neuron is a trivial automaton (one state automaton) from that moment on. So we eliminate the value 0 as the threshold. The threshold value of the 0-neuron cannot be greater than $\mu_{\min}$ either, since otherwise there will exist some excitatory input to the 0-neuron for which the 0-neuron will not fire. This will make the fuzzy neural network unable to realize the given automaton. When the threshold value is in the range $0<T_{0\text{-neuron}}\leq\mu_{\min}$ the neuron can provide both quiet and firing states in accordance with the transition diagram of the automaton.

Now consider the 1-neuron as shown in Fig. 4(b) and Fig. 4(c). The reason for that the threshold value cannot be greater than $1+\mu_{\min}$ is similar to the case where the 0-neuron with threshold value cannot be greater than $\mu_{\min}$, just discussed.

For any 1-neuron, when the input is 0, its next state must be quiet, because the next state of the automaton cannot be in the state corresponding to this 1-neuron. For this reason, the threshold cannot be less than $\mu_{\max}$. When there is *only one* 1-neuron in the network and its threshold value is in the range $\mu_{\max}\leq T_{1\text{-neuron}}\leq 1+\mu_{\min}$, it can provide both quiet and firing states depending upon the state transition of the automaton. However, when there are *more than one* 1-neuron, then the range of the threshold values of 1-neuron is $1<T_{1\text{-neuron}}\leq 1+\mu_{\min}$.

Therefore, step 7 of the synthesis procedure can be replaced by step 7′.

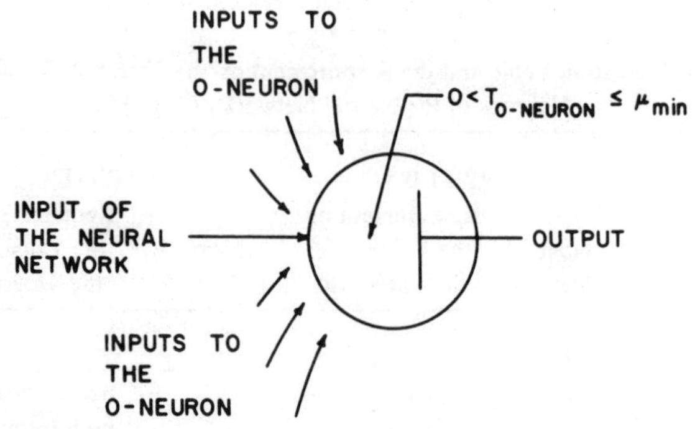

FIG. 4(a). The range of the threshold value of a 0-neuron.

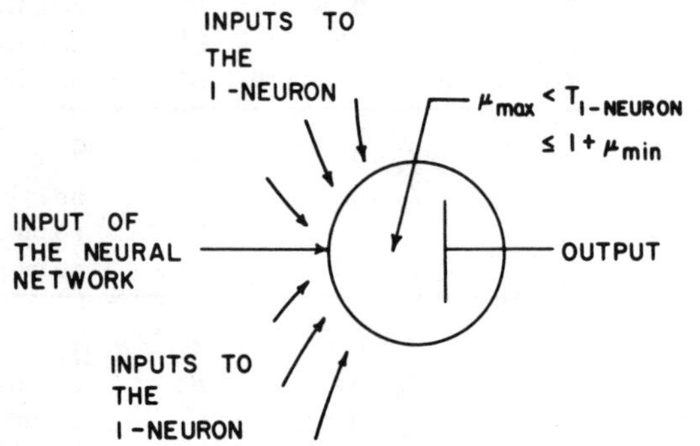

FIG. 4(b). The range of the threshold value of a 1-neuron when there is only One 1-neuron in the neural network.

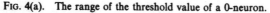

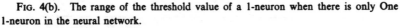

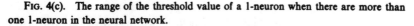

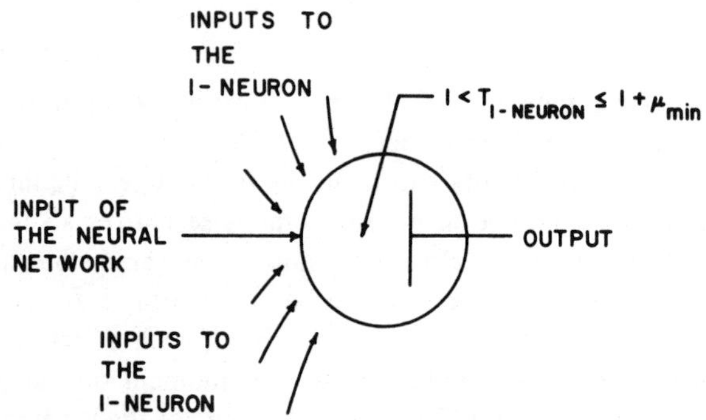

FIG. 4(c). The range of the threshold value of a 1-neuron when there are more than one 1-neuron in the neural network.

(7′) Determine the threshold values of the neurons. The range of the threshold values of a 1-neuron is $\mu_{max} < T_{1\text{-neuron}} \leq 1 + \mu_{min}$ when there is only one 1-neuron in the neural network and $1 < T_{1\text{-neuron}} \leq 1 + \mu_{min}$ when there are more than one 1-neuron in the neural network and the range of the threshold values a 0-neuron is $0 < T_{0\text{-neuron}} \leq \mu_{min}$.

For example, in the neural network of Fig. 3(b), the A neuron is a 1-neuron with threshold T_A; and the B, C, and D neurons are 0-neurons with thresholds T_B, T_C, and T_D, respectively, which agrees with the theorem.

Part A-II. Synthesis of Nonhomogeneous FFA

The synthesis procedure for nonhomogeneous FFA consists of two steps:

(1) Construct a homogeneous automaton which is equivalent to the given automaton. The way of constructing such an equivalent automaton is

to split each nonhomogeneous state into two, a 1-state and a 0-state, which results in a homogeneous automaton.

(2) Synthesize the equivalent homogeneous automaton using the method described in Part A-I.

To show the first step is always feasible, we describe the procedure for obtaining the homogeneous states from a nonhomogeneous state as follows.

(1) Split the nonhomogeneous state into two states. One is a 1-state, and the other is a 0-state.

(2) Consider the following three possible transition lines incident to the nonhomogeneous state:

(2-1) The transition lines coming to the state from other states. Draw all the transition lines driven by input 1 incident to the θ-state with the values of ρ_i's unchanged.

(2-2) The transition lines going out of the state. For each transition line going out of the state driven by an input which is either 0 or 1, if the state to which the transition line is incident, is a homogeneous state, draw two lines driven by the same input to that state with the same membership ρ_i. If the state to which the transition line is incident, is a nonhomogeneous state, draw two lines driven by the same input with the same membership $\rho_p$ut is 1 or 0.

(2-3) The self-looped transition lines of the state. If a self-looped transition line is driven by 1, draw a self-looped transition line driven by 1 at the 1-state and a transition line from the 0-state driven by 1 to the 1-state. If a self-looped transition line is driven by 0, draw a self-looped transition line driven by 0 at the 0-state and a transition line from the 1-state driven by 0 to the 0-state. Again, the membership ρ_i of all the state transitions are kept the same.

This procedure is illustrated by the following example.

Example 2. An automaton M_2 is described by the state transition diagram of Fig. 5(a), in which states A, B, and D are nonhomogeneous states and state C is a homogeneous 0-state. States A, B, and D are split into two states A_1 and A_0, B_1 and B_0, D_1 and D_0, respectively. The subscripts 1 and 0 denote the 1-state and 0-state. The state transition diagram of the homogeneous automaton M_2' in Figure 5(b) is constructed by the procedure just described.

DEFINITION 9.

Two states of a fuzzy automation are equivalent if they are (1) equivalent in the ordinary sense, i.e., for all input sequences applied to the two states outputs are identical, and (2) the grade of acceptance to all input sequences starting from the two states are identical.

DEFINITION 10.

Two fuzzy automata M_a and M_b are equivalent if for every state of M_a, there is at least one equivalent state in M_b and vice versa.

We can easily show the following theorem.

THEOREM 2.

Let M be a nonhomogeneous FFA.

(a) *For any nonhomogeneous state A of M, A_1 and A_0 are always obtainable.*

(b) *States A_1, A_0, and A are equivalent.*

(c) *If B is a homogeneous state of M, then B remains homogeneous under the nonhomogeneous state-to-homogeneous states transformation described above.*

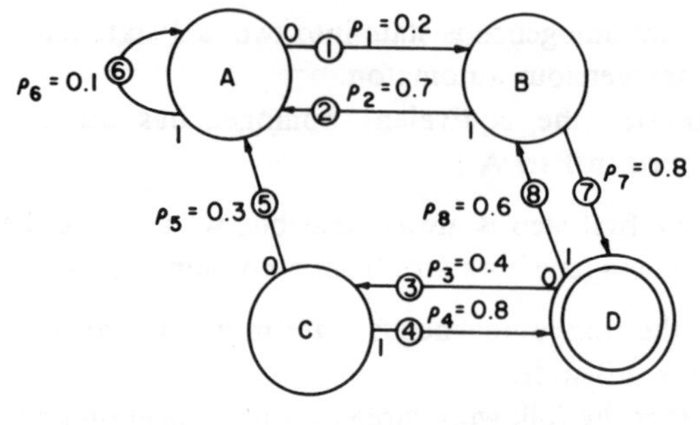

FIG. 5(a). A nonhomogeneous automaton M_2.

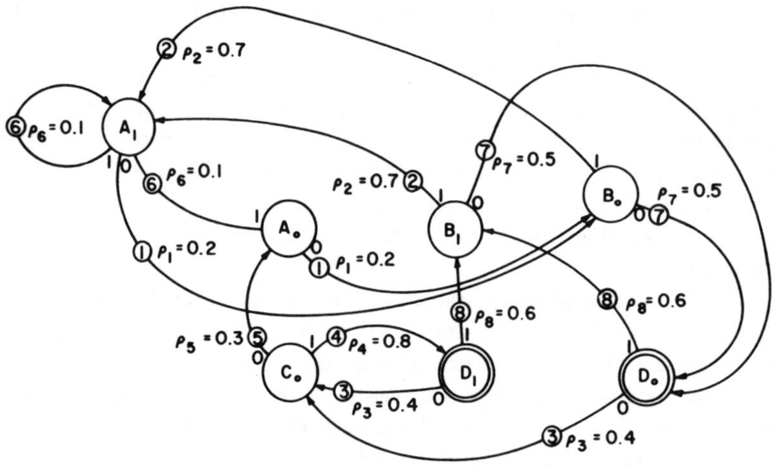

FIG. 5(b). The equivalent homogeneous automaton M_2'.

Example 2 (continued). The equivalence relation among the states of the two automata: Automaton M_2 can be best seen from the state transition tables of the two automata which are shown in Table 3. In this table, besides the next states, the memberships of the state transition are also shown. For example, the entities $A_1/0.1$ at the first row and the first column of the left table means that the membership of the state transition from state A_1 to state A_1 by the input 1 is 0.1. It is seen from Table 3 that states A_1, A_0, and A, B_1, B_0, and B, and D_1, D_0, and D are equivalent states. Since for every state of automaton M_2, there is at least one equivalent state in the homogeneous automaton M_2' and vice versa, hence the two automata are equivalent.

COROLLARY 1.

For any nonhomogeneous automaton, there exists a homogeneous automaton which is equivalent to it.

Example 2 (continued). Realize the nonhomogeneous automaton M_2 of Fig. 5(a) using a fuzzy neural network.

The equivalent homogeneous automaton of M_2 was obtained above. Applying the method described in Part A-I, the realization is shown in Fig. 5(b), in which the output of the neural network is taken from the outputs of neurons D_1 and D_0 feeding to the input of an *OR* neural network. The ranges of the threshold values of the fuzzy neurons are obtained by Theorem 1 which are shown in Table 4.

The following theorem concerns with the lower bound of the number of neurons required for synthesizing an n-state *minimal* automaton, that is, in this minimal automaton no two states are equivalent.

TABLE 3
The state transition tables of M_2 and its homogeneous automaton equivalent M_2'

x_k / q_k	1	0	Equivalent class	x_k / q_k	1	0	Equivalent class
A_1	$A_1/0.1$	$B_0/0.2$	I	A	$A/0.1$	$B/0.2$	I
A_0	$A_1/0.1$	$B_0/0.2$					
B_1	$A_1/0.7$	$D_0/0.5$	II	B	$A/0.7$	$D/0.5$	II
B_0	$A_1/0.7$	$D_0/0.5$					
C_0	$D_1/0.8$	$A_0/0.3$	III	C	$D/0.8$	$A/0.3$	III
D_1	$B_1/0.6$	$C_0/0.4$	IV	D	$B/0.6$	$C/0.4$	IV
D_0	$B_1/0.6$	$C_0/0.4$					

TABLE 4
The Ranges of Threshold Values of the Neurons of the Realization of M_2

Threshold	Lower Bound The threshold is greater than	Upper Bound The threshold is less than or equal to
T_{A_1}	1	1.1
T_{A_0}	0	0.3
T_{B_1}	1	1.6
T_{B_0}	0	0.2
T_{D_1}	1	1.8
T_{D_0}	0	0.5
T_{C_0}	0	0.4

THEOREM 3.

For an n-state minimal automaton, there must be at least $\lceil \log_2 n \rceil^2$ *number of neurons to realize it.*

Proof. Since a neural network containing m neurons can have at most 2^m state, 2^m must be greater than or equal to n. Since m must be an integer $m \geqslant \lceil \log_2 n \rceil$.

COROLLARY 2.

Let m denote the number of neurons required to realize an n-state minimal machine by the method described in this section. Then such a realization with $\lceil \log_2 n \rceil \leqslant m \leqslant 2n$ *can always be obtained.*

PART B. REALIZATION OF THE GRADE OF ACCEPTANCE OF THE FFA

Part A has presented the synthesis of homogeneous and nonhomogeneous state transition diagram using fuzzy neurons. In this part, we shall present the realization of the degree of acceptance of the FFSA obtained in Part A. The grade of acceptance is defined in (7). The problem is to evaluate the grade of acceptance. The method for evaluating the grade of acceptance is best illustrated by the use of an example.

Example 3. Consider the FFA M_2 of Example 2.

$$M_2 = (K, \Sigma, \delta, q_0, F),$$

[2]The symbol $\lceil \log_2 n \rceil$ denotes the least integer which is greater than or equal to $\log_2 n$.

where

$$K=(A,B,C,D),$$

$$\Sigma=(0,1),$$

$$q_0=\{(A,0.6),(B,0.7),(C,0.8),(D,0.9)\},$$

$$F=\{D\},$$

and δ is the fuzzy mapping from $K\times\Sigma$ to K as represented by $M(1)$ and $M(0)$ where

$$M(1)=\begin{array}{c} \\ A \\ B \\ C \\ D \end{array}\begin{array}{c}\begin{array}{cccc} A & B & C & D \end{array}\\ \begin{bmatrix} 0.1 & 0 & 0 & 0 \\ 0.7 & 0 & 0 & 0 \\ 0 & 0 & 0 & 0.8 \\ 0 & 0.6 & 0 & 0 \end{bmatrix}\end{array},$$

and

$$M(0)=\begin{array}{c} \\ A \\ B \\ C \\ D \end{array}\begin{array}{c}\begin{array}{cccc} A & B & C & D \end{array}\\ \begin{bmatrix} 0 & 0.2 & 0 & 0 \\ 0 & 0 & 0 & 0 \\ 0.3 & 0 & 0 & 0 \\ 0 & 0 & 0.4 & 0 \end{bmatrix}\end{array}.$$

We have shown that M_2' of Fig. 5(b) is equivalent to M_2.

$$M_2'=(K',\Sigma,\delta',q_0',F'),$$

where

$$\Sigma=(0,1)$$

$$K'=(A_1,A_0,B_1,B_0,C_0,D_1,D_0),$$

$$q_0'=\{(A_1,0.6),(A_0,0.6),(B_1,0.7),(B_0,0.7),$$
$$(C_0,0.8),(D_1,0.9),(D_0,0.9)\},$$

$$F'=(D_1,D_0),$$

and δ' is the fuzzy mapping from $K'\times\Sigma$ to K' as represented by $M'(1)$ and $M'(0)$, where

$$M'(1)=\begin{array}{c} \\ A_1 \\ A_0 \\ B_1 \\ B_0 \\ C_0 \\ D_1 \\ D_0 \end{array}\begin{array}{c}\begin{array}{ccccccc} A_1 & A_0 & B_1 & B_0 & C_0 & D_1 & D_0 \end{array}\\ \begin{bmatrix} 0.1 & 0 & 0 & 0 & 0 & 0 & 0 \\ 0.1 & 0 & 0 & 0 & 0 & 0 & 0 \\ 0.7 & 0 & 0 & 0 & 0 & 0 & 0 \\ 0.7 & 0 & 0 & 0 & 0 & 0 & 0 \\ 0 & 0 & 0 & 0 & 0 & 0.8 & 0 \\ 0 & 0 & 0.6 & 0 & 0 & 0 & 0 \\ 0 & 0 & 0.6 & 0 & 0 & 0 & 0 \end{bmatrix}\end{array},$$

$$M'(0)=\begin{array}{c|ccccccc|} & A_1 & A_0 & B_1 & B_0 & C_0 & D_1 & D_0 \\ \hline A_1 & 0 & 0 & 0 & 0.2 & 0 & 0 & 0 \\ A_0 & 0 & 0 & 0 & 0.2 & 0 & 0 & 0 \\ B_1 & 0 & 0 & 0 & 0 & 0 & 0 & 0.5 \\ B_0 & 0 & 0 & 0 & 0 & 0 & 0 & 0.5 \\ C_0 & 0 & 0.3 & 0 & 0 & 0 & 0 & 0 \\ D_1 & 0 & 0 & 0 & 0 & 0.4 & 0 & 0 \\ D_0 & 0 & 0 & 0 & 0 & 0.4 & 0 & 0 \end{array}$$

The procedure for evaluating the grade of acceptance is as follows: Suppose $x=100$. The grade of acceptance for $q_0'=(A_1,0.6), (A_0,0.6), (B_1,0.7), (B_0,0.7), (C_0,0.8), (D_1,0.9), (D_0,0.9)$, $x=100$, and $F'=(D_1,D_0)$, $\mu_1=(0.6, 0.6, 0.7, 0.7, 0.8, 0.9, 0.9)$ so

$$\mu_4=\mu_1 M'(100) \qquad \text{[by (A.3)]},$$

$$\mu_4=[[[\mu_1 M'(1)]M'(0)]M'(0)] \qquad \text{[by (A.4)]}.$$

(1) At time $t=1$, set the initial values in the registers $R_{A_1},\ldots,R_{D_0}$ (see Fig. 6) to be the values of the initial designator, namely

$$\mu_1=[r_{A_1}^{(1)},r_{A_0}^{(1)},r_{B_1}^{(1)},r_{B_0}^{(1)},r_{C_0}^{(1)},r_{D_1}^{(1)},r_{D_0}^{(1)}]$$

$$=[0.6,0.6,0.7,0.7,0.8,0.9,0.9]$$

where $r_{A_1}^{(1)}$ is the value in R_{A_1} at time $t=1$, $r_{A_0}^{(1)},\ldots,r_{D_0}^{(1)}$ are similarly defined, the superscript denotes the time. Note that the row vector $[r_{A_1}^{(k)},r_{A_0}^{(k)},r_{B_1}^{(k)},r_{B_0}^{(k)},r_{C_0}^{(k)},r_{D_1}^{(k)},r_{D_0}^{(k)}]$ denotes the grade of membership of the states at time k which is the same as Q_k in (A.5).

(2) At time $t=2$, if the input is 1, set all the excitatory inputs to the 0-neurons to be zero. If the input is 0, set all the excitatory inputs to the

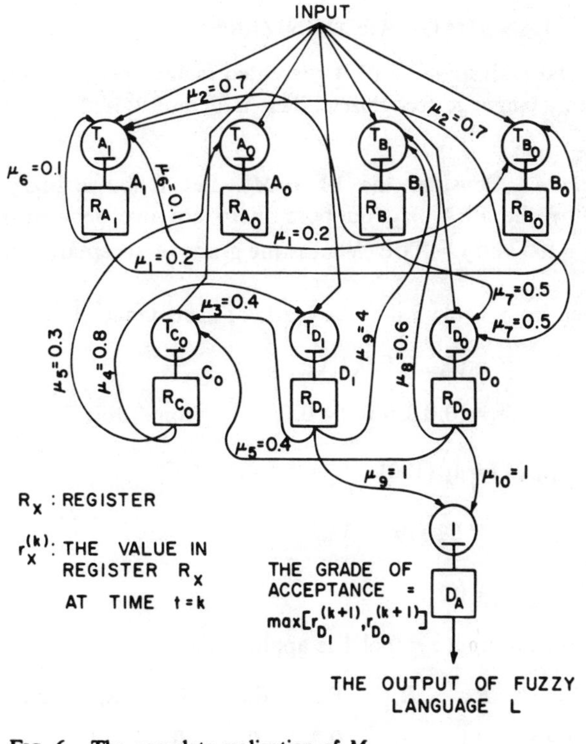

FIG. 6. The complete realization of M_2.

TABLE 5
The Sequences of the Values in the Registers

$$\pi'_k = [r^{(k)}_{A_1}, r^{(k)}_{A_0}, r^{(k)}_{B_1}, r^{(k)}_{B_0}, r^{(k)}_{C_0}, r^{(k)}_{D_1}, r^{(k)}_{D_0}]$$

where $r^{(k)}_{A_1}$ is the value in R_{A_1} at time k.

Time	R_{A_1}	R_{A_0}	R_{B_1}	R_{B_0}	R_{C_0}	R_{D_1}	R_{D_0}	π'_k
$t=0$	0.6	0.4	0.2	0.7	0.8	0.3	0.9	π'_0
$t=1$	0.7	0	0.8	0	0	0.8	0	π'_1
$t=2$	0	0	0	0.2	0.4	0	0.5	π'_2
$t=3$	0	0.3	0	0	0.4	0	0.2	π'_3

1-neurons to be zero. Define

$$(\nu_x)_{\min} = \min[\mu_x, r^{(1)}_x] \tag{13}$$

where μ_x is coming from the register R_x with value $r^{(1)}_x$. Replace the $r^{(1)}_x$ by the maximum of the $(\nu_x)_{\min\text{'s}}$ which are incident to the neuron x. Denote this value by $r^{(2)}_x$.

(3) Repeat step 2 $(K-1)$ times, where K is the length of the input sequence the μ_K is thus obtained. For our example μ_2, μ_3, μ_4 are tabulated in Table 5.

It is of interest to note that if the input at time $t=k$ is 1, the values $r^{(k+1)}_{0\text{-neuron}}$ in all the registers of the 0-neurons are zero. If the input at time $t=k$ is 0, the values $r^{(k+1)}_{1\text{-neuron}}$ in all the registers of the 1-neurons are zero.

After μ_k is obtained, the grade of acceptance can be obtained by using a neuron OR network as shown in Fig. 6. It should be remarked that one additional unit delay is introduced by the OR neural network. The complete realization of M_2 is shown in Fig. 6.

6. FUZZY LANGUAGE RECOGNIZERS

The neural realization of FFA presented in the previous section can be used as fuzzy language recognizers. This is demonstrated by the following example.

Example 4. Consider the FFA M_2. Let L be a fuzzy language generated by the FFA M_2. Suppose there are two sequences of input symbols $x=100$ and $y=1001$. What is the grade of acceptance of x and y in L?

It is seen from Table 5 that the grade of acceptance of x is 0.2 by (A.5).

$$F' = (0,0,0,0,0,1,1),$$

$$Q_4 = (0, 0.3, 0, 0, 0.4, 0, 0, 2) \qquad \text{from Table 5,}$$

$$\mu_M(x) = \mu_M(100),$$

$$= \max_{q_j} \mu_{F' \cap Q_4}(q_j),$$

$$= 0.2.$$

If one additional input symbol 1 is applied, then

	R_{A_1}	R_{A_0}	R_{B_1}	R_{B_0}	R_{C_0}	R_{D_1}	R_{D_0}
$t=5$	0.1	0	0.2	0	0	0.4	0

Thus the grade of acceptance of $y=1001$ is

$$\mu_M(y)=\mu_M(1001)$$

$$=\max_{q_j}\mu_{F'\cap Q_5}(q_j)$$

$$=0.4$$

It should be clear that the fuzzy neural network (Sec. 5) corresponding to the FFA M is the fuzzy language recognizer for the fuzzy language accepted by this FFA M.

7. CONCLUSION

The McCulloch-Pitts cell has been generalized to the fuzzy neuron, which is based on the assumption that the activity of the cell is a "fuzzy" process rather than an "all-or-none" process. It has been shown that any fuzzy automaton can be realized by a fuzzy neural network. The lower and upper bound on the number of neurons to realize an n-state minimal fuzzy automaton are given. The realizations of fuzzy languages using fuzzy neural networks have been presented. The method may be applied to solving problems in many areas involving information processing, pattern recognition, and decision making.

APPENDIX

A fuzzy automaton may be viewed as a generalization of the concept of a nondeterministic automaton. Thus, if on a nondeterministic automaton A the set of possible next states, given the present state and the present input, is a subset Γ of the state-space K, then in its fuzzy counterpart $\mathbf{A}$ the set of next states is a fuzzy subset $\mathbf{\Gamma}$ of K. By this process, which will be referred to as fuzzification, it is a simple matter to define such notion as fuzzy finite-state automaton, a fuzzy push-down automaton, a fuzzy Turing machine, a fuzzy algorithm, a fuzzy Markoff algorithm, etc. [21,22].

FUZZY AUTOMATA

To illustrate this process in more concrete terms, we define a fuzzy finite automaton (FFA) as follows:

DEFINITION A.1.

A fuzzy finite automaton (FFA) over an alphabet Σ is a quintuple (K,Σ,δ,q_0,F) where K is a finite nonempty set of states, Σ is a finite input alphabet, $q_0\in K$ is the initial state, and $F\subset K$ is a set of final states. The symbol δ denotes a fuzzy mapping form $K\times\Sigma$ to K. This means each pair (q_i,a) in $K\times\Sigma$ defines a fuzzy "next state" in K which is characterized by a conditioned membership function $\mu(q_j|q_i,a)$ having as its arguments $q_j\in K$, $q_i\in K$ and $a\in\Sigma$.

If the state of FFA at time n is a fuzzy set Q_n in K defined by a membership function $\mu_n(q_i)$, and an input a is applied, then the state of FFA at time $n+1$ is a fuzzy set Q_{n+1} in K whose membership function is given by

$$\mu_{n+1}(q_j)=\bigvee_{q_i}\left(\mu_n(q_i)\wedge\mu(q_j|q_i,a)\right), \tag{A.1}$$

where $\bigvee_{q_i}$ denotes the supremum over $q_i\in K$. Note that when Q_n is a singleton $\{q_i\}$ the membership function for next state reduces to $\mu(q_j|q_i,a)$.

To simplify the notation, it is convenient to represent (3.1) in matrix form. Specifically, let $M(a)$ denote a matrix whose ijth element is $\mu(q_j|q_i,a)$; let μ_n and μ_{n+1} denote, respectively, row vectors with components $\mu_n(q_1),\ldots,\mu_n(q_{|k|})$ and $\mu_{n+1}(q_1),\ldots,\mu_{n+1}(q_{|k|})$, where $|k|$ is the number of states. Then,

(3.1) may be written as

$$\mu_{n+1} = \mu_n M(a), \quad \text{(A.2)}$$

in which the matrix product is understood in the normal sense, except that the sum (+) is replaced by $\vee$ and the produce $(\cdot)$ by $\wedge$.

More generally, if $x = a_1 a_2 \ldots a_m \in \Sigma^*$ is an input string of length m, thus

$$\mu_{n+m} = \mu_n M(x), \quad \text{(A.3)}$$

where $M(x)$ is given by the matrix product

$$M(x) = M(a_1) M(a_2) \cdots M(a_m), \quad \text{(A.4)}$$

which should be interpreted in the same sense as (A.2).

Equation (A.3) defines the membership function μ_{n+m}, of the fuzzy state at time $n+m$ into which the fuzzy state at time n (characterized by μ_n) is taken by the input string $x = a_1 a_2 \ldots a_m$. It should be noted that (A.3) and (A.4) are analogous to the equations defining stochastic automata, except that they involve membership functions rather than probability distributions and the operations involved in them are $\vee$ and $\wedge$ rather + and $\cdot$.

THE GRADE OF ACCEPTANCE

In what follow, fuzzy automata will be used primarily to characterize fuzzy languages in terms of their acceptance by such automata. For this purpose, we define the *grade of acceptance* of a string $x = a_1 a_2 \ldots a_m \in \Sigma^*$ by a fuzzy automaton. In the case of an FFA, the definition is stated as follows.

DEFINITION A.2.

Let Q_m denote the fuzzy state into which the initial state q_0 (at time $t=1$) is taken by an input string $x = a_1 a_2 \ldots a_m$, $a_1, a_2, \ldots, a_m \in \Sigma$. Let F be a designated set of final states, which may be a fuzzy subset of K. Then, $\mu_M(x)$, the *grade of acceptance* of x by the FFA, is given by the maximal grade in $F \cap Q_m$, the intersection of F and Q_m. More specifically,

$$\mu_M(x) = \max_{q_j} \mu_{F \cap Q_m}(q_j), \quad \text{(A.5)}$$

or

$$\mu_M(x) = \bigvee_{q_j} (\mu_F(q_j) \wedge \mu_{Q_m}(q_j)), \quad \text{(A.6)}$$

where the supremum is taken over all states in K. Note that by (A.3)

$$\mu_{Q_m} = \mu_1 M(x), \quad \text{(A.7)}$$

where μ_1 has only one nonzero component (equal to one) in the position corresponding to q_0.

The authors are indebted to Professor L. A. Zadeh of University of California, Berkeley, for his invaluable comments, suggestions, and encouragement throughout this research.

REFERENCES

1 W. S. McCulloch and W. Pitts, A logical calculus of the ideas imminent in nervous activity, *Bull. Math. Biophys.* 5, 1943.

2 John von Neumann, Probabilistic logics and the synthesis of reliable organisms from unreliable components, *Automata Studies*, Princeton Univ. Press, Princeton, N.J. (1956), pp. 43–98.

3 E. F. Moore, Gedanken-experiments on sequential machines, *Automata Studies*, Princeton Univ. Press, Princeton, N.J. (1956), pp. 129–153.

4 S. C. Kleene, Representation of events in nerve nets and finite automata, *Automata Studies* (Annals of Mathematics Studies, No. 34), Princeton Univ. Press, Princeton, N.J. (1956).

5 M. O. Rabin and D. Scott, Finite automata and their decision problems, *IBM J. Res. Develop.* 3, 114–125 (1959).

6 R. McNaughton and H. Yamada, Regular expressions and state graphs for automata, *Trans. IRE Prof. Group Electron. Comp.* EC-9, no. 1, 39–47 (March 1960).

7 R. McNaughton, The theory of automata, a survey, *Advances in Computers*, Vol. 2, Academic, New York (1961), pp. 379–421.

8 A. Gill, *Introduction to the Theory of Finite-State Machines*, McGraw-Hill, New York (1962).

9 M. A. Harrison, *Introduction to Switching and Automata Theory*, McGraw-Hill, New York (1965).

10 J. Harmanis and R. E. Stearns, *Algebraic Structure Theory of Sequential Machines*, Prentice-Hall, Englewood Cliffs, N.J. (1966).

11 S. Ginsburg, *An Introduction to Mathematical Machine Theory*, Addison-Wesley, Reading, Mass. (1962).

12 A. Ginzburg, *Algebraic Theory of Automata*, Academic, New York (1968).

13 L. A. Zadeh, Fuzzy sets, *Inform. Control* 8, 338–353 (June 1965).

14 L. A. Zadeh, Biological application of the theory of fuzzy sets and systems, *Proc. Symp. Biocybern. Cent. Nerv. Sys.* 1968.

15 W. G. Wee, and K. S. Fu, A formulation of fuzzy automata and its application as a model of learining systems, *IEEE Trans. Sys. Sci. Cybern.* SSC5, No. 3 (July 1969).

16 M. Mizumoto, J. Toyoda, and K. Tanaka, Some considerations on fuzzy automata, *J. Comp. Sys. Sci.* 3, 409–422 (1969).

17 E. S. Santos, Maximin automata, *Inform. Control* 13, 363–377 (1968).

18 M. L. Minsky, *Computation—Finite and Infinite Machines*, Prentice Hall, Englewood Cliffs, N.J. (1967).

19 E. T. Lee and L. A. Zadeh, Note on fuzzy languages, *Inform. Sci.* 1, 421–434 (1969).

20 R. E. Bellman, R. Kalaba, and L. A. Zadeh, Abstraction and pattern classification, *J. Math. Anal. Appl.* 13, 1–7 (1966).

21 L. A. Zadeh, Fuzzy algorithms, *Inform. Control* 12, 99–102 (February 1968).

22 E. S. Santos, Fuzzy algorithms, *Inform. Control* 17, 326–339 (November 1970).

23 R. E. Bellman and L. A. Zadeh, Decision-making in a fuzzy environment, *Management Sci.* 17, No. 4, B141–B164 (December 1970).

24 L. A. Zadeh, Fuzzy languages and their relation to human and machine intelligence, Memorandum No. ERL-M302, Department of Electrical Engineering and Computer Science, University of California, Berkeley, August 1971.

Incorporating Fuzzy Membership Functions into the Perceptron Algorithm

JAMES M. KELLER, MEMBER, IEEE, AND DOUGLAS J. HUNT, STUDENT MEMBER, IEEE

Abstract—The perceptron algorithm, one of the class of gradient descent techniques, has been widely used in pattern recognition to determine linear decision boundaries. While this algorithm is guaranteed to converge to a separating hyperplane if the data are linearly separable, it exhibits erratic behavior if the data are not linearly separable. Fuzzy set theory is introduced into the perceptron algorithm to produce a "fuzzy algorithm" which ameliorates the convergence problem in the nonseparable case. It is shown that the fuzzy perceptron, like its crisp counterpart, converges in the separable case. A method of generating membership functions is developed, and experimental results comparing the crisp to the fuzzy perceptron are presented.

Index Terms—Fuzzy sets, fuzzy 2-means, gradient descent, induced fuzzy membership, iterative training, perceptron algorithm, separating hyperplane.

I. INTRODUCTION

THERE are many cases in pattern classifier design where a linear decision boundary between two sets of sample vectors is desired. One of the common approaches to this problem is to use the perceptron algorithm originated by Rosenblatt [1] as a model of machine learning. This algorithm is one of a class of gradient-descent techniques which play an important role in pattern recognition theory [2].

The classical perceptron technique is an iterative training algorithm which, given two classes of patterns (vectors in Euclidian space), attempts to determine a linear decision boundary separating the two classes. If the two sets of vectors are, in fact, linearly separable, the perceptron algorithm is guaranteed to find a separating hyperplane in a finite number of steps [2]. However, if the two sets of vectors are not linearly separable, not only will the perceptron algorithm not find a separating hyperplane (since one does not exist), but there is no method for knowing when to terminate the algorithm to obtain an optimal or even a good decision boundary. Depending on the values of the sample vectors, the behavior of the perceptron algorithm can be very erratic in the nonseparable case. It is this problem with the nonseparable case that we address by incorporating fuzzy set theory into the perceptron algorithm.

Fuzzy sets were introduced by Zadeh in 1965 [3]. Since that time, researchers have found numerous ways to utilize this theory to generalize existing techniques and to develop new algorithms in pattern recognition and decision analysis [4]–[7]. This paper is concerned with incorporating fuzzy set methods into the classical perceptron pattern recognition technique. In particular, a "fuzzy perceptron" algorithm is developed along with a method of generating fuzzy membership for the training sets. It is also shown that the fuzzy perceptron, like its "crisp" counterpart, converges to a solution in a finite number of steps if the data sets of sample vectors are linearly separable. Finally, the results of both the crisp and fuzzy perceptron are compared on two data sets.

Manuscript received August 6, 1984; revised June 6, 1985.

J. M. Keller is with the Department of Electrical and Computer Engineering, University of Missouri, Columbia, MO 65201.

D. J. Hunt was with the Department of Electrical and Computer Engineering, University of Missouri, Columbia, MO. He is now with the Department of Electrical Engineering, Duke University, Durham, NC 27706.

II. THE CRISP PERCEPTRON AND FUZZY SETS

Suppose we have a set of sample vectors $\{X_1, \cdots, X_n\}$ where each X_k is labeled either class 1 or class 2. If there exists a linear discriminant function g for these two classes then, for each k,

$$g(X_k) = W^t X_k \begin{cases} >0 & \text{if } X_k \text{ is in class 1} \\ <0 & \text{if } X_k \text{ is in class 2} \end{cases}$$

where $W^t = (w_1, w_2, \cdots, w_{p+1})$ is called the weight vector and $X_k^t = (X_{k1}, \cdots, X_{kp}, 1)$ is called the augmented feature vector. If all the class 2 vectors are multiplied by -1, then we have

$$g(X_k) = W^t X_k > 0, \; k = 1, \cdots, n.$$

Geometrically, $g(X) = 0$ defines a hyperplane in R^p where all class 1 vectors lie on one side of the hyperplane and all class 2 vectors lie on the other side of the hyperplane. The perceptron algorithm can be used to attempt to determine a linear discriminant function for the two classes from the sample vectors. If such a linear discriminant function exists (i.e., if the two classes are linearly separable), the perceptron algorithm is guaranteed to find a linear discriminant function in a finite number of iterations [2].

The crisp perceptron algorithm consists of the following steps.

BEGIN PERCEPTRON

Let $X_1, \cdots, X_n \in R^{p+1}$ be the given labeled sample vectors where all vectors have been augmented with a 1 and all class 2 vectors have been multiplied by -1.

Let $W \in R^{p+1}$ be an arbitrary initial weight vector.

Set UPDATE flag to true.

Reprinted from *IEEE Trans. Pattern Anal. Machine Intell.*, vol. PAMI-7, no. 6, pp. 693–699, November 1985.

```
DO WHILE UPDATE flag is true.
   Set UPDATE flag to false.
   DO for all vectors X_j, j = 1, ··· , n.
      If W'X_j ≤ 0 THEN
         Set W to W + cX_j, where c is a positive constant.
         Set UPDATE flag to true.
      ELSE
         {Weight vector W remains the same.}
      ENDIF
   END DO
END DO WHILE
END PERCEPTRON
```

The parameter c in the above algorithm does not have to be constant. If it is constant, the algorithm is called the fixed-increment perceptron. Some other variations, which we will not be considering and in which c is variable, are the absolute-correction algorithm and the fractional-correction algorithm [8].

Notice that if the two classes are not linearly separable, the perceptron algorithm will continue to update the weight vector forever. Terminating the algorithm at an arbitrary point may yield a good weight vector, but it may not, as we shall see later. Several heuristic methods for terminating the algorithm have been suggested, but none has met with universal success [8]. Some even sacrifice guaranteed convergence to a separating hyperplane in the separable case for a guaranteed fairly good solution in both the separable and nonseparable cases. Incorporating fuzzy set theory into the perceptron algorithm is another approach to this problem.

Fuzzy Sets

Given a universe U of objects, a conventional "crisp" subset A of U is commonly defined by specifying the objects of the universe that are members of A. An equivalent way of defining A is to specify the characteristic function of A, $u_A: U \rightarrow \{0, 1\}$ where for all $x \in U$

$$u_A(x) = \begin{cases} 1 & x \in A \\ 0 & x \notin A. \end{cases}$$

Fuzzy sets are obtained by generalizing the concept of a characteristic function to a membership function $u: U \rightarrow [0, 1]$. Most crisp set operations (such as union and intersection) and set properties have analogs in fuzzy set theory. See [9] for a more detailed presentation of fuzzy set theory.

The advantage provided by fuzzy sets is that the degree of membership in a set can be specified, rather than just the binary is/is not a member. This can be especially advantageous in pattern recognition where, frequently, objects are not clearly members of one class or another. Using crisp techniques, an ambiguous object will be assigned to one class only, lending an aura of precision and definiteness to the assignment that is not warranted. On the other hand, fuzzy techniques will specify to what degree the object belongs to each class—information that frequently is useful.

Given a set of sample vectors $\{X_1, \cdots, X_n\}$, a fuzzy c partition of these vectors specifies the degree of membership of each vector in each of c classes. It is denoted by the $c \times n$ matrix U where $u_{ik} = u_i(X_k)$ for $i = 1, \cdots, c$, and $k = 1, \cdots, n$ is the degree of membership of X_k in class i. The following properties must be true for U to be a fuzzy c partition:

$$\sum_{i=1}^{c} u_{ik} = 1$$

$$0 < \sum_{k=1}^{n} u_{ik} < n$$

$$u_{ik} \in [0, 1].$$

III. The Fuzzy Perceptron

As mentioned previously, the main weakness of the crisp perceptron algorithm is that it neither terminates nor necessarily converges to a useful solution when the two classes are not linearly separable. In the nonseparable case, the classes overlap (actually the convex hulls of the vectors in each class overlap [8]). Speaking in nonrigorous terms, the vectors that cause the classes to overlap are primarily responsible for the erratic behavior of the perceptron algorithm. In many cases,these same vectors are also relatively uncharacteristic of the irrespective classes, yet they are given full weight in the perceptron algorithm. This is where fuzzy class membership functions can improve the algorithm. By basing the amount of correction to the weight vector on the fuzzy memberships, vectors whose class is less certain will have less influence in determining the weight vector.

The Algorithm

In order to modify the perceptron algorithm so that vectors of high uncertainty (membership values close to 0.5) have less influence on the results, it is necessary to modify the weight vector correction step that is performed when a vector is misclassified by the current weight vector. In the crisp perceptron, the correction step is $W \leftarrow W + cX_j$. In order to incorporate the membership function values into the correction step, we modify this step so that it becomes

$$W \leftarrow W + |u_{1j} - u_{2j}|^m \, cX_j \qquad \text{where } m \text{ is constant.}$$

This modification has several advantages.

1) It accomplishes the objective of reducing the influence of uncertain vectors in determining the weight vector.

2) It retains the property of finding a separating hyperplane in a finite number of iterations in the linearly separable case (see theorem 1 below).

3) Since $|u_{ij} - u_{2j}|^m = 1$ when $u_{1j}, u_{2j} \in \{0, 1\}$, the fuzzy perceptron reduces to the crisp perceptron when the membership function values are crisp.

Note that if $W'X_j \leq 0$ where X_j is a totally ambiguous vector (i.e., $u_{1j} = u_{2j} = 0.5$), the resulting correction term will be zero since $|u_{1j} - u_{2j}| = 0$. This, however, is legitimate since there is no meaningful way to decide on which side of the decision boundary a totally ambiguous vector should lie. For this reason, the fuzzy perceptron must ignore totally ambiguous vectors in its calculation of W. The choice of the fuzzier m plays an important part in the convergence of the fuzzy perceptron. The way to best utilize the fuzzy membership values is to have the algorithm make major adjustments during the early iterations when it misclassifies "typical" vectors, and then in later iterations only make minor adjustments to the weight vector. Therefore, choices of m less than one should be avoided since that exaggerates the fractional membership differences. The value of m chosen to obtain good results also depends on the method of assigning fuzzy memberships to the sample sets. The general rule is that if vectors in the overlap regions are assigned memberships near 0.5, then almost any value of m greater than one will give good results. Conversely, if these atypical vectors have higher memberships, then larger exponents will be necessary to dampen the oscillations of the decision boundaries. This relationship will be explored more deeply in Sections IV and V.

Like the crisp perceptron, the fuzzy perceptron will find a separating hyperplane in a finite number of iterations in the linearly separable case.

Theorem 1: Let $\{X_1, \cdots, X_n\}$ be a labeled set of vectors in feature space with fuzzy membership assignments in two classes. Assume that $u_{1j} \neq u_{2j} j = 1, \cdots, n$ (i.e., no ambiguous assignments), and assume there exists a weight vector $\tilde{W}$ such that $\tilde{W}'X_i > 0, i = 1, \cdots, n$. Then the fuzzy perceptron algorithm will yield a separating hyperplane in a finite number of iterations.

Proof: The proof is similar to that given in [8] for the crisp perceptron and is included here for completeness. Let $\tilde{W}$ be any separating weight vector. Then $\tilde{W}'X_j > 0$ for $j = 1, \cdots, n$. Let a be a positive scale factor. Denote the kth vector in the sequence of vectors that are misclassified during execution of the algorithm by X^k and denote the weight vector after the kth correction by $W(k + 1)$. Then, from the correction step, for a scale factor a

$$W(k+1) - a\tilde{W} = (W(k) - a\tilde{W}) + |u_1(X^k) - u_2(X^k)|^m \, cX^k$$

Therefore,

$$\|W(k+1) - a\tilde{W}\|^2 = \|W(k) - a\tilde{W}\|^2 + 2(W(k) - a\tilde{W})'|u_1 - u_2|^m cX^k + |u_1 - u_2|^{2m}c^2\|X^k\|^2$$

where $\|\cdot\|$ represents any inner product induced norm on R^{P+1}. But $W'(k)\,X^k \leq 0$ since X^k was misclassified, so

$$\|W(k+1) - a\tilde{W}\|^2 \leq \|W(k) - a\tilde{W}\|^2 - 2a\tilde{W}'|u_1 - u_2|^m cX^k + |u_1 - u_2|^{2m}c^2\|X^k\|^2.$$

Now define

$$b^2 = \max_i |u_{1i} - u_{2i}|^{2m}c^2\|X_i\|^2 > 0$$

$$d - \min_i \tilde{W}'|u_{1i} - u_{2i}|^m cX_i^2 > 0$$

since $\tilde{W}'X_i > 0$ and $u_{1i} \neq 0.5$. Substituting b and d into the previous equation, we have

$$\|W(k+1) - a\tilde{W}\|^2 \leq \|W(k) - a\tilde{W}\|^2 - 2ad + b^2.$$

Now set $a = b^2/d$ (permissible since $b^2, d > 0$). Then

$$\|W(k+1) - a\tilde{W}\|^2 \leq \|W(k) - a\tilde{W}\|^2 - b^2.$$

Therefore, the squared distance from $W(k)$ to $a\tilde{W}$ is decreased by at least b^2 with each correction of the weight vector. Thus,

$$\|W(k+1) - a\tilde{W}\|^2 \leq \|W(1) - a\tilde{W}\|^2 - kb^2.$$

Since $\|W(k+1) - a\tilde{W}\|^2 \geq 0$, the corrections must end after at most k_o corrections where $k_o = \|W(1) - a\tilde{W}\|^2/b^2$. When corrections end, a separating weight vector has been found.

IV. Assigning Fuzzy Membership Values

Now that we have a perceptron algorithm that can handle fuzzy membership values, we need to formulate a method for assigning fuzzy membership values given a set of labeled sample vectors. The approach which we propose is to transform the crisp partition of the vectors (defined by the labels) into a fuzzy partition. The transformation process suggested here was designed so that the membership value of a vector for the class to which it belongs would have several properties as follows.

1) It should be 1.0 if the vector is equal to the mean of its class.

2) It should be 0.5 if the vector is equal to the mean of the other class.

3) It should be near 0.5 if the vector is equidistant from the two means.

4) It should never be less than 0.5.

5) As a vector gets closer to its mean and farther from the other mean, the membership value should approach 1.0 exponentially.

6) It should depend on relative distances from the means of the classes rather than absolute distances.

The following method of assigning fuzzy membership values satisfies the above conditions.

For x_k in class 1:

$$u_{1k} = 0.5 + \frac{\exp(f(d_2 - d_1)/d) - \exp(-f)}{2(\exp(f) - \exp(-f))}$$

and

$$u_{2k} = 1 - u_{1k}.$$

For x_k in class 2:

$$u_{1k} = 1 - u_{2k}$$

$$u_{2k} = 0.5 + \frac{\exp(f(d_1 - d_2)/d) - \exp(-f)}{2(\exp(f) - \exp(-f))}.$$

Here d_1 is the distance from the vector to the mean of class 1, d_2 is the distance from the vector to the mean of class 2, and d is the distance between the two means. The constant f must be positive and it controls the rate at which memberships decrease toward 0.5. It is clear that in using this method of fuzzifying the samples, the value chosen for f is related to that for m in the perceptron algorithm in an inverse fashion, i.e., as f decreases, m must increase to counteract the higher memberships for vectors in the overlap regions. We have found that any combination of m and f, where each number is greater than two, gives excellent results in the experimental data. The results of our experiments will be discussed in Section V. If other methods of creating the fuzzy partition are used, then the role of the fuzzifiers will have to be investigated.

After the fuzzy membership partition is generated, the next step is to run the fuzzy perceptron. Unfortunately, the fuzzy partition generated by this method will not be separable if the original crisp partition was not separable. However, any assignment method that would convert a nonseparable crisp partition into a separable fuzzy partition would either have to violate property 4) above or would have to drop some of the vectors (the ones causing nonseparability) from consideration. Dropping some of the vectors from consideration is undesirable, and relaxing property 4) would have the effect of relabeling the original sample vectors.

Since the new fuzzy partition may be nonseparable, it is necessary to change the stopping criterion for the fuzzy perceptron, since the current criterion—stop when the current weight vector classifies all the given vectors correctly—will never be satisfied in the nonseparable case. Unfortunately, it is difficult to formulate a good stopping criterion for the fuzzy perceptron that is guaranteed to stop in all cases. However, unlike the crisp perceptron, it is possible to formulate a good stopping criterion that will stop in many cases.

The stopping criterion used here is based on the principle that vectors that are fuzzy (i.e., membership value in both classes near 0.5) should not, by themselves, cause the algorithm to perform another iteration. Thus, when the algorithm performs a complete iteration through all the sample vectors, if all the corrections are due to fuzzy vectors, then the algorithm should terminate. This does not mean, however, that a misclassified fuzzy vector should not contribute a correction to the weight vector. It merely means that a misclassified fuzzy vector does not cause the UPDATE flag to be set to true.

Thus, the stopping criterion is implemented by checking the following condition before setting the UPDATE flag to true when a misclassification occurs:

$$W^tX_j \le 0 \quad \text{and} \quad (u_{1j} > 0.5 + \text{BETA} \quad \text{or} \quad u_{1j} < 0.5 - \text{BETA}).$$

In this condition, BETA defines the range around 0.5 in which a vector is considered to be fuzzy.

Clearly, a necessary condition for this stopping criterion to work is that the set of nonfuzzy vectors (those outside the [0.5 − BETA, 0.5 + BETA] range) must be linearly separable. If the nonfuzzy vectors are not linearly separable, no hyperplane will satisfy the stopping criterion that all vectors outside the fuzzy range must be classified correctly. To satisfy this necessary condition, BETA must be such that 0.5 + BETA is greater than or equal to the membership value of vectors that are equidistant from the means of the two classes.

For the method we are using to assign fuzzy membership values, we obtain the following:

$$\text{BETA} = \frac{1 - e^{-f}}{2(e^f - e^{-f})} + \epsilon \qquad \text{where} \quad \epsilon \ge 0.$$

This follows from setting $d_1 = d_2$ in the fuzzy membership equation.

The value of ϵ in this equation is important. If ϵ is too small, the area in which a hyperplane can lie and satisfy the stopping criterion will be too constrained. The result will be that the algorithm may take a long time to terminate or may not terminate. On the other hand, if ϵ is too large, the algorithm may terminate too quickly, producing a nonoptimal decision boundary. In the examples discussed later in this paper, a value for ϵ of 0.02 was found to produce very good results.

V. Results

In order to evaluate the effectiveness of the fuzzy algorithm, the fuzzy perceptron and the crisp perceptron were run on several sets of data and the results compared. The first set of data used was Anderson's IRIS data [5], which are commonly used to test pattern recognition algorithms. The IRIS data set contains three classes, each with 50 sample vectors. Each sample vector has four features. For these tests, only classes 2 and 3, which overlap, were used. Since the two classes overlap, they are nonseparable. The algorithms were run on the IRIS data in two ways: one test of the algorithms used all four features of each vector, while another test used only features 3 and 4 of each vector.

Another set of data used consisted of two classes of sample vectors that were obtained from a multivariate normal distribution generator, and called TWOCLASS. The two classes overlap more than the two classes in the IRIS data set and provide a good test of the stopping criterion used in the induced fuzzy partition approach of the perceptron. Each class contains 121 sample vectors, each with four features. Again, the algorithms were run on this data set using all four features and also using just features 3 and 4 (the best two features).

The induced fuzzy partition approach discussed previously was used to generate fuzzy partitions for the four sets of data. The fuzzy perceptron algorithm was then run for each set of data using the fuzzy partition, while the crisp perceptron was run for each set of data using the original crisp partition. The results are summarized in Tables I and II. In the tables, the value of the fuzzifier f was set at 3.0 and a value of 1.6 was used for the fuzzifier m in the perceptron.

IRIS Data Features 3 and 4

Using features 3 and 4 of the IRIS data, the fuzzy perceptron algorithm produced a very good decision boundary and stopped after 237 iterations. The crisp perceptron

TABLE I
IRIS DATA

Type of Perceptron	Number of Iterations	Number of Misclassifications Out of 100
Fuzzy, features 3-4	237	6
Crisp, features 3-4	200	43
	300	36
	400	41
	500	37
	600	22
	1000	24
	1500	18
	3000	18
Fuzzy, features 1-4	120	2
Crisp, features 1-4	100	3
	110	32
	300	8
	500	7
	700	7
	1000	4
	1500	6
	3000	4

TABLE II
TWOCLASS DATA

Type of Perceptron	Number of Iterations	Number of Misclassifications Out of 242
Fuzzy, features 3-4	2	22
Crisp, features 3-4	2	43
	10	41
	50	118
	100	31
	110	36
	120	22
	130	64
	150	44
	1000	55
Fuzzy, features 1-4	2	21
Crisp, features 1-4	2	62
	10	75
	50	37
	70	107
	100	40
	120	87
	150	29
	152	42
	155	61
	200	67
	300	30

was fairly stable in this case but never produced an acceptable decision boundary, even after 3000 iterations.

IRIS Data, Features 1–4

Using all four features of the IRIS data improved performance considerably. Again, the fuzzy perceptron algorithm produced a very good decision boundary, and in about half as many iterations as when using only two features. The crisp perceptron usually produced acceptable decision boundaries, although never as good as the one produced by the fuzzy perceptron. This case demonstrates the erraticness of the crisp perceptron. After 100 iterations, the crisp perceptron produced an excellent decision boundary which misclassified only 3 sample vectors. However, only 10 iterations later, the decision boundary had deteriorated substantially, misclassifying 32 sample vectors. This illustrates the problems with not having a stopping criterion for the crisp perceptron in the nonseparable case. The algorithm must be terminated at an arbitrary point which may or may not produce a good decision boundary. Another point to keep in mind is that the IRIS data set is fairly well behaved (not much overlap between classes). As we will see when looking at the TWOCLASS data set, a less well-behaved data set can really cause erratic behavior by the crisp perceptron.

TWOCLASS Data, Features 3 and 4

Using features 3 and 4 of the TWOCLASS data set, the fuzzy perceptron algorithm produced a very good decision boundary after only two iterations. The crisp perceptron was very erratic but did come up with a good boundary after 120 iterations. However, after 130 iterations, the misclassification rate was back up to a high level.

TWOCLASS Data, Features 1–4

The results for this case were similar to those using only features 3 and 4. The fuzzy perceptron stopped after only two iterations, and produced a good decision boundary. The crisp perceptron, on the other hand, was very erratic and most of the time did not produce a good decision boundary. It should be noted that the misclassification rate for the TWOCLASS data is comparable to that obtained by using a Bayes' decision function with maximum likelihood estimates of the multivariate normal parameters.

The effect of the values of the two fuzzifiers m and f is demonstrated in Table III. The induced fuzzy partition function and fuzzy perceptron algorithm were run on the 4 feature TWOCLASS data set for a wide range of the two parameters. A sample of those data is displayed in the table. The format of the entries is number of iterations/number of misclassified. The locations in the table where the number of iterations is given as 500 mark runs where the fuzzy perceptron failed to terminate before 500 iterations and was aborted at that point. There are two observations which can be made. First, the fuzzy perceptron converges to an acceptable solution over a wide range of values for the fuzzifiers and in relatively few iterations. Second, the data support our assertion that the fuzzifiers should not be chosen near zero. In particular, numbers less than one should be avoided as those choices allow atypical vectors (memberships near 0.5) to exert considerable influence on the movement of the weight vector. Similar results were obtained for the other data sets.

TABLE III
RUNNING PERCEPTRON AFTER FUZZY TWO-MEANS

m \ f	0.5	1.0	1.5	2.0	3.0	4.0	5.0
1.0	500/75	500/39	500/25	500/24	61/20	2/20	2/22
1.5	500/33	500/23	500/20	122/18	2/21	2/22	2/22
2.0	500/22	500/21	2/20	2/21	2/22	2/23	2/23
2.5	500/24	2/20	2/20	2/23	3/22	2/23	2/23
3.0	34/19	2/20	2/23	2/22	4/22	2/23	2/23
3.5	2/19	2/22	2/22	3/22	7/22	2/23	2/23
4.0	2/20	2/22	2/22	4/22	11/22	2/23	2/23

As a final experiment, the fuzzy two-means algorithm [5] was run on the four data sets. By relabeling the vectors in the class with greatest membership we can create separable sample sets, but with minimal separation. The memberships resulting from this algorithm share many of the same features as those generated by the induced fuzzy partition. Both the crisp and fuzzy perceptron were run on these data, and the results are presented in Table IV. In all four cases, the fuzzy perceptron terminated in fewer iterations than its crisp counterpart, again supporting the claim that the fuzzy perceptron can make efficient use of the degree of how typical each vector is of its class.

VI. CONCLUSIONS

The fuzzy perceptron is proposed as a method to alleviate the main problem with the crisp perceptron—that it does not terminate in the nonseparable case. Other methods have been proposed for doing this, but all have problems of their own. For example, some methods give up the guarantee of finding a solution in the separable case. The rationale behind incorporating fuzzy techniques into the perceptron algorithm is that the sample vectors that cause the two classes to be nonseparable, likely are not typical of their class and, therefore, should not have as much influence as the typical vectors in determining a decision boundary. Fuzzy techniques provide a means for identifying these atypical vectors and weighting them less strongly than the typical vectors in the calculation of a decision boundary. Because the vectors causing the nonseparability have reduced influence, the fuzzy perceptron will not suffer from wild shifts in the weight vector due to a few atypical vectors, as the crisp perceptron frequently does.

One might ask, why not identify the atypical vectors and then ignore them? This is a possibility; however, by ignoring the atypical vectors, the information they possess is lost. Also, there is the question of how atypical a vector must be to be ignored. Using fuzzy techniques allows the amount of a vector's influence to be directly dependent on its typicalness.

We proposed a method of inducing a fuzzy partition on the crisp data based on a function of distance to the mean.

TABLE IV
THE RELATIONSHIP OF THE FUZZIFIERS m AND f ON THE TWOCLASS DATA (FEATURES 1–4)

Data Set	Number of Iterations		Number of Misclassifications/ Number of Vectors
	Fuzzy	Crisp	
IRIS, features 3-4	83	97	8/100
IRIS, features 1-4	874	1456	16/100
TWOCLASS, features 3-4	3	6	22/242
TWOCLASS, features 1-4	4	21	22/242

[a]Entry format is X/Y where X is the number of iterations and Y is the number of misclassified vectors out of 242.

We found, as expected, that the fuzzy perceptron did not suffer the erratic behavior experienced by the crisp perceptron. It also produced good results and terminated fairly quickly, as long as the fuzzifiers are not set too small. When used with data which are "just barely separable," the fuzzy perceptron converged in fewer iterations than did its crisp counterpart. Hence, the fuzzy perceptron appears to be a promising method for generating a decision boundary between the classes, whether or not the two classes are separable.

It should also be noted that, while we chose the perceptron, these techniques could be used in any of the gradient-descent algorithms to produce linear (or nonlinear under appropriate transformation) decision boundaries.

REFERENCES

[1] F. Rosenblatt, "The perceptron: A perceiving and recognizing automaton," Cornell Univ., Ithaca, NY, Project PARA, Cornell Aeronaut. Lab. Rep., 85-460-1, 1957.
[2] J. T. Tou and R. C. Gonzalez, *Pattern Recognition Principles.* Reading, MA: Addison-Wesley, 1974.
[3] L. A. Zadeh, "Fuzzy sets," *Inform. Contr.*, vol. 8, pp. 338–353, 1965.
[4] E. T. Lee and L. A. Zadeh, "Note on fuzzy languages," *Inform. Sci.*, vol. 1, pp. 421–434, 1969.
[5] J. C. Bezdek, *Pattern Recognition with Fuzzy Objective Function Algorithms.* New York: Plenum, 1981.
[6] M. Gupta, R. Ragade, and R. Yager, Eds., *Advances in Fuzzy Set Theory and Applications.* Amsterdam, The Netherlands: North-Holland, 1979.
[7] P. P. Wang and S. K. Chang, Eds., *Fuzzy Sets—Theory and Applications to Policy Analysis and Information Systems.* New York: Plenum, 1980.
[8] R. Duda and P. Hart, *Pattern Classification and Scene Analysis.* New York: Wiley, 1973.
[9] A. Kaufman, *Introduction to the Theory of Fuzzy Subsets*, vol. I. New York: Academic, 1975.

Neurocomputations in Relational Systems

W. PEDRYCZ

Abstract—**Artificial neural nets create a form of new high parallel computational structures used in many areas of applications. Fuzzy sets with all their conceptual capabilities and schemes of knowledge representation are considered as an interesting platform to cope with ambiguity present in human activity, especially decision processes. Relational structures in particular, forming a natural extension of boolean relational systems, play a significant role in building formal relational models of reality. In this correspondence we will indicate strong analogies between relational structures involving some composition operators and a certain class of neural networks. The problem of learning of connections of the structure is addressed and relevant learning procedures are proposed. An optimized performance index proposed here has a strong logical flavor. Some significant implementation details are studied as well.**

Index Terms—**Fuzzy set structures, learning algorithms, neural computations, relational structures.**

I. Introduction

Neurocomputations have already started becoming popular as a tool for completing a large mass of numerical computations in an effective, highly parallel manner. Not tackling problems of rather general philosophical nature (such as, e.g., neural nets as electronic models of brains) we would like to treat these networks as a new paradigm of computation that could replace traditional sequential schemes involved in most computers. To achieve this success two factors of primordial importance have to be taken into account, namely 1) an appropriate way of problem representation which leads to its formulation in terms of a suitable topology of the neural network and 2) an appropriate learning algorithm. The first element solely refers to problem specificity and reflects a common way of handling and solving it by a human being. In other words, the problem of representation is tied with an aspect of a relevant cognitive perspective, refer, for instance, to [3], [4], [7], [12].

Within it, a certain tradeoff between precision and generality of problem description has to be achieved. Moreover all input and output nodes have to get a clear interpretation. This type of interpretation is immediate and easy to carry out for a broad range of problems of image processing where each pixel can be associated with an individual node of the network. Also the values occurring at these nodes are dimensionless having a clear-cut meaning of the level of brightness of the pixel. Unfortunately there is a number of applications in which this simple and straightforward interpretation is not directly available. Usually a kind of preprocessing is necessary to come up with dimensionless and standardized variables which in turn are treated as inputs of the network.

Referring to the second issue, it is desirable to develop new structures of networks in term of nonlinearities involved there as well as different operators. In sequel it induces a need to work out new learning policies.

In this correspondence we will discuss a new neural network structure originating from fuzzy set theory. Fuzzy sets equipped with their own language of knowledge representation form a plausible platform for problem handling, especially in the presence of uncertainty. They offer an interesting tool for adjusting the cognitive perspective [12]. Fuzzy sets utilize set-theoretic operators such as, e.g., of minimum and maximum which have an interesting empirical validation, see for instance [2]. We propose relevant learning algorithms and investigate their properties. Interesting links between these neural networks and relational structures worked out in terms of fuzzy relational equations are also highlighted.

To cast the problem of learning completed with the aid of fuzzy sets and its underlying structures in a certain perspective and refer to some existing interesting results, we can point to some research done in the past [1], [12]–[14]. In comparison to existing topologies already investigated, the proposed system is exclusively based upon set-theoretic operations along with the suitable learning algorithm. The previous studies contained only some elements using fuzzy set techniques either in the learning process or the structure itself, such as, e.g., fuzzy automata studied by Wee and Fu [14].

The correspondence is structured into several sections. In Section II, which is of preliminary character, we discuss some basic relational structures, provide all necessary facts coming from the theory of fuzzy sets and highlight their neural network representation. Afterwords, learning procedures are studied in detail (Section III). In addition to that we consider some modification and enhancements of the generic method studying their impacts on the resulting learning capabilities. Numerical examples illustrate various schemes of learning in relational structures of different levels of complexity.

II. Basic Relational Structures and Their Neural Network Representations

In this section we will set up basic notation that will be used within the correspondence. Let $\boldsymbol{X} = \{x_1, x_2, \cdots, x_n\}$ denote a finite set of input nodes and let $\boldsymbol{Y} = \{y_1, y_2, \cdots, y_m\}$ stand for another set of output nodes. A well-known basic operator realized in fuzzy sets, cf. [2], [8], [11], called max–min composition and denoted by $X \circ R$, is performed on a fuzzy set X and fuzzy relation R giving rise to another fuzzy set Y such that

$$Y = X \circ R \tag{1}$$

i.e.,

$$\begin{aligned} Y(y_j) &= \max_{x_i}(\min(X(x_i), R(x_i, y_j))) \\ &= \bigvee_{x_i \in \boldsymbol{X}} [X(x_i) \wedge R(x_i, y_j)] \end{aligned} \tag{2}$$

where X is a fuzzy set defined in $\boldsymbol{X}$ and Y is a resulting fuzzy set defined in $\boldsymbol{Y}$. Furthermore R is a fuzzy relation R: $\boldsymbol{X} \times \boldsymbol{Y} \to [0, 1]$ describing all relationships (links, connections) between the input and output nodes. Incorporating a usual vector and matrix notation, (2) can be read as the max–min composition carried out with respect to the vector X and individual columns of R, say

$$[X(x_1), X(x_2), \cdots, X(x_n)] \circ \begin{bmatrix} R(x_1, y_1) & \cdots & R(x_1, y_j) & \cdots & R(x_1, y_m) \\ R(x_2, y_1) & \cdots & R(x_2, y_j) & \cdots & R(x_2, y_m) \\ R(x_n, y_1) & \cdots & R(x_n, y_j) & \cdots & R(x_n, y_m) \end{bmatrix}.$$

As is obvious from (2), X forms a vector of activation of all input nodes. Let us fix an output node, say $y = y_{jo}$. Then the grades of activation (grade of membership) $Y(y)$ results by taking maximum over all minima between levels of excitation of input nodes x_i, $X(x_i)$, and relevant connections between these nodes and the output node y which are represented by the corresponding column of the fuzzy relation R, $R(x_i, y)$. In order to get a description of the basic cell

Manuscript received August 25, 1989; revised October 17, 1990. Recommended for acceptance by R. De Mori. This work was supported by the Natural Sciences and Engineering Research Council of Canada.

The author is with the Department of Electrical and Computer Engineering, University of Manitoba, Winnipeg, Man. R3T 2N2, Canada.

IEEE Log Number 9041530.

Reprinted from *IEEE Trans. Pattern Anal. Machine Intell.*, vol. PAMI-13, no. 3, pp. 289–297, March 1991.

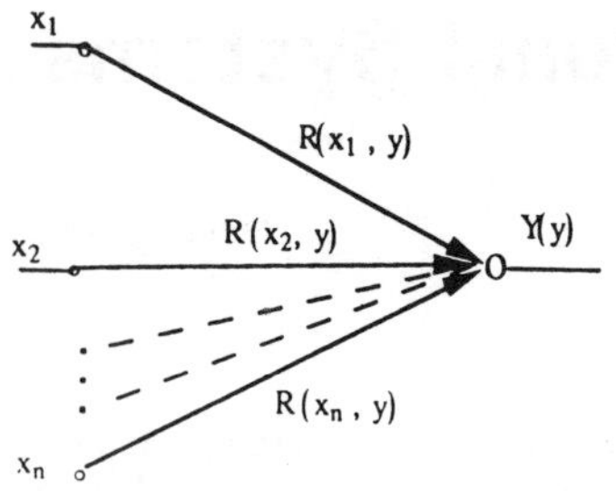

Fig. 1. A basic *n*-input, single output node of the network.

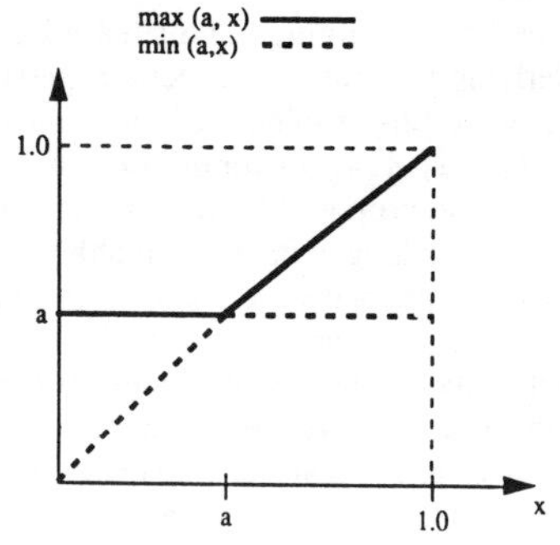

Fig. 2. Graphical illustration of maximum and minimum operators used in relational network.

of the network, it is convenient to consider expression (2) being the entire neural network, as a collection of "*m*" separate *n*-input single-output computational cells. An example of a selected cell is visualized in Fig. 1.

Here small dots represent the minimum operator whereas a big one corresponds to a node where a maximum is taken. It becomes clear that a way in which input nodes contribute (influence) to the output node is realized in a different way in comparison to the ordinary case where minimum is replaced by product and the final aggregation is completed by an ordinary sum. In such a sense the way the output nodes are activated by the max–min composition is less interactive and the particular output node depends on only one appropriate input node.

Also, yet another observation is significant to establish a complete basic element of the network. Following (2), we can deduce that to get the value at the output node, the input nodes should be activated to a certain degree, otherwise because of the lack of summation, the aggregation effect might be too low to activate the output (the output node will never produce a significant value of output). To overcome this shortcoming and obtain the entire unit interval of admissible values at the output node, we will incorporate a bias $\vartheta \varepsilon [0, 1]$ that is added accordingly,

$$Y(y) = \max\left[\max_{x_i}(\min(X(x_i), R(x_i, y))), \vartheta(y)\right]. \quad (3)$$

To derive a complete consistency, the bias might be treated as an auxiliary input node constantly driven by the input value set to 1.0. Due to the form of the node (3), it becomes apparent that all possible values reported at this output node are not lower than this bias. The expression (3) will be viewed as the basic component of the network we are going to work with. It is worthwhile to recall the basic computational structure of the single element of the neural network forming a rough analogy of that discussed above, and described by

$$Y(y) = f\left(\sum_{i=1}^{n} X(x_i)R(x_i, y) + \vartheta(y)\right)$$

where f is a nonlinear function of its argument, e.g., the function f may be considered as a logistic relationship, namely $f(z) = 1/(1 + e^{-z})$. Thus the resulting value of the output node is related to its inputs in a nonlinear form that makes it possible to obtain interesting dynamical properties. The network as described by (3) is obviously a nonlinear one.

To illustrate the character of nonlinearities, we summarize both the minimum and maximum operators in Fig. 2. From a logical standpoint, the structure (3) can be considered as a realization of sum of minterms (products).

Further on, another dual structure representing a product of sums, i.e., a product of maxterms is of interest. The relevant expression reads as

$$Y(y) = \min\left[\min_{x_i}(\max(X(x_i), R(x_i, y))), \vartheta(y)\right]$$

$y \in Y$.

Due to existing duality, we will focus on the previous, max–min structure of the neural network and develop for it a collection of suitable learning algorithms. For the min–max structure they can be obtained in an analogous way.

III. Learning Procedures in Max–Min Structures of Networks

When speaking about learning processes in neural networks in general, it is necessary to discuss some essential components such as performance index optimized within the learning process and specific properties of the learning set of data. The role of the performance index cannot be neglected since it reflects a nature of the framework of the problem at hand being solved. Nevertheless, it is a quite common habit to use a sort of Euclidean distance between target value of the particular output node and the corresponding value generated by the network. One reason standing behind this choice is that this type of distance has a quite transparent energy-like character and it seems to be widely acceptable from a numerical viewpoint. The learning in the network is guided by its values and the minimum (local or global) is looked for. Following a general stream of investigations in fuzzy sets where set-theoretic and logic-based techniques are in common use we will introduce a new performance index called equality index which is strongly tied with these logical aspects. We briefly discuss its properties.

A. Equality Index as Performance Index in Learning Processes

The equality index used for learning purposes and as defined in [8], [9] is given in the following form

$$T(y) \equiv Y(y) = \frac{1}{2}[(T(y) \to Y(y)) \wedge (Y(y) \to T(y)) + (\overline{T}(y) \to \overline{Y}(y)) \wedge (\overline{Y}(y) \to \overline{T}(y))] \quad (4)$$

where $T(y)$ denotes a target value at the node y while $Y(y)$, as before, describes the actual output produced by the same node of the network.

The above definition having a strong logical background requires a careful interpretation. Observing that "→" denotes implication specified between two grades of membership we are going to compare, the first component of this definition describes a degree of equality between $T(y)$ and $Y(y)$: it is viewed as a minimum of degrees to which $T(y)$ implies $Y(y)$ and vice versa. The second component preserves the same structure as the first one with only such a difference that it applies to complements (negations) of the values observed at T and Y; the complement is defined in a usual form, i.e., $\overline{T}(y) = 1 - T(y)$. The implication as it stands in fuzzy sets can be defined in a very general setting and there is more than one simple way to express it. We will recall one possible and flexible approach in which the implications are directly induced by t-norms, cf. [6]. In this light, a formal definition of the implication takes the form

$$T(y) \to Y(y) = \sup\{z \varepsilon [0, 1] | T(y)tz \le Y(y)\} \quad (5)$$

(let us reiterate here that by t-norm we mean a two-argument function t: $[0, 1]^2 \to [0, 1]$ such that it preserves i) monotonicity, i.e., $atb \le a_1tb_1$ if $a < a_1$, $b < b_1$, ii) associativity $at(btc) = (atb)tc$, and iii) commutativity $atb = bta$. Moreover, two boundary conditions are fulfilled: $at0 = 0$, $at1 = a$.

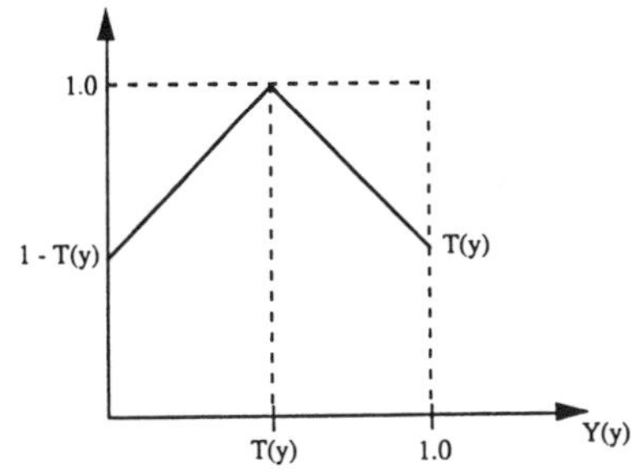

Fig. 3. An illustration of equality index $T(y) \equiv Y(y)$ viewed as a function of one argument, $T(y)$ fixed.

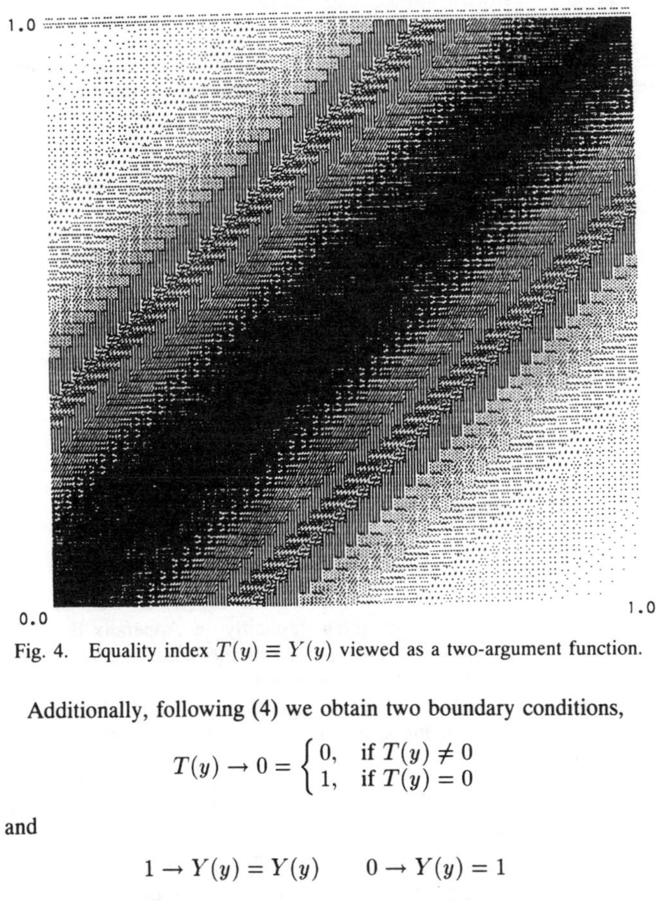

Fig. 4. Equality index $T(y) \equiv Y(y)$ viewed as a two-argument function.

Additionally, following (4) we obtain two boundary conditions,

$$T(y) \rightarrow 0 = \begin{cases} 0, & \text{if } T(y) \neq 0 \\ 1, & \text{if } T(y) = 0 \end{cases}$$

and

$$1 \rightarrow Y(y) = Y(y) \qquad 0 \rightarrow Y(y) = 1$$

So, in fact, for these boundary (boolean) values of the arguments we got an essential implication found in two-valued logic.

As is clear now there is (theoretically) an infinite number of implications induced by *t*-norms. We will select one of them having some plausible properties which are advantageous from implementation point of view as leading to a very simple hardware realization. It is well-known as the Lukasiewicz implication,

$$T(y) \rightarrow Y(y) = \begin{cases} Y(y) - T(y) + 1, & \text{if } T(y) > Y(y) \\ 1, & \text{otherwise} \end{cases} \tag{6}$$

which is induced by *t*-norm given by

$$atb = \max(0, a + b - 1) \tag{7}$$

$a, b \varepsilon [0, 1]$, and known as the Lukasiewicz &-conjunction ("and"-conjunction).

Finally, inserting (6) into (4) we obtain the following expression for the equality index

$$T(y) \equiv Y(y) = \begin{cases} 1 + T(y) - Y(y), & \text{if } Y(y) > T(y) \\ 1 + Y(y) - T(y), & \text{if } Y(y) < T(y) \\ 1, & \text{if } Y(y) = T(y). \end{cases}$$

From a straightforward observation we conclude that it is a piecewise linear function of both the arguments. Obviously, also seen from the above expression, the equality index attains 1 if and only if both of the arguments $T(y)$ and $Y(y)$ are equal. Finally, a graphical illustration of the equality index for $T(y)$ and $Y(y)$ taking all values in their domain is summarized in Figs. 3 and 4.

From this figure one learns that it is highly regular around its maximal value. This fact along with piecewise linear form of the dependency makes this index especially useful for learning purposes as a good candidate for the performance index. Due to its nature, our goal in learning processes will be to maximize its value.

B. Models of Learning in Basic Neural Structures

Since we are already familiar with the equality index as a proper logic-guided candidate for the performance function we are going to optimize, let us study some essential aspects and develop relevant models of learning. Numerical examples will be carefully inspected to point out some of their characteristic features.

First of all, we consider a simple single-input–single-output model (single-input–single-output network) of the following form:

$$y = (x \wedge a) \vee \vartheta \tag{8}$$

where x is viewed as an input while a and ϑ are the parameters we are looking for. For estimation purposes, we have at our disposal a family of input–output pairs (x_i, t_i), $i = 1, 2, \cdots, N$ where t_i stands for the target value the network is going to achieve when being activated by x_i. An overall performance index is formed as a sum of equality indexes $y_i \equiv t_i$, $i = 1, 2, \cdots, N$ with y_i the output of the network where the input value equals x_i; see (8):

$$Q = \sum_{i=1}^{N} (y_i \equiv t_i). \tag{9}$$

The parameters a and ϑ are updated iteratively by taking increments Δa and $\Delta\vartheta$ resulting from deviations reported between all the pairs y_i and t_i, namely,

$$a(k+1) = a(k) + \Psi_1(k)\Delta a$$
$$\vartheta(k+1) = \vartheta(k) + \Psi_2(k)\Delta\vartheta$$

where index k refers to the iteration (learning) step, $k = 1, 2, \cdots$ while $a(1)$ and $\vartheta(1)$ are initial values of the parameters. Ψ_1 and Ψ_2 are nonincreasing functions of k which underline a fact of decreasing influence of increments Δa and $\Delta\vartheta$ on the values of the parameters already being accumulated. Usually in limit, $\Psi_1(k)$ and $\Psi_2(k)$ approach 0. A way of determining the increments Δa and $\Delta\vartheta$ for this single model is presented in Appendix A.

Following detailed formulas the learning algorithm can be concisely summarized as follows:

- Initiate the parameters a and ϑ, i.e., assign the values $a(1)$, $\vartheta(1)$.
- Cyclically process the data $(x_i, t_i)(i = 1, 2, \cdots, N)(k = 1, 2 \cdots)$ updating the values of a and ϑ accordingly (on-line variant of learning)

$$a(k+1) = a(k) + \Psi_1(k)\left[\frac{\Delta a(k+1)}{N} + \eta\frac{\Delta a(k)}{N}\right]$$

$$\vartheta(k+1) = \vartheta(k) + \Psi_2(k)\left[\frac{\Delta\vartheta(k+1)}{N} + \eta\frac{\Delta\vartheta(k)}{N}\right].$$

Note also that the updating procedure is made independent of size of the learning set. First, the values of a and ϑ are updated cyclically with regard to the values x_i and t_i given. The parameter a is adjusted and afterwards all the changes of ϑ apply for this new value of a. In other words, we favor a process of learning of a over possible modifications of the bias ϑ. This is quite straightforward because otherwise the bias, due to the disjunctive way it contributes to (8), could easily override some desired changes of the weight a and the entire process of learning could be remarkably slowed down.

The second component already shown above refers to the addition of a so-called momentum controlled by η. This is a well-known

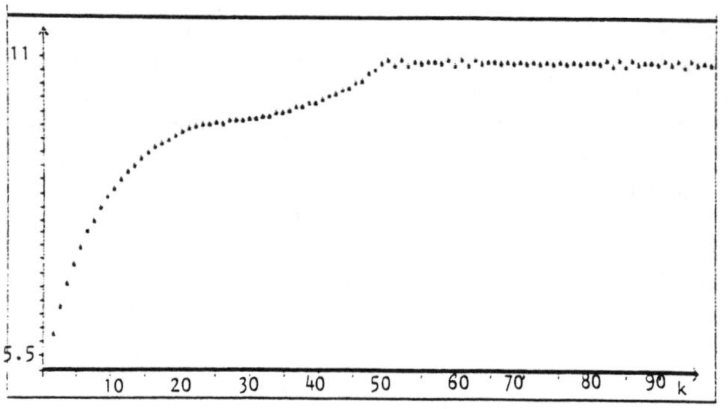

Fig. 5. The values of the equality index obtained in successive learning steps.

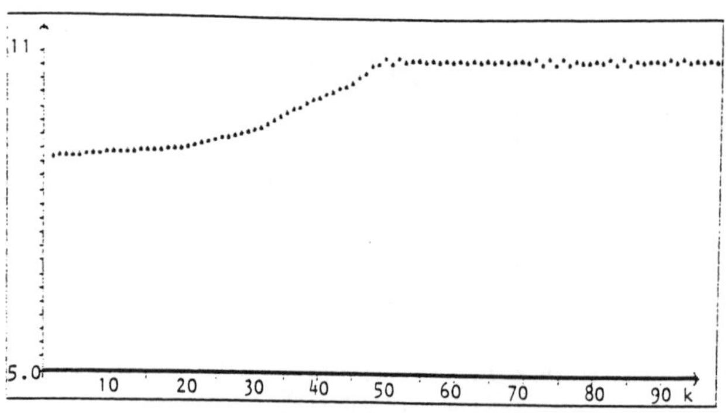

Fig. 6. The values of the equality index versus successive learning steps for different starting conditions (a = 1, $\vartheta = 0$).

idea in neural networks and its goal is to filter out high frequencies associated with the changes of the parameters within the entire learning process, cf., e.g., [5].

The coefficient η specifies a level of modification of the parameters being learned with regard to the values of increment obtained in the previous iteration step (k).

It is also instructive to come up with a straightforward illustration of the performance of the learning method in order to visualize its convergence properties. We will show the following fact:

- for the relationship $x = a$, the updating process of x

$$x(k+1) = x(k) + \Psi(k)\,\frac{\partial Q}{\partial x(k)}$$

with the derivative computed as in Appendix A converges to a in a single step.

Proof: The derivative $\frac{\partial Q}{\partial x(k)}$ is expressed as

$$\frac{\partial Q}{\partial x(k)} = \begin{cases} 1, & \text{if } x < a \\ 0, & \text{if } x = a \\ -1, & \text{if } x > a. \end{cases}$$

Furthermore, let the initial starting value of $x(1)$ be set to zero and $\Psi(k)$ be considered as a harmonic sequence, namely $\Psi(k) = \frac{a}{k}$. Then

$$x(2) = x(1) + \Psi(1) \cdot \frac{\partial Q}{\partial x(0)} = a.$$

In sequel we will consider some numerical examples.

Example 1: In this example we make use of data simulated by a relationship $y = (0.7 \wedge x) \vee 0.5$. The data set consists of 11 pairs with x_i distributed equally along [0, 1] interval, namely $x_1 = 0$, $x_2 = 0.1, \cdots$, and $x_{11} = 1.0$.

In the series of simulations reported below, the functions $\Psi_1(k)$ and $\Psi_2(k)$ are given by

$$\Psi_1(k) = \Psi_2(k) = \frac{1}{5\sqrt[4]{k} + 10}.$$

The contribution of the momentum is specified by setting the parameter $\eta = 0.02$.

1) In the first experiment the starting values of a and ϑ are set to zero, $a = \vartheta = 0$. At each iteration, first, the parameter a has been updated, and afterward the same is completed with ϑ.

The performance of the learning process is visualized in Fig. 5. After 50 iterations, the values of the performance index become stable reaching the value of Q equal to 10.97 with $a = 0.70$ and $\vartheta = 0.497$, so the parameters of the structure have been properly estimated.

2) The second experiment deals with different starting conditions, namely $a = 1$, $\vartheta = 0$; see Fig. 6. The convergence rate is the same as in the previous case, moreover, the same value of the performance index is also obtained, Q = 10.96.

Now we will discuss the learning scheme for the structure of the neural network with n-inputs and single output. To get a concise description, we introduce a vector notation: all weight parameters are collected in a single $\boldsymbol{a} = [a_1, a_2, \cdots, a_n]$. The vectors $\boldsymbol{x}_1, \boldsymbol{x}_2, \cdots, \boldsymbol{x}_N$, and numbers $y_1, y_2, \cdots, y_N$ will denote the learning set, where each $\boldsymbol{x}_i$ is a vector of values observed at the input nodes,

$$\boldsymbol{x}_i = [x_{i1}, x_{i2}, \cdots, x_{in}].$$

Making use of this vector notation, the output of the network is given by

$$y_i = f(\boldsymbol{x}_i; \boldsymbol{a}, \vartheta) = \left(\bigvee_{j=1}^{n} (a_j \wedge x_{ij})\right) \vee \vartheta$$

$$i = 1, 2, \cdots, N.$$

Then the learning process proceeds according to formulas being analogical to those found before, namely

$$\boldsymbol{a}(k+1) = \boldsymbol{a}(k) + \Psi_1(k)\left[\frac{\Delta \boldsymbol{a}(k+1)}{Nn} + \eta \frac{\Delta \boldsymbol{a}(k)}{Nn}\right]$$

$$\vartheta(k+1) = \vartheta(k) + \Psi_2(k)\left[\frac{\Delta\vartheta(k+1)}{Nn} + \eta \frac{\Delta\vartheta(k)}{Nn}\right]$$

$$k = 1, 2, \cdots.$$

The coordinates of the increments of $\boldsymbol{a}$, $\Delta \boldsymbol{a}(k)$ as well as the increment of ϑ, $\Delta\vartheta(k)$ are given explicitly in Appendix B. The parameters of the structure are updated in the same fashion as in the first learning scheme already provided.

Example 2: The data set used for learning in the relational structure with n = 4 input nodes and m = 3 nodes consists of 4 pairs $(\boldsymbol{x}_i, \boldsymbol{y}_i)$ as shown below:

$\boldsymbol{x}_i$	$\boldsymbol{y}_i$
[0.3 1.0 0.5 0.2]	[0.7 0.5 0.6]
[0.1 1.0 1.0 0.5]	[0.7 1.0 0.6]
[0.5 0.7 0.2 1.0]	[0.7 0.7 0.6]
[1.0 0.7 0.5 0.3]	[1.0 0.5 0.6]

As said before, the process of learning is completed separately for each output node. All the weights are summarized in a (4 × 3)-dimensional matrix; see notation in Section II. The values of the biases are collected as entries of a three-dimensional vector.

1) In the first experiment, we consider an initial condition consisting of all 1's and 0's, respectively, such that: $R = \mathbf{1}$ and $\vartheta = \mathbf{0}$. The parameters are set as

$$\Psi_1(k) = \Psi_2(k) = \frac{1}{\sqrt{k} + 1}$$

while the momentum parameter equals 0.2. The process of learning is illustrated in Fig. 7. The values of the obtained weights are equal to

$$R = \begin{bmatrix} 1.00 & 0.48 & 0.60 \\ 0.70 & 0.48 & 0.58 \\ 0.69 & 1.00 & 0.60 \\ 0.70 & 0.70 & 0.60 \end{bmatrix}$$

and the bias vector has all entries equal to 0.

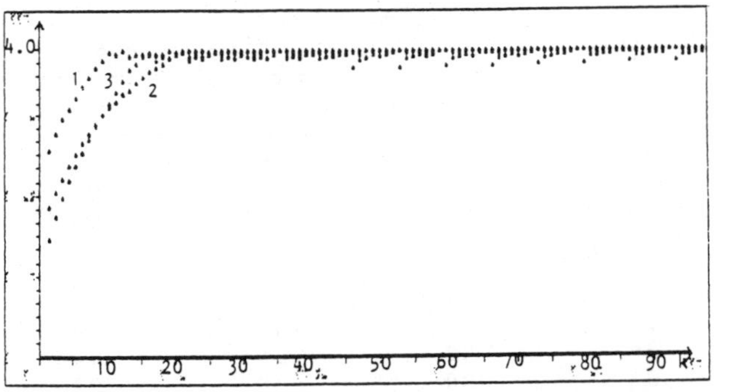

Fig. 7. Learning in the structure with many inputs; initial conditions set as $R = \mathbf{1}$ and $\vartheta = 0$.

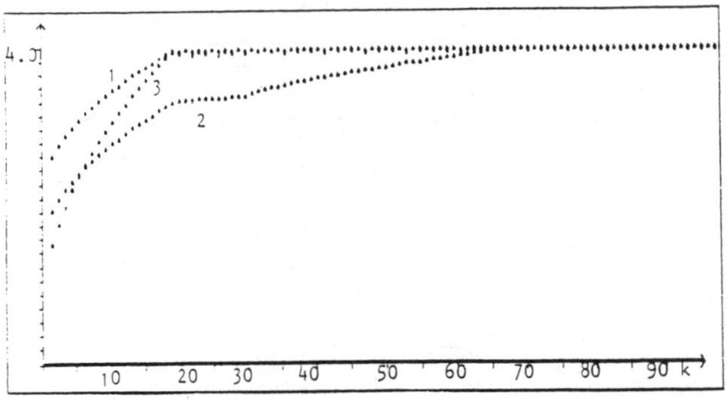

Fig. 8. The results of learning the structure with many inputs; initial conditions set as $R = \mathbf{1}$ $\vartheta = 1$.

The values of the performance index for consecutive coordinates of $\boldsymbol{Y}$, y_1, y_2, and y_3 are equal to 3.99, 3.99, and 3.98, respectively.

2) We slightly modify the initial conditions, setting the biases equal to 1.0, $\vartheta = 1$. The results of learning give rise to the weight matrix and the vector of biases,

$$R = \begin{bmatrix} 1.0 & 0.48 & 0.53 \\ 0.49 & 0.49 & 0.49 \\ 0.53 & 1.0 & 0.53 \\ 0.53 & 0.70 & 0.53 \end{bmatrix}$$

$$\vartheta = [0.70 \quad 0.50 \quad 0.60].$$

As before, the performance index attains maximal values; Fig. 8

Observe that the values of the weights are lower in comparison to the first case. This is primarily caused by nonzero initial conditions of the biases. Additionally the biases are equal to the minimal values observed at the output nodes of the network, compared to the learning set of data.

3) Now the initial conditions for the weights and the biases are set to the minimum observed of the output nodes that is equal to 0.5. The process of learning, as shown in Fig. 9, becomes much faster in comparison to the previous experiment. Nevertheless, for the first output node, the performance index still attains lower value equal to Q = 3.69. For the remaining output nodes, we get maximal possible values of Q. The weights derived in this way are the following:

$$R = \begin{bmatrix} 0.59 & 0.49 & 0.56 \\ 0.70 & 0.47 & 0.59 \\ 0.63 & 1.0 & 0.57 \\ 0.59 & 0.7 & 0.56 \end{bmatrix}$$

and

$$\vartheta = [0.5 \quad 0.5 \quad 0.5].$$

Hence, what might have been expected, for the first output node the learning process is blurred by too high values of the initial values of the biases.

As various results have been derivied, the above example sheds some light on interesting properties of the max–min relational

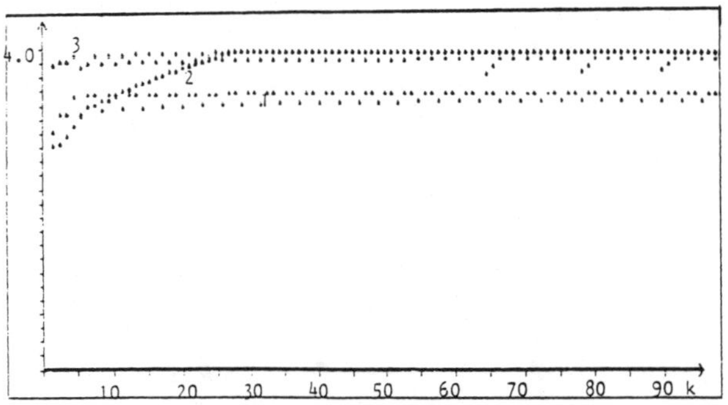

Fig. 9. The results of learning for initial conditions $R = 0.5$, $\vartheta = 0.5$.

structures. We can report that different relations and the biases generate an absolute maximum of the performance index (as it happened in the two first cases, and the third one for the second and third node). In other words, there may exist a certain number of relations satisfying a collection of constraints expressed by the same learning set. This phenomena has a straightforward interpretation arising in a theory of fuzzy relational equations, cf., e.g., [1], [8], [10]. Having this data set (learning set), we can discuss a problem of solution of a system of relational constraint (equations)

$$X_l \circ R = Y_l$$

where $l = 1, 2, 3, 4$ with respect to R. Denote by $\mathfrak{R}_l = \{R | X_l \circ R = Y_l\}$ a family of all fuzzy relations satisfying the lth constraint. If all these families have a nonempty intersection, namely, $\mathfrak{R} = \bigcap_l \mathfrak{R}_l \neq \phi$ (of course each individual family $\mathfrak{R}_l$ is supposed to be nonempty), then the maximal element of $\mathfrak{R}$ (where a term "maximal" is considered in a sense of fuzzy sets (relations) inclusion, see [2]) is determined by taking an intersection of Gödelian implications applied to X_l and Y_l, $X_l \underline{G} Y_l$, where

$$X_l(x_i) \underline{G} Y_l(y_j) = \begin{cases} 1, & \text{if } X_l(x_i) \leq Y_l(y_j) \\ Y_l(y_j), & \text{otherwise.} \end{cases}$$

Of course, the above formula is valid only under assumption of the existence of the family of solutions. Unfortunately, the satisfaction of this assumption is not known in advance. Therefore a blind use of this approach might be extremely misleading, in sequel generating a relation with very small, if not zero, entries. It means that the outcome of this method should be verified by a series of straightforward max–min compositions of the obtained relation and the data. When a collection of equations is solved with the aid of the proposed method, the derived relation R can be viewed as an "approximate" solution and optimal in sense of discussed equality index. In the above example, considering the data as coming from the system of relational equations and completing all relevant computations, the fuzzy relation containing all weights is given as

$$R = \begin{bmatrix} 1.0 & 1.0 & 1.0 \\ 0.7 & 0.5 & 0.6 \\ 1.0 & 1.0 & 1.0 \\ 1.0 & 1.0 & 1.0 \end{bmatrix} \cap \begin{bmatrix} 1.0 & 1.0 & 1.0 \\ 0.7 & 1.0 & 0.6 \\ 0.7 & 1.0 & 0.6 \\ 1.0 & 1.0 & 1.0 \end{bmatrix} \cap \begin{bmatrix} 1.0 & 1.0 & 1.0 \\ 1.0 & 1.0 & 0.6 \\ 1.0 & 1.0 & 1.0 \\ 0.7 & 0.7 & 0.6 \end{bmatrix}$$
$$\cap \begin{bmatrix} 1.0 & 0.5 & 0.6 \\ 1.0 & 0.5 & 0.6 \\ 1.0 & 1.0 & 1.0 \\ 1.0 & 1.0 & 1.0 \end{bmatrix} = \begin{bmatrix} 1.0 & 0.5 & 0.6 \\ 0.7 & 0.5 & 0.6 \\ 0.7 & 1.0 & 0.6 \\ 0.7 & 0.7 & 0.6 \end{bmatrix}.$$

By straightforward calculations (i.e., by performing max–min compositions for all pairs), one can easily verify that the family of solutions is nonempty. According to the developed theory, the weights contained in the relation R are the greatest in their magnitude. Notice that the weights derived in the learning process (especially those obtained for the initial value of R set $\mathbf{1}$) take lower, however very close to the previous, values.

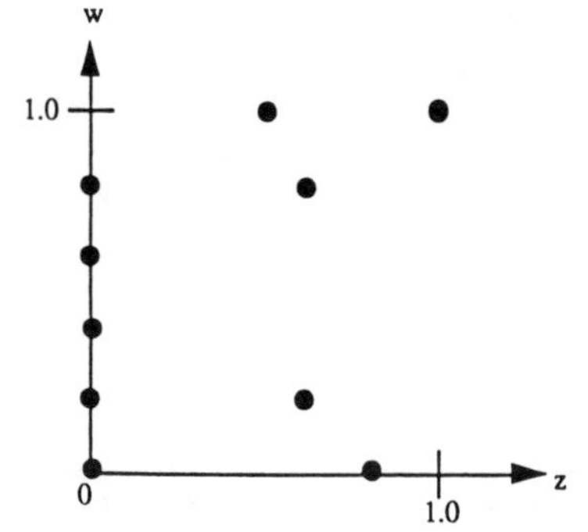

Fig. 10. The learning collection of patterns; see description in text.

TABLE I
LEARNING SET USED IN TWO-OUTPUT NEURAL NETWORKS

z	w	$Y(y_1)$	$Y(y_2)$
0.0	0.0	0.0	1.0
0.0	0.2	0.2	0.8
0.0	0.4	0.4	0.6
0.0	0.6	0.6	0.4
0.5	1.0	0.5	0.5
0.6	0.8	0.4	0.6
1.0	1.0	0.0	1.0
0.6	0.2	0.6	0.4
0.8	0.0	0.8	0.2

IV. Further Modifications of the Learning Algorithm

The learning process already introduced may potentially suffer from the shortcoming deteriorating its convergence properties. Referring to Appendix B, one can observe that the increments causing all changes of the weights a_j, $j = 1, 2, \cdots, n$ or the biases ϑ_i, $1, 2, \cdots, n$ have a strict boolean character being either equal to 0 or 1. It might happen, however, that with a certain configuration of weights and data presented at the inputs of the network, all the increments are equal identically to zero. This, in sequel, may lead to a local lack of convergence. To alleviate the problem we will propose to consider a relaxed version of a strict boolean predicate "being equal" by a multivalued, fuzzy version of a predicate "being included." This predicate will describe a degree of containment.

We will follow some findings contained in [10]. Consider two values in $[0, 1]$, by a and b, respectively. The degree of satisfaction of the predicate

"a is included in b"

(i.e., a is smaller than b) is introduced making use of (5). From a logical standpoint the implication is equivalent to the above stated predicate.

Hence, for instance, a derivative now reads as

$$\frac{\partial}{\partial a}(a \wedge x_i) = a \rightarrow x_i$$

generating a continuum of logical values instead of two boolean truth values resulting from the previous expressions. This yields fuzzy-set specified versions of the predicates Φ and Ψ; see Appendix A. Denote them by Φ_f and Ψ_f.

$$\Phi_f : (i)\vartheta \rightarrow a \wedge x_i \quad \text{and } (ii) a \rightarrow x_i$$

$$\Psi_f : a \wedge x_i \rightarrow \vartheta$$

The above implication may be specified as the Lukasiewcz implication.

Example 3: We will discuss a multivalued version of linearly nonseparable XOR and equivalence problem, both well known in neural networks. The learning collection of patterns is distributed within the unit square as shown in Fig. 10. Additionally, all the patterns are summarized in Table I. On the basis of the two variables of the patterns, say z and w, we build some logical combinations (i.e., their minterms) contributing to the fuzzy set X and forming all inputs of the network

$$X = [z \quad w \quad \bar{z} \quad \bar{w} \quad z \wedge w \quad \bar{z} \wedge \bar{w} \quad z \wedge \bar{w} \quad \bar{z} \wedge w].$$

The learning process is initiated with all connections set to 0.75, $i = 1, 2, \cdots, 8$, $j = 1, 2$ while the learning rate was fixed as 0.125. The momentum term was neglected. The collected series of values of the performance index achieved within the learning process indicates that the learning is fast without any undesired oscillations; see Table II.

The learning is completed separately for each output of the network, while the performance index reported in the table is the sum of the indexes obtained for separate outputs.

TABLE II
RESULTS OF LEARNING IN THE NEURAL STRUCTURE

Iteration Step	Performance Index
1	13.80
2	16.99
3	17.39
4	17.99
5	18.45
6	18.95
7	19.23
8	19.37
9	19.54
10	19.68
16	20.00

The results obtained after 16 learning epochs are the following (the meaning of all input nodes is clearly indicated):

$$\begin{array}{c} \\ y_1 \\ y_2 \end{array} \begin{bmatrix} z & w & \bar{z} & \bar{w} & z \wedge w & \bar{z} \wedge \bar{w} & z \wedge \bar{w} & \bar{z} \wedge w \\ 0.0 & 0.0 & 0.0 & 0.0 & 0.0 & 0.0 & 0.835 & 0.607 \\ 0.0 & 0.256 & 0.0 & 0.184 & 1.0 & 1.0 & 0.03 & 0.22 \end{bmatrix}.$$

This implies that the function realized by the first output node of the network reads as

$$Y(y_1) = (0.835 \wedge z \wedge \bar{w}) \vee (0.607 \wedge \bar{z} \wedge w).$$

The function is nothing but the XOR function slightly modified by the weights. The values of the weights found below 1 are the result of learning in presence of the given learning set not containing extremal situations; see again Table I, i.e., cases where either $z = 0$ and $w = 1$ or $z = 1$ and $w = 0$. For the second output node (y_2) we read the direct logical expression

$$Y(y_2) = (\bar{z} \wedge \bar{w}) \vee (z \wedge w) \vee (0.256 \wedge w) \vee (0.184 \wedge \bar{w}) \vee (0.22 \wedge \bar{z} \wedge w).$$

It is visible that two components of equivalence are prevailing with some residual contribution coming from other variables and products, such as w, $\bar{w}$ and $\bar{z} \wedge w$.

V. Concluding Remarks

We have studied a problem of learning in neural networks with max–min composition operations. Direct links between methodology of fuzzy sets and neural networks become evident. Simultaneously, a straightforward applicational justification of the proposed structure originating in the field of utilization of fuzzy sets (e.g., fuzzy controllers, pattern recognition systems, knowledge-based systems) and easiness of hardware implementations of the neural structure are evident advantages. Once manufactured in hardware, the relational structure can work in a highly parallel mode desired in a broad range of real-time applications. Some relationships that occur to exist between fuzzy relational equations and relational structures of neural networks are of significant value: a formal apparatus of equations can enhance development of new computational structures while on the other hand, the networks can offer new tools for enhancement of efficient implementations of basic models created within a formal framework of these equations.

To address another issue of increased functionality or performance of discussed structure over standard models of nural networks (involving regular product and sum), it is worthwhile to indicate some features.

First the relational model has a straightforward logical interpretation. Any single node realizes a sum of products (minterms) of input logical variables. Thus it is much more plausible to represent a structure possessing logical features. For instance, the multivalued version of the XOR problem discussed in the previous section has an evident logical underlying structure. Then the way of learning in the structure reflecting this topology is much faster than in standard networks. As many recognition problems have a clear geometrical character which can be represented as two (or usually many-valued) predicates, advantages in learning of the structure can be immediately appreciated.

The second aspect is directly associated with hardware implementation. Operations like maximum and minimum fit well requirements of digital implementations, and can be easily connected in fault tolerant structures. Furthermore, they may facilitate processes of learning completed *in situ.*

APPENDIX A

We will derive all formulas for a single-input–single-output computational node as given for instance by (8). Let us take into account the performance index viewed as a sum of equality indexes,

$$Q = \sum_{i=1}^{N} (t_i \equiv y_i).$$

Also introduce $y_i = f(x_i; a, \vartheta)$ which enables us to treat the relationship between x_i and y_i in a more general fashion as already given in (8). The above sum is split into three groups, depending upon the relationship between y_i and t_i.

$$Q = \left[\sum_{i:y_i>t_i} (t_i \equiv y_i) + \sum_{i:y_i=t_i} (t_i \equiv y_i) + \sum_{i:y_i=t_i} (t_i \equiv y_i) \right]$$

Recalling the equality index given by (4) and applying the Lukasiewicz implication there, we get

$$\begin{aligned} Q &= \frac{1}{2} \sum_{i:y_i=t_i} [(f(x_i, a, \vartheta) \to t_i) + (\bar{t}_i \to \bar{f}(x_i; a, \vartheta))] \\ &\quad + \frac{1}{2} \sum_{i:y_i>t_i} [(f(x_i, a, \vartheta) \to t_i) + (\bar{t}_i \to \bar{f}(x_i; a, \vartheta))] \\ &\quad + \frac{1}{2} \sum_{i:y_i<t_i} [(t_i \to f(x_i, a, \vartheta)) + (\bar{f}_i(x_i; a, \vartheta) \to \bar{t}_i)] \\ &= \sum_{i:y_i>t_i} (1 + t_i - f(x_i; a, \vartheta)) \\ &\quad + \sum_{i:y_i=t_i} 1 + \sum_{i:y_i<t_i} (1 + f(x_i; a, \vartheta) - t_i). \end{aligned}$$

Now, a stationary point of Q is searched following a sequence of iterations where the appropriate increments are based upon the derivatives $\frac{\partial Q}{\partial a}$ and $\frac{\partial Q}{\partial \vartheta}$.

They are expressed as

$$\Delta a = \frac{\partial Q}{\partial a} = -\sum_{i:y_i>t_i} \frac{\partial f(x_i; a, \vartheta)}{\partial a} + \sum_{i:y_i<t_i} \frac{\partial f(x_i; a, \vartheta)}{\partial a}$$

and

$$\Delta \vartheta = \frac{\partial Q}{\partial \vartheta} = -\sum_{i:y_i>t_i} \frac{\partial f(x_i; a, \vartheta)}{\partial \vartheta} + \sum_{i:y_i<t_i} \frac{\partial f(x_i; a, \vartheta)}{\partial \vartheta}$$

All remaining derivatives can be computed when the form of the function f is specified. Anyway, even now we can observe that the increments are positive when y_i is lower than the required target value and negative ones when converse situation holds. Thus all increments are driven by the sign of the difference between y_i and t_i. When the form of the function is made more concrete as

$$f(x_i; a, \vartheta) = (a \wedge x_i) \vee \vartheta$$

then the derivatives are calculated as

$$\frac{\partial f(x_i; a, \vartheta)}{\partial a} = \frac{\partial}{\partial a}((a \wedge x_i) \vee \vartheta)$$

and

$$\frac{\partial f(x_i; a, \vartheta)}{\partial \vartheta} = \frac{\partial}{\partial \vartheta}((a \wedge x_i) \vee \vartheta).$$

Notice that for derivatives for minimum and maximum, we have the following expression

$$\frac{\partial}{\partial a}[(a \wedge x_i) \vee \vartheta] = \frac{\partial}{\partial a} \begin{cases} a, & \text{if } (a \wedge x_i) \geq \vartheta \text{ and } a \leq x_i \\ \tau, & \text{otherwise} \end{cases}$$

where τ stands for the expression which does not include the variable a. Bearing this in mind, it becomes apparent that the derivative is either equal to 1 or vanishes, depending exclusively on the satisfaction of the two predicates shown above.

$$\frac{\partial}{\partial a}[(a \wedge x_i) \vee \vartheta] = \begin{cases} 1, & \text{if } \Phi(x_i; a, \vartheta) \\ 0, & \text{otherwise} \end{cases}$$

where Φ stands for conjunction of two predicates (satisfaction of two conditions):

$$\Phi : (i) a \wedge x_i \geq \vartheta \quad \text{and} \quad (ii) a \leq x_i$$

Thus we can speak about exclusively boolean character of the predicate driving any potential increment of the parameter. The same way applies for the second parameter of the function, where now its derivative is controlled by a single predicate $\Psi(x_i; a, \vartheta)$

$$\Psi : \vartheta \geq a \wedge x_i.$$

It Ψ is true then the modification of ϑ is possible. Overall, the increments Δa and $\Delta \vartheta$ are described as

$$\Delta a = -\sum_{i:y_i>t_i} \Phi(x_i; a, \vartheta) + \sum_{i:y_i<t_i} \Phi(x_i; a, \vartheta)$$

$$\Delta \vartheta = -\sum_{i:y_i>t_i} \Psi(x_i; a, \vartheta) + \sum_{i:y_i<t_i} \Psi(x_i; a, \vartheta).$$

Moreover, due to the boolean character of the above predicates, the increments Δa and $\Delta \vartheta$ are bounded by having their values between $-N$ and N.

APPENDIX B

The performance index we are discussing now is again in the form

$$Q = \sum_{i=1}^{N} (t_i \equiv t_i).$$

As we have done before, we split Q into three sums

$$Q = \sum_{i:y_i>t_i} (t_i \equiv y_i) + \sum_{i:y_i=t_i} (t_i \equiv y_i) + \sum_{i:y_i<t_i} (t_i \equiv y_i).$$

Thus, recalling that the output node y_i is expressed as

$$y_i = f(\boldsymbol{x}_i; \boldsymbol{a}, \vartheta) = \bigvee_{j=1}^{n} (a_j \wedge x_{ij}) \vee \vartheta$$

we calculate its derivatives with regard to the lth coordinate of $\boldsymbol{a}$, $l = 1, 2, \cdots, n$

$$\Delta \boldsymbol{a} = \frac{\partial Q}{\partial \boldsymbol{a}} = \begin{bmatrix} \frac{\partial Q}{\partial a_1} \\ \frac{\partial Q}{\partial a_2} \\ \vdots \\ \frac{\partial Q}{\partial a_n} \end{bmatrix}$$

and

$$\Delta \vartheta = \frac{\partial Q}{\partial \vartheta}.$$

For each coordinate of $\boldsymbol{a}$, the increments are calculated similarly as shown in Appendix A, where now the predicate expressing increments of individual coordinates of a_s's, $s = 1, 2, \cdots, n$ are a bit more complicated reflecting relationships existing between inputs and output. Observe that

$$\frac{\partial}{\partial a_s}\left[\left(\bigvee_{j=1}^{n} (a_j \wedge x_{ij})\right) \vee \vartheta\right] = \frac{\partial}{\partial a_s}$$

$$\begin{cases} a_s, & \text{if } \bigvee_{j=1}^{m} (a_j \wedge x_{ij}) \geq \vartheta \text{ and } \bigvee_{\substack{j=1 \\ j \neq s}}^{n} (a_j \wedge x_{ij}) \leq a_s \wedge x_{is} \\ \tau, & \text{otherwise and } \quad a_s \leq x_{is} \end{cases}$$

τ does not depend on the parameter a_s. Hence the predicate $\Phi(x_i;\, a,\, \vartheta)$ reads as a conjunction of three components

$$\Phi : (i) \bigvee_{j=1}^{n} (a_j \wedge x_{ij}) \geq \vartheta \quad (ii) \bigvee_{\substack{j=1 \\ j \neq s}}^{n} (a_j \wedge x_{ij}) \leq a_s \wedge x_{is}$$

$$(iii)\ a_s \leq x_{is}.$$

The predicate for the increment of ϑ is the same as in the previous network:

$$\Psi : \bigvee_{j=1}^{n} (a_j \wedge x_{ij}) \leq \vartheta.$$

References

[1] K. Asai and S. Kitajimo, "Optimizing control using fuzzy automata," *Automatica,* vol. 8, pp. 101–104, 1972.

[2] A. Di Nola, S. Sessa, W. Pedrycz, and E. Sanchez, *Fuzzy Relation Equations and Their Applications to Knowledge Engineering.* Dordrecht, The Netherlands: Kluwer Academic, 1989.

[3] D. Dubois and H. Prade, *Fuzzy Sets and Systems: Theory and Applications.* New York: Academic, 1980.

[4] K. Fukushima, S. Miyake, and T. Ito, "A neural network model for a mechanism of visual pattern recognition," *IEEE Trans. Syst. Man, Cybern.,* vol. 5, pp. 836–834, 1983.

[5] S. Grossberg, (Ed.,) *Neural Networks and Natural Intelligence.* Cambridge, MA: MIT Press, 1988.

[6] R. P. Lippman, "An introduction to computing with neural nets," *IEEE ASSP Mag.,* vol. 4, pp. 4–22, 1987.

[7] K. Menger, "Statistical metric spaces," *Proc. Nat. Acad. Sci.,* vol. 28, pp. 353–357, 1942.

[8] W. Pedrycz, "A fuzzy cognitive structure for pattern recognition," *Pattern Recognition Lett.,* vol. 5, pp. 305–314, 1989.

[9] ——, *Fuzzy Control and Fuzzy Systems.* London: Research Studies Press/Wiley, 1989.

[10] ——, "Direct and inverse problems in comparison of fuzzy data," *Fuzzy Sets Syst.,* vol. 34, pp. 233–236, 1990.

[11] E. Sanchez, "Resolution of composite fuzzy relation equations," *Inform. Contr.,* vol. 30, pp. 38–48, 1976.

[12] M. Serizawa, "A search technique of control rod pattern for smoothing core power distributions by fuzzy automation," *J. Nucl. Sci. Technol.,* vol. 10, pp. 195–201, 1973.

[13] M. Sugeno and T. Terano, "A model of learning based on fuzzy information," *Kybernetes,* vol. 6, pp. 157–166, 1977.

[14] W. G. Wee and K. S. Fu, "A formulation of fuzzy automata and its application as a model of learning system," *IEEE Trans. Syst., Sci., Cybern.,* vol. 5, pp. 215–223, 1969.

[15] L. A. Zadeh, "Outline of a new approach to the analysis of complex systems and decision processes," *IEEE Trans. Syst. Man, Cybern.,* vol. 2, pp. 28–44, 1973.

PARALLEL SELF-ORGANIZING FEATURE MAPS FOR UNSUPERVISED PATTERN RECOGNITION

TERRANCE L. HUNTSBERGER and PONGSAK AJJIMARANGSEE

Intelligent Systems Laboratory, Department of Computer Science, University of South Carolina, Columbia, South Carolina 29208, USA

(Received 11 October 1989)

Neural network research has recently undergone a revival for use in pattern recognition applications.[1] If a training set of data can be provided, the supervised types of networks, such as the Hopfield nets or perceptrons, can be used to recognize patterns.[10,11,18] For unsupervised pattern recognition, systems such as those of the Carpenter/Grossberg ART2 system[8] and Kohonens' self-organizing feature maps[14] are the most commonly used.

The problem of poor separability of input vectors was recently addressed by Keller and Hunt with the fuzzy perceptron model.[13] However, with the exception of the ART2 system, none of these systems are capable of producing continuous valued output, as would be a desirable model for representation of non-distinct input vectors. This paper presents four new algorithms based on the Kohonen self-organizing feature maps which are capable of generating a continuous valued output.[4] We also present the results of some experimental studies run on the NCUBE/10 hypercube at the University of South Carolina.

INDEX TERMS: Clustering, neural nets, pattern recognition.

INTRODUCTION

Image and speech understanding have shown themselves to be difficult problems to solve using traditional techniques. Recent studies have indicated that some portions of the systems needed to address the important concerns for image and speech understanding may be able to be implemented as neural networks.[1] Neural network models use a densely interconnected network of simple computational units. These models are specified by their network topology, unit characteristics, and learning or adaptive rule. The network topology will define how each unit connects to other units. There is a weight associated with each of the connecting paths in the network. The unit characteristics define the function which combines the various inputs and weights into a single quantity as well as the function which then maps this value to an output. The learning rule specifies an initial set of weights and indicates how weights should be adapted during use to accomplish the task at hand.

The early work in neural network models was done by McCulloch and Pitts,[16] Hebb,[9] and Rosenblatt.[18] In the mid 1940s, McCulloch and Pitts[16] started modeling the single nerve cell or neuron in order to create a model of the brain based on anatomical and physiological experimental findings. Hebb[9] introduced some basic ideas about learning in neural network models. Rosenblatt[18] proposed a single layer perceptron capable of learning simple patterns which were linearly separable. A review and some recent work with neural network models can be found in Rumelhart and McClelland.[19]

Neural network models for pattern recognition can be specified as two types, supervised approaches (such as Hopfield net,[11] perceptron[18]) and unsupervised approaches (such as Kohonen,[14] Carpenter/Grossberg[8]). A tutorial review on the use of neural nets for pattern recognition can be found in Lippmann.[15] Multi-layer perceptron[18] and Hopfield[11] types of networks suffer from the problems of convergence to local minima, instability of memory as the training set size increases and the inordinately large number of iterations needed to encode even relatively simple patterns of six variables.[17] A portion of this behavior can be traced to the use of a delta rule for weight updates, which is a steepest descent technique with possible slow convergence properties. Modifications made to the perceptron model by Keller and Hunt[13] are limited to the two class case and are computationally expensive due to the use of exponential functions in the membership value determinations.

Systems such as those of Carpenter/Grossberg[8] and Kohonen[14] are based on

Reprinted with permission from *Int'l. J. General Systems*, vol. 16, no. 4, pp. 357–372, 1990.

biological studies of memory organization and dynamics. The Carpenter/Grossberg design has only recently been extended to describe continuous valued input vectors, but studies indicate that replicable behavior of the system seems to be sensitive to the exact value of the parameters that need to be initialized to run the system.[6] The self-organizing feature map system of Kohonen has previously been shown to be equivalent to the K-means clustering algorithm.[14] As such, it is a strong candidate for continuous valued unsupervised pattern recognition, since the fuzzy c-means algorithm is of the same class. In addition, Kohonens' self-organizing feature maps use a linear update rule for the weights, which makes this model computationally attractive.

This paper presents four new algorithms for generating continuous valued output based on Kohonens' self-organizing feature map model. The first algorithm adds another layer to the network and produces the continuous valued output using the standard Kohonen update algorithm. The second and third algorithms use a new weight update rule which is based on a feedback path from the extra layer. The fourth algorithm demonstrates that a high degree of parallelism can be achieved using a newly developed parallel version of the update algorithm. In the next section, we briefly discuss pattern recognition and fuzzy sets and self-organizing feature maps. This is followed by the presentation of a parallel approach to self-organizing feature maps. Finally, we report the results of experimental studies using this approach, followed by conclusions.

PATTERN RECOGNITION AND FUZZY SETS

Pattern recognition techniques attempt to group a set of units into subsets of classes on the basis of the similarity of their features or properties. Pattern recognition approaches can be categorized as parametric or non-parametric depending on the *a priori* knowledge of the set of patterns. One way to define the pattern recognition process is as follows:

Let $X=\{x_0,x_1,x_2,\ldots,x_{N-1}\}$ denote a set of N objects called units in R^m, where x_i is the kth dimension of feature of unit x_i. Let f be a function whose image on X is $U=f(X)$, i.e. $U=\{u_0,u_1,u_2,\ldots,u_{N-1}\}=\{f(x_0),f(x_1),f(x_2),\ldots,f(x_{N-1})\}$ and $u_{ij}\in\{0,1\}$, where $0\leqq j\leqq c-1$ and c is the total number of clusters. A hard partition of X is a set of subsets of X, $\{X_0,X_1,\ldots,X_{c-1}\}$ that satisfies the conditions:

$$X_i\neq\emptyset,\quad 0\leqq i\leqq c-1,$$

$$X_i\cap X_j=\emptyset,\quad i\neq j,$$

and

$$\bigcup_c X_i=X.$$

For example, a unit can be a pixel in an image and the set of units is the set of pixels in the entire image. A pixel in a color image can be represented by 3 feature values red, green, and blue. In this case $m=3$, and a pixel is in a 3 dimension space (R^3). The task of a segmentation process is to partition a set of pixels into c subsets in which there is a high degree of similarity in the feature values. Suppose there are 4 possible subsets in a particular image to which a pixel could be assigned. If x_i is assigned to the second subset, then the u_i vector would be [0 1 0 0], where $u_{ij}=0$ means that the unit x_i is not a member of subset j and $u_{ij}=1$ means the unit x_i is a member of subset j. The type of partition which classifies pixels in this way is called a hard c partition of X.

When the range of u_i is extended from $\{0,1\}$ to the real interval $[0,1]$, the following properties must also be true for X to be a partition

$$\sum_{j=0}^{c-1} u_{ij}=1,$$

$$0<\sum_{i=0}^{N-1} u_{ij}<N,$$

and

$$u_{ij} \in [0, 1].$$

A form of the partition which assigns the unit in this way is called a fuzzy c partition of X. Details of fuzzy sets and pattern recognition can be found in the monograph by Bezdek.[5]

SELF-ORGANIZING FEATURE MAPS

Kohonen[14] has pointed out that certain laminar networks which consist of interconnected adaptive units have the ability to change their response in a way that the location of the cell in a network becomes orderly in response to a certain characteristic feature in the set of input signals. These results led Kohonen[14] to present an algorithm called self-organization feature mapping, which, it is thought, promotes self-organization in a manner similar to that in the neocortex in the brain. The algorithm will map a set of input vectors onto output vectors, but unlike other mapping algorithms, the output responses will be ordered according to some characteristic feature of the input vectors. Details of this ordering behavior can be found in the monograph by Kohonen.[14]

The basic self-organization feature mapping model consists of two layers. The first layer contains input nodes and the second contains the output nodes. There are adjustable weights which extensively interconnect output nodes to common input nodes as shown in Figure 1.

Let $X = \{x_0, x_1, x_2, \ldots, x_{N-1}\}$ denote a set of N inputs in R^m such that each x_i has m dimensions (or features). X will be viewed as a random vector. Let m be the number of input nodes and c be the number of output (clustering) nodes. The output nodes are arranged as a linear array. W_j is the vector $[w_{0j}, w_{1j} \ldots w_{(m-1)j}]^T$ corresponding to output node j, where $(0 \leqq j \leqq c-1)$. The output $d_{ij} = (x_i - W_j)^T (x_i - W_j)$ is the output of node j when presented with input vector x_i, where W_j is the vector containing all of the weights from the m input nodes to output node j. After the input data x_i has been fed into the system, the weights are updated and tend to partition the input vector space. W_j can be viewed as the center of cluster j and the output d_{ij} is the square of Euclidean distance between the center of cluster j and the input x_i.

Updating of weights in this model for any given input is done only for output units in a localized neighborhood. For each node j, there are NE neighbor nodes on the lefthand side and NE neighbor nodes on the righthand side. The neighborhood is centered on the output node whose distance d_{ij} is minimum. This behavior is included to model the localized lateral interaction of biological neural networks. The neighborhood decreases in size with time until only a single node is inside its bounds. A learning rate must be defined and also decreases with time. Convergence to a cluster center is controlled by the learning rate. Initially, there is large movement of the cluster centers within the feature space. As the learning rate decreases with more iterations, movement becomes restricted to smaller distances around the cluster center. The basic algorithm inolves three steps.

BASIC ALGORITHM

Step 1 Randomly initialize weights W_j for all j and set the neighborhood size (NE) to be $c/2$. Set all weight updates ΔW_j to zero. The learning rate value (*Lrate*) is initialized between 0 and 1.

Step 2 For each input x_i, select the output node $j^*, (0 \leqq j^* \leqq c-1)$, such that d_{ij^*} is a minimum. Update W_j, using the rule:

$$W_j = W_j + Lrate * \Delta W_j,$$

$$\Delta W_j = \Delta W_j + (x_i - W_j),$$

where j includes output node j^* and each of its NE neighbors on the right and left. Repeat Step 2 until there is no change in the weights.

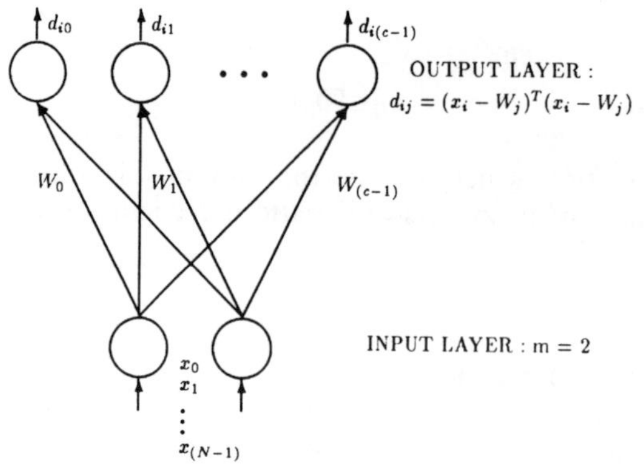

Figure 1 Simple neural net model.

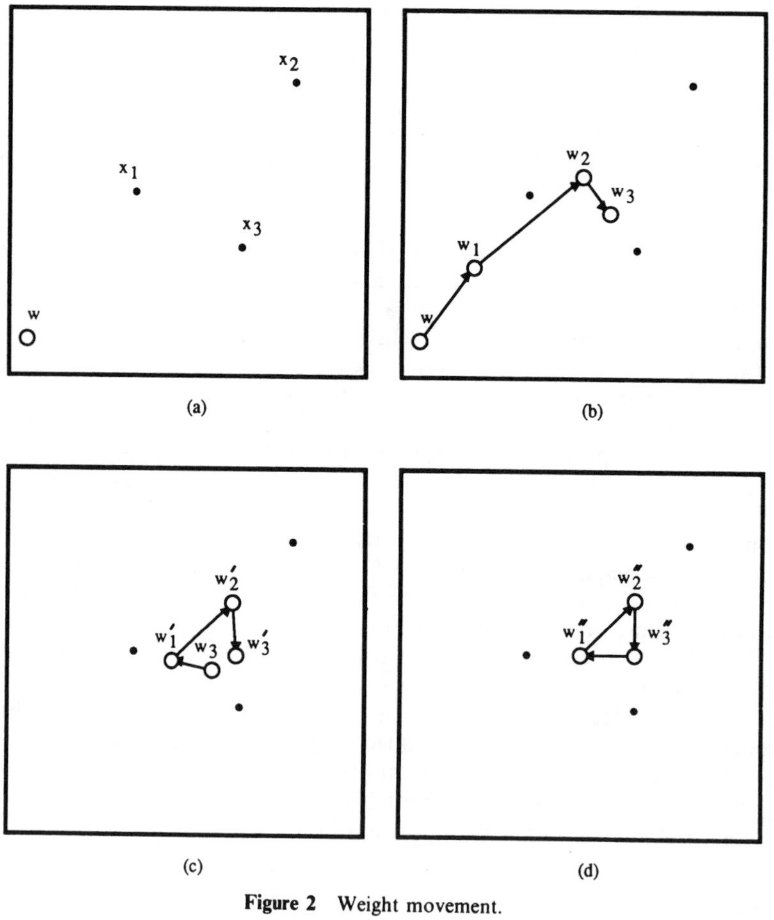

Figure 2 Weight movement.

Step 3 Check if $NE=0$. If this is the case the algorithm is done, otherwise NE will be reduced by 1 and the algorithm returns to Step 2.

The basic idea behind this approach is to move the weights to the center of clusters by updating the weights on each input value. For the sake of simplicity, consider only one cluster and three inputs in 2 dimensions as shown in Figure 2(a).

The filled circle represents the position of input values x_1, x_2 and x_3. The unfilled circle represents a weight which starts at position w. Set the learning rate to 0.5. Once the input x_1 is fed in, the weight is moved to position w_1. When x_2 is input to the net, the weight is moved to position w_2, and so on as shown in Figure 2(b). At the end of the iteration, the algorithm checks to see if a weight has changed within some tolerance on the previous iteration. If there was no change, the last position of the weight will represent the center of a cluster. Otherwise, the process will continue as shown in Figure 2(c). Finally, the process will stop as shown in Figure 2(d). The position w_3'' will represent the center of a cluster. If the value of the learning rate is small, the triangle w_1'', w_2'', w_3'' will also be small and the position of w_3'' will come close to the average of inputs.

Membership Value Assignment

The self-organizing feature map algorithm described above will generate a continuous valued output, but not in the sense of membership values. Another layer is needed to map the distances d_{ij} into membership values. This additional layer does not participate in the weight updates in the algorithm above. The new algorithm is given below, and is essentially a Basic Algorithm with the addition of another Step.

ALGORITHM 1

Step 1 Randomly initialize weights W_j for all j and set the neighborhood size (NE) to be $c/2$. Set all weight updates ΔW_j to zero. The learning rate value ($Lrate$) is initialized between 0 and 1.

Step 2 For each input x_i, select the output node $j^*, (0 \leqq j^* \leqq c-1)$, such that d_{ij^*} is a minimum. Update W_j, using the rule:

$$W_j = W_j + Lrate * \Delta W_j,$$

$$\Delta W_j = \Delta W_j + (x_i - W_j),$$

where j includes output node j^* and each of its NE neighbors on the right and left. Repeat Step 2 until there is no change in the weights.

Step 3 Check if $NE=0$. If this is the case the algorithm can proceed to membership value determination, otherwise NE will be reduced by 1 and the algorithm returns to Step 2.

Step 4 Generate membership values u_{ij} using either one of two possible definitions given below.

For a hard c membership the output value in $\{0, 1\}$ is particularly simple to implement in that we add one more node at the top level as shown in Figure 3. The output function is defined as follows:

$$u_{ij} = \begin{cases} 1 & \text{if } d_{ij} = \min(d_{il}, 0 \leqq l \leqq c-1) \\ 0 & \text{otherwise} \end{cases}$$

which will give the output $u_{ij} \in \{0, 1\}$.

For a fuzzy membership value in the range $[0, 1]$, the system also needs one more level.

However, in this case, each particular node j needs its own top level node to compute its own membership values, as shown in Figure 4. The output functions are defined as:

$$u_{ij} = \begin{cases} 1 & \text{if } d_{ij} = 0 \\ 0 & \text{if } d_{ik} = 0, (k \neq j, 0 \leqq k, j \leqq c-1) \end{cases}$$

otherwise

$$u_{ij} = \left(\sum_{l=0}^{c-1} \left(\frac{d_{ij}}{d_{il}} \right) \right)^{-1}.$$

This form of membership value determination is based on the iterative algorithm developed by Bezdek.[5] This approach to fuzzy membership value assignment has the advantage of the linear update rule as opposed to the traditional fuzzy c-means algorithm, which is quadratic in u_{ij} for a weighting exponent of 2. In

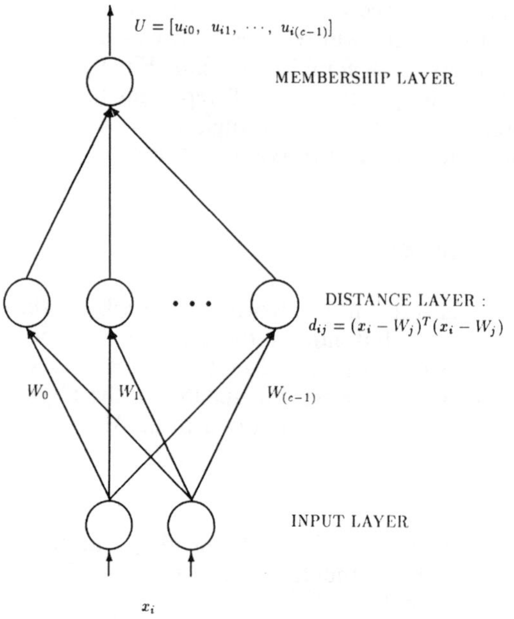

Figure 3 Simple model for membership assignment.

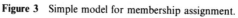

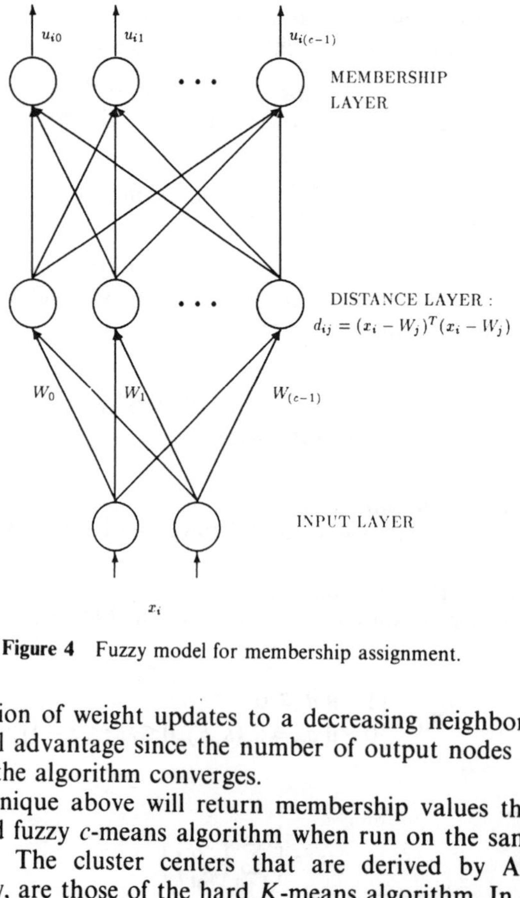

Figure 4 Fuzzy model for membership assignment.

addition, the restriction of weight updates to a decreasing neighborhood, gives an added computational advantage since the number of output nodes involved in the update decreases as the algorithm converges.

Although the technique above will return membership values that are close to those of the standard fuzzy *c*-means algorithm when run on the same data set, the match is not exact. The cluster centers that are derived by Algorithm 1, as mentioned previously, are those of the hard *K*-means algorithm. In order to derive cluster centers that are the same as those of the fuzzy *c*-means algorithm, a feedback path between the new third layer of nodes and the input nodes must be included. This new type of network is shown in Figure 5.

The new algorithm includes the membership values both in the determination of d_{ij}, as well as the weight update rule. The size of the neighborhood of nodes

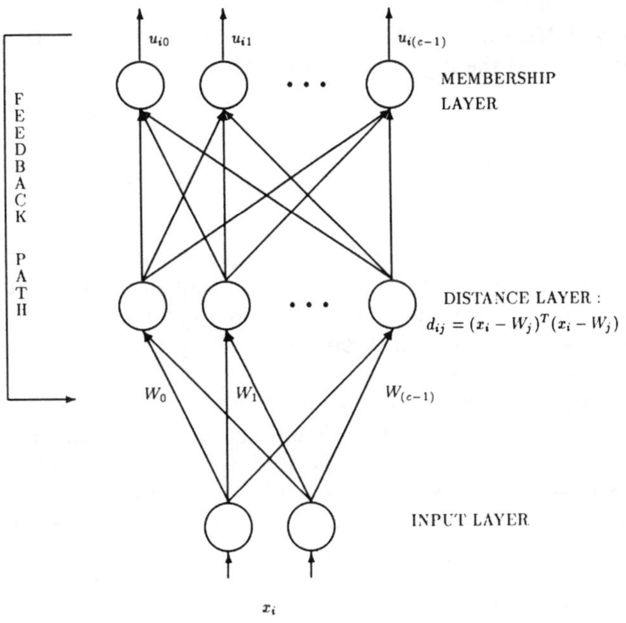

Figure 5 Neural net model with feedback path from membership layer.

remains fixed at $c/2$, which is equivalent to all of the output nodes being involved in the update process. The modified algorithm is given below.

ALGORITHM 2

Step 1 Randomly initialize weights W_j for all j and set the neighborhood size (NE) to be $c/2$. Set all weight updates ΔW_j to zero. The learning rate value (*Lrate*) is initialized between 0 and 1.

Step 2 For each input x_i, define d_{ij^*} as $(x_i - W_j)^T(x_i - W_j)$. Update W_j, using the update rule:

$$W_j = W_j + Lrate * \Delta W_j;$$
$$\Delta W_j = \Delta W_j + u_{ij} * (x_i - W_j),$$

where j includes all of the output nodes. Repeat Step 2 until there is no change in the weights.

Algorithm 2 automatically includes the factor u_{ij}^2 is the definition of d_{ij} with the modification of ΔW_j found in Step 2. The computational complexity is the same as the fuzzy c-means algorithm as far as the number of update calculations, but still has an computational advantage in the linear update rule.

An even greater computational advantage can be gained if the decreasing size neighborhood is included in the algorithm. The neighborhood decreases the total number of update calculations since all of the output nodes are not included each time Step 2 is executed. The new algorithm with both the membership value feedback and variable size neighborhood is given as Algorithm 3.

ALGORITHM 3

Step 1 Randomly initialize weights W_j for all j and set the neighborhood size (NE) to be $c/2$. Set all weight updates ΔW_j to zero. The learning rate value (*Lrate*) is initialized between 0 and 1.

Step 2 For each input x_i, select the output node j^*, $(0 \leqq j^* \leqq c-1)$, such that d_{ij^*} is a minimum. d_{ij} is defined as $(x_i - W_j)^T(x_i - W_j)$. Update W_j, using the rule:

$$W_j = W_j + Lrate * \Delta W_j,$$
$$\Delta W_j = \Delta W_j + u_{ij} * (x_i - W_j),$$

where j includes output node j^* and each of its NE neighbors on the right and left. Repeat Step 2 until there is no change in the weights.

Step 3 Check if $NE=0$. If this is the case the algorithm is done, otherwise NE will be reduced by 1 and the algorithm returns to Step 2.

PARALLEL APPROACH

The sequential versions of the self-organizing feature map modified for a continuous valued output suffer from a lack of parallelism, due to the updating of the weights after each piece of data is fed in. Whereas in the sequential algorithm each input vector is fed into the same m nodes as shown in Figure 1, the parallel algorithm will use N groups with m modes in each group. Weights will be updated by using the average of the distances between W_j to x_i of all N inputs. In order to accomplish this, we let each x_i have its own vector W_{ij}, where $0 \leqq i \leqq N-1$. For example, x_1 has its own W_{1j}. This redefinition of the weights is equivalent to making N copies of the same network and feeding a different m-dimensional input vector into each one. Ideally, there would be N processors in the parallel architecture used for the network. The new parallel algorithm is given below.

ALGORITHM 4

Step 1 **Initialize weights.** Randomly assign weights to $W_{ij}(0 \leqq j \leqq c-1, 0 \leqq i \leqq N-1)$, where c is the number of clustering output nodes and N is the number of input data vectors. Set all weight changes to zero: $\Delta W_{ij}=0$. Initialize neighborhood size (NE) to $c/2$. Initialize leaning rate (*Lrate*) to lie between 0 and 1.

Step 2 **Repeat steps 2.1–2.4 until weights have no change.** Update individual weights for each i

2.1 **Compute distance d_{ij}**
Compute distance d_{ij} between x_i and W_{ij}.
For each j from 0 to $c-1$
$d_{ij}=(x_i-W_{ij})^T(x_i-W_{ij})$.

2.2 **Select minimum distance d_{ij}**
Select j^* such that $j^*=\{j \mid d_{ij}$ is minimum, $0 \leqq j \leqq c-1\}$.

2.3 **Update weight change for node j^* and neighbors**
$\Delta W_{ij}=\Delta W_{ij}+(x_i-W_{ij})$,
where j includes node j^* and its neighbors.

2.4 **Reset weights W_{ij} to the average new weight**
Reset W_{ij} such that
$$W_{ij}=W_{ij}+Lrate * \frac{\sum_{k=0}^{N-1} \Delta W_{kj}}{N},$$
$\Delta W_{ij}=0, (0 \leqq i \leqq N-1)$ for all i.

Step 3 **Reduce neighborhood size.** If size of neighborhood is zero exit, otherwise decrease NE by one and go to Step 2.

The main overhead for this algorithm is found in Step 2.4, where all of the N vectors for W_{ij} are needed in the sum. This combination of information needs to be done simultaneously for maximum efficiency. However, since there are few totally interconnected parallel architectures, the interconnection network and protocols of any particular machine will have a definite impact on the efficiency of the algorithm. The addition of a feedback path and a change in the update rules as was done in Algorithms 2 and 3 will convert Algorithm 4 into the parallel versions of Algorithms 2 and 3.

EXPERIMENTAL STUDIES

A number of experimental studies were done to investigate various aspects of both the sequential and parallel algorithms. Of primary interest are the correct parameter settings for the learning rate and convergence criteria. Also of interest is a comparison between the fuzzy membership value and cluster center determinations of Algorithms 1, 2 and 3. Finally, the computational efficiency and accuracy for cluster center and membership value determination of Algorithm 4 needs to be evaluated.

In the first experiment, Algorithm 1 was run on Anderson's Iris data set, which is commonly used to test clustering algorithms. The Iris data set has 150 four-dimensional items, distributed equally among three classes. We have normalized the data values to have real values between 0 and 1. The nature of the Iris data set is such that data in Class 1 are well separated from Class 2 and Class 3, and data in Classes 2 and 3 are not well separated.

The data was analyzed using Algorithm 1 with a range of learning rates between 0.10 to 1.00 in steps of 0.10. The criterion for weights having no change is determined by the value of the sum of squares of the distance that all weights moved. The weight criteria for convergence was varied between 0.01 and 0.00001 in 4 steps. The number of iterations needed for convergence versus the learning rate for various different convergence criteria are plotted in Figure 6.

The number of iterations is relatively independent of the learning rate for any given weight convergence criteria, generally decreasing with an increase in the learning rate. However, there is a definite trade-off as far as accuracy of classification. The number of misclassified items versus the learning rate for various convergence criteria are plotted in Figure 7.

As is to be expected, the finer the convergence criteria, the better the classification. Figures 6 and 7 suggest that the learning rate should be in the range from 0.50 to 1.00 and the weight criterion should range from 0.001 to 0.0001 to keep the number of misclassified items low and the number of iterations small.

In order to evaluate the effectiveness of the clustering algorithm, we ran the second experiment with the data set from Chiou.[7] This data set has 40 sample vectors. Each sample vector has two features. Table 1 shows the results of applying Algorithm 1 with the addition of the extra output layer for fuzzy membership evaluation, a learning rate of 0.75 and weight criteria 0.001 compared with the results using the fuzzy c-means algorithm.[7]

The membership values from the modified self-organizing feature map are within 0.02, except for data item 38, where the difference is 0.03. The cluster centers reported in the original work[7] are (7.4, 18.0) and (27.0, 18.7). The self-organizing feature map approach yielded (7.20, 18.08) and (26.16, 18.64), both of which are as representative of the input data set as the fuzzy c-mean values. Algorithms 2 and 3 produced results that were identical to the fuzzy c-means algorithm when applied to the same data set.

The experimental studies of Algorithm 4 were conducted on the 1024 element NCUBE/10 hypercube system at the University of South Carolina. Each node in the hypercube analyzed a portion of the test data set, with a global combine step for the updating of the weights. Various size subcubes were used to analyze the efficiency of the algorithm.

Ideally, a neural network for pattern recognition as applied to an image would require as many units as pixels in an image. For example, a typical low resolution image (128 columns and 128 rows) will have 16 384 input pixels. Since each input item requires its own processing unit to do its task, this could require a large number of processing units. In practice, we can perform this algorithm with a limited number of processing units, such as on an NCUBE/10 which has 1024 processing units. This can be done by dividing the input data into subsets and distributing a subset to each unit. Each data subset in the units share the same ΔW_{ij}. Step 2.4 of Algorithm 3 was done using a butterfly combine operation, where the summation is performed as a series of global pairwise additions with a communication overhead of $\log_2 P$ steps.

One measure of the parallel efficiency of an algorithm is given by the ratio of the speedup given by $S_P = TIME_{seq}/TIME_{par}$ versus the number of processors P, where $TIME_{seq}$ is the time taken for the algorithm on a single processor, and $TIME_{par}$ is the time taken for the algorithm running on P processors. Table 2 contains the results of several experiments run with different problem sizes and different size subcubes.

The measure of parallel efficiency given by S_P versus the dimension of the subcube for two different image sizes is plotted in Figure 8.

The efficiency is close to 100% for up to a 9-dimensional subcube (512 processors). As the size of the data subset/node gets larger with image size, the

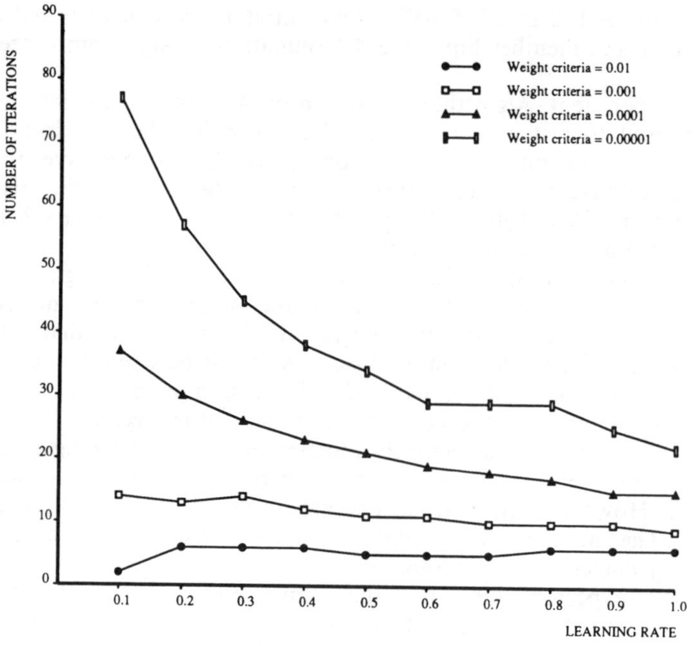

Figure 6 Number of iterations from experiments on Iris data set with different learning rate and weight criteria.

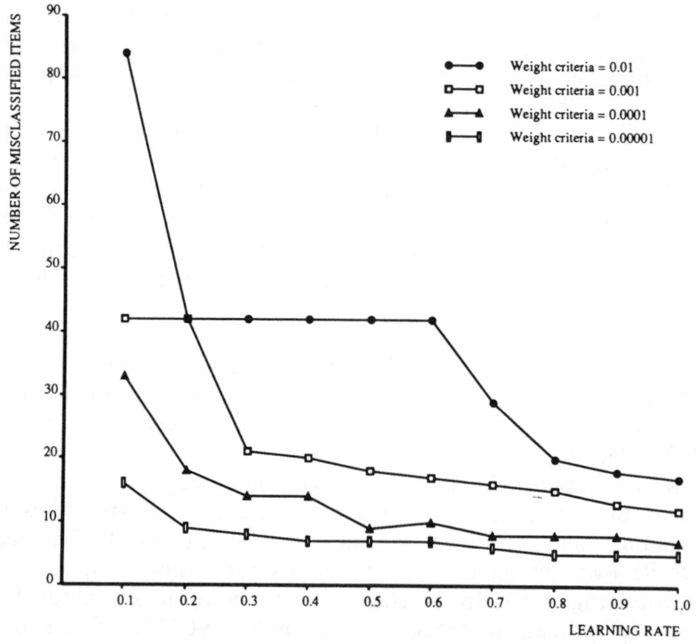

Figure 7 Number of misclassified items from experiments on Iris data set with different learning rate and weight criteria.

efficiency improves for the larger cubes, as seen in Table 2 and in the tail-ends of the two plots.

CONCLUSIONS

We have presented a modified version of the self-organizing feature maps of Kohonen which are capable of generating continuous valued outputs. The addition of another layer of nodes allows membership value determination, with a gain in computational efficiency over the fuzzy c-means algorithm due to the use of a linear weight update rule. This same output layer can also be used to serve as a feedback path to the input layer as was demonstrated in Algorithm 2. Our experimental studies have indicated that Algorithms 2 and 3 will perform an analysis of data sets equivalent to the fuzzy c-means algorithm.

Table 1 Comparing the results with the fuzzy *c*-means algorithm

Items no.	*Input feature*		*Fuzzy c-mean algorithm*		*Parallel algorithm*	
i	x_{i1}	x_{i2}	u_{i1}	u_{i2}	u_{i1}	u_{i2}
0	1	8	0.85	0.15	0.83	0.17
1	−4	15	0.87	0.13	0.87	0.13
2	2	24	0.91	0.09	0.91	0.09
3	3	21	0.95	0.05	0.95	0.05
4	4	18	0.98	0.02	0.97	0.03
5	5	10	0.89	0.11	0.88	0.12
6	21	18	0.16	0.84	0.14	0.86
7	6	24	0.93	0.07	0.93	0.07
8	6	28	0.84	0.16	0.84	0.16
9	7	13	0.94	0.06	0.93	0.07
10	7	15	0.98	0.02	0.97	0.03
11	7	18	1.00	0.00	1.00	0.00
12	8	7	0.80	0.20	0.79	0.21
13	8	20	0.99	0.01	0.99	0.01
14	9	22	0.95	0.05	0.95	0.05
15	10	16	0.97	0.03	0.96	0.04
16	10	19	0.98	0.02	0.98	0.02
17	10	26	0.83	0.17	0.84	0.16
18	13	23	0.80	0.20	0.79	0.21
19	14	20	0.78	0.22	0.78	0.22
20	17	16	0.53	0.47	0.51	0.49
21	17	22	0.51	0.49	0.50	0.50
22	20	20	0.24	0.76	0.22	0.78
23	22	27	0.24	0.76	0.25	0.75
24	23	16	0.09	0.91	0.07	0.93
25	23	22	0.09	0.91	0.09	0.91
26	27	15	0.03	0.97	0.03	0.97
27	25	19	0.01	0.99	0.01	0.99
28	28	17	0.01	0.99	0.01	0.99
29	28	24	0.06	0.94	0.07	0.93
30	29	13	0.07	0.93	0.07	0.93
31	31	17	0.03	0.97	0.04	0.96
32	31	20	0.03	0.97	0.04	0.96
33	26	9	0.18	0.82	0.17	0.83
34	33	25	0.10	0.90	0.11	0.89
35	34	13	0.10	0.90	0.11	0.89
36	36	20	0.09	0.91	0.10	0.90
37	35	29	0.16	0.84	0.18	0.82
38	19	12	0.39	0.61	0.36	0.64
39	15	24	0.65	0.35	0.65	0.35

Table 2 Experimental results from Algorithm 4

Problem size ($Time_{seq}$)	$Time_{par}$	P	S_p	E_p
128 × 128 (874.78)	874.78	1	1.000	1.000
	439.58	2	1.990	0.995
	219.78	4	3.980	0.995
	110.22	8	7.936	0.992
	55.21	16	15.845	0.990
	27.77	32	31.501	0.984
	14.08	64	62.129	0.971
	7.23	128	120.993	0.945
	3.87	256	226.041	0.882
	2.27	512	385.366	0.752
	1.61	1024	543.341	0.530
256 × 256 (3513.20)*	878.30	4	4.000	1.000
	441.55	8	7.959	0.994
	221.56	16	15.856	0.991
	110.88	32	31.684	0.990
	55.66	64	63.116	0.986
	28.21	128	124.536	0.972
	14.27	256	246.192	0.961
	7.41	512	474.116	0.926
	4.32	1024	813.240	0.794

Note: $Time_{seq}$ = Time in seconds on 1 processor. $Time_{par}$ = Time in seconds on P processors. P = Number of processors. $S_p = Time_{seq}/Time_{par}$. * = 4 × 878.30.

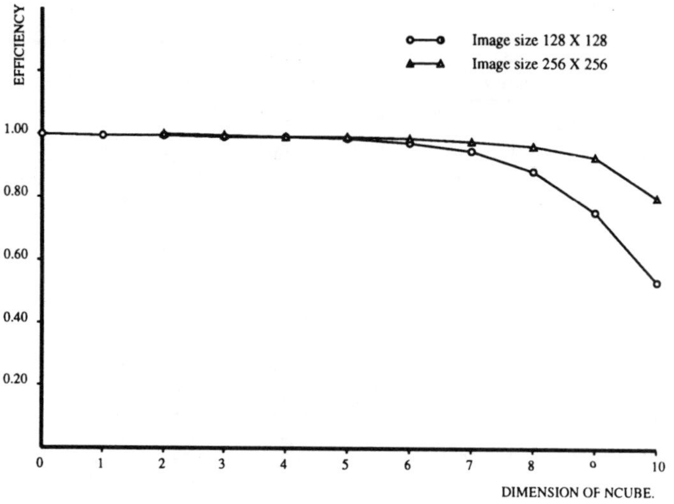

Figure 8 Efficiency plotted on different dimensional subcube.

We also presented a new parallel algorithm, Algorithm 4, which is well suited for implementation on a distributed memory parallel architecture. The efficiency of Algorithm 4 is close to 100% even on a 9-dimensional subcube, with a definite dependence on problem size. Communication overhead in the combine operation used for the updating of the weights is the major cause of the decrease in efficiency as the size of the subcube increases. This effect can be seen in the dependence of the efficiency curve on image size. As the image size grows, the ratio of computational cycles versus communication increases, thus increasing the efficiency relative to a smaller image size. A more efficient use of the hypercube interconnect structure could possibly address this problem.

This new algorithm can be used as a segmentation stage in computer vision systems.[12] The time taken for a full three-class segmentation of a 256×256 image was 4.5 seconds. Previous studies have indicated its utility as the input and output layers for a visible/thermal-infrared sensor fusion system.[3] In addition, studies are currently underway for use of the algorithm for motion analysis.[2]

ACKNOWLEDGEMENT

The authors would like to thank the reviewers whose comments and suggestions have contributed greatly to the readability of this manuscript.

REFERENCES

1. *DARPA: Neural Network Study*. AFCEA, Virginia, 1988.
2. P. Ajjimarangsee, *Multi-Stage Neural Network Model for Dynamic Scene Analysis*. Ph.D. thesis, Department of Computer Science, University of South Carolina, 1989.
3. P. Ajjimarangsee and T. L. Huntsberger, "Neural network model for the fusion of visible and thermal infrared sensor outputs." *Proc. SPIE Cambridge Symposium on Sensor Fusion*, 1988, pp. 153–160.
4. P. Ajjimarangsee and T. L. Huntsberger, "Unsupervised pattern recognition using parallel selforganizing feature maps." *Proc. 4th Conf. Hypercube Concurrent Computers and Applications*, 1989.
5. J. C. Bezdek, *Pattern Recognition with Fuzzy Objective Function Algorithms*. Plenum Press, New York, 1981.
6. M. Caudill, "Neural networks primer—Part VIII." *AI Expert*, 1989, pp. 61–69.
7. E. W. Chiou, *Core Zone Scatterplots: A New Approach to Feature Extraction for Visual Displays*. Master's thesis, University of South Carolina, 1986.
8. S. Grossberg, *Neural Networks and Natural Intelligence*. MIT Press, Cambridge, MA, 1988.
9. D. O. Hebb, *The Organization of Behavior*. John Wiley, New York, 1949.
10. A. Ho and W. Furmanski, "Pattern recognition by neural network model on hypercubes." *Proc. 3rd Conf. Hypercube Concurrent Computers and Applications*, 1988, pp. 1011–1021.
11. J. J. Hopfield and D. W. Tank, "Computing with neural circuits: A model." *Science*, 1986, pp. 625–633.
12. T. L. Huntsberger, C. L. Jacobs and R. L. Cannon, "Iterative fuzzy image segmentation." *Pattern Recognition*, **18**, No. 2, 1985, pp. 131–138.

13. J. M. Keller and D. J. Hunt, "Incorporating fuzzy membership functions into the perceptron algorithm." *IEEE Transactions on Pattern Analysis and Machine Intelligence*, **7**, No. 6, 1985, pp. 693–699.
14. T. Kohonen, *Self-Organization and Associative Memory*. Springer-Verlag, Berlin, 1984.
15. R. P. Lippmann, "An introduction to computing with neural nets." *IEEE ASSP Magazine*, 1987, pp. 4–22.
16. W. S. McCulloch and W. Pitts, A logical calculus of the ideas imminent in nervous activity. *Bulletin of Math. Biophys.*, **5**, 1943, pp. 115–133.
17. M. L. Minsky and S. A. Papert, *Perceptrons*. MIT Press, Cambridge, MA, 1988.
18. R. Rosenblatt, *Principles of Neurodynamics*. Spartan Books, New York, 1959.
19. D. E. Rumelhart and J. L. McClelland, *Parallel Distributed Processing*. Volume 1, MIT Press, Cambridge, MA, 1986.

NN-Driven Fuzzy Reasoning

Hideyuki Takagi and Isao Hayashi
Matsushita Electric Industrial Co., Ltd., Moriguchi, Osaka, Japan

ABSTRACT

A new fuzzy reasoning that can solve two problems of conventional fuzzy reasoning by combining an artificial neural network (NN) and fuzzy reasoning is proposed. These problems are (1) the lack of design for a membership function except a heuristic approach and (2) the lack of adaptability for possible changes in the reasoning environment. The proposed fuzzy reasoning approach solves these problems by using the learning function and nonlinearity of an NN. First, the problems involved in conventional fuzzy reasoning and the NN used in this paper are identified. Then a proposed algorithm is formulated and a concrete explanation using realistic data is developed. An example structure of an NN-driven fuzzy reasoning system is given, and two applications of this method are presented. This new fuzzy reasoning is capable of automatic determination of inference rules and adjustment according to the time-variant reasoning environment because of the use of NN in fuzzy reasoning. This proposed method can be applied to NN modeling and AI and is considered from the standpoint of the explicit incorporation of knowledge into the NN structure.

KEYWORDS: ***fuzzy reasoning, neural network, membership functions***

INTRODUCTION

Fuzzy reasoning can express the qualitative aspect of human logic. Since it realizes the flexible reasoning corresponding to human logical reasoning, extensive research has been conducted into fuzzy reasoning. Its practical applications are now being seen not only in various control fields but also in AI and operation research. However, two problems of conventional fuzzy reasoning have not been solved yet: the method of determining membership functions and the adaptation of reasoning to the environment. The method proposed here is to solve these problems by using an artificial neural network, which we denote by NN. Since this method is an elemental technology, extensive application fields including not only control but also estimation, inference, prediction, and so on can be expected. The aim of this method and its formulation are described, and its effectiveness is explained through several applications.

FUZZY REASONING

Strong Points of Fuzzy Reasoning

The following describes the typical control rules using two-value logic.

AN EXAMPLE OF A TWO-VALUE LOGIC CONTROL RULE

IF the cornering angle is with 20°–40° and
the loading weight is more than 50 kg,
THEN the moving velocity = 3 − cornering angle/20.

Address correspondence to H. Takagi, Central Research Laboratories, Matsushita Electric Industrial Co., Ltd., 3-15 Yagumo-Nakamachi, Moriguchi, Osaka 570, Japan.

Reprinted by permission of the publisher from "NN-Driven Fuzzy Reasoning," by H. Takagi and I. Hayashi, *Int'l. J. Approximate Reasoning*, vol. 5, no. 3, pp. 191–212.

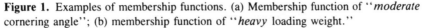

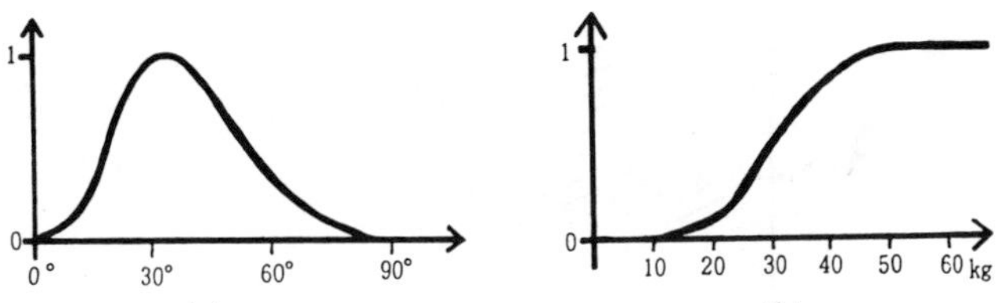

Figure 1. Examples of membership functions. (a) Membership function of "*moderate* cornering angle"; (b) membership function of "*heavy* loading weight."

The problem with this control rule is that it is inapplicable even if the loading weight is 49.9999 kg. Moreover, the control for a cornering of $20 \pm \alpha$ degrees becomes uncomfortable to drive because more than two control rules would be irregularly and alternately applied. There is no way to solve these problems except to chop up the given rules to accomplish smooth control. However, it is impossible to achieve control of perfect smoothness except with infinitely many control rules.

Fuzzy control employs the following rule:

AN EXAMPLE OF A FUZZY CONTROL RULE

IF the cornering angle is a *moderate* degree and
the loading weight is *heavy*,
THEN the moving velocity should be *gradually* decreased.

This is a control rule of human concept expressed in human words. Moreover, the control based on this fuzzy reasoning not only makes the control rules easier to use but also substantially decreases the number of rules.

To execute this inference rule, the corresponding relationship between the input numerical data obtained from sensors and the fuzzy sets such as "moderate," "heavy," and "gradually" must be determined. This mapping relationship is a membership function such as the one shown in Figure 1.

The main strong point of fuzzy reasoning is the accomplishment of distinctive separation between the "logic" and the "membership function." This logic constitutes the backbone of the rule, and the membership function deals with the fuzziness entangled in the logic. When an expert system based on two-value logic is constructed, it very often needs to reconstruct or adjust the rules. The main reason for this lies in the difficulty of fuzziness separation, and this calls for an adjustment of the logic itself. This is one of the reasons that rule construction based on two-value logic is difficult.

Problems with Fuzzy Reasoning

How should we design the membership function that is essential for fuzzy reasoning? The ordinary way is to assume an original membership function to be triangular or trapezoidal at the beginning. If this membership function is found to be unfit, heuristic tuning has to be tried. This means there is no straightforward method for designing a membership function. This is the first problem to overcome.

Since input/output variables are supposed to be independent in fuzzy reasoning, the membership function is designed variable by variable (Figure 2). However, in a case such as *IF the temperature is slightly higher and the humidity is lower*, *THEN the power has to be lowered slightly*, the temperature and humidity cannot be said to be completely independent. In this case, the membership function requires a curved surface in three-dimensional space consisting of the membership value axis and the temperature–humidity plane (Figure 3). Therefore, when a variable number increases, it is nearly

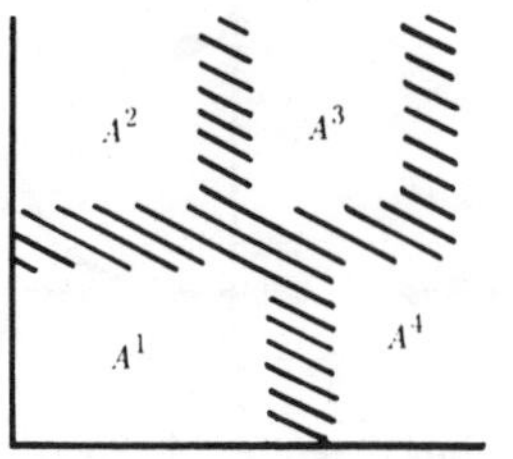

Figure 2. Conventional fuzzy rule partitions.

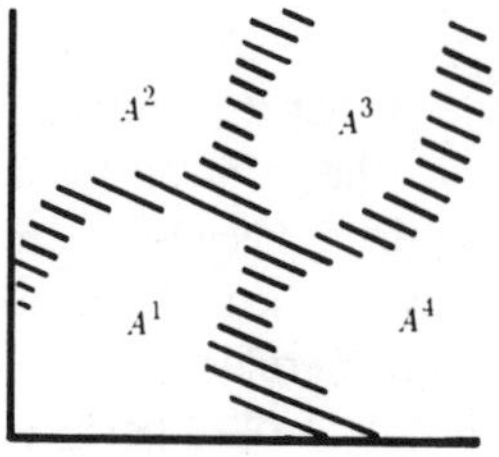

Figure 3. Proposed fuzzy rule partitions.

impossible to design a membership function in multidimensional space by using experience and intuition.

The second problem of fuzzy reasoning is the lack of learning functions. This makes the optimization of reasoning for a time-variant environment such as seasonal changes impossible. In the application of fuzzy reasoning to mass-produced home appliances, it is hard for the producer to adjust them to individual consumer preferences and environments and then ship them. The mass producer has no choice but to adjust them to an average value at the factory. If fuzzy reasoning could have a low-cost learning function, the consumer could tune fuzzy inference rules to fit individual preferences and environments. This could result in an "appliance like a pet that can be trained to read your mind."

PROBLEMS WITH FUZZY REASONING

1. The lack of a definite method to determine the membership function

2. The lack of a learning function or adaptability

COMBINATION OF NEURAL NETWORKS

Introduction to Neural Networks

The brain's mechanism of information processing has been analyzed from the point of view of mathematics and engineering (McCulloch and Pitts [1], Rosenblatt [2]). It is known as associative memory or a learning machine. Recently developed "back-propagation" (Rumelhart et al. [3]) is an effective learning algorithm of multilayer perceptron and has directed attention to the information processing capability of artificial neural networks. This algorithm has been widely employed for various pattern classifications or inference problems expressed in terms of nonlinear functions. Reported in this paper is the application of reasoning and the learning function of the NN for nonlinear problems to fuzzy reasoning. This is started with mathematical analysis made on the NN.

The biological neuron receives signals from various other neurons through each synapse. It fires neural pulses if these input signals exceed a certain threshold value and will not fire for signals below the threshold. An example of engineering models expressing this biological concept is the multi-input, single-output nonlinear circuit shown in Figure 4b. Equation (1) expresses the

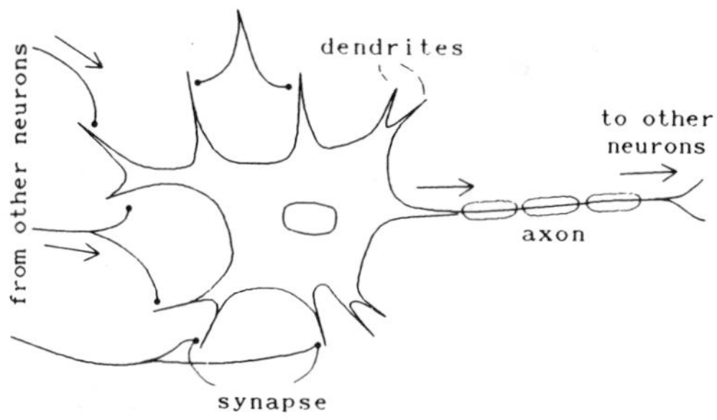

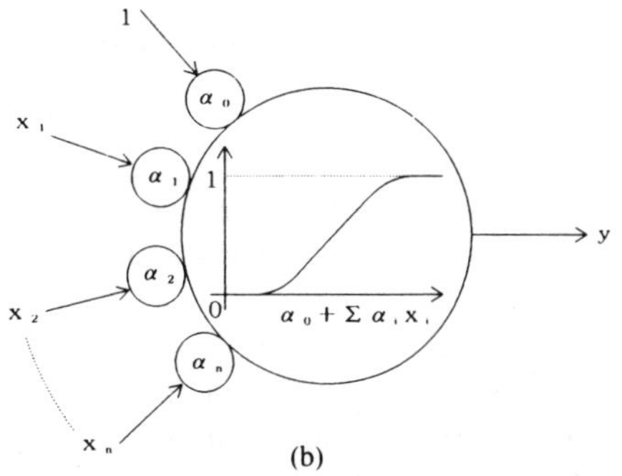

Figure 4. (a) Biological neuron; (b) neuron model.

relationship between the input **x** and the output y of this mathematical model.

$$y_i = f\left(\sum_{j}^{N} \alpha_{ji} x_j + \alpha_{0i} \right) \tag{1}$$

$$f(z) = \frac{1}{1 + e^{-z}} \tag{2}$$

where α is a connectional weight for reflecting the synapse to the model and $f()$ is a sigmoid function expressed in Eq. (2). The reason for employing a sigmoid function is that it is an on/off function and is differentiable; that is the essential condition for back-propagation.

The NN is then a number of these neural models connected to each other to constitute a network. The k-layer perceptron trained by the back-propagation algorithm is employed as the NN in this paper. However, the proposed method does not necessarily limit the application of the NN to the k-layer perceptron.

The following is the definition of NN employed in this paper.

DEFINITION

(*a*) *The k-layer perceptron is a model consisting of one output layer and k − 1 hidden layers.*

(*b*) *The I/O relationship of NN is expressed by the equation*

$$\mathbf{y} = NN(\mathbf{x}) \tag{3}$$

(*c*) *The term k-layers*$[u_0 \times u_1 \times \cdots \times u_k]$ *expresses the model size, where* u_i *is the number of neurons in the input layer, hidden layer(s), and output layer, and k is the number of layers.*

(*d*) *Each input layer and hidden layer has an extra unit of constant 1 in addition to those specified by (c). This unit has no connection to the lower-layer neurons and has connections to the upper-layer neurons.*

(*e*) *All neuron models in the neighboring layers are connected, but*

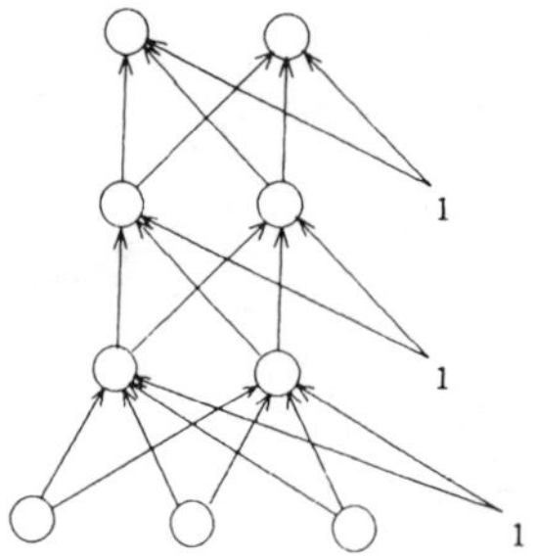

Figure 5. Example structure of neural network.

there should be no connections within layers nor jump connections between layers.

Term (d) in the above definition is to express α_{0i} in Eq. (1). Term (e) is an explanation for the model used in the following section on formulation and is not essential for the NN. As an example, Figure 5 shows a 3-layers[$3 \times 2 \times 2 \times 2$] NN.

An NN can attain the model identification well suited for training data because of its nonlinearity and learning function. This may in turn cause a case where the above condition is very well suited to the learning data but not to the evaluation data. Therefore, it is important to endow the learning data with enough deviation to derive a model that performs well.

Introduction of Neural Network into Fuzzy Reasoning

Two problems inherent to fuzzy reasoning can be handled by the NN. The difference between these two technologies has to do with whether the logic is explicit or implicit. For fuzzy reasoning, stable reasoning can always be attained despite data deviations because the backbone logic is manifested as a rule in IF–THEN form. On the other hand, however, the rule cannot be expressed unless the logic is identified. Since the NN self-organizes the mapping relationship by learning, it is applicable even for unknown logical relationships. Moreover, it is capable of expressing any nonlinear relationship because it is itself nonlinear. However, such a nonparametric method requires a large amount of data. The NN might output a deviated answer if deviated learning data were supplied. From these differences, fuzzy reasoning is employed mainly for well-identified logic cases such as the control, and the NN is used mainly for unidentified recognition rules such as pattern recognition.

Consider now the problem of designing a membership function. Even if it is not clear, the inference rule can be automatically derived from the fuzzy rule partition of learning data using the learning function of the NN. Furthermore, an adaptive modification of the membership function is possible, because the NN has a learning function.

NN-driven fuzzy reasoning is fuzzy reasoning that is driven by an artificial neural network. The fundamental concept is the employment of fuzzy reasoning for the fundamental reasoning and the NN for the determination. Furthermore, the adaptive modification of the membership function becomes possible, replacing conventional experience and intuition.

FORMULATION OF NN-DRIVEN FUZZY REASONING

Outline

The outline of the proposed method is explained by taking as an example the

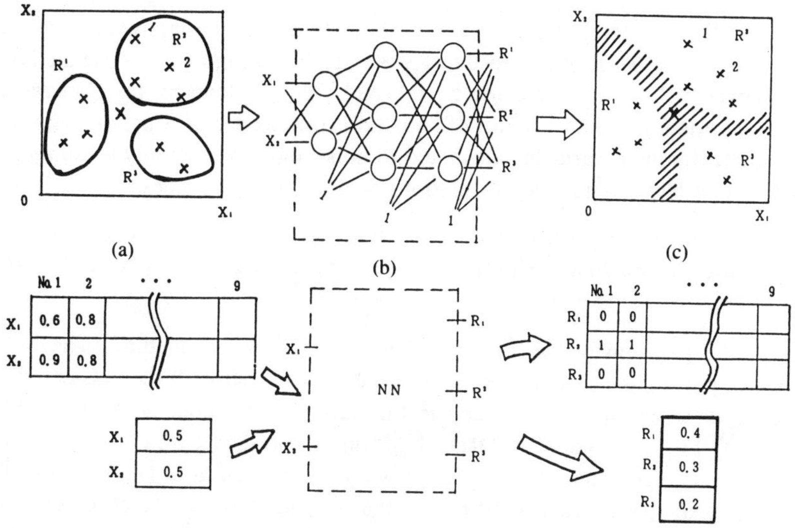

Figure 6. Design of membership functions using an NN. (a) Input data space; (b) NN that determines membership function; (c) data space that is partitioned for fuzzy rules.

control carried out by two inputs, x_1 and x_2, derived from two sensors. The algorithm consists of three major parts:

1. The partition of inference rules
2. The identification of IF parts (the determination of a membership function)
3. The identification of THEN parts (the determination of the amount of control for each rule)

The first part is the determination of the number of fuzzy inference rules and the combination of data belonging to each rule. These data are grouped by a clustering method, and the number of groups equals the number of inference rules (Figure 6a).

The second part is the attribution of arbitrary input for each rule (corresponding to the upper group) to each rule. This derives the membership function for each rule and corresponds to the identification of IF parts (the condition parts) of the rule. It should be noticed that this procedure combines all the fuzzy variables (x_1 and x_2 in Figure 6's case) in the IF part and constitutes a hypersurface membership function. We have used the NN for this determination. The NN can form a continuous membership function governing entire rules internally. It was proved that an arbitrary continuous function can be constituted by an NN having at least one hidden layer (Funahashi [4]).

The third part of the algorithm is the determination of THEN parts (the conclusion parts). The NN is supervised by the learning data and the control value for each rule as in (2). Fundamentally, another control method could be used, but the NN has better adaptability considering the later described systems.

Formulation

The detailed formulation of the NN is explained in the following example of fuzzy modeling included in fuzzy control (Hayashi and Takagi [5, 6]).

The THEN part in the system control is responsible for inferring the exact control value. One of these methods is the fuzzy modeling taking the form of "IF $\mathbf{x} \in A^s$, THEN $\mathbf{y} = u(\mathbf{x})$," wherein $\mathbf{x}$ is an input vector, A^s is the fuzzy set of the sth partitioned rule spaces (Figure 2), and $u()$ appoints an inference function for the control operation. In NN-driven fuzzy reasoning, A^s is partitioned by an NN as shown in Figure 3, and $u()$ is the NN itself. The following shows each step for this.

STEP 1 Define the observed value as y_i, the output, and the input variables as x_j, $j = 1, 2, \ldots, k$. In this step the x_j, $j = 1, 2, \ldots, m$, $m \leq k$, related to the observed value y are selected by the NN. This is done by the backward elimination method using the sum of squared errors as a cost function. This is to eliminate the input variables attributed to noise and to select only those input variables that have significant correlations to the observed values.

STEP 2 The input/output data $(\mathbf{x}_i, y_i)$ are then divided into training data (TRD of n_t) and checking data (CHD of n_c) for model estimation, where $n = n_t + n_c$.

STEP 3 The partition of the TRD is found by a clustering method. The best number of partitions is decided in view of the distance between the clusters in a clustering dendrogram. Each of the TRD divided into r groups is expressed by R^s, $s = 1, 2, \ldots, r$, and the TRD of R^s are expressed by $(\mathbf{x}_i^s, y_i^s)$, where $i = 1, 2, \ldots, (n_t)^s$, and $(n_t)^s$ are TRD numbers in each R^s. The division of m-dimensional space into r here means that the number of inference rules is set to be r.

STEP 4 This step is the identification of the constitution of each IF part in $\mathrm{NN_{mem}}$ (NN generating the membership functions). If $\mathbf{x}_i$ are the values for the input layer, w_i^s in the following are assigned as the supervised data for the output layer:

$$w_i^s = \begin{cases} 1, & \mathbf{x}_i \in R^s \\ 0, & \mathbf{x}_i \notin R^s \end{cases} \qquad i = 1, \ldots, n_t;\ s = 1, \ldots, r$$

The learning of $\mathrm{NN_{mem}}$ is conducted so that these w_i^s can be inferred from the input $\mathbf{x}$. Thus, the $\mathrm{NN_{mem}}$ becomes capable of inferring the degree of attribution $\hat{w}_i^s$ of each training data item $\mathbf{x}_i$ to R^s. We have defined the membership function of the IF part as the inferred value $\hat{w}_i^s$ that is the output of the learned $\mathrm{NN_{mem}}$, that is,

$$\mu_{A^s}(\mathbf{x}_i) \equiv \hat{w}_i^s, \qquad i = 1, 2, \ldots, n$$

STEP 5 This step is the identification of each THEN part. The structure of the THEN part of each inference rule is expressed by the input/output relationship. The TRD input $x_{i1}^s, \ldots, x_{im}^s$ and the output value y_i^s, $i = 1, 2, \ldots, (n_t)^s$, are assigned to the input and output of the NN_s. This NN_s is the NN of the THEN part in R^s. The training of NN_s is so conducted that the control value can be inferred. The CHD input values $x_{i1}, \ldots, x_{im}$, $i = 1, 2, \ldots, n_c$, are substituted in the NN thus obtained to obtain the sum Θ_m^s of squared errors.

$$\Theta_m^s = \sum_{i=1}^{n_c} \{y_i - u_s(\mathbf{x}_i) \cdot \mu_{A^s}(\mathbf{x}_i)\}^2 \tag{4}$$

This estimated value $u_s(\mathbf{x}_i)$ is obtained as the output of NN_s. There is another idea to calculate Θ^s with the weight; this is

$$\Theta_m^s = \sum_{i=1}^{n_c} \mu_{A^s}(\mathbf{x}_i)\{y_i - u_s(\mathbf{x}_i) \cdot \mu_{A^s}(\mathbf{x}_i)\}^2 \tag{4$'$}$$

We have used the following index to decide the best iteration number of NN learning and prevent overlearning.

$$I^s = \frac{n_c}{(n_t)^s + n_c} \sum_{i=1}^{(n_t)^s} \{y_i - u_s(\mathbf{x}_i)\}^2 + \frac{(n_t)^s}{(n_t)^s + n_c} \sum_{j=1}^{n_c} \{y_j - u_s(\mathbf{x}_j) \cdot \mu_{A^s}(\mathbf{x}_j)\}^2$$

If the NN_s has overlearned data, the error of the TRD becomes small but the error of the CHD becomes large. Therefore the number of iterations that gives the smallest I^s, is the best.

STEP 6 This is the simplification of THEN parts by a backward elimination method. Among the m input variables of an NN that infers the control values of the THEN parts for each inference rule, one input variable x^p is arbitrarily eliminated, and the NN of each THEN part is trained by using the TRD as in step 5. Equation (5) gives the squared error Θ_{m-1}^{sp} of the control value of the sth rule in the case of eliminating x^p. This Θ_{m-1}^{sp} can be estimated using the CHD:

$$\Theta_{m-1}^{sp} = \sum_{i=1}^{n_C} \{y_i - u_s(\mathbf{x}_i) \cdot \mu_{A^s}(\mathbf{x}_i)\}^2, \qquad p = 1, 2, \ldots, m \tag{5}$$

By comparing Eqs. (4) and (5), if

$$\Theta_m^s > \Theta_{m-1}^{sp} \tag{6}$$

the significance of the eliminated input variables x^p can be considered minimal, and x^p can be discarded.

STEP 7 The same operations as those performed in step 5 are carried out for the remaining $m - 1$ input variables. Steps 5 and 6 are cyclically repeated in the succeeding step until Eq. (6) would not hold for any remaining input variables. The model that gives the minimum Θ^s value is the best NN.

Thus, steps 1–7 determine the IF parts and THEN parts of each inference rule. The system identification process for the fuzzy model is then completed.

STEP 8 The following equation can derive the final control value y_i^*:

$$y_i^* = \frac{\sum_{s=1}^{r} \mu_{A^s}(\mathbf{x}_i) \cdot \overline{u_s(\mathbf{x}_i)}}{\sum_{s=1}^{r} \mu_{A^s}(\mathbf{x}_i)}, \qquad i = 1, 2, \ldots, n \tag{7}$$

where $\overline{u_s(\mathbf{x}_i)}$ is an inferred value obtained when CHD is substituted in the best NN obtained in step 7.

Detailed Supplemental Explanations

Among the steps shown above, a concrete explanation is supplemented here for step 2 by which the nonlinear membership function can be automatically determined.

It is natural to consider the application of the same control rule to input data that share high similarity. Therefore, the training data are clustered in this way in step 3 (Figure 6a). Each of these clustered groups corresponds to one of the rules such as "**IF** x_1 is small and x_2 is large, **THEN** . . . ." In the case shown in Figure 6a, three rules including R^1 to R^3 exist. These rules make perfect fits at the typical points (training data points) in these clusters. A gradual fitting to multiple rules has to be conducted as one nears the boundary region. The degree of attribution is a membership value. This shape could be the one shown in Figure 6c, which is a top view; the crosshatched area is a region in which the membership functions intersect.

The procedure to derive such a membership function corresponds to step 4. Here we propose to use the NN shown in Figure 6b. The variables of the IF parts (x_1 and x_2 in this case) are assigned to the input. At the output layer, the rule number neuron belonging to input variables and the others are expressed by 1 and 0, respectively. A strong point of the NN is the correspondence of an

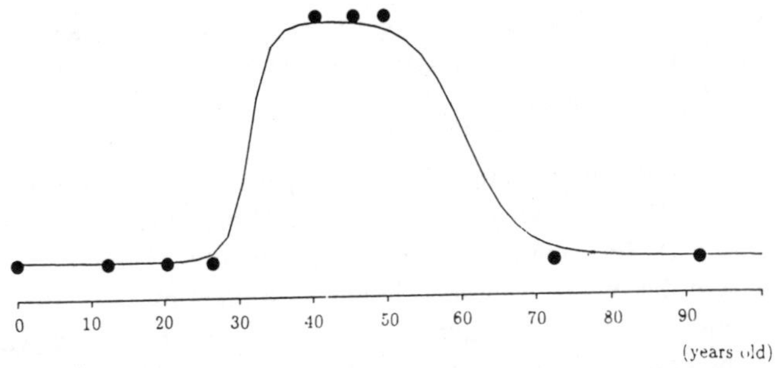

Figure 7. Membership function of "*middle age.*"

analogous output to an analogous input. Only the × points in Figure 6a are used for the training, but the similar output (i.e., the similar control rule) is obtained for the input data that is neighbor to the training data. Moreover, an NN that has finished its training outputs the best balanced attribution value for each rule when those input data are in the intersecting rules. This is the value of membership functions; in other words, this NN comprehends all the membership functions for each rule it contains.

Figure 7 shows an example of membership functions internally formulated by an NN. As a result of NN learning from nine data consisting of "*apparently not middle-aged*" and "*apparently middle-aged*," this NN outputs the membership function "*middle-aged*" (Figure 7). The variable is "age," which is one-dimensional. The membership function shown in Figure 7 can be easily designed by calling on experience and intuition, which would be useless for two-dimensional or multidimensional hypercurved surfaces.

Examples of Concrete Application

Following the above procedures, this formulated NN-driven fuzzy reasoning is applied to the simple previously reported numerical data (Kang and Sugeno [7], Kondo [8]). These data were made from $y = (1.0 + x_1^{0.5} + x_2^{-1} + x_3^{-1.5})^2$ and random noise x_4 (Kondo [8]).

STEPS 1, 2 Table 1 shows the input/output data. Items 1–20 are the training data (TRD) and 21–40 are the checking data (CHD); thus $n_t = n_c = 20$, and $k = 4$. Table 2 shows the result of the training for 15,000 iterations with a 3-layers[4 × 3 × 3 × 1] model that uses all variables and a 3-layers[3 × 3 × 3 × 1] model for the selection of input variables. Both training and checking data were used for these learning models.

The estimation performance of the model that eliminated x_4 was similar to that of the model that used all variables relatively. This means that input variable x_4 is negligible. We abandoned x_4 in the succeeding experiment.

STEP 3 The TRD are partitioned by using a conventional clustering method. The training data thus partitioned are shown in Table 3.

STEP 4 The 3-layers[3 × 3 × 3 × 2] model is trained for 5000 times to infer $w_i^s \in \{0, 1\}$, that is, the degree of attribution of the training data $\mathbf{x}_i$, $i = 1, 2, \ldots, 20$, to A^s, by the value of $\hat{w}_i^s \in [0, 1]$. By this training, the fuzzy number A^s in the IF parts is derived. Table 4 shows the membership values of the fuzzy number A^s of IF parts for the control rule R^s.

STEP 5 The inference formula for determining the control value for the THEN parts in various control rules is identified. Table 5 shows the output errors Θ_3^s derived after the 20,000 iterations of training of the 3-layers[3 × 8 × 8 × 1] model.

STEPS 6 AND 7 The sum of the squared errors Θ_2^{sp} when one of the arbitrary

Table 1. Example Input/Output Data

Training Data (TRD)						Checking Data (CHD)					
No.	y	x_1	x_2	x_3	x_4	No.	y	x_1	x_2	x_3	x_4
1	11.110	1	3	1	1	21	9.545	1	1	5	1
2	6.521	1	5	2	1	22	6.043	1	3	4	1
3	10.190	1	1	3	5	23	5.724	1	5	3	5
4	6.043	1	3	4	5	24	11.250	1	1	2	5
5	5.242	1	5	5	1	25	11.110	1	3	1	1
6	19.020	5	1	4	1	26	14.360	5	5	2	1
7	14.150	5	3	3	5	27	19.610	5	1	3	5
8	14.360	5	5	2	5	28	13.650	5	3	4	5
9	27.420	5	1	1	1	29	12.430	5	5	5	1
10	15.390	5	3	2	1	30	19.020	5	1	4	1
11	5.724	1	5	3	5	31	6.380	1	3	3	5
12	9.766	1	1	4	5	32	6.521	1	5	2	5
13	5.8700	1	3	5	1	33	16.000	1	1	1	1
14	5.406	1	5	4	1	34	7.219	1	3	2	1
15	10.190	1	1	3	5	35	5.724	1	5	3	5
16	15.390	5	3	2	5	36	19.020	5	1	4	5
17	19.680	5	5	1	1	37	13.390	5	3	5	1
18	21.060	5	1	2	1	38	12.680	5	5	4	1
19	14.150	5	3	3	5	39	19.610	5	1	3	5
20	12.680	5	5	4	5	40	15.390	5	3	2	5

Source: Kang and Sugeno [7]; Kondo [8].

Table 2. Results of Backward Elimination Using a Neural Network

	Sum of Squared Errors
When all variables are used	0.0007
When x_1 is eliminated	0.3936
When x_2 is eliminated	0.1482
When x_3 is eliminated	0.0872
When x_4 is eliminated	0.0019

Table 3. Rule Partition of Training Data

Control Rule	Training Data Numbers
R^1	1, 2, 3, 4, 5, 11, 12, 13, 14, 15
R^2	6, 7, 8, 9, 10, 16, 17, 18, 19, 20

input variables is removed from the IF-parts model with control rule R^s is derived. This sum, shown in Table 6, was obtained for control rules R^1 and R^2 after the learning of the 3-layers[2 × 8 × 8 × 1] model for 10,000–20,000 iterations.

Comparing step 5 and step 6 for each control rule, the following conditions are seen to exist:

$$\text{All of } \Theta_2^{1p} > \Theta_3^1 (= 27.86)$$

and

$$\Theta_2^{21} (= 0.93) < \Theta_3^2 (= 1.93)$$

Table 4. Membership Value for Rule R^s

Training Data				Membership Value	
No.	x_1	x_2	x_3	Rule 1	Rule 2
1	1	3	1	0.9970	0.0031
2	1	5	2	0.9972	0.0028
3	1	1	3	0.9972	0.0028
4	1	3	4	0.9973	0.0027
5	1	5	5	0.9974	0.0026
6	5	1	4	0.0028	0.9971
7	5	3	3	0.0028	0.9972
8	5	5	2	0.0027	0.9972
9	5	1	1	0.0027	0.9973
10	5	3	2	0.0027	0.9973
11	1	5	3	0.9973	0.0028
12	1	1	4	0.9973	0.0027
13	1	3	5	0.9974	0.0026
14	1	5	4	0.9973	0.0027
15	1	1	3	0.9972	0.0028
16	5	3	2	0.0027	0.9973
17	5	5	1	0.0027	0.9973
18	5	1	2	0.0027	0.9973
19	5	3	3	0.0028	0.9972
20	5	5	4	0.0029	0.9971

Table 5. Output Errors

Control rule 1: Θ_3^1	27.86
Control rule 2: Θ_3^2	1.93

Table 6. Output Errors After Elimination of Variables

	Rule 1	Rule 2
From Table 5	$\Theta_3^1 = 27.86$	$\Theta_3^2 = 1.93$
When x_1 is eliminated	$\Theta_2^{11} = 42.84$	$\Theta_2^{21} = 0.93$
When x_2 is eliminated	$\Theta_2^{12} = 74.71$	$\Theta_2^{22} = 119.61$
When x_3 is eliminated	$\Theta_2^{13} = 55.27$	$\Theta_2^{23} = 73.28$

Therefore, the NN of step 5 is designated as the conclusion parts model for control rule 1. The computation is continued for control rule 2, and is terminated by the repeated computations in step 2. Thus, the resulting NN, which has the input (x_2, x_3), is designated as the conclusion model. Therefore, the obtained fuzzy model is expressed by the following:

$$R^1: \quad \textbf{IF } \mathbf{x} = (x_1, x_2, x_3) \textit{ is } A^1, \textbf{ THEN } y^1 = NN_1(x_1, x_2, x_3)$$

$$R^2: \quad \textbf{IF } \mathbf{x} = (x_1, x_2, x_3) \textit{ is } A^2, \textbf{ THEN } y^2 = NN_2(x_2, x_3)$$

Figure 8 shows the plot of rule clustering of R^s in the $x_2 x_3$ plane, and Table 7 lists the y_i^* of Eq. (7).

SYSTEM CONSTRUCTION

We now can execute the NN-driven fuzzy reasoning using the above formulation. Figure 9 shows an example of this system executing this reason-

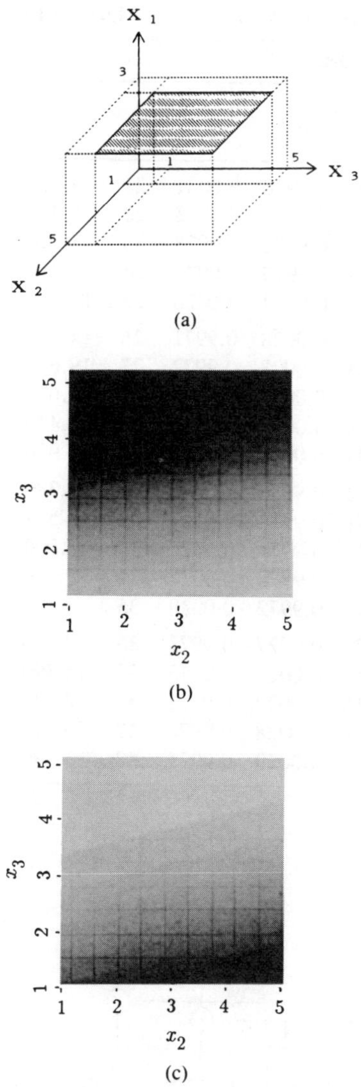

Figure 8. Hypercurved plane of membership function. (a) Display area of membership functional plane for (b) and (c). (b) Membership function of rule 1. (c) Membership function of rule 2.

ing. The NN_{mem} at the left end is the NN of Figure 6b generating the membership functions corresponding to the IF parts derived in step 4. NN_1–NN_r are the NNs of the THEN parts prepared in steps 6–8. This system weighs the output of the THEN part by the membership values of the IF parts and computes the final output value (step 9).

This fundamental system can be developed and expanded. For instance, if the input is not a single defined value but is a fuzzy number, the plural inputs of the NN can be adopted for one of the fuzzy number inputs. Likewise, if the output value is a fuzzy number, the plural outputs can be applied.

This construction is highly suitable for parallel processing, and this is another strong point of this system. Each NN corresponding to the IF part and THEN part of each ruel can be independently processed; furthermore, the NN itself is suitable for parallel processing.

APPLICATIONS

The effectiveness of NN-driven fuzzy reasoning is demonstrated by two reasoning problems. One is the estimation of COD (chemical oxygen demand)

Table 7. Output of Trained NN-Driven Fuzzy Reasoning

Training Data					Checking Data				
No.	y	y^*	W_i^1	W_i^2	No.	y	y^*	W_i^1	W_i^2
1	11.110	11.136	0.9970	0.0031	21	9.545	8.882	0.9974	0.0027
2	6.521	6.534	0.9972	0.0028	22	6.043	6.140	0.9973	0.0027
3	10.190	10.210	0.9972	0.0028	23	5.724	5.712	0.9973	0.0028
4	6.043	6.140	0.9973	0.0027	24	11.250	10.547	0.9971	0.0030
5	5.242	5.370	0.9974	0.0026	25	11.110	11.136	0.9970	0.0031
6	19.020	18.995	0.0028	0.9971	26	14.360	14.334	0.0027	0.9972
7	14.150	14.134	0.0028	0.9972	27	19.610	19.061	0.0028	0.9972
8	14.360	14.334	0.0027	0.9972	28	13.650	13.918	0.0029	0.9971
9	27.420	27.373	0.0027	0.9973	29	12.430	12.293	0.0030	0.9969
10	15.390	15.383	0.0027	0.9973	30	19.020	18.995	0.0028	0.9971
11	5.724	5.712	0.9973	0.0028	31	6.380	7.178	0.9972	0.0028
12	9.766	9.791	0.9973	0.0027	32	6.521	6.534	0.9972	0.0028
13	5.8700	5.747	0.9974	0.0026	33	16.000	11.239	0.9969	0.0032
14	5.406	5.450	0.9973	0.0027	34	7.219	9.018	0.9971	0.0029
15	10.190	10.210	0.9972	0.0028	35	5.724	5.712	0.9973	0.0028
16	15.390	15.383	0.0027	0.9973	36	19.020	18.995	0.0028	0.9971
17	19.680	19.652	0.0027	0.9973	37	13.390	13.892	0.0030	0.9970
18	21.060	21.046	0.0027	0.9973	38	12.680	12.672	0.0029	0.9971
19	14.150	14.134	0.0028	0.9972	39	19.610	19.061	0.0028	0.9972
20	12.680	12.672	0.0029	0.9971	40	15.390	15.383	0.0027	0.9973

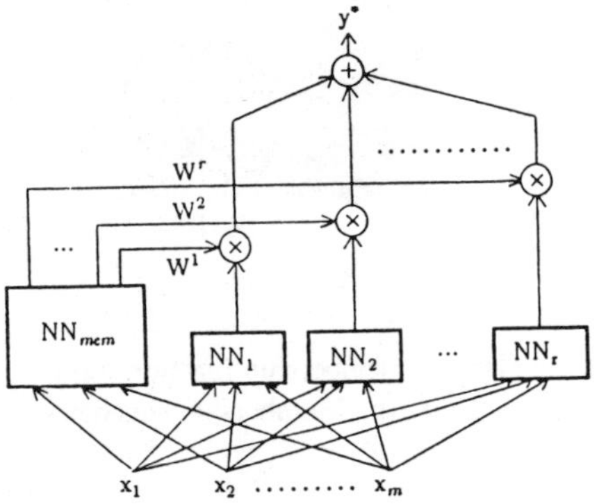

Figure 9. Block diagram of NN-driven fuzzy reasoning system. NN_{mem}, NN that decides membership values of all rules; NN_1–NN_r, NNs that determine control values and output y_i for ith rule; y^*, final control value; x_j, input variable; W^s, membership value.

density in Osaka Bay, and the other is the estimation of the roughness of a ceramic surface finished by a cup-shaped diamond whetstone.

Estimation of COD Density in Osaka Bay

The results of COD density measurements in Osaka Bay conducted between April 1976 and March 1979 were used as input/output data for inference conducted by NN-driven fuzzy reasoning. The input/output variables are as follows:

y	COD density, ppm
x_1	water temperature, °C
x_2	transparency, m
x_3	dissolved oxygen density, ppm

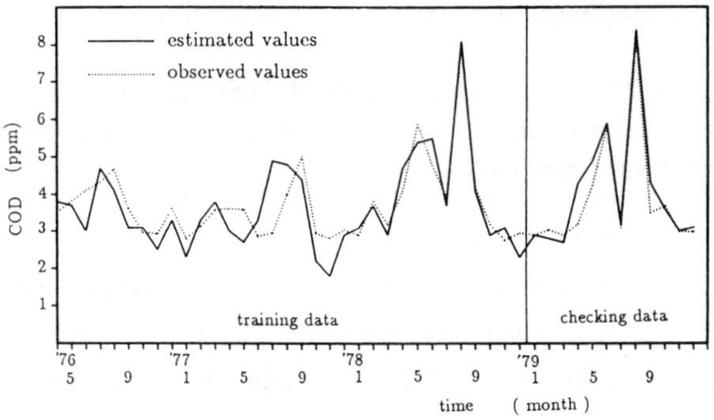

Figure 10. Estimation of COD density in Osaka Bay by NN-driven fuzzy reasoning.

x_4 salty density, %

x_5 filtered COD density, ppm

Fujita and Koi [9] previously reported on the estimation of COD density y by using the GMDH method. They first estimated the filtered COD density x_5 from a diffusion simulation model. Next they estimated output COD density y by using this x_5 and other input variables employed for the GMDH (Group Method of Data Handling) model.

We employed the same data for estimating the COD density y by NN-driven fuzzy reasoning. The model was obtained by the experiments conducted under the following conditions.

1. Thirty-two data points acquired during a period from April 1976 to December 1978 were used for the estimation. Twelve more data points obtained during the period from January to December 1979 were employed for the evaluation. The result of the backward-elimination experiment showed that it was necessary to employ all input variables for estimation.
2. The structure of the NN model employed in the succeeding experiment was as follows:

For the determination of IF-part structure: 3-layers$[5 \times 12 \times 12 \times 2]$

For the determination of THEN-part structure:

3-layers$[\mathrm{m} \times 12 \times 12 \times 1]$, $m = 5, 4, \ldots,$

3. There were 1500–2000 iterations of learning. The resulting NN-driven fuzzy reasoning was as follows:

$$R^1: \ \textbf{IF } \mathbf{x} = (x_1, \ldots, x_5) \ is\ A^1, \textbf{ THEN } y^1 = NN_1(x_1, x_2, x_3, x_4, x_5)$$
$$R^2: \ \textbf{IF } \mathbf{x} = (x_1, \ldots, x_5) \ is\ A^2, \textbf{ THEN } y^2 = NN_2(x_1, x_2, x_3, x_5)$$

Figure 10 shows the estimated value y_i^* and the observed data.

Table 8 shows the comparison between the estimated COD density derived by GMDH and the estimated COD density obtained by the proposed method using the model evaluation index $D = \left[\sum_i (y_i - y_i^*)^2\right]^{1/2}$.

Table 8. Results of Evaluation

	Training Data	Checking Data
GMDH [8]	3.63	2.04
Proposed	3.52	1.58

Estimation of Roughness of a Finished Ceramic Surface

The next is an example of application of NN-driven fuzzy reasoning for estimating the roughness of a surface finished by a diamond grinding wheel. The input/output variables were

y	roughness of ceramic surface, μm
x_1	rim velocity of diamond grinding wheel, m/min
x_2	moving velocity of ceramic plane, mm/min
x_3	cutting depth of diamond grinding wheel, mm
x_4	diamond size
x_5	concentration of diamond grinding wheel

Various whetted surface conditions were assumed by using the above input variables, and the ceramic plane was whetted by using a machining center. The finished ceramic surface was measured by using surface-roughness-measuring equipment. On the other hand, the roughness y was estimated by our proposed method.

Experiments were conducted under the following conditions for obtaining an inference model.

1. Thirteen data points with the following large deviations were used for the estimation:

$$S^2 = \sum_{i,j} \left(\frac{x_{ij} - \overline{x_j}}{\sigma_j} \right)^2$$

$$\sigma_j^2 = \frac{1}{n} \sum_{i}^{n} (x_{ij} - \overline{x_j})^2$$

2. The remaining eight data points were used for the evaluation.
3. The structure of the NN and the number of learning iterations were the same as those in the Osaka Bay problem.

From the experimental results we obtained the following NN-driven fuzzy reasoning:

R^1: **IF** $\mathbf{x} = (x_1, \ldots, x_5)$ *is* A^1, **THEN** $y^1 = NN_1(x_1, x_2, x_4, x_5)$

R^2: **IF** $\mathbf{x} = (x_1, \ldots, x_5)$ *is* A^2, **THEN** $y^2 = NN_2(x_1, x_2, x_3, x_4, x_5)$

R^3: **IF** $\mathbf{x} = (x_1, \ldots, x_5)$ *is* A^3, **THEN** $y^3 = NN_3(x_2, x_4)$

Figure 11 shows the estimated value y_i^* and the observed data.

Despite the limited quantity of available data, these two applications consistently show results better than those obtained by conventional methods.

CONCLUSION

This paper reports the formulation of the determination of fuzzy inference rules and the method of fuzzy reasoning using NN models. The most significant features are the feasibility of (1) automatic partition of a fuzzy rule and the best design of membership function and (2) the automatic adjustment of a membership function for a change of environment achieved by using the learning function of an NN. The experiments proved that the proposed system performed better than conventional reasoning systems.

Problems for future consideration include the verification of these results in extensive application fields. For example, the first point could be the automatic

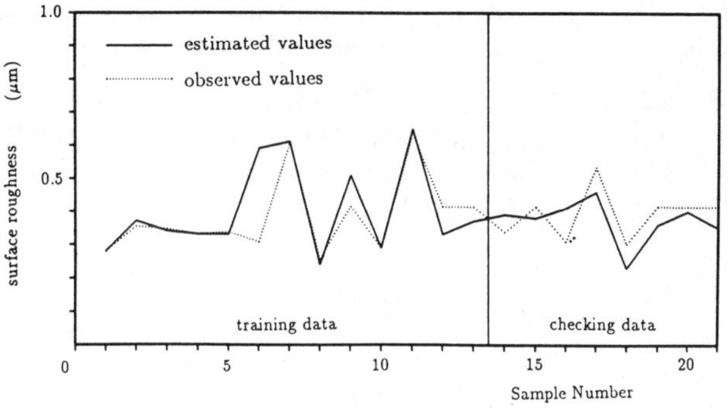

Figure 11. Estimation of roughness of whetted ceramic surface by NN-driven fuzzy reasoning.

preparation of a fuzzy inference rule from the control data manually derived by an expert. The other example could be the automated adaptation of a fuzzy reasoning rule when fuzzy reasoning developed for environment A is to be applied to environment B.

The above considerations were made from the standpoint of fuzzy reasoning. From the standpoint of NNs, this proposed method corresponds to the explicit incorporation of knowledge into the NN structure as a form of fuzzy inference rule. Ways in which knowledge can be incorporated into the NN to improve its capability are being discussed. The conventional methods to incorporate knowledge are (1) the reflection of those on the input pattern, (2) the influence on performance by prewiring the network, and (3) the combination of NNs having different functions. The NN described here includes knowledge expressed in IF–THEN form. This expression is of far higher grade than conventional methods, so there is a possibility to realize powerful NN capability. Furthermore, development of the NN in the AI field as a neural expert system can be also expected.

ACKNOWLEDGMENT

We wish to acknowledge the help of Mr. H. Nomura in our laboratories. The experiments for evaluation were done with his help. We would also like to thank Dr. K. Nagasaka of the University of Osaka Prefecture for his offer of the raw data in the ceramics problem.

References

1. McCulloch, W. S., and Pitts, W., A logical calculus of the ideas imminent in nervous activity, *Bull. Math. Biophys.* 5, 115–133, 1943.

2. Rosenblatt, F., The perception: a probabilistic model for information storage and organization in the brain, *Psychol. Rev.* 65(6), 386–408, 1958.

3. Rumelhart, D. E., Hinton, G. E., and Williams, R. J., Learning representations by back-propagating errors, *Nature* 323(9), 533–536, 1986.

4. Funahashi, K., On the approximate realization of continuous mappings by neural networks, *Neural Networks* 2(3), 183–192, 1989.

5. Hayashi, I., and Takagi, H., Formulation of fuzzy reasoning by neural network, *Proceedings of the 4th Fuzzy System Symposium*, 55–60, May 1988 (in Japanese).

6. Takagi, H., and Hayashi, I., Artificial_neural_network-driven fuzzy reasoning, *Proceedings of an International Workshop on Fuzzy System Applications* (IIZUKA-88), 217–218, August 1988.

7. Kang, G. T., and Sugeno, M., Fuzzy modelling, *Trans. Soc. Instrum. Control Eng.* 23(6), 650–652, 1987 (in Japanese).

8. Kondo, T., Revised GMDH algorithm estimating degree of the complete polynomial, *Trans. Soc. Instrum. Control Eng.* 22(9), 928–934, 1986 (in Japanese).

9. Fujita, S., and Koi, H., Application of GMDH to environmental system modelling and management, in *Self-Organizing Methods in Modeling: GMDH Type Algorithms* (S. J. Farlow, Ed.), Statistics Textbooks and Monographs Ser., Vol. 54, Marcel Dekker, New York, 257–275, 1984.

Implementation of Conjunctive and Disjunctive Fuzzy Logic Rules With Neural Networks

James M. Keller and Hossein Tahani
Electrical and Computer Engineering,
University of Missouri – Columbia,
Columbia, Missouri

ABSTRACT

The use of fuzzy logic to model and manage uncertainty in a rule-based system places high computational demands on an inference engine. In an earlier paper, we introduced trainable neural network structures for fuzzy logic. These networks can learn and extrapolate complex relationships between possibility distributions for the antecedents and consequents in the rules. In this paper, the power of these networks is further explored. The insensitivity of the output to noisy input distributions (which are likely if the clauses are generated from real data) is demonstrated as well as the ability of the networks to internalize multiple conjunctive clause and disjunctive clause rules. Since different rules (with the same variables) can be encoded in a single network, this approach to fuzzy logic inference provides a natural mechanism for rule conflict resolution.

KEYWORDS: ***fuzzy logic, neural networks, uncertainty modeling***

INTRODUCTION

In dealing with automated decision-making problems, and computer vision in particular, there is a growing need for modeling and managing uncertainty. Computer vision is beset with uncertainty of all types. A partial list of the causes of such uncertainty includes

Complexity of the problems
Questions that are ill-posed
Vagueness of class definitions
Imprecisions in computations
Noise of various sorts
Ambiguity of representations
Problems in scene interpretation

Address correspondence to James M. Keller, Electrical and Computer Engineering, University of Missouri, Columbia, MO 65211.

International Journal of Approximate Reasoning 1992; 6:221–240

655 Avenue of the Americas, New York, NY 10010 0888-613X/92/$05.00

Rule-based approaches for handling these problems have gained popularity in recent years (Fikes and Nilsson [1], Barrow and Tenenbaum [2], Brooks et al. [3], Riseman and Hanson [4], Wootton et al. [5], Nafarieh and Keller [6]). They offer a degree of flexibility not found in traditional approaches. The systems based on classical (crisp) logic need to incorporate, as an add-on, the processing of the uncertainty in the information. Methods to accomplish this include heuristic approaches (Shortliffe and Buchanan [7], Cohen [8]), probability theory (Pearl [9], Cheeseman [10]), Dempster–Shafer belief theory (Riseman and Hanson [4], Wootton et al. [5], Li [11]), and fuzzy theory (Wootton et al. [5] Nafarieh and Keller [6], Bonissone and Tong [12], Zadeh [13], Keller et al. [14]).

Fuzzy logic, on the other hand, is a natural mechanism for propagating uncertainty explicitly in a rule base. All propositions are modeled by possibility distributions over appropriate domains. For example, a computer vision system may have rules like

IF the range is LONG

THEN the prescreener window size is SMALL

or

IF the color is MOSTLY RED

THEN the steak is MEDIUM RARE is TRUE

Here, LONG, SMALL, MOSTLY RED, and TRUE are modeled by fuzzy subsets over appropriate domains of discourse. The possibility distributions can be generated from various histograms of feature data extracted from images, fuzzification of values produced by pattern recognition algorithms, or experts expressing (free-form) opinions on some questions, or possibly generated by a neural network learning algorithm.

There are two general approaches to inference in fuzzy logic, the composition rule and truth value restriction. As will be seen the composition rule offers the "purest" extension of crisp logic, whereas techniques based on truth value restriction present the possibility of introducing functional dependencies between antecedents and consequents of rules. In [15] Nafarieh and Keller introduce a truth value restriction inference mechanism that incorporated exponential dependencies between inputs and outputs and later used this scheme in a prototype automatic target recognition (Nafarieh and Keller [6]). It is this work that motivated the current research.

The generality inherent in fuzzy logic comes at a price. Since all operations involve sets rather than numbers, the number of calculations per inference rises dramatically. Also, in a fuzzy logic system, generally more rules can be fired at any given instant. One approach to combatting this computational load has been the development of special-purpose chips that perform particular versions of fuzzy inference (Togai and Watanabe [16, 17]). Artificial neural networks offer the potential of parallel computation with high flexibility. In an earlier paper (Keller and Tahani [18]), we introduced a backpropagation neural network structure to implement fuzzy logic inference.

This network approach performs in a similar fashion to truth value restriction. The technique demonstrated by Nafarieh and Keller in [6] and [15], although it produced excellent results, was not trainable; that is, the inference rule was generated analytically and not from example data. Neural networks approaches offer the flexibility to tailor the response characteristics of each rule to a functional relationship exhibited in a set of training data.

In this paper we demonstrate further properties of the neural network approach to fuzzy logic inference. In particular, we show the insensitivity of the networks to noisy input distributions, their ability to internalize rules with multiple conjunctive and disjunctive antecedent clauses, and their capability for emphasizing one antecedent clause over another. The results will be demonstrated in a simulation study using the same term set as in [6].

FUZZY LOGIC AND NEURAL NETWORKS

The original fuzzy inference mechanism extended the traditional modus ponens rule, which states that from the propositions

$$P_1\text{: IF } \boldsymbol{X} \textbf{ is } \boldsymbol{A} \text{ THEN } \boldsymbol{Y} \textbf{ is } \boldsymbol{B}$$

and

$$P_2\text{: } \boldsymbol{X} \textbf{ is } \boldsymbol{A}$$

we can deduce ***Y* is *B***. If proposition P_2 did not exactly match the antecedent of P_1, for example, ***X* is *A′***, then the modus ponens rule would not apply. However, in [19], Zadeh extended this rule to A, B, and A' modeled by fuzzy sets, as suggested above. In this case, P_1 is characterized by a possibility distribution:

$$\Pi_{(X \mid Y)} = R$$

where

$$\mu_R(u, v) = \max\{[1 - \mu_A(u)], \mu_B(v)\}$$

It should be noted that this formula corresponds to the statement "not A or B," the logical translation of P_1. An alternative translation of rule P_1 that corresponds more closely to multivalue logic is

$$\mu_R(u, v) = \min\{1, \{[1 - \mu_A(u)] + \mu_B(v)\}\},$$

called the bounded sum (Zadeh [19]).

In either case, Zadeh now makes the inference ***Y* is *B′*** from μ_R and $\mu_{A'}$ by

$$\mu_{B'}(v) = \max_u \{\min[\mu_R(u, v), \mu_{A'}(u)]\}$$

This is called the *compositional rule of inference*.

While this formulation of fuzzy inference directly extends modus ponens, it suffers from some problems (Nafarieh [20], Mizumoto et al. [21], Cao and Kandel [22], Schott and Whalen [23]). In fact, using the second translation above, if proposition P_2 is ***X* is *A***, the resultant fuzzy set is not exactly the fuzzy set B. Several authors (Nafarieh [20], Mizumoto et al. [21], Cao and Kandel [22], Schott and Whalen [23], Baldwin and Guild [24]) have performed theoretical and experimental investigations into alternative formulations of fuzzy implications in an attempt to produce more intuitive results.

Besides changing the way in which P_1 translated into a possibility distribution, methods involving truth modification have been proposed (Nafarieh and Keller [15], Nafarieh [20], Baldwin and Guild [24], Yager [25], Hisdal [26], Turksen and Zhong [27]). In this approach, the proposition ***X* is *A′*** is compared with ***X* is *A***, and the degree of compatibility is used to modify the membership function of B to get that for B'.

A fuzzy truth value restriction τ is a fuzzy subset of $X = [0, 1]$ and can be defined by its membership function μ_τ, which is a mapping

$$\mu_\tau\colon X \to [0, 1]$$

For example, we can define truth value restrictions TRUE, VERY TRUE, FALSE, UNKNOWN, ABSOLUTELY TRUE, ABSOLUTELY FALSE, etc.

In the truth value restriction methodology, the degree to which the actual given value A' of a variable X agrees with the antecedent value A in a proposition IF ***X* is *A*** THEN ***Y* is *b*** is represented as a fuzzy subset of a truth space. This fuzzy subset of truth space is what is referred to by the phrase "truth value restriction"; it is used in a fuzzy deduction process to determine the corresponding restriction on the truth value of the proposition ***Y* is *B***. This latter truth value restriction is then "inverted," which means that a fuzzy proposition Y **is** B' in the Y universe of discourse is found such that its agreement with Y **is** B is equal to the truth value restriction derived by the aforementioned fuzzy inference process, that is,

$$\mu_{B'}(v) = \mu_{\tau}(\mu_B(v))$$

It is this formulation of inference that most closely corresponds to the neural network implementation. This is because the layers of a neural network effectively compute the similarity of input data with stored information and modify the output accordingly.

In using fuzzy logic in real rule-based systems, the possibility distributions for the various clauses in the rule base are normally sampled at a fixed number of values over their respective domains of discourse, creating a vector representation for the possibility distribution. Table 1 shows the sampled versions of the "trapezoidal" possibility distributions used in the simulation study, sampled at integer values over the domain [1, 11]. These were the definitions used by Nafarieh and Keller in [6]. Clearly, the sampling frequency has a direct effect on the faithfulness of the representation of the linguistic terms under consideration and also on the amount of calculation necessary to perform inference using a composition rule. For a rule with a single antecedent clause, the translation into a possibility distribution as indicated above becomes a two-dimensional array, and the inference is equivalent to matrix-vector multiplication. As the number of antecedent clauses increases, the storage (multidimensional arrays) and the computation in the inference process grow exponentially.

Neural network structures offer a means of performing these computations in parallel with a compact representation. But the ability of such a network to generalize from an existing training set is the most valuable feature. Recently, there has been considerable interest in the joining of fuzzy logic and neural network technologies. The NASA workshop that gave rise to this special issue and the International Conference on Fuzzy Logic and Neural Networks in Iizuka, Japan, give evidence of this growing commitment. At Iizuka-90, Takagi [28] summarized the current and future trends in the fusion of fuzzy logic and neural networks. Three such contact points are the use of neural networks to learn or tune membership functions for fuzzy logic rules (Takagi and Hayashi [29], Furuya et al. [30]), the use of neural network structures to determine the rules themselves (Saito and Nakano [31], Gupta et al. [32]), and the development of special node combination schemes based on fuzzy set

Table 1. The Meaning of Linguistic Terms Defined on the Domain [1, 11] and Sampled at Integer Points

Label	Membership										
LOW	1.00	0.67	0.33	0.00	0.00	0.00	0.00	0.00	0.00	0.00	0.00
VERY LOW	1.00	0.45	0.11	0.00	0.00	0.00	0.00	0.00	0.00	0.00	0.00
MORL LOW	1.00	0.82	0.57	0.00	0.00	0.00	0.00	0.00	0.00	0.00	0.00
NOT LOW	0.00	0.33	0.67	1.00	1.00	1.00	1.00	1.00	1.00	1.00	1.00
NOISY LOW (1)	1.00	0.70	0.40	0.00	0.00	0.00	0.00	0.00	0.00	0.00	0.00
NOISY LOW (2)	1.00	0.70	0.30	0.00	0.00	0.00	0.00	0.00	0.00	0.00	0.00
NOISY MEDIUM	0.00	0.00	0.30	0.53	0.81	1.00	0.80	0.50	0.20	0.00	0.00
SHIFTED LOW	1.00	1.00	1.00	0.67	0.33	0.00	0.00	0.00	0.00	0.00	0.00
MEDIUM	0.00	0.00	0.25	0.50	0.75	1.00	0.75	0.50	0.25	0.00	0.00
MORL MEDIUM	0.00	0.00	0.50	0.71	0.87	1.00	0.87	0.71	0.50	0.00	0.00
NOT MEDIUM	1.00	1.00	0.75	0.50	0.25	0.00	0.25	0.50	0.75	1.00	1.00
HIGH	0.00	0.00	0.00	0.00	0.00	0.00	0.20	0.40	0.60	0.80	1.00
VERY HIGH	0.00	0.00	0.00	0.00	0.00	0.00	0.04	0.16	0.36	0.64	1.00
MORL HIGH	0.00	0.00	0.00	0.00	0.00	0.00	0.45	0.63	0.77	0.89	1.00
UNKNOWN	1.00	1.00	1.00	1.00	1.00	1.00	1.00	1.00	1.00	1.00	1.00

MORL = more or less.

connectives (Krishnapuram and Lee [33], Keller et al. [34], Yamaka Tomoda [35]). A fourth area of connection, and the focus of this work utilization of neural network structures to perform the fuzzy logic in directly (Keller and Tahani [18], Keller et al. [34], Turksen et al. [36], and Yager [37]).

In [18], we introduced a neural network architecture for fuzzy logic. 1 displays a three-layer feed forward neural network that has been fuzzy logic inference for conjunctive clause rules. It consisted of an inp to receive the possibility distributions of the antecedent clauses, one hidden layer to internalize a representation of relationships, and an output layer to produce the possibility distributions of the consequent. The choice of the linguistic terms (Table 1) and the resolution of sampling were guided by our earlier work on confidence measures in multisensor and temporal imagery (Keller et al. [14]). There is a trade-off between the resolution (and hence the number of distinct terms available) and the number of meaningful terms for a particular application. We chose 11 sampling points based on a set of experiments reported in [14]. There is also a trade-off between the resolution of sampling the domains of the fuzzy variables and the errors generated in the inference procedure (Cao and Kandel [22], Schott and Whalen [23]). This led Schott and Whalen to consider α-level set representations of the fuzzy term set.

The input layer was not fully connected to the hidden layer. Instead, each antecedent clause had its own set of hidden neurons to learn the desired relationship. This partitioning of the hidden layer was done to ease the training burden for multiple-clause rules and to treat each input clause with its hidden units as a functional block. The hidden layer was then fully connected to the nodes of the output layer. All connections were weighted, and each neuron received a net signal that was the linear weighted sum of all its inputs. A bias was added to this sum, and the output or activation of the neuron was given by the logistic function (Rumelhart and McClelland [38])

$$0 = 1/(1 + e^{-net})$$

Standard backpropagation was used to train the weights and biases in the network. It is an iterative procedure whereby an output error signal is

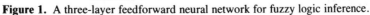

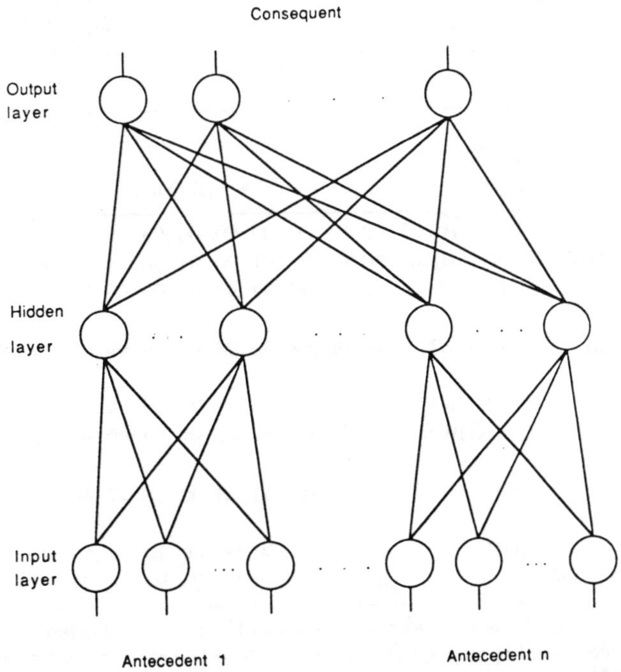

Figure 1. A three-layer feedforward neural network for fuzzy logic inference.

propagated back through the network and is used to modify the parameters. The error signal is defined by

$$e = \frac{1}{2} \sum_j (t_j - u_j)^2$$

where the summation is performed over all output nodes and t_j is the desired (target) value of output u_j for a specified input pattern. In our case, e measures the distance of the output possibility distribution from the desired reaction of the rule to the input possibility distribution. The training procedure modifies weights in proportion to their contribution to the error. This implements a gradient descent algorithm in weight space. The reader is referred to Rumelhart et al. [38] for a complete description of the algorithm. The training continues until the total error is less than some prescribed tolerance.

EXPERIMENTS

The neural network architecture performed very well in generalizing the complex relationships between inputs and outputs. Table 2 (from Keller and Tahani [18]) shows the results of the training and testing of a network to implement the rule IF X is LOW THEN Y is HIGH; whereas Table 3 gives the situation for a rule with two conjunctive antecedent clauses: IF ***X* is LOW** and ***Y* is MEDIUM** THEN ***Z* is HIGH**. In both cases, the performance of the networks matched our intuitive expectation.

As mentioned above, neural networks are finding use in the generation and tuning of membership functions used in fuzzy logic. Noisy input to these

Table 2. Performance of Fuzzy Logic Rule Network with Eight hidden Neurons for Rule IF ***X* is LOW** THEN ***Y* is HIGH**

A. *Training Data*[a]

Input	Output
LOW	HIGH
VERY LOW	VERY HIGH
MORL LOW	MORL HIGH
NOT LOW	UNKNOWN

B. *Testing Results*

Input	Expected Output	Actual Output	Total Sum Squared Error
VERY^2 LOW	VERY^2 HIGH	.00 .00 .00 .00 .00 .00 .03 .10 .27 .56 1.0	0.007
MORL^2 LOW	MORL^2 HIGH	.00 .01 .01 .01 .00 .01 .56 .71 .82 .91 1.0	0.030
MEDIUM	UNKOWN	.99 .99 .99 .99 .99 .99 .99 .99 .99 .99 1.0	0.001
VERY MEDIUM	UNKNOWN	.98 .98 .98 .98 .98 .98 .99 .99 .99 .99 1.0	0.003
MORL MEDIUM	UNKNOWN	.99 .99 .99 .99 .99 .99 .99 .99 .99 .99 .99	0.001
HIGH	UNKNOWN	.99 .99 .99 .99 .99 .99 .99 .99 .99 .99 .99	0.001
NOISY LOW (1)	HIGH	.00 .00 .00 .00 .00 .00 .26 .47 .66 .83 1.0	0.013
NOISY LOW (2)	HIGH	.00 .00 .00 .00 .00 .00 .19 .39 .59 .80 1.0	0.0001
SHIFTED LOW	—	.09 .09 .12 .09 .09 .09 .91 .92 .94 .97 1.0	—

[a] Training terminated when the total sum of squared (TSS) error dropped below $\epsilon = 0.001$. Very$^n A$ is determined by $\mu_{\text{Very}^n A}(x) = \mu_A(x)^{n+1}$; MORL$^n A$ is determined by $\mu_{\text{MORL}^n A}(x) = [\mu_A(x)]^{1/n+1}$.

Table 3. Performance of a Two Antecedent Clause Fuzzy Logic Rule Network with 16 Hidden Neurons (Two Groups of Eight)

A. *Training Data*[a]

Input	Output
(LOW, MEDIUM)	HIGH
(VERY LOW, VERY MEDIUM)	VERY HIGH
(MORL LOW, MORL MEDIUM)	MORL HIGH
(NOT LOW, MEDIUM)	UNKNOWN
(LOW, NOT MEDIUM)	UNKNOWN

B. *Testing Results*

Input	Actual Output											Closest Linguistic Term
(NOISY LOW(1), Medium)	.00	.00	.00	.00	.00	.00	.20	.40	.60	.80	1.0	HIGH
(NOISY LOW(2), MEDIUM)	.00	.00	.00	.00	.00	.00	.19	.40	.60	.80	1.0	HIGH
($VERY^2$ LOW, MEDIUM)	.00	.00	.00	.00	.00	.00	.19	.38	.60	.80	1.0	HIGH
(NOISY LOW(1), NOISY MEDIUM)	.00	.00	.00	.00	.00	.00	.20	.41	.61	.81	1.0	HIGH
LOW, $VERY^2$ MEDIUM)	.00	.00	.00	.00	.00	.00	.05	.17	.36	.64	1.0	VERY HIGH
($VERY^2$ LOW, $VERY^2$ MEDIUM)	.01	.01	.01	.01	.01	.01	.03	.12	.29	.58	1.0	$VERY^2$ HIGH
$MORL^2$ LOW, $MORL^2$ MEDIUM)	.01	.01	.01	.01	.01	.01	.55	.70	.81	.91	1.0	$MORL^2$ HIGH
(NOT LOW, NOT MEDIUM)	1.0	1.0	1.0	1.0	1.0	1.0	1.0	1.0	1.0	1.0	1.0	UNKNOWN
(LOW, SHIFTED MEDIUM	.97	.97	.97	.97	.97	.97	.99	.99	.99	1.0	1.0	UNKNOWN
(MEDIUM, LOW)	1.0	1.0	1.0	1.0	1.0	1.0	1.0	1.0	1.0	1.0	1.0	UNKNOWN

[a] Training converged in 1823 iterations.

"generation nets" or a loss of some internal neurons can produce distorted membership functions. Also, in computer vision applications, the membership functions may be constructed from histograms of a feature value over a region. For example, a normalized histogram of the gray levels in the upper portion of an image may be used as input to a fuzzy logic rule that has an antecedent clause THE SKY is LIGHT. In these cases, it is important to determine the effect of noise in the sensor or calculation process to the outcome of an inference using the data.

Figures 2 and 3 show typical responses of a neural network to noise in the input clause. The network was trained for the rule IF *X* **is MEDIUM** THEN *Y* **is HIGH** using a training set corresponding to the one in Table 2A. It can be seen that the errors in the result are of the same order as the error in the input.

This relationship was examined further as follows. One thousand samples of MEDIUM with 5–50% additive Gaussian noise (100 samples each) were generated and applied to the inference network. The average total-squared-error ($\times 100$) is plotted in Figure 4. The network performed very well until the error

Rule: IF X is MEDIUM THEN Y is HIGH

MEDIUM	.00	.00	.25	.50	.75	1.0	.75	.50	.25	.00	.00
INPUT	.06	.02	.35	.50	.79	1.0	.72	.54	.29	.01	.00

TSS error = 0.020

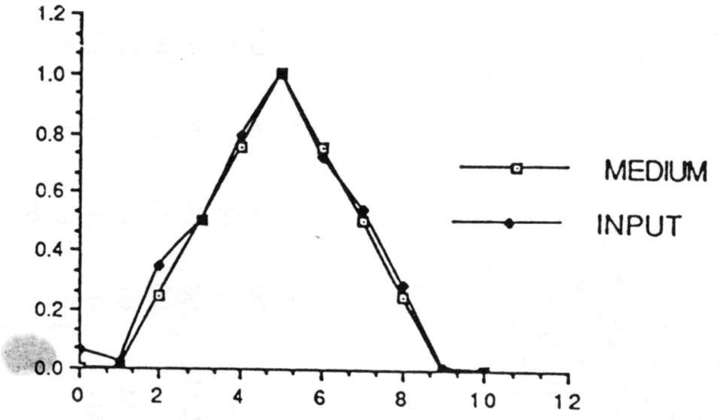

HIGH	.00	.00	.00	.00	.00	.00	.20	.40	.60	.80	1.0
OUTPUT	.00	.00	.00	.00	.00	.00	.28	.48	.67	.84	1.0

TSS error = 0.019

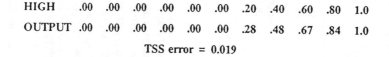

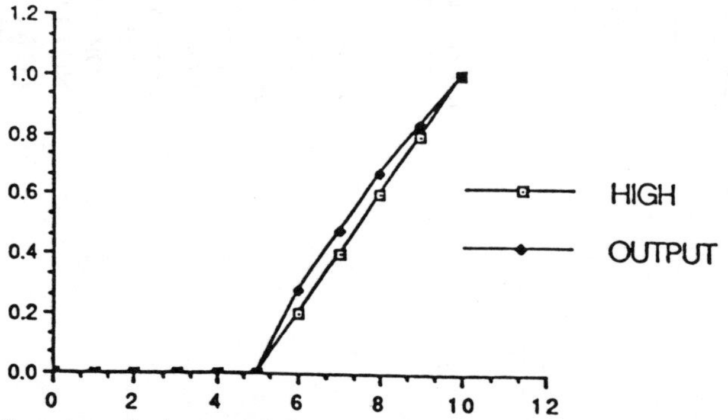

Figure 2. Response of rule network to an input with small amount of additive Gaussian noise.

MEDIUM	.00	.00	.25	.50	.75	1.0	.75	.50	.25	.00	.00
INPUT	.00	.08	.24	.52	.77	1.0	.64	.41	.43	.00	.00

TSS error = 0.060

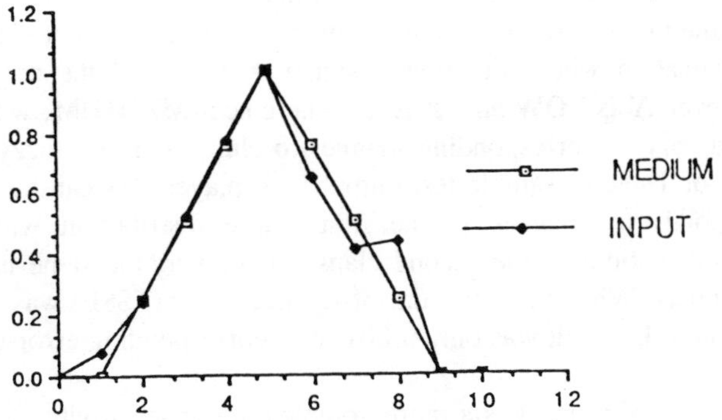

HIGH	.00	.00	.00	.00	.00	.00	.20	.40	.60	.80	1.0
OUTPUT	.00	.00	.00	.00	.00	.00	.25	.46	.65	.83	1.0

TSS error = 0.010

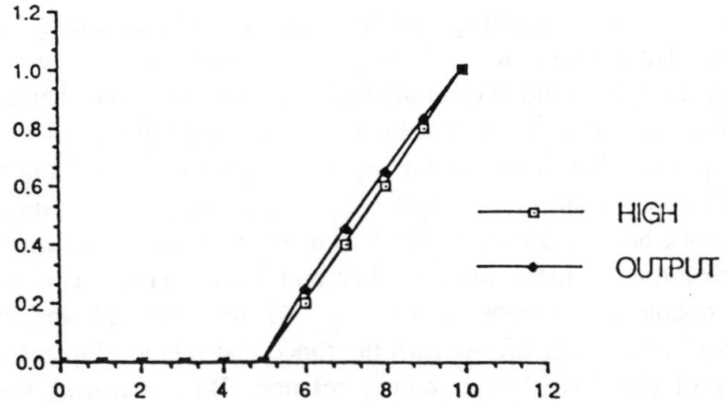

Figure 3. Response of rule network to an input with a larger amount of additive Gaussian noise.

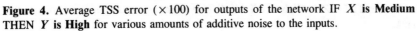

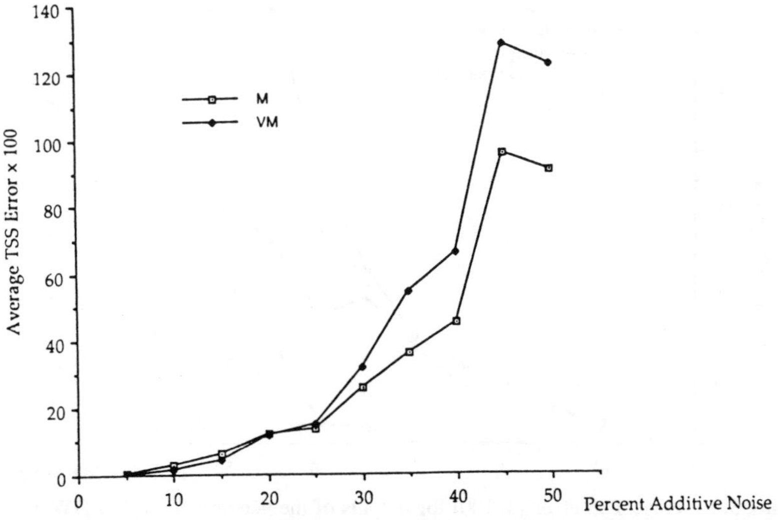

Figure 4. Average TSS error (× 100) for outputs of the network IF *X* **is Medium** THEN *Y* **is High** for various amounts of additive noise to the inputs.

in the input grew quite large. For example, even with 40% additive noise, the average error per output neuron was approximately 0.04. Figure 4 also shows the same error analysis for a noise-corrupted version of VERY MEDIUM as input. Although errors in computer vision are neither all additive nor all Gaussian, the behavior of this network in response to that type of error supports its utility in real fuzzy logic applications.

The same network as in Table 3 was retrained to stress the importance of variations in the first clause. The training set is shown in Table 4A. This would represent a situation where the rule designer would want the output *Z* **is HIGH** whenever *X* **is LOW** and *Y* is anywhere near **MEDIUM**, whereas the output should vary in corresponding manner to changes in the fuzzy variable *X*. In part B of Table 4, sample test output is displayed. As can be seen, the network responds to changes in the first clause distribution while being insensitive to deviations in the second clause. However, the same is true for noise in the inputs. While the total sum-of-squared error (TSSE) was 0.013 for a noisy version of LOW, it was only 0.001 for a corresponding error-corrupted MEDIUM.

Figure 5 graphically displays a more complete noise sensitivity analysis for this rule. Here, as above, 100 samples with each amount of additive Gaussian noise in the inputs were presented to the network in Table 4. What is interesting is that the output error was significantly less for noise in the "unstressed" clause than for noise in the "stressed" clause. This supports the contention that the error in the output of a fuzzy logic network, although low overall, is proportional to the amount of flexibility required of the rule itself.

Table 5 depicts the training of a three conjunctive clause rule network, whereas Table 6 shows training data for a network implementing two double conjunctive clause rules. In [18] we demonstrated that a neural network structure of this type could encode multiple different rules that shared common antecedent clause variables. In a network that encoded two rules, we showed that the response behaved well as the input distributions varied from one rule's antecedent to the second's antecedent. Also, the packing of several rules into a single network has a surprising side benefit of providing a natural means of conflict resolution in fuzzy logic (Keller and Tahani [18]). This is also the cause for double conjunctive clause rules. As we expected, the amount of training required to successfully learn the functional relationship grew with the complexity of the desired input-output relation. Both networks were tested

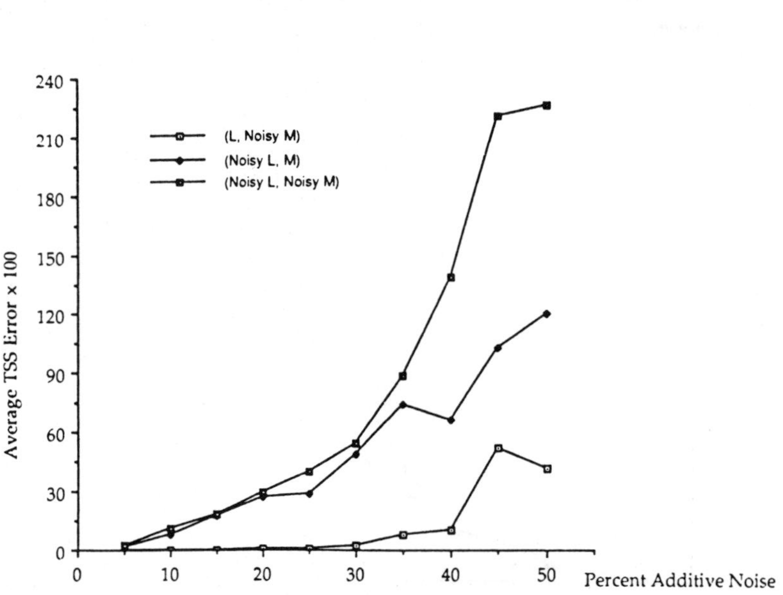

Figure 5. Average TSS error (× 100) for outputs of the network IF *X* **is LOW** and *Y* **is Medium** THEN *Z* **is High** (see Table 4) for various amounts of additive noise to the inputs.

Table 4. Results of Stressing One Clause Over Another in Rule I
X **is LOW** and Y **is MEDIUM** THEN Z **is HIGH**

A. *Training Data*[a]

Input	Output
LOW, MEDIUM	HIGH
VERY LOW, MEDIUM	VERY HIGH
MORL LOW, MEDIUM	MORL HIGH
NOT LOW, MEDIUM	UNKNOWN
LOW, VERY MEDIUM	HIGH
LOW, MORL MEDIUM	HIGH
LOW, NOT MEDIUM	UNKNOWN

B. *Sample Test Results*

Input	Actual Output	Closest Linguistic Term
VERY LOW, VERY MEDIUM	.00 .00 .00 .00 .00 .00 .05 .16 .38 .64 1.0	VERY HIGH
MORL LOW, VERY MEDIUM	.00 .00 .00 .00 .00 .00 .46 .63 .78 .89 1.0	MORL HIGH
N(LOW),[b] MEDIUM	.00 .00 .00 .00 .00 .00 .28 .46 .64 .84 1.0	HIGH (TSSE = .013)
LOW, N(MEDIUM)[b]	.00 .00 .00 .00 .00 .00 .21 .42 .61 .81 1.0	HIGH (TSSE = .001)

[a] Training terminated in 1965 iterations with a TSS error for the entire training set less than 0.001.
[b] For these results, Gaussian noise was added to produce:

N(LOW)	.92	.50	.32	.20	.03	.00	.03	.00	.06	.18	.00
N(MEDIUM)	.00	.08	.24	.52	.77	1.0	.64	.41	.43	.00	.00

with a variety of inputs with results similar to those already discussed for conjunctive clause rules.

In order to implement rules with disjunctive antecedent clauses, networks with two hidden layers were necessary. This was due, in part, to the fact that the network must internalize a considerably more complex decision framework dictated by the inclusive OR structure of the antecedents. In [39] Pedrycz considered the relation between the logical complexity of a fuzzy relation and hidden variables in a neural network. Also, we used standard backpropagation for training. A more sophisticated network training algorithm might have allowed convergence of a single hidden layer network. Table 7 displays training relationships for a two-clause disjunctive rule. Note that there are 23 input-output triples necessary to enable the network to respond appropriately. The training, using backpropagation, of a single hidden layer network, of the

Table 5. Training Data for the Conjunctive Rule IF X **is LOW** and Y **is MEDIUM** and Z **is VERY LOW**, THEN W **is HIGH**

Input	Output
LOW, MEDIUM, VERY LOW	HIGH
VERY LOW, VERY MEDIUM VERY^3 LOW	VERY HIGH
MORL LOW, MORL MEDIUM, MORL VERY LOW	MORL HIGH
NOT LOW, MEDIUM, VERY LOW	UNKNOWN
LOW, NOT MEDIUM, VERY LOW	UNKNOWN
LOW, MEDIUM NOT VERY LOW	UNKNOWN

Training converged in 4548 iterations with TSS error for the entire training set less than 0.001.

Table 6. Training Data for Two Double Conjunctive Antecedent Clause Rules Implemented in the Same Network

Rule 1: IF X **is LOW** and Y **is MEDIUM** THEN Z **is HIGH**
Rule 2: IF X **is HIGH** and Y **is MEDIUM** THEN Z **is VERY HIGH**

Input	Output
LOW, MEDIUM	HIGH
VERY LOW, VERY MEDIUM	VERY HIGH
MORL LOW, MORL MEDIUM	MORL HIGH
NOT LOW, MEDIUM	UNKNOWN
LOW, NOT MEDIUM	UNKNOWN
HIGH, MEDIUM	VERY HIGH
VERY HIGH, VERY MEDIUM	VERY^3 HIGH
MORL HIGH, MORL MEDIUM	HIGH (= MORL(VERY HIGH))
NOT HIGH, MEDIUM	UNKNOWN
HIGH, NOT MEDIUM	UNKNOWN

Training converged in 5922 iterations, with TSS error for the entire training set less than 0.001.

type shown in Figure 1, failed to converge on this complex training set. This caused us to investigate a two hidden layer structure where the first hidden layer was the same as in Figure 1 and the second hidden layer contained six neurons totally connected to those of the first hidden layer and to the nodes of the output layer. This network converged in 4073 passes through the training set with a total sum of squared error of less than 0.001 for the entire training ensemble. We feel that this is a remarkable achievement, given the diversity of the responses to the antecedent possibility distributions that were necessary.

A network with the same structure was trained on the two disjunctive rules

IF X **is LOW** OR Y **is MEDIUM** THEN Z **is HIGH**

and

IF X **is HIGH** OR Y **is VERY HIGH** THEN Z **is MEDIUM**

Table 8 gives the training information for this network. Of the 38 possible input-output triples, seven had to be removed from the training set because they cause direct conflict for disjunctive rules. For example, if Y **is HIGH** then from rule 1 the output should be Z **is HIGH**, assuming that the first clause X **is LOW**; whereas for rule 2 the output should be Z **is MORL MEDIUM** [since HIGH = MORL (VERY HIGH)]. This puts more of a burden on the designer, but the neural network was able to effectively learn a large set of disjunctive clauses.

The disjunctive structure from Table 7 was tested with several additional input pairs, and the match to the expected output in these cases was very good.

Table 7. Training Data for the Two Disjunctive Clause Rule

IF X **is LOW** OR Y **is MEDIUM** THEN Z **is HIGH**

Input	Output
(VERY, MORL) LOW; *	(VERY, MORL) HIGH
*; (VERY, MORL) MEDIUM	(VERY, MORL) HIGH
NOT LOW; NOT MEDIUM	UNKNOWN
MEDIUM; LOW	UNKNOWN
HIGH; LOW	UNKNOWN
HIGH; VERY LOW	UNKNOWN
UNKNOWN; HIGH	UNKNOWN

* = LOW, MEDIUM, HIGH
Training converged in 4073 iterations with TSS error for the entire training set less than 0.001.

Table 8. Training Data for Two Double Disjunctive Antecedent Clause Rules Implemented in the Same Network

Rule 1: IF *X* **is LOW** OR *Y* **is MEDIUM** THEN *Z* **is HIGH**
Rule 2: IF *X* **is HIGH** OR *Y* **is VERY HIGH** THEN *Z* **is MEDIUM**

Input	Output
(VERY, MORL), LOW; *	(VERY, MORL) HIGH[a]
*; (VERY, MORL), MEDIUM	(VERY, MORL) HIGH[a]
NOT LOW; NOT MEDIUM	UNKNOWN
(VERY, MORL) HIGH; *	(VERY, MORL) MEDIUM[a]
*; (VERY, MORL) VERY HIGH	(VERY, MORL) MEDIUM[a]
NOT HIGH; NOT VERY HIGH	UNKNOWN

* = LOW, MEDIUM, HIGH
Training converged in 25751 iterations, with TSS error for the entire training set less than 0.003.
[a] The following input-output triples were omitted from the training of the network because they cause direct conflict for disjunctive rules.

Input	Output
LOW, HIGH	HIGH
LOW, MEDIUM	HIGH
HIGH, MEDIUM	HIGH
LOW, VERY HIGH	MEDIUM
HIGH, MEDIUM	MEDIUM
HIGH, HIGH	MEDIUM
LOW, HIGH	MORL MEDIUM

The previously described error sensitivity analysis was also performed on this network, adding noise to each clause separately and then to both clauses simultaneously. The results are displayed in Figure 6. As can be seen, the average error per output neuron is quite low, even for large amounts of additive noise. Although the overall error is low, it is somewhat surprising that when noise is added to both disjunctive clauses the output error is about twice that for either clause. This would be expected for conjunctive rules more than for disjunctive rules. There are two layers of hidden neurons through which errors can accumulate, but this points out, in a minor way, one of the acknowledged drawbacks of the use of neural networks for computations; that is, after training, the network is a "black box." In most cases it is impossible

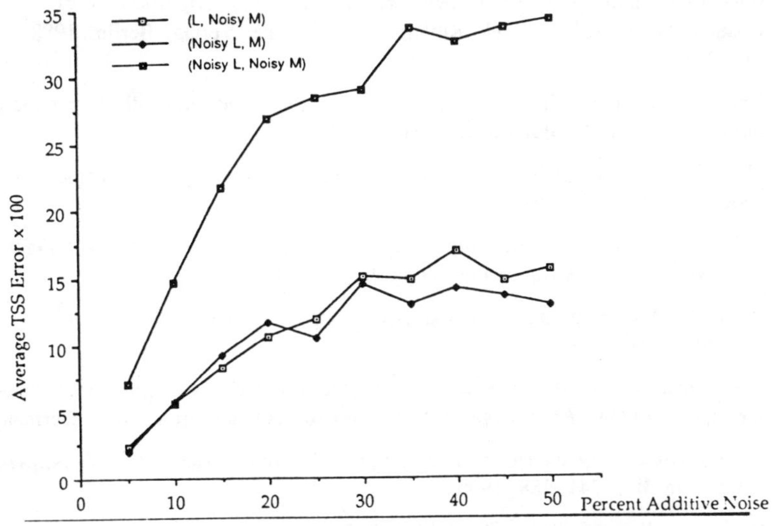

Figure 6. Average TSS error ($\times 100$) for outputs of the network IF *X* **is Low** or *Y* **is Medium** THEM *Z* **is High** (see Table 7) for various amounts of additive noise to the inputs.

to determine the actual algorithm that the network "learned." This is not a serious problem in this case but is pointed out to demonstrate that care should be exercised in extrapolating results. However, in general, the insensitivity to noise coupled with the ability to "share" the network with several rules and the ensuing conflict resolution properties makes these networks a highly desirable mechanism to implement fuzzy logic.

CONCLUSION

Fuzzy logic is a powerful tool for managing uncertainty in rule-based systems but imposes an increased burden on the inference engine. Neural network architectures offer a means of relieving some of the computational burden inherent in fuzzy logic. These structures can be trained to learn and extrapolate complex relationships between antecedents and consequents, they are relatively insensitive to noise in the inputs, and they provide a natural mechanism for conflict resolution.

ACKNOWLEDGMENT

We wish to thank the anonymous referees for their insightful comments and suggestions for the revision of this paper.

References

1. Fikes, R., and Nilsson, N., STRIPS: a new approach to the application of theorem proving to problem solving, *AI*, **2**(3), 189–208, 1971.
2. Barrow, H., and Tenenbaum, J., MSYS: a system for reasoning about scenes, Tech. Note 121, AI Center, SRI International, March 1976.
3. Brooks, R., Greiner, R., and Binford, T., Progress report on a model-based vision system, *Proc. Image Understanding Workshop* (L. Baumann, Ed.), 1978, pp. 145–151.
4. Riseman, E., and Hanson, A., A methodology for the development of general knowledge-based systems, in *Vision, Brain, and Cooperative Computation* (M. Arbib and A. Hanson, Eds.), MIT Press, Cambridge, Mass., 1988, pp. 285–328.
5. Wootton, J., Keller, J., Carpenter, C., and Hobson, G., A multiple hypothesis rule-based automatic target recognizer, in *Pattern Recognition* (Lect. Notes Computer Sci., Vol. 301) (J. Kittler, Ed.), Springer-Verlag, Berlin, 1988, pp. 315–324.
6. Nafarieh, A., and Keller, J., A fuzzy logic ruled-based automatic target recognizer, *Int. J. Intell. Syst.*, 6, 295–312, 1991.
7. Shortliffe, E., and Buchanan, A model of inexact reasoning in medicine, *Math Biosci.* **23**, 351–379, 1975.
8. Cohen, P., *Heuristic Reasoning about Uncertainty: An Artificial Intelligence Approach*, Pitman Advance Publishing Program, 1985.
9. Pearl, J., Fusion propagation and structuring in belief networks, *AI* **29**(3), 241–288, 1986.
10. Cheeseman, P., A method of computing generalized Bayesian probability values for expert systems, *Proc. Eight Int. J. Conf. on AI*, Karlsruhe, West Germany.
11. Li, Z., Uncertainty management is a pyramid vision system, *Int. J. Approx. Reasoning* **3**(1), 241–288, 1989.
12. Bonissone, P., and Tong, R., Editorial: Reasoning with uncertainty in expert systems, *Int. J. Man-Mach. Stud.* **22**, 241–250, 1985.
13. Zadeh, L., Fuzzy logic and approximate reasoning, *Syntheses* **30**, 407–428, 1975.

14. Keller, J., Hobson, G., Wootton, J., Nafarieh, A., and Leutkemeyer, K., Fuzzy confidence measures in midlevel vision, *IEEE T. Syst., Man, Cybern.* **17**(4), 676-683, 1987.

15. Nafarieh, A., and Keller, J., A new approach to inference in approximate reasoning, *Fuzzy Sets and Syst.*, 41, 17-37, 1991.

16. Togai, M., and Watanabe, H., Expert system on a chip: an engine for real-time approximate reasoning, *IEEE Expert* 55-62, 1986.

17. Togai, M., and Watanabe, H., A VLSI implementation of fuzzy logic inference engines: towards an expert system on a chip, *Inf. Sci.* **38**, 147-163, 1986.

18. Keller, J., and Tahani, H., Backpropagation neural networks for fuzzy logic, *Inf. Sci.* to appear, 1992.

19. Zadeh, L., The concept of a linguistic variable and its application to approximate reasoning, Parts 1-3, *Inf. Sci.*, **8**, 199-249; **8**, 301-357; **9**, 43-80, 1975.

20. Nafarieh, A., A new approach to inference in approximate reasoning and its application to computer vision, Ph.D. Dissertation, Univ. Missouri—Columbia, 1988.

21. Mizumoto, M., Fukami, S., and Tanaka, K., Some methods of fuzzy reasoning, in *Advances in Fuzzy Set Theory and Applications* (M. Gupta, R. Ragade, and R. Yager, Eds.), North-Holland, Amsterdam, 1979, pp. 117-126.

22. Cao, Z., and Kandel, A., Applicability of some fuzzy implication operators, *Fuzzy Sets Syst.* **31**, 151-186, 1989.

23. Schott, B., and Whalen, T., Sources of error in fuzzy inference, *Proc. NAFIPS-90*, Toronto, Ontario, **2**, 223-226, 1990.

24. Baldwin, J., and Guild, N., Feasible algorithms for approximate reasoning using fuzzy logic, *Fuzzy Sets Syst.* **3**, 225-251, 1980.

25. Yager, R. R., An approach to inference in approximate reasoning, *Int. J. Man-Mach. Stud.* **13**, 323-338, 1980.

26. Hisdal, E., The IF THEN ELSE statement and interval, fuzzy sets of higher type, *Int. J. Man-Mach. Stud.* **15**, 385-455, 1988.

27. Turksen, I. B., and Zhong, Z., An approximate analogical reasoning approach based on similarity measures, *IEEE Trans. Syst., Man, Cybern.* **18**, 1049-1056, 1988.

28. Takagi, H., Fusion technology of fuzzy theory and neural networks: survey and future directions, *Proc. Int. Conf. on Fuzzy Logic and Neural Networks*, Iizuka, Japan, **1**, 13-26, 1990.

29. Takagi, H., and Hayashi, I., Artificial-neural-network-driven fuzzy reasoning, *Int. J. Approx. Reasoning*, accepted for publication, 1989.

30. Furuya, T., Kokuba, A., and Sakamoto, T., NFS: neuro fuzzy inference system, *Proc. Iizuka-88*, Iizuka, Japan, 219-230, 1988.

31. Saitoh, K., and Nakano, R., Medical diagnostic expert system based on PDP model, *Proc. ICNN'88*, **1**, 255-262, 1988.

32. Gupta, M. M., Pedrycz, W., and Kiszka, J., Fuzzy control: from fuzzy controllers to cognitive controllers, *Proc. 3rd IFSA Congress*, Seattle, Wash., 258-261, 1989.

33. Krishnapuram, R., and Lee, J., Determining the structure of uncertainty management networks, *Proc. SPIE Symposium on Intelligent Robots and Computer Vision*, Philadelphia, 492-599, 1989.

34. Keller, J., Yager, R., and Tahani, H., Neural network implementation of fuzzy logic, *Fuzzy Sets Syst.* to appear 1992.

35. Yamakawa, T., and Tomoda, S., A fuzzy neuron and its application to pattern recognition, *Proc. 3rd IFSA Congress*, Seattle, 30-38, 1989.

36. Turksen, I. B., Guo, L., Lucas, C., and Smith, K., Hardware realization of fuzzy

logic and artificial neural networks, *Proc. Int. Conf. on Fuzzy Logic and Neural Networks*, Iizuka, Japan, **1**, 133-136, 1990.

37. Keller, J., and Yager, R., Fuzzy logic inference neural networks, *Proc. SPIE Symposium on Intelligent Robots and Computer Vision*, Philadelphia, 582-591, 1989.

38. Rumelhart, D., McClelland, J., and the PDP Research Group, *Parallel Distributed Processing, Vol 1*, MIT Press, Cambridge, Mass., 1986.

39. Pedrycz, W., Statistical considerations on solutions of fuzzy relational equations, *Proc. 3rd IFSA Congress*, Seattle, 87-89, 1989.

Epilogue to the Volume

This volume starts with Lotfi Zadeh's original paper on fuzzy sets and ends with a paper that will appear about one month before this volume does. We have tried to carry readers to and through the seminal stops that various scientists and engineers have made on the way to a coherent, well-integrated theory of fuzzy pattern recognition. This theory is certainly incomplete and still in evolution, but it has had enough successes at this point for us to assert, without trepidation, that this branch of science is important, useful, and well founded. We have undoubtedly left out several important papers that deserve to be in this volume while we have included others that may be arguable, either from an historical or technical perspective. Inevitably, authors must accept responsibility for their choices, and we do. It is our hope that the present volume brings to its readers an overall sense of how and why fuzzy models fit into the larger scheme of pattern recognition in particular, and science in general. If this is accomplished for even a few, it will have been worth the effort.

Jim Bezdek
Sankar K. Pal

Author Index

Subject Index

Editors' Biographies

Jim Bezdek received the B.S.C.E. degree from the University of Nevada—Reno in 1969 and the Ph.D. degree in applied mathematics from Cornell University in 1973. He has held academic positions at SUNY/Oneonta, Marquette University, Utah State University, and the University of South Carolina, where he was Chair of Computer Science. Dr. Bezdek was a visiting research scientist at Boeing Aerospace in 1982 and Director of the Information Processing Laboratory at the Boeing Electronics High Technology Center from 1987 to 1989. Dr. Bezdek currently occupies the Nystul Florida Eminent Scholar Chair with the Division of Computer Science at the University of West Florida. His research interests include pattern recognition algorithms, neural networks, image processing and machine vision, medical diagnosis, and expert systems. He is the founding editor of the *International Journal of Approximate Reasoning* and an associate editor of *IEEE Transactions on Systems, Man, and Cybernetics*, and *International Journals of Man-Machine Studies, Applied Intelligence, General Systems, and Fuzzy Sets and Systems.* He is a past president of the International Fuzzy Systems Association and the North American Fuzzy Information Processing Society. Dr. Bezdek is also a Fellow of the IEEE Systems, Man and Cybernetics Society.

Sankar K. Pal is a Professor in the Electronics and Communication Sciences Unit at the Indian Statistical Institute, Calcutta. He obtained the B.Sc. (Hons) in Physics and the B. Tech., M. Tech., and Ph.D. degrees in radiophysics and electronics in 1969, 1972, 1974, and 1979, respectively, from the University of Calcutta, India. In 1982 he received a second Ph.D. degree in electrical engineering along with the DIC from Imperial College, University of London, England. He recieved the Commonwealth Scholarship in 1979 and Medical Research Council (U.K.) Postdoctoral Award in 1981 to work at Imperial College, London. In 1986 he was awarded the Fulbright Postdoctoral Visiting Fellowship to work at the University of California, Berkeley and the University of Maryland, College Park. In 1989 he received an NRC-NASA Senior Research Award to work at the NASA Johnson Space Center, Houston, Texas. He received the 1990 Shanti Swarup Bhatnagar Prize in Engineering Sciences (which is the most coveted scientific award in India) for his contributions to pattern recognition.

Dr. Pal is presently a guest investigator in the Software Technology Branch of the NASA Johnson Space Center, Houston, Texas. He served as Professor-in-Charge of the Physical and Earth Sciences Division, Indian Statistical Institute during 1988–1990. He was also a Guest Lecturer (1983–1986) in Computer Science, Calcutta University. His research interests include pattern recognition, image processing, artificial intelligence, neural nets, and fuzzy sets and systems. He is co-author of the book *Fuzzy Mathematical Approach to Pattern Recognition* (John Wiley & Sons), which received the Best Production Award in the 7th World Book Fair, New Delhi, and has written approximately one hundred and fifty research papers, including ten in edited books and more than eighty in international journals. He has also lectured at different U.S. and Japanese universities/laboratories on his research work. He is listed in *REFERENCE ASIA*, Asia's *Who's Who of Men and Women of Achievements*, vol. IV, 1989.

Dr. Pal is a Reviewer for *Mathematical Reviews* (published by the American Mathematical Society), an Associate Editor for *International Journal of Approximate Reasoning*, a Senior Member of the IEEE, a life Fellow of the IETE, and Treasurer of the Indian Society for Fuzzy Mathematics and Information Processing. He is also a permanent member of the Indo-US Forum for Cooperative Research and Technology Transfer and an organizing/program committee member of various international conferences and meetings.

This volume was completed while S. K. Pal held an NRC-NASA Senior Research Associateship at the Johnson Space Center.